Jewish New Testament Commentary

Books by Dr. David H. Stern:

Jewish New Testament (available in softcover, hardcover, on 20 CDs, and on MP3)

Messianic Judaism: A Modern Movement with an Ancient Past (formerly *Messianic Jewish Manifesto*)

Restoring the Jewishness of the Gospel

Complete Jewish Bible (available in softcover, hardcover, leather, large print)

Jewish New Testament Commentary (available in softcover and hardcover)

Dr. Stern's books have been translated into the following languages:

Complete Jewish Bible
German, Portuguese

Jewish New Testament
German, Polish, Portuguese, Russian, Spanish (coming in 2011)

Jewish New Testament Commentary
German, Italian, Russian

Restoring the Jewishness of the Gospel
Dutch, German, Hebrew, Hungarian, Italian, Japanese, Polish, Spanish, Chinese (2011)

Messianic Judaism: A Modern Movement with an Ancient Past (formerly *Messianic Jewish Manifesto*) Hebrew, Japanese, Portuguese, Russian, Spanish

For a list of the foreign publishers of these books, go to www.messianicjewish.net/jntp. Books are available for purchase through www.messianicjewish.net.

Jewish New Testament Commentary

A companion volume to the
Jewish New Testament

by

David H. Stern

Jewish New Testament Publications, Inc.
Clarksville, Md. USA

The *Jewish New Testament,* copyright © 1989 by David H. Stern, is published by Jewish New Testament Publications, Inc.

Cover illustration by Mickie Klugman-Caspi
Interior design by Now You See it! graphics
Printed in the United States of America

13 12 11 10 19 18 17 16

Hardcover ISBN 13 978-965-359-008-3

Softcover ISBN 13 978-965-359-011-3

Library of Congress Catalog Control Number: 92097129

Published by
JEWISH NEW TESTAMENT PUBLICATIONS, INC.
6120 Day Long Lane
Clarksville, Maryland 21029

Distributed by
Messianic Jewish Resources International
Order Line 800-410-7367
E-mail: JNTP@messianicjewish.net
Website: www.messianicjewish.net

Order Line: (800) 410-7367
E-mail: lederer@messianicjewish.net
Website: www.messianicjewish.net

For the glory of God,
the salvation of Israel
and the edification of the Messianic Community

CONTENTS

INTRODUCTION

COMMENTARY ON BOOKS OF THE NEW TESTAMENT

INTRODUCTION

I WHAT IS THE *JEWISH NEW TESTAMENT COMMENTARY?*

The *Jewish New Testament Commentary* (*JNTC*) deals with "Jewish issues" that confront readers of the New Testament — questions Jews have about Yeshua (Jesus), the New Testament and Christianity; questions Christians have about Judaism and the Jewish roots of their faith; and questions Messianic Jews have about being both Jewish and Messianic. It is a companion volume to the *Jewish New Testament* (*JNT*), my translation of the New Testament from the original Greek into English in a way that brings out its essential Jewishness.

A "Consciousness-Raising" Commentary. Nearly everyone approaches the New Testament with preconceived opinions about its Jewish issues. Sometimes this is the consequence of not having examined them, sometimes it is because of prejudice or childhood training. In any case, my object in the *Jewish New Testament Commentary* is to make people more aware of the New Testament's Jewish issues and thus able to reach new conclusions about them.

For this reason I call the *JNTC* a "consciousness-raising" commentary. It presents information that offers new options. A reader should come away understanding that the New Testament is a Jewish book — written by Jews, largely about Jews, and meant for both Jews and Gentiles. Jews should know that the New Testament presents Yeshua from Natzeret (Nazareth) as the Son of David, Israel's long-awaited Messiah, essential for Jewish individual and corporate salvation. Christians should be certain that they are forever one with the Jewish people, and that the New Testament gives no ground for antisemitism in any form.

II THE COMBINED *JNT—JNTC* PROJECT

This consciousness-raising task is carried out partly by the *Jewish New Testament* and partly by this book. Actually, my original idea, in 1977, was only to write a commentary on the New Testament dealing with Jewish issues. But after drafting notes to a few chapters of the book of Acts I realized that much of what I was writing consisted of objections to the English version I was using: "The translation says 'X,' but the Greek original really means 'Y.'" Rather than waste the reader's time castigating third parties (translators), I decided to try translating the Greek text myself and discovered that I liked the result. Thus the *Jewish New Testament* was born — as an afterthought. From then on I keyed my comments to the *JNT* and dealt with what I considered mistaken renderings in other versions as being distinct from what the New Testament itself says (that is, from what I understand it to be saying).

I intended to publish both translation and commentary in a single volume, not only because they complement each other, but because I believed that some of the more controversial renderings in the *JNT* needed my *JNTC* notes to defend them. Unfortunately the rhythm of my life made it hard for me to finish this project quickly. When the translation was essentially done but I was still working on the commentary, a friend said, "Publish the Jewish New Testament by itself. Both Jews and Christians need to see what a Jewish book the New Testament is. Don't worry about defending it — the Word of God can stand by itself. Later your commentary will serve its purpose." He convinced me, so I published the first edition of the *JNT* in 1989; there have been three subsequent printings.

While the *JNT* was greeted with joy by most Messianic Jews, many Christians, some non-Messianic Jews and a number of reviewers, there were, of course, critics. Whenever I read a negative comment I considered unjustified, I felt frustrated that the commentary was not there to provide a defense. Now it is, and I hope it will stimulate intelligent discussion of the Jewish issues surrounding the New Testament.

The *Jewish New Testament.* Since the *JNTC* is based on the *JNT,* a few words about it seem in order. The *JNT* expresses the New Testament's essential Jewishness in three ways, which I call cosmetic (or superficial), cultural-religious, and theological.

- Cosmetic elements — such as using "execution-stake" instead of "cross," "Ya'akov" instead of "James," and, of course, "Yeshua the Messiah" instead of "Jesus Christ" — are the most obvious; and their frequency has a collective effect.

- Cultural-religious elements embed the Gospel more securely in its Jewish setting; two examples are my use of the word "*tzitzit*" instead of "fringe" at Mattityahu (Matthew) 9:20 to describe what the woman with a hemorrhage touched, and "*Chanukkah*" instead of "the feast of dedication" at Yochanan (John) 10:22.

- Theological elements include translating Messianic Jews (Hebrews) 8:6 so as to show that the New Covenant has been not merely "established" but "given as *Torah*," and rendering Romans 10:4 "...the goal at which the *Torah* aims is the Messiah," not "...Christ is the end of the law."

For a fuller discussion of the character of the *JNT,* see Section V below.

Messianic Jewish Commentaries on the New Testament. The *JNTC* is, so far as I know, only the second commentary on the entire New Testament ever written by a Messianic Jew. The first was by Jehiel Zvi Lichtenstein (1827-1912), whose *Commentary to the New Testament,* written in Hebrew, was published in installments by the Institutum Delitzschianum in Leipzig, Germany, between 1891 and 1904, with the text in the traditional Hebrew block print and the comments in Rashi script (I have cited portions of it in my own notes to the General Letters and the first part of Revelation.) He followed in the footsteps of Joiachim Heinrich Biesenthal (1800-1886), who wrote commentaries on the Gospels, Romans and Hebrews, as well as on Psalms and Isaiah. In this century Victor Buksbazen, Charles Lee Feinberg, Moshe Immanuel Ben-Maeir, Louis Goldberg and Arnold Fruchtenbaum are among the Jewish believers who have produced commentaries to one or more books of the

Bible. The "Netivyah" organization in Jerusalem, under the direction of Joseph Shulam, is preparing a Hebrew commentary on the New Testament which, like this one, draws on Jewish sources and tries to recover Jewish understandings; the first product of this effort will be a substantial commentary on Romans. There remains a need for additional Messianic Jewish commentaries on all the books of the Bible, both *Tanakh* (Old Testament) and New Testament.

The *Complete Jewish Bible.* I produced the *Jewish New Testament* in order to show how Jewish the New Testament is. I never intended to translate the *Tanakh* from Hebrew into English because no one questions its Jewishness. Nevertheless, in response to an expressed demand, I am now preparing the *Complete Jewish Bible,* consisting of the *Jewish New Testament* bound together with a stylistically adapted existing translation of the *Tanakh.* Readers will then have the entire Bible in a single volume, with the *JNT* as its New Testament portion.

III WHAT KINDS OF COMMENTS ARE IN THE *JNTC?*

The *JNTC* draws on a number of approaches, some familiar, some less so, in order to accomplish its purposes. These include:

Historical Notes explaining the situation of the writer, original readers and subjects of the passage, often with particular focus on the Jewish background.

Linguistic Notes explaining points of Greek grammar or the sense of Greek words, and frequently explaining similar points of the Hebrew language, grammar and thoughtforms underlying the Greek text.

Exegetical Notes explaining what a passage means. These are sometimes provided because the text is not clear to a modern reader lacking the original context. But often I write them because the text has typically been *mis*understood by Christians or by Jews or by both; in such cases I must demonstrate that the traditional misunderstanding is wrong, as well as explain why my translation and/or interpretation is right.

Notes Pointing Out the Writers' Jewish Ways of Thinking. Since the writers of the New Testament were all Jewish (Luke is thought to have been a proselyte to Judaism), I often point out their rabbinic patterns of discussion and argument.

Parallels in Jewish Literature. I quote New Testament parallels from ancient, medieval and modern Jewish sources, including the following:

- *The Apocrypha.* A collection of 15 Jewish books written in the 3rd to 1st centuries B.C.E. They are excluded from the *Tanakh*, although Roman Catholics include them in the biblical canon. Among them are Tobit, Judith, Wisdom of Solomon, Sirach (Ecclesiasticus), Baruch, Prayer of Manasseh and 1 & 2 Maccabees. All Catholic English editions and a few Protestant ones include the Apocrypha. There is also a critical edition by R. H. Charles.

- *The Pseudepigrapha.* More than 60 books written between the 3rd century B.C.E. and the 1st century C.E. and usually attributed to *Tanakh* figures by their actual authors. Most either elaborate on *Tanakh* themes or are apocalyptic in character (see my note to Revelation 1:1). There is an older English edition by R. H. Charles and a more recent, more complete one edited by James H. Charlesworth.

- *The Talmud.* Part I is the *Mishna*, a topical presentation of the Jewish Oral *Torah* with rabbinic discussion of it; it was compiled around 220 C.E. by Y'hudah HaNasi (Judah the Prince) and consists of six sections divided into 63 tractates. Hillel, Shammai, Gamli'el and Akiva are among the well-known rabbis whose contributions are included.

  Part II is the *Gemara*, consisting of wide-ranging commentary on Mishna tractates by rabbis who lived in the 3rd to 5th centuries C.E. The Jerusalem Talmud, with Gemara by rabbis mostly from the Land of Israel, is older, smaller and less widely known than the Babylonian Talmud, with its Gemara written largely by Diaspora rabbis living in or near Babylon.

  Blackman's Mishna is a Hebrew-English diglot edition. The Soncino English edition of the Talmud is well known. Adin Steinsaltz's Hebrew edition of the Talmud is now being published volume by volume in English.

- *The Halakhic Midrashim.* The first term means "law-related," the second "discussions, homilies, allegories." These compilations from the 4th century C.E. report much older material and consist of the *Mekhilta* (on Exodus), *Sifra* (on Leviticus), and *Sifre* (on Numbers and Deuteronomy). The Mekhilta has been published in English by the Jewish Publication Society and Sifre on Deuteronomy by Yale University.

- *The Midrash Rabbah.* The final editing was done in the 6th to 10th centuries but most of the material is much older. It includes *midrashim* related to the Pentateuch and the Five Scrolls. Soncino has published an English edition.

Among medieval sources I cite are Rashi (Rabbi Shlomo Yitzchaki, 1040-1105), the most famous Jewish commentator on the Bible and the Talmud, and the *Rambam* (*R*abbi *M*oshe *B*en-*M*aimon, also known as Maimonides, 1135-1204).

There are historical and conceptual connections between what the rabbis wrote and nearly every line of the New Testament. However, I have avoided rabbinic overload in the *JNTC* — since there is no need for it to duplicate what Hermann Strack and Paul Billerbeck did rather exhaustively in their six-volume *Kommentär Zum Neuen Testament Aus Talmud Und Midrasch* (Munich: C. H. Beck'sche Verlagsbuchhandlung, 1926, reprinted 1978), although not all of their references are equally relevant. My own purpose in these notes that draw on Jewish writings is neither to prove that the New Testament copied rabbinic Judaism nor the opposite, but simply to present a sampling of the many parallels; see my note to Mattityahu (Matthew) 6:7.

Modern Jewish Issues. In the Western tradition a scholarly commentary does not discuss modern issues that have no obvious direct relationship to the biblical text. By contrast, I seek them out — first, because Jewish commentators tend to do exactly that, since they see life as a seamless whole; and second, because people's views on modern ethical, political, social and psychological subjects may be presenting symptoms of deeper-lying objections to aspects of the New Testament.

For example, I have a note on when, how and to whom the Gospel should be proclaimed — with specific reference to evangelism of Jewish people — at 1 Kefa (1 Peter) 3:15–16 ("[Be] ready to give a reasoned answer to anyone who asks you to explain the hope you have in you — yet with humility and fear"). At 1 Corinthians 4:1–2 ("We do not use the word of God deceitfully") is a related note on whether Jewish evangelism is inherently a deceitful enterprise; many Jews and not a few Christians have already concluded that it is; while my note, as you might expect, defends Jewish evangelism. Similarly, discussions of Jewish-Gentile intermarriage and Jewish assimilation to Gentile culture are anchored to appropriate verses.

Other Jewish issues arise in Christian settings. Many Christians think that the Church has replaced the Jews as God's people and that the Land of Israel is no longer promised to them. Not a few verses provide opportunities to counter these mistaken views, as well as to show that the New Testament gives no ground for any form of antisemitism and is certainly not antisemitic itself.

Theological Issues Arising in Jewish-Christian Dialogue. The best example is the lengthy note on Romans 5:12–21, which I make the occasion for a theological discussion of "original sin," a notion which, as the average person understands it, is unacceptable in any form to non-Messianic Jews, and seems peculiar to a significant number of Christians. My object is to make sense of an offputting concept and show how it can be useful.

At a number of places I address such questions as, "Is Yeshua God?" and "Is God a Trinity?" With these too I try to push past the reflex responses of "Absolutely" (Christian) and "Absolutely not" (Jewish) in order to discuss the substance of the matter — what positive and negative answers might mean, and whether both Christian and Jewish contexts might admit of less confrontational formulations without compromising the Scriptural data.

Devotional Elements. This is not a devotional commentary, but I feel free to introduce devotional material, partly to give an added dimension to the commentary and partly to enhance spiritual content.

Homiletical Elements. Likewise, while this commentary is neither a collection of sermons nor a guide for preachers writing them, I think its interest and usefulness is increased by containing some material of this kind.

Advocacy and Apologetics. Much of the commentary is intended to promulgate a Messianic Jewish approach to the Scriptures and defend it, sometimes against non-Messianic Jewish viewpoints, sometimes against various Christian theological positions and sometimes against secular attitudes.

God exists. Yeshua is Israel's Messiah. The Bible is God's Word to humanity. Yeshua's atoning death is necessary for everyone's salvation. The Church has not replaced the Jews as God's people. These are propositions that can be defended, and in this commentary I do not hesitate to do so. I have not obligated myself to take a neutral stand on all issues, although I do on some — especially those I do not perceive as closely tied to Jewish questions.

Challenges and Exhortations. Sometimes, taking the role of preacher, I go beyond advocacy and apologetics to challenging and exhorting the reader to take responsible action.

Personal Anecdotes and Illustrations. On occasion I introduce personal anecdotes and information that would be out of place in a more formal type of commentary.

Bible Helps. There are on the market study-Bibles, Bible dictionaries, Bible encyclopedias, introductions to the Bible and many other kinds of reader's helps. They explain how the Bible and its individual books are organized, by and for whom they were written, the general historical context, and details necessary for understanding that the modern reader might lack. The Introduction to the *JNT* includes some elements of this kind; but, for the most part, the *JNTC* does not duplicate what these works do; although it does take on itself this kind of task in relation to Jewish issues. For example, I don't outline every book of the New Testament, but I do outline Romans, because knowing its structure is important for understanding the Jewishness of its message.

Redundancy for Convenience and for Education. I have built a considerable amount of redundancy into the *JNTC*. A reader with the patience to read straight through it might be distressed to see how often I repeat myself. Most of this is purposeful, intended to serve the more typical reader, who looks up a passage and does not know that I may have made the same point elsewhere. I could eliminate the redundancy by referring to other notes, and I have done a great deal of this. Still, I have left some of the repetitious material, partly to save the reader from having to flip through the book overly much, and partly to emphasize ideas I especially hope the reader will embrace and make his own.

Some Things Are Left Out. I don't try to explain everything. For example, at Galatians 3:4 I note that "other interpretations are possible" but don't say what they are. The interested reader should consult a critical commentary.

Also, you will probably be able to identify topics not addressed which you think should have been. If you realize that volumes this size and larger have been written on a single verse of the New Testament and even on a single word, it must be clear that much that might be said has not been said. For example, I have written very little about textual issues. Generally, I accept the United Bible Societies critical text; but, apart from a few remarks in the *JNT* Introduction and footnotes in the *JNT* itself, "lower criticism" (analysis of textual problems with a view to determining which version of a text is authentic) is rarely what the *JNTC* does. Some will spot Jewish issues that I missed or dealt with in a way they consider incomplete or otherwise unsatisfactory. A few issues that have Jewish ramifications I dealt with briefly, even though others have written on them at length — such as on which day of the week Yeshua was executed and whether Communion should be offered daily, weekly, monthly, yearly, or whenever one wishes. I am only one person, and this is only one book. I hope others will fill in my gaps and explore new territory.

Correcting *JNT* Mistakes. The *JNTC* points out errors in early printings of the *JNT* (other than "typos") and corrects them in the appropriate note. See also numbered paragraph 7 of Section V below.

IV THE *JNTC* AND MESSIANIC JUDAISM

Messianic Judaism: 100% Jewish and 100% Messianic. Messianic Judaism defines its aim as being 100% Jewish and 100% faithful to the Bible (which consists of the *Tanakh* plus the New Testament). It thus refuses to conform itself to other people's categories.

Christianity's Main Objection: "You Are Rebuilding the 'Middle Wall of Partition.'" The Christian's main problem with Messianic Judaism is often expressed in these words: "You're rebuilding the 'middle wall of partition' which the Messiah has broken down (Ephesians 2:11–16). Your emphasis on Jewishness will erode the unity of Jews and Gentiles in the Messianic Community (the Church)." I deny that we are doing any such thing. Many of the notes in the *JNTC* are devoted to refuting this mis-impression of Messianic Jewish aims.

Judaism's Main Objection: "You Can't Be Jewish and Believe in Jesus." The most common Jewish problem with Messianic Judaism can be stated as follows: "You are attempting the impossible — you can't accept Yeshua as the Messiah and still be Jewish." The objection assumes what requires proof — whereas the *JNTC* shows that the opposite is true: not only were Yeshua and his first followers all Jewish, but throughout the last two thousand years there have been Jewish people who honored Yeshua as Messiah, Savior and Lord, while remaining as much part of and loyal to the Jewish people as the Jewish community would allow.

The Challenge: Creating a Viable Messianic Judaism. Nevertheless, the task of creating a viable Messianic Judaism that relates seriously to the history and evolution of both Judaism and Christianity during the last twenty centuries remains a largely unaccomplished task. I have written two books that deal with this goal systematically (something the *JNTC* cannot do, because of its verse-by-verse format). My book *Messianic Jewish Manifesto* is meant to help Messianic Jews organize thinking and action as they pursue the exciting challenges facing the Messianic Jewish movement. An abridgement entitled *Restoring the Jewishness of the Gospel: A Message for Christians* is addressed to Christians for whom the Jewishness of the Gospel is an unfamiliar idea. Someday I hope to complete the trilogy with a book explaining Messianic Judaism to non-Messianic Jews.

V GETTING THE MOST OUT OF THE *JNTC*

Use the *JNT*. Since the *Jewish New Testament Commentary* is a companion volume to the *Jewish New Testament,* one of its functions is to explain the *JNT*'s departures from more usual renderings. The *JNTC* can be read with other versions, but the flow of interaction between text and commentary will necessarily be impaired, since the commentary takes the *JNT* renderings as given and frequently explains why other renderings are wrong. Moreover, the footnotes and Scripture Index of the *JNT* give references for all 695 *Tanakh* verses cited in the New Testament, and its glossaries give English equivalents for over 400 Hebrew names and terms found in the *JNT;* the *JNTC* assumes the reader has this information and rarely duplicates it. Therefore, to get the most out of the *JNTC,* use the *JNT.*

Read the Introduction to the *JNTC* Index on page 859 to make best use of this very extensive but non-intensive tool for finding names, topics and words in this book.

Read the *JNT* Introduction. It is an essential part of this Introduction to the *JNTC*. I do not repeat here what I wrote there. However, to stimulate interest and refresh memories I am listing its eight sections with brief annotated contents. The reader can see that it discusses a number of general issues that are inseparable from the subject matter of the *JNTC*.

1. **Why the *Jewish New Testament?*** The *JNT* is needed to show Jews and Christians alike that the New Testament is a Jewish book, to combat Christian antisemitism, to deal with Jewish misgivings about the Gospel, and to help heal history's greatest schism — the separation between the Jewish Community and the Church.

2. **The Bible.** Its central message is that man, both individually and corporately, has sinned and needs salvation; and that God graciously has provided it through Yeshua the Messiah to those who trust and obey him. The *Tanakh* (Old Testament) and the New Testament are interdependent: two testaments, one Bible — given to God's people Israel, the Jews, to whom Gentiles are added without converting to Judaism when they trust in the God of Israel and his Messiah.

3. **The New Testament.** It contains the four Gospels, the Book of Acts, the thirteen letters of Sha'ul (Paul), the eight General Letters, and the Book of Revelation; there are paragraphs on each of these five divisions. There are discussions of the language of the New Testament, dating the New Testament, the canon of the New Testament, and whether tradition and scholarship are in agreement or at odds.

4. **How the *Jewish New Testament* Expresses the New Testament's Jewishness.** Three ways, as explained above (cosmetically, culturally/religiously, and theologically); also by using "Jewish English," defined as including Hebrew and Yiddish expressions which at least some English-speakers who are Jewish incorporate into everyday speech.

5. **Translation Issues.** Two main issues: (1) "literal" versus "dynamic" translations (known to some by the negative-valence term "paraphrases"), and (2) the degree to which the translator's own interpretations should affect his translation (my view is that they do anyway, so he should admit it; not only that, but where there is more than one possible meaning he should not translate ambiguously but choose the best meaning and express that meaning well). The Greek text used for the *JNT* is the United Bible Societies' critical text, 1975 edition, which is the same as Nestle-Aland.

6. **Reasons For Certain Renderings.** Here I gave a preview of the kinds of things I intended to do in the *JNTC*. I chose seven passages and explained why I translated as I did. Three examples: Did Yeshua "fill full" or "fulfill" the *Torah?* (Mattityahu 5:17). Does "binding and loosing" (Mattityahu 18:18) refer to controlling demons or determining Messianic *halakhah* (law, communal practice)? Do Sha'ul's phrases, "works of the law" and "under the law," refer to the *Torah* or to legalism? There I wrote a paragraph on each question; in the *JNTC* I have answered far more extensively.

7. ***Tanakh* Prophecies Fulfilled by Yeshua the Messiah.** A list of 54 *Tanakh* prophecies about the Messiah's first coming, with New Testament passages showing how Yeshua fulfilled them. Of some 50 false Messiahs known to Jewish history, none has fulfilled more than a few; he fulfilled them all. Unfortunately the list contains errors in the first three paperback printings and the first hardcover printing; please correct them as follows:

PAGE	PROPHECY	NOW READS	SHOULD READ
xxvi	1st	"bruise" the serpent's "heel"	"bruise" or "crush" the serpent's "head"
	2nd	18:18, 22:18	[Delete]
	6th	11:23	13:23
	7th	5:11	1:18
xxviii	8th	7:48	[Delete]
	18th	Mattityahu 27:31, 39–44, 67–68	Mattityahu 26:67–68; 27:31, 39–44
xxix	1st	20:25	20:35
	4th	24:31(20)	34:21(20)
	6th	Mattityahu 2:1; Luke 3:1,23	Romans 5:6, 1 Kefa 3:18

8. **Using the *Jewish New Testament.*** The *JNT* text has *Tanakh* quotations in boldface, with book, chapter and verse in footnotes at the bottom of each column. An index of the 695 *Tanakh* citations is found at the end. Two maps show *Eretz-Israel* (the Land of Israel) in the time of Yeshua, and the Eastern Mediterranean and Near East in the Second Temple Period; there is a key to place-names. Glossaries define Hebrew and Aramaic names and terms used in place of the usual English ones; a "reverse glossary" supplies Hebrew and Aramaic equivalents of traditional English words and names.

VI CONVENTIONS USED IN THE *JNTC*

General Abbreviations. Standard abbreviations include "v." and "vv." ("verse" and "verses"), "f." and "ff." ("and the following" verse/verses) and "*ad loc*." (Latin *ad locum*, "at the place" where the same passage is discussed). The *Jewish New Testament* is abbreviated "*JNT*" and the King James Version of the Bible, also known as the Authorized Version, is often referred to as "KJV." Other versions are not abbreviated. The abbreviations "C.E." and "B.C.E." stand for "Common Era" (A.D.) and "Before the Common Era" (B.C.); on these conventions see note at Mattityahu (Matthew) 2:1.

Names and Abbreviations of New Testament Books. Some of the names of New Testament books used in the *JNT* and *JNTC* are the Hebrew names, listed in the following table with their more usual English equivalents. These names are spelled out in full at the beginning of a sentence or when the reference is to a whole chapter (without verse references). When there is a verse reference, the following abbreviations are used:

Ac	Acts of the Emissaries (Acts of the Apostles)	Pp	Philippians
1C	1 Corinthians	Ro	Romans
2C	2 Corinthians	Rv	Revelation
Co	Colossians	1 Th	1 Thessalonians
Ep	Ephesians	2 Th	2 Thessalonians
Ga	Galatians	Ti	Titus
1 Ke	1 Kefa (1 Peter)	1 Ti	1 Timothy
2 Ke	2 Kefa (2 Peter)	2 Ti	2 Timothy
Lk	Luke	Ya	Ya'akov (James)
MJ	Messianic Jews (Hebrews)	Yd	Y'hudah (Jude)
Mk	Mark	Yn	Yochanan (John)
Mt	Mattityahu (Matthew)	1 Yn	1 Yochanan (1 John)
Pm	Philemon	2 Yn	2 Yochanan (2 John)
		3 Yn	3 Yochanan (3 John)

Examples:

See 1C 15:3	See 1 Corinthians, Chapter 15, verse 3
See 1 Corinthians 15	See 1 Corinthians, Chapter 15
See Yd 6	See Y'hudah (Jude), verse 6
Yochanan 1:12 says...	[No abbreviation ("Yn") at the start of a sentence.]

Names, Order and Versification of *Tanakh* (Old Testament) Books. The traditional English names of *Tanakh* books are used, and they are spelled out in full, never abbreviated. When several are listed, the order is that of the Hebrew Bible, which is as follows:

PENTATEUCH
(*TORAH* or *CHUMASH*)

Genesis
Exodus
Leviticus
Numbers
Deuteronomy

FORMER PROPHETS
(*N'VI'IM*)

Joshua
Judges
1 Samuel
2 Samuel
1 Kings
2 Kings

LATTER PROPHETS
(*N'VI'IM*)

Isaiah
Jeremiah
Ezekiel
(The Twelve Prophets)
Hosea
Joel
Amos
Obadiah
Jonah
Micah
Nahum
Habakkuk
Zephaniah
Haggai
Zechariah
Malachi

WRITINGS
(*K'TUVIM*)

Psalms
Proverbs
Job
(The Five Scrolls)
Song of Songs
Ruth
Lamentations
Ecclesiastes
Esther
Daniel
Ezra
Nehemiah
1 Chronicles
2 Chronicles

Chapter and verse references are as in the Hebrew Bible; where the Christian Bible chapter and verse numbers differ, these are shown in parentheses immediately after.

Examples:

See Exodus 20:12–17(12–14), Joel 3:2(2:29), Malachi 3:23–24(4:5–6), Psalm 51:17(15), Ecclesiastes 5:1–2(2–3), Nehemiah 3:38(4:6).

Sequence of Notes in the *JNTC*. Notes to a large group of verses precede notes to a smaller group of verses, which in turn precede notes to individual verses and portions thereof.

Hypothetical example:

CHAPTER 8

8:1–9:6	Note to the passage starting with Chapter 8, verse 1 and ending with Chapter 9, verse 6.
1–13	Note to Chapter 8, verses 1–13
1	Note to Chapter 8, verse 1
2–3	Note to Chapter 8, verses 2–3
3	Note to Chapter 8, verse 3
5a	Note to Chapter 8, first part of verse 5
5b–6	Note to Chapter 8, second part of verse 5 and verse 6
10–12	Note to Chapter 8, verses 10–12

CHAPTER 9

1–6	Note to Chapter 9, verses 1–6
7	Note to Chapter 9, verse 7

References to *JNT* Text and *JNTC* Notes. References to the text of the *JNT* are by book, chapter and verse; *JNTC* notes are referred to by these four abbreviations:

N	note
NN	notes
&N	and note
&NN	and notes

Examples:

See Mt 5:3	See Mattityahu, Chapter 5, verse 3
See Mt 5:3N	See the note to Mattityahu, Chapter 5, verse 3
See Mt 5:3&N	See Mattityahu, Chapter 5, verse 3, and its note
See Ro 10:4–8NN	See the notes to Romans, Chapter 10, verses 4–8
See Ro 10:4–8&NN	See Romans, Chapter 10, verses 4–8, and their notes
See Ro 10:6–8N	See the note (singular) to Romans, Chapter 10, verses 6–8

Use of Boldface Type in the Notes. A citation from the verse(s) being commented on is printed in **boldface** type. At the start of a paragraph it usually indicates that the commentary is on only that portion of the verse(s). Quotations from other parts of the Bible appear in ordinary Roman type.

Pronunciation of Hebrew, Aramaic and Greek Names and Terms. Hebrew and Aramaic names and terms are transliterated in a way that facilitates Israeli pronunciation. Vowels sound like those italicized in the following words: f*a*ther, *ai*sle, b*e*d, n*ei*gh, wh*ey*, *i*nvest (usually not accented) or mar*i*ne (usually accented), *o*bey, r*u*le. As for consonants, "ch" is pronounced as in Johann Sebastian Bach, and so is "*kh*"; "g" is always hard (give); other consonants are more or less as in English. The guttural stop *aleph* is often represented by an apostrophe (') before a vowel (example: Natan'el, pronounced Na-tan-'el and not Na-ta-nel). The stronger guttural stop *'ayin* (deeper in the throat, closer to a hard "g" sound) is usually represented by a reverse apostrophe (') before or after a vowel.

In transliterating Greek names and terms I have made little effort toward helping the reader pronounce the words correctly — by which I mean as they would be pronounced in modern Athens, not as they would be mispronounced in Christian seminaries. I use "*e*" to signify the Greek letter "*epsilon*" and "*ê*" to signify "*êta*," "*o*" to signify "*omicron*" and "*ô*" to signify "*ômega*." I use both "*u*" and "*v*" for "*upsilon*"; this is my one attempt to assist the reader toward correct pronunciation. (However, where "*u*" is written, the correct pronunciation is not "oo" but "ee," as it is also for "*i*," "*ê*," "*ei*," and "*oi*". Also "*e*" and "*ai*" are pronounced "eh," and "*ou*" is "oo." The consonant "*b*" has a "v" sound, "*d*" sounds like "th" in "then," "*th*" is as in "thin," and "*g*" is either a "y" as in "kayak" or a softened hard "g" (a "gh" sound; try voicing the "ch" in "Bach"). For further information consult any modern Greek language text or phrasebook.)

Hebrew and English Names. While in the text of the *JNT* itself I use only the Hebraized forms of personal and place names, in the commentary I allow myself to use both these and the names more familiar to readers of English. Thus I switch between "Avraham" and "Abraham," "Yitzchak" and "Isaac," "Ya'akov" and "Jacob" *(Tanakh)* or "James" (New Testament), etc. See the *JNT* Glossary and Reverse Glossary for clarifications.

VII ACKNOWLEDGMENTS

The word "acknowledgment" pales against the debt of gratitude I owe my parents of blessed memory, Harold Melrose Stern (1892–1981) and Marion Levi Stern (1899–1976) for the love, ethical orientation, upbringing in the Jewish community and other blessings they gave me.

The term also fails to express what I owe to my wife, Martha Frances (Frankel) Stern, who has been not only an *eshet-chayil* ("woman of valor," Proverbs 31:10–31) and an *ezer k'negdi* ("helper standing by me," Genesis 2:18), but who also read through the entire manuscript and offered wise advice; I take full responsibility for any deficiencies due to my stubbornly failing to heed it.

Dr. Paul Ellingworth, translation consultant for the United Bible Societies and editor of its publication *The Bible Translator*, spent three full weeks with me reviewing every word of an earlier version of the *Jewish New Testament*. His advice improved my translation, and if the reader disagrees with some of my renderings even after reading my defense in this commentary, don't blame him.

Joseph Shulam, a Messianic Jew who is very knowledgeable of both Judaism and the New Testament and unique in his manner of relating them to each other, is my close friend and frequent consultant. I am sure this commentary is the better for our conversations.

Martha and I have known Barry and Steffi Rubin since the mid 1970's. Since 1989, Barry, who is the President of Messianic Jewish Communications, has also managed Jewish New Testament Publications. Steffi, a wonderful artist, typeset the *JNTC*. We are grateful for their work and happy in our friendship.

Besides expressing special appreciation to each of these people, I want to add that I have learned and benefited from many others in the Messianic Jewish community of Israel, the United States and the rest of the world. I have also gained knowledge from teachers and friends who are Gentile Christians, non-Messianic Jews, and persons neither Jewish nor Christian. Without my naming them, I hope they will recognize my intention to thank them.

Finally — words can only point — thanks to my God, the God of Abraham, Isaac and Jacob, and to his Messiah Yeshua, my and the Jewish people's savior and Lord. *Barukh attah, Adonai, Eloheynu, Melekh-ha'olam, shehecheyanu v'kimanu v'higi'anu lazman hazeh*! ("Praised be you, Lord our God, King of the universe, who has kept us alive, preserved us and enabled us to arrive at this point in time!")

David H. Stern
78 Manahat, 96901 Jerusalem, Israel
Rosh-HaShanah 5753 (September 1992)

ADDENDUM TO THIRD EDITION (1994)

With this edition I am inaugurating a system for adding new information to the commentary without disturbing the original layout and Index. Where I have something new to say (more than a few words long) I am putting it in an appendix rather than in the original notes. The appendix begins on page 929, immediately following the Index.

David H. Stern
Yom HaAtzma'ut 5754 (April 1994)

ADDENDUM TO SIXTH EDITION (1998)

This is the first edition to appear after the publication of my *Complete Jewish Bible*, my version of the *Tanakh* plus the *JNT*. For stylistic reasons, the *JNT* as it appears in the *CJB* is slightly different from previous published editions of the *JNT*. I have made those changes as few as possible, so that users of the *JNTC* will not have difficulties using it with the *CJB*'s *JNT*.

David H. Stern
Chanukkah 5759 (December 1998)

THE GOOD NEWS OF YESHUA THE MESSIAH,
AS REPORTED BY

MATTITYAHU (MATTHEW)

CHAPTER 1

1–16 The New Testament begins with **the genealogy** of Yeshua in order to show that he meets the requirements set by the *Tanakh* for who the Messiah must be — a descendant of **Avraham** (Genesis 22:18), **Ya'akov** (Numbers 24:17), **Y'hudah** (Genesis 49:10), **Yishai** (Isaiah 11:1), **David** (2 Samuel 7:13; see below on "Son of David") and **Z'rubavel** (Haggai 2:22–23). All these names appear in vv. 1–16. This genealogy recalls the pattern of those in the *Tanakh* (Genesis 5, 10; 1 Chronicles 1–9, etc.).

The genealogy of the Messiah as reported by Luke is different from the one here; see Lk 3:23–38&N.

1 **"Yeshua the Messiah"** is rendered "Jesus Christ" in other English versions, as if the man's first name were "Jesus" and his last name "Christ." Neither is the case. "*Yeshua'*" is Jesus' name in Hebrew and Aramaic, the languages he spoke; in his thirty-some years on earth people called him Yeshua. The word "Jesus" represents the efforts of English-speakers to pronounce the name of the Messiah as it appears in the Greek manuscripts of the New Testament, "*Iêsous*" — yee-**soos** in modern Greek, perhaps yay-**soos** in ancient *Koinê* Greek, which began to displace Aramaic as the *lingua franca* of the Near East after Alexander's conquests (331–323 B.C.E.). In turn the word "*Iêsous*" represents the ancient Greek-speakers' attempts at pronouncing "*Yeshua'*." By using Hebrew "Yeshua" throughout, the *JNT* calls attention to the Jewishness of the Messiah. On the name "Yeshua" itself see v. 21&N.

The Messiah. The Greek word here is "*christos*," which means the same thing as Hebrew "*mashiach*," namely, "anointed" or "poured on." The significance of being known as "The Anointed One" is that both kings and *cohanim* (priests) were invested with their authority in a ceremony of anointing with olive oil. Thus, inherent in the concept of "Messiah" is the idea of being given God's priestly and kingly authority.

The Greek word "*Christos*" is usually brought over into English as "Christ." In two verses of the New Testament (Yn 1:41, 4:25) the Greek text has "*Messias*," obviously, like English "Messiah," a transliteration of the Hebrew word; there the *JNT* uses "*Mashiach*" (see Yn 1:41N).

The *JNT* also renders "*Christos*" as "*Mashiach*" in two narratives where its specifically Jewish significance stands out in bold relief: at 16:15 and at 26:63 (and equivalently at Mk 8:29, 14:61; Lk 9:20, 22:67). Others might have used this criterion to introduce "*Mashiach*" in other passages, for example, at Ac 2:31, 36, 38. A translator's decision to use "Christ," "Messiah" or "*Mashiach*" depends on the purpose of his translation; in the end it may come down to his intuition or personal preference.

But usually in the text of the *JNT* Greek *Christos* is rendered by "Messiah"; "Christ" does not appear even once. This is because "Messiah" has meaning in Jewish religion, tradition and culture; whereas the word "Christ" has an alien ring and a negative connotation because of the persecutions Jews have suffered from those claiming to be his followers. Further, the use of the word "Messiah" more than 380 times in the text of the *JNT* is a continual reminder that the New Testament claims Yeshua to be none other than the promised *Mashiach* for whom the Jewish people have yearned. The English word "Christ" does not point to Yeshua's fulfillment of Jewish hopes and biblical prophecy.

Son of. The Hebrew word "*ben*" ("son," "son of") is commonly used in three distinctive ways in the Bible and in Judaism:

(1) In both the Bible and in Judaism a man is normally identified as the son of his father. For example, if Sam Levine's son Joe is called up to read from the *Torah* scroll in the synagogue, he will be announced not as Joseph Levine but as *Yosef ben-Shmu'el* ("Joseph, son of Samuel").

(2) "*Ben*" can also mean not the actual son but a more distant descendant. as is the case in this verse: **David** and **Avraham** were distant ancestors of Yeshua (also v. 8: Yoram was not the father but the great-great-grandfather of Uziyahu).

(3) Thirdly, "*ben*" can be used more broadly to mean "having the characteristics of," and this too applies here: Yeshua had qualities found both in Avraham and in King David.

Son of David. Avraham and David are singled out because they have unique importance in the Messiah's lineage. The term "**Son of David**" is actually one of the titles of the Messiah, based on the *Tanakh*'s prophecies that the Messiah will be a descendent of David and will sit on David's throne forever (for the *Tanakh* references see Ac 13:23&N). While "Son of David" does not appear as a Messianic title in the *Tanakh* and is first seen as such in the pseudepigraphic Psalms of Solomon 17:23, 36, written in the first century B.C.E., the New Testament records the use of this term some 15–20 times, and it has been used continuously in Judaism till the present.

Son of Avraham. This term is significant in at least four ways:

(1) Both King David and King Yeshua trace their ancestry back to the individual chosen by God as the father of the Jewish people (Genesis 12:1–3).

(2) Yeshua is the promised "seed of Avraham" (Genesis 13:15, explained by Ga 3:16).

(3) The Messiah's mystical identity with the Jewish people (see 2:15N) is hinted at, since every Jew is a son of Avraham (3:9).

(4) Yeshua also has a *mystical* identity with everyone who believes in him, whether Jewish or Gentile (Ro 4:1, 11, 17–20; Ga 3:29).

3, 5, 6, 16 Tamar... Rachav... Rut... the wife of Uriyah (Bat-sheva)... **Miryam.** Women, especially those born Gentiles, were rarely included in biblical genealogies. The first four were Gentile women whom God honored by including them among the recorded ancestors of Yeshua the Jewish Messiah — through whom Gentiles, women and slaves are saved equally with Jews, men and free (Ga 3:28&N). On whether these women became Jews or continued to be Gentiles see Ac 16:1&N.

16 Yosef, the husband of Miryam, from whom was born... Yeshua. The change in language from the litany, "X was the father of Y," signals that Yeshua was not conceived in the usual way; other passages state that the Holy Spirit of God overshadowed Miryam, causing her to become pregnant without sexual union (vv. 18, 20; Lk 1:27, 31, 34–38; also see vv. 18–25&NN, Lk 3:23–38&N).

The Yeshua who was called the Messiah. This somewhat awkward phrase calls attention to the fact that the genealogy leads up to this particular person named Yeshua, the particular Yeshua who was known as the Messiah. There is no implication that he was not the Messiah; **he was called the Messiah** because he was and is.

18–25 On the conception and birth of Yeshua compare Lk 1:26–38, 2:1–7; Yn 1:1–2, 14.

18 Engaged. The Hebrew/Aramaic word for betrothal is "*kiddushin*," which signifies "sanctification, separation," i.e., the setting aside and separating of a particular woman for a particular man. According to the Mishna, adultery during the betrothal period is a more serious sin than adultery after marriage.

The Mishna specifies four kinds of death penalty in descending order of gravity: stoning, burning, beheading and strangling (Sanhedrin 7:1). A man who has intercourse with a betrothed girl is subject to the same penalty as one who has intercourse with his mother, namely, stoning (Sanhedrin 7:4). Someone who has intercourse with another man's wife is liable to death by strangling (Sanhedrin 11:1).

Today, partly in order to eliminate the possibility of committing this grave sin, formal Jewish betrothal (*kiddushin* or *'erusin*) and marriage (*nisu'in*) are generally combined in a single ceremony.

Ruach HaKodesh, Hebrew for "Holy Spirit." The term appears in the *Tanakh* (Isaiah 51:13(11), 63:10–11) and is equivalent to the "Spirit of God" (*Ruach-Elohim*), first seen in Genesis 1:2 as having "moved on the face of the waters" before God said, "Let there be light." From this verse, Isaiah 48:16 and other places in the Bible it can be learned that the Holy Spirit is divine, not less or other than God. Under the terms of the New Covenant, Yeshua sends the Holy Spirit to dwell in any person who trusts God through the Messiah. The Holy Spirit gives such a person power for service, guidance into God's truth, gifts to facilitate holy living, and fruits of righteous behavior. (The King James Version of the English Bible uses the term "holy ghost," which has nothing to do with spooks but is seventeenth-century English for "Holy Spirit.")

Miryam. In English this Hebrew name is usually rendered by the spelling "Miriam" in the *Tanakh* and "Mary" in the New Testament. This unfounded and artificial distinction produced by translators subtly drives a wedge between Yeshua's mother and her own Jewishness. The original Miriam was the sister of *Moshe Rabbenu* ("Moses, our teacher"; Exodus 2:4–8) and a prophet (Exodus 15:20); in some respects she is seen as a role-model for the Jewish woman leader of today. But the name "Mary" evokes in the reader's thinking an otherworldly image of "Madonna and Child," complete with haloes, beatific smiles and angels in array, instead of the New Testament's portrayal of a down-to-earth Jewish lady in an Israel village managing her wifely, maternal and other social responsibilities with care, love and faith.

Yeshua's mother was **discovered to be pregnant by the *Ruach HaKodesh***. Sooner or later everyone discovered she was pregnant. But not everyone discovered that her pregnancy had resulted not from sexual relations but from the Holy Spirit's supernatural activity. The "virgin birth" was a supernatural event (see Section (1) of v. 23N). The God who made heaven and earth is quite capable of causing a woman to become pregnant in a way not possible in nature.

Mattityahu informs his readers of Yeshua's supernatural conception in order to counter the obvious and natural inference that Miryam had misbehaved. The early rabbis developed a tradition that Yeshua was the illegitimate son of Miryam and a Roman soldier named Pantera (in the second-century Tosefta, a collection similar to the Mishna, see Chullin 2:23; in the fifth-century Babylonian Talmud see Sanhedrin 43a, 67a). This calumny, invented, of course, to counter the claims of the Gospel, was worked up further in the sixth-century anti-gospel, *Toledot-Yeshu* (see v. 21N).

20 ***Adonai***, literally, "my lords"; but grammarians consider it the "plural of majesty"; so a slightly less literal translation would be "my Lord." Long before Yeshua's day, however, the word "*Adonai*" had, out of respect, been substituted in speaking and in reading aloud for God's personal name, the four Hebrew letters *yud-heh-vav-heh*, variously written in English as "*YHVH,*" "Yahweh" and "Jehovah." The Talmud (Pesachim 50a) made it a requirement not to pronounce the Tetragrammaton (the word means the "four-letter name" of God), and this remains the rule in most modern Jewish settings. In deference to this tradition (which, in my view, is unnecessary but harmless) the *JNT* uses "*Adonai*" where "*YHVH*" is meant. (Incidentally, the name "Jehovah" is a modern invention, an English hybrid based on the four Hebrew letters as transliterated into German, J-H-V-H, with the individually transliterated Hebrew vowel-points of "*Adonai*," e-o-a.)

The Greek word here is "*kurios*," which can mean (1) "sir," (2) "lord" in the human sense, as in "lord of the manor," (3) "Lord" in the divine sense, or (4) God's personal name *YHVH*. The *JNT* uses "*Adonai*" only when one can be certain that "*YHVH*" is meant; it is not used if there is doubt. So far, editions of the *JNT* are conservative on this score; there are probably additional places in the text where "*Adonai*" could safely be substituted for "Lord." For more on "*kurios*" see 7:21&N.

21 This verse is an example of a "semitism" (an allusion to Hebrew or Aramaic) brought over literally into the Greek text. It provides strong evidence in favor of the theory that there was a Hebrew or Aramaic oral or written tradition behind the extant Greek manuscripts, for only in Hebrew or Aramaic does the explanation here of Yeshua's name make any sense; in Greek (or English) it explains nothing.

The Hebrew word for "**he will save**" is "*yoshia'*," which has the same Hebrew root (*yud-shin-'ayin*) as the name **Yeshua** (*yud-shin-vav-'ayin*). Thus the Messiah's name is explained on the basis of what he will do. Etymologically the name *Yeshua'* is a contraction of the Hebrew name *Y'hoshua'* (English "Joshua"), which means "*YHVH* saves." It is also the masculine form of the Hebrew word "*yeshu'ah*," which means "salvation."

The KJV renders this verse, "…and thou shalt call his name Jesus: for he shall save his people from their sins." But in English, saving people from sins is no more reason for calling someone Jesus than for calling him Bill or Frank. The Greek is no better; only in Hebrew or Aramaic does the explanation explain.

In modern Hebrew Yeshua is usually called *Yeshu (yud-shin-vav*, without an *'ayin)* by nonbelievers. This verse also shows why the name "*Yeshu*" cannot possibly be correct — it does not include all three letters of the Hebrew root of *yoshia'*. However, the matter bears further scrutiny.

According to Professors David Flusser and Shmuel Safrai, Orthodox Jews, "*Yeshu*" was how the name "*Yeshua'*" was pronounced by Galilean Jews in the first century. We know from 26:73 below that Jews of the Galil had a different dialect than those of Judea. According to Flusser (*Jewish Sources in Early Christianity*, p. 15) Galileans did not pronounce the Hebrew letter *'ayin* at the end of a word, much as Cockneys drop "h" at the beginning. That is, instead of saying "Ye-**shoo**-ah" they said "**Yeh**-shoo." Undoubtedly some people began spelling the name according to this pronunciation.

However, that is not the end of the story. In Jewish anti-Christian polemic it became customary not to use Yeshua's correct name but intentionally and consciously to use the distortion "*Yeshu*," because at some point someone realized that "*Yeshu*" is also an acronym consisting of the first letters of the Hebrew insult, "*Yimach sh'mo v'zikhro*" ("May his name and memory be blotted out"; the words adapt and expand the last phrase of Psalm 109:13). Thus "*Yeshu*" was a kind of coded incantation against Christian evangelism. Moreover, since Yeshua came to be regarded in non-Messianic Judaism as a false prophet, blasphemer and idolater wrongly being worshipped as God, and since the *Torah* says, "You shall not even pronounce the names of their gods" (Exodus 3:13), the Messiah's name was purposely *mis*pronounced. Today most Israelis saying "*Yeshu*" suppose this is the man's correct name and intend no disparagement. The *JNT* avoids "*Yeshu*" because of its history and also because in Hebrew it, like "Jesus" in English, carries the valence of "the god the Gentiles worship."

But Yosef Vaktor (see 10:37N) reinterprets the acronym to praise Yeshua, "*Yitgadal sh'mo umalkhuto*!" ("May his name and kingdom be magnified!")

22 To fulfill what *Adonai* had said through the prophet. The New Covenant consistently presents itself as fulfilling prophecies and promises made by God in the *Tanakh*. Such conformity to statements and predictions made hundreds of years earlier, in defiance of all reasonable probabilities, proves beyond reasonable doubt that God "knows the end from the beginning." Moreover, in this case, it proves beyond reasonable doubt that Yeshua is the Messiah. Prophecy fulfillment is the chief rational reason, based on empirical observation of historical events — that is, based on facts — for Jews and others to accept Yeshua as the Messiah.

There have been more than fifty messianic pretenders in the last two thousand years of Jewish history, starting with Todah (Theudas) and Judah HaG'lili (Ac 5:36–37&NN), continuing with Shim'on Bar-Kosiba (died 135 C.E.), whom Rabbi Akiva recognized as the Messiah by changing his name to "Bar-Kochva" ("son of a star"; see 2 Ke 1:19N on "the Morning Star"), and culminating in Shabtai Tzvi (1626–1676), who became a Moslem, and Jacob Frank (1726–1791), who became a Roman Catholic. But none of them met the criteria laid down in the *Tanakh* concerning the identity of the Messiah; whereas Yeshua met all of them that are applicable to his first coming (these fulfilled prophecies are listed in 26:24N and in Section VII of the Introduction to the *JNT*). Of the four gospel writers Mattityahu especially concerns himself with pointing out these fulfillments (see 2:5, 15, 17; 3:3; 4:14; 8:17; 11:10; 12:17; 13:14, 35; 21:4; 22:43; 26:31; 27:9). His object is to demonstrate that Yeshua should be recognized as the Messiah because he fulfilled what *Adonai* said about the Messiah through the prophets of the *Tanakh*.

What *Adonai* had said through the prophet. On this phrase see 2:15N, third-from-last paragraph.

23 The virgin will conceive and bear a son. This verse introduces a major controversy concerning the use of the Hebrew Bible in the New Testament. Following are three objections which non-Messianic Jews and other skeptics often make to Mattityahu's quoting Isaiah 7:14b in this verse, along with Messianic Jewish replies.

(1) *Objection:* A virgin birth is impossible.

Reply: In liberal scholarship miracles are characteristically explained away as natural phenomena in disguise. One might pursue this line here by pointing to observed instances of parthenogenesis in the animal kingdom or modern cloning experiments. But there is no instance of human parthenogenesis. Therefore one must regard a virgin birth as supernatural.

Usually objection to a virgin birth as impossible follows as a logical consequence of objecting to any and all supernaturalism. But the God of the Bible is literally "supernatural," above nature, since he created nature and its laws. Therefore, if it suits his purpose he can suspend those laws. The Bible in both the *Tanakh* and the New Testament teaches repeatedly that God does intervene in human history and does sometimes overrule the natural course of events for his own reasons.

Frequently his reason, as in this instance, is to give humanity a sign of his sovereignty, presence and concern. In fact, Isaiah 7:14a, immediately preceding the portion quoted, reads, "Therefore the Lord himself will give you a sign." The Hebrew word for sign ("*'ot*") means an extraordinary event that demonstrates and calls attention to God's direct involvement in human affairs. The "God" of Deism, pictured as starting the universe like a man winding a watch and leaving it to run by itself, is not the God of the Bible.

(2) *Objection:* Isaiah, in using the Hebrew word "*'almah,*" was referring to a "young woman"; had he meant "virgin" he would have written "*b'tulah.*"

Reply: "*'Almah*" is used seven times in the Hebrew Bible, and in each instance it either explicitly means a virgin or implies it, because in the Bible "*'almah*" always refers to an unmarried woman of good reputation. In Genesis 24:43 it applies to Rebecca, Isaac's future bride, already spoken of in Genesis 24:16 as a *b'tulah.* In Exodus 2:8 it describes the infant Moshe's older sister Miryam, a nine-year-old girl and surely a virgin. (Thus the name of Yeshua's mother recalls this earlier virgin.) The other references are to young maidens playing on timbrels (Psalm 68:25), maidens being courted (Proverbs 30:19) and virgins of the royal court (Song of Songs 1:3, 6:8). In each case the context requires a young unmarried woman of good reputation, i.e., a virgin.

Moreover, Mattityahu here is quoting from the Septuagint, the first translation of the *Tanakh* into Greek. More than two centuries before Yeshua was born, the Jewish translators of the Septuagint chose the Greek word "*parthenos*" to render "*'almah.*" "*Parthenos*" unequivocally means "virgin." This was long before the New Testament made the matter controversial.

The most famous medieval Jewish Bible commentator, Rabbi Shlomo Yitzchaki ("Rashi," 1040–1105), who determinedly opposed Christological interpretation of the *Tanakh*, nevertheless explained that in Song of Songs 1:3 "*'alamot*" (plural of

" *'almah*") means "*b'tulot*" ("virgins") and refers metaphorically to the nations.

Victor Buksbazen, a Hebrew Christian, in his commentary *The Prophet Isaiah*, quoted Rashi as writing that in Isaiah 7:14 " *'almah*" means "virgin." In the first four editions of the *Jewish New Testament Commentary* I cited this Rashi. It has been pointed out to me that Rashi did not write what I represented him as having written, so I have removed the citation from the main body of the *JNTC* and herewith apologize for not checking the original source. For more details, see Appendix, p. 929.

Also, in earlier editions, I referred to a 1953 article in the *Journal of Bible and Religion*, in which the Jewish scholar Cyrus Gordon held that cognate languages support translating " *'almah*" in Isaiah 7:14 as "virgin." However, Michael Brown, a Messianic Jewish scholar with a Ph.D. in Semitics, informs me that Gordon's observations were based on an early incorrect reading of a key Ugaritic text. In this case, my error stemmed from unfamiliarity with recent scholarship.

However, the Bible itself shows us how we can know when an *'almah* is a virgin. Rivkah is called an *'almah* at Genesis 24:43, but it can be deduced from Genesis 24:16 ("Neither had any man known her") that she was a virgin. In the same way, we know that the *'almah* Miryam was a virgin from Lk 1:34, where she asks the angel how she can be pregnant, "since I am a virgin?"

A possible reason for Isaiah's using the word " *'almah*" instead of *b'tulah* is that in Biblical (as opposed to later) Hebrew, "*b'tulah*" does not always unambiguously mean "virgin," as we learn from Joel 1:8: "Lament like a *b'tulah* girded with sackcloth for the husband of her youth." Deuteronomy 22:19 speaks of a woman after her wedding night as a *b'tulah*.

(3) *Objection*: In Isaiah the context (vv. 10–17) shows that Isaiah was predicting as a sign to King Achaz that before the *'almah*'s as yet unconceived and unborn child would be old enough to choose good and refuse evil, Syria and the Northern Kingdom would lose their kings, and Assyria would attack Judah. This prophecy was fulfilled in the eighth century B.C.E. Therefore the prophet was not predicting an event some 700 years in the future.

Reply (for which I am grateful to the Jewish believer Arnold Fruchtenbaum): On the contrary, the context, which includes all of Isaiah 7, not just eight verses, shows that the "sign" of v. 14 was not for King Achaz, who is referred to as "you" (singular) in vv. 11 and 16–17, but for the entire "House of David," mentioned in v. 13, and referred to as "you" (plural) in vv. 13–14.

The sign for Achaz was that before the *na'ar* ("child," at least a toddler, never a newborn baby) should know how to choose good and refuse evil, the events of vv. 16b–17 would occur. That child was Isaiah's son Sh'ar-Yashuv (v. 3), who was with him as he prophesied and at whom he was probably pointing, not the son (Hebrew *ben*) of v. 14. This leaves v. 14 to provide a sign to the whole House of David, including all the descendants of David from that time onward until the prophecy should be fulfilled — which it was by Yeshua's virgin birth.

Occasionally persons unacquainted with Christian tradition, specifically Roman Catholic tradition, confuse the term "virgin birth" with "immaculate conception." The virgin birth of Yeshua — his being conceived by the power of the Holy Spirit of God in

Miryam before she had ever had sexual contact — is accepted by all Bible-believing Messianic Jews and Gentile Christians. The immaculate conception, the Roman Catholic doctrine (first taught by the Church Fathers) that Miryam herself was sinlessly conceived, is not accepted by Protestants because the New Testament makes no mention of it.

Immanu'el is the name given to the Messiah at Isaiah 7:14, 8:8. As Mattityahu himself explains, it means "**God is with us**" — which is how Hebrew *immanu El* is translated at Isaiah 8:10. However, Yeshua was not known by that name during his life on earth; rather, the name gives a hint (*remez*; see 2:15N) at who he is by describing him: he is God-with-us. God's people experience the final fulfillment at Rv 21:3, where in the new heavens and new earth "God-with-them" dwells among them.

In the *Tanakh* names frequently describe an aspect of the person named. In fact the *Tanakh* uses several names to refer to the Messiah, including "Shiloh" (Genesis 49:10), "Branch" (Isaiah 11:1), "Sprout" (Jeremiah 23:5, 33:15), and the longest, "Wonderful Counselor, Mighty God, Everlasting Father, Prince of Peace" (Isaiah 9:5–6(6–7)). All describe the Messiah, yet he was known by just one name, Yeshua.

24–25 Yosef's behavior shows that he accepted Yeshua as his son. According to the Mishna, "If one say, 'This is my son,' he is to be believed" (Bava Batra 8:6). The Gemara explains that he is believed "as regards the right of inheritance" (Bava Batra 134a). Thus Yeshua, as a legally acknowledged son, is entitled to inherit the throne of King David from Yosef, a descendant of David (v. 8). (This point is made in Phillip Goble, *How to Point to Yeshua in Your Rabbi's Bible*, New York: Artists for Israel, 1986.)

25 **Until she had given birth.** Protestants generally affirm that Miryam was a virgin when Yeshua was born, but that "his sisters" (plural: at least two) and four brothers (13:55–56, Mk 6:3) were Miryam and Yosef's natural children. The Roman Catholic Church teaches that Miryam remained a virgin all her life, and that the terms "brothers" and "sisters" are used loosely to refer to more distant relatives (compare Genesis 14:12–16, 31:32, Leviticus 10:4). The Greek phrase "*eôs ou*" ("until") is inconclusive because it does not necessarily imply a change; that is, the Greek could mean either that they did not have relations during the period before she gave birth but did afterwards, or that they remained celibate afterwards as well. But celibacy in particular and asceticism in general, though regarded by pagans as spiritually meritorious, were and are the exception in Judaism and in New Covenant faith, as both Yeshua and Sha'ul teach (see 19:10–12&N, 1C 7:1–40&NN, Co 2:18–23&NN, 1 Ti 4:3a&N).

CHAPTER 2

1 **Yeshua was born** between 8 and 4 B.C.E. The reason he was born "B.C." ("Before Christ") is that Dionysius Exiguus, the sixth-century monk who set up the modern calendar, made a mistake in determining the date which was not corrected till later. Instead of the terms "A.D." ("*Anno Domini*," "in the year of [the] Lord" Yeshua) and "B.C." the Jewish community customarily denotes these periods by "C.E." ("Common Era") and "B.C.E." ("Before the Common Era"), to avoid relating dates explicitly to the Messiah.

In Beit-Lechem. See v. 6&N.

Herod the Great (c. 73–4 B.C.E.) founded the Herodian dynasty (see Lk 3:1N), which ruled the Land of Israel and its surroundings from 37 B.C.E. until the war with Rome in 66–70 C.E. Herod himself was a man of great physical energy and ambition. His career comes to the notice of historians in 47 B.C.E. in Syria and the Galil; a combination of military successes, political machinations and bribery of Roman superiors enabled him to replace the last of the Hasmonean rulers, Antigonus, when the latter died in 37 B.C.E. (possibly in consequence of one of Herod's bribes).

Though technically Jewish by birth, since his family was from the Idumeans (Edomites), who had been forcibly converted to Judaism under the Hasmonean Maccabees in the second century B.C.E. (see 23:15N), neither his religious behavior nor his ethics reflected anything of Judaism. He did, however, reconstruct and enlarge the Second Temple, which had been built under Z'rubavel (see the book of Haggai) in 520–516 B.C.E. The Talmudic rabbis said, "One who has not seen Herod's temple has never seen a beautiful building" (Bava Batra 4a), but also, "It was built by a sinful king, and the building was intended by him as an atonement for having slain Israel's sages" (Numbers Rabbah 4:14).

Herod was consistently paranoid about his power. He had all his rivals exterminated, including those of his wife's family (he had married Mariamne, a Hasmonean, and feared the restoration of the Hasmonean dynasty) and even some of his own children (he had fifteen). He built remote fortresses, Herodion and Matzada, as refuges should he be deposed. The events described in 2:1–17 are entirely in keeping with the man's independently attested character.

Magi were not merely sorcerers or magicians, although the term "magician" comes from this word; nor were they simply astrologers, although they did observe the stars. They were sages, wise men, often in positions of responsibility but sometimes commanding respect because of their wisdom even when not holding office. These Magi came from the Medo-Persian Empire or Babylon.

2 **King of the Jews.** At Yn 1:19N I argue that the Greek word *Ioudaioi* should usually be translated "Judeans" and not "Jews" when the context is the Land of Israel. But the set phrase, "king of the *Ioudaioi*" is used in the New Testament only by non-Jews — here by the Magi, and later by Pontius Pilate and the Roman soldiers (27:37; Mk 15:26; Lk 23:3, 38; Yn 19:19). This argues for making an exception: all of these people were interested not in distinguishing Judeans from Galileans but Jews from Gentiles.

However, one can make a strong case for rendering *Ioudaioi* "Judeans" even here. Not only is the context the Land of Israel, but three times in vv. 1–6 we read of Beit-Lechem in Y'hudah (Judea). The Jewish scholar Solomon Zeitlin so understands the phrase:

> "The gospels according to both Matthew [1:1–16] and Luke [3:24–31] trace the genealogy of Jesus to David, while Mark, who does not give the genealogy, states that Jesus is the son of David [12:35]. John, who stresses the view that Jesus was the son of God, nevertheless wrote, 'But some said, Shall Christ come out of Galilee? Hath not the scripture said, that Christ cometh out of the seed of David and out of the town of Bethlehem where David was?' [7:41–42]. According to the gospels Jesus was greeted with the words, 'Blessed be the kingdom of our father David' [Mark 11:10], 'Hosanna to the Son of David'

[Matthew 21:9]. On the cross on which Jesus was crucified the words 'Jesus of Nazareth, king of the Judaeans' were inscribed in Hebrew, Greek and Latin [*Iesus Nazarenus, Rex Iudaeorum*]. *Mashiah*, messiah, Christ were synonymous in their minds with 'son of David' and 'king of the Judaeans.'" ("The Origin of the Idea of the Messiah," in Daniel Jeremy Silver, ed., *In the Time of Harvest*, New York: The MacMillan Company, 1963, p. 458)

His star. This seems to allude to Numbers 24:17, where Balaam prophesies, "There shall come forth a star out of Jacob." Judaism understands this "star" to be the Messiah. See 2 Ke 1:19N on "the Morning Star."

4 ***Cohanim*** (plural; singular *cohen*), "priests," a word which today evokes the image of clerics in formal Christian denominations or functionaries in eastern or primitive religions. This is because the Jewish priesthood has been dormant since the destruction of the Second Temple in 70 C.E. But in Yeshua's day, when the Temple still stood, Judaism without a priesthood was unimaginable.

The task of a priest, like that of a prophet, is to serve as spokesman and mediator between God and man. The prophet speaks to man on behalf of God, the priest to God on behalf of man. The *cohanim* serving in the Temple were descendents of Moshe's brother Aharon, great-grandson of L'vi, Ya'akov's third son. In terms of practical job-description their primary duty was to offer sacrificial animals on the altar. The ever-bloody altar in the Temple of God was a continual witness to Israel that God's penalty for sin is death (see MJ 10:3). The concepts of priesthood and sacrifice are minimized in today's non-Messianic Judaism (see MJ 9:22N), but the Judaism of the Bible is inoperative without them. Messianic Judaism holds that Yeshua the Messiah is our everlasting *cohen* (MJ 7:23–25) and our everlasting sacrifice (MJ 7:27, Yn 1:29).

***Torah*-teachers.** The Greek word "*grammateus*" translates literally Hebrew *sofer*, which has the literal meaning "scribe" and is usually so rendered in English. But the function of the *sofrim* in Yeshua's day went well beyond copying scrolls or performing secretarial duties; they were the primary students and teachers of the content of Judaism, that is, of *Torah*.

The leading *cohanim*, who were mostly Sadducees, **and *Torah*-teachers**, who were allied with the Pharisees (but see next paragraph), represented the two main concentrations of power within the Jewish religious establishment (see 3:7N). The opinions of the two groups frequently differed, but Herod's question received a single response; from this we learn that all Israel agreed that the Messiah would be born in Beit-Lechem (see v. 6N).

Joseph Shulam, a Messianic Jewish leader in Jerusalem, points out that modern scholars believe the scribes were neither rabbis nor Pharisees but "sages of the *'am-ha'aretz*" (see Yn 7:49N, Ac 4:13N), *Torah*-teachers without *s'mikhah* (ordination; see 21:23N) — but see Mk 2:16&N. For this reason they could not bring *chiddushim* (introduce new interpretations) or *posek halakhah* (make legal judgments). According to Shulam, this is why the people were in shock that Yeshua taught like a rabbi and not like a scribe (7:28–29, Mk 1:22&N).

6 In Judaism the citation of a Scripture text implies the whole context, not merely the quoted words. Thus Micah 5:1(2) reads, in full, from the Hebrew:

"But you, Beit-Lechem Efratah, though small among the thousands of Y'hudah, nevertheless out of you shall one come forth to me who will be ruler in Israel; and his goings-forth are from of old, from ancient days."

Some have taken this verse to mean only that the Messiah is to be descended from King David, who came out of Beit-Lechem (1 Samuel 17:12), also called Efratah (Genesis 48:7). But it is bad exegesis to give this very clear prediction of the geographic origin of the Messiah such a figurative meaning. Instead it is an effort to fudge the obvious reference to Yeshua, the eternal Son of God "whose goings-forth are of old, from ancient days," as noted in Yochanan 1:1–2&N, 14; 8:56–58&N.

It is amazing that in many periods of history significant numbers of Jewish people have fallen for the claims of Messianic pretenders (see 1:22N), not one of whom fulfilled this prophecy by being born in Bethlehem.

There are even rabbinic sources which directly identify Beit-Lechem as the birthplace of the Messiah, for example, the Midrash Rabbah to Lamentations, Section 51 (on Lamentations 1:16):

"A man was plowing when one of his oxen lowed. An Arab passed by and asked, 'What are you?' He replied, 'I am a Jew.' The Arab said to him, 'Unharness your ox and untie your plow [as a sign of mourning].' 'Why?' 'Because the Temple of the Jews is destroyed.' The Jew asked, 'How do you know this?' 'From the lowing of your ox.' While they were talking the ox lowed again. The Arab said, 'Harness your ox and tie up your plow, because the deliverer of the Jews is born.' 'What is his name?' 'His name is Menachem [Comforter].' 'What is his father's name?' 'Chizkiyahu [King Hezekiah is identified in Jewish literature with the Messiah].' 'Where do they live?' He answered, 'In Birat-'Arba, in Beit-Lechem of Judea.'"

The same *aggadah* (story) appears in the Jerusalem Talmud at B'rakhot 5a; there the last line is, "In the royal capital of Beit-Lechem." Moreover, although it does not identify the Messiah as Yeshua, it implies that the Messiah has come already, around the time of the Temple's destruction.

13 An angel of *Adonai*. See Yn 1:14N.

15 Out of Egypt I called my son. Hosea 11:1 clearly refers not to the Messiah but to the people of Israel, who were called God's son even before leaving Egypt (Exodus 4:22). The previous two *Tanakh* quotations (1:23, 2:6) involved literal fulfillment, but this does not. In what sense, then, does Yeshua's flight to Egypt **fulfill what *Adonai* had said through the prophet**?

To answer, we must understand the four basic modes of Scripture interpretation used by the rabbis. These are:

(1) *P'shat* ("simple") — the plain, literal sense of the text, more or less what modern scholars mean by "grammatical-historical exegesis," which looks to the grammar of the language and the historical setting as background for deciding what a passage means. Modern scholars often consider grammatical-historical exegesis the only

valid way to deal with a text; pastors who use other approaches in their sermons usually feel defensive about it before academics. But the rabbis had three other modes of interpreting Scripture, and their validity should not be excluded in advance but related to the validity of their implied presuppositions.

(2) *Remez* ("hint") — wherein a word, phrase or other element in the text hints at a truth not conveyed by the *p'shat*. The implied presupposition is that God can hint at things of which the Bible writers themselves were unaware.

(3) *Drash* or *midrash* ("search") — an allegorical or homiletical application of a text. This is a species of eisegesis — reading one's own thoughts into the text — as opposed to exegesis, which is extracting from the text what it actually says. The implied presupposition is that the words of Scripture can legitimately become grist for the mill of human intellect, which God can guide to truths not directly related to the text at all.

(4) *Sod* ("secret") — a mystical or hidden meaning arrived at by operating on the numerical values of the Hebrew letters, noting unusual spellings, transposing letters, and the like. For example, two words, the numerical equivalents of whose letters add up to the same amount, are good candidates for revealing a secret through what Arthur Koestler in his book on the inventive mind called "bisociation of ideas." The implied presupposition is that God invests meaning in the minutest details of Scripture, even the individual letters.

The presuppositions underlying *remez*, *drash* and *sod* obviously express God's omnipotence, but they also express his love for humanity, in the sense that he chooses out of love to use extraordinary means for reaching people's hearts and minds. At the same time, it is easy to see how *remez*, *drash* and *sod* can be abused, since they all allow, indeed require, subjective interpretation; and this explains why scholars, who deal with the objective world, hesitate to use them.

These four methods of working a text are remembered by the Hebrew word "*PaRDeS*," an acronym formed from the initials; it means "orchard" or "garden."

What, then, is Mattityahu doing here? Some allege he is misusing Scripture, twisting the meaning of what Hosea wrote from its context in order to apply it to Yeshua. Such an accusation stands only if Mattityahu is dealing with the *p'shat*. For there is no question that the *p'shat* of Hosea 11:1 applies to the nation of Israel and not to Yeshua.

Some think Mattityahu is using the *drash* approach, making a *midrash* in which he reads the Messiah into a verse dealing with Israel. Many rabbis used the same procedure; Mattityahu's readers would not have found it objectionable.

Nevertheless, I believe Mattityahu is not doing eisegesis but giving us a *remez*, a hint of a very deep truth. Israel is called God's son as far back as Exodus 4:22. The Messiah is presented as God's son a few verses earlier in Mattityahu (1:18–25), reflecting *Tanakh* passages such as Isaiah 9:5–6(6–7), Psalm 2:7 and Proverbs 30:4. Thus the Son equals the son: the Messiah is equated with, is one with, the nation of Israel. This is the deep truth Mattityahu is hinting at by calling Yeshua's flight to Egypt a "fulfillment" of Hosea 11:1.

This fact, that the Messiah Yeshua stands for and is intimately identified with his people Israel, is an extremely important corporate aspect of the Gospel generally neglected in the individualistically oriented Western world. The individual who trusts Yeshua becomes united with him and is "immersed" (baptized; see 3:1&N) into all that

Yeshua is (see Ac 2:38&N), including his death and resurrection — so that his sinful propensities are regarded as dead, and his new nature, empowered by the Holy Spirit, is regarded as alive (Ro 6:3–6&N). Likewise, just as this intimate identification with the Messiah holds for the individual, so the Messiah similarly identifies with and embodies national, corporate Israel. Indeed it is only because Yeshua identifies himself with the Jewish people, national Israel, the "olive tree" into which Gentile Christians have been "grafted" (Ro 11:17–24), that he can plausibly identify with the Messianic Community, the Church, as "head of the Body" (1C 11:3; Ep 1:10, 22; 4:15, 5:23; Co 1:18, 2:19) and "cornerstone" of the building (below at 21:42, Mk 12:10, Ac 4:11, Ep 2:20, 1 Ke 2:6–7).

Modern readers of the Bible, by using "grammatical-historical exegesis," ignore all modes of interpretation except the *p'shat*, discounting them as eisegesis. This is in reaction to the tendency of the Church Fathers in the second through eighth centuries to over-allegorize, an error which probably resulted from their misunderstanding the limitations of, and therefore misusing, the other three rabbinic approaches to texts. But the New Testament is a Jewish book, written by Jews in a Jewish context; and the first-century Jewish context included all four ways of handling texts. Mattityahu knew perfectly well that Hosea was not referring to Yeshua, to a Messiah, or even to any individual. Yet he also sensed that because Yeshua in a profound yet recondite way embodies Israel, his coming from Egypt re-enacted in a spiritually significant way the Exodus of the Jewish people. Since *remez* and *p'shat* have different presuppositions one should expect fulfillment of a prophecy by *remez* to be different from literal fulfillment. At 1:23 and 2:6 the plain, literal sense of the text, the *p'shat*, suffices to show how the prophecies are fulfilled, but here it does not.

The phrase, "**what *Adonai* had said through the prophet**," takes our attention off the prophet himself and puts it on God who spoke through him. It lets the reader understand that *Adonai* might have been saying more than what the prophet himself understood when he wrote. It prepares him for the possibility that behind Hosea's *p'shat* was God's *remez* to be revealed in its time and lends credibility to the "*PaRDeS*" mode of interpretation.

Recognition that there are four modes of Jewish exegesis also resolves much of the controversy concerning how certain passages in the *Tanakh* ought to be interpreted. For example, most Christians say that Isaiah 53 refers to the Messiah, and some (though not all) traditional Jews say it refers to Israel. But if there is a mystical identification between the Messiah and the people whose king he is (an idea expounded at length by the best-known Christian theologian of the twentieth century, Karl Barth, in his *Church Dogmatics*), then the interpretational conflict vanishes; both claimants hold part of the total truth.

Moreover, the idea that the Messiah personifies or is identified intimately with Israel is a Jewish one. First of all, we see it in the *Tanakh* itself. Compare Isaiah 49:3 ("You are my servant Israel, in whom I will be glorified.") with Isaiah 49:6 ("Is it too slight a thing that you should be my servant... to restore the preserved of Israel?"). The servant is at once Israel and he who restores Israel, that is, the Messiah. In Chapter 12 of Raphael Patai's *The Messiah Texts* he quotes Pesikta Rabbati 161–162, where the Messiah is called Efrayim (a name symbolizing Israel) and is at the same time presented as bearing Israel's sufferings. Likewise the thirteenth-century work which is at the core of the Jewish mystical approach called *kabbalah*, the Zohar (2:212a), links the Messiah's suffering with that of Israel. Patai also retells the eighteenth-century Rabbi Nachman of Bratslav's story of the viceroy and the king's daughter, adding that most interpreters understand the viceroy to represent both Israel and the suffering Messiah.

18 The *p'shat* of this verse from Jeremiah does not refer to the Messiah but to the slaughter of the northern tribes of Israel by the Assyrians. But there is a *remez* here of which Mattityahu makes use: the traditional burial-place of Ya'akov's wife Rachel is in Ramah, just outside Beit-Lechem — one can visit what is called "Rachel's Tomb" there today. Just as Rachel in her grave mourns for her posterity descended from her son Yosef, so the many women of nearby Beit-Lechem mourn for their slain infants.

20–21 What does the New Testament call the Holy Land? Not Palestine but ***Eretz-Israel***, "the Land of Israel." Similarly, the regions north and south of Jerusalem are called not the West Bank but "Y'hudah" and "Shomron" (Judea and Samaria; see Ac 1:8). The New Testament, like the Israelis of today, uses the names the Hebrew Bible uses, not those employed by the Romans or other conquerors. See 5:5&N.

23 This is a problematical verse. In every instance where Mattityahu is showing the fulfillment of a Scriptural prophecy (see list in 1:23N), a specific writer — Isaiah, Jeremiah, David — is named, or "the prophet," or "the *Tanakh*," followed by a verse or passage. Here **the prophets** (uniquely plural) are mentioned, and no text is quoted. This is clear from the fact that Mattityahu leaves out "*legontos*" ("saying"), the Greek keyword he uses to cite Scripture. Rather, he seems to be alluding to a general concept found in several prophets, capable of being fulfilled by the Messiah's being what the Greek text here calls a *Nazôraios* (in some other places the word is "*Nazarênos*"). The questions: Which prophets? What did they actually say? And what is a *Nazôraios/Nazarênos?*

Some have suggested that the verse has to do with Yeshua's taking the vows of a Nazirite (Numbers 6:1–23). But this is improbable, since there is no record that Yeshua, who was not an ascetic (11:16–19), ever did such a thing.

A second possibility is that since **Natzeret** (Nazareth, see Lk 1:26N) was a place people made fun of — as in Natan'el's remark, "Natzeret? Can anything good come from there?" (Yn 1:46) — Mattityahu is referring to the many *Tanakh* prophecies that say the Messiah would be despised (e.g., Psalm 22, Isaiah 52:13–53:12) and is informing us that these prophecies would be fulfilled, in part, by his having the onus of being a ***Natzrati***, a resident of Natzeret.

The third possibility is that Mattityahu is speaking of the prediction that the Messiah will be a *netzer* ("branch") from the stock of Yishai, King David's father (Isaiah 11:1); but compare Jeremiah 23:5, 33:15; Zechariah 3:8, 6:12, where the word is "*tzemach*," ("sprout"). Thus several **prophets** use the idea, though not the word "*netzer*." (For more on "the prophets" see 5:17N.)

What I consider most probable is that Mattityahu is combining the second and third alternatives by means of wordplay, a technique very common in Jewish writing, including the Bible. Yeshua is both *netzer* and *Natzrati*.

Finally, although one of the earliest names for the Jewish believers was "*Notzrim*" ("Nazareth-ites," that is, "followers of the man from Nazareth," Acts 24:5&N), it would be odd for Mattityahu to use the same term for the one they followed. The Talmud refers to him as *Yeshu HaNotzri* (B'rakhot 17b, Sotah 47a). In modern Hebrew "*Notzri*" remains the everyday word for "Christian"; but it is wrong and confusing to speak of "Yeshua the Christian," i.e., the follower of Christ — he could not follow himself! The Talmud's expression should be understood as meaning "Yeshua the *Natzrati*, Yeshua from Natzeret." I use the term "*Natzrati*" instead of "*Notzri*" (both are acceptable modern Hebrew) in order to get away from the modern connotations of "*Notzri*" in Hebrew.

CHAPTER 3

1 **Yochanan the Immerser**, usually rendered "John the Baptist." The name "John," along with numerous variants in many languages — Jan, Juan, Jon, Jean, Ivan, Giovanni — comes from Hebrew *Yo-chanan*, which means, "*YHVH* was gracious, showed favor."

While the Greek verb "*baptizein*" is obviously the source of the English words "baptize" and "Baptist," its root meaning is "to dip, soak, immerse" into a liquid, so that what is dipped takes on qualities of what it has been dipped in — for example, cloth in dye or leather in tanning solution.

But to understand what "*baptizein*" means here one needs the Jewish background. According to the *Torah* one had to be ritually pure before entering the Tabernacle or Temple. Ritual purity could be lost in many ways; the preeminent means of restoring it was through washing. A quick review of Leviticus shows how frequently the matter is mentioned, and one of the six major divisions of the Talmud (*Taharot*, "Cleansings") is devoted to it. Even though there is no longer a Temple, observant Jewish women immerse themselves in a *mikveh* (ritual bath) after each menstrual period, in obedience to Leviticus 15; see MJ 13:4N.

A person who immerses himself participates in an obvious yet living metaphor of purification, with the water, as it were, washing away the impurity. Here Yochanan the Immerser proclaims for the old practice of immersion a new context, cleansing from a life pattern of sin (see vv. 2&N, 6, 11).

Today's ritual baptism in some branches of Christianity does not involve complete immersion of the body in water, but pouring or sprinkling instead. Some scholars believe that at least in some instances, even New Testament baptisms may have been sprinklings or pourings and not actual immersions; verses such as Ezekiel 36:25 (MJ 10:22) and Lk 3:16 with Ac 2:17–18, 10:45 are adduced in support. The various "Baptist" denominations sprang from a movement in the sixteenth and seventeenth centuries that stressed complete immersion of believers, as opposed to sprinkling or pouring baptismal water on infants not yet old enough to have decided consciously to be Christian.

Traditional Judaism has developed its own theology of Christian baptism. Perhaps because a form of baptism (complete self-immersion in a *mikveh*) is required at the point when a non-Jew converts to Judaism, the latter has traditionally understood Christian baptism to be the moment when a Jew removes himself from the Jewish community and adopts a religion alien to, or even in opposition to, Judaism and the Jewish people. Because of these false associations which have become attached to the word "baptism" in the Jewish community, the text of the *JNT* uses the more accurately descriptive word "immersion" throughout.

2 **Turn from your sins to God.** The English language has a perfectly good word for this, "repent," used in the King James and most other versions; but those who image an overwrought, undereducated charlatan yelling it at a frightened and equally illiterate crowd can no longer hear the message in the word. For this reason I have gone back to the original languages to educe the original sense. The Greek word "*metanoiete*," related to "*nous*" ("mind"), means "change your mind, have a complete change of heart." The underlying Hebrew concept is expressed in the word "*t'shuvah*" ("turning, returning"), which in the context of religious behavior means "turning" from one's sins and "returning" to God. Note that there is not only a "from" but a "to," for turning from one's sins is impossible unless at the same time one turns to God — otherwise one only turns from one set of sins to another! The Jewish understanding of repentance, correct on this point, is that each individual must do it, yet it requires God's grace to be able to do it — "Turn us to you, O *Adonai*, and we will be turned" (Lamentations 5:21).

It is not without wisdom that a Jew raised with little knowledge of Judaism who later adopts an Orthodox Jewish lifestyle is termed a "*ba'al-t'shuvah*," literally, a "master of repentance," that is, one who has "turned" from his nonobservant ways and "returned" to an attempt at serving God in the manner prescribed by Orthodox Judaism. My heart's desire is that all Jews become true *ba'alei-t'shuvah* through Yeshua the Messiah, and that all Christians become truly repentant as well (1 Yn 1:9).

Yochanan's message here is identical with Yeshua's at 4:17.

Kingdom of Heaven. The word "Heaven" was used in pious avoidance of the word "God" (see 1:20N); and to this day Hebrew *malkhut-haShammayim* ("Kingdom of Heaven") substitutes in Jewish religious literature for "Kingdom of God," an expression found frequently in the New Testament, first at 6:33 below. In the *Jewish New Testament* "Heaven" is capitalized when it refers to God; "heaven" is in lower-case when it refers to the sky or paradise.

In both Yochanan's and Yeshua's preaching (4:17) the reason for urgency to repent is that **the Kingdom of Heaven is near.** The concept of the Kingdom of God is crucial to understanding the Bible. It refers neither to a place nor to a time, but to a condition in which the rulership of God is acknowledged by humankind, a condition in which God's promises of a restored universe free from sin and death are, or begin to be, fulfilled.

In relation to the Kingdom of God history can be divided into four periods: before Yeshua, during his lifetime, the present age (the *'olam hazeh*) and the future age (the *'olam haba*). There was a sense in which the Kingdom was present prior to Yeshua's birth; indeed, God was king over the Jewish people (see 1 Samuel 12:12). Yeshua's arrival brought a quantum leap in the earthly expression of the Kingdom, "For in him, bodily, lives the fullness of all that God is" (Co 2:9).

The New Testament teaches two seemingly contradictory things about the Kingdom of God: that it is near or present (this verse, 4:17, 12:34; Lk 17:21), and that it is yet to come (25:1, Yn 18:36, Ac 1:6–7). The theologian George Ladd both highlighted and resolved this conflict by calling his book on the Kingdom of God "*The Presence of the Future*."

Today the Kingdom of God comes immediately and truly — but partially — to all who put their trust in Yeshua and his message, thus committing themselves to live the holy lives God's rulership demands. As an example of the "partialness," they have peace in their hearts even though there is not peace in the world. But in the future, at the end of the present age of history, when Yeshua returns, he will inaugurate the Kingdom truly and completely (Rv 19:6); then God will fulfill the rest of his Kingdom promises.

One of the most profound spiritual studies a person can undertake in the Bible is of the Kingdom of God in both the *Tanakh* and the New Testament.

3 This quotation initiates the second part of the book of Isaiah (Chapters 40–66), which offers comfort to Israel and contains many references to the Messiah. The **one who cries** is Yochanan, identified in spirit with the prophet Elijah; see Mk 1:2–3N.

The voice of someone crying out: "In the desert prepare the way of *Adonai*!" KJV has, "The voice of one crying in the wilderness, Prepare ye the way of the Lord"; and most versions, as well as the first two printings of the *JNT*, say that the crier is in the desert. But this is wrong; one learns it by examining the punctuation/cantillation marks in the Masoretic Hebrew text of Isaiah. These show that "in the desert" goes with "prepare the way," not with "someone crying." Although these markings are not God-inspired, they indicate how the text was read and understood at the time they were added (not later than the 8th century C.E.); and without a positive reason for understanding the text differently, it is best to assume these markings are correct.

4 **Camel's hair** was woven into coarse cloth by the poor who could not afford wool garments. While the rich could afford ornate waistbands a poor man would wear a **leather belt.** Thus Yochanan, like many prophets before him, identified with the poor. But the leather belt also elicits association with Elijah (v.3N, 2 Kings 1:8).

Locusts. Leviticus 11:21–22 mentions four species of locusts that may be eaten. Mishna Chullin 3:7 defines the characteristics of *kosher* locusts and in the Gemara, Chullin 65a–66a analyzes these rules at length. Locusts were food for the poor in Yeshua's day; Bedouins cook and eat them to this day, as did the Jews of Yemen before that community was removed to Israel by Operation Flying Carpet in 1950. **Wild honey.** Probably date honey, because oases near Yericho are known for production of dates both then and now, and bees do not live in the desert. (This sentence has been corrected from earlier editions.) The verse tells us that Yochanan lived outside the normal economic framework of the country so that he could be wholly devoted to his prophetic task.

6 **Confessing their sins.** Greek *exomologeô*, "agree, admit, acknowledge, declare publicly, confess," literally, "say the same thing." In the case of confessing one's sins, one is saying the same thing about them that God says, acknowledging the deeds to be wrong, willing to declare publicly one's sorrow, guilt and resolution to change. On *Yom-Kippur* (the Day of Atonement) and other fast days, *s'lichot* (penitential prayers) are recited which can help people who say them with *kavvanah* (intention, devotion) to become more willing to admit their sins and agree with God's opinion of them. See Yn 1:9&N, Ya 5:16&N.

Sins. We live in an age when many people do not know what sin is. Sin is violation of *Torah* (1 Yn 3:4), transgression of the law God gave his people in order to help them live a life which would be in their own best interests as well as holy and pleasing to God. In the so-called Age of Enlightenment, two or three centuries ago, the notion of moral relativism began to gain a hold in Western societies. Under its sway people discarded the concept of sin as irrelevant. In this view there are no sins, only sicknesses, misfortunes, mistakes, or the outworking of one's environmental, hereditary and biological input (western terminology) or of one's fate or karma (eastern). Alternatively, sin is acknowledged to exist, but only as defined in one's culture — cultural relativism thus negates the biblical concept of sin as absolute wrong.

Much of the Bible is concerned with explaining what sin is, what the penalty for sinning is, how we can avoid that penalty and have our sins forgiven, and how we can live a holy life free from the power of sin, pleasing to God and to ourselves. See the book of Romans and especially Ro 5:12–21N.

7 ***P'rushim* and *Tz'dukim*** (plural; singular *Parush, Tzadok*), "Pharisees and Sadducees." These were the two main factions of the religious establishment in Yeshua's time. In 586 B.C.E. Babylon conquered Judea and Jerusalem, laid waste the First Temple, which King Solomon had built, and deported the ruling classes to Babylon. With the Temple, the sacrifices and the *cohanim* no longer functioning, the Jews in exile and after their return seventy years later sought another organizing principle on which to center their communal life. They found it in the *Torah* (the "Law"; see 5:17N), as can be seen already in the report of the reading of the *Torah* by Ezra (Nehemiah 8). The earliest students, developers and upholders of the *Torah* seem to have been of the hereditary priestly caste — Ezra himself was both a *cohen* and a *sofer* ("scribe"). But later, as the *cohanim* were drawn back into caring for the sacrificial system as it developed during the Second Temple period, a lay movement which supported the *Torah* and favored its adaptation to the needs of the people arose and began to challenge the authority of the *cohanim*. The *cohanim* and their backers in the first century C.E. were known as *Tz'dukim*, after the *cohen gadol* appointed by King Solomon, Tzadok (his name means "righteous"; compare 6:1–4&N, 13:17&N).

Meanwhile, under the Maccabees in the second century B.C.E. those whose main concern was not the sacrifices but the *Torah* were called *Hasidim*. (Except for the name, which means "pious ones," there is no connection between these and the various Orthodox Jewish communities that follow the teachings spread by the *talmidim* of the seventeenth-century Eastern European teacher and mystic known as the *Ba'al Shem Tov.*) The successors to the *Hasidim* were known as *P'rushim*, which means "separated ones," because they separated themselves from worldly ways and worldly people. These *P'rushim* not only took the *Tanakh* to be God's word to man, but also considered the accumulated tradition handed down over the centuries by the sages and teachers to be God's word as well — the Oral *Torah* — so that a system for living developed which touched on every aspect of life.

In Yeshua's day the *Tz'dukim* tended to be richer, more skeptical, more worldly, and more willing to cooperate with the Roman rulers than the *P'rushim*. However, the destruction of the Second Temple in 70 C.E. ended the viability of the *Tz'dukim* by destroying the venue of their chief responsibility; and whatever tradition they may have developed has for the most part been lost. See Ac 23:6&N.

The *P'rushim* and their successors were then free to develop further their own received tradition and make it the center of gravity for Jewish life everywhere. Eventually, due to the dispersion of the Jewish people, which separated many from the living flow of tradition, these oral materials were collected and written down in the Mishna (220 C.E.), under the editorship of Y'hudah HaNasi ("Judah the Prince"). The rabbis' discussions about the Mishna during the following two or three centuries in the Land of Israel and in Babylon were collected to form the Jerusalem and Babylonian Gemaras. Combined with the Mishna these constitute the Jerusalem and Babylonian Talmuds.

Centuries of Christian preaching have made the English word "Pharisee" virtually a synonym for "hypocrite" and "stubborn legalist" — witness the entry for "pharisaical" in Webster's Third New International Dictionary:

> "Resembling the Pharisees especially in strictness of doctrine and in rigid observance of forms and ceremonies; making an outward show of piety and morality but lacking the inward spirit; censorious of others' morals or practices; formal, sanctimonious, self-righteous, hypocritical."

While it is true that Yeshua himself lambasted "you hypocritical *Torah*-teachers and *P'rushim"* for having many of these traits (see Chapter 23 and 23:13N), Christians often forget that his hard words were delivered in a family context — as a Jew criticizing some of his fellow Jews. A glance at any modern Jewish community newspaper will show that Jews are still critical of each other and willing to endure such criticism — reproof and rebuke are normal and acceptable behaviors in many Jewish settings. However, Yeshua does not take his fellow Jews to task for being Pharisees but for being hypocrites — the former does not imply the latter. Moreover, Yeshua's criticism was not of all *P'rushim* but only of those who were hypocritical. While some Pharisees were insincere or overly concerned with externals, others were "not far from the Kingdom of God" (Mk 12:34), and some entered it and became followers of Yeshua without ceasing to be *P'rushim* (Ac 15:5). In fact Sha'ul said before the *Sanhedrin*, "Brothers, I myself am a *Parush*" — "am," not "was" (Ac 23:6).

Because of the subconscious negative associations most people have with the English word "Pharisee," the *JNT* text uses the original Hebrew words "*Parush*" (singular) and "*P'rushim*" (plural), and for the sake of parallelism substitutes "*Tzadok/Tz'dukim*" for "Sadducee/Sadducees."

You snakes! Yochanan discerned that these particular Pharisees and Sadducees (see above paragraphs) were insincere. Whether they were dilettantes sampling the latest religious fad or envoys from Jerusalem investigating Yochanan's activities is unclear. Luke 7:28–32 suggests the former, Mt 21:23–27 the latter. In any case, in the end the religious establishment did not accept Yochanan's ministry.

The coming punishment, literally, "the wrath to come." God's wrath is spoken of here and frequently in the New Testament as *the* wrath, emphasizing how certainly — one might even say how automatically — God's wrath must follow sin. Just as God's physical law of gravity makes it certain that the automatic consequence of jumping from a tall building is physical destruction, so God's moral law of sin makes it certain that the automatic consequence of persisting in sins is eternal spiritual destruction in God's wrath.

9 **Don't suppose you can comfort yourselves by saying, "Avraham is our father"!** The Messianic Jewish scholar Alfred Edersheim wrote,

> "[D]id they imagine that, according to the common notion of the time, the vials of wrath were to be poured out only on the Gentiles, while they, as Abraham's

children, were sure of escape — in the words of the Talmud, that 'the night' (Isaiah 21:12) was 'only to the nations of the world, but the morning to Israel' (Jer. Ta'anit 64a)?

"For, no principle was more fully established in the popular conviction than that all Israel had part in the world to come (Sanhedrin 10:1 [quoted in Ro 11:26aN]), and this specifically because of their connection with Abraham." (*The Life and Times of Jesus the Messiah*, New York: Anson D. F. Randolph and Company, 2nd edition [1884], Volume I, p. 271)

God can raise up for Avraham sons from these stones, even as he raised up Isaac from the stone altar in figurative resurrection; compare MJ 11:19&N. The English phrase, "**sons from these stones**" is an attempt to preserve by alliteration the Hebrew wordplay which the Greek text ignores. "Sons" in Hebrew is *banim*, "stones" is written *abanim* (pronounced *avanim*). A less likely possibility is that "from these *stones*" means "from these clods, these *'am-ha'aretz*" (see Yn 7:49N, Ac 4:13N). Wordplay has been common in Jewish speech from ancient times to the present, with many examples in the *Tanakh* itself; see 2:23N.

11–12 Fire. Some commentators see this as a purifying fire that will eliminate the wicked from the Jewish people along lines set forth in Malachi 3:19–21(4:1–3) and Psalm 1:6 ("The way of the wicked will perish"); see Rv 20:15. The same psalm also compares the ungodly with **straw** (Psalm 1:4). Others take it as enthusiasm for holiness, being on fire for God.

He will immerse you in the *Ruach HaKodesh*, the "Holy Spirit," the Spirit of God. A promise made by Yeshua himself (Lk 24:49; Yn 15:26, 16:13–14; Ac 1:8); its fulfillment begins at Ac 2:1ff.

15 We should do everything righteousness requires. Yeshua himself did not have to be immersed for his sins because he committed none (MJ 4:15). Some have suggested he was fully identifying with sinful humanity, who did need purification (see 2:15N, Ro 8:3&N, Pp 2:6–8). On what it is that God's righteousness requires, see Ro 3:24–26.

16 Some ancient manuscripts add "to him" after "opened."

17 Voice from heaven or *bat-kol*; see Yn 12:28&N, Ac 9:4N. "**Heaven**" here has a dual meaning — (1) the sky, (2) God; see v. 2N.

This is my beloved son. While it is true that everyone is in a sense God's son, Yeshua is so in a unique way — his "only" (or "only-begotten") son (Yn 1:18&N). Two other passages come to mind: one in which Adam is referred to as God's son (Lk 3:23), and Psalm 2:7, "*Adonai* said to me, 'You are my son; today I have become your father.'" Combined with 1C 15:45, in which Yeshua is called "the last Adam," and Ro 5:12–21, where Yeshua and Adam are further compared, these texts show us that in thinking about Yeshua's person and ministry one must keep Adam in mind. This is especially important in the verses immediately following, in which Yeshua, like Adam, is tempted by the Adversary, Satan. See also v. 15N.

In whom I am well pleased. The language is reminiscent of Isaiah 42:1, one of the

"Servant" passages; Isaiah 42:1–4 is quoted below (12:18–21); see also 17:5. The "Servant" passages sometimes refer to the people of Israel and sometimes to the Messiah, a fact which strengthens the point made in 2:15N that Yeshua the Messiah represents and stands for the whole Jewish people.

CHAPTER 4

1 **The Adversary.** Greek *diabolos* (usually transliterated "devil") translates Hebrew *satan*, "adversary, opponent, rebel." In Isaiah 14:11–15, between the lines of a taunt against the king of Babylon, can be read the downfall of a creature who was once both powerful and beautiful but who in pride rebelled against God and came to oppose him; Ezekiel 28:11–19 is similar. On the other hand, Job 1–2 is explicit in showing Satan as the opponent of both God and man. In Genesis 3 as the serpent he tempts Adam and Eve to disobey God; equating the Adversary with the serpent is clear from Rv 12:9, which speaks of "that ancient serpent, also known as the Devil and Satan (the Adversary), the deceiver of the whole world." The *satan* is a created being, in no way equal to his Creator; yet he is the background source of all sin, evil and opposition to God. The book of Job teaches that the reason why an omnipotent and good God permits such opposition is a mystery, but that God remains in perfect and unthreatened control. This we see most clearly in Job 40–41, where "Behemoth" and "Leviathan" are seen to be stand-ins for the Adversary, because when God challenges Job to deal with them he repents "in dust and ashes" (Job 42:6). Both the *Tanakh* and the New Testament take for granted the existence of a supernatural realm of good, obedient angels who serve God and evil, rebellious ones (demons) who serve the Adversary.

3 **Son of God.** (See 1:1N on "son of.") This theologically important New Testament term can mean: (1) a godly person (without divine or supernatural overtones); (2) the special one sent by God; (3) the son of God in the flesh, as described in Chapters 1–2 above and Luke 1–2; (4) a human whose presence on earth required a special creative act of God, hence either Adam or Yeshua, who is therefore called "the second Adam" (Lk 3:38 Ro 5:12–21, 1 Corinthians 15); (5) the Yeshua who could in his earthly lifetime relate to God as his personal Father, calling him "*Abba*"; and (6) the divine, eternally existent individual or Word who always has and always will be within the inner "structure" of *Adonai* and, in that structure which is the one God, is in his essence the Son in both equal and subsidiary relationship with the Father (Yn 1:1–3, 14; 10:31; 14:9–10, 28; Pp 2:5–11). Here, from the mouth of the Adversary, it probably carries all six meanings.

The *Tanakh* says little explicitly about these things, yet it does offer strong *r'mazim* ("hints"; see 2:15N) at Isaiah 9:5–6(6–7), Micah 5:1(2), Psalm 2:7, Proverbs 30:4 and Daniel 7:13. In ancient Jewish literature Enoch 105:2 and 4 Ezra 7:28–29, 13:32–52, 14:9 refer to the Messiah as the Son of God. Compare 8:20N on "son of man."

4–10 **The *Tanakh***, the Old Testament — rendered "Scripture" or "it is written" in most translations. The Hebrew word "*Tanakh*" is an acronym formed from the first letters of the three parts of the Hebrew Bible:
(1) *Torah* ("Teaching") — the Five Books of Moses or Pentateuch (Genesis, Exodus,

Leviticus, Numbers, Deuteronomy).

(2) *N'vi'im* ("Prophets") — the historical books (Joshua, Judges, Samuel and Kings), the three Major Prophets (Isaiah, Jeremiah, Ezekiel), and the twelve Minor Prophets.

(3) *K'tuvim* ("Writings") — Psalms, Proverbs, Job, the "five scrolls" (Song of Songs, Ruth, Lamentations, Ecclesiastes, Esther), Daniel, Ezra-Nehemiah and Chronicles.

If you are the Son of God. Satan presents Yeshua with each of the three categories of temptation named by Yochanan (1 Yn 2:15–17&N): "the desires of the old nature" or "flesh" (Ro 7:5&N) — **"If you are the Son of God, order these stones to become bread"**; "the desires of the eyes" — **the Adversary… showed him all the kingdoms of the world in all their glory, and said to him, "All this I will give you if you will bow down and worship me"**; "and the pretensions of life" — the Adversary took him to the holy city, **Jerusalem,** and set him on the highest point of the Temple. **"If you are the Son of God," he said, "jump!"**

Satan was already using the same three kinds of temptations in the Garden of Eden: "When the woman saw that the tree was good for food" (desires of the flesh), "and that it was a delight to the eyes" (desires of the eyes), "and a tree to be desired to make one wise" (pretensions of life), "she took of the fruit and ate" (Genesis 3:6).

The difference is that "the first man" did not resist the Adversary (Ya 4:7), but "the last man" did (Ro 5:12–21&N; 1C 15:21–22, 45–49&NN; MJ 4:15). Yeshua, showing the power of the Word of God in resisting the Adversary (Ya 4:7), quotes the *Torah* in answer to all three temptations — Deuteronomy 8:3 at v. 4, Deuteronomy 6:16 at v. 7, and Deuteronomy 6:13 at v. 10. But Satan, "the inventor of the lie" (Yn 8:44), can misuse Scripture to deceive — Psalm 91:11–12 at v. 6.

12 See 14:3ff.

13 **K'far-Nachum** (Capernaum; the Hebrew name means "village of Nahum") was located on the northwest shore of Lake Kinneret (the Sea of Galilee; see v. 18N) and site of much of Yeshua's activity as described in the New Testament. Now an archeological park supervised by the Roman Catholic Church, it is a standard stop on Christian tours of Israel. An octagonal 5th-century Byzantine structure amidst earlier ruins is said to mark where Kefa lived (8:14); if so, the older remains may be part of the first Messianic Jewish congregation building. The walls of a fourth-century synagogue still stand.

15 Isaiah 8:23–9:1(9:1–2). See Lk 1:79N.

18 **Lake Kinneret** is the name used in Israel for the body of fresh water formed by the River Yarden (Jordan) in the Galil (Galilee); it is so called because it is shaped like a harp (*kinnor* in ancient Hebrew). English versions of the Bible identify it as the Sea of Galilee; at Yn 6:1, 23 and 21:1 the Greek text calls it "the Sea of Tiberias."

Kefa is the name Yeshua gave Shim'on Bar-Yochanan (Yn 1:42&N); it means "rock" in Aramaic. The Greek word for "rock" is "*petros*," which is usually brought into English as "Peter." Occasionally, instead of translating "*Kefa*" as "*Petros*," the Greek text transliterates "*Kefa*" as "*Kephas*"; this appears in English versions as "Cephas."

21 **Ya'akov Ben-Zavdai and Yochanan,** usually rendered "James the son of Zebedee and

John." English-speakers are usually unaware that the name "James" comes from the Hebrew name "*Ya'akov*" ("Jacob"). "*Ya'akov*" was transliterated into Greek as "*Iacobou*"; in Latin this became "*Iacobus*" and later "*Jacomus*," from which comes "James." The seemingly Gentile name "James" thus displays its Jewish roots, as we saw above is also the case with the name "John" (3:1N).

23 **Good News** is the *JNT*'s rendering of Greek *evangelion*, which gives English such words as "evangelism." The more common English translation of the word is "gospel," which means "good news" in archaic English.

24 **Demonized people.** Greek *daimonizomenoi* is sometimes rendered "demoniacs" or "people possessed by demons." As noted in 4:1N above, the Bible takes for granted the existence of a spirit-world. According to the New Testament, demons — also called unclean or evil spirits, lying spirits, and angels of the devil — can affect people by causing physical illness, mental aberrations, emotional malaise and moral temptation. "Demonized" means "affected by demons" in one or more of these ways. Actual "possession" or "ownership" of a human being by a demon is not taught in the Bible.

CHAPTER 5

1 ***Talmidim*** (plural; singular *talmid*), "disciples." The English word "disciple" fails to convey the richness of the relationship between a rabbi and his *talmidim* in the first century C.E. Teachers, both itinerant like Yeshua and settled ones, attracted followers who wholeheartedly gave themselves over to their teachers (though not in a mindless way, as happens today in some cults). The essence of the relationship was one of trust in every area of living, and its goal was to make the *talmid* like his rabbi in knowledge, wisdom and ethical behavior (compare 10:24–25, and see the *JNT* glossary entry on *talmid*).

3 Chapters 5–7 constitute the Sermon on the Mount. Compare the Sermon on the Plain (Lk 6:20–49&N), where many of the same topics are dealt with somewhat differently. For example, where Lk 6:20 simply says "How blessed are you poor" (compare Lk 6:24), v. 4 here says the same of **the poor in spirit**, those who have the humble, dependent, vulnerable attitude of poor people, even if they happen to be rich.

How blessed. Greek *makarios* corresponds to Hebrew *asher* and means "blessed," "happy," and "fortunate" all at once, so that no one English word is adequate. For a Hebrew example, compare Psalm 144:15: "How blessed/happy/fortunate the people whose God is *Adonai*!" Verses 3–12 are known as the Beatitudes because the word "*beatus*" was used in the best-known Latin version, Jerome's "Vulgate" (c. 410 C.E.), to translate "*makarios*." For more on the Beatitudes, see Appendix, p. 930.

Kingdom of Heaven. See 3:2N.

5 **The meek... will inherit the Land.** Or will they, as other versions have it, "inherit the earth"? Christians often think that since the Gospel is for all humanity God is no longer interested in Israel as a nation (even though 23:37–39&N proves the opposite).

This error — known variously as Replacement theology, Dominion theology, Kingdom Now theology, Covenant theology (in some of its forms), Reconstructionism and (in England) Restorationism — with its antisemitic implications, is so widespread that New Testament passages are even mis-translated in conformance with it (see Ro 10:1–8&NN for another such passage). The present verse is one of those passages. Most versions inform the reader that "the meek," presumably all the meek, from all the nations, "shall inherit the earth," ruling the entire planet. While believers will return to rule with the Messiah at his Second Coming (1 Th 4:13–18, Rv 20), here Yeshua is quoting Psalm 37:11, where the context makes it clear that "the meek" refers to the meek of Israel, who, according to God's promises, "will inherit the Land," the Land of Israel, which Mattityahu has already mentioned explicitly (2:20–21&N).

Although Greek *gê* can mean either "earth" or "land," in Psalm 37 the Hebrew word "*eretz*" means "Land" (and not "earth") not less than six times: those of Israel who trust in *Adonai* will "dwell in the Land" (v. 3); and those of Israel who wait upon *Adonai* (v. 9), are meek (v. 11, cited here), are blessed by *Adonai* (v. 22), are righteous (v. 29) and keep his way (v. 34) will "inherit the Land." The term "inherit" in the *Tanakh* refers to the Jewish people's inheritance from God, which includes, in addition to spiritual elements, not the whole earth but a specific small territory on the east shore of the Mediterranean Sea.

Because the Gospel is universal, and because of the false theology teaching that God is no longer interested in the Jews as a nation, Christians have tended to suppose that the New Testament somehow cancels God's promise to give the Jewish people the Land of Israel. No small amount of opposition to the present-day State of Israel on the part of Christians is based on this false assumption. To combat this error it is important for Jews and Christians alike to understand that the New Testament does not alter any of God's promises to the Jewish people; God's literal promises are not somehow spiritualized out of existence "in Christ." See further material in Appendix, p. 930.

Eighteen times in the New Testament the Greek phrase "*ê gê*" refers to the Land of Israel. As mentioned, two are explicit — Mattityahu calls the Holy Land "*Eretz-Israel*" twice (Mt 2:20–21&N). Four are citations from the *Tanakh* — here (Psalm 37:11), Mt 24:30 and Rv 1:7 (Zechariah 12:10, 14), and Ep 6:3 (Deuteronomy 5:17). Five are based on the *Tanakh* without being citations — Lk 4:25 and Ya 5:17, 18 (1 Kings 17:1; 18:1, 41–45), MJ 11:9 (Genesis 12, 13, 15, 20, 23), and Rv 20:9 (Ezekiel 38–39). The remaining eight are implied by the context — Mt 5:13, 10:34, 27:45; Mk 15:33; Lk 12:51, 21:23, 23:44; Rv 11:10. Because Replacement theologians claim that God no longer promises the Land of Israel to the Jews, it is important to see that the New Testament still gives Jewish possession of the physical Land of Israel a significant place in God's plan.

For more on Replacement theology and its refutation, see notes at Mt 24:34; Lk 21:24; Ac 1:6–7, 21:21; Ro 2:28–29; 11:1–32, 11–12, 13–32, 23–24, 28–29; 2C 1:20; Ga 6:16; Ep 2:11–16. Also see my *Messianic Jewish Manifesto*, pp. 109–118.

13–14 Jewish believers are **salt**, a seasoning and a preservative, **for the Land** of Israel (see v. 5N), that is, for the Jewish people, and **light for the world**, for the Gentiles, as taught in Isaiah 49:6. God established a "covenant of salt" (Numbers 18:19), which is applied to King David and his descendants—that is, to the Messiah—in 2 Chronicles 13:5.

The Jewish believers in the Messiah, then, are the righteous remnant (Ro 11), for whose sake God preserves Israel and the world. For more on salt, see Lk 14:34–35&N,

Co 4:5–6&N. Sometimes Israeli Messianic Jews feel they are not part of the "real" Jewish community in the Land. But the reason Messianic Jews are here is to be the righteous remnant, for whose sake God preserves the nation of Israel. This motivates us to keep on trusting God, trying to realize the Messianic Jewish vision and proclaiming Yeshua to our people.

17 **Don't think that I have come to abolish the *Torah* or the Prophets. I have come not to abolish but to complete**, to make their meaning full. The Hebrew word "*Torah,*" literally "teaching, doctrine," is rendered in both the Septuagint and the New Testament by the Greek word "*nomos*," which means "law." Greek has had a more direct and pervasive influence on English and other modern languages than Hebrew has, and this is why in most languages one speaks of the "Law" of Moses rather than the "Teaching" of Moses. It is also part of the reason why the *Torah* has mistakenly come to be thought of by Christians as legalistic in character (see Ro 3:20bN, Ga 3:23bN).

In Judaism the word "*Torah*" may mean:

(1) *Chumash* (the Pentateuch, the five books of Moses); or
(2) That plus the Prophets and the Writings, i.e., the *Tanakh* (known by Christians as the Old Testament; see 4:4–10N); or
(3) That plus the Oral *Torah*, which includes the Talmud and other legal materials; or
(4) That plus all religious instruction from the rabbis, including ethical and aggadic (homiletical) materials.

Here it means the first of these, since "the Prophets" are mentioned separately.

The Prophets. The word "Prophets," capitalized (as here, 7:12, 22:40; Lk 16:16, 28, 31; 24:44; Yn 1:45, 6:45; Ac 13:15, 27, 40; 15:15; 24:14; 28:23; Ro 3:21), refers to the second of the three main parts of the *Tanakh*. When the *Tanakh* prophets as persons are referred to, the word is not capitalized; "prophet" in the singular is never capitalized. By mentioning both the *Torah* and the Prophets Yeshua is saying that he has not come to modify or replace God's Word, the *Tanakh*. Compare Lk 24:44–45.

To complete. The Greek word for "to complete" is "*plêrôsai*," literally, "to fill"; the usual rendering here, however, is "to fulfill." Replacement theology, which wrongly teaches that the Church has replaced the Jews as God's people (v. 5N), understands this verse wrongly in two ways.

First, Yeshua's "fulfilling" **the *Torah*** is thought to mean that it is unnecessary for people to fulfill it now. But there is no logic to the proposition that Yeshua's obeying the *Torah* does away with our need to obey it. In fact, Sha'ul (Paul), whose object in his letter to the Romans is to foster "the obedience that comes from trusting" in Yeshua, teaches that such trusting does not abolish *Torah* but confirms it (Ro 1:5, 3:31).

Second, with identical lack of logic, Yeshua's "fulfilling" **the Prophets** is thought to imply that no prophecies from the *Tanakh* remain for the Jews. But the Hebrew Bible's promises to the Jews are not abolished in the name of being "fulfilled in Yeshua." Rather, fulfillment in Yeshua is an added assurance that everything God has promised the Jews will yet come to pass (see 2C 1:20&N).

It is true that Yeshua kept the *Torah* perfectly and fulfilled predictions of the Prophets, but that is not the point here. Yeshua did not come to abolish but "to make full" *(plêrôsai)* the meaning of what the *Torah* and the ethical demands of the Prophets require. Thus he came **to complete** our understanding of **the *Torah* and the Prophets**, so that we can try more effectively to be and do what they say to be and do. Verses 18–20 enunciate three ways in which the *Torah* and the Prophets remain necessary, applicable and in force. The remainder of Chapter 5 gives six specific cases in which Yeshua explains the fuller spiritual meaning of points in the Jewish Law. In fact, this verse states the theme and agenda of the entire Sermon on the Mount, in which Yeshua completes, makes fuller, the understanding of his *talmidim* concerning the *Torah* and the Prophets, so that they can more fully express what being God's people is all about.

The Anglican Christian writer Brigid Younghughes supports my understanding of this passage in these words:

> "'...I came not to destroy, but to fulfil.' And surely 'to fulfil' means to complete, in the sense of bringing to perfection, not, as Christians have all too often interpreted it, to render obsolete; to fulfil in such a way as to perfect a foundation on which to build further." (*Christianity's Jewish Heritage*, West Sussex: Angel Press, 1988, p. 8)

18 Except at the end of prayers, "**Yes indeed**" and "Yes" are used in the *JNT* to render Greek *amên* (which transliterates Hebrew *'amen*). The Hebrew root '-m-n means "truth, faithfulness," which is why the Hebrew word *'amen* means "It is true, so be it, may it become true" — hence its use in English as well as Hebrew by those listening to a prayer. A speaker's "Amen" to his own prayer is itself superfluous, yet useful as a cue for others to respond with "Amen" (as at 6:13; Ro 1:25, 9:5, 11:36).

In any case, Hebrew *'amen* is always used in reference to something previously said. Yet most versions translate it as if it pointed forward rather than back. For example, the King James Version (KJV) translates this passage as, "Verily, I tell you" what follows. The translators who do this have New Testament internal evidence as grounds; for there are parallel passages in which one gospel writer has, *"Amên* I tell you...," while the other has "Truly (Greek *aleithôs*) I tell you..." (compare Lk 12:44 with 24:47 below, and Lk 9:27 with Mk 9:1). But this solution requires assuming that Yeshua invented a different pattern of speech than can be found in other sources. While one can say that he was originality incarnate, I think it facile to invoke this notion over ordinary conservative scholarship. Instead, one must ask whether his "Amens" make good sense understood traditionally as referring back, not forward. And in fact, they do. (At Yn 16:7 the text does not say, *"Amên, Amên"*; it actually says in Greek what I have put in English, "But I tell you the truth,..."; this does, of course, point forward.)

To be specific, his "Amen" to himself emphasizes his own previous point, sometimes with the force, "You may not think that I really meant what I just said, but I do!" (v. 26; 6:2, 5, 16; 10:15, 42; 13:17; 18:18; 23:36; 24:34, 47; 26:13). His "Amen" to what someone else has just said can be an acknowledgment conveying the sense, "I recognize the problem," (19:28) or even ironic in tone, "Your question/answer shows me that at last you're beginning to catch on!" (21:21, 31), "You can't be serious!" (25:12) or "How I wish it were so (but it isn't)!" (26:34). Sometimes after a speech, or even after an event, it calls attention to what just happened, conveying things like, "That was amazing! Did you notice?" (8:10) or, "Not what you expected, is it?" (a beautiful example at 18:3); at 19:23 it amounts to a sigh; at 25:40, 45 the King's "Amen" means, "You are astounded that things are working out this way, but that's how it is"; at 26:21 Yeshua's

"Amen" means, "Right now you're relaxed and comfortable, but I have news for you!" And sometimes Yeshua's "Amen" is simply affirmative ("I agree") but becomes the take-off for his own reinforcing or contrasting remarks (several of the above examples, and 8:13, where his "Amen" means, "I agree with your unspoken answer to my rhetorical question"). See also Rv 7:11–12N.

The *Tanakh* provides a striking example of "*Amen*" used ironically, even sarcastically, at the beginning of a sentence. In Jeremiah 28 the false prophet Chananyah predicts that within two years God will restore the Temple vessels taken by Babylonian King Nebuchadnezzar. Yirmiyahu replies, "*Amen*! May *Adonai* do so! May *Adonai* perform the words which you have prophesied.... Nevertheless, hear now,... Chananyah: *Adonai* has not sent you. Instead, you are making this people trust in a lie!"

Yud is the smallest letter of the Hebrew alphabet and is used in the *JNT* to render Greek *iôta*, the smallest letter in the Greek alphabet. Only a small **stroke** distinguishes one Hebrew letter from another — for example *dalet* (ד) from *resh* (ר) or *beit* (ב) from *kaf* (כ). KJV transliterates "*yud*" as "jot" and renders "stroke" as "tittle" (the corresponding Hebrew term is "*kotz*," literally, "thorn").

19 ***Mitzvot*** (singular *mitzvah*). A *mitzvah* is a commandment; traditionally in the *Torah* (the Pentateuch) there are 613 *mitzvot* for the Jewish people to obey. In casual Jewish English (see the paragraph "Jewish English" in the Introduction to the *JNT*, Section IV), "doing a *mitzvah*" means "doing a good deed, something nice, something helpful to someone, a favor"; but these meanings derive from the original sense, "a commandment" from God. Elsewhere I have discussed at length whether, and/or in what sense, Messianic Jews are expected to observe the *Torah* and obey the *mitzvot*; see my *Messianic Jewish Manifesto* (Jewish New Testament Publications, 2nd edition, 1991), especially Chapter V.

20 ***Torah*-teachers** ("scribes"). See 2:4N.

21 Sixth of the Ten Commandments (Exodus 20:13, Deuteronomy 5:17). In this commentary I use the Jewish enumeration of the Ten Commandments, in which the first Commandment is, "I am *Adonai*, who brought you out of the land of Egypt, out of the house of bondage." Since this is in fact not a commandment but a declaration, Christian enumerations do not include it. But the Hebrew phrase for "the Ten Commandments" is "*'aseret-hadibrot*," literally, "the ten sayings." This first "saying" is actually the basis for the other nine *dibrot* as well as for all the *mitzvot* (see v. 19N). It is because of who God is ("I am *Adonai*") and because of his benevolent involvement in the ongoing life and history of his people ("who brought you out of the land of Egypt") and his concern for their welfare ("out of the house of bondage") that, in faith, hope, love and gratitude, his people should obey him. Yeshua begins his detailed "filling" of the *Torah* (v. 17N) with one of the Ten Commandments, implicitly alluding to this underlying ground for all obedience to God. "In Judaism the citation of a Scripture text implies the whole context," all Ten Commandments, "not merely the quoted words" (2:6N).

22 ***Sanhedrin***, Hebrew name given to a Jewish court, but the word is Greek in origin. Local courts had three or twenty-three judges; the central *Sanhedrin* in Jerusalem had seventy. See also Appendix, p. 930–931.

Gey-Hinnom, brought over into Greek and English as "Gehenna" and usually translated "hell." Literally, "valley of Hinnom" (a personal name); located both then and now just south of the Old City of Jerusalem. Rubbish fires were always burning there; hence its use as a metaphor for hell, with its burning fire of punishment for the unrighteous, as taught in the Hebrew Bible at Isaiah 66:24. Elsewhere in the *Tanakh* Deuteronomy 32:22 talks about a burning hell; 2 Samuel 22:6, Psalm 18:5 and Psalm 116:3 show that hell is a sorrowful place; Psalm 9:17 says that the wicked go to hell; and Job 26:6 shows that hell is a place of destruction. The Hebrew word in all these verses is "*sh'ol*"; it usually corresponds to Greek "*adês*" ("Hades"). Thus hell is not a New Testament *chiddush* (novelty). When liberals assert that Judaism teaches there is no hell, they are introducing a later doctrine of their own not based on the *Tanakh.*

Since the idea of eternal punishment is at the very least offputting, some seek to soften it by proposing that the final judgment is total annihilation, in which nothing is experienced, either good or bad. Nevertheless, what the Bible teaches about both *sh'ol* (*adês*) and Gey-Hinnom is that there is a state of eternal sorrowful existence to be consciously experienced by those who come under God's ultimate condemnation (see the above passages and Rv 20:15&N). Changing the Biblical concept of hell to non-existence is, unfortunately, wishful-thinking theology.

23–24 Traditional Judaism expresses this idea thusly in the Mishna:

> "*Yom-Kippur* [the Day of Atonement] atones for a person's transgressions against God, but it does not atone for his transgressions against his fellow-man until he appeases him." (Yoma 8:9)

27 Seventh of the Ten Commandments (Exodus 20:13(14), Deuteronomy 5:18). See v. 21N.

28 The believer has "the mind of the Messiah" (1C 2:15) and is not to nurture and cherish improper sexual feelings, desires, urges and lusts. If he does, then, for reasons explained at Ya 1:12–15, he will succumb to the temptations they raise, give sexual fantasizing undue control in his life and finally engage in wrong sexual behavior such as adultery, fornication and homosexuality (on homosexuality see Ro 1:24–28&N).

31 Deuteronomy 24:1 mentions a "writing of divorcement" (Hebrew *sefer-k'ritut*) but does not specify its contents or the conditions under which divorce was permitted. The rabbis call such a document a ***get*** and discuss divorce in the Talmud (for more, see 19:3N).

32 The principle does not prevent believers divorced before coming to Messianic faith from remarrying, since all sins prior to salvation are forgiven when repentance has taken place. Anyone unmarried at the time of his salvation is free to marry (but apparently only to another believer — see 1C 7:39&N).

33–37 Do not break your oath (or: "Do not swear falsely," or: "Do not perjure yourself"). **Keep your vows to *Adonai*.** The distinction between vows and oaths is hazy not only to us, but also within Judaism; and the issue doesn't seem important today. The early believers understood Yeshua not as prohibiting all vows (see Ac 18:5&N, 21:23&N),

but as prohibiting vain oaths — the rabbis of the time did the same. In the Apocrypha compare Sirach 23:9, "Do not accustom your mouth to swearing oaths, and do not habitually use the name of the Holy One." Philo of Alexandria recommended avoiding oaths entirely (Decalogue 84). The Talmud has this parallel to v. 37: "Let your 'no' and 'yes' both be righteous [i.e., straightforward]." (Bava Metzia 49a)

38 Exodus 21:24, Leviticus 24:20, Deuteronomy 19:21, where the context of **eye for eye**, etc. shows that God was not commanding revenge, but controlling and limiting it. Retribution and punishment must be commensurate with the crime; contrast Cain and Lamech's extraction of multiplied vengeance at Genesis 4:24.

The following citation of the Mishna is given at length in order to show that rabbinic thinking on the matter of legal damages goes far beyond the simple *lex talionis* (Latin, "law of retaliation," i.e., eye for eye):

> "If someone wounds his fellow, he becomes liable to compensate the injured party for five different aspects of the injury: damage, pain, healing, loss of time from work, and insult.
>
> "In the case of damage, here is an example of how restitution is determined. Suppose someone blinded someone else's eye, cut off his hand or broke his leg. They value the injured person as if he were a slave for sale in the market, and they appraise his value before the injury and now.
>
> "Here is an example of determining the compensation for pain. Suppose someone burns another with a skewer or nail, even if only on his fingernail, where it doesn't actually produce a wound. They determine how much a man of his position would be willing to be paid to suffer that amount of pain.
>
> "For healing the indemnity is determined in this way. If someone hit another person, he must pay all the expenses of healing him. If he develops ulcers, then if they come about in consequence of the blow, he is liable; but if not, he is not liable. If the wound heals, reopens, heals and reopens again, he is liable for all the expenses. But once it has healed thoroughly, he does not remain liable to pay the expenses of healing him.
>
> "The value of time lost is estimated in this way. They consider what he would earn if he were a watchman over a cucumber field [a job requiring no special skills], for he has already been paid for the loss of his hand or foot. [In practice, this means they determine what kind of work he will be fit for when he fully recovers and evaluate the time lost by this standard.]
>
> "For insult the compensation is determined entirely in accordance with the social status of both the one who caused the indignity and the one who suffered it. If someone insults a person who is naked, blind or asleep, he is liable. But if a sleeping person causes an insult, he is not liable. Someone who falls from a roof and causes injury and insult at the same time is liable for the injury but not for the insult,... because one should not be held responsible for an indignity one did not intend to cause." (Bava Kama 8:1)

41 **If a soldier forces you to carry his pack for one mile, carry it for two.** Literally, "And whoever presses you into service one mile, go with him two." The context is the Roman conquest; soldiers could make subjects do their work for them. Yeshua's advice is a specific application of v. 16.

43 Leviticus 19:18 told **our fathers** to "**love your neighbor** as yourself." While in Psalm 139:21–22 the writer commends himself for hating *God's* enemies, nowhere does the *Tanakh* teach that you should **hate *your* enemy**. Such a teaching must have come from the misinterpretations of those who "teach man-made rules as if they were doctrines" of God (Isaiah 29:13, cited by Yeshua below at 15:9). On "Jacob I loved but Esau I hated" (Malachi 1:2–3) see Ro 9:10–13&N.

44 **Love your enemies!** Some contrast the "realistic" ethics of Judaism with "Christian romanticism" and cite this as an example. However, the command is not to have good feelings about your enemies, but to want and do good for them, and, more specifically, to **pray for those who persecute you.** It is realistic enough to have been flattered by imitation in a well-known medieval Jewish work: "Pray for your enemy that he serve God." (*Orchot Tzaddikim* 15c)

46 **Tax-collectors.** Jews who undertook to collect taxes for the Roman rulers were the most despised people in the Jewish community. Not only were they serving the oppressors, but they found it easy to abuse the system so as to line their own pockets by exploiting their fellow Jews.

47 ***Goyim.*** The Greek word "*ethnê*" (singular "*ethnos*") corresponds to Hebrew *goyim* (singular *goy*), also translated in the *JNT* as "Gentiles," "nations," "pagans" or "non-Jews"; KJV sometimes renders it "heathen." Jews who speak English often use the Hebrew (and Yiddish) word "*goyim*" to refer to non-Jews. Although today "*Goyim*" sometimes carries a mildly pejorative tone linked to the idea that a *goy* is not "one of us" (see Ga 2:15&N), Yeshua here is referring to the fact that the *Goyim* had not received God's revelation as had the Jews, and therefore less was to be expected of them; since this was God's doing, there is no defamatory connotation. See also 10:5N, 24:7N.

CHAPTER 6

1–4 ***Tzedakah***, Hebrew for "righteousness," but in a Jewish context "doing *tzedakah*" means "giving to charity, doing acts of mercy." This is reflected in the Greek text: in v. 1 the Greek word used means "righteousness," but in vv. 2–4 a different Greek word is used which means "kind deeds, alms, charitable giving."

7 Compare the Mishna:

> "Rabbi Shim'on said, '… When you pray, do not make your prayer fixed [repetitive, mechanical], but [appeal for] mercy and supplication before the Omnipresent, blessed be he.'" (Avot 2:13)

Likewise the Gemara:

"When you address the Holy One, blessed be he, let your words be few." (B'rakhot 61a)

New Testament scholars enjoy finding parallels to New Testament teachings in the writings of the rabbis. I enjoy it too — see 5:23–24N, vv. 9–13N, 7:12N and elsewhere throughout this commentary. Nevertheless, it is wise not to take this enterprise too seriously. To explain why I say this, let me present two of the "weighty conclusions" one might be tempted to draw — along with some weightier reasons for being very cautious:

(1) *Conclusion:* Judaism and New Testament religion are really the same, since Yeshua (or Paul, or the gospel writers) and the rabbis teach the same things.
Caution: The logic is faulty, resembling the syllogism, "Grass is green. Money is green. Therefore grass is money." Moreover, traditional Judaism, as it has developed *since* the first century, has consciously distinguished itself over against Christianity, consciously defending itself against the possibility of accepting such a conclusion; and Christianity, throughout most of its history and in most of its expressions, has done the same. There is indeed room to speak of a "Judeo-Christian tradition" consisting of the common elements, but that is a far cry from simplistically proclaiming the identity of two streams which equally stress their differences. I myself expect that in the future these streams will become confluent, but they are not now congruent (see my *Messianic Jewish Manifesto*, Chapter III).

(2) *Conclusion:* The rabbis assimilated or copied Yeshua's teaching without giving him credit. *Opposite conclusion:* Yeshua, Paul and/or the New Testament writers assimilated or copied the rabbis' teachings without giving them credit.
Cautions: The rabbinic writings mostly date from long after Yeshua (the Mishna was compiled in the third century, the Gemaras in the fourth to sixth, other writings still later), so *prima facie* one would suppose the borrowings would be mostly by the rabbis.

On the other hand, these writings report many statements made by persons who lived long before the date of compilation, and sometimes long before Yeshua. Moreover, they also summarize unattributed traditions which may be very old indeed — so that the ideas reported may well predate Yeshua.

Jacob Neusner, a well-known Jewish scholar who deals with New Testament materials as pertinent to establishing the course of Jewish history, stresses the importance of dating any rabbinic or New Testament reference, together with its antecedents, before drawing conclusions about who influenced whom. Since the same first-century Jewish society was the crucible out of which came both Messianic and rabbinic Judaism, often the most reasonable conclusion is that both the rabbis and the New Testament figures and writers drew on a common pool of ideas.

As for giving credit, one can make the case (it is beyond the scope of this commentary) that in fact the New Testament does acknowledge positive contributions made by "tradition" (i.e., the rabbis; see Mk 7:5–13N) and by the *P'rushim* (23:2&N).

8 Compare Isaiah 65:24.

9–13 These verses include what is widely known as the Lord's Prayer, since it was taught by the Lord Yeshua. All of its elements may be found in the Judaism of Yeshua's day, so in this sense it is not original with him; but it is properly revered for its beauty and economy. Its first words, **Our Father in heaven** (*Avinu sh'baShammayim*), open many Hebrew prayers. The next two lines recall the first portion of the synagogue prayer known as the *Kaddish*, which says, "Magnified and sanctified (*Yitgadal v'yitkadash*) be his great name throughout the world which he has created according to his will, and may he establish his Kingdom in your lifetime...." The plural phrasing — "Give us... forgive us... lead us" — is characteristically Jewish, focussing on the group rather than the isolated individual.

The Evil One. The Greek may also be translated simply, "evil," in the sense of "bad things that happen." The Talmud (Kiddushin 81a) reports that "Whenever Rabbi Chiyya ben-Abba fell on his face [in prayer] he used to say, 'May the Merciful One save us from the Tempter.'"

[For kingship, power and glory are yours forever. *Amen*.] This doxology echoes 1 Chronicles 29:11. The oldest New Testament manuscripts lack it, hence the brackets. Roman Catholics do not include it when reciting the Lord's Prayer; Protestants do. On "*Amen*" see 5:18N; here it signals an expected congregational response.

21 Pharaoh understood very well that **where your wealth is, there will your heart be also.** This is why he refused to let the Israelites take their property (Exodus 10:8–11, 24–27).

22–23 **"The eye is the lamp of the body."** Apparently Yeshua quotes a common proverb and comments on it. **If you have a "good eye."** This is in the Greek text, but the explanation, **that is, if you are generous,** is added by me the translator because in Judaism "having a good eye," an *'ayin tovah*, means "being generous," and "having a bad eye," an *'ayin ra'ah*, means "being stingy." That this is the correct interpretation is confirmed by the context, greed and anxiety about money being the topic in both the preceding and following verses. This passage is another link in the chain of evidence that New Testament events took place in Hebrew; I made this point when analyzing v. 23 in Section I of the *JNT* Introduction. See also David Bivin and Roy Blizzard, *Understanding the Difficult Words of Jesus*, Shippensburg, Pennsylvania: Destiny Image Publishers, 1984.

30 **How much more.** This phrase signals a form of argument known in rabbinic literature as *kal v'chomer* ("light and heavy"), corresponding to what philosophers call *a fortiori* reasoning: If A is true, then, *a fortiori* (Latin, "with [even] greater strength"), B must also be true. The English phrase, "how much more," equivalent to Hebrew *kol sh'khen*, expresses this sense and force. Explicit *kal v'chomer* arguments appear in the New Testament twenty-one times, the others being at 7:11, 10:25, 12:12; Lk 11:13; 12:24, 28; Ro 5:9, 10, 15, 17; 11:12, 24; 1C 12:22; 2C 3:9, 11; Pp 2:12; Pm 16; MJ 9:14, 10:29, 12:25.

The fact that the New Testament uses *kal v'chomer* reasoning so often points to a foundational principle of New Testament hermeneutics overlooked by most Christian scholars. The Jews who wrote the New Testament participated in the thoughtforms of their time, and these included certain principles of interpretation (hermeneutical rules, Hebrew *middot*, "measures, norms") widely used to understand the Hebrew Bible. There have been several listings of such *middot* in Judaism; best known are the thirteen *middot* of Rabbi Ishmael. They are found in the introduction to Sifra, a halakhic commentary on the book of Leviticus compiled in the fourth century, but Rabbi Ishmael himself was a *tanna* (a teaching rabbi quoted in the Mishna) who lived in the late first and early second century, and he is undoubtedly summarizing principles "earlier than Hillel" (fl. 10–20 C.E.; *Encyclopedia Judaica* 8:367). They are also included in the *Siddur* (Jewish Prayerbook) to be recited daily as part of the *Birkat-HaShachar*, the "morning blessings" that begin the synagogue service. More than half of the article on "Hermeneutics" in the *Encyclopedia Judaica* (8:366–372) is devoted to them.

I have heard the objection that Yeshua came to bring newness, so that "old" rabbinic principles are not to be taken into account in understanding the New Testament, that its writers had "freed themselves" from rabbinic attitudes and practices and were no longer "bound" by them. Just as at 5:18N I said it was facile to invoke Yeshua's "originality" to justify assuming that Yeshua's "Amen" has a novel meaning, so I say it is likewise facile to invoke his "newness" to justify ignoring the historical, social, religious and intellectual ambience of the time and place in which he lived, and imagining instead a hothouse environment insulated from the Judaism and Jewishness of his surroundings. The *middot* were surely part of everyone's conscious or unconscious background in approaching Scripture, and it is gratuitous to suppose that Yeshua, Sha'ul or the other New Testament writers constituted an exception. Traditional, rabbinic viewpoints are an essential element to take into account in understanding the text of the New Testament.

34 ***Tsuris***, Yiddish adaptation of Hebrew *tzarot*, "troubles." Leo Rosten's informal lexicon, *The Joys Of Yiddish*, lists under "*tsuris*" what he calls a "folk saying": "Don't worry about tomorrow; who knows what will befall you today?" This could be an instance of New Testament material, purged of its origin, resurfacing in a Jewish context (see 5:21N); or, alternatively, Yeshua may in this verse be quoting a proverb already current in the Jewish culture of his own time.

CHAPTER 7

12 The Golden Rule can be found in Jewish writings as early as the Apocryphal book of Tobit (third century B.C.E.), "What you hate, do to no one" (Tobit 4:15); similar sayings are attributed to Isocrates, Aristotle and Confucius. Rabbi Hillel expressed it in the generation before Yeshua; a famous passage in the Talmud comparing Hillel with his contemporary, Shammai, tells the story:

> "A pagan came came before Shammai and said to him, 'Make me a proselyte, but on condition that you teach me the entire *Torah* while I am standing on one foot!' Shammai drove him off with the builder's measuring rod which he had in his hand. When he appeared before Hillel, the latter told him, 'What is hateful to you, do not do to your neighbor. That is the whole *Torah*. The rest is commentary. Go and learn it!'"(Shabbat 31a)

The Golden Rule paraphrases Leviticus 19:18, "You are to love your neighbor as yourself," which Yeshua called the second-greatest commandment (Mk 12:28–31).

Some apologists for Judaism see superiority in Hillel's "negative form" of the Golden

Rule ("do not do to others…") as over against Yeshua's "positive form" ("do unto others…"). One was the well-known Jewish writer, Achad Ha'Am (see discussion and reference in Abba Hillel Silver, *Where Judaism Differed*, New York: The Macmillan Company (1956), paperback edition 1972, pp. 125–126). The point seems to be that others may not react as you do, so that it is unkind and possibly unjust to treat them as you would yourself. But one could take the opposite tack: the goal is to treat people as they want to be treated, and this is better stated as a positive command. Logically there is no substantive difference between the forms, and the spirit of the Golden Rule can emerge from either; likewise, its spirit can be quenched by tedious and tendentious arguments.

21 **Lord**, Greek *kurios*, which can have four possible meanings (see 1:20N). In the present verse, Yeshua seems to say that a day will come when people will address him as the divine Lord — more than human but not necessarily *YHVH*; however, see Pp 2:9–11&N. In the Septuagint "*kurios*" is the most common rendering of "*YHVH*." In Paul's writings and in the General Letters "*kurios*" sometimes refers to Yeshua.

Only those who do what my Father in heaven wants, only those who obey the *Torah* as I have expounded it in this sermon, **will enter the Kingdom of Heaven** (see 3:2N).

22 **That Day** is the Day of Judgment (Hebrew *Yom-haDin*); see Rv 20:11–15&N.

23 **Lawlessness**, Greek *anomia*, "absence of law, absence of *Torah*." Hence **you workers of lawlessness** means "you who act as if there were no *Torah*"; it confirms Yeshua's teaching on the permanence of the *Torah* (5:17–20&NN). The Greek word "*anomia*" can be rendered "wickedness," but doing so here skirts the Jewish context.

28–29 On ***Torah*-teachers**, their **authority** and why **the crowds were amazed**, see 2:4N, 21:23&N, Mk 1:22N.

CHAPTER 8

1–4 By the first century Judaism had developed a list of major signs the true Messiah could be expected to give as proof of his identity (see 16:1–4). Healing a leper was one of them. Another was casting out a deaf, dumb and blind demon (12:22–23&N). Other Messianic signs and references to them are found at 11:2–6 and Yn 6:25–33, 9:1–41, 11:1–52.

2 **Sir**. Greek *kurios;* see 1:20N, 7:21N.

Make me clean, not only free of the **repulsive skin disease** called "leprosy" in many translations (but probably not Hansen's Disease, which is what "leprosy" means today); but also ritually clean (Hebrew *tahor*), so that I will not have to be separated from the community. The rules applicable to "lepers" are specified in Talmud tractate N'ga'im, based on Leviticus 13–14.

4 **Tell no one.** In the early part of his ministry Yeshua did not publicize the fact that he was the Messiah, because the people expected a Messiah who would liberate Israel from

Rome and rule in glory, not one who would die a criminal's death. Had he been publicly identified as the Messiah, the people would have tried to make him king then and there, as they did soon after (Yn 6:15). Had the attempt succeeded, with Yeshua ruling in glory, he would not have fulfilled Isaiah 53's prophecy of a Messiah who must suffer and die. Only at his Second Coming will Yeshua fulfill the prophecies concerning the Messianic Age of world peace.

Go and let the *cohen* examine you, and offer the sacrifice that Moshe commanded in Leviticus 14:1–32. In other words, do what the *Torah* commands after recovery from such a skin disease. This sends a message to the religious establishment that the Messiah has come and is at work, doing what only the Messiah can do (vv. 1–4N). The **testimony to the people** is to go "through channels" — initially to the leadership.

5–13 Replacement theologians (5:5&N) and antisemites might conclude that God is excluding the Jews from his Kingdom (v. 12). However, the point of this story is not exclusion but inclusion: here Yeshua states clearly that Gentiles from all over (**from the east and from the west**), even an army officer of the hated Roman conquerors, can, by virtue of trusting in God (v. 10), join (not replace) God's people Israel and **take their places at the feast in the Kingdom of Heaven with Avraham, Yitzchak and Ya'akov** (v. 11). Verse 12, like many statements of the *Tanakh* prophets pertaining to the Jewish people, is a warning against lack of trust but not an irrevocable prediction. **Those born for the Kingdom**, Jews, **will be thrown outside in the dark, where people will wail and grind their teeth**, only if they fail to heed the warning.

17 This is the first citation in the New Testament from Isaiah 52:13–53:12, the *Tanakh* passage that most clearly portrays the Messiah as a servant of *Adonai* who suffers for the sins of the people. For more on this passage, see Ac 8:34N.

19 **Rabbi** (Hebrew, literally, "my great one") here renders Greek *didaskalos*, "teacher." See 23:7N. Teaching *talmidim* was, and sometimes still is, the chief task of a rabbi.

20 **Son of Man.** One of the titles of the Messiah, based on Daniel 7:13–14, where the text has "*bar-enosh*" (Aramaic). "*Bar-enosh*," like Hebrew *ben-adam*, can also mean "son of man," "typical man," "one schooled to be a man," or simply "man" (see 1:1N on "son of"). Yeshua is all of these: the Messiah, a typical (ideal) man, and one schooled both in heaven and on earth to be a man. Yeshua refers to himself by this title frequently, stressing his full identification with the human condition, as taught in Ro 5:12–21, 8:3–39; 1C 15:21–49; Pp 2:5–11; MJ 2:5–18, 4:15. Compare 4:3N on "son of God."

21–22 **First let me go and bury my father.** Don't suppose this would-be *talmid* is traveling around with Yeshua while his father's corpse is waiting at home, stinking in the sun. The father is not dead yet! If he had been, the son would have been at home, sitting *shiv'ah* (see Yn 11:19–20&N). The son wishes to go home, live in comfort with his father till his death perhaps years hence, collect his inheritance and then, at his leisure, become a disciple. On this and other excuses see Lk 9:57–62&N.

Let the spiritually **dead**, those concerned with the benefits of this world, including inheritances, remain with each other in life and eventually **bury their own** physically

dead. The true *talmid* must get his priorities straight. Note the consequences of not doing so at 13:7, 22; 19:16–26; Lk 14:15–24.

26 Little trust. See Hasidic story cited in Lk 15:15N. **Rebuked the wind and the waves.** See Psalm 107:28–29 and Appendix, p. 931.

29 The appointed time. At the end of history the demons are to be punished eternally by being thrown into the lake of fire (25:41, Rv 20:9–15).

30 Pigs. The Gadarenes were presumably not Jewish and had no compunctions about raising pigs. See Mk 5:11–17&N, Lk 15:1N.

CHAPTER 9

8 Said a *b'rakhah*. A *b'rakhah* ("blessing"; plural *b'rakhot*) in Judaism is a sentence or paragraph of praise **to God**; usually commencing with the formula, *Barukh attah, Adonai* ("Praised be you, *Adonai*," quoting Psalm 119:12); and continuing with a description of the specific reason for praising God at that moment. Thus here God is praised as **the Giver of such authority to human beings.** A similar *b'rakhah* is said by observant Jews upon seeing a person of profound secular learning: "Praised be you, *Adonai* our God, king of the universe, who has given of his wisdom to flesh and blood," i.e., to human beings. Likewise, on seeing an exalted ruler: "Praised be you, *Adonai* our God, king of the universe, who has given of his glory to flesh and blood." For more on *b'rakhot* see 14:19N, 26:27–29N, Lk 5:26&N, 2 Ti 4:6–8N, 1 Ke 1:3–4N.

10 Sinners. This term came to be used by the *P'rushim* to refer to prostitutes, thieves and others of low reputation whose sins were blatant and obvious, not the kind the establishment winked at. Yeshua taught that those who considered themselves not sinners but "righteous" (v. 13) were in fact worse, because they made themselves unteachable (see also Yn 9:38–41).

14 Fast. See Lk 18:12N.

16 This verse and the next speak to the issue of whether faith in Yeshua the Messiah can be combined with Judaism. Here the **old coat** is Judaism. The **unshrunk cloth** is Messianic faith which has not been adapted ("shrunk") to the framework of Judaism as currently practiced. ("Shrinking" here is simply an aspect of Yeshua's "patch" metaphor. It does not imply that Messianic faith must be diminished in order to fit into Judaism.) Combining unadapted Messianic faith with traditional Judaism doesn't work — **the patch tears away from the coat**; that is, faith in Yeshua apart from Judaism — and, later on in the case of Gentiles, faith in Yeshua apart from the foundational truths about God taught in the *Tanakh* — is useless and worthless. Not only that, but it **leaves a worse hole** — attempting to combine unadapted Messianic faith with traditional Judaism leaves Judaism worse off than before. The implication is that one must shrink the new cloth — adapt Messianic faith to Judaism — for Yeshua does not imply that there is anything wrong with patching an old coat! The early Messianic Jews did adapt Messianic faith to Judaism, but the later Gentile Church did not. Instead, some forms of Gentile Christianity became paganized precisely because the *Tanakh* was forgotten or underemphasized. Messianic Jews today are once again trying to bring New Testament faith back to its Jewish roots.

17 Whereas in v. 16 Messianic faith has to be adapted to Judaism, here it is Judaism which must be adjusted to Messianic faith. If one tries to put **new wine**, Messianic faith, into **old wineskins**, traditional Judaism, the faith is lost and Judaism ruined. But if Judaism is **freshly prepared**, reconditioned so that it can accommodate trust in Yeshua the Messiah, both the faith and the renewed Judaism, Messianic Judaism, **are preserved.**

This understanding is undergirded by the writer's careful choice of words: "new" (Greek *neos*) wine, "fresh" (*kainos*) wineskins. "*Neos*" means "new" in respect to time, implying immaturity or lack of development. "*Kainos*" means "new" or "renewed" in respect to quality, contrasting with "old" or "not renewed" and implying superiority. Old wineskins have lost their strength and elasticity, so that they cannot withstand the pressure of new wine still fermenting, although an old wineskin can be restored to service if its useful qualities are renewed.

The meaning of the figure is that the new wine of Messianic living cannot be poured into old religious forms if they remain rigid. But if the old religious forms become "fresh," they can accommodate Yeshua. When "*kainos*" is rendered "new," as in many translations, the implication seems to be that Judaism cannot possibly be a suitable framework for honoring Yeshua the Jewish Messiah — only the "new wineskin" of Gentilized Christianity will work. This is a peculiar conclusion, especially if it is recalled that Yeshua was speaking with his fellow Jews. As rendered here the point is that the only vessel which can hold the new wine of Messianic life in a Jewish setting is a properly renewed, restored, reconditioned and refreshed Judaism, such as Messianic Judaism was in the first century and aims to be now.

Taken together, verses 16 and 17 imply that both Messianic faith and Judaism should adjust to each other. However, the accommodating must be true to God's Word; on that there is no room for compromise. See 13:52&N.

18 **An official.** From the parallel passages (Mk 5:22, Lk 8:41) we know that he was a synagogue official named Ya'ir (Jairus). Compare Psalm 119:46, "I will also speak of your testimonies before kings, and I will not be put to shame."

20 ***Tzitzit*** (plural *tzitziyot*). Observant Jewish men in Yeshua's time and today have worn fringes on the corners of their garments, in obedience to Numbers 15:37–41, the third of the three *Torah* passages recited in the *Sh'ma* portion of the synagogue service. These fringes are made in a special way and have a unique appearance. Their purpose is to remind God's people to obey his commandments. Since they are not merely decorations, the usual renderings of Greek *kraspedon* — "hem," "fringe," "border," "tassel" — are replaced here by "*tzitzit*." Today Jewish men wear *tzitziyot* on a *tallit gadol* ("large *tallit*"), which is not an article of clothing but a ritual cloth donned primarily for synagogue worship, or on a *tallit katan* ("little *tallit*"), which is an undergarment especially designed with corners for the *tzitziyot*. But Yeshua wore his on his **robe,** a heavy blanket-like over-garment similar to that worn by Bedouins today.

A woman who had... a hemorrhage approached him from behind and... touched the *tzitzit*. She was in a state of ritual impurity because of her hemorrhage.

She touched the holiest part of Yeshua's garment. No wonder she approached from behind — she was afraid; this is also why she hesitated to answer Yeshua's question, "Who touched my clothes?" (Mk 5:29–33). For normally the impure defiles the pure (see Haggai 2:11–13; also the Talmud, *Taharot*). But in this case, the opposite happened: the purity of Yeshua the Messiah and of his *tzitziyot* remained uncompromised, while instead the cause of the woman's impurity was instantly removed. In the following incident, the raising of the dead girl, this principle is exemplified even more strongly, since Yeshua himself initiates contact with what is regarded in Judaism as the primary source of all impurity, a dead body (v. 25; compare also above, 8:1–4).

23 **Flute-players and the crowd.** Hired musicians and professional mourners, in keeping with the custom both then and now in Middle Eastern countries.

27 **Son of David.** See 1:1N. By shouting, "Son of David!" the blind men were publicly acclaiming Yeshua as the Messiah.

34 **Ruler of the demons**, that is, the Adversary, Satan. See 4:1N.

35 **In their synagogues.** Whose synagogues? Those of the people in the **towns and villages** of the Galil. See 11:1&N.

CHAPTER 10

2–4 **Emissaries.** Greek *apostoloi,* which means "those sent out," is usually rendered "apostles," a word with a distinctly "churchy" ring I wanted to avoid. I debated using the Hebrew equivalent, "*shlichim*" (singular "*shaliach*"), but decided that "*shaliach*" makes Diaspora Jews think of an Israeli sent to encourage *aliyah* (Jewish immigration to Israel) — not a bad image, in my view, but irrelevant to the New Testament.

Shim'on (Simon), **called Kefa** — see 4:18N. **Andrew** and **Philip** render Greek names. **Ya'akov Ben-Zavdai and... Yochanan** — see 4:21N. **T'oma** (Thomas) means "twin" in Hebrew — see Yn 11:16. **Mattityahu**, identified as L'vi (Mk 2:14, Lk 5:27–29), is believed to be the author of this Gospel. **Bar-Chalfai**, son of Alpheus. **Taddai**; some manuscripts have "Lebbai also known as Taddai" (Lebbeus also known as Thaddeus); he is supposed to be the same as Y'hudah the brother of Ya'akov (Lk 6:16, Yn 14:22, Ac 1:13, Yd 1).

Zealot. The Zealots were the "Jewish Liberation Front" of their day, actively opposing Roman occupation. Their provocations led in 66 C.E. to open rebellion, which was crushed by the Romans with enormous loss of life, destruction of the Temple in 70, and mass suicide of the last holdouts at Matzada in 73 to avoid being captured and enslaved by the Roman army.

Y'hudah from K'riot is known to English-speakers as Judas Iscariot. "Iscariot" is probably not a surname but a rendering into Greek of Hebrew *ish-K'riot*, "a man of K'riot," a town some twenty miles south of Jerusalem.

5 ***Goyim***, "Gentiles" (see 5:47N). In some Jewish circles today "Gentile" and "Christian"

are regarded as interchangeable terms, but this is a mistake, confusing one's people with one's religion. The word "Gentile" means only "non-Jew"; it does not mean "Christian." A member of the Jewish people, a Jew, can opt for a form of non-Messianic Judaism (e.g., Orthodox, Conservative, Reform), or for Messianic Judaism, or for some other religion or none. Likewise a Gentile can decide to follow a form of non-Messianic Judaism and become a proselyte; or he can become a Christian in the same way a Jew becomes Messianic, namely, by putting his trust in God and in his son Yeshua the Messiah; or he can follow another religion or none. Because the religion of Judaism implies membership in the Jewish people, a Gentile who becomes a Jew by religion also becomes a member of the Jewish people, and his children will be Jews. Because Messianic faith — Gentile Christianity and Messianic Judaism — is transcultural and can be held by members of any people, a Jew who becomes a follower of Yeshua remains a member of the Jewish people and does not become a Gentile.

8 You have received without paying, so give without asking payment. The Talmud gives the same advice:

> "Rav Y'hudah said in the name of Rav: Scripture says, 'Behold, I have taught you [statutes and judgments]...' (Deuteronomy 4:5). Just as I teach for free, so you should teach for free. Similarly it has been taught: The next words of this verse are, '...as *Adonai* my God commanded me.' This too implies: Just as I teach for free, so you should teach for free.
>
> "Whence do we deduce that if it isn't possible to find someone who will teach gratuitously, one must pay to learn? A verse says, 'Buy the truth...' (Proverbs 23:23). And whence do we deduce that one who has to pay in order to learn should not say, 'Since I had to pay to learn *Torah*, I will charge to teach it'? From the same text, which adds, '...and do not sell it.'"(Bekorot 29a)

12 *Shalom aleikhem.* The word "*shalom*" means not only "peace" but also tranquillity, safety, well-being, welfare, health, contentment, success, comfort, wholeness and integrity. "*Shalom aleikhem*" means "Peace be upon you" and is a common greeting, as is simply "*Shalom*!" Thus there is a deeper meaning to Yeshua's instruction in v. 13 on when to give or withhold *shalom*, for he refers not only to the greeting but to the whole complex of peace/wholeness/well-being that the Messiah offers through his *talmidim* — and similarly at many places in the New Testament.

15 S'dom and 'Amora were destroyed for their wickedness, Genesis 19.

20 It will not be just you speaking. The word "just" is not in the Greek text; I have added it to avoid the implication that **the Spirit of your heavenly Father** might take control of someone without his knowledge or against his will.

25 Ba'al-Zibbul or Ba'al-z'vuv (the manuscripts differ); usually seen in English as "Beelzebul" and "Beelzebub": derogatory names for the Adversary (see 4:1N). The latter is the name of a Philistine god (2 Kings 1:2) and in Hebrew means "lord of a fly." The Ugaritic root *z-b-l* means "prince," making the former name imply that the Adversary has a measure of status and power; but in post-biblical Hebrew the root *z-b-l* means "dung," with "Ba'al-zibbul" meaning "defecator." Other interpretations are possible.

27 The **housetops** were flat roofs where people gathered when the weather was pleasant (compare Mk 2:4). Since houses were close together, people could shout from their housetops and **proclaim** to an impromptu audience.

28 **Him who can destroy…**, that is, God.

35–36 The Talmud too applies Micah 7:6 to Messianic times:

> "It has been taught: R. Nehorai said, 'In the generation when Messiah comes, young men will insult the old, and old men will stand before the young [to give them honor]; daughters will rise up against their mothers, and daughters-in-law against their mothers-in-law. The people will be dog-faced, and a son will not be abashed in his father's presence.' " (Sanhedrin 97a)

This passage is relevant also at Lk 1:17, where Malachi 3:23–24(4:5–6), "turn the hearts of the fathers to the children," is quoted.

A crude and foolish criticism of the New Testament based on this verse is that Yeshua advocates family strife. Yeshua's purpose is, of course, not to create contentiousness but end it. Yet he knows that tension may result when some members of a family trust him while others do not (see v. 37&N).

37 Yosef Vaktor, a Messianic Jew in Yerushalayim who escaped the Nazis by hiding in a forest and came to faith during the time of the *Sho'ah* (Holocaust), has taught on the subject of loving God more than parents:

> "In choosing between God and relatives, God comes first. Abraham had to leave his family, his kindred and his father's house (Genesis 12:1–3). He had to send his son Ishmael away permanently (Genesis 21:8–13). He had to be willing to sacrifice his son Isaac (Genesis 22:1–19). At the time of the golden calf, Moses told the Levites that because each was willing to be against his son and his brother, with the result that they killed three thousand, God bestowed a blessing (Exodus 32:29–30). One is to stone the false prophet who leads the people into idolatry, even if he is your brother, son, daughter or wife (Deuteronomy 13:6–11). One is to put to death one's rebellious son (Deuteronomy 21:18). In the Sermon on the Mount, Yeshua *machmir* (interprets more stringently); he does the same here. But his method of judging more stringently is different. For example, in the incident of Yn 8:1–11 the *Sanhedrin* might have excused the sin of the woman caught in adultery, that is, it might have not pronounced her guilty. Yeshua does pronounce her guilty, but he lets her go, tempering justice with mercy." (Teaching at Netivyah Congregation, October 29, 1989)

38 **Execution-stake**, Greek *stavros*, usually translated "cross." Actually it was a vertical wooden stake with a crossbar, usually shaped more like a " T " than the Christian symbol, used by the Romans to execute criminals who were not Roman citizens (Roman citizens sentenced to death were given a less painful way to die). It was not a normal Jewish means of execution. *Halakhah* specified four methods of execution — stoning, burning, beheading and strangling (Mishna Sanhedrin 7:1) — but not hanging or being suspended from a cross (see Ga 3:13, 1 Ke 2:24).

However, in Roman-occupied Israel public crucifixions were common: the condemned man carried the crossbar of the stake on which he was to be executed to the place of execution and was nailed to it by his wrists and ankles. Then the stake with him on it was pounded into the ground, where he was left hanging in excruciating torment until he expired, usually many hours later. Also it was a death of utter infamy (Pp 2:8); a modern cultural equivalent would be electrocution. To grasp the enormity of Yeshua's crucifixion process, picture the legitimate and glorious King of the whole world being put to death as a criminal in the electric chair — with too little electricity, so that it took hours for him to die instead of seconds — while crowds gaped and jeered. When the late Jewish comedian Lenny Bruce invited his audience to imagine Gentiles wearing little electric chair models around their necks he was resonating with a deep truth.

Throughout the *JNT* the terms "execution-stake" and "stake" are used instead of "cross"; and "execute on a stake," "nail to the execution stake" and "put to death on the stake" instead of "crucify." These expressions focus attention on the events themselves, particularly their character as judgment; whereas the usual terms explain less and carry church-related associations developed much later in history.

The quasi-Christian cult known as "Jehovah's Witnesses" teaches that Yeshua was tortured on an upright pole without a crossbeam. My rendering of *stavros* as "execution stake" is functional, not symbolic. I want to stress not the cross's shape but its use — in the first century it was not a symbol mounted on a steeple. Weighty archeological and historical evidence confirms that the kind of execution-stake used in Israel then had a crossbeam (Latin *patibulum*), and that it was this which the criminal, and likewise Yeshua, was forced to carry to his place of execution.

To many Christians the cross represents all they hold dear; I do not object to their use of it to symbolize their faith. But for centuries Jews were done to death under the sign of the cross by persons claiming to be followers of the Jewish Messiah. Therefore to me the cross symbolizes persecution of Jews. As a Messianic Jew, still feeling the pain on behalf of my people, I do not have it in me to represent my New Testament faith by a cross.

However, many New Testament references to the cross, or execution stake, are figures for Yeshua's atoning death. If the term "execution stake" or "cross" speaks to us of what Yeshua, the eternal Word of God made flesh, did for us and for all humanity by his death, then the New Testament message is reaching our hearts.

On the message of this verse see Lk 9:23–25&N.

41 ***Tzaddik.*** See 13:17N.

CHAPTER 11

1–30 Having instructed the Twelve and sent them away, Yeshua continues his itinerant healing and preaching; the narrative joins up with 9:36. The disciples of Yochanan the Immerser come to Yeshua with a message "in code," which he also answers in code (vv. 2–6). The interchange piques the crowd's curiosity, on which Yeshua capitalizes by challenging their understanding of Yochanan's ministry and pinning their attention to the chief subject of his preaching, the Kingdom of Heaven (vv. 7–14; see 3:2N). Finding his hearers dull of spirit he provokes them first with irony over failing to penetrate the surface of things (vv. 15–19), then with direct reproach at not turning from their sins even when confronted with evidence that God is present in a new and mighty way (vv. 20–24). Finally Yeshua states plainly that he himself has power and authority directly from God the Father (vv. 25–27), closing with an unexpectedly gentle challenge that they trust Yeshua as the one who can meet their needs (vv. 28–30).

1 **In the towns nearby,** literally, "in their towns." Whose towns? Some say, "the Jews' towns," as if Mattityahu or his redactor were writing specifically for non-Jews or trying to distance himself from the Jews. I prefer to think what is meant is simply the towns of the people with whom Yeshua was then spending his time, the people of the Galil, or possibly the home-towns of his *talmidim*. (Robertson's *A Grammar of the Greek New Testament*, p. 683, takes the Greek word "*avtôn*" ("their") in this verse as being according to the sense of the surrounding words, with the narrative itself being compressed; this supports my understanding.) See 9:35&N.

3–6 **Yochanan the Immerser**, apparently discouraged by being **put in prison** after having announced Yeshua as the Messiah (3:11, 17; Yn 1:27, 29), asks, **"Are you the one who is to come?"** — the one who will put an end to political oppression and get me out of jail? The question is in code, for the phrase, "the one who is to come," would be clear only to those acquainted with Yochanan's teaching. Had they asked, "Are you the Messiah?" it would have been more difficult for Yeshua to send an answer to Yochanan without revealing his identity, which he was not yet wanting to do (see 8:4&N, 9:30).

Yeshua's answer is also in code. He refers to prophecies in the book of Isaiah of six signs which the Messiah will give when he comes: he will make the blind see (Isaiah 29:18, 35:5), make the lame walk (Isaiah 35:6, 61:1), cleanse lepers (Isaiah 61:1), make the deaf hear (Isaiah 29:18, 35:5), raise the dead (implied in Isaiah 11:1–2 but not made specific), and evangelize the poor (Isaiah 61:1–2 in the light of 4:23N above). Since he has done all these things (Chapters 8–9), the message should be clear: Yeshua is the one; Yochanan need not look for another. See 8:1–4N.

But his answer avoids mentioning the Messianic sign of "proclaiming liberty to the captives" (Isaiah 61:1). Added to his remark, **"How blessed is anyone not offended by me,"** Yeshua seems to be saying delicately that even though he is the Messiah, Yochanan will not be set free — as proves to be the case (below, 14:1–12).

Another view of this passage: Yochanan had prophesied that the Coming One would be an instrument of judgment as well as compassion. But in prison he had heard nothing of judgment, only of compassionate miracles. His question thus arises from lacking insight into a first coming in mercy and a second coming for judgment.

9 ***Nu.*** A general-purpose Yiddish word meaning variously, "Well?" "So?" "Indeed!" "I challenge you," or, as in this case, "If not that, then what?" — with many possible inflections and overtones. It translates the similarly flexible Greek particle "*alla*"

(see Paragraph 3 of the entry on "*alla*" in Arndt & Gingrich, *A Greek-English Lexicon of the New Testament*) and in one succinct word captures the dynamic flavor of the exchange between Yeshua and the crowd. See also Lk 12:42N.

10 Malachi 3:1, quoted here, introduces a passage which explicitly states that Eliyahu (Elijah) the Prophet will precede the coming of the Day of the Lord, that is, the Day of Judgment (Malachi 3:23(4:5)). Judaism expects Elijah — who never died but was taken up to heaven by a whirlwind in a fiery chariot (2 Kings 2:11) — to precede the Messiah. See 17:10N.

12 The Greek is difficult. As rendered, it means that **violent ones** (demons and their human vehicles) are trying to keep God from carrying out his plan through Yeshua, e.g., through Herod's having put Yochanan in prison (v. 2). An alternative understanding, "...the Kingdom of Heaven has been advancing forcefully; and forceful people are seizing hold of it," seems inconsistent with vv. 25–30.

14 **He is Eliyahu.** See 11:10N above. Not that Yochanan was Eliyahu reincarnated; on the contrary, MJ 9:27 specifically teaches that reincarnation does not occur; and when asked, Yochanan himself denied that he was Eliyahu (Yn 1:21). Rather, he comes in the spirit of Eliyahu and precedes the Messiah's first coming in the same way that Eliyahu himself is to precede his second coming. Yeshua affirms this understanding at 17:11–12.

20–21 **Miracles.** Modern critics sometimes criticize Christianity for emphasizing Yeshua's miracles as a major ground for believing in him as Messiah and Son of God. They often add that while rabbinic literature frequently reports miracles, they are neither central to the content of Judaism nor taken as proof that God's Law is valid. My response:

(1) The *Tanakh* itself grounds the Israelites' faith in God on one of his most awesome miracles. Exodus 14:31 reports that after the Egyptians had been drowned in the Red Sea, "When Israel saw the great power *Adonai* displayed against the Egyptians, they feared *Adonai* and put their trust in him and in his servant Moshe." Yeshua, showing forth God's power, is only asking from his fellow Jews the same response to God and his servant the Messiah which their mutual ancestors gave.

(2) We have already seen (9:34, 10:25) and will see again (12:24–32; Yochanan 9, 11) that Yeshua's miracles were acknowledged as such even by those who opposed him. To avoid having to decide whether to trust him as God's man, they attributed the miracles to demonic powers. Unlike the modern critics they recognized that miracles require a response, a decision; they just made the wrong one.

(3) Why should it be less noble or sophisticated to predicate faith initially on God's miracles rather than on his Law? Both are from God. One who truly trusts God will acknowledge both his Law and his miracles; can one who withholds belief in either be described as trusting God?

21 **Tzor and Tzidon.** The wickedness of Tyre and Sidon and the predictions of judgment against them are detailed in Isaiah 23:1–8, Ezekiel 26–28, Joel 3:4–8, Amos 1:9–10 and Zechariah 9:2–4.

23 ***Sh'ol.*** Usually brought into English as "Sheol"; Greek *adês* ("Hades"), the place of the dead. In the *Tanakh* Sh'ol is a dim vague state where dead souls wait. Sometimes English versions use "Hell" to translate "*adês*"; this can be confusing, because "Hell" also translates "*gehenna*," a place of torment for the dead (see 5:22N). But see Lk 16:23, where *adês* is also described as a place of torment.

25–27 Yeshua makes known his unique role in history and in establishing mankind's proper relationship with God. The Gospel is spiritually perceived and does not depend on being **sophisticated and educated**; see 1C 1:17–2:16.

28–30 Judaism speaks of the "yoke of Heaven," the commitment any Jew must make to trust in God, and the "yoke of the *Torah*," the concomitant commitment an observant Jew makes to keep the generalities and details of *halakhah*. Yeshua speaks of his own easy yoke and light burden. These two are sometimes contrasted in a way implying that in comparison with Judaism, Christianity offers "cheap grace." But this saying of Yeshua's must be put alongside remarks such as at 10:38 (Lk 9:23–24). The easy yoke consists in a total commitment to godliness through the power of the Holy Spirit. It at once requires both no effort and maximal effort — no effort, in that the necessary moment-to-moment faith can not be worked up from within but is a gift of God (Ep 2:8–9); and maximal effort, in that there is no predeterminable level of holiness and obedience sufficient to satisfy God and let us rest on our laurels.

I am... humble. Can a genuinely humble person even say this about himself? Moses could (Numbers 12:3). True humility implies having neither a higher nor a lower opinion of oneself than one should, and knowing when and when not to speak about oneself at all.

CHAPTER 12

1 ***Shabbat.*** The Hebrew word has entered English as "Sabbath." The biblical concept of a weekly day for resting from workaday purposes has no close parallel in the ancient world. The fourth commandment (Exodus 20:8–11, Deuteronomy 5:12–14) connects *Shabbat* with the fact that God rested after the six days of creation (Genesis 2:1–3); makes it a day of equality in which all, high and low alike, are entitled to rest; and sets it aside as a day which is holy, on which God is to be honored.

2 **Violating *Shabbat*.** The Greek text says, literally, "doing what is unlawful on *Shabbat*," that is, doing something the *P'rushim* considered to be against the *Torah*. The argument was not over whether it was permitted to pick grain by hand from someone else's field, for that is expressly allowed by Deuteronomy 23:26(25), but whether it could be done on *Shabbat*. At issue behind this seemingly minor matter is whether the Pharisaic tradition — which evolved into what rabbinic Judaism calls the Oral *Torah*, later committed to writing in the Mishna, Gemara and other works — is God's revelation to man and binding on all Jews. The question is explored further at 18:18–20&N and Mk 7:5–13&N. According to the Oral *Torah* as we have it now in the Mishna (Shabbat 7:2) thirty-nine categories of *m'lakhah* (work) are prohibited on

Shabbat, while the Tabernacle was being built. One of these was reaping, another threshing. At v. 1 we are told the *talmidim* were reaping; in the parallel passage at Lk 6:1 they were also rubbing the heads of grain together in their hands, which would be defined as threshing. This is the content of the accusation the *P'rushim* were making against them and by implication against Yeshua, responsible as their teacher for their behavior.

3–4 Though Leviticus 24:5–9 allows only ***cohanim*** to eat the bread of the Presence set aside for display before the ark in the **house of God** (Tabernacle), 1 Samuel 21:1–6 (2–7) recounts how King David and the priest Achimelekh violated this *mitzvah* of the Written *Torah* — which the *P'rushim* would accept as more authoritative than a rule in the Oral *Torah*. A *kal v'chomer* argument (6:30N) is implied.

5 The *Torah* itself specifies that some *mitzvot* are more important than others (see Yn 5:22–23&N, Ga 2:12bN). Keeping *Shabbat* is important, but the animal sacrifices required by Numbers 28:1–10 are more so, so that the *cohanim* work on *Shabbat* in order to offer them. ("Temple service takes precedence over *Shabbat*," Shabbat 132b.)

8 For the Son of Man is Lord of *Shabbat*. See Mk 2:27–28N.

10 Is healing permitted on *Shabbat*? See Lk 6:9N.

11 A sheep. One should save an animal's life on *Shabbat*; but whether lifting a sheep out of a pit would, in the first century, have been considered a violation of the rule against work (carrying) on *Shabbat* is not clear. According to modern *halakhah*, it would.

12 How much more. See 6:30N.

18 Isaiah 42:1–4 is the first of several "suffering servant" passages in Isaiah 42–53. Some parts of these passages seem to refer primarily to the people Israel, others to the Messiah yet in Isaiah's future. This fact emphasizes the close identification of the Messiah Yeshua with the Jewish people, as pointed out above, 2:15N.

22–23 While there were Jewish exorcists (v. 27, Ac 19:13), casting out a blind, deaf and dumb demon was a major miracle only the Messiah could be expected to perform (see 8:1–4N), because, unlike the legion of demons (Mk 5:1–20), one couldn't talk with it. Compare Yeshua's answer to Yochanan's disciples (above, 11:5), "the blind are seeing… the deaf are hearing."

27 By whom do your people expel them? The implied answer is: Also by the Adversary. Satanic healings and miracles are possible, and many are led astray by them (Exodus 7:22, 8:7; below, 24:24&N). Those involved in the occult and in false religions because of the miracles and healings they see have found the broad road that leads to destruction, not the narrow gate and hard road that lead to life (7:13–14).

30 Those who are not with me are against me (also at Lk 11:23). Here and in the next seven verses the *P'rushim* are presented with a last chance to stand with Yeshua. More generally, a standard is set by which a *talmid* can test himself: if he is not actively on Yeshua's side, he is on the side of the Adversary. Contrast Mk 9:40, "For whoever is not against us is for us" (similarly Lk 9:50); the seeming contradiction is explained by the context. In Mark the *talmidim* are warned that prior to the final opportunity it is premature to conclude that anyone not on Yeshua's side is against him. The same verse also gives a criterion by which others may be tested in relation to a *talmid's* own work: whoever is not actively opposing the *talmid* is *de facto* an ally, not an enemy.

31–32 Blaspheming (that is, insulting) **the *Ruach HaKodesh*** consists in either (1) wilfully continuing to deny the Gospel when the Holy Spirit has made clear to you that it is true, or (2) attributing the works of the Holy Spirit to the Adversary (Satan); in the present context these amount to about the same thing (other interpretations have been offered).

One can say something against the Son of Man, etc. See Lk 12:8–10&N.

'Olam hazeh… 'olam haba, "this world… the world to come." These concepts are part of rabbinic Judaism. The latter can mean either the Millennial Age (Revelation 19–20; see 1 Th 4:15b-17N) or the Eternal Age following Judgment Day (Revelation 21–22).

38–42 Yeshua never cheapens himself or dilutes his message for those whose interest in him is casual or hostile, and nowhere is this truer than when he predicts his own resurrection. Compare 16:1–4, 26:59–68; Mk 8:27–33, 14:55–64, 15:27–33; Lk 11:29–30&N; Yn 2:18–22.

40 Yonah (Jonah) was sent to prophesy to the non-Jews of Nineveh in Assyria.

42 Queen of the South, i.e., the Queen of Sheba (1 Kings 10:1–10, 2 Chronicles 9:1–12), also not Jewish.

46 Brothers. At 13:55 we are given their names. The Roman Catholic tradition is that these "brothers" were actually more distant relatives; hence their doctrine that Miryam remained a virgin throughout her lifetime (see 1:25N). Hebrew *ach* ("brother") can have a broader range of meaning than Greek *adelphos*, and this broader sense could be read from the Synoptic Gospels, which probably had Hebrew or Aramaic antecedents. But the mention in Paul's letters, written in Greek for Greek-speakers, of Yeshua's brothers suggests that the word was meant to have the narrower Greek meaning. Protestants take the word to refer to children born to Miryam after Yeshua's birth; they would be, actually, half-brothers, since their physical father, but not Yeshua's, would have been Yosef.

48–50 This is the first of several incidents in which Yeshua's treatment of his family is considered by some to be disrespectful and cavalier, even though elsewhere he affirmed the fifth commandment (19:19) and even disputed with the *P'rushim* about it (15:4–6). Why did his family wish to see him? We do not know for sure; we do know that his brothers had little understanding of his ministry (Yn 7:2–9), and that his mother, even though she had been given special insight through the angel Gavri'el (Lk 1:26–56) and through Shim'on and Chanah (Lk 2:25–38), was at times puzzled by his actions (e.g., Lk 2:41–51), although upon being reminded by him, she could summon up a measure of trust (Yn 2:3–5). They may have wanted to bring him food and supplies out of concern for his well-being; or, fearing the opposition, they may have wanted to stop or even seize him (as his friends had wanted to, Mk 3:21). Under such circumstances, when busy ministering to a crowd and fielding opposition, Yeshua may have found it best to communicate that even though blood is thicker than water, spiritual family ties supersede physical ones. His remarks do not come from lack of respect but from his desire to point to the Kingdom of God. Eventually his relatives became members of his spiritual family as well (Ac 1:14, Ga 1:19).

CHAPTER 13

1–52 There are five collections of Yeshua's teachings in Mattityahu, corresponding to the Five Books of Moses. The first, the Sermon on the Mount (Chapters 5–7), was for the multitude; the second, the commissioning (Chapter 10), was for the *talmidim*; this, the third, is for both but is presented at two levels through the medium of the parable (Greek *parabôlê*, Hebrew *mashal).* Chapter 18 is the fourth, and the Olivet Discourse (Chapters 24–25) is the last.

The eight parables reveal the "secrets" (v. 11) of the Kingdom of Heaven (see 3:2N) through comparisons with commonplace things, showing it to be quite unlike what the crowds were expecting — as is clear from their inability to understand him. We learn that the effect of the Word varies, depending on who hears it; and that the visible or institutional church ("Christendom") includes both genuine believers and others. Therefore it is not surprising that throughout the last two thousand years non-Christians who were known as or claimed to be Christians have often behaved un-Christianly.

3–9 Yeshua himself explains this parable in vv. 18–23.

9 **Those who have ears, let them hear!** Some early manuscripts have: "Those who have ears to hear, let them hear!" Yeshua used this phrase at 11:15; he uses it at 13:43; Mk 4:9, 23; 7:16; Lk 8:8, 14:35; Rv 2:7, 11, 17, 29; 3:6, 13, 22; 13:9; and related phrases are found at Mk 8:18; Lk 9:44; Ac 7:51, 28:27; Ro 11:8. It is an invitation to seek Yeshua's deeper meaning and respond with one's whole being (compare above, 7:24, 26). But, as vv. 10–17 show, not everyone is prepared to do so.

10 **Why are you speaking to them in parables?** Till now Yeshua had addressed the crowds in plain speech, except for a few lines in Chapter 11.

11 **Secrets**, KJV "mysteries." Greek *mystêria* means truths hitherto kept secret but now revealed. A number of religions both then and now claim to make available special knowledge or mysteries to an inner circle. Biblical religion is not so. Its truths are available to all who read and believe the Bible. While Yeshua walked the earth there was an inner circle of disciples who received precisely the knowledge necessary to disseminate God's truth to all men throughout all generations. But nothing in Scripture supports the notion, found today in cultish, occult and New Age circles, that true Christianity depends on teachings that are above or beyond the Bible. The extra-canonical books used to support this idea prove themselves both morally and spiritually inferior to the canon of the *Tanakh* and the New Testament. In Yeshua's time the "mystery religions" included the cult of Dionysius and the Orphic Mysteries, as well as various Gnostic approaches ("gnostic," from Greek *gnôsis*, "knowledge," means that these religions claimed to offer a body of secret knowledge which would lead to salvation). Those who today champion a secret Christian tradition available only to initiates have merely revived the heresy of Gnosticism.

It has been given to you to know the secrets... but... not... to them. By itself this is a harsh statement, seemingly out of keeping with the Talmudic epigram of Rabbi Chanina, "Everything is in the hands of Heaven except the fear of Heaven" (B'rakhot 33b), which implies that anyone can turn to God, so that there is not one group to whom "it has been given" and another to whom it has not. In vv. 12–17 Yeshua clarifies his meaning and softens the impact.

13–15 It should not be surprising that there are people who **look without seeing and listen without hearing or understanding**, since Isaiah 6:9–10, quoted here (also at Yn 12:39–40 and Ac 28:26–27), predicts such a phenomenon, as do Jeremiah 5:21 and Ezekiel 12:2. If they were to see, hear and understand, they would **do *t'shuvah*** (in earlier editions of the *JNT*, **return** to God), that is, "repent" (Greek *epistrepho*, see above, 3:2N), and God would **heal them.** But v. 15 says that such people — out of misplaced fear that God might do something bad, whereas actually God does only good — listen selectively (**barely hear**) and perceive amiss (**close their eyes**), or equivalently, as Yochanan puts it, they "love darkness rather than light" (Yn 3:19 and its context).

17 ***Tzaddik***, "righteous one." In Jewish tradition generally, a godly, holy, righteous man. In Hasidic tradition such people, thought to have had supernatural powers, attracted followers and taught their disciples how to live. The implication of vv. 16–17 is that nothing inherent in the *talmidim* earned them the privilege of seeing **the things you are seeing**; the prophets and *tzaddikim* may well have been more meritorious; but God reveals himself not on the basis of human merit but by his own sovereign will (11:25–30, Ro 9:6–18, 1C 1:17–31). In this sense, since Yeshua had to be born at a particular time and place (Ga 4:4–5), there necessarily had to be some to whom "it was given" (v. 11) and others to whom it was not.

18–23 Everyone falls into one of these four categories.

24–30 Yeshua explains this parable in vv. 36–43.

25 **Weeds**, Greek *zizanion*, transliterating Hebrew *zonin*, a poisonous rye-grass which looks like wheat until the heads appear. Judaism understands *zonin* to be not a different plant from wheat but a degenerate form of it. This is seen from the fact that in Mishna Kilayim 1:1, "Wheat and *zonin* do not constitute mingled seeds with each other," in the sense of the biblical requirement that diverse kinds of seeds must not be sown together in the same field (Leviticus 19:19). The surprising legendary explanation of this comes from Genesis Rabbah 28:8 (on Genesis 6:7):

"Rabbi 'Azaryah said in Rabbi Y'hudah's name, 'All acted corruptly in the generation of the Flood: the dog had intercourse with the wolf, and the fowl with the peacock; hence it is written, "For all (flesh) on the earth had corrupted their way" (Genesis 6:12).' Rabbi Julian ben-Tiberius said in Rabbi Yitzchak's name, 'Even the earth debauched itself: wheat was sown and it produced *zonin*, for the *zonin* we find now came from the age of the Flood.'"

In the light of the fact that when Israel turns away from God the *Tanakh* repeatedly describes her with a related word, "*zonah*" ("prostitute"), this understanding of "*zonin*" has implications for understanding the parable.

32 **The smallest of all seeds.** Mustard is a very small seed, but not the world's smallest. Scripture, to be inspired by God, does not require that every fact of nature be woodenly reported. For Yeshua's hearers, mustard might well have been the smallest seed frequently encountered. God used the culture of the age to convey spiritual truth. Apposite is the Talmudic epigram, "The *Torah* speaks in the language of men" (or: "The *Torah* uses everyday human expressions," B'rakhot 31b). The rabbis too used the mustard seed in figures of speech for smallness; see B'rakhot 31a and Leviticus Rabbah 31:9 (on Leviticus 24:2).

In the Bible **birds flying about** are usually symbolic of evildoers, like the weeds in the preceding parable. But alternatively, they represent the nations of the world being sheltered by the Messianic Kingdom, as at Ezekiel 17:23; compare Ezekiel 31:6, 12; Daniel 4:12, 14, 21–22.

33 **Yeast** and leaven usually represent evil (compare 1C 5:6–8). If so it here represents the evil mixed with the good as in the previous two parables. Some interpret the parable to mean that the Church will exert a beneficent influence on the world.

35 **Spoken** by God **through the prophet.** Actually written by King David, but he sometimes functioned as a prophet.

36–43 There will be nonbelievers among those who profess to be Christians. Conclusion: Yeshua puts critics of Christianity on notice that not everything done within Christendom is a product of Christians.

38 **The field is the world**, not only the Jewish people. The Kingdom of God is to involve all of mankind, and this was a change of emphasis from what was usually taught.

39 The enemy is not the Pharisees, but Satan (compare Ep 6:12).

44–46 The first of these parables deals with the unexpected discovery of the Kingdom of God, the second with the successful conclusion to a search for it. In either case the person who comes upon it recognizes its great value and is willing to give up all (he **sold everything he owned**) to have a personal relationship with God (he **bought that field**/the **very valuable pearl**).

A treasure hidden in a field (v. 44). According to *halakhah*, if the treasure is unmarked and found on public land, it belongs to the finder. If it is marked, the owner must be sought. If it is natural (a gold nugget or a diamond) or unmarked and on private land, it belongs to the owner of the land; that's why the finder **bought that field** — to become the owner.

But the story seems to imply that the finder bought the field at the "pre-treasure" price, and that if the owner had known the treasure was there, he wouldn't have sold the field at that price. This raises an ethical question: is the finder obligated either by *halakhah* or morally (if that is different) to notify the owner of the treasure before buying the field? No. Property always has potential beyond what owners know; only God has perfect information. An owner can investigate the opportunities offered by what he owns, and others are not obligated to occupy their time with increasing his knowledge. So if I learn that your land has oil under it, I need not inform you of that fact when I offer to buy it, since ownership should motivate you more than me to find this out for yourself. The seller of this piece of land received a fair price for his land with the potential he knew about; as is often the case, the new owner bought it because he perceived additional potential.

52 **A *Torah*-teacher** (see 2:4N) **who has been made into a *talmid* for the Kingdom of Heaven**, that is, a committed and knowledgeable Jew who has become Messianic, **brings out of his storage room**, out of his treasury of knowledge, **both new things** relating to Yeshua and the New Covenant **and old** things, relating to the pre-Messianic Judaism he already understands. The storage room contains good things, things the house-owner wants and treasures. Some of the good things are new, some of them old. Likewise, the new Messianic and old Jewish things can both be good. Thus the Messianic *Torah*-teacher is uniquely placed to enrich Messianic Judaism by expressing Messianic truth in Jewishly relevant ways, to repair old coats with good patches and restore old wineskins for new wine (9:16–17&N). A good Jewish education, far from being a prophylaxis against believing in Yeshua and the Kingdom he preached, as some opponents of Messianic Judaism suppose, instead ought to provide "rich soil" for bringing forth for Yeshua "grain, a hundred... times what had been sown" (13:8). The outstanding New Testament example is Sha'ul.

53–58 Messianic Jews today often find these verses poignantly relevant to their own families and home towns. But they can take comfort from the fact that although Yeshua himself encountered opposition, indifference and skepticism, in the end his family believed in him (Ac 1:14, Ga 1:19; contrast 12:48–50, Yn 7:3–5), and his home town became a center of New Covenant faith.

55 **Isn't he the carpenter's son?** The language implies that the answer ought to be a plain "Yes." But the real answer is not so simple, as Luke's careful language reveals: "It was supposed that he was a son of the Yosef who was of Eli, of Mattat..." (Lk 3:23–38&N). Yosef the carpenter raised Yeshua and accepted him as his son even though he had no natural human father, since Miryam the virgin was caused to become pregnant by God supernaturally (1:18–25&NN, Lk 1:26–38&NN). As for his **brothers**, see 12:46N.

CHAPTER 14

1 **Herod** Antipas, son of Herod the Great (see 2:1N), ruled over the Galil and Perea, 4 B.C.E.–39 C.E.

Regional governor, Greek *tetrarchos*, "ruler of a quarter" of a country. Herod the Great's kingdom had been divided into not four but three, with one of his sons ruling each part. See Lk 3:1N

3 **Herodias**, daughter of Aristobulus, who was one of the fifteen sons of Herod the Great, although not mentioned in the New Testament. She was married to her uncle Herod **Philip** (not the Philip of Lk 3:1), who fathered her daughter Salomé (v. 6; the name is not given in the New Testament but is known from Josephus). Herodias left Philip to be mistress to his half-brother Herod Antipas (v. 4).

4 **Yochanan**, a true prophet, did not shrink from telling even the most highly placed what they least wanted to hear.

It violates the *Torah* (Leviticus 18:16, 20:21) **for you to have her as your wife**, literally, "for you to have her."

7 **With an oath.** Oaths were far more serious then than now. See 5:37&N.

9 Note Herod's overriding concern for his image here and in v. 5.

12 Josephus reports in *Antiquities of the Jews* 18:5:1, that Herod Antipas was defeated in a war with Aretas, king of Arabia Petrea, and adds:

> "Now some of the Jews thought that the destruction of Herod's army came from God and that very justly, as a punishment of what he did against John, that was called the Baptist; for Herod slew him, who was a good man, and commanded the Jews to exercise virtue, both as to righteousness towards one another, and piety towards God, and so to come to baptism; for that the washing [with water] would be acceptable to him, if they made use of it, not in order to the putting away [or the remission] of some sins [only], but for the purification of the body: supposing still that the soul was throughly purified beforehand by righteousness. Now when [many] others came to crowd about him, for they were greatly moved [or pleased] by hearing his words, Herod, who feared lest the great influence John had over the people might put it into his power and inclination to raise a rebellion, [for they seemed ready to do anything he should advise,] thought it best, by putting him to death, to prevent any mischief he might cause, and not bring himself into difficulties, by sparing a man who might make him repent of it when it should be too late. Accordingly he was sent a prisoner, out of Herod's suspicious temper, to Macherus, the castle I before mentioned, and was there put to death. Now the Jews had an opinion that the destruction of this army was sent as a punishment upon Herod, and a mark of God's displeasure against him." (*Antiquities* 18:5:2, William Whiston translation, 1682)

19 Looking up toward heaven. Yeshua is reported in six places to have prayed with his eyes open (here; Mk 6:41, 7:34; Lk 9:16; Yn 11:41, 17:1). Jews generally do so today; Christians often pray with them closed. There is no command on the subject in the Bible. In an age when people are easily distracted, closing one's eyes may help one to concentrate on God. On the other hand, those who choose to keep their eyes open have the Messiah as their model. The phrase, "toward heaven," can also carry the secondary meaning, "toward God" (see 3:2N).

He made a *b'rakhah*. The Jewish-English phrase means "said a blessing." The Greek here is *evlogeô*, "bless, speak well of"; elsewhere it is often *evcharistô*, "thank." Although the text does not say so specifically, it is reasonable to suppose that he recited the customary *b'rakhah* ("benediction"; see 9:8N) which Jews have said for more than two thousand years before meals that include bread: *Barukh attah, Adonai Eloheynu, Melekh-ha'olam, haMotzi lechem min ha'aretz* ("Praised be you, *Adonai* our God, King of the universe, who brings forth bread from the earth").

Here are two points to note about Jewish blessings at meals. First, the blessing before the meal is short. A longer "Grace" (*Birkat-HaMazon*) is said after the meal. This seems sensible: one thanks God for something received; moreover, on a full stomach one can relax and express appreciation at length; but on an empty stomach, if the prayers become verbose, one's mind easily descends from Heaven to the table. Second, the object of the blessing is God, not the food. It is unnecessary to say, as many Christians do, "Lord, bless this food to our bodies"; since food is already God's blessing to us (Genesis 1:29, 9:3–4)! Rather, we thank him for providing it. See also below, 26:26–27&N.

21 Five thousand men, plus women and children. Elisha, by a similar miracle of creation, fed one hundred people with twenty loaves of bread (2 Kings 4:42–44). Here Yeshua fed perhaps ten thousand with fewer loaves.

31 Such little trust Kefa has, even though a moment before he had much (v. 29). Faith is only present-tense; it does not build up like a bank account (see Ya 1:6–7). Yeshua's rebuke restored it: he walked back to the boat (v. 32). From this we learn the value of well-founded rebuke to the spiritually sensitive, that is, people open to correction.

34 Ginosar (Genessaret), north of modern Tiberias. Site of 1985 discovery of a fishing boat from around the period of Yeshua, now on display at Kibbutz Nof-Ginosar.

36 *Tzitzit.* See 9:20N.

CHAPTER 15

1–20 On these verses, with their very important implications for Messianic Judaism, see the somewhat more complete parallel passage at Mk 7:1–23&NN.

21–28 This passage raises the question: does Yeshua treat Gentiles in a demeaning way? Is he a Jewish chauvinist? The notes to the following verses address this issue. For more, see Appendix, p. 931.

24 I was sent only to the lost sheep of the house of Israel. Yeshua's personal mission prior to his death and resurrection was only to the Jews, God's people. After the Holy Spirit was given, the Gospel would reach Gentiles even in "the farthest parts of the earth" (Ac 1:8), who would be grafted into Israel through the Messiah (Ro 11:16–24).

26 Pet dogs. There are two Greek words for "dog": "*kuôn*," scavenging hounds that roam the streets in packs (7:6, Lk 16:21, Pp 3:2, 2 Ke 2:22, Rv 22:15), and "*kunarion*," small dogs kept as house pets (only in this passage and its parallel, Mk 7:27–28). Yet even if Gentiles are not here compared with wild snarling beasts, are they still not being insulted? The answer can only be: no more than in the *Tanakh* itself, where the people of Israel are taken by God in a special way as his children. And although Judaism teaches that the righteous Gentiles of the world have a share in the world to come, this is not a primary focus either in the *Tanakh* or in rabbinic Judaism.

27 The woman is not offended but understands what she has been told. In humility she accepts not only her own role analogous to that of a house pet being fed crumbs from the master's table, but also the implication that Yeshua's Messianic mission is not for the present directed at Gentiles but at Jews.

28 On these terms Yeshua grants her request. Her case differs from that of the Roman army officer at 8:5–13, an isolated Gentile in a Jewish community. Had Yeshua healed the daughter immediately, this bold talkative woman would surely have spread the news, unleashing an onslaught of Gentiles with needs; and this might well have tempted him to neglect his commission to "the lost sheep of the house of Israel."

39 The boat, last mentioned when left at Ginosar (14:34).

CHAPTER 16

1 Sign from Heaven. A triple wordplay: (1) the appearance of the sky (heaven), which foretells the weather; (2) a sign from God (Heaven); and (3) "signs of the times" (v. 3), where "times" evokes both weather seasons and where we stand in the flow of history. See 3:2N.

4 The sign of Yonah. See 12:39–41.

6 ***Chametz***, "leaven," usually a symbol of sin or evil, as is clear at v. 12 (see 1C 5:6–8&N).

7–8 Alfred Edersheim, a nineteenth-century Hebrew Christian scholar, suggests the disciples thought Yeshua believed they had not brought bread in order to have him do another bread-making miracle. This would have been the same sort of sign-fishing the *P'rushim* and *Tz'dukim* had been doing and would have been an indication of their having **little trust.**

13 Caesarea Philippi, the present-day town of Banyas at the foot of Mount Hermon, where the Jordan River springs forth. Herod Philip (14:3&N) refurbished this town and renamed it in honor of the Emperor and himself.

16 Shim'on Kefa. Or: "Shim'on the Rock" (see 4:19N). The meaning of the Aramaic word "*kefa*," equivalent to Greek "*petros*," is important for this passage, as becomes clear in v. 18&N.

17 Shim'on Bar-Yochanan, Aramaic for "Shim'on, son of Yochanan." The Greek is *Barîona*, usually thought of as transliterating Hebrew *Bar-Yonah* and rendered "Barjona" or "son of Jonah." But at Yn 1:42, 21:15–17 Shim'on is called *Iôannou*, "of Yochanan"; and the Hebrew/Aramaic names Yochanan and Yonah are sufficiently alike that they could become confounded with each other after being transliterated into Greek. Thus Broadus' commentary hypothesizes that *Barîona* represents *bar-ioana*, rendering Aramaic *bar-yochanan* (*ad loc.*, p 354).

Human being, literally, "flesh and blood," corresponding to Hebrew *basar v'dam*, a common expression stressing human limits and weakness.

18 You are Kefa, Greek *Petros*. **Which means "Rock,"** phrase added by me the translator. **And on this rock**, Greek *petra*. *"Petros"* is the masculine form, *"petra"* feminine. See v. 16N. The word "*petra*" appears as a loanword in Hebrew in a most interesting context. *Yalkut Shim'oni*, an anthology of *midrashim* on the Hebrew Bible from the Middle Ages, has in it this passage:

> "When the Holy One wanted to create the world he passed over the generations of Enoch and the Flood; but when he saw Abraham who was to arise, he said, 'Behold, I have found a rock (*petra*) on which I can build and establish the world.' Therefore he called Abraham a rock, as it is said (Isaiah 51:1), 'Look to the rock from which you were hewn.'"(Yalkut 766 on Numbers 23:9, quoting an earlier source, Tanchuma B, Yelamdenu)

We can only speculate on whether this homily was known in Yeshua's day.

Community, Greek *ekklêsia*, which means "called-out ones," and is used in the Septuagint to translate Hebrew *kahal*, "assembly, congregation, community." The usual English translation of *ekklêsia* is "church"; and from it comes the word "ecclesiastical," meaning, "having to do with the church." The *JNT* sometimes uses "Messianic community" or "congregation" to render *ekklêsia*. What is being spoken about is a spiritual community of people based on trust in God and his son the Messiah Yeshua. This can be all people throughout history who so commit themselves, or a group of such people at a particular time and place, such as the Messianic community in Corinth or Jerusalem. The phrase, "the *ekklêsia* that meets in their house" (Ro 16:5), refers to a particular congregation. Unlike "church," *ekklêsia* never refers either to an institution or to a building.

19 In consequence of his confession Yeshua makes Kefa both (1) *shammash* ("steward"; see Ro 16:1N, Pp 1:1N, 1 Ti 3:8–13), with the **keys**, and (2) *dayan* ("judge"), who, as the one who can **prohibit** and **permit**, establishes new covenant *halakhah* (see 18:18–20&N).

21–22 Yeshua teaches his *talmidim* what must happen to him as Messiah and is completely misunderstood, both here and on two later occasions (17:22–23, 20:17–19&N), so different is his scenario from that popularly expected. Even at the Last Supper (Yn 14:28) and after his resurrection (Ac 1:6–7) they did not comprehend God's plan for the Messiah.

23 Even in his closest disciple, Yeshua detected the arch-enemy. We learn that believers can be demonized (on what this means, see 4:24N). Also see Appendix, p. 931.

24 Yeshua's great call to discipleship is his teaching on how to think the way God thinks (v. 23). Dietrich Bonhoeffer, the German Lutheran theologian who was imprisoned in the Buchenwald concentration camp and hanged at age 39 by the Gestapo at Flossenburg, days before the close of World War II, wrote in *The Cost of Discipleship* that there is no "cheap grace," no primrose path to heaven. Jews have often thought Christianity to be offering exactly that; and some Christian theologies, by emphasizing God's work and de-emphasizing man's in the salvation process, encourage this misunderstanding. This verse is the antidote. To follow Yeshua is to say no to oneself, not by practicing asceticisms or developing low self-esteem, but by placing the will of God above one's own feelings, desires and urges. To take up one's execution-stake is to bear the instrument of one's own death (see 10:38N), for, as Bonhoeffer put it, "When Christ calls a man, he bids him come and die." The consequences of wholeheartedly taking this stand are given in vv. 25–26.

CHAPTER 17

2–3 In what is known as the Transfiguration, Yeshua's **face shown like the sun, and his clothing became white as light.** Why? So that his glory would not be less than that of **Moshe and Eliyahu,** who were **speaking with him.** According to Deuteronomy Rabbah 11:10, when God sent the angel Samma'el (see Yd 9N) at the end of Moshe's life to fetch his soul, he "saw Moshe sitting and writing down the Unutterable Name of God, and how the radiance of his appearance was like that of the sun." This is an aggadic extension of what the *Tanakh* itself says about him, "that the skin of his face shone" (Exodus 34:29–35; the New Covenant makes its own *midrash* on this passage at 2C 3:7–18&NN).

5 Another *bat-kol*; see 3:17&N.

Listen to him! because he is the "prophet like Moshe" (Deuteronomy 18:15–19, Ac 3:22–23&N), whom you have just seen.

9 The Transfiguration confirmed Yeshua's "coming in his kingdom" (16:28) to these three *talmidim*, but without the more public confirmation which followed his resurrection (see 1C 15:5–6), the testimony would have been of little value in proving Yeshua's identity and would have raised more questions than it answered. Hence Yeshua advised closedmouthedness for the time being.

10 **The *Torah*-teachers say Eliyahu must come first.** This teaching is based on Malachi 3:1 and 3:23–24 (4:5–6), and it is kept alive in Judaism every Passover, at the Seder meal, when an extra place is set for *Eliyahu HaNavi* ("Elijah the prophet"), and the door is opened to welcome him, should he be there. Three points: (1) Yochanan the Immerser, "if you are willing to accept it," was Eliyahu (11:10–14&N), (2) Eliyahu himself had in fact "come first" by appearing there on the mountain (v. 3), and (3) Eliyahu may yet appear before Yeshua's second coming (see Rv 11:3–6&N).

21 The manuscripts which add v. 21 probably borrowed it from Mk 9:29.

24 A per-capita tax of one **half-shekel** to support the activities of the *cohanim* is specified in Exodus 30:11–16, 38:26. This was equivalent to one or two days' wages for an average worker.

CHAPTER 18

3 **Unless you change.** Greek *strephô* ("turn") can mean inward turning, hence "repent" or "change." KJV renders the phrase, "except ye be converted." The "conversion" needed is not from Judaism but from the sin of self-seeking ambition to be "the greatest" (v. 1). The conversion is not to Christianity or to an "-ism," but to God and relating personally with him through Yeshua the Messiah.

8–9 **Obtain eternal life**, literally, "enter the life."

10 **Their angels in heaven are constantly seeing the face of my Father.** The imagery recalls Oriental court ceremony. The verse does not say that each believer has a guardian angel, but that recent believers as a group have angels in heaven. The apocryphal book of Tobit (c. 300 B.C.E.) speaks of guardian angels; Daniel and Zechariah mention angels of particular countries. The disciples praying for Kefa thought that the knock at the door was that of "his angel" (Ac 12:15), but their ideas were not necessarily correct. There may be guardian angels, but Scripture does not prove it. Angels have many functions in relation to believers: ministering to God on their behalf (MJ 1:14), protecting them (Psalm 91:11, Mt 4:6), overseeing their worship (1C 11:10), in judgment separating them from the wicked (Mt 13:41, 24:31). Their function here is not stated.

11 The manuscripts which add v. 11 probably borrowed from Lk 19:10.

15 **Your brother**, that is, a fellow-believer.
Against you. Some manuscripts have this phrase, others do not.

16 **Two or three witnesses** establish a fact in a Jewish court (Deuteronomy 19:15).

17 **The congregation**, Greek *ekklêsia*; see 16:18N.
Treat him as you would a pagan or tax-collector, i.e., exclude him from fellowship, at least for a while (see the example at 1C 5:1–5 and 2C 2:5–11).

18–20 Contrary to most Christian interpreters, I take the *p'shat* ("plain sense") of this passage to be dealing with making legal judgments and *halakhah*, not prayer.

The words rendered "**prohibit**" and "**permit**" (v. 18) are, literally, "bind" and "loose." These terms were used in first century Judaism to mean "prohibit" and "permit," as is clear from the article, "Binding and Loosing," in the *Jewish Encyclopedia*, 3:215:

> "BINDING AND LOOSING (Hebrew *asar ve-hittir*)... Rabbinical term for 'forbidding and permitting.'...
>
> "The power of binding and loosing was always claimed by the Pharisees. Under Queen Alexandra the Pharisees, says Josephus (*Wars of the Jews* 1:5:2), 'became the administrators of all public affairs so as to be empowered to banish and readmit whom they pleased, as well as to loose and to bind.'... The various schools had the power 'to bind and to loose'; that is, to forbid and to permit (Talmud: Chagigah 3b); and they could bind any day by declaring it a fast-day (...Talmud: Ta'anit 12a...). This power and authority, vested in the rabbinical body of each age or in the Sanhedrin, received its ratification and final sanction from the celestial court of justice (Sifra, Emor, ix; Talmud: Makkot 23b).
>
> "In this sense Jesus, when appointing his disciples to be his successors, used the familiar formula (Matt 16:19, 18:18). By these words he virtually invested them with the same authority as that which he found belonging to the scribes and Pharisees who 'bind heavy burdens and lay them on men's shoulders, but will not move them with one of their fingers'; that is, 'loose them,' as they have the power to do (Matt 23:2–4). In the same sense in the second epistle of Clement to James II ('Clementine Homilies,' Introduction), Peter is represented as having appointed Clement as his successor, saying: 'I communicate to him the power of binding and loosing so that, with respect to everything which he shall ordain in the earth, it shall be decreed in the heavens; for he shall bind what ought to be bound and loose what ought to be loosed as knowing the rule of the church.'"

The article notes that a very different, non-Jewish interpretation, equating binding and loosing with remitting and retaining sins (Yn 20:23), was adopted by Tertullian and all the church fathers, thus investing the head of the Christian Church with the power to forgive sins, referred to on the basis of Mt 16:18 as the "key power of the Church." Needless to say, I reject this later understanding which bears no relationship to the Jewish context.

The usual Christian view of vv. 19–20 is that it defines a "Messianic *minyan*" not as the quorum of ten established by *halakhah* (Talmud, Sanhedrin 2b) for public synagogue prayers, but as **two or three** assembled in Yeshua's name, plus Yeshua himself, who is **there with them** (v. 20). The problem with this is that the passage is not about prayer — although it is not wrong to make a *midrash* on it which does apply to prayer (see below and 2:15N). Rather, Yeshua, speaking to those who have authority to regulate Messianic communal life (vv. 15–17), commissions them to establish New Covenant *halakhah*, that is, to make authoritative decisions where there is a question about how Messianic life ought to be lived. In v. 19 Yeshua is teaching that when an issue is brought formally to a panel of two or three Messianic Community leaders, and they render a halakhic decision here on earth, they can be assured that the authority of God in heaven stands behind them. Compare the Mishna:

"Rabbi Chananyah ben-T'radyon said, 'If two sit together and words of *Torah* pass between them, the *Sh'khinah* abides between them, as it is said, "Those who feared *Adonai* spoke together, and *Adonai* paid heed and listened, and a record was written before him for those who feared *Adonai* and thought on his name" (Malachi 3:16).'"(Avot 3:2)

Curiously, the following extract from the Talmud provides a Jewish setting for both my understanding and the traditional Christian one.

"How do you know that if ten people pray together the *Sh'khinah* ["manifested divine presence"] is there with them? Because it is said, 'God stands in the congregation of God' (Psalm 82:1a) [and a "congregation" must have a *minyan* of at least ten]. And how do you know that if three are sitting as a court of judges the *Sh'khinah* is there with them? Because it is said, 'In the midst of judges he renders judgment' (Psalm 82:1b [taking *elohim* to mean "judges"; compare Yn 10:34–36&N])." (B'rakhot 6a)

Thus, according to vv. 18–20 Yeshua's other *talmidim* join Kefa (16:19) in replacing "the Levitical *cohanim* and the judge who shall be in those days" (Deuteronomy 17:8–12) as the final earthly repository of halakhic authority. However, the new system was not established instantaneously; for later Yeshua could still advise the Jewish public to obey the *Torah*-teachers and *P'rushim* because they "sit in the seat of Moshe" (23:2–3&N). In fact, even today, two thousand years later, the new system has hardly been established at all — Messianic communal practice is far more *ad hoc* and makes far less use of received wisdom and established precedents than one might expect.

The unity of subject matter in vv. 15–20 is also seen in the fact that "two or three" is found in both v. 16 and vv. 19–20. Moreover, it is then evident that v. 21 continues the topic begun in v. 15 (how communal Messianic life is to be lived), without what otherwise is an irrelevant digression to another subject (reassurance about prayer).

The following expansion of v. 19 further clarifies its meaning: "To repeat (Greek *kai*, "and, moreover") [and fortify in other language what I have just said in v. 18], I tell you that if two of you [Messianic community leaders] agree on the answer to any halakhic question or matter of public order that people ask you about, then it [the halakhic decision you make] will be for them [the people who asked the question] as if it had come directly from my Father in heaven." In v. 20 Yeshua strengthens this statement by promising his own presence and authority in such situations.

Nevertheless, one may regard the traditional Christian understanding of vv. 19–20 as a *drash* in which a prayer context is supplied (by allowable eisegesis, see 2:15N) in a homily reassuring believers that their prayers are "powerful and effective" (Ya 5:16&N).

For a fuller discussion of the role of believers in establishing Messianic Jewish *halakhah* and having authority to interpret the *Torah* for God's people, based on this key passage of Mattityahu, see my *Messianic Jewish Manifesto*, pp. 146–151.

21–22 See 6:14–15; contrast Genesis 4:24.

24 **Many millions,** literally, "ten thousand talents." In Roman times one talent equalled 6,000 denarii, a denarius being roughly a day's wages for a common laborer. If a day's wages today is in the neighborhood of $50, 10,000 talents would be $3 billion! In the *Tanakh* a talent weighs 75.6 avoirdupois pounds. This amount of gold, at $350/troy ounce, is worth nearly $4 billion; the same amount of silver, at $4/troy ounce, comes to over $40 million. Haman offered King Achashverosh of Persia 10,000 talents of silver to destroy the Jews (Esther 3:9). The museum in Heraklion, Crete, displays 3,500-year-old Minoan talents — metal ingots used to settle debts.

28 **Some tiny sum**, relatively. Literally, "a hundred denarii," about $5,000 today.

CHAPTER 19

3–9 The only text in the Five Books of Moses dealing with divorce is Deuteronomy 24:1–4, and its discussion of grounds is perfunctory. Hillel and Shammai, who lived in the generation before Yeshua, took opposing sides in interpreting this passage.

> "The School of Shammai say a man may not divorce his wife unless he has found unchastity in her, as it is said, '...because he has found in her *indecency* in a matter.' But the School of Hillel say he may divorce her even if she burns his food, as it is said, '...because he has found in her indecency *in a matter.*'"(Mishna: Gittin 9:10)

Yeshua in v. 9 agrees with the strict-constructionist *Beit-Shammai.* But although *Beit-Hillel*'s lenient position became the halakhic norm, Rabbi El'azar, a member of *Beit-Hillel,* commented in the Gemara to this *mishna,* "When a man divorces his first wife, even the altar sheds tears," citing Deuteronomy 24:13–14 as evidence (Gittin 90b). There is a Jewish tradition that in Messianic times the stricter rulings of *Beit-Shammai* will become the standard.

Yeshua in adducing Scripture harks back to **the beginning**, in Gan-Eden (vv. 4–5), to support his view that a marriage must not be dissolved for anything less than the most direct insult to its one-flesh integrity, **adultery**. Verse 9 may imply that divorce without remarriage is allowable for lesser reasons (see 5:31–32&NN). A second ground for divorce is given at 1C 7:12–16&N.

10–12 Judaism has always considered marriage both normal and desirable — "The unmarried person lives without joy, without blessing and without good.... An unmarried man is not fully a man" (Talmud: Yevamot 62b–63a). On the other hand, some branches of Christianity came to grant abnormally high status to celibacy (on this phenomenon see 1C 7:1–40&NN). Depending on the calling and preferences of the individual, Yeshua allows that either the married or the single life can be one of service to God and humanity; and he takes care to minimize needless guilt on the part of those making the choice.

18–19 Yeshua names the sixth through ninth and fifth of the Ten Commandments (see 5:21N). These deal with interpersonal relationships, as does **"Love your neighbor as yourself,"** which subsumes the others (Ro 13:8–10).

21 **If you are serious about reaching the goal.** Usually, and with equal justification, rendered, "If you want to be perfect." See Ro 10:4N.

24 **Needle's eye.** It is obviously impossible for the largest animal known in the region to pass through the smallest opening normally encountered. Late manuscripts and versions which substitute "cable" or "rope" for "camel," likewise commentaries which suppose the "needle's eye" refers to a small gate kept open in a large gate closed to protect a walled city, are later efforts to tone down Yeshua's starkly incongruous image. (This note has been corrected from earlier editions.)

28 The *Tanakh* speaks of a **regenerated world** at Isaiah 1:25–2:5, 11:1–16, 65:17; Jeremiah 23:3–8, 30:1–31:40; Micah 4:1–5:3; Zechariah 12:1–14:21; Psalms 2, 22, 89; Daniel 7–12. Note also Ro 8:19–23, Rv 21:1–22:5. Rabbinic literature speaks of the *'olam haba* ("world" or "age to come") and describes its time and character in such places in the Talmud as Sanhedrin 96–99.

You... will also sit on twelve thrones and judge the twelve tribes of Israel. An important New Testament verse confirming God's promises to national Israel, e.g., Isaiah 1:26, "And I will restore your judges as at first." See also Ezekiel 48, Isaiah 9:5–6 (6–7). This verse gives a rationale for choosing twelve emissaries (10:2–4) and maintaining that number (Ac 1:15–26); also compare Rv 21:10–14.

CHAPTER 20

1 **Vineyard.** See Yn 15:1&N.

15 **Or do you begrudge my generosity**? Literally, "Is your eye evil because I am good?" See 6:22–23N.

17–19 For the third time Yeshua predicts his coming death. This time he mentions the role of the *Goyim* (see 5:47N), which he avoided before, possibly because he wanted to be able to broach the subject without having his *talmidim* try to dissuade him (16:21–23) or become overwhelmed by grief (17:21–22), even though they might still be terrified at the prospect (Mk 10:32&N). The following incident also helps them understand why the Messiah must die (below, v. 28).

Going up to Yerushalayim here and at Mk 10:32–33, 15:41; Lk 2:42, 18:31, 19:28; Yn 5:1, 11:55; Ac 11:2, 13:31, 15:2, 21:4, 21:12, 21:15, 24:11, 25:1, 25:9; Ga 1:17, 2:1; and compare Yn 7:8; while Lk 10:30–31, Ac 8:26, 15:1, 25:7 report "coming down" from Yerushalayim. Jerusalem is located on top of the Judean hills, some 2,500 feet above sea level and higher than most inhabited places in Israel. This particular ascent was being made from Jericho, 900 feet below sea level. But "going up to Jerusalem" has a spiritual dimension which does not depend on altitude — the earth's spiritual geography is such that from the summit of Mount Everest one still "goes up" to Jerusalem. Today when Jews come to live in Israel they do not "immigrate" but "make *aliyah*" (the word means "going up"), even if they plan to live on the shore of the Dead Sea, the lowest place on earth.

29–30 As they were leaving Yericho... two blind men. Compare the descriptions at Mk 10:46, Lk 18:35. When Gospel witnesses differ, often there is a reasonable way to explain the discrepancies. Only Mattityahu notes the second blind man; presumably there were two, but the one was more prominent than the other — Mark even tells us his name, *Bar-Timai*. Luke places the incident "As Yeshua approached Jericho." But there were two Jerichos; Yeshua may have been leaving the site of still inhabited ancient Jericho, with its archeological remains going back to 7,000 B.C.E., and approaching the more recently developed Roman spa several kilometers nearer Jerusalem.

CHAPTER 21

1 Mount of Olives. Hill one-half mile east of Jerusalem, separated from the Temple site by the Kidron Valley. **Beit-Pagey** (Aramaic, "house of unripe figs," Bethphage) and Beit-Anyah ("house of the poor," Bethany; v. 17) were villages on its south flank, along the road leading up from Jericho. The Mount of Olives is where Yeshua rose to heaven and where he will return at his second coming (Ac 1:9–12&N).

2–7 The key to this passage is the citation from the *Tanakh* in v. 5. It conflates two verses in the *Tanakh*, Isaiah 62:11 and Zechariah 9:9. The former includes the lines,

> "Say to the daughter of Zion,
> 'See your salvation comes!
> See, His reward is with Him,
> but His work lies ahead of Him.'"

The word for "salvation" here is "*yesha'*," identical with the name of the Messiah, Yeshua, except for the optional letter *vav*. Moreover, Isaiah describes this "*yesha'*"as a person, and not just any person, but God — since a person who is salvation must be God. English translations, including Jewish ones, which capitalize pronouns referring to God recognize this fact by capitalizing "His" and "Him" in this passage, as is done above. One may even say that in this verse Isaiah, writing 700 years before Yeshua was born, refers to him in his divine aspect by name.

Zechariah 9:9 has these lines in it:

> "Rejoice greatly, daughter of Zion!...
> See, your king comes to you.
> He is triumphant and victorious,
> humbly riding on a donkey,
> yes, on a colt, the offspring of a beast of burden."

By combining the two verses Mattityahu gives a hint (*remez*; see 2:15N) that God, the Salvation of Israel, the Messianic King and Yeshua of Natzeret are one. Also he hints at the two comings of the Messiah and the difference between them: at his first coming Yeshua is our final atoning sacrifice, bringing salvation by his death; therefore he rides into Jerusalem humbly on a beast of burden, ready to perform the work which lies ahead of him. But he will return, triumphant and victorious, as ruling king, rewarding the faithful — although for those who are faithful now, he has already begun to share the reward which he brings with him.

On a donkey, humbly, reflecting Yeshua's first coming to die for our sins. At his second coming he will be on horseback (Rv 19:11), as befits a king.

On a donkey and on a colt (v. 5).... **Yeshua sat on them** (v. 7). The relationship between these two phrases has given rise to a criticism of Mattityahu which, if justified, impugns his credibility as a divinely inspired writer. In v. 5, Greek *kai*, here rendered "and" (but see below), seems to imply that Zechariah is writing about two donkeys. Then, in v. 7, the phrase, "**and he sat on them**," is ambiguous — did he sit on the **robes**, using them as a cushion, or on both the donkey and the colt?

The argument is that Mattityahu the tax-collector was an ignorant *'am-ha'aretz* (country bumpkin; see Ac 4:13&N) unfamiliar with parallelism in Hebrew poetry, wherein the second line of a couplet sometimes adds no new information but only states differently what the first line has already said. Not knowing this, he supposed that fulfillment of Zechariah's prophecy required both a donkey and a colt and therefore created the ludicrous picture of Yeshua straddling two animals at once.

One can explain it, of course, by saying he did not sit on them simultaneously but in succession, kindly giving the colt rest, since it had never been ridden. One can even find meaning in Yeshua's action: his sitting on not only the donkey but its colt symbolizes his utter humiliation at his First Coming (Pp 2:6–8), since the colt is described as the mere offspring of a beast of burden, even lower in status than the mother animal.

But in fact there is no need to suppose Mattityahu thought Yeshua rode on both animals. Mattityahu was thoroughly familiar with the *Tanakh*, as his many quotations from it attest. Moreover, we know from the parallel passages that Yeshua rode on only one animal (Mk 11:7, Lk 19:35). Perhaps Mattityahu mentions two donkeys for a different reason, namely, to emphasize the immaturity of the colt (see Mk 11:2), too young to be separated from its mother.

Furthermore, the Greek grammar allows a different approach. In v. 5 Greek *kai*, corresponding to Hebrew letter *vav*, makes it possible to replace "and on a colt" with any of these alternative renderings: "yes, on a colt," "indeed, on a colt," "even on a colt," or "that is, on a colt." These eliminate explicitly the *need* for two animals in order to fulfill the prophecy, without excluding the possibility that there were nevertheless two animals there.

The Talmud contains an interesting homily based on Zechariah 9:9, but it obscures the difference between his first and second comings.

> "Rabbi Alexandri said, 'Rabbi Y'hoshua set two verses against each other: It is written, "And behold, one like the son of man came with the clouds of heaven" (Daniel 7:13), while elsewhere it is written, "See, your king comes unto you,... humbly riding on a donkey" (Zechariah 9:9). [He resolved the paradox by saying that] if they deserve it [he will come] with the clouds of heaven, but if not, lowly and riding on an ass.'"(Sanhedrin 98a)

The New Testament explanation, of course, is that at his first coming the Messiah was "humbly riding on a donkey," but his second coming will be "with the clouds of heaven" (24:30). For similar paradoxes cited from the same page of the Talmud see MJ 3:7N and 2 Ke 3:12N.

It has been suggested that Yeshua was an impostor who arranged this and other scenes in order to convince the people he was the Messiah: "Here's an easy prophecy to fulfill: I'll do what it says, and then they'll believe." If riding on a donkey colt were the only qualification for Messiahship, one might take the objection seriously — or we could all be Messiahs. Clearly Yeshua did arrange his entry into Jerusalem to fulfill Zechariah's prophecy. But he also fulfilled many other prophecies which he could not have manipulated, such as the time and place of his birth (Daniel 9:24–26, Micah 5:1(2); see above, 2:1–6&NN), and his resurrection (Psalm 16:10; see Ac 2:24–32&NN). For a fuller listing of these prophecies see 26:24N and Section VII of the Introduction to the *JNT*.

9 **Shouting, "Please! Deliver us!" to the Son of David.** Greek *ôsanna* transliterates Hebrew *hoshia' na* (literally, "Save, please!"). The word, and sometimes the whole phrase, is usually rendered as if it were an acclamation of praise: "shouting, 'Hosanna to the Son of David!'"Actually "*Hoshia' na*" is a prayer addressed to the Messiah, quoted from Psalm 118:25–26; Psalm 118 is Messianic throughout (Mattityahu cites another important passage from it at v. 42 below). The implication is that the crowds recognized and honored Yeshua as the Messiah by shouting, "Please, deliver us, Son of David!" — "Son of David" is a Messianic title (see 1:1N), and the crowds wanted their Messiah to deliver them from the Roman overlords.

Likewise, again quoting Psalm 118:25–26, they were recognizing Yeshua's Messiahship when they shouted, **Blessed is he who comes in the name** — that is, with the power and authority (see Ac 3:16N) — **of *Adonai!*** In other words: blessed is the Messiah, who exercises God's power and authority on earth and at the same time is present **in the highest heaven**, with intimate access to God himself (compare Yn 17:1–26, Pp 2:6–11). That this is the sense is clear from Yeshua's own use of the same passage at 23:39.

12 Pilgrims in Jerusalem turned to merchants for the animals and pigeons they needed for sacrifices; and they had recourse to foreign-exchange dealers because the Temple tax (see 17:24&N) was payable in Tyrian rather than Roman coin, since the latter had heathen markings; see Mishna Sh'kalim 5:3, 6:5, 7:2. Yeshua is fully aware of this but objects to the use of the Temple grounds for these purposes; the Talmud includes curses on the Sadducean priests for their greed. The restrictions placed on business in the Temple area created monopolistic profits for the merchants and revenue for the authorities.

According to the *Tanakh*, "on that day," that is, in Messianic times, "there shall no longer be a merchant in the house of *Adonai* of Hosts" (Zechariah 14:21; the word for "merchant," "trafficker" or "trader" is, literally, "Canaanite," as at Job 40:30(41:6) and Proverbs 31:24).

18–19 See Mk 11:12–14, 20–24&N.

23 Hebrew ***s'mikhah***, rendering Greek *exousia* ("authority"), means "leaning" or "laying" on of hands in the ordination ceremony for a judge, elder or rabbi. Laying on of hands is, in the *Tanakh*, a symbolic act that confers or transfers an office, along with its duties and privileges, by dramatizing God's bestowal of the blessings and giftings needed for the work. In Judaism the practice is traced back to Moses' ordination of Joshua and of the seventy elders (Numbers 11:16–17, 24–25; 27:18–23; Deuteronomy 34:9; see also Ac 8:17, 9:17, 13:3, 19:6, 28:8; 1 Ti 4:4, 5:22; 2 Ti 1:6).

A rabbinic ordinand was granted the right to judge and to decide points of *halakhah* (see 16:19N, 18:18–20N) by a board of three elders, at least one of whom had also received *s'mikhah*. The ***cohanim*** (2:4N) **and elders**, who are also *P'rushim* (v. 45, 3:7N), are asking: "What kind of ordination did you receive that entitles you to teach as authoritatively as you do (7:28–29&N), to decide points of *halakhah* as you do (12:1–15&NN), and to disturb the peace in the Temple courts (vv. 12–17 above)? And who dared give you such an ordination (so that we can interrogate him too)?" Yeshua does not answer their question (although see Yn 5:27, Mk 1:22–27N) but instead puts them on the defensive (21:29–22:46).

33–41 Vineyard. See Yn 15:1&N.

42 Only a few months later Kefa told the *Sanhedrin*, "This Yeshua is the stone rejected by you builders which has become the cornerstone. There is salvation in no one else! For there is no other name under heaven given to mankind by whom we must be saved!" (Ac 4:11–12&NN).

43 The Kingdom of God will be taken away from you. Yeshua is not saying that the Christians will replace the Jews as God's people, as many Christians teach. Rather, he is warning that Jewish leaders who do not look out for God's interests (vv. 33–42) will be deprived of sharing in his rulership; and this task, with its rewards, will fall to a different group of Jewish leaders, the Messianic Jewish *talmidim* caring for Yeshua's Messianic Community (see 18:18–20&N). Before long, of course, this community comes to include Gentile Christians, some of whom become leaders too.

In Sifre, a collection of *midrashim* compiled in the 4th century but including much older material, the rabbis, making a similar point in their discussion of Deuteronomy 32:9, told a similar parable about a king who leased a field to tenants.

44 The manuscripts which have v. 44 probably borrowed it from Lk 20:18.

CHAPTER 22

1–14 Yeshua continues addressing the *P'rushim* and leading *cohanim*. Compare the wedding imagery with Rv 19:7–9&NN, where Yeshua's own marriage and wedding banquet are described.

10–12 Kings would sometimes give banquets for their subjects and invite them all, regardless of status, providing suitable clothing for those unable to afford it. Therefore the one not wearing what the king had provided was without excuse. For the meaning of wedding clothes, see Rv 19:8.

13–14 Outside in the dark, literally, "into outer darkness." This seems to suggest an after-death state different from Gey-Hinnom (5:22N), Sh'ol (Hades, 11:23N) or heaven; the Roman Catholic doctrine of purgatory is partly based on this verse.

In that place…. Verses 13b-14 are Yeshua's comment on the story, not the remarks of the king.

15–16 The *P'rushim* wanted the Jewish theocracy restored and opposed oppressor Rome and its taxes. **Herod's party** — political, not religious — supported the Herodian dynasty set up by Rome and encouraged abiding by the Roman tax laws; they were not usually friendly with the *P'rushim*. The **trap** consisted in putting together an alliance of convenience in which both would ask Yeshua's opinion, hoping his response would alienate him from one group or the other.

21 ***Nu***, Greek *oun*. Paragraph 1 of the entry on "*oun*" in Arndt & Gingrich, *A Greek-English Lexicon of the New Testament*, says, "Inferential, denoting that what it introduces is the result of or an inference from what precedes: so, therefore, consequently, accordingly, then." The all-purpose Yiddish word "*nu*" (see 11:9N, Lk 12:42N) is often used with this meaning, but with the inflection, "Can't you figure it out for yourself?!" — thus conveying precisely the tone of Yeshua's answer.

With the answer itself compare Rav Shmu'el's Talmudic dictum (N'darim 28a), *Dina dimalkuta dina* — "The [secular] law of the [reigning Gentile] government is the Law [binding as *halakhah* on Jews]." And contrast the Messianic pretender, Y'hudah HaG'lili (Ac 5:36&N), who, according to Josephus, said that people who paid Roman taxes were cowards (*Wars of the Jews* 2:8:1).

23 ***Sh'eilah.*** See *JNT* Glossary entry. The word in Hebrew means simply "question," but among Jews speaking English it means "a question about *Torah* or *halakhah*," usually posed to someone expected to be able to give an authoritative answer. Thus "*sh'eilot utshuvot*" ("questions and answers") is the Hebrew term for the Responsa literature in Judaism. Verse 17 contains a *sh'eilah*; see also vv. 35–36, 41, 46.

24 The question posed by the *Tz'dukim* (see 3:7N) is based on the law of *yibbum* ("levirate marriage"), set forth in Deuteronomy 25:5–10 and elaborated in Talmud tractate *Yevamot*, wherein the brother of a man who dies without children is expected to marry his brother's widow in order to maintain the family line (as the *Tz'dukim* correctly state). The firstborn son of the new marriage would count as the dead man's child for inheritance purposes. Should the *yavam* (brother-in-law) refuse to marry his brother's widow, Deuteronomy 25:7–10 provides for a ceremony called *chalitzah* which both humiliates him and releases the widow from her obligation to marry him. The stories of Onan and Tamar (Genesis 38) and of Boaz and Ruth (Ruth 4) are biblical examples of *yibbum* and *chalitzah* respectively. Curiously, rabbinic decrees over the centuries have reversed the *Torah*'s priorities; the Chief Rabbinate of Israel requires *chalitzah* and bans *yibbum* entirely.

31–32 Yeshua derives the doctrine of resurrection from the *Torah* because the *Tz'dukim* accepted only the Pentateuch as absolutely authoritative. This is why he cites Exodus 3:6 rather than the more obvious Scriptural refutations at Isaiah 26:19 (quoted below), Daniel 12:2 (especially) and Job 19:26. Compare the following extract from the Talmud:

> "*Minim* ["sectarians"] asked *Rabban* Gamli'el: 'How do we know that the Holy One, blessed be He, will resurrect the dead?' He answered them from the *Torah*, the Prophets and the Writings, yet they did not accept it [as conclusive proof]. From the *Torah*, as it is written, 'The Lord said to Moses, "Here, you will sleep with your fathers and rise up"' (Deuteronomy 31:16). 'But maybe,' they said to him [by way of objection], 'the verse reads, "and the people will rise up"' [as in fact it does read]. From the Prophets, as it is written, 'Your dead will live and arise with my dead body. Wake up, sing, you who dwell in the dust! for your dew is like the dew on herbs, and the earth will throw out the shades of its dead' (Isaiah 26:19). 'But maybe this refers to the dead whom Ezekiel resurrected?' (Ezekiel 37). From the Writings, as it is written, 'And the roof of your mouth, like the best wine of my beloved, that goes down sweetly, causing the lips of those that are asleep to speak' (Song of Songs 7:9 [taken to refer to Israel]). 'But maybe it means only that their lips will move....' [They did not accept his proof] until he cited this verse: '...which *Adonai* swore to your fathers to give to them' (Deuteronomy 11:21) — not to you, but to them [to your fathers, who are now dead]; hence resurrection is derived from the *Torah*...." (Sanhedrin 90b)

The passage gains interest from the fact that "*minim*" often means Messianic Jews, and *Rabban* Gamli'el is mentioned in the New Testament (Ac 5:34&N, Ac 22:3). Travers Herford suggests they did not reject the doctrine of resurrection but questioned its derivability from the *Tanakh* (*Christianity in the Talmud*, pp. 232–233). I think these *minim* were other sectarians and not Messianic Jews at all, for, Herford's reasoning notwithstanding, there is no reason why Messianic Jews would object to deriving resurrection from the Scriptures.

There are several other passages in the same part of tractate Sanhedrin which derive resurrection from the *Tanakh*. One example:

> "Our rabbis taught: 'It is written, "I kill, and I make alive" (Deuteronomy 32:39). I could understand: I kill one person and give life to a different one, as the world goes on [some die, others are born]. This is why Scripture says [immediately afterwards, in the same verse], "I wound, and I heal." Just as the wounding and healing [clearly] refer to the same person, likewise putting to death and bringing to life refer to the same person. This refutes those who claim that resurrection is not implied by the *Torah*.'"(Sanhedrin 91b)

36 ***Mitzvot,*** literally, "commandments" (see 5:19N), but here better understood as "central principles"; see Mk 12:28N.

37 From the parallel passage at Mk 12:28–34 one learns that Yeshua quoted also

Deuteronomy 6:4, the central affirmation of Judaism, "*Sh'ma Israel, Adonai Eloheynu, Adonai echad*" ("Hear, O Israel, *Adonai* our God, *Adonai* is one"); see Mk 12:29N.

44 All of Psalm 110 is considered Messianic and is quoted or alluded to in the New Testament more than any other passage of the *Tanakh*, namely, here and at 26:64; Mk 12:36; Lk 20:42; Ac 2:34–35; 1C 15:25; Ep 1:20; Co 3:1; MJ 1:3, 13; 5:6, 10; 6:20; 7:17, 21; 8:1; 10:12; 12:2; 1 Ke 3:22.

CHAPTER 23

1–39 Yeshua's denunciation of the establishment (vv. 1–36) is combined with compassionate regret at their rejection of him (vv. 37–39). First he talks about them (vv. 1–12), then he speaks to them (vv. 13–36&N).

2 **The seat** (Greek *kathedra*) **of Moshe.** The Midrash Rabbah says:

> "They made for him [Moses] a *katedra* like that of the advocates, in which one sits and yet seems to be standing." (Exodus Rabbah 43:4)

Pesikta diRav Kahana 1:7 mentions the seat of Moses, and the editors of the English edition comment:

> "The particular place in the synagogue where the leaders used to sit was known metaphorically as the seat of Moses or as the throne of Torah, symbolizing the succession of teachers of Torah down through the ages." (William G. Braude and Israel J. Kapstein, *Pesikta diRav Kahana*, Philadelphia: Jewish Publication Society of America, 1975, p. 17)

A third-century C.E. "Chair of Moses" from Korazin (11:21) is on display at the Israel Museum in Jerusalem; a photograph and description may be found in *Biblical Archeology Review* 13:5 (1987), pp. 32–35. According to the Hebrew University scholarly journal *Tarbitz* I, p. 145, they can also be found in Hamot, Tiberias and Delos (Greece).

The *Torah*-teachers and the *P'rushim*... sit in the seat of Moshe, exercising the power of "the *cohen* or judge in office at that time" (Deuteronomy 17:8–13), officially interpreting the *Torah*. There are some who understand this verse to mean that, according to Yeshua, the Oral *Torah*, as expounded in Orthodox Judaism, is binding on Messianic Jews today. I do not believe this, because I think Yeshua had already initiated a process transferring halakhic authority from the *cohanim*, judges and rabbis to the emissaries and later leaders of the Messianic Community. See 18:18–20&N and *Messianic Jewish Manifesto*, Chapter V.

4 Compare the remarks of the modern Orthodox rabbi H. Loewe:

> "Rabbi Me'ir used to say, 'If I have ruled for others leniently, for myself I decide with stringency.' And conversely, in branding excess, Rabbi Huna describes the

> Pharisee who, lenient to himself, teachers others to obey the hardest rules." (C. G. Montefiore and H. Loewe, *A Rabbinic Anthology*, New York: Schocken Books edition, 1974, p. lxxix)

5 ***T'fillin*** are small leather boxes containing parchment scrolls on which are written excerpts from the *Tanakh* (specifically, Deuteronomy 6:4–9, 11:13–20, Exodus 13:1–16). Observant Jewish men past *bar-mitzvah* age (13) strap one on one arm and the other around the head during the morning weekday synagogue service, in literal obedience to Deuteronomy 6:8, "You shall bind them [that is, God's *mitzvot*] for a sign on your hand, and they shall be for frontlets between your eyes." Other English versions of the New Testament have here the word "phylacteries"; this transliterates the Greek word used in the text, "*phulakterion*," which means "safeguard, amulet, charm," and thus does not reflect the purpose of *t'fillin*.

Tzitziyot. See 9:20N.

7 ***Rabbi*** renders Greek *rabbi*, which transliterates the Hebrew (compare 8:19N). The word means, literally, "my great one," and, less literally, "my master," "my teacher." It became a title of respect used for *Torah* scholars by everyone, even those of the same or higher rank. Thus the Talmud says,

> "Whenever King Y'hoshafat, King of Y'hudah, saw a *talmid chakham* ["wise student," "scholar"] he would rise from his throne, embrace him and kiss him, and call him, '*Avi, avi*' ['My father, my father'], '*Rabbi, rabbi*' ['My teacher, my teacher'], '*Mari, mari*' ['My lord, my lord']." (Makkot 24a; parallel Ketubot 103b)

8–10 But you are not to let yourselves be called "Rabbi"… "Father"… "leaders." The Hebrew Christian scholar Arnold G. Fruchtenbaum holds that this passage prohibits Messianic Jewish congregations from calling their leaders "rabbis" ("The Quest for a Messianic Theology: Statement," in *Mishkan* #2 (Winter 1985), pp. 1–19; with "Response" by myself in the same issue, pp. 20–23; and "A Comment" by him in *Mishkan* #3, pp. 67–68).

My view is that a literalistic approach here is inappropriate, since Yeshua also warns against being called "father" or "leader," terms everyone uses. The context leads me to believe that Yeshua here is prohibiting believers from accepting unearned honors, rather than outlawing three titles. A leader is to be humble, a servant (20:25–28); if he is given any title at all, he is not to become puffed up. Others in the community are to guard against making invidious distinctions between "clergy" and "laity" by bestowing titles.

My own objection to the use of the title "rabbi" today is not theological but ideological and practical. What should a "Messianic rabbi" be? A pastor under another name? I think the term "rabbi" sets up Jewish expectations which ought to be fulfilled. A Messianic Jewish congregational leader who accepts the title "rabbi" without having training adequate to qualify him as a rabbi in a non-Messianic Jewish setting is accepting honor which he has not earned and to which he is not entitled; and this *does* violate Yeshua's injunction.

Should a Messianic rabbi have *s'mikhah* (ordination; see 21:23N)? If so, should it be Messianic or non-Messianic? If Messianic, who is qualified to grant it? Messianic Judaism at present has very few ordained rabbis and no accrediting agency. At present, in order not to embarrass the Messianic Jewish movement, I urge leaders without rabbinic training to resist letting themselves be called "rabbi."

13–36 Nowhere is it clearer than here and at 21:12–13 that the image of "gentle Jesus, meek and mild" falls short of reality. The repeated slashing litany, **Woe to you hypocritical *Torah*-teachers** ("scribes"; see 2:4N) **and *P'rushim!*** angers Jews, mystifies Gentiles and embarrasses Christians, who find Yeshua's remarks intemperate, antisemitic, even "un-Christlike." But Yeshua, like all the prophets, spoke the words of God without fear or favor. He comforted those who were open to him and made repeated invitation to those who opposed him; but when it had become evident that these particular *Torah*-teachers and *P'rushim* were hardhearted, closed-minded and interested only in confuting or trapping him, he seized the initiative, revealing his accusers for what they were. Was he "unloving" toward them? Love must sometimes be tough. Even less was he antisemitic: his within-the-family correction was aimed at making these Jewish brothers of his live up to their high calling (and he partly succeeded; see Ac 15:5, 21:20, 23:6). If Yeshua was unloving or antisemitic, one must say the same of all the Jewish prophets from Moses to Malachi.

A truer measure of antisemitism — as it developed in the Church — is the ease with which the terms "scribes" and "Pharisees" are uncritically equated with "hypocrites," falsely implying that *all* of them were. For Yeshua, in addressing "*you* hypocritical *Torah*-teachers and *P'rushim*" rather than "*the* hypocritical *Torah*-teachers and *P'rushim*," restricts his scathing denunciation to a specific group of them. See 3:7N, Mk 12:38N, 1 Th 2:14–16&NN. The Jewish scholar Menahem Mansoor, writing in the *Encyclopedia Judaica*, also recognizes this:

> "While the Pharisees, as a whole, set a high ethical standard for themselves, not all lived up to it. It is mistakenly held that the New Testament references to them as 'hypocrites' or 'offspring of vipers' (Matt. 3:7; Luke 18:9ff., etc.) are applicable to the entire group. However, the leaders were well aware of the presence of the insincere among their numbers, described by the Pharisees themselves in the Talmud as 'sore spots' or 'plagues of the Pharisaic party' (Sot. 3:4 and 22b)." (*Encyclopedia Judaica* 13:366)

The Mishna remarks that the "plagues" (or "hits" or "self-inflicted wounds") "of Pharisees… ruin the world" (Sotah 3:4). The Jerusalem and Babylonian Talmuds both comment on this in famous passages delineating seven kinds of Pharisees (J. B'rakhot 14b, Sotah 20c; B. Sotah 22b). The following is a hybrid combining elements from both Talmuds with rabbinic expositions; it mentions eight kinds:

> There are seven kinds of Pharisees: the "shoulder" Pharisee, who ostentatiously carries his good deeds on his shoulder so all can see them; the "wait-a-moment" Pharisee, who wants you to wait while he performs a *mitzvah*; the bruised Pharisee, who runs into a wall while looking at the ground to avoid seeing a woman; the "reckoning" Pharisee, who commits a sin, then does a good deed and

> balances the one against the other; the "pestle" Pharisee, whose head is bowed in false humility, like a pestle in a mortar; the Pharisee who asks, "What is my duty, so that I may do it?" as if he thought he had fulfilled every obligation already (compare Pp 3:5–6&NN); the Pharisee from fear of the consequences if he doesn't perform the commandments; and the Pharisee from love — either love of the rewards God promises for performing the commandments, or love of *Torah* itself [no matter which, he is understood here to be the one good kind of Pharisee].

Continuing with B. Sotah 22b:

> "Abaye and Raba said to the teacher [of the above passage], 'Don't mention the Pharisee from love and the Pharisee from fear, because Rav Y'hudah quoted Rav as saying, "A person should always engage himself in *Torah* and *mitzvot* even if not for their own sake [i.e., even if motivated by fear of punishment or love of reward; see above]; because from doing them not for their own sake he will come to do them for their own sake."' Rabbi Nachman ben-Yitzchak said, 'What is hidden is hidden, and what is revealed is revealed — the Great Tribunal will punish those who rub themselves against the walls, simulating humility [that is, God penetrates hypocrisy, reads hearts and judges truly; compare Lk 16:15&N, Yn 2:25].'"

The passage concludes with this quotation from Alexander Yannai, the Hasmonean ruler of Judea (103–76 B.C.E.), who hated the Pharisees:

> "King Yannai said to his wife, 'Fear neither the Pharisees nor those who are not Pharisees; rather, fear the *tsvu'in* who ape the Pharisees, because their deeds are like the deed of Zimri (Numbers 25:14) but they expect a reward like that of Pinchas (Numbers 25:11).'"

The literal sense of the Aramaic word "*tsvu'in*" is "dyed, colored," from which comes the metaphorical meaning, "hypocrites"; it also means "hyenas."

14 The manuscripts which add v. 14 probably borrowed from Mk 12:40 (see note there) or Lk 20:47.

15 You go about over land and sea to make one proselyte. Modern Judaism does not consider itself a missionary religion, and already by the time the Talmud was written Jews had become cautious about receiving converts (see Yevamot 47a). But in the second century B.C.E. the Idumeans were forcibly converted to Judaism, and apparently in Yeshua's time there was still active proselytizing by the Jewish community. For more on this topic, see 1C 7:17–20N, 2C 4:1–2N, Ga 5:3N. Also see Appendix, p. 931.

16–22 The rabbinic elaboration of the laws pertaining to oaths is found in Talmud tractate *Shvu'ot*.

19 **The altar which makes the sacrifice holy.** Exodus 29:37–38: "...the altar will be most holy, and whatever touches the altar will become holy. This is what you are to offer upon the altar: two lambs a year old every day, continually."

23 **Tithes.** The *cohanim* and *L'vi'im* were debarred from owning hereditary land but were to be given a tithe (tenth) of all produce (Leviticus 27:30–33, Numbers 18:21); a second tithe was to be consumed by the owner in Jerusalem (Deuteronomy 14:22–27); and a tithe for the poor replaced the second tithe in the third and sixth year of the seven-year cycle that culminated in the year of *sh'mittah*, in which the land was allowed to lie fallow. The rabbinic elaboration of the law of tithes is found in Talmud tractates *Ma'aserot* and *Ma'aser Sheni.*

The weightier matters of the *Torah* — justice, mercy, trust. Yeshua seems to be alluding to Micah 6:8: "...what does *Adonai* require of you but to do justice, love mercy and walk humbly with your God?"

These... you should have attended to — without neglecting the others! Yeshua clearly upholds keeping even the minutiae of the Law. Those who encourage Messianic Jews to stop observing the *Torah* are ignoring his advice both here and at 5:17–20&NN above. Nevertheless, the main point in this and the following verse is that one should properly order one's priorities so as to live a life pleasing to God.

28 **And far from *Torah***, or: "and wickedness"; Greek *anomia.* An especially cutting denunciation when aimed at those who considered themselves the authoritative expositors of the Law. See 7:23N.

35 **Hevel** (Abel). See Genesis 4:8.

Z'kharyah Ben-Berekhyah, whom you murdered between the Temple and the altar. There is a discrepancy. According to 2 Chronicles 24:20–21, Zechariah, the son of Jehoiada was killed "in the court of the house of *Adonai*"; while Zechariah 1:1 identifies the writer of the book as the son of Berechiah, son of Iddo, but the *Tanakh* does not indicate how he died. Possibly Jehoiada had the additional name Berechiah (it was not uncommon to add names); or Jehoiada, who lived to be 130 (2 Chronicles 24:15), was Iddo's father or was Iddo himself (Ezra 5:1 and 6:14 speak of Zechariah as the "son of" his grandfather Iddo; see 1:1N on "son of"). Josephus speaks of Zechariah the son of Barach as having been killed in the temple, and Targum Yonatan assigns the same kind of death to Zechariah the prophet. Others would explain the discrepancy as a copyist's mistake.

37–39 As if to refute the theology, developed later by the Church, which teaches that God is no longer interested in the Jewish people as such, Yeshua here gives the condition for the salvation of national Israel, as distinct from salvation of individual Jews and Gentiles. In these verses, at the end of his ministry, he addresses the nation of Israel, speaking to its capital, **Yerushalayim**, and thus continues the *Tanakh*'s tradition of corporate salvation, which will come when Israel as a nation blesses the Messiah, **who comes in the name of *Adonai*.** (It is clear from 21:9 in its context that this phrase here refers to Yeshua himself.) The fact that Yeshua will not return until Israel receives national salvation is a powerful motivator for evangelizing Jewish people (see Ro 11:11–12&N,

15&N, 31&N); in fact Jewish evangelism can hasten his coming (2 Ke 3:12&N). For more, see 5:5&N, Ac 4:12&N, Ro 11:23–29&NN, 2C 1:20&N. (Also see Maimonides' "Letter to Ovadyah the Proselyte," quoted in Ro 4:16N.)

Under her wings. Compare the use of such a natural metaphor in the Talmud. A non-Jew comes to Shammai requesting to become a proselyte in order to be appointed *cohen gadol*. Shammai drives him away with a stick, but Hillel receives him and teaches him in a way that enables him to see for himself that the *Torah* prohibits a proselyte from holding that office. He returns to Hillel and thanks him: "Gentle Hillel, blessings on your head for bringing me under the wings of the *Sh'khinah*" (Shabbat 31a). Likewise Moshe is described as being taken to his burial place "wrapped in the wings of the *Sh'khinah*" (Sotah 13b).

God is abandoning your house to you, leaving it desolate. As is clear from the use of the word "house" in Jeremiah 22:5, which Yeshua alludes to, he is not speaking here about the Temple, destroyed forty years later by Roman armies, but to the future generations of Israel, who will be desolate of salvation so long as they seek to achieve it by themselves ("abandoning your house to *you*") and do not welcome God's Messiah Yeshua.

CHAPTER 24

1–39 Chapters 24–25, the "Olivet Discourse" (because it was given on the Mount of Olives, v. 3), discusses the future and constitutes Yeshua's fifth and final teaching in the book of Mattityahu (see 13:1–52N). It is interesting to compare with this chapter a Talmud passage that predicts events prior to the Messiah's coming:

> "Rabbi Yitzchak said that Rabbi Yochanan said, 'In the generation when the Son of David is to come, scholars will be few in number. As for others, their eyes will fail from sorrow and grief. There will be much trouble, and evil decrees will be renewed, with each new evil coming quickly, even before the other has ended.'
>
> "Our Rabbis taught that the following would happen during the seven years at the end of which the Son of David is to come. In the first year, 'I will cause it to rain upon one city and cause it not to rain upon another city' (Amos 4:7). In the second, the arrows of hunger will be sent forth [food shortages, with no one being fully satisfied]. In the third, there will be a great famine, during which men, women, children, pious men and saints will die; and [hunger will cause] the *Torah* to be forgotten by its *talmidim*. In the fourth, there will be surpluses of some things but shortages of others. In the fifth there will be great plenty — people will eat, drink and rejoice; and the *Torah* will return to its *talmidim*. In the sixth year, there will be sounds [in the light of what follows, either rumors of wars (compare Mt 24:6) or heavenly voices or *shofar* blasts (see 8:2N) announcing the Messiah's coming]. In the seventh year there will be wars. And at the end of the seven years the Son of David will come." (Sanhedrin 97a)

This period, with its failing eyes, trouble and evil decrees, is referred to generally in vv. 8, 21; its seven-year duration, following indications in the book of Daniel, is made explicit in the book of Revelation (see Rv 11:1–2N). Hunger and famine appear in v. 7; the death of saints in vv. 9–10; the *Torah* being forgotten by its students in v. 12; eating, drinking and rejoicing in vv. 37–39; the *shofar* in v. 31; wars in vv. 6–7.

7 **Peoples** or "ethnic groups" (Greek *ethnê*; see 5:47N). Recent decades have seen a noticeable increase in both ethnic awareness and ethnic strife. The term is distinct from "**nations**," i.e., political entities (Greek *basileiai*, "kingdoms").

8 The notion that the Messianic Age will be ushered in with a series of convulsions in history referred to as **the "birth pains"** is familiar in rabbinic Judaism; see the quotations in v. 1N, v. 14N; for more examples see Chapter 11, "The Pangs of Times," in Raphael Patai, *The Messiah Texts*, New York: Avon Books, 1979; and compare Revelation 6–18. The "Messianic Age" referred to is the period after Yeshua's second coming (see v. 30), when he will establish peace among the nations and fulfill the prophecies of Isaiah 2:1–4.

10 **Betraying and hating each other.** Similarly, according to the Talmud,

> "Our rabbis taught, 'For *Adonai* will vindicate his people and have compassion on his servants when he sees that their power is gone' (Deuteronomy 32:36). The Son of David will not come until there are many denouncers." (Sanhedrin 97a)

The phrase, "...when he sees that their power is gone," is here understood to mean that the people of Israel will be at the mercy of informers. It is then that God will vindicate his people and have compassion on his servants by redeeming them through the Messiah, the Son of David.

14 Again, a surprisingly similar view of how the Messianic Age will come can be found on the same page of the Talmud:

> "It has been taught that Rabbi Nechemyah said, 'In the generation of Messiah's coming impudence will increase; esteem will be perverted [people won't esteem each other]; the vine will yield its fruit, yet wine will be expensive [because everyone will get drunk and become careless and lazy, so that there will be scarcity]; and the Kingdom will be converted to heresy, and no one will rebuke them.'"(Sanhedrin 97a)

The Soncino English edition of the Talmud has this note on "the Kingdom will be converted to heresy": "Hebrew *minut* [which can mean "heresy" generally or "Christianity" specifically, 22:31–32N]. By 'the Kingdom' is meant the Roman Empire, and the statement is a remarkable forecast by R. Nehemia (150 C.E.) of the conversion of Rome to Christianity under Constantine the Great in 313." However, Travers Herford believes this does not refer to the conversion of Rome but "is merely a way of saying that the spread of heresy and the consequent decay of religion will be universal" (*Christianity in the Talmud*, p. 209). The passage continues:

> "This supports Rabbi Yitzchak, who said, 'The Son of David will not come until the whole world is converted to the beliefs of the heretics.' Raba said, 'What verse [proves this]?' [Answer:] 'It is all turned white: he is clean' (Leviticus 13:13)." (Sanhedrin 97a)

The Soncino Edition's note says, "This [in the light of Leviticus 13:9–17] refers to leprosy: a white swelling is a symptom of uncleanness; nevertheless, if the whole skin is so affected, it is declared clean. So here too; when all are heretics, it is a sign that the world is about to be purified by the advent of Messiah."

15 When Antiochus IV ("Epiphanes") conquered Jerusalem in 167 B.C.E. he erected an altar to Zeus in the Temple. 1 Maccabees 1:54 and 6:7 refer to this as a fulfillment of Daniel's prophecy, but Yeshua is pointing to an additional, future fulfillment.

23–26 The rabbis similarly warn against credulity:

> "Rabbi Shmu'el taught in the name of Rabbi Y'hudah, 'If someone tells you when the day of redemption is coming, don't believe him, for it is written, "The day of vengeance is in my heart" (Isaiah 63:4). If the heart does not tell its secrets to the mouth, how can the mouth tell anything?'"(Midrash on Psalm 9:2(1))

On **false messiahs** see 1:22N.

28 **Wherever there's a dead body, that's where you find the vultures.** Birds preying on carrion seem to refer here to persons used by demonic spirits to carry out evil purposes; they gather around false messiahs (corpses) and draw people away from the truth. Scholars surmise that Yeshua is quoting a folk proverb.

30 **All the tribes of the Land will mourn.** Zechariah 12:10–14 refers to the day when the people of Israel will mourn over God, who has been pierced, as they would mourn over a firstborn son (see Yn 19:37&N).

Here and at Rv 1:7, where the same passage of Zechariah is cited, Greek *gê* in other English versions is rendered "earth," not "Land." Besides obscuring the New Testament's support for the Jewish people's claim to the Land of Israel today, this erroneous translation ignores the fact that Zechariah is clearly speaking of the Land of Israel and not of the whole earth. See 5:5&N and last paragraph of Section VI of the Introduction to the *JNT*.

Coming on the clouds. Again, in the same part of the Talmud we read:

> "Rabbi Nachman said to Rabbi Yitzchak, 'Have you heard when *Bar-Nafle* will come?' 'Who is *Bar-Nafle*?' he asked. 'Messiah,' he answered. 'Do you call Messiah *Bar-Nafle*?' 'Yes,' he replied, 'for it is written, "In that day I will raise up the tabernacle of David *hanofelet* [that is fallen]" (Amos 9:11).'" (Sanhedrin 96b–97a)

The Soncino English edition of the Talmud adds in a note by the general editor, Isidor Epstein, that *bar-nofelet* means "literally, 'son of the fallen.' *Bar-Nafle* is generally assumed to represent the Greek *uios nephelôn,* the 'son of the clouds'; cf. Daniel 7:13, 'there came with the clouds of heaven one like a son of man,' which R. Nachman gave a Hebrew connotation." The passage from Amos is also quoted in Ac 15:16.

31 ***Shofar***, "ram's horn," or, loosely, "trumpet." The ram's horn is blown at the season of the Jewish High Holy Days, one hundred times on *Rosh-HaShanah* (New Year), also called the Feast of Trumpets; and once at the end of *Yom-Kippur* (Day of Atonement). Judaism also understands that the Day of Judgment will be announced by blasts on the *shofar*. Ten *Tanakh* verses mentioning the *shofar* are recited in the *Rosh-HaShanah* synagogue service. See also 1C 15:52&N, 1 Th 4:16&N, Rv 8:2&N.

32 The **fig tree** here is often taken to represent the Jewish people — for example, by the Messianic Jew Paul Liberman, who called his 1976 book on the end-time revival of the Jewish people *The Fig Tree Blossoms* (Tree of Life, P.O. Box 19381, San Diego, CA 92119). See also Mk 11:12–14, 20–24N.

33 **The time is near**. Or: "he is near."

34 **This people will certainly not pass away.** If "this people" is the correct translation of Greek *ê genea avtê*, Yeshua is guaranteeing that the Jews will persist as a people until his second coming. He is echoing the promise of Jeremiah 31:34–36(35–37):

> "Thus says *Adonai*, who gives the sun for a light by day and the ordinances of the moon and stars for a light by night, who stirs up the sea and its roaring waves — *Adonai* of Heaven's Armies is his name: If those ordinances depart from before me, says *Adonai*, then the seed of Israel also will stop being a nation before me forever. Thus says *Adonai*: If heaven above can be measured and the foundations of the earth beneath searched out, then I will also cast off all the seed of Israel for all that they have done."

Thus after proclaiming the New Covenant at Jeremiah 31:30–33(31–34), God immediately states that the Jewish people will last at least as long as the sun and the moon. Both Yeshua and Jeremiah refute Replacement theology (see 5:5N, 5:17N).

However, *ê genea avtê* could mean "this generation." If so, Yeshua must have meant either his own generation or a future one. If his own, then either **all these things** already happened long ago, an interpretation which strains credibility if words mean anything; or they did not happen, in which case the prophecy was false, since his own generation passed away by the early second century at the latest. Those who think he meant that a future generation will see **all these things happen** have the problem of determining how to recognize it, because vv. 4–33 can be variously understood. Thus some believe "this generation" began with the founding of the State of Israel in 1948 or with Israel's recovery of the Old City of Jerusalem in 1967, while others maintain it has not begun yet. Also, what constitutes a generation's passing away? A biblical generation (40 years), the average age at death (70–80 years), or when the last person born at the indicated time has grown old and died (100–plus years)?

Arndt and Gingrich's *A Greek-English Lexicon* is inconclusive. Under "*genea*" it gives the root meaning, "family, descent," and adds: "1. Literally, those descended from a common ancestor, a *clan*; then *race*, *kind* generically.... The meaning *nation* is advocated by some in Mt 24:34, Mk 13:30, Lk 21:32; but see also 2. 2. Basically, the sum total of those born at the same time, expanded to include all those living at a given time — *generation, contemporaries* (cf. Genesis 7:1, Psalm 11:8 [and many New Testament references, including all three cited under '1'])."

36 **But when that day and hour will come, no one knows — not the angels in heaven, not the Son, only the Father.** (In some printings of the *Jewish New Testament* the words "in heaven, not the Son, only the Father" were inadvertently omitted.) Compare Daniel 12:8–10, Acts 1:6 and the following citations, again from Tractate Sanhedrin in the Talmud:

> "Rabbi Shmu'el bar-Nachmani said in the name of Rabbi Yochanan, 'May the bones of those who calculate the end [that is, the time of the Messiah's coming] be blasted away! As soon as the time [which they have determined] arrives and the Messiah has not come, they say, "He will never come!" Rather, wait for him, as it is written, 'Though he tarry, wait for him' (Habakkuk 2:3)." (Sanhedrin 97b; the same phrase from Habakkuk is echoed in Article XII of Maimonides' creed.)

> "Whenever Rabbi Zera' came upon scholars trying [to calculate when the Messiah would arrive], he would say to them, 'It has been taught that three things come when the mind is diverted: the Messiah, finding a lost article, and a scorpion. So don't postpone his coming by thinking about it!'" (Sanhedrin 97a)

According to the Zohar, Rabbi Yose and Rabbi Y'hudah were in a cave, where they found a supernatural book and began studying it, but it disappeared in a flame and a gust of wind. When they came and told Rabbi Shim'on what had happened,

> "he said to them, 'Perhaps you were examining the letters that deal with the coming of the Messiah?... It is not the will of the Holy One, blessed be He, to reveal too much to the world. But when the days of the Messiah approach, even children will be able to discover secrets of wisdom, and through them be able to calculate the time of the end; then it will be revealed to all.'" (Zohar 1:117b-118a)

CHAPTER 25

15 **Talents.** The approximate dollar equivalents would be in six or seven figures. See 18:24N.

31–46 Some take this to refer to the judgment of the Gentile nations on the basis of how they treat **these brothers of mine** (vv. 39, 45), the Jews; compare Genesis 12:3. Others take it to speak of the judgment of those who have not heard the Gospel on the basis of how they treat believers in Yeshua; compare 10:40–42, Ro 8:29.

41 **Go off into the fire prepared for the Adversary and his angels!** See Rv 19:20&N, 20:10&N, 20:15&N.

46 Compare Daniel 12:2.

CHAPTER 26

2 ***Pesach*** ("Passover") is the festival established in Exodus 12:1–13:16 to commemorate the freeing of the Jews from Egyptian slavery and their establishment as a nation and as the people of God. The central event of the original Passover was the slaughter by each Jewish family of a lamb "without blemish or spot," whereupon God spared the firstborn sons of the Israelites but slew those of the Egyptians. When Yochanan the Immerser speaks of Yeshua as the "lamb of God" (Yn 1:29), he is invoking both Temple and *Pesach* imagery (see also 1C 5:6–8&N).

The Last Supper (vv. 17–30 of this chapter) is understood by most scholars to have been a Passover meal or *Seder* (v. 17N). Many *Pesach* themes are deepened, reinforced and given new levels of meaning by the events in the life of Yeshua the Messiah and by his words on this night. However, Joseph Shulam has suggested that it may have been not the *Seder* but a *se'udat-mitzvah*, the celebratory "banquet accompanying performance of a commandment" such as a wedding or *b'rit-milah*.

Here is the background for his argument. When a rabbi and his students finish studying a tractate of the Talmud, they celebrate with a *se'udat-mitzvah* (also called a *se'udat-siyum*, "banquet of completion," i.e., graduation). The Fast of the Firstborn, expressing gratitude for the saving of Israel's firstborn sons from the tenth plague (compare Lk 2:22–24&N), has been prescribed for the day before *Pesach*, Nisan 14, at least since Mishnaic times. When it is necessary to eat a *se'udat-mitzvah*, this takes precedence over a fast. With a modicum of foresight a rabbi can plan to complete a tractate on Nisan 14 and thus avoid having to fast; doing so is not construed as cheating, and in fact it has become the custom.

The tradition of the Fast of the Firstborn dates at least from Mishnaic times. But, Shulam reasons, if it goes back a couple centuries more to the time of Yeshua, and if the *se'udat-siyum* custom applied in the first century to the completing of any course of study, then Yeshua might have arranged to have himself and his *talmidim* finish reading a book of the *Tanakh* on Nisan 14. Or, since Yeshua knew he was to die, he may have regarded it as appropriate to complete his disciples' earthly "course of study" with a banquet. This solution would also resolve the perceived conflict between Yochanan and the Synoptic Gospels over the timing of the Last Supper (see Yn 13:29&N, 18:28N).

However, most of the *Jewish New Testament Commentary* notes on the Last Supper are based on the assumption that the event was in fact a Passover *Seder*.

17 **The first day for *matzah*** ("unleavened bread"). *Pesach* is also known as the Festival of *Matzah* because an essential element in it is eating only unleavened bread throughout its seven days (Exodus 12:15–20). Furthermore, during that period, "no *chametz* ["yeast, leaven"] must be found in your houses" (Exodus 12:19). Traditionally, the day before the Festival begins is the day when the last *chametz* must be removed from the house and burned, and from that moment on the only bread found in the house will be *matzah*. Thus "the first day for *matzah*" is the day before the start of *Pesach*. Since according to the Jewish calendar a day begins at sundown, what this means is that the *chametz* is burned around midmorning, and *Pesach* commences with the *Seder* service after the sun has set.

Seder, literally, "order," but referring here to the ordered ceremony and meal that usher in the week of *Pesach*. Today the sequence of events, prayers, recitals and foods to be eaten is set forth in the *Haggadah* (literally, "telling"), which recounts the biblical story of the Exodus from Egypt with rabbinical embellishments. Many features of today's *Seder* were already present in Yeshua's day, as this passage and Lk 22:14–20&NN reveal.

20 **Reclined.** The last of the "Four Questions" recited in the modern *Seder* service by the youngest person present is, "On all other nights we eat our meals either sitting or reclining; why on this night do we all recline?" The answer is that at the time the questions were fixed in the *Seder* liturgy, slaves ate sitting or standing, while only free Roman citizens reclined. Thus in Roman cultural language reclining represents freedom from Egyptian slavery.

23 **Dips his *matzah* in the dish.** The dish may well have contained *charoset* and/or *maror*, both used in *Seder* services today. *Charoset* is a sweet paste made of fruit, nuts, spices and wine; numerous recipes are in use today in the various Jewish ethnic communities. Its function in the *Seder* is to recall by its appearance the mortar which the Israelite slaves made in Egypt, and it is referred to by the mid-second-century rabbis Me'ir and Eli'ezer bar-Tzadok in the Mishna (Pesachim 2:8, 10:3). *Maror* means "bitter herbs," calling to mind the bitterness of Israelite slavery to Pharaoh; today horseradish root or lettuce is used as *maror*. Rabbi Hillel, in the generation before Yeshua, inaugurated the custom of eating a "sandwich" consisting of a piece of the Passover lamb, together with *matzah* and *maror*, in literal fulfillment of the command, "On (Hebrew *'al*) *matzah* and *maror* shall they eat it" (Exodus 12:8). (Today Ashkenazi Jews do not eat lamb at Passover because it cannot be slaughtered at the Temple; however, the *S'faradim* do.)

24 **The Son of Man will die just as the *Tanakh* says he will.** The *Tanakh* includes the following prophecies of the circumstances and manner of the Messiah's death at his first coming. The New Testament citations or allusions (considered by many to be fulfillments of these prophecies) are given for reference. For a fuller listing of Messianic prophecies see Section VII of the Introduction to the *JNT*.

Prophecy: The Messiah would be	**Location in *Tanakh***	**Fulfillment in New Testament**
Hated without a cause	Isaiah 49:7	Yn 15:24–25
Rejected by the rulers	Psalm 118:22	Mt 21:42, Yn 7:48
Betrayed by a friend	Psalm 41:9, 15(12–14)	Mt 26:21–25, 47–50; Yn 13:18–19; Ac 1:16–18
Sold for 30 pieces of silver	Zechariah 11:12	Mt 26:15
Subject to having his price given for a potter's field	Zechariah 11:13	Mt 27:7
Forsaken by his *talmidim*	Zechariah 13:7	Mt 26:31–56
Struck on the cheek	Micah 4:14(5:1)	Mt 27:30
Spat on	Isaiah 50:6	Mt 26:67, 27:30
Mocked	Psalm 22:8–9 (7–8)	Mt 26:67–68; 27:31, 39–44
Beaten	Isaiah 50:6	Mt 26:67; 27:26, 30
Executed by crucifixion (i.e., having hands and feet pierced; Masoretic text: having a lion at hands and feet)	Psalm 22:17(16)	Mt 27:35; Yn 19:18, 37; 20:35
Executed without having a bone broken	Exodus 12:46, Psalm 34:21(20)	Yn 19:33–36
Thirsty during his execution	Psalm 22:16(15)	Yn 19:28
Given vinegar to quench that thirst	Psalm 69:22(21)	Mt 27:34
Considered a transgressor	Isaiah 53:12	Mt 27:38
Buried with the rich when dead	Isaiah 53:9	Mt 27:57–60

Prophecy: The Messiah would be	**Location in *Tanakh***	**Fulfillment in New Testament**
The one whose death would atone for sins of mankind	Isaiah 53:5–7, 12	Mk 10:45; Yn 1:29, 3:16; Ac 8:30–35
Raised from the dead	Isaiah 53:9–10; Psalms 2:7, 16:10	Mt 28:1–20; Ac 13:33; 1C 11:4–6
Ascended to the right hand of God	Psalms 16:11, 68:19(18), 110:1	Lk 24:51; Ac 1:9–11, 7:55; MJ 1:3
"Cut off, but not for himself," 69 x 7 years after rebuilding of the wall of Jerusalem	Daniel 9:24–26	Ro 5:6, 1 Ke 3:18

26 The **piece of *matzah*** here may have been that eaten immediately prior to the meal. If so, Yeshua said the normal blessing over bread (see 14:19N), followed by, "Praised are you, *Adonai* our God, King of the universe, who has made us holy through his commandments and has commanded us concerning the eating of *matzah*" (see Exodus 12:15–20).

In the modern *Seder* three pieces of *matzah* are placed in a three-part cloth bag called a *matzah tash*. Early in the service the middle piece of *matzah* is broken. Half is divided into enough pieces for everyone at the table and eaten. The other half, called the *afikoman*, is hidden, to be found by children later and eaten by everyone as the last food of the meal (Hebrew *afikoman* may come from a Greek word meaning "dessert"). While in modern Judaism the three *matzot* are taken as representing *cohanim* (priests), *L'vi'im* (Levites) and *Israel* (everyone in Israel not in the first two categories), many scholars believe this ritual was added to the *Seder* service by Messianic Jews, for whom the three *matzot* represent Father, Son and *Ruach HaKodesh*. The second *matzah* — representing the Son, who called himself the "bread of life" (Yn 6:41, 48) and who in the present verse says of the *matzah*, "**This is my body**" — is broken for all and given to all (symbolically representing his death for all mankind). Yet there is a mystery, a hidden part, similar to the hidden *afikoman*: like the middle *matzah* at the Pesach meal, the Messiah appears twice in history, in a first and a second coming. All of these symbolisms are hidden from non-Messianic Judaism, which has suppressed them and substituted others. But, like the *afikoman*, these truths about the Messiah will eventually be found and taken in.

27–29 A cup of wine. See Lk 22:17–20&NN. **The *b'rakhah*** over wine is: "*Barukh attah, Adonai Eloheynu, Melekh-ha'olam, Borey p'ri hagefen* (Praised are you, *Adonai* our God, King of the universe, Creator of the fruit of the vine)." We can be sure Yeshua used the traditional Jewish blessing because in v. 29 he quotes from it the phrase **"fruit of the vine."**

28 The word "**new**" is not found in all the manuscripts of this text and may have been copied from Luke (see Lk 22:20&N). In any case, the Messiah is here establishing the New Covenant promised to the Jewish people in Jeremiah 31:30–33(31–34). This New Covenant does not revoke God's previous covenants. Rather, all five of God's major covenants — made through Noah, Abraham, Moses, David and Yeshua — remain in force today.

(1) God's covenant with mankind through Noah (Genesis 9) is, in Jewish tradition, the basis for the "Noachide Laws" under which Gentiles receive salvation. Although the New Testament asserts that salvation for Jews and Gentiles alike is only through Yeshua, the minimal conditions for acceptance of Gentiles into the Body of the Messiah, as set forth by Jerusalem Conference (Ac 15), parallel the Noahide Laws. For further discussion see Ac 15:20N.

(2) God's covenant with Abraham (Genesis 12, 13, 15, 17) created the Jewish people. Except for the requirement of circumcision it is an unconditional covenant promising that the Jews are to be a blessing to all mankind. This has proved true especially through Yeshua the Messiah, the "seed of Abraham" (Ga 3:16&N), who came forth within the Jewish people and whose just rulership over all nations will extend from Jerusalem the Jewish capital. The covenant now applies to both Jews and Gentiles who follow Yeshua, as explained in Romans 4 and Galatians 3. The Jewish people will one day bless the world in unprecedented ways (Zechariah 8:23; Ro 11:15&N; Revelation 7, 14).

(3) God's covenant with the Jewish people through Moses provided the *Torah* to exhort and guide them into righteous living, to increase their awareness of sin and of their need to repent, and to teach them to accept God's provision for healing the separation from God caused by sin — at first the animal sacrifices, and in the fullness of time Yeshua's sacrifice.

In relation to its blessings and curses the Mosaic covenant is conditional from the Jewish side — but not from God's side, for God is faithful even when his people are not (Ro 3:2–3). According to Scripture, the Jewish people, having broken that covenant (Jeremiah 31:31–32), are currently recipients of its curses and not its blessings (Deuteronomy 28). When Jewish individuals become obedient and cease to break the covenant, God blesses them individually. When the Jewish people as a nation become obedient and cease to break the covenant, God will fulfill his promise to bless them as a nation.

As Judaism correctly holds and most Christian theology incorrectly denies, the *Torah* supplied under this covenant was given forever, has never been abolished, and is still in force. But Yeshua's interpretations of it and other New Testament understandings of it are authoritative, not those of traditional Judaism. For more on this see Ga 6:2&N and Chapter V of *Messianic Jewish Manifesto.*

(4) God's covenant with David (2 Samuel 7) established the throne of his kingdom forever. For this reason the expected Messiah was and is called the Son of David (1:1&N). Messiah Yeshua, a descendant of David, will ascend the throne in God's good time (Ac 1:6–7, Rv 20:2–6).

(5) God's New Covenant with the house of Israel and the house of Judah (Jeremiah 31:30–33(31–34) through Yeshua the Messiah blesses all mankind by providing the final and permanent atonement for sin and by promising that the Holy Spirit of God will write the *Torah* on the heart of anyone with faith. It thus complements the earlier covenants without annulling them (Galatians 3). It was promised in the *Tanakh*, and the books of the New Testament elaborate on it.

30 Singing the *Hallel*. This translates one Greek word which means, literally, "hymning." But since this was the *Seder*, we can know the hymn being sung must have been one of the *Hallel* ("praise") Psalms recited at festivals, Psalms 113–118 or 136.

36 *Gat-Sh'manim*. The name means "oil press"; it is usually brought over into English as "Gethsemane." In the place today called the Garden of Gethsemane are very old, gnarled olive trees; they may have been alive when Yeshua was on earth.

50 Do what you came to do. Or: "Why are you here?"

54 See v. 24N.

61 Yeshua had said earlier (Yn 2:19–22), "Destroy this temple, and in three days I will raise it up again." But Yochanan explains, "The 'temple' he had spoken of was his body," and the fulfillment was in his resurrection.

63a Remained silent. Yeshua's silence here and at 27:12–14 fulfilled the prophecy of Isaiah 53:7, "He is brought as a lamb to the slaughter; and as a sheep before her shearers is dumb, so he does not open his mouth."

63b–64a Tell us if you are the *Mashiach*.... The words are your own. See also Mk 14:61–62&N.

64b Son of Man. See 8:20N. **Coming on the clouds of heaven.** See Mt 24:30&N.

65 Tearing one's garment is a sign of grief and shock; see, for example, Numbers 14:6, Jeremiah 36:24, Job 1:20, Ezra 9:3. It is still Jewish practice to tear one's garment when a close relative dies.

CHAPTER 27

2 Pilate the governor. Pontius Pilate was prefect of Judea from 26 to 36 C.E. and therefore the judge in the trial of Yeshua. An inscription with his name on it has been found in Caesarea, on the coast between Tel Aviv and Haifa. Philo and Josephus characterize him as vile, cruel and cagey; his weak character and lack of concern for truth and justice are clear from the New Testament descriptions of his behavior (see vv. 16–24N). Also see Appendix, p. 932.

9 **Yirmiyahu the prophet.** Although a passing allusion to Jeremiah 32:6–9 may be implied, the reference is to Zechariah 11:12–13, cited loosely or from memory. Why would Mattityahu ascribe the words to Jeremiah? One suggestion is supported by Talmudic references: the scroll of the Prophets may have originally begun with Jeremiah (the longest book, by word count), not Isaiah; if so, Mattityahu by naming Jeremiah is referring to the Prophets as a group, not naming the particular prophet quoted.

16–24 The translation of Aramaic **Bar-Abba**, known to English-speakers as Barabbas, is "son of father" (see Mk 14:36N). Thus two **Yeshua**s: one the son of a human father, the other the Son of God the Father.

It was not out of compassion that Pilate favored releasing Yeshua. Rather, he perceived that Bar-Abba would be a far more dangerous criminal to have on the loose. Pilate was a brutal man (v. 2N, Lk 13:1&N) and a calculating man. He did not escape his share of the responsibility for Yeshua's death (Ac 4:27–28) by merely washing his hands (v. 24).

25 **His blood is on us and on our children.** Or: "His blood be on us…." See Ac 18:6&N. This verse has been used to justify persecution of Jews through the centuries by Christians who presumed that the Jewish people had invoked a curse on themselves and on their posterity, and willingly accepted responsibility for "deicide." But a mob cannot speak in an official capacity for anyone, let alone for a people. Nor, in the light of Ezekiel 18, can anyone invoke a curse on unborn generations. Moreover, even were the curse effectual, Yeshua prayed, "Father, forgive them, for they do not know what they are doing" (Luke 23:34).

Besides, if the Jews were the only ones who killed him, then he didn't die for anyone else. But he died for all, not just for Jews: the righteous Messiah died for everyone who is unrighteous, which is to say, for everyone. Everyone, Jew and Gentile alike, is a sinner. By sinning, everyone, Jew and Gentile alike, killed him. Therefore everyone, Jew and Gentile alike, is guilty of Yeshua's death. See Yn 3:16; Ro 3:23, 5:7–8; 1 Yn 2:1.

30 See Micah 4:14(5:1) and Isaiah 50:6–7.

34 **Wine mixed with bitter gall.** According to the Talmud,

> "When a person is led out to be executed he is given a glass of wine containing a grain of frankincense, in order to numb his senses, as it is written, 'Give strong drink unto him who is perishing, wine to those bitter of soul' [Proverbs 31:6]." (Sanhedrin 43a)

38 Ya'akov and Yochanan wanted to be "one on his right and one on his left" (20:21–23). But who got that privilege? **Two robbers**, in fulfillment of Isaiah 53:12, "He was numbered with the transgressors."

39–44 See Psalm 22:8–9(7–8).

45 Amos 8:9 speaks of the Lord's causing the sun to go down at noon.

46 In Judaism, when a Bible verse is cited its entire context is implied, if appropriate. Thus Yeshua refers all of Psalm 22 to himself; other of its verses are cited at 27:35, 27:39, Yn 19:28 and MJ 2:12.

47 **Calling for Eliyahu.** See 11:10–14&N, 17:10–12&N.

50 **Yielded up his spirit.** Or: "breathed his last."

51 **The *parokhet* in the Temple.** Exodus 26:31–35 describes this curtain as it existed in the desert Tabernacle. It separated the Holy Place from the Holy of Holies. Only the *cohen hagadol* was allowed to pass through it into the Holy of Holies; and that he could do only once a year, on *Yom-Kippur*, to make an atonement sacrifice for his sins and for the sins of the Jewish people. When it was **ripped in two from top to bottom** it symbolized the fact that God was giving everyone access to the most holy place of all in heaven, as taught explicitly at MJ 9:3–9, 10:19–22.

The Talmud bears an amazing witness to the work of Yeshua in altering the system of atonement. The background is that on *Yom-Kippur*, when the *cohen hagadol* sacrificed a goat (Leviticus 16), a piece of scarlet cloth was tied between its horns. If it later turned white, it meant that God had forgiven Israel's sin in accordance with Isaiah 1:18, "Though your sins be as scarlet, they will be white as snow."

> "Our Rabbis taught that throughout the forty years that Shim'on the *Tzaddik* served,... the scarlet cloth would become white. From then on it would sometimes become white and sometimes not.... Throughout the last forty years before the Temple was destroyed... the scarlet cloth never turned white." (Yoma 39a-39b)

Thus in the days of Shim'on *HaTzaddik* the sacrificial system established by God in the *Tanakh* was observed, and it was effective. But afterwards Israel's spirituality declined, so that the sacrificial system was effective only sometimes. Finally, after Yeshua's death, forty years before the destruction of the Temple, it was never effective. The Talmud does not say it, but what had become effective for forgiving Israel's sin was the sacrificial death of Yeshua the Messiah.

57 This **Yosef from Ramatayim** (Joseph of Arimathea) was a member of the *Sanhedrin* (Mk 15:43) who had not voted for Yeshua's death (Lk 23:51) because he was secretly his *talmid* (Yn 19:38).

60 See Isaiah 53:9, "And they made his grave with the wicked" (see v. 38) "and with the rich his tomb."

A large stone, mentioned also at v. 66 and 28:2. See Mk 16:3–4&N.

62–66 It is humiliating to have to confess that in the first two printings of the *Jewish New Testament* these five verses were omitted altogether. Subsequent editions have them as follows:

62 Next day, after the preparation, the head *cohanim* and the *P'rushim* went
together to Pilate 63 and said, "Sir, we remember that that deceiver said while he
was still alive, 'After three days I will be raised.' 64 Therefore, order that the
grave be made secure till the third day; otherwise the *talmidim* may come, steal
him away and say to the people, 'He was raised from the dead;' and the last
deception will be worse than the first." 65 Pilate said to them, "You may have your
guard. Go and make the grave as secure as you know how." 66 So they went and
made the grave secure by sealing the stone and putting the guard on watch.

62 **The preparation.** See Yn 19:31N.

CHAPTER 28

1 **After *Shabbat*, toward dawn on Sunday**, literally, "And late of the *Shabbatot*, at the drawing on toward [number] one of the *Shabbatot* [= weeks]." Jewish days begin at sundown, so that "the first day of the week" includes Saturday night, *Motza'ei-Shabbat* ("the going out of *Shabbat*"); see Ac 20:7&N, 1C 16:2&N. But here the reference is definitely to Sunday morning.

6 **He has been raised.** This is the central fact about the Messiah — he is not dead but alive! Many people think of Yeshua as a great teacher who lived and died two thousand years ago: end of story! But the same documents that tell of his life, teachings and death also tell, in the same matter-of-fact way, of his resurrection — and not merely of a resuscitation only to die again later, but of a new creation by God (Romans 5, 1 Corinthians 15, Messianic Jews 7), so that he can never die but is our brother, savior, king and *cohen gadol* forever. Faith in a dead Messiah is no faith at all. To trust in Yeshua is to trust in someone who is alive and is in intimate, continuing relationship with everyone in his Community (Yochanan 17).

18 **All authority in heaven and on earth is given to me.** See Daniel 7:14.

19 This "Great Commission" of Yeshua is stated with varying emphases at Mk 16:15–20, Lk 24:46–49, Yn 20:21–23 and Ac 1:8.

Make people from all nations into *talmidim*. This must have shocked his hearers, who surely thought that the Messiah was only, or at least primarily, for Jews. Today the situation is reversed, for many Christians think it wrong to evangelize Jews. But their position is inconsistent; for if they really respect Yeshua they should obey his command to make people from all nations, including the Jewish nation, into *talmidim*.

Immersing them (see 3:1N) **into the reality of the Father, the Son and the *Ruach HaKodesh*.** KJV has "baptizing them in the name of the Father, and of the Son, and of the Holy Ghost." Christianity has tended to regard this phrase as a "baptismal formula" to be pronounced when someone is baptized. This understanding leads to such questions as: What is this "name" of the Father, Son and Spirit? Is it Jehovah? Jesus (compare Ac 2:38, 8:16)? or something else? Must all three "persons of the Godhead" be mentioned for a baptism to be valid?

So far as I am concerned, these questions miss the point. First of all, Greek *eis* generally means “into” rather than “in.” Secondly, although “name” is the literal meaning of Greek *onoma*, “immersing into a name” describes no possible literal act. My rendering expresses what I believe to be the intended meaning, since in the Bible “name” stands for the reality behind the name. While “in the name of” can mean “on the authority of,” that seems weak here; more is meant than identifying who authorizes immersion. It is possible that the Greek for “into the name” renders Hebrew *lashem*, “for, for the sake of, with reference to”; if so, the *JNT* renders the sense well.

The Father, the Son and the *Ruach HaKodesh*. This is the closest the New Testament comes to stating the proposition that *YHVH*, *Adonai*, the one God of Avraham, Yitzchak and Ya‘akov, consists of Father, Son and Holy Spirit (compare 2C 13:14). The word “trinity” appears nowhere in the New Testament; it was developed later by theologians trying to express profundities which God has revealed about himself. The New Testament does not teach tritheism, which is belief in three gods. It does not teach unitarianism, which denies the divinity of Yeshua the Son and of the Holy Spirit. It does not teach modalism, which says that God appears sometimes as the Father, sometimes as the Son and sometimes as the Holy Spirit, like an actor changing masks. It is easy to wander astray into error or nonsense in thinking about God, since his ways are not our ways and his thoughts are not our thoughts (Isaiah 55:8). Some Messianic Jews use the term “triunity” in conscious avoidance of the word “trinity,” which has such a non-Jewish, traditionally Christian ring to it, and in order to emphasize the unity of God as proclaimed in the *Sh’ma* without neglecting what this verse highlights. But the bottom line is that it is more important to believe God’s word and to trust him than to argue over particular doctrinal or verbal formulas used in attempting to describe the nature of God.

There is also a textual issue. Although nearly all ancient manuscripts have the trinitarian formula, Eusebius, the Church historian, who may have been a non-trinitarian, in his writings preceding the Council of Nicea in 325 C.E., quotes the verse without it. Most scholars believe the formula is original, but papers by Hans Kosmala (“The Conclusion of Matthew,” *Annual of the Swedish Theological Institute*, 4 (1965), pp. 132–147) and David Flusser (“The Conclusion of Matthew in a New Jewish Christian Source,” *ibid.*, 5 (1966–7), pp. 110–119) take the opposite view.

THE GOOD NEWS OF YESHUA THE MESSIAH,
AS REPORTED BY

MARK

CHAPTER 1

1 **Good News.** See Mt 4:23N. **Yeshua the Messiah.** See Mt 1:1N. **Son of God.** See Mt 4:3N.

2–3 **It is written in the prophet Yesha'yahu.** Only the last two lines quoted are from Isaiah; the first two are from Malachi. The scroll of the Prophets begins with Isaiah, and it was common to refer to a scroll by its first book; but see Mt 27:9N.

Adonai. See Mt 1:20N.

4 **Yochanan the Immerser.** See Mt 3:1N.

An immersion involving turning to God from sin in order to be forgiven, literally, "baptism of repentance," a term to which I gave an expanded translation for better apprehension by modern readers. Traditional Judaism recognizes immersion for purification and for conversion to the Jewish religion, but Yochanan's immersion was neither of these. See Mt 3:1–2&NN.

8 ***Ruach HaKodesh*** ("the Holy Spirit"). See Mt 3:11–12N.

11 **Voice**. See Mt 3:17N.

12 **The Adversary**, Satan, the Devil. See Mt 4:1N.

15 **Kingdom of God.** See Mt 3:2N on "Kingdom of Heaven."

16 **Lake Kinneret**, the Sea of Galilee. See Mt 4:18N.

19 **Ya'akov Ben-Zavdai and Yochanan**. See Mt 4:21N.

21 **K'far-Nachum**, Capernaum. See Mt 4:13N. ***Shabbat***, Sabbath. See Mt 12:1N.

22 ***Torah*-teachers** (scribes) did not have *s'mikhah* (were not ordained as rabbis; see Mt 21:23N) and therefore could not bring *chiddushim* (introduce new interpretations) or *posek halakhah* (make legal judgments; see Mt 2:4N). This is why the people **were amazed** (one could say "were in shock," Hebrew *hishtomemu*): Yeshua taught like a

rabbi and not like a scribe. This was one level of amazement.

The second level of amazement was that he taught **as one who had authority himself**. No rabbi taught (or judged, *pasak*) against the *halakhah* of his own rabbi. But Yeshua, who had no rabbi of his own, appeared to have authority beyond that of any of the rabbis (vv. 23–27&N). By Yeshua's own testimony throughout Yochanan 5–9, and summarized finally at Yn 12:44–50, his authority came directly from his Father, God; see also Daniel 7:14, Mt 28:18).

Finally, at 2:10 below Yeshua claims, uniquely, that he has authority to forgive sins. This is the highest "authority given to human beings" (Mt 9:8), and people "were amazed" at this too (2:12).

23–27 The Talmud says that Rabbi Yochanan Ben-Zakkai, convener of the Yavneh Council which around 90 C.E. developed the structure of post-Temple rabbinic Judaism, studied the speech of the *shedim* (demonic spirits; Sukkah 28a), but not that the *shedim* obeyed him. But Yeshua, unlike the rabbis, **gives orders even to the unclean spirits, and they obey him!** This is why his hearers were **astounded** at his **new teaching.**

32 Influenced by the *P'rushim* (see Mt 3:7N), the people regarded healing on *Shabbat* as a violation of the *Shabbat* work laws (see Mt 12:1–15&NN). Therefore they waited until **that evening, after sundown**. According to *halakhah*, *Shabbat* (v. 21) officially ends when three medium-sized stars become visible.

34 **Because they knew who he was**. See Mt 8:4N on why Yeshua wanted his Messiahship kept a secret.

40 **Serious skin disease**. Usually translated "leprosy," but see Mt 8:2N on "clean."

44 **Tell no one**. See Mt 8:4N. **Go and let the *cohen* examine you**. See Mt 2:4N, 8:4N.

CHAPTER 2

5–12 Yeshua **has authority on earth to forgive sins** (see 1:22N). "All authority in heaven and on earth" has been given to Yeshua (Mt 28:18); see also Co 1:14, 2:9.

10 **Son of Man**. See Mt 8:20N.

14 **Sitting at his tax-collection booth**. See Mt 5:46N.

15 **Sinners**. See Mt 9:10N. ***Talmidim***. See Mt 5:1N.

16 ***P'rushim***. See Mt 3:7N. Some fairly well-attested texts have "the *Torah*-teachers who were *P'rushim*" (literally, "who were of the Pharisees"); if this is the correct reading it poses a problem for the theory expressed in Mt 2:4N that *Torah*-teachers and *P'rushim* were mutually exclusive categories.

18 **Fasting**. See Lk 18:12N.

22 **Freshly prepared wineskins**. See Mt 9:17N.

24 **Violating *Shabbat***. See Mt 12:2N.

25 **What David did**. See Mt 12:3N.

27–28 This passage from the Talmud gives the same message as v. 27:

> "Rabbi Yonatan ben-Yosef said: 'For it [*Shabbat*] is holy unto you' (Exodus 31:14). That is, it is committed into your hands, not you into its hands!" (Yoma 85b)

A similar passage appears in the Mekhilta, Shabbata I:1 on Exodus 31:12–17, where the saying is attributed to Rabbi Shim'on Ben-Menasya.

It may be, therefore, that Yeshua's comment in v. 28, that **the Son of Man is Lord of *Shabbat*,** does not refer only to himself but to everyone, since Hebrew *ben-adam* (literally, "son of man") can mean simply "man, person," with no Messianic overtone: "people control *Shabbat*" and not the other way round.

CHAPTER 3

2 **Heal him on *Shabbat***. See 1:32N above.

5 **And sympathy for them**. Greek *sullupoumenos*, found only here in the New Testament, means "grieving with someone." Such a mixture of two emotions, **anger** and at the same time sympathy, is a normal and appropriate reaction to people whose **hearts** display **stoniness** (Greek *porôsis*; see Ro 11:7–8N) — dullness, insensitivity, intellectual blindness, stubbornness.

6 **Herod's party**. See Mt 14:1N, 22:16N.

16 **Kefa** (Peter). See Mt 4:18N.

17 Most English versions say that Yeshua called the sons of Zavdai "Boanerges, that is, sons of thunder." Greek *Boanêrges* means nothing, so it must be transliterating something in Hebrew. One possibility is ***B'nei-Regesh***, which means, literally, "sons of feeling," hence (in the light of Mt 1:1 on "son of"), "emotional people," "people who get excited easily." Another possibility: "*B'nei-Rogez*," literally, "sons of anger," that is, "people who easily become angry"; for an example of how these "angry young men" expressed themselves see Lk 9:54. The text explains the phrase as meaning "**Thunderers**," which says in poetic Greek about the same thing as either of the Hebrew equivalents.

18 Zealot. Militant opponent of Roman rule; see Mt 10:4N.

19 Y'hudah from K'riot, Judas Iscariot. See Mt 10:4N.

22 Came down from Yerushalayim. See Mt 20:18N. **Ba'al-Zibbul**, the Adversary. See Mt 10:25N.

28 Yes! Greek and Hebrew *amen.* See Mt 5:18N.

CHAPTER 4

8 Even a hundred times. In Genesis 26:12 the Hebrew for "a hundred times" is *meah she'arim*; this makes a nice trans-chronological wordplay, since Meah She'arim (which also means "one hundred gates") is the most Ultra-Orthodox Jewish neighborhood in modern Jerusalem.

CHAPTER 5

1 Gerasenes' territory. Mattityahu 8:28 puts this incident in the "Gadarenes' territory." And some manuscripts have "Gergesenes' territory." There were three towns in the region east of Lake Kinneret and nearby — Gerasa, Gadara and Gergesa — so that the same "territory" might reasonably have been named for all of them. The text does not state which "town" (v. 14) was the one involved.

11–17 The non-Jewish "Gerasenes" (v. 1&N) raised **pigs.** That Yeshua permitted the demons to enter the pigs, destroying harmless animals together with their owners' property, is raised as a moral argument against him. But God has permitted demonic expression with its evil consequences since the Garden of Eden. Job asked why, and God indicated that his dealings with Satanic powers are not to be understood fully by human beings at this time (Job 40–41; see Mt 4:1N). Some have suggested the demons destroyed the pigs in order to prejudice the owners against Yeshua — which is what actually happened. See Lk 15:1N.

19 The Lord. See Mt 1:20N, 7:21N.

22 Synagogue official, Greek *archisunagôgos*, "ruler, head or president of a synagogue."

36 Ignoring. Some texts: "overhearing"; a few, "hearing."

41 ***Talita, kumi!*** "Little girl, get up!" in Aramaic. It is sometimes asked whether Yeshua spoke Hebrew or Aramaic. Though Aramaic and Greek were the international languages in use in the Middle East in the first century, Hebrew was a common household language among Jews at that time and continued to be spoken until the third century C.E. After that time it was used for prayer but rarely for daily communication. In the nineteenth century it was revived for secular literary purposes and consciously developed as a modern language by Eli'ezer Ben-Yehuda and others after 1879. Most people in Yeshua's day probably spoke all three languages in some degree. In the New Testament the Greek word "*Ebraios*" and its cognates can refer to either Aramaic or Hebrew.

On this subject Professor David Flusser, an Orthodox Jewish scholar in Jerusalem, writes:

> "The spoken languages among the Jews of that period were Hebrew, Aramaic, and to an extent Greek. Until recently, it was believed by numerous scholars that the language spoken by Jesus' disciples was Aramaic. It is possible that Jesus did, from time to time, make use of the Aramaic language. But during that period Hebrew was both the daily language and the language of study. The Gospel of Mark contains a few Aramaic words, and this was what misled scholars. Today, after the discovery of the Hebrew Ben Sira (Ecclesiasticus) [a book of the Apocrypha], of the Dead Sea Scrolls, and of the Bar Kokhba Letters, and in the light of more profound studies of the language of the Jewish Sages, it is accepted that most people were fluent in Hebrew. The Pentateuch was translated into Aramaic for the benefit of the lower strata of the population. The parables in the Rabbinic literature, on the other hand, were delivered in Hebrew in all periods. There is thus no ground for assuming that Jesus did not speak Hebrew; and when we are told (Acts 21:40) that Paul spoke Hebrew, we should take this piece of information at face value." (*Jewish Sources in Early Christianity*, POB 7103, Tel Aviv 61070: MOD Books, 1989)

See also Shmuel Safrai, "Spoken Languages in the Time of Jesus," in *Jerusalem Perspective* 4:1 (January/February 1991), pp. 3–8, 13; and William Chomsky, *Hebrew: The Eternal Language* (Philadelphia: The Jewish Publication Society of America, 1957; 4th printing 1969), Chapter 11, entitled "Did Hebrew Ever Die?" (his answer is: No).

CHAPTER 6

14 Herod. See Mt 14:1N.

18 See Mt 14:4N.

30 Those who had been sent out. Or: "The emissaries."

37 Thousands, literally, "two hundred denarii." A denarius was about a day's wages for a common laborer. See Mt 18:24N.

41 Made a *b'rakhah* ("said a blessing"). See Mt 9:8N and Mt 14:19N.

56 Touch… the *tzitzit* on his robe. See Mt 9:20&N.

CHAPTER 7

2–4 The *P'rushim* had interpreted the Written *Torah*, and their sages and rabbis had decreed additional rules. Together these came to be called at first **the Tradition of the Elders** and later the Oral *Torah* (see Mt 5:17N, 12:2–11&NN, 18:18–20&N, 23:2&N); it was committed to writing, notably in the Mishna, in the second and third centuries, expanded in the Gemara in the fourth and fifth (Mishna + Gemara = Talmud), and later in other works.

Mark's explanation of ***n'tilat-yadayim,*** ritual handwashing, in these verses corresponds to the details set forth in Mishna tractate *Yadayim*. In **the marketplace** one may touch ceremonially impure things; the impurity is removed by rinsing **up to the wrist**. Orthodox Jews today observe *n'tilat-yadayim* before meals. The rationale for it has nothing to do with hygiene but is based on the idea that "a man's home is his Temple," with the dining table his altar, the food his sacrifice and himself the *cohen* (priest). Since the *Tanakh* requires *cohanim* to be ceremonially pure before offering sacrifices on the Temple altar, the Oral *Torah* requires the same before eating a meal.

5–13 Many Christians think Yeshua's answer to the question of v. 5 condemns all of Pharisaic tradition. In fact, he objects only to those practices of the *P'rushim* that place **human tradition** above **God's command** (v. 8). He is not opposed to tradition as such, but to **your tradition** (vv. 9, 13) — the operative word is "*your*," as shown by his example (vv. 10–12), where a "tradition" is allowed to nullify the fifth Commandment, "**Honor your father and your mother,**" by letting people devote to Temple worship money which they should use to support their own parents.

On the contrary, Yeshua could not be opposing tradition as such because the New Covenant itself speaks favorably of its own traditions (1C 11:2&N, 2 Th 2:15&N). And at Yn 7:37&N we have an example of Yeshua honoring a tradition spoken of in the Mishna but nowhere in the *Tanakh*.

In fact, traditions are necessary in life. A state cannot be run by a constitution without legislation. Likewise the Jewish nation could not be run by the Written *Torah* alone, without the orderly application of it and addition to it implied in the concept of tradition. But just as a country's legislation cannot contradict or supplant its constitution, so too tradition (Jewish, Messianic, Christian, or whatever) cannot violate or alter God's word (see Mt 12:2–11&NN, Mt 18:18–20&N). The Oral *Torah* comes very close to implying that it can (Bava Metzia 59a, quoted at Ac 9:4N); but according to the present passage this position is inconsistent with Messianic Judaism.

6–7 Isaiah 29:3 is quoted in vv. 8–9 from the Greek Septuagint version. In the Hebrew Bible, the portion corresponding to v. 9 reads, "Their fear of me is a [mere] commandment of men learned" by rote and therefore producing only mechanical outward obedience, unaccompanied by inward faith — an equally serious condemnation. Sometimes the New Testament writers are criticized for not quoting from the Masoretic Hebrew *Tanakh* as we have it today (even though this form of the text did not become fixed until around 800 C.E.). The critics forget that in Yeshua's time there were several different Hebrew texts of most books, and that the Septuagint itself was translated into Greek by Jews some two centuries before Yeshua from an obviously different Hebrew text which they presumably considered authoritative. To Greek-speaking Jews the Septuagint was the normal means of access to the content of the Bible, just as English-speakers today rely on an English version.

11 ***Korban***, literally, "sacrifice," from the Hebrew word for "near." A *korban* is something brought near to God, and it brings the offerer near to God. Mark treats *korban* as a technical term, first transliterating it into Greek and then explaining it as "**a gift to God**."

Yeshua's objection is to bad priorities. Vows and oaths are not to be used selfishly to give a pretext for avoiding doing what God, love and righteousness require. Compare Mt 5:33–37&N, 12:7, 23:16–23&NN, and see how Yeshua continues this teaching in vv. 12–23. The rabbinic elaboration of the formulas and rules concerning oaths and vows can be found in Talmud tractates *Shvu'ot* and *N'darim*.

19 **Thus he declared all foods ritually clean**, even if the participants at the meal have not washed their hands. But Yeshua did *not*, as many suppose, abrogate the laws of *kashrut* and thus declare ham *kosher!* Since the beginning of the chapter the subject has been ritual purity as taught by the Oral *Torah* in relation to *n'tilat-yadayim* (vv. 2–4&N) and not *kashrut* at all! There is not the slightest hint anywhere that **foods** in this verse can be anything other than what the Bible allows Jews to eat, in other words, *kosher* foods. Neither is *kashrut* abolished in Ac 10:9–28 or Ga 2:11–16; see notes there.

Rather, Yeshua is continuing his discussion of spiritual prioritizing (v. 11&N). He teaches that *tohar* (purity) is not primarily ritual or physical, but spiritual (vv. 14–23). On this ground he does not entirely overrule the Pharisaic/rabbinic elaborations of the laws of purity, but he does demote them to subsidiary importance. See Yn 7:22–23&N on the halakhic process of assigning ranks to potentially conflicting laws. Yeshua here is making Messianic *halakhah*.

The Greek text at this point is a dangling participial clause, literally, "cleansing all the foods." There is no "Thus he declared"; I have added these words for the sake of clarifying the one meaning I believe this passage can have, namely, that it is Mark's halakhic summary of Yeshua's remarks (see Section V of the Introduction to the *JNT*, paragraph on "The Translator and His Interpretations"). However, some believe this phrase is not a comment by Mark but part of what Yeshua himself said and render it: "a process which cleanses all food." According to this understanding, Yeshua is explaining that the body's ordinary digestive process makes all foods clean enough to be eaten, so that handwashing is of minor importance and the *P'rushim* shouldn't be giving it so much attention. Conclusively against such a rendering is that it suddenly puts the focus on hygiene instead of ritual purity, which is the topic of the rest of the passage. It does not answer the halakhic *sh'eilah* ("question"; see Mt 22:23N) about ritual purity posed by the *P'rushim*, because food can have in it not a single germ and yet be ritually unclean.

Moreover, the nominative masculine form of the Greek participle "*katharizôn*" ("cleansing") agrees grammatically with "*legei*" ("he replied," literally, "he says") in v. 18, so that on the basis of the linguistic evidence it makes better sense to suppose that "cleansing all the foods," like "he replied," is a comment by Mark and not part of what Yeshua said.

24–30 See Mt 15:21–28&NN.

CHAPTER 8

6–7 The ***b'rakhah*** over the bread (v. 6; see Mt 14:9&N) would have also sufficed for the fish, according to Jewish law. Therefore the ***b'rakhah*** in v. 7 must have been the spontaneous words of a faithful Son to his Father at the moment of performing a creative miracle.

15 ***Chametz*** ("leaven, yeast"). See Mt 16:6N.

CHAPTER 9

1–13 See Mt 11:10–14&N, 17:10–12&N.

29 **Only by prayer**. Some manuscripts add: "and fasting."

40 **Whoever is not against us is for us**. Apparently inconsistent with Mt 12:30, but see note there.

43 **Gey-Hinnom** ("Gehenna," "hell"). See Mt 5:22N.

48 Isaiah 66:22–24 teaches the existence of a "new heaven and a new earth" (confirmed in 2 Ke 3:13, Revelation 21–22), in which God's people will worship him, "and they will go forth and look upon the carcasses of those who have transgressed against me; for **their worm** will **not die, and** their **fire** will **not** be **quenched**."

49–50 **Salt** is used to **season** (Co 4:5–6&N) and as a preservative, producing permanence (Mt 5:13–14&N). "It is forbidden to offer any sacrifice without salt" (*Rambam, The Commandments*, Negative Commandment #99; see Leviticus 2:13); hence it is appropriate for *talmidim*, who are to offer themselves as living sacrifices (Ro 12:1–2), to be **salted with fire**. Observant Jews sprinkle salt on bread before reciting the *b'rakhah* over it (Mt 14:19N); this follows from the rabbinic equating of the home dining table with the Temple altar (7:2–4&N). See Lk 14:34–35N.

CHAPTER 10

2–12 See Mt 5:31–32&N, 19:1–12&N.

16 **Made a *b'rakhah* over them**. We do not know in what manner Yeshua blessed the children; but today, every *erev-Shabbat* (Friday evening), at the dining table, the father of the family says to his sons, "God make you like Efrayim and M'nasheh," the sons of Yosef and grandsons of Ya'akov; and to his daughters he says, "God make you like Sarah, Rivkah, Rachel and Leah," the wives of the Patriarchs. Then, placing his hand on the child's head, he pronounces the Aaronic Benediction (Numbers 6:24–26):

> *Adonai* bless you and keep you!
> *Adonai* make his face shine on you!
> *Adonai* lift up his face on you and give you *shalom* [peace]!

18 There are those who take Yeshua's remark to mean, "You should not be calling me good, because only God is good, and I am not God." But it does not say that; rather, it challenges the man to consider who Yeshua really is, whether he may indeed be more than an ordinary human being.

19 "**Don't defraud**" summarizes the ninth and tenth Commandments (see Mt 5:21N), which prohibit bearing false witness and coveting. Some manuscripts omit this phrase, and it is not found in Mattityahu's or Luke's version of the incident.

25 **Needle's eye**. See Mt 19:24N.

30 ***'Olam hazeh… 'olam haba.*** See Mt 12:31–32N.

32 **Going up to Yerushalayim.** See Mt 20:17–19N.

Yeshua was walking ahead of them. This connects with v. 31. His *talmidim* **were amazed** at Yeshua's boldness and **afraid** of what might happen to Yeshua (vv. 33–34) and to themselves in Yerushalayim.

33 ***Goyim.*** Gentiles. See Mt 20:19N.

47 **Son of David,** a Messianic title. Therefore by his shout **Bar-Timai** was identifying Yeshua as the Messiah. See Mt 1:1N on "Son of David" and Mt 20:29–30N on the incident itself.

CHAPTER 11

9 See Mt 21:9N.

12–14, 20–24 If Yeshua's cursing and drying up the fig tree had been a petulant reaction to disappointment because he couldn't satisfy his hunger, it would be unworthy of anyone, let alone the Messiah. But Yeshua is making a point by means of prophetic drama, acted-out parable (possibly Lk 13:6–9). *Tanakh* examples include Yirmiyahu, who bought and then broke a clay bottle (Jeremiah 19), and Yechezk'el, who made and then burned up a model of Jerusalem (Ezekiel 4–5); for a later New Testament instance see Ac 21:10–11.

Even out of season a fig tree **in leaf** — it must have been in leaf to be seen **in the distance** (v. 12) — holds forth the promise of fruit. The normal early season for figs in Israel is June, but the early unripe fruit (Song of Songs 2:13) begins to show itself even before the spring leaves appear on the branches, often before Passover.

We know that Yeshua expects God's people to put forth the fruit of righteousness, and that unproductive branches are thrown in the fire (Mt 7:16–20; 12:33; 13:4–9, 18–23; Yn 15:1–8). Thus the drying-up of the fig tree is an acted-out warning. In keeping with Proverbs 27:18 ("He who tends a fig tree will eat his fruit, and he who serves his master will be honored") Yeshua here is teaching his followers what it means to serve their master, God: it means simply to **have the kind of trust that comes from God** (v. 22), and that they will wither away if they don't. Yeshua neither acts from pique nor performs arbitrary miracles like a magician; every one of his supernatural acts has spiritual significance.

Also see Mt 24:32N.

15 See Mt 21:12N.

28 ***S'mikhah*** ("ordination"). See Mt 21:23N.

CHAPTER 12

1 See Mt 20:1N.

13–19 See Mt 3:7N, 22:15–16N, 22:23N, 22:24N.

24–27 See Mt 22:31–32N.

28 **Which is the most important *mitzvah*?** Although the literal meaning of "*mitzvah*" is "commandment," what the inquirer is really asking is: "What is the most important basic principle, the one on which all the rest of the *Torah* depends?" The rabbis, too, used to epitomize the *Torah*. For example, in the Talmud we find:

> "Rabbi Simlai said, 'Six hundred thirteen commandments were given to Moses — 365 negative, equalling the number of days in the year, and 248 positive, equalling the number of a man's members. David came and reduced them to eleven [Psalm 15]. Then Isaiah reduced them to six [Isaiah 33:15–16], Micah to three [Micah 6:8], and Isaiah again to two, as it is said, "Keep judgment and do righteousness" [Isaiah 66:1]. Then Amos reduced them to one, "Seek me and live" [Amos 5:4]. Or one could say Habakkuk: "The righteous shall live by his faith" [Habakkuk 2:4].'"(Makkot 23b-24a, abridged)

For the famous Talmudic example of the pagan who wanted to be taught the whole *Torah* "while standing on one foot" see Mt 7:12N.

29 ***Sh'ma Israel, Adonai Eloheynu, Adonai echad.*** How can God be one and yet be

Father, Son and Holy Spirit? Doesn't that make God three? Nowhere does the New Testament say that God is three, but here it does say that God is one, unique, the only God there is — so that his Word is the only authoritative word about God, man and the relationship between them.

Also the *Tanakh* in several places gives a *remez* ("hint"; see Mt 2:15N) that the "inner structure" of the one true God involves Father, Son and Holy Spirit. Isaiah 48:16 uses three different terms to speak of the divine: "...from the time that it was, there am I; and now *Adonai* God and his Spirit has sent me." At Genesis 1:26 God uses the plural to speak of himself: "Let us make man in our image, after our likeness..."; the rabbinic explanation that this means God and the angels has no contextual support, and there is no reason for a "plural of majesty" at this point. Likewise, here in the *Sh'ma* (Deuteronomy 6:4) there are two such *r'mazim*: (1) the triple reference to God, and (2) the use of the word "*echad*," which often means a multiple unity (such as "one" cluster of grapes or "one" bundle of sticks) instead of "*yachid*," which nearly always excludes multiple oneness.

30 Yeshua cites the central affirmation of Judaism, God's unity as proclaimed in the *Sh'ma*, with its immediately following command to love God with all one's being. For him the two go together and constitute a single principle; compare Ro 13:8–10, Ga 5:14, and 1 Yn 4:8 ("God is love").

With all your understanding. This phrase does not appear in the Hebrew of Deuteronomy 6:5. It may have been added by the translator of Mattityahu's Gospel, which was probably originally in Hebrew, in order to convey in a Greek cultural setting the full sense of the commandment — that everything one is, does and has must be used to love God. If so, the translator was doing "dynamic equivalence translation" (see Section V of the Introduction to the *JNT*), catering to the Greek mentality, which so highly valued intellectual activity. Alternatively, Yeshua is appealing to his questioner, who as a *Torah*-teacher made constant use of his understanding in his work.

31 **Love your neighbor as yourself** (Leviticus 19:18). See Lk 10:25–37, Mt 7:12&N.

36 See Mt 22:44N.

38 **Watch out for the kind of *Torah*-teachers who....** Most English versions translate this passage in a way that makes it appear Yeshua is talking about *all Torah*-teachers (see Mt 2:4N), e.g., KJV, "Beware of the scribes, which...." But the Greek construction does not justify a comma after "scribes" in KJV; a comma there makes it appear that Yeshua is condemning all of them. The comma makes such a rendering antisemitic, because it prejudges a whole class of Jews where Yeshua does not. Yeshua, rather, is condemning only those *Torah*-teachers who exhibit certain objectionable behaviors. In so doing he is expressing the prophetic tradition of the *Tanakh*, not the anti-Jewish tradition of Christendom. See also Mt 23:13–36&N and 1 Th 2:14–16&NN, where the same issue arises.

40 ***Davvening*** (Yiddish): praying. The term usually refers to praying the liturgical prayers of the synagogue. Today's traditional Jew *davvens* three times a day, adding extra prayers on *Shabbat* and *yom tov* (festivals). In the synagogue the *chazan* (cantor) chants the first few words of each prayer or blessing, and each person recites the prayer softly at his own speed, until the cantor signals the end of that prayer by chanting its last few words. One can call attention to oneself by reciting the prayer loudly or with florid chanting which gives an appearance of deep piety.

Although the specifics of first-century *davvening* were different, Yeshua here inveighs against such religiosity — possible in any era and in any religion — particularly when coupled with behavior that highlights its hypocrisy, such as exploitation of the poor and helpless. In this Yeshua, like the prophets before him, was concerned about right social action, a perennial Jewish theme.

42 **Two small coins**, literally, "two *lepta*, which equals a *quadrans*," the smallest Roman coin; 64 of them equalled a denarius, which was a day's wages for a common laborer.

CHAPTER 13

1 **What huge stones! What magnificent buildings!** The First Temple, built by King Solomon and destroyed by the Babylonians in 586 B.C.E., was a building of great magnificence (1 Kings 6–7). The Second Temple, built under Z'rubavel in 516 B.C.E., could not compare with it (Haggai 2:3). King Herod the Great, to ingratiate himself with the Jewish people, undertook its renovation and expansion. According to Yn 2:20 it took 46 years, but it was successful, and the remodeled Second Temple dominated all Jerusalem. A scale model of first-century Jerusalem on display at the Holyland Hotel in West Jerusalem impressively demonstrates the majesty of the Temple Yeshua's *talmidim* saw.

2 **Not one stone will be left on another, absolutely everything will be demolished.** This prophecy was fulfilled literally in 70 C.E., when Rome overwhelmed the First Jewish Rebellion by capturing Jerusalem and sacking the Temple. Excavations made after the Six-Day War revealed enormous stones from the Western Wall of the Temple Court (of which the still-standing "Wailing Wall" is part) lying helter-skelter, not one left on another.

8 **Birth-pains** of the Messianic Age of peace. See Mt 24:8N.

14 See Mt 24:15N.

22 **False messiahs**. See Mt 1:22N.

26 See Mt 8:20N.

29 **The time is near**. Or: "he is near."

30 **This people**. See Mt 24:34N.

CHAPTER 14

1 ***Pesach*** (Passover) is also called the **festival of *Matzah*** (unleavened bread). See Mt 26:2N, 26:17N.

5 **A year's wages**, literally, "300 denarii."

7 See Yn 12:8N.

12 See Mt 26:17N.

18 See Mt 26:20N.

20 **The dish**, perhaps of *charoset*. See Mt 26:23N.

22–28 See Mt 26:23–30&N. See also Appendix, p. 932.

32 ***Gat-Sh'manim***, Gethsemane. See Mt 26:36N.

36 ***Abba*! (that is, "Dear Father!").** Hebrew has incorporated the Aramaic word "*Abba*," which is a familiar way of addressing one's father. It is the equivalent of "Dad" or "Daddy"; like all Israeli children, my own call me "*Abba*." Judaism teaches that anyone can address God, and that God is close to each one; many prayers commence with, *Avinu sh'bashammayim* ("Our Father who art in heaven"; see Mt 6:9–13&N). Nevertheless, Judaism regards it as unacceptable to appear overly familiar with God. Thus the Mishna tells this story about the winsome, offbeat first-century B.C.E. rabbi known as Honi the Circle-Maker:

> "Once they asked Honi the Circle-Maker to pray for rain. He said to them, 'Go out and bring in the *Pesach* ovens [which were made of clay], so they won't be softened [by the rain].' He prayed, but no rain fell. So what did he do? He drew a circle, stood inside it and said to God, 'Master of the Universe, your children have turned to me because they consider me a son in your household. I swear by your great name that I will not move from here until you show compassion on your children!' A few drops fell. 'I didn't pray for that kind of rain, but for rain that will fill the ditches, caves and water cisterns.' Rain began falling violently. 'I didn't pray for that kind of rain either, but for good, pleasant rain that will be a blessing.' Then it began to rain normally [and kept on so long they had to ask him to pray it would stop]....
>
> "Shim'on ben-Sh'tach sent a message to him: 'If you were anyone except Honi, I would have pronounced a ban of excommunication on you! But what can I do to you? You beg God and he does what you want, like a son who cajoles his father and he does what he wants.'"(Ta'anit 3:8; and see the Gemara on it at Ta'anit 23a)

Shim'on ben-Sh'tach's reason for being ready to excommunicate Honi was his acting too familiar with God. This we know from B'rakhot 19a, which asks, "What about excommunicating someone who behaves familiarly with Heaven?" and then quotes the same paragraph about Honi and Shim'on ben-Sh'tach.

The article on "*Abba*" in Gerhard Kittel's *Theological Dictionary of the New Testament*, I:6, says:

> "As concerns the usage of Jesus, the probability is that He employed the word *Abba* not merely where it is expressly attested (Mark 14:36) but in all cases, and particularly in address to God, where the Evangelists record Him as saying *o patêr, pater* ["Father"], *patêr mou, pater mou* ["my Father"], and even perhaps *pater êmôn* [our Father]."

Notes give Mt 11:26, Mk 14:36, Yn 5:36, Ro 8:15, Ga 4:6; Mt 11:25, Lk 11:2, 23:34, Yn 11:41, 12:27f., 17:5; Mt 11:27, 26:53; Mt 26:39, 42; and Mt 6:9, respectively, for the five Greek terms.

Elsewhere in the New Testament the word "*Abba*" is always associated with the Holy Spirit and with adoption (Ro 8:14b–17&N, Ga 4:6). For different but related discussions see Mt 2:15&N and Mt 27:16–24&N.

55 ***Sanhedrin***, the "supreme court" of seventy judges (see Mt 5:22N). This nighttime meeting was illegal; some scholars believe this particular "*Sanhedrin*" was not even the official one at all. Nevertheless, there seems to be little doubt that this body, whoever it consisted of, included important establishment figures and in condemning Yeshua carried out an action which expressed the desire of many *P'rushim* and *Tz'dukim*.

61–62 **"Are you the *Mashiach, Ben-HaM'vorakh*** ("the Messiah, the Son of the Blessed One," i.e., the Son of God)**?" "I AM."** Some scholars assert that in the Synoptic Gospels Yeshua does not claim to be the Messiah. Such an assertion requires explaining away the plain sense of these verses. Here, in response to the direct question of the *cohen hagadol*, Yeshua does not hesitate; moreover, he uses the very word "*Adonai*" used to identify himself to Moses at the burning bush, when he said, "I AM who I AM" (Exodus 3:14; there are other possible translations of God's Hebrew words, "*Ehyeh asher ehyeh*," such as, "I will always be what I am now.") Thus Yeshua not only affirms that he is the Messiah, the Son of God (see Mt 4:3N), but hints that he is to be identified with *Adonai* himself. Yochanan reports other instances of such hints; see Yn 4:26&N, 18:6&N.

It is true that at an earlier stage of his ministry Yeshua did not want it known that he was the Messiah (see Mt 8:4N), but in these final days there was no "Messianic secret."

At Mt 26:64 Yeshua's answer to the *cohen hagadol* is reported as, "The words are yours." The literal translation of the Greek text there is, "You have said," and the phrase is taken as the equivalent of a straight "Yes" answer, much like the English phrase, "You said it!" (see Lk 22:70N, 23:3N).

HaG'vurah ("the Power"). A euphemism for "God." See MJ 1:3N on "*HaG'dulah BaM'romim*."

63 **Tore his clothes**. See Mt 26:65N.

72 Throwing himself down, or possibly, "beating his breast." Greek *epibalôn*, "throwing oneself upon," "beating upon."

CHAPTER 15

1 Pilate. See Mt 27:2N.

2 The words are yours. See 14:61–62N.

4–5 On Yeshua's silence before the accusations of the head *cohanim* see Mt 26:63N.

13 Put him to death on the stake! Greek *Stavrôson avton* is usually translated, "Crucify him!" See Mt 10:38&N.

34 See Mt 27:46N.

37 Gave up his spirit. Or: "breathed his last"; likewise in v. 39.

38 See Mt 27:51N.

40 Miryam from Magdala. See Lk 8:2N.

42 Preparation Day. Mark explains to non-Jewish readers that it means **the day before a *Shabbat***. See Yn 19:31N.

43 Yosef of Ramatayim. See Mt 27:57&N.

46 A stone, large and flat.

CHAPTER 16

1 When *Shabbat* was over. Mark means *Motza'ei-Shabbat* (the "going-out of Sabbath"), that is, Saturday evening, when *Shabbat* was over (see 1:32N). At *Pesach* season this would be after 7 PM. In Israel today many stores open on Saturday evening after being closed all day; evidently the same custom prevailed then.

3–4 The two Miryams were stymied as **they went to the tomb. They were asking each other, "Who will roll away the stone from the entrance to the tomb for us?"** Such stones were too large for them to move. **Then they looked up and saw that the stone, even though it was huge, had been rolled back already**. An atheistic lawyer named Frank Morison investigated Yeshua's resurrection, intending to write a book disproving it. Instead, the evidence convinced him that it had happened. After coming to faith in God and his Messiah he wrote *Who Moved The Stone?* (London: Faber & Faber, 1958), proving that Yeshua's resurrection actually took place.

6 Yeshua from Natzeret, Greek *Iêsoun ton Nazarênon*, "Yeshua the Nazarene." See Mt 2:23N.

9–20 These verses do not appear in the two oldest Greek manuscripts, their style differs from the rest of Mark, and the transition from v. 8 is awkward. Therefore some scholars believe them to be scribal additions. Others consider them apostolic in origin and inspired by God, but not written by Mark, having been added by an editor to bring closure to the otherwise abrupt ending. And others believe Mark wrote them. They are included in the *JNT* text, but with a footnote pointing out their problematical character.

15–18 This is Mark's version of the Great Commission; see Mt 28:19–20&N.

16 Logically there are four possibilities:

(1) **Whoever trusts** in God, in his Messiah Yeshua, in the Good News, in God's Word, **and is immersed will be saved**.

(2–3) **Whoever does not trust**, whether (2) immersed or (3) not, **will be condemned** because he refuses to come to God in God's way, that is, by faith. Case (2) shows that baptism in and of itself has no saving value.

(4) The case of someone who trusts but is not immersed is not mentioned. However, immersion following faith is the norm (Ac 8:36); and refusal to be immersed is disobedience to God's command (Ac 2:38) — it demonstrates *de facto* lack of trust, since trust is supposed to lead to obedience (Ro 1:5). Luke 23:43, telling of the repentant thief executed along with Yeshua, is sometimes cited to show that immersion is not required for salvation. Since in his circumstances the thief could not possibly have undergone immersion, what the incident shows is that the un-immersed believer is a possible case but definitely the exception to the rule.

17–18 Those who trust in the Good News can expect God's power to work through them. Verse 20 says that this promise was fulfilled anciently, and numerous modern instances may be found as well, even though centuries of anti-supernaturalism predispose Westerners not to believe it. On the other hand, there are extreme sects (e.g., the "snake-handlers") who take these verses out of context and make of them a foolish standard for measuring their own and others' faith, thereby tempting God (against Mt 7:1–5, Ya 1:13).

19 Sat at the right hand of God. This fulfills Psalm 110:1 and Yeshua's own prediction about himself at 14:62.

THE GOOD NEWS OF YESHUA THE MESSIAH, AS REPORTED BY

LUKE

CHAPTER 1

1 **Theophilos**, addressed in v. 3 as "Your Excellency," was probably an upper-class Greek for whom Luke wrote this book and the book of Acts (see Ac 1:1N) with the purpose he himself states in v. 4. Alternatively, since the name means "lover of God," Luke may be writing to a generic and typical disciple.

5 **Herod** the Great. See Mt 2:1N.

Cohen, priest (see Mt 2:4N). The *cohanim* were partitioned into 24 divisions, the names of which appear at 1 Chronicles 24:7–18; the **Aviyah division** was the eighth. Each served for a week at a time; thus the members of a division did Temple duty twice a year. All divisions were present for *Sukkot* (see Yn 7:2N, 7:37N, 8:12N).

His wife was a descendent of Aharon. A *cohen* must marry a woman from a family of *cohanim*. Elisheva was not only from a priestly family but descended from Moses' brother, the first *cohen gadol*.

6 ***Mitzvot***. See Mt 5:19N. ***Adonai***. See Mt 1:20.

Contrary to some Christian theologians, the New Testament teaches that the *Torah* of Moses offers righteousness. To be considered **righteous before God**, Z'kharyah and Elisheva had to love God and fellowman, trust God and believe his word. As evidence of this love and trust they observed all the rules of behavior God had revealed, including those which demanded repentance and a blood sacrifice as a sin offering when they fell short of full obedience. For more, see Ro 9:30–10:10&NN.

7 **Elisheva was barren; and they were both well along in years.** Barrenness was often considered a sign of God's displeasure and judgment (as can be inferred from Elisheva's reaction at v. 25). The stage is set for another in the series of miraculous births of important men that began with the births of Isaac to 100-year-old Abraham and 90-year-old Sarah (Genesis 18:1–5, 21:1–7), Samson to Manoah and his wife (Judges 13) and Samuel to Elkanah and Hannah (1 Samuel 1:1–2:10). After the birth of Yochanan to Elisheva (v. 57) the series culminates and concludes with the birth of Yeshua the Messiah to the virgin Miryam (2:7).

15 **He is never to drink wine or other liquor**. It may be that Yochanan, like Samson, was to be a Nazirite, dedicated to God in the special way outlined in Numbers 6:1–21. The

outward requirements included eating no grapes or grape products, not cutting the hair, and not going near a dead person. See also Appendix, p. 932.

17 **He will go out ahead of *Adonai***, in the sense of Isaiah 40:3–5, which he himself quotes at 3:4–6 below. Though Yochanan is not Elijah, he will function with his same **spirit and power** to "clear the way before" God (Malachi 3:1) and announce the Messiah's coming. See Mt 11:10–14&N, Mt 17:10–12&N, and below, 1:76–78&N.

To turn the hearts of fathers to their children. See Mt 10:35–36N.

19 **Gavri'el**, one of the two angels mentioned by name in the *Tanakh* (Daniel 8:16, 9:21); the other is Mikha'el (see Rv 12:7&N).

25 **Removed my public disgrace**. Elisheva invokes the words of Rachel, another woman of the Bible, whose barrenness was ended by God's direct involvement; see Genesis 30:22–23.

27 **Of the house of David**, i.e., descended from King David. See 3:22–38&N, Mt 1:1–16&N, Ro 1:3–4&N.

31 **Yeshua**. See Mt 1:1&N, 1:21&N.

32 ***HaElyon***, Greek *upsistos*, "highest, most high." The Hebrew name *Elyon* is used by itself at Numbers 24:16 and elsewhere. God is first called *El elyon* ("God most high") at Genesis 14:18–20, where Avraham tithed to the priest Malki-Tzedek. That phrase is found in the New Testament at Mk 5:7, Lk 8:28, Ac 16:17, MJ 7:1; the first three of these are spoken by demoniacs. *Upsistos* appears in the plural to denote places ("in the highest [heavens]") at Mt 21:9; Mk 11:10; Lk 2:14, 19:38. "**Son of *HaElyon***" means "Son of God," as is clear from v. 35. The language of vv. 32–33 is entirely in line with the *Tanakh* and very Messianic.

The throne of his forefather David was promised for the Messiah to King David in 2 Samuel 7:12–13, 16; see Mt 1:1N.

33 **There will be no end** (see Daniel 2:44; 7:14, 18, 27) **to his kingdom**, the Kingdom of God (see Mt 3:2N).

35 **The *Ruach HaKodesh* will come over you**. Compare Mt 1:18–23, 1:16N and this strange passage from the Zohar:

> "The Faithful Shepherd said, 'At that time [there will come] pangs and pains upon the woman in childbirth, that is, the Shekhina.... And through these pains, which will make her cry out, seventy supernal Sanhedrins will be aroused, until her voice reaches the Lord.... And from those voices which she gives forth... her womb opens... to give birth to two Messiahs.... In that time the forests will be denuded, and the Serpent will pass from the world.'" (Ra'aya Mehemna 3:67b-68a, in Raphael Patai, *The Messiah Texts*, pp. 129–130)

Son of God. See Mt 4:3N.

37 **With God nothing is impossible.** Compare Mt 19:26; also Genesis 18:13–14, where the Lord responds to Sarah, who is too old to bear a child, "Is anything too hard for *Adonai?*"

42 **How blessed**. See Mt 5:3N.

43 **Lord**. See Mt 7:21N.

46–55 These verses are known in the western world as the *Magnificat*, from the section's first word in the Vulgate, Jerome's translation of the Bible into Latin around 400 C.E. They resemble Hannah's song of praise to God at the dedication of her son Samuel (1 Samuel 2:1–10). Many lines are quoted exactly or approximately from the *Tanakh*; compare vv. 46 (Psalm 34:2), 47 (Psalm 35:9), 48 (1 Samuel 1:11), 49 (Psalm 111:9), 50 (Psalm 103:17), 51 (Psalm 89:11(10)), 52 (Job 12:19, 5:11), 53 (1 Samuel 2:5, Psalm 107:9), 54 (Psalm 98:3), 55 (Genesis 17:7, 19; Micah 7:20).

59 **On the eighth day, they came to give the child his *b'rit-milah*.** Circumcision is the sole condition for a Jew's being under the covenant God made with Abraham (Genesis 17:10–14). It is to be done on the eighth day of a boy's life (Genesis 17:12, Leviticus 12:3).

They were about to name him Z'kharyah after his father. Anyone acquainted with Jewish religious practice knows that a Jewish boy is named at his *b'rit-milah.* But whence do we know of this custom? In a series of lectures over Israel Army Radio Professor David Flusser said:

> "From early Christian literature we can learn about Jewish customs not recorded in early Jewish sources. Take an example: the Jewish custom of giving a boy his name during his circumcision ceremony is not known in our Talmudic literature, but in one of the Gospels (Luke 1:59–64) we are told that John the Baptist's father gave him his name during this ceremony." (*Jewish Sources in Early Christianity*, MOD Books, P.O.B. 7103, Tel Aviv 61070, Israel, 1989, p. 10, condensed)

Among Ashkenazic Jews today it is not customary to name a child after a living relative, but this is not always the case with Sephardics, and it was apparently not so in Israel two thousand years ago.

63 **Yochanan**. See Mt 4:21N.

64 **And his first words were a *b'rakhah*** (blessing) **to God**. The experience of Z'kharyah was that of a righteous man (v. 5) with deficient faith (v. 18), whom God chastised (vv. 19–20) in order to deepen his faith (Proverbs 3:11, MJ 12:5–15). This verse shows that the chastening had the desired result.

68–79 These verses are known in the west as the *Benedictus* (which is the section's first word in the Vulgate; see 1:46–55N). As with the *Magnificat* there are many references to the *Tanakh*, and the entire prophecy is couched in Tanakhic language. Verse 71 is quoted from Psalm 106:10.

76–78 Verse 76 recalls Malachi's prophecy that Elijah precedes the Messiah (compare also above, 1:17&N). **Sunrise** in v. 78 alludes to Malachi 3:20(4:2), where the Messiah is called "the Sun of Righteousness… with healing in his wings."

79 Those who are in darkness... living in the shadow of death. Because in rabbinic literature the citation of a line of Scripture frequently implies reference to the entire passage of which it is a part (see Mt 2:6N), it is appropriate to point out that Isaiah 8:23–9:1 (9:1–2), quoted more fully at Mt 4:15–16, leads into one of the *Tanakh*'s most important Messianic passages, Isaiah 9:5–6 (6–7):

> 5 "For unto us a child is born,
> Unto us a son is given,
> And the government shall be upon his shoulder,
> And his name shall be called
> *Pele Yo'etz El Gibbor Avi Ad Sar Shalom*;
>
> 6 "So that the government may grow
> And peace be unbounded
> Upon the throne of David
> And upon his kingdom,
> To establish it
> And uphold it
> In justice
> And righteousness
> From now
> Until eternity.
>
> "The zeal of *Adonai* of Hosts will do this."

Verse 5 explains that the "great light" of Isaiah 9:1 (see also Isaiah 58:8, 60:1–2) is a person, the child born to us, the son given us (see Mt 1:23&N), on whose shoulder the government shall be, and whose character and properties are defined by his Hebrew name, which means "Wonder Counselor, Mighty God, Father of Eternity, Prince of Peace." Verse 6 explains v. 5; it shows why there is a need for a son with such names to rule Israel. The reason is that it requires nothing less than a divine human to establish forever the government of the world from David's throne, with peace, justice and righteousness prevailing.

This passage has been understood from ancient times to be a reference to the Messianic King. For example, the first-century B.C.E. Aramaic translation of the *Tanakh* called the *Targum Yonatan* rendered this passage: "From ancient times his name was given as Wonderful Counselor, Mighty God, He who lives forever, the Messiah in whose days peace shall increase."

Later, however, Jewish commentators sought vigorously to avoid referring the passage to Yeshua and therefore gave it a different meaning. To appreciate how they went about it, we must understand that the long Hebrew name is not to be taken as the actual name by which the Messiah was to be known, but (like "Immanu'el" in Isaiah 7:14 and Mt 1:23&N, and see Mt 28:19N) as an indication of his character and as a sign of his being the Messiah. Isaiah understood that a name could function as a sign: "And it shall be to *Adonai* for a name, for an everlasting sign that shall not be cut off" (Isaiah 55:13).

So, consider the name. Jewish versions of the Bible often translate it as a sentence about God: "A wonderful counselor is the mighty God, the Eternal Father, the Prince of Peace." The purpose of translating the name thus is to detract from its function as descriptive of the person bearing it and make it rather (and only) a description of God. But such a translation makes it irrelevant to the context. For the verses tell us that in order for the son on whose shoulder the government shall be to have the properties of being increasing, eternal and entirely peaceful, just and righteous, that child, that son, must be a Wonder Counselor — one whose counsel is vastly beyond that ordinarily found in the world's governments, so far beyond as to be worthy of the appellation "*pele*," a term which in the *Tanakh* is reserved for God alone and refers to his miracles. And he must be a prince of *shalom*, which means not only peace but harmony, well-being, integrity and health (see Mt 10:12N). Yeshua is a Father of Eternity, one whose perspective covers all of history and goes beyond into eternity (Yn 1:1–18, MJ 1:1–3). And finally, although he is distinct from the Father and has different functions, he is in his essence, without decreasing his humanity, Almighty God (Jeremiah 23:5–6; Yn 1:1&N, 1:14&N, 10:30&N; Co 2:9&N).

CHAPTER 2

1 **Augustus**. Title with overtones of divinity given by the Roman Senate in 27 B.C.E. to Gaius Julius Caesar Octavianus, founder of the Roman Empire. He ruled the Mediterranean world until 14 C.E.

2 There is an historical problem because, according to Tacitus and others, **Quirinius** did not begin **governing in Syria** until 6 C.E. But he was in charge of Syria's defense and foreign policy under Varus around 7 B.C.E. and later, so he could have supervised the **registration** (for tax purposes) in Herod's territory.

This registration, the first of its kind, or: "this first registration," before the better-known one of 6 C.E. referred to in Ac 5:37.

6 See Appendix, p. 932.

8 **Shepherds** derived little income from their unskilled work, so that they were held in low esteem. As such they were at the opposite end of the social scale from the Magi of Mt 2:1ff. Both came to honor the Messiah of high and low alike.

10 The coming of Yeshua the Messiah is **good news that** brings **great joy to all the people**; the "people" is Israel (as in v. 32 below).

11 **A deliverer** or "savior." Greek *sôtêr*, corresponding to Hebrew *moshia'*, which is another form of the word "*hoshia'*"(see Mt 21:9&N) and is related to Yeshua's own name (see Mt 1:21&N). The word "*sôtêr*" is first used in the New Testament at Lk 1:47, where it refers to God (i.e., the Father); here it refers to Yeshua as having functions which are exclusively God's.

A study of the word "*yasha'*"("save") in the *Tanakh* reveals several senses in which it is used in connection with God. God saves Israel (Exodus 14:30) his people (2 Samuel 3:18) from the hand of her enemies (1 Samuel 4:3), and he promises to save them also from their uncleannesses (Ezekiel 36:29). He saves afflicted ones (Psalm 18:28(27)), those of a contrite spirit (Psalm 34:19(18)), the children of the needy (Psalm 72:4), the poor from the sword (Job 5:15), and the humble (Job 22:29). He saves not with sword and spear (1 Samuel 17:47) but with his right hand (Psalm 138:7), in his mercy (Psalm 31:17(16)), and for the sake of his own name (Psalm 106:8). He can save directly (1 Samuel 10:19) or through a human agent such as King Jeroboam (2 Kings 14:27), and in one instance the credit is given to "the angel of his presence" (Isaiah 63:9). In conclusion, salvation may be from outward enemies or inward uncleannesses (sins), and it may apply to a people or to an individual.

Thus the New Testament, which uses the word "*sôtêr*" 24 times and the related verb "*sôzô*" ("save") 44 times, builds on the foundation already established in the *Tanakh*. When inquiry is made as to whether someone is "saved," the question has roots in the *Tanakh* as well as in the New Testament.

14 This verse commences the liturgical passage known in the western world as the *Gloria*. **People of good will** are people whom the will of God favors and whose own wills desire what God wills. The latter is itself a consequence of God's favor (Ep 2:8–10; compare Ro 11:31&N).

21 **On the eighth day, when it was time for his *b'rit-milah*, he was given the name Yeshua**. See 1:59N, Mt 1:21N.

22–24 These verses record the observance of two points of Jewish law, *pidyon-haben* (redemption of a firstborn son) and the purification of a mother after childbirth.

The ceremony of redeeming the **firstborn male** son reminds the Jewish people of their redemption from slavery in Egypt (Exodus 13:2–16) and of avoiding the last of the Ten Plagues to afflict the Egyptians, the slaughter of their firstborn sons (Exodus 11:45, 12:29–30), by slaughtering a lamb in accordance with God's command and placing its blood on the doorposts; on seeing it the angel of death passed over the Israelite families (Exodus 12:3–14, 21–28).

Each family therefore dedicates its firstborn son to God's service but then redeems the boy for a payment of five sanctuary-*shekel*s (Numbers 18:16). In consequence God accepts instead the Levites, the descendants of Ya'akov's son L'vi, for service in the Tabernacle or Temple (Numbers 3:12–13, 45; 8:14–19).

Pidyon-haben takes place after the son is thirty days old (Numbers 3:14). Today it is normally done on the thirty-first day, but that is not a biblical requirement. The narrative in v. 22 suggests either that Miryam and Yosef went up to Jerusalem at the time of *pidyon-haben* and remained there ten days until it was time for Miryam's purification, or that they delayed the *pidyon-haben* until the purification.

Purification of a mother is described in Leviticus 12:1–8. The mother of a son remains ceremonially unclean for forty days after childbirth. On the forty-first day a sacrifice is offered,

> "a one-year-old lamb for a burnt offering and a young pigeon or turtledove for a sin offering.... But if she cannot afford a lamb, then she shall take a pair of doves or two young pigeons..., and the *cohen* shall make atonement for her, and she shall be clean." (Leviticus 12:6, 8)

From Luke's quotation of this in v. 24 we learn that Yosef and Miryam were relatively poor. Today's Orthodox Jewish women cannot offer a sacrifice, since there is no Temple; but they immerse themselves in a *mikveh* in partial observance of the purification rite.

Their purification. Only Miryam was ritually impure, so the plural is unexpected. Luke may be thinking of her purification together with Yeshua's redemption rite. Or Yosef may have undergone ritual purification with Miryam; it was permitted though not commanded (compare Sha'ul's purification at Ac 21:22–27&NN). In our own times, even though neither the Written nor Oral *Torah* requires it, some Orthodox Jewish men immerse themselves in a *mikveh* on Friday afternoon in order to be ritually pure before the commencement of *Shabbat*.

Torah, see Mt 5:17N. **Up to Yerushalayim**, see Mt 20:18N.

25 He waited eagerly for God to comfort Israel. This "comforting" is the main subject of the latter portion of the book of Isaiah (Chapters 40–66), to which Shim'on makes a number of allusions in vv. 29–35. The comforting was prophesied by Isaiah to come about through the Messiah (see Isaiah 40:1, 49:13, 52:9).

29–32 These verses are known in the West as the *Nunc Dimittis;* like Miryam's *Magnificat* (1:46–55&N) and Z'kharyah's *Benedictus* (1:68–79&N), it draws heavily on the *Tanakh* for its style and subject matter. Verses 30–31 are closely tied to Isaiah 40:5 in the Septuagint version, which reads, "all flesh will see the salvation of God," and to Isaiah 52:10.

30 *Yeshu'ah*. This renders Greek *sôtêrion;* both words mean "salvation." But there is a wordplay here, because Hebrew *yeshu'ah* is also the feminine form of the Messiah's name, Yeshua (see Mt 1:21&N).

32 A light that will bring revelation to the *Goyim*. Compare Isaiah 42:6, "I am *Adonai*..., and I will appoint you as a covenant to the people," i.e., to the Jews, "and as a light to the *goyim*" (Gentiles, nations, pagans; see Mt 5:47N). Likewise Isaiah 49:6, "I will also make you a light of the *goyim*," and Isaiah 51:4.

34 Compare Isaiah 8:14.

36 Tribe of Asher, one of the "ten lost tribes of Israel" which vanished after the conquest of the Northern Kingdom in 722 B.C.E. (see Yn 4:9N), leaving only the tribes of Y'hudah and Binyamin on the Land, plus the tribe of L'vi serving in the Temple. But individual families could preserve their identities and transmit their genealogies.

37 Now she was 84. Or, obviously with lower probability, "she had been a widow for 84 years."

38 Waiting for Yerushalayim to be liberated or "redeemed." Compare Isaiah 52:9, "For *Adonai* has comforted his people; he has redeemed Yerushalayim." All the Isaiah passages quoted above in vv. 25–28 draw heavily on the portions of Isaiah that identify the Messiah with the people Israel; see v. 25N, Mt 2:15N.

41 His parents went to Yerushalayim for the festival of *Pesach*. There were three "pilgrim festivals" in the Jewish calendar when all Israel was supposed to appear at "the place where *Adonai* chooses to establish his name" (Deuteronomy 16:2) — *Pesach* ("Passover"; see Mt 26:2N), *Shavu'ot* ("Weeks," "Pentecost"; see Ac 2:1N), and *Sukkot* ("Tabernacles," "Booths"; see Yn 7:2N). Not all Jews obeyed the requirement, especially those as far away as Natzeret; but, being observant and pious Jews, Miryam and Yosef went **every year**.

42 When he was twelve years old. This single incident from Yeshua's "silent years" (see 2:52N) took place near the age at which a Jewish boy today undergoes his *bar-mitzvah* ceremony and becomes a "son of the commandment," personally responsible for keeping the *Torah* given by God to Moses on Mount Sinai. At this time he dons *t'fillin* for the first time officially (see Mt 23:5N), and for the first time he is given an *aliyah* (call-up) to come to the *bimah* (lectern) and read from the *sefer-Torah* (*Torah* scroll) in a synagogue service. Verses 46–47 suggest a comparable "coming out" for Yeshua, but there the parallel ends. *Bar-mitzvah* did not start to become a major ceremonial event in the Jewish life-cycle until the Middle Ages, and only in modern times has it become the focus of grandiose celebrations. Moreover, the age for *bar-mitzvah* is not twelve but thirteen.

46–47 Questioning what they said... his responses. This questioning or "putting *sh'eilot*" (see Mt 22:23N) was not one-sided querying but dialogue, since Yeshua answered the rabbis' return-questions. Thus, there was a real intellectual exchange going on, and the listeners were amazed at how well this twelve-year-old was holding up his side of it.

48 Why have you done this to us? Miryam's question is misplaced. Upset as she and Yosef may have been while searching several days for their child, they should, according to Yeshua's response in the following verse, have known where to look, especially in the light of what had already been revealed to them about their son (Mattityahu 1–2, Luke 1–2). The narrative does not suggest that Yeshua, by "getting himself lost," had misbehaved, but that Miryam, like many worried mothers, had overreacted.

52 In this verse and v. 40 we are told everything the New Testament has to say about Yeshua's life between the ages of about two (Mt 2:16) and thirty (below, 3:23), except for the single incident at age twelve (vv. 41–51) and the fact that he was known in Natzeret as a carpenter (Mk 6:1–4). Humanly he **grew in wisdom**, even though divinely he *is* Wisdom. God was gracious and sensible enough not to burden us with too much to read or with unnecessary details, for "of making many books there is no end; and much study is a weariness of the flesh" (Ecclesiastes 12:12); moreover, "there are also many other things Yeshua did; and if they were all to be written down, I don't think the whole world could contain the books that would have to be written!" (Yn 21:25). A biographer would have told more; since the writers of the Gospels were not primarily biographers but communicators of the Good News, they wrote only what people needed to know for their own spiritual well-being.

But that has not dispelled curiosity about the most famous human being in history; so that a number of false gospels were written in ancient times, purporting to describe Yeshua's life during this "silent period"; many of them have been collected in Wilhelm Schneemelcher, ed., *New Testament Apocrypha* (English translation by R. McL. Wilson, 2 volumes, Philadelphia: The Westminster Press, 1963). Not only that, but in modern times new religions have attempted to undermine the truth of the New Testament by co-opting "the Christ" into their own value systems. In their spiritual equivalent of gossip-sheets they have invented stories that Jesus travelled to India, studied yoga with Far Eastern "masters," was visited by extraterrestrial beings, and performed various miracles and works of magic.

All of this satisfies the "itching ears" of those "ever learning and never coming to the knowledge of the truth" (2 Ti 4:3, 3:7). There is not the slightest evidence that Yeshua did anything between ages 12 and 30 other than live the life expected of the Jewish son of a Jewish carpenter in the Galil (Mt 13:55, Mk 6:3). On the contrary, had he been absent for eighteen years his contemporaries would not have been as familiar with him as Yn 6:42 shows they were. The purpose of these elaborate fabrications is, on the one hand, to cater to people's pride in having some supposedly superior knowledge, and, on the other, to draw attention away from the central message of the New Testament — the Bad News that human beings are separated from God by their sins and stand in need of atonement, and the Good News that the Messiah Yeshua has made that once-for-all atonement and offers it to anyone who will trust him and his word.

CHAPTER 3

1 Luke roots in world history the world-shaking and world-transcending events he describes. **Tiberius** was **Emperor** of Rome from the death of Augustus in 14 C.E. (see 2:1N) until 37 C.E. After Hordos (Herod) the Great died in 4 B.C.E. (see Mt 2:1N), his kingdom was divided. The region of **Y'hudah** was at first ruled by Herod's son Archelaus (Mt 2:22) until he was deposed in 6 C.E. After that it was ruled by a Roman "procurator"; this office was held by **Pontius Pilate** (see Mt 27:2N) from 26 to 36 C.E. North of Y'hudah the region of **the Galil** was ruled by another of Herod the Great's sons, **Herod** Antipas, from 4 B.C.E. until 39 C.E. East of the Galil a third son of Herod the Great, Herod **Philip**, ruled **Iturea and Trachonitis** from 4 B.C.E. until 34 C.E. And to the north, northwest of Damascus, the region around the city of **Abilene** was ruled by one **Lysanias**, mentioned in inscriptions but not clearly identified.

2 **With Anan** (Annas) **and Kayafa** (Caiaphas) **being the *cohanim g'dolim*** (high priests). Could there be two high priests? No, Anan was *cohen gadol* for some years until 15 C.E. and was then deposed by the Romans — the office was no longer held for life but was manipulated by the Romans for political purposes. Anan's son-in-law Kayafa attained the office in 25 or 26 C.E. and was deposed in 36; he is mentioned in all four gospels as the *cohen gadol* presiding over Yeshua's two trials and archaeologists in Jerusalem have recently unearthed his tomb. Nevertheless Anan remained a powerful figure (see Yn 18:12–24&NN), and it was natural to continue calling him *cohen gadol* (compare Ac 4:6), since for Jews, this office was held for life.

3 **Immersion**. See Mt 3:1N. **Turning from sins**. See Mt 3:2N.

4–6 Isaiah 40:3–5 is quoted as describing the ministry of Yochanan the Immerser. See also 2:25N above.

All humanity will see God's deliverance. This is quoted from the Septuagint; the Hebrew Bible has: "All flesh will see it together." The Hebrew text underlying the Septuagint would have had the word "*yeshu'ah*" for "deliverance." There is a pun here, for *yeshu'ah* is the feminine form of the Messiah's name *Yeshua'*; this seems to be the point of Luke's more extended quotation (compare Mt 3:3, Mk 1:3).

8 **Sons from these stones**. See Mt 3:9N.

12 **Tax-collectors**. See Mt 5:46N.

16 **In the *Ruach HaKodesh***. See Mt 3:11–12N.

19–20 See Mt 14:1–12&N.

22 **A voice came from heaven**. See Mt 3:17N.

23–38 A literal translation of the Greek text starting at v. 23 would be: "And Yeshua himself was beginning about thirty years, being son, as was supposed, of Yosef, of the Eli, of the Mattat, of the L'vi," etc. The questions raised here are: What does it mean to be "of" someone? and which person is described as being "of the Eli"? — Yosef or Yeshua?

If Yosef is here reported to be the son of Eli, there is an apparent conflict with Mt 1:16, which reads, "Ya'akov was the father of Yosef, the husband of Miryam, from whom was born the Yeshua that was called the Messiah." But the genealogies of both Mattityahu and Luke employ unusual language in connection with Yeshua — and with good reason, since both assert that he had no human father in the ordinary sense of the word, but that the virgin Miryam was caused to bear Yeshua by the Holy Spirit of God in a supernatural way; see Mt 1:16N.

If this is so, what do the genealogies mean? The simplest explanation is that Mattityahu gives the genealogy of Yosef, who, though not Yeshua's physical father, was regarded as his father by people generally (below, 4:22; Yn 1:45, 6:42); while Luke gives the genealogy of Yeshua through his mother Miryam, the daughter of Eli. If so,

Yeshua is "of the Eli" in the sense of being his grandson; while Yeshua's relationship with Yosef is portrayed in the words, "son, as supposed" — implying not actually; see numbered paragraph (2) of note on "Son of" at Mt 1:1N.

Luke's language also distinguishes Yosef from Yeshua's direct ancestors by not including the word "the" before "Yosef" in the original Greek. "By the omission of the article, Joseph's name is separated from the genealogical chain and accorded a place of its own" (F. Rienecker, *Praktisches Handkommentär Zu Lukas Evangelium)* 1930, p. 302, as cited in *A Jewish Christian Response* by the Messianic Jew Louis Goldberg).

A different explanation of these anomalies is to make not Yeshua but Yosef the grandson of Eli on his mother's side. In the *JNT* text as it stands I have opted for this explanation; that is the significance of my reintroducing the word "the" as a demonstrative: **It was supposed that** Yeshua **was a son of *the*** particular **Yosef who was**, on his mother's side, the grandson **of Eli**, son **of Mattat**, son of **L'vi**.... But I have no strong attachment to this explanation; the other is equally satisfying and equally problematical.

The two genealogies also raise the question of how Yeshua can claim the throne of his ancestor King David (see Mt 1:1N on "son of David"). The argument against him is that even if Luke's genealogy is of Miryam and goes back to David, it doesn't help Yeshua; because descent, for purposes of inheriting kingship, cannot be counted through the mother. And if Yosef is not Yeshua's physical father, his legal status as Yeshua's adoptive father, even though adequate for establishing Yeshua's legal right to King David's throne (see Mt 1:24–25N), is insufficient to fulfill the prophecy of 2 Samuel 7:12 to David, "And when your days are fulfilled and you sleep with your fathers, I will set up your seed after you, who will issue from your bowels." But there is a descent from David, whether it applies to Yosef or to Miryam, and no genealogy could cope with the radically unique circumstances of Yeshua's birth as God's "only and unique" son (Yn 1:18&N), with no human physical father. Such circumstances transcend pedestrian application of genealogies. Yeshua was the seed of David, physically from his loins, in the manner and to the degree that these circumstances admit; also see Mt 1:16N.

A fifth- or sixth-century non-Messianic Jewish "anti-gospel" called *Toledot-Yeshu* ("Generations of Yeshu"; see Mt 1:18N), apparently written for Jewish popular consumption after several centuries of Church persecution, represents Yeshua as the product of an illegitimate union between Miryam and a Roman soldier named Yosef ben-Pandera. A more attenuated version of this story appears in the Talmud (Shabbat 104b, Sanhedrin 67a) and the Tosefta (Chullin 2:22–23); see Herford, *Christianity in Talmud and Midrash*). The obvious motive for such a fable is to neutralize the Gospel narratives of heavenly intervention with a more earthy explanation for an unmarried woman's bearing a son.

CHAPTER 4

2 The Adversary. See Mt 4:1N.

16–17 ***Shabbat***. See Mt 12:1N. **He went to the synagogue as usual**, like any good Jew. **He stood up to read** publicly from a scroll. The custom in the synagogue now is to read through the *Torah* (i.e., the Pentateuch; see Mt 5:17N) each year, with portions of several chapters read on Monday, Thursday and *Shabbat* mornings, ending and beginning over again on *Simchat-Torah* ("Rejoicing of the *Torah*"), which comes at the end of *Sukkot* (Yn 7:2N). At an earlier stage in Jewish history three years were taken to read through the *Torah*.

There is a second reading called the *haftarah* ("conclusion"); it consists in portions from the Prophets and Writings related to the *parashat-hashavua'* ("[*Torah*] portion for the week"). While there is uncertainty over exactly what the first-century customs were, it seems clear that if Yeshua **was given the scroll of the prophet Yesha'yahu**, he was being offered the *haftarah* reading. Since there is uncertainty about the practices of the time, it is not clear whether **he found the place** set by the lectionary for that *Shabbat*, or the place he himself chose, or the place where the scroll happened to open.

18–21 Verses 18–19 quote Isaiah 61:1–2a but do not include the immediately following words, "...and the day of vengeance of our God." Although normally a citation of Scripture implies the surrounding context (Mt 2:6&N), here Yeshua may have stopped short so that he could say, **Today, as you heard it read, this passage of the *Tanakh*** (up to but not including the "day of vengeance") **was fulfilled** — as described at 7:20–23, Mt 11:2–6&N. For at his first coming he healed and brought Good News of the Kingdom and salvation (Mt 4:17); it was not his time to take vengeance or judge (Yn 8:15, 12:47).

20 ***Shammash*** in Hebrew or *shammes* in Yiddish. A synagogue attendant or caretaker, the "servant" of the congregation (which is what the word literally means). The Greek word here is "*upêretês*" ("attendant, servant").

24 **Yes!** Hebrew *amen*, transliterated in the Greek. See Mt 5:18N.

25 **For three-and-a-half years.** Early *JNT* editions mistakenly have "for a year-and-a-half."

25–26 The incident is described in 1 Kings 17:1, 7, 9–24; 18:1.

27 **Serious skin diseases**. See Mt 8:2N. **Elisha** and **Na'aman the Syrian**. The story is told at 2 Kings 5:1–14.

33 **Unclean demonic spirits**. See Mt 4:24N.

40 **With the setting of the sun**. See Mk 1:32N.

CHAPTER 5

1 **Lake Kinneret**. The Sea of Galilee (see Mt 4:18N).

5 **Rabbi**, Greek *epistatês*, "overseer, superintendent, taskmaster, inspector, leader, chief"; by etymology it means "one who stands over"; most English versions render it "master." According to Oepke in Kittel, ed., *Theological Dictionary of the New Testament* (Volume 2, pp. 622–623), the word, used in the New Testament only by Luke (here, 8:24, 45; 9:33, 49; 17:13) translates Hebrew "*rabbi*," which the other synoptic writers transliterate.

8 In vv. 3–5 Luke called him merely Shim'on, but here he pointedly notes that **Shim'on Kefa** (Shim'on the Rock; Mt 4:18N, 16:18&N) **fell at Yeshua's knees**. Catch the irony.

Sir. See Mt 1:20N, 7:21N, 8:1–4N.

12–14 See Mt 8:1–4&N.

17 ***P'rushim***. See Mt 3:7N. ***Torah*-teachers**. See Mt 2:4N.

26 **Amazement seized them all, and they made a *b'rakhah* to God** (literally, "they glorified God"). Many Jews familiar with the concept of "*b'rakhah*" (Mt 9:8N) and the blessings said over wine (Mt 26:27–29N) and bread (Mt 14:19N) may nevertheless be unaware that by the time of the Talmud (5th century) Judaism specified formulas for dozens of blessings to be said on all kinds of occasions. Some examples (with today's wording):

> Upon smelling fragrant herbs, grasses or flowers: "Blessed are You, *Adonai*, our God, King of the universe, who creates fragrant vegetation."
>
> Upon seeing a rainbow: "Blessed are You, *Adonai* our God, King of the universe, who remembers the covenant, is faithful to his covenant and fulfills his word." The reference is to Genesis 9:8–17.
>
> Upon seeing unusually beautiful people, trees or fields: "Blessed are you, *Adonai* our God, King of the universe, who has such phenomena for himself in his universe."
>
> Upon seeing unusually strange-looking people or animals: "Blessed are you, *Adonai* our God, King of the universe, who makes his creatures different."
>
> Upon hearing especially good news that benefits both oneself and others: "Blessed are you, *Adonai* our God, King of the universe, who is good and does good."
>
> Upon eating seasonal fruits for the first time in their season, purchasing oneself a new garment of value, or performing a seasonal *mitzvah* (e.g., celebrating Passover or *Chanukkah*): "Blessed are you, *Adonai* our God, King of the universe, who has kept us alive, sustained us and enabled us to reach this time."

Of the standard *b'rakhot* I know, this one most fires my imagination:

Upon seeing six hundred thousand or more Jews together: "Blessed are you, *Adonai* our God, King of the universe, Knower of secrets."

And so on in connection with many things and events, some ordinary and some extraordinary, some good, some bad (see 2 Ti 4:8N).

While it is known that blessing formulas along these lines predate Yeshua, there is uncertainty over first-century customs (as with *Torah*-reading practices, 4:16–17&N), so it is impossible to know to what degree everyday consciousness of God's doings would have been channeled into *b'rakhot* like those found in the Talmud and in today's Judaism. But I find no difficulty in supposing that on the occasion of Yeshua's healing a paralytic and forgiving his sins in a public setting, the people's amazement and subsequent glorifying of God was poured into the available Jewish molds. Perhaps someone thought to pronounce the sixth blessing of the *'Amidah*, which ends, "Blessed are you, *Adonai*, who is gracious to forgive abundantly," or the eighth, which ends, "Blessed are you, *Adonai*, who heals the sick of his people Israel." But in addition, I am sure there was spontaneous praise, and possibly one or more persons invented new *b'rakhot* along such lines as: "Blessed are you, *Adonai* our God, King of the universe, who cures the incurable." To which, as I see the scene in my mind's eye, the crowd would have responded with enthusiastic "*Amens*" (Mt 5:18&N) amid shouts and cheers.

27 **A tax-collector named L'vi** seems to be the same as Mattityahu (Mt 9:9). At Mk 2:14 he is called L'vi Ben-Chalfai (Levi, son of Alpheus); but this Chalfai is apparently different from the Chalfai who was father of Ya'akov (Mt 10:3, Mk 3:18, Lk 6:15, Ac 1:13). Since people then as well as now often had more than one name, it is not surprising to find differences between the several lists of the Emissaries (Mt 10:2–4, Mk 3:16–19, Lk 6:14–16, Ac 1:13).

Being named L'vi, he was almost certainly a descendant of Ya'akov's son L'vi and therefore a member of the tribe set aside to do the work connected with the Temple. Another member of this tribe who came to trust in Yeshua was Bar-Nabba (Ac 4:36). Acts 6:7 informs us that "a large crowd of *cohanim* were becoming obedient to the faith" (the *cohanim* or priests are a clan within the tribe of L'vi). In today's non-Messianic Judaism *cohanim* and Levites still retain certain rights and responsibilities distinct from those of other Jews. For example, in the public reading of the *Torah* in an Orthodox synagogue a *cohen* reads first and a Levite reads second; the third to seventh readings may be done by any Jewish man.

30 ***Talmidim***, disciples. See Mt 5:1N. **Sinners**. See Mt 9:10N.

33 **Fasting**. See 18:12N.

38 **Freshly prepared wineskins**. See Mt 9:17N.

CHAPTER 6

1–5 See Mt 12:1–8&N.

9 **What is permitted on *Shabbat*?** Mattityahu 12:10 reports the question as: "Is healing permitted on *Shabbat?*" The answer of modern *halakhah* is threefold:

(1) On *Shabbat,* healing to save life is not only permitted but a duty.

(2) Caring for the seriously ill (e.g., those with a high fever or pain affecting the whole body) is allowed, within certain constraints.

(3) Treating minor ailments is prohibited by *g'zerah* (rabbinical decree) — the reason being that most treatments require grinding to prepare medicine, and grinding is a prohibited form of work (see 12:2N).

Since a shriveled hand is neither life-threatening nor "serious," this healing, on the face of it, violates today's *halakhah* concerning *Shabbat.*

However, since Yeshua did not use medicine and hence no grinding was done, a case could have been made — in the fluid halakhic environment of the first century — that no violation had taken place (but compare Yn 9:6&N).

Presumably the Mishna reflects the halakhic situation among the *P'rushim.* It prohibits healing on *Shabbat* through medical means but allows healing which comes as a byproduct of some other activity:

> "They may not set a fracture. If someone's hand or foot is dislocated, he may not pour cold water over it; but he may wash it in the usual way; and if it heals, it heals." (Shabbat 22:6)

In v. 10 the man holds out his shriveled hand, and it is restored to soundness. This is in no sense a medical cure, but clearly he held out his hand in response to Yeshua's instruction for no other reason than to be healed, so that by the logic implicit in the Mishna the cure was not a byproduct and was therefore a violation of *Shabbat.*

Actually, Yeshua brings five arguments against the way in which the *P'rushim* use their *halakhah*:

(1) In the parallel passage at Mt 12:11–12 Yeshua attacks the premise underlying the Oral *Torah* as understood by the *P'rushim* with an argument about priorities: "doing good deeds" is more important than observing the details of the *Shabbat* work rules. Determination of priorities is a legitimate form of halakhic ruling (see Yn 7:22–23N).

(2) He strengthens his case with a *kal v'chomer* argument (see Mt 6:30N): if it is permitted to rescue a sheep on *Shabbat*, how much more is it permitted to heal a man on *Shabbat*!

(3) In the parallel passage in Mark he adds that "*Shabbat* was made for man, not man for *Shabbat*" — which is to say that God's rules are to serve man and enable him better to glorify God, not to enslave man and require him to glorify the rules (see Mk 2:27&N).

(4) At Yn 5:17–18 he says, "My Father has been working until now, and I too am working," which his hearers correctly interpreted as Yeshua's claim to divinity and thus his need and right to work on *Shabbat.*

(5) Finally, at Yn 7:22–23, where he has just healed a man on *Shabbat*, he brings another *kal v'chomer* argument: if his opponents allow circumcision on *Shabbat*, how much more should they allow healing (see Yn 7:22–23N).

The common thread in these five arguments is that the rules of the *P'rushim* for

Shabbat are generally good guides to behavior, but they must not be allowed to become oppressive — there are circumstances when one should break them in order to obey God's will and be an active participant in his Kingdom (for more, see Ac 4:19N, Ga 2:11–20&NN). "Breaking the rules" for the right reasons is an essential element in Messianic *halakhah*!

13 Emissaries. See Mt 10:1N.

14 Bar-Talmai. The sixth emissary in Luke's list is identified as the son (Aramaic *bar*) of "Talmai," a Hebrew transliteration of the name "Ptolemy" given to several Egyptian kings after the Alexandrian conquests of 336–323 B.C.E., which brought Israel under Egyptian rule and influence for many decades. Thus it is not surprising that a Jew would have an Egyptian name. In other English versions this emissary is called Bartholomew.

16 Y'hudah from K'riot. See Mt 10:2–4N.

20–49 These verses are known as the Sermon on the Plain, i.e., the "level place" of v. 17. A comparison with the Sermon on the Mount (Mt 5:3–7:29) has led critics to suppose that either Mattityahu or Luke is unreliable — starting with the different venues reported by the two writers for what the critics suppose must have been the same speech. Overzealous harmonizers, on the other hand, also assuming that Yeshua made but one such speech, have suggested, for example, that Luke's "level place" was located on Mattityahu's "mount" or "hill" (Mt 5:1). A more likely explanation, which takes into account the common experience of public speakers, is that Yeshua preached the same message many times, with variations in length, emphases and illustrations, depending on the needs of his audience. Luke reports one such event and Mattityahu another. For comments on the content of the sermon, see Mt 5:3–7:29NN.

40 See Mt 5:1N for the cultural context of this verse.

CHAPTER 7

5 He loves our people — in fact, he built the synagogue for us! The normal relationship between Romans and Jews, as is usual between conquerors and conquered, was not one of love and trust — from either side. But this pagan Roman officer had demonstrated a love for the Jewish people which moved the Jewish leaders to plead on his behalf before Yeshua, whose primary ministry was not to Gentiles but to Jews (Mt 10:5, 15:26; Yn 1:11). Love was demonstrated to be a matter of deeds — "he built the synagogue for us!" — not mere words or feelings; and this is its primary meaning throughout Scripture. Similarly, in modern times "Righteous Gentiles" have been honored by trees planted along the road to Israel's *Yad VaShem* Memorial of the Holocaust because they risked their own death to save Jewish lives.

11 Na'im means "pleasant" in Hebrew; the Greek here is *Nain*. An Arab village near Nazareth retains the ancient name.

13 Luke calls Yeshua **the Lord** here to point up the significance of this miracle.

15 **Gave him to his mother**. The citation from the *Tanakh* reminds us that the entire story resembles Elijah's raising from the dead the son of the widow from Tzarfat (1 Kings 17:17–24).

16 **A great prophet has appeared among us**. The people's reaction is the same as that of the Tzarfat widow. From this miracle readers are to conclude that (at the very least) Yeshua is as great a prophet as Elijah.

22 See Mt 11:2–6N.

26 ***Nu***. See Mt 11:9N, Lk 12:42N.

35 **The proof of wisdom is in all the kinds of people it produces**, which is more or less parallel to Mt 11:19. Alternatively, but less clearly parallel, are two other possible understandings of this difficult Greek sentence: "The proof of what is purveyed as wisdom is the character of the people who hold to it," and, "Everyone tries to justify his own brand of wisdom."

36 **Sinner**. See Mt 9:10N.

49 **Who is this fellow that presumes to forgive sins?** In Isaiah 43:25 it is *Adonai* himself whom the prophet quotes as saying, "I, yes, I, am the one who blots out your own transgressions, for my own sake." Compare 5:17–26 and Mk 2:5–12N.

CHAPTER 8

2 **Miryam (called Magdalit)**, that is, Miryam from the village of Magdala, on the west shore of Lake Kinneret north of Tiberias and south of Ginosar.

13 **Apostatize**, Greek *aphistêmi* ("go away, desert, fall away"). The word used in the parallel passages (Mt 13:18, Mk 4:17) is "*skandalizo*" ("fall into a trap, be caught in a snare"). Yeshua's point is that poorly rooted believers, whose commitment is inadequate to carry them through times of temptation, harassment and persecution, "fall away" from faith.

26 **Gerasenes**. See Mk 5:1N.

31 **The bottomless pit**, Greek *abussos*, "abyss," found also at Ro 10:7; Rv 9:1–2, 11; 11:7; 17:8; 20:1, 3. The word is used in the Septuagint to translate Hebrew *tehom*, as in Genesis 1:2, "Darkness was over the abyss." At a later period in Judaism "*tehom*" referred to the place where renegade spirits were confined.

44 ***Tzitzit***, ritual fringe. See Mt 9:20&N.

CHAPTER 9

5 Wherever they don't welcome you, shake the dust from your feet when you leave that town as a warning to them. Jews would shake the ritually impure dust of a Gentile city from their feet upon leaving it and returning to the Land of Israel; a secondary effect was to demonstrate to the city's inhabitants that the Jew had no fellowship with them; compare Ac 10:28N. When Yeshua's *talmidim* did the same to Jews (here, Ac 13:51; compare Ac 18:6), it symbolized their refusal of the Kingdom of God and consequent refusal to be part of genuine Israel (see Ro 9:6).

16 Made a *b'rakhah*. See Mt 14:19N.

18–23 See Mt 16:13–23&NN.

23–25 Most "how-to" books advise the ambitious to look out for Number One in order to get ahead in the world. Yeshua's advice is exactly the opposite: put aside selfishness in order to get ahead in heaven; advancement in this world will follow as a consequence (12:31, Mk 10:29–30). His follower must treat his life apart from God as the life of a capital criminal, to be nailed on the stake and put to death.

Execution-stake. See Mt 10:38N.

31 Exodus, Greek *exodos*, literally, "departure" and translated "death" in some versions. While Yeshua was indeed to "die" and then, after his resurrection, "depart" into heaven, the use of the word here, after the appearance of Moshe, brings to mind everything connected with the Jewish Exodus from Egypt. The word "*exodos*" appears in the New Testament in only two other places — MJ 11:22, where it specifically refers to the Exodus from Egypt; and 2K 1:15, where it means Kefa's own death.

50 Whoever isn't against you is for you. See Mt 12:30&N.

51 He made his decision, literally, "he established/strengthened his face"; KJV has, "He set his face to go to Jerusalem." The *JNT* rendering implies the same fixity of determination.

53 The people there would not let him stay because his destination was Yerushalayim. Arab nations today will not admit tourists whose passports show that they have been in Israel. The conflict between the people inhabiting Shomron (Samaria) and the people of Israel was as sharp then as it is between the Israelis and some of the Arab inhabitants of Samaria today (see Yn 4:9N). Often accommodation and friendship can be arranged privately between people who publicly are enemies, but the publicity surrounding Yeshua's proposed trip made this impractical.

54 Fire from heaven to destroy them. Yeshua had given his *talmidim* power (v. 1), and they were eager to duplicate Elijah's feat (1 Kings 1:10, 12).

57–62 Yeshua challenges the excuses of those whose commitment is weak. To the excuses of those who reject him altogether, as at 14:18–20, he responds with fury and withdraws his offer. In perspective, either kind of excuse seems foolish, like the excuses people put forth today: "I can't believe in Yeshua because I'm Jewish" — but all the early believers were Jewish, as well as many since. "I'll have to give up too much" — yet far less than what is to be gained. "I'll lose my friends" — see Yeshua's answer to this one at Mk 10:29–30. To all the excuses the Bible has answers, but there is no guarantee people will accept them.

59–60 Let me… bury my father. See Mt 8:21–22&N.

CHAPTER 10

1 **Seventy**. The emissaries numbered twelve to correspond with the twelve tribes of Israel; this is made explicit at 22:30 (Mt 19:28) and Rv 21:12–14. These seventy correspond to the seventy elders Moshe appointed in the wilderness, who received of the Spirit and prophesied (Numbers 11:16, 24–25). The high *Sanhedrin* numbered seventy for the same reason.

4 **Don't stop to *shmoose* with people on the road**. KJV translates *mêdena aspasêsthe* as "Salute no one," but the Yiddish word "*shmoose*," which means "talk in a friendly way, chit-chat, engage in idle conversation, gossip" and is derived from Hebrew *shmu'ot* ("things heard, rumors"), conveys precisely the sense of Yeshua's instruction not to waste time on the road but to hasten to the destination and get on with the work to be done. Elisha similarly instructed Gehazi as he left to lay Elisha's staff on the face of the Shunammite woman's dead child: "If thou meet any man, salute him not; and if any salute thee, answer him not again" (2 Kings 4:29, KJV).

5–6 **Shalom!** See Mt 10:12N.

8–11 The message of truth is to be proclaimed whether it is welcomed or not. Why should people uninterested in the Gospel and unreceptive to it be evangelized? Because the message itself is powerful, since it comes from God; it may cause them to change their minds. Note that Yeshua's *talmidim* are not merely to take opposition in stride, but to condemn it (vv. 10–11a; see 9:5N).

12 **On the Day of Judgment**, literally, "on that Day." **S'dom**. See Genesis 18:20–19:29.

13 **Tzor and Tzidon**. See Mt 11:21N.

15 The *p'shat* ("simple sense") of Isaiah 14:12–15 (see Mt 2:15N) refers to the actual King of Tyre, but many interpreters see in this passage a *remez* ("hint") alluding indirectly to the Adversary, Satan (Mt 4:1N), as the "bright star, son of the morning" (rendered "Lucifer" in KJV).

16 **Whoever rejects me** (Yeshua) **rejects the One who sent me** (God). The same idea,

that belief in God necessarily implies belief in Yeshua, is expressed in variously different ways also at Yn 14:6, Ac 4:12, 1 Yn 2:23.

17 With your power, literally, "in your name." See Ac 2:38N.

19 You can trample down snakes and scorpions. This is a preview of the Messianic Age which accompanies Yeshua's return in glory to rule on earth: "The suckling child shall play on the hole of the cobra, and the weaned child shall put his hand on the viper's nest" (Isaiah 11:8). See also Mk 16:17–18&N.

20 Be glad your names have been recorded in heaven. Judaism features prominently the idea that the names of the forgiven are recorded in heaven. The liturgy for *Rosh-HaShanah* (Jewish New Year) includes a prayer for being written in the Book of Life, and the *Yom-Kippur* (Day of Atonement) liturgy nine days later has a prayer for being "sealed" in the Book of Life, the idea being that the decision is made final on that day (but see Yn 7:37N). For more see Rv 20:12bN.

25 An expert in *Torah*. Greek *nomikos*, which would be rendered "lawyer" in a non-Jewish context, here means a specialist in Jewish law, including both the Written *Torah* and the Oral *Torah* ("Tradition of the Elders" in Mk 7:2–4&N).

32 L'vi. See 5:27N.

33 A man from *Shomron*, that is, a Samaritan, specifically the "Good Samaritan." There had been enmity for centuries between the Jews and the Samaritans (see Yn 4:9N), so that Yeshua's questioner would probably have subscribed to the prevailing low opinion of Samaritans among Jews and could be expected to think that if a *cohen* and a *L'vi* refused the man aid, how much more would a mistrustful Samaritan also refuse him aid. Yeshua himself had recently traveled through Shomron (9:51–53).

34 Oil and wine were considered medicine.

35 Two days' wages, literally, "two denarii."

41–42 There is only one thing that is essential, namely, paying attention to Yeshua. Or the Greek may be translated, "One thing is needed"; so that **Marta**, instead of **fretting and worrying about so many things**, could have served Yeshua just one dish and then been able to relax and join her sister.

CHAPTER 11

1–13 Teach us to pray. In today's secular society people often feel unable to pray and assume that the ability to pray is natural to some and lacking in others. But Yeshua's *talmidim*, even though they too felt inadequate in prayer, were on the right track in supposing that Yeshua could teach them how to pray. His teaching consisted of four parts:

(1) What to pray for (vv. 2–4),
(2) The importance of persistence (vv. 5–10),
(3) The certainty of a positive answer because of God's love and goodness (vv. 9–13), and
(4) The ultimate gift, the Holy Spirit, who is the source and power for all right prayer (v. 13b; see Ro 8:26–27).

2–4 This version of the Lord's Prayer is briefer than Mattityahu's, but it contains the same topics for prayer. See Mt 6:9–13&N.

8 ***Chutzpah***. A colorful Hebrew and Yiddish word that means "boldness, audacity, effrontery, insolence, gall, brazen nerve, presumption, arrogance, persistence and just plain 'guts,'" in varying combinations, proportions and intensities. To me it seems the ideal rendering of Greek *anaideia*, which Arndt & Gingrich's *A Greek-English Lexicon of the New Testament* translates as "impudence, shamelessness."

13 Ephesians 5:18 commands Yeshua's followers to "keep on being filled with the Spirit." The *Ruach HaKodesh* first came upon believers after they had been praying persistently (Ac 1:4, 2:4) in response to Yeshua's own promise (this verse, 24:49, Ac 1:8). Those filled with the Holy Spirit may expect to receive gifts (Ro 12:6–8, 1C 12:28–30, Ep 4:11–12), display fruits of righteousness (Ga 5:22–23), and have the desire, love and power to communicate effectively the Good News of Yeshua by word and deed to those who have not yet believed it (the entire book of Acts centers on this theme). Moreover, "anyone who doesn't have the Spirit of the Messiah doesn't belong to him" (Ro 8:9).

14 **Ba'al-Zibbul**. See Mt 10:25N.

23 See Mt 12:30N.

29–30 **Yonah became a sign to the people of Nineveh**. This is understood in rabbinic writings as follows: the news that Yonah had spent three days and three nights in the belly of the fish (Mt 12:40, Yonah 1:17) preceded Yonah's arrival at Nineveh, which is why Yonah's reluctant and lackluster preaching ("Nineveh will be destroyed in forty days") was sufficient to awaken in its inhabitants fear and a need to repent before the God capable of performing such a miracle for the preacher.

31 **Queen of the South**, i.e., the Queen of Sheba. See Mt 12:42N.

34 **When your eye is good** or **bad**. See Mt 6:22–23N.

38 **Doing *n'tilat-yadayim* before the meal**. See Mt 15:2–3N.

39–52 In general see the notes to Mt 23:13–36.

41 **Give as alms what is inside**. A difficult text in the original Greek. One possibility:

"Give to the poor what is inside your cups and dishes," here understood no longer as robbery and wickedness (v. 39) but food, good things in general. Another: "Give truly, from your heart," i.e., from what is inside. A third: Luke, working from an Aramaic source, misread "*zakki*" ("give alms") for "*dakki*" ("clean," as in the parallel passage, Mt 23:26).

42 See Mt 23:23N.

51 **Hevel… Z'kharyah.** See Mt 23:35N.

CHAPTER 12

1 ***Chametz***. See Mt 16:6N.

3 See Mt 10:27N.

5 **Gey-Hinnom**. See Mt 5:22N.

6 **Next to nothing**, literally, "two assarions." The assarion was the smallest Roman coin.

8–10 Luke is the only writer who places all this material in one passage (compare Mt 10:32–33, 12:31–32; Mk 3:28–29 corresponds to v. 10 only). In the context of counseling his followers against fear generally (vv. 4–7) Yeshua encourages them not to be afraid to acknowledge their faith publicly. One need not be a behavioristic psychologist to understand his means: reward (v. 8) and punishment (v. 9). Verse 10 explains what v. 9 means by "disowning Yeshua": a person unenlightened by the working of the Holy Spirit in him may **say something against the Son of Man**, but he **will have it forgiven him** because he doesn't really grasp the full import of his words. But if the Holy Spirit has caused genuine knowledge of Yeshua to enter his spirit, then in speaking against Yeshua he may well be **blaspheming the *Ruach HaKodesh*** (the Greek word "*blasphêmia*" means "slander, defamation, reviling judgment, scurrilous talk, calumny, reproach, railing, impious and irreverent speech").

That is, if a person knows that Yeshua is "the way, the truth and the life; no one comes to the Father except through" him (Yn 14:6); if he knows that "he who disowns the Son disowns the Father, but he who acknowledges the Son has the Father too" (1 Yn 2:23); if he knows that "there is no other name under heaven given to men by whom we must be saved" (Ac 4:12) — then his denial of Yeshua as Messiah, Savior, Lord and Son of God becomes the ground for his "not being forgiven" (v. 10), apparently "neither in the *'olam hazeh* nor in the *'olam haba*" (Mt 12:32).

What conclusions are to be drawn? On the one hand, believers in Yeshua should note that nonbelievers may "say something against the Son of Man" without incurring God's wrath, because they are "unaware of what they are doing" (Ac 3:17; also Lk 23:34), since the Holy Spirit has not brought the significance home to them. Although "the love and kindness of God has been revealed to every human being" (Ti 2:11; compare Ro 1:19–20), and "the *Torah* and the Prophets give their witness" to God's way of putting people right with him (Ro 3:21–22), nevertheless there are literally millions of Jewish people who have never in their lives heard the Gospel. That is, the Good News about Yeshua has never been presented to them in a way that made sense to them, given their training and backgrounds, and given the unpleasant fact that so much evil has been perpetrated against the Jewish people "in the name of Christ" — in his name but without his authority, of course. Thus when a Jew — or, for that matter, a non-Jew — who is thus ignorant of the true message of the Gospel "says something against the Son of Man," it may have no significance. In fact, if he has been taught, as some Jews are, that Yeshua is a false god, or a pretender, or an unfaithful Jew who led others astray, he may believe he is doing a good deed in denouncing Yeshua. What people who are prejudiced against Yeshua need is to be presented with the Good News in a way that shows it is truly good news, a fulfillment of the prophecies of the *Tanakh* and the best expression of the truths of Judaism.

Only when a person understands the Gospel in his mind and heart and spirit yet still rejects it is he blaspheming the Holy Spirit and risking eternal punishment (see MJ 6:4–6&N).

On the other hand, no one reading these words can excuse himself for speaking against Yeshua by saying, "The Holy Spirit has not enlightened me," for he may be doing so right now. In other words, it is the reader's responsibility to be open to the working of God's Spirit and to "check the *Tanakh*" and the New Testament "to see if these things are true" (Ac 17:11). In summary, vv. 8–10 show that disowning Yeshua does not consist merely in speaking words against him but in fighting against the Holy Spirit when he is holding the truth about Yeshua in front of you.

11–12 The ruling powers and the authorities include both Jewish and Gentile tribunals. Yeshua continues to comfort believers concerning fear: they need not be anxious about committing the unpardonable sin of blaspheming the Holy Spirit when under investigation by hostile officialdom, because the Holy Spirit himself will provide the words they need to glorify God in such dire moments.

13–34 No passage could be more to the point for modern man than these verses about the nature, origin and cure of greed.

13–14 Rabbi, tell my brother…. Traditionally a rabbi was not a clergyman but a teacher of Jewish values and customs, and as such the authoritative judge or arbitrator who decided points of law and ethics central to people's lives. Only since the secularly inspired *Haskalah* ("Enlightenment") of the eighteenth and nineteenth centuries have rabbis in the West been viewed alongside Catholic priests and Protestant ministers as marginal figures in a supposedly secular "real world." But, alluding to Exodus 2:14, where Moshe appointed himself ruler and judge over his fellow Israelites, Yeshua rejects the role of arbitrator in order to probe the attitude motivating his questioner while implicitly rejecting his request.

15–21 He addresses his remarks **to the people;** apparently Yeshua regards the questioner's attitude as typical.

22–34 To his *talmidim* he goes into the matter more deeply, as was his practice (Mt 13:10–17). He identifies fear as the source of greed (v. 22). The one certain way to relieve anxiety over material matters is by seeking God's **kingdom** (v. 31) and its eternal **riches**. This is accomplished through doing ***tzedakah*** (literally, "doing righteousness," but understood as "giving to charity"), that is, by not being selfish but sharing the wealth (v. 33). Yeshua is not against having wealth but against making wealth the be-all and end-all of life (vv. 21, 31, 34).

27 Shlomo. See 1 Kings 10:47, 2 Chronicles 9:3–6.

42 *Nu.* Yiddish, rendering Greek *ara*, which Arndt and Gingrich call an "interrogative particle indicating anxiety or impatience,... usually incapable of direct translation." That may be true of English; but if the Greeks had a word for it, so do the Jews. See also Mt 11:9N.

46 Disloyal, Greek *apistoi*, "unbelievers, unfaithful."

48 Entrust or "deposit." If the latter, then "**they ask still more**" continues the financial imagery: they want interest on their deposit.

49 Fire. Primarily the refining fire of holiness and the ultimate fire of judgment against sin (compare Isaiah 66:24; Malachi 3:2–3; 1C 3:13–15; Rv 19:20, 20:14–15). Secondarily a fire of hostility between unbelievers and believers (below, 12:53).

50 This **immersion** (see Mt 3:1N, 3:15N) involves Yeshua's total identification with sinful mankind in which he bears our sins and their punishment, in keeping with Isaiah 53:6, "*Adonai* has laid on him the iniquities of us all." He thus becomes a sacrifice for our sins, giving up his very life and immersing himself into death, paying the death penalty we owe for our sins "like a lamb brought for slaughter" (Isaiah 53:7).

51 Yeshua is not to rule in glory at his first coming; he is not at that time to fulfill the Messianic prophecies of world peace, e.g., "They shall beat their swords into plowshares…" (Isaiah 2:4, Micah 4:3). For this reason he will **bring… division**: some will acknowledge him as Messiah, while others will not, so that families will be split down the middle over this issue (vv. 52–53, on which see Mt 10:35–36N).

54 Once again Yeshua speaks differently **to the crowds** than to his *talmidim* (vv. 22–53). To his own disciples he entrusted information about his ministry and about how to obey him in a manner reflecting their already existing commitment to him. His only task with the crowds was to awaken them to their need to commit their lives to him, to become *talmidim*. This is the message of 12:54–13:9.

CHAPTER 13

1 Men from the Galil whom Pilate had slaughtered just as they were slaughtering

animals for sacrifice, literally, "Galileans whose blood Pilate had mixed with their sacrifices." These verses exemplify Pilate's brutality (see Mt 27:2&N, 16–24&N).

3, 5 Unless you turn to God from your sins (repent, do *t'shuvah*, Mt 3:2N), **you will all die as they did**. The "Bad News" (Ro 1:18–2:8&NN) is explicit, the Good News implicit (Ro 3:19–3:26&NN). Then as now people did not want to think about their own evil ways, so they put their attention on current events to distract them. News is the opiate of the people. Most of us cannot affect world events very much, but all of us can worry about them and criticize the sins of others — instead of focussing on our own lives and our own sins.

6–9 In these verses Yeshua shows how patient God is with wayward humanity in general. However the **fig tree** metaphor is frequently used in the *Tanakh*, and also at Mt 21:18–22, to represent the Jewish people, who were expected to **bear fruit** (v. 9) by leading righteous lives and by communicating God's truth to the other nations of the world (Isaiah 49:6). So, has the "**one more year**" ended? — are the Jewish people **cut down** or set aside by God? Certainly not! (Jeremiah 31:34–36 (35–37)) Heaven forbid! (Ro 11:1–2, 11–12) Some Jews, having trusted in Yeshua the Messiah and remained united with him, bear fruit (Yn 15:1–8, also a "plant" metaphor, in that case a vine); while God patiently preserves the Jewish people as a whole until "all Israel will be saved" (Ro 11:26).

14–17 Concerning healing on ***Shabbat*** see 6:9N.

19 A mustard seed... grew and became a tree, and the birds... nested in its branches. The mustard plant is always small (Mt 13:31–32&N); it never becomes a tree. But by God's special intervention the first shall be last and the last first (v. 30). God can make the mustard plant grow great; likewise he can exalt the unwanted and humiliated Messiah (Isaiah 53:1–12, Psalm 118:22–23, Pp 2:6–11). Yeshua uses the imagery of Ezekiel 17:23–24, 31:6 and Daniel 4:9–11, 18 (4:12–14, 21), passages which identify the birds with the nations of the world. Thus the Kingdom of Heaven honors Yeshua, the rejected Messiah; and the nations of the world find protection in him.

28 But yourselves thrown outside. Yeshua is trying to wake up people who think their own good works or their Jewishness will guarantee them entry into the *'olam haba* ("the world to come"). Not only in Messianic Judaism but also in non-Messianic Judaism there is little ground for such a hope. True, the Mishna says, "All Israel has a share in the *'olam haba*" (Sanhedrin 10:1, quoted more fully at Ro 11:26aN). But the subsequent material, which names many categories of Israelites excluded from the world to come, makes clear that the sense of this declaration is that although all Israelites have a special opportunity to share in the future life (as Sha'ul puts it, Jews have an "advantage," Ro 3:1–2, 9:4–5), they can lose it by not living up to their calling. While neither kind of Judaism offers hope to those who expect God to overlook their sins without their trusting him, only Messianic Judaism offers the content of trust that solves the sin problem.

31–35 Some interpreters believe these ***P'rushim*** were trying to frighten Yeshua into Judea, so that the *Sanhedrin* would be able to exercise control over him. Compare the attempt of Amaziah, priest of the golden calf at Beit-El, to frighten the prophet Amos out of Israel into Judea; he too failed (Amos 7:10–17). But such devious motivation need not have been present, for not all Pharisees wanted to do him in; these may have thought enough of him to warn him. In fact, some were "not far from the Kingdom of God" (Mk 12:34); and some came to faith in Yeshua and remained Pharisees (Ac 15:5), among them Sha'ul (Ac 23:6&N).

The threat of Herod Antipas (Mt 14:1N) was real. Although he wanted to see Yeshua perform a miracle (23:8), he regarded him as a dangerous leader like Yochanan the Immerser (Mk 6:14–16), whom he had killed.

Yeshua's answer, like Sha'ul's to Agav (Ac 21:13), is that negativism will not dissuade him from following God's plan.

35 See Mt 23:37–39&N.

CHAPTER 14

1–6 See 6:9N.

8–10 Proverbs 25:6–7 gives the same advice, some of it in the same language.

14 **The resurrection of the righteous** is clearly distinguished from that of the unrighteous, both in the *Tanakh* (Daniel 12:2) and in the New Testament (16:26&N; Rv 20:4–6, 12, 15).

16–24 God invites sinners to his salvation **banquet** (vv. 16–17) and receives a chorus of ridiculously transparent and insulting excuses (vv. 18–20). See 9:57–62N for a comment on flabby excuses; however, these, unlike those, reflect not weak commitment but intentionally ignoring the invitation and despising the host, coupled with hypocritically refusing to say so forthrightly. The host is angry but invites others (vv. 21–24); similarly God is angry with Jews and Gentiles who are so busy being self-sufficient or fulfilling their life programs that they spurn salvation. Nevertheless God's offer continues going out to all who will hear, notably those less well-fixed, who can realize how needy they are.

23 **Insistently persuade people to come in**. KJV reads, "Go out into the highways and hedges, and compel them to come in." The Greek word translated "compel" or "insistently persuade" is "*anangkason*," which has a range of meanings from physically forcing to verbally convincing; throughout this spectrum of significations is a tone of intensity and urgency.

In times past this verse was used to justify forcing Jews to be baptized against their will. Yet nowhere in the Bible does God say or suggest that he wants people to be forced to accept his love and kindness. From the outset, in the Garden of Eden, where Adam could freely choose whether or not to obey God, there has been only one message, and it is a message of persuasion: "Turn from sin to God and trust in the Good News" (Mk 1:15). In fact, it is impossible to force people to repent or believe, for these things are matters of the heart. Thus "forced conversion" is a contradiction in terms, since true "conversion" means inwardly turning from sin to God through Yeshua, not outwardly transferring from one religious institution to another. Likewise, attempting to force "conversion" is not obeying God; quite the contrary, the coercion and cruelty involved constitute gross *dis*obedience. But "insistent persuasion" that respects the hearer's dignity is commanded and can produce good results.

26–33 If anyone... does not hate his father [and] ... mother... he cannot be my *talmid*. One hears v. 26 selectively misquoted in exactly this way, and on this basis a case is made that Yeshua is a cruel madman. But the key to his warning is, of course, the phrase, "**and his own life besides**." The theme of these verses is not alienation from one's family but the cost of discipleship: nothing, not love for father or mother or even one's own life, is to take precedence over loyalty to God and his Messiah (see Mt 16:24&N). He must **renounce all that he has** (v. 33), acknowledging that if God is to be primary in his life, possessions and even social relationships, in and of themselves, must be secondary. Being Messianic is more than merely acknowledging facts about Yeshua.

28 Estimate the cost. Spiritual cost-benefit analysis is taught in the Mishna also:

> "Be thinking about the loss of a *mitzvah* against its reward, and the reward of a transgression against its loss." (Avot 2:1)

The sense is: Compare the relatively small cost of observing the *mitzvah* with the great and eternal benefit obtained by fulfilling it; likewise, compare the fleeting reward gained by transgressing a command with its great and eternal cost.

A famous Christian application of this principle was formulated in the seventeenth century by Blaise Pascal (1623–1662), a founder of mathematical probability theory; it is known as Pascal's Wager. His idea is that, rationally, whether or not to believe in Yeshua's Messiahship, Lordship and atonement should depend on two factors: the *value* of what you stand to gain or lose by believing or not, and the *probability* that it is true — which determines the probabilities of your receiving those gains or losses.

The Bible states that if you believe in Yeshua you will have some finite costs (forgoing "the passing pleasures of sin" (MJ 11:24), the effort of striving to do good); but you will have eternal life with God, a benefit of infinite value. On the other hand, if you reject Yeshua you will have some finite benefits (enjoying whatever happiness the world and the Devil offer); but you will go to hell and be separated forever from God and all goodness, an infinite cost.

Suppose there is only one chance in a billion that Yeshua is who the Bible says he is. Then it is still absolutely worthwhile to believe in Yeshua; because, although you have a very high chance of paying some finite cost, nevertheless a tiny chance at an infinite reward still has infinite value — one-billionth of plus-infinity is still plus-infinity. And it is equally un-worthwhile to disbelieve, because, although you have a very high chance of gaining some finite amount of benefits, even a one-billionth chance of minus-infinity has a value of minus-infinity, which outweighs all finite benefits. Only those who are *absolutely* certain that the Bible is false, who can give absolute zero probability to its truth, can rationally choose to disbelieve. For others faced with Pascal's Wager (and everyone is), the rational way of counting the cost always leads to trusting in Yeshua.

Why are so few rabbis (or functionaries in other religions) believers? One reason is that most have never heard the Gospel presented in a Jewish way. The *Jewish New Testament* and the *Jewish New Testament Commentary*, attempt to do so. But even if the Gospel is understood as the Good News it is, and not as a Gentile religion or a pagan reworking of Judaism, another reason is that rabbis (and functionaries in other religions) are usually unwilling to pay the cost — which in their case would be exchanging the honor and privileges given them in the Jewish (or other religious) community for dishonor and shame, for the status of outcast and *meshummad* ("apostate"; literally, "one who has been destroyed"). A third reason is that they do not accurately perceive the benefits. Even apart from the heaven-hell question, few can imagine the rewards of helping shape a new and true Judaism faithful to God, the Jewish Messiah, the Jewish people and the rest of humanity. It is hard for them to envision the excitement of devoting their rabbinical training to uniting the two great streams of world history that for two thousand years have grown apart (see Mt 9:16–17&NN, 13:52&N).

One who did catch this vision, and accordingly reevaluated the costs and benefits, was Sha'ul of Tarsus. He wrote,

> "But the things that used to be advantages [benefits] for me, I have, because of the Messiah, come to consider a disadvantage [a cost, or at most a finite benefit]. Not only that, but I consider everything a disadvantage [cost, finite benefit] in comparison with the supreme value [infinite benefit] of knowing the Messiah Yeshua as my Lord. It was because of him that I gave up everything and regard it all as garbage [at most a finite benefit, worthless by comparison], in order to gain the Messiah [infinite benefit]." (Pp 3:7–8)

He counted the cost rationally and correctly. He understood Pascal's Wager a millennium-and-a-half before Pascal formulated it and drew the appropriate conclusion.

In fact there have been rabbis throughout history who have followed in Sha'ul's footsteps, and their stories make fascinating reading; see, for example, John During, ed., *Good News: Special Rabbis' Edition* (P.O. Box 7847, Johannesburg, RSA), which describes the lives of fourteen 19th- and 20th-century rabbis who became Messianic Jews. Also see the story of Daniel Zion, Chief Rabbi of Bulgaria, in Ac 4:13N.

34–35 Several interpretations have been offered; the one that appeals to me is that **salt** represents a person's willingness to do what Yeshua demands of his *talmidim* (vv. 26–33). But if his willingness turns into unwillingness, if a *talmid* returns to worldly ways after experiencing the truth and joy of following God's way, what else is left to restore him? Nothing. Compare MJ 6:4–6&N.

CHAPTER 15

1 Sinners. See Mt 9:10N.

2–3 This fellow... welcomes sinners...! All three **parable**s in this chapter deal with God's love for the open sinner who repents. This idea is not unique to Yeshua or the New Testament; here is an excerpt from the *Rambam*'s *Mishneh-Torah*, Maimonides' comprehensive summary of Judaism's requirements, completed in 1178:

> "Let not the *ba'al-t'shuvah* ["Jew who repents/returns to [Orthodox] Judaism"; see Mt 3:2N] suppose that because of the iniquities and sins he has committed he is kept at a distance from the level attained by the righteous men. It isn't so. He is loved as tenderly by the Creator as if he had never sinned. Not only that, his reward is great, since he experienced the taste of sin and nevertheless rid himself of it by conquering his *yetzer* ["[evil] impulse"]. The sages said, 'Where the *ba'al-t'shuvah* stands, the completely righteous men cannot stand' (B'rakhot 34b). That is, the level attained by the *ba'al-t'shuvah* is higher than that of someone who never sinned at all, because the former had to strive harder to subdue his *yetzer* than the latter."

There are significant differences between this paragraph from the *Mishneh-Torah* and the parables in this chapter. First, the New Testament does not recognize "completely righteous men," except for Yeshua (also see v. 7&N). Second, it does not recognize differing "levels" of persons who have not come to faith in Yeshua — all are equally saved by his death. Third, the New Testament does recognize that the sinner who has been forgiven more will love God more (7:41–43 above). Fourth, the emphasis in Yeshua's parables is not on the penitent's effort but on God's love. However, in Scripture these are two sides of a coin: "Turn us to you, *Adonai*, and we will be turned" (Lamentations 5:21; see Mt 3:2N).

4–7 The sheep metaphor echoes Ezekiel 34.

7 Righteous people who have no need to repent, literally, "who are such as to have no need to repent." There is joy in heaven over an open sinner who has obvious need to repent and does so at last. But there is also joy over those who have maintained a condition of righteousness by always and regularly turning to God in repentance (1 Yn 1:9), who do not need the thorough and soul-shaking experience of repentance which a lost person, a "lost sheep," often goes through when he turns to God from a life pattern of sin. Clearly Yeshua does not regard the grumbling *P'rushim* and *Torah*-teachers to whom he is speaking (v. 2) as having maintained such a condition of righteousness; so he is trying to shake their mistaken supposition that righteousness can consist in following a set of rules apart from genuinely trusting God in one's heart (compare Yn 9:40–41&NN).

8 A Greek **drachma** was approximately equal to a Roman denarius, a laborer's daily wage.

11–32 The parable of the Prodigal Son who leaves his loving father with his fortune, squanders it and then returns home in repentance is so widely referred to that those unfamiliar with the New Testament are often surprised to learn that the story originates here. Some say its only point is that the love of the father (i.e., God) is so all-embracing that he joyfully welcomes anyone who turns to him from sin. Certainly the parable shares this theme with the previous two.

But in vv. 25–32 we see the "older son," who considers himself righteous but rejects his father's generosity by resenting the reason for which it is offered. Some take the older son to be "the Jews" and the younger "the Gentiles," but context makes it more reasonable to think of the older son as anyone who supposes God owes him something, and the younger as anyone who knows he has sinned and therefore throws himself on God's mercy, accepting Yeshua as his only hope for salvation and forgiveness.

15 What is a nice Jewish boy doing, feeding **pigs**? Well, he's not so nice any more, and, for that matter, not so Jewish either. He left his Jewish father and home and went to "a distant country" (v. 13), where the people were Gentiles and therefore had no compunction about raising pigs. He assimilated himself into that culture, first living recklessly and now of necessity performing that society's less pleasant tasks.

What does it mean to "stop being Jewish"? Consider that the word "Jew" is the English transliteration of Hebrew *Y'hudi*, from the root "*yadah*," which means "to give thanks, to praise, to confess openly and freely." To be a true Jew is to be someone who gives thanks to God, praises God, and confesses God, his Word, his truth and his love, openly and freely, who is in a close relationship with him (compare Ro 2:28–29N). This is what *Adonai* meant when he said to the Israelites, "I will take you to me for a people, and I will be to you for a God" (Exodus 34:7).

Assimilation is a serious problem today; intermarriage rates in some American Jewish communities exceed 50%. But the essence of assimilation is not intermarriage, nor is its root cause lack of Jewish education. Rather, it is a lack of closeness to God, obtained truly through his Messiah Yeshua, so that the individual Jew can thank, praise and confess him.

A Jew who comes to faith in Yeshua frequently becomes far more interested in his own Jewishness, not less so. Least of all should one think of assimilation as leaving the Jewish community to become a Christian; on the contrary, accepting the Jewish Messiah Yeshua and believing God's word, written by Jews, is as Jewish an act as a Jew can do.

No Jew has to "feed pigs." He can come home to Father as soon as he realizes he ought to — see the rest of the parable.

Raphael Patai cites a Hasidic story with many similar details but in the service of a different moral, the importance of not having "little trust" (Mt 8:26), especially in "hastening the end" (2 Ke 3:12&N):

> "A parable about a prince who sinned. And his father expelled him from his house. And he went erring about, aimlessly, in the company of cardplayers and drunkards. And all the time he sank lower and lower. Finally he joined a group of peasant villagers. Of their bread he ate and at their work he worked.

One day the king sent one of his lords to search for his son, for perhaps he had improved his ways and was worthy of being returned to his father's house. The lord found him plowing in the field. And he asked him: 'Do you recognize me?' 'Yes,' answered the prince. And the lord said: 'And what is your request of your father the king? I shall tell him.' The prince answered, 'How good would it be if my father took pity on me and sent me a garment like those the peasants wear, and also heavy shoes which are suitable for a villager.' 'O, you fool, you fool,' cried the lord, 'it would have been better for you to ask of your father that he should take you back to his house and his palace. Is, perchance, anything lacking in the house of the king?'

"Thus they [the Jews] cry, 'Give us this and give us that....' It would be better to request and to pray that He should lead us back to our country and build our Temple, and there we shall have everything we need." (Abraham S. B. H. Michelsohn, *Sefer Shemen haTov* ("The Book of Good Oil"), Piotrkov, 1905, p. 142, as translated and quoted in *The Messiah Texts*, p. 79)

21 The son began his prepared recitation confessing his sins; but the father, reading his heart (16:15&N, Yn 2:25), didn't even wait till he was finished (Isaiah 65:24) before receiving him as fully his son once more.

28 **Pleaded**. The father has not given up on his petulant and self-righteous older son but entreats him lovingly and courteously.

32 The parable leaves open whether the older son will respond to his father's appeal. In present-day reality whether self-righteous people will respond to God's salvation offer also remains open; "it is not his purpose that anyone should be destroyed, but that everyone should turn from his sins" (2 Ke 3:9).

CHAPTER 16

8 ***Sekhel***, "common sense, practical intelligence, 'smarts'" in both Hebrew and Yiddish. "**Have more *sekhel*"** translates Greek *phronimôteroi eisin*, "are more prudent." Yeshua is not praising this corrupt manager's goal of "looking out for Number One," but his cleverness and intelligence in pursuing his mistaken goal. Further, his comment that the worldly are more creative in working toward their aims than those enlightened by trusting God are in pursuing the goals God has set forth for them seems to be true today as well as then. Many well-intentioned people are bound, when seeking solutions, by lack of imagination, freedom and grounding in reality.

9 Yeshua urges his followers not to use the materials of this world in a wicked way but for noble ends, so that their **friends**, God the Father and Yeshua the Son, may welcome them into the **eternal home**, just as the manager can expect his newly purchased "friends" to welcome him into their worldly homes.

11 Worldly wealth, literally, "unrighteous *mammon*" (Greek *mammônas*, transliterating Aramaic *mammona* and Hebrew *mammon*, "wealth, riches").

14 They ridiculed him, literally, "they turned up their noses at him."

15–18 Some commentators regard these four verses as disconnected remarks placed together by an editor. I see them as Yeshua's response to the Pharisees' reaction (v. 14) to his parable and teaching (vv. 1–13). Verses 15–18 are therefore all connected, and connected with the following story (vv. 19–31); note especially that vv. 16 and 31 deal with the *Torah* and the Prophets (see v. 16N). Thus there is a cumulative effect to what Yeshua is saying, with v. 18 presenting a telling example of how the *Torah* cannot become void, all the more when the Kingdom of God, God's active present rulership, is so near (see v. 18N).

15 God knows your hearts (as did Yeshua himself, Yn 2:25). Compare 1 Samuel 16:7, "A man looks on the outward appearance, but *Adonai* looks on the heart"; and 1 Chronicles 28:9, "*Adonai* searches all hearts and understands all the imaginations of the thoughts."

16 Up to the time of Yochanan the Immerser **there were the *Torah* and the Prophets** giving their prophetic and predictive witness to the coming of **the Kingdom of God**. The verse does not mean that the authority of the *Torah* and the Prophets came to an end when Yochanan appeared (an error even the notable Hebrew Christian thinker David Baron made). But **since then**, in addition to their witness (v. 31, Yn 5:46, Ro 3:21), **the Good News of the Kingdom of God**, which is now "near," **has been proclaimed** directly, first by Yochanan (Mt 3:1–2) and now by Yeshua (Mt 4:17, Mk 1:15), with the result that **everyone is pushing to get in**.

18 See Mt 19:3–9&N on **divorce**; but this pronouncement of Yeshua's is not primarily a teaching on divorce. Rather, it is an example demonstrating that the *Torah* and the Prophets continue to have authoritative force, as v. 17 has explicitly stated. The *P'rushim* are not to use their position of power to interpret Scripture in ways that contradict its intent.

22 Avraham's side. A rare phrase in early Jewish writing, but not unknown. The *talmid* whom Yeshua loved reclined at his side at the Last Supper (Yn 13:23–25). A Jewish work dating from around the time of Yeshua says, "After this suffering of ours, Avraham, Yitzchak and Ya'akov will receive us, and all our ancestors will praise us" (4 Maccabees 13:17). Thus being at "Avraham's side" suggests both being in *Gan-Eden* (Paradise) and being present at the Messianic banquet (Mt 8:11, Rv 19:7–9).

23 Sh'ol, Greek *Adês*, the "place" of the dead until the final judgment. It is not wholly a place of punishment, but from this passage we learn that it includes one. In the end Sh'ol itself will be thrown into the lake of fire (Rv 20:13–15).

26 A deep rift, and no one can cross. Yeshua, like Daniel 12:2, teaches distinct fates after death for the wicked and the righteous. See 14:14&N.

30–31 Moshe (that is, the *Torah*) **and the Prophets**; the phrase means the entire *Tanakh* (compare 24:44–45&N, Mt 5:17&N), which Yeshua says is sufficient to warn people to trust God. Later (24:25–27&N) Yeshua shows specifically how the *Tanakh* points to himself.

CHAPTER 17

3 If your brother sins, rebuke him: advice which goes against the grain of a self-centered and permissive society in which the standard is "I'm OK, you're OK."

If he repents, forgive him. Forgiveness is a command (Mt 6:14–15, 18:21–35); one is to forgive from one's heart, overruling one's feelings if necessary — since this too goes against the grain.

10 We're just ordinary slaves, not deserving of thanks or reward. It is not that God wants the groveling appropriate to slaves, but the absence of pride expected of those who know that obeying him is a matter of **duty.**

12 They stood at a distance because the *Torah* requires people with serious skin diseases to separate themselves from the rest of the people (Leviticus 13:45–46, Numbers 5:2).

14–19 This is an interesting story, and here is one way to understand it. All ten trusted Yeshua enough to obey his command, **"Go and let the *cohanim* examine you"** (v. 14), knowing that examination by a priest was necessary after healing, and they had not been healed yet (see Mt 8:1–4&NN). All ten had enough trust in Yeshua to be healed, but only one showed gratitude to Yeshua and praise to God; his kind of trust not only healed him but **saved** him (v. 19).

16, 18 From Shomron... this foreigner. See 9:53N, 10:33N, Yn 4:9&N.

21 The *P'rushim* of v. 20 expect a physical kingdom whose beginning can be dated with some precision. Yeshua replies by noting that he brings a spiritual kingdom, a spiritual rulership consisting in new modes of relationships among believers. But to his *talmidim* he expands on the subject of the Kingdom and points to a day when he will indeed rule (v. 24; compare Mt 24:30–31).

The Kingdom of God (see Mt 3:2N on "Kingdom of Heaven") **is among you**, or, alternatively, "...within you," referring to the inner change that takes place when people trust in God.

26 See Genesis 6–9.

28 See Genesis 18:16–19, 29.

32 Lot's wife looked back toward Sodom and became a pillar of salt, Genesis 19:26.

37 See Mt 24:28N.

CHAPTER 18

1–7 Yeshua depicts an Oriental judge who can be approached without the bureaucratic entanglements of the modern West, a man without conscience but with a human weakness that ultimately leads him to grant genuine justice in spite of himself. If a corrupt judge finally gives in to a widow's pestering, how much more will God, who is altogether just, respond to his chosen people's continual prayers (as opposed to the widow's occasional visits), such as, "*Adonai,* how long will you look on? Rescue me from their destructions, my only one from the lions" (Psalm 35:17), or, "O God, how long will the adversary insult? Will the enemy blaspheme your name forever?" (Psalm 74:10).

5 **Because this widow is such a *nudnik***, literally, "because this widow causes me trouble, bothers me." The Yiddish word "*nudnik*" means "someone who persistently bores, pesters, nags." It captures precisely the particular kind of bothering and trouble the corrupt judge experiences.

7 **Is he delaying long over them?** It would seem so — the words were spoken nearly two thousand years ago, and the final vindication is yet to come. But 2 Ke 3:8–9 sets things in the right perspective: God is not slack in his dealings with humanity in the sense that people understand the term "slackness," for with him "one day is like a thousand years" (Kefa quotes Psalm 90:4). And God's motive for delaying? To bring people to repentance (Ro 2:4–6).

10–14 Because those who reject the Gospel sometimes accuse evangelists of acting "holier-than-thou," it is noteworthy that it was Isaiah who first used that phrase, referring to Israel in rebellion against God: "[They] say, 'Stand apart, don't come near me, for I am holier than thou'"(Isaiah 65:5). Unfortunately, God's people are susceptible to this most offensive of sins, against which both *Tanakh* and New Testament severely warn, religious pride.

10 The ***Parush*** had high social status, while the **tax-collector** was despised (see Mt 5:46N).

11 **Prayed to himself** and not to God, in spite of his addressing God. He wasn't in contact with God at all but merely boasted and justified himself. Alternatively, "prayed about himself."

12 **I fast twice a week**. There is no evidence that the Pharisees as a group fasted twice a week, although they did fast "frequently" (Mt 9:14). The Talmud speaks of one who "undertakes to fast every Monday and Thursday throughout the year" as not unusual but nevertheless not the norm (Ta'anit 12a). Within the framework of trusting God, fasting was and is a normal part of a believer's life (Isaiah 58:1–12, Mt 6:16–18, 9:14–17).

I pay tithes on my entire income. The requirement to pay ten percent of income is based on Leviticus 27:30–33 and Numbers 18:21–26; and it is discussed in tractate Ma'aserot of the Talmud, which sets forth which products must be tithed and states the principle that only tithed produce may be eaten (thus untithed produce is not *kosher*). The Mishna says, "A person who undertakes to be reliable must tithe what he eats, what he sells and what he buys; and he may not stay as a guest with an *'am-ha'aretz* (an unlearned man)" (Demai 2:2). But in general tithing all of one's income was regarded as beyond the call of duty. I would suppose this *Parush* felt he was doing something special and unique for God, for which God owed him thanks and reward. Such a mentality is, of course, neither peculiar to Pharisees in particular nor unbelievers in general; on the contrary, it is those who consider themselves believers who seem to be especially susceptible to this sort of false pride.

13 **Sinner that I am**, literally, "the sinner." He experienced the depth of his own sin and was utterly remorseful and repentant, and as a result God forgave him (v. 14).

15 **People brought him babies to touch**. Yeshua was to lay hands on them and bless them. See Mk 10:16N.

18–19 See Mk 10:18N.

20 Yeshua cites the sixth through ninth and the fifth of the Ten Commandments (see Mt 5:21N), the ones concerning relationships with other people.

22–23 **Sell whatever you have** and **distribute the proceeds to the poor**. Rabbi Yitzchak of Troki, the sixteenth-century Karaite polemicist whose *Chizzuk-Emunah* remains the most comprehensive summary of traditional Judaism's arguments against the New Testament, writes that although Christians claim the Law of Moses was too demanding and Yeshua's law is easier to observe, his decree that this young ruler should give away his entire inheritance to the poor is far more strict than the *Torah*, which requires only that he give a tenth of the income the inheritance produces and nothing from the capital.

But why should Rav Yitzchak assume that Yeshua's prescription for this man was intended for everyone? A doctor does not ask all his patients to take the same medicine. Yeshua was making known not God's will for all men at all times, but his will for this man then. The man **became very sad** precisely because he had a different will of his own. On the other hand, for those whose attachment to their wealth stands in the way of their faith God's will today may be the same as for this rich man.

You will have riches in heaven. Compare Sirach 29:11, "Lay up treasure for yourself according to the commands of the Most High, and it will bring you more profit than gold."

38 See Mt 1:1N on **Son of David**.

CHAPTER 19

1 **Zakkai**. The name, ironically, means "innocent" in Hebrew. On **tax-collector** see Mt 5:46N.

8 **Four times as much**. When a person confessed to fraud and made voluntary restitution the *Torah* required him to return the amount stolen plus twenty percent (Leviticus 5:20–24(6:1–5), Numbers 5:5–7). An apprehended thief had to pay the victim double (Exodus 22:3, 6(4, 7)). But a man stealing what is essential and showing no pity was required to pay back fourfold (Exodus 21:37(22:1), 2 Samuel 12:6). Zakkai, fully repentant, not only acknowledged the heartlessness and cruelty of his behavior but voluntarily imposed upon himself the whole restitution required by the *Torah* for such acts.

9 **Salvation**, Hebrew *yeshu'ah*, which is the feminine form of Yeshua's own name. Thus there is a wordplay: Yeshua/salvation has literally **come to this house** (compare 2:30&N, Mt 1:21&N).

10 **To seek... what was lost**, as in Chapter 15, and echoing Ezekiel 34:16, where God seeks his lost sheep.

35 Yeshua on the colt entering Yerushalayim fulfills the prophecy of Zechariah 9:9, quoted at Mt 21:5; see Mt 21:2–7N.

38 See Mt 21:9N.

43 This mode of punishment for Yerushalayim is spoken of in Isaiah 29:3, Jeremiah 6:6 and Ezekiel 4:2. The very explicit prophecy of this and the following verse was fulfilled in the Roman conquest of Yerushalayim, 66–70 C.E. With v. 43 compare 21:20 below; with v. 44 compare Mt 24:2, Mk 13:2.

45 See Mt 21:12N.

CHAPTER 20

2 ***S'mikhah***. See Mt 21:23N.

9 **Vineyard**. See Yn 15:1N.

10–12 Compare 2 Chronicles 36:14–16.

16 **Heaven forbid!** See Ro 3:4N.

18 **Whoever falls on that stone**, Yeshua, **will be broken in pieces**, his erect pride will be done away with, and in his humiliation he may recognize his sin and need for forgiveness, so that he repents. **But if** he persists in his own way, apart from God, and the stone **falls on him he will be crushed to powder**, totally destroyed (compare Yn 3:16). Less traumatic than either is to accept the stone without having to fall or be crushed.

A *midrash* in the Talmud uses similar imagery:

> "'And they stood under the mount' (Exodus 19:17). Rabbi Abdimi ben-Chama said: This teaches that the Holy One, blessed be He, turned the mountain upside down over them like an inverted cask, and said to them, 'If you accept the *Torah*, it will be good. But if not, this will be your burial place!'"(Shabbat 88a)

That is when the people said, "We will do and we will hear" (Exodus 24:7), obligating themselves to obey the whole *Torah* even before they knew what it required.

20 As an excuse to hand him over to... the governor for expressing anti-Roman sentiment. By adding this phrase (Mattityahu and Mark do not have it) Luke makes their deviousness explicit.

21 ***sh'eilah*** ("question"). See Mt 22:23N.

28 See Mt 22:24N.

46 See Mk 12:38N.

47 ***Davvening*** ("praying"). See Mk 12:40N.

CHAPTER 21

20–23 Here Yeshua predicts the destruction of Yerushalayim by the Roman armies in 66–70 C.E. The **days of vengeance** (v. 22) are spoken of in Deuteronomy 32:35 as the time when *Adonai* "will judge his people" for being wicked and forsaking him; however, the context there is that ultimately God will "forgive his land and his people" (Deuteronomy 32:43). Such vengeance is also spoken of in Jeremiah 46:10 and Hosea 9:7.

Although the historical evidence is not absolute, it is widely thought that the Messianic Jews of Jerusalem heeded Yeshua's words here and moved in 66 C.E. to Pehel (Pella), east of the Jordan River. It is also understood that this act of foresight based on the Messiah's own warning and instruction was taken by the non-Messianic Jews as an act of disloyalty to the nation in time of war, and it became a major cause for resenting Jewish believers and taking sanctions against them.

One such sanction was the *Birkat-HaMinim* ("blessing relating to the *minim*"), twelfth of the nineteen blessings in the *'Amidah*. In its present form it says nothing about Messianic Jews:

> "For the slanderers let there be no hope. Let all wickedness perish in an instant. May all your enemies be quickly cut off. Uproot, break, throw down and humble

the kingdom of arrogance speedily, in our days. Blessed are you, *Adonai*, who breaks enemies and humbles the arrogant."

But the Talmud says that the original form of this blessing had, instead of "*lamalshinim*" ("for the slanderers"), the term "*laminim*" ("for the sectarians"), understood to be heretics in general or Messianic Jews in particular (see Mt 22:31–32N):

> "The *Birkat-HaMinim* was instituted in Yavneh [in the general council of rabbis around 90 C.E.].... It was composed by [Rabbi] Shmu'el HaKatan.... If a *chazan* [leader of synagogue prayers] makes a mistake in any other of the blessings they do not remove him, but if he makes a mistake when saying the *Birkat-HaMinim* they remove him because he is suspected of being a *min* himself." (B'rakhot 28b)

The Talmud is clear and explicit about how the *Birkat-HaMinim* could be used against Messianic Jews. A Messianic Jew could gladly and gratefully pray the other eighteen blessings of the *'Amidah*, but he could hardly invoke a curse on himself. Persons not reciting the *Birkat-HaMinim* were suspected of *minut* and subject to *cherem* (exclusion from the community; see Yn 9:22&N).

The *Encyclopedia Judaica* (4:1035f.) says that Shmu'el HaKatan revised a previously existing blessing that had been used against the Gnostics, the Sadducees and the Roman Empire as well as the Messianic Jews.

24 Many believe the prophetic message in the final part of this verse has been fulfilled in our own days, after nearly two thousand years. If so, it constitutes a powerful argument for believing in Yeshua.

The verse's opening passage, "**Some will fall by the edge of the sword**," was initially fulfilled in the rebellion of 66–70, when over a million Jews may have perished (see below). Moreover, its fulfillment was grievously repeated throughout history, often by those who called themselves Christians and claimed to be acting in the name of the Jewish Messiah. The phrase, "the edge of the sword." is found also in Jeremiah 21:7 and Sirach 28:18 (in the Apocrypha).

The second clause, "**Others will be carried into all the countries of the *Goyim*,**" could stand as a heading for a history of the Jewish Diaspora. Josephus (*Wars of the Jews* 6:9:3) states that 1,100,000 Jews were slain and 97,000 carried away captive as slaves by the Romans in the war of 66–70. The Diaspora is predicted as early as in the words of Moses (Deuteronomy 28:63–68) and dates at least to the Assyrian conquest of Israel (722 B.C.E.) and the Babylonian Captivity (586 B.C.E.; see Ezra 9:7). But the Roman slaughter and destruction brought the Jewish nation to an end: the Diaspora, in a national sense, had previously been partial; now and in the Second Rebellion (132–135 C.E.) it became all but total.

And Yerushalayim will be trampled down by the *Goyim* until the age (literally, "seasons") **of the *Goyim* has run its course**. Consider this prophecy in the light of Psalm 79:1 ("O God, *Goyim* have come into your inheritance; they have defiled your holy Temple; they have laid Yerushalayim in heaps"), Isaiah 63:18 ("...our adversaries have trampled down your sanctuary") and Daniel 9:26 ("After sixty-two sevens Messiah will be cut off, with nothing left to him; and the people of a prince yet to come will destroy the city and the sanctuary....").

The Romans permitted Jews to continue living in Jerusalem after 70 C.E., but in the wake of the Second Rebellion under the false messiah Shim'on Bar-Kosiba all Jews were expelled, and the city, now entirely Gentile, was renamed Aelia Capitolina. (However, Jews continued to live in B'nei-B'rak, Yavneh, Tzippori, Tiberias and other locations throughout the Land of Israel. In fact, there has been a Jewish presence in *Eretz-Israel* continuously since the time of King David.)

Roman rule continued until 324, the Byzantine Empire controlled Jerusalem until 614 and the Persians governed briefly until 629. In 638 Muslim Arabs conquered the Holy City; and the Ummayads, ruling from Damascus, built the Dome of the Rock mosque on what was believed to be the site of the Jewish Temple, completing it in 691. The Abbasid Arabs took over in 750; their capital was Baghdad. The Egyptians imposed their rule in 878. The Crusaders, thinking they were acting in the name of Yeshua, came to the Holy Land in 1096 "to reclaim it from the infidels." In 1099 they not only defeated the Muslims but massacred all the Jews they could find. The Crusaders in turn were driven out in 1187 by the Kurdish Ayyubid leader Salach-ed-Din (Saladin).

Battles between Crusaders and Muslim Arabs continued until 1244, with dominion being established by the Egyptian Mamluks in 1250; formerly military slaves of the Ayyubids, they had overthrown their masters. Suleiman (= Solomon) the Great displaced them in 1517, and his Ottoman Turks held sway in the Holy Land for 400 years until they were defeated by Britain's General Allenby in World War I. The British Mandate given by the League of Nations lasted until 1948, when, in the wake of the Nazi Holocaust, the world's conscience was momentarily pricked enough to permit the State of Israel to be established by a just-over-two-thirds vote of the United Nations General Assembly. By the U. N. plan of 1947 Jerusalem was to have been an internationalized city, but when five Arab countries attacked Israel within hours of her independence she fought back and conquered the western, more modern part of Jerusalem. Nevertheless the Old City of Jerusalem, the portion the present verse speaks about, which includes the Temple site, was occupied by Jordan until the Six-Day War. On June 8, 1967, the Israeli army entered the Old City and converged on the Western ("Wailing") Wall, liberating Yerushalayim at last.

Many regard that as the moment when Yeshua's prophecy was fulfilled — 1,897 years of Gentile rule over Yerushalayim came to an end, and she is no longer "trampled down by the *Goyim*," because "the age of the *Goyim* has run its course"; at last Yeshua's words have come true. Others date the fulfillment from Israel's 1980 proclamation that Jerusalem is a united city under Israeli sovereignty. Still others will not consider it fulfilled until Muslims no longer control the Temple Mount.

Those who adhere to Replacement theology — also called Covenant theology, Dominion theology, Kingdom Now theology, Christian Reconstructionism, and (in England) Restorationism — hold that the Church is the "new" or "spiritual" Israel, having replaced the "old" Israel, the Jews, as God's people. According to this view the Jewish people no longer have promises from God, only curses; therefore they deny any significance after 70 C.E. to the "times of the Gentiles." The falseness of this interpretation follows logically if Replacement theology itself is refuted — for which see references in Mt 5:5N.

In the Talmud a lengthy series of speculations on when the Messiah will come includes the following paragraph, which resembles Yeshua's prediction in the present verse:

> "Rabbi Chama bar-Chanina said, 'The Son of David will not come until even the pettiest [*hazola*] kingdom stops having power over Israel, for it is written, "He will cut off the shoots [*hazalzalim*, a related word, understood here as a metaphor for "petty kingdoms"] with pruning hooks, and he will hew down and remove the branches." And this is followed by, "In that time shall *Adonai* of heaven's armies be presented with the gift of a people scattered and peeled" (Isaiah 18:5, 7).'"(Sanhedrin 98a)

What follows may seem a digression, but it is tied to the present verse by the concept of waiting two thousand years to see something happen. Messianic Jews hold that Messianic Judaism is the modern continuation of a Jewish stream which began in the first century with the Jewish followers of Yeshua. Opponents claim we ignore the intervening centuries of historical conflict between the Church and the Jewish people — as Israel High Court Justice Meir Shamgar wrote in the Esther Dorflinger verdict:

> "For this purpose [to convince the Court she was a Jew entitled to make *aliyah* (immigrate) under Israel's Law of Return] she made exaggerations with long and tortuous arguments concerning the possibilities of her being a Jew who believes in Jesus' being the Messiah, as if we are still living in the beginning of the first century of the Christian Era, as if since then nothing had occurred in all that relates to the crystallization of the religious frameworks and the separation from Judaism of all those who chose another path." (Israel High Court of Justice Case #563/77)

I have two comments. First, the entire Zionist enterprise has had a virtually identical premise. For two thousand years the Jews had no home in *Eretz-Israel*. Those who opposed Zionism criticized its "long and tortuous arguments concerning the possibilities of" recreating a Jewish state, "as if we were still living in the first century of the Christian Era, as if since then nothing had occurred in all that relates to the crystallization of" political, social and "religious frameworks." Fortunately, the anti-Zionists were wrong — as is Justice Shamgar. (My thanks to Israeli Messianic Jews Menahem Benhayim and Ari Sorko-Ram, who both suggested this parallel.)

Second, if "religious frameworks" have "crystallized" in a way that separates "from Judaism all who chose another path," then it is a task of Messianic Judaism to persuade Christians and Jews alike to decrystallize the frameworks so as to bring them into line with reality. Jews who honor Yeshua remain Jewish. It is God who made us Jewish; and neither the rabbis, the Jewish people nor Israel's High Court of Justice can overrule God's reality and de-Jew us.

25 Signs in the sun, moon and stars. Understand this to refer to the Great Day of *Adonai* (Joel 3:1–5(2:28–32), Isaiah 13:9–10).

27 Son of Man. See Mt 8:20N. At his second coming Yeshua will fulfill the remaining unfulfilled prophecies of the *Tanakh* concerning him.

32 This people. See Mt 24:34N.

CHAPTER 22

1 The festival of *Matzah*, known as *Pesach*. See Mt 26:2N, Mk 14:1N.

3 The Adversary (see Mt 4:1N) **went into Y'hudah**. God's Adversary can act through people who by their sin and failure to turn to God open themselves to the influence of him and his demons (Mt 4:24N, 12:43–45). From such an entrenched position he can influence people to carry out his will and oppose God's will.

7 The day of *matzah*. Not the day on which *matzah* is first eaten, but the day before *Pesach* begins, when *chametz* ("leaven") must be removed from the house. See Mt 26:17N.

On which the Passover lamb had to be killed in the Temple Court. The laws of Passover then mandated slaughtering and eating a lamb to memorialize the lamb slain and consumed by each family the night of the Exodus from Egypt (Exodus 12:3–14). After the Temple was destroyed in 70 C.E. and it became impossible to slaughter a lamb there, the custom arose of placing a lamb shankbone on the *Seder* plate at each family table to recall the sacrifice. Today, some Sephardic traditions allow or even mandate a lamb entrée at Passover; but the Ashkenazic custom is to avoid eating lamb, since it cannot be slaughtered at the Temple.

8 *Seder*. See Mt 26:17N.

10 A man carrying a jar of water. An unusual sight, as this was ordinarily women's work.

11 Where I am to celebrate *Pesach* with my *talmidim*. A rabbi's follower would consider it an honor to have his rabbi request the use of his home for him and his students to observe Passover.

12 Furnished, already outfitted with what was needed for the Passover meal.

14 Reclined. See Mt 26:20N.

16 Given its full meaning, Greek *plêrôsai*, sometimes translated figuratively as "fulfilled"; but see Mt 5:17N. Yeshua at this meal, the "Last Supper," added considerably to the familiar symbolism of *Pesach* (vv. 17–20&NN). The final and fullest meaning for *Pesach* will be revealed after the return of Yeshua the Messiah to rule in glory.

17a A cup of wine. Luke is the only one of the four writers describing the establishing of the New Covenant (*B'rit Chadashah*) who mentions both a cup of wine before the meal (here) and another after (v. 20); compare Mt 26:26–29, Mk 14:22–25, Sha'ul at 1C 11:23–25, and see also Yn 6:51–58, 13:1–20. The *Seder* requires four cups of wine, two before the meal and two after. Each is identified with one of God's promises in Exodus 6:6–7:

> "Therefore say to the children of Israel: 'I am *Adonai*, and (1) I will bring you out from under the burdens of Egypt; (2) I will deliver you out of their bondage; (3) I will redeem you with an outstretched arm and great judgments; and (4) I will take you to me for a people, and I will be to you a God.'"

The cup of this verse must have been the first or second one, since the breaking of bread (v. 19) comes just after the second cup. The third cup is mentioned in v. 20&N.

17b–18 Made the *b'rakhah*... "fruit of the vine." See Mt 26:27–29N.

19 See Mt 26:26N on the breaking of the middle **piece of *matzah*** for the *afikoman* and how this represents the death of Yeshua the Messiah.

20 The cup after the meal, the third of the four cups (see v. 17aN), corresponding to Exodus 6:6, "I will redeem you." Thus Yeshua used the "cup of redemption," as the third cup is called, to inaugurate the **new covenant,** which redeems from the "Egypt" of bondage to sin all who trust in God and his Messiah. The New Covenant is spoken of in the *Tanakh* at Jeremiah 31:30–33(31–34), but Greek *kainê diathêkê* can also be rendered "renewed covenant" (Mt 9:17N). Even though it is "not like" the Covenant through Moshe (Jeremiah 31:31(32)), the New Covenant renews and restores what the Mosaic Covenant promised to the Jewish people. For more see Mt 26:28N, MJ 8:8–13&NN.

Ratified by my blood. Biblical covenants were always ratified by shed blood (Genesis 8:20–9:17, 15:7–21; Exodus 24:3–8).

One of the horrendous manifestations of Christian antisemitism was the infamous "blood libel" against the Jews, in which Jews were accused of murdering a Christian baby in order to use the blood in the Passover service! Many Jewish lives were lost as a result of the inflamed feelings of non-Jews against Jews produced by this patent falsehood. I know of no evidence that blood libel arose because Yeshua gave the Passover wine the significance of blood. On the contrary, it is well known that the laws of *kashrut* prohibit Jews from drinking blood (this impinges on the New Testament at Yn 6:51–66&N, Ac 15:20&N). See the article, "Blood Libel," in *Encyclopedia Judaica*, 4:1120–1131.

22 The Son of Man is going to his death according to God's plan, literally, "as it has been determined." See Mt 1:22N on the significance of prophecy fulfillment; Mt 26:24N lists not less than twenty *Tanakh* passages prophesying that the Messiah would suffer and die for the sins of mankind and be raised from the dead. His death establishes the New Covenant, which itself fulfills a *Tanakh* prophecy (v. 20&N).

24–30 Yeshua resolved the **argument… as to which of them should be considered the greatest** with two points. First, the Kingdom of God functions differently from worldly kingdoms; those who would be great must be not power-seekers but servants (vv. 25–27) like Yeshua himself (v. 27; Mk 10:41–45; Yn 13:4–5, 12–17). Second, those who have been loyal (v. 28) will indeed be rewarded with power (vv. 29–30). Yeshua does not condemn ambition, only its worldly aims and methods.

31 **To sift you like wheat**, to put you through trials as he did Job. In sifting the wheat is shaken as the chaff is separated; Yeshua alludes to future testings for the emissaries. Compare Amos 9:9, which speaks of Israel's being "sifted" by God.

32 **Once you have turned back in repentance**, literally, "when you have turned again" or "turned around" or "turned back." KJV's "when thou art converted" speaks to the modern ear of conversion to a religion, perhaps even from Judaism to Christianity (which is, of course, on principle anachronistic in New Testament times, since Christianity as such did not exist then). But in Judaism "turning" (*t'shuvah*) is not conversion but repentance (see Mt 3:2N). Here it refers to Kefa's returning to unshakable trust after denying Yeshua three times (vv. 34, 54–62).

Strengthen your brothers. Compare Yn 21:15–17. Kefa fulfilled this commission gloriously in the early Messianic Community (see Acts 1–15).

35–38 Henceforth the emissaries will still be protected, but the circumstances will differ. Prudence and practical considerations will play a more important role: **wallet, pack** and a Roman short **sword** are to be standard equipment, especially on the road, where highwaymen pose a threat to life itself.

37 **He was counted with the transgressors**. Yeshua applies this phrase from Isaiah 53:12 to himself. For more on Isaiah 52:13–53:12, the *Tanakh* passage that most clearly prophesies the Messiah's first coming, see Ac 8:34N.

What is happening to me has a purpose. Or: "what is written about me [in the *Tanakh*] has its fulfillment."

38 **"Enough!"** Yeshua is not inventorying his disciples' arsenal but saying, "You have taken me too literally. I'm not talking about swords. End the conversation! Enough already!"

41 **Knelt down and prayed**. Except for the *'Aleinu* prayer when recited on *Rosh-HaShanah* and *Yom-Kippur*, Jews no longer kneel to pray because they regard the custom as alien — to be specific, as Christian. But Christianity adopted it from Judaism! The *Tanakh* gives many examples of Jews kneeling in prayer (e.g., Psalm 95:6, Daniel 6:11(10), 2 Chronicles 6:13); indeed Hebrew *b'rakhah* ("blessing") comes from *berekh* ("knee").

42 **Not my will but yours.** If Yeshua the Messiah and God the Father are one (Yn 10:30), how could their wills ever differ? They can differ because Yeshua, even though "in the form of God,… appeared as a human being" and became "obedient even to death" (Pp 2:6–8). As a human being Yeshua was "in every respect… tempted just as we are, the only difference being that he did not sin" (MJ 4:15). "Even though he was the Son, he learned obedience through his sufferings" (MJ 5:8). It was as a human being, not as God, that he experienced the process of learning to conform his will to his Father's will, since as God, who is omniscient, he did not need to "learn."

As Yeshua prayed in the *Gat-Sh'manim* garden on the Mount of Olives, he was exposed to the temptation of not being executed on the stake but letting himself be rescued by "a dozen armies of angels" (Mt 26:53). Nevertheless he subjected himself to the will of God the Father. Every believer in Yeshua is expected to make his obedience his model, drawing on the power of the Holy Spirit to conform ever more closely to it (2C 3:17–18).

47–54 This report of Yeshua's arrest is truncated. Further details are found in Yn 18:1–12, Mt 26:47–50; Mk 14:42–52.

51 **Just let me do this**. Or (to his *talmidim*): "Stop! No more of this [resistance]!" Or: "Let them [the officers of the Temple guard] do what they came to do." The Greek is consistent with any of these renderings.

66 In this case the **people's council of elders** seems to refer not to a separate group but to the *Sanhedrin* members who met to discuss what to do with Yeshua. **The *sanhedrin*** then refers to the building where they met. See Mt 5:22N. On ***cohanim*** and ***Torah*-teachers** see Mt 2:4N.

67–70 See Mk 14:61–62N.

67 ***Mashiach***, Greek *Christos*. See Mt 1:1N on "Messiah."

69 **At the right hand... of God**. Yeshua applies Psalm 110:1 to himself. See Paragraph (7) of MJ 1:2–3N and Mt 22:44N.

70 **You say I am**, literally, "You say," with the same import here as the modern English idiom, "You said it!" Yeshua's meaning here is, "Yes, I am indeed the Son of God, just as you have asked in your question." That Yeshua's inquirers understood him is clear from their response in v. 71. See also 23:3N.

CHAPTER 23

1 **The whole *Sanhedrin***, literally, "the multitude of them." The context (22:66–71) shows that it is the *Sanhedrin*.

Pilate. See Mt 27:2N.

3 **King of the Jews**. Or: "king of the Judeans." In favor of the latter is the fact that Pilate was governor of Judea only, so that for him "our nation" could very well have meant only "the Judeans." This could explain why in v. 5 the elders tailor their accusation to his frame of reference: "He started in the Galil," which you, Pilate, do not rule, and which, for you, is not relevant, "and now he's here," that is, "throughout all Judea," which makes him very relevant indeed. Verses 6–7 then support "king of the

Judeans," inasmuch as there Pilate, on learning that Yeshua is from the Galil, sends him to Herod in the hope that Herod can find some reason for dealing with him. But Herod finds no cause of action, since Yeshua is accused of being king not of the Galileans but of the Judeans, so he is sent back to Pilate. On the other hand, and to my mind the more weighty argument, is the context, which favors "king of the Jews." The mention of "our nation" in v. 2 and of the Galil in v. 5 suggests a broader geographical reference than Judea — along with the points made in Mt 2:2N.

The words are yours. The Greek is the same as five verses above (see 22:70&N). Here Yeshua means that Pilate has hit upon the truth.

7 **Herod** Antipas. See Mt 14:1N.

23–25 Some argue that Pilate's protestations against putting Yeshua to death (vv. 14–16) show that he did not really want to do it, and that therefore little blame rests with him. To this is added the argument that Yeshua himself says there is one whose blame in the matter is greater than Pilate's (Yn 19:11&N). If these arguments are true, they support antisemitism: the Jews and not the Gentiles (as represented by Pilate) are responsible for the death of Jesus.

But in these verses Luke takes pain to show just how weak-willed and unconcerned for justice Pilate was. The **yelling** and **shouting** of a mob **prevailed** over him. He **decided** (the Greek can mean "passed judgment") **to grant their demand** rather than the righteous demand of justice. He **released** a man whose black character Luke paints with the words "**insurrection and murder**." And he **surrendered** not only his feeble intentions but his commission under Rome and under God (for Genesis 9:5–6, which establishes human government to protect human life, applies to Gentiles as well as to Jews) not to the **will** of the Jewish people but to the will of an unruly crowd. Thus Luke makes clear that Pilate's share of guilt is great.

26–31 See Appendix, page 933.

26 **Grabbed hold of a man from Cyrene**. No Roman soldier would think of carrying a sentenced criminal's cross, nor would any Jew willingly do so. Yeshua's strength apparently gave out; the soldiers pressed into service the first adequate person they could find.

30 Since the citing of a Bible quotation in a Jewish text is meant to call to mind the entire context of the passage, it is worthwhile considering all of the tenth chapter of the prophet Hosea. In it Israel is described as a "luxuriant vine," very prosperous (v. 1), but ungrateful to God (v. 2). Therefore, says Hosea, "Surely now they will say, 'We have no king because we did not fear *Adonai*. And as for the king, what can he do for us?'"(v. 3); given distrust of God and his son, what good can King Yeshua do? "They swear falsely,… their judgment springs up like hemlock" (v. 4), like poison, as when the irregular meeting of *Sanhedrin* members illegally condemned Yeshua. As punishment, "Israel will be ashamed" (v. 6), so that "they will say to the mountains, 'Cover us!' and to the hills, 'Fall on us!'"(v. 8) rather than suffer such shame. Not only that, but "When it is my desire," that is, God's desire, "I will punish them, and the peoples," the Gentile nations, "will be gathered against them" (v. 10). The solution for a people in such a miserable state is to "Sow for yourselves according to righteousness, reap according to mercy, break up your fallow ground; for it is time to seek *Adonai*" (v. 12). In other words, repent, return to God. The advice is sound for all eras, as much in our own day as in Yeshua's or Hosea's, especially in the light of v. 31 of our present text, which says that if such terrible things happen when the wood is green and cannot burn well, that is, on the day when innocent Yeshua is put to death as a criminal, how much worse it will become as the years pass and resentment of the Messiah and his followers hardens (especially when that resentment is inflamed by evil deeds done in the Messiah's name by those claiming to be his followers). See Appendix, page 933.

33 KJV renders Greek *kranion* (**skull**) by the word "Calvary," which means nothing in English but is an adaptation of Latin *calvaria*, "bare skull."

34 Yeshua said, "Father, forgive them: they don't understand what they are doing." Antisemites cannot stand this verse, for it destroys the ground on which they suppose they stand. They would rather remember Mt 27:25, where the rabble brought together by those Jewish leaders intent on destroying Yeshua usurped authority to announce, "His blood is on us, even on our children!" They cannot bear to think that the Messiah Yeshua asked his father to forgive those Jewish brothers of his, specifically on the ground that they were ignorant of the significance of what they were doing. It is the shame of the Christian Church through the centuries that many who claimed to be speaking in the Jewish Messiah's name could still bring a charge of "deicide" against the Jewish people, sanctimoniously anchoring their accusation in Scripture (Mt 27:25) while failing to imitate the Messiah (1C 11:1) in forgiving those who were unaware of what their acts and shouts meant. How much more severe must be the punishment of those who knowingly violated Yeshua's own condition for salvation, "If you do not forgive others their offences, your heavenly Father will not forgive yours" (Mt 6:15; compare Mt 18:35).

Some early manuscripts lack this verse, but the weight of scholarly opinion favors the view that Yeshua did indeed say these words.

There is also an interpretation which says that these words did not apply to the Jews at all but to the Gentile Roman soldiers, since vv. 32–34 are about them. But the particular Jews who had a hand in seeing that he was put to death were as much unaware of what they were doing as the Roman soldiers; indeed, the *talmidim*, who had been told at least three times exactly what would happen by Yeshua himself (9:21–22, 44–45; 18:31–34), were likewise entirely undone when it did happen. Also note the parallel with Ac 7:60, where the same author, Luke, reports that Stephen similarly asked God's forgiveness for the *Sanhedrin* members, obviously Jewish, who were at that moment stoning him to death.

Did God answer Yeshua's prayer? Did he forgive these Jews? The answer is "Yes," but we must understand that he forgave specific sins, not all their sins. On the ground of their unawareness of what they were actually doing, God forgave them the sin of judging Yeshua a criminal worthy of death and possibly even the sin of complicity in having him executed (this is arguable). But he did not grant them salvation, forgiveness for all their sins and entrance into the Kingdom — unless they repented of all sins and came to genuine faith, as Kefa urged at Ac 2:38, 3:19–20. Support for this understanding comes from Kefa's speech at Ac 3:13–20, where he accuses his Jewish audience:

"...you handed over [Yeshua] and disowned [him] before Pilate, even after he had decided to release him. You denied the holy and innocent one, and instead asked for the reprieve of a murderer! You killed the author of life!... Now, brothers, I know that you did not understand the significance of what you were doing, neither did your leaders.... Therefore, repent and turn to God, so that your sins may be erased...."

Ignorance is cited as an ameliorating factor, but they must still repent and turn to God in order to have their sins erased. Similarly Ac 2:38 in the light of Ac 2:23, 36. And likewise Stephen's words, "Lord! Don't hold this sin against them!" (Ac 7:60), refer to forgiveness of the specific sin of wrongfully putting Stephen to death, not to salvation in general.

In conclusion, the knowledge of God's forgiveness indicated in this verse ought to have forestalled completely the charge of "deicide."

They divided up his clothes by throwing dice (literally, "by casting lots"), thus fulfilling a prophecy in Psalm 22's numerous prophecies of the Messiah's atoning death.

35 Fulfills the prophecy of Psalm 22:8(7).

36 Fulfills the prophecy of Psalm 69:22(21).

38 Some manuscripts, apparently borrowing from Yn 19:20, add that the inscription was written "in Greek, in Latin and in Hebrew."

43 ***Gan-Eden***, literally, "Garden of Eden" in Hebrew, is also Hebrew's expression for "Paradise," which is the English transliteration of Greek *paradeisos*, the term used in the Septuagint at Genesis 2:8 to translate *Gan-Eden. Paradeisos* itself comes from the Persian word "*pardes*," which has been taken into Hebrew; it means "enclosure, preserve, garden, park, citrus orchard," as well as "Paradise" in the Talmud. See Mt 2:15N.

44 **Darkness**. Amos 8:9 says,

"'On that Day,' declares *Adonai*, God, 'I will make the sun go down at noon and darken the earth in broad daylight.'"

This is one of several *Tanakh* references to darkness as a symbol of and accompaniment to God's judgment; another is Joel 2:31(3:4), quoted at Ac 2:20. And compare Yn 3:19. At Yeshua's death God was judging sin.

45 See Mt 27:51N.

46 Yeshua quotes from Psalm 31, which is a prayer for deliverance from troubles and adversaries. God answered this prayer not by preventing Yeshua's death, which was necessary for our sakes, but by raising him from the dead.

Gave up his spirit. In the light of the previous quotation, this is a better translation than the equally possible "breathed his last." (Hebrew *ruach* and Greek *pneuma* can mean either "spirit" or "breath.") In either case, the sense is that in that moment he died.

53 Wrapped it in a linen sheet. See Yn 19:39b-40N.

54 Preparation Day. See Yn 19:31N.

A *Shabbat* was about to begin as soon as the onset of night was signalled by the appearance of three medium-sized stars (Talmud: Shabbat 35b).

55 The women... saw the tomb and how his body was placed in it. This is important evidence to be taken together with Yn 20:5–8; see note there.

56 Spices and ointments. See Yn 19:39b-40N.

It is sometimes claimed that the New Testament says nothing about keeping the fourth commandment (see Mt 5:21N). This verse contradicts that claim, so it is important for a Jewish understanding of the New Testament. **On *Shabbat* the women rested, in obedience to the** fourth **commandment** (Exodus 20:8–11, Deuteronomy 5:12–15; also Exodus 16). Of course they did! They observed *Shabbat* every week. The writer mentions it only to explain why they didn't go to Yeshua's tomb the very next day. "[B]ut on the first day of the week, while it was still very early" — as soon as it was practical to do so — "they went to the tomb" (24:1). The Greek has the correlative conjunctions "*men... de*" in this sentence; the sense is not easily translated word-for-word, but it implies the just-explained "of course... but" relationship between the parts of the sentence: "Of course [they observed *Shabbat*], but [as soon as they could, they went]." Arndt and Gingrich's Lexicon explains "*men... de*" similarly at Mt 3:11, "To be sure, [I baptize you with water], but [one is coming...]."

CHAPTER 24

6–7 See 9:22, 17:25, 18:32–33; Mt 16:21, 17:22–23, 20:18–19; Mk 8:31, 9:31.

10 Miryam the mother of Ya'akov. Or: "the wife of Ya'akov" or "the daughter of Ya'akov." The Greek says only "of Ya'akov."

13 Two of them. These two were *talmidim* but not among the twelve emissaries.

19 He was a prophet. For the reasons given in the rest of the verse the *talmidim* had at this point settled on this description of Yeshua; compare Mt 21:11, Ac 3:22–23&N.

21 And we had hoped that he was the one who would liberate Israel. In other words, these Zealot-sympathizers had hoped he would turn out to be the Messiah — for they had not yet grasped the notion of a suffering Messiah who would die for sins. Even after the *talmidim* had seen the resurrected Yeshua a number of times and been taught by him for forty days they still expected him to "liberate Israel" without delay (Ac 1:6). Yeshua answered their question about when and how he will consummate the setting up of the Kingdom in Ac 1:7–8; see Ac 1:6–7N.

25–27 Throughout the *Tanakh* are prophecies about the Messiah that are fulfilled in Yeshua and reported in the New Testament. See Section VII of the Introduction to the *Jewish New Testament* for a list of 54 of them, including several indicating that **the Messiah** had **to die like this**; see also Mt 26:24N. Yeshua, walking with the two *talmidim* toward Amma'us, certainly referred to many of these prophecies as he **explained to them the things that can be found throughout the *Tanakh* concerning himself**. Yet they still did not get the point; only when he "broke the *matzah*... and handed it to them" were "their eyes... opened" (vv. 30–31).

39–42 Look at my hands and my feet, pierced by the nails (23:33). **"Have you something here to eat?" They gave him a piece of broiled fish.** Apparently people in the first century had trouble believing in a physical resurrection from the dead. Heretics solved the problem by proclaiming that Yeshua didn't really die on the cross but only swooned (for a recent resurrection of this non-resurrection theory see Hugh Schonfield's *The Passover Plot*). Others claimed he died a normal death and stayed dead (Mt 28:11–15). Others simply couldn't understand how it could happen and thus became doubters; Sha'ul dealt with this problem in 1 Corinthians 15. But Yeshua dealt with it by demonstrating that he was not merely a ghost, a vague "spiritual" entity, but fully present physically, with special capacities not available to unresurrected persons, such as becoming invisible (v. 31) and passing through walls (vv. 36–37; Yn 20:19–20).

44–45 The *Torah* of Moshe, the Prophets (*N'vi'im*) **and the Psalms** (standing for the Wisdom books or *K'tuvim*), in other words, the entire *TaNaKh* (see vv. 25–27&N). Note especially Isaiah 52:13–53:12 and Hosea 6:2.

46 See vv. 25–27&N, 1C 15:3–4&N.

47 This is the Great Commission. See Mt 28:19&N.

48–49 What my Father promised was the *Ruach HaKodesh* (Joel 3:1–5(2:28–32); Ac 1:8; 2:1–4, 16–21). The Holy Spirit gives the **power** necessary for being **witnesses**.

50 Raising his hands he blessed them. To this day there is a portion of the synagogue service wherein a *cohen* raises his hands and pronounces over the congregation the Aaronic benediction of Numbers 6:24–26.

52 They bowed in worship to him because they now understood who he was, the Son of God, divine and worthy of worship yet without being a "second god"; see Isaiah 9:5(6), Jeremiah 23:5, Proverbs 30:4, Micah 5:1(2). Worshipping something less than God would have been considered idolatry by every one of these highly religious Jewish disciples (compare Ac 10:25–26, Rv 22:8–9). Yochanan's version of the Good News contains much more of Yeshua's own teaching concerning his divine nature than Luke's (for example, Yn 8:58, 10:31, 14:6, 16:28, 17:5).

53 They spent all their time in the Temple courts praising God. The early believers had a living faith and a close relationship with God; being Jews they expressed that faith by praising God at his Temple. We pick them up praising God at Ac 1:14. As we will see (Ac 1:1&N), the book of Acts could also be called “Luke, Part II.”

THE GOOD NEWS OF YESHUA THE MESSIAH, AS REPORTED BY

YOCHANAN (JOHN)

CHAPTER 1

1–18 In his prologue to the Good News Yochanan sets forth both the divine and human origin and nature of the Messiah. Contrary to modern Jewish opinion, which holds that the Messiah is to be human only, numerous Jewish sources speak of the supernatural features of the Messiah; see below on specific verses in this prologue and also 17:5N.

The passage consists of groups of couplets separated by prose explanations. Pliny the Younger, one of the first pagans to mention Christians, wrote that they would meet on a fixed day before daylight "and recite by turns a form of words" (or: "sing an antiphonal chant") "to Christ as a god" (Letter to Emperor Trajan, around 112 C.E.).

Besides the prologue to Yochanan, additional New Testament passages lending themselves to "antiphonal chant" or other liturgical use are found in Lk 1–2 and at Ro 11:33–36, Pp 2:6–11, 1 Ti 3:16 and 2 Ti 2:11–13. The Hebrew parallelism of the Psalms and other books in the *Tanakh* was probably designed for antiphonal chanting.

1a In the beginning was the Word. The language echoes the first sentence of Genesis, "In the beginning God created the heavens and the earth." The **Word** which **was with God and... was God** is not named as such in Genesis but is immediately seen in action: "And God *said*, 'Let there be light'"(Genesis 1:3). "And God *called* the light Day" (Genesis 1:5). And so on, through Genesis and indeed throughout the whole *Tanakh*. God's expressing himself, commanding, calling and creating is one of the two primary themes of the entire Bible (the other being his justice and mercy and their outworking in the salvation of humanity). This expressing, this speaking, this "word" *is* God; a God who does not speak, a Word-less God is no God. And a Word that is not God accomplishes nothing. In the *Tanakh* God himself puts it this way:

> "For as the rain comes down, and the snow from heaven, and returns not there, but waters the earth, and makes it bring forth and bud, that it may give seed to the sower, and bread to the eater: so shall my word be that goes out of my mouth: it shall not return to me void, but it shall accomplish that which I please, and it shall prosper in that for which I sent it." (Isaiah 55:11)

Thus the *Tanakh* lays the groundwork for Yochanan's statement that the Word was *with* God and *was* God. In v. 14 we learn that this Word is Yeshua the Messiah himself; moreover, at Rv 19:13 Yeshua is explicitly called "the Word of God."

"**Word**" translates Greek *logos*. While "*logos*" had a role in pagan Gnosticism as one of the steps through which people work their way up to God and as such found its way into numerous Jewish and Christian heresies, here it does not bespeak a pagan intrusion into the New Testament, as some suppose. Rather, it corresponds to Aramaic "*memra*" (also "word"), a technical theological term used by the rabbis in the centuries before and after Yeshua when speaking of God's expression of himself. In the Septuagint *logos* translates Hebrew *davar*, which can mean not only "word" but "thing" or "matter"; hence the Messianic Jew Richard Wurmbrand has suggested this midrashic understanding of the initial phrase of this verse: "In the beginning was the Real Thing."

Thus the Messiah existed before all creation (compare 17:5). In fact, he was involved in creation (Co 1:15–17, MJ 1:2–3). The Talmud too teaches the Messiah's pre-existence. According to a *baraita* (an unattributed teaching from the Mishnaic period rabbis, who are known as *Tanna'im*),

> "It was taught that seven things were created before the world was created; they are the *Torah*, repentance, the Garden of Eden, Gey-Hinnom, the Throne of Glory, the Temple, and the name of the Messiah.... The name of the Messiah, as it is written: 'May his name [as understood here, the name of the Messiah] endure forever, may his name produce issue prior to the sun' (Psalm 72:17)." (Pesachim 54a, N'darim 39a; also Midrash on Psalm 93:3)

And see 19:17N.

1b–3 Is Yochanan speaking about two (**the Word was *with* God**) or one (**the Word *was* God**)? Yochanan's answer expresses Hebraic rather than Greek thinking: it is a matter of both/**and**, not either/or. We learn in these verses that the Word was not a created being, as the fourth-century heretic Arius taught and as Jehovah's Witnesses teach today.

4–9 Yeshua as the **true light** for the world is a major theme of Yochanan. See 8:12&N.

6 **Yochanan** the Immerser; see Mt 3:1N.

11 **His own homeland... his own people**, literally, "his own things [neuter]... his own people [masculine]." His own homeland and people could be either the world and all humanity, or the Land of Israel and the Jewish people; the latter seems more relevant, since he spent his entire life in or near *Eretz-Israel*. A still narrower interpretation, Natzeret and the people who knew him there, conforms to Lk 4:16–30 and Mk 6:1–6 but seems out of context here. In any case the majority of those he reached did not become his followers.

12 **Put their trust in his person and power**, literally, "put their trust in his name." The concept of "name" in the Ancient Middle East included everything a person was. We retain the sense today when we say someone speaks "in a person's name," meaning with his authority and expressing his views. To "trust in the name of Yeshua the Messiah" certainly does not mean to attribute magic properties to the name itself.

The right to become children of God. Isn't everyone a child of God? In a sense, yes (Ac 17:28); indeed, all are created "in his image" (Genesis 1:26–27, Ya 3:9). In numerous places God reveals himself as a Father (and in at least one place, Isaiah 49:14–15, as a Mother) to Israel. But here being a "child of God" means having an intimate personal relationship with him, as did Avraham, Yitzchak, Ya'akov, Moshe and David. God spoke to them personally and they spoke to him. It is exactly the same way with everyone who comes to trust in the Messiah, meeting the conditions of the New Covenant: the believer is able to be in touch with God his Father; see below, Chapters 15–17 and numerous places in Sha'ul's letters.

14 **The Word became a human being**, literally, "the Word became flesh." It is not that a man named Yeshua, who grew up in Natzeret, one day decided he was God. Rather, the Word, who "was with God" and "was God," gave up the "glory [he] had with [the Father] before the world existed" (17:5) and "emptied himself, in that he took the form of a slave by becoming like human beings are" (Pp 2:7). In other words, God sent "his own Son as a human being with a nature like our own sinful one" (Ro 8:3), so that "in every respect he was tempted just as we are, the only difference being that he did not sin" (MJ 4:15). It is God the Word, then, who decided to become man, not the other way round.

But can the one God, whose ways are as high above our ways as the heavens above the earth (Isaiah 55:8–9), "become a human being" and still be God? Does not the assertion that the Creator becomes the creature contradict the very essence of what it means to be God? The New Testament writers were aware that the concept of God becoming human needed unique treatment. For example, Sha'ul writes that in Yeshua the Messiah, "bodily, lives the fullness of all that God is" (in Co 2:9); likewise, see v. 18&N. Such circumspect language points to the extraordinariness of the idea. Mattityahu writes that when the Son of Man will come "no one knows — not the angels in heaven, not the Son, only the Father" (Mt 24:37): God is omniscient, yet there is something the Son does not know. Instead of rejecting the incarnation because it contradicts his prejudices about God, an open-minded person tries to discover what the concept means in the New Testament. Its writers are pointing to and attempting to describe a mystery which God has revealed in considerable measure but not altogether, for "now I know partly; then I will know fully" (1C 13:12).

The *Tanakh* reports many instances of God's appearing as a man — to Avraham in Genesis 18, to Ya'akov (Genesis 32:25–33), Moshe (Exodus 3), Y'hoshua (Joshua 5:13–6:5), the people of Israel (Judges 2:1–5), Gid'on (Judges 6:11–24), and Manoach and his wife, the parents of Shimshon, (Judges 13:2–23). In all of these passages the terms "*Adonai*" and "the angel of *Adonai*" (or "*Elohim*" and "the angel of *Elohim*") are used interchangeably, and in some of them the angel of *Adonai* (or *Elohim*) is spoken of as a man. The *Tanakh* itself thus teaches that the all-powerful God has the power, if he chooses, to appear among men as a man. The New Testament carries this already Jewish idea one step farther: not only can God "appear" in human form, but the Word of God can "become" a human being — and did so.

Non-Messianic Judaism has generally taken a defensive theological position against Christianity and its concept of incarnation. Thus the *Rambam*'s thirteen-point creed has as its third article:

"I believe with perfect faith that the Creator, blessed be his name, is not a body, that he is free from all material properties, and that he has no form whatsoever."

Maimonides clearly did not mean to contradict the *Tanakh*'s own descriptions of God as having physical features such as a back, a face (v. 18N) and an outstretched arm; rather, he meant to exclude incarnation. In the light of the New Testament a Messianic Jew can simply pronounce him wrong. However, for the sake of retaining a traditional Jewish formulation, he can preserve the words but reinterpret them against Maimonides' purpose. For example, a New Testament believer can agree that God's nature is not physical or material, but he would insist that the article does not exclude the incarnation of the Word as Yeshua if it is understood as an occasional, rather than essential, attribute of God, an event necessitated because sin occurred in human history.

On the other hand, the *Malbim* (*M*eir *L*oeb *B*en-Yechiel *M*ichael), writing in the middle of the nineteenth century, though a staunch defender of Orthodoxy against Reform Judaism, had a concept of *hitgalmut* ("incarnation") surprisingly close to the Christian idea of incarnation; it is found in his commentary on Genesis 18, where *Adonai* appears to Avraham. (The word "*hitgalmut*" is related to *golem* — recall the Yiddish play, "The *Golem*," based on a folktale about a clay body which its maker caused to come alive.)

Sh'khinah, God's manifest presence. See paragraph (3) of MJ 1:2–3N.

15 See v. 30.

16 **Grace**, Greek *charis*, is equivalent to Hebrew *chen* ("grace, favor") or *chesed* ("loyal love and kindness").

17 On ***Torah*** see Mt 5:17N. On "**Yeshua**" and "**Messiah**" see Mt 1:1N. Another passage comparing Moshe and the *Torah* with Yeshua and the New Covenant is 2C 3:6–16. It is sometimes thought that the present verse demeans Moshe, but this is not the case. On the contrary, that a mere man for whom no claim to divinity has ever been made should even be compared with the Word of God incarnate shows how highly Yochanan regards Moshe.

Nor does he demean the *Torah*, God's eternal "teaching" about himself as given to Israel, by comparing it with **grace and truth**. Elsewhere Yeshua himself says that he did not come to abrogate the *Torah* but to fill it out (Mt 5:17–20&NN), and proceeded to follow this program by interpreting the *Torah* in ways that make its meaning and commands even clearer (Mt 5:21–48).

Grace and truth are personal attributes of God which Yeshua not only revealed in a unique way during his brief earthly lifetime, but, in his eternal capacity as the Word of God, has been continually bestowing on humanity since the dawn of creation. Grace, truth and the *Torah* are all from God, supreme expressions of who he is; see Rv 19:11N.

18 **No one has ever seen God**. Yet many who saw the angel of *Adonai* thus saw God (v. 14N). Moreover, Moshe saw "God's back" (Exodus 33:19–23), Isaiah "saw *Adonai* sitting on a throne, high and lifted up" (Isaiah 6:1), and the seventy elders of Israel "saw the God of Israel…and ate and drank" (Exodus 24:9–11). Therefore this passage must be taken to mean that the ultimate glory and nature of God are hidden from sinful humanity. As Exodus 33:20 puts it, "And [God] said, 'You cannot see my face, for no one can see me and live.'"

The only and unique Son, who is identical with God. Greek *monogenês theos* is to Jewish people a shocking and problematical phrase. "*Theos*" means "God," and "*monogenês*" can mean either "only-begotten" or "only, unique." If "*monogenês*" is an adjective, the phrase may be rendered, "the only-begotten God" or "the only and unique God." The former concept is alien to the *Tanakh* and the rest of the New Testament and inconsistent with the remainder of Yochanan's Gospel as well; while the latter does not make sense in the context of the sentence.

The *JNT* takes "*monogenês*" as a substantive, with "*theos*" ("God") standing in apposition and describing it. In this case the phrase means either "the Only-Begotten One, who is God" or "the Only and Unique One, who is God." The word "Son" is supplied and is not in the Greek text used for the *JNT*, although some manuscripts do have "*uios*" ("son") instead of "*theos*."

What, then, does it mean to call the only and unique son "God," especially when the Son, who is God, **has made him**, the Father, who is also God, **known**? Is there more than one God? Again, refer to v. 1N: this "Only and Unique One" is fully identified with God, yet not in such a way as to negate the basic truth of the *Sh'ma* that "*Adonai* is one" (Deuteronomy 6:4, Ro 3:30). For this reason I have supplied the words, "**who is identical with**," in order to reflect the delicacy of the incarnation concept (see v. 14&N) when the predicate "**God**" is applied to "**the only and unique Son**": throughout his Gospel Yochanan teaches that the Father is God, and the Son is God; yet he distinguishes between the Son and the Father, so that one cannot say that the Son is the Father. I submit that the chief difficulty in our understanding this lies neither in the Greek text nor in my translation of it, but in the very nature of God himself.

19 **Judeans**. Is the New Testament antisemitic? Here, with the word "Judeans" (rather than "Jews" as in most English translations) being used to translate Greek *Ioudaioi* the first time it is used in Yochanan's Gospel, we must go beyond what is found in Mt 2:2N, 3:7N, 23:13N and Lk 23:3N, and aim for the heart of the subject.

The charge usually takes the form of accusing the New Testament in general and Yochanan's Gospel in particular of making statements about "the Jews" that not only are negative, unfriendly, misleading and false, but are intended by the authors to induce dislike and hatred of "the Jews" as a class and as individuals. After all — to use the language of KJV, which is echoed in most later English versions — was it not "the Jews" who "did persecute Jesus" (John 5:16), "sought the more to kill him" (5:18), "murmured at him" (6:41), again "sought to kill him" (7:1), induced people to fear him (7:13, 19:38, 20:19), spoke against him (8:22, 48, 52, 57), "did not believe" (9:18), "took up stones again to stone him" (10:31, 11:18), said that Jewish law required Jesus to die (19:7), and exerted political pressure on Pilate to kill Jesus (19:14)? If the charge is true either Christianity and Messianic Judaism stand condemned, or the New Testament must be discounted as not inspired by God and untrustworthy as a guide to Messianic behavior.

The matter cannot be decided by pointing to antisemitic acts committed through the centuries in the Messiah's name or claiming New Testament justification, because that assumes what must be proved; but I intend to disprove the charge by showing that, to the contrary, Yeshua and the New Testament condemn antisemitism.

Nor will I acknowledge that a scholarly commentary asserting or assuming that there is antisemitism in the New Testament carries weight if its author's theology and presuppositions have not been examined for antisemitic bias or for misconstruction of the relationship between Israel and the Messiah's Body (the Church). As an example of such, consider these remarks of Rudolf Bultmann (1884–1976), the distinguished liberal Christian theologian:

> "The term *oi Ioudaioi*, characteristic of the Evangelist [John], gives an overall portrayal of the Jews, viewed from the standpoint of Christian faith, as the representatives of unbelief.... The Jews are spoken of as an alien people.... Jesus stands over against the Jews.... *Oi Ioudaioi* does not relate to the empirical state of the Jewish people [e.g., currently unsaved], but to its very nature." (*The Gospel of John: A Commentary*, Philadelphia: The Westminster Press, 1971, pp. 86–87)

So, instead of relying on other commentators or on how the Church has historically applied its understanding of the New Testament's "*oi Ioudaioi*," I will look at the linguistic and historic-cultural contexts surrounding the uses of the word "*Ioudaioi*" in the New Testament to see if it really means "Jews."

A non-Messianic Jewish neurologist named Jack Epstein wrote an article, "Roots of Religious Prejudice" (*Journal of Ecumenical Studies* 5:4, pp. 697–724), in which he categorizes the 197 instances of the word "*Ioudaioi*" and 5 instances of cognate words in the New Testament as being used positively 16 times, negatively 80 times and neutrally 106 times. His solution is to replace the word "Jews" in the 80 negative uses by other words — "Pharisees," "High Priests," "bystanders," "moneylenders," "chief priests," "a band" (Ac 23:30), or "old wives' tales" (in place of "Jewish fables," Ti 1:14&N).

Obviously the intent of this exercise is to modify the harsh and antisemitic sound of the text in the light of modern sensitivities. Its justification is that the opposition attributed supposedly to "the Jews" was aimed at the Jewish man Yeshua and his Jewish followers; thus it could not have been *all* "the Jews" who opposed them but some subgroup. Epstein compares the attribution of these negative acts to "the Jews" as a whole with speaking of "the whites" as opposing Abraham Lincoln, plotting against him and killing him at the theater: such a misreporting of American history would inflame black-white racial tensions no less than the mis-translating of the New Testament has inflamed tensions between Jews and Christians. A similar rationale seems to underlie the Living Bible's use of the phrase "Jewish leaders" instead of "Jews" at a number of points in John's Gospel and Acts.

But Epstein's analysis, though interesting as far as it goes, lacks authority because it does not address the basic question of how the word "*Ioudaioi*" should be exegeted. Malcolm Lowe, in an article called "Who Were The *Ioudaioi*?" (*Novum Testamentum*, 18:2, pp. 101–130), has done the analysis necessary for a reliable answer to this question, and the *Jewish New Testament* reflects most of his conclusions.

Lowe argues that three distinct meanings may be presumed possible for "*Ioudaioi*" and its Hebrew precursor "*Y'hudim*":

(1) Members of the tribe of Judah (Hebrew *Y'hudah*, Greek *Ioudas*).

(2) Followers of the Jewish religion, that is, Jews.
(3) People living in or originating from Judea (Hebrew *Y'hudah*, Greek *Ioudaia*). Since Judea's boundaries did not remain fixed, three possible regions may reasonably have been referred to in Yeshua's time:
  (a) Judea "in the strict sense," approximately the territory assigned to the tribe of Judah, and not including Shomron (Samaria) or the Galil (Galilee).
  (b) The procurate of Pontius Pilate, namely, Judea as in (a) plus Shomron and Idumea.
  (c) The kingdom of Herod the Great and the last Hasmoneans, that is, the whole of the historic Land of Israel, which means Judea as in (b) plus the Galil and territory north of the Galil (in modern Lebanon) and east of the Yarden River (the Golan Heights and parts of modern Jordan and Syria).

While "*Ioudaioi*" today means only the second of these three possibilities (Jews by religion), in Yeshua's time all three meanings were possible. This is not a new discovery, and I dare suggest (but do not assert) that only implicit antisemitic bias on the part of translators and their intended audiences can account for the continued and unrelieved use of the word "Jews" to translate "*Ioudaioi*" in most English translations until this day. (A few occasionally note "Judeans" as an alternate translation in the margin.)

Throughout all four Gospels and Acts 1–8 "*Ioudaioi*" in nearly all instances means "Judeans" and not "Jews." In these books when Jews refer to "*Ioudaioi*" they are generally distinguishing Judean Jews from Galilean or other Jews; for when Jews of this period wanted to refer to Jews in the religious sense they invariably spoke of the "people of Israel" — one finds this in the Mishna as well as the New Testament (see Ro 9–11&NN, and especially Ro 11:26a&N; also Ep 2:12&N). Judean Jews were characterized as being more committed than other Jews to the forms of Judaism taught by the two parties headquartered in Yerushalayim, the *P'rushim* and the *Tz'dukim*, who included most of the *cohanim*. It was these Judean Jews (and, it should be emphasized, even of them only a subgroup, not every single one) who spearheaded the opposition to Yeshua, as reported by Yochanan. Thus Lowe's sense (3)(a) is most common when Jews are the speakers.

But when non-Jews refer to "*Ioudaioi*" in the Gospels and Acts 1–8, it is often sense (3)(b) or (3)(c) that is meant, for the term is used in a political sense: the territory of the tribe of Judah is rarely in mind, and what is meant is the province of Judea as the Romans had to deal with it. One could even render "king of the *Ioudaioi*" as "king of the Judeans" in the Gospels, since the phrase is used largely by Gentiles for whom the primary interface with the Jewish people was political and not theological; however, since the concept of "Messiah" was known to the Gentile rulers as a religious concept, I have preserved the more common "king of the Jews" (see Mt 2:2&N, Lk 23:3&N).

The several festivals which Yochanan identifies as being "of the *Ioudaioi*" (2:13, 5:1, 6:4, 7:2, 11:55) are specifically Judean festivals. Of course they are Jewish too; that goes without saying. But all the festivals Yochanan names — *Pesach* at 2:13, 6:4 and 11:55, and *Sukkot* at 7:2 — are pilgrim festivals, that is, festivals during which all Jews-by-religion were required by the *Torah* to go up to Yerushalayim in Judea (see 5:1N). Moreover, in 10:22 *Chanukkah* is *not* identified as a festival "of the *Ioudaioi*," since it is not a pilgrim festival.

At 2:6, 11:19, and Mk 7:3 customs are spoken of that today have the force of *halakhah* (Jewish religious law). But in New Testament times, before these practices became binding on all Jews, it would have been the Judeans who would have been most insistent on their observance.

From Acts 9 onward "*Ioudaioi*" usually means "Jews" and not "Judeans" or "Judahites," since the context is no longer the Land of Israel but the Diaspora, where the word is used to distinguish Jews from the *Goyim* — Gentiles, pagans, followers of other religions. For example, at Ga 2:13–15 Sha'ul calls himself, Kefa and the other believers "Jews," not "Judeans" (and certainly not "former Jews"; see notes there). Also, Paul calls himself a Jew even though he was from the tribe of Benjamin, not Judah (Ac 13:21, Ro 11:1, Pp 3:5). The exceptions to this rule occur in Ac 12, Ac 21–28 and the very important case of 1 Th 2:14 (see note there); in these instances the context is the Land, and "Judeans" is the proper rendering.

So then, has the locus of difficulty merely been shifted from the Gospels to the latter portions of the New Testament? Are the Gospels exonerated from the charge of antisemitic tendency but the Book of Acts and the Letters convicted? For — again using KJV — it is clear that it was "the Jews" who "took counsel to kill" Paul in Damascus (Ac 9:23); in Pisidian Antioch they "were filled with envy, and spake against those things which were spoken by Paul, contradicting and blaspheming" (Ac 13:45), and eventually they "stirred up the devout and honourable women, and the chief men of the city, and raised persecution against Paul and Barnabas, and expelled them out of their coasts" (Ac 13:50); in Berea "the Jews of Thessalonica...came...and stirred up the people" (Ac 17:13); in Corinth "the Jews made insurrection with one accord against Paul, and brought him to the judgment seat, Saying, This fellow persuadeth men to worship God contrary to the law" (Ac 18:12–13); in Greece "the Jews laid in wait for" Paul (Ac 20:3); in Ephesus Paul himself is quoted as speaking of "the lying in wait of the Jews" (Ac 20:19); and he writes the Corinthians that "Of the Jews I received forty stripes save one" (2C 11:24). These *Ioudaioi* cannot be only Judeans; they must be members of *'am-Israel* (the people of Israel), followers of Judaism, Jews.

Nevertheless, are they "Jews in general"? or must they be some limited portion of the Jewish people? I don't believe it prejudices my case to admit beforehand that I want to arrive at the latter conclusion, because at the same time I commit myself to do so only if there is evidence for it in the text of the New Testament and not merely in my own wishings. Fortunately, there is such evidence. In the synagogue at Iconium Paul and Barnabas

> "so spake, that a great multitude both of the Jews and also of the Greeks believed. But the unbelieving Jews stirred up the Gentiles, and made their minds evil affected against the brethren...and part held with the Jews, and part with the apostles. And when there was an assault made both of the Gentiles, and also of the Jews with their rulers, to use them despitefully, and to stone them, They were ware of it, and fled unto Lystra and Derbe...." (Ac 14:1–6, KJV).

We see here that it was the *unbelieving* Jews who caused the trouble (the Greek word translated "unbelieving" in KJV, "*apeithêsantes*," may also be rendered "disobedient").

Likewise, although "the Jews" came from Thessalonica to stir up the Bereans, which Jews were they? It was "the Jews who believed not" who, "moved with envy took unto them certain lewd fellows of the baser sort, and gathered a company, and set all the city on an uproar…" (Ac 17:5, KJV); the preceding verse informs us that other Jews did believe.

From the first Diaspora presentation of the faith (Ac 9:20–22) to the end of the book of Acts (Ac 28:24–25a&N) the story is the same: the Gospel of Yeshua the Messiah divided the Jewish community, so that some Jews believed it and were obedient to its truth; while other Jews did not believe it and were disobedient, opposing it and its followers. The believing Jews, while still Jews, are referred to as God's people, members of the Body of the Messiah or the Messianic Community (Greek *ekklêsia*, "called-out ones," "church"; see Mt 16:18N). The unbelieving Jews, explicitly called this in Ac 14:2 and Ac 17:5, are elsewhere called "the Jews"; but this term should be taken as a kind of shorthand for "the unbelieving Jews" or "the disbelieving Jews." To apply to New Testament times modern sensitivities concerning statements about "the Jews" produces bad exegesis. It is clear from the New Testament that those who refuse to believe the Gospel, whether Jewish or Gentile, fall under God's condemnation; while those who trust and obey, whether Jewish or Gentile, receive his blessing.

For this reason, whenever a negative statement is made about the *Ioudaioi* and the referent is properly Jews and not Judeans, the *JNT* adds the word "unbelieving," even when it does not appear in the text; see Ac 9:22–23N for a complete listing of these places. The purpose, of course, is to make clear that the reference is not to the Jewish people as a whole but to a subgroup who opposed the Gospel, and that therefore none of the references to *Ioudaioi* in the New Testament are antisemitic.

Cohanim. See Mt 2:4N.

L'vi'im. See Lk 5:27N.

21 **Are you Eliyahu?** That is, are you the Prophet Elijah, who is to come before the Great Day of *Adonai*, according to Malachi 3:23(4:5)? See notes at Mt 11:10, 14; 17:10, where Yeshua makes clear that Yochanan the Immerser is not Eliyahu reincarnated but does come in his spirit for those who will accept him.

Are you the prophet? That is, are you the "prophet like me" whom Moshe promised would come to the people of Israel, and whom they were to heed (Deuteronomy 18:15, 18)? For more, see Ac 3:22–23&N.

23 ***Adonai***. On the use of this word in lieu of God's name, *YHVH*, see Mt 1:20N.

24 ***P'rushim***. See Mt 3:7N.

25 **Immersing people**, Greek *baptizeis*, usually rendered, "baptize." See Mt 3:1N.

29 **God's lamb**. Yochanan identifies Yeshua with the dominant sacrificial animal used in connection with Temple ritual, and particularly with the sin offerings, since he is **the one who is taking away the sin of the world**. Elsewhere in the New Testament Yeshua the Messiah is equated with the Passover lamb (1C 5:7&N). The figure of the lamb connects Yeshua with the passage identifying the Messiah as the Suffering Servant in Isaiah 53 (Ac 8:32); and his sacrificial death by execution on a stake is compared with "that of a lamb without a defect or a spot" (1 Ke 1:19), as required by the *Torah* (e.g., Exodus 12:5, 29:1; Leviticus 1:3, 10; 9:3; 23:12). In the book of Revelation Yeshua is referred to as the Lamb nearly thirty times. On God's requiring a human sacrifice for sins, see 1C 15:3N, MJ 7:26–28N, and indeed the entire book of Messianic Jews.

30–34 This is Yochanan's version of the events reported in the Synoptic Gospels at Mt 3:11–17, Mk 1:7–11, and Luke 3:15–17, 21–22.

32 **Spirit**, i.e., the Holy Spirit.

33 ***Ruach HaKodesh***. See Mt 1:18N.

34 **Son of God**, a title descriptive of the Messiah. See Mt 4:3N.

35 ***Talmidim***. See Mt 5:1N.

38 **"Rabbi!" (which means "Teacher!")**. The Greek text first transliterates the Hebrew word "*rabbi*" and then gives the meaning, "Teacher" (Greek *Didaskale*). "*Rabbi*" appears 15 times in the Greek text of the New Testament, always in reference to Yeshua, except at Mt 23:7–10&NN, where Yeshua discusses the word itself.

40 **Kefa**. See v. 42N.

41 ***Mashiach*.... The word means "one who has been anointed."** See Mt 1:1N on "Messiah." This is one of the two places in the New Testament where the Hebrew word for "Messiah" is transliterated into Greek as "*Messias*" (the other is at 4:25). It shows that the author wanted to reflect the Jewish or Hebraic character of the speaker's words. KJV renders this phrase, "Messias, which is, being interpreted, the Christ."

42 **You are Shim'on Bar-Yochanan** — that is your name in Aramaic, Simon the son of John. "Bar-Yonah" is the majority reading, but mostly from late witnesses; Bruce Metzger, *A Textual Commentary on the Greek New Testament*, considers it a scribal assimilation to Mt 16:17; see note there.

You will be known as Kefa, Greek *Kephas*, transliterating Aramaic *Kefa*, and usually given in English as "Cephas." **The name means "Rock,"** Greek *Petros*, usually given in English as "Peter." See Mt 4:18; 16:16, 18 and notes there.

45 **The one that Moshe wrote about in the *Torah*.** See v. 21&N, Deuteronomy 18:15–18, and Ac 3:22&N, which quotes this passage. Yeshua fulfills Moshe's prophecy.

Also the Prophets wrote about Yeshua. See Section VII of the Introduction to the *Jewish New Testament*, Mt 26:24N and Lk 24:25–27N.

Yeshua Ben-Yosef, Yeshua the son of Yosef. This would have been his official Hebrew name, by which he would have been known. Yosef the carpenter was not physically his father, as we know from Mt 1:18–25 and Lk 1:26–38, 2:1–7; but he was legally his father and functioned as a father, raising him so that he "grew both in wisdom and in stature" (Lk 2:52). To call him *Yeshua Ben-Elohim* ("Yeshua, the Son of God") would be correct, and he is called that in v. 34 above and at other places in the New Testament. But this theological truth would obviously not have been a practical means of identifying Yeshua in the society of his time.

51 **Yes indeed!** Greek *Amên, amên*, which reproduces the Hebrew words. See Mt 5:18N on this important word and Yeshua's characteristic use of it.

The ladder imagery recalls Jacob's dream (Genesis 28:12–15).

The Son of Man. An important title for the Messiah, used by Yeshua in reference to himself. See Mt 8:20N.

CHAPTER 2

4–5 **Mother, why should that concern me? — or you?** Literally, "What to me and to you, woman?" This translates into Greek a Hebrew idiom found a number of times in the *Tanakh*, and we are thereby reminded of the Hebraic roots necessary to proper understanding of the New Testament. The meaning of this idiom is flexible; renderings include: "What do we have in common?" "Why do you involve me?" "You must not tell me what to do," "Why turn to me?" "Your concern is not mine."

Greek *gunê* means "woman," but saying "*Gunê*!" to a woman in Greek is not nearly as cold an address as "Woman!" in English; this is why I have rendered it "Mother." Nevertheless Yeshua's answer, *in toto*, no matter how translated, puts distance between him and his mother Miryam. Why does he do this? Is he disobeying the commandment to honor his father and mother (as opponents of the Gospel suppose)?

The answer comes with the following remark, **My time** (literally, "my hour") **hasn't come yet.** Yochanan's Gospel often has Yeshua speaking about his time (7:30; 8:20; 12:23, 27; 13:1; 17:1), and each occasion has a reason. Here the reason is that Yeshua's mother had been informed, even before he was born, that he was meant for greatness (Lk 1:35, 43); she had heard others prophesy about him (Lk 2:25–38); she had observed his development (Lk 2:40, 51), although not always with understanding (Lk 2:41–50); and she had known that future generations would bless her (Lk 1:48). Yeshua's comment is meant to aid her in the transition from seeing him as her child to seeing him as her Lord, to keep her from undue pride, and to indicate that he as Lord sovereignly determines when he will intervene in human affairs — he does not perform miracles on demand merely to impress his friends, or even to give *naches* (a Yiddish word that means "the kind of joy a mother feels") to his mother. See v. 11&N on the purpose of his miracle.

Actually he both honored and cared for his mother: in the agony of being executed he entrusted his mother to the *talmid* whom he especially loved (19:25–27). And in the end she did come to regard him as Lord, for she was present and praying with the other *talmidim* in the upstairs room after his resurrection (Ac 1:14).

From Miryam's response, **Do whatever he tells you**, it is evident that she was neither dissatisfied nor put off by her son but received his communication in the right spirit. Moreover, Yeshua did not ignore the problem to which she had called attention but granted far more than she asked or imagined (Ep 3:20). Finally, v. 12, conveniently ignored by those who seek to prove there was a rift between Yeshua and his family (compare Mt 12:48–50&N), says that he left with "his mother and brothers."

6 **Jewish ceremonial washings**, literally, "the cleansings of the *Ioudaioi*," who in this verse seem to be the Jews by religion, not the Judeans by geography or origin (see 1:19N), if Yochanan is explaining the situation for non-Jewish readers. Alternatively, "Judean ceremonial washings" — on the assumption that the wedding brought guests from all over, including Judea, and in deference their customs were observed (compare 1C 10:29). "Cleansings" (Hebrew *Taharot*) is the title and subject of one of the six sections of the Talmud; this is a measure of their importance in traditional Judaism (see also Mk 7:2–4N).

Twenty or thirty gallons, literally, "two or three *metrêtas*," a *metrêtes* being estimated by Josephus at about 8 1/2 gallons and corresponding approximately to the Hebrew *bat*.

11 This verse states the purpose of Yeshua's miracle: to anchor the trust of his new *talmidim* in the glory of God as manifested through him.

13 **The festival of *Pesach* in Y'hudah**, or "the Judean festival of *Pesach*" or, literally, "the *Pesach* of the Judeans" (but probably not "...of the Jews" for reasons detailed in 1:19N and 5:1N).

Went up to Yerushalayim. See Mt 20:17–19N.

14–17 **Those who were selling cattle, sheep and pigeons**. See Mt 21:12N.

20 **It took 46 years to build this Temple**. King Herod the Great (see Mt 2:1N) began the remodeling of the Second Temple complex around 19–20 B.C.E. About two years were spent in preparation, which may not be included in the "46 years" of the present verse; so that this incident could have taken place any time between 26 and 30 C.E. Herod's Temple may not have been entirely finished when it was destroyed by the Romans in 70 C.E.

21 **But the "Temple" he had spoken of was his body**, not the building (compare 1C 6:19). Yeshua often spoke obliquely to those he knew lacked faith (for another example, see v. 25). At Mt 13:10–17 he answered at length the question of his *talmidim*, "Why do you speak to them in parables?" Like Nechemyah he did not waste time in futile conversation with closed-minded people (Nehemiah 2:19–20, 6:2–3).

22 **They trusted in the *Tanakh***, or "trusted in that verse of the *Tanakh*." If the former, it means the *talmidim* came to believe in all the passages referring to or hinting at the Messiah's resurrection, such as Hosea 6:2, Isaiah 53:7–12, Jonah 1:17 (which Yeshua alluded to at Mt 12:39–41, 16:4; Lk 11:29–32) and Psalm 16:8–11 (quoted and expounded by Kefa at Ac 2:24–32); see Section VII of the Introduction to the *Jewish New Testament*, Mt 26:24N and Lk 24:25–27N.

But if the latter, it means that at the end of Yeshua's ministry, when he overturned the money-changers' tables a second time (Mt 21:12), the *talmidim* recalled Yeshua's quoting Psalm 69, "Zeal for your house will devour me" (above, v. 17). This would show that Yochanan's Gospel attributes to the later overturning of tables in the Temple a major immediate-causative role in Yeshua's being brought to trial and death.

23 **There were many people who "believed in his name"** but not in him (vv. 24–25). His **miracles** excited them, but they were not ready to acknowledge their sin and repent. In contrast, Nakdimon (3:1ff.) was a sincere seeker, and eventually he came to genuine faith.

25 See Lk 16:15&N.

CHAPTER 3

1 **Nakdimon** (Greek *Nikodemos*), who held "the office of teacher in Israel" (v. 10&N), must have been a very important figure; but he is not mentioned in traditional Jewish literature. However, some have identified him with Nakdimon ben-Gurion, mentioned in the Talmud as a wealthy merchant at the time of the Second Temple and its destruction. Even if he is not the same, we learn at least that this Greek name was used by Jews. Nakdimon is called **a ruler**, which implies he was a rabbi and a member of the *Sanhedrin*, as confirmed by 7:50 below. Eventually Rabbi Nakdimon got "born again from above" (vv. 3–8) and came to trust in Yeshua (19:39).

2–3 Yeshua neither criticizes Nakdimon for fearing to seek him openly nor praises his insight in perceiving that Yeshua has come **from God**. Rather, he deals with him at his point of need, which is to be **born again from above**. Greek *gennêthê anôthen* is sometimes rendered "born again" and sometimes "born from above"; my rendering reflects my conclusion that both aspects are relevant; also see 1 Ke 1:3–4&N. While the widespread currency since the 1970's of the expression "born-again Christian" originates here, the concept itself is Jewish, as demonstrated by this example from the Talmud: "Shim'on Ben-Lakish said, '…a proselyte is like a newborn infant'"(Yevamot 62a); likewise Rabbi Yosi (Yevamot 48b). The idea resembles that of the "new creation" (2C 5:17&N), which too is found in rabbinic literature (e.g., in Genesis Rabbah 39:11).

5 **Born from water and the Spirit**. Immersion in water is connected with ritual cleansing of the body (see above, 1:26–34, and Mt 3:1–17), while the Holy Spirit gives power for turning from sin and living a holy life; both bespeak aspects of purification. This is why "born from water" does not mean ordinary human birth; moreover, since everyone is "born from water" in that sense, it would be silly for Yeshua to make a condition out of it with the word "**unless**."

8 **The wind**. There is a wordplay here, since both the Greek word "*pneuma*" and the Hebrew word "*ruach*" may mean either "wind" or "spirit," depending on context.

10 **You hold the office of teacher in Israel**, literally, "You are the teacher of Israel." The use of the definite article implies that Nakdimon's position was uniquely important, although it is difficult to reconstruct precisely what it was.

11–13 It is sometimes asserted that Yeshua never claimed to be more than an ordinary human being. But here he affirms his heavenly origin; and indeed, throughout

Yochanan's Gospel he presents himself as divine as well as human, both in function and in essence.

We speak… we give evidence. Sir Edwin Hoskyns in his commentary on John, *The Fourth Gospel*, explains the plural here as Yeshua associating himself with other witnesses: Yochanan the Immerser (1:7, 32–34), Isaiah (12:41), Abraham (8:56), Moses (5:46), and the writers and subjects of the *Tanakh* (5:39).

14–15 Just as the Israelites were saved from the plague of serpents when they gazed on the brass **serpent** raised by **Moshe** (Numbers 21:6–9), so all people are saved from eternal death, torment and separation from God by gazing with spiritual eyes on the person of the Messiah Yeshua **lifted up** in death on the execution-stake. Compare 8:28&N, 12:32.

16 This perhaps most famous and most quoted of verses in the New Testament epitomizes the truth of God that has come to Jews and Gentiles alike in Yeshua the Messiah. It teaches that (1) God loves his creation, the world; (2) to love is to give, to love much is to give much, and God loves the world so much that he gave what is most precious to him; (3) Yeshua was fully aware in advance that he would die as God's own sacrifice; (4) Yeshua knew that he was uniquely God's son; (5) the destiny of man when he relies on himself and does not trust in Yeshua is total destruction (Greek *apollumi*, "be ruined, destroyed, lost") — not cessation of conscious existence, but the eternal suffering that is the inevitable consequence of sin; and (6) the destiny of an individual who trusts in Yeshua is everlasting life — not only in the future but right now — not just survival beyond the grave, which everyone has (5:28–29; Rv 20:4–5, 12–15), but positive life "in" Yeshua (1:4, 11:25–26). Trusting in Yeshua is not mere intellectual acknowledgement but adherence to, commitment to, trust in, faith in, reliance upon Yeshua as fully human, completely identified with us, and at the same time fully divine, completely identified with God.

17 The world is subject to condemnation and in the end will have its sinfulness condemned. But Yeshua's first coming was not for that purpose. In the Day of Judgment he will be the Judge who condemns the world (5:27).

18 **Those who do not trust**. Clearly those who, upon hearing the Good News and understanding it, nevertheless refuse to trust **are judged already**. But what about those who have never heard of Yeshua? or who have heard but not understood? See Ro 2:14–16N and Lk 12:8–10N.

19–21 This passage echoes Isaiah 59:2, "Your iniquities have made a separation between you and your God, and your sins have hidden his face from you, so that he will not hear."

23 **Einayim**. The Greek text has "*Ainon*," possibly a corruption of Hebrew *Einayim* ("Two Springs"); its location is uncertain but is thought to be in the eastern hills of Shomron (Samaria).

24 **Yochanan's imprisonment** is reported in Mt 14:3–12, Mk 6:17–29.

26 **Here he is, immersing**. Actually not Yeshua but his *talmidim*, as clarified at 4:2.

30 Yochanan's humility is no less genuine than that of Moshe, who, though raised to prominence by God, proclaimed himself "the meekest man on the face of the earth" (Numbers 12:3). The verse cautions believers against calling attention to themselves instead of Yeshua.

31–36 Yochanan the Immerser closes with an either-or challenge, still applicable to every Jew and every Gentile: trust in Yeshua and have **eternal life** (on which see 17:3&N), or disobey him and experience **God's wrath** (on which see Ro 1:18–2:8&NN).

CHAPTER 4

5–6a **Sh'khem, near the field Ya'akov had given to his son Yosef**. See Genesis 33:19, Joshua 24:32. *Tel-Sh'khem* (the archeological site of Sh'khem) is just outside modern Nablus in Shomron (Samaria), and **Ya'akov's Well,** not far away, is a tourist site to this day.

6b **Yeshua, who had become exhausted from the trip**. As a human being he experienced human exhaustion; as Son of God he worked continuously (5:17); compare MJ 4:15. At Mt 24:36 is a similar puzzle: Yeshua does not know when he will return, only the Father knows. We can note these facts, based on Scripture; but to explain them transcends human knowledge. This is why one speaks of the incarnation as a mystery (see 1:14&N).

9 **A Jew**, as distinct from a Samaritan. See 1:19N. Enmity between Jews and people from **Shomron** (Samaritans) is at least as old as the return of the southern tribes from the Babylonian Exile in the sixth and fifth centuries B.C.E. and has its roots in the division of Israel into the Northern and Southern Kingdoms after the death of King Solomon (931 B.C.E.; see 1 Kings 11–12), with the result that the Southern Kingdom worshipped in Jerusalem but the Northern did not.

Assyria conquered the Northern Kingdom of Israel in 722 B.C.E. and deported many of its people, who belonged to the ten northern tribes, replacing them with pagans; they intermarried with the remaining Jews to produce the Samaritans. Their descendants were not idolaters, but they acknowledged only the Pentateuch as inspired by God. They also denied Jerusalem as the religious center, opting instead for Mount Gerizim (v. 20 below); this explains why they tried to obstruct Nechemyah's rebuilding of Jerusalem (Nehemiah 2:19, 4:2). See Lk 9:53N, 10:33N.

10–15 In Hebrew, *mayim chayyim* (literally, **living water**) means running water from a stream or spring, in contrast with water stored in a cistern. Figuratively, with Yeshua, it means spiritual life; compare 7:37–39.

19 **I can see that you are a prophet** because you supernaturally knew about my sin. The *Tanakh* prophets spoke forth God's word in relation to the sins of Israel and other nations; prediction was a secondary aspect of their ministry. See paragraph (6) of Ac 12:8–10N.

20 See v. 9N, Deuteronomy 11:29, Joshua 8:33–35.

22 **Salvation comes from the Jews**. Compare 11:16–24, 15:27. Christians should acknowledge their Jewish roots and present close involvement with the Jewish people (Ep 2:13&N). Jews should acknowledge more specifically that only through Yeshua comes *yeshu'ah*, "salvation" (see notes at Mt 1:1; Lk 2:11, 3:4–6). Because Yeshua is speaking to a Samaritan, a non-Jew, I think it appropriate to translate "*Ioudaioi*" here as "Jews" and not "Judeans" (see 1:19N).

24 This verse is sometimes misappropriated to support the mistaken idea that the *Torah* is inferior or is no longer in force, having been replaced by worship "in spirit and in truth" (the literal rendering of **spiritually and truly**). But spiritual and true worship is not to be set alongside or compared with the *Torah*. Rather, true, spiritual worship is God's universal standard, which he also commands in the *Torah* itself. The *Torah* opposes legalism and the mere performance of acts and routines without true, spiritual involvement.

25 ***Mashiach***. See 1:41N.

26 **I, the one speaking to you, am he**, literally, "I am, the one speaking to you." Thus he answers everyone who questions whether Yeshua proclaimed his own Messiahship. The declaration, "I am," echoes *Adonai*'s self-revelation, "I am who I am" (Exodus 3:14). Yeshua says this "I am" nine times in Yochanan's Gospel (here; 6:20; 8:24, 28, 58; 13:9; 18:5, 6, 8), implying a claim even greater than being the Messiah. See Mk 14:61–62&N.

27 **Yeshua himself said, "A prophet is not respected in his own country."** He said it at Mt 13:57, Mk 6:4, Lk 4:24.

46–54 This passage has elements in common with Lk 7:1–10, but this is clearly a different story. Both the Roman centurion of Luke and this official had extraordinary faith. The text does not state explicitly that the **officer in the royal service** (Greek *basilikos*) was not Jewish, but, given Roman practice, it would have been exceptional if he was.

54 Or: "This was the second time that Yeshua came from Y'hudah to the Galil and performed a miracle."

CHAPTER 5

1 **A Judean festival**, rather than "a Jewish festival," for reasons detailed at 1:19N. Yochanan uses this phrase at 6:4 and 11:55 (and a similar phrase at 2:13) in connection with *Pesach* (Passover) and at 7:1–3 in connection with *Sukkot* (Tabernacles). These are two of the three *regalim* (pilgrim festivals), the third being *Shavu'ot* (Weeks, Pentecost; see Ac 2:1&N). The focus here is not on the Jewishness of these festivals but on the fact that the *Torah* required all Jewish men to come to "the place *Adonai* your God shall choose" (Deuteronomy 16:16), which proved to be Yerushalayim in Y'hudah (Judea). Only in this verse is the festival not named. *Chanukkah*, a Jewish festival but not a pilgrim

festival tied to Judea, is mentioned at 10:22 but is not called a Judean festival. See 1:19N.
Went up to Yerushalayim. See Mt 20:17–19N.

2–16 A *Shabbat* healing by Yeshua. Three others are at Mt 12:9–14 (Mk 3:1–6, Lk 6:6–11), Lk 13:10–17, and Lk 14:1–6. Yochanan reports a fifth at 9:1–41 below. See notes to these passages.

3–4 The manuscripts with the extra words are inferior, but v. 7 seems to require some such explanation. Concerning this pool the *Encyclopedia Judaica* notes its mention in the New Testament and adds that "excavations of the site have revealed that a health rite took place there during the Roman period" (9:1539).

10 It's against *Torah* for you to carry your mat, that is, against the Judeans' (see 1:19N) or Pharisees' (see Mt 3:7N) understanding of the *Torah*, against their tradition, against what later became Jewish *halakhah*. Jeremiah 17:21–22 speaks against bearing a burden on *Shabbat*, but the context suggests that the prohibition is against working for profit, as at Nehemiah 13:19. The Mishna makes carrying in a public area on *Shabbat* unlawful. But in a walled city like Yerushalayim a special legal arrangement called an *'eruv* makes it legal to carry on *Shabbat*. Perhaps the man had his home outside the walls of Yerushalayim, beyond the range of the *'eruv*; or he may have been homeless and slept on his mat each night outside the city. Another possibility: he had not yet left Yerushalayim and was still in the Temple area, but the Judeans perceived that he was about to leave and were warning him not to violate *Shabbat* by carrying his mat through the gates. Note, however, that the Judeans ignored the miraculous healing and concerned themselves only with the infringement of their version of the Law; they could not see that the formerly crippled man's ability to carry his mat attested to God's glory.

14 Stop sinning, or something worse may happen to you. While disease is not invariably a consequence of sin, as Yeshua himself affirms (9:3), it can be. Also compare Mt 12:43–45.

17–18 "My Father, God, **has been working** on *Shabbat* since the beginning of time, **and** therefore **I too am working** on *Shabbat*." Here is an interesting alternative understanding: in the larger scheme of things, there is a "*Shabbat*" yet to come (MJ 4:9–11), so that the present era of history can be thought of as "weekdays." The Talmud too recognizes this by dividing history into six 1,000–year "days" (Psalm 90:4, and see 2 Ke 3:3–9&N), after which comes the Messianic millennium, the seventh "day" (Sanhedrin 97b). Since it is now still a 1,000–year "weekday," even the *Torah* "permits" the Father and Yeshua to work; and they will continue working until the "day" comes that is entirely *Shabbat*. (But in what sense they will cease working then is not evident.)

Yeshua's Judean opposition immediately perceived that **by saying God was his own Father he was claiming equality with God**. Some Jews would like to reclaim Yeshua for the Jewish people by regarding him as a great teacher, which he was, but only human, not divine. Yeshua's claim here makes that option impossible. A merely human "great teacher" who teaches that he is equal with God would be, as C. S. Lewis put it, either "a lunatic — on a level with a man who says he's a poached egg — or else He would be the devil of hell. You must make your choice. Either this man was, and is, the son of God: or else a madman or something worse." (*Mere Christianity*, New York: MacMillan, 1958, p. 41)

Yeshua's words produced the first reported effort to kill him. If he had been blaspheming God, as the Judeans thought, it would have been proper to be **intent on killing him**, since "Anyone who blasphemes the name of *Adonai* shall surely be put to death" (Leviticus 24:16; see below, 8:58&N). Yeshua's healing and his claim to equality with *Adonai* occasioned his discourse in the rest of this chapter.

19 **The Son cannot do anything on his own**. Those who find Yeshua's claim to divinity unpalatable are quick to point out that with these words Yeshua seems to describe himself in a way inconsistent with being divine. They say it is essential to God's nature that he does everything on his own and is answerable only to himself. But they miss the point, for Yeshua here is teaching something important about the inner nature of God, about how the Son and the Father relate to each other within the eternal unity of *Adonai*. Yeshua is teaching that he is capable, humanly, of disobeying God and of having his own contrary will (compare Mt 26:39). For this reason the divine Son "learned obedience" (MJ 5:8) and became completely submissive to the Father's will through the power of the *Ruach HaKodesh*, who is with him "in unlimited measure" (3:34). Yeshua is not inferior to his Father: to submit and obey perfectly demonstrates one of God's perfections; to will what is not God's will is to be inferior to God.

What he sees the Father doing. Yeshua's sight, whether spiritual only or physical as well, uniquely enables him to perceive what his Father does and wants.

Whatever the Father does, the Son does too. Yeshua is teaching that he has divine power. Specifically, he has power to raise the dead (v. 21) and the authority to render divine judgment (v. 22).

22 **The Father does not judge anyone**; rather, he has given judgment over to his Son (v. 27). Yet the *Tanakh* tells us that God will one day judge all humanity; and if it is the Father who entrusts judgment to the Son, then the Father does, after all, have a role in judgment as the delegator. From all this it follows that the Son is included in what is meant by "God." This is one of the many ways Yochanan deals with the mystery and paradox of Yeshua's simultaneous humanity and divinity; see also v. 30, 12:48–49.

23 **Whoever fails to honor the Son is not honoring the Father who sent him**. Compare Mt 22:33–46, 1 Yn 2:23, which also teach against the idea that one can honor, worship and believe in God without believing in Yeshua the Messiah, the Son of God.

29 **Resurrection of life… resurrection of judgment**. There are two kinds of deaths and resurrections; this is taught in the *Tanakh* at Daniel 12:2 and by Sha'ul at Ro 2:5–8. One is for those God considers righteous because they **have done good**. In the light of 6:28–29 below and Ep 2:8–10, this means they have trusted in Yeshua's execution as atonement for their sin, been immersed into his death, risen to eternal life (Ro 6:3–11, 23), and been granted a share in the "first resurrection" (Rv 20:4–6). The other is for **those**

who have done evil, who have not trusted in Yeshua; they are subject to the "second death" (Rv 20:12–15). See Ac 24:15&N.

31–47 After discounting his own witness (v. 31) Yeshua names five witnesses to who he is: Yochanan the Immerser (vv. 32–35), Yeshua's works (v. 36), the Father (vv. 37–38), the *Tanakh* (v. 39) and Moshe (vv. 45–47).

37–39 The Father who sent me has himself testified on my behalf. Similarly at 8:18.

Compare Jeremiah 29:23, "'I am the one who knows, and I am witness,' says *Adonai*."

But these Judeans cannot receive the Father's witness because **his word does not stay in** them. This is due to their hard hearts that do not believe God. A person with **love for God** would receive Yeshua. The main element of God's witness is his Word, Scripture, the *Tanakh*. Yeshua invites those who do not have the Word staying in them to search the Scriptures, just as the Jews of Berea later did (Ac 17:11).

40–44 On the strength of what Yeshua has said till now he now argues: (1) You do not have God's love in you. (2) Instead, you seek honor from men and from each other. (3) You refuse to come to me (Yeshua) to have life because you prefer honor from each other and because you want to honor those who come in their own name, not in God's name.

45–47 Yeshua saves for last the argument which would be the most meaningful to his hearers: Moshe wrote of Yeshua (Lk 16:31, 24:44; MJ 11:26). Traditional Judaism denies this, but the early Messianic Jews often based their case for Yeshua's Messiahship on passages of Scripture, including those written by Moshe, such as Genesis 49:10, Numbers 24:17 and Deuteronomy 18:15–18. Even within non-Messianic Judaism all three are widely regarded as referring to the Messiah. Therefore, says Yeshua, it is not even necessary for me to make a special accusation because Moshe has done it already: if you don't believe him, why would you believe me? Compare Lk 16:31.

CHAPTER 6

1–15 The third of Yeshua's miracles reported by Yochanan, the feeding of five thousand people, is told in the Synoptic Gospels in essentially the same way (Mt 14:13–21, Mk 6:32–44, Lk 9:10–17).

4–5 Judean festival of *Pesach*. See 5:1N.

Where will we be able to buy bread? Perhaps people had begun to reduce bread supplies in anticipation of Passover (see Mt 26:17N, 1C 5:6–8N). If so, it adds to the drama of vv. 7ff.

7 Half a year's wages, literally, "200 denarii."

12 According to *halakhah*, destruction of food is prohibited (Shabbat 50b, 147b). Also, before a meal, if the attendant sweeping the floor

> "is a scholar, he removes crumbs [of bread] the size of an olive and leaves those that are smaller. This supports what Rabbi Yochanan said: 'It is permissable to destroy wilfully crumbs smaller than an olive.'"(B'rakhot 52b)

In other words: waste not, want not; the rule is better thought of as a practical guide for housekeepers than a compulsive legalism. This is Jewish background for Yeshua's command to **gather the leftover pieces, so that nothing gets wasted**.

14 Not just any prophet, but **"the prophet"** of Deuteronomy 18:15, 18. Compare 1:21&N, 7:40; Ac 3:22–23&N, 7:37; Mt 21:11.

15 **They were on the point of coming and seizing him, in order to make him king**. The crowd wanted freedom from Roman rule and peace for Israel, and they thought Yeshua was the man for the hour. But his own view was different: "My kingship does not derive its authority from this world's order of things" (18:36). Had they succeeded, they would have nullified God's way of making Yeshua the Messiah, which was through his being the Suffering Servant dying for the sins of humanity, being resurrected, ascending to God's right hand and returning in future glory to assume the throne. The hope then as now among traditional non-Messianic Jews was for a conquering hero.

16–21 Compare Mt 14:22, Mk 6:45–52.

21 **Instantly the boat reached the land**. Another miracle, one not reported by Mattityahu or Mark.

26–71 The attitude of the crowd generates Yeshua's lengthy discourse.

26 **Miraculous signs** should awaken consciousness of God, but these people are conscious only of their own physical needs.

27 **The food which passes away** and **the food that stays on into eternal life** are opposites and constitute the theme of Yeshua's remarks.

28–29 **What should we do in order to perform the works of God?** The people are probably not asking how to do miracles but how to please God. Nevertheless Yeshua's answer surprises them.

30–32 **What miracle will you do?** A strange question for people who have just seen him do one (vv. 10–14). But they seem set on diminishing its importance by presenting one equally great or greater: **Our fathers ate manna in the desert**; see also Exodus 16:4, 15; Numbers 11:8; Psalm 105:40. Yeshua corrects his questioners' exegesis of the *Tanakh* — they think **"he"** refers to **Moshe**, but Yeshua says its antecedent is **my Father**, God.

36 **You have seen but still don't trust**. For this refusal to trust Yeshua their sin is all the greater; compare 15:24, also 20:29.

37 Everyone the Father gives me will come to me... whoever comes to me I will certainly not turn away. This is as forthright a statement of the paradox of predestination and free will as can be found. The Father has given certain people to Yeshua. How do I find out if I am one of them? By coming to Yeshua: I have free will and can choose to come, and I have Yeshua's word that he will not turn me away. Some claim that New Testament faith is exclusivist, but here we see that Yeshua is available universally (see also Ro 10:11–13).

41 Judeans in sense (3)(c) of Lowe's classification (see 1:19N); likewise at v. 52. Alternatively, *Ioudaioi* means something like "unbelievers" in these two verses. The questioning has now escalated to **grumbling**.

42 Yeshua Ben-Yosef... his father. See 1:45N.

44 No one can come to me unless the Father... draws him. Another insight into the framework of free will (see v. 37&N).

51–66 The bread that I will give is my own flesh, and I give it for the life of the world.... Unless you eat the flesh of the Son of Man and drink his blood, you do not have life in you (vv. 51, 53). Because of what Yeshua said here the grumbling (v. 42) quickly became disputing (v. 52), then a **hard word** they couldn't **bear to listen to** (v. 60), and finally an insuperable barrier for **many of his *talmidim*** (not merely his casual hearers), who **turned back and no longer traveled around with him** (v. 66).

The most literal sense of the text implies cannibalism, which, were it what Yeshua meant, would certainly be an insuperable barrier to faith in him. But even a high view of the inspiration of the Bible does not require the elimination of metaphorical and symbolic language. Although Yeshua's particular hearers may have been either shocked at what he said or seeking an excuse for not obeying his call to repentance and loyalty, not every Jewish audience would have reacted that way. For the same kind of metaphor is used in the Midrash Rabbah to Ecclesiastes 2:24 ("There is nothing better for a man than that he should eat and drink"). The *Midrash* quotes rabbis from the 3rd–4th centuries C.E.:

> "Rabbi Tanchuma said in the name of Rabbi Nachman ben-Rabbi Shmu'el ben-Nachman, and Rabbi Menachma said (according to another version Rabbi Yirmiyahu and Rabbi [Y'hudah HaNasi] said in the name of Rabbi Shmu'el ben-Rabbi Yitzchak): 'All references to eating and drinking in the book of *Qohelet* [Ecclesiastes] signify *Torah* and good works.' Rabbi Yonah said, 'The clearest proof for this is Ecclesiastes 8:15, "A man has no better thing under the sun than to eat, drink and be merry, and that this should accompany him in his labor." The word for "his labor" is "*'amalo*," but it should be read "*'olamo*" ("his world"), that is, in this world. The verse continues, All "the days of his life"; and that alludes to the grave. So are there food and drink in the grave that accompany a person to the grave? Of course not. Therefore "food and drink" must mean *Torah* and good works.'"

The point is that Jewish understanding allows for symbolic interpretation of "food and drink." To eat the flesh of the Son of Man is to absorb his entire way of being and living. The Greek word "*sarx*" ("flesh") is also used to refer to human nature in general, to the physical, emotional, mental and volitional aspects of human existence. Yeshua wants us to live, feel, think and act like him; by the power of the *Ruach HaKodesh* he enables us to do so. Likewise, to drink his blood is to absorb his self-sacrificing life-motivation and indeed his very life, since "the life of the flesh is in the blood" (Leviticus 17:11). Jews and Gentiles open to the truth of who Yeshua is will find this interpretation acceptable.

This passage in Yochanan and the statement of Yeshua about the *matzah* at the Last Supper (Mt 26:26), "This is my body," have led to much theologizing about the nature of the identification between the bread and Yeshua's body. But even the Roman Catholic doctrine of "transubstantiation" of the bread, which says that it "becomes" his body, is not meant to be taken in the crude sense of transformation of one physical substance into another. While it is true that the language of such theologizing is alien to Jewish ears, as, for example, when it speaks of the "real presence" of Yeshua's body in the bread, still the overall intent of the discussion is not distant from what was said in the paragraph quoted from the Midrash. And despite academic debate over what is meant by the "real presence," none would assert Yeshua's "real absence" from believers and the bread they eat at the common meal.

59 **A synagogue in K'far-Nachum.** Yeshua spoke here on another occasion; see Mk 1:21–29.

62 Compare 1:51, 3:13, 17:5.

63 **The flesh is no help**. This is not a downgrading of the body in some Greek dualistic sense, but rather a typically Jewish assertion that without the Spirit of God the physical things have no value of their own.

64–65 See vv. 37&N, 44&N; also compare 2:25.

66 Yeshua succeeded in winnowing out those who were not sincere or who found too high the cost of eating his flesh and drinking his blood. Compare Lk 14:25–33, also addressed to a crowd.

68–69 Kefa's confession of faith in Yeshua may be compared with Mt 16:16, Mk 8:29 and Lk 9:20.

70 **An adversary**, Greek *diabolos*, which gives us the English word "devil." See Mt 4:1N. Yet this is *remez*, not *p'shat* (Mt 2:15N) — Yeshua does not simply equate Y'hudah from K'riot (v. 71) with Satan.

CHAPTER 7

1 **Avoiding Y'hudah because the Judeans** (not "the Jews") **were out to kill him. Y'hudah** (Judea, Greek *Ioudaia*) is mentioned three times in vv. 1–3; this is overwhelming evidence in favor of translating "*Ioudaioi*" here as **Judeans** and not "Jews." And if this is the case here, there is no good reason to translate differently in many other places where Judea is not explicitly mentioned. See 1:19N for more on this subject.

2 Judean festival of *Sukkot*, that is, the Feast of Tabernacles (temporary dwellings), when Jewish males were required to go to Yerushalayim (see v. 1N, 5:1N). Leviticus 23:33–43, Numbers 29:12–39 and Deuteronomy 16:13–16 prescribe details of *Sukkot*. It commences on the 15th day of Tishri, five days after *Yom-Kippur* (the Day of Atonement), and lasts seven days, with an eighth day, *Sh'mini Atzeret*, an added day of rest; this means it comes during late September or October. Families build booths of palm branches, partly open to the sky, to recall God's providence toward Israel during the forty years of wandering in the desert and living in tents. The festival also celebrates the harvest, coming, as it does, at summer's end, so that it is a time of thanksgiving. (The Puritans, who took the Old Testament more seriously than most Christians, modeled the American holiday of Thanksgiving after *Sukkot*.) To observe the festival people brought to the Temple an *etrog* ("citron"), a citrus fruit representing the fruit of the Promised Land, and waved a *lulav*, which is a palm branch, a myrtle and a willow bound together; today the same is done in the synagogues.

The festival is prophetically connected with the fate of the Gentiles, for Zechariah writes:

> "It shall come about that everyone left of all the nations who came against Yerushalayim shall go up from year to year to worship the King, *Adonai* of Heaven's Armies, and to keep the festival of *Sukkot*. For whoever does not come up from all the families of the earth to worship the King, *Adonai* of Heaven's Armies, there will be no rain. If the family of Egypt does not go up, if it does not come, then they will have no overflow [from the Nile River]. This will be the plague with which *Adonai* will smite the nations that do not come up to keep the festival of *Sukkot*. This will be the punishment of Egypt and of all nations that do not come up to keep the festival of *Sukkot*." (Zechariah 14:16–19)

This refers to the Messianic Age, after the whole world has come against Yerushalayim and been defeated; in the light of the New Testament it should be understood as taking place after the second coming of Yeshua the Messiah. The rabbis of the *Talmud* recognized the connection of this festival with the Gentiles: speaking of the seventy bulls required by Numbers 29:12–34 to be sacrificed during the seven days of the festival, "Rabbi El'azar said, 'To what do these seventy bulls correspond? To the seventy nations'"(Sukkah 55b). In rabbinic tradition, the traditional number of Gentile nations is seventy; the seventy bulls are to make atonement for them.

The festival of *Sukkot* is the background for Chapters 7–8 of Yochanan's Gospel. Further details of its customs are needed to understand 7:37–39 and 8:12; see notes there.

3–8 Yeshua's **brothers... had not put their trust in him** (v. 5). It is sometimes argued that if his brothers did not believe in him, why should we? But one of them, Ya'akov, not only came to trust in him later but became leader of the Messianic Jewish community in Yerushalayim (Ac 2:17; 15:13; 21:18; Ga 1:19; 2:9, 12); and he is usually credited with authorship of the book of Ya'akov. Likewise another brother, Y'hudah, is thought to be the author of the New Testament book bearing his name.

Yeshua was not swayed by his brothers' challenge, which seems to have stemmed from a reasonable and friendly — yet entirely human — motive, the desire to see their brother succeed and become famous. Yeshua had performed miracles in the Galil; his brothers apparently felt he should not delay in developing his reputation in Judea too and even gave a plausible argument (v. 4). But Yeshua had another agenda. **My time has not yet come** (v. 6), either to go to the festival or to do miracles in Judea. Underlying the repeated mentioning of Yeshua's "time" (see 2:4N) is the theme of his basic mission, to die for the sins of mankind; this was to take place exactly at God's right moment and was not to be precipitated by any human challenge.

8 **I am not going up... now**. (On "going up to Yerushalayim" see Mt 20:17–19N.) There is a textual question. The preferred reading has *ouk* ("not"), which yields as the simplest rendering, "I am not going up." *Oupô* ("not yet"), found in some manuscripts, is considered by Bruce Metzger (*A Textual Commentary on the Greek New Testament*) as having been introduced later by scribes uncomfortable with v. 10, which says he *did* go up. I have no reason to doubt *ouk*. But the Greek present tense, which often has ongoing force, allows this understanding: "I am not at present in the process of going up," or, more simply, "**I am not going up now** but may do so later — I'm not telling."

12 At 5:17–18N I pointed out that the option of regarding Yeshua as merely a great teacher is illusory and not in keeping with what he taught. It is similarly impossible to regard him merely as **a good man**, although he certainly was one.

15 **Without having studied**, that is, without having attended any of the usual *yeshivot*, sitting under the rabbis and *Torah*-teachers who inculcated the Pharisaic oral tradition of *Torah*. The implication is that the speakers regarded Yeshua as an *'am-ha'aretz*, that is, a "hick" (see v. 49N, Ac 4:13&N; compare Mt 13:54–55, 21:2–7&N; Mk 6:2; Lk 4:22). Actually, Talmudic tradition reports that "Yeshu" (see Mt 1:21N) learned from Rabbi Y'hoshua ben-Perachyah, who was the chief teacher of his day (Sanhedrin 107b, Sotah 47a). Although this is historically impossible, since the rabbi lived about a hundred years earlier, we see that Jewish tradition does not regard Yeshua as religiously ignorant. The New Testament reports demonstrate that he had not only wide knowledge of both biblical and traditional materials, but wisdom from God transcending academic credentials.

17 **If anyone wants to do his will**. This refers not merely to feelings, attitudes or mental assent but to having decided to obey God. Such a person will come to know whether Yeshua is the Messiah, the Son of God, as he himself teaches.

19 Two quick punches: (1) the people are not obeying the *Torah* Moshe gave them, even though they suppose they are; for if they were, they would welcome Yeshua (see 5:45–47). (2) Yeshua was spiritually discerning: he spoke what they felt in their hearts (2:25) but did not want to admit (see next verse).

20 A godly person reacts to having his sin exposed by admitting it, being sorry at having done wrong and resolving, with God's power, to change. Here we see the normal reaction of a worldly person to having his sin exposed: accusation of the exposer and denial of the sin.

21 **I did** only **one thing**, literally, "one work," the miracle of 5:9, **and because of** merely **this all of you are** in fact **amazed** in spite of yourselves, even though at the same time you are out to kill me because I did it on *Shabbat*.

22–23 **Moshe gave you *b'rit-milah*** in the *Torah* at Leviticus 12:3. **Not that it came from Moshe but from the Patriarchs**, Avraham, Yitzchak and Ya'akov; for God gave the command of circumcision to Avraham in Genesis 17:1–27, and he carried it out on Yitzchak at Genesis 21:4, all centuries before Moshe.

A boy is circumcised on *Shabbat* so that the *Torah* of Moshe will not be broken. The *Torah* states that a Jewish male child is to be circumcised on the eighth day of his life (Genesis 17:12, Leviticus 12:3), but it also prohibits work on *Shabbat* (Exodus 20:9–10, 23:12, 31:14–15, 34:21, 35:2; Leviticus 23:3; Deuteronomy 5:12–14). Therefore, if the eighth day of a boy's life falls on *Shabbat*, is circumcision to be put off till the ninth day, or is *Shabbat* to be broken by doing the work of tool-carrying and cutting needed for the operation? The Judeans (the Jewish religious authorities centered in Judea; see 1:19N) of Yeshua's time had already decided the question, and their decision stands on record in the *Talmud*.

The following is from my discussion in *Messianic Jewish Manifesto*, p. 159:

> "In this passage Yeshua presents a *din-torah* that the *mitzvah* of healing takes precedence over that of refraining from work on *Shabbat*. In making this decision as to which of two conflicting laws holds in a particular situation, he was doing much the same thing as did the rabbis who developed the Oral *Torah*. In fact, Yeshua referred in this passage to a well-known such decision which can be found in the *Talmud*, tractate *Shabbat*, pages [128b-137b].
>
> "The rabbis were confronted with the conflict between the law against working on *Shabbat* and the commandment that a man should circumcise his son on the eighth day of his life. The conflict arises from the fact that cutting and carrying through a public domain the tools needed to perform a *b'rit-milah* are kinds of work forbidden by the rabbis on *Shabbat*. They decided that if the eighth day falls on *Shabbat*, one does the necessary work and circumcises the boy; but if the circumcision must take place after the eighth day, say, for health reasons, it may not be done on *Shabbat* in violation of the work prohibitions — one waits till a weekday.
>
> "Yeshua in defending his ruling used what Judaism calls a *kal v'chomer* ('light and heavy') argument, known in philosophy as reasoning *a fortiori* ('from greater strength'). Its essence is the expressed or implied phrase 'how much more…!' Yochanan 7:23 says, in effect, 'You permit breaking *Shabbat* in order to observe the *mitzvah* of circumcision; how much more important it is to heal a person's whole body, so you should permit breaking *Shabbat* for that too!'"

In fact traditional Judaism makes use of reasoning identical with Yeshua's in regard to this matter. The Talmud records that to the question of why saving life suspends the *Shabbat* work prohibitions,

> "Rabbi El'azar answered, 'If circumcision, which involves only one of the 248 parts of the human body, suspends *Shabbat,* how much more must [saving] the whole body suspend *Shabbat!"* (Yoma 85b)

These verses of Yochanan are important because they prove that Yeshua did not oppose the Pharisees' tradition *per se*. He was not against legislation needed to apply the *Torah* to particular times and circumstances, but against attributing to that legislation inspiration by God (Mk 7:5–13&N). In v. 24 Yeshua gives his standard for developing "oral law": "Stop judging by surface appearances, and judge the right way!"

27 **We know where this man comes from**, that is, from Nazareth and from ordinary human parents (6:42). **But when the Messiah comes, no one will know where he comes from**. This expectation that the origins of the Messiah must be shrouded in mystery contradicts Micah 5:1, which predicts the Messiah's birth in Bethlehem (as cited in Mt 2:1–8). See vv. 41–42&N.

35 **Greek-speaking Jews**. The word in the text is *"Ellênôn"* ("Greeks"). Did the Judeans wonder if Yeshua would teach Gentiles? The word "Greek" often means "Gentile" in the writings of Luke and Sha'ul. But I think that since the text explicitly refers to **the Greek Diaspora** ("dispersion"), which has meaning with respect to Jews and not with respect to Gentiles, the Judeans have in mind either Greek or Greek-speaking Jews. Of these two it seems much more likely that **the Greek Diaspora** refers to the entire territory conquered by Alexander, where Greek had become the *lingua franca*, than to Greece specifically. See also 12:20–21&N, Ac 6:1&N.

37 **On the last day of the festival, *Hoshana Rabbah***, literally, "on the last day, the great, of the festival." Greek *megalê* ("great") corresponds to Hebrew *rabbah*. The seventh, last day of *Sukkot* was its climax. Throughout the seven days of the festival a special *cohen* had carried water in a gold pitcher from the Pool of Shiloach (Siloam) to be poured into a basin at the foot of the altar by the *cohen hagadol*. It symbolized prayer for rain, which begins the next day, on *Sh'mini Atzeret*; and it also pointed toward the outpouring of the *Ruach HaKodesh* on the people of Israel. The rabbis associated the custom with Isaiah 12:3, "With joy shall you draw water from the wells of salvation." (In a suggestive reflection of how the holiday used to be celebrated, today's Moroccan Jews pour water on each other at *Sukkot*.) On the seventh day the water pouring was accompanied by *cohanim* blowing gold trumpets, *L'vi'im* singing sacred songs, and ordinary people waving their *lulav*s and chanting the *Hallel* (Psalms 113–118), which includes in its closing verses:

> *"Adonai*, please save us! [Hebrew *Hoshia' na* or *Hoshana*]
> *Adonai*, please prosper us!
> Blessed is he who comes in the name of *Adonai!*

> We have blessed you out of the house of *Adonai*.
> God is *Adonai*, and he has given us light." (Psalm 118:25–27)

The words, "Please save us!" led to the day's being called *Hoshana Rabbah*, the Great Hosanna. This prayer had Messianic overtones, as is seen from its use when Yeshua made his triumphal entry into Yerushalayim a few days before his execution (Mt 21:9, Mk 11:9–10). It was also a prayer for salvation from sin, for *Hoshana Rabbah* was understood to be the absolutely final chance to have one's sins for the year forgiven. On *Rosh-Hashanah* one asks to "be inscribed in the Book of Life" (see Rv 20:12bN), and on *Yom-Kippur* one hopes to have that inscription "sealed"; yet in Jewish tradition there remained opportunity for forgiveness up to *Hoshana Rabbah*.

In addition,

> "A connection between the possession of the *Ruach ha-Kodesh* and ecstasy, or religious joy, is found in the ceremony of water drawing, *Simchat Beit-HaSho'evah* ["feast of water-drawing"], on the festival of *Sukkot*. The Mishnah said that he who had never seen this ceremony, which was accompanied by dancing, singing and music (Sukkot 5:4), had never seen true joy (Sukkot 5:1). Yet this was also considered a ceremony in which the participants, as it were, drew inspiration from the Holy Spirit itself, which can only be possessed by those whose hearts are full of religious joy (Jerusalem Talmud, Sukkot 5:1, 55a)." (*Encyclopedia Judaica* 14:365)

From this passage we also learn that Yeshua and his *talmidim*, like other Jews, observed at least portions of the Oral *Torah* and did not utterly reject it as "traditions of men" (see Mk 7:5–13&N) — since the water-drawing ceremony is specified not in the *Tanakh* but in the Mishna.

It was in the midst of this water pouring, trumpet blasting, palm waving, psalm chanting and ecstatic joy on the part of people seeking forgiveness — and in the presence of all 24 divisions of the priesthood (see Lk 1:5N) — that Yeshua cried out in the Temple courts, **"If anyone is thirsty, let him keep coming to me and drinking! Whoever trusts in me, as the *Tanakh* says, rivers of living water will flow from his inmost being!"** Compare Isaiah 44:3, 55:1, 58:11; also the woman at the well, above, 4:6–15; and the ultimate fulfillment at Rv 22:17. In effect Yeshua was declaring, "I am the answer to your prayers." His dramatic cry, supported by the full panoply of Temple ritual, was not misunderstood, as vv. 40–43 make abundantly clear. His subsequent proclamation, "I am the light of the world," also based on the passage of Psalm 118 quoted above, provoked an even more agitated reaction (8:12&N, 58–59&N).

39 The Spirit had not been given, because Yeshua had not yet been glorified. See 14:26, 15:26, 16:7–15 and 17:5 for an explanation of this verse; see also Ac 1:8 and its fulfillment at Ac 2:4ff., when the Holy Spirit did come.

40 The prophet. See 1:21N.

41–42 But others said, "How can the Messiah come from the Galil? Doesn't the

***Tanakh* say that the Messiah is from the seed of David and comes from Beit-Lechem?"** Yes, the *Tanakh* does say that (2 Samuel 7:12–13; Jeremiah 23:5–6; Micah 5:1(2)); Psalms 89:36–38(35–37), 132:11; 1 Chronicles 7:11, 14). Chapter 2 of Mattityahu explains how the Messiah could come from both Beit-Lechem in Y'hudah and Natzeret in the Galil: he was born in Beit-Lechem, taken to Egypt to escape the massacre of infants ordered by Herod, and by God's command returned to Natzeret. Luke 2:1–7 further explains why a family from Natzeret happened to be in Beit-Lechem for Yeshua's birth: the Romans ordered a census and required everyone to return to his own city for it. Doubters could have inquired and learned these things, but, as is common with people whose minds are made up, they did not wish to be "confused by the facts."

43 So the people were divided because of him. Yeshua the Messiah always divides people into two camps: those who are with him and those who are not. The middle ground quickly disappears.

47 The *P'rushim* think their guards are deceived, but their answer (v. 46) suggests more that they are bemused.

48 Has any of the authorities put their trust in him? Or any of the *P'rushim*? The questioners suppose a negative answer, but Nakdimon may have already trusted in Yeshua (see vv. 50–52); by 19:39 he surely had. Have any of the modern era's Jewish authorities put their trust in Yeshua? See Ac 4:13N.

49 These *'am-ha'aretz* do, but they know nothing about the *Torah*, they are under a curse! The critical Judeans, although trained in the *Torah*, which teaches love, not only despise the *'am-ha'aretz*, the "people of the land" (see v. 15N, Ac 4:13&N), but regard them as under a curse because of their lack of education.

52 Study the *Tanakh* and see for yourself that no prophet comes from the Galil! One need not study it deeply to find that the prophet Jonah came from Gat-Hefer in the Galil (2 Kings 14:25). On this subject the *Talmud* agrees: "Rabbi Eli'ezer... said..., 'There was not a tribe in Israel which did not produce prophets'"(Sukkah 27b). But the Greek text also allows the meaning that no future prophet comes from the Galil and does not refer to the past. See also vv. 41–42&N.

7:53–8:11 See the note on this passage in the *JNT* itself. Bruce Metzger, in *A Textual Commentary on the Greek New Testament, ad loc.*, writes that

> "the account has all the earmarks of historical veracity. It is obviously a piece of oral tradition which circulated in certain parts of the Western church and which was subsequently incorporated into various manuscripts in various places,"

namely, into Yochanan's Gospel after 7:36, 7:44 or 7:52, and into Luke's Gospel after 21:25 or 21:38. On the strength of its apparent "historical veracity" the *JNT* includes it here in its traditional location, with the asterisked note explaining that some scholars doubt whether it was originally part of this Gospel.

Then they all left, each one to his own home (7:53). If this remark is in chronological order, it seems to refer to the return of the pilgrims at the end of the *Sukkot* holiday to their homes in regions and countries distant from Jerusalem (see 5:1N), while **Yeshua went to the Mount of Olives** (8:1) instead of going down to Nazareth. Perhaps he stayed in Bethany, on the flanks of the Mount of Olives, at the home of his friends Miryam, Marta and El'azar (11:1–2&N) at least until *Chanukkah* (10:22) and probably until he left to go to the East Bank of the Jordan River (10:40). The interchange with the woman caught in adultery took place after **daybreak** (8:2) the next day, which was still *Hoshana Rabbah* (7:37&N), since Jewish days begin at sunset. Later the same day he said, "I am the light of the world," which relates to *Hoshana Rabbah* customs (8:12&N).

CHAPTER 8

1–11 See 7:53–8:11N.

5 **In our *Torah* Moshe commanded that such a woman be stoned to death**. Leviticus 20:10, Deuteronomy 22:22–24; see also Numbers 5:11–31. Under Roman rule it was illegal for Jewish courts to enforce a death sentence, but that did not always succeed in preventing stonings (Ac 7:58–59) or attempts thereat (v. 59, 10:31).

7, 11 Yeshua's response showed four things: he was not against the *Torah*, he was merciful toward the woman, he opposed her sin (Exodus 20:13(14)), and he could silence hecklers and put them to shame (compare Mt 22:46).

12 **Yeshua spoke to them again**, still on the last day of *Sukkot*, *Hoshana Rabbah* (7:37&N, 7:53–8:11N).

I am the light of the world: whoever follows me will never walk in darkness but will have the light which gives life. Compare Isaiah 9:1(2), "The people who walked in darkness have seen a great light," and Malachi 4:2(3:20), "But to you who fear my name the sun of righteousness will arise with healing in his wings"; both are alluded to at Lk 1:78–79. Also see Isaiah 49:6 (quoted at Ac 13:47); Yn 1:4–5, 7–9; 3:19–21; 5:35; 9:5; 12:35–36, 46; Ac 9:3, 13:47&N; 1 Ke 2:9; 1 Yn 1:5–7, 2:8–10. All of these texts have been understood as referring to Yeshua as the light or in connection with light.

His remark was specifically suited to the feast of *Sukkot*; for, according to the Mishna, at the Temple

> "there were four golden *menorah*s with four golden bowls at the top of each, and four ladders each leading to a bowl. Four strong young *cohanim* would climb up with pitchers each holding 9 liters of oil which they would pour into the bowls. From the worn-out drawers and girdles of the *cohanim* they made wicks, and with them they lit the *menorah*s; and there was not a courtyard in Jerusalem that was not lit up by the light of the *Beit-HaSho'evah* [festivities]. Pious men and men of good deeds would dance around [the *menorah*s] with lit torches in their hands, singing songs and praises, while the Levites played harps, lyres, cymbals, trumpets and innumerable other musical instruments...." (Sukkah 5:2–4)

The Gemara on this passage says the *menorahs* were 75 feet high (Sukkah 52b). Thus, the water-drawing festival was accompanied by bright lights and dancing — for *Sukkot* is specifically a festival of rejoicing. As before, when the water from Shiloach was being poured and Yeshua used the occasion to invite people to come to him and drink, now he uses the fact that the feast is accompanied by a blaze of light to announce, "I am the light of the world," adding a promise with implications for both this life and eternity. For background see 7:2N, 7:37N.

15 **I pass judgment on no one**. Not now, during his human life, during his first coming. In the future he will judge everyone (5:22, 27–30).

17 **Your *Torah***. Some, perhaps to cast suspicion on whether Yeshua considered himself a Jew, suppose that with these words he distanced himself from the *Torah*, that by calling it **your *Torah*** he meant that it belonged to the Judeans or *P'rushim* but not to him. But there is no such implication, for Yeshua too is part of the Jewish people to whom the *Torah* was given. Rather, the sense is that since the *Torah* is theirs, as they themselves have already claimed (v. 5), they should heed it. (Compare President John F. Kennedy's famous inauguration address challenge, "Ask not what your country can do for you, but what you can do for your country." Needless to say, Kennedy considered America his own country too.)

The testimony of two people is valid. Deuteronomy 17:15, 19:15.

18 Obviously Yeshua is not using the texts referred to in the previous verse in a literal sense to prove, as he would if it were actually a court hearing, that he has two acceptable witnesses. He is using them midrashically: he and his Father have independent wills (5:19N) and are therefore "two" witnesses.

19 Yeshua never speaks of Yosef as his father in any of the Gospels; always he speaks of God as his Father. See 1:45N.

21 **And you will die in your sin**. A new teaching. Until now Yeshua has not said you must trust in him unless you are prepared to die in your sin.

24 **I am who I say I am**, literally, just "I am." Yeshua is intimating here and in v. 28 that he is to be identified with God; see 4:26N.

28 **When you lift up the Son of Man**. Yeshua is predicting the manner and instrumentality of his death: these Judeans will have him crucified by the Romans. See 3:14N, 12:32.

30–32 There is a kind of trust which falls short of making one **really** a *talmid* (see 2:23–25, Mt 5:1N) of Yeshua. Real ***talmidim*** **obey** Yeshua, which is more than mentally acknowledging who he is. The popular quotation, "**You will know the truth, and the truth will set you free**," is conditioned on obeying what Yeshua says.

33 **We are the seed of Avraham**. See Yochanan the Immerser's response to a similar claim (Mt 3:9&N); also Ga 3:16&N, 3:29&N.

We… have never been slaves. True for the speakers but not for the nation, which was redeemed from slavery in Egypt. The "Four Questions" of the *Haggadah* read on Passover are answered by a passage which begins, "*'Avadim hayinu*" ("We were slaves"). The speakers are avoiding Yeshua's challenge by invoking extreme literalism.

34 **Slave of sin**. See the exposition of this concept by Sha'ul at Ro 6:14–23.

36 Contrast the well-known line in the Passover *Haggadah*, "Now we are slaves; next year may we be free!" Why next year, why not now? But also note Ro 8:18–25.

41 **We're not illegitimate children**, like you (implied)! Apparently they knew something about the unusual circumstances of Yeshua's birth. Compare 9:34; also Mattityahu 1–2, Luke 1–3 and notes there.

44 **You belong to your father, the Adversary** (Greek *diabolos*, "devil," used in the Septuagint to translate Hebrew *satan*, "adversary"; see Mt 4:1N). Yeshua is through playing games: he has listened to these people claim Avraham and God as their father; he is no longer interested in wrong answers.

46 **Which one of you can show me where I'm wrong?** Or: "Which one of you can convict me of sin?" In either case the answer is: No one.

48 **You are from Shomron**. Of course he wasn't, but they are insulting him; see 4:9N, 7:20N.

57 **You're not yet fifty years old.** The implication is that he appears close enough to fifty for the statement to be meaningful as a reasonable upper limit to his estimated age; yet we know that he was "about thirty" when he began his public ministry (Lk 3:23) and that his ministry lasted no longer than three years. Conclusion: he must have looked older than he was. Other commentators take fifty as the upper limit of the active life span, as, for example, in Numbers 4:3, 39; 8:24–25; but to me this seems arbitrary and irrelevant to the context.

58–59 **Before Avraham came into being, I AM.** This and 10:30 are Yeshua's clearest self-pronouncements of his divinity. On **"I AM"** see 4:26N. It was very clear to the Judeans exactly what Yeshua's claim was, because they immediately took up stones to put him to death (v. 59) for blasphemy. Claiming to be God and, specifically, pronouncing God's name (as Yeshua had just done) were punishable by death (Leviticus 24:15–16 and Mishna Sanhedrin 7:5, "The blasphemer is not guilty until he pronounces the Name.").

CHAPTER 9

2 Yeshua's *talmidim* were not the first to attribute all human misfortune and disability to immediately traceable sin: the entire book of Job is devoted to combatting this misunderstanding of how sin has come to affect the present world. Verses 1–5 of this chapter correspond to Chapters 1–2 of Job; both set the scene for teaching about sin.

6 **Made some mud with the saliva**. Building is one of the thirty-nine kinds of work prohibited on *Shabbat* according to Mishna Shabbat 7:2; Mishna Shabbat 24:3 also says that on *Shabbat* "it is permitted to put water into the bran" of animals, "but they must knead it." It requires kneading to make clay, and clay is a building material; so there are two possible violations of *Shabbat*, according to Pharisaic understanding — building and kneading.

Put the mud on the man's eyes. If this was done as a means of healing and with the intention of healing, this too would have been regarded as a violation of *Shabbat*; see Lk 6:7N, but also Yn 7:22–23&N.

7 **Shiloach**, Greek *Siloam*. Hebrew *shiloach* means "sent," as Yochanan says. The Pool of Shiloach still exists, in the neighborhood of East Jerusalem called Silwan (which is the Arabic transliteration of "*shiloach* "). It marks the end of Hezekiah's Tunnel, constructed by the Judean king around 700 B.C.E. to bring water from the Gichon spring in the Kidron Valley to the Pool of Shiloach in the City of David (2 Kings 20:20, 2 Chronicles 32:30).

16 **He doesn't keep *Shabbat*.** A false accusation (see 7:22–23&N), which the accusers take as a fact. **So there was a split among them**, as before; see 7:43&N.

17 **He is a prophet** and more — see the man's response to additional information about Yeshua (vv. 35–38).

22 **Banned from the synagogue**, here, 12:42 and 16:2; in Greek a single word, "*aposunagogos*," literally, "de-synagogued." Judaism has three degrees of excommunication, though none is common today. The lightest, *n'zifah* ("rebuke"), could be declared by one person and normally lasted seven days. The next, *niddui* ("casting out, rejection"), usually required three people to declare and lasted thirty days, and people were required to stay four cubits (six feet) from him. The most severe, *cherem*, was a ban of indefinite duration; and a person under *cherem* was treated like one dead. (In the Talmud see Mo'ed Katan 16a–17a, N'darim 7b, Pesachim 52a.) For a family so poor as to allow their son to beg — begging charity was to be avoided as much as giving charity was to be practiced — being de-synagogued would have been a dreadful disaster. For Messianic Jews today social ostracism by family and/or the Jewish community — that is, being treated as if under a *cherem* — can be a cost to be counted when committing one's life to Yeshua (see Lk 14:26–33&N).

24 **Swear to God that you will tell the truth!** (literally, "Give glory to God!"). **We know that this man is a sinner**. Reading with a twentieth-century mentality, the sense one would arrive at is: "Give the glory to God, not to the person who put mud on your eyes; he doesn't deserve glory and couldn't have been responsible for your healing, because we know he is an open sinner." But the phrase, "Give glory to God," often precedes a solemn judicial statement; here it is an adjuration to admit as true the conclusion these

P'rushim have reached (compare Joshua 7:19 and 1 Samuel 6:5). Who deserves credit for the healing is not at issue.

34 Why, you *mamzer*! (literally, "In sins you were born, entirely!"). The Hebrew and Yiddish word "*mamzer*" is often rendered "illegitimate son," although technically it refers specifically to the offspring of a marriage prohibited in Leviticus 18; according to *halakhah*, a *mamzer* may not marry a legitimate daughter of Israel, only a *mamzeret*. Here the Jewish English term "*mamzer*" is used colloquially (like the English word "bastard") to convey with precision and force the hot-tempered and insulting valence of the Judeans' response.

And they threw him out, carrying out the threat of v. 22.

35–38 Yeshua meets the newly outcast formerly blind man, who has exchanged exclusion from the world of seeing for exclusion from society, and brings him to faith in himself as Messiah. Clearly the man was ready to believe.

39 It is to judge that I came into this world. Not a contradiction with 5:22&N, 8:15&N. The "judging" that Yeshua did at his first coming consisted in making clear to people where they really stood in respect to God, as the rest of the verse explains. Only at his second coming does he judge the world (5:22, 27–30).

40–41 Compare Jeremiah 2:35, where *Adonai* speaks almost identically to his people Israel.

CHAPTER 10

1–21 Yeshua changes the metaphor. He is the **good shepherd** (vv. 11–14); compare 21:15–17, MJ 13:20, 1 Ke 5:4; see also Ezekiel 34:23, 37:24 and Psalm 23.

8 Those who have come before me have been thieves and robbers. Compare Jeremiah 23:1–2, Ezekiel 34:1–22; also Ac 5:36–37&NN.

16 I have other sheep which are not from this pen, namely, Gentiles, whom Yeshua says he will combine with the Jews into **one flock** under himself, the **one shepherd**. Although at first he sent his *talmidim* only to "the lost sheep of the house of Israel" (Mt 10:5) and spoke of his own commission in the same way (Mt 15:24), this limitation applied only to his life before resurrection. Moreover, he intimated the coming inclusion of Gentiles when he healed the Roman army officer's orderly (Mt 8:5–13) and the daughter of the woman from Cana'an (Mt 15:22–28), ministered to the woman at the well in Shomron (4:1–26), and prophesied that many would come from the east and the west to sit with the Patriarchs (Mt 8:11) and that some nations (or Gentiles; see Mt 5:46N) would be judged favorably (Mt 25:31–46&N).

This joining of non-Jews to God's people is alluded to again at 11:52 and is the major subject of the book of Acts, of Sha'ul's letters to the Romans, Galatians and Ephesians, and of the book of Revelation. The ingathering of Gentiles has begun but has not been completed. Portions of the Bible have been translated into more than 1,800 languages, but there are some 5,000 languages spoken (depending on what is defined as a language). There are believers in the Messiah and in God's Word among hundreds of peoples, but hundreds of other peoples are virtually unreached. The "other sheep" will continue to be added "until the Gentile world enters in its fullness" (Ro 11:25).

The *Tanakh* often has the salvation of Gentiles in view; see, for example, Genesis 12:3, 18:14, 22:18, 26:4; Isaiah 11:10, 19:6, 54:1–3, 60:1–3; Hosea 1:10; Amos 9:11; Malachi 1:11; Psalms 72, 87. Isaiah 45:23 is quoted by Sha'ul in this connection (Pp 2:10). The strongest impact of this idea on the consciousness of observant Jews comes from Zechariah 14:9, recited daily in the synagogue in the *'Aleinu* prayer: "And *Adonai* will be king over all the earth; on that day *Adonai* will be one and his name one." While Zechariah 14:16–19 proves that eventually New Testament worship will be far more Jewish in character than it is now (see 7:2N), the present verse and the New Testament references given in this note show that the final form of God's chosen people includes Gentiles who have not converted to Judaism.

17–18 I lay down my life.... No one takes it away from me: on the contrary, I lay it down of my own free will. Yeshua was neither the victim nor the perpetrator of any "Passover plot" but was the fulfiller of God's eternal plan that the eternal Word (1:1–2) humble himself by taking human form and dying for the sins of humanity (1:14, Pp 2:6–11). Yeshua's several predictions of his impending death for this purpose (here, 12:23–36, 13:33, 16:28; Mt 10:28, 16:21, 17:22–23, 20:17–19; and parallel passages in Mark and Luke), as well as *Tanakh* passages indicating the Messiah would die and be resurrected (Isaiah 53:1–12, Psalm 16:8–11) provide ample proof.

I have the power to take it up again. It is the Father who raised up Yeshua (Ro 8:11); but according to this verse Yeshua had the power, even in death, to resurrect himself.

19–21 Again a division; see 7:43&N, 9:16. On attributing the works of the Holy Spirit to Satan, see Mt 12:31–32&N, Lk 12:8–10&N.

20 He's *meshuggah*, Hebrew and Yiddish equivalent of Greek *mainetai* ("he is out of his mind, insane, crazy, mad, not in control of himself"), often used colloquially, as here, to discredit the content of what someone says because of the person's supposedly irresponsible condition.

22 *Chanukkah*, the Feast of Dedication, in which Jews since 164 B.C.E. have celebrated the victory of the *Makkabim* over Antiochus IV, king of Syria. This is the earliest mention of the holiday in all literature and the only mention of it in the Bible, since the *Tanakh* was completed before that date (the book of Daniel contains prophecy about the event celebrated). The apocryphal books, 1, 2, 3, and 4 Maccabees, present historical and other perspectives on what happened.

Antiochus, recently defeated in Egypt, expressed his frustration by attacking Judea, ruthlessly slaughtering men, women and children, and invading the Temple. There he carried off the golden altar, *menorahs* and vessels; and to show his contempt for the God of Israel he sacrificed there a pig to Zeus. He forbade circumcision, observing *Shabbat* and keeping *kosher*, and commanded that only pigs be sacrificed in the Temple; he himself cooked a pig in the Temple and poured its broth on the holy *Torah* scrolls and on the altar.

Syrian officers were dispatched to enforce these cruel and blasphemous decrees. One day when the Syrian officer in Modi'in commanded Mattityahu *HaMakkabi* (Mattathias the Maccabee or Hammer), head of a family of *cohanim*, to sacrifice a pig, he and his five sons killed the first Jew to comply (see Ac 6:1N) and then killed the officer and his soldiers. This was the start of a rebellion. After Mattityahu's death his son Y'hudah (Judas Maccabeus, about whom Handel wrote his oratorio so named) assembled a number of courageous Jews and led them to victory over the Syrians, first in guerilla warfare, then later in open battle. On the 25th of Kislev they rededicated the Temple and consecrated a new altar. The *ner tamid* ("eternal light") was relit, but there was only enough consecrated olive oil to keep it burning for one day, and it would take a week to prepare more. By a miracle of God reported in the book of 2 Maccabees the light burned for eight days, by which time a new supply had been prepared. For this reason Jews celebrate *Chanukkah* for eight days, starting on Kislev 25, which can fall between November 27 and December 27.

The Bible does not state when Yeshua was born, perhaps as a prophylactic against our worshipping the day instead of the One who is worthy. But it is interesting that the early believers in the Messiah apparently saw a link between *Chanukkah* and the birth day of the Messiah: the one is concerned with an earthly building, the other with the living Temple of God who came down from Heaven — for Yeshua himself made the comparison when he said, "Destroy this temple, and in three days I will raise it up again" (2:19). So, since the end of the third century December 25, the Roman calendar date corresponding to Kislev 25, has been the generally accepted date for Christmas in the Western churches (the Greek Orthodox observe January 6, the Armenians January 19).

In secular America both Christmas and *Chanukkah* become distorted. Christmas turns into a commercial extravaganza, thereby expressing the "American civil religion" of pious platitudes and meaningless customs, such as trees, Santa Claus, reindeer, and obligatory exchanges of cards and presents. At best it becomes a time for family togetherness (although a byproduct is that the suicide rate is highest then, for that is when people who miss their families or have none become most despairing), but little thought is given to God or Yeshua.

Likewise *Chanukkah* has become a Jewish refuge and defense against absorption into and assimilation by the Gentile majority: "We don't celebrate Christmas; we celebrate *Chanukkah*, because we're Jewish." Gift-giving at *Chanukkah* (one gift each night) is a relatively modern Jewish tradition, obviously developed in response to the older tradition of gift-giving at Christmas. Messianic Jews use *Chanukkah* as an occasion for re*dedication* to God and his Messiah.

Chanukkah is celebrated using a special *Chanukkah menorah* with nine lights. One uses a match to light the *shammash* ("servant"), and it is then employed to light one candle the first night, two the second, and so on until on the eighth night all eight lights and the *shammash* are burning brightly. For Messianic Jews the imagery is rich: Yeshua, the "light of the world" (8:12&N), came as a servant (Mk 10:45) to give light to everyone (1:4–5), so that we might be lights to others (Mt 5:14).

But Christmas itself is not a biblical holiday at all. If it is to be celebrated, it should be observed as a Jewish holiday; for what is more worthy of voluntary celebration than the coming of the Jewish Messiah into the world, by whom all may have the light of life? (Much material in this note is drawn from the chapter on *Chanukkah* in *The Gospel In The Feasts Of Israel*, by the Hebrew Christian, Victor Buksbazen.)

23 **Shlomo's Colonnade**, also referred to at Ac 3:11, 5:12. The eastern part of the walkway surrounding the outer court of Herod's Temple, mentioned in the writings of Josephus.

24 See Mt 8:4&N.

25 **The works I do... testify**. Same argument as at 5:36.

28 **I give them eternal life**. Contrast this story from one of the "minor tractates" appended to the Talmud:

> [Once Rabbi Akiva, in order to persuade a woman to reveal certain sensitive information,] "said to her, 'My daughter, if you will tell me the answer to the question I am going to ask you, I will bring you to eternal life.' 'Swear it to me,' she said. Rabbi Akiva swore the oath with his lips but cancelled it in his heart." (Kallah 18b in some editions; Kallah 16 in *The Minor Tractates of the Talmud*, Soncino edition)

Akiva swore falsely in order to accomplish his own purpose, the end justifying the means. Yeshua spoke truly, because he in fact has authority (Mk 1:22&N) to grant eternal life.

30 **I and the Father are one**, the same One as in the *Sh'ma*: "*Adonai*, our God, *Adonai* is One" (Deuteronomy 6:4). Yeshua's self-assertion of his own divinity is occasioned by his regard for his followers: "no one will snatch them from" Yeshua's (v. 28) or the Father's (v. 29) hands. "*Ani veha'av, echad anachnu*" ("I and the Father are one"); therefore we who are in Yeshua's care have complete assurance that nothing "will be able to separate us from the love of God which comes to us through the Messiah Yeshua, our Lord" (Ro 8:31–39). See also v. 38&N.

31–33 **The Judeans once again picked up stones in order to stone him**, as at 8:59 and for the same reason, self-identification as God, which they understood as blasphemy (v. 33). See 8:5N, 8:58–59N.

34–36 **Your *Torah***. See 8:17N, Mt 5:17&N. Here "*Torah*" means "*Tanakh*," since the passage quoted is from the Psalms, not the Pentateuch.

You people are *Elohim*, here Greek *theoi* ("gods"). But in the Hebrew text of Psalm 82 the word "*elohim*" may be translated "God," "gods," "judges" or "angels." Yeshua's rabbinic mode of Bible citation implies the context of the whole psalm (Mt 2:6N), which plays on these meanings:

> "*Elohim* [God] stands in the congregation of *El* [God]:
> He judges among the *elohim* [judges/angels/gods]:

'How long will you judge unjustly?...
I have said, "You are *elohim* [judges/angels/gods],
All of you are sons of the Most High."
Nevertheless you will die like a man
And fall like one of the princes.'
Arise, *Elohim* [God (the Judge)], and judge the earth,
For you will inherit all the nations." (Psalm 82:1–2, 6–8)

The first and last "*Elohim*" mean "God," but the others should be rendered "judges," "gods" or "angels." To remind the reader to reach back through the Greek to the Hebrew wordplay I rendered *theoi* by its Hebrew equivalent.

Yeshua's wordplay implies a rabbinic-style *kal v'chomer* argument (Mt 6:30N): if humans, who do evil works as they "judge unjustly" are *elohim*, how much more is Yeshua, who does good works (vv. 25, 32–33, 37–38) *Elohim*; and if "all of you are sons of the Most High," how much more does the description "Son of God" apply to Yeshua.

38 **The Father is united with me and I am united with the Father**. This explains v. 30; also see 17:21–23&N.

42 **Many... put their trust in him**, as at 2:23, 7:31, 8:30, 11:45, 12:11.

CHAPTER 11

1 Like a number of the incidents Yochanan reports, the events of this chapter presume knowledge of material found in the Synoptic Gospels. **Beit-Anyah** is mentioned in Mk 11:11–12 as the place where Yeshua and his *talmidim* stayed after making their triumphal entry into Yerushalayim. **Miryam** and **Marta** are introduced at Lk 10:38–42.

2 **Miryam... poured perfume**, etc. Reported by Yochanan at 12:3–8; Mt 26:6–13 and Mk 14:3–9 say this occurred in the home of Shim'on, the man whom Yeshua healed of a serious skin disease; perhaps he shared quarters with the three siblings. A similar incident took place earlier (Lk 7:36–38).

4 **This sickness will not end in death**. In fact El'azar did die (v. 14), but Yeshua raised him, so that the illness did not "**end**" in death.

7 **Let's go back to Y'hudah** from the east side of the Yarden River (10:40).

16 This **T'oma** is the famous "doubting Thomas," and his pessimism here already foreshadows the events of 20:24–29 which give him his nickname.

17 **El'azar had already been in the tomb for four days** and had already begun to decay (v. 39). Yeshua raised others from the dead — Ya'ir's daughter (Lk 8:41–42, 49–56) and the son of the widow in Na'im (Lk 7:11–17). The *Tanakh* reports that Elijah and Elisha had raised people from the dead (1 Kings 17:17–24, 2 Kings 4:17–37). And

indeed doctors today bring back people who have been "clinically dead" for many minutes, perhaps hours. But nowhere in biblical or secular history is there an instance of anyone medically dead for four days — to the point where there would be an odor — being physically raised from the dead.

The incident is reported in such a way that no one misses its significance: Yeshua has physically brought back to life a four-days-dead, cold, stinking corpse; and this miracle crowns Yeshua's career prior to his own death and resurrection. This is what produced the profound reaction among the populace and authorities reported in the rest of this and the following chapter.

19–20 Many of the Judeans had come... to comfort them at the loss of their brother.... Miryam continued sitting *shiv'ah* in the house. The word "*shiv'ah*" means "seven," and the phrase, "sitting *shiv'ah*," refers to the Jewish custom of sitting in mourning for seven days following the death of a deceased parent, spouse, sibling or child. The Greek here says only "sitting," which is an unusual word if all that is meant is that Miryam stayed in the house when Marta went out. Because it is so clear from the context that Miryam was mourning her brother I have added "*shiv'ah*" in the text to show that her "sitting" was in fact specifically "mourning." The Orthodox Jewish mourner sits unshod on the floor or on a low stool in the home of the deceased or his near relative and abstains from all ordinary work and diversions and even from required synagogue prayers, while friends visit him to comfort and pray with him. Both sisters observed the practice, which was not significantly different then from now; but Marta, who evidently had digested Yeshua's counsel at Lk 10:41–42, was now the one willing to set custom aside and leave **the house** in order to meet him.

24 I know that he will rise again at the Resurrection on the Last Day. How did she know this? From the *Tanakh*, which teaches it at Daniel 12:2. This was standard doctrine among the *P'rushim* (but not the *Tz'dukim*; see Mt 3:7N, 22:23–32&NN, Ac 23:6–9&NN).

25 I AM the Resurrection and the Life. In addition to Yeshua's absolute "I AM" statements (see 4:26&N) Yochanan reports seven predicated "I AM" statements: I AM the bread of life (6:35), the light of the world (8:12, 9:5), the gate (10:7), the good shepherd (10:11, 14), the resurrection and the life (here), the way and the truth and the life (14:6), and the real vine (15:1). The book of Revelation adds that Yeshua similarly spoke of himself after the resurrection as the "A" and the "Z" (Rv 1:8) and as the first and the last (Rv 1:17).

39 Before medicine could distinguish clearly between being comatose and being dead, people were occasionally buried alive. Jewish burial practices attempted to eliminate this grisly possibility. According to a post-Talmudic tractate compiled in the eighth century,

> "We go out to the cemetery and examine the dead [to see if they are still alive and have been buried by mistake] for a period of three days and do not fear being suspected of engaging in the ways of the Amorites [i.e., superstitious practices]. Once a man who had been buried was examined and found to be alive; he lived

for twenty-five years more and then died. Another such person lived and had five children before he died." (S'machot 8:1)

The title of this tractate is the plural of "*simchah*" ("joy") and is a euphemism for mourning.

Marta's remark confirms, then, that she has given up all hope that her brother is still alive — the three-day period has passed: **It has been four days since he died**.

41 **Yeshua looked upward**. He prayed with his eyes open, as Jewish people do today. Christians usually pray with eyes closed; the reason most often given is in order to screen out visual distractions and concentrate on God. Which to do is a matter of individual choice; the Bible does not require either.

47 **The head *cohanim* and the *P'rushim***, the two foci of opposition to Yeshua in the Judean establishment, **called a meeting of the *Sanhedrin***, the ruling council (see Mt 5:22N), but it was apparently an illegal meeting (Mk 14:55N).

48 The establishment had a working relationship with Rome even though it was an oppressing foreign power. This relationship was perceived as threatened by anyone whom Rome might regard as intending to lead a revolt and set up an independent government.

Everyone will trust in him as the longed-for Messianic king who would restore Israel's national glory.

The Temple, Greek "the place" (compare 4:20; Ac 7:46, 49).

49–52 **On behalf of the people**. Kayafa's intended sense is "instead of the people." That is, "Better for us to ensure that Yeshua is put to death than that thousands of our people die at the hands of Romans suppressing a rebellion." But **Kayafa... was *cohen gadol* that** fateful **year**, and for this reason, even though he was an evil man, God used him to prophesy. As v. 51 explains, this is why his words carried a significance deeper than Kayafa's intended sense. The deeper significance involves exchanging Kayafa's meaning for one implying that Yeshua would fulfill Isaiah 53:6,

> "All of us, like sheep, have gone astray;
> we have turned every one to his own way;
> and *Adonai* has laid on him
> the iniquity of us all."

Yeshua would pay the death-penalty for sin in lieu of and **on behalf of the people** of Israel (the "all of us" of Isaiah 53:6), and also on behalf of non-Jews (v. 52, 10:16&N). For a discussion of how this works, see Ro 5:12–21&NN.

55 **The Judean festival of *Pesach***. See 5:1N.

The purification ceremony prior to *Pesach*. Those who had become ritually unclean because of having touched a dead body had to purify themselves by immersion (Numbers 9:10, 13). Sometimes the purification required seven days (Numbers 31:19–20). On *Pesach* see Mt 26:2N.

56 What do you think? That he simply won't come to the festival? That is, since he knows the authorities seek his death, will he disobey the *Torah* and not show up, in order to save his skin?

CHAPTER 12

7 She kept this. Or: "Let her keep it." But she does not have any left over, she poured it all out (Mk 14:6–8); moreover the actual anointing of Yeshua's body for burial is described below (19:39–40). See other commentaries *ad loc.*, e.g., Edwyn C. Hoskyns, *The Fourth Gospel*, pp. 415–417.

8 You always have the poor with you, as Deuteronomy 15:11 teaches, **but you will not always have me**. While Yeshua's point is to call the attention of his *talmidim* to the importance of his brief remaining time on earth, some, noting the stress Judaism puts on charity, have regarded his remark as callous and selfish. It is not, for two reasons: (1) Miryam's timely act of love toward the Messiah is valued by God precisely for its *un*selfishness, and (2) the marginal significance of the resources here withheld from the poor is negligible compared both with their need and with the opportunities available to potential givers.

10 The head *cohanim* were Yeshua's main opposition; they sought not only to kill him but to obliterate all signs of his work.

11 Because of him, that is, because El'azar had been raised from the dead by Yeshua, **large numbers of Judeans were leaving their leaders**, the *P'rushim* and the head *cohanim* (11:47&N), **and putting their trust in Yeshua**, who by demonstrating God's power and holiness commends himself as the true leader of Judeans in particular and Jews generally.

12–16 See Mt 21:1–11&NN.

20–21 Greek-speaking Jews (see 7:35N) who had come to Yerushalayim in obedience to the *Torah* (see 5:1N). Since the text simply says "Greeks," many think they were Gentiles. Sha'ul often uses "Greeks" to mean "Gentiles" (Ro 1:16, 10:12; Ga 3:28; Co 3:11), but here and at 7:35 the context implies Greek-speaking Jews; compare Ac 6:1&N, 9:29.

These approached Philip, whose name was Greek and who was probably himself a Greek-speaker.

We would like to see Yeshua. Yeshua's answer (vv. 23ff.) suggests that their purpose was to offer him new opportunities for ministry in their part of the world. Yeshua says that the time for expanding his activities in the world is over, but that his effect in the world will nevertheless be all the greater.

24 Compare the Talmud paragraph quoted at 1C 15:35–36N.

25 This message, as it applies to others, is found in Mt 16:25, Mk 8:35 and Lk 9:23–24; here Yeshua applies it to himself, since it is he who pioneers and finishes our trust (MJ 12:1).

26 Compare Mt 20:28, Mk 10:45.

27 Compare Yeshua's prayer in the garden of Gat-Sh'manim (Mt 26:38–39, Mk 14:34–36, Lk 22:41–43).

28 ***Bat-kol*** (literally, "daughter of a voice"). Voice from heaven. The phenomenon is well-known in Jewish literature, which uses the term to mean a voice or message from God, as in this excerpt from the Tosefta (a 2nd-3rd century collection of rabbinic material similar to the Mishna):

> "After the death of Haggai, Zechariah and Malachi, the last of the prophets, the Holy Spirit ceased from Israel; nevertheless they received communications from God through the medium of the *bat-kol*." (Tosefta Sotah 13:2)

For more, see Ac 9:4N.

31 **The ruler of this world**, the Adversary, Satan. See 8:44N.

32 **When I am lifted up**. See 3:14&N, 8:28&N.

38 Given the customary method of citing the beginning of a passage to call to mind the whole (Mt 2:6&N), the inference is that all of Isaiah 53:1–12 applies to Yeshua.

39 **They could not believe**. God offers everyone the opportunity to "believe" or "trust" him. Greek *pistis* and the equivalent Hebrew, *emunah*, may be translated by either word (see Ac 3:16N) or by both (Ga 2:16c&N). But if they reject him, he may eventually make belief impossible: he hardens hearts (Ro 9:18). In this case God blinded them (vv. 40–41), just as he hardened Pharaoh's heart (Exodus 9:12, 11:10) after Pharaoh hardened his own heart (Exodus 8:32), so that it became impossible for Pharaoh to trust in God. Even when he asked Moses for a blessing (Exodus 12:32), it was but a momentary aberration from his self-determined and God-confirmed hardness. Perhaps his pain over the loss of the firstborn sons of Egypt, or his fear that Moses would inflict worse punishment filled him briefly with sorrow. But it was not the godly kind of sorrow that leads to repentance (2C 7:10), for within a day he sent the whole Egyptian army to bring Moses and the people back.

I dwell on this because occasionally I am asked, "If Hitler repented on his deathbed, do you think God forgave him?" Sometimes I refuse to answer, on the ground that it's a trick question meant to test God and predicated on the false assumption that the questioner has the right to judge whether God is fair. When I do answer, my answer, insofar as it pertains to the nature of God, is: Yes —conditional upon genuine repentance (and it is beyond my ability to imagine what that could possibly have meant in Hitler's case).

However, in my view the question is probably vain. I think God had long before hardened Hitler's heart, since Hitler had hardened his own heart, so that he **could not believe** (see Ro 9:17–21&NN). We know that God wants everyone to repent (Ro 2:4, 2 Ke 3:9), but we also know that at death God confirms the unbeliever in the way he chose when alive (3:16–21, 5:21–30; Ro 2:5–8; Rv 20:13–15). From this verse and from Exodus, we must acknowledge that sometimes God, who knows the end from the beginning, finalizes the unbeliever's unbelief before he dies.

40 Do *t'shuvah* (in earlier editions of the *JNT*, **turn from their sins**). See Mt 3:2N, 13:13–15N.

41 Yesha'yahu... saw the *Sh'khinah* of Yeshua. Greek, "his glory." On *Sh'khinah* ("manifest glory") see paragraph (3) of MJ 1:2–3&N. Yochanan refers to Yeshua's glory, not that of God the Father. Yet the allusion is to Isaiah 6:1–3, where the prophet reports that he

> "saw *Adonai* sitting upon a throne, high and lifted up, and his train filled the temple. *S'rafim*...cried to each other, '*Adonai* of heavenly armies is holy, holy, holy! The whole earth is full of his glory!'"

Yochanan apparently means that in this heavenly vision Yesha'yahu had a glimpse of Yeshua's future manifest glory; and since Yeshua is to be included in the concept of *Adonai*, there is no *a priori* reason to suppose that Isaiah's vision was of God the Father.

42–43 Many of the leaders did trust in Yeshua; **but because of the *P'rushim* they did not say so openly, out of fear of being banned from the synagogue** (see 9:22N); **for they loved praise from other people more than praise from God.** Believers in Yeshua are not to hide their faith but confess it openly. One hears of "secret believers" who acknowledge to a small circle of friends that Yeshua is the Messiah but refuse to let it be known or even deny it. What they have is a powerless intellectual assent that cannot save them (Ya 2:14–26&N). See Ro 10:8b-10&N. Also compare Lk 12:8–9 (Mt 10:32–33), Mk 8:38, 2 Ti 1:7–8.

44–50 This summary of Yeshua's public message and challenge encourages "secret believers" to become public witnesses who let their words and lives proclaim fearlessly that they are relying on God and his truth. To reject Yeshua is to reject God,and his message will stand to judge all humanity.

CHAPTER 13

1 Loved them to the end. Or: "loved them into the goal/consummation." See Ro 10:4N.

5 He began to wash the feet of the *talmidim*. Footwashing was a courtesy shown to guests in a home, usually performed by a servant or the host's wife when the guests entered the house or while they were reclining at table (see Lk 7:44, Mk 1:7). Here Yeshua acts out his teaching of Mk 10:43–44 that the greatest must be a servant.

8–10 Compare Exodus 30:20: "Aaron and his sons are to wash their hands and feet...when they come near the altar to minister..., so that they will not die." The *cohanim* were already cleansed from impurity, but even so they had to wash their hands and feet.

Once sins of the past have been forgiven we need not have them forgiven again; the initial confession and immersion that washes away past sin need not be repeated. But there is continual need to repent of newly committed sins, make reparation for them and seek forgiveness for them. Compare these verses with the more explicit teaching on this subject at 1 Yn 1:5–2:2.

14–17 A *talmid* is not above his rabbi but can become like his rabbi. This pattern was standard in both first-century and later Judaism. See the *JNT* glossary entry on "*talmid*," Mt 5:1N and the midrash extract cited in 19:17N.

16 **An emissary**, Greek *apostolos* ("one sent"); see Mt 10:2–4N.

17 **If,** as is the case, **you know these things** (vv. 13–16), **you will be blessed if you do them**, or: "you will find happiness/joy in behaving accordingly."

19 Another "I AM" statement; see 4:26N.

20 Compare Lk 10:16, Mt 10:40.

23 **One of his *talmidim*, the one Yeshua particularly loved**. This is Yochanan, the author of the Gospel. See 19:26–27&N, 21:20.

26 **Piece of *matzah***, Greek *psômion*, "small bit of bread." We know from Mt 26:17, 23; Mk 14:1, 12, 20; and Lk 22:1, 7 that the "bit of bread" was unleavened.

Dip it in the dish, perhaps of *charoset* and/or *maror* (see Mt 26:23N). *Maror* ("bitter herbs"), which in the Passover service recalls the bitterness of Israelite slavery in Egypt, is appropriate to the present occasion as well.

29 As noted in 18:28N, some scholars believe Yochanan reports a different date for the Last Supper than the synoptic Gospels. Part of their reasoning is that if it were the *Seder* meal as the Synoptics say (but see the suggestion in Mt 26:2N that it was a *se'udat-siyum*), no one would have **thought that… Yeshua was telling** Y'hudah, "**Buy what we need for the festival**." Following are three supporting arguments, along with points against them:

(1) *Argument: Halakhah* prohibits financial transactions on *Shabbat* and festivals. *Against:* The Oral Law as we know it today was not yet finalized in Yeshua's time.

(2) *Argument:* Therefore the stores would be closed, so there would be no place to buy anything. *Against:* If argument (1) does not hold, neither does (2). According to C. H. Lenski's commentary, *St. John's Gospel*, stores were shut on Nisan 13 (the day before *Pesach*) but open all night on Nisan 14, as preparations were made for the *chagigah* the following morning (see 18:28N); he does not give the source for this information.

(3) *Argument:* If it was already *Erev-Pesach* ("Passover eve"), it was too late to buy what was needed for it. *Against:* The directive may have been to buy for the rest of the seven-day festival, not for the *Seder*.

30 **And it was night**. Words of heaviness, with symbolic as well as literal import. Compare 9:4–5, 12:46; Lk 22:53.

34 Why is this a **new commandment**? Doesn't Leviticus 19:18 already say, "Love your neighbor as yourself"? The difference is this: Leviticus says, "as yourself"; Yeshua says, **"In the same way that I have loved you,"** which presupposes that God's way of loving can be ours. Humanly this is impossible. But Yeshua gives us a new nature, a new spirit, in fulfillment of *Tanakh* promises (Ezekiel 36:26, 37:14; Jeremiah 31:32(33)), God's Spirit, the Holy Spirit. This is how we can love as God loves; God makes it possible.

35 **Everyone will know that you are my *talmidim* by the fact that you have love for each other**. I personally bear witness to the truth of this statement. I became willing to investigate the truth claims of the New Testament not because I was overwhelmed by irrefutable arguments but because I met believers whose love for each other went beyond what I had experienced. It was not even their love toward me which impressed me (although they treated me well), but their self-sacrificing and cheerful willingness to give themselves fully for each other without any trace of self-serving motivation. This is what those who claim to be trusting Yeshua are called to do and can expect God's power to enable them to do. God can be counted on to fulfill his promise that the world will recognize such people as true disciples of Yeshua.

37 Kefa, ebullient as always (e.g, vv. 8–9), makes a rash promise, also reported at Mt 26:33–34, Mk 14:29–30, Lk 22:33–34.

CHAPTER 14

5 **T'oma**, who trusts only what he can see (11:16, 20:24–29), picks up the challenge of the preceding verse, "You know the way."

6 **Yeshua said, "I AM the Way — and the Truth and the Life; no one comes to the Father except through me."** This challenge strikes at the heart of non-Messianic Judaism's denial of Yeshua as Messianic mediator. Some try to ignore this challenge by denying its authenticity: either the Gospel of Yochanan is historically untrustworthy or the words are not Yeshua's but placed in his mouth by early church theologians. This view, of course, denies the divine inspiration of the New Testament.

More interesting is Two-Covenant theology, originated by Rabbi Moshe Ben-Maimon ("The *RaMBaM*," Maimonides, 1135–1204), pioneered in this century by the non-Messianic Jewish philosopher Franz Rosenzweig (1886–1929), and since elaborated by such liberal Christian theologians as Reinhold Niebuhr and James Parkes. This theory holds that the Jewish people were brought close to God by means of the covenant with Avraham and the *Torah* of Moshe, so that they have no need to "come" to the Father through Yeshua or anyone else, because they are already with him. Accordingly, Yeshua's word is not for Jews but for Gentiles and is to be understood thusly: "I am the way, the truth and the life; and no Gentile comes to the Father except through me."

The Two-Covenant theory may be understood as a modern variant of the Talmudic doctrine stating that Jews are bound by the *Torah* of Moshe, but Gentiles share in the world to come if they obey the seven "Noachide laws" given after the flood to Noah for all mankind — prohibitions against idolatry, murder, incest, theft, blasphemy and eating the flesh of a living animal; and the positive command to promote justice, i.e., to institute government (Sanhedrin 56a, cited and discussed in Ac 15:20N).

The Two-Covenant theory enables the Jewish Community to live in apparent peace (from its own point of view) with its Christian neighbors by alleviating the pressure on Judaism to downgrade Jesus, the New Testament and Christianity; for a non-Messianic Jew can say, "We Jews have our way, Judaism; and you Gentiles have your way, Christianity. We will each serve God best by following the way provided for us. It is a manifestation of God's grace that he has provided Jesus for you Gentiles and *Torah* for us Jews." Thus Jesus can be held in high regard, because his claims are not taken as posing any threat to the structure of non-Messianic Judaism.

Unfortunately for this theory, it does not fit the New Testament facts at all. The "tolerance for Christianity" that it produces is not tolerance of what the New Testament states is true. For Yeshua was a Jew who presented himself to Jews, and these Jews remained Jewish after they came to trust in him. He rarely presented the Gospel to Gentiles; indeed, it was only with difficulty and supernatural intervention that his Jewish disciples came to realize that Gentiles could join God's people through trusting Yeshua without converting to Judaism (see Acts 10–11, 15). In the book of Acts Kefa's initial sermons presented Yeshua to Jews as the Jewish Messiah (Ac 2:14–40, 3:12–26; especially Ac 2:36&N, 3:25–26), as did Sha'ul's (Ac 9:20–22, 13:16–43). In his letter to the Romans Sha'ul states that salvation through Yeshua is God's Good News "to the Jew especially"; however, since he is stressing that Gentiles too may be part of the people of God, he immediately adds, "but equally to the Gentile" (Ro 1:16). In sum, replacing Yeshua's "No one comes to the Father except through me" with "No Gentile comes…" does unacceptable violence to the plain sense of the text and to the whole New Testament.

Actually Rosenzweig's theory reflects his own personal history. A German Jew raised in an assimilated family, he seriously considered the claims of Christianity, particularly in an exchange of letters with a Jewish Christian named Eugen Rosenstock. He was on the verge of "converting to Christianity" — I put the phrase in quotation marks to emphasize that conversion in Europe, with its state churches, could never have been perceived as a Jewish thing to do — when he decided to give traditional Judaism one last chance. He went to a synagogue on *Yom-Kippur*, experienced the resonant depths of meaning in the liturgy of the *Machzor* (prayer book for the High Holy Days), and decided to cast his lot with his ancient heritage and with his own people. A noble sentiment, but what a pity that there did not exist in his society a vibrant Messianic Judaism which he could have perceived as being just as Jewish as what he did participate in, while being coupled with the efficacious spiritual power that God gives only through Yeshua, who is the Way, the Truth and the Life!

If the words of this verse are authentically Yeshua's, and if the Two-Covenant theory does not fit the facts, then we are left with a statement whose audacity, breadth, apparent arrogance and sheer *chutzpah* pose a serious problem. What exclusivity, what intolerance for a religion to accept Yeshua's claim to be the only way to God! It requires a decision either to acknowledge Yeshua's position as the Messiah, the Son of God, or to reject him as a madman or a fraud and to reject religion centering on him as deceptive at best. There is no *tertium quid* (see 5:17–18N). For if one holds that Yeshua was a "great teacher," the unavoidable question is, "Then why don't you believe and act on his 'great teaching,' **'I AM the Way — and the Truth and the Life; no one comes to the Father except through me'?"**

Messianic Judaism and Christianity, which accept this teaching, are indeed in a sense exclusive, for they deny that there are other men, other religious leaders, who have come from God and paid the death penalty for mankind's sins. In this sense, then, Yeshua is *the* way; and it is not true that "on the mountaintop all paths meet," for only Yeshua's path arrives there. Nevertheless this exclusivity is tempered by three factors:

(1) The path is open to everyone (Ro 10:9–13).

(2) Yeshua's path sets no precondition except turning from sin to the one true God. In particular it does not require Gentiles to stop being Gentiles or Jews to stop being Jews.

(3) It is God's one true path; it exists. This simply means that, rather than complaining about exclusivity, one should be profoundly grateful to God for providing a way out of the sinful condition that besets every human being.

True exclusivity would be either God's providing no path whatsoever, instead of one which suffices for all, or providing it for some but not for everyone. To want some way other than that which God has offered is simply to want to play God, to design one's own remedy for sin, and ultimately not to take the evil of sin seriously (on the New Testament's remedy for sin, see Ro 5:12–21&N). This is true arrogance and *chutzpah*.

Messianic Judaism and Christianity, properly taught and practiced, are intolerant of sin and of the just mentioned varieties of arrogance and *chutzpah*, but not of other religions, in the sense usually meant. Messianic Jews and Gentile Christians acknowledge not only the freedom of religion guaranteed by the constitutions of nations but also the *de facto* right and capacity each individual has to seek the truth as best he can. Other religions have the right, within the framework of law, to communicate their views, to seek, gain and hold adherents, and to minister to them. This is tolerance. But tolerance does not and cannot mean agreeing that other religions are true.

The positive message of this verse is available to everyone. Yeshua is the Way by which everyone comes to the Father: his work and his very person both show us and give us all we need to be in a right personal relationship with God. More than that, he is not merely a way, a path, but the goal itself — Truth and eternal Life. And all this is conditioned only on our holding to our trust in him, so that we keep God's commands.

For more see the pamphlet by the Messianic Jew Louis Goldberg, *Are There Two Ways of Atonement?* (Baltimore: Lederer Publications, 1990).

9 Whoever has seen me has seen the Father. This apparently contradicts 1:18 ("No one has ever seen God") and 5:17–30, which focuses on the distinctions between the Father and the Son. The paradox is resolved by Co 2:9: "In him," Yeshua, "bodily, lives the fullness of all that God is." The human mind is stretched beyond its limits in trying to cope with the idea that the Creator of the universe and one of his creations, a human being named Yeshua, are to be identified with each other. The language of the New Testament, as it treats this issue, shows that God has great respect for our difficulty in apprehending this. The New Testament never says, directly, "Yeshua is God." Nor does it say, "Yeshua is only a man and not God," except in the mouths of his opponents. The New Testament adds insights in one place and another, "line on line, precept on precept, here a little, there a little" (Isaiah 28:10, 13).

10–11 **I am united with the Father and the Father united with me**. This adds to what v. 9 has taught; see 17:21–23&N.

12 **Whoever trusts in me will also do the works I do**, in fact even **greater ones**. What follows explains how this astounding promise is to be fulfilled.

14 **If you ask me for something in my name, I will do it**. The word "me" is missing in the first three editions of the *Jewish New Testament*, but the textual evidence for including it is convincing, even though a number of later manuscripts, among them those underlying KJV, omit it. Including it creates a "Jewish problem," because it makes it appear that the New Testament teaches people to "pray to Jesus and not to God," in denial of Judaism's correct doctrine that prayer should be to God alone.

However, there is no contradiction. Elsewhere Yeshua instructs his followers to pray to the Father (16:23, Mt 6:9). But here Yeshua has just taught that he is one with the Father, who is living in him and doing his own works through him (vv. 10–11; also 10:30, 17:21–23); we also know that Yeshua does just what the Father tells him to do (5:17–30). So petitioning Yeshua is tantamount to petitioning the Father. Yeshua the divine Son is the divine agent of the Father, no less God than the Father, and therefore justifiably addressed in prayer.

We are to make our requests in Yeshua's name, that is, as his followers, on his authority. This is necessary because he alone is sinless (Ro 3:23); and, except for prayers of repentance, God does not obligate himself to hear the prayers of sinners (Isaiah 59:1–2, quoted in Ro 3:23N).

Finally, we know from 1 Yn 5:14 that in order to expect our prayers to be answered the **something** we ask for must accord with God's will.

Thus the sense of the verse *in toto* is that Yeshua tells his disciples: You are my followers; and the Father has given me authority to receive your requests, which are at once communicated to him. He has also given me authority to grant your requests without presenting them to him formally. Asking me is the same as asking him. If your requests are godly, in accord with God's plan, I need no further grant of authority from the Father to fulfill them, and I *will* fulfill them.

In order to justify from this verse the Christian pattern of praying to Jesus, one must understand that the moment Jesus, the eternal Son of God and "part of" *Adonai*, hears the prayer, the Father, who is also "part of" *Adonai*, hears it too. In this way the verse is consistent with the Jewish idea that prayer must be to *Adonai* alone.

But perhaps the whole question is moot now, because below, at 16:23, Yeshua says a day will come when *talmidim* will no longer ask Yeshua but the Father, as he earlier taught in the Lord's Prayer (Mt 6:9&N). One can argue that that day came when Yeshua rose from the dead, or when he sent the Holy Spirit (see 16:20–22, 14:26, 15:25–26). If so, then praying to Yeshua is already out of date, and the "Jewish problem" of this verse is no longer so pressing. Perhaps one should construe the behavior of those who still pray to Jesus as demonstrating their belief that that day has not come yet.

15 **If you love me, you will keep my commands**, my *mitzvot*. It is wrong to think of Messianic Judaism or Christianity as "easy," requiring only pleasant feelings of love but no actions to prove it. *Dake's Annotated Reference Bible* lists 1,050 New Testament commands which, according to this verse, are to be obeyed by those who love Yeshua. The distinction drawn between Old Testament Judaism as a religion of law and New Testament faith as a religion of love is unfounded. In both the *Tanakh* and the *B'rit Chadashah* biblical religion is based on both love and law, both mercy and justice; it has always been so and always will be.

16 **Another comforting Counselor**. Greek *paraklêtos* means "counselor, comforter, exhorter," or, literally, "one called alongside." There are two words in Greek for "another" — "*allos*" ("another of the same kind"), and "*eteros*" ("another, of a different kind"). Here the word is "*allos*": a comforting counselor just like Yeshua, namely, the *Ruach HaKodesh* (vv. 17, 26). Compare the Talmud:

> "What is [the Messiah's] name?... [Some] say: His name is Menachem the son of Hezekiah, since it is written, 'Because *Menachem* [a comforter] that could relieve my soul, is far from me' (Lamentations 1:16)." (Sanhedrin 98b)

17 **The Spirit of Truth**, God's Spirit, the Holy Spirit,... **will be in you**. This is an amazing promise for a Jewish person to read, because the *Tanakh* speaks of only a few persons as having the Holy Spirit "with" or "upon" them (among them Moshe and the seventy elders (Numbers 11:17–29), Gid'on (Judges 6:34), Yiftach (Judges 11:29), Shimshon (Judges 14:6), Sha'ul (1 Samuel 11:6), David (1 Samuel 16:13, Psalm 51:13 (11)), and Sha'ul's messengers (1 Samuel 19:20)), and even fewer as having the Holy Spirit "in" them (Yosef (Genesis 41:38) and Betzal'el (Exodus 31:3)).

26 **The Father will send** the Holy Spirit **in my** [Yeshua's] **name**. At 15:26 we read, "I [Yeshua] will send you [the Holy Spirit] from the Father." Whether the *Ruach HaKodesh* proceeds from the Father and the Son jointly or from the Father alone seems an issue rather removed from everyday life. Nevertheless it was over this point of doctrine that the Greek Orthodox Church, headquartered in Constantinople, and the Roman Catholic Church, headquartered in Rome, finally split apart in the year 1054. See 17:21–23N on the scandal of denominationalism.

27 **I am giving you my *shalom***, my peace. "If Jesus is the Messiah, where is world peace?" The question is often asked as if the implied negative answer proves that Yeshua's claim to Messiahship is false. For it is true that the swords have not yet been beaten into plowshares, and nations still learn war (Isaiah 2:4). The answer is that Yeshua is indeed fulfilling his promise, but not all at once. Peace does not come to those who refuse it, to those who, as it were, fight peace, but to those who gladly receive it.

Within every believer is a *shalom* (which means not only "peace" but also "health, wholeness, integrity"; see Mt 10:12N) that comes from God himself. It is not a self-satisfied false peace that ignores suffering, but a compassionate peace that longs for God's *shalom* to be present with everyone and motivates action to help bring it about.

When the Messiah returns to rule with a staff of iron (Rv 12:5, 19:15) he will compel cessation of hostilities between nations. Meanwhile, where is world peace? In the lives of believers; so that in Yeshua blacks and whites, Israeli Jews and Palestinians, indeed members of any groups at enmity can experience in themselves and in each other Yeshua's *shalom.*

28 **The Father is greater than I**. Yeshua here is speaking of himself in his limited capacity as a human being. For as the Word he had glory equal to the Father's (17:5), but as a human being he humbled himself (Pp 2:6–8) — there were times when he grew tired (4:6) and things he did not know (Mk 13:32). Yet in his essence, he and the Father are One (1:1–3, 5:23, 6:62, 10:30, 14:9).

30 **The ruler of this world**. See 12:31N.

31 **Get up! Let's get going!** It's time to leave the Passover meal and go to the *Gat-Sh'manim* garden (Mt 26:36).

CHAPTER 15

1 **I am the real vine**. Israel is also God's vine or vineyard; see Isaiah 5:1–7, 27:2–6; Jeremiah 2:21, 12:10; Ezekiel 17:5–6; Hosea 10:1; Joel 1:7; Psalm 80:8–16; and compare Yeshua's parables at Mt 21:33–43, Mk 12:1–12, Lk 20:9–19. The fact that "vine" describes both the Jewish people and its Messiah reinforces the close identification of Yeshua with Israel (Mt 2:15N). The Messianic Jewish remnant (Ro 9:6ff., 11:1–10) will obey Yeshua's commands, stay attached to the real vine, and have the real vine's power and strength to bring forth good fruit (Mt 7:16–19). And so will the grafted-in Gentile Christian branches (Ro 11:17–24).

2 **Fruit**, what grows naturally out of a plant or situation. At Ga 5:22–23 it refers to character qualities given by the Holy Spirit, at Mt 13:1–23 perhaps to other people who trust Yeshua, at Ro 6:21–22 to righteousness.

Prunes. The Greek word means, literally, "cleans." To clean of excess foliage is to prune, but the context also calls to mind cleansing from sin (see 13:7ff.).

10 **I have kept my father's commands**. This probably refers to 14:31. The context gives no ground for considering it an assertion that Yeshua obeyed the *Torah* perfectly.

14–15 Yeshua's *talmidim* are no longer his **slaves** but his **friends**. Later, *talmidim* are his brothers, God's sons by adoption (Ro 8:14–17, Ga 3:27–4:8).

16 **Go and bear fruit** (v. 2N). Staying (vv. 1–8) and going are consistent with each other: the Messianic lifestyle is, on one hand, passive and receptive and, on the other, active, transmissive and productive.

18–25 The world's hate for Christians and Messianic Jews stems from its hate for the Messiah. Those of whom Yeshua was speaking actually saw and experienced what he did and hated him anyway because they did not want to give up their sin and live righteously (16:7–11).

23 **Whoever hates me hates my father also**. See 1 Yn 2:22–23&N.

25 The *Talmud* asks,

> "Why was the Second Sanctuary destroyed, seeing that in its time they occupied themselves with studying *Torah*, obeying *mitzvot* and practicing charity? Because in it prevailed hatred without a cause." (Yoma 9b)

CHAPTER 16

2 **They will ban you from the synagogue**. See 9:22N. The vast majority of Jewish people are staunch supporters of the principle of free speech. But in many synagogues, if a Jewish believer in Yeshua makes his faith public, speaks about it, and attempts in conversation to persuade others to acknowledge the Messiah, he may be asked to leave the synagogue and not come back. In fact, I once attended a synagogue for the first time and in a *private* conversation told its rabbi about my faith; his response was to make it clear I would not be welcome to return. The price a Messianic Jew is asked to pay for worshipping God with his own people is often silence about God's most important historical work! The reason for such behavior is given in v. 3.

Fortunately, there are many social situations, both in synagogues and in other settings, where this does not happen, where Jewish people are open to hearing the Gospel explained. I have found this true in Israel more than in the Diaspora, because Diaspora Jews often use their conception of Jewishness without Yeshua to defend against assimilation into the surrounding Gentile culture.

7 **But I tell you the truth**. See Mt 5:18N.

8–9 **The world is wrong… about sin, in that people don't put their trust in me.** Instead, they have other theories about sin, theories which downgrade the horribleness of sin and upgrade their own holiness. Thus they find no need to accept for themselves Yeshua's atoning death.

10 God comes to consider sinners righteous only because Yeshua has done his work on earth and is now with the Father, alive and interceding with him on our behalf (Ro 8:34, MJ 7:25, 1 Yn 2:1).

12–15 The Messianic life is lived by attentiveness to the Holy Spirit. Moreover, by telling his *talmidim* that **the Spirit of Truth** will **guide** them **into all the truth** and **announce the events of the future** (see Ac 11:27N, 1C 12:8–10N) Yeshua virtually pre-authenticates the New Testament Scriptures which they will write as the product of the Holy Spirit.

16–22 The world of nonbelievers will rejoice at Yeshua's death, but his return after being resurrected will turn the sorrow of the *talmidim* into joy.

30–32 The *talmidim* have at last come to the point of simple, childlike faith (compare Mt 18:3). Nevertheless, Yeshua does not permit them to bask in it but at once calls their attention to its fickleness. The moment you feel secure, certain your faith is strong, may well be the very instant **when you will be scattered, each one looking out for himself; and you will leave me** (Yeshua) **all alone**.

33 **In the world you have *tsuris*** (see Mt 6:34N). The life of a believer in the Messiah is not the proverbial rose garden, except, perhaps, for the thorns. Nevertheless, Yeshua encourages us: **Be brave! I have conquered the world!**

CHAPTER 17

1–26 Yeshua as our *cohen gadol* (MJ 6:20) prays on our behalf to his Father. In this intercessory prayer we see deeply into the Messiah's heart — into the intimacy of the relationship between the Son and the Father, on the one hand, and between the Son and his *talmidim*, on the other. The depth of this prayer exceeds that possible to any mere human; it presupposes that Yeshua came forth from God, had the Father's glory before the world existed (v. 5), shares all that belongs to the Father (v. 10), can give the Father's glory to believers (v. 22), is eternal (vv. 5, 24) and has uniquely intimate knowledge of the Father (v. 25).

3 **Eternal life is this: to know....** Eternal life is not merely survival after death, which everyone shares (3:16N, 5:29&N; Daniel 12:2), but having intimate "knowledge" of the Father and the Son. The Hebrew word for "knowledge," "*da'at*," denotes not only the comprehending of the acts and circumstances of the world, but also the most intimate experiencing of the object of knowledge (hence its use in Hebrew to mean sexual intercourse in such expressions as, "And Adam knew Chavah his wife" (Genesis 4:1)). Here the word "know" is used exactly as in Jeremiah 31:33(34), in the passage promising Israel a new covenant: "And no longer will each one teach his neighbor and his brother, 'Know *Adonai*,' for they will all know me."

5 This verse teaches the pre-existence of the Messiah; see 1:1aN.

6 **I made your name known**. This signifies that in his own person (1:18, 14:9) Yeshua revealed more directly than ever before God's authority, power and character. A literalistic understanding of the phrase, "I made your name known," became the theme of the scurrilous *Toledot-Yeshu*, the 6th-century C.E. anti-gospel (see Mt 1:18N) which said that the offense "Yeshu" committed that earned him the death penalty for blasphemy was the unauthorized use of the "72–letter name" of God to perform magic (see *Encyclopedia Judaica*, 7:711).

12 **So that the *Tanakh* might be fulfilled**. See Psalm 41:10(9), cited in connection with

Y'hudah from K'riot at 13:18 above; Psalm 55:13–16; and Psalm 109:8–9, cited at Ac 1:20. Prefiguring Y'hudah in these Psalms may be Achitofel, who turned traitor to King David (2 Samuel 16:14–17).

15 Believers are expected to be involved in what Judaism calls *tikkun-ha'olam*, repairing the world. *Tikkun-ha'olam* is deeply embedded in the Jewish ethic; for this reason even secular Jews usually find themselves concerned with bettering society. Believers in Yeshua the Messiah are not to separate themselves altogether (1C 5:10) but to act like yeast causing the world's dough to rise (Lk 13:21), caring for widows and orphans while remaining unspotted through participation in the world's sins (Ya 1:27), not being conquered by evil but conquering it with good (Ro 12:21).

17 **Separate… for holiness,** Greek *agiason*, equivalent to Hebrew *kadesh*, "sanctify." (I avoid the word "sanctify" in the *JNT* because it seems archaic and removed from most people's reality today.) To sanctify is to separate for holiness, to set apart for God. This separateness is not a physical removal from other people and their concerns (see v. 15&N) but a spiritual relocation into God's sphere of being.

20 **I pray not only for these** twelve *talmidim*, my *shlichim* ("messengers," "emissaries," "apostles"), **but also for those who trust in me because of their word**. Here Yeshua is praying for all the millions down through the centuries who have come to trust in him because these twelve faithfully communicated the Gospel. The ensuing verses are Yeshua's one prayer specifically for us.

21–23 **That they may all be one**. The content of Yeshua's one prayer for today's believers is for their unity "in" the Father and the Son: **Just as you, Father, are united with me and I with you, I pray that they may be united with us**.

The Greek preposition "*en*" is most often rendered "in" in this passage and in 10:38; 14:10–11, 17, 20; 15:4–7; and 16:33; but its sense is hard to convey by a single English word, for it can mean "in the sphere of, in connection with, within, inside, by, on, near, among, with." Overall, the word conveys intimacy and involvement: Yeshua and the Father are intimately involved and concerned with each other's existence, even to the point of being "one" (here, 10:30). Yeshua uses this word "*en*" frequently, as does Sha'ul in his letters, to get across the notion of deep mutual concern and participation.

Thus Yeshua prays that the unity between believers and himself, between believers and the Father and between believers and other believers will have the same character as the unity between himself and the Father. The history of the Christian church offers all too ample proof that his prayer was needed! Most Jewish people are at least confused, if not scandalized, by the distinctions between various kinds of Christians which seem to divide more than unite: Eastern Orthodox versus Western, Roman Catholic versus Protestant, hundreds or thousands of Protestant denominations (most of which are "versus" at least some of the others), and thousands of one-church "denominations" with no organizational affiliation. How many lives have been sacrificed over the centuries in wars between Christians? How often do the media report loveless castigations of one Christian group by another?

Jewish people look on this display of disunity with disgust or disdain, while the less virulent expressions may provoke mild amusement. For the Jewish community functions rather differently. It has a built-in unity partly based, like that of the Messianic Community, on God's having chosen them for himself. But Jewish unity is also based on a common history involving common social patterns, religious practices, persecution by outsiders (both Christian and non-Christian), and the biological element of descent from a common ancestor. A common expression is the feeling among many Jews, "We're all family to each other." While there are Jewish denominations — three major ones and several minor — and even some friction between them, this does not prevent unified community action when basic issues are concerned, such as support for the survival of the State of Israel or opposition to antisemitism. Only the Hasidic sects seem to produce the sort of discord between themselves that other Jews can regard as slightly ridiculous (but only rarely vicious). Thus Jews consider themselves largely immune from the kinds of divisions that seem endemic to the Christian Church, with such unpleasant consequences for both themselves and the rest of humanity.

It is no wonder, then, that Yeshua prayed as he did. While Scripture declares that there already exists a spiritual unity between believers in the Messiah (Ro 12:4–8&NN, 1C 12:12–27&NN), what we see is, to put it mildly, a very imperfect reflection of it. The modern ecumenical movement is a cross-denominational effort to create unity, although anxiety to achieve the goal can lead to generating an appearance of unity at the institutional level which glosses over real differences in doctrine and practice as well as unhealed relationships between people. On the other hand, opposition to ecumenism is sometimes voiced by those who, in the name of doctrinal purity, refuse to work through the crises of resolving differences with their brothers in the Lord.

However serious the schisms between the various Christian denominations, the greatest schism in the world is that between the Jewish people and the Body of the Messiah. The Jews are God's people, and so is the Messianic Community (the Church). It was never God's intent that there be two separated peoples of God; for the Body of the Messiah, consisting of saved Jews and Gentiles, is built on a Jewish foundation; it springs from a Jewish root. And conversely, non-Messianic Judaism is a broken-off branch, although one with enough life to flourish if grafted in again to the living tree (Ro 11:17–26&NN). Messianic Judaism, by striving to be one hundred percent Jewish and one hundred percent Messianic, offers itself as one means to help heal this schism. If the schism between the Jews and the Church can be healed, how much more easily the schisms within the Church!

Finally, healing of these splits is given an evangelistic purpose in Yeshua's prayer: may they be one in us **so that the** unsaved **world may believe that you** (God the Father) **sent me** (Yeshua).

CHAPTER 18

4 Yeshua… knew everything that was going to happen to him. See 10:17–18N.

5–8 I AM. There is a double meaning. Yeshua was both identifying himself and voicing God's authority (see 4:26N). Apparently he was demonstrating God's power as well, so that it was in direct consequence that **they went backward from him and fell to the ground.**

9 **"I have not lost one…."** Quoted from 6:39; compare 17:12.

10–11 Yochanan's description complements that of the Synoptic Gospels. We learn who "one of the men with Yeshua" (Mt 26:51) was, namely, **Kefa**. We are told that the "servant of the *cohen hagadol"* (Mk 14:47) was named **Melekh**. Yeshua's remark to Kefa, **"This is the cup the Father has given me: am I not to drink it?"** fits perfectly his prayers at *Gat-Sh'manim* (Lk 22:42).

13 **First they led him to Anan**. Only Yochanan tells us of this irregular preliminary hearing. Anan had been *cohen gadol* (high priest) from 6 to 15 C.E. Many members of his family became *cohen gadol* after him, including five of his sons as well as his son-in-law **Kayafa**. He retained his title after leaving office (vv. 15, 16, 19, 22; but not vv. 10, 13, 24, 26, which refer to Kayafa) and obviously remained a powerful behind-the-scenes figure; perhaps this is why his advice on how to deal with Yeshua was sought first.

14 See 11:49–52.

20 **In the Temple where all Jews meet together**. Or: "…all Judeans…." Since the Temple was the religious center for the whole Jewish people, "Jews" seems a more appropriate rendering than "Judeans"; hence the exception to the general rules of 1:19N on *Ioudaioi*.

22 **This is how you talk to the *cohen hagadol*?** Yeshua was not answering disrespectfully but pointing out that even though this late night meeting was most irregular, normal legal procedure requires the obtaining of independent witnesses. Yeshua was willing to trust public reports of his public behavior, as is clear from v. 23. "These things… didn't happen in some back alley" (Ac 26:26). Compare Ac 22:30–23:10.

24 **Anan sent him… to Kayafa**. Yochanan does not report the trial before Kayafa, but it is reported in Mt 26:59–68 and Mk 14:55–65. Nor does he report the meeting of the Sanhedrin the next morning as do Mt 27:1–2, Mk 15:1 and Lk 22:66–23:1; presumably his readers know about these from other sources.

28 **They didn't want to become ritually defiled**. This defilement is not the same as that spoken of at 11:55 but results from entering the home of a Gentile, in this case the Governor's Headquarters. The *Torah* does not mention such a defilement; it is a rabbinic addition (see Ac 10:28N).

And thus unable to eat the *Pesach* meal, literally, "unable to eat the *Pesach*." Some scholars believe "the *Pesach*" refers to the Passover lamb and conclude that Yochanan, unlike the Synoptic Gospels, places the *Seder* (the first evening of Passover) on Friday evening after the execution of Yeshua in the afternoon. I do not believe that Yochanan's Gospel reports a different date for the crucifixion from the Synoptics (but see 13:29&N); rather, the meal of 13:1 was the *Seder*, and it took place on Thursday night; but "the *Pesach*" in this verse refers to other food eaten during *Pesach*, specifically the *chagigah* (festival sacrifice), which was consumed with great joy and celebration on the afternoon following the *Seder*. This is the *Pesach* meal which the Judeans gathered outside Pilate's palace would have been unable to eat had they entered, because their defilement would have lasted till sundown. If "the *Pesach*" meant the Passover lamb, defilement in the morning might not have been a problem, since the *Seder* meal took place after sundown.

31 **We don't have the legal power to put anyone to death**. Although the *Torah* prescribes the death penalty for a number of offenses, and although the Romans permitted the Judeans a measure of self-government, they did not allow the execution of a death sentence; capital punishment was reserved for Rome.

32 **How he was going to die**, by being "lifted up" (3:14, 8:28, 12:32) on an execution-stake, a cross, which was a Roman, not a Jewish, method of capital punishment.

36 **My kingship** (or: "kingdom") **does not derive its authority from this world's order of things**, literally, "is not of this world." This is not to say that the Messianic kingdom and Yeshua's rulership is only "spiritual," not to be expressed really and physically in this world, fulfilling the prophecy that Israel will become "the head and not the tail" (Deuteronomy 28:13); but that the present aspect of his kingship is in believers' hearts and lives (see 16:27&N), not in international politics (which is the framework of Pilate's question). Thus Yeshua, without denying his office as the Messiah, the King, claims he has done nothing against Rome.

38a **What is truth?** The cynical and worldly Pilate shrugs off him who is the Truth (14:6) with a flippant question, to which he is uninterested in knowing the answer. Alternatively, it was a philosophical question divorced from practicality, the kind asked by people "who are always learning but never able to come to full knowledge of the Truth" (2 Ti 3:7&N).

18:38b–40, 19:4–16 This corresponds to the Judean mob scene reported at Mt 27:15–27. The passage below at 19:4–15 presents material found only in Yochanan. Pilate is portrayed as repeatedly seeking an excuse to set Yeshua free (v. 39; 19:4, 6, 10, 12, 15) but also as too weak to initiate his release. Therefore he shares the guilt for putting Yeshua to death, although the guilt of Y'hudah from K'riot is greater (19:11&N).

40 **Bar-Abba**. See Mt 27:16–24N.

CHAPTER 19

6 **Put him to death on the stake!** Usually rendered, "Crucify him!" See v. 15N.

7 **We have a law**, or: "We have a *Torah*," which specifies the death penalty for blasphemy (see 8:58N).

8 **Pilate became even more frightened**, either because his efforts to avoid taking responsibility for Yeshua's death (18:38bN) were not succeeding, or because the Judeans' accusation (v. 7) made him think Yeshua might actually be (in some pagan sense) a "son of the gods."

11 The one who handed me over to you is guilty of a greater sin. It was an unspeakably great sin for Pilate to fail to exercise his power to prevent Yeshua's execution. But it was a still greater sin for Judah from K'riot — for whom it would have been better had he never been born (Mt 26:24) — to deliver Yeshua, with full knowledge of who he was and of his innocence, to an unjust death penalty.

12 "Friend of the Emperor." This was a technical term sometimes used as a title of honor for provincial governors and here as a sign of loyalty.

14 Preparation Day. See v. 31N.

15 Execute... on a stake like a common criminal. This gives the full sense of the Greek word usually translated "crucify." See Mt 10:38N.

16 Handed him over to them, to the Roman soldiers (Mt 26:26–31, Mk 15:16–20), not to the Judeans.

17 Carrying the stake himself until Shim'on of Cyrene took it (Lk 23:26). Compare with Yeshua's suffering this extract from a *midrash* compiled in the 9th century C.E.:

> "In the seven years prior to the coming of the son of David, they will bring iron beams and load them on his neck until his body doubles over and he cries and weeps. Then his voice will rise to the highest places of heaven, and he will say to God, 'Master of the Universe, how much can my strength endure? How much my spirit, my soul, my limbs? Am I not flesh and blood?' It was because of this suffering of the son of David that David wept, saying, 'My strength is dried up like a potsherd' (Psalm 22:16(15)). During this ordeal the Holy One, blessed be he, will say to the son of David, 'Efrayim, my true Messiah, you took this suffering on yourself long ago, during the six days of creation. And right now, your pain is like my pain [due to the destruction of the Temple].' At this the Messiah will reply, 'Now I am at peace. It is enough for a servant to be like his master.'"(Pesikta Rabbati 36:2)

Several other features of this passage echo the New Testament. The seven years is taken from Daniel in the *Tanakh*, but the New Testament refers it to Yeshua's second coming (Rv 12:14; compare Daniel 7:25, 9:24–27, 12:7). Psalm 22 is frequently cited in the New Testament, notably its initial words by Yeshua himself on the execution-stake (Mt 27:46&N). On the pre-existence of the Messiah see 1:1a&N. On a servant's being like his master, see Yeshua's remarks to his *talmidim* at 13:14–17 above.

20–22 In Yochanan only. We see Pilate unwilling to bother himself over the point that offended the head *cohanim*, distinguishing between Yeshua's supposedly erroneous claim to kingship and the implication of Pilate's sign that Yeshua was in fact the king of the Jews (or: "of the Judeans"; see 1:19N, Mt 2:2N). Yochanan therefore reports the incident to show that God used Pilate's sign, intended by him to mock the people in general and only incidentally to mock Yeshua in particular, to announce an eternal truth to the whole community and, by implication (and by inclusion here), to the whole world.

24 Ten books of the New Testament quote or allude to various portions of Psalm 22; it is one of the most important Messianic Psalms.

26–27 Yochanan alone reports this incident involving Yeshua and himself (**the *talmid* whom he loved**); it demonstrates Yeshua's filial love (see 2:4&N).

28–29 In response to Yeshua's **"I'm thirsty,"** people offer him a **sponge** soaked in what Mattityahu calls "vinegar" (Mt 27:48) and Yochanan calls **cheap sour wine** (a little earlier he had been offered "bitter gall," which he had refused, Mt 27:34). They pass it up to him on what Mattityahu calls a "stick" and Yochanan a **hyssop branch**. Hyssop is a variety of oregano with a pungent cooling taste; it grows wild on the hill by my house, and its branches are 12–18 inches long.

30 **Delivered up his spirit**, or, putting euphemism aside, "died."

31 **Preparation Day**. The day before a *Shabbat* or festival when food is cooked and other preparations made, since no work is to be done on the holyday itself. This particular Preparation Day was also the first day of *Pesach* (see 18:28N).

But may one cook for *Shabbat* on a festival day? Yes; the *halakhah* requires an *'eruv tavshilin*, which is a special agreement allowing cooking for *Shabbat* to be done on the festival day, provided it was commenced before the festival began.

The Judeans did not want the bodies to remain on the stake after nightfall (when the *Shabbat*, or any next day, begins), because of Deuteronomy 21:22–23 (see Ga 3:13&N).

An especially important *Shabbat*, or, possibly: "*Shabbat HaGadol*" (the "Great Sabbath"); since the Greek text reads, "great was the day of that *Shabbat*." But what is today called *Shabbat HaGadol* is the *Shabbat* immediately preceding Passover week, not the one that falls during its seven days, as is the case here; and I am unaware that the terminology was different in Yeshua's day. Obviously the *Shabbat* of *Pesach* week, when millions of Jews were in Jerusalem on pilgrimage, would be an important one. The modern synagogue ritual for this *Shabbat* calls for reading Ezekiel 37:1–14, the vision of the Valley of Dry Bones, as the *haftarah* (the concluding Scripture reading, from the Prophets); the passage links *Pesach* with Messianic times by speaking of a future redemption for Israel just as Passover itself celebrates a past one.

34 **Blood and water flowed out**. Apart from whatever symbolism may suggest itself, such as of immersion or communion, the *p'shat*, the simple sense of the text, is that Yeshua, who had been a living man, was now dead. According to medical opinion, the "blood and water" are signs that the final cause of death was massive heart failure. Thus refuted are teachings, already current among heretical groups when Yochanan wrote, that Yeshua had not been a flesh-and-blood human being (see 1 Yn 4:2&N). This false doctrine (docetism) is echoed by modern cults that speak of a "Christ-figure" who only faked being human.

At the same time this report disproves the "swoon theory," probably equally ancient, that Yeshua did not die but only lost consciousness and was later revived by his *talmidim*, who then invented the "resurrection myth." The most imaginative recent restatement of this ancient canard is *The Passover Plot*, by the apostate Messianic Jew Hugh J. Schonfield (1901–1988).

35 **The man who saw it**. Either Yochanan is writing of himself in the third person, or friends are affirming his honesty, as at 21:24. The purpose of reporting that Yeshua actually did die is the same as the purpose of the whole Gospel (20:31) — so that **you too can trust**.

36 Exodus 12:46 specifies that no bone of the Passover lamb is to be broken; Numbers 9:12 says the same thing. Yeshua is himself "the lamb of God" (1:29, 36), our Passover lamb (1C 5:8&N). Psalm 34:21(20) says: "Many are the afflictions of the righteous, but *Adonai* delivers him out of them all. He keeps all his bones; not one of them is broken."

37 Yochanan quotes a most important Messianic prophecy, in which *Adonai says*,

> "I will pour out upon the house of David and upon the inhabitants of Jerusalem the spirit of grace and of supplication; and they will look upon me whom they have pierced, and they will mourn for him as one mourns for an only son, and they will be in bitterness over him as one that is in bitterness for a firstborn." (Zechariah 12:10)

Adonai is the "me" who is pierced and the "him" who is mourned over, but Yochanan identifies the latter as Yeshua; thus, by implication, Yeshua is once again in some sense equated with *Adonai* (see 14:9&N).

The "they" of "they have pierced" is the house of David and the inhabitants of Jerusalem. Some Jewish translations into English go back to Zechariah 12:9, where the Hebrew word "*goyim*" is used, and explicitly substitute "the nations" for "they" in v. 10. In my judgment this is an instance of an overdetermined translation in the service of defensive theologizing against Messianic Jewish and Christian recognition of this text as a prophecy of Yeshua. It is most natural to understand "they" as referring to the closest preceding plural noun ("the house of David and...the inhabitants of Yerushalayim") and unnatural to skip over it and go back to "the nations" for the referent. Moreover, at least one Talmudic source regards this passage of Zechariah as being Messianic in application (Sukkah 52a; for more see Ga 3:13N, also Rv 1:7&N).

Nevertheless, it may be that Yochanan understands this piercing as involving both Jews and Gentiles. It was done directly by the "nations" in the persons of Pilate and the Roman soldiers, yet it would not have happened without pressure from the Judeans (see Ac 2:22–23&N). If this understanding is correct, then both Jews and Gentiles pierced Yeshua, share responsibility for his death, and will regret what they did when they look upon him — whether spiritually now or literally when he returns.

Zechariah 12:10 also points to the future salvation of national Israel, which the New Testament confirms by Sha'ul's words, "...all Israel will be saved" (Ro 11:26a&N).

38–39a Yosef of Ramatayim (Mt 27:57, Mk 15:43, Lk 23:50) and **Nakdimon** (3:1, 7:50) were two highly placed Messianic Jews, both members of the *Sanhedrin* (Lk 23:50–51, Yn 7:50–52); both secret believers. Yochanan does not disparage them for hiding their faith (see 9:22&N, Lk 12:8–9). But their period of secrecy was brief, for the act reported here made their beliefs known. While no one is required to make a public announcement of his convictions the moment he comes to faith, he should, after acquiring some knowledge enabling him to defend his views (1 Ke 3:16), be willing to set fear aside and stand openly with Yeshua the Messiah.

39b–40 They took Yeshua's body and wrapped it in linen sheets. It continues to be **Jewish burial practice** to wrap the body in a shroud, but **spices** no longer are. Spices function against the rapid deterioration of the body in a hot climate and may serve an embalming function.

41 In the garden was a new tomb. The Church of the Holy Sepulchre, in the Old City of Jerusalem, was built on the site venerated as Yeshua's burial location at least since the early fourth century, when it was found by Helen, the mother of Roman Emperor Constantine, as she investigated local traditions. It was outside the "first" and "second" walls surrounding Jerusalem in Yeshua's day, but inside the "third" wall; it is inside the present-day wall built by sultan Suleiman I "the Great," who ruled the Ottoman Empire from 1520 to 1566.

Some identify Yeshua's burial location with a spot outside today's walls called the Garden Tomb. It was not advocated as a possible site until the nineteenth century, by the British Colonel Gordon; few archeologists are convinced. The place has been made into a garden and is open to tourists; it does have a tomb, perhaps from the first century and probably much like the one in which Yeshua was buried, which one can enter and see.

Occasionally evidence is credibly marshalled for other locations.

CHAPTER 20

1 **Early on the first day of the week, while it was still dark.** Here, definitely Sunday morning before dawn; see Mt 28:1&N.

5–8 The burial clothes consisted of a shroud around the body and a head-cloth (compare 11:44). Yochanan's painstaking description of their undisturbed location, especially the separate position of the still folded head cloth (v. 7), tells us that Yeshua's body was miraculously loosed from the burial clothes, so that they collapsed in place. This is why **the other *talmid*… saw, and he trusted.**

9 **The *Tanakh* teaches that the Messiah has to rise from the dead** at Isaiah 53:9–12 and Psalm 16:10 (cited at Ac 2:24–32).

15 Thinking he was the gardener. Gardening is the oldest profession — Adam was to be a gardener (Genesis 2:15). Yeshua, the "second Adam" (1C 15:45, Ro 5:12–21), is also perceived as a gardener.

16 "Rabbani!" (That is, "Teacher!"), literally, "My great one!" or "My teacher!" As a title "*rabban*" was conferred only on the heads of the central academy and of the *Sanhedrin*. Gamli'el I, quoted at Ac 5:34–39, is known in Jewish history as *Rabban* Gamli'el. Apparently the term was used more broadly in informal conversation. Although there is no evidence that Yeshua was ever ordained a rabbi, it is implied at Mt 23:8 that he and his *talmidim* regarded him as one.

17 Stop holding onto me, not, as in KJV, "Do not touch me," which suggests a fragility about his post-resurrection physical state contradicted by the rest of Yochanan's gospel. Yeshua had work to do and was not to be kept from it even by Miryam's joyful attention.

19 The *talmidim* were hiding **behind locked doors out of fear of the Judeans**, concerned that the Judeans would not be satisfied with the death of their leader but would pursue the followers as well. The rendering found in most versions, "for fear of the Jews," besides being misleading in the first-century context (1:19N), reinforces the stereotype of Jews as bogeymen.

Messianic Jews and Christians who are paranoid that if they witness clearly to Jewish people they will be persecuted, who find it easier to remain ghettoized **behind locked doors out of fear of** "the Jews," would do better to obey the Great Commission (Mt 28:19&N), relying for confidence on God, "our help and our shield" (Psalm 33:20).

Yeshua miraculously appears but greets them in the usual way, ***"Shalom aleikhem!"*** Yeshua's post-resurrection appearances combine the supernatural with the ordinary in a way that makes the mixture seem normal rather than mysterious and otherworldly.

21 I… am sending you into the world with my message of Good News.

22 Breathed… the *Ruach HaKodesh*. Yeshua's breathing was meaningful (see 3:8N) but symbolic. The *talmidim* actually received the Holy Spirit's power a month and a half later, at *Shavu'ot*(Ac 2:4); see also Lk 24:49, Ac 1:8.

24 T'oma. See 11:16&N.

26 The *talmidim* came together again **eight days later**. By Jewish reckoning the first and last days are counted; therefore this was a week later (circumcision "on the eighth day" is performed one week after a male baby is born). Apparently from the very beginning the believers took note of the fact that Yeshua rose from the dead on *Yom Rishon* ("the first day of the week"), that is, between Saturday sunset and Sunday sunset, which is why Gentile Christians, using a midnight-to-midnight calendar, celebrate Sunday, though not the biblical Sabbath, as a special day in the week. But the Jewish believers evidently met on Saturday nights (Ac 20:7&N, 1C 16:2&N). Also see Rv 1:10N.

28–31 These verses taken together summarize the purpose of Yochanan's Gospel. There is a textual problem: the phrase in v. 31 rendered "**so that you may trust**" appears in two forms in the ancient manuscripts. The one means, "so that you may continue trusting" and implies that the book is intended to strengthen and confirm the faith of believers. The other means, "so that you may, at a point in time, come to trust" and implies that the book is for unbelievers. In either case, what is to be trusted in is Yeshua's identity with God and consequent power to give us the blessing of eternal life.

28 My Lord and my God! "Doubting Thomas's" confession is as close as the New Testament comes to asserting that Yeshua "is God" (with the possible exception of Ti 2:13; see note there). Yet it is not a propositional statement, but an exclamation by a *talmid* who had just seen with his own eyes the opposite of what he had dared hope for, namely, Yeshua resurrected. This is important for Jewish readers for whom the declaration, "Yeshua is God," is unpalatable. It is not that Yeshua "is not God"; rather, the precise way in which Yeshua is regarded as divine is not so simply expressed in the New Testament as "is" or "is not." See 1:1–3, 14, 18, 45; 4:26; 5:17–19; 8:24, 58–59; 10:30, 34–36; 11:25; 14:6, 9–11, 14, 28; 17:1–26; 18:6 and notes in all these places for further elaboration of just how Yeshua is to be identified with God without being any less a human being. In this connection note that the *Tanakh* prophesies or hints at this identification of the Messiah with God at Isaiah 9:5–6(6–7), Jeremiah 23:5–6, Micah 5:1(2) and Proverbs 30:4.

30 Many other, similar kinds of **miracles** comparable with those recorded, **which have not been recorded in this book**. Yochanan's gospel differs from those of the Synoptics in many respects. Why? Because his purpose is different. He chooses the incidents he reports to suit his purpose. Also he presumes knowledge of the events reported in the Synoptics; see 6:1–15&N, 11:1&N and 18:10–11&N. He could write more (see 21:25N), but he recognizes the value of brevity (compare Ecclesiastes 12:12).

CHAPTER 21

1–15 The Synoptics had mentioned that Yeshua would appear to the *talmidim* in the Galil (Mt 28:7, 10; Mk 16:7), and Mt 28:16–20 reports one such appearance. Here Yochanan describes another, earlier appearance.

3 Shim'on Kefa said, "I'm going fishing." He was going back to his old way of life, apparently unaware of what Yeshua's commission (20:21) meant. The others followed his example and went with him. The result of this self- rather than God-determined activity was that **they didn't catch anything**. When they allowed the Messiah to determine what they should do, they caught a netful (v. 11); compare Lk 5:3–7.

15–17 Two Greek verbs with related meanings are used in this passage. Greek *agapaô* is selfless, self-giving love, the kind of love God has for his human creations; "*phileô*" is the love friends or brothers have for each other (Philadelphia, the city of brotherly love). Scholars are divided on the degree to which the use of these two different words for "love" affects the sense of this exchange between Yeshua and Kefa. The exchange goes like this: "Do you *agapaô* me?" "I *phileô* you." "Feed my lambs. Do you *agapaô* me?" "I *phileô* you." "Shepherd my sheep. Do you *phileô* me?" "You know I *phileô* you."

"Feed my sheep." Some translators use "love" throughout, believing the two words are used only for variety.

The books of Acts, 1 Kefa and 2 Kefa demonstrate that Kefa more than rose to the occasion and fulfilled Yeshua's calling.

19 **The kind of death by which Kefa would glorify God**. Tradition has it that he was crucified upside-down, because he said he was unworthy to be crucified in the same position as his Lord. He is believed to have died in Rome in the mid-60's C.E.

20 **The *talmid* Yeshua especially loved**, Yochanan. See 13:23, 19:26–27&N.

22 Yeshua rules out curiosity about matters that do not concern us or help us live a holy life, although he does not rule out scientific inquiry into how the world works. Likewise he excludes unhealthy, jealous competition concerned with comparing our lives, tasks, gifts, accomplishments, interests and calling with those of others. In both matters Yeshua's central point is: **You, follow me!**

25 **Many other things Yeshua did**. For the purpose given in 20:31 a complete biography of Yeshua is not needed, yet this has not prevented wild speculation about his "silent years"; see Lk 2:52N. But a full biography would suffocate the earth. As Buckminster Fuller used to say, "Less is more."

THE

ACTS

OF THE EMISSARIES OF YESHUA THE MESSIAH

CHAPTER 1

1 **The first book** is the Gospel of Luke, also addressed to **Theophilos** (see Lk 1:1&N). This "second book" could be called "Luke, Part II."

Everything Yeshua set out to do and teach is the content of the Gospel of Luke. Luke's subject in the present book is the accomplishments of the early believers, in particular how they succeeded in bringing Gentiles into the framework of Messianic faith without their having to convert to Judaism, so that trust in Yeshua would not be for Jews only. Today the problem is exactly the opposite: the cultural and religious superstructure of faith in Yeshua the Jewish Messiah has become so "Gentilized" that most Jews find it hard to believe that the New Testament is as much for them as for Gentiles; see 11:18&N, 15:1&N. On the name "Yeshua" ("Jesus") see Mt 1:1N.

2 See Lk 24:44–51. **Emissaries**. See Mt 10:2–4&N.

3 **He… gave many convincing proofs that he was alive**. See 1C 15:3–8&NN; also Mattityahu 28, Mark 16, Luke 24 and Yochanan 20–21.

He spoke with them about the Kingdom of God. This was the central topic of Yeshua's post-resurrection teaching. See vv. 6–7&N, also Mt 3:2N on "the Kingdom of Heaven."

5 **Immerse** or "baptize." See Mt 3:1N. Yochanan's water immersion accomplished ritual purification of the body for *chozrim bitshuvah* ("persons who turn from sin to God in repentance"). Yeshua's promised immersion in the Holy Spirit would give power from God to continue living a holy life and to bring the Gospel effectively to others. This verse condenses Lk 3:16.

6–7 **Self-rule**. According to Arndt and Gingrich's *A Greek-English Lexicon of the New Testament*, Greek *tên basileian* here means "the kingship, royal power, royal rule," and not "the kingdom" in the sense of the territory ruled by a king.

Lord, are you at this time going to restore self-rule to Israel? The expectation of virtually all Jews was that when the Messiah came he would deliver Israel from Roman oppression and become king over a Jewish nation reunited and sovereign as it had been under Kings Saul, David and Solomon, and again under the Maccabees (see Yn 10:22N) and their Hasmonean descendants (164–63 B.C.E.). This is seen clearly at Yn 6:15, when "they were on the point of coming and seizing [Yeshua], in order to make him king," to force God's promise concerning the Messiah that "the government shall be upon his shoulders" (Isaiah 9:5–6(6–7), Lk 1:79N). No one grasped Yeshua's teaching that he had not come this first time to rule, but to die "a ransom for many" and be resurrected the third day (Mk 10:33–34, 45). Even his *talmidim* misunderstood and continued to do so after the predicted events had taken place. At vv. 7–8 Yeshua filled this gap in their knowledge, focussing their attention not on his return but on their task; and we learn later (3:21) that Kefa got the point.

Nevertheless, there is a different point which many Christians need to learn from Yeshua's answer, namely, that God will indeed restore self-rule to Israel. There is an ancient, widespread and pernicious Christian teaching that the Church is the "New" or "Spiritual" Israel, having replaced the Jews as God's people. In this view — known variously as Replacement theology, Covenant theology, Kingdom Now theology, Dominionism, Reconstructionism and (in England) Restorationism — God's promises to Israel were nullified when "the Jews" refused to accept Jesus (never mind that all the first believers were Jews). This false theology, impugning the character of God by suggesting that he will welch on his promises, has provided apparent justification for many antisemitic acts in the Church. It also lies behind most Christian protestations that the present-day regathering of the Jewish people to the Land of Israel is without theological or biblical significance.

Yeshua's answer to his disciples' question as to whether he will now restore self-rule to Israel is, **"You don't need to know the dates or the times; the Father has kept these under his own authority."** From this we learn, contrary to the teaching of Replacement Theology, that the kingdom certainly *will* be restored to Israel. The only question is when, and that is not presently ours to know. "The secret things belong to *Adonai* our God" (Deuteronomy 29:28(29)).

For a modern presentation of the Replacement theology heresy see David Chilton, *Paradise Restored* (Fort Worth, TX: Dominion Press, 1985). A book by a popular Christian author refuting Reconstructionism and revealing its antisemitism is Hal Lindsey, *The Road to Holocaust* (New York: Bantam Books, 1989); another refutation is H. Wayne House and Thomas Ice, *Dominion Theology: Blessing or Curse?* (Portland, Oregon: Multnomah Press, 1988).

8 To be Yeshua's **witnesses** in both word and deed means communicating the verbal content of the Gospel and living God's way and not our own (Lk 9:23–25&N). This is the central task of the people of God, but it can be accomplished only with power from the ***Ruach HaKodesh***. Compare the Great Commission (Mt 28:18–20, Mk 16:15–18, Lk 24:47–49, Yn 20:21–23).

The *talmidim* are to start evangelizing where they are, **in Yerushalayim**, the center of the Jewish people. Then they are to move out into **all Y'hudah** (Judea, the Jewish countryside) **and Shomron** (Samaria, populated by half-Jews; see Yn 4:9N), and finally, **in fact**, to go **to the ends of the earth**, that is, to reach Gentile peoples. The verse serves as a table of contents for the book of Acts. Chapters 1–6 deal with Yerushalayim, 6:1–8:3 shows how the Yerushalayim community was forced into the surrounding area, and Chapters 8–9 include several instances of ministry in Y'hudah and Shomron. Beginning with Chapter 10 we are introduced to the gradual spread of the Gospel among the Gentiles, first through Kefa but especially through Sha'ul. Numerous successes are reported, and the book concludes with Sha'ul's successfully communicating the Gospel in the very heart and center of Gentile civilization, Rome.

The Body of the Messiah has for the most part not taken seriously Yeshua's injunction to communicate the Gospel first to the Jewish people; see Ro 1:16&N. In one sense the Gospel has already reached **the ends of the earth** — the Bible, or at least parts of it, have been translated into some 2,000 languages. Yet this does not excuse what has been, by and large, the Messianic Community's failure to reach the Jewish people with the Gospel. The Church, instead of developing mistaken theology to excuse its neglect (Yn 14:6N) or becoming exasperated when Jews reject their message, should communicate God's love and truth while seeking his wisdom on how to address issues Jewish people raise in connection with Yeshua, the New Testament, Christianity and religion in general. My own books, including this one, aim to forward the endeavor.

9–11 A cloud hid him.... Yeshua... will come back in just the same way, fulfilling Daniel 7:13 and Yeshua's predictions (Mt 26:64; Mk 14:62; Lk 21:27; Rv 1:7, 13; 14:14). In the *Tanakh* a cloud often expresses God's glory (e.g., the pillar of cloud, Exodus 13:21), his *Sh'khinah* ("manifest presence," MJ 1:2–3N).

The reply of the **two men dressed in white**, evidently angels (see 7:53N, MJ 13:2N), supports our hope (Ti 2:13) that Yeshua is coming back and at the same time implies a partial answer to the disciples' question in v. 6: Yeshua will restore self-rule to Israel and bring peace to the earth when he comes **back to you in just the same way as you saw him go into heaven.**

12 The *Shabbat*-walk distance from the Mount of Olives. The Mount of Olives is east of what is today called the Old City, which corresponds (very approximately) to what was meant anciently by Yerushalayim. The rabbinic rules for *Shabbat*, with certain exceptions, limit walking outside a walled city to 2,000 cubits (about 0.57 mile). According to Lk 24:50–51 Yeshua left his *talmidim* and ascended into heaven from Beit-Anyah, which is on the mount's south slope. The olive grove in the garden of Gat-Sh'manim, on its west slope, has trees that may have been living in Yeshua's time. Jewish tradition, based on Zechariah 14:3–5, says that the Messiah will appear on the Mount of Olives; vv. 9–12 tie Yeshua's first coming and his departure with his reappearance in a manner that will fulfill that expectation.

13 The upstairs room where they were staying, possibly the same as in Lk 22:12, possibly another house or apartment in the city (2:2 below), or possibly a room in the Temple complex made available for meeting (Lk 24:53).

The traditional English names of the eleven emissaries named are Peter, James, John, Andrew, Philip, Thomas, Bartholomew, Matthew, James the son of Alpheus, Simon the Zealot and Judas the brother (or son) of James.

14 Singlemindedly. Greek *omothumadon*, used 10 times in Acts. The community of believers must be united in heart and mind in order to have power in prayer. The word is used in the Septuagint at Exodus 19:8, where the people of Israel "answered together [Hebrew *yachdav*, Greek *omothumadon*], 'All that *Adonai* has said we will do.' "

Along with the women. Judaism always granted an important place to women; however, in the synagogue men and women are traditionally separated by a dividing wall or curtain (*m'chitzah*; see Ep 2:14N). The reason given is that it diminishes sexual attention and passion, which interfere with prayer. But in a powerful prayer meeting such concerns vanish as all turn to God. Moreover, this group functioned more like a family than a congregational assembly. Nevertheless, it is not clear that the phrase, "**along with the women**," implies that women and men were together.

Miryam (Yeshua's mother), and his brothers. See Mt 1:16–2:11, Lk 1:26–2:52, Yn 2:4, 7:3–5 and notes there. Yeshua's family, however uncertain they may have been before, were convinced of Yeshua's Messiahship after his resurrection.

18 **Fell to his death** (or: "swelled up"). At Mt 27:3–10 we read that the *cohanim* bought the **field** and used it as a cemetery for foreigners, hence its name (v. 19), and that **Y'hudah** from K'riot died by hanging himself. The differences between the two accounts can be resolved thus: the *cohanim* considered the money Y'hudah returned as his and bought the field in his name. The Greek for "fell to his death" means, literally, "having become prone." Augustine harmonizes by suggesting he hanged himself and then fell.

19 ***Chakal-D'ma*** is Aramaic.

Their language. People spoke both Aramaic and Hebrew; the New Testament quotes words from both languages.

Field of Blood, bought with blood-money, where Y'hudah spilled his own blood, and/or where foreigners were buried. All three explanations are apposite.

23 **Yosef Bar-Sabba, surnamed Justus**. Like many Jews today he had both a Gentile name (Latin), meaning "righteous," and a Jewish one (Aramaic), meaning "son of the elder"; or possibly it should be rendered "Bar-Shabba," "son of *Shabbat*."

24 **Lord**. See Mt 1:20&N, 7:20&N.

26 **They drew lots**. This was a recognized way of ascertaining God's will. Proverbs 16:33 says, "The lot is cast into the lap, but the whole decision is from *Adonai*," which means that what is attributed to chance, fate, luck or coincidence is determined by God. As Albert Einstein put it in objecting to quantum theory's use of probability mathematics, "God does not play dice with the universe."

This second **Mattityahu** (the first we encounter at Mt 9:9), **was added to the eleven emissaries,** not Sha'ul (Paul), as some Christians suppose. Sha'ul was indeed an emissary (see the first verse in most of his letters), but not one of the Twelve because he did not meet the requirements (vv. 21–22).

CHAPTER 2

1 **The festival of *Shavu'ot*** ("Weeks") is one of the three *regalim* ("pilgrim festivals"), when every Jewish male goes up to Yerushalayim (see Mt 20:17–19N). The others are *Pesach* and *Sukkot*; see Mt 26:2N; Yn 2:13N, 7:2N.

The name "*Shavu'ot*" comes from Exodus 34:22 and Deuteronomy 16:9–10, which, along with Leviticus 23:15–16, determine that the festival is to be seven weeks after the start of *Pesach*. The Bible also says, "You shall number fifty days" (Leviticus 23:16); hence in the New Testament the Greek name for the holiday is "*pentêkostês*," which means "fifty" and is usually transliterated into English as "Pentecost." Two other names for the festival are found in the *Tanakh*: "*Yom-HaBikkurim*" ("Day of the Firstfruits," Numbers 28:26) and "*Chag-HaKatzir*" ("Feast of the Harvest," Exodus 23:16).

On *Shavu'ot* the firstfruits of the wheat harvest were presented to *Adonai* in the Temple. The offering consisted of two loaves of bread baked with leavened flour (Leviticus 23:17). Thus was celebrated God's providence at the start of the wheat season.

Besides its primary agricultural significance *Shavu'ot* later came to be understood as commemorating the giving of the *Torah* to Moshe. The earliest references to this reinterpretation date from the 2nd and 3rd centuries C.E. (Talmud: Shabbat 86b, Pesachim 68b); but Louis Jacobs, using material from Louis Finkelstein's *The Pharisees*, theorizes that "the transformation into a historical feast took place before the present era" (*Encyclopedia Judaica* 14:1420–1421). Exodus 19:1 says that the Israelites came to the foot of Mount Sinai "in the third month"; from this and other biblical data the rabbis deduced that God actually gave the *Torah* on *Shavu'ot*. Thus each Pilgrim Festival was associated with a major historical event in the forming of the Jewish people, and also with a major religious theme. *Pesach*, celebrating the Exodus from Egypt, has creation as its theme, the creation of the Jewish people. The theme of *Shavu'ot* is revelation; and the theme of *Sukkot*, associated with the forty years of wandering culminated by entering the Promised Land, is redemption. These three themes — creation, revelation and redemption — reappear in other aspects of Jewish life, for example, the three meals of *Shabbat* (see Ro 11:36N).

Because *Shavu'ot* recalls God's revelation of himself, his power and his *Torah* to the Jewish people, the synagogue readings for this holiday include Exodus 19–20 (Moshe's ascent of Mount Sinai and the Ten Commandments) and two passages celebrating other theophanies (appearances of God), Ezekiel 1–2 and Habakkuk 3. Also read at this festival is the book of Ruth, appropriate because it is a story about a harvest; but in addition, since it tells about the joining of the Moabite woman Ruth to God's people, it gives a *remez* ("hint"; see Mt 2:15N) about a then future aspect of God's work on earth, the joining of Gentiles to God's people the Jews through the Messiah Yeshua.

Finally, *Shavu'ot* is the traditional date on which King David died, a point to be remembered when reading vv. 25–32; see v. 29&N.

It is in this framework of Jewish thought and custom, in which *Shavu'ot* is celebrated as a festival of harvest and *Torah*, that the events of Acts 2 must be understood. Because it was God's intention to bring the Jewish New Covenant (Jeremiah 31:30–33(31–34)) to the Jewish people in a Jewish way, he made maximal use of the Jewish festivals to convey new truths in ways that emphasized their connection with old truths (see Mt 13:52&N).

Thus God promised through Jeremiah, "I will write my *Torah* on their hearts." This he does as he gives his Holy Spirit (v. 4). The same one God gives both *Torah* and Spirit (which thus are in a sense one) on the same one holiday, *Shavu'ot*, to the same one people, the Jewish people, stretching through history from the fire on Mount Sinai to the tongues of fire at Jerusalem (vv. 2–3&N).

Yeshua himself is called the "firstfruits" at 1C 15:23 (compare Ro 8:29), and he speaks of a "harvest" of people with prepared hearts at Mt 9:37–38 and Yn 4:35. Later in the present chapter, at v. 41, three thousand persons become the "firstfruits" of the Spirit-empowered activity of Yeshua's *talmidim*; while at Ro 8:23 what believers have now of the Holy Spirit is said to be only the "firstfruits" in comparison with what is to come.

Yeshua spoke of himself as the "bread of life" (Yn 6:35). Since leavened stuff (*chametz*) symbolizes sin in the *Tanakh*, Yeshua represented himself as sinless by using unleavened bread, *matzah*, to inaugurate the New Covenant (Lk 22:20&N). The *Shavu'ot* bread offering is made with leaven, symbolizing God's people as having sin before Yeshua's atoning death; later Sha'ul writes the Messianic Community in Corinth that "in reality you are unleavened. For our *Pesach* lamb, the Messiah, has been sacrificed" (1C 5:6–8&N; see 1 Yn 1:5–10&N). The two loaves of the offering can now be understood as representing God's expanded people comprised of Jews and Gentiles (see Yn 10:16N, Ro 11:17–26&NN, Ga 3:28&N, Ep 2:14&N).

The book of Ruth points up a lesson not to be ignored. Ruth the Moabitess was added to the Jewish people with her noble confession, "Your people shall be my people, and your God shall be my God" (Ruth 1:16). This woman, who became an ancestor of Yeshua (Mt 1:5), expressed her loyalty to the Jewish people even before she spoke of God. But over the centuries, many calling themselves Christians have done just the opposite, hating the Jews, accusing them of deicide, ignoring the New Testament's warning not to boast against the Jewish root (Ro 11:16–26). The book of Acts shows that Gentiles may now become part of God's people without becoming Jews themselves. But no Gentile can become a Christian if he cannot say to Jews, "Your people shall be my people," at the same time as he says, "Your God shall be my God."

It is also no accident that God chose the holiday connected with the *Torah* to send the *Ruach HaKodesh*, the Holy Spirit, to empower the life of each *talmid* and to empower the entire Messianic Community. Achad Ha'Am's epigram, "More than that Israel has kept *Shabbat*, *Shabbat* has kept Israel," implies that it is the power of the *Torah* which has preserved the Jewish people through the centuries. Likewise, it is the power of the Holy Spirit which has changed the lives of millions for the better and enabled them to testify to God's life-changing power even in the face of great persecution. One need only compare Kefa's own ineffectiveness prior to receiving the *Ruach HaKodesh* (Mt 16:21–23, 26:69–75; Yn 21:15–17) with the inspiring sermon quoted in this chapter (vv. 14–40). Just as the *Torah* (the Hebrew word means "teaching" not "law") teaches God's truth, so the Holy Spirit teaches God's truth (Yn 14:26, 15:26, 16:13). The truth of the *Torah* set forth in the *Tanakh* is not different from the truth of the *Torah* set forth in the New Testament. The Messiah's *Torah* is not different from or an improvement over God's *Torah* in the *Tanakh*, for "the *Torah* of *Adonai* is perfect" (Psalm 19:7) and does not need improvement. Sha'ul calls it "holy, just and good" (Ro 7:12); what more could one ask? What is different is the receptiveness of those for whom the *Torah* is meant, due to having a new spirit and a heart of flesh (Ezekiel 36:26) on which the

Torah is written (Jeremiah 31:32(33)), a heart receptive to the Holy Spirit (1C 2:14). Thus the Holy Spirit in a believer's life makes the *Torah* even more real to him (2C 3:6–18), and the giving of the *Ruach HaKodesh* on *Shavu'ot* only heightens the significance of the giving of the *Torah* on *Shavu'ot*.

The parallels between Sinai and Pentecost continue: (1) At both the *Torah* was delivered to God's people. At Sinai the Ten Commandments were written on tables of stone by the "finger of God" (Exodus 31:18), while at Pentecost the *Torah* was written on tables of the heart (2C 3:6–18), in fulfillment of the prophecies of Jeremiah 31:32(31) and Ezekiel 36:26. Far from replacing, canceling, or contradicting the *Torah* of Moses, the Holy Spirit confirms it for Messianic believers (Ro 3:31). (2) Both took place at *Shavu'ot*. (3) Both were accompanied by theophanies. (4) Both were accompanied by many languages (voices, tongues); see vv. 4b–13&N. (5) Both were accompanied by fire. The fire at Sinai was one fire visible by all; the fire at Yerushalayim divided itself and rested on each one individually. Thus at Sinai the *Torah* was given externally to the people as a whole, while at Yerushalayim the *Torah* was put within each individual believer. (6) At Sinai a mixed multitude (*erev rav*, Exodus 12:38) accompanied the people, just as people from many countries were present at Pentecost. (7) *Torah* means teaching, and the Holy Spirit is the Teacher (Yn 14:26, 15:26, 16:13). (8) It is customary in the Jewish celebration of *Shavu'ot* to eat milk foods. The Holy Spirit provides the "milk of the Word" (1 Ke 2:2, MJ 5:12–13).

How do we know that *Torah* can come from Jerusalem as well as from Sinai? Several *Tanakh* prophecies confirm it, but best known is Isaiah 2:3, featured on the title page of the *Jewish New Testament*: "For out of Tziyon shall come forth *Torah*, and the Word of *Adonai* from Yerushalayim." Pentecost fulfilled this prophecy in a powerful way; and I hope that in a modest, emulative way the *Jewish New Testament* and this commentary contribute to the process of *Torah* emanating from Jerusalem.

Because *Shavu'ot* commemorates the giving of the *Torah* it is sometimes thought of as the day on which Judaism was born. Likewise, because God gave the Holy Spirit to his people on *Shavu'ot*, it is sometimes regarded also as the birthday of the Messianic Community. But one could equally think of *Pesach* as the "birth of a nation" for the Jews, who are first portrayed as a unified people in Exodus 12, at the time of the first Passover. Similarly, it can be argued that the Messianic Community too came into being on *Pesach*, since that is when Yeshua died and was resurrected, and we as a community have died and been resurrected with him (Ro 6:1–8).

2–3 Roar of a violent wind…. tongues of fire which separated. God emphasized the connection between the *Torah* and the *Ruach HaKodesh* by giving both with similar miraculous signs. The roar and fire in Jerusalem recalled the fire, smoke and sounds at Sinai (Exodus 19:18–19, Deuteronomy 5:19–21). However, instead of God's people being kept away (Exodus 19:21–23; Deuteronomy 5:22–24), God's glory, represented by the tongues of fire, came to each individual.

4a They were all filled with the *Ruach HaKodesh*. In *Tanakh* times certain individuals had the Holy Spirit "in" or "with" them (Yn 14:17N); here he fills them all, bringing to pass what Moshe had prayed for long ago, that *Adonai* would put his Spirit on all his people (Numbers 11:29), and fulfilling Yeshua's promise (Lk 24:49; Yn 14:16, 20:22; Ac 1:8).

4b–13 The miraculous event accomplished through the Holy Spirit amounts to a reversal of Babel (Genesis 11:1–9). Then God confounded the speech of people misusing their unity for sinful purposes (the English word "babble" comes directly from the Hebrew). Here God enabled people whose different languages separated them to understand each other praising God, which is the proper use of unity.

There were two reactions to what God did — as usual (Yn 7:43&N). **Religious Jews** (v. 5) were **amazed and confused** (v. 12) but open to being taught. **Others** (v. 13) ridiculed the *talmidim.*

Everyone heard them speaking in his own language (v. 6), and a representative list of Roman Empire nations is given (vv. 9–11). This corresponds closely to a Talmudic concept of how God dealt with the nations:

> "Rabbi Yochanan said, 'What is meant by the verse, "*Adonai* gives a word; those spreading [it] are a great army" (Psalm 68:12(11))? It means that every single word going forth from the Almighty was split into seventy languages. The school of Rabbi Ishmael taught that the verse, "[Is not my word...] like a hammer that breaks a rock into pieces?" (Jeremiah 23:29), means that just as a hammer is divided into many sparks [when it hits a rock or piece of metal], so every single word that went out from the Holy One, blessed be he, split into seventy languages.'"(Shabbat 88b)

In rabbinic thought seventy is the traditional number of Gentile nations and the traditional number of languages of mankind. Although the number of tongues mentioned in the present passage falls short of seventy, enough are mentioned to allow the understanding that God is speaking here through Yeshua's faithful *talmidim* to all humanity.

But there is more. In Exodus 19:16, what the people heard was not "thunders," as in most translations, but "voices" (Hebrew *kolot*). So just as from the above *midrash* we can learn that at Sinai God's "great voice" (Deuteronomy 5:19(22)) was divided into the seventy languages of the Gentiles, so also from the present passage we learn explicitly that at Pentecost the praises of God were similarly heard in the various Gentile languages.

Midrash Tanchuma 25 says that at Sinai the people were confused when they heard God's "voices" coming from every direction (as masterfully portrayed in Arnold Schoenberg's opera, *Moses und Aron*). Similarly, the people hearing the languages of the nations at Pentecost were confused, overwhelmed and amazed (vv. 5–13) — as is always the case when God appears; compare Psalm 18:7–15 and Job 38–42.

11 Jews by birth and proselytes, literally, "both Jews and proselytes." Gentile proselytes to Judaism were a sizeable component of the Jewish people in Yeshua's day, perhaps even the majority (see Mt 23:15&N); therefore in the book of Acts the theme of bringing the Gentiles to faith in the Jewish Messiah (1:8N) has in a sense already appeared. However, the gathered crowd did not consist of Gentiles from these countries, since vv. 5–6 state that it was composed of religious Jews — that is, Jews sufficiently observant of Jewish religious requirements to have come from far away to be in Jerusalem for the pilgrim festival of *Shavu'ot* (v. 1&N, 20:16&N).

Arabs. Not the ancestors of today's Arabs but Jews from Arabia. Gentiles are not added to the Messianic community until the Samaritans of Chapter 8; see 1:8&N.

15 Kefa disposes of the closed-minded skeptics and scorners before addressing the open-minded but bewildered remainder.

17–21 In the Last Days, in Messianic times. Kefa explains that the Last Days have already begun (see also MJ 1:2, 1C 10:11, 1 Ke 1:20). They are continuing now (1 Yn 2:18, Yd 18); and they will culminate in a Last Day (Yn 6:39ff., 12:48), here called **the great and fearful Day of *Adonai*** (compare Rv 1:10&N).

The sun will become dark. This one of Joel's portents occurred: the sun became dark when Yeshua was hanging on the execution-stake (Mt 26:45). But the others, spoken of at length in the book of Revelation, are meant for the future.

Whoever calls on the name of *Adonai* will be saved (cited also at Ro 10:13). This is the key sentence of Joel's prophecy. The rest of Kefa's speech shows that one can call on *Adonai* for salvation only by acknowledging Yeshua as the Messiah.

22–23 Men of Israel,... you killed him! Like a knife the accusation pierced their hearts, as it does today the heart of any Jew who has ever been told, "You Jews killed Jesus!" But Kefa's true charge to his listeners and the false charge that the Jewish people committed deicide are worlds apart. This verse places the responsibility very precisely.

First, the Messiah's death was **in accordance with God's predetermined plan and foreknowledge.** It was not an accident, not a miscalculation on the part of Yeshua and his *talmidim*. God knew and planned Yeshua's death as atonement for humanity's sins. But that provides the killers no excuse; they had free will and could have chosen to act differently. Compare Lk 22:22, "The Son of Man is going to his death according to God's plan, but woe to that man by whom he is being betrayed!" Thus the Bible teaches both predestination and free choice; and the antinomy has never been expressed more succinctly than in Rabbi Akiva's Mishnaic epigram, "All is foreseen, yet free will is given" (Avot 3:15). Yeshua's death is neither God's fault (compare Ro 9:6–29&NN) nor Yeshua's mistake.

Second, Gentiles — Pontius Pilate and Roman soldiers — were directly involved in killing Yeshua. Kefa does not measure the degree of their guilt because he is not speaking to them. But Pontius Pilate's very act of washing his hands (Mt 27:24) showed he recognized his own guilt, and the way the Roman soldiers mocked and savaged Yeshua shows us their depraved mentality. The issue is not Gentile innocence versus Jewish guilt.

Third, the "**you**" who "**killed him**" were Jews who had seen that **Yeshua... was a man demonstrated... to have been from God.** They were well aware of it (**you yourselves know this**), and they were aware of the factual basis for this conclusion, **the powerful works, miracles and signs that God performed through him in** their actual **presence** (compare Yn 10:32–38). This distinguishes them from the Jewish people who throughout history have been maliciously charged with deicide. We may suppose that in the audience were some who had taunted Yeshua, "If you are the Son of God, come down from the stake" (Mt 27:41). Others had called for freeing the murderer and rebel Bar-Abba instead of the Messiah, whom they had wanted executed (Mt 27:16–26). Still others were members of the illegally convened *Sanhedrin* which had sentenced him and hypocritically turned him over to the Romans, **men not bound by the *Torah***, to be put to death (Mt 26:57–27:2). Jews more distant in space and time did not commit these specific sins.

Although Kefa was a fellow Jew who addressed his hearers as "brothers" (v. 29), he nevertheless used the strongest possible language to motivate repentance — as did Moshe and the Prophets. Although Kefa's words, like theirs, were meant in the first instance for contemporaries, they can move us if we hear with our hearts as well as our minds.

For we have a responsibility to know and respond. The New Testament's position is that all humanity, Jews and Gentiles, then and now, killed Yeshua. We did it by disobeying God, for which the penalty is death (Genesis 2:17). Because Yeshua loved us he died in our place. In this sense we killed him, and the blame rests on each one of us until we accept his atoning sacrificial death and God forgives us (see Ro 5:12–21&N).

24 **But God has raised him up**. It is of the essence of Messianic faith that Yeshua is alive (1C 15:12–19). If he were not, we could feel sorry but could do nothing to repair the relationship between him and us, and Kefa would not have delivered this sermon.

Suffering of death. The Hebrew phrase, "*matzrei-Sh'ol*" ("pains of Sh'ol"), is found in Psalm 116:3. Some people unfamiliar with the Bible think of death as an end to the agonies of life; they say of an ill person, "It was better for him that he died." But the Bible regards death as the ultimate tragedy. Only for those who have eternal life through Yeshua the Messiah has the sting of death been removed (Ro 6:23, 1C 15:55–56, Pp 1:21).

25–36 Psalm 16:8–11 (cited in vv. 25–28) is a key text, along with Lk 24:44–46 and 1C 15:4, showing that the Messiah must rise from the dead; and it would be hard to improve on Kefa's exposition of it (vv. 29–36).

27 **Sh'ol**, "Hades, hell." See Mt 11:23N, Lk 16:23&N.

29 **The patriarch David died**. According to Jewish tradition he died on *Shavu'ot*, as Kefa's *Shavu'ot* audience was undoubtedly aware.

And was buried. The *Tanakh* says he was buried in the City of David, southeast of the present Western Wall (1 Kings 2:10).

His tomb is with us to this day.

> "The tomb of David was probably destroyed at the time of the Bar Kokhba revolt (135 C.E.). However, various sites were suggested by popular traditions over the ages and the one which became generally accepted was the place now called Mt. Zion. This tradition is about 1,000 years old, first being recorded in Crusader times…." (*Encyclopedia Judaica* 5:1330).

In other words, the site now called King David's Tomb isn't.

30 **God had sworn to him with an oath that one of his descendants would sit on his throne**, according to Psalm 132:11 and 2 Samuel 7:12–13; also see 13:23N.

35 On Psalm 110:1, cited here, see Mt 22:44N and Mk 16:19N. The earliest extant rabbinic interpretations apply this verse to Abraham (Talmud: N'darim 32b and Sanhedrin 108b). But in the Midrash on Psalms, compiled in the 11th century, we find that

> "Rabbi Yudan [c. 350 C.E.] said in the name of Rabbi Hama [ben-Hina, c. 260 C.E.], 'In the time to come, when the Holy One, blessed be he, seats the King, the Messiah, at his right hand, as it is said, "*Adonai* said to my Lord, 'Sit at my right hand,'"and seats Abraham at his left, Abraham's face will grow pale, and he will say to God, "My son's son sits at the right, while I sit on the left!" God will then comfort him by saying to him, "Your son's son is indeed at my right, but I myself, in a manner of speaking, am at your right, since 'The Lord is at your right hand' (Psalm 110:5)."'"(Midrash on Psalm 18, Section 29)

This passage shows that there were *'Amora'im* (Talmudic period rabbis, 3rd to 5th centuries C.E.) who applied Psalm 110 to the Messiah.

36 Let the whole house of Israel know beyond doubt that God has made him both Lord and Messiah. How can the Two-Covenant theory survive this climax to Kefa's sermon? The Two-Covenant theory says, in effect, that Jesus is for Gentiles and Moses is for Jews (see Yn 14:6&N). But Kefa's central point is that all *Jews*, **the whole house of Israel**, should acknowledge Yeshua as **Lord and Messiah** because **God has made him** fulfill those roles in Jewish life and human history. See also 4:12&N.

God has made him Lord and Messiah. From the viewpoint of God and eternity the Word became a human being (Yn 1:1, 14; Pp 2:5–11). Under the aspect of time, in Kefa's experience, Yeshua had just been revealed as who he really is. Non-Messianic Judaism objects that the New Testament says Yeshua, who is only a man, became a god. But the New Testament never says such a thing, not even here. What it says is that God had, from eternity, made him who was already equal with God before the universe was created (Pp 2:6–8&NN, Co 1:15–17&NN, MJ 1:1–3&NN), **both Lord** of all humanity **and** the promised **Messiah**, king of the Jewish people.

Whom you executed on a stake. See vv. 22–23&N, Mt 10:38N.

37–41 Although Kefa came down harder on his Jewish audience than any Christian preacher today would dare, so that **they were stung in their hearts**, nevertheless **three thousand people** responded to his call to **turn from sin** and **return to God**. It is the Holy Spirit acting in the giver of the message and in its receivers who brings about genuine trust. Moreover, the Good News that God forgives makes sense only against the background of the bad news that you have grievously sinned. The people were so affected that they asked, **"Brothers,"** — they were not offended personally by the bringers of the bad news, but still considered them brothers — **"What should we do?"** They took the initiative.

38 Kefa's answer: **Turn from sin, return to God**. Six English words to translate one Greek word, "*metanoêsate*," which means "repent" and expresses the Hebrew concept of *t'shuvah* (see Mt 3:2N).

And be immersed (or "baptized"; see Mt 3:1N) **on the authority of Yeshua the Messiah** (literally, "on/upon the name (Greek *onoma*) of Yeshua the Messiah"). The command is to absorb completely and accept totally the work, power, authority and person of Yeshua the Messiah; on "*onoma*" see 3:16N, Mt 28:19N.

40 This perverse generation. Yeshua called them wicked and adulterous (Mt 16:4). Now Kefa calls them perverse, because despite having seen and heard Yeshua, most had rejected him. Some had even attributed the Messiah's works to Satan (Mt 12:27–32), which is as perverse as you can get.

Kefa begs his hearers to **save yourselves** from them, since they are destined for particularly severe judgment and punishment (Lk 12:48). Some consider this to have been the destruction of the Temple and the slaughter of vast numbers of them by the Romans in 66–70 C.E., at least partially fulfilling Lk 21:20–24 (see notes there).

41 Three thousand people. Some think it unspiritual, or at least *gauche*, to keep statistics on how many persons come to trust in Yeshua and join congregations of believers. God thinks otherwise. In the book of Acts Luke traces the growth of the Messianic Community from at least 120 (1:14) to some 3,120 (here). "About five thousand men," not counting women and children, were added soon after (4:4&N). Some twenty years later there were "many tens of thousands... among the Judeans" of Jerusalem alone (21:20&N). Besides these statistics we read that "the Lord kept adding to them" (v. 47), "the number of *talmidim* was growing" (6:1), "the number of *talmidim* in Yerushalayim increased rapidly" (6:7), "their numbers kept multiplying" (9:31), and "a great number of people trusted and turned to the Lord" (11:21). Moreover, Luke takes note of key subgroups: "a large crowd of *cohanim* were becoming obedient to the faith" (6:7); "some of those who had come to trust were from the party of the *P'rushim*" (15:5).

These data imply that early Jewish evangelism was successful. A genuine "people movement" arose in which hundreds of thousands of Jews came to faith in Yeshua the Jewish Messiah (see Ac 21:20&N). It was still going on at the close of the book of Acts (28:24–25&N).

42–47 This picture of the Messianic Community empowered by the Holy Spirit and obedient to God remains the model for his people today.

42 The teaching of the emissaries. Greek *didachê* means either the act of teaching or the doctrine taught. Since Hebrew *Torah* also means "teaching," the phrase can be translated, "the *Torah* of the emissaries" (although the *JNT* usually reserves the word "*Torah*" to render Greek *nomos* ("law") when it refers to the Law of Moses). To the Jewish mind the *Torah* is not something dead, fixed forever, but a living **teaching** to be applied in the light of circumstances to the lives of individuals.

That this is so is implied by Deuteronomy 17:8–13, which gives to "the *cohanim*, the *L'vi'im* and the judge who shall be in those days" the right to "declare unto you the sentence of judgment." This passage is a key biblical ground for the Jewish claim that there is such a thing as an Oral *Torah* in addition to the written one. Unfortunately what is accepted in traditional Judaism as the Oral *Torah* — the Mishna, the Gemara, and the rabbinical discussions and court judgments since then — does not take into account Yeshua's exposition of the *Torah* (Mt 5:17&N, 1C 9:21&N, Ga 6:2&N); **the teaching of the emissaries**, whose authority in the matter comes from the Messiah himself

(Mt 18:18–20&N); or the New Testament, which itself "has been made *Torah*" (MJ 8:6&N).

This is the first time the New Testament portrays the emissaries teaching, giving out the true *Torah sh'be'al peh* ("Oral *Torah*"). Why only now? Because only now were they filled with the *Ruach HaKodesh*, able to have the mind of the Messiah (1C 2:16), to be reminded of everything Yeshua had said to them (Yn 14:26) and to be guided into all the truth (Yn 16:13). What traditional Judaism calls the Oral *Torah* can certainly be mined for its treasury of truths (Mt 13:52&N). But as it stands the Oral *Torah* cannot be authoritative; because its writers and expositors have ignored the Messiah's coming, his interpretations of *Torah* and the interpretations of those he appointed, as well as the New Testament itself, which constitutes one-quarter of the written Word of God.

Fellowship (Greek *koinônia*, "community, commonness, communion, fellowship") includes two elements, each of which fosters the other, as explained below: (1) deepening friendship, and (2) developing a common vision, goals and priorities.

Breaking bread. Many Christians assume that this refers to "taking communion" and have an image of the early believers meeting in homes (v. 46) to eat a tiny wafer of bread and drink a symbolic amount of wine or grape juice, just as Christians do today in their churches. However, the context is not twentieth-century Christianity but first-century Judaism; and for Jews then as now, fellowship was mediated by meals. To say that the early Messianic Jews broke bread is to say neither more nor less than that they ate together.

The meaning of eating together must be grasped. First of all, when possible, religious Jews begin a meal with bread and say over it a *b'rakhah* (cited in 14:19&N, and see Mt 9:8N). Then they break off a piece of the loaf and eat it, so that the blessing of God specifically for his provision of bread to eat will not have been said in vain.

Yeshua knew and observed this practice, but he also gave an additional meaning to the act of breaking bread when he said, as he broke the *matzah* at the Last Supper, "This is my body, which is being given for you; do this in memory of me" (Lk 22:20; compare 1C 11:24). This practice clearly became part of the "*Torah* of the emissaries," so that the early believers were to recall Yeshua's death for them as they began their meal — though some fell short of the standard (1C 11:20–34). Then, after that, the entire meal time was to be devoted to fellowship, "communion" in the ordinary sense of the word (see above, on "fellowship"), not in the technical Christian sense (wafer of bread, cup of wine).

Yet this fellowship was not mere worldly socializing that ignores God. Consider the Mishna:

> "Rabbi El'azar ben-'Azaryah [1st–2nd century C.E.] said, '... If there is no meal there is no [study of] *Torah*, and if there is no [study of] *Torah* there is no meal.'"(Avot 3:17)

Maimonides explains that each aids in bringing about the full expression of the other and completes it (*Commentary on Pirkey-Avot, ad loc.*). In other words, if one becomes preoccupied with religious studies and ignores normal social interaction, the individual's study does society little good. But, conversely, if at the main time of socializing, the meal, one ignores the things of God, it is a sign that religious truth has not penetrated deeply into the life of the individual. Yeshua, by his identification of himself with the bread, focuses the meal on himself and enables this reworking of Rabbi El'azar's epigram: If there is no time of interacting with fellow believers, one's identification with Yeshua and study of God's *Torah* is incomplete. But if the time of interacting with fellow believers does not relate itself to Yeshua's death on our behalf and to encouraging one another in living the life God wants us to live, the time has been wasted. See note to 1C 11:17–34 in the Appendix, pp. 929–930.

The prayers, both the statutory Jewish prayers, as at 3:1 below, and times of pouring out one's heart to the Lord spontaneously, as at 4:24–30. See notes at both places.

44–46 Since many of the first believers were visitors from other countries who had not come to Yerushalayim prepared to take up life there, an immediate need arose for those with local property and resources to use them to care for their new brothers and sisters in the Messiah. These verses certainly teach unselfishness, unpossessiveness and hospitality as traits to be cultivated everywhere and always, but I don't think they constitute God's special seal of approval on communal living as lifestyle or socialism as politics.

46 Continuing... in the Temple. They remained Jews.

47 Having favor with all the people. They were not excluded from the Jewish community.

The Lord kept adding... those being saved. This is the climax of the picture painted in vv. 42–47. Because of the believers' Holy Spirit-empowered obedience to the *Torah* (that is, to the *Torah* as expounded by the emissaries), God blessed the Messianic Community with growth in numbers of truly saved persons, all of them Jews. This significant and rapidly growing community of persons honoring Yeshua the Messiah and believing the Gospel is described not as an alien "Christian Church" but as a movement within Judaism; the first Gentiles without a prior "Jewish connection" do not join the Messianic Community until Chapter 10.

CHAPTER 3

1 One afternoon at three o'clock, the hour of *minchah* prayers. The Greek for this verse reads, literally, "And Kefa and Yochanan were going up to the Temple at the hour of the prayer, the ninth." By Roman reckoning the day began at sunrise, so the "ninth hour" would have been around 3 PM. According to one Talmudic source (B'rakhot 26b) the three prayer services were instituted after the fall of the First Temple to replace the sacrifices (see Daniel 6:11 for a comparable custom during the Babylonian Exile). The three services are called *Shacharit* ("morning"), ***Minchah*** ("afternoon"; the word means "gift, offering") and *Ma'ariv* ("evening").

2 Beautiful Gate. The Hebrew word for "beautiful" is "*yafeh*," and any tourist can enter the Old City of Jerusalem by the "Jaffa Gate"; it is the end of the road from the port of Yafo (Jaffa, Joppa), named for its beauty, on the seacoast south of Tel Aviv. The gate spoken of here may be the Nikanor Gate referred to in the Mishna (Middot 2:3), which led from the Court of the Gentiles to the Women's Court of the Temple.

11 Shlomo's Colonnade. See Yn 10:23N.

12 A personal reaction: the start of Kefa's speech is so Jewish! The crowd had just witnessed an unbelievable miracle, and he asks, deadpan, "What are you all acting so surprised about?"

13 The God of Avraham, Yitzchak and Ya'akov, the God of our fathers. This phrase is not accidental in Kefa's sermon. Its two parts are found in the first paragraph of the *'Amidah*, the central section of the *Minchah* prayer service (see v. 1N), which begins, "Praised be You, *Adonai* our God and God of our fathers, God of Avraham, God of Yitzchak and God of Ya'akov,..." and which his hearers would just then have been reciting in their *minchah* prayers in *minyan*s throughout the Temple grounds, much as is done today at the Western Wall ("Wailing Wall") in the Old City of Jerusalem.

Kefa's point: the very God to whom you have just now been praying in these words **has glorified his servant Yeshua**. In using the word "servant" Kefa identifies Yeshua as God's suffering servant spoken of in Isaiah 42–53; he makes the same identification at 1 Ke 2:21–25 by citing Isaiah 53.

16 His name is not a magic word. Greek *onoma* corresponds to Hebrew *shem*, which, biblically, means not just a name but everything that the named individual is and represents — his work, personality, power, authority and reputation. See 2:38N, Mt 28:19N.

Trust, Greek *pistis*. "belief, trust, firm reliance, firm conviction, faith," corresponding to Hebrew *emunah*. The Jewish philosopher Martin Buber, though he honored Yeshua his "elder brother," tried in his book, *Two Types of Faith*, to demonstrate that the *pistis* of the New Testament and the *emunah* of the *Tanakh* are different. He claimed that *pistis* is primarily mental assent to doctrines and facts, while *emunah* is a heart attitude of trust that expresses itself in righteous acts. In fact, however, the latter is the only kind of faith God honors, in both the Old Testament and the New. True Messianic faith is not different in character from that of the *Tanakh*; it means acknowledging who God is and what he has done, believing his promises, relying on him for power to live a holy life, and then living that life.

The *Jewish New Testament* generally uses the word "trust" instead of "faith" to translate "*pistis*," because "trust" more clearly signifies to English-speakers the confident reliance on God that generates holy deeds, as opposed to mere mental acknowledgement of facts and ideas. The book of Galatians uses the awkward phrase, "trusting faithfulness," because the message of that book is so dependent on keeping the correct meaning of "*pistis*" in the forefront of consciousness (see Section (1) of Ga 2:16cN).

17–18 After inculpating his fellow Jews in vv. 13–15 (see 2:22–23&N, 2:36&N) Kefa again calls them **brothers** (as at 2:29; also see 2:37–41&N) and mitigates his words: **you did not understand the significance of what you were doing**. In the *Torah*, atonement avails only for unintended sins; for sins committed presumptuously there is no atonement (see Numbers 15:22–31, Leviticus 4–5). Even the *cohanim* and *P'rushim* involved in the events leading up to Yeshua's execution may be forgiven through trusting Yeshua, and some availed themselves of the opportunity (6:7, 15:5). Also compare 7:60, Lk 23:34.

A second cushion for the shock: **this is how God fulfilled what he had announced in advance**. The Messiah's death does not end all hope; on the contrary, God intended him to die, be resurrected and return. See 2:22–23&N.

God... announced... through... all the prophets... that the **Messiah was to die**. In not specifying the *Tanakh* passages Kefa assumes his audience is aware of the relevant passages already and has their agreement that they apply to the death of the Messiah; otherwise at this point he would have lost his audience. See Mt 26:24N for a list of these *Tanakh* prophecies and their New Testament fulfillments.

19 **Repent and turn to God**, literally, "Change your mind and turn." KJV has "Repent and be converted"; but to the modern reader this suggests changing religions, *e.g.*, from Judaism to Christianity, which is not what Kefa was talking about. For at that time "Christianity" as such did not exist; there was Judaism with Yeshua and Judaism without him (the same choice, along with the possibility of rejecting both, faces Jews today).

20 **Times of refreshing**, that is, the Messianic Age. Compare the Mishna:

> "Rabbi Ya'akov used to say, 'Better is one hour of repentance and good deeds in this world than the whole life of the world to come; and better is one hour of contentment (*korat-ruach*, "cooling of spirit") in the world to come than all the life of this world.'" (Avot 4:17)

In these "times of refreshing" self-rule will be restored to Israel (see 1:6–8&NN), and **the Messiah appointed in advance for you**, namely, **Yeshua**, will return. Kefa's audience, like today's Orthodox Jews, expected the Messiah in the future. Kefa says that the very Messiah they expect will turn out to be Yeshua, and he goes on in the following verses to explain why he doesn't come at once.

21 **He has to remain in heaven** at the right hand of God (Psalm 110:1, quoted above at 2:35) **until the time comes for restoring everything**, both social and natural (Isaiah 11:1–12, Ro 8:18–23), when Yeshua will come on the clouds of Heaven (Daniel 7:13–14). Yeshua said the same thing at least twice, quoting Daniel (Mt 24:30, 26:64).

22–23 The same passage, Deuteronomy 18:15–19, is also cited in Stephen's sermon at 7:37. The *P'rushim* asked Yochanan the Immerser if he was "the prophet" foreseen in this passage (Yn 1:21&N). The five thousand whom Yeshua fed wondered the same thing (Yn 6:14&N), as did some of the crowd to whom he offered living water (Yn 7:40). Evidently this passage from the Five Books of Moses was widely understood then as Messianic, and people were looking for its fulfillment.

But in later rabbinic literature this passage of the *Torah* is minimized in numerous instances of what I call "defensive theology," interpretations developed specifically to counter its New Testament application to Yeshua. Here are five:

(1) The commentary of Rashi (1040–1105) says it means that God will raise up a prophet in Moshe's place, "and so on, from prophet to prophet." That is, the passage does not speak of only a single individual prophet to come, but of the

Tanakh's many prophets, of whom Malachi was the last.

(2) The *Midrash Rabbah*, compiled in the 6th to 12th centuries, has nothing on the passage at all, allowing silence to deflect curiosity.

(3) The Talmud (5th century) has an interesting paragraph (Yevamot 90b) which applies it to prophets in general in order to prove that they could abrogate a command of *Torah* if the need was great enough — using as an example Elijah's building an altar on Mount Carmel, near present-day Haifa and not in Jerusalem where God authorized one, in order to save Israel from idolatry (1 Kings 18:31ff.).

(4) Typical in our age is a popular commentary on the *Torah* by the former chief rabbi of England, Dr. J. H. Hertz, who says of the phrase, "like me": "Not of the same rank as Moses, but of the line of Prophets of which Moses is the 'father'." In support he cites Deuteronomy 34:10, "And there has not risen a prophet since in Israel like Moses, whom *Adonai* knew face to face." Of course, that verse was written centuries before Yeshua and therefore is irrelevant in proving whether or not Moses was prophesying about him.

(5) Perhaps the most obvious well-known example is in the 12th-century creed of Maimonides, especially as epitomized in the poem *Yigdal*, recited daily in the synagogue. The seventh of the *Rambam*'s creedal statements reads,

> "I believe with perfect faith that the prophecy of Moshe *Rabbenu* [Moses our teacher], peace be unto him, was true, and that he was chief of the prophets [literally, "father to the prophets"], both of those who preceded him and those who came after him."

The *Yigdal* rephrases it,

> "There has not arisen in Israel another like Moshe, a prophet who saw his vision clearly."

Was Yeshua "a prophet like Moshe"? Yes, and more. A prophet speaks for God, which Yeshua did; but he also spoke as God. He spoke what the Father gave him to say, as did all the prophets; but he and the Father are one (Yn 10:31). Moshe explained the sacrificial system for atonement; Yeshua was the final sacrifice for sin, the eternally effective atonement. Moshe established the system of *cohanim*, with his brother Aaron as the first *cohen gadol* of the Tabernacle; the resurrected Yeshua is the eternal *cohen gadol* in the heavenly Tabernacle that served as model for the earthly one (Messianic Jews 7–10). At no point did Yeshua contradict what Moshe said; rather, he clarified and strengthened the *Torah* (Mt 5:17–20&NN), made its application plainer (Mt 5:21–7:29), and sometimes himself *was* the application. See also 2:42N.

You are to listen to everything he, Yeshua, the prophet like Moshe, **tells you. Everyone who fails to listen to that prophet will be removed from the people and destroyed.** But what if the nation as a whole fails to listen? Then this becomes the kind of *Torah* violation which leads to the curses of Deuteronomy 28:15–68 (see Ga 3:13&N). The destruction of the Temple (70 C.E.), the expulsion from Jerusalem (135 C.E.) and the centuries of exile typify the punishments suffered by the Jewish people not for deicide and not directly for rejecting Yeshua but for violating the *Torah*'s injunction to listen to the prophet like Moshe, who is Yeshua, "the goal at which the *Torah* aims" (Ro 10:4&N). But he can still be heard. He speaks through the *Tanakh* and the New Testament. Those who heed him become part of Israel's remnant (Romans 9–11&NN) and are not **removed from the people.**

24 All the prophets announced these days. See the lists of prophecies at Mt 26:24 and in Section VII of the Introduction to the *JNT*.

25–26 You are the sons of the prophets and of the covenant with… Avraham. The point is that for this very reason **it is to you first that God** sent Yeshua the Messiah. The Gospel is "to the Jew first" (Ro 1:16, KJV). And it is with the Gospel of Yeshua that the promise of v. 25 is fulfilled; for that promise was made to Avraham and his son Yitzchak; and Yeshua is himself, in a midrashic sense, the promised **seed** who brings the blessing (Ga 3:16&N). The blessing consists in **turning each one of you from your evil ways.** On the one hand, you must turn (v. 19); on the other hand, God does the turning. Compare Lamentations 5:21, "Turn us to you, *Adonai* and we shall be turned"; and see Paragraph 2 of 2:22–23N above. Unlike more self-defensive audiences today, the people do not seem to object to being told that their **ways** are **evil**; apparently they accept this assessment of themselves and continue listening to Kefa and Yochanan (4:1).

CHAPTER 4

1–2 ***Cohanim***. See Mt 2:4N. ***Tz'dukim***, "Sadducees," who denied **resurrection from the dead**. See Mt 3:7N, 22:31–32&N.

4 The number of men (Greek *andrôn,* "men," i.e., not women) **came to about five thousand**. Since Kefa was addressing men who had just been praying *minchah* (3:1&N), not women, this seems to mean that 5,000 men came to trust in Yeshua as a result of this sermon. A less likely interpretation is that at this time the number of men in the Messianic Community totalled 5,000, including those who had come to faith earlier. In either case there would have been additional women and children, thousands of them. See 2:41N.

5 Rulers, elders and *Torah*-teachers (see Mt 2:4N), that is, the *Sanhedrin* (see Mt 5:22N).

6 On **Anan** and his **family** see Yn 18:13&N.

11 At Mt 21:42 Yeshua too quoted Psalm 118:22.

12 There is salvation in no one else! For there is no other name under heaven given to mankind by whom we must be saved! Like 2:36 (see note there) this verse contradicts the Two-Covenant theory, which posits that Jews don't need Yeshua for salvation as they are already "with the Father" through the covenant with Abraham (Yn 14:6N). It is true that the covenant with Abraham assures a special place for the Jewish people as a nation, and there are great and valuable promises associated with that covenant (see Sha'ul's discussion of the subject at Romans 4, 9–11; Galatians 3–4; and notes to these chapters). But it does not guarantee salvation for the individual Jew; that is not among its terms. Kefa, here addressing Jews, not Gentiles, and speaking by inspiration of the Holy Spirit of God (v. 8), asserts that Yeshua is the only person by whom **we** (the Jewish people, both individually and collectively) **must** (there is no alternative) **be saved** (from eternal destruction and God's fury due us for our sins). And if there is no other salvation for Jews, who already have wonderful promises from God, how much more (Mt 6:30N) is there no other salvation for Gentiles.

Moreover, since he is speaking to the leaders of the Jewish nation, he may also be asserting that *national* salvation can come only through Yeshua. See Mt 23:37–39&N, Ro 11:23–29&NN, 2C 1:20&N.

13 **When they saw how bold Kefa and Yochanan were,... they were amazed.** These "hicks" from the Galil (see next paragraph) dared to address the core of the establishment and tell them they were wrong! It was the *Ruach HaKodesh* at work in believers who gave such boldness (see vv. 23–31&NN), and he does the same today.

Untrained *'am-ha'aretz*, literally, "people of the land," ordinary folks, not systematically educated in the Bible and the traditions of either the *P'rushim* or the *Tz'dukim* (who together constituted the *Sanhedrin*'s membership). Jewish people have always had high regard for education, and "education" used to mean primarily education in religious matters. Thus an "untrained *'am-ha'aretz*" would be guaranteed low social status, and little would be expected of him. The members of the *Sanhedrin* could easily spot these Galileans by their up-country accents as persons unlikely to be delivering religious truth. (I recall from my youth in America northerners who were surprised when a person with a southern accent turned out to be well educated.) But the Galileans' lack of training did not affect the truth of their message: there are uneducated savants and educated fools. For more, see Yn 7:15&N.

Messianic Jews are sometimes disdained by the Jewish community as being untrained in Judaism. "If you had a good Jewish education, you wouldn't believe this nonsense about Jesus." Like other Jews some Messianics have received a Jewish education, and some have not. But deciding whether Yeshua is the Messiah is not so abstruse a question as to require intensive Jewish education. The *Tanakh* lays down some criteria the Messiah is to meet, and the New Testament demonstrates that Yeshua has fulfilled some of them already and promises that at his return he will fulfill the rest (see Section VII of the Introduction to the *JNT*). Furthermore, no matter how much Jewish education a Jew might have, it would not be enough to change his mind if he is determined to reject Yeshua.

For example, Daniel Zion was Chief Rabbi of Bulgaria from 1928 to 1948. He authored over twenty books, including the first translation of the *Siddur* (the Jewish prayerbook) into Bulgarian. Sometime in the 1930's he came to faith in Yeshua the Messiah (see 9:4N). When Hitler wanted to deport the Jews of Bulgaria to the Polish death camps, *Rav* Daniel prevailed on King Boris II not to permit it. As a result, 86% of Bulgaria's 50,000 Jews survived World War II, a record proportionally better than in any other country reached by the Nazis except Denmark, whose Jewish community was one-tenth as large. Later, leading most of Bulgarian Jewry, *Rav* Daniel made *aliyah* (immigrated to Israel) and became rabbi of a synagogue in Yafo. On *Shabbat* he would conduct regular services in the morning and teach from the New Testament at home in the afternoon. He retained the respect of Israel's Bulgarian Jewish community, even though his faith in Yeshua was well known. I met him in 1974; he died in 1979, aged 96. How will those who derogate Messianic Jews as *'am-ha'aretz* explain *Rav* Daniel's open and bold proclamation of Yeshua as the *Mashiach* of Israel? Will they say he did not have "enough Jewish education" to make an informed decision? See Mt 13:52&N. For more on *Rav* Daniel see Joseph Shulam, "Rabbi Daniel Zion, Chief Rabbi of Bulgaria Jews During World War II," in *Mishkan* #15 (1991), P.O. Box 116, Jerusalem, pp. 53–57.

16–17 How can Luke know what went on behind locked doors? We know that Yosef of Ramatayim was both a believer and a member of the *Sanhedrin* (Mk 15:43); Nakdimon, also a secret believer, was probably in the *Sanhedrin* too (Yn 7:50). Luke in his researches (Lk 1:3) would have consulted them or other *Sanhedrin* members who came to faith later.

19 **You must judge whether it is right in the sight of God to listen to you rather than God**. Also 5:29, "We must obey God, not men." These verses constitute a solid basis for civil disobedience in a wicked state, but no rationalization at all for illegal behavior grounded in selfishness.

24 Why, at the beginning of their prayer, do these Messianic Jews remind God that he **made heaven, earth, the sea and everything in them**? Not only because it is pointless for mere human beings to fight God (vv. 25–28), but because the *talmidim* are praying that God will sovereignly give the Messiah's "slaves" power "to speak [God's] message with boldness" (vv. 29–31). Similarly, in the *Siddur*, a morning prayer asking God to regather the Jewish people from the four corners of the earth alludes to the same passage of Psalm 146:6 because it so clearly requires God's sovereign power to do it (Hertz edition, pp. 30–31). But at 14:15 below, the passage is used differently, to point pagans away from manmade idols to the Creator of all.

25–26 The book of Acts quotes the Greek of the Septuagint. The Hebrew for Psalm 2:1–2 reads:

"Why are the nations in an uproar?
And why do the peoples mutter in vain?

"The kings of the earth arise
And the rulers take counsel together
Against *Adonai* and against his Messiah" [or: "and against his anointed one"].

Jewish writings often call attention to a text by citing its beginning; therefore the reader should understand that the believers' prayer of vv. 24–30 is permeated by all of Psalm 2, not just its initial verses. Jewish as well as Christian expositors have seen Psalm 2 as Messianic. However, Rashi, the greatest of the Jewish commentators, says,

> "Our rabbis expound it as relating to king Messiah; but according to its plain meaning it is proper to interpret it in connection with David, in the light of the statement, 'And when the Philistines heard that David was anointed king over Israel, all the Philistines went up to seek David' (2 Samuel 5:17)."

Yet even if the plain sense *(p'shat*, Mt 2:15N) does refer to David, the writings of the Scripture and the events of salvation history often contain a deeper meaning to be clarified only when later history plays on the theme already revealed. The theme of Psalm 2 is that while men may devise plans according to their own purposes, it is God who will have his way. This is why the *talmidim* addressed God as "Master" (v. 24) and reminded themselves in the prayer that he created earth, sky, sea and all living creatures. This gives them the necessary assurance that despite the *Sanhedrin*'s warning (v. 17) and opposition, God will vindicate his Messiah and those who proclaim his message. The prayer is answered immediately (v. 31).

27 Herod Antipas, son of Herod the Great (Mt 2:1–22, Lk 1:5). Ruler of the Galil. See also Mt 14:1–12&NN, Mk 6:14–29, 8:15; Lk 3:1, 19–20; 8:3, 9:7–9, 23:7–15; Ac 13:1.

Pontius Pilate, procurator of Judea (Mt 27:2N), is singled out, along with Herod, as having unique responsibility in bringing about Yeshua's death (see Mt 27:16–24N).

Goyim, "nations, pagans, non-Jews"; see 5:47N. In the Hebrew of Psalm 2:1 (vv. 25–26N) the word rendered "nations" is "*Goyim.*"

The peoples of Israel. Usually the singular, "people," is used; here the plural along with "*Goyim*" implicates all humanity as having been **assembled against... Yeshua.**

Servant. See 3:13N.

Whom you made Messiah or, literally, "whom you anointed" (Greek *on echrisas*). But here it refers back to Psalm 2 and shows, like the rest of v. 27, fulfillment of its prophecies (see vv. 25–26N). See Mt 1:1N on "**Messiah**."

31 They were all filled with the *Ruach HaKodesh*. Some of them had been filled before (2:4), but Ep 5:18 instructs believers to keep being filled with the Holy Spirit.

They spoke God's message with boldness. This is a sure sign of being filled with the Holy Spirit (compare vv. 8, 13&N), and it is also the purpose of the filling (1:8).

33 They were all held in high regard by the nonbelieving Jews, as at 2:47. Nevertheless, thinking highly of believers is not enough to save unbelievers. Or, saying the same thing in the words of Israel's former prime minister, Menachem Begin, "There is a great difference between gathering a good impression and taking the correct view" (*The Revolt*, Dell, revised edition 1977, p. 395).

34 See 2:44–45N.

36 Yosef, whom the emissaries called Bar-Nabba (which means "the Exhorter"). "The Exhorter" translates Greek *uios paraklêseos,* which can mean "son of counsel," "son of comfort," "son of exhortation," "son of encouragement." Aramaic *bar* ("son, son of") often has the sense, "one who has the quality of" (see Mt 1:1N). The word "*nabba*" is apparently related to the Hebrew root meaning "prophet," and a prophet is one who counsels, comforts, exhorts and encourages. Apparently Yosef was always comforting and exhorting his fellow *talmidim*, so the emissaries gave him this nickname. He becomes an important figure in Chapters 9–15.

CHAPTER 5

1–2 The sin of Chananyah and Shappirah was not that they reserved some of the proceeds for themselves but that they tried to create the impression that they had not (v. 4).

3–4 The Adversary, Satan. See Mt 4:1N.

You lie to the *Ruach HaKodesh*…. you have lied… to God. The Holy Spirit is thus identified with God.

5 One sometimes hears presented as Christian doctrine the second-century heresy of Marcion that the New Testament preaches a superior God of love, while the Old Testament God is an inferior deity concerned with judgment, wrath, justice and the carrying out of the details of the Law. In the present incident and at vv. 10–11 we see that the New Testament is, so far as justice and judgment are concerned, the same as the *Tanakh*. God is One. He cannot abide sin. Fraud is sin, and it is punished. Sometimes the punishment for sin is delayed, but in this instance the immediacy of the judgment showed everyone that God is real and means business (compare 1C 5:5, although the context is very different). New Testament love is not a feeling but right action, as Judaism has always taught. "Children, let us not love with words and talk, but with actions and in reality!" (1 Yn 3:18)

15–16 What sounds to modern ears like a charlatan's stunt not only reflected genuine faith but was rewarded by complete healing success. Does God heal miraculously today? Some people suppose that all healing ministries are run by fakers pursuing easy money. But even physicians who believe neither in God nor in miracles will attest to extraordinary and inexplicable cures for which they deserve no credit, and they will agree that the label "psychosomatic" will go only so far in accounting for them. In other words: yes, God still heals.

27–39 At the time of Herod Agrippa all but three of the seventy members of the *Sanhedrin* were *Tz'dukim*. Therefore in suppressing the Gospel the *Sanhedrin* was judging it by two Sadducee criteria: (1) it proclaimed resurrection, which the *Tz'dukim* denied, and (2) it proclaimed "another king, Yeshua" (17:7), which, if true (compare Yn 18:33–38), would be politically subversive, as well as destructive of the cozy working relationship the Sadducees had with the occupying Romans. The Gospel is political in other ways too — it says to love your enemies, to return good for evil, and to go to war (but our weapons are not carnal, 2C 10:3–5; and our adversaries are not human but demonic, Ep 6:10–17).

28–29 In this name… this man's death. The name of Yeshua is not mentioned in the direct quote from the *cohen hagadol*. Today some Orthodox Jews refuse to speak the names "Yeshua," "Jesus," or even "Yeshu," but say only "that man." See Mt 1:21N.

29–32 Kefa never wastes an opportunity to proclaim the Gospel. Here he knows he must be brief (as at 4:8–12), for the *Sanhedrin* will not patiently endure a sermon. Yet his message always, even to these determined opponents, is one of hope, one which offers salvation.

We must obey God, not men. See 4:19N.

You… killed him. See 2:22–23N.

30 Stake, Greek *xulon*, which KJV renders "tree" here and at four other places (10:39, 13:29; Ga 3:13; 1 Ke 2:24), all referring to what Yeshua was hanged on until he died. Yeshua was not hanged on a tree, but on a *stavros*, usually translated "cross" and in the *JNT* translated "execution-stake," as explained in Mt 10:38N. The word "*xulon*" is used instead of *stavros* in these five places because all of them quote or allude to Deuteronomy 21:22–23, where the Hebrew word is "*'etz*," normally rendered into Septuagint Greek as "*xulon*." Both Hebrew *'etz* and Greek *xulon* can mean "tree, wood, stake, stick," depending on context. In Deuteronomy 21:22–23, where the subject is hanging, an *'etz* is any piece of wood on which a person can be hanged, i.e., a stake (perhaps if metal gallows had existed, a different word would have been used). If Luke had meant a tree and not a stake, the Greeks had a word for it, "*dendron*," which he could have used but didn't. Therefore, while at Mt 26:47 and Mk 14:48 *xulon* means "stick," at Lk 23:31 and Rv 18:12 it means "wood," and at Rv 2:7 it has to mean "tree," here it means "stake." See also Ga 3:13N and 1 Ke 2:24N.

34 Gamli'el (Gamaliel) I, known in Jewish history as *Rabban* Gamli'el the Elder. He was the first to carry the title "*Rabban*" ("our master, our great one") rather than the more common "*Rabbi*" ("my master, my great one"). His name means "God is also for me." He is "the Elder" because he was the first of six Gamli'els, of whom his grandson Gamli'el II was best known.

Gamli'el I was the grandson of Hillel and the leader of his school of disciples, *Beit-Hillel* (see Mt 19:3N). At one point, as may be inferred from his title, "*Rabban*," he was head of the *Sanhedrin*, although at the time of the present verse he was only **a member**. He was **a *Parush*** ("Pharisee"; see Mt 3:7N) and **A teacher of the *Torah*** (Greek *nomodidaskalos*, "law teacher"), at whose feet Sha'ul of Tarsus (Paul) sat (22:3&N). That he was **highly respected by all the people** is confirmed in the Mishna:

> "When *Rabban* Gamli'el the Elder died, the glory of the *Torah* came to an end; and purity and holiness [Hebrew *p'rishut*, "separation," related to *Parush*] came to an end." (Sotah 9:15)

While the Second Temple still stood Gamli'el laid the groundwork for the triumph of liberal Pharisaism under Rabbi Yochanan ben-Zakkai after the Second Temple's destruction. Among his *takkanot* (Rabbinic regulations modifying and applying the written *Torah*; literally, "improvements, repairs") were decrees allowing greater movement to certain groups on *Shabbat* (Mishna, Rosh HaShanah 2:5), forbidding a husband to annul divorce proceedings without his wife's knowledge (Gittin 4:2), and permitting a widow to remarry after only one witness (rather than two) testifies to her husband's death (Yevamot 16:7). He was in close touch with Diaspora Jews, for three of his letters to various communities outside Israel are preserved in the Talmud.

Gamli'el's counsel for moderation (vv. 35–39) was accepted this time (vv. 39–40) but abandoned under what was perceived as greater provocation (7:51–58). His moderation may have been due to a generous spirit, a desire to protect the Pharisees from Sadducean hostility, or a genuine sensitivity to God's spirit at work, even though he himself was not a believer. Christian apocryphal literature, seizing on his relatively sanguine treatment of the Messianic Jews, reports that he came to faith in Yeshua, but there is no independent evidence for it.

36 Todah (English versions: "Theudas"). Not the Todah mentioned by Josephus (*Antiquities of the Jews* 20:5:1), since this would imply a double error by Luke the careful historian, for that Todah lived after Y'hudah HaG'lili (v. 37) and after Gamli'el was speaking. The Todah mentioned in this verse, otherwise unknown to history, led one of the many uprisings during the years following the death of Herod the Great in 4 B.C.E.

37 Y'hudah HaG'lili, "Judas the Galilean"; according to Josephus, he was known as Judas of Gamla on the Golan Heights. In consequence of his revolt **at the time of the enrollment for the Roman tax**, which took place in 6 C.E. (see Lk 2:2&N), the Zealot Party (Mt 10:4N) formed itself and became a major provocation leading to the Roman destruction of Jerusalem in 66–70 C.E. Or, as F. F. Bruce wrote in *The Acts of the Apostles*, "Gamaliel was unduly optimistic if he thought it [Y'hudah's revolt] had come to naught" (p. 148). According to Josephus (*Wars of the Jews* 7:8:1) Y'hudah HaG'lili was the grandfather of El'azar ben-Ya'ir, defender of Matzada (73 C.E.) — evidently revolution ran in the family.

38–39 Christian polemicists have used these verses to show that the mere fact of the Church's survival and growth is a fulfillment of Gamli'el's prophecy. Jewish polemicists, on the other hand, assert that the Jewish community's survival under pressure and persecution for two thousand years proves that the Jews are God's people. Of course, mere survival of a group of people does not prove it is **from God**; but I believe that in fact both are right.

At least one Christian writer applies these verses — midrashically, one may say — to today's Messianic Judaism:

> "It is too early to assess the full significance of this growing movement. The Jewish community inevitably sees it as a threat and, coming at a time of insecurity in so many other ways, it has created a certain amount of unease. Some Gentile Christian churches and groups who would normally be very much in support of Jewish Christians have found this new development equally disturbing. Some have felt it right to attack the new movement, others to accept it with a certain amount of reluctance. One thing is certain: nothing quite like it has been seen since the days of the Acts of the Apostles. Gamaliel's advice to the leaders

of the Jewish people (Acts 5) might be equally good advice for Gentile Christians at this time: 'If this undertaking is of men it will fail, but if it is of God you will not be able to overthrow them.'"(Walter Barker, *A Fountain Opened: A Short History of the Church's Ministry Among the Jews, 1809–1982*, London: Olive Press, 1983, p. 4)

41 **On account of him**, literally, "over the name," and therefore, alternatively, "for the sake of *HaShem*." *HaShem* ("the Name") is a euphemism for *YHVH*. Alternatively, "the name" here stands for Yeshua; see vv. 28–29&N. See also 3 Yn 7&N. Suffering for the sake of God is discussed at 7:59–60N.

CHAPTER 6

1 ***Talmidim***. See Mt 5:1N.

Greek-speaking Jews... those who spoke Hebrew. The Greek words are "*Ellênistôn*" and "*Ebraious*" ("Hellenists" and "Hebraists"), and their precise meaning is debatable. The emphasis could be less on language than on culture, or even on geography — whether these Jews were native to the Diaspora or to *Eretz-Israel*. And even if the primary referent is language, some believe that Hebrew was no longer commonly spoken in Yeshua's time and that Aramaic, the related Semitic language originally spoken in Babylon and learned by many Jews during the Babylonian Exile, is what is meant. While it could be either or both, I am convinced that Hebrew was still widely spoken in New Testament times; see Mk 5:41N.

The division between Greek-speaking and Hebrew-speaking (or culturally Greek and culturally Hebrew) Jews dates from the conquest of *Eretz-Israel* by Alexander the Great in 323 B.C.E. He and his successors introduced the Greek language and Greek culture into the lands they ruled. While Hellenistic influence produced such fruits as the Septuagint, Philo of Alexandria and Josephus, "Hebraists" considered the "Hellenists" to have developed an adulterated Judaism which had assimilated elements of the pagan cultures around them — although the Judaism of the Hebrew-speakers had not avoided these influences either. The Maccabean Revolt (see Yn 10:22N) contains elements of intra-Jewish struggle related to this issue. In any case, groups which are different from each other can usually find excuses for deprecating each other.

2 **To serve tables**. Understand this phrase as metonymy: "to see that widows' needs are met," or: "to occupy ourselves with financial and administrative matters."

5 **What they said was agreeable to the whole gathering**, including the Hebrew-speakers, who apparently joined in protecting the interests of the Greek-speakers, for all seven appointees have Greek names. On "**Nicholas**" see Rv 2:6N; on "**proselyte**" see Mt 23:15N and notes cited there.

6 **Laid their hands on them**, conferring the duties and privileges of their office; see Mt 21:23N on "*s'mikhah*" ("laying on of hands").

7 On the growth of the Messianic Community see 2:41N.

A large crowd of *cohanim* ("priests"; see Mt 2:4N) **were becoming obedient to the faith.** Although most of the *cohanim* are presented in the New Testament as being opposed to Yeshua, this was not true of all. There were holy men in the priesthood such as Z'kharyah the father of Yochanan the Immerser (Lk 1:5–25, 57–59).

There is a theory that the *cohanim* who came to believe in Yeshua were not part of the establishment but those who had become disenchanted with it and had gone off to join the Essenes in Qumran. The reasoning is that the theology of the Dead Sea Scrolls is much closer to the New Testament than that of the *Tz'dukim* who controlled the Jerusalem priesthood. But the theory lacks New Testament evidence to support it. Moreover, since the activity of the Messianic believers had not yet spread to other parts of the Land than Jerusalem, it seems more likely that the *cohanim* becoming obedient to the faith at this time were those who made it their business to be in Jerusalem, rather than retreat to the desert. For God can reach the hearts even of people whose usual ties and associations might be expected to lead them to an opposing stance. At 15:5 we are also informed of believing *P'rushim*.

9 **Synagogue of the freed slaves**. People with similar cultural and social backgrounds often choose to worship together. The **freed slaves** were probably Jewish **Cyrenians, Alexandrians and people from Cilicia and the province of Asia** who had been captured and enslaved by the Romans, or their descendants; General Pompey, who captured Jerusalem in 63 B.C.E., took a number of Jews prisoner and released them in Rome. Some, however, may have been Gentile converts to Judaism; the phenomenon of proselyte zeal is familiar in all religious communities.

11 **To allege, "We heard him speak blasphemously against Moshe and against God."** What would have been the content of the alleged blasphemy? The two most likely possibilities: (1) Yeshua is greater than Moshe (see 3:22–23N), (2) the *Torah* has been changed (see vv. 13–14&N).

13–14 **Against this holy place**, the Temple, where the *Sanhedrin* (v. 12) met. **For we have heard him say that Yeshua... will destroy this place.** To show how such a misunderstanding could arise see Lk 21:5–6 and Mk 14:57–59, where, although Yeshua did not say that he personally would destroy the Temple, he did correctly predict its destruction; also Yn 2:19–22&NN, where he used the term "temple" metaphorically to speak of his own body but was thought to be referring to Herod's structure. Likewise Stephen's words could be taken in a way he did not intend (see 7:44–50).

Against the *Torah*. Elsewhere I have explained how Messianic Judaism recognizes that the *Torah* is eternal, and Yeshua did not abrogate it (2:42N; Mt 5:17N, 12:12N, 15:2–3N).

But what of the more specific charge, that Stephen said **Yeshua... will change the customs Moshe handed down to us**? I. Howard Marshall, a Christian scholar, is correct in stating,

> "The *customs* are no doubt the oral traditions giving the scribal interpretation of the law; these were regarded as stemming from Moses, just as much as the

written law was. An attack on the oral law was thus tantamount to an attack on the law as a whole." (*Acts: An Introduction and Commentary*, p. 130)

The first words of Mishna Pirkey-Avot are:

"Moshe received the *Torah* from Sinai and handed it down to Y'hoshua, and Y'hoshua to the Elders, and the Elders to the Prophets; and the Prophets handed it down to the Men of the Great Synagogue. They said three things: be deliberate in judging, raise up many *talmidim*, and make a fence around the *Torah*." (Avot 1:1)

The *Torah* spoken of in this quotation is the Oral *Torah*; thus handed down it is regarded as unchangeable. Even the "fence" of rules and customs which the rabbis are instructed here to continue producing in order to prevent inadvertent violation of the Written *Torah* is thought of as already contained "organically" in what Moshe received from God on Mount Sinai:

"Every interpretation of the *Torah* given by a universally recognized authority is regarded as divine and given on Sinai, in the sense that it is taken as the original divinely willed (*gottgewollte*) interpretation of the text; for the omniscient and all-wise God included in His revealed *Torah* every shade of meaning which divinely inspired interpretation thereafter discovered.... Therefore, every interpretation is called *derash*, 'searching' for what God had originally put there.... Every interpretation given by the scholars of the Talmud, Moses had received on Mt. Sinai, for he had received the *Torah*, and the interpretation was contained in it, not mechanically, but organically, as the fruit of the tree was contained in the seed from which the tree had grown...." (Saul Kaatz, *Muendliche Lehre und Ihr Dogma*, Berlin, 1923, p. 48, as quoted in George Horowitz, *The Spirit of the Jewish Law*, New York: Central Book Company, 1973, p. 92).

Nevertheless there is in Judaism a persistent strand of thought which says that when the Messiah comes he will expound the *Torah* more fully and even change it. Here are three quotations to this effect from the Midrash Rabbah, redacted in the 6th–12th centuries but containing material which is much earlier, some of it predating Yeshua. The first is from Genesis Rabbah 98:9 (on Genesis 49:11, "his foal and his colt"):

"When he comes about whom it is written, 'Lowly and riding upon an ass, even upon a colt the foal of an ass' [Zechariah 9:9, cited at Mt 21:2–7&N, Yn 12:15], he will compose for them words of *Torah*... and point out to them their errors [in understanding *Torah*].... Rabbi Chanin said, 'Israel will not need the teaching of king Messiah in the future, because it says, "Unto him [the Root of Yishai] will the *Goyim* seek" (Isaiah 11:10) — the Gentiles and not Israel.' If so, why will the Messiah come, and what will he do.? He will come to gather the exiles of Israel and to give them thirty *mitzvot*."

The passage goes on to derive the number thirty from the thirty pieces of silver of Zechariah 11:12 (cited at Mt 26:15, 27:9). There follows a discussion of whether the thirty commandments are for the Gentiles or for the Jews. Leviticus Rabbah 9:7 (on Leviticus 7:11–12) says that

> "Rabbis Pinchas, L'vi and Yochanan said in the name of Rabbi Menachem of Galatia, 'In the Coming Time all the sacrifices will be abolished, except the thanksgiving offering. All the prayers will be abolished, except the thanksgiving prayer,'"

which is the next-to-last prayer of the *Shmoneh-Esreh*. See MJ 13:15–16&N. Ecclesiastes Rabbah on Ecclesiastes 11:8, "All that comes is vanity," simply states,

> "The *Torah* which one learns in this world 'is vanity' in comparison with the *Torah* of the Messiah,"

that is, in comparison with what one will learn when the Messiah comes and teaches his understanding of *Torah*. His way of interpreting *Torah* will constitute and produce substantive "change" in the eternal and unchangeable *Torah*. This is also what is meant by the same phrase, "*Torah* of the Messiah" (KJV: "law of Christ") when Sha'ul uses it (Ga 6:2&N).

Raphael Patai has summarized material relating to the Messianic alteration of the *Torah* in the chapter "New Worlds and a New Tora," in *The Messiah Texts* (Avon, 1979). He quotes the 9th-century *Alphabet Midrash of Rabbi Akiva*:

> "In the future the Holy One, blessed be He,... will expound to [the pious] the meanings of a new Tora which He will give them through the Messiah."

Drawing on this tradition the Midrash Talpiyot (c. 1700 C.E.) explains that the "new Tora"

> "means the secrets and mysteries of the Tora which have remained hidden until now. It does not refer to another Tora, heaven forfend, for surely the Tora which He gave us through Moses our Master, peace be upon him, is the eternal Tora; but the revelation of her hidden secrets is called 'new Tora.'"

It then explains that the very same letters found in the *Torah* of Moshe will be rearranged, and that in this way the "new Tora" will be the "unchanged" Mosaic Law. Another writer, L'vi Yitzchak of Berditchev (c. 1740–1810) is quoted as offering the same explanation. Also an undated Yemenite *midrash* is cited:

> "In the future the Holy One, blessed be He, will seat the Messiah in the supernal Yeshiva, and they will call him 'the Lord,' just as they call the Creator.... And the Messiah will sit in the Yeshiva, and all those who walk on earth will come and sit before him to hear a new Tora and new commandments and the deep wisdom which he teaches Israel.... [A]nd the Holy One, blessed be He, will reveal... rules of life, rules of peace, rules of alertness, rules of purity, rules of

> abstinence, rules of piety, rules of charity.... And no person who hears a teaching from the mouth of the Messiah will ever forget it, for the Holy One, blessed be He, will reveal Himself in the House of Study of the Messiah, and will pour his Holy Spirit upon all those who walk the earth, and His Holy Spirit will be upon each and every one. And each one in His House of Study will understand the *Halakhot* [laws, rules] on his own, the *Midrashot* [studies, interpretations, legends] on his own, the *Tosafot* [annotations, often referring to the 12th–14th-century commentaries on the Talmud and Rashi] on his own, the *Aggadot* [stories, folk tales] on his own, the traditions on his own, and each one of them will know on his own [compare Jeremiah 31:32–33(33–34)].... And even the slaves and the slave-women of Israel who were bought for money from the nations of the world, the Holy Spirit will rest upon them, and they will expound on their own."

These texts do not "prove" that normative Orthodox Judaism necessarily expects a new *Torah* when the Messiah comes, but they do show that such expectations have been accepted within an Orthodox Jewish framework during a period covering at least 1,500 years. If this stream of thought existed in the first century as well, it is not unreasonable to expect Yeshua the Messiah might rightfully "change the customs handed down to us by Moshe."

Yet such changes, whether according to Orthodox Jewish understandings of *Torah* or according to the explanations of *Torah* offered in this commentary, take place within the Jewish framework of thought which says that there is but one eternal *Torah* given to Israel. It is this one eternal *Torah* which the Messiah expounds and applies, and even his "changes" are organically contained within it. For more, see Mt 5:17&N, 1C 9:21&N, Ga 6:2&N.

CHAPTER 7

2–53 Stephen has been charged with having taught against Moshe, God, the Temple and the *Torah* (6:11–14&NN) — in other words, against everything Judaism stands for. Demonstrating that the best defense is a good offense, he indicts the religious leaders after the manner of the Prophets, saying it is they who have abandoned each one of these four sacred trusts.

2 **Brothers and fathers**. Stephen, like Kefa (2:29, 3:17), speaks as a fellow Jew, one of the family. His critique is no more antisemitic than those of his predecessors the Prophets.

The God of glory. His first words refute the charge that he has "spoken blasphemously... against God" (6:11). His regard for the one God is demonstrated consistently throughout his speech.

Avraham avinu, "Abraham, our father," a phrase common in Jewish discourse.

In Mesopotamia, in "Ur of the Chaldees" (Genesis 15:7), not in the better-known city, also called Ur, at the mouth of the Euphrates River, which is not in Mesopotamia.

3 Stephen quotes Genesis 12:1, words recorded as spoken by God to Avraham in Charan but presumably also spoken in Ur.

4 **After his father died**. Was Stephen biblically uninformed? Genesis 11:26 seems to say that Terach, Avraham's father, was 70 when Avraham was born; and Genesis 12:4 clearly says that Avraham was 75 when he left Charan; these data imply that Terach was 145 at the time. But Genesis 11:32 says that Terach died at 205, sixty years later. Two explanations of the inconsistency have been offered:

(1) Genesis 11:26 may mean Terach was 70 not when Avraham was born but when his brother Nachor was born. It is not implausible that Nachor was considerably older than Avraham, since his granddaughter Rivkah married Avraham's son Yitzchak.

(2) Stephen was using a text of the Pentateuch in which Terach's age was given as 145, not 205. The Samaritan text of the Pentateuch does say 145, so we are not dealing with a *deus ex machina*. Moreover, there are scholars, Avraham Spero and Jakob Jervell among them, who believe Stephen himself was a Samaritan. This would also explain v. 16, which says that Avraham was buried in Sh'khem, since this too follows Samaritan tradition. It explains a possible anti-Temple tendency in vv. 47–50 (compare Yn 4:20–22&NN) and gives logic to placing the story of the spread of the Gospel to Shomron in the immediately following passage (8:4–26). At worst, if under pressure Stephen erred, his errors would be what are known in Judaism as *ta'uyot b'tom-lev*, honest mistakes.

The first century Alexandrian Jew Philo, in *De Migratione Abrahami*, also speaks of Avraham's leaving Charan after Terach's death.

6–44 Stephen paints a picture of the majority in Israel refusing to honor those whom God chose to bring them the salvation he had promised them — especially Yosef (vv. 9–16), who was recognized by Pharaoh, a Gentile, but not by his own brothers, and Moshe (vv. 17–44).

14 **Seventy-five**, according to the Septuagint, but seventy according to the Masoretic Hebrew text (Genesis 46:27, Exodus 1:5). Genesis 46:20 accounts for the discrepancy. In this verse the Septuagint names four grandsons and one great-grandson of Joseph, whereas the Masoretic text does not.

16 According to the Hebrew text of the *Tanakh* Avraham bought a burial cave in Hevron (Genesis 23:2–20), in which Ya'akov was buried by Yosef (Genesis 49:29–50:13). Ya'akov bought a field from Chamor in Sh'khem (Genesis 33:18–19), in which the bones of Yosef were placed centuries later (Joshua 24:32). Non-biblical sources (the pseudepigraphical books of Jubilees and Testaments of the Twelve Patriarchs, the Mekhilta and Josephus' *Antiquities of the Jews*) say Joseph's brothers' bones eventually were removed and buried in Israel; most sources say in Hevron. Either Stephen is telescoping these events in his quick and pressurized review, or he is using something other than the Hebrew text, perhaps the Samaritan one (see v. 4N).

29 **Two sons**, Gershom and Eli'ezer (Exodus 2:22, 18:3–4).

30 According to Jubilees 1:27, 29; 2:1, "the angel of the Presence" talked with Moshe on Mount Sinai. This seems to be the angel of *Adonai*, referred to over and over in the *Tanakh* (for example at Genesis 22:11, 48:15). Some believe the angel of *Adonai* was a pre-incarnation appearance of the eternal Word who became flesh in Yeshua the Messiah. See vv. 35, 38, 53&N, and especially Yn 1:14N.

35–38 These verses refute the charge that Stephen spoke against Moshe (6:11). Here Stephen lauds him as **ruler, ransomer,** one who spoke with the angel, miracle-worker, prophet and receiver of **living words**.

37 See 3:22–23N.

38 **Assembly**, Greek *ekklêsia,* translated "church" in KJV, despite its inappropriateness in speaking of the Jewish people. The word means, literally, "called-out ones," whether called out from Egypt or from sin; satisfactory renderings are "assembly," "congregation" and "community."

The angel that had spoken to him at Mount Sinai from the burning bush (v. 30&N), not the angels understood to have mediated the giving of the *Torah* (v. 53&N).

Living words, that is, the *Torah.* Clearly Stephen does not teach against the *Torah;* this refutes the third charge (6:13–14&N).

42–43 **God... gave them over...** See Ro 1:24–28N.

The book of the prophets, that is, the book of the twelve "minor prophets," regarded as a single book in Jewish reckoning of the *Tanakh.* Stephen's citation of Amos conforms closely to the Septuagint, which differs in details from the Masoretic text. However, **"beyond Babylon"** in place of "beyond Damascus" may be Stephen's *midrash* pointing out that the penalty for turning away from the one true God will be worse than the Babylonian Exile.

44–50 Stephen refutes the final charge, that he has spoken improperly against the Temple (6:13–14&N), by showing that it was the people, not God, who wanted a **dwelling place** or **house** more substantial than the **Tent of Witness** or "Tabernacle" originally authorized in the *Torah.* The establishment has tended toward "Temple-olatry" instead of adopting God's attitude. He cites Isaiah in support of his criticism.

45b–47 See 1 Kings 8:12–21; Psalm 132:5, 7.

51 **Stiffnecked**. This term is used six times in the *Tanakh*: Exodus 32:9; 33:3, 5; 34:9; Deuteronomy 9:6, 13. Always it is *Adonai* portraying the Israelites to Moshe, or Moshe portraying them to God or to themselves. Gentiles cannot call Jews stiffnecked without subjecting themselves to the charge of being antisemitic. But Jews can — in intra-family fights different rules apply.

Uncircumcised hearts (Leviticus 26:41; Deuteronomy 10:16, 30:6; Jeremiah 4:4, 9:25(26); Ezekiel 44:7, 9) **and ears** (Jeremiah 6:10). These too are the *Tanakh*'s characterizations of Israel: God's people outwardly bear the sign of the covenant with Avraham

(v. 8) but inwardly are heathen, impure, rebellious (compare Ro 2:17–3:2&NN).

You continually oppose the *Ruach HaKodesh*. See Mt 12:31–32&N, Lk 12:8–10&N.

52 Yeshua made the same accusation (Mt 23:29–32, 35). Yochanan the Immerser was the last prophet; he too was put to death (Mt 14:1–12). On the application of the *Tanakh* prophecies to Yeshua, see Section VII of the Introduction to the *JNT*, and Mt 26:24&N.

Of the *Tzaddik*, Greek *tou dikaiou*, literally, "of the Righteous One." See Mt 13:17N.

You have become his betrayers and murderers, not directly — as they are about to become of Stephen — but through Pontius Pilate and the Roman government. See 2:22–23&N.

53 The verse of the *Tanakh* which comes closest to stating outright that **the *Torah*... was delivered by angels** is found in Moshe's final speech before his death: "*Adonai* came from Sinai and rose from Seir to them; he shone forth from Mount Paran; and he came from the holy myriads;... at his right hand *eshdat lamo*" (Deuteronomy 33:2). Hebrew *eshdat lamo* is taken by some Jewish commentators to mean, "was a fiery law (*esh-dat*) for them." The Septuagint translates the passage, "at his right hand were his angels with him." Rashi says that the "holy myriads" were angels. Strack and Billerbeck, in their six-volume *Commentary on the New Testament from the Talmud and Midrash* (Munich: C. H. Beck'sche, 1975 reprint of 1926 original, in German), give several dozen citations from rabbinic literature showing that the idea of angelic mediation of the *Torah* was widespread. For example, the Midrash Rabbah does a wordplay on the text of Psalm 68:

> "Rabbi Abdimi of Haifa said, 'Twenty-two thousand [angels] descended with God on Sinai, as it says, "The chariots of God are twenty thousand, thousands of *shin'an*" [often translated "angels"] (Psalm 68:18(17)). The very best, the choicest (*sh'na'an*) went down.'"(Exodus Rabbah 29:2)

The psalm continues, "*Adonai* is among them, Sinai in the holy place."

But the rabbis are not united in asserting angelic mediation of the *Torah*. The following takes a defensive theological position (see 3:22–23N) against Gnosticism and against what the rabbis supposed Christianity taught:

> "When [God] gave the commandments on Mount Sinai, at first he uttered them loudly all at once, as it is said, 'And God spoke all these words [simultaneously; see last paragraph of 2:4b–13N], saying,...' (Exodus 20:1). Then [the angel] Mikha'el said, 'He will commission me to explain his words.' And [the angel] Gavri'el said, 'He will commission me to explain them.' But as soon as he continued, saying, 'I am *Adonai* your God' (Exodus 20:2), they said, 'As he gives his children the *Torah* he is committing his commandments, fully explained, directly to his son Israel." (Pesikta Rabbati 21:5)

In two other places the New Testament makes reference to angelic mediation of the *Torah* (Ga 3:19&N, MJ 2:2&N). In the present verse the mention of angels emphasizes that even though the *Torah* came through supernatural mediation — which demonstates Stephen's high regard for the *Torah* — his hearers, who are sitting in judgment of him, **have not kept it!**

You have not kept it! Stephen has cast all caution to the winds, and this is the resulting climax to his speech. The *Sanhedrin* was the final authority in matters of *Torah*, so it is as if Stephen were to stand before the Supreme Court and call its members criminals. He does not address the question of whether "Yeshua from Natzeret... will change the customs Moshe handed down to us" (6:14). Why should he? If the leaders do not observe them now, what difference will it make if Yeshua changes them? Compare Yeshua's criticisms of a group of *P'rushim* and *Torah*-teachers in Mt 23:13–36&NN.

54 On hearing these things they were cut to their hearts. Obviously Stephen's remarks were designed to produce a reaction, as was Kefa's *Shavu'ot* sermon, when the crowds were "stung" in their hearts (2:37). But there the message produced repentance and faith, here rage and fury.

55–56 A portion of v. 55 was inadvertently omitted from the first three printings of the *Jewish New Testament*. Verse 55 should read:

> "But he, full of the *Ruach HaKodesh*, looked up to heaven and saw God's *Sh'khinah*, with Yeshua standing **at the right hand of** God."

On **God's *Sh'khinah***, his manifest glory, see Paragraph (3) of MJ 1:2–3N.

Standing at the right hand of God. The text of Psalm 110:1 (see Mt 22:44N) says, "*Adonai* said to my Lord, 'Sit at my right hand...'," but Stephen sees him standing. Since Yeshua's function in heaven with God is to be the *cohen gadol* for all believers and intercede for them (MJ 2:16–18&N, 7:25&N and *passim*), possibly his posture indicates that Stephen sees him performing his high-priestly duties, for which sitting would be inappropriate. Against this is MJ 10:11–14&N.

Son of Man, that is, Yeshua the Messiah. This is the last use of this title in the New Testament. See Mt 8:20N.

57 They began yelling...; and with one accord (or: "singlemindedly"; see 1:14N), **they rushed at him.** This is hardly the behavior expected from the supreme tribunal of the land. It is not clear whether those who rushed at Stephen included some of his Greek-speaking accusers along with the angrier members of the *Sanhedrin* (which had not delivered a verdict). In any case, experienced jurists should have sensed the danger latent in the circumstances and taken steps to protect Stephen instead of joining the mob. Either the *Sanhedrin* had already decided to put Stephen out of the way without an honest trial, or the judges allowed emotion to overrule reason after his inflammatory speech.

58 Threw him outside the city and began stoning him. And the witnesses.... Deuteronomy 17:2–7 states that stoning was to take place outside the city gates, and that the witnesses to the criminal act were to be the first to stone the convicted criminal. Leviticus 24:24 makes the same point: "Bring forth him that has cursed outside the camp; and let all that heard him lay their hands upon his head, and let all the congregation stone him." The Mishna deals with the punishment of stoning:

> "The place of stoning was as the height of two men. One of the witnesses pushed him down by his hips. If he turned over face downward, he turned him on his back. If he died from the blow and the fall, that was enough. But if not, the second witness took a stone and dropped it on his chest. If he died from this, that was enough. But if not, his stoning had to be carried out by all Israel, as it is said, 'The hand of the witnesses shall be first upon him to put him to death and afterward the hand of all the people' (Deuteronomy 17:7)." (Sanhedrin 6:4)

Laid down their coats. Compare what the Talmud says about carrying out the sentence of stoning:

> "When the trial is over, they take him [the condemned person] out to be stoned. The place of stoning was at a distance from the court, as it is said, 'Take out the one who has cursed' (Leviticus 24:14). A man stands at the entrance of the court; in his hand is the signalling flag [Hebrew *sudarin* = *sudar*, "scarf, sweater"]. A horseman was stationed far away but within sight of him. If one [of the judges] says, 'I have something [more] to say in his favor,' he [the signaller] waves the *sudarin*, and the horseman runs and stops them [from stoning him]. Even if [the condemned person] himself says, 'I have something to say in my favor,' they bring him back, even four or five times, only provided that there is some substance to what he is saying." (Sanhedrin 42b)

At the feet of a young man named Sha'ul. This is the first mention in the New Testament of Paul of Tarsus ("Saint Paul"). Acts 13:9 gives both his names; see note there. Sha'ul himself recalls this event at 22:20.

One more piece of information completes the ground for an interesting speculation. According to the Talmud, the court must provide the *sudarin*, not the accused (Sanhedrin 43a, commenting on the above quoted paragraph). Joseph Shulam thinks *sudar* in later Hebrew can also mean "coat." Thus, he conjectures, the Greek translator of Acts from a presumed original Hebrew text didn't understand the Jewish context and therefore wrote of laying coats at Sha'ul's feet, whereas actually Sha'ul was a member of the *Sanhedrin*, specifically, the one who held the *sudar*. (For more on Sha'ul's possibly being a member of the *Sanhedrin* see 8:1&N, 9:1–2N, 23:1&N, 26:10&N; Ga 1:14&N.) On the other hand, the stoning of Stephen was so disorderly that it seems improbable that provision was even made for signalling.

59–60 Lord Yeshua, receive my spirit!… Don't hold this sin against them. Stephen was the first Messianic Jew to die *'al kiddush-HaShem* (literally, "in sanctification of the Name" of God), that is, as a martyr to his faith.

Readiness for martyrdom is seen already in the *Tanakh*: Chananyah, Misha'el and 'Azaryah (Shadrakh, Meishakh and 'Aved-n'go) preferred being thrown into "the burning fiery furnace" over bowing down to King Nevukhadnetzar's idols (Daniel 3). In the Apocrypha, 2 Maccabees tells that when ordered by Antiochus IV to renounce

Judaism, seven sons and their mother, one after the other, chose death. "These figures," comments the *Encyclopedia Judaica*, "became the prototypes for and symbols of martyrdom and martyrs in both Judaism and Christianity" (10:982). Through the centuries countless Jews persecuted in Christendom have died *'al kiddush-HaShem*; likewise innumerable Christians have endured death for their faith.

Stephen learned how to face death from Yeshua the Messiah himself, who was not a martyr at all but came to earth from equality with God (Pp 2:6–8) "to give his life as a ransom for many" (Mk 10:45). Nailed to the execution-stake, Yeshua said, "Father! Into your hands I commit my spirit" (Lk 23:46, quoting Psalm 31:6(5)). He also prayed, "Father, forgive them, for they don't understand what they are doing" (Lk 23:34&N). The Jewish scholar Claude G. Montefiore writes that he knows of no comparable sentiments in any of the rabbinic martyrologies, that this statement of forgiveness constitutes "a religious advance" (*Rabbinic Literature and Gospel Teachings*, p. 372). Martyrdom for one's faith is always noble, and Stephen's death *'al kiddush-HaShem*, in loyal imitation of his Lord, was altogether noble.

At the same time, it must be noted that martyrdom does not, as some Jewish writers suppose, constitute a "Christian value." Martyrdom for its own sake is a cultish value which is neither Christian nor Jewish. The *Musaf* service for *Yom-Kippur* includes a martyrology of Rabbis Ishmael, Akiva and eight others who died *'al kiddush-HaShem* under Roman Emperor Hadrian in 135 C.E., at the end of Bar-Kosiba's rebellion. *Foxe's Book of Martyrs*, a 17th-century work describing many Christians put to death because of their faith, is still in print. Both Judaism and Christianity honor their martyrs, but without making martyrdom a virtue or a goal.

CHAPTER 8

1 **Sha'ul gave his approval**, apparently through his vote in the *Sanhedrin*. See 7:58&N, 26:10&N.

3 This verse and 9:1–2, along with the background of 7:58 and 8:1, show that Sha'ul in his zeal for traditional Judaism (Ro 10:2&N; Ga 1:13–14&NN, 4:18) was a formidable persecutor of Messianic Jews (Pp 3:6), possibly their worst persecutor (1 Ti 1:13–16&NN).

4–26 See Paragraph (2) of 7:4N.

4 For the Messiah's stated purposes (1:8) the scattering of the believers (v. 1), which seemed a disaster, proved a blessing; because **they announced the Good News of the Word**, telling about Yeshua, **wherever they went**. As Yosef said to his brothers after an earlier persecution, "You intended evil for me, but God meant it for good" (Genesis 50:20). Compare Ro 8:28.

5 **Philip**. Not the emissary but the Greek-speaking Jew (6:5), because the emissaries remained in Yerushalayim (v. 1).

Shomron. See Yn 4:9N.

10 This man is the power of God called "The Great Power." Shim'on may have been just a magician who liked having powers and controlling people. Or he may have been the leader of a heretical Jewish Gnostic sect. Gnostics usually postulated various spiritual entities in a hierarchy leading to God and prescribed ascetic or orgiastic practices as means for attaining higher spiritual levels in the hierarchy. **"The Great Power"** would have been one of the levels in his doctrinal system. He may well have been in touch with the supernatural; but it would have been with demons, not **the power of God**. Shim'on's sin (vv. 18–23) confirms his ungodliness.

13 Shim'on... came to believe and was **immersed**. Some would say he had "believed" only intellectually and had not been truly born again (see Ya 2:14–26), so that, having fooled Philip, he was immersed by mistake. Others would regard him as genuinely saved but still "carnal"; that is, he had not yet renounced obviously sinful behavior patterns. One's opinion on this might affect one's attitude toward v. 24&N.

24 It is not clear whether Shim'on's words sprang from genuine repentance or were themselves only more sham, deception and hypocrisy. See v. 13&N.

26 The road that goes down from Yerushalayim to 'Aza. 'Aza Road is an important thoroughfare in modern Jerusalem; the ancient road continued toward the sea west-southwestward below Manahat (1 Chronicles 8:6), where I now live, through 'Emek Refayim (the Valley of Rephaim). There the Philistines assembled against King David before he defeated them (1 Chronicles 14:8–16).

27 An Ethiopian, from Greek *aethein* ("to burn") and *ips* ("face") — a "burnt-face." The New Testament takes special note of this prominent black man, who was Jewish (see below).

Eunuch. Throughout the ancient Near East men in positions of power were often castrated. The *Tanakh* has a number of examples including 'Eved-Melekh the Cushite (Ethiopian) at Jeremiah 38:7. The term may also refer generally to a high official.

The Kandake (KJV "Candace," without "the"). Like "Pharaoh" or "Caesar," this is a title not a name; it means "queen" or "queen mother." The monarchy of Ethiopia claims to trace its genealogy from King Solomon and the Queen of Sheba (1 Kings 10) through their son Menelik I to King Haile Selassie, who was deposed in 1974, some three thousand years later. Ethiopian Jews, who call themselves "Beta Israel" ("house of Israel") but are also known as Falashas (the Amharic word for "exiles"), consider themselves descended from Jews who came with Menelik I. This is legend, but "Ethiopian chronicles show that Judaism was widespread before the conversion to Christianity of the Axum dynasty during the fourth century" (*Encyclopedia Judaica* 6:1143).

He had been to Yerushalayim to worship. Chapter 8 deals with two categories of persons in one sense joined to and in another sense separated from the Jewish people. The Samaritans (vv. 4–24) were not Jews but had Jewish ancestry (Yn 4:9N); they did not worship in Jerusalem (Yn 4:20–21). This Ethiopian was born Jewish or a Jewish proselyte, since the first full Gentile was not reached with the Gospel until Chapter 10 below. But because he was a eunuch he was prohibited from worshipping in the congregation of God's people (Deuteronomy 23:1). His travelling so far to worship, even though debarred, attests to his godliness. In later Scriptures God took special note of godly eunuchs (Isaiah 56:4–5, Mt 19:10–12).

29 Reading from Yesha'yahu the prophet. God is having this man read from one of the key Messianic prophecies pointing to Yeshua, Isaiah 52:11–53:12.

30–31 Do you understand what you're reading? It is amazing how one can read and reread the Bible without seeing in it the reality of God and his son Yeshua; that was my own experience until age 37. It is my hope that the *Jewish New Testament* and this commentary will aid Jews and Gentiles everywhere to understand better what they are reading. My special concern is for sincere seekers whose response to the question, like that of the Ethiopian eunuch, is: **How can I unless someone explains it to me?**

32–33 The quotation conforms to the Septuagint. The book of Acts has already referred to Yeshua four times as the servant of God (3:13, 26; 4:27, 30). Four passages in Isaiah 42–53 mention God's suffering servant. Much modern Jewish interpretation understands this servant to be the people of Israel, not the Messiah; although this seems to me to be defensive theology (3:22–23N), since many of the earlier Jewish expositors did not see it that way. Polemics have been exchanged over this question, and especially over the fourth "servant" passage, Isaiah 52:11–53:12.

My view is that the passage points both to Israel and to Yeshua, and that any interpretation that excludes either is inadequate. At Mt 2:15N I explained how Mattityahu's quotation of Hosea 11:1, the *p'shat* ("simple sense") of which clearly refers to Israel, could be "fulfilled" by Yeshua. In my book *Messianic Jewish Manifesto*, in a section entitled "Yeshua Is Identified With the People of Israel," which deals with individual and corporate aspects of the Gospel, I explained how Israel and Yeshua the Messiah can both be the suffering servant. The rest of this note is largely quoted from there.

An interesting way to think about the Gospel as simultaneously individual and corporate is to consider the ways in which the Messiah Yeshua stands for and is intimately identified with his people Israel. Just as the individual who trusts Yeshua becomes united with him and is "immersed" (baptized) into all that Yeshua is, including his death and resurrection — so that God regards his sin nature as dead, and his new nature, empowered by the Holy Spirit, as alive — just as this intimate identification with the Messiah holds for the individual, so the Messiah similarly identifies with and embodies national Israel.

In the New Testament one encounters this notion first at Mt 2:15&N. The idea that one stands for all can be found throughout the Bible, sometimes for weal and sometimes for woe — in the story of Achan's sin (Joshua 7), in the relationship between Israel and her king (many places in the *Tanakh*, for example, 1 Kings 9:3–9), in the relationship between Adam and Yeshua on the one hand and all humanity on the other (Ro 5:12–21, 1C 15:45–49), and in the debate over the "servant passages" (Isaiah 42:1–9, 49:1–13, 50:4–11, 52:11–53:12). Consider, for example, these phrases from Isaiah 49:1–6:

"*Adonai*… said to me, 'You are my servant, Israel, in whom I will be glorified.'

> ... And now *Adonai* says,... 'It is too light a thing that you should be my servant, to raise up the tribes of Ya'akov and to restore the preserved of Israel; I will give you as a light to the nations, that my salvation may reach to the end of the earth.'"

Does "Israel" restore "the preserved of Israel"? Who is the "light to the nations"? Judaism understands this as a goal to be fulfilled by the Jewish people. Christians think at once of Yn 8:12, where Yeshua said of himself, "I am the light of the world." I believe that the Jewish people will be the light to the nations that we ought to be only when we have in us him who is the light of the world, Yeshua.

This concept, that the Messiah embodies the Jewish people, should not seem strange to Christians, for the New Testament teaches precisely that about Yeshua and the Church. What else does it mean to talk of the Church as a body of which the Messiah is the head (Co 1:18)? Or a temple of which he is the chief cornerstone (Ep 2:20–22)? The concept of one standing for all is familiar. But the Church has not clearly grasped that the Holy One of Israel, Yeshua, is in union not only with the Church (Yochanan 17), but also with the Jewish people. When Christians have fully digested this and can communicate to Jews that through Yeshua the Messiah, by virtue of his identification with Israel, the Jewish people will achieve their destiny (2C 1:20&N), then the Jewish people will have been presented a less alien and more attractive Gospel. And the Church will have become more faithful to it.

Nor have Jews reading the New Testament grasped this concept any better. If they had, the controversy over whether Isaiah 53 was referring to the Jewish people or to a then unborn Messiah would dissolve, because it would be understood that Israel's Messiah embodies his people and the people of Israel are epitomized in their Messiah.

The above paragraphs are addressed to Christians estranged from their Jewish roots and from the Jewish people. However, Philip told the Ethiopian eunuch not about the interrelationship between Israel and Yeshua, but simply what he needed to know at that point, namely, "the Good News about Yeshua" (v. 35&N).

33 **Who will tell about his descendants?** That is, since he is dead, as we can all see from the previous quoted lines, he will have no progeny, no posterity. This is a lament. But the lament proves unwarranted in Yeshua's case, because he is raised from the dead, and in him are many spiritual sons, as Isaiah foretold a few verses later (Isaiah 53:11), "He shall see his seed." God does the unexpected, providing seed for one who died with neither wife nor children.

34 **Is the prophet talking about himself or someone else?** Isaiah himself does not meet the requirements of the passage, even though he is a servant of God. See vv. 32–33N.

35 Philip is called an evangelist (21:8), and, like any wise evangelist, he began communicating **the Good News about Yeshua** at the point of interest and concern of his hearer. Unwise evangelists, like unwise salespeople, sometimes use a prepared "pitch" that does not speak to the concerns of their "customer"; their message proves irritating, like scratching where it doesn't itch.

36 On immersion and Yeshua's command that *talmidim* be immersed see Mt 3:1N,

28:19&N; Mk 16:16&N.

39 **The Spirit of the Lord snatched Philip away**, evidently miraculously, as suggested by the ensuing words, **Philip showed up at Ashdod**. Ashdod today is one of Israel's three port cities, along with Haifa and Eilat; it is located about 25 miles south of Tel Aviv.

40 Philip continued doing the work of an evangelist **as he went through all the towns** of the coastal plain northward **until he came to Caesarea**, some 40 miles north of Tel Aviv. There he married and settled down (21:8–9).

An old city rebuilt by Herod the Great, with a harbor, Caesarea became the capital city of the Roman procurators. Riots between Jews and Gentiles here marked the start of the Jewish war with Rome in 66 C.E. Partly unearthed by archeologists, the only inscription with the name of Pontius Pilate was found here. Today its amphitheater, built by Herod, is used for concerts; while nearby have been built homes for the well-to-do.

CHAPTER 9

1–2 Sha'ul was so incensed against the Messianic Jews (8:3) that he was not satisfied to conduct his inquisitions and persecutions only in Yerushalayim. Letters from the *cohen hagadol* would carry weight in the Diaspora. Under Roman rule the *Sanhedrin* did not have temporal power; but in internal Jewish matters it was honored even beyond the borders of Israel, for example, in Damascus (v. 3).

People… who belonged to "the Way." Evidently this is how the early believers referred to themselves (19:9, 23; 22:4; 24:14&N, 22). Other Jews, in calling them *Natzratim* or *Notzrim*, identified them as one Jewish school or sect among many (24:5&N); but the term "The Way" is a claim to universal validity for Yeshua's doctrine and practice. Indeed, Yeshua called himself "the Way" (Yn 14:6).

Bring them back to Yerushalayim for trial and punishment (22:5). Apparently Sha'ul had become the *Sanhedrin*'s prosecuting attorney (on his *Sanhedrin* membership see 7:58&N, 8:1&N, 26:10&N).

He wanted to extradite people from Damascus across two borders to Jerusalem. The basis in Roman law for doing such a thing might have been that Messianism was not a *religio licita*, a "legal religion" given certain protections by the Romans, whereas Judaism was. Against this idea is the fact that Roman Emperors Nero and Claudius saw the Messianics as a Jewish sect, hence would have included them in the protection given Jews.

3–19 The story of how Sha'ul came to trust in Yeshua is told again at 22:5–16 and a third time at 26:13–18, with varying details. See 26:13–14N on reconciling the differences. Compare also the visions described in Rv 1:9–20, Daniel 10:4ff.

4 **A voice**. The best known of many rabbinic stories about a *bat-kol* (voice from heaven, literally "daughter of a voice"; see Yn 12:28&N) is found in the Talmud. One time, in a dispute over a point of *halakhah* (Jewish law),

"Rabbi Eli'ezer adduced in defense of his opinion all the arguments in the

> world, but the audience of rabbis did not accept them. He said, 'If I am right about this point of *halakhah*, let this carob tree prove it!' Whereupon the carob tree moved two hundred feet from its place. 'A carob tree,' they retorted, 'doesn't prove a thing!'
>
> "So he said to them, 'If the *halakhah* agrees with me, let the stream of water prove it!' And the stream flowed backward. 'Water proves nothing,' they said.
>
> "Again, he said, 'If the *halakhah* agrees with me, let the walls of this *beit-midrash* ["house of study"] prove it!' Then the walls of the house bent inward, as if they were about to fall down. But Rabbi Y'hoshua rebuked the walls and said, 'If scholars debate *halakhah*, what business is it of yours?' So to honor Rabbi Y'hoshua the walls did not fall down, but to honor Rabbi Eli'ezer they didn't straighten up altogether, and they stand inclined to this day.
>
> "Then Rabbi Eli'ezer said to the other rabbis, 'If I am right, let it be proved from heaven!' Whereupon a *bat-kol* was heard, 'Why do you fight Rabbi Eli'ezer? He is always right about the *halakhah*!' But Rabbi Y'hoshua stood up and said, '"It is not in heaven!" (Deuteronomy 30:12)' What did he mean by this? Rabbi Yirmiyahu explained that he meant the *Torah* had already been given from Mount Sinai; therefore we don't pay attention to a *bat-kol*, since God long ago said in the written *Torah*, 'You are to decide by a majority' (Exodus 23:2, as interpreted in Jewish tradition). Rabbi Natan met Eliyahu the Prophet and asked him, 'What did the Holy One, blessed be He, do when this happened?' Eliyahu replied, 'He laughed and said, "My children have gotten the better of me!"'"(Bava Metzia 59b)

The sense of the reply attributed to God is: "I gave them an opinion by means of a *bat-kol* (either as a test, or by way of new revelation); but they found a way, based on the logic implicit in my previous revelations, to negate the impact of the *bat-kol*, and I have to admit that logic is logic!" The point of the passage as a whole is that God, like a chief executive who has delegated authority to subordinates, acquiesces to rabbinic rulings which apply *Torah* to ongoing Jewish life.

But it is wrong to conclude, as some opponents of the New Testament do, that after Mount Sinai God no longer reveals truth directly. In the *Tanakh* God is reported as having spoken not only with Avraham, Yitzchak, Ya'akov and Moshe, but with many of the Prophets and with others centuries after Sinai. In the New Testament a *bat-kol* was heard at Yeshua's immersion (Mt 3:17), on the Mount of Transfiguration (Mt 17:5) and in response to Yeshua's request that God glorify his own name (Yn 12:28).

Here the *bat-kol* turns out to be the voice of Yeshua himself, and apparently nothing less would have sufficed to turn Sha'ul 180 degrees around from his zealous persecution of Messianic Jews to becoming one himself. Many since then have testified that their own coming to faith in Yeshua followed on seeing or hearing him themselves.

One of the most remarkable of these appearances of Yeshua the Messiah was to the former Chief Rabbi of Bulgaria, Daniel Zion (see 4:13N). One morning at sunrise, as he was praying *Shacharit* (3:1N), he saw Yeshua. The vision repeated itself on several occasions; and in the period following he, like Sha'ul, came to trust Yeshua as Israel's Messiah.

5 Sir, who are you? Or: "Lord, who are you?" The Greek word "*kurios*" may mean either (see Mt 1:20N, Mt 7:21N). The correct rendering here depends on to what degree, at that moment, Sha'ul was aware of who was speaking with him. Obviously he was not fully aware, or he wouldn't have needed to ask!

You are persecuting me. How? By persecuting the Messianic Jews. This demonstrates how closely the Messiah identifies with his people (see 8:32–33N and Yochanan 17). Yeshua is "head" of the "Body of the Messiah"; when the body is pained, the head says so.

7 Compare Daniel 10:7, Yn 12:28–29.

10 Chananyah ("Ananias") is described at 22:12 as being "an observant follower of the *Torah* who was highly regarded by the entire Jewish community" of Damascus. A *Torah* zealot like Sha'ul (22:3, Ga 1:13–14; also Ac 21:20, Ro 10:2) would not have found anyone else credible.

"Here I am," Greek *Idou egô* ("Behold, I"), corresponding to Hebrew *Hineni*. Chananyah joined a select company when he gave this answer expressing ready and expectant submission to God. Avraham answered, "*Hineni!*" when God told him to sacrifice his son Yitzchak (Genesis 22:1), and also when the angel of *Adonai* told him to stay his hand (Genesis 22:11). Moshe answered, "*Hineni!*" to God's call from the burning bush (Exodus 3:4). Shmu'el did the same when God first spoke to him (1 Samuel 3:4–10), likewise Yesha'yahu when the voice of *Adonai* asked, "Whom shall I send?" (Isaiah 6:8). Today anyone can say "*Hineni!*" to God by agreeing that he speaks to us through the Bible, repenting of his sins, accepting God's forgiveness through Yeshua's death as atonement, and offering himself to God unconditionally in obedient, holy service.

13–14 Although Chananyah had offered himself to God he still had reservations about carrying out God's command — just like Moshe (Exodus 3:13; 4:1, 10, 13) and Yesha'yahu (Isaiah 6:5). God does not demand uncomprehending obedience, or obedience in the face of overwhelming fears; if we are humble in turning to him, he will calm our fears and make us fit instruments for his use, as he did Moshe, Yesha'yahu, the prophet Yirmiyahu (Jeremiah 1:4–19), Chananyah and others. Yeshua's answer to Chananyah's reservation is given in vv. 15–16. That Chananyah was reassured is proved by his greeting Sha'ul as "Brother" (v. 17).

15 To carry my name to the *Goyim*, Greek *ethnê*, "nations, pagans, Gentiles" (see Mt 5:47N). This astounding turn of events, after two thousand years in which God's working in human history was largely mediated through the Jewish people, is the main theme of the book of Acts (see 1:8&N).

20–22 See Mt 13:52&N.

22–23 Jews... nonbelieving Jews. Greek *Ioudaioi* in both cases, and "nonbelieving" is not in the Greek text. See Yn 1:19N, where the argument is made that when the context is the Land of Israel "*Ioudaioi*" should usually be translated "Judeans," and when the context is the Diaspora it should be translated "Jews." But here confusion arises in v. 24 if the word "Jews" is left unmodified, because both the believers and the objectors were Jewish. Therefore here and in eleven other places in Acts (13:45, 50; 14:4, 19; 17:5, 13; 18:12, 28; 20:3, 19; 21:27) the word "nonbelieving," "unbelieving" or an equivalent phrase is added to "Jews" in order to make clear precisely which Jews were involved; also see 14:2&N. To the original readers the unmodified word "*Ioudaioi*" was probably clear enough; but today's readers, because of twenty centuries of history, might easily read out of the unmodified word "Jews" an antisemitic tendency not present in what Luke wrote. See also Section V ("Translation Issues") of the Introduction to the *JNT*.

23–31 On the differences between the story of Sha'ul's life as reported here and as reported in Ga 1–2:11 see notes there.

Sha'ul created an uproar wherever he went, whether he opposed the Gospel (7:58–8:3) or proclaimed it (here and henceforth). The brothers sent him to Tarsus so that other aspects of Sha'ul's spiritual life could grow to match his zeal (v. 30). Only then did the Messianic Community enjoy peace (v. 31).

29 Greek-speaking Jews. See 6:1N.

32 The narrative returns to Kefa. The last reference to him was in connection with his return from Shomron (8:25).

Lud or Lod; in other English versions Lydda. On the plain below Yerushalayim, about 10 miles east of Yafo (v. 38&N) and modern Tel Aviv and less than two miles from David Ben-Gurion Airport. Today it has a mixed Arab and Jewish population.

35a A mass movement among Jewish people toward faith in Yeshua, likewise at v. 42 in the Yafo area. **The Sharon** is the flat plain between and north of **Lud** and Yafo.

35b–36 Tavita (which means "gazelle"). Most English versions do not translate Greek *dorkas*, which is the Greek equivalent of the Hebrew name ***Tavita***, but simply transliterate it "Dorcas."

Doing *tzedakah*, charitable works; see Mt 6:1–4N.

38 Yafo or Jaffa; in other English versions Joppa. A coastal city adjoining modern Tel Aviv to the south, where a promontory forms a natural harbor protected from the strong southwest winds that can whip up 15-foot seas during winter storms.

41 Shim'on the **leather-tanner** stank all the time; his profession guaranteed it. **Kefa**'s unpretentiousness, his straightforward identification with ordinary folks, is demonstrated by his staying **on in Yafo for some time with** him; in modern Hebrew slang Kefa would be called "'*amkha*" ("your [kind of] people").

CHAPTER 10

2 **A "God-fearer."** Greek *phoboumenos ton theon*, "one who fears God," is regarded by most scholars as a technical term describing a Gentile who attached himself to Judaism but chose not to undergo formal conversion, which included circumcision and public immersion (proselyte baptism). This class of Gentiles, known in Judaism as "proselytes of the gate," was quite large at this time. They were attracted to the nobility of Jewish worship and to the truth of the one God who had revealed himself in the Bible, but for various reasons did not become Jews. See 13:16N.

He gave generously to help the Jewish poor. The text does not say "the Jewish poor" but "the people," Greek *laos*. However "*laos*" is frequently a technical term referring to the Jewish people, the people of God, not people in general; hence this rendering.

And prayed regularly to God. Like Ruth in the *Tanakh* (Ruth 1:16) this God-fearing Gentile had accepted the two essentials of true worship (see above, 2:1N): (1) "Your people shall be my people." Although Cornelius did not officially join the Jewish people, he cared for them as his own. (2) "And your God shall be my God." He prayed to the God of Israel. Or, looking at it another way, he had works stemming from faith (Ro 1:5, 16:26; Ga 5:6; Ep 2:10; Ya 2:14) — which is how the New Testament defines true religion (Ya 1:27), as does the *Tanakh* (Micah 6:8, Ecclesiastes 12:13).

5 **A man named Shim'on, also called Kefa**. See Mt 4:18N. Early printings of the *JNT* are missing the important words, "named Shim'on."

12–14 Leviticus 11 specifies that only those four-footed animals that chew the cud and have split hoofs are *kosher* ("fit") for Jewish people to eat. No reptiles are allowed, and permitted birds are listed by name. In Kefa's vision **all kinds** of creatures appeared, including those that are non-*kosher* or ***treif***. The word "*treif*" means "torn" and actually refers to animals slain by predators and not slaughtered in accordance with Jewish practice; modern "Jewish English" (see Section IV of the Introduction to the *JNT*) extends its meaning to include food that for any reason is not *kosher*.

17–19 **Kefa was still puzzling over the meaning of the vision he had seen.... Kefa's mind was still on the vision.** What could it possibly mean? Would God, who established his covenant with the Jewish people and gave them an eternal *Torah* at Mount Sinai, and who is himself unchangeable (Malachi 3:6), change his *Torah* to make unclean animals *kosher*? This is the apparent meaning, and many Christian commentators assert that this is in fact the meaning. But they ignore the plain statement a few verses later which at last resolves Kefa's puzzlement, "God has shown me not to call any person unclean or impure" (v. 28&N). So the vision is about persons and not about food.

God has not abrogated the Jewish dietary laws. Yeshua said, "Don't think that I have come to do away with the *Torah*" (Mt 5:17–20&NN). The specific issue of whether Yeshua abolished *kashrut* has already arisen at Mk 7:19&N; the conclusion there is that he did not. In Kefa's vision the sheet lowered from heaven contained all kinds of animals, wild beasts, reptiles and birds; yet I know of no Bible interpreters who insist that eagles, vultures, owls, bats, weasels, mice, lizards, crocodiles, chameleons, snakes, spiders and bugs must now be considered edible. God specifies in Leviticus 11 what Jews are to regard as "food." Later, the way in which the laws of *kashrut* fit into the New Covenant is clarified for Kefa and for us (Ga 2:12b&N, 14b&N).

20 **Have no misgivings about going with** a group of Gentiles. See v. 28N.

21 **Here I am**. See 9:10N.

25–26 **Fell prostrate at his feet** to welcome him, also to honor him as God's messenger, but not to "worship" him (as some English versions have it). As a "God-fearer" Cornelius would have known better — like Rabbi Akiva's wife, who prostrated herself and kissed his feet when he returned after twelve years' *yeshivah* study but certainly did not worship him (Talmud, Ketubot 63a). However, Kefa's response, "**Stand up! I myself am just a man**," shows that he misread what Cornelius did as an act of idolatry to be expected from a pagan: the fisherman from the Galil had probably never had such a thing happen to him before.

28 **You are well aware that for a man who is a Jew to have close association with someone who belongs to another people, or to come and visit him, is something that just isn't done.** Before examining whether Jews did in fact keep themselves aloof from Gentiles, take note of Kefa's careful word choices. He does not use "*ethnê*," the usual New Testament word for "Gentiles" and equivalent to Hebrew *Goyim*; for it could be interpreted as having a deprecatory nuance (Mt 5:47N). The word here is "*allophulos*," "someone who belongs to another tribe," used only here in the New Testament. Also the word "*athemitos*," used only twice in the New Testament, does not mean "unlawful, forbidden, against Jewish law," as found in other English versions, but rather "taboo, out of the question, not considered right, against standard practice, contrary to cultural norms."

It is not difficult to find evidence in Jewish sources for what these Gentiles were "**well aware**" of, that although nothing in Jewish law says that Gentiles themselves are **common or unclean**, many of their products and practices were regarded as conveying ritual impurity or were for other reasons forbidden to Jews. At one point the Mishna says, straightforwardly,

> "The dwelling-places of Gentiles [literally, "Canaanites," meaning Gentiles in the Land of Israel] are ritually unclean." (Ohalot 18:7)

Most of Mishna tractate 'Avodah Zarah ("Idol Worship") is devoted to limiting the contacts Jews may have with Gentiles (literally, "idol-worshippers"). For example, according to Chapter 2, Jews may not remain alone with Gentiles, leave cattle at their inns, assist them in childbirth, suckle their children, do business with them when they are travelling to idolatrous festivals, drink their milk or vinegar or wine (which is why there is such a thing as "*kosher* wine"; the *Tanakh* says nothing about it), or eat their bread or oil or pickled vegetables or (in the Gemara on this section) their cooked food. The Bible itself limits Jews to *kosher* food (Leviticus 11), slaughtered according to

Jewish law (Deuteronomy 12:21), on which the tithe has been paid (Leviticus 22:15). In the Gemara, Sanhedrin 104a says that King Hezekiah, by inviting heathens into his house to eat at his table, caused his children to go into exile. However, the Mishna regards table fellowship between Jews and Gentiles as not unheard of, since one section commences with the phrase, "If an Israelite was eating with a Gentile at table," before stating a law about which wine may be drunk on such an occasion ('Avodah Zarah 5:5).

Two points should be noted. First, throughout most of the period covered by the *Tanakh* the main way in which the Jewish people rebelled against God was by going after idols. Although the *Tanakh* requires Jews to treat well the Gentiles in their midst, Jews who go after Gentile ways risk being cut off from their people and God's promises. This is why Nechemyah insisted that Jewish men divorce their Gentile wives (Nehemiah 13:23–31). By the Second Temple period, when the majority of Jews lived in Gentile environments (that is, in the Diaspora), and Israel itself was ruled by Gentiles, the threat from assimilation to Jewish identity, in both its national and its religious aspects, had become even stronger. Thus, while obedience to the details of the ritual impurity laws was not widespread, the overall tone of life in Jewish society vis-à-vis Gentile society did indeed produce the kind of self-imposed separation from Gentiles of which Kefa speaks.

Second, while I had no difficulty finding passages in Jewish writings supporting the assertion that Jews kept themselves separate from Gentiles, I have quoted selectively from the Talmud in order to make the point. During the Middle Ages such selective quoting was abused by Christian authorities, with dire results for the Jewish communities of that time. People were not taught that the Talmud, like the ocean, contains a little of everything, but that it teaches xenophobia and downgrades non-Jews. Passages teaching the equality of all persons before God were overlooked, as were those upholding high and impartial ethical standards. This biased portrait of Judaism inflamed professed Christians to carry out acts of violence against Jews; for the same reason thousands of copies of the Talmud were burned.

But God has shown me not to call any person common or unclean. If Jewish law made Gentile products and practices unclean, it would have been only human, all too human, for people to have extended the description, "unclean," to Gentiles themselves. Such attitudes would have been not so much taught as caught, absorbed from the total milieu; and the influence of these attitudes would have quickly become pervasive. This is why it took direct intervention from God to shake Kefa loose from them.

Also, as explained in vv. 17–19N, this verse proves that the meaning of Kefa's vision had nothing to do with abrogating the laws of *kashrut*.

With this statement and it expansion in vv. 34–35 Kefa puts his dealings with Cornelius and his friends on a new footing: a barrier that both sides might have thought insuperable, that would have made true spiritual communion impossible, is removed altogether.

30 I was at *minchah* prayers in my house. Literally, "I was at the ninth hour praying in my house." See 3:1N.

34–35 God does not play favorites, but… whoever fears him and does what is right is acceptable to him, no matter what people — or, as we might say today, no matter what ethnic group — **he belongs to**. The Judaism of the rabbis has a comparable teaching that among the nations there are righteous people "who have a share in the world to come" (Tosefta, Sanhedrin 13:2), where righteousness for Gentiles is often defined as keeping the seven Noachide laws (see 15:20&N).

36–43 The points of Kefa's sermon to these God-fearing Gentiles: Yeshua is sent by God and is still alive. He will be the final judge of all human beings. The *Tanakh* points to him. Those who trust in his mercy will be forgiven their sins **through his name**, that is, because of who he is and what he has done.

38 God anointed Yeshua... with the *Ruach HaKodesh*: The verse mentions Father, Son, and Holy Spirit.

40–41 Pinchas Lapide is unique among Orthodox Jewish scholars in that he believes Yeshua's resurrection was an historical event, that it actually took place. Why, then, is he not a believer? Because, he says, the resurrection was **seen, not by all the** Jewish **people, but by** relatively few **witnesses**. In contrast, he points out, the entire Jewish people saw God descend on Mount Sinai and consequently said, "We will do and we will hear" (Exodus 24:7). Joseph Shulam's comment: Even though they did all see God at Sinai, they didn't follow him but slipped right back into idolatry; in other words, their profession of loyalty did not produce it. My comment: God's choice to reveal the risen Yeshua to only a few does not excuse disbelief, because the evidence is sufficiently weighty to convince a reasonable and open-minded person (see 1C 15:5–8&NN).

42 Jewish people renders Greek *laos*; the word "Jewish" is not in the text but is implied (see v. 2N).

44–48 Had Kefa and company not seen for themselves that the Holy Spirit came on these non-Jews exactly as on themselves, with the manifestation of speaking in other languages (2:4), they would not have immersed them. As with Kefa (vv. 9–29), it took a supernatural act of God to dislodge their resistance to bringing Gentiles into the Body of the Messiah, accomplished and symbolized by immersion. Cornelius and his friends were the first full Gentiles to enter the Messianic Community without becoming Jews first.

45 The believers from the Circumcision faction. Or, more literally, "the believers from the Circumcision," which could mean not a faction but all Jewish believers. Which is it?

At 15:5, 21:20; Ga 2:12; and Ti 1:10 "the Circumcision" refers to a subgroup of Messianic Jews, namely, those who insisted that Gentiles could not join the Messianic Community merely by trusting in God and his Messiah Yeshua; they had to become Jewish proselytes. This faction would have consisted of saved Jews who, in their former life as non-Messianic Jews, considered "God-fearers" (10:2) fence-straddlers that ought to convert to Judaism. Faith in Yeshua would not have made them change their opinion, because the possibility that Gentiles could be members of the Messianic Community without becoming Jews had never arisen.

But at Ro 4:9, 4:12, 15:8; Ga 2:7–9 and Ep 2:11 "the Circumcision" is used merely to distinguish Jews from Gentiles. While this sense works well in the present verse, at 11:2 the same expression appears where that meaning does not fit — there were no Gentile believers in Jerusalem, so it would be superfluous to speak of the believers there as Jewish. In two passages so close to each other the same phrase should mean the same thing.

Whether it means all Messianic Jews or the faction that wanted Gentile believers to convert to Judaism is elucidated by what it was that bothered them. It is not reasonable to suppose that *all* Messianic Jews, or even a significant majority of them, would have both experienced amazement at God's giving the Holy Spirit to Gentiles (this verse) *and* criticized Kefa for entering Gentiles' homes and eating with them (11:2–3). Only Jews (Messianic or non-Messianic) concerned with Gentiles would have had such reactions. Therefore my rendering, "**of the Circumcision faction**." For more on them see 15:1&N, Ga 2:12cN, Ti 1:10N.

CHAPTER 11

2 Those of the Circumcision faction. See 10:45N.

8 Nothing unclean or *treif* has ever entered my mouth (as at 10:12–14&N). Kefa's hearers, the strict Circumcision faction, "zealots for the *Torah*" (21:20), are no more *Torah*-observant than Kefa himself. God chose Kefa as his instrument to bring Yeshua to the Gentiles precisely because he was an observant Jew; in this way all would know that God's hand was in it. Had a less *Torah*-true Jew seen the vision, it would have been no less of God, but observant Jews might have dismissed him as being self-serving and antinomian, as such people later regarded Sha'ul (for different reasons; 21:21, Ro 3:8).

18 The observant Jews in the Messianic Community were amazed that Gentiles could become part of God's people, part of the Body of the Messiah, without first becoming Jews. But today the situation is exactly the opposite: many Gentile Christians are amazed at a movement of Messianic Jews that claims Jews can accept the Jewish Messiah, Yeshua, without taking on the lifestyle of Gentiles. The more things change, the more they stay the same! In both cases it is the expectations of the "in-group" that God overturns. See 1:1N, 15:1N.

Do *t'shuvah*. For some American Jews this expression is "Jewish English" (see Section IV of the Introduction to the *JNT*); its underlying meaning is "repent," although some use it to mean "return to Orthodox Judaism" (which, of course, is not its sense here). Like the phrase, "do penance," it should be understood as involving a genuine inner change of heart and attitude and not merely as an outward act; see Mt 3:2N.

19–21 We have seen the Gentile Cornelius and his friends come to faith. Here we see a people-movement among Gentiles in a large city, Antioch.

19 The persecution that had arisen over Stephen. See 8:1–4&NN.

20–23 The Lord Yeshua. An examination of the evangelistic contexts of the book of Acts shows that to Gentiles Yeshua was not usually proclaimed as Messiah, because the concept of "Messiah" (Mt 1:1N) was meaningful only to Jews (2:31, 36, 38; 3:18, 20; 4:10; 5:42; 8:5, 12; 9:22, 34; 17:3; 18:5, 28; 24:24; 26:23) or to Gentiles who knew Judaism well (10:36). Rather, he was announced to Gentiles as Lord, an authoritative figure who is the final judge and through whom, if they have faith, come forgiveness and incorporation into God's people (here; 13:12, 48–49; 14:3; 15:35–36; 16:14–15, 31–32; 17:24; 19:10, 24). Later, after they had been taught about Yeshua's role as the Jewish king of the Jewish nation to whom they had joined themselves by their trust (Ro 11:17–24&NN), they could be expected to understand communications about him as the Messiah (15:26, 20:21).

26 "Messianic," or "Messianics," Greek *Christianoi*, which could also be rendered, "Messiah people" or, as in other translations, "Christians." I think the name "*Christianoi*" was applied to Gentile believers by Gentile nonbelievers. Why? Because Jewish believers would have designated their Gentile brothers in faith by the same term they used for themselves, "people belonging to the Way" (see 9:2&N); while the Jewish nonbelievers of Antioch wouldn't have thought enough about Gentile believers in Yeshua to have given them a special name. Probably the Gentiles of Antioch kept hearing about *Christos* ("Christ"); and being unacquainted with the Jewish notion of "Messiah" (see vv. 20–23N, Mt 1:1N), they designated Yeshua's followers by what they supposed was their leader's name. In all likelihood the term was deprecatory, like "Moonies" in referring to the disciples of Sun Myung Moon. But in time Jewish and Gentile believers in Yeshua learned to bear proudly the name that began as an epithet (1 Ke 4:16&N; see also 26:28&N). The name nonbelieving Jews gave to Jewish believers was "*Natzratim*" or "*Notzrim*" ("Nazarenes"), that is, followers of the man from *Natzeret* ("Nazareth"); the word in modern Hebrew for "Christians" remains "*Notzrim*" (see 24:5&N, Mt 2:23&N).

Should a Jew who has put his trust in Yeshua as the Messiah call himself a Christian today? Most people, Jews and Christians alike, would answer in the affirmative on the ground that the very definition of "Christian" is "one who believes in Jesus Christ," regardless of whether his family background is Jewish, Christian, Moslem, pagan or something else. But many Jewish believers disagree; in fact, the relatively small community of Jews who believe in Yeshua is split into two camps, the Messianic Jews (I use this term here in a narrower sense than usual) and the Hebrew Christians.

A Hebrew Christian might say, "I call myself a Christian because I have come to believe in Jesus Christ, my Savior and my Lord; and my first loyalty must be to him and to his Church, the community of the saved. Nevertheless, I was born a Jew and will die a Jew, so I speak of myself as not just a Christian but as a Hebrew Christian, in order to testify to all, nonbelieving Jews and Gentile Christians alike, that I continue to identify with my Jewish brothers, including those who do not share my faith."

A Messianic Jew might say, "I call myself Messianic for the same reason that my Hebrew Christian friend calls himself Christian, namely, to make it clear that I follow Yeshua the Messiah, my Savior and my Lord, and identify with his Body, the Messianic Community, which he calls the Church. I prefer the word 'Messianic' because it comes from 'Messiah,' which has meaning to Jews; whereas the words 'Christ' and 'Christian' are not only alien to Jewish culture and religion but represent the banner under which the Jewish people experienced centuries of discrimination, persecution and murder. And although 'Hebrew' may have had an elegant ring in the nineteenth century, today it sounds quaint — no Jew today calls himself a 'Hebrew,' and neither do I."

To this the Hebrew Christian could reply, "You're fooling yourself. You think your 'Messianic' terminology will win Jews to Jesus, but they will simply think you are devious. As soon as they find out that your 'Yeshua' is Jesus and that to be 'Messianic' is to be a Christian, they will drop you like a hot potato. Meanwhile, you are alienating your Gentile Christian brothers in the Lord, who think you are a coward and not straightforwardly standing up for Christ and the Gospel."

And the Messianic Jew might return, "Untrue! I tell one and all that I am part of the Messiah's Body, consisting of all believers in Yeshua, Jewish and Gentile. In fact, it is precisely because I am zealous for the Gospel that I will not make words with a negative valence for Jews a barrier to their accepting its truth. Further, if I say I am a Christian they will, first, think I have conformed myself to the image of Gentile Christians they have in their head, and, second, think I have abandoned Judaism and the Jewish people. But I have done neither: accepting Yeshua the Jewish Messiah is the most Jewish thing a Jew can do, and I am committed to expressing my love for him in a Jewish way, within the framework of Judaism — except where Judaism specifically takes a stand against him and against the New Testament."

The Hebrew Christian: "But if you say you have not abandoned Judaism, do you accept the authority of the rabbis, their interpretation of Jewish law? A Christian is free from the details of Judaism as the rabbis expound it. If you identify with Judaism and not with Christianity you are abandoning Christ, and your professed faith is empty."

The Messianic Jew: "No, I identify with Judaism and the *Torah*, but not as interpreted by rabbis who do not accept Yeshua as the Messiah, even though I think much that they have said is true and should be evaluated on its merits, not discarded *en bloc*. What I uphold is the *Torah* as expounded by Yeshua the Messiah (see Mt 5:17–20&NN, 1C 9:21&N, Ga 6:2&N)."

To which the Hebrew Christian would reply that he too accepts the Law of Christ as authoritative. And so the discussion would go on; for more see my book *Messianic Jewish Manifesto*.

Though the single word "Christian" is too fragile a peg on which to hang a debate between competing ideologies, each of which can rightly claim to bring out elements of truth, it should not be surprising that the word serves exactly that function — names and slogans have always focussed and energized controversies.

27 **Prophets** among the believers are mentioned here and at 13:1, 15:32 and 21:9–10, as well as in 1C 12:28–29, 14:29–37; Ep 4:11; and possibly 2 Ke 3:2. Non-Messianic Jews maintained then and maintain still that prophecy ceased in Israel soon after the Return from Babylon. For example, 1 Maccabees 9:27 says, "So there was terrible distress in Israel; there had not been anything like it since the time prophets stopped appearing among them." (Compare 1 Maccabees 4:46, 14:41; Josephus, *Against Apion* 1:8). But according to the New Testament, prophecy recommenced with Yochanan the Immerser (Mt 11:9).

The title, "prophet," is applied frequently to Yeshua (3:22–23&N, 7:37; Mt 21:11; Lk 24:19; Yn 7:40, 9:17). In the Messianic Community prophets ranked after emissaries (1C 12:28, Ep 4:11). Since Yeshua promised his *talmidim* that the Holy Spirit "will…

announce to you the events of the future" (Yn 16:13), all believers are urged to seek the gift of prophecy (1C 14:39), which is promised to everyone (2:17–18, fulfilling Joel 3:1–2(2:28–29)). Prophecy may mean either prediction of things to come, as in this passage, or, more often, clearly and boldly speaking forth the word God wants spoken (see 1C 12:8–10N).

28 **It took place while Claudius was** still **Emperor**, that is, quickly. Claudius ruled the Roman Empire from 41 to 54 C.E.; see 18:2&N.

CHAPTER 12

1 **King Herod** Agrippa I (11 B.C.E.–44 C.E.), ruler of all Israel, 41–44 C.E.; grandson of Herod the Great (Mt 2:1) through a son (Aristobulus) not mentioned in the New Testament; father of Herod Agrippa II (25:13–26:32). On his death, see vv. 22–23.

2 **Ya'akov, Yochanan's brother** (Mt 4:21), the first of the twelve emissaries to die *'al kiddush-HaShem* (see 7:59–60&N on Stephen's martyrdom). According to tradition, of the twelve emissaries only Yochanan survived to die a natural death.

3 **Judeans**. See Yn 1:19N. Herod Agrippa's consistent policy was to conciliate the majority.

Days of *Matzah*. See Mt 26:17N.

4 ***Pesach***, Greek *pascha*. It appears 29 times in the New Testament, but for some inexplicable reason KJV here translates it "Easter" — here alone! Of course the reference is to Passover (see Mt 26:2N).

Herod did not want to arouse public opinion against himself by trying a leader of a significant Jewish minority community during the holy season.

5 A five-point teaching on **prayer**: Prayer must be (1) **intense**, not casual; (2) ongoing (**was being made**; the Greek verb tense implies continuing activity); (3) **to God** — in genuine contact with the living God (possible only through Yeshua, Yn 14:6), not with empty repetition (Mt 6:7) and not in unbelief (MJ 11:6); (4) specific, not vague (**on his behalf**); "you don't receive because you don't ask" (Ya 4:2–3); and (5) communal (**by the Messianic community**) — the believer is not called to an isolated life; even his private prayers should be not self-centered but reflective of his membership in the Body of the Messiah.

12 **The house of Miryam**. Believers met in each other's homes for prayer, worship and fellowship arising from their common trust in Yeshua (2:46, 8:3). New-Testament-based prayer groups, home Bible studies and house congregations reflect this emphasis today. Within Judaism the *chavurah* (friendship-group) movement similarly fosters awareness of one another.

Yochanan (surnamed Mark). According to Co 4:10 he was a cousin of Bar-Nabba (see 4:36–37; 13:5, 13; 15:37–39). A marginal note in an early manuscript identifies him with Mark, author of the second Gospel, and Lucius from Cyrene (13:1) with Luke himself; and this is the prevailing opinion among scholars.

15 **"You're out of your mind!" they said to her.** God is real, and he answers prayer. Many of us can grasp this concept intellectually, but when the evidence is knocking at the door we find it hard to believe.

It is his guardian **angel.** The concept of guardian or ministering angels is also found at Mt 18:10, but it is not exclusively a New Testament idea. "For he will give his angels charge over you, to keep you in all your ways" (Psalm 91:11). And from the Talmud (Soncino Edition):

> "On entering a bathroom one should say: 'Be honored, you honored and holy ones who minister to the Most High.... Wait for me until I enter, take care of my needs and return to you.'"(B'rakhot 60b)

A note in the Soncino English edition explains that these words are addressed to the angels thought of as accompanying a man to the privy, which was regarded as the haunt of evil spirits. Also from the Talmud:

> "'...I, Daniel, alone saw the vision, for the men with me did not see the vision; instead a great quaking fell upon them....' (Daniel 10:7).... Since they did not see it, why were they terrified? Because, although they themselves saw nothing, their guardian angel did see it. Rabina said, 'This proves that when a person is terrified and doesn't know why, it is because his guardian angel has seen something, even though he hasn't.'"(Sanhedrin 94a)

In the Soncino edition one note explains that according to the Talmud (Chagigah 16a), everyone has a guardian angel accompanying him. Another note speculates that there might be a connection between this "guardian spirit" and the modern idea of the "subconscious mind."

17 **Ya'akov** (James). On the name itself see Mt 4:21N. This Ya'akov is called the "brother" of Yeshua at Mt 13:55, Mk 6:33; see also Mt 1:25N. Not a believer during the Messiah's earthly ministry (Yn 7:3–8&N), he came to faith later, perhaps as a result of seeing Yeshua resurrected (1C 15:7). He was among the 120 present in the "upstairs room" (1:14). He became leader of the Messianic Jews of Yerushalayim (15:13, 21:18; Ga 2:9, 12). Tradition considers him the author of the New Testament book of Ya'akov (Ya 1:1). Apparently Kefa had already turned over the leadership in Yerushalayim to Ya'akov and was himself establishing congregations elsewhere (8:14, 9:32–11:18; 1C 1:12, 9:5).

22–23 The description here of Herod Agrippa's death is consistent, though not identical, with that of Josephus:

> "Agrippa came to Caesarea, where there was a festival for him. On the second day he put on a garment made entirely of silver and came into the theater early in the morning, at which time the silver of his garment reflecting the sun's rays shone so resplendently as to spread a horror on those gazing at him. Presently his flatterers exclaimed that he was a god, adding, 'Be merciful to us; for

> although till now we have reverenced you only as a man, henceforth we will regard you as superior to mortal nature.' But the king neither rebuked them nor rejected their impious flattery. However, as he looked up, he saw an owl and immediately understood that this bird was the messenger of ill tidings. Suddenly and violently a severe pain arose in his stomach. Therefore he looked at his friends and said, 'I, whom you call a god, am commanded now to leave this life; while Providence thus reproves the lying words you just now said to me.' After five days, exhausted by the stomach pain, he died, aged fifty-three." (Adapted from *Antiquities of the Jews* 19:8:2)

The report is similar enough to confirm the reliability of the New Testament, yet different enough to show that the descriptions are independent of each other.

24 Another growth report; see 2:41N.

CHAPTER 13

1–4 The passage demonstrates the central importance for believers of congregations in mediating God's will to individuals; likewise 14:26–28&NN, 15:40&N.

1 **Menachem (who had been brought up with Herod the governor)**. Josephus may have been referring to him when he wrote,

> "There was one of these Essenes whose name was Menachem, of whom it was said that not only did he conduct his life excellently, but God had given him the ability to predict the future. This man once saw Herod when he was a child, going to school, and saluted him as king of the Jews. But Herod, either thinking that Menachem did not know him or that he was joking, reminded him that he was only a private person. Menachem smiled to himself, slapped him on the backside with his hand and said, 'However that may be, you will be king. You will begin your reign happily, because God finds you worthy of it. But remember the blows Menachem gave you; they are a sign that your fortune will change. Now it will be most reasonable for you to love justice towards men, piety towards God, and clemency towards your subjects. But I also know what your overall conduct will be, that you won't behave this way. You will outdo everyone in happiness and obtain an everlasting reputation, but you will forget piety and righteousness. And these crimes will not be hidden from God at the end of your life; you will find out then that he will remember them and punish you for them.'"(*Antiquities of the Jews* 15:10:5)

Compare 12:22–23&N.

4 Acts 13:4–14:26 describes the first of four trips by Sha'ul. The others are recounted at 15:40–18:22, 18:23–21:15 and 27:1–28:16.

5 **They began proclaiming the word of God in the synagogues** (literally, "...in the assemblies (Greek *sunagôgais*) of the Jews"; the English word "synagogues" already implies "of the Jews"); see also Ya 2:2&N.

Although Sha'ul was called to be Yeshua's emissary to the Gentiles (9:15, 22:21; Ro 15:13; Ga 1:16, 2:7–9; Ep 3:8), he invariably made it his practice throughout his life to bring the Good News of Yeshua the Messiah to the Jews first, wherever there were any (here; 13:14; 14:1; 16:13; 17:1–2, 10, 17; 18:4; 19:8; 28:17 — ten instances). This accords both with his teaching (Ro 1:16&N) and his heart's longing that Israel should be saved (Ro 9:1–5, 10:1, 11:26). With both argument and practice he thus refutes Two-Covenant theology, which asserts that Jews can be saved without trusting in Yeshua (Yn 14:6N). Unfortunately, few Gentile Christians have seen fit to obey Sha'ul's exhortation to be imitators of him (1C 11:1) in this area. Instead, if they evangelize at all, they usually reach out to everyone but the Jews, who are often the last to have the Gospel properly explained to them, so that they are left to rely on hearsay and half-truths, or, worse, are presented with error and evil in the name of the Gospel.

Yochanan (Mark). The name **Mark** is not in the text but is known from 12:25.

6–8 No one is quite sure what is the connection between the names **Bar-Yeshua** ("son of Yeshua"), **Elymas** (possibly related to Hebrew *chalom*, "dream," or *'alim*, "wise"), and the fact that he was a **sorcerer**.

9 **Sha'ul, also known as Paul**. In this verse we are given **Sha'ul**'s Roman name, and from this point on (except at 22:7, 13 and 26:14, where he recounts the incident that led him to faith) the New Testament always speaks of him as **Paul** (Greek *Pavlos*), undoubtedly because his ministry was primarily among Gentiles. The name "**Paul**" appears 132 times in Acts 13–28, 30 times in his 13 letters and once at 2 Ke 3:15. However, except in the present verse, the *JNT* uses "**Sha'ul**" for all of them, to highlight the Jewishness of the New Testament and its major figures. I choose by this means to remind the reader that **Sha'ul/Paul** remained a Jew all his life, indeed, an observant Jew (16:3, 17:2, 18:18, 20:16, 21:23–27, 25:8, 28:17; and see 21:21N), even a Pharisee (23:6, Pp 3:5), while nevertheless sparing no effort to bring to Gentiles the Gospel of Yeshua the Messiah.

Some object to my decision on the ground that at this point, they claim, Sha'ul gave up his old Jewish name and took on a new Christian name, which he kept for the rest of his life in order to identify himself henceforth as no longer a Jew but a Christian. But, as explained above, he did no such thing. Rather, Sha'ul, like "Yochanan surnamed Mark" (12:12, 25), like "Hadassah, that is, Esther" (Esther 2:7), and like many Jews today in the Diaspora, had two names all his life — a Hebrew name and a name in the local language. Lutheran commentator R. C. H. Lenski is correct in writing (*ad loc.*), "The child had both names from infancy." But it does not necessarily follow that the names were used as suggested in his next sentence, "When his father called him he shouted, 'Saul, Saul!' but when the Greek boys with whom he played called him they shouted, 'Paul, Paul!'"

I see no theological or spiritual significance in the New Testament's calling Sha'ul "Paul" from this verse onward. There is only the practical value, at the time the New Testament was written, of calling the emissary to the Gentiles by the name he used with them. For the *JNT*, with its very different audience and purpose, this value is, in my opinion, outweighed by the value of reinforcing the reader's perception of Sha'ul's

Jewishness. See Section V of the Introduction to the *JNT* on "Translation Issues." Also see Lk 23:33N and Ac 12:4N for two instances where the KJV, with far less reason or logic, renders a Greek name by an English name completely unrelated to it.

13 Yochanan left them. See 15:39N.

15 After the reading from the *Torah* and from the Prophets. Then as now, on *Shabbat* there was added to the liturgy a reading from the *Torah* (the Pentateuch) and a *haftarah* ("conclusion"), which consisted of a reading from the *N'vi'im* (Prophets) or *K'tuvim* (Writings). Following this would be a *drashah* (literally, "investigation," that is, a teaching or sermon), depending on who was available to teach or preach. Hospitality often dictated offering this honor to a visitor, if he was competent. Compare Lk 4:16–17&N.

16–46 Sha'ul's sermon in the synagogue of Pisidian Antioch illustrates how he went about presenting the Gospel to Jews. As with Stephen's speech (7:2–53), the appeal is through the history of God's dealings with the people of Israel. Yeshua is presented as the "Son of David"; a term everyone understood to mean the Messiah (see Mt 1:1N).

16 God-fearers. See 10:2N. Besides Sha'ul's conviction that it was right to present the Gospel first to Jews (v. 5N), he also knew that it was in the synagogues where he would find the Gentiles most likely to be responsive, since "proselytes of the gate" were already interested in the one true God. One aspect of communicating the Gospel consists in determining which people are likely to respond favorably to it. Sha'ul wasted little time trying to convince those who closed themselves off but invested much time in reaching persons open to it. In this regard the Jewish community is no different from Gentile communities: there is a full spectrum of receptiveness, from persons implacably opposed to those whose hearts are waiting and aching for God's Good News.

17 The God of this people Israel chose our fathers. While it is possible that some Jews, like some Christians, become proud of being "chosen," I think many find it embarrassing and wish, like Tevye in "Fiddler on the Roof," that God "would choose somebody else, for a change." But only if I take chosenness to imply superiority do I become either embarrassed or proud. The right attitude, the one taken by Sha'ul and by the writers of the *Tanakh*, is that Israel's election by God is not predicated on any special quality in Israel but entirely on God's "grace," rightly defined as "undeserved favor." Being aware that his favor is undeserved should make us humble without embarrassing us (see 20:18–19N on "humility").

> "*Adonai* did not set his love upon you or choose you because you were more numerous than any people, for you were the fewest of all peoples; but rather because *Adonai* loved you, and because he wanted to keep the oath he had sworn to your fathers." (Deuteronomy 7:7–8)

So long as God's act of choosing Israel is seen as a means whereby God glorified himself by creating opportunities to express his love, it causes neither conceit nor discomfiture. When our attention is diverted from God to ourselves, then enter the sins of pride and embarrassment (a kind of pride in reverse). Sha'ul proceeds to state some of the ways in which God has expressed his love.

With a stretched-out arm. A phrase the *Tanakh* uses repeatedly to describe God's judgment on those who rebel against him and against his people Israel (Exodus 6:6; Deuteronomy 4:34, 5:15, 7:19, 9:29, 11:2; 1 Kings 8:42; 2 Kings 17:36; Jeremiah 32:21; Ezekiel 20:33–34; Psalm 136:11–12; 2 Chronicles 6:32).

18 Took care of them, or: "bore with them" — two different Greek words are found in the various manuscripts, reflecting two possible ways of understanding the Hebrew word "*nasa*" found in Deuteronomy 1:31, to which this verse alludes (see I. Howard Marshall's commentary, *ad loc.*).

20 450 years, consisting of 400 years in Egypt, 40 in the Wilderness and 10 until Joshua divided up the Land.

21–22 After forty years God removed him. The *Tanakh* does not state how long King Saul reigned. Josephus says 40 years in one place but 20 years in another (*Antiquities of the Jews* 6:14:9, 10:8:4), perhaps reflecting 1 Samuel 7:2. Another theory: the years of Samuel (v. 20) and Saul are brought together into one sum.

23 In keeping with his promise to raise up **from this man's** (King David's) **descendants a deliverer**. See 2 Samuel 7:12–13, 16; Isaiah 11:1 in the context of Isaiah 7–12; Jeremiah 23:5–6; Zechariah 3:8; Ezekiel 37:24 (in the context of Ezekiel 36–37); Amos 9:11–12; Psalms 89:4–5(3–4), 36–37(35–36), 132:11; Lk 1:32–33; Ro 1:4. The fifteenth blessing of the *'Amidah* prayer takes this promise as given:

> "Speedily cause the Branch [i.e., Offspring, Son] of David your servant to flourish. Exalt his horn [or: his ray; i.e., increase his glory] by your salvation, because we hope for your salvation all the day. Praised be you, *Adonai*, who causes the horn of salvation to flourish."

See Lk 2:11N on "deliverer" (Greek *sôtêr,* "savior," equivalent to Hebrew *moshia',* which is related to "*yeshu'ah*" ("salvation") used three times in the above prayer, and to the name Yeshua, Mt 1:21N).

24 Yochanan the Immerser. See Mt 3:1–17, 11:2–19, 14:1–12; Mk 1:2–11; Lk 3:1–22; Yn 1:6–8, 19–34; Ac 19:1–7; and notes to these passages.

27–29 See 2:22–23N, Mt 26:24N, Lk 24:25–27N.

33–34 Raising up Yeshua from death is explicitly meant in v. 34, but in v. 33 what is meant is **raising up Yeshua** to prominence. This took place at his immersion by Yochanan, when the voice from Heaven also quoted Psalm 2:7, "**You are my Son**" (Lk 3:22), and Yeshua began his public ministry as Savior of the world.

From the words, "**Today I have become your Father**," some of the early Messianic Jews, known as Adoptionists, developed the view that Yeshua was not God's son in any special way different from the rest of us until the day of his immersion, at which time he "became" the Son of God, so to speak, "by adoption." Adoptionism does not conflict with Yn 1:1, 14, which says that the eternal Word of God became flesh, because the Word could be eternal without having eternally been the Son. But it does conflict with Ro 1:3–4 and Co 1:15 (see notes there), from which one concludes that Yeshua's Sonship is eternal and not datable within history. On the Messianic significance of the title, "Son of God," see Mt 4:3N.

The holy and trustworthy things of David. See Mt 1:1N on "Son of David."

35 Sha'ul's argument is the same as Kefa's at 2:25–36; see note there.

38–39 Let it be known to you... is proclaimed to you... everyone who puts his trust. Sha'ul is polite and not coercive in his presentation of the Good News. He makes knowledge available and directs it to the individual but leaves him free to act or not act on the information. This remains the essence of ethical evangelism. See Lk 14:23&N, 2C 4:1–2&N.

Through this man, Yeshua, **forgiveness of sins is proclaimed to you.** Yeshua has authority to forgive sins, even though no one can forgive sins but God (Mk 2:5–12&N). Conclusion: Yeshua is divine. "Through him," that is, with him as the only available mediator (4:12, Yn 14:6, 1Ti 2:5&N).

That is,... Verse 39 clarifies why forgiveness of sins is important even for people who have the *Torah*. It summarizes Romans 7–8 and Messianic Jews 7–10 in a single sentence. The *Torah* provides a means of temporary atonement through repentance plus the Temple sacrifices (see the books of Romans and Messianic Jews), but it does not provide the permanent atonement or the power for right living which the individual needs. Yeshua and the Holy Spirit do this, and they are necessary for anyone who wishes to keep the *Torah* properly (Ro 4:25, 6:7, 10:4).

The things concerning which you could not be cleared by the *Torah* of Moshe. According to the Mishna, "There are thirty-six transgressions for which the *Torah* specifies the punishment of *karet*," that is, being "cut off" from Israel (K'ritot 1:1). For these the *Torah* provides no "clearing": no sacrifice or punishment named in the *Torah* provides atonement or restores fellowship. These transgressions include the prohibited sexual unions of Leviticus 18, blasphemy (Numbers 15:30), idolatry, necromancy (Leviticus 20:6), profaning *Shabbat* (Exodus 31:14), certain violations of ritual purity laws, eating *chametz* during *Pesach* and eating or working on *Yom-Kippur*.

The transgression must be committed "wantonly" to be subject to *karet*; if committed by mistake or in ignorance, a sin offering may be brought. In fact, according to the plain sense of Numbers 15:30, the key element in any unpardonable sin is acting "with a high hand"; and the New Testament is equally clear that the New Covenant provides no remedy for those who intentionally sin (see Ro 3:7–8, 6:1–2; MJ 6:4–6; and especially Ya 2:10–11N).

Karet means excision from the Jewish people (Leviticus 18:29 and the verses cited above); the Talmud explains it more specifically as premature death (Mo'ed Katan 28a). Regardless of its exact meaning, *karet* is regarded as a punishment administered directly by God; no human court determines it. But according to the Talmud,

> "Rabbi Akiva says that if those subject to the punishment of *karet* repent, the Heavenly *beit-din* [court] grants them remission." (Makkot 13b)

However, this is not specified in the Written *Torah*; and I speculate that Rabbi Akiva, who lived in the second century C.E., was developing defensive theology (3:22–23N) against Sha'ul's teachings.

42–44 The initial effect of Sha'ul's sermon was to arouse interest, not opposition. He did not alienate his Jewish hearers by denouncing them as opposing God or following manmade religion, as some zealous but mistaken Christian evangelists do today; rather, he urged those who in the past had held **fast to the love and kindness of God** to **continue** doing so. Doing so, of course, then as well as now, implied accepting the Good News of Yeshua the Messiah.

45 What upset the unbelieving Jews? The vast **crowds** of Gentiles, "nearly the whole city" (v. 44). The opposition was initially not to the content of the Gospel but to the fact that outsiders were attracted to it.

The phrase, "**who had not believed**," is absent from the Greek text; I have added it in order to clarify which Jews are meant, as explained in 9:22–23N. The addition is especially justified here because v. 43 speaks of Jews who *did* believe Sha'ul's message.

46 There is no point in arguing against blasphemous passion. This was the first of Sha'ul's several experiences, while traveling on his four journeys, of partial or total rejection by the synagogue and the first time he turned to Gentiles apart from the Jews. On the word "***Goyim***" see Mt 5:47N.

47 Isaiah 49:6, quoted here, is, essentially, the Great Commission (see Mt 28:19–20&N), as given to the Jewish people. The phrase "light for the *Goyim*" (also found at Isaiah 42:6) recalls Isaiah 60:1–3:

> "Arise, shine, for your light has come, and the glory of *Adonai* has risen upon you.... And *Goyim* will walk in your light...."

The "light" who "has come" is Yeshua, the "light of the world" (Yn 8:12&N, which gives other references). Only when the Jewish people shine forth this light can we be the **light for the *Goyim*** that we are supposed to be.

50–52 That a minority co-opts influential members of the majority to accomplish its purpose is neither unusual nor the point. Rather, we observe that divisions fade away when unbelievers unite to persecute God's people (v. 50). Fortunately, persecution produces no lasting effects. The Gospel continues to spread (v. 51), and the believers are **filled with joy and with the *Ruach HaKodesh*** (v. 52). This is not surprising, since even the gates of Sh'ol cannot overcome the Messianic Community (Mt 16:18). History shows that persecution strengthens believers' resolve and increases their joy in the Holy Spirit.

CHAPTER 14

1–7 The same thing happened in Iconium as in Pisidian Antioch (see 13:46N); it became a pattern. Sha'ul and Bar-Nabba preach in the synagogue, winning Jews and Gentiles to Yeshua. This brings about opposition from unbelieving Jews, who stir up the unbelieving Gentiles. So long as the challenge is nonviolent, Sha'ul and Bar-Nabba stay on to meet it, and the Holy Spirit confirms the Word with signs following (v. 3, Mk 16:20). They show themselves brave (v. 3), prudent (vv. 5–6) and singleminded in spreading the Good News (v. 7); while the division among the people of the city proves good for the Gospel (v. 4, Yn 7:43N).

8–18 A new situation: how to preach to thoroughgoing pagans, Gentiles who are in no sense "God-fearers" (10:2&N)? They acknowledge the miracle of vv. 8–10 but attribute it neither to God, of whom they know nothing, nor to the Adversary, Satan, as did some *P'rushim* with Yeshua (Mt 12:24), but to false gods. Sha'ul's solution is (1) to identify God as the source of blessings they have experienced, (2) to point out that for this reason he is to be worshipped, and (3) to note the passing of the age in which the Gentiles were free to walk in their own ways (see Micah 4:5), implying that now they too must turn to God. Compare 17:22b–31&N.

14 Tore their clothes. See Mt 26:65&N.

15 Men! Why are you doing this? We're just men, human like you! Compare 3:12.
Turn from these worthless, powerless **things** which create nothing **to the living God who made heaven and earth and the sea and everything in them**, who created and has power over everything. See 4:24N.

19–20 It is not clear whether the **unbelieving Jews** (see 9:22–23N) in fact stoned Sha'ul to death, so that he actually arose from the dead, or only thought he was dead — in which case there is still an implied miracle of healing, for someone apparently dead would not normally be in condition to walk back to town.
Why did he go back? To prove that he could not be intimidated. The next day he did indeed leave, but on his own terms. Compare his similar behavior at 16:35–40.

21–23 Sha'ul's "follow-up work": (1) strengthening the new disciples, spiritually; (2) urging them to use that strength to hold fast to the faith; (3) giving fair warning of what to expect — troubles but also the Kingdom of God (see Mt 3:2N), so that it's all worth it. Finally, he (4) appointed **elders** (leaders; see 1 Ti 3:1–7&NN, 1 Ke 5:1–4&NN) to guide the young congregations; in order to do this he and Bar-Nabba retraced their steps.

26–27 Luke carefully ties together the end of the journey with its beginning at 13:1–4. Note the model of order for responsible persons entrusted with tasks by a local congregation: (1) they are prompt, (2) they report to the congregation the details of what happened (in this case they also take on themselves the responsibility of assembling the congregation), (3) they give God the glory for it, and (4) they interpret the significance of what happened, emphasizing what is most important — in this case, that **God… had opened**

a door of faith to the Gentiles — thus building understanding and therefore unity in pursuit of common goals.

28 Bar-Nabba and Sha'ul spent a year in Antioch (11:26), left (11:30), returned (12:25), left again (13:4) and have now again returned. They leave for the Jerusalem Conference (15:2) and return together (15:22), but they leave Antioch separately (15:36–40). Sha'ul returns once more and spends time there (18:22–23). See also Ga 2:11&N.

CHAPTER 15

1–29 Certain New Testament chapters are uniquely important for Messianic Jews because they bear directly on the central issue of Messianic Judaism, which is: What does it mean to be at the same time both Jewish and a believer in Yeshua, and how does one go about doing justice to both? This is one of those chapters, along with Acts 21; Romans 7, 9–11; Galatians 2–4; Ephesians 2; Messianic Jews 7–10; Ya'akov 2; and others.

1 **Some men… from Y'hudah** (Judea). Verse 24 tells us they were from the Messianic community in Yerushalayim but had not been authorized to be **teaching the brothers.** Unauthorized teachers are also discussed at Galatians 2:11ff.; it may have been the same situation, or earlier, or later (scholarly opinions differ), but in any case it was at least similar.

Came down. See Mt 20:17–19N on "going up to Yerushalayim."

You. The "you" are Gentiles who have come to faith in God and his Messiah Yeshua without becoming proselytes to Judaism. The question of whether Jewish believers should have their sons circumcised is not raised here at all, but it *is* raised at 21:21&N.

Unless you undergo *b'rit-milah* in the manner prescribed by Moshe. The condition named for salvation is actually shorthand for something far more comprehensive. These men from Y'hudah are insisting that Gentiles must become in every sense Jews. At v. 5 they make this clearer by adding explicitly that the Gentile believers should be directed "to observe the *Torah* of Moshe," by which they mean both the Written and Oral *Torah*.

This condition goes beyond the requirements for individual salvation set forth in the *Tanakh*, in Judaism or by the emissaries. The *Tanakh* says, and Kefa quotes it at 2:21, "Everyone who calls on the name of *Adonai* will be saved." Judaism teaches that to be saved Gentiles need only obey the seven Noachide laws (see v.20N). The New Testament books of Romans, Galatians and Ephesians have as a central issue the equality of Jews and Gentiles before God, insofar as salvation is concerned; they make it clear that observance of the *Torah*, as it applies to Jews, is not a condition for the salvation of a Gentile.

Thus the requirement that Gentiles convert to Judaism and the teaching behind this requirement constitute a serious threat to the Gospel. For if individuals not born into Jewish culture and society are each required to become Jews before God will recognize their faith in him, far fewer Gentiles will trouble themselves to accept the Gospel. The real issue is: can faith in God and his Messiah transcend Jewish culture? Can a Gentile become a Christian without also becoming a Jew?

It is one of the supreme ironies of life on this planet that the issue today has become precisely the opposite: can a Jew become a follower of Yeshua the Messiah without becoming a *Goy?* Much of the opposition within the Jewish Community to Jews' coming to trust in Yeshua takes it for granted that the answer is No. It is assumed that when a Jew accepts Yeshua he abandons his people, adopts a Gentile lifestyle and is lost to the Jewish community. While some Jews who became Christians have done exactly that, the very existence of the early Messianic Jewish communities proclaimed from the beginning that it did not have to be so. These communities lasted, some of them, at least until the fourth and fifth centuries of the Common Era, when Epiphanius wrote about them.

Why, in the past, did many Jewish believers, in practice, leave their people? Because in the fourth century, when Roman Emperor Constantine converted to Christianity and the Gentile-dominated Church gained political power, it began to require Jews who accepted Yeshua as the Messiah to give up all ties with Judaism, Jewish practices, Jewish friends and anything Jewish. During most of the last 1,500 years a Jewish believer in Yeshua had to take on Gentile religious and cultural ways, first, because the Jewish community excluded him, and second, because of Christendom's social pressure and distaste for Jewish ways. Concerning the latter, it is as if "men from Rome came down and began teaching the Jewish brothers, 'Unless you totally ignore your circumcision in the manner prescribed by Moshe, you cannot be saved!'"Much of the Church continues to insist on this view, unscriptural though it is, basing their opinion on isolated passages misinterpreted, particularly Ep 2:11–15, 1C 10:31 and Ga 3:28; see notes to these passages and the rest of Acts for further discussion. The correct conclusion is: a Jew who becomes Messianic remains a Jew, and a Gentile who becomes a Christian remains a Gentile.

Circumcision (Hebrew *milah*) antedates Moshe by more than 400 years. It is the sign of the covenant (*b'rit*) God unilaterally made with Avraham (Genesis 12:1–3, 13:14–17, 15:1–7, 17:1–19, 22:16–18, 26:2–5, 28:13–15, 31:13, 35:9–12). The instruction to Avraham to circumcise everyone in his household, and all male descendants when one week old ("on the eighth day") is found at Genesis 17:9–14 and confirmed to Moses at Leviticus 12:2–3. Circumcision has always been considered indispensable by virtually all Jews. When a male Gentile becomes a Jewish proselyte he must be circumcised.

It is not only that these believers from Judea wanted the Gentile believers circumcised, but they wanted it done in accordance with the Oral Law, in accordance with Jewish tradition. Three points support this understanding:

(1) Circumcision by itself is not enough for them; they want it done in this specific way, **in the manner prescribed by Moshe**.

(2) The written *Torah*, the Pentateuch, specifies hardly anything about the "**manner**" in which Jewish circumcision is to be done.

(3) The Oral *Torah* was also understood to have been given by God to Moshe on Mount Sinai at the same time as the Written Torah (see 6:13N); and it *does* specify the "**manner**" in which Jewish circumcision is to be done.

Many Near Eastern peoples practiced circumcision; that is not the point. Within Judaism circumcision is done in a certain way, with a certain ceremony; only then is it a *b'rit-milah* ("covenant of circumcision"). Even a Jew who has been circumcised in some other way — for example, as is common today, in a hospital by a doctor before the eighth day — is required by *halakhah* to undergo symbolic circumcision in which a drop of blood must be drawn. The **manner prescribed by Moshe** was codified in the Mishna some 170 years later than the events described here and is contained largely in these sections: Shabbat 9:3, 18:3, 19:1–6; Pesachim 3:7; Megillah 2:4; N'darim 3:11; Arakhin 2:2; K'ritot 1:1 and N'ga'im 7:5. See also Yn 7:22–23&N and Ac 16:1–3&NN.

One final point: these **men from Y'hudah** seem to have been unaware that Cornelius and his friends had been received into the Messianic Community without being circumcised (10:1–11:18); or they were aware of it but opposed (see 10:45N), and unwilling to accept this *fait accompli*, so that they decided on their own to do something to limit the influx of Gentiles.

2 **Discord and dispute with Sha'ul and Bar-Nabba** arose because their mission in life was to bring the Gospel to as many Gentiles as possible, and they were altogether unwilling to have needless barriers put in their way.

Some non-Messianic Jews side with the "men from Y'hudah" in this matter. They take the view that Christianity has been made an "easy" religion that requires "mere faith," whereas Judaism is a meaty and tough religion that demands action. But the objection misses the point altogether. The point is, what has God required? God has required Jews to be Jews, and he has made Gentiles Gentiles, but he has required both Jews and Gentiles to trust him, obey him and follow him through his Messiah Yeshua. Such obedience and trust and day-by-day following are not easy; such faith is not "mere." It too demands action (Mt 3:8, Ep 2:10, Ya 2:19–20). Gentiles entering the New Covenant have plenty to do without also having to convert to Judaism.

Sh'eilah. See Mt 22:23N.

The emissaries and the elders up in Yerushalayim. Jerusalem was not only the source of Messianic faith but its center, for the emissaries were still there (8:1&N), and other experienced elders were there too. Since Sha'ul and Bar-Nabba had come from there (4:36, 9:26–30, 12:25), they would be subject to Jerusalem's jurisdiction and would accept their verdict.

5 **Some of those who had come to trust were from the party of the *P'rushim*** (on which see Mt 3:7&N). Many Jews are offended at the commonly held Christian view of the Pharisees as invariably stubborn and prideful hypocrites who substituted legalism and outward appearances for true worship and service to the living God. But there were in fact some Pharisees who believed in Yeshua. They were not "former Pharisees" but Messianic Jewish Pharisees, just like Sha'ul (23:6, Pp 3:5).

"But," some may object, "these *P'rushim* were wrong. Their Judaizing view was roundly defeated." Yes, but they were still believers; not every believer is right about everything! Further, the text does not tell us that all the Pharisees who were believers took this position; but, on the contrary, it does tell us that Sha'ul, who was a Pharisee, took the opposite stand.

7 Kefa recalls the incidents of 10:1–11:18. Though Sha'ul is known as the emissary to the Gentiles (22:21, Ro 11:13, Ga 2:8), it was through Kefa that the Gentiles — Cornelius and his household — first heard the Gospel and received the Holy Spirit.

8 **God, who knows the heart** (like Yeshua at Yn 2:25). Kefa emphasizes that heart-

religion (meaning not merely outward show but genuine inner turning to God) is true religion. The *Tanakh* too puts more emphasis on "circumcised hearts" than on literal circumcision (see references in 7:51N).

9 Kefa's version of the Gospel is the same as Sha'ul's: cleansing of the heart by trust is the one and only condition for salvation.

10 **A yoke… which neither our fathers nor we have had the strength to bear**. Much Christian teaching contrasts the supposedly onerous and oppressive "yoke of the Law" with the words of Yeshua, "My yoke is easy, and my burden is light" (Mt 11:30&N). This is a mistake, on two counts. First, observant and knowledgable Jews do not consider the *Torah* a burden but a joy. If a person regards something as pleasant, you will not be able to convince him that it is unpleasant! (An entirely different question: how many observant and knowledgeable non-Messianic Jews actually experience and exhibit God's joy?) Second, and much more importantly here, such teaching misidentifies the yoke which Kefa says has proved so unbearable.

The term "yoke" in this context is certainly Jewish enough. For example, the Mishna explains with these words why Deuteronomy 6:4–9 precedes Deuteronomy 11:13–21 in the *Sh'ma Israel* portion of the synagogue liturgy:

> "For what reason does the [paragraph beginning with the word] '*Sh'ma*' precede the [paragraph beginning with] '*V'hayah im shamoa*'? So that one should first accept upon oneself the yoke of the Kingdom of Heaven, and [only] after that accept upon oneself the yoke of the *mitzvot*." (B'rakhot 2:2; the phrase "yoke of the *mitzvot*" also occurs in Sifra 57b).

In this *mishna* the term "yoke" does not imply an oppressive burden any more than Yeshua's yoke does. Accepting the "yoke of the Kingdom of Heaven" means acknowledging God's sovereignty and his right to direct our lives. Once one acknowledges his right to direct our lives, it is obvious that if he has given commandments we should obey them. The same is true of Yeshua, who put it this way (Yn 14:15): "If you love me" (compare the first paragraph of the *Sh'ma*), "you will keep my commands" (compare the second).

So then, if the "yoke of the commandments" is not burdensome, what is Kefa talking about? He is speaking here of the detailed mechanical rule-keeping, regardless of heart attitude, that some (but not all!) *P'rushim*, including, apparently, the ones mentioned in v. 5, held to be the essence of Judaism. This was not the "yoke of the *mitzvot*" prescribed by God, but a yoke of legalism prescribed by men! The yoke of legalism is indeed unbearable, but the yoke of the *mitzvot* has always required, first of all (Mk 12:28–34), love of God and neighbor; and it now implies love toward Yeshua the Messiah. But love can *never* be legalistic! Sha'ul too spoke of legalism as a "yoke of slavery" (Ga 5:1&N); see his detailed exposition of the subject in Romans 1–11, and see Ga 2:16bN.

11 This verse sums up Kefa's speech: equality of Jews and Gentiles before God. The question arises, did he fail to live up to his principles in Galatia (Ga 2:11ff.)? If the

Galatian incident occurred before the Jerusalem Council (see v. 1N on "some men... from Y'hudah"), then Kefa's speech here reflects his change after Sha'ul's chastening. If the confrontation in Galatia occurred after the Jerusalem Council, it illustrates once more Kefa's weakness in applying his doctrine to his own personal life (compare Mk 14:27–31, 66–72).

13 Ya'akov, the half-brother of Yeshua the Messiah; see 12:17N.

14–18 Ya'akov's contribution is to point out that God decided in ages past not only to have Israel as his people, but also to take **from among the *Goyim* a people to bear his name** (v. 14), that is, to be identified with him and to honor him. The Greek word "*laos*" ("people") refers to a people elected by God. Although at 10:2 and 10:42 it refers to the Jewish people (see notes there), here the implication is that Gentiles do not have to become Jews in order to be included in the *laos*, because God is now doing something new for **the rest of mankind** (v. 17).

Kefa has described recent events; Ya'akov ties them to received prophecy **in the *Tanakh***. The quotation itself (vv. 16–18) is Amos 9:11–12, approximately as found in the Septuagint. The Masoretic text has, in lieu of our v. 17, "...so that they [Israel] may possess the remnant of Edom and of all the nations who are called by my name." Its Hebrew has "*yireshu... 'Edom*" ("possess... Edom"), while the Hebrew underlying the Septuagint Greek must be "*yidreshu... 'adam*" ("seek... mankind"). Concerning **I will rebuild the fallen tent of David**, see paragraph headed "coming on the clouds" in Mt 24:30N.

The complete fulfillment of Amos's prophecy will take place when the undivided realm of King David's time is restored. Meanwhile, this is a beginning.

19 My opinion. As chairman Ya'akov sums up the discussion and sets forth a plan.

The *Goyim* who are turning. Or: "the *Goyim*, while they are turning." Joseph Shulam expounds the second alternative thusly: Do not put obstacles in the way of the Gentiles while they are going through the process of turning from idolatry to God. Instead, let them use their spiritual energy in repentance. There will be plenty of opportunities later for them to absorb what Moses has to say (v. 21&N).

20 Abstain from things polluted by idols, defined in v. 29 as food sacrificed to false gods, especially meat (see 1C 8:4–13, 10:25).

Fornication, any form of sexual immorality. In the first-century pagan world (as, unfortunately, in the twentieth-century Western world) sexual unions outside of marriage were regarded very lightly, along with homosexual behavior, temple prostitution and other improper practices. In Judaism, on the other hand, these were abominations (Leviticus 18).

What is strangled, that is, meat from animals not slaughtered in a way that allows the blood to flow out. According to the Oral *Torah*, Jewish *sh'chitah* (slaughtering) requires that an animal be killed with a single knife stroke across the neck. The animal dies instantly, that is, humanely, and the blood drains quickly.

And blood. This could be either literal, referring to drinking animals' blood or failing to remove it from meat, or figurative, a metaphor for murder.

Here are three possible interpretations of what the Jerusalem Council required from

Gentile believers:

(1) The four prohibitions are a variant of the Noachide laws, presented in the Talmud as what God has required of all mankind since the days of Noah (i.e., before "Jew" and "Gentile" were defined):

> "Our rabbis taught, 'The sons of Noah were given seven commandments: practicing justice and abstaining from blasphemy, idolatry, adultery, bloodshed, robbery and eating flesh torn from a live animal.' Rabbi Chananyah ben-Gamli'el said, 'Also not to drink blood taken from a live animal.'"(Sanhedrin 56a)

There follows the scriptural basis for these laws in the form of a *midrash* on Genesis 2:16. Thus Judaism is not only a particularistic national religion specifying God's requirements for Jews but also a universalistic religion that states what God demands of non-Jews as well. Possibly the Jerusalem Council based its prohibitions on this tradition, although its four requirements neither state nor imply anything about practicing justice or eschewing robbery. On the other hand, the Council may have specified only minimum requirements, with the expectation that other moral attributes would be acquired later, possibly as a result of Gentiles' attending synagogue services and learning there the Jewish moral tradition (v. 21&N).

(2) Some manuscripts lack "from what is strangled." If this is the correct reading, the three remaining prohibitions correspond to the three acts a Jew must die rather than commit:

> "Rabbi Yochanan said in the name of Rabbi Shim'on ben-Y'hotzadak, 'By a majority vote it was decided in the upper chambers of the house of Nitza in Lud that in every law of the *Torah*, if a man is commanded, "Transgress, or you will be put to death," he may transgress in order to save his life — with these exceptions: idolatry, fornication and murder.'"(Sanhedrin 74a)

In other words, Gentile believers must avoid idolatry, fornication and murder because they are such serious moral transgressions that a Jew would die *'al kiddush-HaShem* (7:59–60N) rather than commit them.

(3) The requirements were only secondarily ethical; they were primarily practical social requirements for fellowship between Jewish and Gentile believers. A Gentile who did not immediately observe all four prohibitions would so offend his Jewish brothers in the faith that a spirit of community would never be able to develop.

Why don't today's Gentile Christians avoid eating blood-sausage and purchase only *kosher* meat?

(1) If the first interpretation is correct, then they should, because the prohibitions are understood, like the Noachide laws, as binding forever.

(2) If the second interpretation is the right one, then they needn't, since there never were food prohibitions in the New Testament, not in Acts 15 and not now.

(3) But if the third interpretation is correct, then these food laws were given only as practical guides to avoid disruption of fellowship between believing Jews and Gentiles in the social context of the first century. Today, when Messianic Jews are a

small minority in the Body of the Messiah, and few if any of them take umbrage at Gentiles' eating habits, the issue is irrelevant, and there is no need for Gentile Christians to obey a command never intended as eternal. However, in Israel, Gentile believers may find it convenient to keep at least a semblance of *kosher*, simply to fit in with a pattern widespread in the Land, or to be able to invite tradition-keeping Jews to dinner; and there are not a few Gentile Christians who do so.

21 This is a difficult verse. Of the following possible meanings a good case can be made for any of the first four, and I find it hard to choose between them.

(1) "Since Moses has disciples everywhere, that is, since there are Jews throughout the Roman Empire, their scruples are to be respected. This is why we are setting up these general rules." This corresponds to Sha'ul's injunction not to offend Jews (1C 10:31) and in particular reflects sensitivity to the concerns of the believing *P'rushim* (v. 5).

(2) "In every city Gentiles are responding to public proclamation of Judaism in the synagogues by becoming proselytes and 'God-fearers.' This will continue, and Judaism will lose nothing if some Gentiles, who never belonged to Moses anyway, are not required to become Jews." In other words, if the Circumcision faction is anxious that allowing Gentiles to become Christians without becoming Jews first will seriously reduce the number of Jewish proselytes — not to worry.

(3) "These Gentile Christians have been hearing the *Tanakh* in the synagogues but have chosen not to convert to Judaism. Why press them now and put this obstacle in their way (v. 19) precisely when they have made a heart commitment to follow the God of Israel and his Messiah Yeshua?" This is the other side of the coin of (2). The Gentile believers, who never belonged to Moses anyway, should be encouraged along the new path of faith and participation in God's people opened for them by Yeshua the Messiah.

(4) "Let Gentiles enter the Messianic Community without becoming Jews, and don't be troubled over it, because, no matter where these Gentile believers live, they will continue visiting the local synagogue and hearing what Judaism teaches about living a godly life." This acknowledges the value of non-Messianic Judaism in its ethical aspects. It is a "temporal" interpretation applicable to first-century conditions, not an "eternal" one, since Gentile Christians have long ceased to visit synagogues in significant numbers.

(5) A more extreme version of (4): "Don't worry about converting Gentile believers to Judaism, because as they keep going to the synagogues they will eventually become Jews anyway." But this contradicts other New Testament teachings.

(6) "Since Moses, that is, the *Torah*, is read in the synagogues every *Shabbat*, Gentile believers who attend synagogue will keep hearing the three or four points of v. 20 emphasized over and over and will keep being sensitized to them." I think v. 21 has a broader focus than this.

22 **Y'hudah Bar-Sabba**, perhaps related to Yosef Bar-Sabba (1:23&N).

Sila, referred to in English translations as Silas and Silvanus, was a prophet (v. 32, 11:27N) and a companion of Sha'ul on his second journey (15:40–18:22). Sha'ul mentions him in three of his letters; he is also mentioned at 1 Ke 5:12.

23 To: The brothers from among the Gentiles. Again, the decision does not affect Messianic Jews, who presumably were themselves faithfully keeping the Law (see v. 1N, paragraph on "you").

Throughout Antioch, Syria and Cilicia, the areas where Sha'ul had ministered (13:4–14:27) and taught the Gentiles they need not keep the Law of Moses as Jews observe it.

24 Without our authorization. See v. 1N on "some men... from Y'hudah." The men did not violate orders not to teach; rather, they had not been commissioned to teach at all. However, now that the issue has been resolved, if they or anyone else teaches circumcision and Jewish law-keeping for Gentile believers, they are culpable.

Upset you with their talk, unsettling your minds, or: "unsettling your consciences." These false teachers mis-trained the Gentiles' consciences, so that they felt guilty for not having been circumcised and for not keeping the details of the *Torah* as it applies to Jews. These Gentiles may have been made to feel guilty, but they have committed no sin for which they need forgiveness; by understanding that they have been misled their burden of guilt will depart.

There are today all kinds of sects and denominations that likewise create false guilt by nonscriptural teaching — for example, that attending a movie is a sin, or that observing one day rather than another as a day of worship is a sin, or that drinking even a small amount of alcoholic liquor is a sin for everyone. Fundamentalist Christianity gets a bad name from misguided teachers who lay a heavier yoke on believers than our Lord Yeshua has done (see v. 10N).

27 They will confirm in person what we are writing. A letter by itself could be a forgery; see 2 Th 2:2&N.

29 Shalom! Farewell. See Mt 10:12N.

39 Sha'ul was unwilling to be burdened by a companion he considered unreliable (13:13; see 12:12N), but Bar-Nabba was willing to put up with his nephew. While unreconciled **sharp disagreement** is a sin, differences of opinion, calling, personality and modes of working are not. Sha'ul and Bar-Nabba could have decided amicably to go their separate ways, each doing the Lord's work. After this, however, although we hear no more of Bar-Nabba's ministry, we do hear enough to conclude that Sha'ul eventually made up with both Bar-Nabba and Mark (1C 9:6, Co 4:10, 2Ti 4:11, Pm 24).

40 After being committed to the love and kindness of the Lord by the brothers. As before (13:1–4&N), Sha'ul and his partner were sent out by the local congregation; they did not merely decide on their own what to do. There are no "loners" in the New Testament. This commences Sha'ul's second journey, which ends at 18:22 (see 13:4N).

CHAPTER 16

1 **He was the son of a Jewish woman** and therefore a Jew, not a Gentile. Many Christians suppose he was a Gentile for at least these two reasons: (1) At Numbers 1:2 God calls for a census of Israel "by their families, by their fathers' houses." (2) The genealogies in the *Tanakh* always mention the men and only rarely the women.

Nevertheless, while legal responsibilities and entitlements are passed from father to son (see Mt 1:1N on "Son of" and "Son of Avraham," Mt 1:24–25N, Lk 3:23–38N), Jewish and non-Jewish descent are invariably traced through the mother, not the father. The child of a Jewish mother and a Gentile father is Jewish, the child of a Gentile mother and a Jewish father is Gentile. If a Gentile woman converts to Judaism, she is a Jew, and her subsequent children are likewise Jewish. The questions for us are, first, whether this was the case in the first century, and, second, even if it was, is it authorized biblically?

In his interesting book, *Who Was A Jew? — Rabbinic and Halakhic Perspectives on the Jewish Christian Schism* (Hoboken, New Jersey: Ktav Publishing House, Inc., 1985), Lawrence H. Schiffman has a chapter, "The Jew By Birth," in which he dates matrilineal Jewish descent to at least the second and probably the first century C.E., adducing as evidence Mishna Kiddushin 3:12, Tosefta Kiddushin 4:16, and Josephus. Among the supportive biblical passages is Ezra 10:2–3:

> "And Shechanyah… answered Ezra, 'We have trespassed against our God and taken foreign wives from the people living in the Land…. So, let us make a covenant with our God to put away all the wives and such as are born to them….'"

The phrase, "and such as are born to them," implies that the children of Jewish fathers and Gentile mothers are Gentiles and not Jews; otherwise they would not be excluded from the Jewish people in this covenant. Oved, the son of Bo'az and Ruth the Moabitess, is Jewish not because of his father Bo'az but because Ruth became Jewish first, not by some formal conversion process (there was none at the time) but with her confession, "Your people shall be my people and your God my God" (Ruth 1:16; 4:9–10, 21–22). Schiffman discusses these and other relevant biblical passages, concluding that inheriting Jewishness and non-Jewishness through the mother goes "back as far as the mid-fifth century B.C.E." (*Who Was A Jew?*, p. 16). In other words, the practice is biblical.

Former Chief Rabbi of Israel Shlomo Goren gives evidence that not only is it biblical but many centuries older; see his article on pp. 32–37 in Baruch Litvin, compiler, and Sidney B. Hoenig, editor, *Jewish Identity: Modern Responsa and Opinions on the Registration of Children of Mixed Marriages* (Jerusalem & New York: Feldheim Publishers, 1970).

The importance of tracing Jewishness through the mother increased when Jewish life became disrupted and Jewish families were broken apart by conquerors and persecutors. The rabbis reasoned, first, that where Jewish women were being abused it might be impossible to determine who the father was and therefore whether he was Jewish; and, second, that since a child's loyalties are often determined by the mother because she spends more time with him, a child raised by a Jewish mother and a Gentile father is more likely to be brought up loyal to Judaism than the child of a Jewish father and a

Gentile mother who will not give him the early training that builds such devotion.

The conclusion that Timothy was a Jew and not a Gentile is important for understanding v. 3&N.

Timothy was the son of a Jewish woman **and a Greek father**. Since exogamy violates Jewish law, an explanation is called for, although any conclusion must be a conjecture. I think the most likely reason for Timothy's mixed parentage is that Timothy's mother, Eunice (2 Ti 1:5), like many Jews today, was assimilated into the dominant Gentile culture around her and simply did not observe *halakhah*. Before coming to New Covenant faith she married a non-Jew, but afterwards her pagan and nonbelieving husband left or died; whereupon she raised her son in the faith "from childhood" (2 Ti 3:15). Possibly she and Timothy went to live with her Messianic Jewish mother Lois (2 Ti 1:5).

Many Messianic Jews like to say that believing in Yeshua "makes us even more Jewish." One result, in some cases, is that we become more attentive to Jewish laws and customs. But if the above explanation of why Timothy's father was Gentile is correct, it is clear that coming to faith did not make Eunice more observant. For if she had been observant, she would have seen to it herself that her son got circumcised. In Judaism the responsibility for circumcising a Jewish boy rests with his Jewish father but not, of course, with a Gentile father. If the father is unwilling or, as in this case, unable to take responsibility for his son's circumcision, the *beit-din* (Jewish religious court) sees to it, acting on behalf of the Jewish commmunity as a whole. If a boy has not been circumcised by the time he reaches thirteen, *bar-mitzvah* age, the obligation to get circumcised becomes his own. While the mother is not directly accountable for her son's circumcision, nothing prevents her from urging the boy's father or the *beit-din* to act. Unlike Moses' wife Zipporah (Exodus 4:25), Eunice did not take this responsibility on herself, which is why Timothy was still uncircumcised when Sha'ul arrived on the scene, so that he, himself an observant Jew (see 13:9N), acted *in loco patris* (v. 3&N).

Here are other possible reasons, likewise speculative, why Timothy had a Jewish mother and a Gentile father:

(1) It was not a marriage but the rape of an observant Jewish woman. This is not impossible, given the antisemitism and level of violence in ancient Roman society. This explanation has appeal for Messianic Jews who would like to paint a picture of every Jewish believer as *Torah*-true and gloss over the fact that the Gospel has appeal for assimilated Jews too.

(2) Eunice came to faith before her marriage and therefore considered herself no longer Jewish but Christian, therefore not subject to the *Torah*, so that she had no scruples about marrying outside her people. Those who think accepting Yeshua decreases Jewish loyalty or frees a Jew from the Law might prefer this explanation, but the New Testament evidence is against it. Jews who accepted Yeshua as the Messiah did not suddenly consider themselves ex-Jews; everything in the book of Acts demonstrates exactly the opposite. Moreover, accepting Yeshua as the Jewish Messiah does not free a Jew from the Law; this point is made in numerous notes in this commentary. A different point: although there is no specific evidence that the teaching had yet been promulgated, we know that believers in Yeshua were encouraged to marry other believers (1C 7:39&N).

(3) She simply fell in love with the man. But this explanation reflects twentieth-century fantasy, not first-century reality.

3 **Sha'ul... took him and did a *b'rit-milah***, which can imply that he had an expert *mohel* ("circumciser") perform the operation. While Sha'ul had both Jewish ritual knowledge (22:3) and at least some manual dexterity (18:3), circumcising an adult is not a simple operation and normally requires a specialist.

Because of the Jews living in those areas. A number of non-Messianic Jewish thinkers have a high regard for Yeshua. Even if they don't acknowledge him as the Messiah they consider him to have been a good Jew whose teachings were well within the rubric of Judaism and whose life can serve as an example to all (but see Yn 5:17–18N, 14:6N). It was Paul, they say, Sha'ul, who was "the villain of the piece," he who paganized Judaism by presenting Yeshua as a man-god, diluted it by throwing out the Law, and whose opportunism stopped at nothing as he tried to win Gentiles to himself after failing to convince the Jews. The present verse can help put this canard to rest.

Sha'ul's detractors would say that his circumcising Timothy was motivated by sheer opportunism, that he did not care a whit about the commandment itself (see 15:1N) and in fact explicitly taught that circumcision didn't matter at all (1C 7:19; Ga 5:6, 6:15), and that he circumcised Timothy only "because of" the Jews, that is, to conciliate them, so that they would not raise the issue.

But this theory conflicts with the New Testament evidence. Sha'ul himself observed the *Torah* to the end of his life (see 13:9&N for references), and he never taught Messianic Jews to stop observing it (21:20–27&NN.).

So, if "because of the Jews" does not mean to conciliate them, what does it mean? It means that even though it was not Sha'ul's responsibility to have Timothy circumcised (see v. 1N), he took it upon himself because he did not want Timothy's uncircumcision to provoke questioning that would impede the Gospel. The Gospel itself contains the stumblingblock of the Messiah's death (1C 1:23), and a good proclaimer of the Gospel will remove all other stumblingblocks if he can. That is the point: Sha'ul anticipated the problem and solved it.

Had Timothy been a Gentile there would have been no problem. Jews were glad to welcome Gentile "God-fearers." It is because Timothy was in fact Jewish by virtue of having a Jewish mother, yet uncircumcised because his Gentile father had not had him circumcised (v. 1N), and because this was widely known (**they all knew that his father was a Greek**, or: "had been a Greek," which may imply that the father was already dead), that there was danger of the Gospel's being misrepresented as contrary to Judaism.

4 **Decisions**, those of 15:20–29, perhaps best understood as halakhic *dinim* ("legal rulings"); see my *Messianic Jewish Manifesto*, Chapter V ("*Torah*").

6–10 The Holy Spirit can give specific instructions where not to go (vv. 6–7) and where to go (vv. 9–10).

10 **We concluded**. The author, Luke, was with Sha'ul and reports his own experiences. The "'we' passages" continue until 16:17 and resume at 20:5.

12–13 We spent a few days in the city; then on *Shabbat* we went outside the gate to the riverside, where we understood a *minyan* met. The Greek words "*prosevchê einai*" mean "where a prayer-place was"; here it is translated "where a *minyan* met." *Prosevchê* often denotes a synagogue building, and synagogues were frequently built by running water in order to eliminate the need for constructing a *mikveh* for ritual immersion. But in this instance there is reason to suppose that there was no synagogue at the river's edge. For when the Roman Emperor Claudius expelled the Jews from Rome (18:2&N), the Roman-controlled city of Philippi followed suit. In consequence, it is likely that a few Jews passed over by the expulsion order, along with other Jews who formerly lived in Philippi but now lived outside it nearby, did not have a building in which to meet and instead gathered together at the river's edge. A *minyan* ("quorum" of ten men) would have been enough for a regular synagogue service, and a modified version of the service could proceed with fewer men, or even with no men and only women, as is the case here, since Sha'ul and his companions spoke **to the women who had gathered there**.

16–18 From this passage we learn: (1) Demons can perform apparently useful services (v. 16). (2) They can tell the truth if it serves their purpose (v. 17), even though their ruler, Satan, is "the inventor of the lie" (Yn 8:44). (3) Nevertheless, their object is to interfere with the Gospel (v. 18). (4) Powerful and remarkable as they are, demons must submit to the authority of Yeshua the Messiah (v. 18, Mk 1:23–27). Note that in expelling the demon Sha'ul does not address the girl but the demon, and he does not rely on his own authority but that of Yeshua (contrast 19:13–16&NN).

20–22 Since they are Jews (see Yn 1:19N). The charges, that they are **causing trouble** and **advocating customs… against the law for… Romans,** are both false and vague. Their purpose is only to stir up a **mob:** thus antisemitism throughout history. Nevertheless, these Gentile pagans were right about one thing: Jews for Jesus are **Jews,** not *Goyim*.

22 The judges tore their clothes off them and ordered that they be flogged. No mention of a trial or a defense. When antisemitic feelings run high, as in this city which had already ejected its Jews (vv. 12–13N), justice also flees.

31 Trust in the Lord Yeshua (see 11:20–23N), **and you will be saved.** There are five conditions for the salvation of individuals stated in the New Testament:

(1) Believing that Yeshua is Lord and trusting in him (here, Ro 10:9).
(2) Acknowledging him publicly (Ro 10:9, Lk 12:8).
(3) Turning from sin to God (Mk 1:15, Ac 2:38).
(4) Being immersed (Ac 2:38, Mk 16:16). See v. 33&N.
(5) "Holiness, without which no one will see the Lord" (MJ 12:14). A person who meets the first four conditions but leads an ungodly life gives public evidence that he is not saved.

Sha'ul names only the first condition, the touchstone, sensing that the jailer is ready to meet all of the conditions as soon as they have been explained, which Sha'ul then does (v. 32).

You and your household. In the Bible a man and his family are considered as a unit far more than in the individualistic twentieth-century West; and some use this verse in advocating infant baptism (see v. 33&N). Nevertheless, the jailer's faith will not save the members of his household. Rather, Sha'ul is stating a general principle: if one trusts in Yeshua, one will be saved. This principle applies not only to the jailer, says Sha'ul, but also to his household. Another view: "and your household" is a word of knowledge (1C 12:8–10&N), a correct prediction given Sha'ul by the Holy Spirit, that the jailer's entire household would come to faith after hearing the Gospel (v. 32). See v. 33&N.

33 He and all his people were immersed. Including the babies? Christian denominations split on this. Catholics, Eastern Orthodox, Anglicans (Episcopalians), Lutherans, Presbyterians and Methodists baptize babies, while Baptists and most smaller Protestant denominations do not. I personally believe that the New Testament evidence favors immersion of believers only, which is to say that "**all his people**" means that every person old enough to hear the Gospel message and respond to it with faith did so, with the consequence that they obeyed it and immersed themselves. Nowhere does the New Testament state that babies were ever immersed, but also nowhere does it say they were not. So, because of the unknowns, different interpreters have reached opposite conclusions.

Such disputes have divided the Body throughout its history. As a Messianic Jew I believe that Messianic Jews should interest themselves in these matters as much as other believers do. But also as Messianic Jews, living bridges of the greatest schism in the history of the world, that between the Church and the Jewish people, we should be especially aware that the Adversary uses such differences of opinion to turn one part of the Messiah's Body against another. Messianic Jews must remain in fellowship with each other and with the rest of the believers, no matter on which side of this issue or any other they stand, so long as it is clear that the basics of the faith are being preserved. Our Lord Yeshua prayed "that they" — meaning we — "may be one" (Yn 17:20–23&NN). It is far more important to live out that unity and avoid the scandal of "the Messiah… split in pieces" (1C 1:13) than to insist that one's own interpretation must be accepted (even though, when all is known, it may prove correct) at the expense of fellowship with believers who disagree.

35–40 Believers in Yeshua are sometimes expected to be "meek and mild" and behave like "doormats." While we are not to sue each other (1C 6:1–8), and we are to turn the other cheek and go the second mile (Mt 5:39–42), there is one situation where we are expected to stand adamantly, refusing to give ground; and that is where the Gospel itself is at stake. If the Gospel can be served better by fighting back, we should fight back — the fighting, of course, to be conducted ethically and by spiritual means (2C 10:3–5, Ep 6:10–18). We are to obey God rather than people (4:19&N, 5:29).

In these verses we see Sha'ul using several legitimate means: he mentions his own Roman citizenship, he points out the officials' illegal behavior — public flogging and imprisonment without a trial or conviction of any crime — and he demands public redemption of public insults. He does all this to insure his proper treatment, but not because of personal pride. His concern is for the Gospel only: he wants to ensure that no one in Philippi will come away from the incident with the impression given by Sha'ul's accusers (vv. 20–23), that the message of the Messiah is not for Romans.

CHAPTER 17

1 **A synagogue**. The text has: "an assembly of the Jews." See 13:5N.

2 Being an observant Jew (13:9N), it was **his usual practice** to attend synagogue, not an occasional event when it suited him.

Gave them *drashot*, literally, "lectured to them." A *drash* or *drashah* is, literally, a "searching"; the word denotes a sermon, exegesis, exposition or homiletical interpretation of a text. The word "*midrash*" is related. The normal form for a *drash* in the midrashic period (100 B.C.E. to 500 C.E.) was: (1) introduction, consisting of a biblical verse with illustrations and parables, leading up to (2) the particular text to be explained, now expanded by stories, allegories and associations with other texts, and (3) conclusion, consisting of exhortations and words of comfort and ending with the *Kaddish* prayer (see Mt 6:9–13N). That Sha'ul frequently used Talmudic and *midrashic* thought patterns is illustrated by Ro 10:5–13; 1C 9:9–14; 2C 3:3–18; Ga 3:16, 4:22–31.

3 **Explaining and quoting passages to prove**, literally, "opening up and setting before them." One hears opposition to "proof-texting," a term that means explaining and quoting Scripture passages in order to prove something, just like Sha'ul. The main argument against proof-texting is that it can be misused: passages can be quoted out of context or invested with a meaning the author never intended. These are indeed abuses; "nevertheless, God's firm foundation stands" (2 Ti 2:19): when passages are quoted with regard to context, with terms properly translated and explained, and with account taken of the culture and background of the author and his intended readers, the method is perfectly proper. It was used by the rabbis throughout Jewish history, and it is reasonable to suppose that Sha'ul's methods of using Scripture were well within Jewish tradition.

The fact that the *Tanakh* is cited some 695 times in the New Testament shows that its writers were convinced that although God had done something unique and radically new in Yeshua, the meaning of what he had done could be adequately expressed only in relation to the *Tanakh*. This conviction set the first believers to reading the *Tanakh* with new eyes, which led to understanding how it relates to New Covenant truth. For some purposes it was sufficient to refer generally to "the Scriptures" or "the *Tanakh*" (*e.g.*, 1C 15:3–4); but frequently major events in the life of Yeshua were related to individual texts. However, one seldom finds in the New Testament the kind of far-fetched allegory common in later rabbinic and Christian interpretation; and there is rarely the kind of sustained verse-by-verse commentary on a *Tanakh* passage that can be found already at Qumran and later in both Jewish and Christian traditions (but MJ 3:7–4:11 has this character). In conclusion, what is seen in the New Testament is individual verses used with restraint to express the writers' underlying confidence that Yeshua the Messiah's coming is central to fulfilling God's purposes for Israel and the world.

The Messiah had to suffer and rise again from the dead. Sha'ul had to show this from the *Tanakh*, e.g., from Isaiah 52:13–53:12 and Psalm 16:8–11 (see 1C 15:3–4&N), because the Jewish people were expecting that the first and most important act of the Messiah would be political liberation (1:6–7&N).

This Yeshua... is the Messiah (See Mt 1:1&N). The first task was to re-order

Jewish expectations. The second, here, is to show that these new expectations are fulfilled in Yeshua.

4 **Some of the Jews were persuaded and threw in their lot with Sha'ul and Sila.** The normal consequence of trusting Yeshua is to remain in fellowship with those who led you to faith. Sha'ul and Sila, unlike many of today's evangelists, never left new believers to flounder for themselves; and we are not told of new believers who went off by themselves, eschewing the company of other members of the Body.

"God-fearers." See 10:2N.

5 **Unbelieving Jews** here and at v. 13. See 9:22–23N.

Jason was probably Jewish, for Sha'ul and Sila would not have needlessly offended the Jewish community by lodging with a Gentile. Many Greek-speaking Jews had Greek names; see 13:9N. In his commentary I. Howard Marshall speculates (*ad loc.*) that if he was Jewish, "his Jewish name may have been Joshua, with Jason as a somewhat similar-sounding Greek name for use in a Greek environment." Like thinking prevails in today's Jewish Diaspora: Hebrew and local-language names are often chosen to resemble each other, e.g., Bruce and Baruch. Josephus writes of a 2nd-century B.C.E. *cohen gadol*, Joshua, who "changed his name to Jason" (*Antiquities of the Jews* 12:5:1).

7 **They assert that there is another king, Yeshua.** Compare 16:20–23&NN, also the accusations made against Yeshua at his own trial (Yn 18:33–38, 19:12) and his responses. He is King. He will rule the world. However, at present his rulership is not in this world (Yn 18:36), so that Sha'ul taught believers to obey temporal laws (Ro 13:1–7) and Kefa wrote, "Honor the king" (1 Ke 2:17). In the light of the emissaries' own teaching, the accusation against Sha'ul and his companions is false.

10–12 **Berea.... As soon as they arrived, they went to the synagogue. Now the people here were of nobler character than the ones in Thessalonica; they eagerly welcomed the message, checking the *Tanakh* every day to see if the things Sha'ul was saying were true. Many of them came to trust.** Today such openmindedness is similarly welcomed by Messianic Jews and is praiseworthy. We are confident that when the Good News is given this sort of a fair hearing, and the hearers rely on the facts, including **the *Tanakh***, to verify the message, the response today will often be like that in Berea, where many Jewish people came to trust in Yeshua — a clear success for Sha'ul's Jewish evangelism.

17 In Athens, Sha'ul discussed the Gospel **in the synagogue with the Jews**, as usual (13:5N). **And with the "God-fearers"**, the people most likely to respond favorably (10:2N, 13:16N). **And in the market square**, the most prominent public gathering place, **with the people who happened to be there** — he tried to reach anyone he could, so he went to where people had time to talk with him and listen (this is the New Testament's example of street evangelism). He did not expect others to approach him but went to them, and he was tireless about it — he went **every day**.

18 Epicurean and Stoic philosophers. The followers of Epicurus (341–270 B.C.E.) denied the existence of a purposeful God and believed the universe originated by chance from a falling rain of atoms. They mocked the popular (pagan) gods and mythology. Their view of the soul was materialistic: it dissolved and dissipated at death. Thus the aim of life was gratification, not pursuit of higher or externally given moral and spiritual interests. Gratification could be gross and sordid if one was so inclined, or esthetic and refined. Today's successors to the Epicureans speak of "doing your own thing," and their unabashed selfishness is rarely ameliorated by the common qualification usually honored in the breach, "so long as it doesn't hurt anybody else."

Stoics were pantheists for whom "God" was merely a word standing for some vague spirit of reason in the universe. They understood the soul to be corporeal and at death somehow absorbed into this blurry "God." All the major Eastern religions and certain seemingly Western offshoots have at bottom a similar theology, that there is no transcendent God who created and rules the universe independently of human beings and their imaginings. The Stoic moral code was in some ways higher than that of the Epicureans, but for them the highest morality was an austere apathy and unconcern which regarded itself as superior to passion as well as circumstance. Many alienated people today repress the genuine hurt and guilt they ought to feel and attempt to elevate their alienation into philosophy, thus ending up with a version of Stoicism. In this philosophy pleasure is not good and pain is not evil, for nothing really matters. "Reason" becomes a guide, but when "reason" finds nothing left to live for, suicide becomes the "reasonable" action — the first two leaders of Stoicism died by their own hand. In this century Albert Camus's novel, *The Stranger*, and his essay, "The Myth of Sisyphus," deal with this question from a nonbeliever's standpoint (see my discussion in *Messianic Jewish Manifesto*, pp. 35–41, on history and the meaning of life).

Both Stoicism and Epicureanism (and their successors) oppose biblical religion. In the present verses we see how Sha'ul, expressing God's love, dealt with people — sinners like everyone else — whose primary channel of life-expression was intellectual.

Babbler, or: "dilettante"; literally, "seedpicker," like a bird that picks from here and there.

He sounds like a propagandist for foreign gods. The task of people who work with their minds is to classify into comprehensible categories. The ever-present pitfall is classifying wrongly or too quickly. Yeshua the Messiah is not "foreign gods." The right response to him is not to put him in a readymade box, but have one's entire viewpoint changed, categories and all. "Don't be conformed to this world's standards, but be transformed by the renewing of your minds" (Ro 12:2).

19–22a High Council (v. 19), **Council meeting** (v. 22a). Greek *Areios pagos* in both places, rendered "Areopagus" and "Mars' hill" in KJV (the god of war was called Ares by the Greeks and Mars by the Romans). The place-name referred colloquially to the High Council, which had once met there.

22b–31 To those who approach life intellectually Sha'ul offers knowledge in lieu of **ignorance** (v. 23). He does not use the Scriptures at all, since these would carry no weight with these highly educated pagans (contrast vv. 2–3&NN, 10–12&N). Instead, he quotes from Greek poets in v. 28 (first Epimenides, then Aratus or Cleanthes); elsewhere he quotes Menander (1C 15:33) and Epimenides of Crete (Ti 1:12). He presents God as Creator, Giver of all, and Ruler of nations and history (vv. 24–26), and as One who seeks our love (vv. 27–28), which consists not in idol-worship (vv. 24–25, 29) but in turning from sins (v. 30), because a day is coming when everyone will be judged by God through the resurrected Yeshua (v. 31). His resurrection gives public proof that the Gospel is true and therefore objectively demands belief (see 26:8N).

32 The same division noted earlier between open- and closed-minded Jews (Yn 7:43N) is now seen among Gentiles.

34 Although it is said occasionally that Sha'ul was unsuccessful in Athens, this verse proves the contrary: the persons named became the core of that city's Messianic community.

CHAPTER 18

2 **Claudius had issued a decree expelling all the Jews from Rome** in 49 C.E. The expulsion is usually connected with the remark of Suetonius, "Since the Jews were continually making disturbances at the instigation of Chrestus, he [Claudius] expelled them from Rome" (Claudius 25:4); and it is presumed that the pagan Suetonius was speaking not of some otherwise unknown Chrestus but of *Christos* ("Christ," see Mt 1:1N) and misspelled the word. If so, Suetonius (75–160 C.E.) is one of the earliest writers outside the New Testament to mention Yeshua the Messiah, and his expression, "instigation of *Christos*," would refer to disputes between Messianic and non-Messianic Jews. However, the possibility remains that "Chrestus" was someone else altogether. See 28:24–25N.

3 Sha'ul earned his own living (see also 1C 9:1–19), even though he taught that those who proclaim the Good News are entitled to be supported by their fellow believers (1C 9:14). In observing the Mishnaic admonition, "Do not make of the *Torah*... a spade with which to dig" (which means, don't use your knowledge of spiritual things as a means of getting rich), he went beyond the call of duty.

6 **Your blood be on your own heads** (compare Mt 27:25&N). **For my part, I am clean.** At Ezekiel 3:16–19 God tells the prophet that he will be blameworthy if he fails to warn the wicked person to leave his wicked ways, but if he does warn him he will be guiltless. Sha'ul is, in effect, applying the passage to himself and saying, "I have done what I could to bring you the message of salvation; you choose to reject it at your peril, but I have discharged my responsibility. I would not leave you and **go to the *Goyim*** (13:46&N) if you were responsive, but you leave me no other choice. The Gospel is for you especially, but it will also save them" (Ro 1:16).

7 **Whose house was right next door to the synagogue.** Definitely a confrontational tactic. Sha'ul had no intention of being intimidated or dropping out of sight. He still intended his and the Gospel's presence to be very visible in the Jewish community. Believers today should consider following his example and making the saving message of Yeshua clearly evident to Jewish people. The wisdom of Sha'ul's policy is shown in the following verse and in the reassurance of vv. 9–10.

8 **Crispus, the president of the synagogue**, or: "the synagogue-ruler," meaning one of several (see v. 17N). Sha'ul himself **immersed** Crispus (1C 1:14).

12 **Gallio** was proconsul of Achaia between 51 and 53 C.E., according to an inscription from Delphi; this is an important factual landmark in determining the chronology of Sha'ul's travels (see Ga 1:17–2:2&NN.).

Unbelieving Jews here and at v. 28. See 9:22–23N.

13 **Against the *Torah***, or: "against the [Roman] law." It seems that Jewish complainants would mean the former; moreover, Gallio takes it this way and acts accordingly (v. 15). But it is possible that the latter is meant, as at 16:21–22, 17:7.

17 **Sosthenes, the president of the synagogue** (Greek *archisunagôgos*, "synagogue ruler," also at v. 8, 13:15; Mk 5:22, 35–38; Lk 8:49, 13:14). Probably the new president, after Crispus, the former president, became a Messianic Jew (v. 8&N). But it is not impossible that Crispus and Sosthenes were both "synagogue rulers," two among several, and that Crispus continued to hold office even after becoming Messianic. This Sosthenes may be the same as the one at 1C 1:1 — which would mean that he later became Messianic himself, perhaps in consequence of this incident.

They all grabbed him and **gave him a beating.** Either the other Jews did this to Sosthenes because he had led them into public humiliation; or the Greeks, observing that Gallio the governor was not interfering, "proceeded to indulge their anti-Jewish feelings" (I. Howard Marshall, *Acts*, *ad loc.*).

18 **Sha'ul remained for some time**. Except where his own life was in immediate peril Sha'ul never left at a time of crisis or under duress.

Having his hair cut short in Cenchrea because he had taken a vow, and with him were Priscilla and Aquila. Priscilla is mentioned first; she may have been the more notable of the couple. Some suggest, and the Greek text allows, that it was Aquila and not Sha'ul who took the vow; but since the overall narrative is about Sha'ul, this is unlikely.

Yeshua rules out oaths for Messianic believers (Mt 5:33–37) but not vows, although the distinction between them is not a clear one (see Mt 5:33N). The Greek word for "vow" occurs only here and at 21:23. What kind of vow did Sha'ul take, and what did cutting his hair have to do with it? Nothing is said of what he vowed to do, but Numbers 6:1–21 describes the Nazirite vow, which involves allowing the hair to grow during the days of the vow; and Mishna tractate Nazir spells out the details of such vows, including their minimum length, thirty days. Strictly speaking, however, this cannot have been a Nazirite vow; for if it had been, Sha'ul would not have been shaved in Cenchrea but would have waited till he arrived in Yerushalayim (v. 22) to shave his head and offer the obligatory sacrifice at the Temple (compare 21:23–24&NN). Furthermore, if we assume that the patterns described in the Mishna, compiled around 220 C.E., were already being followed in Sha'ul's time, he would have had to spend at least thirty days in Israel to validate his vow (Nazir 3:6, 7:3), since a Nazirite vow undertaken in a "land of the Gentiles" is invalid. Perhaps this was a Diaspora adaptation of the Nazirite vow.

No matter what the details of Sha'ul's vow were, this verse proves that he did not abandon the *Torah*; on the contrary, even when he became as a Gentile among Gentiles he continued to observe Jewish practices. See 13:9N, 1C 9:20–22&NN.

21 Some manuscripts add at the beginning of Sha'ul's farewell, "I must by all means keep this coming feast in Yerushalayim." If the words are genuine, they surely refer to one of the pilgrim festivals (Yn 5:1N), perhaps *Shavu'ot* (as at 20:16), and would account for Sha'ul's wanting to go there at this time, since no other reason is given. However, the prevailing view among scholars is that the sentence was added later. The similar statement at 20:16 is genuine (see note there).

22–23 **Went up… came down**. See Mt 20:18N. Sha'ul's second journey (see 13:4N) ends with his return to **Antioch**, where he naturally **spent some time** in his home congregation (13:1–4&N, 14:26–28&NN, 15:40&N).

His third journey, described in 18:23–21:16, commenced with his passing **systematically through the region of Galatia and Phrygia, strengthening all the *talmidim*** he had won to the Lord — this was part of his calling as an emissary and congregation-planter. His second journey began the same way (15:41), and compare Ro 1:10–12.

24 **Alexandria** was the chief center of Diaspora Hellenistic Judaism. The great Jewish intellectual, Philo, lived there and possibly was still alive at the time of these events. Jews occupied two of the five districts of the city, named for its founder, Alexander the Great, who established it on the Mediterranean Sea near the mouth of the Nile River in 331 B.C.E. Its great library, destroyed in 699 C.E., made it a major center of learning. It developed its own variety of Judaism which made accommodations to Greek culture — it was a kind of "Reform Judaism" in its day. Alexandria even had its own Temple. The Septuagint was translated there around 200 B.C.E.

25 **He knew only the immersion of Yochanan** (Mt 3:1–12), so that even though **he accurately taught the facts about Yeshua**, he had not experienced the full significance of Yeshua's life, death and resurrection and had not been filled with the *Ruach HaKodesh* (see 19:1–7&NN).

Likewise today there are those whose knowledge of the things of God is good as far as it goes, and who even can present the facts about Yeshua accurately; but they have not experienced his salvation and his Holy Spirit for themselves. If they are as open to truth as Apollos, it should be enough for their salvation to have **the way of God explained in fuller detail**, emphasizing the person and work of Yeshua the Messiah, since they already know who God is. I suspect that many well-informed Jews belong to this category.

28 Apollos was useful in Achaia because he made use of the *Tanakh* and focussed his efforts on showing that the promised Messiah is indeed Yeshua, rather than dealing with secondary issues that satisfy curiosity but do not lead people to salvation.

CHAPTER 19

1–7 A special group of people are considered here, those who, like Apollos (18:25&N), had known of God's involvement in "salvation history" up to the time of Yochanan the Immerser but had not known of Yeshua. After instruction, they are **immersed into the name of the Lord Yeshua**, that is, into all that he is (2:38&N, Mt 28:19&N). Thereupon the Holy Spirit, of whom they had **never even heard**, visits them in power and with the same charismatic phenomena as were manifested in the one hundred twenty at *Shavu'ot* (2:4), in the people of Shomron (8:17), probably in Sha'ul (9:17), and in Cornelius and his household (10:44–48).

8–10 In Ephesus the development of opposition to the Gospel within the synagogue was relatively slow in coming — it took three months. But when it did come and grew strong enough to obstruct communication of the Gospel, Sha'ul did a strategic withdrawal **to Tyrannus's *yeshivah*.** The Hebrew word "*yeshivah*" comes from the word that means "sit"; it signifies a place for learning *Torah.* The Greek word so rendered, "*scholê,*" which gives us English "school," means "study hall," a place where students and teachers meet; it appears as a loanword in rabbinic literature, and probably no English word comes as close to its proper meaning as "*yeshivah*" — or, alternatively, "*midrashah*" ("school, college, academy, seminary"); the Yiddish word "*shul*" ("school") would also serve.

But these Hebrew words, because they are "Jewish English" (see Section IV of the Introduction to the *JNT*), foreclose on a question worth exploring, namely, whether Sha'ul withdrew from the synagogue to a Jewish environment or a Gentile one? Or even more strongly, was he forgetting about the Jews altogether and instead "turning to the *Goyim*" (13:46, 18:6)?

The answer to the second question is definitely No, because the text states that he continued evangelizing all who would listen **for two years; so that everyone, both Jews and Greeks… heard the message about the Lord.** But the answer to the first depends on how one understands the social dynamics of the situation and on whether or not **Tyrannus** himself was Jewish; this will determine whether his *scholê* is properly thought of as a *yeshivah*/*midrashah.*

As in most of his synagogue forays, Sha'ul's message split the congregation into those who agreed with him and those opposed (see 20:3N). The latter **began hardening themselves and refusing to listen.** Then they **started defaming the Way** of life proclaimed in Sha'ul's Gospel **before the whole synagogue.** In any given location Sha'ul normally began by evangelizing in the synagogue (13:5&N). But he also had a "Plan 'B'"ready for use if the synagogue environment should become too heated for effective communication of the Gospel, whereby he would take with him prominent Jews and others whom he had won to the Messiah and move out of the synagogue to a different center that would still impact the Jewish community. I learn this from the mention of Jason in Thessalonica (17:4–8&NN) and Crispus in Corinth (18:8&N), and it suggests to me that Tyrannus is named here because he was a prominent Jew whose property Sha'ul was able to use. If Tyrannus was Jewish, his *scholê* can properly be called a *yeshivah.* On the other hand, Luke may be telling us that at this point Sha'ul shifted from a Jewish base to a non-Jewish one, as he did in Corinth, when he moved to the house of the Gentile, Titius Justus (18:7&N).

Regardless of whether Tyrannus was Jewish or a Gentile "God-fearer," he would have been attuned to Jewish ways, since Sha'ul presumably met him in the synagogue. The Gentile scholar S. F. Hunter explores the options:

> "Tyrannus may have been (1) a Greek rhetorician or (2) a Jewish rabbi.
> (1) This is the common opinion, and many identify him with a certain Tyrannus, a sophist, mentioned by Suidas....
> (2) Meyer thinks that as the apostle had not passed wholly to the Gentiles, and Jews still flocked to hear him, and also that as Tyrannus is not spoken of as a proselyte, this *scholê* is the *beth Midhrash* of a Jewish rabbi. 'Paul with his Christians withdrew from the public synagogue to the private synagogue of Tyrannus, where he and his doctrine were more secure from public annoyance.' (Meyer *in loc.*)
> (3) Another view (Overbeck) is that the expression [Tyrannus's School] was the standing name of the place after the original owner."
> (*International Standard Bible Encyclopedia*, p. 3030)

I discount "the common opinion" because it probably reflects "the common bias" of New Testament scholars against giving sufficient weight to the Jewish context of the Gospel when it was presented in the first century. I am satisfied that Tyrannus was a Jewish rabbi, and that what he had was a *yeshivah* — or, as above, a *beit-midrash* ("house of study") or *midrashah* (same). While one should not superimpose the modern Orthodox Jewish cultural concept of *yeshivah* on the New Testament, it is reasonable to suppose that Sha'ul, who had studied with *Rabban* Gamli'el (22:3&N), used methods developed in first-century Judaism, although he presented the content of the Gospel to Gentiles in a way that transcended Jewish culture (see 11:20–23N, 1C 9:20–22&NN).

It is important for modern Messianic Judaism to have available the concept of a Messianic *yeshivah* or *midrashah*. Restoring the Jewishness of the Gospel should involve presenting the eternal Gospel in a Jewish religious, cultural and social environment. While today the word "*yeshivah*," to most Jewish people, means a school for Jewish studies, particularly *Torah*, Talmud, *halakhah*, etc., it is right for Messianic Judaism to appropriate this term and apply it to Messianic Jewish institutions of learning that relate seriously to the Jewish as well as the New Testament materials. This is one way to meet the challenge of Mt 13:52&N.

11–12 An aim of the book of Acts is to show that in every way Sha'ul, the emissary to the Gentiles, had a ministry equal to that of Kefa, the leading emissary to the Jews (see Ga 2:7–9&N). With these verses compare Kefa's healing miracles of 5:15–16. Of course it is God who heals, not Sha'ul or Kefa.

13 Jewish exorcists (Greek *exorkistês*, used only here in the New Testament). Josephus speaks of King Solomon's having learned

> "that skill which expels demons.... And he left behind him the manner of using exorcisms, by which they drive away demons so that they never return, and this method of cure is of great force unto this day. Indeed, I have seen a

> certain man of my own country, whose name was El'azar, releasing people who were demoniacal in the presence of Vespasian, his sons, his captains and the whole multitude of soldiers. The manner of cure was this: he put a ring that had a root of one of those sorts mentioned by Solomon to the nostrils of the demoniac, after which he drew out the demon through his nostrils...." (*Antiquities of the Jews* 8:2:5)

Exorcism of *shedim* (Hebrew, "demons") is a theme in the Talmud. In medieval Jewish literature the term "*dibbuk*" becomes commoner. There are descriptions of Jewish exorcisms dating from the present century.

Given that demons are regarded as real and not imaginary phenomena (see Mt 4:1, 24; 9:34; 11:20–21; Mk 5:11–17 and notes), it may be surprising that it is sometimes possible to use magical means, that is, demonic means, to expel them. Apparently there is some degree of order even in the demonic hierarchy, so that some demonic powers can expel other demonic powers. Nevertheless, ultimately "a house divided against itself cannot stand" (Mt 12:22–29&NN). And there are demons that do not respond to the means used by exorcists but only to prayer (Mk 9:14–29).

Tried to make use of the name of the Lord Yeshua, as if the name itself had magical powers. They were attempting to use the Messiah as a means to their own ends. But Yeshua himself is always the end, never the means to other ends.

I exorcise you demons **by the Yeshua that Sha'ul is proclaiming**. Obviously these exorcists, though knowing nothing about Yeshua, had noticed that those who spoke of their faith in him had power (Mk 16:20). Like Shim'on (8:19) they were power-hungry, but they did not understand that the power comes from the Holy Spirit (1:8), who is given only to those putting their trust in Yeshua as Messiah, Lord and Savior. When used by those with such trust, his name is powerful in expelling demons (3:6, 9:34; Mk 16:17–18).

Compare this interesting story from the Jerusalem Talmud; it probably took place before 130 C.E.:

> "The case of Rabbi El'azar ben-Damah, whom a serpent bit. There came in Ya'akov, a man of K'far-Sama, to cure him in the name of Yeshua ben-Pandira; but Rabbi Ishmael did not allow it. He said, 'You are not permitted, Ben-Damah.' Ben-Damah replied, 'I will bring you proof that he may heal me.' But before he had finished bringing proof, he died. Rabbi Ishmael said, 'Happy are you, Ben-Damah, for you have departed in peace and have not broken through the ordinances of the wise; for on everyone who breaks through the fence of the wise, punishment comes at last, as it is written, "Whoever breaks down a fence, a serpent will bite him" (Ecclesiastes 10:8).' The serpent only bit him that a serpent might not bite him in the future. And what could Ben-Damah have said? '...Which, if a person do, he shall live by them' (that is, not die in them; Leviticus 18:5)." (Shabbat 14d)

Yeshua ben-Pandira is Yeshua from Natzeret (compare Tosefta Chullin 2:24 with Babylonian Talmud 'Avodah Zarah 16b–17a). The 5th–6th century Jewish anti-Gospel, *Toledot-Yeshu*, is clearer about this: it presents "Yeshu" (see Mt 1:21N) as the illegitimate son of Miryam and a Roman soldier named Pandira.

Obviously Ya'akov from K'far-Sama (or K'far-Sechanyah; see below), whose role in the story is passive, was a Messianic Jew. What is important in connection with our verse is that it is taken for granted that Ya'akov would in fact have healed Rabbi El'azar Ben-Damah in Yeshua's name. That is, if a non-Messianic Jew does not allow a colleague's life to be saved through the power Yeshua gives his followers, he implicitly acknowledges that the power exists.

A variant of this story told in Babylonian Talmud is even more explicit about this:

> "A man is to have no dealings with the *minim* nor may he be cured by them, even to gain one hour of life. The case of Ben-Damah, Rabbi Ishmael's sister's son, whom a serpent bit. There came Ya'akov the *min* of K'far-Sechanyah to cure him...." ('Avodah Zarah 27b)

Later the text comments on the quotation from Ecclesiastes,

> "It is different in regard to *minut* [the heresy of the *minim*, i.e., in this case, Messianic Judaism], which bites a man, so that he comes to be bitten afterwards."

Thus the last half of the story means this: Ben-Damah did not transgress the ordinances of the rabbis, he did not break down the "fence" around the *Torah*, by allowing a heretic (a Messianic Jew) to minister to him. So the literal serpent which bit him and caused his death saved him from being bitten by the figurative serpent of heresy and from suffering in the *'olam haba* punishment worse than death.

This same story appears in three additional places in rabbinic literature: Tosefta Chullin 2:22–23; Jerusalem Talmud 'Avodah Zarah 40d–41a; and Midrash Rabbah Ecclesiastes 1:8.

14 **A Jewish *cohen gadol* named Skeva** (Greek *Skevas*). There is no record of a high priest with that name. Perhaps if his Hebrew name were known (see 13:9N) he could be identified.

15 Demons know who Yeshua is and recognize his power; see Mt 8:29, Ya 2:19.

16 Mark 5:4 gives another instance of a demoniac with supernatural strength.

17 Compare 5:11.

18 Trust consists not merely in verbal professions of belief but in turning from sin. Often public confession of sin is the key, for the prayers and exhortations of other believers, as well as the fear of being ashamed in front of them, can keep one from giving in to temptation and returning to the sin one has confessed. The notion that sin can be kept private is surely a delusion: what is whispered now will one day be shouted from the rooftops.

19 A drachma was a day's wages for common labor; therefore think of **fifty thousand**

drachmas as at least two million dollars. On the other hand, books and scrolls, since they were individually produced, were relatively much more expensive than now. Speculation: if the average believer had $200 worth of occult books to burn, the congregation numbered ten thousand. Ephesus was a major center for occult religion (vv. 23–35).

The destruction of these books was one of the best investments believers have ever made. Not only did they forsake publicly their former pagan ways, but the demonic contents of these books went up in flames, never to poison the minds of anyone again. We are not told that anyone suggested selling the books to pagans and "laundering" the proceeds by using them to advance the Gospel.

23–41 Luke shows that there was opposition to the Gospel not only from nonbelieving Jews, but also from nonbelieving Gentiles acting on their own without Jewish instigation. It is necessary to point this out because some Jewish scholars, for example, Joseph Klausner (*From Jesus to Paul*, Boston: Beacon Press, 1961; p. 229), maintain that the book of Acts was written late, around 95 C.E., at a time when there was presumably no longer hope for reaching Jews with the Gospel, so that nothing would be lost by depicting Jews in the worst possible light. But Luke is reporting events in the history of the spread of the Gospel and has no reason to do such a thing. Rather, he gives examples of the kinds of problems that arose from all three relevant groups — Jews, pagans and the ruling Romans.

25–29 Demetrius' real motive, greed, is to be concealed for propaganda purposes by a veneer of civic pride. The flavor of his empty rhetoric is faithfully reproduced in v. 27. Verses 28–29 show that the scheme worked: the rabble were roused.

34 As soon as they recognized that he was a Jew. As in Philippi (16:12–13&N, 16:20–22&NN.), antisemitism was at home among these pagans. Pagan antisemitism is not directed specifically only at Sha'ul or his particular version of Judaism but at all Jews and at Judaism generally.

35 The temple of the great Artemis. Artemis is the same as Diana in the Roman pantheon; Ephesus was the center of Artemis-worship. This temple was considered one of the seven wonders of the ancient world. Perhaps the **sacred stone** was a meteorite.

CHAPTER 20

3 A plot against him by the unbelieving Jews. "Unbelieving" is not in the Greek text; see 9:22–23N. We have read of a number of plots, some originated by Jews, some by Gentiles. We have seen in general that sometimes people receive the Gospel and sometimes they reject it (see Yn 7:43N). Their rejection can be either active or passive, the latter expressing itself as indifference, apathy or a feeling of superiority even while approving of the believers. The following table presents instances of each, showing the verses in the book of Acts and the locations of the Jewish and Gentile responses to the Gospel:

RESPONSE	JEWS	GENTILES
Believing the Gospel	2:41. Jerusalem 13:43. Pisidian Antioch 14:1. Iconium 17:4. Thessalonica 17:11–12. Berea 18:8. Corinth 19:9. Ephesus 28:24. Rome	14:1. Iconium 16:14, 30. Philippi 17:4. Thessalonica 17:11–12. Berea 17:34. Athens 18:8. Corinth 19:17–20. Ephesus
Rejecting the Gospel (active opposition)	4:1ff., 5:17ff., 6:11–14, 7:54–8:3, 9:29, 12:3–4, 21:27ff. Jerusalem 9:23–24. Damascus 13:45, 13:50, 14:19. Pisidian Antioch 14: 2, 5, 19. Iconium 17:5–8, 13. Thessalonica 18:6, 12–13. Corinth 19:9. Ephesus 20:3. Greece	12:1–4. Jerusalem 14:5, 19. Iconium 16:16ff. Philippi 19:23ff. Ephesus
Rejecting the Gospel (passive opposition, indifference, etc.)	2:47, 4:21?, 5:34–39. Jerusalem 28:24. Rome	17:32. Athens 26:24, 28. Caesarea

6 **After the days of *Matzah***, that is, after Passover. See Mt 26:2N, 26:17N; 1C 5:6–8&N. Sha'ul, the observant Jew (13:9N), kept *Pesach*.

7 ***Motza'ei-Shabbat*** in Hebrew means "departure of the Sabbath" and refers to Saturday night. The Greek text here says, "the first day of the *sabbaton*," where Greek *sabbaton* transliterates Hebrew *Shabbat* and may be translated "Sabbath" or "week," depending on the context. Since *Shabbat* itself is only one day, "the first day of the *sabbaton*" must be the first day of the week.

But what was meant by "the first day of the week"? Or, to make the question's relevance to Messianic Judaism clearer, were the believers meeting on Saturday night or on Sunday night? (It is clear from the verse that the meeting was in the evening.) A Saturday night meeting would fit more naturally with Jewish *Shabbat* observance, wherein the restful spirit of *Shabbat* is often preserved into Saturday evening, after the official end of *Shabbat* itself, which occurs after sunset when it gets dark enough to see three stars. It would be natural for Jewish believers who had rested on *Shabbat* with the rest of the Jewish community to assemble afterwards to celebrate their common faith in Yeshua the Messiah. The Gentile believers who came along later would join in the already established practice, especially since many of them would have been

"God-fearers" (10:2N) already accustomed to following the lead of the Jews in whose company they had chosen to place themselves. And since by Jewish reckoning days commence after sunset, the sense of the Greek text seems best rendered by *"Motza'ei-Shabbat,"* not "Sunday."

In various places this commentary notes the Christian Church's tendency to expunge Jewish influences, and I think an instance arises when the present verse is understood to refer to Sunday night. A Sunday night meeting would imply a break of one full day of work between the Jewish *Shabbat* and the gathering at which Sha'ul spoke. Although Sha'ul cautions Gentiles against being "Judaized" into legalistic observance of the Jewish Sabbath (Co 2:16–17&NN, and possibly Ga 4:8–10&N), although he asks the believers in Corinth to set aside money for the Jewish poor of Jerusalem also on "the first day of the *sabbaton*" (1C 16:2&N), and although Yochanan at Rv 1:10 speaks of what most translators render as "the Lord's day" (I translate it "the Day of the Lord"; see note there), nevertheless the meeting in Ephesus must have been on Saturday night. For in this city, as in other places, Jewish believers constituted the core of the congregation — Sha'ul "took the *talmidim* with him" from the synagogue (19:8–9), with many Gentiles coming to faith later (19:17, 20). The Jewish believers, as explained, would have been accustomed to prolonging *Shabbat*, so that they would probably not have minded Sha'ul's **talking till midnight.** A Saturday night meeting would continue the God-oriented spirit of *Shabbat*, rather than require the believers to shift their concern from workaday matters, as would be the case on Sunday night.

I do not find the New Testament commanding a specific day of the week for worship. There can be no objection whatever to the practice adopted later by a Gentile-dominated Church of celebrating "the Lord's Day" on Sunday, including Sunday night; but this custom must not be read back into New Testament times. On the other hand, Messianic Jews who worship on Saturday night rather than Sunday can find warrant for their practice in this verse.

8–9 The **many oil lamps burning** made the room smoky and stuffy and depleted the oxygen. I suppose **Eutychus** was **sitting on the window sill** to get some air. Unfortunately it still didn't keep him from going **sound asleep** and falling to his death.

10 Compare Kefa's raising Tavita from the dead (9:35–41; see 19:11–12N) and Yeshua's raising three people from the dead; see Yn 11:17N.

16 ***Shavu'ot*** ("Weeks," Pentecost; see 2:1N). Sha'ul's desire to hurry to Yerushalayim for *Shavu'ot* shows that as a Messianic Jew he remained devoted to the *Torah* and to Jewish practice (see 13:9N). We can see this also from the fact that on another occasion he felt he had to justify a decision to remain in Ephesus and *not* go up to Jerusalem for this pilgrim festival (1C 16:8–9&N).

18–19 You yourselves know how… I was with you… serving… with much humility. Sha'ul does not indulge in self-praise but appeals to the judgment of the Ephesian congregation's elders, who had known and experienced him for three years (v. 31). While often accused, even in the New Testament itself (2C 10:1–13:10), of pride in his accomplishments, nevertheless, like Moses, who could write that he was "the meekest of all men on the face of the earth" (Numbers 12:3, Mt 11:28–30&N), Sha'ul had reached a point where he could speak of himself without either undue praise or undue modesty. (He had also learned not to be unduly affected by physical circumstances and possessions, Pp 4:12.)

21 The Gospel is the same for Jews as for non-Jews: repentance and trust in God through Yeshua the Messiah. The Two-Covenant theory (see Yn 14:6&N) is wrong.

22–23 See 19:21 for Sha'ul's first statement of this intention, and 21:4, 10–14 for further interaction with the Holy Spirit on the matter. The rest of the book of Acts deals with the dramatic outworking of this plan and premonition.

26–27 I am innocent of the blood of all. To the unbelieving Jews of Corinth Sha'ul had said, "Your blood be on your own heads; for my part, I am clean" (18:6&N). At the outset the Corinthians had refused to hear him; these Ephesian elders, attentive till now, still risk falling away and having **blood** guilt on their heads. The serious problems that will arise in Ephesus after he leaves (vv. 28–31) he has tried to avert by proclaiming **the whole plan of God**; their responsibility is to remain in "the care of the Lord and the message of his love and kindness" (v. 32).

33–35 Sha'ul earned his own living and did not become a burden to the Ephesians (see 18:3&N).

35 The words of the Lord Yeshua himself, "There is more happiness in giving than in receiving." These words of Yeshua's appear nowhere else in the New Testament — that is, they are not found in the Gospels. There are many apocryphal New Testament books which contain numerous purported other sayings of Yeshua. See Lk 2:52N.

36 Sha'ul kneeled down with them all and prayed. See Lk 22:41&N.

CHAPTER 21

4 Guided by the Spirit, they told Sha'ul not to go up to Yerushalayim. Is God divided? Does he speak from both sides of his mouth? Can the Holy Spirit tell Sha'ul to go to Yerushalayim (20:22) and also speak through others telling him not to go? First, the two events are not at the same time. God can give an order and then rescind it, as he did in the case of Abraham's sacrificing Isaac (Genesis 22), or make a promise to destroy Nineveh and then change his mind because its inhabitants repent (Jonah 4). But here the *Ruach HaKodesh* is giving the believers of Tzor a word of knowledge (1C 12:8–10&N) that in Yerushalayim Sha'ul will meet with trouble. This word, already sensed by Sha'ul (20:23), is confirmed again shortly afterwards (vv. 10–14&N). But it is their own inference, not the Holy Spirit's command, that Sha'ul should therefore not go on. Their urging seems reasonable, and it appeals to sentiment. But it is not the Lord's will for Sha'ul, whom he told at the beginning that his ministry would involve suffering (9:16).

7 Ptolemais, named after the Ptolemys, the rulers of Egypt. Modern Akko (Acre), north of Haifa.

8 Philip the proclaimer of the Good News, not the emissary but **one of the Seven** appointed *shammashim* (6:5, 8:5), settled in **Caesarea** (8:40&N). Although it was the Roman capital, Philip must have won only Jews to the Lord at first; since Kefa later brought the first Gentile to faith in that very city (10:1–11:18).

10–14 A prophet named Agav, mentioned earlier (11:28; see also 11:27N). Facing a similar situation Yeshua said to Kefa, "Get behind me, Satan!" (Mt 16:23). Yeshua was angry at the Adversary; here Sha'ul is sorrowful over his friends' efforts to dissuade him from doing what the Spirit wants him to do (see v. 4&N). In the end the others assent, subordinating their feelings to the Lord's will.

18 Ya'akov, the half-brother of Yeshua and leader of the Messianic Community in Yerushalayim (see 12:17N).

19 Sha'ul does not mention the great collection he and his companions were bringing with them for the Jewish poor in Yerushalayim; we assume it was duly delivered (see 24:17&N). His concern is rather with **the things God had done among the Gentiles** through him. He is not boasting; the elders need to be brought up to date on how the Lord is moving in places abroad (compare 14:26–27&N).

20 On hearing it they praised God. An attempt is sometimes made to prove that the believers in Yerushalayim opposed Sha'ul's efforts to reach Gentiles with the Gospel. These words prove the contrary: these believers, who were intensely committed to their Jewishness, praised God for what Sha'ul was doing and addressed him as "**brother**"; compare Ga 2:6–10.

Many tens of thousands. Most English versions render Greek *muriades* as "thousands"; but the word, like its Hebrew equivalent, *r'vavot*, means, literally, "tens of thousands." Although "*muriades*" gives English its word, "myriads," which is not specifically quantitative, there is no reason here to turn a word which *is* specifically quantitative into one which is not, let alone into a different quantity. The matter is important because there is a theory common in non-Messianic Jewish circles that Messianic Jews constituted a negligible proportion of first-century Jewry. This assumed quantitive insignificance is then used to explain the relatively infrequent mention of Yeshua in Jewish sources and their almost complete neglect of Sha'ul.

It is hard to develop a defensible estimate of the number of Messianic Jews in the first century. I occasionally read in Messianic Jewish publications that there were half a million or a million, but I have yet to see anyone take responsibility for these numbers in print by naming primary sources. Nevertheless, there are some benchmarks. The *Encyclopedia Judaica*'s article on "Population" states:

> "...a census of the Jewish population taken by Emperor Claudius in 48 C.E.... found no less than 6,944,000 Jews within the confines of the empire.... It stands to reason, therefore, that shortly before the fall of Jerusalem the world Jewish

population exceeded 8,000,000, of whom probably not more than 2,350,000–2,500,000 lived in Palestine." (13:871)

The article also notes that Jews constituted some 40% of the 500,000–1,000,000 inhabitants of Alexandria, "in which case the Alexandrine [Jewish] community may well have exceeded in size that of Jerusalem in its heyday." Thus the Alexandrine Jewish community numbered 200,000–400,000, and the Jerusalem community "may well have" been smaller.

What proportion of the Jews of Jerusalem were Messianic? The word "*muriades*" in this verse, if taken literally, necessarily means at least 20,000 Messianic Jews. Twenty thousand, the minimum number of Messianic Jews, is 5% of 400,000, the maximum population of the city. Thus at least 5% of the Jews of Jerusalem were Messianic. If we carry this exercise in mathematical logic one step further and assume that 5% of the world Jewish population was Messianic, we can deduce that there were at least 400,000 Messianic Jews alive in the world before the fall of Jerusalem.

Moreover, archeological data yield much lower figures for city populations. Magen Broshi, curator of Jerusalem's Shrine of the Book, which houses the Dead Sea Scrolls, estimates the city's population at the end of King Herod the Great's rule (c. 4 B.C.E.) at 40,000, and before the destruction of the Second Temple (c. 66 C.E.) at 80,000; these figures do not include the "suburbs" outside the city walls ("Estimating the Population of Ancient Jerusalem," pp. 10–15 in *Biblical Archeology Review* 4:2 (1978)). If there were 80,000 Jews and 20,000 Messianic Jews, the Messianics constituted a quarter of the city's population! But I find this unimaginable — a minority constituting a quarter of the Jewish population of Jerusalem could not have sunk into the oblivion suffered by the early Messianic Jewish community.

Another factor enters, although its consideration implies changing the word "**Judeans**" to "Jews" (see next part of this note, on "Judeans"). The population of both Messianic and non-Messianic Jews in Jerusalem was swollen by pilgrims who, like Sha'ul, had come for *Shavu'ot*, or who, like the Jews in 2:5–11, had stayed over since *Pesach*. Josephus wrote how the population of Jerusalem swelled up for the pilgrim feasts. If Magen Broshi's estimate should be tripled for *Shavu'ot*, 20,000 is about 8% of 240,000; and applying this to the world figure yields 640,000 Messianic Jews in the world.

But there were **many** *muriades*, which must mean more than the minimum of 20,000. There could have been 30,000, 50,000 or more Messianic Jews in Jerusalem when Sha'ul arrived. In this case the world figure could well approach the million mark.

On the other hand, if it can be shown that *muriades* is not used literally to denote "tens of thousands" but figuratively to mean merely "very many," then we can conclude next to nothing about the Messianic Jewish population in the first century. However, the burden of proof falls on those wanting to discount the word's literal meaning, since Luke employs numbers literally when describing the size of the Messianic Community and uses nonnumerical terminology when speaking less precisely about its growth (see 2:41&N). The word "*muriades*" can be satisfactorily rendered "tens of thousands" in all three places where Luke uses it (Lk 12:1, Ac 19:19, here), and likewise at its three other New Testament appearances (MJ 12:22; Yd 14, where I render it "myriads"; and Rv 9:16).

Judeans, or "Jews." Normally I render Greek *Ioudaioi* "Judeans" when the context is the Land of Israel, but when the context is the Diaspora, I translate it "Jews" (see Yn 1:19). Here both contexts are present, and one can make a case either way. The location is Yerushalayim, obviously in the Land, so I have put "Judeans" in the text. Moreover, the Judeans were the Jews most likely to be **zealots for the *Torah*.** But the social context of the pilgrim feast brings in the Diaspora, as noted above and at 2:5; see 2:11N. Moreover, the textual context includes both "Gentiles" (v. 19) and "*Goyim*" (v. 21), which would argue in favor of rendering "*Ioudaioi*" "Jews" by way of contrast. In my view, a close call.

And they are all zealots for the *Torah*, or "jealous on behalf of the *Torah*." God himself is described as "jealous" at Exodus 20:5 and elsewhere. On "*Torah*" as a translation of Greek *nomos* see v. 21N. Nowhere in this narrative are these "zealots for the *Torah*" condemned for their devotion or for their adherence to the *Torah*. On the contrary, it was normal for Messianic Jews in Jerusalem to observe the Jewish Law. Not only were they Jews (not ex-Jews), but they behaved Jewishly, which means that they observed the *Torah* and were zealous for it. Their self-identification and their identification by others was as loyal Jews concerned for preserving the Jewish people, as the next verse demonstrates.

And so it is today. Messianic Jews today too regard themselves as loyal Jews. Most have increased their Jewish consciousness as a result of coming to trust in the Jewish Messiah, Yeshua; and most are actively concerned for preserving the Jewish people. The model fostered in parts of the non-Messianic Jewish community that when one believes in Yeshua one leaves the Jewish people is false and misleading. There is no ground for it in the New Testament, which time and again demonstrates exactly the opposite. Churchmen who spread the lie that Jewish believers in Yeshua are no longer Jewish do incalculable harm to the Gospel, to the Jewish people and to the Church — not least by lending credibility to non-Messianic Jews who have their own defensive reasons for holding the same view.

21 **What they have been told about you**. Not, "They know that you…." Ya'akov's careful choice of the verb "*katêchêthêsan*" (from which comes the English word "catechism"), in the passive voice, means that he was fully aware that what these zealous Messianic Jewish brothers had heard about Sha'ul was not true. They had been told a lie, a rumor had spread, gossip had circulated. The problem, as becomes evident immediately, was not what Sha'ul had done (for he had not done the thing these people had been told), but how to deal with a situation where people are misinformed and feelings run high because they are **zealots**.

What had they been told? **That you are teaching all the Jews living among the *Goyim***, living among the Gentiles, in the nations outside Israel, in the Diaspora, **to apostatize** (Greek *apostasia* means, literally, "standing apart" and implies rebellion) **from Moshe**, that is, from the *Torah* God gave to Moses on Mount Sinai, from the Jewish Law. This apostasy consists of two parts, **telling them not to have their sons circumcised and not to follow the traditions.** These were also the issues in Acts 15.

The importance of circumcision has already been discussed at 15:1&N, 16:1–3&NN. Opposing the command that embodies Jewish distinctiveness would be tantamount to teaching that the Jewish people as such are unimportant and have no future (which is exactly what Replacement theology does teach; see Mt 5:5N and other references there). Not following the traditions means not observing the *Torah*, probably including the Oral Law as well as what is written in the *Tanakh*.

The accusation against Sha'ul, then, was that he was a traitor to the Jewish people who taught Jews all over the Diaspora to cease functioning as Jews. Here are three points to refute the charges:

(1) Sha'ul himself did not violate the *Torah* but continued to keep it after coming to trust in Yeshua. He had Timothy circumcised (16:3). He kept numerous Jewish customs — taking a vow (18:18&N), observing festivals (20:16&N), paying for the vow-ending sacrifices of four men at the Temple (vv. 23–27 below), evidently fasting on *Yom-Kippur* (27:9&N). He regularly attended synagogue services and was welcome to teach in them (17:2, etc.). As a Messianic Jew he remained a Pharisee (23:6&N). Thus he could say that he believed everything that accords with the *Torah* (24:14), that he had committed no offense against the *Torah* (25:8), and that he had a clear conscience in the sight of God and man (24:16); against his claims his accusers failed to make a case in court (26:31–32). At the end of his ministry he continued to assert exactly the opposite of what he is charged with here, saying, "I have done nothing against either our people or the traditions of our fathers" (28:17). For still more evidence see 13:9N.

(2) Sha'ul's teaching not to circumcise (1C 7:18&N; Ga 5:2–6&NN, 6:12–15&NN) and not to observe Jewish laws and customs (Ga 4:8–11&NN, Co 2:16–23&NN) were never directed to Jews but invariably and only to Gentiles. Gentiles had to be reassured that they were saved and incorporated into the people of God by trusting God through the Messiah Yeshua, not by observing this or that set of Jewish practices or by converting to Judaism; for, although Judaism acknowledged that the righteous Gentile had a share in the world to come, there was in the first century a strong movement for Jewish proselytism (see Mt 23:15&N and references there).

(3) Sha'ul did not need to instruct Diaspora Jews to observe the Law, for there was no shortage of rabbis and teachers to exhort them (Ac 15:21). Moreover, what in the *Tanakh* could be clearer than that Jews are expected to keep the *Torah*? The New Testament does not repeat truths already evident from the *Tanakh*; it assumes them. Sha'ul assumed them too.

Thus we dispose of the indictment against Sha'ul. But this verse also hints at a crucial question for today's Messianic Judaism: should Messianic Jews keep the Law? Many Orthodox and Conservative Jews with a strong commitment to their religion, who consider obedience to the Law the central distinctive of Judaism, **have been told** that Christianity teaches Jews **to apostatize from Moshe, telling them not to have their sons circumcised and not to follow the traditions.** Believing it, they are likely to consider Messianic Judaism not Judaism at all. How Messianic Jews should relate to the Law is far too broad an issue to discuss in this commentary, but I have dealt with it throughout my book, *Messianic Jewish Manifesto*, especially in Chapter V ("*Torah*"); see particularly pp. 136ff. (On the other hand, when Messianic Jews do circumcise their sons and follow the traditions, there are non-Messianic Jews who accuse them of deception — see 2C 4:1–2&N. A "Catch–22" if there ever was one!)

22–24 Action is necessary in order to head off a violent confrontation with the "zealots" due to their believing the false rumor of v. 21.

In spite of the arguments of v. 21N confirming Sha'ul's loyalty to Judaism and the *Torah*, many Christians suppose that when Sha'ul came to faith in Yeshua he stopped being Jewish, stopped observing the Law and began teaching other Jewish believers to do likewise. But those who hold this mistaken opinion have a serious problem with the ethics of these verses. If Sha'ul was not really *Torah*-observant, if he really did teach the Jews in the Diaspora not to have their children circumcised and not to follow the traditions, than he and Ya'akov are exposed orchestrating a charade to deceive the Jewish believers zealous for the *Torah* into discounting the truth they had been told and believing a lie instead. Nothing in the whole New Testament justifies this understanding of how Ya'akov, Sha'ul or any other believer functioned.

23 **A vow**. A voluntary vow; the terms are set forth in Mishna Nazir (see also 18:18N). Generally such vows were from one to three months in length. The outward elements consisted in not touching anything dead, refraining from any product of the grapevine and not cutting one's hair (see Numbers 6:1–21). At the end of the vow the Nazirite had his hair cut and burned it on the Temple altar, and certain prescribed sacrifices were offered.

24 The exact details of this procedure, presumably a common one, are uncertain. However, the *Torah* states the central requirements:

> "This is the *torah* of the *nazir* on the day when the period of his vow is completed. He is to be brought to the entrance of the Tent of Meeting and is to present his offering to *Adonai*: a yearling male lamb without blemish as a burnt offering, a yearling ewe without blemish as a sin offering, a ram without blemish as a peace offering, a basket of *matzah*, loaves of fine flour mixed with oil, *matzah* spread with oil, and their grain offering and drink offerings." (Numbers 6:13–15)

Clearly the four men were poor; otherwise they could have bought their own sacrificial animals and gifts. Sha'ul as patron must do more than merely **pay the expenses**; he too must be accepted by the *cohanim* and be ritually purified. The process took seven days (v. 27).

Everyone will know, Greek *gnôsontai*, which implies certain knowledge of what is true, in contrast with what they "have been told" (v. 21). This means that Ya'akov already understood perfectly, and the zealous Jerusalem believers would soon see, **that there is nothing to these rumors they have heard about** Sha'ul; **but that, on the contrary**, in Ya'akov's words to Sha'ul, **you yourself stay in line** (Greek *stoicheis*, "walk, stand in line; are in the ranks") **and keep the *Torah*.** The authority of Ya'akov stands behind the assertion that Sha'ul was *Torah*-observant.

25 This repeats the *din* (Hebrew for "ruling," halakhic decision) of 15:19–20&NN and 15:28–29, reassuring Gentiles that the preceding three verses dealing with the situation of Messianic Jews do not affect the earlier determination that Gentiles can become Christians without becoming Jews.

27 **Unbelieving Jews**. See 9:22–23N. The unbelieving Jews from Asia stirred up **all the crowd**, which included many Judean unbelieving Jews. Sha'ul had long been concerned about them (see 1 Th 2:14–16&NN, Ro 15:31&N).

28 Five lies. Sha'ul did not teach **against the people** or **against the *Torah*** or **against this place** (the Temple); nor had he **brought some *Goyim* into the Temple** or **defiled this holy place**. The accusations were precisely the ones most likely to stir up feeling against him. A Gentile entering the Temple's inner court would ceremonially defile it.

29 **Trophimus from Ephesus**, whom Sha'ul had brought with him (20:5). People "from the province of Asia" (20:4) would have been the ones most likely to recognize him.

30–32 The Roman battalion was stationed in the Antonia Fortress, immediately adjacent to the Temple grounds; so it did not take long for them to arrive and prevent the mob from lynching Sha'ul.

37–40 A dramatic and inspiring instance of what Ep 5:16 (KJV) calls "redeeming the time": Sha'ul turns his rescue into an opportunity for proclaiming the Gospel to his would-be killers.

38 **That Egyptian**. The first-century historian Josephus reports that he came to Jerusalem around 54 C.E., during the time of Felix (23:24N):

> "At this time someone came out of Egypt who said he was a prophet and advised the masses of the common people to go with him to the Mount of Olives, where he would show them how, at his command, the walls of Jerusalem would fall down; and he promised he would enable them to enter the city through those walls after they had fallen down. When Felix was informed of these things, he ordered his soldiers to take their weapons, and he came against them from Jerusalem with a great number of horsemen and footmen. He attacked the Egyptian and the people with him, slaying four hundred of them and taking two hundred alive. The Egyptian himself escaped from the battle but did not appear any more." (Condensed from *Antiquities of the Jews* 20:8:6)

40 **In Hebrew**, literally, "in the Hebrew language," which could have been either the Aramaic heard more often in public or the Hebrew still spoken in public but more often at home. See Mk 5:41N.

CHAPTER 22

1 **Brothers and fathers**. Stephen, Sha'ul's former enemy, used the same words to address an unfriendly audience (7:2&N); see also 23:1&N. The fact that Sha'ul's circumstances here and his speech have several other features in common with Stephen's gives a certain sense of closure (see 7:58).

2 In Hebrew. See 23:40N.

3 Born in Tarsus. Sha'ul was born a Hellenistic Jew; by announcing this he increases his identification with his Asian accusers.

But brought up in this city. He also identifies with the Jerusalemites, probably the majority.

And trained at the feet of Gamli'el. On Gamli'el himself see 5:34N. Jewish tradition says nothing about Sha'ul's apprenticeship with the most distinguished rabbi and scholar of his time. In fact neither the Talmud nor any early *midrash* says anything about him at all — a fact that cries out for an explanation. In an article called "Paul and the Law — 'All Things to All Men,'" the Messianic Jewish scholar H. L. Ellison writes of Elisha ben-'Avuyah, who was one of the great rabbis of the early 2nd century and who is quoted in the Mishna (Avot 4:20) but later apostatized:

> "He was excommunicated and is almost always referred to as *Acher* (The Other One). There was never any danger of tradition's keeping his memory green, for it told also of how he had deliberately profaned the Sabbath. In other words, his false teaching had been sterilized and rendered harmless, not so much by his excommunication but rather by his notorious breach of the law. With Paul, however, his memory had to be forgotten, for there were no stories that could be told about him that would neutralize his teaching." (Included in W. Gasque and R. Martin, editors, *Apostolic History and the Gospel*, Grand Rapids, Michigan: Eerdmans, 1970, p. 199)

This is because Sha'ul, unlike Elisha ben-'Avuyah, kept the Law all his life, as the rest of Ellison's article proves and as I have shown at 13:9N, 16:3N and 21:21N. Aware of this, and heeding the principle that "the only bad publicity is having your name misspelled," the rabbis said nothing about Sha'ul. The principle is still in use; often the non-Messianic Jewish community's response to Messianic Judaism, especially the forms of it which are willing to grapple seriously with relating to the *Torah*, is to ignore it publicly, to pretend it doesn't exist — in the hope that it will go away, which it will not.

Trained... in every detail of the *Torah*... and I was as zealous for God as all of you are today. Sha'ul completes the recitation of his credentials by reminding his hearers that he too knows the *Torah* and has stood in their shoes, as zealous as they (compare Ga 1:13–14&NN). It is said that a fool learns from his own experience, but a wise man can learn from the experience of others. Sha'ul hopes that even among this zealous mob there will be some who are wise and can profit from hearing where their present path leads.

5–16 This second report of Sha'ul's coming to trust in Yeshua diverges in some details from those at 9:3–19 and 26:13–18. See 26:13–18N on reconciling the differences.

12 Chananyah, an observant follower of the *Torah* who was highly regarded by the entire Jewish community, or: "...who[se character] is witnessed to by all the Jews living there." In other words, the fact that he was a *Torah*-true Jew can be verified by whoever wants to do so. This fact about Chananyah, not reported at 9:10–17, is relevant for Sha'ul's present audience. (Another instance of Sha'ul's appealing to objective verifiability is when he answered those who doubted whether Yeshua had actually been resurrected; see 1C 15:5–8&NN.)

14 The *Tzaddik*, or "the Righteous One"; see 7:52&N, where Stephen too used this term for Yeshua the Messiah. At Isaiah 53:11 God speaks of "my righteous servant," who will "make many righteous."

16 Immerse yourself, Greek *baptisai;* the verb is in the middle voice, which means that it has reflexive force. If the word were in the passive voice here, "be immersed" would be appropriate. Jewish practice in the *mikveh*, for proselyte baptism as well as for other ritual purifications, is self-immersion, in contrast with the common present-day Christian baptismal practice of being immersed by someone else.

17 It happened that as I was praying in the Temple, I went into a trance, Greek *ekstasis*, "standing outside oneself." The ecstasy was unusual, but Sha'ul's praying in the Temple area was normal Jewish behavior. This fact, which Sha'ul mentions casually, without emphasis, all the more strongly evidences that Sha'ul continued his usual Jewish practices after coming to faith in Yeshua (see 13:9N, 21:21–24&NN).

18–21 The Lord tells Sha'ul to leave Jerusalem because the Jewish people there will not respond to his message. Sha'ul immediately trots out his Jewish credentials, objecting that the Jews of Jerusalem ought to accept what he says now because they know how diligently he opposed the believers in the past (vv. 4–5). But Yeshua repeats his command, **"Get going!"** (v. 21).

Why won't the Jews of Jerusalem hear Sha'ul? Because a believer's having opposed the Gospel in the past is not what makes a nonbeliever believe. On the contrary, the believer's faith now outweighs everything else about him. No matter how reasonable his beliefs seem to himself now, a believer cannot substitute his own stormy process of coming to faith for that of someone else.

Therefore, in instructing Sha'ul to get on with his task of evangelizing the Gentiles (v. 21) Yeshua is saving Sha'ul years of fruitless endeavor which would have been the outcome of following his own natural desire to devote all his energy to winning his Jewish brothers (Ro 10:1). Sha'ul's earthly wisdom would not have led him to the specific mission Yeshua had designed for him. The Lord knows better than we how we can best serve him. Moreover, the book of Acts shows that Sha'ul experienced no small measure of success with Jews as well.

21 I am going to send you far away, to the *Goyim*. The Messianic Community in Jerusalem sent Sha'ul home to Tarsus (9:30), where for some thirteen years he had the opportunity to proclaim the Gospel to the Gentiles. Later, with this experience behind him, he set out on his travels to reach non-Jews throughout the Eastern Mediterranean area.

22 The objection was to Sha'ul's message, which grants Gentiles equality with Jews as part of God's people; see Ep 2:11–16&NN. That this was the objection is proved by 21:27–30.

23 Waving their clothes gave their anger a visible dimension. Likewise they probably were

throwing dust only because there were no stones handy (compare 7:58, Yn 8:59). My guess, based on thirteen years of living in the Middle East, is that the **dust** was not thrown **in the air** vaguely or ceremonially but purposefully and vigorously in Sha'ul's direction!

24 The commander, still convinced Sha'ul must be a dangerous criminal, since he had not understood Sha'ul's message in Hebrew (v. 2), was determined to whip the truth out of him.

25 As in Philippi (16:36–40&N) Sha'ul makes full use of his legal rights not merely to save his hide but also to protect the honor of the Gospel. Both whipping him and binding him in chains (v. 29) would violate his rights as a Roman citizen. Since Sha'ul had not been charged, nor had the commander been informed of grounds for a charge, whipping Sha'ul prior to a trial would have been a misuse of authority for which the commander would have been liable. By questioning the whipping Sha'ul was saving the commander as well as himself an unpleasant experience.

27 Sha'ul's "**Yes**" is certainly true; summary death awaited anyone falsely claiming Roman citizenship.

30 The only way the commander can now find grounds for holding Sha'ul is to receive an accusation from others, in this case the *Sanhedrin*.

CHAPTER 23

1 **Sha'ul looked straight at them** and probably recognized many familiar faces in the *Sanhedrin*, since he may well have once been a member himself (26:10&N). In any case, it is clear from vv. 6–10 that he understood his audience.

Brothers. These people are still Sha'ul's brothers (compare 22:1&N). However, this is not a formal meeting of the *Sanhedrin*, for "Brothers" is not a mode of address appropriate for a court in regular session (rather, it is appropriate for old friends; see above paragraph). Instead, this is the gathering summoned by the Roman commander (22:30). In no other *Sanhedrin* session does the person being questioned commence the proceedings with a speech of his own (compare 4:5–22, 5:21–40, 6:12–7:60; Lk 22:66–71). Also, in a formal session the identity of the *cohen hagadol* would have been clear to Sha'ul (vv. 2–5; but see note there).

2–5 Sha'ul's outburst is certainly not the behavior of a man who had heard and understood Yeshua's command to turn the other cheek (Mt 5:39). Yeshua himself, when struck, argued the injustice of it without vexation or irritation (Yn 18:22). But no claim of perfection is made for Sha'ul. Like the heroes of the *Tanakh*, whose failings are reported faithfully along with their victories, he is shown to be a man who has not yet achieved the goal, as he himself admits (Pp 3:12–13, 1C 9:25–27). God saves imperfect people.

I didn't know, brothers, that he was the *cohen hagadol*. It has been suggested that this line drips sarcasm, that Sha'ul knew perfectly well who the *cohen hagadol* was but means that he wasn't acting like one!

6 On the ***Tz'dukim*** and ***P'rushim*** see Mt 3:7N.

I myself am a *Parush* (a Pharisee), Greek *egô Pharisaios eimi*. "*Egô*" ("I") adds emphasis ("I myself"), and the verb "*eimi*" is present tense ("am"). Though a Messianic Jew for some twenty years, Sha'ul still considers himself a Pharisee (compare Pp 3:5). This fact alone invalidates equating "Pharisee" with "legalist" or "hypocrite"; see 15:5&N, Mt 23:13–36N.

It is concerning the hope of the resurrection of the dead that I am being tried. Compare Yeshua's correction of the *Tz'dukim* on this point (Mt 22:23–32). A Pharisee could believe in Yeshua and his resurrection and remain a Pharisee like Sha'ul; Luke refers to other believing *P'rushim* at 15:5. But it is difficult to see how a Sadducee could remain a Sadducee after coming to faith in the risen Yeshua (see v. 8&N), and the New Testament makes no mention of believing Sadducees. It does mention believing *cohanim* (6:7&N), and some of these may well have been *Tz'dukim* before coming to faith.

8 The *Tz'dukim* believed the human soul disappeared with the body; only God's Spirit remained. One hundred fifty years later belief in **resurrection** of the dead had become an essential ingredient of normative Judaism, for Mishna Sanhedrin 10:1 says:

> "These have no part in the *'olam haba* [the world to come]: those who say the resurrection of the dead cannot be inferred from the *Torah*...."

For more, see Mt 22:31–32N.

The existence of angels and spirits is an issue because of what Sha'ul said in his earlier address (22:6–11, 17–21); see v. 9. On angels, see 7:53&N; Ga 3:19&N; MJ 1:4–2:18&NN, 13:2b&N.

9 **What of it?** Compare *Rabban* Gamli'el's similarly restrained reaction to the believers' claims (5:39).

10 Sha'ul's tactic of diverting the *Sanhedrin*'s attention away from himself and his supposed crime to a long-standing dispute among themselves succeeded.

12 **Judeans** (see 21:20N, Yn 1:19N), or possibly "unbelieving Jews" (see 9:22–23N).

Took an oath, saying they would neither eat nor drink till they had killed Sha'ul, which they failed to do (vv. 16–35). But they didn't starve to death, for such an oath could be dissolved by the rabbis.

> "The sages have allowed four kinds of vows to be nullified: vows of urging, vows of exaggeration, vows made in error and vows made under duress" (Mishna N'darim 3:1).

See Numbers 30:3–16(2–16) and Deuteronomy 23:22–24(21–23) on vows; and compare 18:18&N, Mt 5:33–37&N.

15 The conspirators would have overcome the Roman guard bringing Sha'ul across the Temple court from the Antonia Fortress to the *Sanhedrin* chambers.

16 We know a bit about Sha'ul's parents — they were Hellenist Jews who also were Pharisees; they were of the tribe of Benjamin; and they spoke Hebrew as well as Greek (23:6, Pp 3:5) in the town where they lived, Tarsus in Cilicia. But we know nothing about his sister or about his nephew, who was visiting or living in Jerusalem and who helped save him. How his nephew became privy to the plot is uncertain. Either Sha'ul's enemies included members of his own family, in which case the nephew's presence would not have alarmed them; or his relationship to Sha'ul was unknown to the plotters.

24 **Felix the governor**, or, more exactly, the procurator of Judea. He was governor of Shomron (Samaria) from 48 to 52 C.E., while Cumanas ruled Judea. When the latter was removed from office for failing to suppress rioting between the Jews and Gentiles of Caesarea, Felix replaced him. About him Tacitus wrote, "With all cruelty and lust he exercised the power of a king with the spirit of a slave," referring to his being a freedman of Emperor Claudius' mother Antonia. Felix had three wives in succession, the last being Drusilla (24:17).

25 **The following letter**, literally, "a letter having this form." Luke must have had access to the document itself in order to quote it exactly.

30 **I immediately sent him to you and ordered his accusers to state their case against him before you.** Claudius Lysias knows that these accusers have nothing against Sha'ul worthy of judgment in a Roman court (compare 18:12–16, 25:19&N) — he has already learned that and just said so (vv. 28–29). But he wants to extricate himself from a bad situation which he has already bungled several times.

31 **Antipatris**, currently being excavated by archeologists at Tel Afek, northeast of Tel Aviv. It is 42 miles from Jerusalem and 26 miles from Caesarea. On a visit there I saw the capital of a Roman column that had been discovered accidentally by a farmer plowing his field; it was still in place, just six inches below the surface.

34 **Cilicia** was ruled by the propraetor of Syria, and Sha'ul might have to be heard before him.

35 **Under guard in Herod's headquarters building** (the Praetorium). Sha'ul is placed in military custody for his protection but not put in a prison cell, since no charges have yet been brought against him.

CHAPTER 24

1 **Chananyah**. See 23:2–5&N.

Tertullus. Probably Jewish ("we," vv. 5–6); but his having a Latin name suggests that he may have had good Roman connections.

2 It was customary to begin a presentation in court with a compliment, in this case flattery so excessive as to contradict the facts (see Tacitus' remark at 23:24N).

5 Tertullus presents the accusation against Sha'ul briefly but not well. Being a **pest** is hardly an indictable crime. "**World**" renders Greek *oikoumenê,* "the inhabited earth"; but Felix is not Caesar and does not have jurisdiction beyond his own district.

The sect of the *Natzratim*, a Hebrew word derived from "*Natzeret*" (Nazareth), the town where Yeshua the Messiah lived most of his life. The Greek word used here is "*Nazôraios*"; it is used six times in Acts and five times in the Gospels as descriptive of Yeshua himself, and in these places the *JNT* renders it "from Natzeret." Today a similarly derived Hebrew word, "*Notzrim,*" is the ordinary word for "Christians"; after two thousand years it no longer refers to a group considered to be within Judaism. Most English translations use the term "Nazarenes" in this verse. See also Mt 2:23&N.

Greek *airesis* gives us the English word "heresy," but its meaning here is "**sect.**" It is used in Jewish literature to refer to other groups, including the *P'rushim* — it does not necessarily have a negative connotation.

Tertullus wants Felix to understand the *Natzratim* as a Messianic group, and that any group supporting a Messiah is loyal to a different king and subversive of Roman hegemony.

6 **He tried to profane the Temple.** The Asian Jews thought he had actually done so (21:28), but by this time even his accusers realized he had not. Attempted profanation of the Temple is a reduced charge.

We arrested him. This is a gross understatement — they wanted to lynch him (21:30–32&N).

6b–8a Even in the manuscripts which provide this additional information Tertullus avoids mentioning *why* **Lysias the commander intervened**, namely, to save Sha'ul from the plot on his life (23:12–24).

10–21 Sha'ul's defense before Felix responds to each of Tertullus' three points: (1) During his twelve days in Jerusalem he incited no insurrection (vv. 5, 11–13), (2) his being a *Natzrati*, a follower of Yeshua from *Natzeret*, is no ground for complaint (vv. 6b, 14–16), and (3) he did nothing wrong, either in the Temple or elsewhere (vv. 6a, 16–18). Finally, he challenges his accusers to bring against him any charge that will stand up (vv. 19–21).

12 Sha'ul raised no commotion in the Temple but went about his business quietly, in a manner consistent with his purpose of placating those Messianic Jews who were "zealots for the *Torah*" (21:20ff.). It would have been counterproductive for him to have done anything which did not demonstrate that he "stays in line and keeps the *Torah*" (21:24).

14 **The Way**. See 9:2&N; 18:25–26; 19:9, 23; 22:4, where "the Way" is used in the same technical sense to refer to the beliefs and practices of Yeshua's followers. The term implies that "the Way" is the *right* Way. "**Which they call a sect**" implies that his accusers regard it as one way among several, and a way they do not like. Sha'ul refers back to Tertullus' use of the word "sect" and neutralizes any possible negative overtone (v. 5&N).

I worship the God of our fathers. This is precisely the response a present-day Messianic Jew makes to Jews who consider him apostate. The God we worship is the only God, *Elohey-avoteynu*, "the God of our fathers" (the phrase is found in the first blessing of the *'Amidah*, the central synagogue prayer). Likewise today's Messianic Jew, with Sha'ul, believes **everything that accords with the *Torah*** "as upheld by the Messiah" (1C 9:21&N, Ga 6:2&N) **and everything written in the Prophets**, including the prophecies pointing to Yeshua as the Messiah (see Section VII of the Introduction to the *JNT*, Mt 5:17&N, Lk 24:25–27&N).

15 Which they too, the *P'rushim* but not the *Tz'dukim*, **accept** (see 23:6N).

A resurrection of both the righteous and the unrighteous. Only here does Sha'ul mention the resurrection of the unrighteous. For his teaching on the resurrection of the righteous see 1C 15&NN, 1 Th 4:12–17&NN. Yeshua teaches the resurrection of the righteous and the unrighteous at Yn 5:29&N; it is mentioned clearly in the *Tanakh* at Daniel 12:2. This dual resurrection underlies all passages speaking of future judgment, including Mt 25:31–46, Yn 12:48, Ro 14:10, 2C 5:10 and Rv 20:4–6, 11–15. Also see v. 21N below.

16 Sha'ul **makes a point of always having a clear conscience** precisely because he has a clear awareness of coming judgment; see 1C 3:10–15, 9:25–27; Pp 3:12–17.

17 To bring a charitable gift. Not mentioned in Chapter 21, but confirmed by Sha'ul in his own letters (Ro 15:25–31, 1C 16:1–4, 2C 8:1–9:15, Ga 2:10).

The gift was not only for Messianic Jews but for unbelieving Jews as well, since they too are included in "**my nation**" (see Ro 15:25–31&NN and Ga 2:10&N, where believing Jews and Gentiles are enjoined to show kindness and charity toward Jews specifically.) That Sha'ul considered the Messianic Jewish community in Jerusalem part of the Jewish **nation** is not even an issue, nor should there be any question today that Messianic Jews are part of the Jewish people. (In spite of this the State of Israel's High Court of Justice in 1989 made Messianic Jews Israel's *refuseniks* — the only Jews in the world not to be considered Jews for purposes of Israel's Law of Return, which allows any Jew anywhere to immigrate to Israel and be a citizen.)

19 But some Jews from Asia — they ought to be here.... Sha'ul interrupts his own more accurate report of what transpired in the Temple, perhaps to gain control of his hot temper before discussing in front of a non-Jewish judge the misbehavior of his fellow Jews. See 23:2–5&N.

21 Other than this one thing...: "I am on trial... because I believe in the resurrection." See 23:6–10&NN. Sha'ul not only believes in but has seen and heard the resurrected Yeshua. His point is that a Jewish community divided on whether resurrection takes place at all is in no condition to judge him or other Messianic Jews on whether Yeshua is the Messiah. It would be as if Ferdinand Magellan's crew were to stand trial for claiming to have circumnavigated the globe before judges who differed on whether the earth is round or flat.

The principle can be applied today. For example, if a group of people, Jewish or not, is divided over whether or not the Bible is God's inspired word to humanity, with most "right-wing" people, *e.g.*, Orthodox Jews and Evangelical Christians, saying it is, and most "left-wing" people, e.g., Reform Jews, Liberal Christians and secularists, saying it is not or hedging, it would be confounding issues for a Messianic Jew to try to defend his faith before them all together; since they would already, for their own reasons, be in disagreement over a point that Messianic Judaism takes as given.

22 **When Lysias the commander comes down**. There is no evidence that he ever did. Felix is simply putting off a decision in Sha'ul's favor that would alienate the leaders of the people he is ruling. See v. 26 for a clearer picture of Felix's motives.

24 **Drusilla**, the youngest daughter of Herod Agrippa I (see 12:1N). Since she **was Jewish**, it may have been from her that Felix acquired "a rather detailed knowledge of things connected with the Way" (v. 22). She died with her son in the eruption of Mount Vesuvius that destroyed Pompeii in 79 C.E.

25 **Righteousness, self-control and the coming Judgment**. Sha'ul delivered a complete salvation message suited to the condition of his hearer: the past, when Yeshua through his atoning death made righteousness available to everyone (Ro 3:21–26, 5:8); the present, when the Holy Spirit empowers believers to lead increasingly holy lives, with self-control being not only necessary but possible (Ga 5:22–23); and the future, when everyone — including Felix, you and me — will be judged (1C 3:10–15).

Felix was **frightened** enough not to want to hear more about judgment, but not frightened enough to believe the Gospel, which offers an alternative to the divine penalty for sin, death. "How will we escape if we ignore such a great deliverance?" (MJ 2:3)

26 **He hoped Sha'ul would offer him a bribe.** The "charitable gift" (v. 17) piqued his interest. Perhaps he thought the Gentiles who contributed to the Jewish nation might provide the funds to buy Sha'ul's freedom.

27 **Porcius Festus**, procurator of Judea from 59 to 62 C.E. The Porcia family had attained senatorial rank in Rome centuries earlier.

CHAPTER 25

1 Festus had just arrived from Rome, was unfamiliar with Judea and went to Jerusalem as soon as he could to acquaint himself with the leaders and the current issues.

2–3 The Judean leaders did not make a demand but made use of the opportunity to ingratiate themselves with Festus by giving him the pleasure of granting an apparently minor and harmless request. They counted on his ignorance of the reason why Sha'ul had been sent down from Yerushalayim in the first place, namely, because of a plot not unlike the one described here. They hoped Festus would send Sha'ul with a small guard that could be easily overcome.

4 Perhaps Festus was in fact familiar with why Sha'ul was in Caesarea; or he preferred to adhere to the normal course of Roman justice, rather than make an exception that could produce untoward consequences for which he would be blamed. Maybe he was simply too busy to deal with this special request so early in his term of office, or he may have suspected not all was *"kosher."* He plays safe, offers standard procedure, and the Judean leaders can only accede.

6 Festus remained in Jerusalem only long enough to get his bearings (v. 1&N), **eight or ten days.** The very next day after returning to Caesarea he arranged for Sha'ul's retrial.

7–8 Once again no good case was made against Sha'ul, and once again he defended himself against the three major possible accusers — the Pharisees, concerned with **the *Torah***; the Sadducees and *cohanim*, concerned with **the Temple**; and the Roman state, embodied in **the Emperor**. Luke omits the specifics of both accusation and defense.

9–11 Progress on Sha'ul's case ceased for two years while Felix waited, perhaps for a bribe (24:26). Now, with Festus showing himself uninterested in justice, Sha'ul decides to enter his appeal to be tried by the highest authority, a right available to Roman citizens since 509 B.C.E. Yeshua had promised that Sha'ul would one day go to Rome (23:11), and he himself had long wanted to go there (Ro 1:10–15&N). His dream is fulfilled at 28:16.

13 **King Agrippa**. Herod Agrippa II, the last Herodian king, was raised in Rome and made king in 50 C.E., six years after the death of his father Herod Agrippa I (see 12:3N). His capital was Caesarea Philippi (modern Banyas), at the foot of Mount Hermon, some 40 miles northeast of Caesarea, where modern Israel, Lebanon and Syria meet.

Bernice was Agrippa's sister, so their relationship was incestuous. Felix's wife Drusilla (24:24) was sister of both. Bernice was later mistress of two emperors, Vespasian and Titus, and almost became Empress. Obviously she had long since given up whatever vestiges of Jewish religion and morals she might have once had.

14 Agrippa and Bernice made an official visit to welcome the new procurator but stayed on longer than necessary for the purpose. Festus used the time discuss the perplexing but not pressing issue of Sha'ul.

19 Gallio in similar circumstances had refused to sit in judgment on a matter of internal concern among Jews (18:12–16). Festus was less wise. Nevertheless this Gentile's description of the dispute as one **about certain points of their own religion** is additional evidence that Messianic Judaism is a form of Judaism.

CHAPTER 26

1 Sha'ul **began his defense**, not in a judicial sense, for he is not being tried before Herod Agrippa II (see 25:13N). Since he has already appealed to Caesar (25:11), it is before him that he will be making a formal defense in court. Rather, Sha'ul is "defending" his whole life, his Gospel, his Lord. From Sha'ul's (and Luke's) viewpoint he is doing even more than that: he is making use of an extraordinary opportunity to proclaim the Gospel to yet another kind of audience, the ruling elite (compare Lk 21:12–15). His hearers see him as a prisoner, but he sees himself as a bringer of Good News. That Sha'ul's picture of the situation is correct is seen in the responses of Festus (v. 24) and Agrippa (vv. 25–29), for they relate not to Sha'ul's guilt or innocence but to the Gospel message.

Sha'ul's speech may be outlined thus: (1) Introduction (vv. 2–3), (2) Sha'ul the zealous Pharisee (vv.4–8), (3) Sha'ul the zealous persecutor of Messianic Jews (vv. 9–11), (4) Sha'ul confronted by Yeshua the Messiah (vv. 12–18), (5) Sha'ul the zealous preacher of Yeshua (vv. 19–20), (6) Sha'ul's arrest by zealous unbelieving Jews (v. 21), (7) Sha'ul focussing his own zeal on the I-thou encounter of the moment, as he offers his hearers salvation through trusting Yeshua the Messiah (vv. 22–23, 25–27, 29). The pivot-point in Sha'ul's life, as well as in his speech, is part (4), his confrontation by Yeshua. The pivot in the lives of his hearers is part (7), his present proclamation of the Gospel, with its choice between obeying God or not. Sha'ul's zeal, his singleminded pursuit of his purpose in life, contrasts with the effete and indifferent dilettantism of the Roman aristocrats, as portrayed in Chapter 25 and in vv. 24–32 below.

2–3 **By Jews**; or possibly "by Judeans," who are also Jews (see 21:20N, Yn 1:19N). But not "by the Jews," as if "the Jews" were alien to Sha'ul; moreover, in the Greek there is no article before "*Ioudaioi*" here or in vv. 3, 4 or 7.

Agrippa himself was a Jew (his father Agrippa I wasn't but his mother was, since his mother's mother's mother was Mariamne, the Hasmonean princess and second of King Herod the Great's ten wives; see 16:1N). The reason Sha'ul says he **considers himself fortunate** to be making his defense before him is that Agrippa, who is not only Jewish by birth but **well informed about all the Jewish customs and controversies**, will appreciate the situation. Sha'ul is talking to a *landsman* (Yiddish: "fellow Jew") and knows he can dispense with the sort of detailed explanations that would be necessary to get himself understood by pagans. The irony of vv. 6–7 would be lost on Festus.

Nevertheless, Sha'ul knows that he will be able to communicate with Festus and the rest of the assembly too, because when the king pays close attention they too will pay close attention (I can't help thinking of the song: "When the *rebbe* laughs/cries, all the *Hasidim* will be laughing/crying…").

Sha'ul's introduction, which is complimentary yet free of fabricated flatteries (contrast 24:2–4), sets the tone for the rest of the speech.

4–5 Sha'ul can take it as a given that **all Jews know,… and if they are willing, they can testify** about him (for evidence of this see 21:21 and possibly 28:21–22). There had not yet been an effort to expunge Sha'ul from the history of the Jewish people (see 22:3N), although, by implication, some Jews would already have refused to vouch for him.

In my own country, Cilicia — and in particular, the city of Tarsus.

In Yerushalayim, where Sha'ul had studied under *Rabban* Gamli'el (22:3).

I lived as a *Parush*, a Pharisee. The Greek verb is in the aorist tense, which implies action accomplished in the past that has effects continuing into the present. Sha'ul lived as a Pharisee in the past, and he continued doing so after he became a believer (see 23:6&N, Ga 1:14&N, Pp 3:5&N). By emphasizing, for the benefit of the gallery (Agrippa already knew it; see vv. 2–3N), that the *P'rushim* are **the strictest party of**

our religion, all the more does he imply that as a Messianic Jew he remained *Torah*-observant (see 13:9N, 21:21N).

6–7 **How ironic**! An informed Jew like Agrippa can appreciate the irony; this is why Sha'ul calls his attention to it by addressing him directly. Agrippa himself may not cherish the hope of resurrection, but he knows very well that **our twelve tribes** do.

8 **Why do you people consider it incredible that God raises the dead?** There is a tendency among liberal scholars to regard Yeshua's resurrection not as an event in verifiable human history but as a subjective event in the realm of faith. This is not the Bible's approach at all. J. Warwick Montgomery writes,

> "On the Areopagus [Paul] presents Christ's resurrection as the capstone of his case for the truth of the gospel (Acts 17:19–31). In 1 Corinthians 15 he blends *kerygma* [proclamation] with *apologia* [proof] by offering a list of eyewitness testimonies to the evidential fact of the resurrection. In his stand before Agrippa and Festus (Acts 26), he not only assumes that these sin-blinded sinners can evidentially arrive at the facticity of the resurrection ('Why should it be thought a thing incredible with you, that God should raise the dead?'), but also appeals to a common ground of evidential knowledge ('The king knoweth of these things, before whom also I speak freely: for I am persuaded that none of these things are hidden from him; for this thing was not done in a corner' [v. 26 below, KJV])... Christian [and Messianic Jewish] faith is not blind faith or credulity; it is grounded in fact. To talk about a real but unprovable resurrection is as foolish as to talk about suprahistorical or spiritual resurrections. They are all cop-outs — sincere, certainly, but terribly harmful in an age longing to hear the meaningful affirmation, 'He is risen.'" (*Faith Founded on Fact*, Nashville, Tennessee: Thomas Nelson, 1978, pp. 78–79).

For more, see 1C 15:2–8&NN.

9 F. F. Bruce paraphrases: "Pharisee though I was, and thus in theory a believer in the resurrection of the dead, I yet judged it incredible in this particular case, and thought it my duty to oppose such a heresy," then adds, "In later years Paul thought himself unfit to form any judgment by himself (2 Corinthians 3:5)." (*Commentary on Acts*, p. 442)

10 **I cast my vote against them.** This phrase, taken literally, constitutes evidence that Sha'ul was at one time a member of the *Sanhedrin* (see 7:58N, 8:1&N, 23:1&N; Ga 1:14&N). But the expression may be literal in a context other than the Great *Sanhedrin*; or it may be figurative, meaning only that he too favored punishing Yeshua's followers with death.

11 **Trying to make them blaspheme**, that is, trying to make them denounce Yeshua, by threatening them with death unless they recanted. See 7:59–60N on *kiddush-HaShem*, martyrdom for God's sake.

13–18 This is Sha'ul's third version of his encounter with Yeshua on the road to Damascus, the others being at 9:3–19 and 22:5–16. Some details in the reports differ. In Chapter 9 the light is said to have flashed around Sha'ul and his companions; in the other tellings it surrounded Sha'ul. In Chapter 9 his companions stood speechless, hearing the voice but seeing no one; in Chapter 22 they saw light but did not hear the voice of the speaker; and here, in Chapter 26, they all fell to the ground. Each telling, having its own purpose and being directed to a particular audience, emphasizes different aspects of what happened. Here is a composite consistent with all three versions. The light surrounded both Sha'ul and his companions. They all saw the light, but only Sha'ul saw Yeshua. They all heard some sort of sound, but only Sha'ul heard distinct words. All fell to the ground, but Sha'ul's companions got up again.

Understood as what it is described as being, a supernatural event, no further explanation is needed. But some who do not believe in supernatural events have attempted to "demythologize" Sha'ul's "conversion experience" as a combination of coincidences, psychotic or epileptic seizures, and embellishments. (The very term "conversion experience" subtly prejudges the matter by focussing on subjective aspects, whereas in all three reports Sha'ul emphasizes the objective.)

Phillip Goble, in his one-man play, *The Rabbi From Tarsus* (Wheaton, Illinois: Tyndale House, 1981), depicts Sha'ul in a Roman dungeon at the end of his life, with his physician and chronicler friend Luke peering down at him through a hole in the roof. Paul is dictating information for the book of Acts:

> "Now let me pause to clear up one thing, Luke — for the benefit of the scoffers you must refute. What exactly made me switch… not religions, but vocations, from that of persecutor to that of advocate and apostle? What was the problem, Doctor? Are the scoffers right? Was it really just a case of sunstroke? Nervous collapse? Hallucination? Guilt catharsis? 'What is truth for you, Saul, is not truth for me,' they say. 'There are natural explanations for everything.'"
>
> (Paul reclines on the stone bench like a man talking to his psychiatrist.)
>
> "Yes, yes, Doctor. Here is the natural explanation. One day, on the road to Damascus, while I tried to enforce the Law of Moses, piously serving my God with all my heart, I — the arrestor — was arrested… by a naive superstition. Quite naturally, a meteor just *happened* to blaze across the sky. At the very same time, it just *happened* to thunder, so that the other rabbis quite naturally did see and hear *something*. At the very same time — clumsy me — I just *happened* to fall off my horse. And at the very same time, I just *happened* to hallucinate with a nightmare vision, complete with face, fire and voice, that just *happened* to be my enemy, who just *happened* to want me to go to work for him! — among people who just *happened* to be my enemies, the Gentiles. At the very same time, I just *happened* to have tissues form over both my eyes with a purely accidental case of coincidental cataracts."
>
> (Rising)

"Yes, Doctor, there are natural explanations for everything, if one has enough bad blind faith to go his own way. (Many, like Nero, are lords of their own lives who want to go their own way, even if it may lead to hell.) But, Luke, I had to trust God, and like any other disciple, take a step of faith into the *mikveh* waters and into the Damascus synagogue."

14–15 I heard a voice saying to me in Hebrew,... "I am Yeshua." See Mk 5:41N on whether Hebrew or Aramaic was spoken in Yeshua's time, and Mt 1:1N on the name "Yeshua." The movement by English-speaking Messianic Jews to call the Messiah by his Hebrew name, "Yeshua," which the Savior and his friends would have used during his lifetime, instead of the more common "Jesus," has actually been denounced by a few Gentile Christians as being "separatist," "rebuilding the middle wall of partition" (Ep 2:14) between Jews and Gentiles in the Messianic Community. But this verse gives more than adequate ground for the practice: if it was good enough for Yeshua to call himself "**Yeshua**," it is good enough for us too. It is perverse to regard adoption of Yeshua's own custom as separatist.

16–18 Chananyah is not mentioned (contrast 9:10–17, 22:12–16), for Agrippa would not have been interested in the role played by "an observant follower of the *Torah*" (22:12&N).

16 Stand on your feet. The same words as used by *Adonai* in calling Ezekiel to service as a prophet (Ezekiel 2:1) suggest that Sha'ul too was being called to speak for God.

When I appear to you in the future. For other appearances of Yeshua to Sha'ul see 18:9–10, 22:17–21, 23:11, 27:23–24; 2C 12:1–9.

17 The people, Greek *laos*, which refers to the Jews (10:2&N, 10:42&N).

20 That they should turn from their sins to God and then do deeds consistent with that repentance. On "turn from sins" and "repentance" (Greek *metanoieô* and *epistrephô,* corresponding to Hebrew *shuv*) see Mt 3:2N. Sha'ul's message was the same as that of Yochanan the Immerser (Mt 3:2, 8) and Yeshua (Mk 1:15, Mt 23:3); compare Ep 2:8–10&NN, Ya 2:14–26&NN. The New Testament in general, and Sha'ul in particular, are sometimes thought to proclaim an easy and painless salvation which makes no demands on the individual. This verse shows that Sha'ul expected followers of Yeshua not merely to assent to a creed but to do good works.

21 Jews. Not "the Jews" (see 26:2&N). Sha'ul is still occupied with the paradox that it is Jews, not Gentiles, who are opposing him. The usual translation, with the definite article, which is not present in the Greek text, pits Sha'ul against "the Jews" as a whole; it is therefore effectively antisemitic, even if not deliberately so (see Ro 10:4&N, 10:6–8&N).

22–23 I stand... saying nothing but what the Prophets and Moshe said would happen. Yeshua had done the same (Lk 24:25–27&N, 44–45), showing how the *Tanakh* pointed to himself. See Section VII of the Introduction to the *JNT*, which lists 54 *Tanakh* prophecies and their New Testament fulfillments. Sha'ul dealt particularly with two questions still raised by many Jewish hearers of the Gospel: Why must the Messiah suffer and die? and, How are the Gentiles included with the Jews as equal sharers in God's promises?

24 Festus could no longer contain himself. Sha'ul had not even been talking to him, but to the King, whom he had addressed no less than four times. Perhaps Festus thought Sha'ul was wasting the king's time with nonsense and felt embarrassed at having arranged the session, so that he was trying to excuse himself by pre-empting the critic's role. A more likely explanation of his interruption is that he was troubled by the Gospel message itself and attempted to blunt its impact by discrediting its proclaimer. The same tactic is often used today by hearers of the Gospel, both Jewish and Gentile, who would rather not relate seriously to it. Sha'ul's calm and measured reply (vv. 25–27) gives the lie to Festus' charge and in fact makes *him* sound like the **crazy** one!

One hears much about "deprogramming" people whose beliefs and practices, like Sha'ul's, have suddenly changed. One justification offered by deprogrammers and those who hire them is that the person being deprogrammed is **out of** his **mind,... crazy** — exactly what Festus thought of Sha'ul. It is true that sometimes transformations of belief-systems turn out for the worse. But can that justify capturing an adult Jew whose life has noticeably improved because he has come to faith in Yeshua and subjecting him to involuntary psychological manipulation and abuse, in order to change him from being a supposedly **crazy** believer in the Gospel into a supposedly sane unbeliever? One such horror story is reported by the person to whom it happened, Ken Levitt, writing with Ceil Rosen, in the book *Kidnapped For My Faith* (Glendale, California: Bible Voice, 1978). Fortunately these ill-advised and illegal efforts usually fail, since faith is not acquired by force, and people do not trust Yeshua the Messiah because they are crazy but because they are convinced that the Gospel is true.

26 Sha'ul senses that the level of his discourse has been beyond Festus' spiritual capacity. Sha'ul does not have time to explain everything to him just then. Rather, aware that he wishes to be well thought of by his superiors, Sha'ul can relieve Festus' anxiety by assuring him that Agrippa will not think Sha'ul insane. (For another aspect of this verse, see v. 8N.)

In some back alley, literally, "in a corner."

28–29 In short, you're trying to convince me to become Messianic (Greek *Christianos*, usually rendered "a Christian"). See 11:26N, which explains that the word "Christian" referred to Gentile believers, since the Jewish believers were called *Natzratim* (24:5&N). Agrippa's remark shows that he has become aware of Sha'ul's evangelistic purpose (see 26:1N). But his use of the word "*Christianos*" instead of "*Natzrati*" may carry a mildly twitting overtone: "you're trying to convince me to become a Gentile as well as a believer in Yeshua" — a response heard to this day from Jewish people presented with the Gospel. No Messianic Jew wants an unbelieving Jew to stop being Jewish and become a Gentile, he only wants him to trust in Yeshua. This is what Sha'ul implies in his answer: refusing to relate to Agrippa's term "*Christianos*," he instead points with earnest intensity to himself as an example of the kind of faith he covets for Agrippa and for all the rest of his audience.

32 The appeal to the Emperor cannot be annulled because Festus accepted it publicly before Sha'ul's accusers.

CHAPTER 27

1–44 This account of Sha'ul's trip to Rome is considered one of the finest ancient descriptions of a sea voyage.

2 **Aristarchus** from Thessalonica was with Sha'ul in Ephesus (19:29) and accompanied him with the collection from the Gentile congregations to Yerushalayim (20:4). He went with Sha'ul to Rome (Co 4:10, Pm 24).

9 **It was already past *Yom-Kippur*,** literally, "past the Fast." It is as a matter of course that Luke writes of the Jewish holiday *Yom-Kippur* (the Day of Atonement). This is evidence that Sha'ul continued observing Jewish practices, keeping the Law until the end of his life (see 13:9N, 21:21N, 22:3N). It also lends strength to the contention that Luke himself was Jewish or a proselyte to Judaism; he would otherwise be unlikely to measure time for his Gentile reader (1:1–4) by the Jewish calendar.

Shipping became increasingly risky after mid-September and was rarely engaged in after mid-October because of the likelihood of storms. *Yom-Kippur* can occur between September 14 and October 14.

For a Jewish believer *Yom-Kippur* has a different significance than for the unbeliever. A Messianic Jew knows that Yeshua the Messiah, by his death on behalf of all sinners (Yn 3:16; Ro 3:21–26, 5:8), has become the final *kapparah* ("atonement," literally "covering"; the word is a cognate of "*kippur*"). For this reason no further sacrifices for sin are necessary; this is the subject of Messianic Jews 7–10&NN.

10 It is possible that Sha'ul was prophesying, in the sense of giving forth a word of God. Or he may simply have been offering his opinion as an experienced sea-goer who had seen disasters before — he had been shipwrecked three times and been adrift overnight on wreckage (2C 11:25). But his advice went unheeded.

14 **A full gale**, Greek *anemos tuphonikos* (the first means "wind"; the latter gives us the English word "typhoon"). They tried to hug the south coast of Crete; but the **northeast** wind, blowing from shore, drove them out to sea, where the larger waves were more difficult to deal with.

22 **You should have listened to me.** We cannot know whether Sha'ul was indulging himself in a well-earned but all-too-human "I told you so," or reminding his hearers of their mistake so that they would be more willing now to hear his message of hope.

23–26 Even in a storm at sea, as cargo is being thrown overboard, Sha'ul loses no occasion to communicate the Gospel, or at least to arouse the curiosity of his shipmates. Verse 26 is predictive prophecy, fulfilled at v. 41.

31 **Unless these men remain on board the ship, you yourselves cannot be saved.** But hadn't God already promised that not one life would be lost (vv. 22, 24)? Think of it this way: the prophecy includes God's foresight concerning decisions which are nevertheless made by free will. If the sailors had left the boat, would the centurion's and his soldiers' lives have been saved? This is a hypothetical question which need not be answered, since that is not what happened, and we have no framework for dealing with such questions. Once again we are reminded of Rabbi Akiva's summary of the paradox, "All is known, yet free will is given" (Avot 3:15).

Moreover, in the Holy Scriptures, even what appears to be an absolute prediction ("X will happen") may be implicitly conditional ("If you disobey God, X will happen"). Jonah's apparently unconditioned prediction of Nineveh's destruction (Jonah 3:4) is a good example — the prophet was wrong (and angry about it) because the people of Nineveh repented (which, rather than the city's ruin, is what God actually wanted).

Why did the sailors have to stay on board? It was a practical matter: had they left, there would not have been enough skilled personnel left to operate the ship in the storm.

35 **Said the *b'rakhah*** which Jews normally make over bread, "*Barukh Attah, Adonai Eloheynu, Melekh-ha'olam, haMotzi lechem min ha'aretz*" ("Praised be you, *Adonai* our God, King of the universe, who brings forth bread from the earth"). See Mt 14:19N.

41 This verse says, literally, "And coming upon a place between two seas they drove the vessel; and while the prow, having run aground, remained immovable, the stern was broken by the force." The sense is not exactly clear from the text. I have surfed for over thirty years; and this gives me some knowledge of how the sea works, which, I hope, helps solve the mystery. When a swell reaches an island, its waves split to pass it, and they may meet head-on at the far end of the island. At this place, the sand carried along by the currents from both directions is deposited as a sandbar or sand spit, on which the waves break from two nearly opposite directions, sometimes even running straight into each other. Such a spot makes for lively surfing but is very treacherous for ships and boats. My translation reflects this understanding, based on my experience surfing the islands off the coast of Southern California.

CHAPTER 28

6 The deliverance confirms justice, refutes superstition and fulfills Yeshua's promise that believers can expect miracles (Mk 16:17–18, Lk 10:19).

They said he was a god. Compare 14:11–12.

8 Yeshua often laid his hands on the person to be healed (Mk 5:23, 6:5, 16:18; Lk 4:40, 12:13). Chananyah laid his hands on Sha'ul that he might regain his sight (9:12, 17). See also 5:12.

13–14 **Puteoli** had a strong colony of Jews, so it is not surprising that some of them were Messianic.

16 We arrived in Rome, where Sha'ul had appealed to be tried before the Emperor (25:9–11&N).

17–31 The concluding passage of the book of Acts contains very important material for understanding the relationship between Judaism and Christianity, Gospel and *Tanakh*, Messianic and non-Messianic Judaism, Jewish and Gentile Christians. The conclusion is that Sha'ul had a very successful evangelistic ministry among the Jewish community of Rome, and that entire synagogues became Messianic. It is one of the high points of Messianic Jewish history.

17 The local Jewish leaders. In his **three days** Sha'ul had arranged with the brothers in the Roman community, of whom he knew many (see Romans 16), to draw up a list of Jewish community leaders; for he would quickly have ascertained what these leaders later said themselves (vv. 21–22), that they knew very little about the Gospel. Thus Sha'ul saw an evangelistic opportunity. The believers in the Roman congregation had apparently not done much to evangelize the 10,000 or more Jews living in Rome (*Encyclopedia Judaica* 14:242), or they had tried but been ineffective. Perhaps they wished to avoid the sort of persecution some of them might have already experienced in Yerushalayim when they came to faith at or shortly after *Shavu'ot* (2:10), or after the martyrdom of Stephen (8:1–3). Or the persecution alluded to in 18:2&N might have shocked them into silence.

19 When the Judeans (Greek *Ioudaioi*) **objected**. At 26:2, 7, 21 the same word is rendered "Jews," because there the contrast is between Jews and Romans. Here, speaking to Jews, Sha'ul is referring specifically to the Jews of Judea, not "the Jews" in general. See 26:2N, 26:21N; Yn 1:19N.

21–22 These Jewish leaders were very open-minded, more so than today's usually are. The situation in Rome was different from the others described in the book of Acts, where very quickly the non-Messianic Jewish community took a hostile position against the Messianics. Somehow the Roman believers avoided such a clash with the non-Messianic synagogues, so that at Sha'ul's arrival they were willing to listen and not immediately opposed.

23 Surely this all-day session in which **large numbers** of "local Jewish leaders" (v. 17) of the capital of the world came to visit the world's leading evangelist in order to hear about Messianic Judaism must be unique in world history.

Sha'ul's procedure with them was the same as with Jewish people everywhere: he appealed to the *Tanakh*, **making use of both the *Torah* of Moshe and the Prophets to persuade them about Yeshua.** Sha'ul could use the Scriptures freely, since many of the Jewish leaders probably knew them by heart.

But Sha'ul's central topic was **the Kingdom of God.** This term (and its equivalent, "Kingdom of Heaven") is used frequently in the Gospels (see Mt 3:2N); but it appears in Acts only at 1:3, 8:12, 14:5, 19:8 and here (compare also 1:6). At 15:10N a paragraph from the Mishna was cited in which Jews are enjoined to accept "the yoke of the Kingdom of Heaven" (acknowledging God and who he is) even before accepting "the yoke of the *mitzvot*." Rather than presenting the Gospel as something alien or superior to Judaism, Sha'ul discusses a topic well known to his audience of Jewish leaders; and his object is to expand their conception of it by his **thorough witness**. Sha'ul must have spent hours explaining what the whole New Testament teaches, namely, that at this point in history accepting "the yoke of the Kingdom of Heaven" implies accepting the entire Gospel. God's active and present rulership is expressed through the Messiahship and Lordship of Yeshua, the salvation he brings to humanity, and the improvement he brings to the inner lives and outward behavior of believers through the continuing work of the Holy Spirit ("sanctification").

24–25 Some were convinced by what he said, while others refused to believe (Greek *apisteô*, "disbelieve, refuse to believe, be unfaithful"). Of the "large numbers" of Jewish leaders present (v. 23), "some" (Greek *oi men*, "these, on the one hand") were persuaded and "some" (*oi de*, "these, on the other") disbelieved, refused to believe. The "some" and the "some" are correlative, of comparable size, of more or less the same order of magnitude. What may reasonably be concluded, therefore, is that the whole leadership of Rome's Jewish community was well represented by the "large numbers," and that a sizeable proportion of them, though not necessarily half, were persuaded of the truth of Messianic Judaism then and there. This is why I say that the meeting must be unique in world history (v. 23N) — I know of no other reported instance of a sizeable proportion of a major Jewish community's leadership coming to faith in the Gospel in one day.

So they left, disagreeing among themselves. The Gospel properly proclaimed always causes division, because those who believe it and those who do not have different world-outlooks (see 20:3N, Mt 10:35–36, Yn 7:43N). Since those who were persuaded were leaders, they surely returned to their synagogues and communicated the Gospel themselves; so that in due time, especially with Sha'ul's continued teaching over the next two years (v. 30), entire synagogues must have become Messianic. A "people-movement" took place in Rome, a movement in which entire families and communities were won to the Lord Yeshua the Messiah. Though we are not told this directly, the indications are present: an openness to the Gospel rather than a predisposition against it, leaders being persuaded, substantial numbers being involved, broad community participation, respect for the evangelist and Spirit-blessed ministry.

25–27 Sha'ul's **final statement** quoting Isaiah 6:9–10 is not an imprecation, an anathema, or a curse, but a warning to the **some** who **refused to believe**, a last word of persuasion recalling the events that took place in Yesha'yahu's day and which are repeated whenever people harden their hearts. Like Pharaoh, who hardened his heart too often, God eventually seals and makes final the hardening, so that it becomes impossible for the person to **do *t'shuvah*** (in earlier editions of the *JNT*, **return** to God), that is, "repent"; see Mt 3:2N, 13:13–15N, Yn 12:40N, Ro 9:17–21&NN. Heeding the quotation prevents suffering its consequences.

28 This salvation of God has been sent to the *Goyim* and they will listen! From 1:8&N we have seen that one purpose, perhaps the main purpose, of the book of Acts has been to show that the Gospel would spread "to the ends of the earth" and permeate the Gentile peoples. Some Christians have gone beyond this and claimed to see in the book of Acts the rejection of the Gospel by "the Jews," so that God rejected them and turned to the Gentiles, who gladly received the message. It is a fact that God's truth and his promises became available to Gentiles in a new way as a result of what God did during the early years of the Messianic Community, as reported in the book of Acts; for it was decided that Gentiles did not have to become Jews in order to become Christians (10:1–11:18&NN, 15:1–29&NN, 21:20–27&NN). Also it is a fact that Gentiles in substantial numbers believed the Gospel. Nevertheless, as we have just seen, Jews continued accepting Yeshua as Israel's Messiah right up to the very day on which the words of this verse were spoken. God had not rejected Jewish people as unworthy of the Gospel (see Ro 11:1ff.).

Some argue that the destruction of Yerushalayim in 70 C.E. closed the age of God's dealings with the Jews, and that Rome, the Gentile capital of the world, was to be the new center for propagating God's truth. Cited as evidence is that the book of Acts starts in Yerushalayim and ends in Rome. Certainly Rome became and remains the center for the largest Christian denomination, the Roman Catholic Church. But Jerusalem has never ceased to be the holy city, "beautiful for situation, the joy of the whole earth" (Psalm 48:3(2)), reverenced by three monotheistic religions. Now, after being "trampled down by the *Goyim*" for 1,897 years, it is at last once more in the hands of the Jewish people (since 1967); and with the apparent fulfillment of Yeshua's prophecy concerning this (Lk 21:24&N) it should, at the very least, be clear to all that God is continuing his work with the Jewish people.

The proper perspective is this: the Gospel was to move out from Jerusalem and the Jews to the Gentiles in "the ends of the earth," that is, to Rome and beyond. This was a new work of God, though not without antecedents, since Jews had been making proselytes for centuries (see Esther 8:17, Mt 23:15&N). It is not that "the Jews" were rejected but that the Gentiles were accepted (Ep 2:11–16&NN). This message shocked many Jews, and some Jews today still look down on Christianity as an "easy religion" not worthy of Jewish credence. This is why it was necessary to have the longest book in the New Testament deal with the question; and the answer of the book of Acts is that despite some Jewish resistance, God is bringing his truth to Gentiles and they are being included in the people of God without converting to Judaism. Yet the Jews are no less God's people — "with respect to being chosen they are loved for the Patriarchs' sake, for God's free gifts and his calling are irrevocable" (Ro 11:28–29).

29 This verse, not found in the best manuscripts, adds little, since we know that "they left, disagreeing among themselves" (v. 25), and obviously Sha'ul's parting shot did nothing to mute the debate!

30 As always, Sha'ul supported himself and did not rely on others, especially not on young and struggling Messianic congregations. In this respect he was like other rabbis of his day. See 18:3N.

31 **Openly and without hindrance proclaiming the Kingdom of God and teaching about the Lord Yeshua the Messiah** (see v. 23&N). The perfect note on which to end the book, whose purpose is secondarily historical and primarily inspirational. Even though under house arrest awaiting trial, Sha'ul was free — free for the one thing that gave meaning to his life, proclaiming the Gospel. By his life as well as his words he showed forth the Messiah in him; he was "a light to the Gentiles" (Isaiah 49:6) and to Jews too.

From prison (though possibly elsewhere) he wrote the letters to the Philippians, Ephesians and Colossians. Scholars are divided over whether he was ever set free. Some believe he eventually reached Spain, as was his desire (Ro 15:24); this would imply he was freed at least once. During his time of freedom he might have again visited the congregations he had established in Greece and Asia Minor; then, after a second arrest, he would have written his last letter, 2 Timothy, in which he anticipates his pending execution by writing, in the perfect tense, "I have fought the good fight, I have finished the race, I have kept the faith" (2 Ti 4:7). Tradition has it that he was condemned to death and executed in Rome between 64 and 68 C.E. Some think Luke intended to write a third book describing Sha'ul's life after the point at which Acts ends, since the story does not seem to be finished. But Luke's perspective in these last verses seems to be one of not knowing more. However, all this is based on inferences; there is no conclusive evidence.

THE LETTER FROM YESHUA'S EMISSARY SHA'UL (PAUL) TO THE MESSIANIC COMMUNITY IN ROME:

ROMANS

CHAPTER 1

1 Here is an outline of the book of Romans, Sha'ul's consummate epitome of the Gospel and its consequences.

CHAPTERS, VERSES	CONTENTS
1:1–15	Introduction, greetings.
1:16–17	Theme: The Gospel brings salvation to Jews especially and also to Gentiles, and its benefits are acquired by trusting.
1:18–11:36	I What the Gospel is: what God has done already and what He will yet do.
1:18–3:20	A. Everyone is guilty in God's sight.
1:18–2:16	1. Gentiles are guilty
2:17–3:20	2. Jews are guilty
3:21–5:21	B. The guilty will be regarded by God as forgiven and righteous if they trust in Yeshua's atoning sacrificial death.
6:1–8:39	C. Being united with the Messiah enables believers to lead increasingly righteous lives pleasing to God and to have eternal life.
9:1–11:36	D. Believers can trust God to keep his promises to them. The chief obstacle to such trust is God's apparent failure to keep his promises to the Jewish people, accompanied by Jewish unbelief. But God will keep his promises to the Jews as individuals; and as a

	nation, the Jewish people will accept Yeshua as the Messiah; thus "all Israel will be saved." See 9:1–11:36N for detailed outline.
12:1–15:33	II What believers should do because of what God has done. Ethical behavior and right heart attitudes.
16:1–25	Conclusion, greetings.

A motif running through the entire book, perhaps even the point of the letter, is that, in contrast with the historical period covered by the *Tanakh*, when the Jews alone were God's chosen people, now, united with Yeshua the Messiah of Israel, believing Gentiles and Jews are fully equal members of God's people in respect to every element of salvation (see v. 16N).

I wish to call attention to a massive work in progress which I hope will soon be ready for publication: Joseph B. Shulam and Hilary Le Cornu, *A Jewish Commentary on the New Testament: Romans*. For information write Netivyah, POB 8043, 91080 Jerusalem, Israel.

Sha'ul, "also known as Paul" (Ac 13:9&N), was a Messianic Jew who, as **a slave** (or: "servant") **of the Messiah Yeshua** (Mt 1:1N) and as **an emissary** (Mt 10:2–4N), **called and set apart** (Ac 9:3–19, 22:5–21; Ga 1:13–2:10), showed how Gentiles become part of God's people without having to become Jews through believing and obeying **the Good News** (or: "Gospel"; see Mt 4:23N) **of God** — both from God and about God.

2 God promised this Good News in advance (see Ga 3:8&N). In his letter to the Romans Sha'ul is always showing how the great truths he is expounding are derived from God's **prophets in the *Tanakh*** (what Christians call the Old Testament). As Edith Schaeffer put it in a book title, "*Christianity is Jewish*."

3–4 His Son, i.e., the Son of God (on which see Mt 4:3N). The Greek text of v. 4 is difficult and can be rendered differently; but its form suggests that Sha'ul is quoting a hymn, a fact reflected in the *JNT* by the three parallel clauses describing Yeshua:

(1) **He is descended from David, physically** (literally, "of seed of David according to flesh"), through his mother Miryam (Lk 3:23–38&N). Her husband Yosef was also descended from King David (Mt 1:1–16&N) but was not Yeshua's physical father; for Miryam was caused to give birth by God's Holy Spirit (Mt 1:18–2:12&NN; Lk 1:26–56&NN, 2:1–38&NN). While God is in one sense father to everyone, and in a more intimate sense to the people of Israel (Exodus 4:22, Mt 2:15N), he is father in this unique sense only to Yeshua (8:3&N, Yn 1:18&N, MJ 5:7–10).

(2) He is **Son of God spiritually.** Yeshua is therefore a man **set apart** (or: "designated," "determined"), different from other people in that he alone was qualified to bring salvation to humanity. This is **powerfully demonstrated** less by his manner of birth than **by his having been resurrected from the dead**, since that happened after a widely known ministry and was a public fact witnessed on a number of occasions (1C 15:3–8&NN). Moreover, his resurrection also powerfully demonstrates that

believers are assured of their own resurrection (8:28–39, 1C 15:12–57); this too is in consequence of his being the Son of God, spiritually.

(3) **He is Yeshua the Messiah, our Lord.** His being "Son of David" makes him the Messiah (see Mt 1:1N on both terms). His being Son of God implies that he shares God's very nature (Mt 4:3N) and is worthy to be called **our Lord.**

5a Grace or "undeserved favor," Greek *charis*, which incorporates attributes of God which the Hebrew of the *Tanakh* calls *chesed* ("loving-kindness") and *rachamim* ("mercy").

Sha'ul's commission from Yeshua is to promote **trust-grounded obedience**, often translated literally, "the obedience of faith" (on Greek *pistis*, "trust, faith," see Ac 3:16N). But this expression is ambiguous. Sha'ul does not mean "the obedience which *is* faith," he is not saying that obedience *consists in* having faith in Yeshua. Rather, he is speaking of the *good works* which flow from obeying God — the right deeds which are the necessary consequence of truly putting one's trust in God, his Word and his Messiah. This needs to be said because Sha'ul is often portrayed as promoting "faith" and opposing "works." The wrongness of such an oversimplification is discussed at 3:27–28&N, Ep 2:8–10&NN and Ya 2:14–26&NN.

Sha'ul's self-definition of his ministry at this early point in the letter and again at the end of it (16:26) must be kept in mind when reading Romans. With passion he opposes both legalism (works stemming from prideful self-sufficiency that ignores **trust** and regards performing good deeds as doing God a favor) and antinomianism (undisciplined living that ignores the **obedience** which leads to right action).

5b–6 Among all the Gentiles, including you. Greek *ethnê* corresponds to Hebrew *goyim* and may be translated "nations, ethnic groups, Gentiles, non-Jews, pagans, heathen"; see Mt 5:47N, 10:5N. If "Gentiles" is correct, Sha'ul is writing mostly to Gentiles; if "nations," he is writing to a mixed congregation of Gentiles and Jews. His addressing a Jew at 2:17 is inconclusive, since this is a rhetorical device. But his self-identification as "an emissary… among all the Gentiles" (v. 5; see also v. 13) and his specifically addressing Gentiles at 11:13 means that he is in this letter indeed speaking primarily to them. Thus, while his teaching in Romans is true (and truth is the same for both Gentiles and Jews), much of what he writes is directly applicable only to Gentiles. Understanding the book of Romans properly depends on determining which portions of it apply to everyone and which apply directly only to non-Jews.

7 Grace to you and *shalom* (more than merely "peace"; see Mt 10:12N) **from God our Father and the Lord Yeshua the Messiah.** This is Sha'ul's usual greeting, found in one form or another at the beginning of all his letters.

10–15 Sha'ul longed to reach Rome himself. He finally did so — in bonds (Ac 28:16; see Ac 25:9–11&N). The theme returns at 15:14–33.

14 Narrowly religious people, whether ultra-fundamentalist Christian or ultra-Orthodox Jewish, in their eagerness not to be contaminated by worldly, secular influences, sometimes forgo gaining knowledge which could enlarge their universe of experience and their understanding of how things and people work. Sha'ul was not like this.

He was a cosmopolitan who gladly acknowledged his **debt** to whoever had enriched his life.

16 **I am not ashamed of the Good News.** How often believers hide the Good News of the Messiah out of fear or shame — fear of being rejected or opposed (see Pp 1:27–28N), shame or embarrassment at being thought foolish or "different"!

How can such unworthy motives be overcome? By remembering Sha'ul's reason: **since it is God's powerful means of bringing salvation. Salvation** implies escape, safety, preservation, soundness, healing and deliverance from the consequences of sin, chief of which is death (Genesis 2:17). The Hebrew word for "**salvation**," "*yeshu'ah*," is the female form of the Messiah's name, Yeshua; for more see Mt 1:21N and Lk 2:11N. While the **Good News** is **powerful**, it can seem weak; but it is the weak and foolish things of God that confound the worldly-wise (1C 1:18–31).

To everyone who keeps on trusting. This renders the Greek more accurately than the usual translation, "to everyone who believes," not only because "trust" is closer to the biblical concept than "believe" (see Ac 3:16N), but also because the present tense of a Greek verb implies ongoing activity, not a once-and-for-all event.

To the Jew especially, but equally to the Gentile, literally, "both to Jew firstly and to Greek." A major theme of the book of Romans — some would say the main theme — is that, so far as salvation is concerned, Jews and Gentiles are equal before God (2:7–12; 3:9–31; 4:9–12; 5:12, 17–19; 9:24; 10:12–13; 11:30–32). By stating that the Gospel is the same for Jew and Gentile, this verse contradicts the Two-Covenant theory, which says that Jews and Gentiles have different ways to God, so that Jews do not need the Gospel (for further explanation and refutation see Yn 14:6&N).

Nevertheless, in spite of Jewish-Gentile equality before God, I have taken the Greek word "*prôton*," which has the literal meaning, "firstly," to mean "especially" in this verse. At 2:9–10 the same Greek phrase is twice translated, "to the Jew first, and then to the Gentile." My justification for the different rendering in this verse has to do with what sort of "firstly" is meant. I discussed this in my book *Messianic Jewish Manifesto* (pp. 259–261), from which the remainder of this note, except for the last paragraph, is taken (with minor changes):

Mitch Glaser, of Jews for Jesus, in his 1984 Covenant Theological Seminary lecture trenchantly entitled, "'To the Jew First': The Starting Point For The Great Commission" (lecture given at Covenant Theological Seminary, 1984), presented three options for understanding this phrase. He concluded that it does not refer only to "historical priority," to the historical fact that Yeshua brought the Gospel to Jews before Gentiles knew about it, or to Sha'ul's always proclaiming it to Jews prior to focussing on Gentiles — although both are historically true.

Nor does it refer only to "covenant priority," the idea that — as John Murray put it in his commentary on Romans,

> "Salvation through faith has primary relevance to the Jew… aris[ing] from the fact that [he] had been chosen by God to be the recipient of the promise of the Gospel and that to him were committed the oracles of God,"

although this too is true. Rather, "to the Jew first" means that there is a "present priority" to proclaim the Gospel to Jews, and the Church should acknowledge it. This does not necessarily mean that every single believer should seek out the Jews in the community and witness to them before telling any Gentiles about Yeshua — although that is exactly what Sha'ul did throughout the book of Acts. As Mitch Glaser puts it, believers today should have

> "a priority of Gospel concern for the Jewish people.... Perhaps the most lucid explanation of the Present Priority view of Romans 1:16 can be found in the statement of the Lausanne Consultation on Jewish Evangelism, Occasional Papers #7:
>
>> 'There is, therefore, a great responsibility laid upon the church to share Christ with the Jewish people. This is not to imply that Jewish evangelism is more important in the sight of God, or that those involved in Jewish evangelism have a higher calling. We observe that the practical application of the scriptural priority is difficult to understand and apply. We do not suggest that there should be a radical application of "to the Jew first" in calling on all the evangelists, missionaries, and Christians to seek out the Jews within their sphere of witness before speaking to non-Jews! Yet we do call the church to restore ministry among this covenanted people of God to its biblical place in the strategy of world evangelization.'"

Christians pray in the Lord's Prayer, "Thy kingdom come, thy will be done on earth as it is in heaven." Jews pray in the *Kaddish*, "May he establish his kingdom in your lifetime and in your days, and within the life of the whole house of Israel, speedily and soon." 2 Kefa 3:12 says that believers in Yeshua should work to hasten the coming of the Day of God. Could it be that one reason for the "present priority" of preaching the Gospel **to the Jew especially** is that neglecting Jewish evangelism delays the coming of the Kingdom of God on earth?

Thus it is because of the need to understand "*prôton*" as underlining the "present priority" of bringing the Gospel to the Jewish people that I translate it here by the word "especially."

17 The Gospel discloses **how God makes people righteous in his sight**; these eight words render two Greek words which mean, literally, "God's righteousness." This is the theme of the first eleven chapters of the book of Romans.

From beginning to end it is through trust (see Ac 3:16N). Without trust in God one cannot understand God's means of making people righteous in his sight. The eleventh-century theologian Anselm put it simply and straightforwardly: "I believe so that I may understand." Sha'ul quotes the prophet Habakkuk in the *Tanakh* to prove his point, and in so doing he proves mistaken narrowminded Christians who regard Judaism as lacking the element of faith.

A literal rendering of this verse is: "For in it is revealed God's righteousness from faith to faith; as it has been written, 'And the righteous one by faith will live.'"

18–32 These verses depict the dreadful consequences of rejecting God. One must understand the "Bad News" before one can properly appreciate the Good News and the central role of trust (faith) in appropriating it.

18a **God's anger** or "wrath." It is not popular these days to point out that God is a God of wrath. People would rather quote 1 Yn 4:8 ("God is love") and look no further. But it is in the context of God's holiness, meaning his hatred for sin, and his justice, meaning his dispensing the punishment that sin brings on itself, that his love, mercy and grace become so precious. The paradox of how God can be both just and merciful has been a theme in Jewish writing. "If you want the world to endure there can be no absolute justice, while if you want absolute justice the world cannot endure" (Genesis Rabbah 39:6). The solution to the paradox is Yeshua's atoning death, as summed up in Ro 3:19–26&NN and Yn 3:16.

The wrath **is** continuously being **revealed**, because people keep on sinning. Note the passive verb. God's delight is in his mercy, not in actively pouring out wrath. But the moral laws of the universe he created are such that God's anger automatically goes on being revealed to those who go on disobeying him.

Wrath is revealed **against all godlessness.** Humanists and legalists, ignoring the most important "X" in the equation, suppose they can become righteous by their own efforts without trusting God. **And wickedness**. Antinomians, persons who oppose law and eschew discipline, who overrate inner experience and underrate outward behavior, can easily make the opposite error, imagining that they can have a good relationship with God while disobeying his commands. Such people's lives, lacking adequate moral restraints, can all too easily degenerate into wickedness.

18b–20 If you do not know God, it is not God's fault but yours. The characteristics of God that make his existence self-evident, **his eternal power and his divine nature**, are **known** to you, because **God has made it plain** to you.

"The heavens declare the glory of God,
and the firmament proclaims his handiwork.

"Each day utters speech,
and each night expresses knowledge." (Psalm 19:2–3(1–2)

Therefore only "The fool has said in his heart, 'There is no God'"(Psalms 14:1, 53:2(1)) — meaning not "No God exists," but "No God exists who actively concerns himself with people's thoughts and deeds and judges them."

This is as close as the Bible comes to "proving the existence of God," for there is no reason why it *should* prove it. Rather, it takes effort for sinners to ignore God; defense mechanisms require active energy for their maintenance by **people who in their wickedness keep suppressing the truth.** Or, as the prophet Yesha'yahu put it centuries earlier, "Your iniquities have made a separation between you and your God" (Isaiah 59:2). In sum, since you already know enough to trust God and obey him, you **have no excuse** for not doing so.

21 Whether you acknowledge God's existence is not the question. Even demons believe in

God, but their "belief" makes them tremble (Ya 2:19), because they know they cannot avoid his punishment for their evil deeds and thoughts. So it is taken as axiomatic that you **know who God is** (vv. 18–20) and are aware of his existence. The issue, rather, is that you **do not glorify him as God or thank him**, you do not relate to him personally as who he is. It is this initial failing that produces the long downhill slide. Once God is no longer in your **thinking**, everything becomes **futile** or "vain." Your **heart** becomes spiritually **undiscerning**; and, lacking God's light (Yn 8:12&N), it can only be **darkened**.

22 The next stage of downfall consists, as in Orwell's novel, *1984*, in asserting as truth its opposite — darkness is really light, futility is really wisdom. **Claiming to be wise**, though perhaps masking your pride by a false humility, you nevertheless **have become** a **fool**.

23 Jews seeing Christians at worship are frequently offended by **images**. The Eastern Orthodox Church uses icons, and the Roman Catholic Church uses crucifixes (statues of Yeshua on the execution-stake) and other representations. Protestants generally reject the practice as violating the second Commandment, "You are not to make for yourself any carved idol" (Exodus 20:4).

The theology of the denominations that use images makes clear that they are not themselves objects of worship and that God is not present in them in the sense that heathens attribute divine power to their idols or in any other way. The unsurpassed sarcasm directed at idol-worshippers in Psalm 115 and Isaiah 44:8–20 is divinely inspired and accepted by these denominations too.

Yet it cannot be denied that many unlettered believers treat images as idols or magical amulets — superstition, like any other sin, unless guarded against, can find its way into God's people. In the same way, Jewish customs such as touching the *Torah* scroll as it is carried around the synagogue or kissing the *mezuzah* on the doorpost can be subjectively converted from reminders of God into superstitious practices.

24–28 When people stray from God, he eventually gives them over to the consequences of their horrific error — in physical (v. 24), emotional (v. 26) and mental (v. 28) dimensions, that is, in every aspect of their lives. Sexual sin (v. 24) and, in particular, homosexuality (vv. 26–27) are singled out as punishments from God, punishments which themselves are sins.

Homosexuality was rife throughout the first-century Roman Empire, as it is today. This is why the Gay Liberation movement can gain a wide hearing as it seeks equality, acceptance and approval of homosexuals and their behavior. It is why the Metropolitan Community Church, with tens of thousands of members in the United States, many of them openly active homosexuals, can refuse to condemn homosexual behavior as sin, yet seek acceptance as a Christian denomination. It is why outsiders condemn the Christian community when it rejects the MCC's claim and refuses to recognize homosexuality as an "alternative lifestyle."

The basic attitude of people who believe the Bible should be to love sinners while hating their sins. But believers must accept the Bible's judgments on what is and what is not sin. Moreover, denouncing the sin is an aspect of loving the sinner; this is what enables him to repent, be forgiven, and change. All of this can be done compassionately and effectively; the real tragedy is that few Christian churches try to minister to homosexuals.

Homosexuals who have put their trust in Yeshua the Messiah, acknowledged their homosexual behavior and fantasies (see Mt 5:28N) as sin, and become part of a community of believers in the Messiah who love, for care and pray for them, have found that the Holy Spirit gives them strength to flee their temptations, turn from their sin and live godly lives, either in heterosexual marriage or in celibacy. Like former substance-abusers, many recognize that they are weak in the area of their former sin but rely on God day by day to keep them free of it (compare 2C 12:9–10).

Those who refuse God's offer of help receive **in their own persons the penalty appropriate to their perversion** — vice becomes self-perpetuating, self-avenging, and productive of its own punishment.

25 **The Creator — praised be he forever.** ***Amen.*** See paragraphs on "Praised be *Adonai* forever" and "*Amen*" in 9:4b–5N.

28 Compare Jeremiah 2:5.

29–32 The downward slide gathers speed. With the necessary changes, the above description applies to all kinds of sins. Verses 29–31 are the Bible's most comprehensive list of the evils people invent for themselves, and v. 32 shows the state of man in deepest depravity, in which **not only do they keep doing** these things, **but they applaud others who do the same**, thus forming a godless society opposing everything God wants from his beloved creation, humanity.

Even so, in each one a voice of conscience still protests that it is **God's righteous decree that people who do such things deserve to die**, as has been the case from the days of Adam and Eve (Genesis 2:17) until now. Thus the "Bad News."

CHAPTER 2

1–5 But the Bad News is not over. Perhaps you are not caught in the mire of 1:18–32 but perceive the condition of others who are and rightly condemn them. Your sin is pride, and Sha'ul has a word for you: spotting the evil in others has not rooted out the evil in you — or, as the folk saying has it, "It takes one to know one." Sha'ul accuses you, who have made yourself a judge, less for passing judgment on others than for not passing equally severe judgment on yourself (compare Mt 7:1–4, Ya 4:11–12). You cannot take a stand outside humanity, supposing you are special; you too must **turn from your sins** (v. 4; see Mt 3:2N). This is the only reason God in his mercy has held back his anger against you. True, he has always shown such mercy: Adam and Eve did not die on the day they ate from the tree of the knowledge of good and evil but hundreds of years later (Genesis 2:17, 3:1–22, 5:1–5); Noah's generation heard him warn them and was given 120 years to repent (Genesis 6:1–7:6, 2 Ke 2:5); Jonah announced doom to the inhabitants of Nineveh, but they turned from sin and were spared (for awhile). Nevertheless there is urgency, because the Day of Judgment will surely come, with its solemn consequences (vv. 7–8), and you do not know when that will be (1 Th 5:2). The Talmud expresses the same concern:

"Rabbi Eli'ezer said, 'Repent one day before you die.' His disciples asked him, '[How can we do that?] Who knows on what day he will die?' He answered them, 'All the more reason to repent today, because you might be dead tomorrow!'"(Shabbat 153a)

6 This idea is found also in the *Tanakh* at Job 34:11, in the Apocrypha at Sirach 16:14, and in the New Testament at Mt 16:27, Yn 5:29 and 2C 5:10.

7–8 The Bad News concludes where it began in 1:18, with God's paying back **wrath and anger** (v. 8) to those whose deeds display their lack of trust in him. But v. 7 offers a ray of hope; indeed, it gives the kernel of the Gospel.

9–12 The Bad News, like the Good News, is universal: "All have sinned and fall short of earning God's praise" (3:23). To prove this, Sha'ul must show that it applies to Jews as well as to Gentiles; this is his subject from here to 3:20. Some Jewish people, he says, may think that belonging to God's chosen people or having detailed knowledge of the *Torah* may save them from God's wrath and guarantee them eternal life — they may consider 1:18 true for Gentiles but not for themselves. That such a view was not uncommon among Jews in the first century is suggested by Mt 3:9–10, Ac 10:28&N and Ga 2:15. I have found this attitude without apology among a few ultra-Orthodox Jews, but it seems safe to say that the vast majority of today's Jews would find such a position uncongenial, if not repulsive, just as Sha'ul does. Moreover, there are non-Jews with the same attitude — people proud of calling themselves Christians or of their religious knowledge, but whose lives fail to demonstrate what their mouths proclaim.

Sha'ul starts in vv. 9–10 by relating the summary in the preceding two verses **to the Jew first, then to the Gentile** — to the Jew first and foremost because his *Torah* knowledge ought to make him more aware of how God functions; also see 1:16&N. On "***shalom***" see Mt 10:12N. Since God is impartial (v. 11), the criterion he uses in judgment is not whether an individual's life situation places him **within the framework of *Torah*** as a Jew, but whether or not he has **sinned** (v. 12).

12 **Outside the framework of *Torah***, Greek *anomôs*, literally, "apart from law," "a-legally."

Within the framework of *Torah*, Greek *en nomô,* literally, "in-connection-with law," "in law." Some translations (New International Version, Revised Standard Version) have "under the law" here, even though they use the same phrase elsewhere to translate *upo nomon*, which means something else (see Ga 3:23bN).

13 Jews may be **hearers of the *Torah*** (rather than "readers," because scrolls were rare and *Torah* knowledge came from hearing them read aloud and memorizing them), but if they don't do what it says they are sinners who will die; Ya 1:22 expresses the same thought.

14–16 To stress the priority of deeds over head-knowledge of the *Torah* or status as a Jew, Sha'ul pointedly speaks of **Gentiles, who** by definition **don't have *Torah*** but nevertheless **do naturally what the *Torah* requires**, as being **for themselves** already ***Torah*** because **their lives show that the conduct the *Torah* dictates is "written in their hearts."** The quotation from Jeremiah 31:32(33) speaks of the "new covenant" which

Adonai is to make with Israel, when he says, "I will put my *Torah* in their inward parts and write it in their hearts" (see MJ 8:8–12).

That non-Jews have knowledge of the eternal moral law of God set forth in the *Torah* is further proved when they come to explicit and conscious faith in God — **on a day when God passes judgment on people's inmost secrets,** which, **according to the Good News as** Sha'ul **proclaims it** and as Yeshua himself proclaimed it (Yn 5:22–29), **he does… through the Messiah Yeshua.** On the day people come to faith they at last admit that God was right and they were wrong. Some of their behavior may prove not blameworthy, so that their **consciences… sometimes defend them**; but some of their behavior they will then perceive is falling short of God's standard, and their consciences will **accuse them.**

The above interpretation of these verses takes the "day" of v. 16 to be the day of an individual's salvation, the day he truly puts his trust in God. But an equally plausible understanding is that the "day" is the Day of Judgment at the end of history.

Just below the surface of these verses is the question of whether it is possible for a person to be saved without explicitly having put his faith in God through the Messiah Yeshua. For vv. 14–15 speak of doing what the *Torah* requires and having the conduct the *Torah* dictates written in one's heart; and it sounds very much as if such a person would in fact be trusting and loving God with all his heart and soul and strength (Deuteronomy 6:5, Mt 22:37). Skeptics sometimes ask, "How can God be so unfair as to condemn to hell some 'primitive tribesman' who hasn't even heard of the Bible?" They often raise the issue not out of concern for the "pitiful lost heathen" but as a dodge to justify their own unbelief; the very form of the question assumes that God is unjust and not worthy of their trust, that the "primitive tribesman" is an innocent "noble savage" and God the guilty party.

Sha'ul carefully skirts answering conclusively. On the one hand, the New Testament explicitly states, "Whoever trusts and is immersed will be saved; whoever does not trust will be condemned" (Mk 16:16); this can be understood to mean that anyone who does not explicitly acknowledge Yeshua will be condemned and not saved, including all "primitive tribesmen." Such a reading strengthens the motivation to evangelize.

On the other hand, the present verses suggest this line of reasoning: if non-Jews, without the *Torah*, live up to the light they have, obeying whatever of the *Torah* God has written in their hearts, then their consciences will sometimes defend them and sometimes accuse them. When their consciences accuse them, they will admit their sin, ask forgiveness from God and from the people sinned against, make restitution where possible, and throw themselves on God's mercy. If they keep doing that, "Will not the Judge of all the earth do right?" (Genesis 18:25), even if these people have never heard of Yeshua? Yes, he will, although they will have no *assurance* of their salvation, since they will not know that Yeshua has made a final atonement for their sins.

I will not pursue the matter further, except for this one caution: no one reading the above can be in the condition of the person just described and therefore excused from trusting God and his Messiah Yeshua. For anyone reading the *Jewish New Testament* and this commentary is being presented with the Gospel, and he cannot evade responsibility for deciding what to do with it. If he rejects it, any reading of Mk 16:16 puts the blame for the eternal consequences on his shoulders alone.

17–23 Having shown that being without the *Torah* does not necessarily place the Gentile at a disadvantage, Sha'ul demonstrates with cutting sarcasm derived from his own experience as a very zealous Pharisee (Ac 22:3, 26:5; Ga 1:13–14; Pp 3:4–6) that a Jew can waste his advantage (3:1–2) by misusing his Jewish status and *Torah* knowledge to justify boastfulness (vv. 17–20) and hypocrisy (vv. 21–23). The picture drawn is not antisemitic; rather, it applies the universal truth of vv. 1–3 in a specifically Jewish context.

24 The result of the behavior described in vv. 17–23 is that, far from being a "light to the Gentiles" (Isaiah 42:6, 49:6), as he is supposed to be, such a Jew plunges them further into darkness, causing them to harden their hearts: **because of you… God's name is blasphemed by the *Goyim*** (Greek *ethnê,* 1:5b–6N). One may add that, with the necessary changes, the same accusation can be made of some who "call themselves" (v. 17) Christians: by leading lives that shame God they cause Jewish people to despise the Messiah and distance themselves even farther (example: the televangelist scandals of the late 1980's). Fortunately, God's truth does not depend on them, and there are others whose lives are a better testimony.

In the thirteenth century the moralist, Rabbi Moses of Coucy, wrote,

> "Those who lie freely to non-Jews and steal from them, are worse than ordinary criminals. They are blasphemers; for it is due to their guilt, that some say, 'Jews have no binding law, no moral standards.'"(From *Semag*, as quoted by Hertz in his *Prayerbook*, p. 723)

25–26 On the one hand, **circumcision**, taken as symbolic of being Jewish but recalling the covenant with Avraham in particular, **is indeed of value**, as explained in 3:1–2, 9:4–5, 11:11–32 — but only **if you do what *Torah* says. But if you are a transgressor of *Torah*, your circumcision has become uncircumcision!** You have thrown away everything your Jewishness stands for. By despising God and his Law you have cut yourself off from his promises and from his people, spiritually, even though biological and cultural attachments remain. The reality behind the symbol has departed. (On the significance of circumcision see Ac 15:1N, 16:3N.)

On the other hand, **if an uncircumcised man**, a Gentile, **keeps the righteous requirements of the *Torah*,… his** physical **uncircumcision** will **be counted as** spiritual **circumcision**, "circumcision of the heart" (v. 29; the imagery comes from Leviticus 26:41; Deuteronomy 10:16, 30:6; Jeremiah 9:24–25(25–26); compare Ac 7:51&N). He will then become an heir to promises of the covenant with Avraham (this theme is resumed in Chapter 4; also in Ga 3:6–29). See vv. 14–16N.

27 Sha'ul presses his case against sanctimoniousness in general and its Jewish form in particular. The Greek word "*krinei*" may be rendered "will judge," "is judging," or, as here, "**will**, by his very existence and manifestly righteous behavior, **stand as a** continual **judgment**."

28–29 Following is a very literal rendering of these Jewishly significant verses:

"For not the in-the-open [a] Jew is, and not the in-the-open in flesh circumcision. On the contrary, the in-the-secret [is a] Jew; and circumcision of heart, in spirit not letter; of whom the praise [is] not from people but from God."

This passage is significant for Messianic Judaism because it answers authoritatively the perennial question facing the Jewish community at large and the State of Israel in particular, "Who is a Jew?" The English word "Jew" and the Greek word "*Ioudaios*" transliterate Hebrew *Y'hudi*, which is related to the word "*hodayah*" ("praise"). Thus, by etymology a Jew is a God-praiser; and conversely, the **praise** he should seek and value comes **not from other people but from God.** This wordplay, surely present in the mind of a Hebrew-speaking religious Jew like Sha'ul but not conveyed either in the English translation or in the Greek text, underlies this passage.

For the real Jew is not merely Jewish outwardly. Here are four possible interpretations; I think Sha'ul would disagree with the first, agree with the ideas of the second and third, but say that in this passage he means the fourth.

(1) "*Being born to a Jewish family does not make one a Jew.*" Moishe Rosen, leader of the organization Jews for Jesus, is fond of quipping, "Being born to Christian parents doesn't make you a Christian any more than being born in a bagel factory makes you a bagel." This is true because being a Christian or a Messianic Jew requires faith, which is not transmitted biologically; trusting Yeshua makes anyone a child of God (8:14–15), but, as a Protestant cliché has it, "God has no grandchildren." However, this interpretation of our text contradicts the halakhic definition of a Jew as the child of a Jewish mother or a person converted to Judaism. While Sha'ul does not necessarily bind himself to the rulings of the *P'rushim* or the rabbis, it does not appear that he questioned this particular point but that he agreed with it (Ac 16:1–3&NN). Therefore, and also because nothing in the book of Romans questions the halakhic definition of a Jew, this cannot be the meaning.

(2) "*Being born to a Jewish family does not guarantee that one will be a good Jew, a real Jew, one who praises God.*" Sha'ul would certainly endorse this, but in context such a statement seems weak. The Greek phrase literally translated "in-the-open" can indeed mean "passively in the open, concerning externals," hence, "being born to a Jewish family," which is the passive external distinctive of Jews. But it can also mean "actively in the open, making a public display," which leads to:

(3) "*The born Jew who puts on a show of his Jewishness is not behaving the way a Jew should; he is not a good Jew, a real Jew, one who praises God.*" Sha'ul would agree with this too, but the context suggests he goes further and says:

(4) "*The born Jew who puts on a show of his Jewishness is not a Jew at all!*" He is not a God-praiser in any sense and therefore forfeits his right to be considered a Jew in God's sight. Instead he boasts about God's gifts as if they were his own achievements (vv. 17–20) and hypocritically teaches God's *Torah* to others while violating it himself (vv. 21–23, 25, 27). God will exclude such a one from the promises he has made to the Jewish people (see Chapters 9–11). (However, if he repents, gives up his pride and sanctimonious cant, and comes to acknowledge Yeshua as his Savior, Lord and Messiah, he will be "grafted back into his own olive tree" (11:24) — so there is a sense in which his Jewishness remains, because it is still "*his own* olive tree." But in his present state he is a branch cut off from the tree, hence not a Jew.

See 11:23–24N.) This radical sense is concordant with v. 25 ("your circumcision has become uncircumcision") and with Sha'ul's opposition to a Jew's relying on his Jewishness for assurance of salvation (see vv. 9–12N).

True circumcision is not only external and physical. Or: "Circumcision is not a matter of boasting about the fact that a physical operation has been performed."

On the contrary, the real Jew is one inwardly (compare Mt 6:5–6, 23:3–7); **and true circumcision is of the heart, spiritual not literal.** (The metaphor of heart circumcision is from the *Tanakh*; see vv. 25–26N above.) It is obvious that in v. 28 the people spoken of as *not* real Jews are in fact born Jews, for no one needs to be told that Gentiles are not Jews. But in this passage, exactly who *is* a real Jew? Is Sha'ul talking about born Jews who are also born again (Yn 3:3), that is, about Messianic Jews? Or is he making a radical and dramatic assertion that some Gentiles (as well as some born Jews) are actually Jews in God's sight by virtue of being Jews inwardly, having circumcised hearts that offer praise to God? In other words, is he saying that both Messianic Jews and Gentile Christians are Jews?

In favor of the latter idea, that born-again Gentiles are real Jews, real God-praisers and inheritors of promises made to the Jewish people, are the following arguments:

(1) The most immediate context (vv. 24–27) deals with Gentiles and presents a series of points that lead naturally to that conclusion. Verse 26 says that an uncircumcised man who keeps the righteous requirements of the *Torah* will have his uncircumcision counted as circumcision. Verse 27 says that the uncircumcised man who obeys the *Torah* stands as a continual judgment against the circumcised man who has the *Torah*'s guidance available to him but disobeys it. Thus a certain class of Gentiles is doing what a real Jew should do; it is then but a short step to asserting that, since the essence of the matter is "spiritual not literal," such Gentiles are in fact Jews. (A point of formal support: v. 25 stands in the same complementary logical relationship to v. 26 as v. 28 does to v. 29.)

(2) If the book of Romans as a whole is the context, we find throughout it the theme that Jews and Gentiles are equal before God in regard to salvation (1:16&N). So if "real Jew" means the same thing as "saved person," then a Gentile can be a real Jew.

(3) The equality of Jews and Gentiles before God recurs as a theme in Sha'ul's other letters. In the Messiah "there is neither Jew nor Gentile" (Ga 3:28, Co 3:11). The *m'chitzah* ("wall of separation") between Jew and Gentile has been broken down (Ep 2:14). Galatians, Ephesians and Colossians deal especially with the subject and show that Sha'ul was at pains to establish this point. Would it not make Messianic Jewish and Gentile Christian equality "more equal" if both could be called real Jews?

(4) In two other passages (in other letters) Sha'ul makes very similar assertions. At Pp 3:3, after criticizing certain Messianic Jewish heretics, he says, "For it is we who are the Circumcised, we who worship by the Spirit of God and make our boast in the Messiah Yeshua! We do not put confidence in human qualifications...." At Ga 6:15–16, at the end of an entire letter devoted to the issue of salvation by faith, he writes, "Neither being circumcised nor being uncircumcised matters; what matters is being a new creation. And as many as order their lives by this rule, *shalom* upon them and mercy, and upon the Israel of God." (See notes to both passages.)

In favor of the idea that, in the sense of these verses, the only real Jews are born-again Jews, and that born-again Gentiles are indeed saved but not by virtue of that fact Jews, are these arguments:

(1) The intermediate context (2:17–3:20) is discussing not Gentiles but Jews. At 2:17–24 Sha'ul describes a Jew who ought not to be considered a Jew. Although he does bring in the effect of such a person on Gentiles in v. 24 and continues talking about Gentiles in vv. 25–27, this discussion of Gentiles is subordinate; for the verses following this passage return to analyzing the significance of being Jewish (3:1–20). Since v. 28 has already returned to the subject of born Jews, v. 29 too should be understood as referring to born Jews — especially since 3:1–2 clearly refers to born Jews ("What advantage has the [born] Jew [not the saved Gentile]?... Much...!").

(2) Although Jews and Gentiles are equal as regards salvation, there are other distinctions between them, as Sha'ul acknowledges immediately (3:1–2) and later (9:4–5, and especially 11:28–29). One distinctive (Sha'ul does not deal with it, but Yeshua does at Lk 21:20–24), for example, is that the Jewish people are to inherit the Land of Israel in perpetuity. This is a promise to physical or national Israel that has not yet been entirely fulfilled, but it will be. No one expects the Land to be inherited by all believers, Jews and Gentiles alike. Another distinctive is the Jew's relationship with the *Torah*. About this Sha'ul has much to say, both in this letter and elsewhere. But it is clear from the Jerusalem Council (Ac 15:20) that the Gentile believer's relationship with the *Torah* was different from that of the Jewish believer. Many notes in this commentary address this matter. Because of these distinctives remaining to the Jewish people Sha'ul would not cloud the question by such a peculiar assertion as, "Some Gentiles are Jews."

(3) The two passages quoted above (in argument (4)) are as ambiguous as the present one as to whether they refer to born-again Jews or to all believers; for detailed discussion see Pp 3:3N, Ga 6:16N.

This leaves us at an impasse, which the modern interpreter finds unsatisfying because he assumes that any passage, properly understood in its linguistic and historical contexts, has one and only one meaning (puns and the like aside). However, Sha'ul was not a modern but a Pharisee who grew up in the home of Hebrew-speakers and had his mind steeped in rabbinic modes of thought at the feet of *Rabban* Gamli'el I (Ac 22:3, 23:6; Pp 3:5).

Carrying many new ideas in his head, Sha'ul could produce a sentence that had both a simple sense (*p'shat*) and a hint (*remez*) of something more profound; furthermore, he would not be averse to making an allegorical or homiletical application (*drash*) of his own words or looking in them for a secret meaning (*sod*); because these four ways of interpreting texts were well known among educated Jews and were part of Sha'ul's thinking equipment. For more on these four levels of rabbinic interpretation see Mt 2:15N.

Thus a born-again Gentile, one who has come to faith in the God of Israel through trusting Yeshua the Messiah, is indeed a Jew inwardly; his heart is circumcised even though his flesh is not; he is a true God-praiser, whose praise comes from God and not from other people — in many senses a real Jew. In the present verse we find a hint (*remez*) of such ideas which Sha'ul will develop in the rest of Romans.

Elements of *drash* are present in the implicit challenge and exhortation to Jews who make a show of their Jewishness to change their ways and repent, and not risk being overtaken or even replaced by Gentiles (compare 11:11–25).

One can perceive a *sod* (secret truth), in that Yeshua, the Son of God identifying with all mankind by his atoning death, overthrows human categories by divine intervention.

But the simple sense of the text, the *p'shat*, the meaning arrived at by linguistic and historical analysis, even though in some senses less profound than the other levels which rest upon it, is that the only real Jew is the born Jew who has been born again by trusting in Yeshua the Messiah, for only he lives up to what the name "Jew," conferred on him at birth and confirmed by physical circumcision, implies and demands.

CHAPTER 3

1–2 Then what advantage (or "prerogative" or "superiority") **has the Jew**, that is, the born Jew or the Jewish proselyte? **What is the value of being** physically **circumcised** according to Jewish law, a member of the covenant people? After the squeeze of 2:17–29 one might expect the answer, "None," and there has been no shortage of antisemites who have decided they know better than Sha'ul.

But Sha'ul's answer is: **Much in every way,** not just in one way or some ways, but every way, of which **in the first place** (or "most importantly" or "especially"; the Greek word is again "*prôton*"; see 1:16&N) is the fact that **the Jews were entrusted with the very words of God**, his *logia*, his divine communications (not limited to his promises or prophecies, as the word "oracles" in KJV implies). This is of first importance because any other advantage of being Jewish stems from God's having chosen and spoken to the Jewish people. To imagine that the Jews are special because they have a finer ethical sense than others, or a land, or some sort of "racial genius" is to put the cart before the horse. The Jews were "the fewest of all peoples" (Deuteronomy 7:7), yet *Adonai* loved them, chose them and separated them for himself. "He declares his Word to Ya'akov, his statutes and his judgments to Israel. He has not done so with any other nation; and as for his judgments they have not known them" (Psalm 147:19–20). In sum, having the very words of God is no cause for Jewish pride, since the initiative was entirely God's; yet it is "in every way" a great advantage.

3–4 "If the New Testament is true, why doesn't my rabbi believe it?" Sha'ul, the rabbi from Tarsus, gives the correct answer to this common Jewish question: the veracity of God's Word (v. 2) does not depend on who believes it; truth stands by itself. **If some of them were unfaithful** to God's words (or "did not believe" them), **so what? Does their faithlessness** (or "unbelief, lack of trust") **cancel God's faithfulness? Heaven forbid! God would be true even if everyone were a liar!** Even the socially and religiously sanctioned unbelief of the Jewish community as a whole from Sha'ul's day to the present does not take one iota away from the truth of God's Word. Over against Jewish communal rejection of God's Word as expressed in the books of the New Covenant, the individual may discover for himself its truth and stability; the outcome of his search is not in doubt: God would be true even if everyone were a liar.

Sha'ul invites such individual search of the Word by quoting from the great penitential psalm provided for anyone ready to turn from sin, Psalm 51. Verse 6(4) is quoted; in the *Tanakh* it reads,

> "Against you, you alone, have I sinned
> and done what is evil in your sight,
> so that you are justified in your word
> and declared innocent when put on trial."

In presenting one verse Sha'ul, following normal rabbinic methods of citing Scripture, is calling attention to the whole psalm in which it appears (see Mt 2:6N), including the portions full of hope for any Jew who has been unfaithful and unbelieving:

> "Create in me a clean heart, O God....
> Restore to me the joy of your salvation....
> Then I will teach transgressors your ways,
> and sinners will return to you.
> O Lord, open my lips,
> and my heart will declare your praise....
> O God, you will not despise a broken and contrite heart."

Only then, after the individual has gotten himself right with God, can his prayer for the Jewish community as a whole be offered:

> "In your will, do good to Zion:
> build the walls of Yerushalayim!"

4 **Heaven forbid!** Greek *mê genoito*, which some modern versions render literally, "Let it not be!" But this loses the force of the idiom, used in the Septuagint to translate the Hebrew expression, "*Chalilah!*" (Genesis 44:7, 17; Joshua 22:29, 24:16), which means "Profanation!" "A curse on it!" "Away with it!" "*Chalilah!*" may be Hebrew's most intense wish for negation; therefore KJV's "God forbid!" conveys the sense well. I substitute "Heaven" for "God" in this expression because neither the Hebrew nor the Greek refers to God at all; and Jewish sensibility tends to remove words like "God" or "Lord" from curses, perhaps to avoid breaking the Third Commandment by taking God's name in vain (Exodus 20:7; compare Mt 5:33–37, also Mt 4:3N). The phrase occurs fifteen times in the New Testament, ten of them in Romans (here, 3:6, 31; 6:2, 15; 7:7, 13; 9:14; 11:1, 11), the others at Lk 20:16; 1C 6:15; Ga 2:17, 3:21, 6:14.

5–8 Sha'ul counters a specious argument based on carrying the point of vv. 3–4 to an absurd extreme. Compare the similar self-justification of 6:1–2.

9 **So**, given the advantage of being Jewish (vv. 1–2), **are we** Jews (note that Sha'ul considers himself a Jew, not an ex-Jew) **any better off?** (Literally, "Do we excel?") **Not entirely.** Most versions, following the Vulgate of Jerome, give the answer to this rhetorical question as, "Not at all." In *A Textual Commentary on the Greek New Testament* (*ad loc.*) Bruce Metzger writes,

> "The unexpected sequence... of *ou pantôs* (which ought to mean 'not entirely,' but which in the context must mean 'not at all') accounts for the deletion of the

words in some witnesses... and their replacement by *perisson* in others...."

Here I believe Metzger's theological presuppositions lead him to dismiss the straightforward translation, "**Not entirely**," which says Jews have *some* advantage, and replace it with the idea that Jews have *no* advantage. For what Metzger calls "the context" has to include vv. 1–4, where Sha'ul specifically called attention to the advantages Jews *do* have. C. E. B. Cranfield, after noting that "*ou pantôs* properly means 'not altogether'," concludes, as I do, that this is indeed the correct understanding (*Romans, ad loc.*).

Why, then, are Jews not entirely advantaged? Because, as Sha'ul has **already** said, **all people, Jews and Gentiles alike, are controlled by sin.** True, having God's very words is an advantage Jews do have (vv. 1–2); and the infallibility of God's promises, even if no one believes them (vv. 3–4), is another. But the same Word of God, the ***Tanakh***, reminds us of the Bad News that everyone sins, Jews included (see also vv. 22–23); in this regard Jews have no advantage. As Sha'ul later explains, the *Torah* lacks power in itself to change people's lives (8:3). The commentator C. K. Barrett, although he translates "*ou pantôs*" "by no means," is correct in writing, "The advantage of the Jew is real, but it is an advantage which is (or may at any moment become) at the same time a disadvantage. It consists in knowing (out of Scripture) that before God all talk of 'advantages' is folly and sin" (*The Epistle to the Romans*, p. 68).

10–18 The proof-texts from the Hebrew Bible for the idea presented in v. 9 show that no one is righteous or kind (vv. 10–12), that everyone sins by both word (vv. 13–14) and deed (v. 15), because of a lifestyle that is evil and disastrous (v. 16) rather than good (v. 17), since they lack the fear of the Lord which is the beginning of wisdom and knowledge (v. 18; Psalm 111:10; Proverbs 1:7, 9:10).

19–26 Many profound ideas are brought together in these eight verses as Sha'ul sets forth with masterly brevity God's ultimate solution to man's ultimate problem, sin. Whether his succinctness posed difficulty to Sha'ul's original readers we cannot know, but today we find many ambiguities and uncertainties in his compressed phrases. The concepts introduced here are so important that a seemingly small difference in interpretation can have enormous consequences for the Jews, for the Church and for the Jewish-Christian interface. For this reason I have in several places included phrases not found in the Greek text in order to make as clear as possible what I believe to be the correct interpretation. This accords with my translation philosophy of deciding what a text means and expressing that meaning as clearly as possible (as explained in the *JNT* Introduction, Section V). But since there are other plausible understandings it seems fair to offer the reader a literal rendering as well:

> [19] And we know that whatever things the law says, to the ones in-connection-with the law it speaks; so that every mouth may be stopped and under judgment may become all the world to God; [20] because by works of law will not be justified all flesh before him; for through law full-knowledge of sin.
>
> [21] But now, without law God's righteousness has been manifested, being witnessed to by the law and the prophets, [22] moreover, God's righteousness

through faithfulness [or: trust] of Messiah unto all the ones trusting (for there is no difference, [23] for all sinned and come short of God's glory); [24] being justified without cost by his grace through the redemption which is in-connection-with Messiah Yeshua, [25] whom God set forth a propitiation [or: mercy seat] through faithfulness [or: trust] in-connection-with his blood, for a showing-forth of his righteousness because of the passing-by of the sins that had previously occurred [26] in-connection-with the forbearance of God, for the showing-forth of his righteousness in the present period unto his being just and justifying the one from faithfulness [or: trust] of Yeshua.

The key to understanding these verses properly is realizing that they are a *midrash* on Psalm 143, as explained in v. 20aN. Other verse-by-verse notes deal with other issues raised by this passage.

19 Whatever the *Torah* (here the whole *Tanakh*, from which vv. 10–18 has given quotations; see Mt 5:17N) **says, it says to those living within the framework of the *Torah*** (see 2:12N), that is, to Jews; **in order that every** self-justifying **mouth may be stopped**, Jewish included (Gentiles have already had their guilt pinpointed in 1:18–2:16); **and** thus **the whole world be shown**, proven by God's own words, **to deserve God's adverse judgment**. There is also this implicit *kal v'chomer* argument (see Mt 6:30N): if Jews, who have the *Torah* to guide them, turn out to be guilty before God, how much more will Gentiles, who do not have this guidance, also prove worthy of punishment.

20a For in his sight no one alive will be considered righteous, quoted from Psalm 143:2. Greek *dikaioô,* corresponding to Hebrew *hatzdik*, is to be understood in a legal sense as "declare righteous or innocent," rather than "cause to behave righteously." God does the latter too, as part of his work in believers after they trust in Yeshua the Messiah; and it is a lifelong process. But being declared innocent by God and considered righteous, no longer regarded by him as a sinner deserving of his adverse judgment (v. 19), happens instantaneously at the moment a person gives up his self-righteousness, accepts God's assessment of him and means of forgiveness (through Yeshua), and depends entirely on God's mercy.

As with other rabbinic citations from the *Tanakh*, the phrase quoted is meant to call to mind the entire context, Psalm 143:1–2 (see vv. 3–4N). This is the passage on which vv. 20–26 constitute at once *midrash* (vv. 19–26N), commentary and fulfillment:

"A psalm of David:

"Hear my prayer, *Adonai*; give ear to my supplications;
in your faithfulness answer me with your righteousness;

"and do not enter into judgment with your servant;
for in your sight no one alive will be considered righteous."

The Psalmist is aware that no one's works suffice to earn him being declared righteous by God (v. 20a; see first paragraph of this note), and therefore he pleads to be answered with God's righteousness (vv. 21–26). And he expects a positive answer because God is faithful (vv. 22&N, 25–26). Verses 24–26 provide assurance that God will not enter into judgment with his trusting servants. In the rest of Psalm 143 the Psalmist acknowledges his dreadful condition and continues to plead for God's mercy. This must be the attitude of all who truly turn to God.

20b Legalistic observance of *Torah* commands. I use this phrase to render Greek *erga nomou* because the briefer and literal "works of law" has almost always been misunderstood and made the underpinning of some dreadful theology. "*Nomos*" ("law") is correctly taken by most interpreters to mean the Jewish Law, the Law of Moses, the *Torah*. But from this point on, interpreters have usually riveted themselves to one of the following three misinterpretations of this verse:

(1) *"No one will be considered righteous by God on the ground of doing the good works the Torah requires."* This is manifestly wrong because the most important good work the *Torah* requires is trusting God, loving him with all one's heart and soul and strength (Mk 12:28–30). Who can read the *Torah* without seeing that? Therefore, on the face of it, this interpretation is absurd. After all, the *Torah* was given by God to be obeyed; so why should obeying it not lead to being considered righteous by God? Moreover, Sha'ul quotes with approval Moses' pronouncement that "the person who does these things," who performs the righteous deeds commanded by the *Torah*, "will attain life through them" (10:5, quoting Leviticus 18:5). Surely attaining life and being considered righteous by God are equivalent.

(2) *"No one will be considered righteous by God on the ground of doing the good works the Torah requires, because no one is able to live up to the Torah's demands (Yeshua excepted)."* Those who hold to the interpretation of Paragraph (1) in spite of the difficulty raised there defend their position by implicitly adding the clause about human inability. But such a teaching is not found in Sha'ul's argument here, or elsewhere in Romans, or, for that matter, anywhere in the Bible.

On what biblical evidence might one base the conclusion that no one is capable of obeying the *Torah*? Ya'akov 2:10 says that "a person who keeps the whole *Torah*, yet stumbles at one point, has become guilty of breaking them all." But the "stumbling" spoken of here is rebellion against keeping a particular command of the *Torah* while claiming to uphold it. Ya'akov is not saying that anyone necessarily rebels (see Ya 2:10–11&N). Acts 15:10 speaks of Kefa's objecting to placing on the Gentiles "a yoke which neither our fathers nor we were able to bear." But this "yoke" meant "detailed mechanical rule-keeping, regardless of heart attitude, that some… held to be the essence of Judaism. This was not the yoke of the *mitzvot* prescribed by God, but a yoke of legalism prescribed by men" (I am quoting Ac 15:10N). Yeshua himself objected to this (Mt 23:2–4, Mk 7:5–13&N).

The *Torah* was given to be obeyed, and God expected people to obey it. That is why Moses said,

> "This commandment which I command you today is not too difficult for you, nor is it beyond your grasp…. The word is very near you, in your mouth and in your heart, to do it." (Deuteronomy 30:11–14).

Sha'ul himself quotes from this passage at 10:6–8&N. It is unthinkable that God instructed the Jewish people to observe a Law that was impossible to keep, for which the penalty of violation was death. The God of love does not play cruel games.

True, the people fell short of keeping the *Torah*; they sinned. But the *Torah* itself includes a procedure for dealing with sins, provided they were not committed "with a high hand," that is, in rebellion, after the manner of Ya 2:10&N. This procedure was the sacrificial system, and in fact the greater part of the Five Books of Moses is devoted to it. This system offered forgiveness to a repentant person who brought the required sacrifice. (How Yeshua affected this part of the *Torah* is touched on at v. 25 and developed more fully in Messianic Jews 9–10.) Thus, at the time the Messiah died, the *Torah* provided a framework within which a person might be saved (Mt 19:16–22, Lk 1:6&N, MJ 11:1–40), provided he trusted God in everything and in no way relied on his own self-righteousness.

In conclusion, this understanding is wrong because there is no reason for supposing a person cannot live up to what the *Torah* demands. The *Torah* does not set an impossible standard. Rather, it sets a standard of faith, trusting in God, and of following its system of repentance and sacrifice for obtaining forgiveness from God and restoring a condition of being considered righteous in his sight.

(3) "*No one will be considered righteous by God on the ground of the* bad *works the* Torah *requires.*" Even more ridiculous than the first mistaken interpretation, what this means is that the *Torah* itself supposedly requires prideful, self-justifying, legalistic rule-following. But the *Torah* itself inveighs vigorously against such behavior, and the New Testament quotes portions of the *Tanakh* which make that very point! Furthermore, Sha'ul calls the *Torah* "holy, just and good" (7:12), which could not be true of a *Torah* that demanded bad works or self-righteousness.

So then, why even mention such a peculiar understanding? Because many Christians seem to have the idea that the *Torah* was an inferior product of God, that the Messiah is in some sense "better" than the *Torah*, and that therefore the *Torah* is relatively "bad." But such an interpretation impugns the character of God. It is tantamount to the second-century heresy of Marcion, who regarded the Old Testament as inferior to the New Testament and the God of the Old Testament as inferior to the God of the New.

Theology based on one or the other of these misinterpretations has taught Christians that the Jewish Law is inferior, inadequate, legalistic, a producer of pride, something separate from God's grace, superseded now that Yeshua has come, and of value only insofar as it points to the Messiah. If this were true, anyone who would uphold such a Law must obviously be blind, foolish or misled. Since Jews uphold the Mosaic Law, it follows from these premises that Jews are blind, foolish or misled. In this way antisemitism is made virtually a pillar of Christian faith! No wonder a "gospel" with such implications is unacceptable to Jews!

But there is an alternative. While sometimes Sha'ul uses the word "*erga*" ("works," in the plural) neutrally, nineteen times he employs it as a technical term with negative valence, signifying:

> "actions stemming from a boastful, self-righteous belief that by doing them, by following a set of rules in one's own strength, without any trust in God or

faithfulness towards him, one can earn God's praise and applause and obligate him to grant one a berth in heaven."

The word "*erga*" is used by itself in this sense at 4:2, 6; 9:11; 11:6 (three times); Ep 2:9; 2 Ti 1:9; and Ti 3:5. It is used with "*nomou*" ("of law") in the present verse, 3:27, 28; 9:32; Ga 2:16 (three times); and Ga 3:2, 5, 10.

This is also the sense understood for "*erga*" ("works") in the third misinterpretation above. The difference between it and my understanding is that I do not take "*erga*" with the modifier "*nomou*" ("of law") to mean "bad self-strength works prescribed in the *Torah*," but rather:

> "bad self-strength works produced when sinful people misuse and pervert the *Torah*, so that instead of regarding it as God's gracious gift intended both to orient people toward righteous, God-motivated behavior and at the same time to show them how far short they fall of achieving it, they regard the *Torah* as a rulebook containing requirements they can meet mechanically, without trusting God or even caring about him, and can therefore take great pride in their own achievements and have great self-satisfaction over how much they have pleased God."

In other words, "works of law" are indeed "works produced by the *Torah*," but *through its being used improperly*. This is what I have tried to convey in my rendering, "**legalistic observance of *Torah* commands.**"

This is a good place to call attention to a book clarifying these issues: Daniel P. Fuller's *Gospel And Law: Contrast Or Continuum?* (Grand Rapids, Michigan: Eerdmans, 1980).

20c **What the *Torah* really does is show people how sinful they are**, literally, "for through law is full-knowledge of sin." Greek *amartia* corresponds to Hebrew *chet*; both are usually translated "sin," but both also convey the sense, "missing the mark," like an archer who shoots off-target. Thus, what the *Torah* gives to anyone who lets himself be affected by it is ever fuller awareness of how much he is missing the target of righteousness which the *Torah* sets before him. This is, of course, not the *Torah*'s only task — it also offers positive guidance toward right behavior. In theory a Jew, with the *Torah* to direct him, might possibly be able to aim nearer the target than a Gentile without it. Nevertheless, his achievement will always fall short of the goal; and unless he realizes this and becomes appropriately humble he will surely not be saved. The subject is analyzed at length in Chapter 7.

21 **Quite apart from *Torah***, Greek *chôris nomou*, literally, "apart from law"; KJV's archaic "without the law" does not mean "lacking it" but "outside it." What this phrase means is that God's righteousness has nothing to do with our obeying the *Torah* and its prescriptions but goes back to the underlying axiom of such obedience, faith.

God's way of making people righteous. An alternative rendering for this phrase is "God's righteousness," that is, as in vv. 25–26&NN, his "moral integrity," to use the phrase of Leander E. Keck (*Paul and His Letters*, Philadelphia: Fortress Press, 1979, pp. 118–123). God's moral integrity is demonstrated directly by Yeshua's atoning death;

it does not depend on the constitution of the Jewish nation, the *Torah*.

Nevertheless, **The *Torah* and the Prophets give their witness to it.** Throughout the *Tanakh* God's holiness and moral integrity are proclaimed, as also is the truth that human beings cannot attain God's standard of righteousness by striving for it. As Isaiah 64:5(6) puts it, "All our righteousnesses," those we achieve by mere human effort without genuine reliance on and trust in God, "are as filthy rags." Moreover, not only do the Scriptures attest to God's way of making people righteous, but non-Messianic Judaism is aware of it too. The eleventh-century Midrash to Psalm 44:1 says,

> "When the children of Israel went out from Egypt, they could not offer any works of their hands whereby they might be redeemed. And so, it was not because of the works of their fathers, nor was it because of their own works, that the sea was divided before them; rather, it was only so that God might make a name for himself in the world."

The *Siddur* quotes Daniel 9:18 in the preliminary morning prayers:

> "Sovereign of all worlds! Not because of our righteous acts do we lay our supplications before you, but because of your abundant mercies,"

and then continues by expounding on this verse in the spirit of Ecclesiastes:

> "What are we? What is our life? What is our piety? our righteousness? our helpfulness? our strength? our might? What shall we say before you, *Adonai*, our God and God of our fathers? Are not all the mighty men as nothing before you, the men of fame as though they had never existed, the wise as if without knowledge, and those with understanding as if without discernment? For most of their works are void, and the days of their lives are vanity before you, and the preeminence of man over beast is nothing, for all is vanity."

So, like Sha'ul, the rabbis have recognized human inability to meet God's standard for righteousness, even with the guidance of the good *Torah* that God gave.

22 Through the faithfulness of Yeshua the Messiah, Greek *dia pisteôs Iêsou Christou*, in other translations virtually always rendered, "through faith in Jesus Christ." This implies that God considers an individual righteous because he believes in Yeshua. But George Howard ("Romans 3:21–31 and the Inclusion of the Gentiles," *Harvard Theological Review* 63 (1970), pp. 223–233) has made a strong case for regarding this Greek phrase not as an objective genitive but as a subjective genitive, with the word "*pistis*" meaning "faithfulness" rather than "faith, belief" (on this see Ac 3:16N and Section (1) of Ga 2:16cN). For the relevant quotation from Howard's article see section (2) of Ga 2:16cN, all of which constitutes an essential complement and sequel to the present note.

Sha'ul uses the same expression, "*dia pisteôs Iêsou Christou*," not only here but in v. 26; Ga 2:16 (twice), 3:22; Ep 3:12 and Pp 3:9. Somewhat similar constructions are found at Co 2:12 and 2 Th 2:13. The issue is important enough to make it worth understanding what subjective and objective genitives are. In Greek grammar *pisteôs* ("faithfulness of" or "faith of") is the genitive case of "*pistis*" ("faithfulness" or "faith"); broadly speaking, the genitive case adds the "of." The question, then, is: what kind of an "of" is it? H. E. Dana and Julius R. Mantey, in *A Manual Grammar of the Greek New Testament* (The MacMillan Company, 1927; 1957 printing) deal with the matter on pp. 78–79. With a noun of action,

> "We have the subjective genitive when the noun in the genitive *produces* the action, being therefore related *as subject* to the verbal idea of the noun modified,"

and the example given is "the preaching of Jesus Christ" (Ro 16:25). In contrast, there is the objective genitive.

> "We have this construction when the noun in the genitive *receives* the action, being thus related *as object* to the verbal idea contained in the noun modified."

The example given is: "But the blasphemy of the Spirit shall not be forgiven" (Mt 12:31). In the first example (the subjective genitive), Yeshua *does* the preaching and does not receive it. In the second (the objective genitive), the Spirit does not *do* the blaspheming but receives it, is the object of it. In our present verse, if "*pisteôs*" is subjective, Yeshua *does* the *pistis* ("the faithfulness of Yeshua"); if objective, Yeshua *receives* the *pistis* ("faith in Yeshua") and someone else does it.

In addition to the grammatical points presented by Howard, a key argument for regarding "*pisteôs Iêsou*" as "faithfulness of Yeshua" arises from taking vv. 20–26 as a commentary on Psalm 143, as explained above in v. 20aN. The psalm speaks not of our faith in God but of God's faithfulness to us.

As noted, the same phrase appears in v. 26, and the decision made here and in that verse controls how to translate "*pisteôs*" in v. 25 also.

But E. D. Burton, whose *Commentary on Galatians* I elsewhere quote with approval (at Ga 2:16b&N), writes (p. 121),

> "The evidence that *pistis*, like *elpis* and *agapê,* may take an objective genitive is too clear to be questioned (cf. Mark 11:22, Acts 3:16, Colossians 2:12, 2 Thess 2:13)."

Nevertheless I do question it, at least in all but one of the verses he cites. Mark 11:22 I render, "Have the kind of trust that comes from God," instead of "Have faith in God;" I take the construction as a genitive of origin, as when one identifies Paul *of* Tarsus (having Tarsus as his origin); the genitive of origin has more affinity with the subjective genitive than with the objective genitive. Colossians 2:12 is a subjective genitive (see Co 2:11–13aN), while 2 Th 2:13 is another genitive of origin (see note there). Burton's case for taking Sha'ul's "*pisteôs*" as objective genitive is thus reduced to Ac 3:16 and is further weakened by its being a very difficult verse, no matter how translated, and by its not having been written or spoken by or about Sha'ul.

23 All have sinned and therefore **come short of earning God's praise** (literally: "come short of the glory of God"). On sinning and falling short of the target of earning God's praise, see v. 20cN. The principle that everyone is a sinner is taught in the *Tanakh*:

> "There is no one who does not sin." (1 Kings 8:46)
>
> "For there is not a righteous person on the earth, who does good and does not sin." (Ecclesiastes 7:20)
>
> "Behold, *Adonai*'s hand is not shortened, so that it cannot save;
> nor is his ear heavy, so that it cannot hear.
> Rather, your iniquities have made a separation between you and your God
> and your sins have hidden his face from you, from hearing." (Isaiah 59:1–2)
>
> "We are all like one who is unclean, and all our righteousnesses are like filthy rags." (Isaiah 64:5(6))

The question of why it is true, and how it comes about, that everyone sins — in other words, the question of so-called "original sin" — is discussed at 5:12–21N.

The truth of this verse, which epitomizes the Bad News of 1:18–3:20, is basic to understanding both the inherent problematic condition of all mankind and the Good News that God offers the only solution to the problem through Yeshua the Messiah.

24 **By God's grace, without earning it, all** who continue faithfully trusting (understood from v. 22) **are granted the status of being considered righteous before him** (God), **through the act redeeming us from our enslavement to sin** (literally just "through the redemption"; see vv. 19–26N) **that was accomplished by the Messiah Yeshua.** Sha'ul gives detailed examination to this theme in Chapter 6.

25a ***Kapparah* for sin**. Greek *ilastêrion* appears twice in the New Testament; at MJ 9:5 it means the "mercy seat" which formed the cover of the Ark of the Covenant in the Holy of Holies of the Temple, where the *cohen hagadol* entered once a year, on *Yom-Kippur*, to offer a sacrifice for the sins of the people (Leviticus 16; see MJ 9:5N). In the present verse it means "propitiation, expiation, atonement" and corresponds to Hebrew *kapar*, which has the same meaning in the *Tanakh* and has the root sense of either "cover" or "wipe clean." These two root meanings both express what God does when he accepts expiation for sin: he covers the sin from his sight and/or wipes or washes it away.

Non-Messianic Jews are hard pressed to give an answer to the question: "Now that the Temple has been destroyed, so that sacrifices can no longer be offered in the manner God requires in the *Torah*, what is the *kapparah* for sins?" The customary answer, that the sacrifices have been replaced by repentance, prayer and works of charity, finds no basis in the *Tanakh*, even though all three are worthy activities and the first two are surely essential elements of the atonement process. The correct answer to the question is given in this verse: Yeshua is the *kapparah*. See also Messianic Jews 9–10&NN.

25b **Through his faithfulness in respect to his bloody sacrificial death**, Greek *dia pisteôs en tô autou aimati*, literally, "through faithfulness in his blood." On understanding *pisteôs* as Yeshua's faithfulness to God and not our faith in him, let alone "in his blood," see v. 22N. The Greek preposition "*en*," which often means simply "in" or "by," is here better rendered "in the sphere of" or "**in respect to**."

"Blood" must be understood as a metaphor for "death" and not as a special, magical substance. KJV's "through faith in his blood" suggests that Yeshua's blood magically atones for sin if we have faith in it. There have been enough pagan intrusions into Christianity without adding this one. For proof that "blood" means "bloody sacrificial death," as rendered here, see Leon Morris, *The Apostolic Preaching of the Cross* (Grand Rapids: Eerdmans, 1955), pp. 108–124. See also Yn 6:51–66N.

Thus Sha'ul is referring here to Yeshua's faithfulness to God in being willing, even though sinless and not deserving execution, to undergo a painful, horrible, bloody sacrificial death on our behalf (see Pp 2:5–11). He is not speaking about our trust, faith or belief in Yeshua, or in his death, or in his blood.

25c–26 This vindicated (or: "demonstrated") **God's righteousness**, etc. From here to the end of v. 26 Sha'ul continues his *midrash* on Psalm 143 (see v. 20aN) by analyzing exactly how Yeshua's atoning death relates to God's righteousness. The Greek text is difficult, and there are other interpretations; I have given weight to Barrett's commentary in arriving at my understanding.

On "**faithfulness**" see v. 22N, where George Howard's article was cited. In that article he also writes (p. 231):

> "It is not through the Law of Moses that the promise to Abraham is fulfilled but through the faithfulness of Christ. Only in this way has God devised to bring all nations to himself."

Thus it is God's faithfulness to his own promise made to Abraham that all the nations of the world would be blessed through him (Genesis 12:3) that produces God's redemption of humanity through Yeshua and Yeshua's faithfulness to God. This is what is meant by "**God's righteousness**."

But the central issue of this passage is the justice/mercy paradox. We know that God is altogether just and altogether merciful, even though it is hard for us to understand *how* he can be righteous and just, exacting due punishment for sin, but yet at the same time be merciful, forgiving people who trust in Yeshua. The answer is that individual righteousness begins and ends with trusting God, neither more nor less (1:17). This means (1) trusting that God has justly poured out the full measure of his wrath (1:18) on Yeshua, the sacrificed lamb of God who takes away the sins of the world (Yn 1:29), and (2) trusting that in his great mercy God regards anyone who identifies fully with Yeshua as already fully punished for his past sins (6:3).

But how does this make God both just and merciful? How can an individual rely on someone else's taking the punishment which he himself deserves for his sins? This question bothers many thoughtful people, Jews and Gentiles alike. The following parable, whose source I do not know, does not fit the theological realities at every point, but it is suggestive.

Once upon a time there was a king who was strong, brave and possessed of all other good qualities. He ruled his country justly, loved his people and was loved by them.

Because of this there was no crime in his kingdom — until one day it was discovered that a thief was loose in the land.

Knowing that wrongful behavior would multiply unless he took a strong stand against it, the king decreed that when caught the thief would receive twenty lashes. But the thefts continued. He raised the punishment to forty lashes in the hope of deterring further crime, but to no avail. Finally, he announced that the criminal would be punished with sixty lashes, knowing that no one in the country could survive sixty lashes except himself. At last the thief was caught, and it turned out to be — the king's mother.

The king was faced with a dilemma. He loved his mother more than anyone in the world, but justice demanded that the punishment be carried out. Moreover, were his subjects to see that it was possible to commit a crime and not be punished for it, social order would eventually be completely undermined. At the same time, he knew that if he were to subject his own mother to a punishment that would kill her, the people's love would turn to revulsion and hate toward a man so lacking in compassion and ordinary affection, and he would be unable to govern at all. The whole nation wondered what he would do.

The day arrived for administering the prescribed punishment. The king mounted a platform in the capital's central square, and the royal flogger took his place. Then the king's elderly mother was brought forward, fragile and trembling. On seeing her son the king, she burst into tears. "I'm... so sorry... for what I did!" she wailed, between sobs. Then, recovering, the bent, white-haired figure made her way toward the flogging harness. The people gasped as the flogger raised his muscled arm with the leather whip.

Just as it was about to crack down on the exposed back of the woman who had given him birth, the king cried "Stop!" The arm poised in mid-air, the whip fell limp. The king rose from his seat, removed his robe, walked to the harness, embraced his mother, and, with his broad frame covering his mother and his bared back exposed to the flogger, commanded him, "Execute the sentence!" The sixty stripes fell on the back of the king.

> "He was wounded for our transgressions,
> bruised for our iniquities;
> his suffering was for our well-being,
> and by his stripes we are healed.
> We all, like sheep, have gone astray;
> we have turned, each one to his own way;
> and *Adonai* has laid on him
> the iniquity of us all." (Isaiah 53:5–6)

27–28 Literal translation of these verses:

> "Wherefore therefore the boasting? It was shut out. Through what law? of works? No, rather through a law of trusting. For we reason that a person is justified by trusting, apart from works of law."

The **boasting** spoken of is that of 2:17–21. The reasons for rendering "works" as **legalistic observance of rules** are given in v. 20bN.

The KJV rendering of v. 28, "Therefore we conclude that a man is justified by faith without the deeds of the law," raises the question of whether Sha'ul and Ya'akov are inconsistent with each other, because Ya'akov writes that faith apart from the actions is barren (Ya 2:20), and that "a person is declared righteous because of actions and not because of faith alone" (Ya 2:24); see Ya 2:14–26&NN for my answer, showing that Sha'ul and Ya'akov do not contradict each other. Also see Ep 2:8–10&N, where Sha'ul himself ties faith to works and explains how they are related to each other. And see 4:1–2N below.

29–30 Sha'ul argues: If you still think that only Jews can be saved because only they have the *Torah* to follow, ask yourself, **is God the God of the Jews only? Isn't he also the God of the Gentiles** (Greek *ethnê*, see 1:5b–6N)? **Yes, he is indeed the God of the Gentiles; because, as you will admit, "God is one"** (*Adonai echad*), quoted from the most important verse in Judaism, the *Sh'ma* ("Hear, O Israel, *Adonai* our God, *Adonai* is one," Deuteronomy 6:4).

Christians are sometimes asked: "If the *Sh'ma* says that 'God is one,' how can you believe in the Trinity, which says that God is three?" If the question is a rhetorical way of stating that God's oneness is inconsistent with the notion that he is Father, Son and Holy Spirit, then Sha'ul's quoting of the *Sh'ma* should demonstrate that at least one educated Jew found no contradiction. If the question is asked seriously, it must first be insisted emphatically that trinitarian theology does not say that "God is three"; beyond that, it is my hope that the *Jewish New Testament* and this commentary on it will help supply an answer.

The conclusion to be drawn from God's oneness is, **Therefore he will consider righteous the circumcised on the ground of trusting** (*ek pisteôs*) **and the uncircumcised through that same trusting** (*dia tês pisteôs*). I am grateful to Joseph Shulam for pointing out the significance of the Greek terms "*ek*" ("out of") and "*dia*" ("through") in this verse; the rest of this note builds on his analysis.

As Jews grow up faithfully "out of" the soil of faith, trusting in Yeshua, God will regard them as righteous. And he will do exactly the same thing for Gentiles as they go "through" the process of coming to have the same faith that faithful Messianic Jews have. Gentiles do this when they take Jewish history, which is salvation history, as their own. They thus come into union with this Jewish faith-stream; and this Jewish faith-stream, as they encounter the Jewish Messiah, carries them on into salvation.

Thus there is a difference between Jews and Gentiles — though not in their salvation; for, as the whole book of Romans is at pains to point out (1:16&N), in the Messiah, so far as salvation is concerned, there is "neither Jew nor Gentile" (Ga 3:28). But for historical reasons there is a difference between Jews and Gentiles in the process which leads to their salvation. Only the Jews have salvation history as their own, so that they come "out of" the matrix of faith and salvation history. Gentiles must appropriate that history to themselves, for it is not theirs naturally. But it is theirs, and fully so, as they identify with it and go "through" to become one with the faith experiences and salvation history of the Jewish people.

In conclusion, I will repeat, in order to avoid any misunderstanding: the righteousness which God confers through Yeshua is absolutely the same for Gentiles as for Jews.

In the Kingdom of God, wherein God rules the saved, there are no second-class citizens, no "separate but equal"; rather, there is "neither Jew nor Gentile."

31 **Does it follow that we abolish *Torah* by this trusting?** Sha'ul follows the rabbinic method, found throughout the Talmud, of anticipating a hypothetical questioner — and not so hypothetical, if one reads the literature of Jewish attitudes toward Christianity. Here is his argument: You might think the assertion, "'Works of law' are of no avail for salvation," is tantamount to overthrowing the *Torah* itself — if you were used to thinking of the *Torah* as a rulebook capable of being followed mechanically without trusting God (see v. 20bN). For this very reason Sha'ul, in order to keep the attention of those who would otherwise reject anything more he has to say, addresses the issue head-on, answering in the negative as strongly as possible, **Heaven forbid!** (on this expression see 3:4N, last paragraph) and adds: **On the contrary, we confirm *Torah*** (or "uphold" it, "establish" it or "place" it "on a firm foundation"). Why does trusting, which is the exact opposite of mechanical rule-keeping, "confirm *Torah"?* Because trusting God, and not mechanical rule-keeping, is the very basis, foundation and essence of *Torah*, it is what the *Torah* is all about. In saying so, Sha'ul does not exhaust the subject; far from it. It is his literary style, however, to introduce a topic briefly, allowing the reader to be filled with questions about it, and then return to it later. That is what he does here; he returns to the matter of how faith and *Torah* fit together in Chapters 7 and 9–11.

CHAPTER 4

1–2 **Then what should we say Avraham, our forefather, obtained by his own efforts?** Having offered reassurance to his hypothetical Jewish questioner that the Gospel's focus on faithful trusting does not destroy *Torah* but confirms it (3:31&N), Sha'ul addresses a second objection he might raise: What about *z'khut-avot*, the "merits of the fathers"? (See 11:28–29N.)

There can be no doubt that in the 1st century C.E. the doctrine was widespread that descendants can benefit and even can claim salvation on the ground of their ancestors' righteousness. Yeshua's opponents made exactly such a claim at Yn 8:33, Sha'ul's own opponents obviously were making use of the idea at 2C 11:22, and Yochanan the Immerser rebuked his investigators before they had a chance to say, "Avraham is our father" (Mt 3:9&N).

There is a kernel of biblical basis for this belief: "And because he loved your fathers he chose their offspring after them" (Deuteronomy 4:37; see also Exodus 32:13). Moreover, there is a perfectly correct application of this idea not to the rights of the descendants but to the faithfulness of God, that he will fulfill his own promises to the forefathers (11:28–29&N).

Rabbinic literature does well in pointing up Avraham's faithful and trusting attitude toward God. For example, the Midrash Rabbah:

> "In the *'olam haba* [world to come] Israel will sing a new song, as it is said, 'Sing unto *Adonai* a new song, for he has done marvelous things' (Psalm 98:1). By whose *z'khut* [merit] will they do so? By the merit of Avraham, because he

> trusted in the Holy One, blessed be he, as it says, 'And he trusted in *Adonai*' (Genesis 15:6)." (Exodus Rabbah 23:5)

But even Avraham's trust is of no avail to his descendants; they must have trust of their own. Romans 9–11 can be viewed as an elaboration of this principle. The present chapter investigates the nature of Avraham's own "merit": what is it that he **obtained by his own efforts?** (The phrase translates one Greek word which means "found, discovered" or even "achieved.") Didn't he have "works," meritorious "deeds" that earned him his salvation? This is what Sha'ul's hypothetical questioner is asking.

In one sense the answer is "Yes" — if trusting can be counted as a "work," or if trusting in its proper sense implies appropriate good works that stem from it, which is what Sha'ul himself speaks about at Ep 2:8–10 and Ya'akov at Ya 2:14–26 (see 3:27–28N). But, as explained at 3:20bN, "works" here are understood in contradistinction to "faith" as **legalistic observances.** If Ya'akov's point is that "faith without works is dead" (Ya 2:26), Sha'ul's point here is complementary and equally true: works without faith are dead.

3 Sha'ul quotes the same verse as cited in the Midrash Rabbah above (vv. 1–2N). The one "deed" that "earned" Avraham being declared righteous by God was not a deed at all, but the non-act (the heart attitude) of trusting God.

6 **Legalistic observances**, Greek *erga*, "works." See 3:20bN.

9–12 Sha'ul finishes destroying the argument that physical circumcision (i.e., being a member of the Chosen People) is the Jews' big advantage (refer back to 2:25–29). He consistently maintains that the advantage of Jews is spiritual, not physical (3:1–2, 9:4–5, and most explicitly at 15:27). At the same time he shows that the righteousness that comes from trusting God is available equally to Jews and Gentiles not merely because it antedates the Mosaic Law, but because it antedates even the Abrahamic Covenant, when **circumcision** was given **as a sign** of Abraham's already demonstrated faith and **as a seal** guaranteeing God's promises, but not as something to boast about.

Thus ***Avraham avinu*** ("Abraham, our father" — a common phrase in rabbinic writing and in today's *Siddur*; v. 12) is "our" father not only to Jews but also to trusting Gentiles, hence, to "all of us" (v. 16&N). Galatians 3:6–18 develops the same theme, as do vv. 13–22 below.

13–15 In these three verses the Greek word "*nomos*" occurs four times. In each case, does it mean *Torah* in general, the legal portions of the *Torah*, law in general, or legalism? My rendering reflects my own understanding (see Introduction to *JNT*, Section V) — legalism the first two times (3:20&N), law in general the last two times (v. 15N).

13 **The promise to Avraham and his seed that he would inherit the world**. The Greek word for "**world**" here is "*kosmos*"; Kittel's *Theological Dictionary of the New Testament* explains that here it means "inhabited world," but its sense "merges into that of the nations of the world" (III, p. 888), as found in such passages as Genesis 12:1–3, 15:3–5, 17:2–7, 18:18 and 22:17–18. These passages are not the same as the ones in which it is promised that Avraham and his descendants would inherit the Land of Israel (Genesis 12:7, 13:14–17, 15:7–21, 17:7–8, 24:7); when the New Testament wishes to refer to the Land, it uses the word "*gê*" (see Mt 5:5N and *JNT* Introduction, Section VI, last paragraph).

At 9:7 Sha'ul takes "**seed**" to mean Yitzchak, Avraham's son; and at Ga 3:16 he makes a *midrash* applying the word "seed" to Yeshua. In the present passage Sha'ul uses "seed" in its ordinary figurative sense to mean Avraham's descendants — not only his physical seed, but (at v. 16) his spiritual seed. See 9:7–9N and, for a discussion of the various possible meanings of "seed," Ga 3:16N.

15 For what law brings is punishment. But where there is no law, there is also no violation. Cranfield (commentary on Romans, *ad loc.*) disagrees; but to me this seems to be a statement about law in general rather than about the *Torah* in particular: although moral behavior is absolute, unless a statute makes a particular act illegal and punishable, there is no violation and the act goes unpunished. This general principle is applied specifically to the *Torah*, insofar as it contains elements of law, at 5:13 and 7:7–10.

16 *Avraham avinu* for all of us, Gentiles as well as Jews. Can a Gentile speak of Avraham as his father? The following, condensed from the *Rambam*'s well-known "Letter to Ovadyah the Proselyte," is quoted at length because its sentiments are so precisely appropriate, provided one imagines it as written to a Gentile follower of Yeshua instead of a convert to Judaism.

> "You ask me if you are permitted to say in the prayers, 'God of *our* fathers,' and 'You who worked miracles for *our* fathers.' Yes; you may say your blessing and prayer in the same way as every born Jew. This is because *Avraham avinu* revealed the true faith and the unity of God, rejected idol-worship, and brought many children under the wings of the *Sh'khinah* [see Genesis 18:19]. Ever since then whoever adopts Judaism and confesses the unity of the Divine Name, as prescribed in the *Torah*, is counted among the disciples of *Avraham avinu*, peace unto him. In the same way as he converted his contemporaries through his words and teaching, he converts later generations through the testament he left his children and household after him. Thus *Avraham avinu* is the father of his pious posterity who keep his ways, and the father of his disciples and of all proselytes who adopt Judaism.
>
> "Since you have come under the wings of the *Sh'khinah* and confessed the Lord, no difference exists between you and us, and all miracles done to us have been done, as it were, both to us and to you. Thus it is said in the book of Isaiah, 'Let not the son of the stranger who follows *Adonai* say, "*Adonai* has completely separated me from his people"' (Isaiah 56:3). There is no difference whatsoever between you and us.
>
> "Know that our fathers, when they came out of Egypt, were mostly idolaters; they had mingled with the pagans in Egypt and imitated their way of life, until the Holy One, blessed be he, sent *Moshe Rabbenu* [Moses our teacher], who

separated us from the nations, brought us under the wings of the *Sh'khinah*, us and all proselytes, and gave all of us one *Torah*.

"Do not consider your origin inferior. While we are the descendants of Avraham, Yitzchak and Ya'akov, you derive from him through whose word the world was created. As Isaiah writes, 'This one will say, "I belong to *Adonai*," while that one will call himself by the name of Ya'akov' (Isaiah 44:5)."

17–24 "I have appointed you to be a father to many nations." Avraham is our father. See vv. 9–12N.

Avraham... trusted God as the one who gives life to the dead. That God quickens the dead is a major tenet of Judaism; the second benediction of the *'Amidah*, the prayer recited three times every day in the synagogue, reads:

"You are mighty forever, *Adonai*. You cause the dead to live, you are great to save. With loving-kindness you sustain the living; with great mercy you cause the dead to live, support the falling, heal the sick, free the bound and keep faith with those who sleep in the dust. Who is like you, Master of mighty deeds? Who resembles you, O King? You cause death, you cause life, and you cause salvation to sprout forth, so you can be trusted to cause the dead to live. Blessed are you, *Adonai*, who causes the dead to live."

Resurrection faith distinguished the *P'rushim* from the *Tz'dukim* (Mt 22:23–33&NN, Ac 23:6–10&NN). Today it distinguishes Orthodox Judaism from liberal elements in other branches of Judaism. Avraham's resurrection faith was both literal and figurative, and both senses are indicated in this chapter.

Figuratively, so far as procreation and fulfillment of God's promise of descendants was concerned, Avraham's **body... was as good as dead, since he was about a hundred years old** (ninety-nine, to be exact; see Genesis 17:17, 24), and **Sarah's womb was dead too** (she was about ninety). Yet, although **past hope**, with resurrection faith he trusted **that what God had promised he could also accomplish** (a theme that returns at 8:31–39, and see 9:1–11:36N). For at Genesis 15:5–6, after wondering how God would fulfill his promise to make him a great nation when he was old and childless, God

"brought him outside and said, 'Now look at the sky and count the stars — if you can count them!' Then he said to him, '**so many will your seed be**!' And Avraham put his trust in God, and it was credited to his account as righteousness,"

as quoted in v. 3.

But Avraham also had literal resurrection faith. It was necessary for what Judaism regards as his greatest "work," his willingness to sacrifice his only son Yitzchak, through whom God had said the promise would be fulfilled (Genesis 17:21, 22:1–19). This act is referred to throughout the High Holy Day services, and Genesis 22 is one of the statutory *Torah* readings on *Rosh-HaShanah*, a feast on which the *shofar* is blown one hundred times — and the *shofar* is associated with the resurrection of the dead (see

Mt 24:31&N, 1C 15:52&N, 1 Th 4:16&N, Rv 8:2&N). The act is mentioned twice in the New Testament explicitly as an example of great faith (MJ 11:17–19&NN, Ya 2:21).

Here it constitutes the background for the conclusion of our passage, which says that we who have become followers of Yeshua have the same kind of resurrection faith as Avraham because **we have trusted in him who raised Yeshua our Lord from the dead** (v. 24), just as Avraham "had concluded that God could even raise people from the dead" (MJ 11:19). That is why **the words, "it was credited to his account..." were not written for him only**, but **also for us, who will certainly have our account credited too** (vv. 23–24). This is a radical statement, for it says that Avraham was not special. Whereas Jewish *midrashim* attribute unique ability, holiness and power to Avraham, enabling him to have trust far beyond what ordinary people can attain to, Sha'ul insists that such trust is available to everyone. This is the Good News, that through Yeshua the Messiah anyone can have the same close personal relationship with Almighty God that Avraham had! Indeed, many believers have received promises from God just as Avraham did and have seen God fulfill them.

25 The content of our "hope" (v. 18; 5:2, 4, 5) is that because we have fully identified with Yeshua, **who was delivered over to death because of our offences and was raised to life in order to make us righteous**, we too will be resurrected to sinless eternal life with God (6:5, 23; 8:23). Chapter 5 elaborates this theme.

CHAPTER 5

1–4 Chapter 5 develops the ideas of 4:25. Verses 1–2 speak of the past, present and future aspects of salvation.

Let us continue to have *shalom* (peace, integrity, wholeness, health) **with God**. The textual evidence favors this reading, but some manuscripts read, "We have [or: "We continue to have"] *shalom* with God." This descriptive statement is true, but the exhortation fits the context better; for v. 2 exhorts us to **boast about the hope of experiencing God's glory** (instead of coming short of it, 3:23&N) when we are resurrected, and v. 3 exhorts us to **boast in our** present **troubles** (see 8:18), because by a roundabout route (vv. 3–4) they lead to the same **hope** as in v. 2. Boasting about oneself (1:22, 2:17–21) is excluded (3:27, 4:2); the proper content of boasting is God's work through Yeshua the Messiah (1C 1:31&N).

5 **This hope does not let us down**, literally, "...make us ashamed" (compare Psalms 22:6(5), 25:21(20)), as we would be if we had a false hope; **because God's love for us** (v. 8) **has** already **been poured out in our hearts through the *Ruach HaKodesh*** (the Holy Spirit), **who** is fully God (2C 3:17–18&N) and **has been given to us** in fulfillment of a different promise (Ezekiel 36:27; Yn 14:16, 26; 15:26; 16:7, 13; Ac 1:8, 2:4), and thus guarantees that God will also keep this present promise to resurrect us. For additional assurance that God will keep his promises and not let our hope be disappointed, see 8:31–39&N, 9:1–11:36N. Chapter 8 discusses the role of the Holy Spirit.

6 **At the right time** (compare Ga 4:4) **the Messiah died on behalf of ungodly people**, as

Isaiah 53 (especially vv. 6, 12) indicated he would, and as he himself said he would (Mk 10:45; Yn 10:12, 17–18; 1 Yn 3:16).

9–10 By means of his bloody sacrificial death, literally, "by his blood"; see 3:25N.

The truths of 4:25 are restated in these two verses in a *kal v'chomer* argument (see Mt 6:30N). If Yeshua's death accomplishes so much, **how much more** his life accomplishes! The same kind of argument is used in Romans at four other places: vv. 15, 17; 11:12, 24; also see 3:19N.

12–21 This is one of the great theological passages in the Bible; but because upon it Christians have erected the doctrine of original sin, it is for Jewish people one of the most problematic. Pivotal in Chapters 1–8 of Romans, it looks backward to 3:21–5:11, where God's means of considering people righteous (first mentioned at 1:17) through Yeshua is proclaimed, and forward to 6:1–8:39, where Sha'ul elaborates the consequences for the individual believer of what Yeshua has accomplished.

The purpose of these ten verses in their context is not to teach about the origin of human sin but to give assurance that the Messiah has truly redeemed us human beings from bondage to sin by paying its full penalty on our behalf. Sha'ul makes his case by developing the parallel between the effects on mankind of Adam and of Yeshua (vv. 12, 14, 18–19, 21), while stressing that what Yeshua accomplished by his obedience to God was far greater and better than what Adam wreaked by his disobedience (vv. 15–17) and simultaneously dispelling any suspicion that focussing on these two men minimizes the importance of the *Torah* (13–14a, 20).

But the whole argument is built on a premise which Sha'ul assumes can be taken for granted, as axiomatic, namely, that it was the one man Adam who brought sin and death upon all humanity (on the role of the woman, Chavah [Eve], see 1 Ti 2:13–15&N). After a paragraph on some points of the text itself I will examine what Judaism and Christianity have made of this proposition and see if I can discern where Messianic Judaism might take its stand.

Sin entered the world through one individual, Adam, who disobeyed God's command in the Garden of Eden not to eat from the tree of the knowledge of good and evil (Genesis 2:17, 3:6); **and through sin, death**, because God decreed certain death as the punishment for sin (Genesis 2:17, 3:19, 5:5). While death may have been possible before Adam sinned, had he chosen not to eat from the tree of life (Genesis 2:9, 3:22), it apparently was not a necessary consequence of being human. **And thus death passed through to the whole human race, inasmuch as** (or "because") **everyone sinned.** It can hardly be questioned that this says, on the one hand, that Adam's transgression caused death to come to everyone and also, on the other, that each person deserved death because each person sinned — that is, each person dies for his own sin, as Ezekiel 8:4 says, "The soul that sins, it shall die." But how these facts are related to each other and applied to understanding the existential condition of mankind forms the kernel of my inquiry in this note. Sha'ul himself is less concerned to explain the precise mechanism of how death **passed through** than to defend the justice of death's coming to those who did not consciously violate a God-given command (vv. 13–14a, based on the argument of 4:15). **In this**, in having direct contact with God, being directly responsible to him and having the consequences of his acts pass through to others in the future, **Adam**

prefigured the one who was to come, Yeshua (v. 14b). But there are very significant differences between these two men (vv. 15–17) which are brought out through *kal v'chomer* arguments (see vv. 9–10N). **In other words**: vv. 18–19 repeat and elaborate the point of vv. 12, 14b. **Will be made righteous** (v. 19): while being declared righteous before God is still in view, the use of the future tense suggests the ongoing extension of that declared righteousness into actual righteousness (sanctification; see Ga 2:16aN). The future tense could refer to the fact that many people in years to come will be declared righteous as they come to faith, but it can also imply the future total sanctification of the saved. **The *Torah* came into the picture so that the offense would proliferate** (v. 20) — see 3:20, 4:15 and 7:7–25 on this function of the *Torah*, which non-Messianic Judaism tends to minimize. **Where sin proliferated, grace proliferated even more** — see 6:1ff. for prophylaxis against misusing this idea to justify sin. Verse 21 sums up not only this passage but all that has been said since 3:21.

Before assessing the doctrine of original sin, we must see what it actually says. Otherwise we will find ourselves dealing with oversimplified abstractions — "Judaism says man is a sinner because he sins, Christianity that man sins because he is a sinner," "Judaism is less concerned with where sin comes from than struggling against it," "Christianity alone regards sin as fatal; Judaism takes it for a minor illness." Slogans substitute both for thinking and for fair dealing.

A. Content of the Doctrine of Original Sin.

The analysis commences with a summary of the content of one version of the doctrine of original sin — I say one version because there are at least six; see A. H. Strong, *Systematic Theology*, on which I am relying for much of this portion of my note. Augustine (354–430 C.E.) was instrumental in developing this version; a modified modern form of it would make these points (objections to them can be found in Section C of this note):

(1) *Terminology. Original sin* involves two components: *original pollution*, which is the sinful state and condition into which people are born, in consequence of which they have a sinful nature that makes it impossible for them to do what God will regard as spiritual good; and *original guilt*, which makes everyone worthy of condemnation and death from the moment he comes into existence. These are "original" because they (a) are derived from the original root of the human race, Adam; (b) are present in the life of every individual from his origin (birth or before) and not merely the result of imitation; and (c) are the origin, the inward root, of all the sinful inclinations and sinful deeds that defile a person. However, they are not original in the sense of having been present when God created man in his image and pronounced him good (Genesis 1:26–31).

(2) *Locus of responsibility for sin in the universe.* Although God created the universe and everything in it, even evil (Isaiah 45:7), he is not to be considered the author of sin and is not to be held responsible for it. Sin originated in the angelic world, with Satan (the Adversary, represented in the Garden of Eden by the serpent); and in man it originated with Adam.

(3) *What was "the" original sin?* Although in a formal sense Adam's sin was eating the forbidden fruit, the essence of it was his apostatizing from God, opposing him,

rebelling against him personally, substituting his own will for God's will. This he did out of pride, unbelief, desire to be like God (self-exaltation) and unholy satisfaction in doing what had been prohibited. It is this apostasy which is "the" original sin that has been passed on from Adam to us and for which we are held accountable, not the act of eating forbidden fruit.

(4) *Original pollution.* The word "*sin*" means not only actual *sinful deeds* but also *sinful inclinations* and having a *sinful nature*. Having a sinful nature means that one's very nature is corrupted and polluted, so that one is bound to develop sinful inclinations and desires that will lead one to commit actual sinful deeds as soon as one reaches the age of moral responsibility. It means that one is in a condition of "*total depravity*" — which is not to say that the sinner has no innate knowledge of God's will, no ability in his conscience to discriminate between good and evil, no admiration for virtue, no capability to act for others' good, no capacity to do deeds that may produce some external good, or that his every deed is as bad as it can possibly be; rather, what total depravity means is that the corruption extends to all of man's nature, so that nothing the sinner does will be credited to his account by God as good, because it is not and cannot be motivated by true, unadulterated love of God and desire to do his will.

(5) *Transmission of original pollution.* Original pollution is transmitted from Adam to his descendants by propagation. At the risk of introducing anachronistic imagery, I will compare Adam's sin with a cosmic ray that penetrates the genetic material of one person and brings about a fatal mutation which is completely dominant, so that all his descendants receive the "defective gene" that "causes sinful nature" and eventually die of this "congenital disease."

(6) *Original guilt.* Adam's original sin of apostasy from God resulted not only in our having his pollution (sinful nature) transmitted to us, but also in our having his guilt imputed to us, so that we are born guilty and worthy of death as the penalty for our own sin. We are guilty on three accounts. First, we are guilty of Adam's sin of apostasy itself, even though we did not exercise individual moral choice in the matter. Second, we are guilty of having a sinful nature, even though we were born with it and did not choose it; because this is a nature inherently in a state of apostasy from God, and such apostasy is condemnable. And third, of course, we are guilty of all the actual sinful deeds we commit as individuals.

(7) *Imputation of original guilt.* Original guilt is not transmitted by propagation but justly imputed to us on the ground that we are organically one with Adam. That is, even though we did not exercise individual moral choice when he sinned, we were present "in him" (compare MJ 7:9–10, where L'vi "in Avraham" paid tithes to Malki-Tzedek). Responsibility for someone else's sin conflicts with the individualistic philosophy of Hobbes, Locke, Rousseau and the American founding fathers; but in biblical times the notion that one individual's guilt could involve his whole family or even his entire people was more current; for example, Achan's sin (Joshua 7). Even today Americans traveling abroad find themselves held accountable for decisions made by leaders they may actually have voted against; "Yankee, go home!" proclaims the perceived "organic unity" of the American people, of which most Americans are part not by choice but by birth. Our oneness with Adam, our natural head and first father, means that his punishment is justly ours.

(8) *Death is the penalty for sin.* The penalty for sin is death: death is not merely the natural end of human life, but a punishment. This death is threefold: physical, spiritual and eternal. Physical death comes at the end of the physical lifespan. Spiritual death means lack of communion with God, separation from him — as Isaiah 59:2 puts it, "Your sins have made a separation between you and your God." Finally, if one remains in spiritual death throughout one's physical lifespan, this condition is, upon physical death, confirmed by God and becomes eternal death in Gey-Hinnom (hell), that is, eternal and irremediable separation from God and all goodness.

(9) *The remedy for original sin.* There is only one remedy for the pollution and guilt of original sin, and that is to trust in God, to turn away from sin and self-pleasing to God and his will, to accept that the sacrificial death of Yeshua, who never sinned but paid by his death the penalty we owe for our sin, reconciles us with God and removes the separation. No amount or kind of striving in our own strength, apart from trusting God through Yeshua, can remove original sin.

B. Other Versions of the Doctrine of Original Sin.

We can gain some insight into the "competition" with the Augustinian version of the doctrine of original sin by seeing how it and the other five versions listed by Strong interpret the seminal statement of v. 12, "**Death passed through to the whole human race, inasmuch as everyone sinned.**"

(1) *Augustinian*, which says we are born with both original pollution (for which we are guilty) and original guilt connected with Adam's sin of apostasy: "Death physical, spiritual and eternal passed through to the whole human race, because all sinned in Adam their natural head."

(2) *Mediate imputation (Placeus (1596–1665))*, which says that the original pollution we are born with is a ground for our guilt, but that we are not guilty of Adam's sinful act of apostasy: "Death physical, spiritual and eternal passed through to the whole human race, because all sinned by possessing a depraved nature."

(3) *Federal (Cocceius (1603–1669))*, which says the opposite of the above, namely, that the original pollution we are born with is not a ground for our guilt, but that Adam's apostasy is imputed to us because he was our "representative" in Eden, our "federal head": "Death physical, spiritual and eternal passed through to the whole human race, because all were regarded and treated as sinners."

(4) *Uncondemnable vitiosity (the "New School," 18th-century New England)*, which says that the original pollution we are born with is not a ground for guilt, and also that we are not guilty of Adam's act of apostasy, but become guilty only when we commit sinful acts, and that physical death is a natural phenomenon: "Spiritual and eternal death passed to all, because all have actually and personally sinned."

(5) *Arminian-Methodist (Arminius (1560–1609) and John Wesley (1703–1791))*, which says that although man is born physically and intellectually depraved, his will can cooperate with the Holy Spirit, so that he becomes guilty only when he "ratifies" his sinful nature by committing sinful acts: "Physical and spiritual death is inflicted upon all, not as the penalty of a common sin in Adam, but because, by divine decree, all suffer the consequences of that sin, and because all personally consent to their inborn sinfulness by acts of transgression."

(6) *Pelagian (Pelagius, c. 410)*, which says man is born innocent and able to obey God but sins by following the bad examples around him: "All incurred spiritual and eternal death by sinning after Adam's example."

As a rough approximation, we may say that the farther down the above list we move, the closer we come to what traditional Judaism can accept as a satisfactory theology of sin.

C. Objections to "Augustinian" Original Sin, and Answers.

But before turning to closer examination of the positive assertions about sin found in Jewish materials, I wish to look at some of the objections made to the Augustinian version, the most "extreme" version, of the doctrine of original sin; and it will be clear from even the above minimal presentation of the alternatives that many Christians as well as Jews find aspects of it unpalatable. The list of objections, with possible answers, is organized according to the nine paragraphs summarizing the doctrine itself in Section A above.

(1) Objections to terminology. In this brief summary I present none. However, Judaism, following biblical and Middle Eastern thought patterns, prefers to build inductively from particular examples to more general principles; whereas Christian theology, heavily influenced by Greek ways of thinking, tends to start with general principles and work deductively to implications for particular situations. For this reason, Jewish thinkers find themselves uncomfortable not so much with particular terminology as with the whole theologizing enterprise.

(2) Objections to the doctrine that Adam originated human sin:

(a) God originated human sin; if he made man able to sin, God is the ultimate origin. *Answer*: The logic may seem reasonable, but we are dealing with what Judaism, Christianity and secular philosophy acknowledge as a paradox or antinomy. Scripture is clear that God does not do wickedness, is perfectly holy, has no unrighteousness in him, cannot be tempted by evil and tempts no one to do evil, created man good, hates sin, and provided (in the Messiah) for deliverance from sin (Deuteronomy 25:16, 32:4; Isaiah 6:3; Zechariah 8:17; Psalm 5:4, 11:5, 92:16; Job 34:10; Lk 16:15; Ya 1:13). Furthermore, our consciences witness that we are responsible for sin, not God.

(b) Satan originated human sin; he is responsible, the ultimate origin. *Answer*: Christianity does not accept this either as a means of removing responsibility from man or as a setting-up of an independent creator in the universe. Christianity has been accused of being dualistic, of setting up two gods, one (God) being holy and the other (Satan) being evil. But Christianity accepts the clear teaching of Job 1–2 that Satan's activities are thoroughly under God's control, and that Satan has already been defeated by Yeshua.

(c) Man is not responsible for sin because sin is only man's creaturely limitation. *Answer*: No; Adam could have chosen not to sin, but he willed otherwise. We too choose to sin, and we are responsible for our choice.

(3) Objection that turns on a wrong understanding of what "the" original sin was: Adam's sin was minor; thus death is a disproportionate punishment. *Answer*: Had Adam's sin been merely eating some fruit, itself a morally neutral act, this objection would hold. But, as explained, Adam's sin was disobeying God's

single express command and thus rejecting God's authority, his will, his very person, apostatizing from God and rebelling against him, wilfully creating the very separation that is death.

(4) Objections to the notions of original pollution and total depravity:

(a) There is no such thing as original pollution, because sin is not a state or a collection of inclinations but actual sinful deeds.
Answer: Both experience and Scripture contradict this limited notion of what sin is. Our conscience convicts us, so that we feel guilty when we contemplate our sinful desires and our great distance from the holiness of God; and Scripture speaks of God's looking at mankind in the days before the Flood and seeing not only "that the wickedness of man was great in the earth," but also "that all the inclination of the thoughts of his heart was only evil all day long" (Genesis 6:5).

(b) There is no such thing as original pollution, because there can be no sin prior to conscious intent. Therefore Adam's act of apostasy, which surely was not his conscious intent, is not condemnable; and also our own having a sinful nature and sinful inclinations, also not consciously intended, is not condemnable.
Answer: Common sense and conscience tell us that violating a command implies rebellion against the one who commanded. Furthermore, we feel guilt for things we have done even unintentionally — and Scripture provides for sacrifices in such cases (Leviticus 5:17). Also Psalm 19 indicates that people properly feel remorse for unintended sins — "Who can discern errors? Cleanse me from secret faults," contrasted with the following verse, "Also keep your servant back from presumptuous sins; let them not have dominion over me" (Psalm 19:13–14(12–13); also Psalm 51:8(6)). The objection rests on the false premise that the law must be published or recognized; but if law is identical with the constituent principles of existence and binds human nature to conformity with God's nature (since man is created in his image), then right volitions are demanded not arbitrarily but properly as manifestations of a right state of being. Verses 13–14a confirm this understanding.

(c) There is original pollution, but it is not total; it affects only man's mind, emotions and body, but not his will, so that he can conquer his sinful inclinations by himself. (This is the Arminian position; see Section B(5) above.)
Answer: Man is not compartmentalized; the rot affects all of him. Though he can do some things of moral value, in the sense of things which prove beneficial in some measure to some, these have no spiritual value for him and do not constitute spiritual good to be credited to his account.

(d) A more specifically Jewish form of the previous objection: there is indeed an evil inclination *(yetzer ra')* in man, but it can be conquered and even turned to good use by following the *Torah*.
Answer: Apart from God man can do nothing good; he cannot even obey the *Torah* properly, although he may be able to perform certain specific commands, because apart from God he cannot love God. Following the *Torah* today implies accepting Yeshua as the Messiah and as the *kapparah* (covering, atonement, expiation; see 3:25aN) for one's sin.

(e) The doctrine of original pollution and total depravity leads to unacceptable consequences, including these:

1) It denies free will — if one has a sinful nature that compels one to sin, one is no longer free to choose not to sin.
Answer: Even the sinner remains free to choose better rather than worse courses of action; further, and more importantly, he is free to turn to God in repentance from sin and accept God's remedy for his condition — "Everyone who calls on the name of *Adonai* will be saved" (10:33 and Ac 2:21, quoting Joel 3:5(2:32)).
2) It neutralizes appeals to conscience, making ethical conduct unimportant.
Answer: Ethical conduct is critically important for saved people, as Chapters 12–15 make clear. But for the individual himself, salvation is more important than ethical behavior because it makes communion with God possible and enables him to will God's will. Moreover, salvation is not in conflict with ethical behavior — it is not as if a person could help others by sacrificing his own salvation (see 9:2–4a&N). Quite the contrary, it is only God's grace that makes the deeds of an unsaved person of value to anyone; God deserves all the credit, the rebellious unsaved person none.
3) It makes a blasphemous charade of God's command to "turn from evil and do good" (Psalm 34:15(14), quoted at 1 Ke 3:11).
Answer: It is true that God commands sinners, who can do no good, to do good. But this means that they should turn from evil to God in repentance and acknowledge that God considers them righteous only because of what Yeshua has done for them. Only then, believing God, they will be able to do the good he has commanded them to do.
4) It makes God's grace more important than man's conduct.
Answer: In a sense it is true that God's grace is above man's conduct — nothing man can do apart from God can force God to consider man righteous; in fact, the very idea is a contradiction. And apart from the great grace he has shown through Yeshua he never considers anyone righteous. Thus God's grace is indeed more important than man's conduct. Nevertheless, the conduct man should display is that of first turning to God and trusting him and his son Yeshua, and then doing what he has commanded. God's grace and man's conduct are not alternatives or opposites; the proper relationship between them is this: man's conduct should emerge from gratitude to God for his grace (see Ep 2:8–10).
5) It is static and depressing, encouraging lethargy and discouraging struggle against sin.
Answer: The struggle against sin, apart from trusting God through Yeshua, is doomed to failure, because it is actually a struggle against God. The battle against sin will ultimately succeed, but only when it is carried out in God's way, with the resources he provides. Life apart from God is indeed static and depressing, and a certain amount of self-motivated struggle *ought* to make one tired and lethargic after a while, since no amount or intensity of such struggle can lead to victory. But once one acknowledges God's remedy, the desire to do his will is more than sufficient motivation to lead to both enthusiasm and effectiveness in the struggle against sin.

(5) Objections to the transmission of original pollution by propagation:

(a) Genetic transmission of sin is too materialistic a notion.
Answer: Modern heredity theory explains transmission of physical traits and psychological dispositions from generation to generation, but the concept of propagation is broader than this. My example using scientific language was meant metaphorically, not literally.

(b) If Adam's descendants inherit a sinful nature, then either the Messiah inherited from his mother Miryam a sinful nature and is not sinless as claimed; or his human nature was specially created, so that he is not truly one with us, and therefore his atonement is ineffective.
Answer: While not an objection that would be raised by Judaism, this is a serious objection within Christianity. It arises out of the assumption within the Augustinian version that human souls are not individually created by God for each person but are somehow passed on from the "original soul-stuff" God created at the beginning. The objection does not arise in connection with some of the other versions of the original sin doctrine.

(6–7) Objections to the notion of original guilt and its imputation to Adam's posterity:

(a) If God counts me guilty for a sin I did not commit, he is neither fair nor just.
Answer: This is the immediate gut-reaction of most people who object to the doctrine of original sin in any of its forms except Pelagianism. The objection has several components which can be separated from each other; paragraphs (b)–(e) deal with some of them. Here I make these points: (1) Could there have been a fairer test of the common human nature we share with Adam than what is reported of him in the Garden of Eden? He was created sinless, was fully aware of God's single command, and was not subjected to a dependent childhood immersed in evil examples. Could we, with inborn depravity and examples of sin all around us, have done better? (2) An alternative is to attribute the imputing of original guilt to God's sovereignty rather than his justice. But this pits his sovereignty against his justice. (3) There is a spiritual union with the Messiah that assures our salvation, and this is considered just (3:26); so, by analogy, the physical and natural union that causes our guilt is also just. (See more on this in paragraph (b) and at the end of this Section C.)

(b) Organic unity with Adam is at best a theoretical construct, certainly not a proven fact, and hence no ground for imputing guilt.
Answer: This was dealt with in paragraph (7) of the presentation of the doctrine itself; here we add that sin has a self-isolating character which closes us off to the bonds uniting us with others. People feel united with their families, professional colleagues, nation or the unfortunate in proportion to the breadth of their sympathies; and if their sympathies are broad enough they feel united with all mankind — which would include Adam and his apostasy. The self-isolated and self-contained see themselves as responsible only for their own personal acts, but those with broad sympathies identify with the human race. Most Jewish prayers, for instance, are composed in the first-person plural; a notable example in the *Tanakh* is Daniel 9:1–19.

(c) A person should not be considered responsible for a sinful nature he did not personally originate.
Answer: Conscience and experience say we are responsible for what we are, even

if we did not originate it. Being responsible for having a sinful nature is not like being told one is guilty of some external wrong done by someone else one never heard about; the sinful nature is not external to us — it is our own inmost selves.

(d) Given that one cannot repent of someone else's sin, Adam's sin cannot be imputed to us, because we cannot repent of it.
Answer: This should be included with paragraph (3) above, because it misunderstands what Adam's sin was. True, we cannot repent of his eating forbidden fruit; but we can repent of apostasy from God, both as an act he committed and as a state that we are in. In fact, people who have turned to God in faith are continually finding in themselves unsuspected evil pockets of apostasy and rebellion which call forth the deepest repentance.

(e) If we are held responsible for Adam's first sin, then we should be held responsible for all his later sins — and for those of our immediate ancestors as well. But the Bible clearly repudiates such a notion: "Fathers shall not be put to death for children, nor shall children be put to death for fathers; everyone shall be put to death for his own sin" (Deuteronomy 24:16; see also Ezekiel 18:1–4).
Answer: The first sin of Adam, the apostasy, was unlike his later sins or anyone else's sins. This first apostasy of human nature occurred but once, and for this we are responsible, because it is our apostasy. However, the passages from Deuteronomy and Ezekiel apply to all later sins, since these are personal acts.

(8) Objections to death as the penalty for sin:

(a) Death is not a penalty but a natural phenomenon.
Answer: It can be debated whether death was a natural phenomenon for animals in Eden (where neither men nor animals were carnivorous); but Genesis 3:22 implies that Adam had the potential to be immortal, and Genesis 2:17 states that God decreed death as the penalty for human sin. The fact that we find it hard to imagine life on earth if everyone lived forever does not mean that God would be unable to control overpopulation or rule other aspects of such an ecology.

(b) The death penalty is inappropriately large for Adam's sin.
Answer: If based on the idea that Adam's sin was minor, see my answers at (3)(a) and (7)(d); if on the idea that unconscious sins are uncondemnable, see my answer at (4)(b).

(9) Objections to accepting Yeshua's sacrificial death as the only remedy for original sin:

(a) The *Torah* specifies many different kinds of sin offerings, guilt offerings and other sacrifices for various kinds of sins, but none was ever commanded for original sin, original pollution or original guilt. Therefore there is no need to atone for such sin or remedy it.
Answer: The whole sacrificial system itself can only hint at the seriousness with which God regards sin. By his mercy he did not require Adam's immediate physical death, but God did cause a death, the first sacrifice, that of the animal with whose skin he clothed Adam and Chavah, immediately following Adam's transgression (Genesis 3:21). The unceasingness of the sacrifices is also suggestive (MJ 10:1), as are the stories of Avraham's offering Yitzchak (Genesis 22) and God's preferring Abel's animal sacrifice over Cain's offering of grain and/or vegetables (Genesis 4:1–8). To see only sins and be blind to sin is to miss the forest for the trees.

(b) How can believing this or that fact about someone who died two thousand years ago change the inner core of a person's being?
Answer: It is not intellectually accepting facts which saves (Ya 2:14–26&NN), but putting one's complete trust in God and in his having solved man's basic problem already. As Sha'ul puts it, what saves is being "immersed into the Messiah Yeshua" and "into his death" (6:3). Also, as he explains in Chapters 6 and 8, it is not that our sinful inner nature is *changed* but that we *receive a new nature* that loves God and is able to do spiritual good.

(c) Trusting in Yeshua is unnecessary; it is enough to trust in God.
Answer: "*The God who is there*" (to use a book title by Francis Schaeffer), the God who really exists, is the God who in fact sent Yeshua. Trusting in God necessarily implies trusting in Yeshua his Son. To suppose that one can trust in God without trusting in Yeshua and his atoning death is to trust only in the god of one's imagination and not in the God of Avraham, Yitzchak and Ya'akov. "Everyone who denies the Son is also without the Father, but the person who acknowledges the Son has the Father as well" (1 Yn 2:23&N).

(d) We can conquer sin by obeying the *Torah*.
Answer: At this point in history, obeying the *Torah* implies trusting in Yeshua and his sacrificial death for us. See 10:4&N, MJ 8:6&N.

(e) We can conquer sin by doing good deeds.
Answer: Even though our acts can have external benefits to others and to ourselves, God will not regard these acts as good in regard to our own spiritual well-being if they are not based on our trust in God through Yeshua.

(f) If Adam's sin is ours by propagation, then so can Yeshua's righteousness and faith be ours by propagation.
Answer: Propagation does not transmit personal guilt, only the guilt of the species. Since grace, righteousness and faith are personal, these are not transmitted.

Finally, to the entire undertaking of producing such a thing as the doctrine of original sin there is the objection that it goes beyond what Scripture actually and clearly says into realms of vague, unnecessary and misleading speculations that serve no useful purpose but divert energy into searching for the origins and causes of sin that ought to be used in the struggle against it. Closely related is the question of why Christianity has devoted such effort to this matter, while traditional Judaism has not.
Answer: The reason Christianity has developed the thought-structure of original sin may be found in the passage under discussion, Romans 5:12–21, and also in 1C 15:21–22, 45–50; for in these places Sha'ul develops the parallel between the Messiah and Adam, thus elevating Adam's role in human history above what was clear to writers who had only the *Tanakh* to rely on. In answering the question, "How can the Messiah's death save us?" with "The same way Adam's sin killed us," Sha'ul inevitably opened up the question, "How did Adam's sin kill us?" Christian theology's varied answers to this last question necessarily "go beyond Scripture," because Scripture, though it gives true information, gives limited information. And the answers are varied because even though the best minds have wrestled with the problem there is left a remainder of uncertainty, since all of us still "see through a glass, darkly" (1C 13:12, KJV). To be sure, it is possible to misuse theology, just as one can misuse anything else; but the proper use of the doctrine of original sin is to make one ever more aware of how filthy and unholy sin

is and how vital it is to pursue the struggle against it, with the help of the Holy Spirit given to us because we have trusted in Yeshua.

D. The Tanakh, *Judaism and Original Sin.*

But is it true that the notion of original sin "goes beyond Scripture"? See what the *Tanakh* itself says, quite apart from anything added by the New Testament. Numbers 15:28 speaks of sinning unwittingly; Leviticus 5:5–6 of the trespass offering for sins of omission; Leviticus 4:14, 20, 31 of the sin offering for sins of ignorance; and Leviticus 1:3 of the burnt offering for general sinfulness, "that he may be accepted before *Adonai*" — no other reason is given. In Psalm 19:13(12) the writer begs God, "Cleanse me from secret faults," which not only shows that sin may be a state as well as an act (for faults are not acts), but also suggests that sin is pollution, defilement, impurity, uncleanness. This is confirmed in Psalm 51:4(2), "Wash me thoroughly from my iniquity and cleanse me from my sin," and in Leviticus 16:16, 19, where on *Yom-Kippur* the *cohen hagadol* must make atonement for the Holy Place and cleanse the altar because of "the uncleannesses of the children of Israel" — with the word "uncleannesses" being used together with the words "transgressions" and "sins." The idea of the defiling force of sin is brought out in A. Buechler's indispensable *Studies in Sin and Atonement in the Rabbinic Literature of the First Century* (New York: Ktav, 1967). Isaiah 1:5 proves that sin affects a person's entire being: "The whole head is sick and the whole heart faint." Jeremiah 17:9 makes the same point: "The heart is deceitful above all things and is exceedingly wicked; who can fathom it?" In addition this verse suggests that sin has power beyond man's capacity to understand, let alone conquer, without God's help. Psalm 51:7(5), "Behold, I was shaped in iniquity; and in sin did my mother conceive me," together with Job 14:4, "Who can bring a clean thing out of an unclean? No one," strongly suggest transmission of original pollution through the generations, so that each person is born with it. The verses quoted by Sha'ul at 3:10–18, together with 1 Kings 8:46 and Ecclesiastes 7:20 (both quoted in 3:23N), establish at the very least that sin is universal.

With such broad support in the *Tanakh* for the doctrine of original sin, how has Judaism avoided accepting it? By giving greater weight to passages that stress human free will and the efficacy of ethical behavior, such as Genesis 4:6–7 ("And *Adonai* said to Kayin, 'Why are you angry? Why your downcast face? If you do well, won't you be accepted? And if you don't do well, sin is crouching at the door; it lusts after you, but you can rule over it.'") and Deuteronomy 30:15, 19 ("See, I have today set before you life and good, death and evil. Therefore choose life, so that you may live"). But ruling over sin and choosing life begin and end with trusting in God and relying on his strength (1:17, quoting Habakkuk 2:4); such victory is unattainable apart from God, which means apart from God and Yeshua.

Judaism, in its effort to avoid the conclusion that it is essential to trust in Yeshua's atoning sacrificial death, sometimes produces a picture of man as self-reliant to the point of caricature. For example, Trude Weiss-Rosmarin's *Judaism and Christianity: The Differences*, which frequently becomes a polemic against Christianity, says,

"The Jew *rejoices* when he can prove his ethical mettle in the *unaided* battle

> against the temptations of sin.... The Jew is taught to regard himself always and ever as *stronger* than sin and the power that draws him to it. He is bidden to glory in that strength." (Pp. 50–51, all emphases hers)

She says the Jew regards sin as a challenge to be exhilaratingly overcome by ethical effort, whereas the Christian regards sin as an inescapable fate from which the only deliverance is the passive receipt of grace through a savior, and concludes,

> "There is no bridge that could span the gulf separating the Jewish doctrines of free will and freedom of ethical choice from the Christian dogmas of 'original sin' and 'grace.'"(P. 52)

I hope my note demonstrates how wrong she is, that the "unaided battle" will certainly be lost by the individual who chooses to attempt establishing his own righteousness apart from God (see 9:30–10:10) and refuses the helping hands which God holds out to him (10:21, quoting Isaiah 65:2).

For I do not see an unspannable gulf between traditional Jewish and Christian doctrines, but a difference in emphasis, encouraged and exaggerated by the prolonged conflict between the Synagogue and the Church. This becomes clearer if we turn to Jewish writings outside the *Tanakh*, such as the Apocrypha:

> "Do not say, 'It is through the Lord that I fell away,'
> for you are not to do the things he hates.
> Do not say, 'It was he who made me go astray,'
> for he has no need for a sinful person.
> The Lord hates all abomination,
> and those who fear him do not love it either.
> He made mankind at the beginning
> and left him in the hand of his own decision.
> If you will, you can keep the commandments;
> and to act with faithfulness is a matter of intention.
> He has set before you fire and water:
> stretch forth your hand to whichever one you want.
> Before man are life and death,
> and whichever he likes will be given to him....
> He has not commanded anyone to do wickedly,
> and he has not given anyone license to sin."
> (Sirach (Ecclesiasticus) 15:11–17, 20)

A Messianic Jew can agree with all of this, provided it is understood that the "decision," "will" and "intention" which lead to "water" and "life" commence with trusting in Yeshua the Messiah.

These ideas also find expression in the Talmud:

> "Everything is in the hands of God except the fear of God." (B'rakhot 33b)

> "Whoever desires to defile himself will find all the gates open, and whoever wants to purify himself will be able to do so." (Shabbat 104a; compare Rv 22:11)

and in the *Rambam*'s *Mishneh-Torah*:

> "Every human being can become as righteous as Moses or as wicked as Jeroboam." (On Repentance 5:2)

Thus the traditional Jewish view is that man, created in the image of God, is good. "My God, the soul which you have given me is pure" (B'rakhot 60b). He has free will and can choose to sin or be righteous; he is not compelled by a "sin nature" to sin. Instead the rabbis postulated that in each individual is the *yetzer ra'* ("evil inclination"). The biblical basis for such an idea is Genesis 6:5, "And *Adonai* saw that… all the inclination (*yetzer*) of the thoughts of his heart was only evil (*ra'*) all day long," and Genesis 8:21, "…for the inclination (*yetzer*) of man's heart is evil (*ra'*) from his youth." But they did not consider the *yetzer ra'* to be an unmitigated woe. The Midrash Rabbah presents it as providing motivation for necessary life activities:

> "Nachman said in the name of Rabbi Shmu'el: 'And behold it was very good' (Genesis 1:31) refers to the *yetzer ra'*. But can the *yetzer ra'* be 'very good'? Amazingly enough, yes — were it not for the *yetzer ra'* no man would build a house, take a wife and father children, or engage in business; as Solomon said, 'I considered all labor and excellence in work and concluded that it comes from a man's rivalry with his neighbor' (Ecclesiastes 4:4)." (Genesis Rabbah 9:7)

Far from considering it essentially Satanic and able to produce only evil results, they concluded it could even be turned to God's service. Sifre to Deuteronomy 6:5 ("You shall love *Adonai* your God with all your heart….") says that loving with "all" one's heart includes with the *yetzer ra'* (see more on this in Chapter 7). But the *yetzer ra'* so understood is not as irredeemably evil as the Bible makes clear sin is.

Turning to the role Judaism gives to Adam, one can find in rabbinic materials passages that recognize his seminal role in bringing sin and death to humanity.

> "Rabbi Yose said, 'If you want to know about the reward of the righteous in the world to come, consider Adam. He was given one single negative command. He violated it, and see how many deaths have been decreed for him and for all his generations forever. Now which is greater, the attribute of reward [literally, of goodness] or that of punishment? Surely the attribute of reward is greater. So if the attribute of punishment, which is less, caused so many deaths, then think how much more the person who repents from sin and fasts on *Yom-Kippur* will cause *z'khut* [being declared innocent] to himself and to all his generations forever.'"(Sifra 27a)

If "Yeshua the Messiah" is substituted for "the person who repents from sin and fasts on *Yom-Kippur*" we have virtually a reproduction of Sha'ul's argument in 5:14–19. Also see the Talmud, Shabbat 55a–55b.

If we move beyond rabbinic Judaism to the apocalyptic Judaism of the Pseudepigrapha, which was not expunged from the accepted tradition of Judaism until many decades after Sha'ul, we find ideas even closer to the doctrine of original sin. Consider 2 Baruch 54:14–15, 19, which says, in the context of Baruch's praying for the meaning of a vision,

> "It is just that those who do not love your *Torah* perish;
> the torment of judgment awaits those who have not submitted themselves
> to your power.
> For although Adam first sinned and brought untimely death upon all,
> yet of those born from him each has prepared future torment for his
> own soul;
> also each of them has chosen for himself future glories....
> Adam is therefore not the cause, except for his own soul,
> but each of us has been the Adam of his own soul."

Responsibility for sins is on each individual, yet Adam is the original cause of death. These ideas are spelled out further in 4 Ezra, from which I quote only a small selection of relevant passages:

> "[You gave the] *Torah* to Jacob's seed and the Commandment to the generation of Israel. And yet you did not take away from them the evil heart, that your *Torah* might bring forth fruit in them. For the first Adam, clothing himself with the evil heart, transgressed and was overcome; and likewise also all who were born of him. Thus the infirmity became inveterate; the *Torah* indeed was in the heart of the people, but in conjunction with the evil seed; so what was good departed, and the evil remained." (4 Ezra 3:19–22)

This says much the same thing as Sha'ul does below (7:7–25) but contrasts with rabbinic theology, which emphasizes the power of the *Torah* to keep the *yetzer ra'* in check and overcome it — "The *Torah* wears away the *yetzer ra'* as water wears away stone" (Talmud, Sukkah 52b), which is true if it be understood that the *Torah* today requires faith in Yeshua the Messiah.

> "A grain of evil seed was sown in the heart of Adam from the beginning; how much ungodly fruit it has produced until now and will yet produce until the threshing-floor comes! Calculate it in your own mind: if a grain of evil seed has produced this much ungodly fruit, then when once the innumerable ears of good seed have been sown, how large a floor will they fill?" (4 Ezra 4:30–32)

This resembles the Sifra passage quoted above. Compare also Mt 13:39.

> "Who of those who have come into the world has not sinned? Or who among the earth-born has not transgressed your covenant? Now I see that the coming age will bring delight to the few but torment to many. For the evil heart has grown up in us which has estranged us from God, brought us to destruction,

> made known to us the ways of death, showed us the paths of perdition and removed us far from life! And this is true of not merely a few, but of virtually all who have been created!" (4 Ezra 7:46–48)

This again expresses the universality of sin; see also Mt 7:13–14, 20:16, 22:14.

> "And I replied, 'This is my first and last word: It would have been better if the earth had not produced Adam, or, alternatively, having once produced him, for you to have kept him from sinning. For how does it profit any of us that in the present age we must live in grief and after death look for punishment? Adam, what have you done! For although it was you who sinned, the fall was not yours alone but ours also who are your descendants! How does it profit us that we have been promised the eternal age, when we have done the works that bring death?'"(4 Ezra 7:116–119)

The word "fall" here translates Latin *casus*, which may also be rendered "fate, destruction." In any case, of all Jewish writings, 4 Ezra comes closest to expressing the idea that the whole human race shares in Adam's sin.

Finally, the Midrash on Psalm 51:

> "Healing comes from you [God]. Because the wound is large, put a large poultice on it for me, as it is said, 'Wash me thoroughly from my iniquity' (Psalm 51:4(2)). From this you learn that everyone who commits a transgression is as unclean as though he had touched a dead body and must be purified with hyssop. So too, David said, 'Purge me with hyssop, and I shall be clean' (Psalm 51:9(7)). Did David actually fall into uncleanness and thus require purging with hyssop? No, but into an iniquity whereby his soul was wounded unto death. Thus also in another Psalm, he said, 'My heart is wounded unto death within me' (Psalm 109:22)."

Contamination by a dead body is the severest form of ritual impurity; here sin is spoken of as equally defiling. Compare the passages from the *Tanakh* on defilement quoted above.

E. Messianic Jewish Theology of Sin.

I do not propose to construct a Messianic Jewish theology of sin in this note. My purposes in this survey have been to show that there is not a single monolithic, fixed and settled Christian theology of sin; that Jewish objections to the doctrine of original sin have often been more against a slogan than against the content of the doctrine properly understood; and that there are many Jewish sources that dovetail well with New Testament approaches to the subject, even if mainstream Judaism ignores them today. If Judaism stresses man's effort while Christianity focuses on God's grace, are these not two aspects of one truth? Man's effort apart from God's grace is ineffective, but the New Testament urges those who are saved by grace to continue struggling against sin by the power of the Holy Spirit and to do the good works God has prepared for him to do. There is room for a Messianic Jewish expression of the theology of sin that does justice to traditional Jewish emphases without departing from the truths of Scripture as set forth in both the *Tanakh* and the New Testament.

CHAPTER 6

1–2 These verses, reiterating what was said at 3:5–8, introduce the theme of Chapters 6–8 and are Sha'ul's answer to all who accuse the New Testament of offering "cheap grace." He is more radical than those who merely exhort us to subdue our sinful impulses; for he asserts that by virtue of being united with the Messiah (vv. 3–6) our old self and its sinful inclinations have actually **died**. Dead people do not sin; rather, the dead are "cleared from sin" (v. 7). Chapters 6–8 explore how believers are to make these truths real in their own lives. On **Heaven forbid!** here and at v. 15 see 3:4N.

3–6 **Immersed** translates a form of the Greek word "*baptizô*," usually transliterated "baptized." The root meaning of "*baptizô*" is "dip, soak, immerse" into a liquid so that what is dipped takes on qualities of what it has been dipped in — such as cloth in dye or leather in tanning solution (see Mt 3:1N). This is why being **immersed into the Messiah** (v. 3) is equated with being **united with him** (v. 5). These verses support the case that immersion is the preferred form of baptism, since baptism is compared here with burial, and burial resembles immersion but does not resemble pouring or sprinkling. On "**execution-stake**" see Mt 10:38N.

7 Literally, "For the one having died has been justified [or "declared innocent"] from the sin." The deathbed confession in the *Siddur* includes the words, "May my death be an atonement for all the sins, iniquities and transgressions of which I have been guilty against you" (Hertz edition, pp. 1064–1065), following the pattern of a prayer in the Talmud (B'rakhot 60a) and the Mishna (Sanhedrin 6:2). Yoma 86a also speaks of death as "finishing" the punishment for sin and quotes Isaiah 22:14, "Surely this iniquity shall not be atoned for [Hebrew *y'khupar*, "covered"] until you die." Sha'ul here is drawing on the Jewish tradition that says an individual's own death atones for his sin. He applies it by affirming that our union with the Messiah and with his death (vv. 3–6) means that we have effectively died: in union with the Messiah's death we died, and that atones for our sin.

8 As life is stronger than death, there is an implicit *kal v'chomer* argument (Mt 6:30N): **since we died with the Messiah**, how much more do **we trust that we will also live with him!**

9 **Never to die again**. Yeshua raised people from the dead, as did Elijah and Elisha; but they all died again. Yeshua's resurrection is the firstfruits of a new creation (1C 15:20, 23), in which believers have a share (2C 5:17, Ga 6:15, Ya 1:18), a new creation from which death has been eliminated (1C 15:50–57, Rv 20:14, 21:4). Mekhilta to Exodus 20:19 says:

> "If it were possible to do away with the angel of death, I would. But the decree has long ago been decreed. Rabbi Yosi says, 'It was on this condition that Israel stood before Mount Sinai, on condition that the angel of death would not rule over them. For it is said, "I said: You are gods (*Elohim*), etc." But you corrupted your conduct. "Surely you will die like men" (Psalm 82:6–7).'"

Yeshua has gone beyond this; he has conquered death, so that **death has no authority over him** or over those united with him.

14 You are not under legalism (Greek *upo nomon*; Sha'ul's use of this phrase discussed in depth at Ga 3:23bN). The word "*nomos*," literally "law" and often translated "*Torah*" in the *Jewish New Testament* (Mt 5:17&N), must here be rendered "**legalism**," which is defined in 3:20bN as perversion of the *Torah* into a system of rules for earning God's praise without trusting, loving or communing with God the Giver of the *Torah.*

Under legalism... under grace. The word twice translated "under," Greek *upo*, means "controlled by" (as at 3:9) or "in subjection to" (compare 7:14; also see 1C 9:20–22&NN) and opens the path to the slavery metaphor in the following verses. But in what sense are believers "in subjection to" grace? In the sense that they have accepted Yeshua's "yoke," which is "easy" and "light" to be "under" (Mt 11:28–30&N), in contrast with the "yoke" of legalism, which is not (Ac 15:10&N). Being "under grace" is a subjection which, because of the nature of grace itself, does not have the usual oppressive characteristics of subjection.

God's people are to live *en* ("within the framework of," 2:12N) *Torah*, but they are not be *upo* ("in subjection to," Ga 3:23bN) legalism. God's giving the *Torah* was itself an act of grace which the New Testament compares with his sending Yeshua (Yn 1:17&N). God's people, the people who are in a trust relationship with him, are and always have been under grace and under *Torah* (a gracious subjection) but never under legalism (a harsh subjection).

15 The perverse suggestion of 3:5–8 and 6:1–2 is restated a third way.

16–23 Sha'ul expounds Yeshua's saying, "No one can be slave to two masters" (Mt 6:24). The **slaves to sin** (v. 17; compare Yn 8:34) get no **benefit** (v. 21) but **earn** their wages, **death** (v. 23). But when **enslaved to righteousness** (v. 18), **eternal life is what one receives as a free gift from God** (v. 23). Such slavery is true freedom.

Verse 23 is Sha'ul's classic expression of the idea that the only place you can work your way to is hell; no one can work his way to heaven. To reach heaven one must acknowledge the futility of striving in one's own strength and accept God's **free gift** of **eternal life** as being offered **in union with the Messiah Yeshua our Lord** by his grace when one responds with faith or trust.

CHAPTER 7

1–14 Sha'ul has explored the meaning of dying with the Messiah (6:1–14) and the concept of human enslavement to sin (6:15–23, building on the groundwork laid in 5:12–21).

Now, in relating these ideas to the *Torah*, he introduces a new analogy, marriage. Throughout this chapter it must be kept in mind that Sha'ul was not anti-*Torah*, as some suppose, but had a high view of the *Torah*; see v. 12&N.

In v. 1 Sha'ul specifies that he is writing these verses **to those who understand *Torah*,** primarily Jews, even though the letter as a whole is addressed in the main to Gentiles (see 1:5b–6N).

1–3 There is no reason to limit Greek *nomos* in these verses to the *Torah*, for the principle that death discharges an individual from his obligations under law applies to all kinds of law (see 4:15&N). One can find this same teaching applied specifically to the *Torah* in a rabbinic source:

> "Rabbi Yochanan said, 'What is meant by the phrase, "With the dead, free" (Psalm 88:6)? That when a man dies he becomes free from the *Torah* and from the commandments.'"(Shabbat 30a; similar passages are found at Shabbat 151b, Niddah 61b, and in one of the oldest collections of *midrashim*, the *Pesikta diRav Kahana*, Supplement 1:20)

4 You have been made dead with regard to the *Torah*. It is not the *Torah* that has been made dead (abrogated), nor is a believer made dead in the sense of no longer responding to its truth. Rather, he has been made dead not to all of *Torah,* but to three aspects of it: (1) its capacity to stir up sin in him (vv. 5–14), (2) its capacity to produce irremediable guilt feelings (vv. 15–25), and (3) its penalties, punishments and curses (8:1–4). A few remarks on each in turn (and also see v. 6N):

(1) How the *Torah* has the capacity to stir up sin in an individual, alluded to earlier (2:18; 3:20; 5:13, 20), is analyzed carefully in vv. 5–14 and on through 8:13. This capacity of the *Torah* to make us sin is not a fault in the *Torah* but a fault in ourselves. A healthy person thrives in an environment deadly to someone who is ill; likewise the *Torah*, beneficial to a believer living by faith, is an instrument of death to those controlled by their sinful nature. The fault in ourselves is that we have a sinful propensity (5:12–21&N) to misuse the *Torah*, making it into a framework of legalism instead of what it is, a framework of grace (6:14–15&N, 8:2&N).

(2) The *Torah* can still produce guilt feelings in a believer — as it rightly should whenever he contemplates how his behavior falls short of the standard God sets in the *Torah*. But these feelings are not irremediable. The remedy is once-and-for-all trust in Yeshua the Messiah's final atonement for sin (3:21–26), followed by ongoing confession of and repentance from sins (1 Yn 1:9–2:2) coupled with restitution to injured parties and reliance on the power of the Holy Spirit (7:25–8:39).

(3) It is **through the Messiah's body**, through his atoning death (3:21–26), that believers **have been made dead** to the penalties set forth by the *Torah* for disobeying it. "The Messiah redeemed us from the curse pronounced in the *Torah* by becoming cursed on our behalf" (Ga 3:13&N). This is clarified in v. 6&N.

Sha'ul's metaphor switches directions at several points in this verse. It is **through the Messiah's body**, through our union with him that includes union with his death, that believers **have been made dead** (see 6:2–11) to the aspects of *Torah* on which Sha'ul is concentrating. Because a death has taken place they are now free to **belong to**

someone else. That is, using Sha'ul's analogy of vv. 2–3, they are no longer "married" to legalism but free to marry and be united with **the one who has been raised from the dead**, Yeshua the Messiah (the wedding is coming, Rv 19:6–9). Now they can **bear fruit for God** (Mt 13:8, Yn 15:1–8); this means either doing good deeds (Ep 2:8–10), which better fits the contrasting phrase in v. 5, "fruit for death," or proclaiming the Gospel, so that the unsaved are born again, which better fits the marriage context of vv. 2–3.

5 **Living according to our old nature**, literally, "in the flesh." Greek *sarx* is rendered "old nature" here, at 7:14, 18, 25 and eleven times in 8:3–13. The problem with translating "*sarx*" as "flesh" is that it reinforces the mistaken popular notion that the New Testament sets up a dualism between the soul or spirit, regarded as higher and better, and the body, regarded as lower and worse. Is this not what today's reader gathers from KJV's rendering of v. 18a, "For I know that in me (that is, in my flesh) dwelleth no good thing"? Celibacy and other ascetic practices found in some Christian denominations are taken as proof that the New Testament teaches this, even though in reality this teaching comes straight from paganism (see Co 2:16–23&NN).

Sha'ul had a highly developed psychology. By "flesh" he did not mean the physical body alone, but all the thoughts, emotions and physical urges that comprise human nature — and especially human nature as found in people before they are saved. Elsewhere Sha'ul says, "If anyone is united with the Messiah, there is a new creation" (2C 5:17) — that is, he has a second, new human nature controlled by the Holy Spirit. The old nature has died with Yeshua (6:5); and by the power of the Spirit it will stay dead — we owe nothing to it, that we should obey its corrupted and misguided passions (8:1–13). Instead, as a result of being united with Yeshua, we owe God obedience to his desires and commands. This is how to understand "*sarx*" in these passages. The idea that the spirit is good and the body bad may be Greek or Gnostic, but it is neither Jewish nor Christian.

6 Because Yeshua paid the penalty for our disobedience to the *Torah*, death, **we have been released** (*katargeô,* as in v. 2) **from this aspect of the *Torah***, the aspect of it which causes unbelievers to produce "fruit for death" (v. 5). The phrase, "this aspect of," is not in the Greek text; I have added it because believers have *not* been released from *every* aspect of the *Torah*, as explained below and in v. 4N. In v. 3 the phrase, "that part of," is likewise not in the Greek text, yet it is obviously what the text means, since the death of a woman's husband does not free her from obedience to other aspects of the *Torah*. The present verse is analogous in this regard. (On the legitimacy of the translator's adding a phrase, see *JNT* Introduction, Section V, on "The Translator and His Interpretations.")

We have been released from this aspect of the *Torah* because (using the argument of vv. 1–3) **we have died to**, and therefore been released from, (1) our own propensity to turn it into a framework of legalism, (2) irremediable guilt feelings which follow disobeying it, and (3) the *Torah's* penalties and curses for disobeying it — the three ways (v. 4&N) in which the *Torah* once **had us in its clutches**. In the following verses Sha'ul focuses on the first of these, our propensity to make the *Torah* into a legalistic system because of the deadly interaction between our passions and sinfulness with the *Torah* itself.

As a result of our release from the aspect of *Torah* that produces fruit for death, **we are serving in the new way provided by the Spirit**, who has written the *Torah* in our hearts (MJ 8:8–12, quoting Jeremiah 31:30–33(31–34), and MJ 10:15–22, alluding to Ezekiel 36:26–27) **and not in the old way of outwardly following the letter of the law** (literally, "in newness of Spirit and not in oldness of letter"); compare 2:29 and 2C 3:6. Clearly, if the *Torah* has been written in the hearts of believers they are not released from *every* aspect of it.

7–25 Some commentators believe that the "Romans 7 experience" described in these verses applies only to people who are as yet unsaved, and that as soon as a person has trusted in Yeshua he moves on permanently to the "Romans 8 experience" of conquering sin by the power of the Holy Spirit, advancing "from glory to glory" (2C 3:18). I don't think this reflects reality. Saved people too fail to practice what they preach.

Here is what I consider a better model: when a person comes to trust in Yeshua he surrenders to him all of himself that he can. But as he grows in his faith he finds previously hidden portions of himself, areas of sin he was formerly unaware of, which he must then surrender as well. Preceding each such surrender is a "Romans 7 experience," and the surrender takes place only when he is willing to move into Romans 8 with respect to that part of his life.

7 **Therefore, what are we to say? That the *Torah* is sinful** (literally, "is sin")? At 2:18, 3:20, 5:13, 20 and the last few verses Sha'ul has indicated that the *Torah* makes people sin. His concern is that readers might jump to the unwarranted conclusion that the *Torah* itself "is sin," that is, sinful. So he answers his own question in the strongest possible negative language, **Heaven forbid!** (on which see 3:4N) and proceeds in vv. 7–14 to analyze how a "holy, just and good" *Torah* can stir up sin. The answer is that it is not the *Torah*'s fault but our own.

"Thou shalt not covet." The tenth commandment (Exodus 20:14(17), Deuteronomy 5:18; see Mt 5:22N) can be transgressed without an external act: entertaining envy in one's heart is already sin. Thus this example is well suited to proving that the *Torah* cannot be construed as a set of behavior rules to be followed mechanically (legalistically). (The archaic rendering, **"Thou shalt not...,"** constitutes a "stylistic crutch" which I chose because it strikes the modern reader as more distant, less inward, and hence more suited to generating legalism.)

8 **Sin, seizing the opportunity.** Here Sha'ul's meaning for "sin" comes very close to the rabbinic notion of the *yetzer ra'*, the "evil inclination." Unlike the rabbis, however, he pictures sin here and on through v. 25 not as conquerable by man, but as "sinful beyond measure" (v. 13) and therefore beyond control through man's unaided will. For more on the *yetzer ra'* see paragraph C(4)(d) and Section D of 5:12–21N.

Apart from *Torah*, sin is dead. This is both an outward application of and an inward parallel to the principle of 4:15b, "where there is no law, there is also no violation." The outward application is that the *Torah*, as a species of law, "creates" violations (see Ga 3:21&N), even though it is holy. The inward parallel is that the *Torah*, as God's teaching and as his provocation to conscience (compare 2:14–15), "creates" sin, as clarified in the following verses.

9 See v. 4N. Claude G. Montefiore writes,

"The Rabbis insist that the only effective remedy for the Evil Inclination is the study of fulfilment of the Law. Yet they sometimes seem to realize (in this, at least, like Paul!) that the *yetzer ha-ra* is stirred up by the prohibitions of the Law. Such perhaps would seem to be the suggestion of the following story:

"'The evil inclination desires only that which is forbidden. Rabbi Mena (on the Day of Atonement, when drinking is forbidden) went to visit Rabbi Haggai, who was ill. Rabbi Haggai said, "I am thirsty." Rabbi Mena said, "Drink." Then he left him. After an hour he came again and said, "How about your thirst?" He said, "No sooner had you permitted me to drink than the desire left me."' (Jerusalem Talmud Yoma VI, Sec. 4, 43d, line 21)." (*Rabbinic Anthology*, p. 302)

10 **The commandment that was intended to bring me life was found to be bringing me death.** Sha'ul is not unique among Jewish writers in pointing out that the life-giving *Torah* produces death when rejected or misused (compare 1 Ti 1:8–9):

"Rabbi Tanchuma said, 'The Voice of the Lord went forth from Sinai in two ways — it killed the heathen, who would not accept it; but it gave life to Israel, who accepted the *Torah.*'"(Exodus Rabbah 5:9)

"Rabbi Y'hoshua ben-L'vi said, 'What is the meaning of the verse, "And this is the *Torah* which Moses set before the children of Israel" (Deuteronomy 4:44)? It means that if a person is meritorious, it becomes for him a medicine that gives life; but if not, it becomes a deadly poison.' That is what Raba meant when he said, 'If he uses it the right way it is a medicine of life for him, but for someone who does not use it the right way it is a deadly poison.'"(Yoma 72b)

See also 2C 2:16, MJ 4:12, Rv 1:16.

12 **So the *Torah* is holy; that is, the commandment is holy, just and good.** Those who think Sha'ul sought an escape from the Jewish Law in order to make Christianity easy for pagan converts must find this verse difficult. It proves that Sha'ul neither had an un-Jewish view of the Law nor desired to abrogate it. The verse witnesses to Sha'ul's lifelong high regard for the *Torah*, which corresponds to his lifelong observance of it (see Ac 13:9N, 21:21N). This attitude would have been with him from his youth, since his parents were Pharisees (Ac 23:6); it would have been strengthened by his studies with *Rabban* Gamli'el (Ac 22:3); and there is no reason to suppose that his coming to faith in Yeshua — who did not "come to abolish the *Torah*" (Mt 5:17) — would have changed it. So many errors about Sha'ul's opinion of the Law could have been avoided had this verse been understood as constraining everything he writes about it. God's holy *Torah* for holy living does not change. Why? Because God himself does not change (Malachi 3:6) and holiness does not change. Moreover, this verse is not alone: vv. 10, 14, 16, 22 and 8:2, 4, 7–8 all show that Sha'ul had a high regard for the *Torah*.

14 **For we know**, without needing evidence, **that the *Torah* is of the** Holy **Spirit**. This remark shows that Sha'ul as a Messianic Jew retained a high view of the *Torah*, because

in support of his main argument he presents the statement undefended, expecting his readers not to demand proof. It is a given, an axiom to which all can agree without requiring further demonstration.

I am bound to the old nature, literally, "I am fleshly" or "carnal." See v. 5N.

15–25 Sha'ul explores the frustration of everyone who has ever failed to live up to principles which he knows are right. Anyone with a "bad habit" such as smoking or overeating knows the truth of these verses only too well. As Yeshua put it, "The spirit is willing, but the flesh" — that is, the "old nature" (v. 5N) or "human nature" — "is weak" (Mt 26:41, KJV).

"Sin" is presented throughout this chapter, but especially in this passage, as some alien entity that acts in us apart from and in opposition to our own will, bringing us ultimately to defeat and despair (v. 24). (Actually, this is not quite the case: only when we do not use God's way of conquering sin — by the Holy Spirit through Yeshua the Messiah (7:25–8:39) — does sin conquer us.) A similar personification of sin can also be found in Jewish sources, for example:

> "Rabbi Yitzchak said, 'At first sin is like an occasional visitor, then like a guest who stays awhile, and finally like the master of the house.'"(Genesis Rabbah 22:6; the same teaching is attributed to Raba in the Talmud, Sukkah 52b; compare Ya 1:14–15)

As brought out in 5:12–21N, Judaism stresses that the individual is responsible and able to defeat this alien entity, sin (or the *yetzer ra'*), and that the means for doing so is obedience to the *Torah*. To this Sha'ul agrees, but he adds that it is impossible unless we stop trying to conquer sin by our own strength and accept God's rescue through Yeshua (vv. 24–25); in relation to overcoming sin, this is what obedience to the *Torah* means.

17–19 But now it is no longer "the real me" doing it, literally, "But now I no longer work it" (similarly at v. 20), **but the sin housed inside me.** One of Flip Wilson's best-known lines used to be, "The Devil made me do it." He could get away with blaming the Devil for his misdeeds because he's a television comedian. But if I am serious about my transgression I cannot blame the Devil or the sin housed inside me or **my old nature** (literally, "my flesh"; see v. 5N); I must take the responsibility myself: I did it. Sha'ul's purpose in drawing the distinction between "the real me" and "the sin housed inside me" is not to excuse me but to point up the fact that salvation brings one a new nature attuned to the Holy Spirit. He continues developing the implications through 8:13.

21–23 The rule, a kind of perverse "*torah*." The whole phrase translates Greek *nomos*, which can have at least these three meanings: (1) "law" in the sense of "legislation, statute"; (2) "law" in the sense of "rule, norm"; and (3) "Mosaic Law, *Torah*"; see 3:20bN. In these verses Sha'ul is engaging in wordplay drawing on all three meanings. Sin is personified as having, so to speak, organized its own Mount Sinai and there given its own "*torah*" which, willy-nilly, we find ourselves devotedly obeying with our old nature ("flesh," v. 5N). Similarly at v. 25 and 8:2.

24 The anguished cry of the defeated person torn apart by this inner conflict leads to a desperate question seemingly addressed to blank walls and an empty sky: **Who will rescue me**, "the real me" (v. 17&N) or "my mind" (8:1), irretrievably bound together with "my old nature" (v. 18) and therefore hopelessly impotent in opposing the old nature's obedience to sin's "*torah*," **from this body bound for death**, literally, "from the body of this death"?

25 As rendered here, this verse answers the question of v. 24: **Thanks be to God, he** (God) **will** rescue me from my sin-controlled, death-bound body. How will he? **Through Yeshua the Messiah, our Lord.** The words, "He will," are not in the Greek but added to convey the sense.

A more literal rendering of the Greek which means almost the same thing would be: "The grace of God, through Yeshua the Messiah our Lord." This too answers the question.

But the more usual literal rendering, which depends on a different understanding of the Greek grammar, "Thanks be to God, through Yeshua the Messiah, our Lord," focuses on our thanks to God being directed through Yeshua. This is true (see 1:8) but irrelevant at this point, since it leaves unanswered the pregnant question of v. 24.

CHAPTER 8

1 This chapter crowns the first half of the book of Romans, resolving the issue raised in Chapter 7 and solving humanity's overriding problem, sin. The answer is the *Ruach HaKodesh*, who is in us if we are living **in union with the Messiah Yeshua**. In vv. 5–13 Sha'ul expands on what it means to live in union with him.

Therefore. Bible interpreters' office humor: when you see a "therefore," you'd better find out what it's there for. This "therefore" is a weighty one; it sums up the first seven chapters and means: "Because of who Yeshua is and everything he has done in history on behalf of sinners."

No longer any condemnation from the *Torah* (7:4&N).

I believe that the structure of Sha'ul's argument relating Chapters 7 and 8 is reflected best if 7:25 and this verse are joined, with the words "although" and "nevertheless" added, thusly:

> "To sum up: *although* with my mind I am a slave of God's *Torah*, but with my old nature a slave to sin's "*torah*," *nevertheless*, therefore [i.e., because of Yeshua, as explained above], there is no longer any condemnation awaiting those who are in union with the Messiah Yeshua."

The Greek, however, does not justify putting this rendering in the text itself; for this reason I have consigned it to the notes.

2 ***Torah* of the Spirit… *"Torah"* of sin and death.** What are these two? Here is the wrong answer: Yeshua gave a good *Torah* of the Spirit which produces life, in contrast with the bad Mosaic Law that produces only sin and death. But this interpretation not only contradicts Sha'ul's arguments in Chapters 3 and 7, but is implicitly antisemitic as well (see 3:20bN).

The right answer is that the *Torah* of the Spirit is the Mosaic Law properly apprehended by the power of the Holy Spirit in believers, what Sha'ul elsewhere calls "the *Torah*'s true meaning, which the Messiah upholds" (usually rendered, "the law of Christ," Ga 6:2&N). The second "*torah*" is written in lower-case and put in quotation marks, because it is "sin's '*torah*'"(7:21–23&N), in other words, not a God-given *Torah* at all but an anti-*Torah*. More specifically, it is the Mosaic Law improperly understood and perverted by our old, sinful nature into a legalistic system of earning God's approval by our own works (3:20b&N).

This interpretation of v. 2 can be paraphrased and expanded (on the basis of 7:4N) as follows:

> "The *Torah*, as understood and applied through the Spirit, thereby giving life in union with Messiah Yeshua, has set me free from the aspects of the *Torah* that stimulate me to sin (7:5–14), fill me with irremediable guilt (7:15–24) and condemn me to death."

3–4 For what the *Torah*, taken here, apparently, to mean merely a collection of words, **could not do by itself, because it lacked the power to make the old nature**, the "flesh" (see 7:5N), **cooperate, God did**. All power resides in God, and he did what his own teachings, instructions and commands could not of themselves do **by sending his own Son as a human being with a nature** just **like our own sinful one**, literally, "God sending his own Son in likeness of flesh of sin." Although Yeshua was a human being and had a truly human nature (Greek *sarx*, "flesh"; see 7:5N), his "flesh" or "nature" was not like that of other humans because it was not sinful, and he did not sin. He encountered temptations just like those we face, but he conquered them without sinning by the power of the Holy Spirit (MJ 2:17–18, 4:15; Mt 4:1–11; Yn 3:34).

God did this (sent his Son) **in order to deal with sin**, because sin is such a serious disturbance in creation that nothing less could overcome it. In the *Tanakh* the central purpose of the whole book of Job is to show that only God can solve the problem of sin in the universe. God gives Satan (the Adversary; see Mt 4:1N) permission to test Job (Chapters 1–2); Job loses his possessions, children and health and spends most of the book protesting his fate, justifying himself and fending off the counterproductive advice of his friends. Even God's appearing to him personally as the Creator (Chapters 38–39) merely silences him. Only when he perceives that God alone can handle Behemoth and Leviathan, who are stand-ins for Satan (Chapters 40–41), does he "repent in dust and ashes," and his well-being is restored.

The phrase could also be translated, "[God sent his Son] as a sin offering." While true, and while such a rendering evokes *Tanakh* imagery, it fits the context less well.

And in so doing he, God, **executed the punishment against sin in human nature**, literally, "he condemned sin in the flesh," **so that the just requirement of the *Torah*** that sin against a perfectly holy God must be punished by death **might be fulfilled in us** and not merely in Yeshua, because we are united with him and have died with him (6:3–6). Also, being united with him means that we **do not run our lives according to what our old nature wants but according to what the** Holy **Spirit**

wants, literally, we "walk not according to flesh but according to Spirit."

This completes the explanation of why believers are no longer under the *Torah*'s condemnation (v. 1). But a new question is raised: why is it important to do not what the old nature wants but what the Spirit wants? The answer follows in vv. 5–13.

5–8 In 6:11 Sha'ul proposed a radical solution to humanity's problems: "Consider yourselves to be dead to sin but alive for God, by your union with the Messiah Yeshua." The present verses explain the radical psychology underlying his radical solution. The primary psychological fact of life — deeper than any analysis of id, ego and superego; or of genetic, physiological, behavioral, environmental or educational conditioning; or of birth traumas, complexes, sexual experiences, interpersonal communication, family background or games people play — is that the sinful "old nature" (the "flesh," 7:5&N) is utterly irredeemable. This is why no self-help measures, psychotherapeutic methods, educational programs, environmental changes or resolutions to improve can enable us to **please God**; all of them are based on **having the mind controlled by the old nature**, which **is death**, rather than **by the Spirit**, which **is life and *shalom*** — not only "peace" but "tranquillity, safety, well-being, welfare, health, contentment, success, comfort, wholeness and integrity," in short, everything secular and popular psychology promise but cannot deliver. This is why Yeshua said, "You must be born again from above" (Yn 3:7), and Sha'ul wrote, "If anyone is united with the Messiah, he is a new creation — the old has passed; look, what has come is fresh and new!" (2C 5:17). If there were no new nature, Sha'ul's psychology would offer the most pessimistic picture of the human condition — as he himself admits (1C 15:16–19). But since there is a new nature, only Sha'ul's solution of letting one's mind be controlled by it, through the Holy Spirit, offers any real hope to mankind; all other psychologies offer palliatives and ultimate failure. Verses 7–8 explain why this so. These two verses also undergird the claim that Sha'ul had a high regard for the *Torah* (see 7:12N).

9 **The Spirit of God** and **the Spirit of the Messiah** are equated with each other in at least one Jewish source (see citation in MJ 3:2–4N).

11 God's powerful Holy Spirit, living in believers, guarantees that God will fulfill his promises and gives believers rock-solid hope even when passing through times of distress and apparent despair. See vv. 14–27&N, Ep 1:14.

13 **If by the Spirit you keep putting to death the practices of the body, you will live.** KJV says, "...mortify the deeds of the body...." This is not a mandate for "mortification of the flesh," in the sense of asceticism or masochism, which Sha'ul elsewhere says have no spiritual value (7:5N, Co 2:16–23&N). Rather, he is only restating what he has been urging since v. 5. The phrase, "practices of the body," refers to the body's bad habits which the sinful old nature has produced; previously Sha'ul wrote similarly of the body's "various parts" which a believer should not "offer... to sin as an instrument for wickedness" (6:12–13, 19; 7:5, 23). Unless you, the believer, continually and actively, by the power of the Holy Spirit, "put to death" your body's bad habits to which it has become accustomed and conditioned by your old nature, these bad habits will certainly find expression, so that

you will certainly die, spiritually and eternally as well as physically. By actively and continually setting the mind on the Spirit (v. 6), **you will live**, as explained in vv. 10–11.

14–27 How do we know that the Spirit will empower us to obey the *Torah*, as promised in vv. 1–13? From his yet more fundamental ministry as guarantor of our Good News-inspired hope that we who trust Yeshua will one day share in the very glory of God. The theme of this passage, then, is that God's Spirit in believers gives all the assurance and confidence we need for victory, no matter what sufferings, discouragements and doubts we meet along the way.

14a The first point of assurance is that the Spirit is **God's Spirit**, he who moved over the face of the waters on the first day of creation (Genesis 1:2), he who inspired the prophets (e.g., Isaiah 61:1). It is **by** him, coequal with God the Father and Yeshua the Son (Mt 28:19&N, 2C 3:17–18N), that we **are led**.

14b–17 Second, our assurance is built on our being adopted as **God's sons**. We do not come in a **spirit of slavery**, implying alienation, but one of deep intimacy, like children who lovingly call their father "Daddy" — which is what ***Abba*** really means (see Mk 14:36N). Moreover, the filial relationship to the Father is not only personal but legal, so that we are **heirs of God and joint-heirs with the Messiah**, our brother (v. 29; see also Ep 3:6).

This adoption as God's sons is only for those **who are led by God's Spirit**, that is, only for those who have put their trust in Yeshua, because it is he who sends the Spirit (Yn 14:26), and those who do not have Yeshua do not have the Father either (1 Yn 2:23). But in the case of believers, **the Spirit** of God **himself bears witness with our own spirits that we are children of God.** The adoption process will become complete when "our whole bodies are redeemed and set free" (v. 23). Other verses on adoption: Yn 1:12, Ga 4:4–5, Ep 1:5. Adoption is an aspect, along with reconciliation, of being restored to God's favor from our former condition as his enemies (5:10–11).

Many Western societies stigmatize persons who have been adopted, but God's view of adoption is very positive: believers who are adopted become first-class **sons**, even **joint-heirs with the Messiah.** Moreover, first-century attitudes toward adoption must have been very positive too, else this passage would not have resonated with its readers. Were this biblical perspective more prevalent today, adoption could become a major solution to the problem of abortion. The confrontation between "right to life" and "freedom of choice" would not be altogether eliminated, but its scope would be greatly reduced. Then pregnant women not able or not wanting to raise their children could be grateful to the adoptive parents and to a changed society for resolving their situation in a way that allowed a life to continue instead of being cut off. The children could grow up gratified at having been chosen by their adoptive parents, just as believers are thankful to have been adopted and transferred from death to eternal life by God the Father, whom we are to imitate (Mt 5:48).

18 Of what are we **heirs**? We don't fully know yet: **the glory… will be revealed to us in the future**. But we do know that to obtain it we must share in the Messiah's sufferings (including his death — but also see Co 1:24&N).

19–25 Our inheritance involves an ecologically ruined world that will one day be restored (Ac 3:21, 1C 15:23–28, MJ 2:8–11, Rv 21:1). It **was made subject to frustration** because of human sin (Genesis 3:16–19) — the intractability of the physical world is not merely a natural law, and one day it will end (for an imaginative fictional portrayal of such a phenomenon see the final two chapters of C. S. Lewis's *The Last Battle*, in his series, "The Chronicles of Narnia"). Of this we have a **certain hope**, for which we are **waiting eagerly, but with patience**. This is the larger context of whatever suffering, discouragement and doubt we experience — a context of **hope**.

26–27 Should we feel overwhelmed by being trapped in an as yet unredeemed universe, we have a third assurance (see 14aN, 14b–17N) provided by the Spirit: he prays properly our heart's deepest yearnings, even when consciously we don't know how to do it.

28–30 With the reminder that the Spirit's pleadings "for God's holy people accord with his will" (v. 27) we leave the ministry of the *Ruach HaKodesh* and move on to the assurance offered by God the Father himself in having an unthwartable **purpose** (Greek *prothesis*, which can also be rendered "plan") for his people (v. 28).

This purpose or plan originated in the unfathomable past: **knew in advance... determined in advance** (v. 29; compare Ep 1:3–14&NN; on the issue of predestination versus free will see 9:19–21&N). It expresses itself in present history: **called... caused to be considered righteous** (v. 30). And it continues on into the world to come: **glorified** (v. 30) — in the past tense, showing that even though from our limited human viewpoint glorification is still in the future, from God's viewpoint it is already accomplished, hence for us a certainty on which we can rely.

Throughout all of this, the believer's responsibility is to **love God** (v. 28), as always (Deuteronomy 6:5), and to be sure, through faith in Yeshua, that he is included among the **called** (v. 28).

31–39 The chain of assurances provided in vv. 28–30 makes Sha'ul confident enough even to challenge his own argument. **If God is for us, who can be against us?** Not God (vv. 31–33), not **his Son... the Messiah Yeshua** (vv. 34–37), and in fact no one, nothing (vv. 35, 38–39), **will be able to separate us from the love of God which comes to us through the Messiah Yeshua our Lord.** The certainty is absolute — except for a very important nagging question raised in 9:1–5 and requiring three chapters to answer (see 9:1–11:36&N).

36 If we, Yeshua's followers, **are considered sheep to be slaughtered** by trouble, hardship, persecution, hunger, poverty, danger and war (v. 35), so too he was "led like a sheep to the slaughter" (Isaiah 53:7).

Psalm 44, quoted in this verse, speaks of Israel as oppressed by enemies and scattered among the nations, yet faithful to God's covenant; the psalmist prays for God's deliverance and acknowledges the futility of self-effort ("I do not trust in my bow, nor shall my sword save me," v. 7(6)). In quoting one verse Sha'ul implicitly is applying the entire psalm to those who have come to trust in the Gospel, thus expanding on what he wrote in v. 18 above.

CHAPTER 9

9:1–11:36 Chapters 9–11 of the Book of Romans contain the New Testament's most important and complete discussion of the Jewish people. In them God promises that "all Israel will be saved" (11:26) and commands that Gentile Christians show the Jews God's mercy (11:31). In the face of what these chapters teach, every form of Christian antisemitism stands condemned; and every claim, whether by Jews or Christians, that the Gospel is not for Jews must collapse.

This discussion of the Jews arises from what might seem an unrelated topic, Sha'ul's assurance to believers in Yeshua the Messiah that God's love for them will see them through every distress and can never be overpowered or withdrawn (8:14–39). In fact, some theologians fail to find this connection, notably those Dispensationalists who hold that Romans 9–11 is merely a "parenthesis" in an argument that moves from Chapter 8 directly to Chapter 12.

But this is a serious mistake. Chapters 9–11 do proclaim the eventual salvation of the Jewish nation as an integral part of God's "Good News promised in the *Tanakh*" (1:2) "to the Jew especially" (1:16&N). Yet in context these chapters serve another function, which is to answer the burning question any of the original readers would have asked at this point in Sha'ul's letter: "Sha'ul, if God is as powerful and faithful as you portray him (in Chapter 8), then why, as more and more Gentiles accept the Gospel, are more and more Jews rejecting and opposing it? Didn't God say repeatedly in the *Tanakh* how much he loves Israel — 'with an everlasting love' (Jeremiah 31:2(3))? If God's love for the Jews is everlasting, how can it be that, despite centuries of experience with God himself and despite having God's Word with its Messianic promises (3:1–2), so many of the Jews individually and the Jewish nation as an entity are refusing this love as expressed through his Messiah? Apparently they, with all their advantages, are being lost, and God's 'everlasting love' won't do them any good. That worries us: how can *we* be sure of your promise that 'no created thing will separate *us* from the love of God' (8:39)?"

Therefore, it is because a believer (either Gentile or Jewish), seeing the response of most Jewish people to the Gospel, might doubt God's faithfulness to his own promises or his capacity to fulfill them and thus call into question God himself, that Sha'ul is compelled at precisely this point in his letter to deal at length with how the salvation of the Jewish people will indeed be accomplished and thereby vindicate God.

Chapters 9–11 are organized as follows:

CHAPTERS, VERSES	CONTENTS
9:1–6a	Introduction: *The problem:* by rejecting the Gospel, Israel, with her many advantages, makes it appear that God's promises have failed.
9:6b–11:32	*The solution.*
9:6b–29	I Is God to blame? No.
9:30–10:21	II Is Israel to blame? Yes. What was Israel's

mistake? Misconstruing the *Torah*, regarding it as requiring not trust but legalistic works. This is why Israel has not received what God has promised her.

11:1–32 — III Nevertheless, Israel's failure is not permanent. God has not rejected his people the Jews, and he will fulfill his promises to them. Furthermore, the fulfillment will be even more glorious because Israel's temporary stumbling has been God's means of bringing salvation to the rest of mankind. Because all Israel will be saved, Gentile Christians should not boast but should show Jews God's mercy. Indeed, it is through Gentile Christian mercy that salvation will come to the Jewish people.

11:33–36 — Conclusion: Hymn of praise to God marvelling at the grandeur of his plan for world history.

1 Since Sha'ul's ministry was to Gentiles (1:5b–6&N, 11:13), perhaps some people thought he would no longer be interested in the Jews. Therefore in this verse he affirms in three different ways the sincerity of his great grief over Israel's failure, as a people, to honor their Messiah. Actually, even as an emissary to the Gentiles, whenever he came to a new place he brought the Gospel "to the Jew first" (1:16&N, Ac 13:5&N).

2–4a The anguish Sha'ul experiences as he considers Jewish rejection of Yeshua shows him following in the footsteps of *Moshe Rabbenu*. When Israel apostatized and built the golden calf, Moses prayed, "This people has sinned a great sin and have made themselves gods of gold. Yet now, if you will forgive their sin — and if not, blot me, I pray, out of your book which you have written" (Exodus 32:32).

God's answer to Moshe was, "Whoever has sinned against me, him will I blot out of my book. Therefore, now, go; lead the people to the place of which I have spoken to you; behold, my angel will go before you" (Exodus 32:33–34). This angel has been identified with Yeshua the Messiah himself (see Yn 1:14N, Ac 7:30N), and the book is none other than the Book of Life (Rv 20:12b&N). Every *Rosh-HaShanah* and *Yom-Kippur* the synagogue liturgy calls for Jews to pray that their sins will be forgiven and their names written in the Book of Life; Revelation 20:15 says that those whose names are not written in it will burn eternally in the lake of fire and sulfur.

Thus Moshe, like Sha'ul after him, was willing to be under God's curse if it would help his fellow Jews.

3 **My brothers, my own flesh and blood, the people of Israel**. Sha'ul is not speaking of all Jews but only of those who have not come to trust in Yeshua. "If five of your sons are faithful and two are not, you may cry, 'Woe is me, for *my sons* are unfaithful!'"

4b–5 The tragedy of Israel's present apostasy is compounded because Israel has so many advantages over Gentiles. This subject was broached at 2:17–20 and again at 3:1–2, 9. Now Sha'ul lists eight advantages Jews have.

(1) **They were made God's children**, stated explicitly at Exodus 4:22 and understood throughout the *Tanakh*. The Greek word used here for "children" is the same as the one used to describe believers in Yeshua at 8:15.

(2) **The *Sh'khinah* was with them**. The usual rendering, "theirs was the glory," does not capture the Jewish flavor of Sha'ul's remark. "*Sh'khinah*" is a word used in the Mishna to mean "the glorious presence of God" which was visible in the pillar of fire and smoke in the wilderness (Exodus 13:31, 33:9; Numbers 12:5, 14:14; Deuteronomy 31:15), and which was present in the Tabernacle (Exodus 40:36–38) and in the Temple (Ezekiel 1:28; 3:23; 9:3; 10:4, 18–19; 11:22–23; 43:2–5; 44:4). Having God visibly present was an obvious advantage to the Jewish people in helping them be aware of his work and ways. See MJ 1:2–3N.

(3) **The covenants are theirs**, not only those with Avraham (Genesis 17) and Moshe (Exodus 19–24), but also the New Covenant (Jeremiah 31:30–36(31–37)) inaugurated by Yeshua (Mt 26:28&N). God made the New Covenant with Israel, although its terms extend to include Gentiles.

(4) The fourth advantage consists of two parts. First, **the *Torah*** itself, containing God's very words for the guidance and edification of the Jewish nation, had been its constitution for more than 1,300 years when Sha'ul wrote (by comparison, America's has been in force for just over 200 years).

But second, and more important, is **the** actual **giving of the *Torah*.** This was the formative event which, together with the Exodus from Egypt, has shaped the destiny of the Jewish people through history. In that moment when God gave the *Torah* to Moshe on Mount Sinai, the divine and eternal met the human and temporal in a way equalled only by the incarnation, death and resurrection of Yeshua the Messiah himself (see Yn 1:17&N). Note that the New Covenant too has been "given as *Torah*" (MJ 8:6b&N).

(5) **The Temple service** was not merely a daily reminder to the Jewish people of God's concern for them, but was also God's provision for their spiritual survival and continued existence, cleansing them from sin through the sacrificial system (see notes at 3:20b, 3:25a, Mt 26:28, Lk 1:6, Ac 13:38–39, MJ 9:22) and maintaining them until the Messiah came.

(6) **The promises** of redemption, reconciliation and ultimate victory through the Messiah were made to Israel — for the *Tanakh* is nothing if not a record of God's promises to the Jewish people.

(7) **The patriarchs are theirs**. Avraham, Yitzchak and Ya'akov founded the nation and received the aforementioned promises; and God's faithfulness to them guarantees the fulfillment of those promises (see 2C 1:20N, Mt 5:5N and references in its last paragraph). Non-Messianic Judaism traditionally banks on their upright behavior ("the merits of the Fathers") as being advantageous to them, though this is not the point here (but see 11:28–29N).

(8) Finally, **from them, as far as his physical descent is concerned, came the Messiah**.This is no cause for chauvinistic pride, since the Messiah is for all mankind and not Jews only; yet it is a great honor and advantage which one would not have

expected the Jewish people to ignore. Also, since he **is over all** (Isaiah 9:5–6(6–7), 1C 15:27–28, Co 1:15–19) — which means that he is in charge of everything, and therefore greater than all seven previously named advantages — all the more should Israel have heeded and accepted him.

Praised be *Adonai* forever (compare 1:25). This is the language of a Jewish *b'rakhah* (blessing); in Hebrew it would be "*Barukh Adonai l'olam va'ed.*" In Jewish liturgies a recital of God's attributes or deeds, such as here, elicits a blessing; for example, the Aramaic "*B'rikh hu*" ("Blessed be he") in the *Kaddish.*

Amen. As at 1:25, this word instructs the congregation hearing Sha'ul's letter being read aloud to affirm the *b'rakhah* with their own "*Amen,*" just as "*V'imru, Amen*" ("And say ye, *Amen*") serves the same function in the *Kaddish.* (For more on "*Amen*" see Mt 5:18N.)

There is a debate over the meaning of the last half of v. 5. A literal rendering of the text, without punctuation (because first-century Greek had none), is:

> "...and from whom [came] the Messiah the according to flesh the [one] being over all God blessed unto the ages *Amen.*"

There are three possible interpretations:

(1) The whole phrase describes the Messiah himself, stating that he came from the Jews and "is over all, God, blessed for ever. *Amen.*" If this understanding is right, we have here one of the relatively few statements in the New Testament that the Messiah is God (verses widely agreed to have this import are Yn 1:1 taken together with Yn 1:14, 10:30 and 20:28; other verses state or imply it less directly). One can understand the desire of Christians to find Scriptural support for affirming Yeshua's divinity. But although such a strong and surprising theological statement — especially shocking to Jews — would enhance Sha'ul's argument, it craves more than simple expression without any explanation whatsoever; for any Jewish hearer of the letter would immediately have so many questions that he would be unable to concentrate on Sha'ul's following discussion. Furthermore, it makes the "*Amen*" irrelevant, since it no longer is a congregational response to a *b'rakhah.*

(2) At the other extreme, in which no part of the phrase describes the Messiah, is the rendering, "and from them, physically, came the Messiah. Forever praised be God, who is over all. *Amen.*" Although much of Chapter 9 deals with God's sovereignty, that is not the subject of what Sha'ul has just been speaking about, so that there is no obvious reason to bless God at this point specifically for his being "over all," even though it is true.

(3) My own position, expressed in the translation, is that the phrase first speaks of the **Messiah** as being **over all.** After this, **God** is to be **blessed forever** for having chosen a people for himself and given them these many advantages, crowned with the advantage of having the Messiah, who is in charge of everything, be one of their number.

6a But none of this means that the Word of God has failed. This completes the explicit statement of the problem Sha'ul is dealing with in Chapters 9–11 — "In the case of the Jews, has the Word of God failed?" (see 9:1–11:36N). But the question is raised in a way that anticipates the happy conclusion, "No, it has not failed."

6b–29 The first of the three major parts of Chapters 9–11 (see 9:1–11:36N) asks whether God is in any degree at fault for Israel's currently rejecting the Messiah. This is the logical place to start, for it was the questioning of God's ability to fulfill his promises that raised the issue. The passage establishes — on the unshakable ground of God's sovereignty (vv. 19–23), justice and mercy (vv. 14–18) — not only that the promises apply to but a limited "seed" (vv. 6–13) or "remnant" (vv. 27–29) of Israel, but also that at least some of them apply to certain Gentiles who never were part of Israel (vv. 22–26).

6b The Word of God has not failed; rather, the failure has been on the part of those **from Israel** who are **not truly part of Israel.** In his earlier discussion of this same issue at 2:28–29&N, Sha'ul was speaking of individual Jews. Here, where his focus is on the Jewish nation as a whole, in its capacity as God's people, **Israel** (on this important term, see 11:26aN), he introduces the concept of the faithful "remnant," an idea which pervades the *Tanakh* (see vv. 27–28&N, 11:1–6&NN). In fact, the *Tanakh* warns that in certain cases of disobedience a person may be "cut off from among his people" (see Ac 13:38–39N). That the notion was accepted in non-Messianic Judaism can be inferred from the fact that in the Mishna the well-known statement, "All Israel has a place in the world to come," (Sanhedrin 10:1, quoted more fully at 11:26aN) is immediately followed by a list of Israelites who have no place in the world to come.

It should not be thought that God is quick to cast away his sons, meaning the Jewish people (Exodus 4:22). Keeping in mind 8:14–15, 9:24–25 and 11:1–6, consider this passage from the Talmud:

> "Abaye and Raba interpret the verse, 'You are sons of *Adonai* your God…' (Deuteronomy 14:1) in this way: 'When you behave like sons you are called sons, if you do not behave like sons you are not called sons.' This is Rabbi Y'hudah's opinion. Rabbi Me'ir said: 'In both cases you are called sons, for it is said, "They are stupid sons" (Jeremiah 4:22). Also it is said, "They are sons in whom there is no faith" (Deuteronomy 32:20); also, "…a seed of evildoers, sons who deal corruptly" (Isaiah 1:4); and also, "It shall come to pass that in the place where it was said to them, 'You are not my people,' it will be said to them, 'You are sons of the living God.'"(Hosea 2:1(1:10))' Why quote so many verses to make the point? So that if you say, 'They may indeed be called sons when they are stupid but not when they lack faith,' you are faced with the verse, 'They are sons in whom is no faith.' And if you say, 'They may be sons and lack faith, but if they serve idols they are not called sons,' there is the verse, '…a seed of evildoers, sons who deal corruptly.' And if you say, 'They may be called sons when they deal corruptly, but not good sons,' then listen: 'It shall come to pass that in the place where it was said to them, "You are not my people," it will be said to them, "You are sons of the living God."'"(Kiddushin 36a)

7–9 God decides what his promises mean and how they are to be carried out. Although the phrase, "**seed of Avraham**," seems self-explanatory, God decided that **what is to be called your "seed,"** for purposes of the promise, **will be in Yitzchak**, not in Yishma'el, of whom the same word, "seed," is used in the following verse of the *Tanakh*, Genesis 21:13, but not in connection with the promise. (Some Muslims claim that the Land of Israel belongs to the Arabs on the ground that they are "Abraham's seed" through Ishmael. These verses of Romans, in passing, refute that claim.)

10–13 **The case of Rivkah** is **even more to the point** in demonstrating God's absolute sovereignty in determining such matters independently of anything human beings do. For **both** Ya'akov and Esav were **her children**, whereas the fact that Yishma'el's mother was Hagar and Yitzchak's was Sarah might lead one to conclude that Sarah's greater worthiness had *earned* Yitzchak the promises. Nor can one look for a difference in deservedness on the father's side, **for both were conceived in a single act by Yitzchak**; the Greek word "*koitê*" does not mean merely that both had the same father, which is, of course, true, but that both were conceived in the same act of sexual intercourse.

Also, in the case of Yishma'el and Yitzchak, you might say that Yishma'el, who was fourteen years old when Yitzchak was born, had already proved himself unfit. But in the present instance the decision was made by God **before they had been born, before they had done anything at all, either good or bad.** Sha'ul makes as explicit as possible God's motivation: **so that God's plan might remain a matter of his sovereign choice, not dependent on what they did but on God, who does the calling**.

God's decision, contradicting the normal rules of that society, was that **the older will serve the younger**, which is consistent with the pronouncement made centuries later, **Ya'akov I loved but Esav I hated** (in which "hated" is a relative term meaning "loved less"; see Lk 14:26&N). This is quoted from Malachi 1:2–3, and as the context there shows, it not only looks back to those two brothers, but forward to their posterity as well; for God punished the Edomites, who were descended in part from Esav (Deuteronomy 2:4; Obadiah 1, 6), and blessed Israel, Ya'akov's seed.

14 That a loving God can hate (v. 13; Psalm 139:21–22) and that his hatred can seem arbitrary might tempt one to say, **"It is unjust for God to do this."** Sha'ul, concentrating on both God's sovereignty and his justice, replies, **"Heaven forbid!"** (on this phrase see 3:4N). "He is the Rock, his work is perfect; for all his ways are justice; a God of truth and without iniquity, just and right is he." (Deuteronomy 32:4)

15–16 In quoting Exodus 33:19 Sha'ul brings into focus God's mercy along with his sovereignty and justice. Though God is within his rights to hate whom he will, so that standing with God **doesn't depend on human desires or efforts**, God nevertheless does have **mercy** and does show **pity**.

Non-Messianic Judaism understands God's attribute of mercy as even greater than his attribute of justice. Although this seems a very beautiful idea, it can lead to the false hope that God in his mercy will somehow overlook the just punishment for sins. It is easy to see why such a hope is sought — people who do not have Yeshua to satisfy God's demand for justice by being the *kapparah* (atonement) for their sins, know that they need God's mercy desperately. The wish, then, is father to the thought that God is more merciful than judgmental.

Messianic Judaism does not have to elevate mercy over justice, because Yeshua the Messiah combines in himself God's perfect justice with his perfect mercy and demonstrates how they dovetail and coincide (see 3:25–26&NN). This is why Sha'ul can quote Exodus 33:19 in answer to a question about God's justice, thereby placing God's mercy alongside his justice and not above it.

17–18 Exodus 4:21, 7:3, 9:12, and especially 14:4 speak of God's hardening Pharaoh's heart. Sha'ul sees history repeating itself. Israel's rejection of Yeshua, like Pharaoh's rejection of Moshe, provides the circumstances for God to **demonstrate** his **power** through an act of deliverance from the "Egypt" and "bondage" of sin and death. Further, knowledge of this deliverance continues to be publicized: just as the Exodus became known through the *Tanakh* and the annual reading of the *Haggadah* at *Pesach*, so the Messiah's atoning death and resurrection are being made known through evangelism (and now, after Sha'ul's day, through the New Testament). All this is a direct result of Israel's apostasy (a point reiterated at 11:11–12, 15, 19, 25, 30–32) — for Israel's self-will, like Pharaoh's, serves God's merciful ends.

19–21 "Hardens" (v. 18) is a hard word which easily provokes one to question the moral justice of the universe. "If God makes me hard, why does he blame me for being hard?" Sha'ul offers little comfort as, in his Jewish manner, he answers this question with a question, **Who are you, a mere human being, to talk back to God?** Lest one think Sha'ul is being arrogant, he lets God himself be the one to whom objection must be made by quoting Isaiah in v. 20 and using the image of **the potter** and the **clay** from Jeremiah 18:6 in v. 21. Traditional Judaism takes the same viewpoint, as can be seen in this quotation from the weekday morning prayers in the *Siddur* (Prayerbook): "Who is there among all the works of your hands, among those above or among those below, who could say to you, [God,] 'What are you doing?' "

However, against Sha'ul's refusal to budge on the matter of God's sovereign **right to make from a given lump of clay this pot for honorable use and that one for dishonorable** must be placed his insistence that "Everyone who calls on the name of *Adonai* will be saved" (10:13). Similarly, Rabbi Akiva taught, "All is foreseen and free will is given" (Avot 3:15). Sha'ul does not let go of either side of the apparent paradox of predestination versus freedom of choice (see also Pp 2:12–13&N). Rather, he is action-oriented, steering us away from idle and destructive questioning of God's governance, toward the practical solution, which is coming humbly to God through Yeshua the Messiah — this path is closed to no one. Rashi (1040–1105) notes that Pharaoh was given five chances to repent (in connection with the first five plagues) but hardened his own heart, and only after that did God confirm Pharaoh's decision by hardening Pharaoh's heart (commentary on Exodus 7:3). God does not harden the heart of anyone but a confirmed rebel (Yn 12:39&N); he wants all to turn from sin to him (2:4, 2 Kefa 3:9).

22–24a These verses thus show that God's mercy is more evident and more wonderful, more glorious, more "mercy-full," when the background of judgment is clearly perceived. See vv. 15–16N.

24b Salvation of Gentiles as well as Jews, a major theme in Chapters 1–4, is reintroduced in the context of showing how God will fulfill his promises to the nation of Israel in spite of her present apostasy in rejecting Yeshua the Messiah. Just as God in his mercy **called** people **from among the Gentiles**, who **deserved punishment and were ripe**

for destruction, so that he might **make known the riches of his glory**, so, as we will see in Chapter 11, he will once again turn to Israel in mercy.

25–26 Sha'ul uses these texts from **Hoshea** midrashically. Hosea was not referring to Gentiles but to Israel itself; he meant that one day Israel, in rebellion when he wrote, would be called God's people. Sha'ul's meaning, which does not conflict with what Hosea wrote but is not a necessary inference from it, is that "God's people" now includes some Gentiles. How this has come about and for what purpose are examined at 9:30–10:4 and 11:17–32, as well as in the book of Ephesians.

27–28 The first part of Hosea 2:1(1:10), quoted in vv. 25–26, includes God's promise — originally made to Avraham (Genesis 22:17) and Ya'akov (Genesis 32:17) — that "the number of the sons of Israel will be as the sand of the sea, which cannot be measured or numbered." Turning on this part of Hosea's prophecy, Sha'ul cites **Yesha'yahu** to show that its fulfillment does not, as one might think, imply the salvation of every single Jew, for **only a remnant will be saved.** This idea has already been expressed in v. 6b&N, and it will be expanded on at 11:1–6&N.

29 **As Yesha'yahu said** nine chapters **earlier** in his book, **"If *Adonai-Tzva'ot*** [*Adonai* "of hosts, of armies"; Greek *Sabaoth* transliterates the Hebrew; see Rv 1:8N on this title of God] **had not left us a seed** (v. 7&N), **we would have**" been destroyed altogether, like **S'dom** and **'Amora** (Genesis 19). The **seed** is the "remnant" of v. 28. By referring back to concepts presented in vv. 6–7, vv. 27–29 give closure to Part I of Chapters 9–11, on God's role in Israel's apostasy (see 9:1–11:36N). God cannot be blamed for the nation of Israel's failure to accept Yeshua as her Messiah; on the contrary, God must be thanked for showing enough mercy to preserve a "seed" or "remnant" of individual Jews who did accept him, namely, the Messianic Jews.

9:30–10:21 In Part II of Chapters 9–11 (see 9:1–11:36N), Sha'ul turns from God's role in Israel's apostasy to the human aspect. The majority in Israel missed the Messiah because they did not grasp that the first requirement of the *Torah* is faith (trusting God), not "works" (actions undertaken on one's own, apart from God; see 3:20bN). Israel has had the right goal (vv. 30–31) but has pursued it in the wrong way (vv. 32–33). Chapter 10 (which must not be separated from 9:30–33) analyzes what Israel's misunderstanding was (10:1–13) and proves that there was no excuse for it (10:14–21), so that the blame rests entirely with Israel.

Essential to correctly understanding Part II is realizing that the *Torah*, the Mosaic Law, is a covenant based not on "works" but on trusting God. All major English translations and most commentators present 9:30–10:21 as if Sha'ul were contrasting two paths to righteousness authorized by God, the Mosaic Law and the New Covenant, and showing the advantages of the latter over the former. But there is only one path, for the *Torah* of Moshe requires faith and offers righteousness by faith, just like the New Covenant; so that any interpretation which denigrates the Law of Moses is not only antisemitic but insulting to God, the Giver of the "*Torah* of righteousness" (v. 31). The notes below provide support for this strong assertion.

30–32a **So**, in the light of vv. 24–29, **what are we to say,** what are we to conclude? That there is a monumental paradox (vv. 30–31) crying for explanation (v. 32a)!

Verses 31–32a say, literally,

> [31] "But Israel, pursuing *nomos* (a law) of righteousness, did not arrive at *nomos*.
> [32a] Why? Because not from trust but as from works."

Here are three possible interpretations, mine being the third:

(1) Christians who believe that the New Covenant offers righteousness in a new way not provided by the Mosaic Law generally take v. 31 to mean: "But Israel, pursuing the Mosaic Law, which stems from God's righteousness, defines God's righteousness, and (most importantly) demands God's righteousness, but does not offer God's righteousness, did not arrive at the righteousness demanded by the Mosaic Law."

This understanding, however, renders v. 32a superfluous; for if Israel pursued the wrong goal, a Law that does not offer God's righteousness, no further explanation is needed as to why they did not arrive at it. One also is led to ask what advantage God would gain from putting the people of Israel through the useless busy-work of such a pointless charade.

(2) A second way of construing vv. 31–32a: "But Israel, pursuing not the Mosaic *Law* but a (perfectly proper) *principle*, namely, righteousness, did not arrive at expressing that principle. Why? Because their pursuing it did not stem from trust but from works."

But there is no compelling reason why *nomos* should mean "principle" here when it means *"Torah"* in 10:4–5 (and throughout most of Romans). More importantly, the "as" of v. 32 ("as from works"), which suggests something contrary to fact, is ignored; for this interpretation says that Israel's pursuit did in fact stem from works.

(3) My interpretation is expressed in my expanded rendering that excludes other interpretations (see the *JNT* Introduction, Section V, for a defense of this translation procedure). *Nomos* is the ***Torah***, the Mosaic Law. The *Torah* is "of righteousness" in at least four senses — it stems from, defines, demands *and offers* God's righteousness; in context, what should be stressed is that it **offers** the same **righteousness grounded in trusting** that **Gentiles… have obtained.** But **Israel, even though they kept pursuing** the right goal, the ***Torah*** and the righteousness it offers, **did not reach** what they were pursuing, namely, the *Torah* (literally, "teaching") that righteousness must be grounded in trusting God and is never an earned payment for **legalistic works**. That is, they did not reach the *real meaning of the Torah*, and therefore they also did not reach the *righteousness that the Torah offers through trusting*.

Why? Sha'ul's answer is elliptical, and any interpretation must supply missing words. I take "from trust" and "as from works" to be modifiers of "righteousness"; because the same phrase, "from trust," modifies "righteousness" in v. 30 (my translation in both places: **grounded in trusting**). Contrary to the other two interpretations, mine implies that Israel was correct in believing that the *Torah* offers righteousness. But they were wrong in thinking that righteousness could be obtained on the ground of works apart from trusting, for God honors only "trust-grounded obedience" (1:5&N, 16:26). Further support for this interpretation is that Sha'ul spends 10:1–13 explaining how the *Torah* of Moshe is grounded in trusting.

I have met Orthodox Jews who make this same mistake by asserting that performing *mitzvot* (*Torah* commandments), even if done mechanically and without faith, earns a Jew acceptance with God, sometimes justifying their position by maintaining that God is interested in actions, not feelings. Insofar as they value deeds over mere emotions they are right; but normative Orthodox Jewish teaching on the subject is at odds with them and instead is virtually equivalent to what Sha'ul says here, that deeds performed without *kavvanah* (literally, "direction," that is, conscious devotion to God) gain the doer no merit with God, even though other people may benefit from the deed.

Many Jews and some Gentiles claim to "trust in God" but don't define "God" as the one who sent his Son Yeshua to atone for their sins by his death. Thus they trust in a god of their own imaginings instead of the God who exists. The trust of which Sha'ul speaks is always in the God who was and is and will be, the God of the Bible, the God who created all; trust is never in a god that one shapes for oneself.

32b–33 The **stone that will make people stumble** was proclaimed by Isaiah 7:14; 8:8, 10 to be a person named Immanu'el ("God-With-Us"), who was identified at Mt 1:23&N as Yeshua the Messiah. Luke, after quoting Psalm 118:22, "The stone which the builders rejected has become the chief cornerstone," added, "Whoever falls on this stone will be broken in pieces, but if the stone falls on someone he will be crushed to powder!" (Lk 20:18&N). Elsewhere Sha'ul speaks of the Messiah as a stumbling-stone to the Jews (1C 1:23&N; see also Genesis 49:24, Exodus 17:6, 1C 10:4, 1 Ke 2:6–8).

Therefore the Greek words rendered "**on it**," interpolated by Sha'ul into the *Tanakh* text, may refer to the Stone; or they may be translated, "on him," as at 10:11, where the passage is cited again and refers explicitly to the Messiah.

Will not be humiliated (or "disappointed" or "put to shame") on the Day of Judgment.

CHAPTER 10

1 Compare 9:1–4a. As a first approximation, in Chapter 10, Sha'ul writes mainly about the **salvation** of Jewish individuals, while in Chapter 11 he is more concerned with the salvation of the Jewish nation as a whole. On the word "**salvation**" see Lk 2:11N.

2 **Zeal for God** is good, not bad (Ga 4:17–18); "who will hurt you if you become zealots for what is good?" (1 Ke 3:13) Thus not all zeal is fanaticism. True, zeal can be abused, as Sha'ul **can testify**; because before he came to faith, he zealously persecuted believers in Yeshua (Ac 7:58–8:3, 9:1–6, and especially 22:3–4, where he describes to the Jewish establishment his former attitude by saying, "I was a zealot for God, as all of you are today").

Why does non-Messianic Jewish zeal for God go astray? Because **it is not based on correct understanding** of the *Torah*, God's word about himself (literally, "it is not according to knowledge") — a statement designed at least to pique the curiosity of Jews who spend their lives studying *Torah*. Paul goes on to explain what he means (see vv. 3–10N).

3–10 These verses analyze the "ignorant zeal" of non-Messianic Jews (v. 2), and the structure of the argument is of critical importance. Verses 3, 4 and 5 each start with the word "**for**"; thus there is a set of nested explanations — v. 3 explains v. 2, v. 4 explains v. 3, and vv. 5–10 explain v. 4.

3 This verse is really just an expansion of what was said at 9:32a, but it has to be restated here in order to establish the chain of reasons noted in vv. 3–10N.

4 The evidence that non-Messianic Jews "have not submitted themselves to God's way of making people righteous" (v. 3), which itself shows that their "zeal for God" is "not based on correct understanding" (v. 2), is that they have not grasped the central point of the *Torah* and acted on it. Had they seen that trust in God — as opposed to self-effort, legalism, and mechanical obedience to rules — is the route to the righteousness which the *Torah* itself not only requires but offers (9:30–32a&N), then they would see that **the goal at which the *Torah* aims is** acknowledging and trusting in **the Messiah, who offers** on the ground of this trusting the very **righteousness** they are seeking. They would see that the righteousness which the *Torah* offers is offered through him and only through him. They would also see that he offers it **to everyone who trusts** — to them and to Gentiles as well (vv. 11–13 below; 3:29–4:25 and 9:24–30 above).

Is Sha'ul guilty of stereotypical thinking and prejudice? Does he accuse *all* non-Messianic Jews of relying on self-effort and having an attitude of legalism? No, rather, he considers this to be the prevailing establishment viewpoint in the non-Messianic Jewish community of his time. Stereotypical thinking and prejudice (which when applied to Jews is called antisemitism) arises when an attribute possibly predicated truly of a community is applied uncritically, often falsely, to each individual in it. This Sha'ul does not do.

An error made by all major English versions and by most commentators — and one with profound antisemitic implications even when none are intended — is the rendering here of the Greek word "*telos*" as "end," in the sense of "termination." The King James Version is ambiguous — in it the verse reads, "For Christ is the end of the law for righteousness to every one that believeth"; this leaves to the reader the decision whether "end" means "termination" or "purpose" (as in "the end justifies the means"). But other versions decide the matter for him, and they decide it wrongly. The New English Bible says, "For Christ ends the law and brings righteousness for everyone who has faith"; and the margin gives as an alternate, "Christ is the end of the law as a way to righteousness for everyone who has faith." The (Roman Catholic) Jerusalem Bible goes even farther: "But now the Law has come to an end with Christ, and everyone who has faith may be justified." Likewise Today's English Version (the "Good News" Bible): "For Christ has brought the Law to an end, so that everyone who believes is put right with God."

However, the Messiah has not brought the Law to an end, nor is he the termination of the Law as a way to righteousness. The *Torah* continues. It is eternal. God's *Torah*, properly understood as the very teaching which Yeshua upholds (1C 9:21&N, Ga 6:2&N), remains the one and only way to righteousness — although it is Yeshua the Messiah through whom the *Torah*'s righteousness comes. For the Good News that righteousness is grounded in trust is proclaimed already in the *Torah* itself; this is the central point of 9:30–10:21. In seed form this was already stated at 1:16–17; Sha'ul declares it directly at Ga 3:6ff. To such a *Torah* there is no cessation, neither in this world nor in the next.

This truth is not peripheral but central to the Gospel, and it cannot be compromised, even if the whole of Christian theology were to oppose it! While there is a recent and valuable strand of modern Christian scholarship which acknowledges that Sha'ul is neither anti-Jewish nor anti-*Torah*, very little of this has penetrated popular Christianity. To Jews with even a modest amount of Jewish training the *Torah* is correctly understood as a central and eternal element of God's dealing with mankind in general and with Jews in particular. Therefore, the idea that "the law has come to an end with Christ" is for them both shocking and unacceptable. Fortunately the idea is also untrue!

According to Arndt and Gingrich's *A Greek-English Lexicon of the New Testament*, the Greek word "*telos*," used 42 times in the New Testament, has to mean "finish, cessation, termination" in four or five places (Mk 3:26, Lk 1:33, 2C 3:13, MJ 7:3, 1 Ke 4:7). But in the great majority of cases its meaning is either (1) "aim, purpose, goal" toward which a movement is being directed (1 Ti 1:5, 1 Ke 1:9), or (2) "outcome, result, consummation, last part" of a process not obviously being directed and which may or may not terminate (6:21–22 above, Mt 26:58, MJ 6:8). These meanings are reflected in the English word "teleology," the branch of philosophy dealing with goals and purposes. Then why is "*telos*" regularly regarded as meaning "termination" here? Because theology gets in the way of exegesis, wrong theology that falsely understands the Mosaic Law as not offering God's righteousness through trust, wrong theology that denigrates God's *Torah* and thereby both the God who gave it and the Jewish people to whom he gave it.

Even the paraphrases of the Living Bible ("Christ gives to those who trust in him everything they are trying to get by keeping his laws. He ends all of that") and Phillips ("Christ means the end of the struggle for righteousness-by-the-Law for everyone who believes in him") miss the point. The verse is not about our struggle but about God's *Torah*. It is true that whoever comes to trust in Yeshua relies on Yeshua for salvation and thus ends his self-effort. But this verse does not speak of ending anything. It says that the great sweep of God's purpose in giving the *Torah* as a means to righteousness achieves its goal and consummation in the coming of the Messiah.

It therefore follows, Sha'ul says, that a person who has the trust in God which the *Torah* itself requires will — precisely because he has this trust, which forms the basic ground of all obedience to the *Torah* (1:5) — understand and respond to the Gospel by also trusting in God's Messiah Yeshua. It is in this way and only in this way that he will be deemed righteous in the sight of the God he wants to serve and whose *Torah* he wants to obey. Only by believing in Yeshua will he be able to obey the *Torah*. By disbelieving in Yeshua he will be disobeying the *Torah*. This is because **the goal at which the *Torah* aims is the Messiah, who offers** the *Torah*'s **righteousness**, which is God's **righteousness, to everyone who trusts.**

5–10 The chain of reasoning begun in v. 2 continues (see vv. 3–10N). Providing evidence for what was said in v. 4, these six verses deal with Jews who trust; the extension to Gentiles who trust is discussed in vv. 11–13. The sequence of "Jew, then Gentile" is dictated by the fact that the New Covenant was made with Israel, that is, with the Jewish people.

In these verses Sha'ul quotes not from the *Tanakh* generally but specifically from the *Torah* "proper," the Five Books of Moses (see Mt 5:17N), in order to prove that **the**

righteousness grounded in the *Torah* (v. 5) is nothing other than **the righteousness grounded in trust** (v. 6). (The purpose of these verses has been too often misunderstood; see below.)

5 The quotation is from Leviticus 18:5, "You shall therefore keep my statutes and my judgments, which, if a person does them, he will live by them." Should there be any doubt whether the righteousness that results from obeying God's statutes and judgments leads to eternal life, the verse says, "he will live by them," on which Rashi (quoting the Sifra, a fourth-century collection of *midrashim* related to Leviticus), comments: "It refers to the world to come; for if you say it refers to this world, doesn't everyone die sooner or later?" Thus I translate the phrase, **he will attain life through them** — eternal life.

The word for "live" or "attain life" is the same as that used at 8:12–13 to describe what will happen to the believer who "by the Spirit" keeps "putting to death the practices of the body." Conclusion: Sha'ul affirms that the *Torah* and the *Ruach HaKodesh* offer one and the same eternal life. This is consistent with and suggested by the fact that the Holy Spirit came to the first believers on *Shavu'ot* (Pentecost), the same day the *Torah* was given to Moses (see Ac 2:4&N).

The two most important of the "statutes and judgments" referred to in Leviticus 18:5 are stated by Yeshua at Mark 12:28–31: (1) loving God (the *Sh'ma*, Deuteronomy 6:4–5) and (2) loving one's neighbor as oneself (Leviticus 19:18). Both are predicated on trusting in God: you can't love God if you don't believe in him as who he says he is, and since both you and your neighbor are made in God's image you can't love your neighbor as yourself in the sense that the *Torah* demands without believing in the God who made both of you. Therefore, Leviticus 18:5, quoted here by Sha'ul, backs up his point that obeying the *Torah* requires trust, not legalistic works.

6–8 Verse 6 commences with "**Moreover**." Conjunctions are little words easily ignored, but in a closely reasoned argument they can be of critical importance, even to the point of changing its entire sense. This is an instance. The Greek conjunction "*de*," used here, is confusing to English-speakers because it can have any of these three very different meanings:

(1) "*And, moreover, furthermore,*" implying that what follows continues the thought already begun. Example: "I love you, *and* I will love you always."

(2) "*But, rather, in contrast, on the contrary,*" implying that what follows is different from and contrasts with the preceding thought. Example: "I love you, *but* you don't love me."

(3) "*But, but only if,*" implying that what follows is not in contrast with the preceding thought but does limit, condition or modify it in some way. Example: "I love you, *but* I need you to return my love."

Greek could use "*de*" in all three sentences.

Again, erring for the same reason as in v. 4, namely, deeply rooted antisemitism, all the major English translations and most commentators take "*de*" as "but" in sense (2). This makes vv. 6–8 contrast with v. 5 instead of continuing or modifying its thought, thusly: "The righteousness based on the *Torah* says one thing (v. 5), *but, in contrast*, the righteousness based on faith says something else (vv. 6–8)." This interpretation, like the one that makes v. 4 speak of terminating the Law, is antisemitic, even if today it is unintentionally so. It flows out of the Christian theology which mistakenly minimizes the importance of the Mosaic Law. This, in turn, is the fruit of the Church's effort during the second through sixth centuries of the Common Era to eliminate, hide or finesse the Jewishness of Christianity (see my *Messianic Jewish Manifesto*, Chapter III, especially pp. 52–55). It is crucial, therefore, to insist that vv. 6–8 do not present the righteousness based on faith in the Messiah Yeshua as *different* from the righteousness based on the *Torah*, but as *the same* — the same righteousness based on the same trust and leading to the same eternal life.

The chief reason vv. 6–8 should be seen as explaining v. 5 and not as presenting something new is that the quotation from Deuteronomy 30:11–14 which Sha'ul uses to make his point is from the *Torah* itself, the very *Torah* that is wrongly understood to teach legalism (both by the non-Messianic Jews Sha'ul is opposing and by the Christian interpreters I am opposing). Sha'ul quotes from the *Torah* in order to show that **the righteousness grounded in trusting** (v. 6) is exactly the *same* as "the righteousness grounded in the *Torah*" (v. 5). He proves this by showing that the very trust implicit in the *Torah* quotation of v. 5 (as explained in v. 5N) is taught explicitly as well — the *Torah* itself commands the very trust Sha'ul is talking about, trust in God and in his Messiah when he comes. Thus vv. 6–8 sharpen the meaning of v. 5, which is then seen to imply that the person who practices "the righteousness grounded in the *Torah*" (v. 5) will necessarily have **the trust** in Yeshua the Messiah **that we proclaim** (v. 8). That is, he will see that the *Torah* itself guides him toward the goal of trusting in the Messiah Yeshua (v. 4). Therefore, understanding "*de*" (v. 6) in sense (1), I have rendered it "**Moreover**" in the *JNT*, so that vv. 6–8 *add* to the point already made in v. 5 instead of *contrasting* with it.

But I would not oppose taking *de* as conveying sense (3), *limiting* what "the righteousness grounded in the *Torah*" (v. 5) can mean. Specifically, this would make v. 6 limit the righteousness grounded in the *Torah* to being nothing other than **the righteousness grounded in faith.** If this is the correct understanding, then vv. 4–6 are to be taken thusly:

> "For the goal at which the *Torah* aims is the Messiah, who offers righteousness to everyone who trusts. For Moshe writes about the righteousness grounded in the *Torah* that 'the person who does these things will attain life through them.' *But* that very righteousness which the *Torah* offers is itself limited by the *Torah* itself to being a righteousness grounded in trusting, because the *Torah* itself says, 'Do not say in your heart, "Who will ascend to heaven?"' — that is, to bring the Messiah down by means of works not grounded in trusting...," etc.

That is, the righteousness grounded in *Torah* (v. 5) says that you must trust, not that you must do legalistic works. It is true that the person who "does these things" (v. 5) will attain life and righteousness, but the "doing" of "these things" can only be accomplished in faith; it is by definition impossible to do them by self-effort, for that would contradict what the *Torah* itself requires. Thus vv. 6–8 *limit* the meaning of "righteousness grounded in *Torah*" (v. 5) to "righteousness grounded in trusting" (v. 6) and exclude from God's righteousness those Jews (and non-Jews) who think Leviticus 18:5 authorizes self-effort or legalism as a means of earning that righteousness. (That there were such people is clear from Ga 3:12&N, where Sha'ul quotes the same verse of Leviticus in the context of showing how legalists misuse it.)

Both this alternative rendering and the one found in the *JNT* are consistent with Sha'ul's overall reasoning in these verses and in Ep 2:8–10&N.

Perhaps the most cogent reason for rejecting sense (2) for "*de*" is that Greek has a different word, "*alla*," which is a strong adversative, which Sha'ul could have used had he meant to present an alternative way of being considered righteous by God. Had he written "*alla*," it could only have been translated, "but, on the contrary, in contrast." As it is, the word "*de*," in the light of all that has been said, should be understood in either sense (1) or sense (3) but not in sense (2). No matter which of these two is chosen, vv. 6–8 must be taken as advancing the thought of v. 5, not as contrasting with it a second path to righteousness. Sha'ul is building on v. 5 to support his point of v. 4 and 9:32, that the *Torah* itself requires trust.

As I said, I believe Sha'ul quotes Deuteronomy to prove the *Torah* itself teaches that righteousness requires trust. But some think Sha'ul misuses the *Torah* by quoting selectively in order to apply the passage to the Messiah, whereas the original refers clearly and only to the *Torah*:

> "For this commandment which I command you this day is not hidden from you, nor is it far away. It is not in heaven, which might make you say, 'Who will go up to heaven for us and bring it to us, so that we may hear it and do it?' Nor is it beyond the sea, which might make you say, 'Who will cross the sea for us and bring it to us, so that we may hear it and do it?' On the contrary, the word is very near you, in your mouth and in your heart, so that you can do it." (Deuteronomy 30:11–14)

However, Sha'ul is not picking and choosing. He plays by the rules. According to the canons of rabbinical citation, the context is assumed as given — even a brief quotation is supposed to call to the reader's mind the entire passage of which it is a part (Mt 2:6N). Sha'ul knows this; he knows his readers cannot be "deceived" into ignoring the context, particularly the words adjacent to the ones he cites. Therefore, far from changing the *p'shat* ("simple sense," Mt 2:15N) of the text, Sha'ul is assuming his readers know the *p'shat* already, so that he can base upon it a *drash* ("teaching") which should win the acceptance of anyone who approaches *Torah* in a spirit of trust.

Christian theologians who think the Mosaic Law offers only "works-righteousness" and not "faith-righteousness" (and Jewish critics of the New Testament who wrongly but understandably suppose that they can rely on such Christian commentators to expound the New Testament correctly) say that in v. 8 Sha'ul intentionally stopped short of quoting the phrase, "so that you can do it," at the end of the passage, because he knew they *couldn't* do it. In other words, these theologians think that Sha'ul knew something Moses didn't, namely, that no one was capable of keeping the *Torah*; and that therefore he extracted phrases from context and gave them the opposite meaning from the one they have in their original setting. Can Jewish critics be blamed for calling Sha'ul deceptive, if this is what he did?

But Sha'ul certainly was not a deceiver, as he himself protested when so accused (1C 9:20–22&N, 2C 4:2&N). Rather, in his *drash* he is referring the "commandment" and "word" of the Deuteronomy passage to God's requirement that Israel is to trust in the Messiah when he comes, the "prophet like me" whom Moses wrote about (Deuteronomy 18:15–19; see Ac 3:22–23&N). Furthermore, even though he doesn't quote the words, "so you can do it," he implies them by including this "doing" in his *drash* at vv. 8b–10&N. This is not deception but midrashic exposition.

In v. 7 Sha'ul's substitution of "**descend into Sh'ol**" for "cross the sea" does not seriously alter the underlying thrust of the *p'shat*, but it does make its application to the Messiah clearer. Just as no human effort is needed to bring the *Torah* from heaven, where, according to Jewish tradition, it existed from eternity past, before God gave it to Moses on Mount Sinai; so likewise no one needs to **ascend to heaven**, where the Messiah once was (Yn 6:36, Pp 2:6–8) — even, according to Jewish tradition, from eternity past (compare Micah 5:1(2)) — in order **to bring the Messiah down.** Nor need one **descend into Sh'ol**, according to the *Tanakh* the place of the dead, where Yeshua also was (for three days; Psalm 16:10, Mt 12:39–40, Yn 2:19–22, 1 Ke 3:19), **to bring the Messiah up from the dead**, because God has already done it (Acts 2:24–32). If there is no need to bring the Messiah from where he has once been (Sh'ol), all the more is there no need to bring him from where he has not been ("beyond the sea"); this is an implied *kal v'chomer* argument (see Mt 6:30N). In any case, the purpose of both the Deuteronomy passage and this one is to show that self-effort is neither necessary nor possible: both *Torah* and Messiah were given by God's grace, without human assistance, so that Israel might "hear… and do."

8b–10 The thing Israel is to "do" is **the word**, which is **near you, in your mouth and in your heart.** That **word** is not about following rules legalistically but is **the word about trust that we** emissaries of the Messiah **proclaim**. What is this "trust"? According to Sha'ul's analysis it consists of two components, **trusting** (in a narrower sense of the term) and **acknowledging publicly**; and for these activities one employs, respectively, the **heart** and the **mouth**. Only on the basis of such trust can our efforts to obey God's directives (1:5) lead to being made righteous (1:16–17) and to **deliverance** (or "salvation") from the death penalty which sinners (that is, all people, 3:23) have earned (6:23).

In fact, v. 9 plus the last two verses cited constitute the whole Gospel in brief, so far as the individual is concerned. As a sinner, you not only fall short of earning God's praise (3:23) but have earned death as your wages (6:23a). Nevertheless, God's free gift to you is eternal life through Yeshua the Messiah, our Lord (6:23b). If you put your trust in him inwardly (heart) and outwardly (mouth), you will be delivered from death to life (v. 9).

The Greek word for "to **acknowledge publicly**" is "*omologein*," usually translated "to confess" but meaning, literally, "to say the same thing" — in this case, to agree with what God has revealed in his word about himself and his Son. The public, open aspect of this agreeing is essential; this can be seen from the contexts elsewhere in the New Testament where the word "*omologein*" is used — Mt 10:32; Lk 12:8; Yn 1:20, 9:22, 12:42; 1 Ti 6:13; 1 Yn 4:2–3, 15; 2 Yn 7.

An important consequence, especially for Jewish people, is that there are no "secret believers." The term refers to persons who believe that Yeshua is the Messiah but do not tell their family and friends and have little fellowship with other believers. True, trusting in Yeshua is often a process and not an instantaneous event, and during this period a person may not yet be "ready to give a reasoned answer to anyone who asks you to explain the hope you have in you, with humility and fear" (1 Ke 3:15–16&N). If the person is in touch with other believers and being taught properly, this period should rarely be longer than a few days or weeks. In unusual cases it could last a few months, but it should never take years. Without exception, those who fail to acknowledge their faith publicly are aborted in their spiritual growth; in the end Yeshua will not acknowledge them before his Father in Heaven (Lk 12:8).

Trusting God means trusting that he will provide the spiritual resources needed to deal with trials of your faith (Mt 10:19–20). God normally uses more experienced believers to channel these resources to you — the religion of the Bible is not found alone in the lotus position. If you do not consider yourself "ready to give a reasoned answer," you should seek out other believers to help you.

I will make my appeal even more direct. I know a number of Jewish people — some are Orthodox Jews, some *Hasidim* — who agree mentally that Yeshua must be the Messiah but have gone for years without telling family, friends and colleagues. They are leading double lives; but the hidden life is not a life of faith, only a life of hiding. Behind their reticence is fear, but beneath the fear is lack of trust in God's ability to care for and protect them. According to v. 9 (and Ya 2:14–26), their mental assent is not saving faith. There are no secret believers. If this description fits you, I urge you to "come out of the closet" without delay. God will help you weather the crisis.

The Greek tense of the verbs in v. 9 speaks of action at a specific time, but in v. 10 the tense often implies continuing action, although the majority of scholars believe that Sha'ul is not actually emphasizing it here. Nevertheless, it is a fact that one usually comes to trust at an identifiable point or period of time; but in order to **continue toward righteousness** and **deliverance**, it is necessary that **one goes on trusting** and **keeps on acknowledging publicly** one's faith.

Finally, and most importantly, what is the significance here of naming Yeshua's Lordship and his resurrection as the two "articles of faith" essential to righteousness and salvation? Here "**Lord**" (Greek *kurios*) could be equivalent to either Hebrew *Adon* ("Lord," applied to God in the sense of "Ruler") or to God's personal name *YHVH* (represented in Jewish liturgy as "*Adonai*" and in English writing sometimes as "Jehovah" — see Mt 1:20&N, 7:21&N). To **acknowledge... that Yeshua is** *Adon* implies committing oneself to obeying him (1:5); this is the meaning of "*kurios*" at Mt 7:21–23. To acknowledge that he is *Adonai* means not only that, but also affirming that he is one with the Father (see Yn 10:30N), fully divine, with all of God's attributes and authority; this is the meaning of *kurios* at Pp 2:9–11&N. A case can be made for either meaning here. It must be pointed out that to acknowledge Yeshua the Messiah as *Adonai* is not to deny that the Father and the Holy Spirit "are" *Adonai* too, or to believe in anything but one God (Deuteronomy 6:4), or to believe anything that conflicts with the *Tanakh*.

But this acknowledgement of Yeshua's divine authority is meaningless unless, with respect to his humanity, he has been **raised... from the dead**. Further, only a resurrected Lord can be our *cohen gadol* interceding with the Father on our behalf (8:34; MJ 4:14, 7:25), only a resurrected man can be the firstfruits of the resurrection promised to us (8:23, 29; 1 Corinthians 15), and only a resurrected Messiah can come to rule in glory and fulfill the universal Jewish expectation of final deliverance for the nation of Israel (11:25–27; Isaiah 2:1–5, 9:5–6(6–7); Lk 21:27–28; Ac 1:6–7; 1C 15:51–52;

1 Th 4:13–18). Faith in Yeshua must be accompanied by the conviction in one's heart that he has been resurrected. An unresurrected Messiah can perform none of the Messianic tasks, and such "faith" is in vain (1C 15:12–28&NN).

11–13 Although Sha'ul has been speaking of the *Torah*, which was given only to Jews, his analysis of trust in vv. 8b–10 implies that trusting is something that non-Jews are equally able to do (as we know already from Chapter 4). So he pivots on those verses to return to the theme of Gentile salvation raised at 3:27–4:25 and again at 9:24–30, and smooths the transition by citing **the verse quoted** at 9:33, the most recent appearence of this topic. There the stress was on "**will not be humiliated**"; here it is on "**whoever**" — Jew or Gentile — **rests his trust** on the Messiah. Verse 12 supports this truth by restating the argument of 3:28–31; and v. 13 gives as evidence yet another Scripture, with emphasis on the word "**everyone**."

14–15 The short digression on the Gentiles (vv. 11–13) is followed by a return to the case against Israel. Sha'ul now utilizes a method he has employed before (3:1; 6:1, 15), one used by the rabbis throughout the Talmud — he introduces an imaginary opponent to make objections and forwards his case by answering them. This opponent is perhaps best thought of as a non-Messianic Jew defending Israel and looking for the flaws in the argument of 9:30–10:13. He appears five times — by implication here (vv. 14–15), and explicitly at v. 18, v. 19, 11:1–2 and 11:11.

His first objection is to Sha'ul's use of the quotation from Joel in v. 13. His position is: "That verse about calling on the name of *Adonai* should not be applied to Jews in the way that you have done. It is not our fault if we don't call on the name of *Adonai* through Yeshua, because no one was sent to proclaim him to us." His four questions detail the links: calling requires trusting, which requires hearing, which requires a proclamation, which requires that someone be sent — and the sender, in this case, would have to be God. In the end, therefore, he blames God: "If God had sent someone **announcing good news about good things**, we would have welcomed him, we would have thrilled to the sound of his **feet**" — that is the import of his quoting Isaiah.

A similar objection is heard today when it is claimed that the *Tanakh* does not contain Messianic prophecies fulfilled by Yeshua (or at best is unclear about them), so that Jews cannot be blamed for not receiving him as the Messiah. Again, the blame is laid on God — he didn't send us anyone, his message isn't clear; it's his fault, not ours.

16–17 Blaming God for human sin is as old as Adam (Genesis 3:12), and Sha'ul will have none of it. **No**, he says, your analysis is wrong, **the problem is that** only some (the Messianic Jews), not **all**, have **paid attention... and obeyed** (the two English verbs translate the single Greek word "*upêkousan*" ("hearkened").

Sha'ul supports his assertion with a quotation from the same portion of Isaiah as was cited by the imaginary opponent; implicitly Sha'ul admonishes him to pay attention to the context. The phrase, "***Adonai*, who has trusted in what he has heard from us?**" (KJV, "Lord, who has believed our report?"), addresses all four of the opponent's questions (vv. 14–15). "From us" emphasizes that people were indeed *sent* to *proclaim*, and "what he has heard" suggests that Israel did indeed *hear* (but Sha'ul returns to secure this point in vv. 18–21). Thus the only missing link in the chain is **trust** (v. 17), which

Israel has refused to supply.

In quoting Isaiah 53:1 and 52:7 Sha'ul, like any rabbi, expects his readers to recall the context. Here the context extends through Isaiah 53:12 and includes the most extensive and detailed prophecy in the whole *Tanakh* of the Messiah's first coming, when he would die an atoning sacrificial death for sins. Also, in v. 15 the Greek word "*evangelizomenoi*," translated "those announcing good news" and corresponding to Isaiah's Hebrew word "*m'vasser*," is the cognate to the word for **Good News** or "Gospel" in v. 16 (Greek *evangelion*, Hebrew *b'sorah*). Thus Sha'ul is telling his imaginary opponent, "Israel has had the Good News that should have led them all to trust in Yeshua — they have had it in Isaiah 53, but they didn't believe it." That is the point of v. 17 — the **word** has already been **proclaimed about the Messiah** (see also vv. 8–10 above), and it has been **heard**. Therefore, since **trust comes from what is heard**, Israel ought to have trusted. An application for today: do evangelism! Proclaim the Gospel! Unless people hear the Good News of Yeshua, they cannot come to trust in him; for "trust comes from what is heard."

18 The opponent counters Sha'ul: "You say Israel should have trusted. I am willing to admit for argument's sake that people were sent to proclaim, but the problem is not Israel's failure to trust. **Isn't it, rather, that Israel didn't hear?**" Sha'ul replies, **No, they did hear**, as is proved by Psalm 19:2–5(1–4), of which the final verse is quoted:

> "The heavens declare the glory of God,
> The firmament proclaims his handiwork.
> Each day announces it to the next,
> Each night expresses this knowledge.
> There is no speech, nor are there words,
> Their voice is not heard,
> Yet **their voice has gone out throughout the world**
> **And their words to the ends of the earth.**"

Implied here is a *kal v'chomer* argument (see Mt 6:30N) that if everyone in the world, including, of course, Gentiles, has had the kernel of the Gospel proclaimed by the heavens, so that anyone can respond by trusting in God; how much more should Israel, who have had the written *Torah* (3:2, 9:4; the same Psalm 19 calls the *Torah* "perfect, restoring the soul"), have paid attention and trusted! Sha'ul made the same point at 1:19–20 (see also Ti 2:11).

19 Thrust and parry continue. "Granted that they may have heard," replies the opponent, "it still is not their fault that they have not come to faith in Yeshua. The sound waves may have struck their eardrums, **But, I say, isn't it rather that Israel didn't understand** the message they heard?" Sha'ul does not deny the possibility that Israel failed to understand, but he does not admit it as an acceptable excuse. Israel should have understood. The poetic parallelism of Deuteronomy 32:21 quoted in v. 19 implies another *kal v'chomer* argument: If **a non-nation**, that is, **a nation void of understanding**, understood the message declared without words by the heavens (see v. 18N), how much more should Israel have understood it from the written word of God! But the argument is even stronger, for Sha'ul quotes this passage to show that God predicted long ago that he would use precisely this circumstance to **provoke you** (Israel) **to jealousy** and **make you angry**; in fact, this jealousy becomes the very means of Israel's deliverance (11:11, 14). The context of Deuteronomy 32:21, cited here, shows that God is using eye-for-eye justice with Israel — the rest of the verse says that because Israel has made God jealous and angry, therefore God will make Israel jealous and angry. But the final words of the poem reveal that in the end, God "will forgive his land and his people" (Deuteronomy 32:43).

20–21 (See 9:1–11:36N for an outline of Chapters 9–11.) Sha'ul concludes Part II (9:30–10:21) the same way he did Part I (9:6–29) — by recalling its opening verses. Isaiah 65:1 (v. 20) echoes 9:30, and Isaiah 65:2 (v. 21) echoes 9:31.

CHAPTER 11

1–32 Part III of Chapters 9–11 (see outline of these chapters in 9:1–11:36N) shows how God will fulfill his promises to the nation of Israel. Although Replacement theology wrongly claims the contrary, Jewish "disobedience" (v. 30) does not annul God's promises to Israel, because "God's free gifts and his calling are irrevocable" (v. 29). Sha'ul therefore cautions Gentile believers in Yeshua against antisemitism and false pride (vv. 13–26), while showing them what should be their active role in hastening the salvation of the Jewish people (vv. 30–36&NN).

1–6 Sha'ul's imaginary non-Messianic Jewish opponent, introduced at 10:14–15&N, has given up trying to prove that Israel is not responsible for its unbelief. His new tack is to try to show that Sha'ul's message, with its accusation of Jewish culpability for failing to heed it, is not merely unpleasant to Jewish ears but inconsistent with Scripture and therefore unworthy of being heeded. If the opponent can make his point stick, Sha'ul's case will be discredited on the ground that it contradicts what God has already revealed. **"In that case,"** says the opponent, "if Israel has, as you say, 'kept disobeying and contradicting,' (10:21) **isn't it** a necessary implication **that God has repudiated** (or: "cast aside" or "abandoned") **his people?**" The opponent wants the reader to admit this; but if he does he must also admit an unacceptable implication, that God has broken his word, as promised in the *Tanakh*, "God will not repudiate his people." If Sha'ul's message entails believing in a God who breaks his word, it is not God but Sha'ul's message that must be rejected.

Sha'ul's reply is couched in the strongest possible denial language (see 3:4N), **Heaven forbid!** Sha'ul's logical method here begins with a *reductio ad absurdum*: God at least cannot have cast aside every single Jewish individual, **for indeed I myself am a son of Israel**, and he hasn't rejected me. More specifically, I am from the **seed of Avraham** as defined in 9:6–13; and lest the imaginary opponent suppose I am spiritualizing that phrase and letting it include Gentiles (which it does in Galatians 3–4; compare 9:24 above and Mt 3:9), I mean here that I am a literal physical descendant, **from the tribe of Binyamin** — a claim which, at the time Sha'ul wrote, could probably have been independently verified. Sha'ul refers elsewhere to his Jewishness (2C 11:22; Ga 1:13–14, 2:15; Pp 3:5–6; see also Ac 22:3, 23:6, 26:5) and does so again here, not in order to boast (2:17) but to advance his argument.

Having begun with himself, he will prove in the rest of the chapter that — using the very words of the *Tanakh* which the opponent implies are contradicted by Sha'ul's message — **God has not repudiated his people** (1 Samuel 12:22, Psalm 94:14; the first four printings of the *JNT* cite "Isaiah 12:22" by mistake), **whom he chose in advance** (Greek *proegnô,* rendered "knew in advance" at 8:29). Sha'ul is not falling for his opponent's trick of trying to set the Gospel message in opposition to God's word. In fact, Sha'ul agrees with his opponent that God does not renege on his promises; later Sha'ul himself insists that "God's free gifts and his calling are irrevocable" (v. 29 below).

If you (the opponent) think otherwise, **Don't you know what the *Tanakh* says about Eliyahu** the prophet, who thought he was the only Jew of his time who had not apostatized? God disabused him of his melancholy conclusion by saying, **"I have kept for myself seven thousand men who have not knelt down to** the false god ***Ba'al***" to worship him. Sha'ul's point is that **it's the same way in the present age** as it was then: **there is a remnant** (same word as at 9:27) of Israel, the Messianic Jews, **chosen** not by themselves but **by** God's **grace** (see 6:23N). Thus does Sha'ul recapitulate Part I of these three chapters (see 9:1–11:36N), that God is sovereignly, justly, and, most of all, mercifully (see vv. 30–32 below, as well as 9:6b–29&NN) at work fulfilling his promises in history, even when our eyes and ears seem to tell us differently.

Then in v. 6 he recapitulates what he said in Part II (9:30–10:21&NN), that **legalistic works** (self-efforts apart from trust in God; see 3:20bN), are incompatible with **grace**, which requires no effort or prior deeds, only trust. But here the emphasis is on the relationship between good works and being chosen: works that please God must follow election by him, not precede it (Ep 2:8–10&NN).

7–8 Returning to the main thrust of his argument, Sha'ul summarizes: **What follows is that Israel** as a nation **has not attained the goal for which she is striving** (not: "was striving," as in most translations, for this suggests that Israel is no longer striving for righteousness). **The ones chosen**, the Messianic Jews, **have obtained it** through trusting in the atonement God has provided in Yeshua, **but the rest have been made stonelike**.

Made stonelike. The Greek verb *"pôroô"* is found here and at Mk 6:52, 8:17; Yn 12:40 and 2C 3:14. The related noun, *"pôrôsis,"* is used at v. 25 below, Mk 3:5 and Ep 4:18. In most versions the verb is rendered "hardened" or "blinded"; the *JNT*'s literal translation points up the allusion to Ezekiel 36:26, where God, speaking of what he will do for Israel in the Latter Days, says, "I will take away the stony heart out of your flesh, and I will give you a heart of flesh."

As at 10:14–21 Sha'ul does not give a tough answer without Scriptural support. Here three of Israel's major figures writing in the three main sections of the *Tanakh* (Moses in the *Torah*; Isaiah in the Prophets; David in the Writings) are shown to bear witness to Israel's **dullness**, blindness and deafness to God, and consequent bondage. Sha'ul, who might otherwise be accused of arrogance or antisemitism, is seen instead to be in the tradition of the great prophets of our people, on whom he is relying.

9–10 The **dining table** refers not to the laws of *kashrut*, which, although complicated to the outsider, are hardly sufficiently complex to **become a snare and a trap**, but to fellowship at meals, which is highly valued in Judaism, especially if "words of *Torah*" are exchanged. In the Mishna we read:

> "Rabbi Shim'on said: 'If three have eaten at one table and have not spoken there words of *Torah*, it is as if they had eaten from the sacrifices of the dead; since it is said, "For all their tables are full of vomit and feces, without God present" (Isaiah 28:8). But if three have eaten at one table and have spoken there words of *Torah*, it is as if they had eaten from the table of God, blessed be he; since it is said, "And he said to me, this is the table which is before *Adonai*" (Ezekiel 41:22).'"(Avot 3:3)

(In Isaiah 28:8 the Hebrew phrase, "*b'li makom*," means, literally, "without a place"; the verse really means, "For all their tables are full of vomit and feces, without a place [to eat]." But Rabbi Shim'on relies on wordplay to make his point: by Mishnaic times the word "*Makom*" ("place") had also become a euphemism for "God," probably referring particularly to his omnipresence; hence above I twice render "*Makom*" as "God.")

But if Jews who reject Yeshua have conversation purporting to be "words of *Torah*," then the dining table has indeed **become for them a snare and a trap, a pitfall and a punishment** — in the sense that when the worldview of non-Messianic Jewish life pervades the relaxed atmosphere of mealtimes, it becomes difficult for an individual Jew to recognize Yeshua and come to trust in him.

Backs that are **bent** symbolize slavery, in this case slavery to sin and its consequences. Sha'ul quotes the Septuagint Greek version, but the Hebrew original has, "make their loins continually totter," "loins" being understood as a center of strength.

Greek *dia pantos*, corresponding to Hebrew *tamid*, is rendered "**continually**," not "forever," as in some English versions. "Continually" means "all the time, at present," while "forever" implies "always — now, in the future, and till the end of time." Here "forever" would be inconsistent with God's promises to Israel and also with what is said in vv. 11–32 immediately following.

On Psalm 69 see 15:3–4N.

11–12 Sha'ul's imaginary non-Messianic Jewish opponent (see 10:14–15N) makes his fifth and final attempt to overturn Sha'ul's reasoning. "**In that case**, that is, if, as you, Sha'ul, claim, it is Israel's own fault that they do not trust Yeshua as the Messiah (10:14–21), and if, as you claim, this rejection does not signify that God has repudiated his people (11:1–10), then, **I say, isn't it that they**, Israel, **have stumbled with the result that they have permanently fallen away?**" This is not, as some commentators think, a repetition of the question in v. 1. There it was whether God had acted to abandon Israel; here it is whether Israel's rejection of Yeshua has as its necessary consequence the permanent self-exclusion of the Jewish people from the purview of God's promises, without any positive action on God's part. If Sha'ul answers, "Yes," his whole Gospel will be unacceptable to Jews, again not because it offends them, but because it contradicts the *Tanakh*, which presents God's promises to Israel as unconditional (vv. 28–29).

As at v. 1, Sha'ul's shocked disclaimer, **Heaven forbid!** (see 3:4N), highlights how unthinkable he regards the notion that the Jewish people might not receive what God has promised them. That would be bad, but the reality is **quite the contrary**, good, on four counts:

(1) **By means of** Israel's **stumbling** (the word sometimes implies stumbling to one side of a path, getting off the track), **deliverance has come to the Gentiles**, and that is a good thing in itself.

(2) This deliverance for Gentiles is intended to fulfill the prophecy of Deuteronomy 32:21, quoted at 10:19 above, that God will **provoke** Israel **to jealousy** "over a non-nation, over a nation void of understanding." It is good when God fulfills one of his prophecies, for it vindicates God's name and character.

(3) Israel's eclipse is not permanent, she is only **temporarily placed in a condition less favored than that of the Gentiles**. Although in itself this may seem bad, in the context of God's long-range plan it is good; as will be shown, it is part of how God brings salvation to the Jewish people.

(4) Israel's forthcoming full commitment to Yeshua the Messiah, which is what **Israel in its fullness** implies, will **bring** even **greater riches**, even greater good, to humanity than their temporary abasement has brought (point 1 above).

Here is a literal translation of Sha'ul's answer in these verses:

> [11b] "May it not be! Rather, on the contrary, by the stumble of them [is] the deliverance to the Gentiles, unto the provoking-to-jealousy of them; [12] and if the stumble of them [is] riches of world, that is, [if] the defeat [or: "inferior status"] of them [is] riches of Gentiles, by how much more the fullness of them."

By means of their stumbling. The Greek word "*paraptôma*" is elsewhere rendered figuratively as "trespass," but in vv. 11–12 it has for its context the related verb "*ptaiô*," which means "**stumbled**" in v. 11; the prefix "*para-*" means "next to, alongside." The passage recalls 9:32–33 and portrays Israel tripping over the "stone that makes people stumble" (9:33), Yeshua, and falling alongside the path of *Torah* (which has trust in the Messiah as its "goal and fulfillment," 10:4&N), off to the side, where the light of God's glory does not shine (Psalm 119:105).

The deliverance. What deliverance? That which had been promised in the *Tanakh* to Israel, nothing less than deliverance (or: "salvation") from sin and its consequences, including all the evils in the world. **Has come,** meaning it has begun and will certainly be completed, but not meaning that its full implications (such as world peace) have already happened in history (see 8:14–39, especially 8:28–30&N). **To the Gentiles**, the *Goyim*, the nations (see Mt 5:47N). The deliverance was meant for Israel (Mt 10:6, 15:24); but as a nation, Israel failed to receive it. Individuals did accept it, but the majority, including the establishment, did not. This led to its being offered to the Gentiles, as the book of Acts documents (see especially Ac 13:42–47&NN), although God has never stopped holding out his hands to his "disobeying and contradicting" people (10:21).

The traditional non-Messianic Jewish counterclaim is that the righteous of all nations have always had a place in the world to come, and therefore Christianity is essentially unnecessary, although it deserves credit for helping to lead Gentiles out of idolatry toward monotheism. However, it does not lead them to true monotheism because it "teaches that a man is God." Moreover, in this view, Christianity is not only unnecessary for Jews but a positive evil, since it leads them away from their more perfect monotheism.

I have dealt with these arguments at various places in this commentary. For example, at Yn 14:6&N it was pointed out that Yeshua is the only route to righteousness for Jews as well as for Gentiles, so that monotheism which excludes Yeshua as the Messiah is mistaken. Here I wish to focus on the question of whether Israel's failure to acknowledge her Messiah when he came had positive consequences for the Gentiles. It is a fact that in the first century, Gentiles as a rule did not know, fear and obey God (Ep 2:11–12&NN). Thus they did not meet the Jewish criterion for having a place in the world to come (1:18–2:16), so that if the Gospel had not been proclaimed to them, very few of them would have received "the deliverance." It is pointless to speculate how God might have brought them that deliverance, had the leaders and the majority of Israel obeyed the Gospel when it was first offered; what we do know is that God did in fact use Israel's disobedience as a **means**, causing Messianic Jews (notably Sha'ul, v. 13) to evangelize Gentiles as well as Jews, and we know that many Gentiles responded positively.

The deliverance has come to the Gentiles. This is, of course, a good in itself. But just as God used Israel's decline as a **means** of bringing that deliverance to the Gentiles, so God is now using the Gentiles' deliverance **in order to provoke them** (Israel) **to jealousy**, in fulfillment of Deuteronomy 32:31, which was quoted above at 10:19. That is, the Gentiles' deliverance is itself a **means** of bringing that same deliverance to Israel, to whom it was promised (see vv. 30–32&NN below).

To provoke them to jealousy. Is there anything about Gentile Christians that would make non-Messianic Jews jealous of them? Throughout most of the last two thousand years, the Church, to its great shame, not only has not provoked Jews to jealousy but has engendered repugnance and fear; so that Jewish people, instead of being drawn to love the Jewish Messiah Yeshua, have usually come to hate or ignore him, remaining convinced that their non-Messianic Judaism or secularism or agnosticism is superior to Christianity.

If this seems a harsh judgment, then let us hear of which Christians Jews are expected to be jealous. Of the "Christians" who trapped Jews in their synagogues and burned them alive (which happened when the Crusaders conquered Jerusalem in 1099, as well as in several European cities)? Of the "Christians" who forced Jews to hear conversionary sermons against their will and expelled from the country those who did not respond (which took place for centuries during the Middle Ages and the Inquisition)? Of the "Christians" who invented the "blood libel" that Jews murder a Christian child and use his blood in their Passover *matzah*? Of the cross-carrying "Christian" priests leading murderous mobs in pogroms? Of the "Christians" who remained silent while six million Jews perished in the Holocaust? Or perhaps of the "Christians" who murdered them — including Hitler himself, who was never excommunicated from the Roman Catholic Church? Of "Christian" members of the Ku Klux Klan and other white "Christian" supremacy gangs and their brutish demonstrations? Of "Christians" that support Palestinian organizations whose terrorists kill and maim Israeli Jewish children? Of Greek Orthodox Archbishop Capucci, convicted of gun-running for those same Palestinian terrorist organizations? (These horrific events are further chronicled by Messianic Jew Michael L. Brown in his book, *Our Hands Are Stained With Blood: The Tragic Story of "The Church" and the Jewish People*, Shippensburg, Pennsylvania: Destiny Image Publishers, 1992.) Of which of these "Christians" are we Jews supposed to be jealous? After such a recital, it is kinder not to dwell on what these people provoke us to — but jealousy it is not.

The Jews' pain would have been the same regardless of whether these people called themselves Christians; and the name "Christian" is not copyrighted, so that anyone who chooses can apply it to himself, whether his behavior entitles him or not. But the Church's shame is not only in not having taken a stand consistently repudiating every one of these and other horrors committed against the Jews, but in having actually authorized and encouraged some of them. There is no way of silencing every individual who misuses the name of the Messiah, falsely claiming his authority for their evil deeds. But there is a way for a community to withdraw its approval and fellowship from such people and condemn them publicly; instead, through much of its history, the Church did exactly the opposite. Of this Jews are to be jealous?

Nevertheless, there is another side. The point is not to cite merciful deeds done for the Jews in Christ's name, to "balance the ledger"; that is no consolation at all. Rather, it is that Gentile Christians should understand the words, "**provoke them to jealousy**," as a command, or at least as a challenge. Non-Messianic Jews ought to be able to look at saved Gentiles in the Church and see in them such a wonderful change from their former selves, such holy lives, such dignified, godly, peaceful, peace-bringing, honorable, ethical, joyful and humble people, that they become jealous and want for themselves too whatever it is that makes these Gentiles different and special. Many Jews — myself among them — have been won to trust in Yeshua through the jealousy-provoking behavior of Gentile Christians, behavior that overcomes with its love all the pent-up antipathy, distrust and pain which a Jewish person can feel, even when these feelings are justifiable by objective historical reality. Not natural? Yes, the Good News is not natural, but supernatural. Its work is done in people and through them by the *Ruach HaKodesh*, the Holy Spirit, who can remove every shred of antisemitism and falseness and replace them with the transparent love that truly "fulfills the whole *Torah*" (13:10). The rest of Chapter 11 expands on this theme, and Chapters 12–15 are nothing if not a manual on how to provoke Jews — and unbelieving Gentiles — to jealousy (see 12:1N).

Being placed temporarily in a condition less favored than that of the Gentiles. This phrase gives the sense in context of the single Greek word "*êttêma*" ("inferior status, defeat, diminishing"); in particular, the word "**temporarily**" is added because a future, different *plêrôma* ("**fullness**") is foreseen. It is possible to understand Sha'ul in terms of quantity rather than **condition**: "If the diminishing of remnant Israel's numbers is bringing riches to the Gentiles, how much greater riches will their full numbers bring!" This interpretation is rejected in v. 25N on the word "*plêrôma*." The comparison, **than that of the Gentiles**, is implied, not stated, in the text.

The idea of a temporary eclipse of Israel by the Gentiles can be found in rabbinic writings too. In the Talmud the passage, "But if you will not hear it, my soul will weep in secret for the pride" (Jeremiah 13:17) is examined:

> "What is the meaning of the phrase, 'for the pride'? Rabbi Shmu'el ben-Yitzchak said, 'For the glory [Hebrew *gaveh*, literally, "pride"] has been taken away from them and given to the nations of the world.'"(Chagigah 5b)

Also in the Talmud, the saying of Rabbi Papa, "When the ox runs and falls, the horse is put in the ox's stall" (Sanhedrin 98b), is explained by the Jewish commentators, such as Rashi, as referring to Israel and the Gentile nations. Thus the Soncino English edition of the Talmud explains that the horse is allowed to replace the ox, but when the ox recovers it is hard to remove the horse. Likewise, the Israelites fell and the Gentiles were given power, but when Israel recovers it will be hard to remove the Gentiles from their position of power without inflicting much suffering (see *Sanhedrin*, p. 667, note 3).

One difference between Sha'ul and the rabbis is that in Sha'ul's understanding, it is the spiritual element in the "glory" or "power" which has passed to the nations from that part of Israel which has remained "stonelike" (vv. 7, 25); whereas for the rabbis, the spiritual glory and power remain with Israel even when the temporal outward aspects pass to others.

How much greater riches will Israel in its fullness bring them! Here Gentiles are offered a "selfish" motive for evangelizing Jews: if Jewish spiritual failure has brought riches to the Gentiles, but Jewish spiritual success will bring them even greater riches, it pays spiritually to win Jews. God, who created humanity, knows human nature very well and does not shrink from using self-interest to motivate right behavior. There are numerous examples of it in the *Tanakh*; two of the best known are the second paragraph of the *Sh'ma* (Deuteronomy 11:13–21) and the fifth commandment (Deuteronomy 5:16).

13–32 But to those of you who are Gentiles (literally, "But to you the Gentiles"). Sha'ul is writing to the Messianic Community in Rome, a body of Messianic Jews and Gentile Christians (in Chapter 16 he sends greetings to both believing Roman Jews and believing Roman Gentiles), and he calls the Gentile Christians "Gentiles." Thus he refutes the theology which claims that when a Gentile becomes a Christian he is no longer a Gentile. Similarly Ga 2:13&N show that a Jewish believer in Yeshua remains a Jew. The passages which say that in the Messiah "there is neither Jew nor Gentile" (Ga 3:28&N, Co 3:11) refer to equality of status in the Body of the Messiah and not to the obliteration of all distinctions.

I say this. Everything up through v. 32 is directed to Gentile believers specifically. Sha'ul shifts his remarks from one audience to another, as he did at 2:17. Since 10:14 he has been addressing an imaginary non-Messianic Jew whose first three objections (10:14–15, 18, 19) would not have interested Gentiles much, but whose last two (vv. 1, 11) might well provoke in some of them a prideful antisemitic response: "Yes indeed, God has repudiated his people the Jews and replaced them with us the Christians. Yes indeed, the Jews have stumbled so as to fall away permanently from ever receiving what God has promised, and we Christians will get those blessings instead." Curiously, much of the Christian Church through the centuries (and not excluding today) has managed to believe this Replacement theology lie of their own invention instead of what Sha'ul says to refute it. The irony of this is dwarfed by the tragedy of what its consequences have been for the Jews.

For this very reason it is especially important for both Jews and Gentiles — Messianic and otherwise — to understand these twenty verses well. They demonstrate to Gentiles that Christianity and antisemitism are absolutely incompatible. More than that, they prove that God is not — as some think — "finished with the Jews." More than that, they prove that any Christian teaching that speaks of the Church as the "New Israel" (a phrase found nowhere in the New Testament but invented by the theologians) which has replaced the "Old Israel" (by which they mean the Jews) is vastly oversimplified and liable to abuse (see vv. 23–24N, Ga 6:16N). More than that, these verses demonstrate again that Sha'ul himself was not an antisemite and did not teach that the Church had supplanted Israel; instead, he had a deep and concerned love for his own Jewish people, warned very severely against antisemitism, and confirmed the promises God made in the *Tanakh* with his light-bearing words of hope, "**All Israel will be saved**" (v. 26).

13–14 Since I myself am an emissary sent to the Gentiles (as he said at 1:13; see also Ga 1:16, 2:7–9, and Ep 3:8; while Ac 9:15, 22:17–21 and 26:17–20 report this commission from Yeshua himself), **I make known the importance of my work** (literally, "I glorify my work"), I make a point of letting Jewish people know about it, **in the hope that somehow I may make some of my own people jealous** of saved Gentiles (vv. 11–12&N) **and** by this roundabout method, as an indirect byproduct of my ministry to Gentiles, **save some of them** too — not that Sha'ul by himself saves anyone, for Yeshua the Messiah does that; rather, Sha'ul, by obeying God, participates in God's work (1C 3:6; Mt 9:36–38).

One hears little these days about this principle of evangelism. Most Christians do not have a ministry to Jewish people, so they suppose that they have no particular responsibility toward them. They are rarely exhorted to make their ministry to Gentiles known among Jews as a means of provoking them to jealousy, the way Sha'ul did.

Sha'ul is very circumspect about what he hopes to accomplish — he has the **hope** that **somehow** he **may** make **some** of them jealous and save **some** of them. Actually, he spent considerable time among Jews (see Ac 13:5N) and in at least one instance, in Rome, the very city to which this letter was written, he seems to have had, a few years later, a notable evangelistic success with them (Ac 28:24–25&N).

15 Why does Sha'ul persist in using his energy to make his ministry known among people whom he expects to be unreceptive? Because **if their rejecting Yeshua means reconciliation for the world, what will their accepting him mean if not life from the dead!** The phrase, "life from the dead," can be taken in three ways; the first offers the weakest motivation for Sha'ul's behavior, the last the strongest:

(1) *Vaguely.* Reconciliation for the world, meaning "individual believers' salvation and **reconciliation** with God," is the downpayment we have now; while "**life from the dead**," meaning, in some vague symbolic sense, "something even more wonderful," is what we will have when the Messianic Age has fully come.

(2) *Metaphorically.* Since Yeshua alone can bring spiritual life to the spiritually dead (Yn 1:4–5, 8:12, 14:6), Sha'ul, always aware of this truth and feeling such pain for his own flesh and blood (9:1–4), uses every opportunity to make the Gospel known and a topic of discussion among Jews everywhere. This interpretation makes the verse a *midrash* on Ezekiel 37, which uses the valley-of-dry-bones figure to speak of the people of Israel's being metaphorically "resurrected," first physically, that is, being regathered as a united nation to inhabit the Land forever (Ezekiel 37:1–12, 15–22), and then spiritually (Ezekiel 37:13–14, 23–28; in the light of the New Covenant this can be understood as the Jewish people's coming to faith in God and his Messiah Yeshua). Jeremiah 24:6–7 presents the same sequence: God first brings

the Jews to the Land and then gives them a heart to know him.

(3) *Literally*. "**Life from the dead**" is to be taken at its face value. It is nothing less than the consummation of salvation in bodily resurrection (as in 8:11–24), a hope Pharisees held then, as Orthodox Jews do now. The resurrection will be delayed until the Jewish people, as a nation, come to faith in Yeshua; therefore Sha'ul feels duty-bound to follow the Jewish pattern of hastening the Messiah's (second!) coming (see 2 Ke 3:12&N) by evangelizing the Jewish people indirectly (vv. 13–14) as well as directly (Acts 9–28, 1C 9:19–23).

Of these three interpretations my preference is for the last. "**Life from the dead**" should be understood literally, since there is no reason to prefer a vague or metaphorical interpretation when the context is well served by a literal one. However, the second interpretation also provides strong motivation for Jewish evangelism.

Their casting Yeshua aside... their accepting him. The Greek words "*apobolê avtôn*" mean, literally, "their rejection" or "the rejection of them." The Greek grammatical form of *avtôn* is known as the genitive, and two interpretations are possible: (1) the objective genitive, "their being the object of rejection," so that the question for exegetes is, who rejects them? — and (2) the subjective genitive, "their being the ones who do the rejecting," and the interpretative issue is, whom or what do they reject? Other places where an important subjective/objective genitive issue arises are 3:22, 26&NN and Ga 2:16c&N (section (2)).

Most translations opt for the first, "their being rejected," understood to mean that God rejects the Jews now but will later include them. I went along with this, unconsciously projecting the implied antisemitism, until a reader called my attention to the problem with the genitive. Therefore, in the first printing of the *Jewish New Testament* v. 15 reads: "For if their being cast aside means reconciliation for the world, what will their acceptance mean? It will be life from the dead!" I now repudiate this rendering because I now understand that it contradicts Sha'ul's continuing point that "God has not repudiated his people" (vv. 1–2), and that "they have not permanently fallen away" (v. 11). Even "their being placed temporarily in a condition less favored than that of the Gentiles" (v. 13) is not equivalent to their being rejected or cast aside, not even temporarily. And finally, vv. 28–29 completely rule out the possibility of the Jews' being rejected, because "God's free gifts and his calling are irrevocable."

Rather, in this verse it is the unbelieving Jews, not God, who are doing the rejecting; because whether God rejects the Jews has already been answered in the negative (vv. 1–10). Whom or what are the Jews rejecting? It can only be Yeshua, or, more or less equivalently, the Gospel. Hence I interpolate "**Yeshua**" and "**him**" into the text as the object of rejection and acceptance. Making humans and not God the ones rejecting and accepting also fits the context of vv. 17–24 which follow, where Sha'ul explains that human "branches" who lack faith and therefore reject Yeshua cannot share in the "cultivated olive tree."

16 The metaphor of the olive tree, beloved of Messianic Jews everywhere, extends through v. 24 but is introduced by a different image, taken from Numbers 15:20–21: **If the *challah* offered as firstfruits is holy, so is the whole loaf.** Today "*challah*" means the special braided loaves of bread served in Jewish homes on *Shabbat* and during festivals. In the Bible the word describes a small "cake" baked from dough set aside for God; this must be done first (hence the term "firstfruits"). Only afterwards may the loaf made from that dough be eaten, so that the loaf is then "holy" in the sense of being usable at all. Talmud tractate Challah gives details of the procedure.

Also, to illustrate the same principle another way, **if**, as is the case, **the root is holy**, then **so are the branches**, for they are connected to the root, so that the same sap flows through to the branches from the root.

But in Sha'ul's metaphor, who or what is the **root**, or, in the earlier metaphor, the **firstfruits**? Three distinct possibilities are:

(1) The believing remnant of Israel that is truly Israel (9:6–7), that is, the Messianic Jews (11:1–15),
(2) Avraham (4:12) or all the Patriarchs (11:28),
(3) Yeshua the Messiah (8:29, 1C 15:20), who alone makes Israel holy.

Any of these fits the context of vv. 17–18; but the material in Chapter 4 about Avraham (alluded to again in v. 28), as well as the truism that firstfruits are offered first, suggest something chronologically anterior, hence the people who trusted first, either Avraham or all the Patriarchs. Although some of the Church Fathers and Karl Barth opted for possibility (3), I suspect that this idea gained currency in the early Church because of its tendency to want to deprive the Jews of their place as God's people, the root and firstfruits of faith. For a more extended discussion see the comment on this verse in C. E. B. Cranfield, *The International Critical Commentary: Romans.*

And who are the **branches** growing from this **root,** the **loaf** made from the dough from which the **firstfruits** came? Four options are:

(1) Every single Jew, past, present and future.
(2) Every single Messianic Jew, past, present and future.
(3) The Jewish people, as a nation, though not necessarily every Jew.
(4) All believers, Jewish and Gentile, past, present and future.

In v. 26aN, I will show why it must be the third of these, the Jewish nation.

17–18 If some of the branches, that is, unbelieving individual Jews but *not* the whole Jewish people, **were broken off**, removed (temporarily, not permanently! — vv. 11–12, 23–24) from being eligible to receive what God has promised, **and you** Gentiles (v. 13), **a wild olive, were grafted in among them**, among the branches which are still part of the tree, the Messianic Jews, the Jewish nation as represented by its Messianic Jewish community, **and have become equal sharers in the rich root of** God's cultivated **olive tree**, then **don't boast as if you were better than** (literally, "don't boast against") **the** natural **branches**, neither the ones still in place (the Messianic Jews) nor the ones broken off (the non-Messianic Jews). Gentile pride in having been joined to the "chosen people" is utterly out of place, particularly when directed against those very people! As Sha'ul writes elsewhere, "After all, what makes you so special? What do you have that you didn't receive as a gift? And if in fact it was a gift, why do you boast as if it weren't?" (1C 4:7)

However, if you do boast, for whatever reason — carelessness, thickheadedness, or actual malice — it ought to help you stop if you **remember that you are not supporting the root**, but **the root is supporting you.** Or, to make Sha'ul's point as clear as it can be, whether the root is Yeshua, Avraham, the Patriarchs, the Messianic Jews or all the Jews (see v. 16N), it is a Jewish root, and don't you forget it! The Jewish community sometimes draws a picture of the Jew who comes to faith in Yeshua as someone doubly unwelcome, rejected both by other Jews and by the Gentile majority in the Church as well. It's easy enough to understand why a Messianic Jew might be rejected by some in the Jewish community, but why did the image of his being rejected by the Church even arise? It came from Gentile Christians who forgot Sha'ul's warning and regarded the Jewish believer in their midst not as a natural branch of the olive tree into which they were grafted, but as an alien.

Shifting the perspective slightly, notice that Sha'ul is reminding Gentile Christians that trusting God also means joining God's people. It is no different now than it was with Ruth: "Your people shall be my people and your God my God" (Ruth 1:16). Gentile Christians have joined Israel, not the reverse (see also Ep 2:11–16&NN). For a Gentile Christian to look down on the people he has joined is not only *chutzpah* and ingratitude but also self-hate.

19–21 **So**, seeking an excuse for pride, **you**, a new imaginary opponent (see 10:14–15N), a prideful boastful Gentile Christian, **will say, "Branches were broken off so that I might be grafted in,"** the implication being that God prefers Gentiles to Jews. Sha'ul's answer is, literally, "[It is] well"; my rendering, **True, but so what?** brings out the implicit irony, the point being that the opponent's statement, though true, cannot be made into a ground for boasting against the branches. For even though **They were broken off because of their lack of trust**, nevertheless, the only reason **you stay in place** is **because of your trust** in the God of the Jews and in the Jewish Messiah. **So don't be arrogant; on the contrary, be terrified** of letting pride in having been included with God's people replace trust in God. This was the very sin Sha'ul found unbelieving Jews prone to at 2:17–29, and compare Mt 3:9. "Stand in awe" or even "fear," as some translations have, are not strong enough; you are to **be terrified**, once you face the fact that **if God did not spare the natural branches** when they apostatized through lack of trust in him, **he certainly won't spare you**, a grafted-in branch, when you, through antisemitic pride, demonstrate that same lack of trust.

22 Some people think that if they have given mental assent to the proposition that Yeshua is the Messiah, they have "eternal security" with God, no matter how they live their lives. This parody of genuine trust is rightly called "cheap grace." The truth of the matter is that "faith" without actions to match is dead (Ya 2:14–26); in other words, salvation is conditional: **provided you maintain yourself in that kindness! Otherwise you too will be cut off!** This involves taking care that faith "works itself out in love" (Ga 5:6, Ep 2:10).

23–24 Conversely, the only condition non-Messianic Jews must meet in order to become sharers in the promises God made them is **not** to **persist in their lack of trust.** Then they **will** most certainly **be grafted in; because God is able to graft them back in.** This means that God can keep his promises, which is specifically the issue behind Chapters 9–11 (see 9:1–11:36N).

God's ability to graft them back in is proved by another *kal v'chomer* argument (see Mt 6:30N), that if **you** Gentiles **were cut out of what is by nature a wild olive tree**, a nation of pagans separated from God's promises (Ep 2:11–12&NN), and were

grafted, contrary to nature, that is, contrary to normal agricultural practice, contrary to what makes economic sense, **into a cultivated olive tree**, the Jewish people, enabling God's "foolishness" (1C 1:17–31) to highlight his sovereign control over his purposes (9:6b–29); then (the climax of the argument), **how much more will these natural branches be grafted back into their own olive tree!** How much easier it will be to bring an understanding of spiritual truth to those who belong to the people God has been dealing with for thousands of years than to those who do not! The analogy does not apply to every single Jew over against every single Gentile — especially today, when some Jews are raised without any Jewish identification, while many Gentiles, particularly those raised in Christian homes, have been exposed to spiritual truth as much as or more than many Jews. But, leaving modern exceptions aside, it ought to be easier for a Jew to believe in Yeshua as the Messiah than for a Gentile (and this would certainly have been so when Sha'ul wrote), since "Messiah" is a concept which is part of Jewish culture, whereas a Gentile has to be introduced to an idea alien to his culture (see Ac 11:20–23N.) Furthermore, a Jew, as a member of the Jewish people, has the advantages enumerated at 9:4–5. This is why a "Jews for Jesus" broadside says, in a lighthearted vein, "You don't have to be Jewish to believe in Jesus — but it helps!"

The "olive tree" analogy of vv. 17–24 casts new light on the important theological question, "Who are God's people?" The most common theology in non-Messianic Judaism would answer this question, "The Jews." The most common theology in Christendom answers, "The Church." But from the olive tree we learn that there are three distinct groups at present who are all in some sense part of God's people, and no proper theology can ignore any of them:

(1) Messianic Jews, who are the natural branches that are part of the cultivated olive tree.
(2) Gentile Christians, the wild olive branches which have been grafted into the cultivated olive tree.
(3) Non-Messianic Jews, the natural branches which have fallen off the cultivated olive tree but can easily be grafted back in again.

What I call "olive tree theology" must take into account all three groups, all three kinds of "branches," in defining and describing the past, present and future of God's people.

But theologians, like other people, want a simple life. The most widespread Christian oversimplification is found in some forms of Covenant theology and is most correctly called Replacement theology. This erroneous theology says that the Jews used to be God's chosen people; but when they spurned Jesus, God spurned them and chose a new people, the Church, to replace them — so that now, the Church receives all of God's promises and blessings, while the Jews get only the curses. Were this thinly disguised antisemitism true, Sha'ul would have to picture a cultivated olive tree with its root, trunk and branches all dead, and the wild olive branches living by themselves, grafted into nothing alive.

Unfortunately, Replacement theology is currently gaining strength in several growing movements in Christendom: Dominionism, Reconstructionism, "Kingdom Now," and in England, Restorationism. These movements are spreading the correct idea that the Church should not retreat into a ghetto or a fortress mentality, but should bring the presence of the Kingdom into the world, actively attempting to improve life here on earth — actually a very Jewish idea. It is truly a shame that these movements propagate Replacement theology, since they don't need it to make their point; indeed, many Christians who could benefit are driven away by it. I wish these movements would see that there is no logical connection between their program for improving life on this planet and Replacement theology, and would repudiate the latter. For additional discussion of Replacement theology see notes at Mt 5:5, 24:34; Lk 21:24; Ac 1:6–7, 21:21; Ro 2:28–29; 11:1–32, 11–32, 11–12, 28–29; 2C 1:20; Ga 6:16; Ep 2:11–16.

In reaction to Replacement theology, the Jews, first the *Rambam* (Maimonides, 1135–1204), later Franz Rosenzweig (1886–1929), and after him many Jewish and Christian thinkers seeking good relations between the two faith communities, came up with Two-Covenant theology. This says that Jews are saved by the covenants with Avraham and Moshe, while Christians are saved by the covenant with Jesus. Messianic Jews have no place in this picture, even though Yeshua's first followers were Jewish. Were this correct, Sha'ul would have to describe two separate olive trees, both cultivated, but cultivated differently, with no grafting of branches, and presumably no fallen branches. The main flaw in Two-Covenant theology is that it confuses Jewish national salvation with the personal salvation of individual Jews. The covenants with Avraham and Moshe guarantee Jewish national salvation, but only the covenant with Yeshua brings individual salvation, and it is needed today for national salvation as well (2C 1:20&N). For further discussion, see Yn 14:6N, my *Messianic Jewish Manifesto*, pp. 256–259, and the journal *Mishkan*, No. 11 (1989), P. O. Box 116, Jerusalem 91000, Israel (the entire issue is devoted to this topic).

In the first half of the nineteenth century there was also a Christian reaction to Covenant theology which has come to be known as Dispensationalism. In this view, both the Jews and the Christians are peoples of God, but their promises differ. There are varieties of Dispensationalism, but in one form the Church's promises are heavenly and the Jews' earthly. Sha'ul would have to picture two different kinds of trees — an olive tree and, say, a pear. Messianic Jews leaving God's people of earthly promise and joining God's people of heavenly promise would, I suppose, be olive branches grafted into the pear tree — a horticultural and spiritual monstrosity and impossibility! This view arose from a well-meaning attempt to deal with the main problem created by Replacement theology, namely, that there are obviously promises in the *Tanakh* which God made to the Jewish people that were unconditional, not depending on the faithfulness of the Jewish people, promises which God intended to fulfill in the process of returning the Jewish people to faith (see Ezekiel 36 and Jeremiah 31:30–37). Replacement theology overlooks these or misconstrues them. But Dispensationalism, by separating the futures of the Jews and the Christians, falls short of saying what needs to be said.

To change the metaphor, let theology picture God as a juggler. Traditional Jewish theology sees God as throwing one ball into the air, the Jews. Christian Replacement theology sees him as having thrown the Jewish ball into the air in the past, but now he has let it fall and is juggling the Christian ball. Two-Covenant theology and Dispensationalism see God as somewhat more coordinated — he can juggle two balls at a time, both the Jews and the Christians. But only "olive tree theology" credits God with being able to juggle all three balls at once, Gentile Christians, Messianic Jews and non-Messianic Jews, without letting any of them drop to the ground.

At this point "olive tree theology" is relatively undeveloped. But it is in ferment: theologians are proposing solutions to the problem of who is God's people that include all three groups and allow for both universal personal salvation and Jewish national salvation only through Yeshua — although no one of these solutions is widely known and taught. Walter Kaiser's "promise theology" is one effort in this direction, while the Jewish believer Arnold Fruchtenbaum has done a monumental piece of research on the subject in his *Israelology: The Missing Link in Systematic Theology* (Ariel Ministries, P. O. Box 3723, Tustin, California 92681, 1989, 1104 pages). Undoing the work of centuries of misunderstanding will require substantial efforts not only in theology but in the reeducation of the components of God's people (however defined!) to understand who they really are and how they relate to each other and to the Almighty.

25 **For**. The word points forward to the reason, given immediately, why Sha'ul has presented the olive-tree metaphor (vv. 17–24).

Brothers. He emphasizes that he considers not only Messianic Jews but also Gentile Christians his brothers in faith, because some of them might have taken umbrage at the sharpness of his immediately preceding remarks (compare Ac 3:17&N).

Truth which God formerly concealed but has now revealed. This whole phrase translates the single Greek word "*mustêrion*," which does not mean "mystery" either in its modern sense of "riddle" or in its ancient Greek "mystery-religion" sense of a secret disclosed only to initiates.

Why is what Sha'ul says here a secret truth that was not understood until he explained it? Because one would have expected Israel to be the first nation to be saved. Israel has had advantages enjoyed by no other people (3:1–2, 9:4–5), the Gospel itself is "to the Jew especially" (1:16&N), and God has promised Jewish national salvation (Ezekiel 36:24–36, Mt 23:37–39&N, Ac 1:6–7&N). Why, then, is he doing the unexpected, making the Gentiles "joint-heirs" (Ep 3:3–9) with the Jews? In order to give the fullest possible demonstration of his love for all humanity and not Jews only (vv. 30–32 below).

So that you won't imagine you know more than you actually do, literally, "lest you be wise in yourselves," conceited, so that you Gentiles might separate yourselves from Jews and imagine you are better than they are. "Do not be wise in your own eyes; but fear *Adonai* and depart from evil" (Proverbs 3:7).

Stoniness, or "hardness" (Greek *pôrôsis*). See v. 7N on "made stonelike."

To a degree, Greek *apo merous*, "from part." The literal sense could yield this rendering: "Stoniness has come upon Israel, stemming from part of it." Though close to Sha'ul's point, grammatical considerations exclude it; because in the four other places where the phrase is found in the New Testament, it has descriptive force. Therefore it should be understood here as modifying "stoniness"; so that translations which read, "Hardness has come upon part of Israel" (the part that rejects Yeshua) are wrong, even though the statement is true. Sha'ul is focussing not on parts but on wholes. "No man is an island, entire of itselfe" (John Donne) — all Israel, including the part that accepts Yeshua, is affected by this partial stoniness; for, as the next two clauses show, it delays Israel's national salvation.

The stoniness is not total, because there are and always have been Jews trusting Yeshua. It is wrong to see in the term "partial stoniness" a veiled approval of non-Messianic Judaism as superior to the "total stoniness" of paganism; that is the opposite of Sha'ul's point, which is that rejection of Yeshua by people with so many advantages (9:4–5) demonstrates utter stoniness. (This is no new problem for the Jewish people — in the *Tanakh* God frequently called us stubborn and stiffnecked.)

The passage does not say that God caused the stoniness, as he hardened Pharaoh's heart (9:17–18); but it does imply that God knew it would happen. Nevertheless, this does not provide an excuse for anyone to remain stone-hearted (see 10:13).

The Gentile world... in its fullness. Greek *plêrôma* ("fullness") probably refers not to number (the full complement of Gentiles to be saved throughout history) but to breadth of representation. Sha'ul wrote when the Gospel mission to the Gentiles was just beginning; but already he foresaw what Yeshua had prophesied, that "this Good News about the Kingdom will be announced throughout the whole world as a witness to all nations [or: "to all Gentiles"]. It is then that the end will come" (Mt 24:14). Later Yochanan would see in his vision countless multitudes "from every nation and tribe and people and language" (Rv 7:9). The fullness of the Gentile world comes in when all components and subgroups of humanity are contributing people to the Kingdom.

The language here recalls Lk 21:24, where Yeshua prophesied distress in the Land and judgment on the people of Israel, with Jerusalem being "trampled down by the Gentiles until the times of the Gentiles have been fulfilled." (*Plêrôthôsin*, "have been fulfilled," is related to *plêrôma*; see Lk 21:24N).

Enters, not "has come in." Greek *eiselthê* speaks simply of an event that will take place, not of the moment when it will have finished taking place. The latter interpretation would excuse laziness in evangelizing the Jewish people, for it implies that little can happen in Israel's salvation timetable until Gentiles have finished entering the Kingdom. But the entering of the Gentiles in their fullness, like any other major historical process, such as the Renaissance or the Industrial Revolution, is an event that necessarily must occupy a considerable period of time. Sha'ul's prophecy is being fulfilled at this very moment. The Gentiles are entering in their fullness right now. Evangelism has been worldwide for several centuries; parts of the Bible have been translated into some 2,000 languages; a quarter of the world's population count themselves part of Christendom; and although many unreached peoples remain, the breadth of representation has never been greater. So it is not surprising that with the rise of Messianic Judaism as a conscious worldwide movement within the Jewish people, we are starting to see all Israel saved. Also see Appendix, p. 933.

26a In this way. Greek *outôs* means "thus," not "then" (as in some versions) — the emphasis is on the *manner* in which all Israel will be saved, not the *time* when it will happen, for the time is "now" — see v. 25N (last three paragraphs) and v. 31&N (last paragraph). In what manner will Israel be saved (what kind of "thus")? Sha'ul says it four different ways in this chapter — vv. 11–15, 16–24, 25–29 and 30–32. The story is always the same: most of Israel rejects Yeshua, forcing the Gospel to be presented to the more responsive Gentiles. This goes on until their numbers and manifest godliness provoke more and more Jews to jealousy, whereupon the stoniness of their hearts breaks down, Israel receives Yeshua with a new "heart of flesh" (Ezekiel 36:26), and God fulfills his promise of national salvation.

All Israel. Of whom is Sha'ul speaking when he uses the term, "all Israel"? Before addressing this question, we must examine the word "Israel."

The name "Israel" was given to the third Patriarch, Ya'akov, after he wrestled with "a man" who was "*Elohim*" (God) (Genesis 32:25, 31). This is a fact of utmost importance in interpreting the New Testament. God, who knows everything before it happens, gave Ya'akov this name at this time to symbolize the Jewish people's future wrestling match with him, as recorded in the *Tanakh* and culminating in two thousand years of wrestling with Yeshua the Messiah. Read the entire passage (Genesis 32:25–33) with the understanding that this mysterious "man" who was God may have been Yeshua in a pre-incarnation appearance (see Yn 1:14N for a discussion of this and other such appearances). Think of him as still waiting to hear the Jewish people say to him, as did Ya'akov, "I will not let you go unless you bless me" (compare Mt 23:37–39&N), and, "I have seen God face to face, yet my life is preserved." Just as Ya'akov feared death at the hands of his enemy-brother Esav but grew confident that because he had seen God his life would be preserved, so those who have seen God in the face of Yeshua the Messiah know that they have eternal life despite anything the Adversary may do; also Messianic Jews no longer approach their Gentile brothers in fear as enemies.

Likewise, it is significant for the Church — especially in the light of the current Middle East situation — to note that when God gave the name Israel to Ya'akov a second time, he reaffirmed promises previously made to Avraham and Yitzchak, particularly the promise that the Land would belong to Ya'akov and his descendants the Jewish people (Genesis 35:9–13). Also in this passage is a *remez* ("hint"; see Mt 2:15N) of what Sha'ul in vv. 17–24 above calls the grafting-in of Gentiles: God says to Ya'akov, "There shall come from you a nation," the Jewish people, the root, "and a company of nations," Hebrew *kahal goyim*, which can also be rendered "a congregation of Gentiles," the branches (Genesis 35:11).

Thus throughout the rest of the *Tanakh*, Ya'akov's descendants are called the "house of Israel"; this means that the Jewish people are the people of God. As "God's chosen people" they are the object of his special concern and affection; they are called his "first-born," his "son," his "beloved." But at the same time they are obligated by covenants to obey him in a unique way not required of other nations. The vicissitudes of God's people Israel, as recorded in the *Tanakh*, demonstrate over and over that when God's people refuse to obey him, punishment inevitably follows. In his mercy God provides two mitigations: (1) delaying the deserved punishment, thus providing an opportunity for his rebellious and stiffnecked people to repent, and (2) allowing a "righteous remnant" to escape the corporate penalty altogether. These ideas pervade the writings of the Prophets; see, for example, Amos 3:2, 11; 9:7–9; Jeremiah 29:7; Isaiah 10:5–14, 20–23; 43:14–25.

The election of Israel by God raises the question of particularism versus universalism. Despite the particularism implied in the election of Israel, a strain of universalism runs through the *Tanakh*, showing that God has not neglected the other nations (see, for example, Isaiah 2:1–4 and the books of Ruth and Jonah). However, once Israel is chosen, God's universalism is never divorced from Israel; from Genesis 12 onwards it is through Avraham and his seed that the other nations of the world will be blessed, that is, through the Jews. The Gentiles of Nineveh trusted the Jewish prophet Jonah that the God of the Jews was offering them one last chance to repent; Ruth joined herself to the Jewish woman Naomi and her Jewish people and God. Likewise, today Gentiles must trust in a Jewish Messiah in order to be saved. If they insist on a separate blessing, there is no blessing; but if they will join themselves to the Jews, saying with Ruth, "Your people shall be my people," then blessings are theirs in abundance.

A variant of insisting on separate blessing is to claim that Israel is some other people than the one God says it is — to ask, "Which people is actually God's chosen?" and give an answer other than the Jews. This issue first arose at the time of the Samaritan schism (2 Kings 17:24–41), and it was still current seven hundred years later, when the Samaritan woman at the well spoke with Yeshua (Yn 4:20–24). In terms of that incident, we may rephrase the question, "To which people — the Samaritans or the Jews — flows the living water from the spiritual well of Ya'akov, who is also named Israel?"

It is inevitable that people without faith in the whole of God's revealed Word — Samaritans then, all kinds of unbelievers today — will dispute the election of the Jewish people or even the concept of election itself. The idea that God should choose some over others is intolerably offensive unless understood within the framework of God's overall plan as set forth in the *Tanakh* and the New Testament. But as soon as a person puts his trust in God's Word, the concept of Israel's election loses its offensiveness and becomes instead the means of blessing everyone, Jew and Gentile alike, according to the promise of Genesis 12:3.

It is the Church's fault that the question of who is God's people became a point of contention and separation between Judaism and Christianity. For the Church began claiming, over against the Jews, to be the "New Israel," the "true Israel," the "Israel of God," and regarded the Jewish people as merely the "Old Israel," no longer eligible to receive God's promises because of having rejected Yeshua. How ironic that the Church claimed to supplant the Jewish people as Israel when it behaved instead like Israel's old name, Ya'akov, which means "supplanter"! This perverted understanding of election, ignoring everything Sha'ul writes in Chapters 9–11, raised between Jews and Christians an unnecessary barrier — which I hope the *Jewish New Testament* and this commentary can help to eliminate.

On the other hand, the answer of some non-Messianic Jews, as reported in the New Testament (for example, at Mt 3:9), that merely being a physical descendant of Ya'akov suffices to guarantee membership in God's elect, is equally a perversion of God's revealed truth (see 9:6 above).

From theology we turn to a linguistic question relevant to understanding the meaning of the term "all Israel": how was the term "Israel" used in Sha'ul's day? Who used it, and for what? Examination of Jewish and Greek literature shows that Jews used the word "Israel," rather than "Jews," to refer to themselves as a nation, and especially when speaking of themselves as God's people.

Gentiles, on the other hand, never used the term "Israel" at all, since the concept of a people elected by God was foreign to them. They used the term "*Ioudaioi*" ("Jews" or "Judeans," see Yn 1:19N), which for them signified primarily the country of origin, Judea; they took for granted that each country had its own religion, the Jews too; but apart from that the word had no more religious significance than "Italians" or "Americans." Diaspora Jews used the term "Jews" more than did Jews in the Land of Israel in referring to themselves, since they lived among Gentiles who used only that term (compare 2 Maccabees, a Diaspora book, with 1 Maccabees, written in Israel).

Most of the 71 instances of the word "Israel" in the New Testament clearly refer to the Jewish people. Besides this verse, problems arise only in Ro 9:6, 1C 10:18, Ga 6:16, and Rv 7:4; see the notes to those verses.

Sha'ul used the term "Jew" eleven times in Chapters 1–8 of Romans, always in contrast with "Gentiles" or "Greeks." He uses the term "Israel" only in Chapters 9–11, where it appears twelve times. Why did Sha'ul switch? Because in Chapters 1–8 he wanted to emphasize that through trust in Yeshua, Gentile individuals are equal with Jewish individuals before God (he also uses "Jews" for that purpose at 9:24 and 10:12); but in Chapters 9–11 his purpose is to bring out that the Jews as a nation remain God's people — that is, they remain Israel — even if some of them disobey, and God's promises to Israel, the Jewish nation, remain valid (9:1–11:36N). In conclusion, "Israel" means the Jewish people, but with attention called to their being God's chosen people, his "firstborn," his "beloved," his "son," and as such, the recipients of the advantages enumerated in 9:4–5.

Now we are ready to ask who **all Israel** is. This term has the same four possible meanings as "loaf" and "branches" in v. 16: (1) every single Jew, past, present and future; (2) every single Messianic Jew, past, present and future; (3) the Jewish people, as a nation, but not necessarily including every individual Jew; and (4) all believers, both Jewish and Gentile, past, present and future. As we will see, the third is correct.

Many Christians are unaware of how peculiar it sounds to a Jew to hear the term "Israel" used to refer to Gentiles; such an idea would never enter his mind. Yet meaning (4) is the most important of the mistaken views, because, as noted above, the Gentile-dominated Church has claimed throughout most of its history that she is the "New Israel" and the "True Israel," and that the Jews are only the "Old Israel," excluded from God's promises. But none of these terms can be found in Scripture; they are an antisemitic effort, though sometimes not intentionally so, to go beyond what Scripture says and remove the Jewish people from the place which God has given them.

And in fact, meaning (4) is impossible in the present context, for several reasons. First, "Israel" has clearly meant only Jews throughout Romans 9–11, right up to the preceding verse. Second, Sha'ul uses the word "Jews," not "Israel" when he wants to emphasize Gentile participation in God's promises, as noted above. Third, the subject of Chapters 9–11 is how God will make good his promises to the Jewish people, not to a combined Jewish-and-Gentile people (9:1–11:36N). Fourth and last, the story of how God will in fact do this is told four times in 11:11–32 (see first paragraph of this note), and in the other three tellings there is no question that Sha'ul is speaking about Jews only (vv. 15, 24, 31).

Nevertheless, some branches of Christianity attempt to impose this sense, applying reasoning which can perhaps bear up better at Ga 6:16, where the term "God's Israel" appears — but see my comments there. The effect of such an understanding is to deny that God will fulfill his specific promises to the Jewish people and thus to contradict Sha'ul's whole purpose in writing Chapters 9–11. Proponents of this view answer that objection by saying that all God's promises are fulfilled "in Yeshua" (true in a sense) and that he stands for the whole Jewish people (also true in a sense; see Mt 2:15N). To show what wrong conclusions this reasoning can lead to, an application of it would be that the Land of Israel belongs to Yeshua; therefore, since he represents Israel and now owns the Land, so that the promise that the Land will be Israel's forever is fulfilled "in him," no further return of the Jews to the Land should be expected. But the promises in the *Tanakh* to the Jewish people are directly to them, not to the Messiah. If the Messiah receives what was promised to the Jewish people and then prevents the Jewish people from receiving it, the promise has been effectively cancelled; God has reneged on it. We must rule out the interpretation which says that **all Israel** includes Gentiles.

But **all Israel** is also not every single Jew (meaning (1)). Not only do Chapters 9–11, with their emphasis on the Jewish people as a corporate whole being the recipient of God's promises, not require that, but such an interpretation conflicts with the "remnant" notions brought in at 9:6, 27 and 11:1–6.

With even more certainty, **all Israel** is not merely all Messianic Jews (meaning (2)), even though 9:6 implies that only the Messianic Jewish subset of Israel is truly Israel. For this would make the "truth which God formerly concealed but has now revealed" (v. 25), and which Sha'ul has spent three chapters leading up to, an anticlimactic tautology — it is obvious that all saved Jews will be saved.

Rather, the word "**all**" is used here figuratively, not literally. In the *Tanakh*, that is to say, in Hebrew thinking, the word "*kol* " ("all") in reference to a collective does not mean every single individual of which it is composed, but rather the majority, or the essential part, or even a significant or highly visible component possibly much smaller than a majority. New Testament examples include Mt 2:3 (KJV: "When Herod… heard…, he was troubled, and all Jerusalem with him") and Mt 3:5 (KJV: "Then went out to him… all Judea and all the region round about Jordan"). Clearly the writer does not mean that every single person in Jerusalem was troubled, or that Judea and the Jordan regions were emptied of their populations; his words do not even imply that a majority were so affected.

All Israel, then, is the Jewish nation as a corporate whole (meaning (3)), including every Messianic Jew (by tautological necessity) but not necessarily every individual Jew. Whether the proportion of Jews saved will be a majority, or ten percent or ninety, is a matter of pointless speculation; however, I do expect that when this prophecy is fulfilled, the "establishment" of the Jewish people will consist mostly of Messianic Jews, and Messianic Jews will not be at the periphery of the nation but at its center, leading, setting the tone and providing the vision for the Jewish public — "the head and not the tail" (Deuteronomy 28:13).

This interpretation of **all Israel** as the Jewish nation taken corporately accords with vv. 17–24 on the grafting in of broken-off non-Messianic Jewish branches (but not necessarily all of them), with v. 12 on Israel "in its fullness" (the same word, *plêrôma*, as used in v.25 for the Gentiles; see note there) and with the idea that only a remnant (less than the totality) will be saved (v. 5, 9:6&N, 9:27).

Moreover, oddly enough, it also accords with one of the most famous paragraphs in the Mishna, although the latter's emphasis is very different:

> "All Israel have a portion in the world to come, as it is said, 'Your people, all of them righteous, will inherit the Land for ever — the branch of my planting, the work of my hands, in whom I glorify myself' (Isaiah 60:21). But these have no share in the world to come: he who says that resurrection from the dead cannot be proved from the *Torah*, he who says the *Torah* is not from Heaven [i.e., not inspired by God but merely a human product], and a heretic [of which there are many categories]. Rabbi Akiva says: also one who reads the heretical books…."
> (condensed from Sanhedrin 10:1)

In this *mishna* the phrase, "all Israel," similarly does not mean every individual, since the Jews to be excluded from the world to come are named immediately (Rabbi Akiva's remark apparently refers to believers in Yeshua, among others).

Will be saved or "delivered," both spiritually — saved from the eternal consequence of sin, and also, in the end, from sinning at all — and physically or nationally — restored to possession of the Land of Israel under the kingship of the Messiah himself (Ac 1:6–7&N). For more on what being "saved" means, see Lk 2:11N on "savior."

All Israel will be saved. How can a Jew read these words and not realize that the New Testament holds out the same exalted hope for the Jewish people as does the *Tanakh*? How can a Gentile Christian not see in them a command from God to love the Jewish people and pray for their spiritual and physical well-being? A Messianic Jew experiencing the poignancy of rejection by his own Jewish people, perhaps even by his own family, makes these glorious words his expectation and refuge and prayer. For him it is a joy to contemplate God's answer to the plea of the *Kaddish*, "May he [God] establish his Kingdom during your life and during your days and during the life of all the house of Israel, speedily and at a near time; and say ye, *Amen*." For he has God's irrevocable promise (v. 29) that **all Israel**, the nation of which God has made him an inseparable part, **will** turn to Yeshua the Messiah and **be saved**.

26b–27 Sha'ul combines two passages of Isaiah that speak of Israel in the *Acharit-HaYamim* ("End of Days"), that is, in Messianic times. The Hebrew of Isaiah 59:20–21a reads: "And there will come to Zion a Redeemer, to those who turn from transgression in Ya'akov, says *Adonai*. And as for me, this is my covenant with them, says *Adonai*." Sha'ul quotes the Septuagint version, which, instead of having Jews themselves turning from transgression, has the Redeemer turning away ungodliness from Ya'akov. Despite the textual difference there is no conceptual difficulty, for biblical understanding makes the two go hand in hand: "Turn us, and we shall be turned" (Lamentations 5:21).

The Hebrew of Isaiah 27:9a says, "Therefore by this shall the iniquity of Ya'akov be atoned for" (*y'khupar*, "covered"), "and this is all the fruit of taking away his sin." The Septuagint reads, "Therefore shall the iniquity of Ya'akov be taken away, and this is his blessing when I take away his sin."

Both passages call attention to God's role in taking away sin from Ya'akov, a sin Sha'ul identifies as "stoniness" toward the Messiah. The passages are appropriate, since Sha'ul's object in Chapters 9–11 is to show that despite appearances to the contrary, God's promises will not fail of fulfillment. Thus we are led to the summing-up of vv. 28–29.

28–29 With respect to the Good News they, Israel (v. 26), **are hated** (or: "they are enemies"). Hated by whom? Enemies of whom? Clearly, God — by whom also **they are loved**. Lance Lambert, a Messianic Jewish writer living in Jerusalem, points out that Replacement theologians, who say that "Israel" today means the Church, do not apply their theology to the first clause in this verse! If they did they would have to conclude that God hates the Church!

Clearly it is the Jews who, **with respect to the Good News... are** temporarily **hated** by God **for your sake**, for the sake of you Gentiles, **so that the** Good News can come to you (vv. 11–12&N, 15, 17). **But with respect to being** permanently **chosen** as God's people (v. 26aN), **they are** permanently **loved** by God.

Moreover, if v. 28 speaks of the Jews, then also v. 29 speaks of the Jews: **God's free gifts and his calling** *to the Jews* **are irrevocable**, no matter how much Replacement theologians sputter over it.

Why is God's people permanently loved? Without thinking, a Christian might answer, "Because God *is* love (1 Yn 4:8), it simply flows out of God's essential nature to love his people." Sha'ul's answer may come as a surprise and seem "unspiritual": **for the patriarchs' sake**. God made promises to the Patriarchs, Avraham, Yitzchak and Ya'akov, which he is honor-bound to keep. Protecting his honor is also an essential attribute of God.

The Patriarchs still have a "sake," because they are still alive (Mt 22:32). But the phrase, "**for the patriarchs' sake**," does not express the rabbinic notion of *z'khut-avot*, the "merit of the Fathers." The rabbinic idea is that the good deeds of the ancestors add to the welfare of their descendants. The expression, "*zokher chasdei-avot*" ("You remember the good deeds of the Patriarchs") appears in the first blessing of the *'Amidah*. The concept draws on the fact that the *Torah*, in the second of the Ten Commandments, indicates that the benefits of a person's good deeds extend into the indefinite future.

While it is true that good deeds yield ongoing good consequences, nevertheless, Sha'ul is not saying that the Patriarchs earned God's favor by their meritorious actions, neither for themselves nor for their descendants. Rather, he is speaking of the Patriarchs not as doers of meritorious works but as receivers of God's gracious promises. God made wonderful promises to them concerning their descendants the people of Israel; and he must keep those promises in order to vindicate his own righteousness (3:25–26) and faithfulness (3:3). **For**, given that God is forever righteous and faithful, **God's free gifts**, those promises and indeed all the gifts mentioned at 9:4–5, **and his calling** the Jews to be a people dedicated to God, a holy nation (Exodus 19:6), a light to the Gentiles (Isaiah 42:6, 49:6), **are irrevocable**; because God cannot deny his own eternal nature as a faithful fulfiller of promises.

In the light of Chapters 9–11 in general and these verses in particular, any Christian theology which teaches that God no longer loves the Jews, or that the Jewish people will not receive all the good things God has promised them, contradicts the express teaching of the New Testament (see 9:1–11:36N). Furthermore, such teaching necessarily portrays God as unfaithful and thus less than God, unworthy of being trusted by anyone, Jew, Christian or "other."

30–32 Sha'ul makes a final restatement of his theme, Israel's salvation in history, this time in terms of God's mercy. These three verses look back to 9:15–18, where God's mercy was presented as an aspect of his sovereignty, and forward to 12:1, where his mercies (plural, to Jews and to Gentiles, as seen in these verses) are made the basis and motivation for right action, as prescribed in the next four chapters.

31 By your (you Gentiles') **showing them** (Israel, the Jews) **the same mercy that God has shown you**. These twelve English words render the Greek phrase, "*tô umeterô eleei*," literally, "by your mercy." Grammatically there are three possible ways of understanding these three simple words:

(1) Objective genitive ("by the mercy that has been shown to you Gentiles"),
(2) Subjective genitive ("by the mercy you Gentiles show toward Israel"),
(3) Possessive genitive ("by the mercy you Gentiles have in your possession").
See 3:22N for a discussion of subjective and objective genitive in Greek grammar.

Most translations opt for the first; but by itself this could lead a Gentile reader to conclude that his own role in Israel's salvation is passive. He might conclude, "Somehow, by the mercy God has shown to me, God will show mercy to Israel. I wonder how; I'll wait and see." Or he might remember vv. 11–12 and say, "The mercy God has shown me will make Israel jealous. There isn't much I can do to speed up the process, but I'll be really happy when it happens" — without realizing it will never happen so long as that is his attitude. I do not believe Sha'ul in this verse is promoting Gentile Christian inaction and passivity with regard to the Jews.

On the other hand, the second by itself might cause a Gentile to busy himself with what *he* considers mercy, so that he does not really communicate *God's* mercy. He may decide that it is "mercy" not to "offend" Jews by presenting the Gospel to them. But *God's* mercy centers on what Yeshua the Messiah has done, is doing, and will do; so that showing God's mercy to Israel cannot exclude communicating the Good News of Yeshua to them by word as well as by deed.

The third by itself is too abstract and static — one wonders if it means anything at all.

The normal rules of interpretation require choosing between the grammatical alternatives, because people don't usually mean more than one thing at a time, puns and double-entendres excepted. However, in this case, the nature of God's mercy itself leads me to a rendering which does combine all three senses, because all three are relevant to what Sha'ul is saying.

I am taking here an organic, systemic or holistic approach to grammar, rather than an analytic one, reflecting my conclusion that Sha'ul at this point did the same. Instead of choosing one of the three genitive structures named above, I think he spoke or wrote without analyzing which one would best express his meaning. If you could ask him, I think he would say that all three genitives contribute to and intensify his intended message. And here is why.

A key fact about God's mercy is that it contains within itself a moral imperative not to hold it back. God himself does not withhold his mercy; and anyone who has truly received God's mercy cannot but let himself be a channel for communicating that mercy from God to others. Therefore, the import of what Sha'ul is telling Gentiles is this: "Everything you have from God — your salvation, your righteousness, your hope — comes from God's having shown you his mercy by grafting you into Israel, through your trusting Israel's Messiah. You have that mercy in your possession, and it is wrong for you to hold it back. Therefore, both because you owe it to the people of Israel to display God's mercy toward them, and because God's mercy is in its essence not something that can be hoarded, you are always to be **showing them** (Israel) **the same mercy that God has shown you**.

"But more than that, God has given you Gentiles a unique blessing. The means whereby mercy came to you was 'Israel's disobedience' (v. 30). This implies that non-Messianic Jews played no conscious and intentional part in your coming to trust in Yeshua the Messiah; rather, God used their disobedience for his own purposes. But, in contrast with that, you have the opportunity to be yourselves the conscious and intentional means of blessing Israel. The word '**by**' implies this means. Indeed the very reason that **Israel has been disobedient now** is **so that** ***by means of*** **your showing them the same mercy that God has shown you, they too may now receive God's mercy**. God has blessed you Gentiles by choosing you as his instrument for willingly blessing the Jews."

Sha'ul specifically exhorts Gentiles along these lines at 15:27, and indeed most of the rest of this letter is devoted to instructions about how to express God's mercy to others. And the operative word is "**now**"; used twice in this verse, it gives urgency to the exhortation: Gentiles should show mercy **now** so that unbelieving Jews, **now** disobedient (and therefore headed toward a bad destiny), may **now**, through you, receive God's mercy (and be headed toward a good destiny). Israel's salvation does not depend on some future event for which Christians must passively wait. All that is needed is for Gentile Christians (and Messianic Jews) to show God's mercy to the unsaved of Israel. They can and should do it **now**. *Then*, as well as *thus*, "all Israel will be saved" (first paragraph of v. 26aN).

32 This verse epitomizes simultaneously Chapters 1–8, Chapters 9–11 and the preceding two verses. That **God has shut up all mankind together in disobedience** (compare 3:23) was detailed in regard to Gentile individuals in 1:18–2:16, in regard to Jewish individuals in 2:17–3:20, 5:12–21 and 7:1–24, and in regard to the Jewish people as a nation chosen by God for obedience in most of 9:30–11:29. God's **mercy to all** through Yeshua the Messiah is the topic of most of the rest of Chapters 1–11; in the preceding verse Sha'ul explains that that mercy is transmitted through the Messiah's people, through his Body, through the saved.

God has not caused people to disobey. Rather, once they have disobeyed, God has limited their privileges, "imprisoned" them (Ga 3:21–29&NN), made them subject to punishment (as required by his attribute of perfect justice).

The verse centers on the words, "**so that**," which tell us that the central purpose of all human history is for those who love God to be a vehicle for God's mercy. In the context of vv. 30–31 what this verse says is that while God sovereignly chooses to show mercy to all, he does not act alone but uses means. His preferred means in this present age is to use saved people to convey his mercy to the unsaved.

Thus the expository section of Chapters 9–11 closes by relating God's fulfillment of his promises in history (the *raison d'etre* for these chapters; see 9:1–11:36N) to his purpose in having history at all, which is so that God can manifest his mercy to his creatures. The delay in the fulfillment of the promises to the Jews is so that God can be merciful to Gentiles too.

33–36 The greatness of God's sovereignty, mercy, faithfulness and ordering of history, so that not one of his promises will go unfulfilled, causes Sha'ul to burst into song. He — and we — have caught a glimpse of the working of God's mind and are overwhelmed. Only a hymn of praise to God can escape our lips; it is a fitting climax to Chapters 9–11 in particular and to the first eleven chapters in general.

34–35 In v. 34 Isaiah 40:13 is quoted in the Septuagint version (it is also cited at 1C 2:16). Verse 35 cites Job 41:3(11) to the effect that no one can put God in his debt. In Job 38–41 God not only displays his omnipotence to Job but also intimates that God alone can deal with the forces of evil that would otherwise overwhelm humanity; therefore Job should trust God's inscrutable judgments and unsearchable ways (see 8:3–4N, 9:19–21&N). Indeed, the main point of Chapters 9–11 has been that those who have had doubts about God should set them aside.

36 The three chief areas in which God manifests his nature and his power are alluded to here: creation (**from him**), revelation (**through him**) and redemption (**to him**). Orthodox Judaism has observed that these same themes pervade the whole Bible and find expression in the traditional ways of celebrating *Shabbat* and the other Jewish holidays (see Ac 2:1N).

Amen. As explained in 9:5N (paragraph on "Praised be *Adonai* forever. *Amen*."), this word instructs the congregation hearing the letter read aloud to say, "*Amen*," in response to and agreement with Sha'ul's praise of God.

CHAPTER 12

1 **Therefore** (see 8:1N), because of everything God has done and is doing in Chapters 1–11, **I exhort you** to do everything in Chapters 12–15, all of which is epitomized in the instruction to **offer yourselves as a sacrifice.** Compare Ep 4:1&N.

God's mercies were spoken of throughout Chapters 1–11, especially in Chapters 9–11, and explicitly at 11:30–32&N. God's mercies form the pivot of the book of Romans, on which Sha'ul turns from doctrine to the practical advice introduced by the Greek word "*parakalô*" ("**I exhort**" or: "I advise, counsel, encourage, request, comfort").

Offer yourselves (literally, "your bodies") **as a sacrifice** — a striking metaphor when animal sacrifices were still being made twice daily in the Jerusalem **Temple worship**. At 6:1–14 and 8:13 Sha'ul explained what kind of death is required: the believer is not to live by his old nature but by the Spirit: then he will be **living** with the Messiah's life (8:10–11) and thereby be **set apart for God**.

It is the logical "Temple worship" for you. KJV has "...which is your reasonable service." Greek *latreia* corresponds to Hebrew *'avodah*, which can mean "work, service," in the everyday sense (the cognate *'eved* means "slave"); and this is what today's reader mistakenly picks up from the archaic expression in KJV. But "*'avodah*" is also the technical term for the religious "service" performed in the Temple; and the context demands this meaning here.

2 Presenting God your body for right action commences with **your mind**. Turn from **the standards of the *'olam hazeh*** ("this world"), rooted, as they are, in everything but God and his word; and learn **what God wants**. After consideration you will **agree** that what he wants is morally **good**, psychologically **satisfying** and in practice **able to succeed** (or: "able to reach the goal," Greek *teleion*, sometimes rendered "perfect" but here strongly connoting the goal-orientation and accomplishment inherent in the related word "*telos*," as explained in 10:4N).

3 The warning to Gentiles against boasting and conceit (11:18, 25) is extended to **every single one of you**, because a person committed to doing God's will (v. 2) is easy prey to delusions of grandeur.

The standard which God has given to each of you, namely, trust. Or: "the standard of trust" (or: "faithfulness"), namely, that of Yeshua, "that God has given to each." Or: "the amount and particular pattern of trust that God has given to each."

12:4–13:10 This passage carries on the thought introduced in v. 3. Compare 1 Corinthians 12–14, which covers much the same subject matter. God's people are an organic unity, a body (vv. 4–5). Each member of the body is given gifts (vv. 6–8) meant to be used properly and not abused (vv. 6–21), within an overall framework of love (vv. 9–13, 13:8–10) in which evil is to be overcome with good (12:14–13:7).

Or, looking at it from a different perspective, Sha'ul is setting up general guidelines for Messianic communal life. The Jewish people already had such guidelines in the *Torah*; here transcultural elements (see Ga 1:17N) are extracted and applied. Even today the Church can learn much about communal consciousness, caring and belonging from the Jewish community's way of functioning.

4–5 People often think of membership in a synagogue or church as a matter of personal choice. But biblically, membership is organic, comparable with the relationship which members (**parts**) of the natural body have with each other, each with its own **function** but needing for its well-being the services of parts having other functions, and all contributing to the good of the entire body, whose life-energy is supplied by God. Compare 1C 7:4, 12:12; Ep 4:11–16.

6–8 God gives **gifts** (Greek *charismata*; see 1 Corinthians 12:8–10&N) to all believers and **grace** (*charis*) suited to each gift. For example, the grace accompanying **leadership** is **diligence** and **zeal**. In the context of v. 3, it is clear that boasting about one's gifts is altogether out of place (compare 3:27; 1C 1:29–31, 4:7). Boasting kills unity.

Prophecy, literally, "speaking on behalf of," in this case on behalf of God: the *Ruach HaKodesh* either gives supernatural insight or makes use of one's own natural talents. Prophecy may be, but need not be, predictive.

Counselor... comfort and exhort. See on "*parakalô*," v. 1N.

8–21 It is easy to find Jewish parallels to Sha'ul's ethical teachings (but on what they signify, see the cautions in Mt 6:7N). Compare the end of v. 8 with this passage from the Mishna:

> "The world is upheld by three things — *Torah*, temple worship and acts of mercy." (Avot 1:2)

Compare v. 15 with this citation from the Gemara:

> "A person should share in the distress of the community." (Ta'anit 11a)

Compare v. 17 with this *mishna*:

> "One should be guiltless before other people as well as before God, for it says, 'You shall be guiltless before God and before Israel' (Numbers 32:22)." (Sh'kalim 3:2)

Verses 19–20 quote from the *Tanakh* itself. Furthermore, the very grammar of vv. 9–13, which contains only participles and no finite verbs, is what is found in Hebrew codes, not Greek; this suggests a very early Hebrew source.

In connection with Yeshua's Sermon on the Mount I pointed out that there is no reason to expect New Testament ethics to differ from *Tanakh* ethics, since God does not change. All the advice found in these verses is implicit in the *Torah* and the Prophets, and frequently explicit as well. Because Gentiles are not bound by *Torah* in the same way as Jews, and because the Holy Spirit does his work from within, Sha'ul draws out for believers the core principles of right action, confident that persons with transformed minds (v. 1) will, by the power of the *Ruach HaKodesh*, be able to apply those principles in particular situations.

Most of the teaching is self-explanatory and yields its implications to anyone who will think. Example: v. 21, **Do not be conquered by evil** — retaliation means you have been conquered both by your enemy, whom you have allowed to take the initiative and provoke you to give tit for tat, and by your own old nature's evil impulses, which you ought to be suppressing (8:1–13).

CHAPTER 13

1–7 Having discussed believers' relationships with each other and with nonbelievers (12:4–21), Sha'ul naturally turns to how they should relate to the chief external institution, the state (see also 1 Ke 2:13–17). His advice, which can be seen as an application of 12:21, corresponds to Judaism's "*Dina dimalkuta dina*," Aramaic for "The law of the kingdom is Law," *Torah* to be obeyed as if God had commanded it (see Mt 22:21N).

Does this mean that believers should obey the wicked laws of an evil government — the Nazis, the Communists, other totalitarian regimes? No, because this rule does not stand by itself in Scripture; it must be set against Ac 5:29 ("We must obey God, not men") when the will of the state and the will of God conflict (see v. 7N). The early Christians refused to offer incense to statues of the Roman emperor because such idolatry would have been disobedience to God; they paid with their lives. Jews too have been martyred *'al kiddush haShem* ("for the sake of sanctifying the Name" of God; see Ac 7:59–60N) when they refused conversion to a Christianity which was incapable of communicating either its truth or its Jewishness, with the result that Jews perceived it as idolatry. The implications of Scripture for civil disobedience in the modern sense — that is, for a moral cause, presumably also a selfless one — deserves attention that cannot be given here.

7 Compare Mt 22:21 (KJV), "Render therefore unto Caesar the things that are Caesar's, and unto God the things that are God's." Richard Wurmbrand, a Jewish believer in Yeshua who was imprisoned and tortured for his faith for fourteen years in Communist Romania, says that what such an evil government should be rendered is a hard kick in the pants. But, he adds, the officials of that government should be loved, since they are created in God's image, the Messiah loves them, and we are to imitate the Messiah (1C 11:1). (His ministry consists in smuggling Bibles into countries that restrict their production, import or use — a good example of obeying God rather than man.)

8–10 Yeshua said that all the *Torah* and the Prophets depend on two commandments — loving God, as commanded in the *Sh'ma* (Deuteronomy 6:5), and loving one's neighbor as oneself (Leviticus 19:18); see Mk 12:28–34&NN. Sha'ul quotes four of the five commandments in the "Second Table" of the Law, those which concern behavior toward other people; Yeshua did the same (Mt 19:16–20). Rabbi Chiyya equated Leviticus 19:18 with one of the "Second Table" commandments, the prohibition against coveting (Leviticus Rabbah 24:5); likewise Rabbi Akiva recognized Leviticus 19:18 as a great principle of *Torah* (Genesis Rabbah 24:7). Sha'ul's point in these verses is not to abrogate specific commands but to show that the principle of loving one's neighbor, which is the pervading theme of everything from 12:9 till here, must underlie all halakhic applications and will, when appropriated by the power of the *Ruach HaKodesh*, lead to right behavior in daily life. This is how **love is the fullness of *Torah***— not by superseding it, but through being the beginning, the end and the motivating force at work in it. (See also Ga 5:14N.)

The discussion over whether Messianic Jews should keep the Law (see Ac 21:21N and *Messianic Jewish Manifesto*, Chapter V, entitled "*Torah*") must consider these verses. On the one hand, Jewish critics say that feeling love is no guarantee of right action, so that halakhic rules for specific situations are necessary. Without them, they say, people will abuse the principle of love by ignoring precedents and even God's specific commands on the ground that love has "replaced" them, and this will ultimately lead to disobeying the command to love as well! As "Exhibit A" these critics point to the notable lack of love of Christians toward Jews at various times in the last two thousand years.

On the other hand, certain Christian theologians, especially those who follow Lutheran tradition, such as Helmut Thielicke and Dietrich Bonhoeffer, will have nothing to do with specific guidelines. They fear these could "quench the Spirit" (1 Th 5:19), reducing obedience to mere rule-following, legalistic "works of law" that cannot save (3:28; 3:20aN).

Messianic Jews live with that tension. But so do Gentile Christians, and likewise non-Messianic Jews. For even the most orthodox Jew, even one who, for the sake of argument, knows every halakhic decision ever made, would, as a practical matter, have to reach his own conclusions as to what the Law requires of him, at least in boundary-line situations; and if, at such moments, he is not operating in love, his decisions will be wrong. Conversely, an approach which disregards legal rules and precedents guarantees a lower standard of ethical action, since each individual will have to "reinvent the wheel" as he rediscovers for himself accumulated wisdom and expertise.

I think the best position avoids both the wooden application of law and the unreliability of subjective love-feelings. It combines the sensitivity of Spirit-inspired love (which is more than a mere feeling; it implies loving action) with respect for ethical instruction, *halakhah* and other law, seeking to draw from the full complement of God-given human and supernatural resources the right and loving responses in all circumstances.

Moreover, the supposed conflict between traditional Jewish doctrine and New Testament is sometimes illusory. Consider Sifre to Deuteronomy 79b (4th century C. E.), which asks why Deuteronomy 11:13 (the verse commencing the second paragraph of the *Sh'ma*) includes the phrase, "to love *Adonai* your God":

> "It is because you might otherwise say, 'Look, I learn *Torah* in order to get rich,' or '...in order to be called "Rabbi,"' or '...in order to earn a salary.' But Scripture says, '...to love *Adonai* your God.' In other words, all that you do should be done only out of love."

11 The urgency of the historical moment makes right behavior all the more important. Jewish writings of the period too regarded the **final deliverance** as imminent:

> "In those days the Elect One will arise and choose the righteous and holy from among them, because the day for their being saved has come near." (Enoch 51:1b–2)
>
> "For truly my redemption has drawn near; it is not far distant as it was before." (2 Baruch 23:7)

12–13 **Night** and **day**, also **darkness** and **light**, as metaphors for evil and good are found in the Gospel of Yochanan (see Yn 8:12&N), in the *Tanakh* (for example, Isaiah 60:1ff.), and in the Dead Sea Scrolls of the Essenes, who separated themselves from what they considered the decadent and immoral life fostered by the establishment Judaism of their time. In addition, **day** and **daytime** are metaphors for the *'olam haba*, the age to come.

14 **Clothe yourselves with the Lord Yeshua**. Compare Isaiah 61:10:

> "I will greatly rejoice in *Adonai*;
> my soul will be joyful in my God.
>
> "For he has clothed me with the garments of salvation,
> he has covered me with a robe of righteousness."

The Hebrew word for "salvation" in this passage is "*yesha'*," related to "Yeshua," which also means "salvation." Compare Rv 19:8.

CHAPTER 14

14:1–15:6 Among believers there are two groups, those with "strong trust" and those with "weak trust." The latter are depicted in this passage as feeling they must abstain from meat or wine and/or observe certain days as holy, while the former feel no such compunctions.

On the basis of this passage Messianic Jews are sometimes asked by Gentile Christians to stop observing Jewish holidays or keeping *kosher*. Or they are criticized as having "weak faith" if they adhere to Jewish practices. But the specifics of the passage are clearly in a Gentile cultural and religious context, not a Jewish one. It does not teach that following Jewish practices is a sign of "weak faith." Rather, it exhorts believers, Jewish or Gentile, whose trust is "strong" not to look down on those whose trust they consider "weak" — precisely the opposite of the behavior described above.

The passage also teaches the "weak" not to pass judgment on the "strong" for failing to observe practices the "weak" consider important, since all believers are equal before the God who has delivered them. Invidious distinctions and disputes should give way to caring for one another and mutual upbuilding, in imitation of the Messiah. The rabbis too teach that the gifted, the rich and the learned should not boast against those who have not received those blessings from God. They too teach against having a "holier-than-thou" attitude. They too teach that all in Israel should care for each other and build up the community.

The problem in the passage does not come from the behavior it teaches but from identifying precisely who are the "strong" and the "weak" and drawing out the implications. The four most frequently offered candidates are these (of them, (4) is correct):

(1) The weak are Gentile Christians who abstain from what has been sacrificed to idols, as in 1 Corinthians 8 and 10. But Sha'ul does not deal here with idol-worship as a problem, even though there are at least a dozen parallels between this passage and that one.

(2) The weak are legalists, either Gentile or Jewish believers, either Judaizers (Ga 2:14b&N) or of some other stripe, who believe they earn a righteous status before God by their works. But a major point of the book of Romans is precisely that such persons are not merely "weak" in trust but utterly lacking in it, unbelievers not believers; whereas here the weak in trust are clearly portrayed as believers.

(3) Many interpreters bring to this passage a presupposition that the New Testament abrogates the ceremonial and ritual details of the Jewish Law, such as *kashrut* and the Jewish holidays. They see the weak as Messianic Jews who still observe these "Jewish details" because they have not yet realized that there is no longer any need to do so. According to this understanding Gentile Christians, along with Jewish believers who have "freed themselves from the Law," are not to look down on their "weaker brothers" for abstaining from pork, celebrating Passover or fasting on *Yom-Kippur*. On the other hand, Messianic Jews who do practice these customs have no ground for a "holier-than-thou" attitude toward those who do not. Quite the contrary: not only have they a direct command not to pass judgment on their brothers who do not keep the Law, but there is implicit in this interpretation an indirect, subliminal message to aspire to the "strong faith" that will "free them from the Law."

In Chapter V of my *Messianic Jewish Manifesto* I have explained why I do not believe the New Testament abrogates the *Torah*. It is true that Yeshua's sacrifice alters the meaning of Temple sacrifices and perhaps eliminates the need for at least some of them (see Messianic Jews 7–10&NN). But it is also true that the New Testament itself "has been given as *Torah*" (MJ 8:6b&N); as a result *Torah* itself has been transformed (MJ 7:12&N). In particular, Gentiles have been brought into an expanded Messianic people of God (above, 11:23–24&N); and the relationships between Jews and Gentiles in this new Messianic people of God have been spelled out (e.g., in Acts 15, in the book of Galatians, and at 15:27 below). Yet the major changes are not in the *Torah* itself but in how to apply it, how to establish priorities among conflicting commands that might govern a particular situation (see Yn 7:22–23&N, Ga 2:12b&N). Such changes are not so much in the content of *Torah* as in the hearts of those entrusted with determining how to use it (Mt 18:18–20&NN). Yeshua himself said he did not "come to abolish the *Torah*" (Mt 5:17&N); it distorts his statement if it is interpreted to mean that he came to abolish the ritual, ceremonial and civil aspects of the Law and to preserve only the moral aspects.

In any case, it is clear from the passage itself that the "weak" cannot be equated with observant Messianic Jews. For nothing in Judaism requires a Jew to be a vegetarian (v. 2). It is argued that *kosher* food might not have been available. But

Rome had a large Jewish colony (Ac 28:17N); it is unthinkable that it would not have had a *shochet* (ritual slaughterer). It is argued that the *shochet* might have been unwilling to sell to Messianic Jews. But this is a gratuitous assumption for which there is no evidence, and the willingness of the Jewish leaders of Rome to come and listen to Sha'ul (Ac 28:17ff.) argues against it. Also nothing in Judaism requires a Jew to refrain from wine (v. 21); the only exceptions are Nazirites during the period of their vow and *cohanim* on duty. On the contrary, wine-drinking is so much a part of Jewish ritual that it is lent an aura of sanctity which, at least until recently, made alcoholism very uncommon among Jews.

For these many reasons we conclude that the "weak" cannot be Messianic Jews who are "not yet free from the Law."

(4) The weak are believers, either Gentile or Jewish, who have not yet grown sufficiently in their faith to have given up attachment to various ascetic practices and calendar observances. Their tie to these activities, however, is not supported by a rational though mistaken ideology, as with the legalists of (2) above. Rather, it is irrational and emotional, linked to psychological needs, social pressures or superstition, or it may simply be a matter of habit. When their activities in these areas are questioned in "arguments over opinions" (v. 1), they are not "fully convinced in their own minds" (v. 5), not "free of self-doubt" (v. 22), but rather easily "upset" or even "destroyed" (v. 15) and thus able to "fall away" or "stumble" (vv. 20–21). This is why Sha'ul calls them "weak."

At least four distinct groups of people fit the description:

(a) First are Gentiles who, as in (1), want to avoid the appearance of evil by maintaining physical and emotional distance from anything that reminds them of their previous idolatrous practices. In this category should also be included anyone, Jewish or Gentile, who wants to avoid the trappings of his former sinful way of life.

I once met a musician who had been addicted to heroin and under its influence had used his guitar to express the anguish of his existence in desperate, despondent blues. On coming to faith he not only stopped using drugs but destroyed his record collection and his guitar; two years later he still felt himself too "weak" in his faith to play his instrument. Making music is obviously not a sin, but he was afraid that playing guitar might resuscitate his habits of the "bad old days." For the sake of his own soul and sanity he constructed this "fence around the law" for himself.

(b) Second are Gentiles who adopted elements of Jewish practice as part of their faith along with believing in Yeshua. They have, as it were, bought what they considered a whole package and have not yet unwrapped it and decided what is really important for them. In the first century the phenomenon was common enough to require considerable attention in the New Testament (Acts 15 and the whole book of Galatians, for starters). Today it rarely happens in relation to Jewish practices, but it is very common for someone to accept Yeshua in a particular Christian setting and only afterwards discover that some of the practices he has picked up in that setting are not essential to his faith.

(c) Third are Gentiles or Jews who have brought into their faith practices found in other religions with which they are familiar. These practices often appeal to their religiosity but are irrelevant or even contrary to the Gospel. I have known people saved out of New Age religions who continued yoga-style meditation until they realized it was harmful.

(d) Fourth are Messianic Jews who have not grasped how the incorporation of the New Covenant into God's *Torah* and the presence of the Holy Spirit in themselves alters the way in which the *Torah* is to be applied. They therefore feel a compulsiveness about observing ceremonial and ritual details. When their faith grows stronger they will be free not from the Law but from this compulsiveness.

But "weak" is the wrong word for Messianic Jews who have decided out of conviction to observe the Law as interpreted by the rabbis in the same way as a non-Messianic Jew would, except for such parts of it as they believe might conflict with the Gospel. Their reasons might be, for example, in order to strengthen their sense of Jewish identity, or to demonstrate that believing in Yeshua does not turn a Jew into a Gentile, or to help preserve the Jewish community by upholding its distinctives publicly. Or they might simply be satisfied that in most instances the rabbinic directives and principles adequately express God's will. So long as they do not impose their pattern on others but uphold the unity of Jews and Gentiles in the Body of the Messiah, neither passing judgment nor looking down on those who behave or believe differently, they are among the "strong in trust," not "weaker brothers."

1 To **welcome** someone only in order to lure him into a futile dispute, or, equally, to welcome someone who comes only to argue, is not the "love" of 12:8–10 and 13:8–10 but the "quarreling" condemned at 13:13.

2 **Eats anything... only vegetables**. Sha'ul is not proposing that the Jewish dietary laws have been abrogated. See 14:1–15:6N above and also Mk 7:19N, Ac 10:17–19N, Ga 2:11–16&NN.

3–4 Sha'ul chooses his words carefully in order to pinpoint the sin of each. **The one who eats anything** might take pride in having thought the matter through and freed himself from his fears and compulsions; therefore he might **look down on** his duller, weaker brother, with his self-created fence around his self-created law. But **the abstainer** is more likely to develop a "holier-than-thou" attitude and **pass judgment on** the other as careless or a libertine. In this letter, boasting has already been condemned at 1:22, 30; 2:17–27; 3:27–4:2; 11:18, 25; 12:3ff.; and judging at 2:1–3.

5 **One person considers some days more holy than others**. The reference is not specifically to Jewish holidays but to any days that any believer might have come to regard as especially holy. This is because the "weak" are not specifically Jewish believers, but any believers attached to particular calendar observances (see Section (4) of 14:1–15:6N).

Each should **be fully convinced in his own mind**. This principle for dealing with doctrinal and practical disputes applies to *adiaphora* (matters about which the Bible is indifferent) and must be balanced against 2 Ti 3:16, "All Scripture is God-breathed and is valuable for teaching the truth, convicting of sin, correcting faults and training in right living." Where Scripture gives a clear word, personal opinion must give way. But where the Word of God is subject to various possible interpretations, let each be persuaded in his own mind while at the same time "outdoing one another in showing respect for each other" (12:10).

6–12 Judging and boasting do not befit people whose standing before God is equal. Verse 11 quotes Isaiah 45:23, also cited by Sha'ul at Pp 2:10 in a similar context (and compare 15:1–3 below with Pp 2:1–8).

12 Compare the Mishna:

> "[Rabbi El'azar HaKappar (late 2nd century C.E.)] used to say, 'Those who are born will die, and the dead will be raised to life again, and the living [that is, the resurrected] will be judged, so that people will know, make known and understand that he is God, the Maker, the Creator, the Discerner, the Judge, the Witness and the Plaintiff; and that it is he who will judge; and with him there is no guile, forgetfulness, respect of persons or taking of bribes; for everything is already his. Understand that everything is according to the reckoning of the account — do not let your *yetzer* [(evil) inclination] lull you in to hoping that the grave will be a refuge for you [that is, that there will be no future judgment]. For it is not by your own will but in spite of yourself that you were created and born, that you go on living, that you will die, and that you will have to give account before the King over kings of kings, the Holy One, blessed be he.'"(Avot 4:22)

13 The teaching of this verse, which expresses the central point of this chapter, is a *midrash* on Leviticus 19:14, which says, "You are not to place a stumblingblock before the blind," or, more generally, you are not to bring cruel intended harm upon someone who is helpless. The rabbis interpreted "blind" metaphorically to mean those unlearned in *Torah* (Sifra to Leviticus 19:14, Bava Metzia 75b, 'Avodah Zarah 21b–22a). This meaning for "blind" would include both those whom Sha'ul calls weak in trust and those whom he considers strong in trust but inclined to pride; until their attitudes change both are relatively helpless, and it is wrong to cause them to commit sin, either in fact or in their own opinion.

14 **Nothing is unclean in itself**. Sha'ul is certainly not espousing moral relativism. His remark has to do not with human behavior but with *tum'ah* ("ritual uncleanliness"). It is not surprising that Sha'ul, having alluded in the previous verse to Leviticus 19, a chapter full of commandments about *tum'ah*, continues with a dictum on that subject. It is, nevertheless, a surprising conclusion for a Jewish scholar who sat at the feet of *Rabban* Gamli'el to reach; indeed he had to be **persuaded by the Lord Yeshua the Messiah** himself. For the concept of *tum'ah* pervades not only the Mishna, one of whose six major divisions, *Taharot* ("Ritual Cleanlinesses"), has this as its central topic, but the Pentateuch itself, especially Leviticus 11–17. The Bible does not always explain why some things are pure and others not. Hygiene is not the issue; for if it were, there would be no reason to exclude Gentiles from the application of these laws. And the rabbis do not speculate much on the reasons. Since the laws of ritual purity apply to Jews only, the statement that nothing is unclean in itself should suffice to free any Gentile whose conscience still bothers him in regard to such matters. As for Jews, even in rabbinic Judaism most of the purity laws gradually fell into disuse (see *Encyclopedia Judaica* 14:1412). Developing a comprehensive Messianic Jewish theology of ritual impurity is beyond the scope of this commentary. For related issues see Mk 7:1–23&NN, Ac 21:24&N, Ga 2:12bN, MJ 13:4&N.

16 **Do not let what you know is good**, that one need not be in bondage to rules about food, **be spoken of as bad**, as a result of your flaunting your freedom to eat as you wish.

21–22 Compare the Talmud:

> "It was taught: If there are things which are allowed but which some treat as prohibited, you must not permit them in their presence." (N'darim 15a)

23 **Anything not based on trust is a sin**. One could call this the principal axiom of New Covenant thinking and behavior.

CHAPTER 15

1–6 The discussion of Chapter 14 is concluded (see 14:1–15:6N) by upholding Yeshua himself as our example.

3–4 Psalm 69, cited here, is prophetic and Messianic throughout and is the third most frequently quoted Psalm in the New Testament (after Psalms 110 and 118) — see Mt 27:34, 48; Mk 15:35; Lk 23:36; Yn 2:17, 15:25; Ac 1:20; Rv 3:5, 16:1; and above, 11:9–10. In the original, a persecuted servant of God is addressing God; in the present context that servant is seen to be Yeshua the Messiah.

Sha'ul sees behind the *p'shat* ("plain sense") of the text of Psalm 69:10(9) a *remez* ("hint"; see 2:28–29N, Mt 2:15N) about Yeshua. This shows one of the ways in which **everything written in the past was written to teach us**, where "us" notably includes Gentile Christians, even though the *Tanakh* was not originally written for them (compare 1C 10:5–11, 1 Ti 3:16).

Christian seminarians under pressure sometimes make jokes about "sermons based on Leviticus," implying that they consider much of the *Tanakh* boring, with little to say to Christians. (Were they familiar with Jewish literature they would realize how rich the book of Leviticus is for everyone; see, for example, the popular commentary on it by the Messianic Jewish scholar Louis Goldberg). Many Christians go further and simply discard the Old Testament in favor of the New. They are not usually explicit about it. Instead they acknowledge verbally that the Old Testament is inspired by God, but in practice they ignore most of it. No wonder Jews often regard the *Tanakh* as the Jewish Bible and the New Testament as the Christian Bible — Christians have fostered that impression by their own attitudes and behavior!

But Christians who weight the New Testament above the Old not only disparage Sha'ul's teaching and ignore the example of himself, the other New Testament authors and Yeshua; but they deprive themselves of the **encouragement**, comfort and good counsel (12:1N) that **the *Tanakh*** offers in helping believers **patiently to hold on to** their

hope of complete salvation (as spelled out earlier, 8:17–30). Also, they are the ones most likely to fall prey to antisemitism in the Church, since they remove themselves from three-quarters of God's inspired Word, which gives the fundamental and unshakeable ground for their identifying with the Jews as God's people (see vv. 7–33&NN).

7–33 Gentile Christian identification with and service to God's people the Jews is a major theme of this section.

7–9a Verse 7 makes a transition between the previous topic (14:1–15:6&N) and what follows; vv. 8–9a present the proposition forming the basis of the discussion which continues to the end of the chapter.

The Messiah became a servant of the Jewish people. It is not true that Yeshua is the Christian Messiah, while the Jews are waiting for someone else. He is the Messiah of the Jews. If he is not the Jewish Messiah, the Christians have no Messiah.

Sha'ul focuses on two reasons for Yeshua's becoming a servant of the Jews: **to show God's truthfulness** and **to show** God's **mercy**. God's truthfulness, faithfulness and reliability are certain (8:31–39). Though one might question this because not all Jews have followed Yeshua, God will make **good his promises to the Patriarchs** (11:28–29), and he will do this through his **servant of the Jewish people**, Yeshua the Messiah. This has already been thoroughly discussed in Chapters 9–11.

9–12 God's **mercy** is demonstrated by **causing the Gentiles to glorify God.** Sha'ul has not yet treated this, so he opens, as he did with God's truthfulness, by citing Scripture texts as evidence. He adduces them from all four major sections of **the *Tanakh***: from the Former Prophets (2 Samuel 22:50), the Pentateuch (Deuteronomy 22:43), the Writings (Psalm 117:1) and the Latter Prophets (Isaiah 11:10). Every part of the *Tanakh* witnesses to the inclusion of Gentiles in the people of God.

14–33 The passages quoted in vv. 9–12 illustrate two themes that opened this letter (1:5–16) — his own ministry (including his projected visit to Rome and Spain) and his readers' role in it.

17–19 Sha'ul does not disobey his own injunction against boasting, because his boasting is never about himself but about **what the Messiah has accomplished.**

21 The quotation of one verse implies the quotation of the entire passage that forms its context, as explained at 3:3–4N. Here the context is Isaiah 52:13–53:12, the passage of the *Tanakh* which most clearly foreshadows Yeshua.

24, 28 Why **Spain**? Because apparently "the Messiah was not yet known" in that province (v. 20). Scholars differ over whether he succeeded in getting there (see Ac 28:31N).

25–26 Years earlier the leaders of the Jerusalem Messianic community had enjoined Sha'ul to "remember the poor" (Ga 2:10). He wrote about the present collection on their behalf at 1C 16:1–4 and 2C 8:1–9:15. So well did he succeed in making Gentile *tzedakah* ("charity"; Mt 6:1–4N) toward the Jewish poor a part of his Gospel that this project was initiated not by him but by the believers in **Macedonia and Achaia.** The gift was duly delivered (Ac 24:17).

27 Obedience in doing *tzedakah* should be with joy — **they were pleased to do it**, "God loves a cheerful giver" (2C 9:7) — for this reflects the fellowship between Messianic Jews and Gentile Christians that Sha'ul is at pains to inculcate (11:11–32). In v. 26 the word translated "contribution" (in this and all versions) is "*koinônia*," literally, "fellowship"; genuine fellowship implies a willingness to give and share.

But there is a more basic ground, **duty** (compare 1C 9:14, Ga 6:6). Because **the Gentiles have shared with the Jews in** the **spiritual matters** listed in 9:4–5, Gentile believers have an obligation **to help the Jews in material matters**, simply out of gratitude (Sha'ul makes the same point at 1C 9:11). This verse does not restrict the material help only to Jews who believe; there is no creedal test for Jews to be eligible for help from Gentile Christians. Many Gentile Christians obey this broader understanding, contributing generously to the State of Israel and other Jewish causes and charities not in the hands of Jewish believers.

On the other hand, in vv. 25 and 31 the word for "God's people" is "*agioi*" ("holy ones" or "saints"), always used by Sha'ul to denote believers; so that in context the "Jews" of the present verse are believers. On this point Gentile Christians have a less clear record, for they are rarely taught to assist the Messianic Jewish community. Nowhere in the world do Messianic Jews operate from a position of numerical or material strength. Among Israel's 4,200,000 Jews (1992), not more than 3,000 are Messianic, by most estimates. Among the United States' 250,000,000 people, of whom 5,800,000 are Jewish, the Messianic Jews number perhaps 100,000. At the risk of being labeled a *shnorrer* (Yiddish for "beggar" and sometimes applied to fundraisers), I entreat Gentile Christians who believe God's Word to obey Romans 15:27 by assisting Messianic Jewish congregations, organizations and individuals.

31 Sha'ul urged the Romans to pray **that I may be rescued from the unbelievers** (literally, "the disobedient") **in Y'hudah**. According to 1 Th 2:14–16&NN it was especially the Judean nonbelievers who took affront at Sha'ul (see also Ac 21:27&N). His prayer was answered, perhaps more literally than Sha'ul had wished, at Ac 21:32ff.; and it was in direct consequence that he eventually realized his desire to come to Rome (Ac 28:16).

And that my service (or possibly "Temple worship" in the sense of 12:1&N) **for Yerushalayim may be acceptable to God's people there.** Why would they refuse a gift? Aside from aversion to "becoming a charity case," there was resentment even among believers at Sha'ul's ministry to the Gentiles, even though the Jerusalem leadership stood solidly with him. In the 19th century Tübingen School of Christian theologians developed the idea that there was a sharp conflict between the Jewish-oriented leaders in Jerusalem and the Gentile-oriented Paul, and the idea continues cropping up in the works of scholars to this day; but the New Testament does not support it; see Acts 10–11, 15, 21; Ga 2:1–10. Nevertheless the relationship between Sha'ul and some of those not in leadership positions had its frictions, and his temper may have added to the heat. Yet from Ac 21:17–19 and 24:17 it is reasonable to infer that the Messianic community in Yerushalayim "received this fruit" (v. 28).

CHAPTER 16

1 Phoebe, *shammash* of the congregation. She was either its only *shammash*, or one among several. It is possible that the Greek word *"diakonos,"* with the root meaning "runner of errands," should be taken here to mean "servant" or "worker" in a general sense, as is usually the case in the New Testament. But there is good reason to think that in this instance it is a technical term denoting someone ordained to a recognized office in the congregation and having the duty of caring for its practical affairs, as at Ac 6:6. The usual English term for this office is "deacon," which transliterates the Greek word; and the closest Hebrew equivalent is "*shammash*" (Yiddish "*shammes*"), the person who handles the day-to-day practical tasks of keeping a synagogue going.

In an age where feminism is an issue, it should be noted not only that this woman held a prominent office in the Cenchrean congregation, but that the word *"diakonos"* is a masculine, not a feminine, form. Phoebe was a "deacon," not a "deaconess" (as some English versions render the word). See 1 Ti 3:8–13 for the qualifications of a *shammash*.

3–5 Priscilla and Aquila. See Ac 18:1–3. Continuing the theme of v. 1N, the mention of the woman first may indicate her greater prominence (see Ac 18:18&N). It is not known on what occasion they **risked their necks** for Sha'ul; they may have had such a role in the Ephesus disturbance of Ac 19:23–40, since it seems to have been there that they hosted a congregation in their home (see 1C 16:19, Ac 19:10), just as they did in Rome.

The congregation that meets in their house. The Greek word for "congregation" is "*ekklêsia*," which most English translations render "church" (see Mt 16:18N). "*Ekklêsia*" means "called-out ones" and thus refers to the people, not a building, as is clear from this verse. It sometimes means the entire number of believers united with the Messiah throughout history, or all the believers in a particular city (either at a particular time or over a period of time), but here it means a local congregation. The New Testament considers it the norm for believers to meet together regularly (compare 1C 16:1–2, MJ 10:24–25).

7 Relatives (family members) or, alternatively, "fellow-kinsmen, fellow-countrymen" that is, other Messianic Jews; compare 9:3.

Junia, perhaps the wife of **Andronicus**; some think the name is masculine, but this is unlikely (the masculine-form name is Junius). The matter takes on importance from the remark that they were **well known among the emissaries**, which may mean not that they were well known *to* the emissaries, but that they were themselves well-known emissaries. If so, this would be the only instance of a female emissary in the New Testament.

12 Three more women are singled out here and another two in vv. 13, 15.

13 At Mk 15:21 Shim'on of Cyrene is called "the father of Alexander and Rufus." This **Rufus** may be the same.

16 Greet each other with a holy kiss — a Middle-Eastern custom. In recent years hugging and holy kissing has come back in vogue in some other countries as well, after centuries of being out of fashion (a handshake is obviously a much weaker expression of body language). When between members of the opposite sex, care must be taken that it is a holy kiss and not an unholy one! More generally, in an age of transition when customs are changing, the principle of Chapter 14, not causing distress to another for whom the Messiah died, applies here: those who experience discomfort from a given form of body expression should not be made to suffer it against their will.

17 **Those who cause divisions**, either by "looking down" or "judging" (14:3) or by opposing the sound doctrine set forth in this letter.

18 **By smooth talk and flattery they deceive the innocent**, because, as Proverbs 14:15 puts it, "The simple believe every word."

19 **Be innocent concerning evil**, "harmless as doves" (Mt 10:16). There is no need for a believer to occupy himself with the details of evil or how it is accomplished. Folk wisdom is rightly suspicious of the censor who spends hours poring over pornography, ostensibly to protect the public from it.

20 **God, the source of *shalom*** (peace, wholeness; the same phrase is used at 15:33) **will soon crush the Adversary**, Satan, the ultimate source of all opposition to God (see Mt 4:1N) **under your feet**. This imagery draws on Genesis 3:15; compare Lk 10:19, MJ 2:7–9, and a Jewish work written around 108 B.C.E., the Testament of Levi 18:12:

> "And Beliar [a variant of B'liya'al, another name for Satan, as at 2C 6:15] will be bound by him [the "new priest" that the Lord will raise up, 18:2], and he will give power to his children to tread on evil spirits."

According to Genesis 3:15 it is the "seed of the woman," understood at Ga 4:4 to be the Messiah, who will "bruise" or "crush" the serpent's "head." But here it is ***God*** who **will... crush the Adversary under *your* feet**. Therefore, by implication Yeshua is identified both with God and with those who trust in him (see Mt 2:15N).

21 **Timothy**. See Ac 16:1–3&NN and Sha'ul's two letters to him.

22 **Tertius, the one writing down this letter**. Sha'ul's secretary.

25–27 A final poetic greeting which sums up the message of the whole book. Sha'ul repeats his reference to the **secret truth... kept hidden for ages** (see 11:25&N, Ep 1:9&N, 3:3–9) and once again uses the phrase, "**trust-grounded obedience**" (1:5a&N), which expresses what he hopes to foster by writing this letter. Important as is the work of **Yeshua the Messiah** (Chapters 3–8), he is nevertheless subordinate to God the Father: **To... God, through Yeshua the Messiah, be the glory forever and ever. *Amen.***

THE FIRST LETTER FROM YESHUA'S EMISSARY SHA'UL (PAUL) TO THE MESSIANIC COMMUNITY IN CORINTH:

1 CORINTHIANS

CHAPTER 1

1 **Sha'ul** (Paul, Ac 13:9&N) founded the Messianic community of Corinth (Ac 18:1–18). He refers to an earlier letter (5:9), but this is the first of the two that are extant. He wrote it in the mid–50's C.E., both because of reports he had received (1:10–12, 5:1, 11:18) and questions the Corinthians had raised (7:1, 8:1). While at least one problem in this community was doctrinal (Chapter 15), most concerned attitudes and behavior.

Here is an outline of this letter:

CHAPTERS, VERSES	CONTENTS
1:1–9	Greeting. Thanksgiving.
1:10–6:20	I Reported disorders.
1:10–4:21	A. Spirit of divisiveness.
5:1–13, 6:12–20	B. Sexual misbehavior.
6:1–11	C. Appeals to pagan law courts.
7:1–15:58	II Problems raised by the Corinthians.
7:1–40	A. Celibacy, Marriage, Divorce.
8:1–11:1	B. Food sacrificed to idols — used to teach self-control and consideration for others. Rights of emissaries and self-control (9:1–18). Evangelism and empathy (an aspect of self-control) (9:19–23).
11:2–14:40	C. Disorders in public worship.
11:2–16	1. Veiling of women in public worship.
11:17–34	2. Disorder at the Lord's Supper (Communion, Eucharist, Mass).
12:1–14:40	3. Charismatic gifts from the Holy Spirit and their use in public. Love, the "better way" (12:31–14:1a).
15:1–58	D. Resurrection of the dead.
16:1–20	Conclusion. Organizing the charitable collection. Greetings.

I was called by God's will and did not achieve my office through my own efforts (Ac 7:57–8:3, 9:3–31, 22:3–21).

Brother Sosthenes, perhaps successor to Crispus (v. 14) as president of the synagogue in Corinth (Ac 18:8, 17). Formerly a vehement opponent of Sha'ul and his Gospel, he grew so close to him as to be his partner in writing this letter, so that those in Corinth who deprecated Sha'ul's authority (Chapters 4 and 9, 2 Corinthians 10–12) might at least respect a prominent fellow-Corinthian. Sha'ul himself is an even better example of a virulent adversary who became a strong supporter of Yeshua.

2 **Everyone everywhere**. This refutes the view that Sha'ul's letters, since they were written to specific congregations with specific problems, are not normative for us. However, the manner in which they are normative depends on right interpretation.

3–9 Before dispensing advice that could antagonize some of his readers, Sha'ul establishes a basis of trust by expressing his underlying confidence in the Corinthians.

3 See Ro 1:7N.

10–11 **Factions**. The Corinthian leaders wrote asking certain questions (7:1) but said nothing of this much more important matter, schisms rending the community asunder. Rather, it took **some of Chloe's people** to make this known to Sha'ul. The implication is that the leaders should have reported it themselves.

12 **I follow Sha'ul... Apollos... Kefa**. The Gospel has been perverted into a cult of personality; but loyalty to leaders, thinkers or denominations must not supersede loyalty to the Messiah. Yet "**I follow the Messiah**" is no better a boast than the others, since it proudly disparages all teachers and, supposedly in the name of faithfulness to Yeshua, tries to justify heeding no one. **Apollos** was Sha'ul's successor in Corinth and an effective teacher (Ac 18:24–28). Having lived in Hellenized Alexandria, he may have offered a Greek approach similar to that of the Alexandrian non-Messianic Jew, Philo. **Kefa**, on the other hand, would have emphasized Jewish elements (compare Acts 10–11, Ga 2:11–16). But doctrinal differences and preferences for one person over another must not degenerate into infighting.

13 **Immersed into the name of**, that is, made to partake of the quality and character of; see Mt 3:1N.

14–17 **I didn't immerse... Oh yes, I did... I can't remember** — showing that the Messiah charged Sha'ul to proclaim the Gospel (v. 17), with the act of immersing normally being done by others (Yn 4:2, Ac 10:48).

Luke writes that **Crispus** was "the president of the synagogue" (Ac 18:8). Three other people in the New Testament had the common name **Gaius** (Ac 19:29, 20:4; 3 Yn 1); this Gaius is probably the same as at Ro 16:23. **Stephanas** is mentioned again at 16:15, 17.

22 **Jews ask for signs** of God's power as proof of Messianic profession. But Yeshua, during his time on earth, repeatedly refused to give one on demand, except for predicting his own resurrection (Mt 12:38, 16:1; Yn 2:18), so that disbelieving Jews asserted that no sign of Yeshua's messiahship had been given. Professor David Flusser, an Orthodox Jewish scholar in Jerusalem, writes, "Until the Messiah does the works of the Messiah we cannot call him the Messiah." But Mt 11:2–6 and Yn 10:32–38, 12:37 refute this objection by showing that he did perform such works. Indeed some of his miracles were regarded in Judaism specifically as Messianic signs, such as healing a leper (Mt 8:1–4&N) and restoring sight to a man born blind (Yochanan 9). Others seek a sign not from Yeshua directly but from those who claim to act in his name. However, a miracle is not proof that Yeshua is the Messiah, for there are demonic miracles (Mt 24:24, 2 Th 2:9, Rv 13:3–4). Nor are miracles necessary for faith (Yn 20:28); no one has to wait for a sign before trusting Yeshua the Messiah (although sometimes, in his grace, God gives one).

Greeks try to find wisdom. Sha'ul frequently uses the word "Greeks" as a synonym for "Gentiles"; but here he is probably speaking of a trait characteristic of the ancient Greeks, their desire to increase control over their surroundings through acquiring knowledge. Though useful if properly applied (the scientific advances of Western civilization are predicated upon it), the presumption that God can be contacted, sin forgiven or ultimate meaning attained through wisdom is itself an act of faith and a misplaced one at that; known as gnosticism, it is targeted in the New Testament as an enemy of the Gospel.

Today there is a recrudescence of gnosticism in what is loosely called the New Age Movement. Also there are many, both Jews and Gentiles, who hold the supposedly secular presupposition that knowledge ("this world's wisdom," v. 20) is the key to everything; to deal with their concentric layers of intellectual objection requires endless rounds of philosophical demonstration. But no amount of it suffices to bring them to trust in God and his Messiah. On the contrary, the intellectual objections will melt away once the intellect itself has been brought to obey God's truth; for God, who created the intellect, has not set it in opposition to faith (2:16&N, Ro 1:17&N).

23 **A Messiah executed on a stake as a criminal!** (The last seven words translate Greek *estavrômenon,* literally, "crucified." See Mt 10:38N.

To Jews this is an obstacle (or "stumbling-stone"; Greek *skandalon*, from which comes the English word "scandal"), because all Jewish hopes in the Messiah centered on his restoring self-rule to Israel (Ac 1:6–7&N) and bringing peace to the earth (Isaiah 2:1–5). Given such expectations, a Messiah crucified by Roman oppressors seems an insuperable obstacle. But careful reading of the *Tanakh* shows that the obstacle is removed by understanding that the prophets predicted an inglorious first coming of the Messiah to die for the sins of the world (Isaiah 52:11–53:10; Zechariah 9:9, 12:10) before being resurrected (Isaiah 53:10, Psalm 16:10), returning to the Father in Heaven (Psalm 110:1) and coming again in glory to fulfill these hopes (Isaiah 53:10–12).

At the same time, **to Greeks it is nonsense**. The entire concept of a Messiah who acts in history even to bring peace, let alone to be an atonement for sin, is foolishness to those whose gnostic "wisdom" leads them to a more abstract, pseudo-spiritual concept of God, or whose skepticism makes them deny God altogether. As noted above, many of today's Jews and Gentiles are, in this regard, "Greeks" in their thinking.

24–25 God's power, for which Jews are said to want the evidence of "signs" (vv. 22–23), is better expressed in apparent "**weakness**" (12:9, 2C 13:4) that proves **stronger than humanity's strength**.

26 Not many of you are wise,... wield power or boast noble birth. Those who consider themselves wise, powerful or well-born often despise Christianity because of its humble origins; but the teachings of Yeshua lend no support to such conceit and arrogance. The Kingdom of God is for the "poor" (Lk 6:20) and the "poor in spirit" (Mt 5:3) who are willing to set aside vested economic and academic interests in order to come as little children (Mt 18:1–3). Simple people often have less mis-education to overcome and less attachment to the status quo that might raise the cost of their coming to faith (see Lk 14:26–33&N).

Uniquely, Jews have a Scriptural reason not to hold the powerless in contempt. Moses told the Israelites,

> "*Adonai* did not set his love upon you or choose you because you outnumbered other peoples, for you were the fewest of all people. Rather, it was because *Adonai* loved you, and because he wanted to keep the oath he had sworn to your fathers, that *Adonai* brought you out with a mighty hand and redeemed you…." (Deuteronomy 7:7–8)

Nevertheless, one finds some non-Messianic Jews looking down on Messianic Judaism as attracting only Jews who are ignorant (Jewishly or generally), emotionally unstable or economically distressed — only *'am-ha'aretz* ("rabble," "hicks," literally, "people of the earth") are "taken in" by it. In answer: (1) some Messianic Jews are wealthy, socially prominent, well-adjusted, and well-educated; a number of rabbis have come to faith (see Ac 4:13&N). More importantly, (2) although one can find in Jewish writings some prejudice against the *'am-ha'aretz*, as a whole Judaism gives little ground for making invidious comparisons with other people (see v. 31N) and no ground whatever for judging the truth of something by who believes it.

29 The reason God chooses the lowly is to forestall boasting about anything other than himself. Compare Ep 2:8–9.

31 The entire passage from which this quotation comes is worth citing, since its three false bases for boasting are precisely those of v. 26 above:

> "Thus says *Adonai*: 'Let not the wise man boast about his wisdom, and let not the powerful man boast about his power, and let not the rich man boast about his riches. Rather, let anyone who wants to boast, boast about this: that he understands and knows me, that I am *Adonai* who exercises loving-kindness, justice and righteousness on the earth, because I take pleasure in these things,' says *Adonai*." (Jeremiah 9:22–23(23–24))

Also Psalm 34:3(2): "My soul will boast in *Adonai*; the humble shall hear of it and be glad."

CHAPTER 2

1,7 Wisdom... secret wisdom. See 1:22–23&NN, 6:12–13&NN, 8:1&N, 15:33–34N.

8 This world's leaders, including both the Jewish and the Roman individuals who had a part in putting Yeshua to death.

16 A friend's six-year-old boy, a third-generation Messianic Jew, announced, "I'm smarter than anyone in the whole world." "How's that?" I asked. "Because I have **the mind of the Messiah**." Through apprehending God's Word we can think his thoughts after him.

CHAPTER 3

1–3 "**Worldly**" in v. 1 renders Greek *sarkinos*, but in v. 3 it renders "*sarkikos*." Both are adjectives derived from "*sarx*" ("flesh"; see Ro 7:5N). The first adjective refers to literal, physical flesh; the latter is more figurative. Understand these verses in this sense: "I couldn't talk to you as people who had spirits capable of responding spiritually. Instead, I had to talk to you as one talks to babies made only of flesh, who can understand what is said to them only in the most literal way, whose spirits will develop later but are developmentally incapable of being so addressed now. And I must still talk to you that way, because you are still worldly, thinking only about the world and its things, so that your spirits, though in principle mature enough to respond, are underdeveloped; your IQ is normal, but your 'SQ' is way below par because of the way you run your life."

8–15 This passage speaks of the judgment of believers. Although all who put their trust in Yeshua will be delivered from the final judgment of unbelievers (Rv 20:11–15), their rewards in Heaven will depend on their works as believers on behalf of the Kingdom (5:5, 9:25; Mt 16:27, 25:14–30; Lk 14:13–14; Ro 14:10–11; 2C 5:10; Ep 2:10; 2 Ti 4:8, 14; 1 Ke 5:4; 2 Yn 8).

13 On **the Day** of Judgment, **the Day** of *Adonai*, God's **fire** will reveal and refine what is worthy to remain in his Kingdom and destroy what is not.

16 You people as the Body of the Messiah **are God's Temple and... God's Spirit lives in you**. In Jewish understanding God lives in his Temple; that is where his glory dwells, his *Sh'khinah* (MJ 1:2–3N), his Spirit. The Samaritan woman knew that Jerusalem was where Jews worshipped (Yn 4:20), where the Temple was; but Yeshua replied that the time would come when "the true worshippers will worship the Father in spirit and truth" (Yn 4:23). According to the present verse, that time has come. Sha'ul uses the word "temple" in another sense at 6:19 below; there it means the physical body of the individual believer.

CHAPTER 4

3–4 Though the Spirit gives me the capacity to do it (2:14–15), and I affirm its appropriateness (11:31), **I don't even evaluate myself**. I give no objective significance to my introspective judgments, for despite my being unaware **of anything against me,... this does not make me innocent** (Psalm 19:13(12)). Only one evaluation matters: that of **the Lord**.

7 Compare Ep 2:8–9. Together with 1:29–31 and 3:18–23 the sense is: everything belongs to you believers, and at the same time you belong to the Messiah; you own all, yet you did not earn it but received it as a gift; therefore boasting is utterly out of place, except for boasting about the Lord.

12 **Working with our hands for a living**. Sha'ul was a tentmaker (Ac 18:3).

14 **To confront you and get you to change**. The phrase translates the single Greek word "*noutheteô*," often rendered "warn" or "admonish." Jay Adams, in his book *Competent To Counsel*, has popularized the term "nouthetic counseling," which has as its purpose confronting people with what Scripture has to say about a matter and getting them to change their behavior and attitudes so as to conform with God's command and advice. Because such counseling is based on absolute standards of right and wrong it is at odds with methods of clinical psychology that rely on the values of the client. Since 1970 even secular psychology has felt pressed to move away from ethical relativism (see the works of Herbert Mowrer and Karl Menninger's book, *Whatever Became of Sin?*).

17 **Timothy**. See Ac 16:1–3.

20 **The Kingdom of God**. Or, "God's rulership." See Mt 3:2N.

CHAPTER 5

1 **Stepmother**. More literally, "the wife of his father"; there is no reason for Sha'ul to use this roundabout expression to refer to the person's own mother. From 2C 7:12 ("the one wronged") some conclude that the man's father was still alive at the time. Reuben, the firstborn son of Jacob, committed this sin with his father's concubine Bilhah (Genesis 35:22); therefore, although he had some good characteristics, he was deprived of significant blessing in Jacob's final prophecies (Genesis 49:3–4).

5 **The Adversary**, Greek *Satanas*, transliterating Hebrew *Satan*. English-speakers use the words "Satan" and "Devil" interchangeably; in the Bible Satan, though always depicted as inferior to God, is adversary to both God and humanity (as in Job 1–2). See Mt 4:1N.

His old nature, literally, "the flesh," which in the New Testament does not refer to the body only but to the entire physical, emotional, mental and spiritual nature that a person has acquired in his years of attachment to the things of this world, apart from God (see Ro 7:5N).

Hand over such a person to the Adversary for his old nature to be destroyed. "The nakedness of your father's wife you shall not uncover; it is your father's nakedness" (Leviticus 18:8). In Sanhedrin 7:4 the Mishna prescribes stoning as the penalty for this sin; K'ritot 1:1 says, "There are thirty-six who are to be cut off from Israel:... he who lies with his mother or with the wife of his father." (Also see Yn 9:22N on excommunication in Judaism.) Thus it may be that Sha'ul was recommending to the Corinthians that they apply the traditional Jewish punishment for this sin.

Critics who find his prescription too severe should note that the excommunication is not permanent (see below), and that it has two positive purposes. The first is **that his spirit may be saved in the Day of the Lord** (even if he only "escapes through the fire," 3:15). The object of depriving the offender of fellowship with other believers (v. 11) and exposing him to the afflictions that God will permit Satan to cause him because of his sin is to bring him to his senses, so that he will repent. When he does, giving up his immoral behavior, he should be accepted again, as can be seen from 2C 2:5–10, where the believers are urged to welcome him back into their company, in order not to discourage him beyond measure. The second purpose is to protect others in the Messianic community from being drawn into sin; v. 13 cites the *Tanakh* as ground for using excommunication in this way.

6–8 I question the common assumption that Sha'ul's Passover language here is entirely figurative. I see no compelling reason in the context to excise the plain sense (*p'shat*) from the phrase, "**Let us celebrate the *Seder*.**" Instead, it seems that the early believers, Gentiles included, observed the Jewish feast of ***Pesach***. As we will see, their service combined traditional Jewish Passover symbolism with new symbolism relating to Yeshua the Messiah's central role in Jewish and world history. Evidently the Corinthian congregation observed Passover without supposing that, as many of today's Christians might think, they were "going back under the Law."

Chametz, Hebrew for "leavening agent." The evening before *Pesach*, Jews must **get rid of the old *chametz*** (found in bread, flour products of all kinds, and grain liquor). The last bits of bread containing *chametz* must be burned the following morning (the Hebrew for "getting rid of leaven" and "burning leaven" is the same, "*bi'ur-chametz*"). That evening, after sundown, the family will celebrate the *Seder* (see Mt 26:17N), eating the special meal during which the *Haggadah* (the liturgy recalling the Exodus from Egypt) is read. At this meal and throughout the week of *Pesach* the only kind of bread that may be eaten is ***matzah*** (unleavened bread; see Mt 26:17N), in obedience to Exodus 12:15–20, 13:3–7; Deuteronomy 16:3. It may be significant that the prescribed punishment for violating this ordinance is the same as that for sexual misbehavior with one's stepmother, being cut off from one's people (Exodus 12:19; compare vv. 1–5&NN). Even today, many Jews who consider themselves rather religiously unobservant nevertheless eat only *matzah* during Passover or at least at the *Seder* on the first night of Passover.

In the New Testament, *chametz* often symbolizes **wickedness and evil** (Mt 16:6–12, Mk 8:15, Lk 12:1), with *matzah* representing **purity and truth**. This accords with the *Tanakh* and Jewish tradition as well and is thus explained by a Jewish writer:

> "*Matzah* was used in the sacrificial system of the Temple. Offerings had to be absolutely pure, and anything leavened (*chametz*) was considered impure

> because it had fermented, or soured. (The word *chametz* literally means 'sour'.) *Matzah* — unleavened bread — on the other hand, was a symbol of purity. The Talmud says, 'leaven represents the evil impulse of the heart'" (Alfred J. Kolatch, *The Jewish Book of Why*, Middle Village, NY: Jonathan David Publishers, Inc., 1981, p. 187)

Leviticus 2:4–11 spells out the requirement that baked goods offered in the Temple had to be unleavened. The passage in the Talmud to which Kolatch refers is:

> "After reciting the *'Amidah* Rabbi Alexandri used to add the following: 'Sovereign of the Universe, you are well aware that our will is to perform your will. What keeps us from doing it? The yeast in the dough….' "(B'rakhot 17a)

In the Soncino translation a note explains that "the yeast in the dough" is "the evil impulse, which causes a ferment in the heart." Another Jewish writer puts it this way:

> "Some Jewish thinkers see *chametz*, that which rises and becomes leaven, as symbolically representing those tendencies in a man which arouse him to evil. They see the whole process of searching for the *chametz* and eliminating it as a reminder to man that he should search through his deeds and purify his actions. Mere renunciation of the imperfect past, one's own *chametz*, is not sufficient; it must be destroyed. The pieces of *chametz* that are placed around the house before the ritual search should then remind a person of the fact that 'there is not a person in the world who does only good and never sins.' [Ecclesiastes 7:20]" (Mordell Klein, ed., *Passover*, Jerusalem: Keter Books, 1973, p. 38)

However, **The saying, "It takes only a little *chametz* to leaven a whole batch of dough,"** quoted in a similar context at Ga 5:9, here tells the Corinthians not only that each individual should guard against personal sin, but also that permitting a promiscuous sinner who professes to be a fellow-believer (see vv. 9–10) to remain in their midst is a sure way to infect the entire Messianic community with sin.

And **leftover *chametz***, left over after the search should have removed it — not the search of the house for physical *chametz* but the symbolic introspective search for sinful passions and behavior patterns left over from one's former life in the world apart from God — is inappropriate for people who **in reality… are unleavened**, already purified by the Messiah, **our *Pesach* lamb**. Such passing back and forth between the literal and the figurative, the seen and the unseen, is of the essence in celebrating Jewish holidays; this is how spiritual realities become individually and communally real.

For our *Pesach* lamb, the Messiah, has been sacrificed. In the New Testament Yeshua the Messiah is portrayed frequently both as a lamb and as a sacrifice. At Yn 1:29, 36 he is called "the lamb of God, who takes away the sins of the world." At Ac 8:32, Luke quotes Isaiah 53:7–8, which speaks of the Messiah as a slaughtered lamb, and explicitly connects it with Yeshua. And the book of Revelation is full of passages about the Lamb that was slaughtered (Rv 5:6–13; 6:1, 16; 7:9–17; 12:11; 13:8, 11; 14:1–10; 15:3; 17:14; 19:7–9; 21:14, 22–23; 22:1–3). Messianic Jews 9:1–10:20 says that Yeshua's death effectively replaces the sacrifices for sin. (Romans 3:25 implicitly connects Yeshua's sacrificial death with a different Jewish holiday, *Yom-Kippur*; for there he is called the "*kapparah*," the covering, or atonement, "for sin." And this is not inconsistent with his also being the Passover lamb; in fact, he gives new meaning to all the Jewish holidays.)

But here Yeshua's death is understood as that of the Passover lamb, as at Yn 19:33, 36: "But when they got to Yeshua and saw that he was already dead, they didn't break his legs.... For these things happened in order to fulfill this passage of the *Tanakh*: 'Not one bone of his will be broken' [Exodus 12:46, which refers to the Passover lamb]." Likewise, at the Last Supper, which is generally understood to have been a Passover meal, Yeshua referred to the broken *matzah* as his body and the wine as his shed blood which establishes the New Covenant (11:23–26; Mt 26:26–29). And 1 Ke 1:19 should be considered an allusion to Yeshua as the Passover lamb, because it speaks of "the costly bloody sacrificial death of the Messiah, as of a lamb without defect or spot"; whereas the Passover lamb too was to be "without blemish" (Exodus 12:5).

On the night of the Exodus from Egypt, at the original Passover, each family sacrificed and ate a lamb, after smearing its blood on the doorposts of the house, so that the angel of death would "pass over" that house and not kill that family's firstborn son when he killed the firstborn sons of the families of Egypt (Exodus 11:4–7; 12:3–13, 21–23, 29–30). Thus, the most straightforward significance of the Messiah's being our Passover lamb is that because of his death, the angel of death will pass over us at the final judgment and instead we will have everlasting life. "For God so loved the world that he gave his uniquely-born Son, so that everyone trusting in him may have eternal life instead of being utterly destroyed" (Yn 3:16). The Greek of our passage does not have in it the word for "lamb" but says, literally, "For the Messiah, our *Pesach*, has been sacrificed." This echoes Exodus 12:11 ("It is *Adonai*'s *Pesach*") and 12:21 ("...and kill the *Pesach*"), where the absence of the word "lamb" from the Hebrew calls attention to the total identification between the Passover event and the Passover lamb — neither exists without the other. Likewise, there is no escape from the utter destruction of eternal death at the Last Judgment apart from trust in the Messiah, who is our Passover.

At the original Passover, an annual feast was prescribed in which each family would slaughter and eat a lamb as a remembrance of the Exodus (Exodus 12:3–14, 21–28). In Yeshua's time the central event of Passover was the slaughter of the lamb for each household in the Temple court; and when Sha'ul wrote, this was still the custom. At a modern Ashkenazic *Seder* there is no Passover lamb, because the rabbis decreed that if the lamb could not be slaughtered at the Temple (impossible after its destruction in 70 C.E.), lamb should not be eaten during Passover at all. Instead, a lamb shankbone is placed on the "*Seder* plate," along with the other ceremonial items needed for the meal, as a reminder that these sacrifices did once take place. (Sephardic Jews, however, do eat lamb at Passover.) Today, when a Messianic Jew observes *Pesach*, his identification of Yeshua the Messiah with the Passover lamb gives him a rich treasure of new significance to add to the traditional layers of meaning for this festival.

9 **My earlier letter**. This letter has not survived except in the reference to it here. From this we learn that not everything Sha'ul wrote became Holy Scripture.

11 **With such a person you shouldn't even eat**. But you should eat with persons inquiring

into the faith (Ac 10:1–11:18&NN) and with fellow-believers in good standing (Ga 2:11–16&NN).

CHAPTER 6

1 Verses 1–8 clearly forbid lawsuits between believers in secular courts. Although embarrassment at airing dirty laundry **before pagan judges** is a reason (v. 6, 10:32), one which Christians share with Jews ("What will the Gentiles think?"), there should be greater embarrassment at the failure of the Messianic community to function as it should (vv. 2–8). Also, those who are not **God's people** and therefore lack the Holy Spirit are incompetent to apply believers' principles properly. Compare the Talmud:

> "It was taught that Rabbi Tarfon [2nd century C.E.] used to say, 'In every place where you find pagan law courts, you must not make use of them, even if their laws are the same as the laws of Israel; because the *Tanakh* says, "These are the judgments which you shall set before them" (Exodus 21:1) — "before *them*" and not before pagans.'"(Gittin 88b)

2–3 Believers, because they are united with the Messiah, will share in his exaltation to rulership (4:8, Psalm 8:7(6), 2 Timothy 2:12), which implies that they will **judge the universe**, including **angels**; however, curious though we may be, Sha'ul does not focus on the details of how we will judge angels. Y'hudah 6 speaks of a future judgment for evil angels; and Chapters 13–16 of the Book of Enoch, a Jewish writing from the 1st century B.C.E., show that the Judaism of that time recognized the idea that human beings will judge angels.

9–11 Unrighteous people will have no share in (literally, "will not inherit") **the Kingdom of God**, or, "God's rulership," a translation that perhaps fits the context here better, since very great prerogatives of rulership have just been discussed (judging the universe, including angels, vv. 2–3). In 4:20 the Kingdom of God is thought of as present, but in this verse and at 15:50 it is future; actually it is both (see Mt 3:2N).

Sha'ul is not saying that a single infraction will cause a person to lose his salvation; but that people who continue to lead a life of sin, who are habitual thieves, who intentionally go on committing one or more of the four enumerated varieties of sexual immorality, who refuse to give up the other egregious sins named, show by their behavior that they are not part of God's people (compare 1 Yn 3:9). Mere mental assent to doctrines or to the fact of Yeshua's Messiahship is not sufficient for salvation, for "faith without actions is dead" (Ya 2:26).

The idea that a person can profess belief in God or in Yeshua and still highhandedly go on sinning is repugnant to the writers of Scripture. Overly easygoing congregations bring shame on the Messianic Community by softpedaling the need for believers to change their lifestyles. Such congregations produce complacent pseudo-believers. Some take advantage of the notion that God is gradually changing them, thereby justifying continued indulgence in their sins. God, who has made his will clear, has provided **through the power of the Lord Yeshua the Messiah and the Spirit of our God** everything needed to overcome known grievous sins like the ones named in these verses. We are not to presume on God's patience (Ro 2:3–6).

On homosexuality, see Ro 1:24–28N. Many in the modern world do not consider the activities listed to be sins, and perhaps many in the ancient world didn't either. God does.

Some of you used to do these things. But you have cleansed yourselves, etc. (v. 11). Although uncompromisingly opposed to sin (vv. 9–10), Sha'ul is equally open to and loving toward the repentant sinner. Because God forgives, we are to do the same (Mt 6:14–15, 18:21–35).

12 **"For me, everything is permitted"** (the words, "**You say**," are not in the Greek text but are added to show that this was not a central principle of Sha'ul's teaching but a saying in use among a group of Corinthians who would later have been called gnostic libertines. Sha'ul does not deny the principle, but he cautions against its misuse by pointing out that **not everything is helpful** and that **I am not going to let anything gain control over me**. He taught the same lesson in another context at Ga 5:1, 13 and returns to the topic at 10:23, where a different criterion is brought to bear, edification of the community as a whole, as opposed to considering only oneself (see also 8:1–13N).

13 **"Food is meant for the stomach and the stomach for food"** (approximately equivalent to, "If it feels good, do it"), apparently another gnostic saying. This is not said in order to oppose the Jewish dietary laws. Rather, the libertines offer it as a euphemistic argument against sexual self-restraint, in the context of Chapters 5–7. At the same time its literal sense previews the issue taken up at 8:1, eating food sacrificed to idols. According to the Talmud,

> "A favorite saying of Rav was: 'In the *'olam haba* there is neither eating nor drinking… but the righteous… get their enjoyment in the glory of the *Sh'khinah*, as it says, 'They beheld God, and ate and drank' (Isaiah 32:9)." (B'rakhot 17a)

15 **Heaven forbid!** See Ro 3:4N.

19–20 Sexual immorality has been the subject of vv. 12–20; but these two verses go beyond that subject to remind us that a surprising number of believers fail to take care of their bodies, so that they become overweight, run-down, drug-dependent, out of shape, or otherwise insufficiently healthy to carry on the Lord's work effectively.

CHAPTER 7

1 **The questions you wrote about**. From here at least through 15:58 and perhaps through 16:9 Sha'ul is answering questions raised by the leaders of the Corinthian Messianic community (see 1:10–11&N).

Is it good for a man to keep away from women, that is, to be celibate? From Sha'ul's remark, "I wish everyone were like me" (v. 7), many infer that he regarded celibacy as the preferred condition for believers; and from vv. 8–9, 26–27, 32–34, 38 and 40 one can build a case that Sha'ul had a rather jaundiced view of marriage. Some critics of Christianity, basing their judgment on this chapter and the Christian tradition of celibate monastic orders and a celibate Roman Catholic priesthood, find Christianity inferior to Judaism on the ground that its teaching on marriage contravenes both nature and *Torah.* Moreover, demographic statistics provide supportive evidence; for even today, when Jewish teaching has less influence on Jewish young people, 98% of Jewish men in the United States marry, as compared with only 93% for the population as a whole.

However, in evaluating Sha'ul's teachings here, one must keep in mind the circumstances for which he wrote, particularly these three points:

(1) The Messianic community in Corinth had emerged from a wildly pagan background and even at the time of this letter was not fully able to control its impulses toward sexual license (vv. 2, 5, 9; not to mention Chapters 5–6). Sha'ul's immediate purpose was to remedy this deficiency.

(2) Sha'ul tailored his remarks to his audience, who were still "babies, so far as experience with the Messiah is concerned" (3:1), even though he did intend his letter to be read by others (1:2). This means that he had to provide clear-cut rules, since he could not count on their spiritual discernment to develop appropriate responses in each individual case. It is risky to entrust "babies" with decisions beyond their capacity.

(3) Most importantly, the tone of the whole chapter is governed by an underlying sense of urgency — "there is not much time left" (v. 29) in "a time of stress like the present" (v. 26). Apparently the Corinthians required no proof of this, since Sha'ul gave none. What was this urgency? Many commentators think they were looking toward the Lord Yeshua's imminent return (compare v. 31); however, elsewhere Sha'ul cautioned against over-preoccupation with that subject and pointed out that certain events must take place first (2 Th 2:1–3). My conclusion is that the urgency pertained to the particular situation in Corinth; and although the specifics are not stated, Sha'ul and the Corinthians agreed that there was a need to act quickly, put forth extra effort and take special measures in order to deal with it (vv. 29–35). Therefore, some of Sha'ul's strictures should be regarded as special responses suitable to situations of great urgency. One may reply that believers ought to consider all situations urgent, and there is truth in that; nevertheless, the truth in it is not so overwhelming as to turn every one of Sha'ul's remarks on marriage into ironclad rules for all times and all places. Rather, the applicability of each rule to believers generally must be examined in context; and this we shall do.

Also see Rv 14:4N.

3–9 Concerning celibacy, then, Sha'ul's overall counsel is against it. When he says, "**I wish everyone were like me**" (v. 7), he is not wishing that everyone were celibate. Were that his meaning, then — *reductio ad absurdum* — he would be wishing (depending on the assumed context) that the Messianic Community or the human race would die out from not reproducing itself.

What he actually wishes is that everyone were as little distracted by wayward sexual impulses as he is. Then they would have **self-control** (vv. 5, 9) and would be able to devote themselves to the Lord's work with undivided attention (vv. 33–35). However, he realizes that such a disposition cannot be willed into being but is a **gift from God** (v. 7) which has not been given to everyone. Therefore, if single people **can't exercise**

self-control, they should get married; because it is better to get married than to keep burning with sexual desire (v. 9; literally, as in KJV, "better to marry than to burn"). At 1 Ti 5:14 he specifically counsels widows under age 60 to remarry.

Marriages should be monogamous (v. 2) and should provide sexual satisfaction to both parties (vv. 3–4); indeed, this is a matter of entitlement; and special note should be taken of this teaching by those who think of Christianity as "anti-sex." Moreover, Sha'ul's counsel here is surprisingly "modern" in that he insists that spouses be "considerate of each other's needs" (to use today's terminology).

Apparently there was in Corinth a movement toward celibacy *within* marriage (see also vv. 36–37) — extremes spawn extremes, so where libertinism flourishes one often finds asceticism as a reaction. Therefore, in v. 5 Sha'ul finds it necessary to advise married couples against such sexual abstinence, **except by mutual agreement, for a limited time, and then only so as to have extra time for prayer**, which is to say that the practice has no merit in itself but only insofar as it facilitates greater devotion to the Lord; **but afterwards, come together again**, lest you **succumb to the Adversary's** (Satan's) **temptation** to engage in illicit sex. And even after all this, Sha'ul adds that he is **giving you this as a suggestion, not as a command** (v. 6&N), so that no one should think sexual abstinence within marriage is ever required. It may be, however, that the early believers observed the Jewish practice of *niddah*, abstinence from sexual relations during the period of the wife's menstrual flow and for one week thereafter (Leviticus 15; see MJ 13:4&N).

6, 10, 12, 17, 25, 40 In no other chapter of the New Testament is the writer so at pains to state precisely the degree of authority to be attributed to each of his pronouncements. **I am giving you this as a suggestion, not as a command** (v. 6). **For those who are married I have a command, and it is not from me but from the Lord** (v. 10). **To the rest I say — I, not the Lord** (v. 12). **This is the rule I lay down in all the congregations** (v. 17). **I do not have a command from the Lord, but I offer an opinion as one who by the Lord's mercy is worthy to be trusted** (v. 25). **In my opinion,... and in saying this I think I have God's Spirit** (v. 40).

Although the word "Lord" in these passages refers not to God the Father but to Yeshua, nevertheless if God inspired the entire Bible, how can there be such variations in authority? My answer is that one need not think of inspiration by God as being so heavy-handed as not to admit of refinements. God created everything, including nuances in authority. From the quotations cited here we learn that Sha'ul himself can be humble when giving his opinion, since he is apparently unaware that he is writing what will be accepted by future generations as Scripture inspired by God. God's authority is discovered to have been behind his opinions and suggestions by virtue of the letter's becoming recognized by believers as God-inspired and accepted into the canon of the New Testament.

10–11 Sha'ul was taught this **command from the Lord** by Yeshua himself (Mt 5:31–32, 19:3–9; Mk 10:1–12; Lk 16:18). The terms "**separate herself**" and "**leave**" include both "separation" and "divorce" in the modern sense of those terms. This teaching applies to a marriage in which both partners are believers, members of God's people (this was also the context of Yeshua's remarks). In the two passages of Mattityahu's Gospel, Yeshua gave an exception to this rule: adultery. Adultery is the only explicitly stated ground for divorce between believers.

A woman is not to separate herself from her husband. But if she does… This is "second-best" advice — "Don't do this! But if you do, then proceed as follows:…" Another example is seen in 1 Yn 2:1. Christianity tends to be more black-and-white than Judaism, less willing to deal with real-life situations wherein the best solutions are impossible or unlikely, so that it is necessary to deal with second-bests. Judaism, because its ethical perceptions have been shaped by legal questions brought for judgment concerning who should do what in specific circumstances, has been more willing to consider "second-bests." However, on this matter the New Testament itself demonstrates its affinity with Judaism.

12–16 The New Testament teaches a second ground for divorce, besides adultery (vv. 10–11&N), but it applies only in the case of a marriage between a believer and a nonbeliever. Since a believer is expected not to marry a nonbeliever (v. 39&N, 2C 6:14&N), such a marriage should arise only if one of two married unbelievers becomes a believer. The ground is stated explicitly in v. 15, and it is clear that **if the unbelieving spouse separates himself**, the believing spouse can get a divorce and remarry, because **in circumstances like these, the brother or sister is not enslaved**. Anything less than freedom to obtain a divorce and remarry would be enslavement to a marriage that retains only formal existence. On the other hand, for a believing spouse to leave his or her unbelieving partner would be a clear violation of vv. 12–13.

The meaning of v. 14 is obscure. In what sense are the **children** of believers or of a mixed marriage between a believer and an unbeliever **set aside for God**? Christians who favor infant baptism (for example, Roman Catholics, Lutherans, Episcopalians, Methodists and Presbyterians) use this text as justification. Those who oppose it (Baptists and most Pentecostals) understand the verse to mean only that such children have a "head start" toward salvation, in that they can be brought up "in the fear and admonition of the Lord" (Ep 6:4, KJV).

17 **Let each person live the life the Lord has assigned him**, whether single or married, and let him **live it in the condition he was in when God called him**. Sha'ul applies this to two "conditions" — being Jewish or Gentile (vv. 18–20), and being enslaved or free (vv. 21–24), repeating at the end of each of these sections his admonition not to seek unnecessary change in one's religious, social or economic status when the time can be better spent serving the Lord.

18a **Someone already circumcised when he was called**, that is, a Jewish believer, **should not try to remove the marks of his circumcision**. From this we can reasonably infer that he should not assimilate into Gentile or so-called "Christian" culture but should remain distinctly Jewish. For Sha'ul is obviously talking about more than physical circumcision, although the specific operation of "de-circumcision" was actually performed by Jewish Hellenizers in the days of King Antiochus IV (whose desecration of the Temple in 165 B.C.E. resulted eventually in the feast of *Chanukkah*; see Yn 10:22N). Of this Josephus writes:

> "Menelaus and the sons of Tuvyah were distressed, so they went to Antiochus and informed him that they wanted to leave the laws of their country and the Jewish way of living according to them, and to follow the king's laws and the Greek way of living; and in particular, they desired his permission to build themselves a gymnasium in Jerusalem. After he gave them permission, they also hid the circumcision of their genitals, so that even when they were naked they might appear to be Greeks. Accordingly, they discontinued all the customs of their own country and imitated the practices of the *Goyim*." (*Antiquities of the Jews* 12:5:1)

The same event is described in the Apocrypha as one of the causes of the Maccabean revolt (1 Maccabees 1:11–15), and allusions to the phenomenon are found in Assumption of Moses 8:3 and in the Mishna (Avot 3:11).

Curiously, when a Jew comes to believe that a fellow Jew, Yeshua, is the Jewish Messiah promised in the Jewish Scriptures, today's Jewish community considers it the very epitome of assimilation into the Gentile world. Yet here is a verse from one of the books of the New Covenant with Israel, inaugurated by this same Yeshua, which strongly discourages a Messianic Jew from assimilating. This dissonance results from several historical factors which in the past have made it all but impossible for a Jewish believer to obey Sha'ul's instruction:

(1) First, since New Testament times (Yn 9:22) a Jew who acknowledges Yeshua as the Messiah has usually been excommunicated by his own Jewish people, or at best regarded with suspicion; so that even if he wants to follow Jewish customs or remain loyal, it isn't easy for him to do so in isolation.

(2) Second, no longer welcome in the Jewish community, he enters the community of believers. But here, although Jews and Gentiles are equal in God's sight, Gentiles are the vast majority. He finds himself a lone Jew in a sea of Gentiles, or vastly outnumbered, with few or no other Jewish believers to support him in his efforts to preserve his Jewishness. Gentile believers rarely try to make up for this lack; and even if they try, as a practical matter they seldom have enough knowledge of Judaism to be truly helpful.

(3) Third, the Church has usually maintained a mistaken view of conversion. Instead of understanding that a Jewish believer converts from sin to righteousness (the same as a Gentile believer), it has thought he converts from Judaism to Christianity. By the 4th century C.E. the Church was requiring Jewish believers to sign documents in which they had to agree to stop following Jewish customs or associating with unsaved Jews. Further, since the Church promulgated this view, one is not surprised to find that the Jewish community regarded it as authoritative and used it as evidence that a Jewish believer is no longer Jewish. Were this view correct, it would be proper to urge Jewish believers to eliminate Jewish practices. But it is not true, as I point out throughout this commentary, showing that the first Jewish believers remained fully Jewish and encouraging today's Jewish believers to do the same.

(4) Fourth, the Church has misunderstood the New Testament's teaching about the unity of Jews and Gentiles in the Messianic Community (12:13 below, Ga 3:28&N) and therefore misused it to force Messianic Jews to assimilate. Members of every other ethnic group are encouraged to maintain their culture and express their faith within it. But when a Messianic Jew does so he may be accused of "legalizing"

(Ro 6:14&N), "Judaizing" (Ga 2:14b&N) and "raising again the middle wall of partition" (Ep 2:11–16&NN).

(5) Fifth and last, it cannot be denied that some Jewish believers have had a measure of self-hate (although this unfortunate phenomenon is also found among non-Messianic Jews). In their desire to be accepted by their new Gentile friends in the Church they may have said or done things that depreciate Judaism or Jewishness. On the one hand, Judaism's failure to recognize Yeshua as the Messiah is a sin of grievous dimension. On the other, no Messianic Jew should ingratiate himself with Gentile Christians by appealing to antisemitic impulses. Jewish self-hate is simply not a concomitant of the Gospel.

The challenge to today's Messianic Jews is to establish, despite these factors, a community in which we express fully the ties we have with our Jewish people and also with our Gentile Christian brothers in the Lord.

18b Someone uncircumcised when he was called shouldn't get circumcised. That is, a Gentile believer should not convert to Judaism. This does not speak of a Gentile Christian who wants to give up his faith in Yeshua and convert to non-Messianic Judaism — of course Sha'ul would not countenance that. Rather, he says that Gentile believers should not undergo conversion to Judaism while retaining their faith in Yeshua. At the time Sha'ul was writing there was a strong Judaizing movement, but Sha'ul does not deal here with this error (elsewhere he does; see Acts 15&NN and the whole book of Galatians). Here his chief concern is with the use of time (see vv. 25–40N); his advice to Gentiles is not to waste time converting to Judaism when it is unnecessary (v. 19) and there are more important things to do, namely, serving the Lord.

On the controversial question of whether there might ever be circumstances under which Gentile Christians could legitimately convert to Judaism in the light of what the New Testament teaches, see Ga 5:2–4&N, which continues the present discussion.

19 Being circumcised means nothing. By themselves, out of context, these words are a slap in the face of Judaism, in which circumcision confirms a man's membership in God's people under the covenant with Abraham (Genesis 17:1–14). But in context, with the rest of the verse, the meaning is that in God's Messianic Community, Jews and Gentiles have equal standing before God (12:13; Ro 3:22–23, 29–30; Ga 3:28, 5:6, 6:15; Co 3:11). On this ethnic ties, cultural expressions, customs and social or religious status have no bearing; in this regard, being Jewish or Gentile does not matter. What matters is **keeping God's commandments**, elsewhere in similar contexts equated with "faith working itself out in love" (Ga 5:6) and "being a new creation" (Ga 6:15). One may argue that God's commandments to Jews differ from his commandments to Gentiles. Determining whether that is true requires lengthier analysis, for which see my *Messianic Jewish Manifesto*, Chapter V (entitled "*Torah*"). But the requirement to keep the applicable commandments is identical for Jews and Gentiles, and the trust in Yeshua which forms the basis for being acceptable in God's sight is also identical for Jews and Gentiles. For this, "being circumcised means nothing" (see Ro 4:9–12).

25–40 The principle of remaining in the condition in which one is called to faith, which Sha'ul has repeated three times and illustrated by two extraneous examples (vv. 17–24), is now applied to **the question** at hand, the one **about the unmarried** (v. 25). In a **time of stress like the present** (v. 26) when **there is not much time left** (v. 29), **because the present scheme of things in this world won't last much longer** (v. 31), **it is good for a person to stay as he is** (v. 26). One should decide in favor of a major change in one's life only if the change will help one to **be free of concern** (v. 32) for **the world's affairs** (vv. 33, 34) and more able to give **undivided devotion** (v. 35) to **the Lord's affairs** (vv. 32, 34).

But Sha'ul takes extraordinary pains to show that he is not opposed to marriage. He assures his readers that he does **not have a command from the Lord** but only **an opinion** (v. 25), which he offers in the most tentative language (**I suppose**, v. 26), **that if a man is unmarried, he should not look for a wife** (v. 27). He then not only hastens to add that **if you marry you do not sin** (v. 28), but also makes his suggestion but one instance of how people should generally not be preoccupied with their temporal activities. In other words, he is not discriminating against the unmarried, for the **married**, the **sad**, the **happy**, and **those who deal in worldly affairs** should all live as if unattached to these conditions (vv. 29–31). He is not opposed to marriage or to sexual fulfillment therein, his object is **not to put restrictions on you** (v. 35); rather, he wants to **spare you the normal problems of married life** (v. 28) that **split** a person's concern and divide his energies (vv. 32–34). See also 9:4–6.

36–38 Several ambiguities in the Greek render this passage particularly obscure. The **man** may be the girl's fiancé (my understanding) or her father, since the word rendered "**fiancée**" is, literally, "virgin." If he is her father, the issue is whether he should marry off his daughter. (In the Dead Sea Scrolls, the "man who gives his virgin" is the girl's father).

If there is strong sexual desire, so that marriage is what ought to happen, literally, "if he/she is overripe, and thus it ought to be." This may speak of either his or her passions, or the phrase may be rendered, "If she is past the best age for marriage and therefore is entitled to get married."

The idea that the man (whether fiancé or father) should decide for the woman is certainly not "politically correct"; although it makes sense that if it is the fiancé that the passage is speaking about, and if it is his choice to remain celibate "for the sake of the Kingdom of Heaven" (Mt 19:10–12), he certainly won't be doing her a favor by marrying her and forcing her to live celibately too! But in any case, the decision is not to be imposed against her will; for either her passions are explicitly taken into account (see above); or, if not, Sha'ul's attitudes about how a husband should behave toward his wife ("Husbands, love your wives, just as the Messiah loved the Messianic Community," Ep 5:25) and a father toward his daughter ("Fathers, don't irritate your children and make them resentful," Ep 6:4), as well as his tone throughout this chapter, militate against his meaning here to condone sexual oppression or "male chauvinism" in any form.

39 **Provided he is a believer in the Lord**. The plain sense of this verse limits widows who remarry to marrying believing men. There is no direct instruction to believers who have never married (but see 2C 6:14–7:1&N). However, it is usually supposed that if Sha'ul had dealt with the subject in relation to them, he would have given the same advice. If this is a reasonable assumption, then both the New Testament and non-Messianic

Judaism prohibit exogamy ("marrying out"). A believer is to marry a believer, and a Jew is to marry a Jew. But may a Gentile believer marry a Jewish believer? This verse of the New Testament permits it, while non-Messianic Judaism prohibits it

But if the New Testament "has been made *Torah*" (MJ 8:6&N), should a Messianic Jewish understanding of *halakhah* permit Messianic Jews to marry Messianic Gentiles? The question is controversial, and cases can be made for both "Yes" and "No." A marriage between Jewish and Gentile believers demonstrates to all the unity of Jew and Gentile in the body of the Messiah. But if a Messianic Jew chooses to restrict his marriage pool to other Jewish believers, he testifies to the Jewish community that he wants to preserve the Jewish people, and that Messianic Judaism does not imply assimilation (the chief expression of which is intermarriage).

In this regard there is an asymmetry between the woman and the man, because a Messianic Jewish woman who marries a Messianic Gentile man will still have Jewish children, but a Messianic Jewish man with a Messianic Gentile wife will have non-Jewish children. (See Ac 16:3N on the status of mixed-marriage children, also a controversial subject).

Another consideration for a Messianic Jewish woman concerned for the salvation of other Jewish people is that her ability to pursue her concern will be largely in her husband's hands, since "the head of a wife is her husband" (11:3). If her Gentile husband is called by God to work in an area other than Jewish ministry, she may have little opportunity for it herself. In contrast, a Messianic Jewish man with a call to the Jews normally would not be prevented from pursuing it by his wife's not having such a call herself, since, as a rule, a wife's call is to help her husband (Genesis 2:18; in this first approximation I am skirting individual circumstances and sexual equality issues). Intermarriage between Jewish and Gentile believers is discussed further in *Messianic Jewish Manifesto*, pp. 180–181.

CHAPTER 8

1 **About food sacrificed to idols**. The question raised in this chapter is whether a believer is free to eat meat which he knows or suspects may have been part of an offering in a pagan temple. This apparently minor issue pervades the next three chapters (through 11:1). Though the details relate to another era of history, the underlying principles are very relevant for life in today's world.

The structure of these three chapters is:

(1) Presentation of the question and the new underlying elements being misused, "knowledge" (vv. 1–6) and "freedom" (6:12, 10:23);

(2) A principle for resolving such questions — limiting oneself in order to edify others (vv. 7–13);

(3) Illustrations of the principle (9:1–10:22);

(4) Application of the principle to the question at hand (10:23–11:1).

The former pagans of Corinth who became believers knew that even though they once worshipped idols, offering similar sacrifices in the same shrines, God has forgiven their past sins. Further, as believers they do not offer such sacrifices now; rather, they know that the idols to which they sacrificed have "no real existence" at all (v. 4).

Therefore, since they have this "**knowledge**" (vv. 1, 4–6), and since "everything is permitted" (6:12, 10:23), is there any reason why they should have scruples against buying meat in the public meat-markets — as some of them, whom Sha'ul considers "weak" (vv. 7–12), do have?

The key to Sha'ul's answer (vv. 7–13, 10:23–11:1) is doing what **builds up** or "edifies." (The Greek word is "*oikodomeô*," a word whose literal sense has to do with putting up houses but which, like "constructive" in English, has a metaphorical meaning too; the word is so used ten times in this letter — vv. 1, 10; 10:23; and seven times in Chapter 14). What **builds up** is **love**; whereas **knowledge** — unless it is governed by love (13:2) — only **puffs up**, or, worse, "builds up wrongly" (v. 10; "wrongly" is not in the Greek but is implied by the context; KJV's rendering, "emboldened," captures the sense but misses the connection with the other instances of "*oikodomeô*"). Likewise, in union with the Messiah we have freedom; therefore, in a sense, "everything is permitted"; but, as Sha'ul puts it, "not everything is edifying" (10:23; see also 9:1ff. and 6:12–13N).

The portions of these chapters dealing explicitly with the food question (8:1–13, 10:23–11:1) closely resemble Ro 14:1–15:6&NN. In that passage, one must consider the possibility that "weak" refers to Messianic Jews "not yet free of the Law" (it doesn't); but here the "weak" can only be former pagans, not Jewish believers.

6 **One God, the Father**, as the *Tanakh* teaches. The New Testament does not teach that there is more than one God, nor does it teach that the one God is Yeshua the Son. **From whom all things come and for whom we exist**. The Father is the final source and final goal (Ro 11:36); at the close of history even Yeshua becomes subject to the Father (15:28).

One Lord. Greek *kurios;* see Mt 1:20N, 7:21N. Here "*kurios*" cannot mean "*Adonai*" or *YHVH* (the personal name of God); it must mean "*Adon*," Hebrew for "Lord," not a name but a title of God bespeaking the fact that everyone owes him allegiance and obedience. The assertion that the Lord is **Yeshua the Messiah** means that the allegiance and obedience owed to God are also owed to Yeshua. Why? Because **through** him **were created all things**, for Yeshua is the Word who "became a human being" (Yn 1:14), the same Word as when "God said" the things by which the universe was created (Genesis 1:3–31); and also because Yeshua is he **through whom we have our being** — from which we learn that God the Father exercises his function as maintainer and provider by continuing to speak our existence through him, the living and ongoing Word. Compare Ro 11:36, Co 1:15–19.

7 **Knowledge**. Should the word be in quotation marks or not? If not, Sha'ul's emphasis is that true knowledge, as set forth in vv. 4–6 and v. 8, should suffice to set a person free of overscrupulousness. But he may still be using the word ironically, as in vv. 10–11, pointing out that his questioners' self-proclaimed "knowledge" is still not enough to keep them from prideful, inconsiderate behavior that will damage others.

13 **I will never eat meat again, lest I cause my brother to sin**. Sha'ul's readers are left to think about this for a chapter and a half, but this is not his final disposition of the question, which he takes up again at 10:23.

CHAPTER 9

1–3 Sha'ul moves on from the Corinthians' misuse of knowledge to their misuse of the freedom they have in union with the Messiah (see 8:1N). By the saying, "Everything is permitted" (6:12, 10:23), they justify eating food offered to idols, without thinking about the harm it may cause others (Chapter 8&NN). But, **Am I not a free man** too? Yet I don't behave thus inconsiderately.

Moreover (and what follows is a *kal v'chomer* argument; see Mt 6:30N), unlike yourselves, as **an emissary of the Messiah**, I am entitled to something much more substantial than merely eating pagan sacrifices — I'm entitled to stop working for a living and to be supported by you (vv. 4–14; the particular example was chosen for his readership, who were sensitive about money matters, as is clear from 2 Corinthians 8–9).

For those of you who dispute my entitlement by challenging my credentials as an emissary (2 Corinthians 10–12), **my defense when people put me under examination** is, first, that **I have seen Yeshua our Lord** (Ac 22:18, 21, where Yeshua specifically commissioned Sha'ul to evangelize the Gentiles), and, second and more to the point in your own case (v. 2), that **you yourselves are the result of my work for the Lord** as an emissary (4:15, 2C 3:1–3).

This defense is placed precisely here in order to establish as incontestable his right to be supported; so that his claim to be relinquishing it voluntarily (vv. 12–27), which he sets forth as an example to be imitated (11:1), cannot be undermined by a counter-claim that he had no such right in the first place.

4 **We** emissaries **have the right to be given food and drink** by the believers whom we serve (see also v. 14). Sha'ul, building an airtight case, supplies four arguments as proof:
(1) An analogy from everyday occupations (v. 7);
(2) A *midrash* on Deuteronomy 25:4 (vv. 8–10);
(3) An analogy from the Temple priesthood (v. 13);
(4) A teaching of the Lord Yeshua himself (v. 14).
By way of contrast, consider an excerpt from the Mishna:

> "Rabbi Tzadok said, 'Do not make of [the *Torah*] a crown with which to advance yourself or a spade with which to dig.' Also Hillel used to say, 'He who makes worldly use of the crown [of the *Torah*] will waste away.' From this you learn that whoever derives a profit from the words of the *Torah* removes his life from the world." (Avot 4:5)

In times past rabbis and other Jewish religious functionaries supported themselves in secular occupations, as did Sha'ul (v. 12, Ac 18:3), but today it is normal for congregations to pay their rabbis a salary, so that invidious comparison between Judaism and Christianity on this point is unwarranted. Elsewhere the New Testament too warns against money-grubbing (1 Ti 6:7ff.).

5–6 **Don't we**, that is, don't **Bar-Nabba and I**, as emissaries, not only "have the right to be given food and drink" (v. 4) at the expense of the other believers, but also **have the right to take along with us a believing wife** and have the believers also take care of her? **The**

other emissaries have this right; and by implication at least some of them are married. Eusebius' *History of the Christian Church* (written around 320 C.E.) quotes Papias (early 2nd century) as authority that the emissary Philip was married. **The Lord's brothers** are mentioned by name at Mt 13:55 and Mk 6:3, but only from this passage do we learn that they may have been married. However, we know **Kefa** was married from the fact that he had a mother-in-law (Mt 8:14, Mk 1:30, Lk 4:38); perhaps Sha'ul singles him out here from the other emissaries because he had been in Corinth with his wife or because he was the hero of one of the Corinthian factions (1:12), possibly the one in which were gathered most of Sha'ul's adversaries (compare Ga 2:11–14).

The passage confirms my understanding in Chapter 7 that Sha'ul was not opposed to marriage.

Kefa (Peter) is regarded by Roman Catholics as the first Pope, yet he was married. The Catholic rationale for a celibate priesthood draws on Mt 19:10–12 and elements of Chapter 7 above.

9–10 If God is concerned with cattle, all the more does he say this for our sakes. A literal rendering of this would be: "Is God concerned about cattle? Or is it all because of us that he says it? Because of us." The literal rendering would suggest that God is *not* concerned with cattle; animal rights activists would have a legitimate complaint against Sha'ul! But in fact God is concerned with cattle; indeed this is why the *Torah* forbids muzzling an ox, and this law exemplifies kindness to animals. Nevertheless God's *primary* concern is with human beings, a point Sha'ul makes by going beyond the *p'shat* (simple sense of the text, Mt 2:15N) to make a *drash* giving the significance for us through allegory. Alternatively, one may say (and this is the basis of my translation) that Sha'ul brings out an implicit *kal v'chomer* argument (see Mt 6:30N): "If, as is the case, God is concerned with cattle, how much more is he concerned with people!"

11–12 Sha'ul interrupts his listing of proofs to preview the content of vv. 15–27.

13 See Numbers 18:8–24 on the portions for the *cohanim* and the Levites. The passage may refer not just to the Temple priesthood but to priesthoods in general, including idolatrous ones, with which his readers would be more familiar.

14 See 9:4N, Mt 10:10, Lk 10:7–8; also 1 Ti 5:18.

15–18 Although Sha'ul has the right to live from preaching the Gospel, he does not; rather, he supports himself through his trade, tentmaking (Ac 18:3). He regards his keeping himself independent as its own reward, because it means that he can make the Gospel **available free of charge** and not expose himself to the slightest risk of abusing his right to be supported by the believers.

19 For although I am a free man (v. 1), **not bound to do anyone's bidding** (7:22), **I have** voluntarily **made myself a slave to all**. This principle is to "freedom" (countering license) as 8:13 is to "knowledge" (countering pride). In vv. 20–22 Sha'ul illustrates the principle of making himself a slave to others. He says, in effect, that although he could behave in a selfish way that would feel natural and comfortable, he goes out of his way to empathize with and serve others and their needs (see vv. 20–27&NN). He does this **in order to win as many people as possible** to trust in the Messiah — Sha'ul's central goal in life (vv. 16–17).

20–22 Since my translation of these three controversial verses embodies my interpretation of them (in keeping with the principles of the *JNT* Introduction, Section V, on "The Translator and His Interpretations"), it is only fair to offer a literal rendering as well:

> 20 That is, I became to the Jews as a Jew, in order that I might gain Jews; to those under law as under law, not being myself under law, in order that I might gain those under law; 21 to those apart from law as apart from law, not being apart from God's law but "en-lawed" of Messiah, in order that I may gain those apart from law. 22 I became to the weak, weak, in order that I might gain the weak. To all people I have become all things, in order that in all circumstances [or: "by all means," or: "at least"] I might save some.

I will deal with the issues clause by clause.

20a That is, Greek *kai*. Because these verses illustrate v. 19, explaining how Sha'ul "made [himself] a slave to all," KJV's "and" is not a good translation.

With Jews, what I did was put myself in the position of a Jew, literally, "I became to the Jews as a Jew." Three times in these verses Sha'ul says he "became as," and once that he "became," the distinctive attribute of a group of people; lastly he summarizes by saying that he has "become," as KJV puts it, "all things to all men" (v. 22) — a phrase which today connotes being a deceiver or a chameleon who changes his behavior to suit his audience for the sake of an ulterior goal. We know that Sha'ul rebuked Kefa for behaving in this way (Ga 2:11–16&NN), but did he play the hypocrite himself? To the same Corinthian readership Sha'ul later wrote, "We refuse to make use of shameful underhanded methods" (2C 4:1–2&N), and then used three chapters of that letter to defend himself against such charges (2 Corinthians 10–12). He could hardly expect them to believe him there if in the present passage they were to understand him as teaching that the end justifies the means.

More specifically, modern critics take this passage to mean that Sha'ul observed the *Torah* when he was with Jews but dispensed with it when with Gentiles. And not only those with an axe to grind say this of him; well-meaning Christian commentators friendly to him often appear to have an ethical blind spot which Sha'ul's critics can exploit. However, I believe the commentators' deficiency is not in the area of ethics but in the area of exegesis. Their misunderstanding of these verses forces them into a cul-de-sac from which their only escape is to appear to justify, or at least overlook, dissembling for the sake of the Kingdom of God. For they give his circumcising Timothy (Ac 16:1–3) as an example of "becoming as a Jew to the Jews" and "as under law to those under law"; and they cite his eating with Gentiles, whose food, presumably, was non-*kosher* (Ga 2:11–14&NN), to illustrate his "becoming as apart from law to those apart from law." They reveal thereby three misinterpretations:

(1) They think "becoming as" means "behaving like,"

(2) They think "under law" means "expected to obey the *Torah*" and as a consequence

equate "the Jews" with "those under law,"

(3) They seem unaware of the fact that being Jewish is not something one can put on or off at will.

In regard to the last of these, I have pointed out that Sha'ul never considered himself an ex-Jew (Ac 13:9N, 21:21N). So even if he had not been a man of integrity, even if he had been willing to put on a façade of observing Jewish customs among Jews but not among Gentiles, he could hardly have flouted Jewish law among Gentiles without having his duplicity discovered and his credibility undone.

Since Sha'ul remained a Jew all his life, we can eliminate another misinterpretation of "becoming as" — "becoming something that one formerly was not." In principle such exegesis could apply to Sha'ul's becoming as "outside the *Torah*" (v. 21) or "weak" (v. 22), but not to his becoming as a Jew, since he already was one. One Gentile believer who converted to Judaism in order to evangelize Jews argued that by becoming "as a Jew to the Jews" he was only imitating Sha'ul. This I reject, for Sha'ul does not mean he changed his religious status or philosophical outlook to that of his hearers (but see 7:18&NN, Ga 5:2–4&N).

No, Sha'ul did not play charades in "becoming as" the people around him. What he did was *empathize* with them. He put himself in their position (hence the lengthy phrase I use to translate "became as"). He entered into their needs and aspirations, their strengths and weaknesses, their opportunities and constraints, their ideas and feelings and values — in short, to use the current vernacular, he tried to understand "where they were coming from." In addition he made a point of doing nothing to offend them (10:32). Having established common ground with those he was trying to reach, he could then communicate the Good News in patterns familiar to them, using rabbinical teaching methods with Jews, philosophical thought-forms with Greeks. With the "weak" he could bear with their overscrupulousness, because he understood its origin (8:7–12). He did everything possible to overcome all barriers — psychological, social, and especially cultural; for he knew that the task of communicating the Good News had been entrusted to him (vv. 15–18, 23), and he could not expect others to meet him halfway. But he never condescended by imitating or feigning ungodliness or legalistic compulsiveness or "weak" scrupulosity, for the degree to which he would change his behavior to make them feel at ease was always constrained by his living "within the framework of *Torah* as upheld by the Messiah" (v. 21).

Moreover, Sha'ul's strategy of removing unnecessary barriers between himself and those whom he hoped to win to faith, far from being outside the pale of what Judaism can consider ethical behavior, was anticipated by Hillel when he accepted as a proselyte a Gentile who insisted on being taught the *Torah* "while standing on one foot" (Shabbat 31a, quoted in Mt 7:12N; but on this also see David Daube's *The New Testament and Rabbinic Judaism*, University of London: The Athlone Press, 1956; reprinted by Arno Press, 1973; Part III, Chapter 11).

In order to win Jews. In v. 19 Sha'ul announced that his goal was "to win as many people as possible," that is, as many of all kinds of people as he could. By "winning" them, of course, he means getting them to realize that they are sinners who need God's forgiveness and can obtain it only by accepting Yeshua's atoning death on their behalf. For a discussion of the Jewish antecedents of the Greek word for "win," *kerdainô,* see Part III, Chapter 12 of Rabbi Daube's book cited above.

Note that Jews are not exempt from needing God's forgiveness through Yeshua; if they were, Sha'ul would not be making efforts "to win Jews." Those in the Jewish community today who object to evangelistic targeting of Jews should be aware that Sha'ul gave "winning Jews" as one of his specific goals; and at the end of this section of his letter he exhorts believers to imitate him (11:1). Those who urge followers of Yeshua to desist from evangelizing Jewish people are either unaware of what this verse means or consciously inciting them to violate a religious precept.

20b People in subjection to a legalistic perversion of the *Torah*, literally, "those under law." The two questions here are: (1) Who are "those under law"? and (2) what is meant by "under law"? The first question will be easier to address after we have glanced briefly at the second.

I say "briefly" because my detailed remarks on "under law" are in Ga 3:23bN. Here I note that Greek *upo nomon* does not mean under "law" in a general sense, or even under "the *Torah*." Rather, it means "under something that is *not* the *Torah* but a perversion of it, specifically, a perversion that tries to turn it into a set of rules that supposedly one can obey 'legalistically,' that is, mechanically, with neither faith nor love for either God or men, yet nevertheless thereby earn God's applause and approval." This is why I use the phrase, "**a legalistic perversion of the *Torah***."

Further, people are not "under" it merely in the sense of "having to obey" it, but "under" it in an oppressive sense, "**in subjection to**" it as to a slavemaster (a metaphor Sha'ul uses wherever the phrase "*upo nomon*" appears, that is, in both Galatians and Romans). The legalistic perversion refers to both (1) aspects of the objective system of law developed within Jewish society, and (2) the subjective phenomenon that takes place when an individual turns God's *Torah*, which is based on grace and trust, into rules and compulsiveness. For more, see especially Ga 3:23bN and also Ro 3:20bN, 6:14–15N; Ga 2:16bN.

"Those under law" are, in my judgment, not Jews but Gentiles who have been Judaized. My reasoning is as follows: Sha'ul has already spoken about Jews and has no need to repeat himself by calling Jews "those under law"; to do so adds nothing; instead it raises the bogus issue of why he should mention the same group of people twice. The distinction some commentators make between nationality ("a Jew") and religion ("under law") did not exist for first-century Jews; Jews began thinking in this way only in the late eighteenth and nineteenth centuries (with disastrous results in the Holocaust, when Jews who considered themselves "good Germans" by nationality remained in Germany under the Nazis and perished by the hundreds of thousands). Further, there is not another Greek *kai* here to be translated epexegetically as "that is" (first paragraph of v. 20aN) and thereby justify understanding the sentence this way.

Rather, after mentioning Jews once and only once, Sha'ul now talks about three groups of Gentiles. The first have subjected themselves to a legalistic perversion of the *Torah*. The second have no involvement with the *Torah* at all (v. 21&N). And the third are the "weak," who subject themselves to their own overscrupulous conscience as if it were *Torah* (v. 22&N). Of the better-known English versions only the Living Bible's rendering of vv. 20–21 clearly delineates these three groups of Gentiles.

The legalistic perversion of the *Torah* that Judaized Gentiles subjected themselves to was not always non-Messianic Judaism. In fact, more often it was a watered-down form of it, perhaps binding them to observe certain Jewish holidays (Co 2:16–17, Ga 4:10), or binding the men to get circumcised but not to obey the rest of the Jewish law (Ga 5:3, 6:13). Unsaved Gentiles who subjected themselves to some but not all of Jewish practice were called God-fearers (Ac 10:2N), but not all God-fearers became legalistic about their observance of Jewish customs. With Gentiles who put themselves "under law" Sha'ul had to apply the principles of Acts 15 and the book of Galatians; and to do so he "became as" they, he "put himself in their position."

Be warned that the New Covenant can be perverted into legalism as easily as the *Torah*! How many millions of Christians have mistakenly supposed that they can guarantee themselves a niche in heaven by forcing themselves to obey rules such as, "Don't swear," "Don't drink," "Don't go to movies," "Say your Rosary every day" (for Catholics), "Read the Bible every day" (for Protestants), "Speak in tongues every day" (for Pentecostals), or even, "Confess Jesus as your Savior and Lord." And how many others have been immunized against the true Gospel by exposure to this false one! Thus, to make a *midrash*, "those under law" can easily be people who think they are Christians but are really "people in subjection to a legalistic perversion of the New Testament"!

Under this legalism... under such legalism. Abbreviated translations of *upo nomon*, understood as explained above.

I myself am not in subjection to a legalistic perversion of the *Torah*. If "*upo nomon*" meant "required to obey the *Torah*," Sha'ul could not have written this. Sha'ul was a Jew (Ac 13:9N), and Jews are required to obey the *Torah* — the true *Torah*. The next verse reveals what Sha'ul understood about himself in relation to the true *Torah*; this verse tells only about his relationship to legalistic perversion of it.

21 **With those who live outside the framework of *Torah***. Greek *tois anomois* can mean "to the lawless," in the sense of "wicked," or, as here, "to the un-lawed," those outside the framework of law, apart from law. The "law" spoken of here is, of course, as throughout this passage, the *Torah*; so, we could say, "the un-*Torah*ed." In some contexts (for example, Ro 2:12–16), this would be synonymous with "the Gentiles"; but here, as we have indicated in v. 20bN, it means only a particular group of Gentiles, those who have neither subjected themselves to a legalistic perversion of the *Torah* nor made their overscrupulous consciences into a self-created "*torah*" of their own (compare Ro 7:21–23&N).

This group tends toward libertinism and lack of discipline, though this need not be the case for any particular individual. Some of the people to whom Sha'ul is writing were once in this category (6:9–11), and the tone of the whole section (8:1–11:1) and indeed of the entire letter suggests that this was the mindset Sha'ul was dealing with among many leaders of the Corinthian Messianic community.

I put myself in the position of someone outside the *Torah*, literally, "as un-lawed," "as un-*Torah*ed," in the position of someone who does not relate to the *Torah* at all.

Though being myself not outside the framework of God's *Torah* but within the framework of *Torah* as upheld by the Messiah, literally, "not being un-*Torah*ed of God but (on the contrary) en-*Torah*ed of Messiah," or, as one commentator has rendered it (with a peculiarly irrelevant but for that reason memorable overtone), "not being God's outlaw but Messiah's inlaw." Greek *anomos theou* ("un-lawed of God") is contrasted with *ennomos Christou* ("en-lawed of Messiah") by the use of the strong adversative "*alla*" ("but on the contrary"), and the whole phrase is strongly tied to the previous one by the use of the participle "*ôn*" ("being"). Combined with Sha'ul's earlier remark that he is not "*upo nomon*" ("under law"), this gives us a very precise picture of exactly where he stands in relation to the *Torah*.

He is not in subjection to a legalistic perversion of the *Torah* but lives within the framework of God's true *Torah*, which he defines as being the one and only *Torah* that there is, the *Torah* of Moses, understood and modified in accordance with what the Messiah has said and done in establishing the New Covenant. The *Torah* of the Messiah is not something that abrogates and supersedes the *Torah* of Moses; rather, as Yeshua said, "Do not think that I have come to do away with the *Torah* or the Prophets. I have not come to do away with them but to fill them out," to make their full import clearer than ever (Mt 5:17&N). Thus even though the Pharisees and *Torah*-teachers (scribes), and the rabbis after them, teach many things about the *Torah* that are true, they are off-target to the extent that non-Messianic Judaism makes of the *Torah* a legalistic system that perverts its true intention, which is to be a framework for receiving God's grace through faithful trusting (Ro 10:4–8&NN).

The Messiah has made this true purpose of the *Torah* stand out as never before in three ways:

(1) By expounding its teaching correctly (numerous examples in all the Gospels);

(2) By demonstrating, through his faithful trusting of the Father even to the point of dying in order to atone for everyone's sins, how great is God's grace and love for mankind, appropriated through faithful trusting, as the *Torah* says (Ro 3:21–31&NN, 9:30–10:10&NN; Ga 2:16–3:29&NN);

(3) By making the New Covenant itself part of *Torah* (MJ 8:6b&N), which has the effect of modifying, reinterpreting or re-applying some of its specific provisions without changing its overall framework (see Yn 7:22–23&N, Ga 2:11–14&NN). Such modifications not only conform to Jewish expectations of what happens to the *Torah* when the Messiah comes (as explained in Ac 6:13–14N), but also are part of an historical sequence of changes in the *Torah* that begin in the *Tanakh* itself (for example, celebrating Purim was a new *mitzvah* given some 800 years after Sinai (Esther 9:27–28)).

Sha'ul does not say he is "in subjection to" (*upo*) the *Torah* of Messiah, for, in contrast with the framework that results from perverting the *Torah* of Moses into legalism, there is no oppressiveness, no subjection, in being within the framework of the *Torah* as set forth by the Messiah ("My yoke is easy, my burden is light," Mt 11:28–30&N; Ac 15:10&N). When Sha'ul wants to emphasize oppressiveness or compulsion in relation to something abstract, such as the law, he uses "*upo*" ("under"); if that is not his intention, he uses "*en*" ("in, within, in the framework of"). Thus, for example, at Ro 3:19, "We know that whatever the *Torah* says, it says to those living within the framework of the *Torah*," the last seven words translate Greek *en tô nomô,* "in the law"; similarly at Ro 2:12. A number of English translations, including the KJV, fail to bring out this important distinction.

The essential elements of ***Torah* as upheld by the Messiah** are clear from a number of passages. In Mk 12:28–34 Yeshua was asked what was the most important *mitzvah*; and his reply was to quote the *Sh'ma*, "Hear, O Israel, the Lord our God, the Lord is One; and you shall love the Lord your God with all your heart and with all your soul and with all your strength" (Deuteronomy 6:4–5). Then he volunteered that the second most important *mitzvah* is, "Love your neighbor as yourself" (Leviticus 19:18); this Sha'ul affirmed by declaring that love sums up all the *mitzvot* and "fulfills the whole *Torah*" (Ro 13:9–10, Ga 5:14; see also the great "love chapter," 12:31–14:1a, in the present letter). To the Galatians he said the same thing in different words, "Bear one another's burdens — in this way you will be fulfilling the *Torah* as set forth by the Messiah" (Ga 6:2&N). In the "*Torah* as set forth by the Messiah," Yeshua's atoning death becomes the final and permanently effective sacrifice for sin (Messianic Jews 9–10). Another *mitzvah* of the *Torah* as set forth by the Messiah is spreading the Good News throughout the world among Jews and Gentiles alike (Mt 28:19&N, Ac 1:8&N), a consequence of which is that unity between Jews and Gentiles in the Body of the Messiah is a more important principle of *Torah* than keeping *kosher* (Ga 2:11–14&N). Yet much of the *Torah* stands without alteration. For more, see especially Ga 6:2N.

22 With the "weak" I became "weak," in order to win the "weak." In relation to its context (8:1–11:1), here is the chief point of vv. 20–22. Sha'ul has made himself "a slave to all" (v. 19). Examples from his past include Jews and Judaized Gentiles, the "un-lawed" Gentiles include his Corinthian questioners, and now he speaks of the group those questioners are willing to ignore and ride roughshod over — the "weak," those with overactive but misguided consciences (8:7–12). Their scruples are not to be despised but understood, so that they may be won to faith (the immediate context) or their life in the Lord strengthened (the larger context; see 8:7–12). A deeper understanding of God's truth will free the "weak" (Yn 8:32) from the bondage of overscrupulousness.

With all kinds of people I have become all kinds of things, so that in all kinds of circumstances I might save at least some of them. This is the point of vv. 20–22 considered by themselves; it sums up the passage and restates v. 19. For the refutation of the criticism that Sha'ul's being "all things to all men" means he was a deceiver or a chameleon, see v. 20aN.

In all kinds of circumstances. Or: "at all events," "by all means," "at least," "certainly," "wholly." The Greek text uses the word for "all" or a derivative of it four times in this sentence and the beginning of the next.

23 Because of the rewards promised by the Good News, so that I may share in them along with the others, literally, "for the sake of the Good News, so that I might become a joint sharer in it." Verses 23–27 continue elaborating the principle of v. 19. One of Sha'ul's motives in making himself everyone's slave is altruistic, the desire to win them to trust in Yeshua (vv. 19–22). The other is, in a manner of speaking, selfish (see last paragraph of Ro 11:11–12N) — the desire to share in the benefits promised by the Good News. However, neither the *Tanakh* nor the New Testament ever considers it selfishness for a believer to desire eagerly all the good things God promises; indeed, one of the good things promised is freedom from selfishness.

24–27 Sha'ul disabuses readers who might think his having won some people to the Lord assures his place in heaven. One can never rest on one's salvation laurels; on the contrary, having invited others to enter the competition, one must oneself continue to fight temptation and run the harder. However, the competition is not against other people but against one's old nature (Ro 8:9–13). He reinforces this message at Pp 3:7–14; compare Ro 12:1–2, MJ 12:1–13).

25 **Submits himself to strict discipline**, or: "exercises self-control in everything."
Crown. See 2 Ti 4:8.

27 **I treat my body hard** (literally, "I give my body a black eye") **and make it my slave**; Sha'ul himself is the Messiah's slave (Ro 1:1, Pp 1:1) and everybody's slave (v. 19). Not that Sha'ul deprecates the flesh — the Greek word is not "*sarx*" ("flesh"), but "*sôma*" ("body"). Rather, the body makes a good servant but a bad master (compare Ro 8:13&N).

Sha'ul is probably speaking here of being **disqualified** from the rewards due faithful workers (3:8–15&N), not from salvation itself. However, compare the Apocrypha, "There is such a thing as a man who is wise and teaches many and yet is unprofitable to himself" (Sirach 37:19).

CHAPTER 10

1 **I don't want you to miss the significance of what happened to our fathers** as they left Egypt on their way to the Land of Israel. This introduces an illustration showing that the risk of rejection by God (9:27) is real; compare Psalms 78 and 106. For even though **all of them** had extraordinary advantages that might have led them to suppose their status with God was secure (vv. 1–4, compare Ro 9:4–5, Mt 3:9), "the majority of them" met with God's disapproval and died as a result (v. 5); let this be a warning to you (vv. 6–14). Compare MJ 2:3, 6:4–6.

They were **guided by the pillar of cloud** (Exodus 13:21–22) and they **passed through the sea** (Exodus 14:19–31; Psalms 105:39, 136:13–15).

2 **They… immersed themselves**. Some manuscripts read, "they were immersed"; but this is less likely, since the Jewish practice was self-immersion. Either translates a form of the Greek word "*baptizô*," usually rendered "baptized," but whose root meaning is "dip, soak, immerse" into a liquid, so that what is dipped takes on qualities of what it has been dipped in — for example, cloth in dye or leather in tanning solution (Mt 3:1N). Thus immersion **into Moshe** means being united with him, accepting his vision, goals and leadership. The Israelites did this by trusting him **in connection with the cloud and** in connection **with the sea**. Translations which have the Israelites being baptized *in* the cloud and *in* the sea are misleading — according to the *Tanakh* they were next to or under the cloud, and they passed on dry ground between walls of sea water on either side of them. Rather, as an anonymous critic has pointed out, it was the Egyptians who were "baptized *in* the sea, well and truly!"

Nevertheless, there is an analogy here between immersion into Moses and immersion "into the Messiah" (Ro 6:3, Ga 3:27; in this letter compare 1:13–15, 12:13) — just as in the following verses the "food" and "drink" are in some measure analogous with the bread and wine of Communion (Eucharist, Mass, the Lord's Supper). Whether the concept of "immersion into Moses" is original with Sha'ul or borrowed from an existing *midrash* is debated; no such *midrash* has come to my attention, although other parts of Sha'ul's illustration are found in *midrashim* (see vv. 3–4N).

3–4 The **food** (manna, Exodus 16:4–36), the **drink** (water) and the **rock** (Exodus 17:1–7; Numbers 20:7–13; Psalms 105:41, 114:8) were all **from the Spirit,... Spirit-sent**. Both phrases translate the Greek word "*pneumatikos*," used only by Sha'ul in the New Testament; he uses it 15 times in this letter, more than in all his other letters put together. I believe its meaning here is "pertaining to the Holy Spirit" (Hebrew *Ruach HaKodesh*), but in this context it could also mean "spiritual" in the sense of either "supernatural" or "conveying spiritual sustenance." The former (as in Psalm 78:24–25) makes these verses mean that even with supernatural advantages, Israel failed the test. The latter idea, that the manna and the water somehow gave spiritual nourishment, sounds strange to modern ears, but it may have roots in the Judaism of Philo, who allegorized the miraculous food and drink (or its source, the rock) into the word and wisdom of God (*Legum Allegoriae* 2:86; *Quod Deterius Potiori*, p. 176). If this is the correct interpretation, then, in context, it may bear on how the bread and wine of Communion "are" the body and blood of the Messiah (Mt 26:26&N).

The rock **followed them**.

> "According to the Aggadah [the legendary and midrashic material woven about the *Tanakh*], the Children of Israel were accompanied in the desert by a rolling stone that poured forth water." (Avraham Chill, *The Minhagim*, New York: Sepher-Hermon Press, Inc., 1979, p. 322)

This statement draws on such sources as Rashi, who comments that the Well of Miriam, mentioned in the Talmud at Ta'anit 9a, was "a rock, and... it rolled and went along with Israel, and it was the rock Moses struck"; at Shabbat 35a it is spoken of as "a moveable well." Thus it is likely that the notion of the rock's following the Israelites was already established in Judaism.

But where does Sha'ul get the idea that **that rock was the Messiah**? Suggestive but not decisive are Ro 9:33–10:11, where Yeshua is identified with the "stone that causes people to stumble" of Isaiah 28:16; and Lk 20:17–18, where he is the "stone which the builders rejected," now "the cornerstone" (Psalm 118:22) that breaks believers when they fall on it but grinds unbelievers to powder when it falls on them; see also Mt 16:18&N. In the same category are the many references to God as a Rock in the *Tanakh* (Deuteronomy 32:4, 15, 18, 30, 31; 2 Samuel 22:47; Isaiah 26:4; Psalms 18:32(31); 19:15(14); 28:1; 31:3–4(2–3); 42:10(9); 62:3(2), 7–8(6–7); 78:35; 89:27(26); 92:16(15); 94:22; 95:1; 144:1) and in Jewish prayers and songs. One of the best known *z'mirot* (songs) sung in Jewish homes on *Shabbat* is "*Tzur Mishelo Achalnu*" ("The Rock From Which We Have Eaten"). Since it may date back to as early as the second century, and because so many of its ideas parallel those of these verses, I quote two stanzas:

> The Rock, from whom we have eaten —
> Bless him, my faithful friends!
> We have eaten our fill without exhausting the supply,

Which accords with the Word of *Adonai.*
He nourishes his world, our Shepherd, our Father;
We have eaten his bread and drunk his wine....
With nourishment and sustenance he has sated our souls....
May the Merciful One be blessed and exalted!

Of seventeen traditional tunes for this *z'mirah* listed in Neil Levin's *Z'mirot Anthology* (Cedarhurst, New York: Tara Publications, 1981), my favorite is #3, a Sephardic melody popular in Israel. Some Messianic Jews in Israel sing this *z'mirah* to this melody when celebrating the Lord's Supper.

Nevertheless, none of the above fully explains why Sha'ul identified the rock following the Israelites in the wilderness with the Messiah; possibly there is a Jewish source for this, but if so, it is unknown to me. However, the idea of the pre-existence of the Messiah is found in numerous Jewish writings (see Yn 1:1N).

5 **The majority**. An understatement; of all the Israelites over 20 years old, only Joshua and Caleb were permitted to enter the Promised Land (Numbers 14:27–38, 26:63–65).

6 **Prefigurative historical events** or object lessons (Greek *tupoi*, "types"). Like us, the Israelites had numerous advantages; let **us not set our hearts on evil things as they did**, so that we may prevent the negative aspects (vv. 5, 7–10) from prefiguring our destinies too.

7–8 This refers to the making of the golden calf. **"Indulge in revelry"** means sexual play or idolatry or — as in v. 8, alluding to Numbers 25:1–9 — the former in the service of the latter.

Twenty-three thousand died in a single day. Numbers 25:9 says 24,000 died in the plague. Harmonizers suggest that both numbers are approximations to an exact figure between the two; or, alternatively, that of the 24,000 who died of the plague, 23,000 died on the same day. Some think that Sha'ul forgot the correct figure and gave an approximation from memory (and not a bad one at that); the acceptability of this explanation depends on one's theory of inspiration: could God, inspiring the Bible through fallible human beings, have permitted even a relatively small factual error to be included in the text?

9 See Numbers 21:4–6; compare Yn 3:14, which refers to the same event.

10 Numbers 17:6–15 (16:41–50) and possibly other incidents. **Destroying angel**, Exodus 12:23, 2 Samuel 24:16, 1 Chronicles 21:15, 2 Chronicles 32:21; compare also Ac 12:23. The Midrash Rabbah to Ecclesiastes 4:3 speaks of "five destroying angels," each with its own name.

11 **To us who are living in the *acharit-hayamim***, the *Tanakh*'s "latter days" (Numbers 24:14; Deuteronomy 4:30, 31:29; Jeremiah 23:20, 30:24, 48:47, 49:39; Ezekiel 38:16; Daniel 2:28, 10:14; Hosea 3:5) and "end of days" (Daniel 12:13). Since the Messiah has already come once, we are at least living in the beginning of the End

Times, awaiting his return at the end of the End Times. This translation accords also with rabbinic usage, for they used Hebrew *ketz* ("end") to mean the end of this age and the beginning of the Messianic Age. A more literal rendering is: "upon whom the goals and fulfillments of the ages has come," and this is not inconsistent with what has been said here.

13 Temptation, or "testing." If the latter, then the question arises whether God ever puts people to the test (see Ya 1:13&N), and the answer is that he does. The most famous testings were of Avraham (Genesis 22), Job (the whole book) and Yeshua (in the desert, Mattityahu 4). In Revelation 2–3 those who overcome, who pass the test, will receive rewards.

14–22 Building on the warnings of vv. 6–13, Sha'ul presents a new reason for not eating food sacrificed to idols (the issue raised at 8:1), that it just doesn't make sense for **sensible people** (v. 15) to **drink both a cup of the Lord and a cup of demons** (v. 21). This is the capstone of the argument supporting and leading up to the conclusion at v. 23.

16 The "cup of blessing." The third cup of the Passover *Seder* is called the "cup of blessing"; and since vv. 16–21 are about the Lord's Supper, which is based on the Last Supper that Yeshua ate, which was a Passover meal, this may be the meaning. Or, because of the following phrase, "**over which we make a *b'rakhah***" (Hebrew for "blessing"; see Mt 9:8N), it may refer to a special blessing beyond the normal blessing over wine (see Mt 26:27N), said in order to consecrate the wine and make it "be," for our **sharing** (or: "communion"), the Messiah's **bloody sacrificial death** (literally, "blood"; see Ro 3:25N; compare Ro 6:3–5). The Lord's Supper is the subject of 11:23–34 below.

17 Since we all partake of the one loaf of bread, Yeshua, who said, "I am the bread of life" (Yn 6:35), **we who are many constitute one body**. This becomes the seed-idea of Chapter 12.

18 Physical Israel, literally, "the Israel according to flesh." This is a key verse for evaluating the traditional Christian claim, formalized as Replacement theology, that the Church has supplanted the Jews as "the true Israel" or "the new Israel." In the present verse the issue takes this form: does Sha'ul's use of the phrase, "according to flesh," imply the existence of a different Israel "according to Spirit"? Sha'ul contrasts these two modifiers at Ro 1:3–4, 8:4–5, and Ga 4:29; and these are the only places where the phrase, "according to Spirit," appears at all in the New Testament; although in 19 other places where the phrase "according to flesh" is found, one can usually imagine an alternative "according to Spirit." But it is at Ro 11:17–24, in his analogy with cultivated and wild olive trees, that Sha'ul expresses most clearly his understanding of Israel in the present era as consisting of three groups — branches of the cultivated tree which have been cut off and remain cut off (non-Messianic Jews), branches of the cultivated tree which have been cut off and grafted back into their own tree (Messianic Jews), and wild olive branches that have been grafted into the cultivated tree (Gentile Christians); see Ro 11:23–24N. Thus **physical Israel** is a subset of Israel consisting of the first two of these three groups: non-Messianic Jews plus

Messianic Jews. At no place in the New Testament is the Church called the new Israel or the true Israel. More on this at Ro 11:26aN and Ga 6:16N.

10:23–11:1 The question of freedom, raised at 6:12 in the same words, is answered here in terms of the effect not on oneself but on one's **fellow**, and the criterion is: is it **edifying**? Verses 25 and 27–29a give three rather specific instructions relating to freedom, in answer to the question raised at 8:1 (see 8:1N, 8:13N); vv. 26 and 29b–31 provide the underlying rationale; and vv. 32–33 and 11:1 sum up the applicable principles of Messianic living, key elements of the "*Torah* as upheld by the Messiah" (9:21&N).

32 Is this a threefold division of humanity? Non-Messianic **Jews** are mentioned, pagan **Gentiles** (literally, "Greeks"), and **God's Messianic Community**, consisting of Messianic Jews and Messianic Gentiles. Some draw the inference from this verse that a Jew who gets saved is no longer a Jew. The reasoning is that just as when a Gentile comes to faith in the Messiah he leaves his paganism behind, so also when a Jew comes to such faith he leaves his "legalistic Judaism" behind; that in God's Messianic Community both lose their former identity — "there is neither Jew nor Gentile" (Ga 3:28), the Messiah "has made us both one and has broken down the *m'chitzah* which divided us" and created "from the two groups a single new humanity" (Ep 2:14–15) for whom "neither being circumcised nor being uncircumcised matters — what matters is being a new creation" (Ga 6:15).

Though it is true that Jews and Gentiles are equally in need of salvation, and in this regard there is no difference between them, nevertheless salvation does not wipe out their identity as Jews and Gentiles. Besides what I have written on this at Ga 3:28N and Ep 2:11–22&NN, I should observe here that Sha'ul referred to saved Gentiles as "Gentiles" (Ro 11:13&N, Ep 2:11&N) and to saved Jews as "Jews" (Ga 2:13&N); also he spoke of himself as still a Pharisee (Ac 23:6&N), which implies, of course, that as a believer he considered himself still Jewish. God's Messianic Community, his Church, consists of saved Jews who remain Jews and saved Gentiles who remain Gentiles.

CHAPTER 11

11:2–14:40 A new section begins, dealing with public worship. There are three topics: (1) veiling of women in public worship (vv. 3–16), (2) disorder at the Lord's Supper (vv. 17–34), (3) charismatic gifts from the Holy Spirit and their use in public (12:1–14:40); this section also includes the famous "love chapter" (12:31–14:1a). Tactful Sha'ul commences with a compliment, as at 1:4–5.

2–16 Three issues for today raised by this passage:

(1) Male chauvinism: does Sha'ul teach an unacceptable male dominance?

(2) Cultural relativism: are the prescriptions set forth here laws for all times and places, or are they meant only for first-century Corinth?

(3) Messianic Judaism: if the rules about head covering apply today, does this keep Messianic Jewish men from wearing *kippot* (*yarmulkes*)?

2 **I passed on** (Greek *paradidômi*) the **traditions** (the related Greek word *paradoseis*). At v. 23 and 15:3 the words "received" and "passed on" are used of two of these "traditions" — the Lord's Supper and the evidence of Yeshua's resurrection. "Tradition" in this sense simply means "that which has been carefully and faithfully 'passed on' by one generation and 'received' by the next." This corresponds to Jewish understanding; for example, as the Mishna puts it:

> "Moses received the *Torah* from Sinai and passed it on to Joshua, and Joshua to the elders, and the elders to the Prophets, and the Prophets to the men of the Great Synagogue…." (Avot 1:1, quoted in full at Ac 6:13–14N)

Clearly Judaism places a high value on citing the authority for what one teaches — this is evident from virtually any page of the Talmud. Perhaps this is why Sha'ul dwells on the process of "receiving" and "passing on." Contrast Yeshua's, "You have heard…. But I tell you…." (Mt 5:21, 27, 31, 33, 38, 43), which made his listeners conclude that "he did not instruct them like their *Torah*-teachers but as one who had authority himself" (Mt 7:28–29&N).

The New Testament speaks of three kinds of "traditions":

(1) The traditions of the Messianic Community, here and at 2 Th 2:15, 3:6;
(2) "Human traditions," meaning pagan traditions, Co 2:8;
(3) Jewish traditions, that is, the Oral *Torah* as set forth by the Pharisees — Sha'ul, at Ga 1:14; and Yeshua, eight times in Mt 15:2–6 and Mk 7:3–13. Some of these Jewish traditions are regarded in the New Testament as bad (Mk 7:5–13&N); but others are, by implication, good (Yn 7:37–39&NN).

It seems clear that in passing on traditions Sha'ul expected them to be observed, so that in a sense he was establishing a kind of Oral *Torah* for the Messianic congregations. At the same time, he expected the governing principle for the observance of this Oral "*Torah* as upheld by the Messiah" (9:21) to be love, not legalism, and certainly not the greed that was replacing love when the Corinthians celebrated the Lord's Supper (vv. 17–22).

3 The presenting symptom seems to be the forwardness and insubordination of Corinthian women (see also 14:33b–35&N). They followed worldly fashions and did not dress modestly, as befits people of God (see 1 Ti 2:9–15&NN). Even in the Messianic Community, where "there is neither male nor female" (Ga 3:28&N; see 10:18N above), there remain distinctions between the roles of men and women; and these straightforwardly have to do with headship, authority, and submission. How should moderns sensitized to the demeaning of women understand this passage? By relating it to the last phrase of the verse, which says that **the head of the Messiah is God** (compare 15:24–28), a relationship that Yeshua presumably does not find demeaning. Nor do we expect a man to chafe when taught that **the head of every man is the Messiah** (compare 3:21–23, Ep 4:15). So Sha'ul expects wives to receive with equanimity the comparable word that **the head of a wife is her husband** (compare Genesis 3:16, Ep 5:22–25&N).

However, Sha'ul's reasoning presents a problem. True, he balances "male chauvinist" elements (vv. 4–10, 13–15) with "feminist" elements (vv. 11–12), though not in equal quantity. So long as he bases his counsel of propriety on theology and Scripture

(vv. 7–12), the Corinthians' cultural norms (vv. 4–6, 13), or the practice in other congregations (v. 16), his arguments are acceptable. But an appeal to "nature" is harder for the modern reader to receive; see vv. 14–15&N.

4 Every man who prays in public worship meetings **or prophesies** (see 12:10).

Wearing something down over his head. This is the literal translation, and it is used here to show that Sha'ul is talking about wearing a veil, not a hat. The usual translation, "with his head covered," obscures this fact, and as a result an issue has arisen in Messianic Judaism that should never have come up at all, namely, whether it is proper for a Messianic Jewish man to wear a *kippah* ("skullcap" or, in Yiddish, *yarmulke*) in public worship. Of course it is proper, since objection to it is based only on a mis-translation of this verse. For more, see my *Messianic Jewish Manifesto,* pp 170–171.

Generally speaking, Orthodox Jews wear *kippot* at all times, Conservative Jews in religious contexts only, and Reform Jews rarely if at all. The custom of wearing a *kippah* has no Scriptural basis and is not required even in the Talmud; it did not acquire mandatory status (from an Orthodox Jewish viewpoint) until the writing of the *Shulchan Arukh* in the 16th century, though it had become customary some centuries earlier. In the synagogue a Jew saying his prayers will sometimes pull his *tallit* (prayer shawl) up over his head; he does it in order to create privacy and intimacy between himself and God and this distinguishes his situation from the public praying or prophesying Sha'ul is writing about.

5 Concerning an adulteress Moshe commands, "The *cohen* is to stand the woman before *Adonai* and let the hair of the woman's head go loose" (i.e., he removes the headdress symbolizing her faithfulness to her husband; Numbers 5:18). And in the Mishna we read:

> "These are the women who may be divorced and not given the marriage settlement specified in their *ketubah* [marriage contract]: she who transgresses the Law of Moses and Jewish custom.... And what is meant here by Jewish custom? If she goes out (into public areas) with her hair loose, or spins cloth in the street (that is, with her arms exposed), or spends time talking loosely (or flirting) with all kinds of men." (Ketubot 7:6)

Here Sha'ul is not imposing Jewish standards; rather, his concern with decorum and **shame** leads him to want women who believe in the Messiah to conform to customs found throughout the Eastern Mediterranean (v. 16). Both in early Semitic and later Greek society chaste women wore their hair up or under a veil. However, in v. 10&N he introduces a transcultural element as well.

7–12 He is the image... of God. Genesis 1:27 says that man (that is, humanity), made in the image of God, was "created male and female." But Genesis 2:21–23, reflected in v. 8, explains how God did this, by making Eve from Adam's side as a helper suitable for him (Genesis 2:18, alluded to in v. 9). Verses 11–12 balance out the picture. Of interest is this quotation from the Midrash Rabbah:

> "[Rabbi Simlai] said to [his *talmidim*], 'At first Adam was created from dust and

Eve from Adam; but from now on it will be "in our image, after our likeness" (Genesis 1:26); not man without woman, and not woman without man, and neither of them without the *Sh'khinah* (God's glorious presence).'"(Genesis Rabbah 8:9).

10 A difficult verse, perhaps to be understood from Isaiah 6:2, where the angels cover themselves in the presence of a higher authority, God; or perhaps that even if a woman cares little about shocking men, she should care about shocking the angels, who are present at public worship.

14–15 Does **the nature of things itself**, Greek *phusis*, "nature" (from which come English words such as "physics" and "physical"), really **teach you that a man who wears his hair long degrades himself**? Whether scientific measurement would uphold the assumption that men's hair naturally grows shorter than women's is not precisely the point; rather, there are natural distinctions between men and women which should not be obscured. Sha'ul is probably in some measure campaigning against homosexuality and transvestism. "Nature" here seems to include not only physical but social and cultural elements; we can theorize that in a culture where men wear their hair long without compromising their male identity and women with short hair are still considered feminine, Sha'ul might not press the issue as he does. We know from 9:19–23 that he was sensitive to cross-cultural interaction, but further speculation is probably fruitless. This leaves open the question of whether his strictures apply today or were only meant for first-century Corinth. But see 1 Ke 3:3N.

17–34 Since Sha'ul's letters were written before any of the Gospels, this is the oldest record of the Last Supper in the New Testament. The subject of the Lord's Supper was raised at 10:16–21 and is now the second matter concerning public worship to which Sha'ul addresses himself in this section of the letter (11:2–14:40; see v. 2N). Compare the reports of the Last Supper in the Gospels: Mt 26:20–30, Mk 14:17–26, Lk 22:14–20, Yn 13:1–14:31. Also see Appendix, p. 933.

18 Cliques. Compare 1:10–17, 3:4–23.

20 A meal of the Lord. See Rv 1:10N.

23 I passed on, Greek *paradidômi;* see v. 2N. The Greek has a wordplay not effectively brought over into English: the word translated "**betrayed**" is also a form of *paradidômi* (**Yeshua, on the night he was** "passed on [to the authorities]").

24 After he had made the *b'rakhah*. See Mt 9:8N, 26:26N.

25 The cup after the meal, the "cup of blessing" in the Passover Service, as reported by Luke. See 10:16&N, Lk 22:20&N.

The New Covenant spoken of in Jeremiah 31:30–33(31–34), Mt 26:28&N.

26 At Passover Jews all over the world retell the story of the plagues and the Exodus and thus proclaim the central fact on which their peoplehood is founded (see 5:6–8N).

Likewise, members of the Messianic Community are to **proclaim the death of the Lord** as their exodus from sin and as the basis for their existence. Both proclamations look not only back toward a past redemption but also forward to a future one; hence the proclamation is **until he comes** the second time.

27–31 Failure at self-judgment (vv. 27–29, 31) opens one to demonic attack (compare 5:5, 10:20–22), which can cause sickness or death (v. 30). This is a good place to be reminded that the root meaning of the Hebrew word for "to pray," *l'hitpallel*, is "to judge oneself."

30 Sin can lead to sickness. This resembles the modern theory of psychosomatic illness but points to spiritual rather than emotional roots of disease.

32 Compare MJ 12:3–14.

CHAPTER 12

1 **Things of the Spirit**, Greek *pneumatika*, not "spiritual gifts," as in some translations; although the gifts (Greek *charismata*, vv. 4, 9, 28, 30, 31) of the Holy Spirit are the subject of these three chapters. Sha'ul first deals with the diversity of gifts in the one body of the Messiah (12:1–12:31a), apparently addressing the problem of people's taking pride in having this or that gift from the Spirit, or feeling inferior because they don't have it. In the "love chapter" (12:31b–14:1a) he describes the "best way" to live a Messianic life, even better than possessing spiritual gifts. Finally, in 14:1b–40 he addresses the problem the Corinthians had with disorderly use of the gifts of the Spirit in public worship (see 11:2N).

2–3 **Idols, which can't speak at all** (Psalm 115:4–9), in contrast to **speaking by the Spirit of God**, by the ***Ruach HaKodesh*** (Holy Spirit), who speaks through human beings in various ways (vv. 7, 10).

No one… says, "Yeshua is cursed!" — literally, "*Anathema* Yeshua!" On curses, see Ro 9:3N. Since saying "**Yeshua is Lord**" is not merely making sounds with one's mouth, but truly believing, it requires the presence of the Holy Spirit (Ro 8:9); likewise to curse Yeshua is a sure sign of the absence of the Holy Spirit and the likely presence of some other spirit that opposes God (1 Yn 3:24–4:8). Compare 16:22 below.

4–6 The word "Trinity" is never used in the New Testament, but the elements which led theologians to develop such a concept are seen in passages like this one, where **Spirit, Lord**, and **God** refer respectively to the Holy Spirit, Yeshua the Messiah, and the Father. There seems to be less significance in the attribution of the three activities — **giving** to the Spirit, **being served** to the Lord, and **working** to God (the Father) — than in the oversight of all the activities by **the same** one God.

I agree with the following paragraphs, written by a Roman Catholic:

"The Corinthians, it seems, had been disputing about the relative value of the different charismatic graces, and valued some of them, such as speaking in tongues, more highly than others. In his teaching in response to these disputes, Paul deliberately lumps all the charismatic graces together, and to describe them uses four different words as though these four words were synonyms. Each of the words is used to describe all the graces given by the Spirit for building up the community. Each of the words brings out a different characteristic of one same reality:

> 'Now concerning spiritual gifts (*pneumata*).... There are varieties of gifts (*charismata*), but the same Spirit; and there are varieties of service (*diakonia*), but the same Lord; and there are varieties of working (*energemata*), but it is the same God who inspires them all in every one.'

"In this passage, 'gifts,' 'services,' 'workings' are but different words for '*pneumata*,' the 'inspirations' or spiritual 'gifts' which build up the body of Christ. And 'Spirit,' 'Lord,' 'God' are... the one source of all the gifts." (Paul Hinnebusch, *Community In The Lord*, Notre Dame, Indiana: Ave Maria Press, 1975, p. 169)

7, 11 **The particular manifestation of the Spirit** that each person receives is due not to his own merit but to **the Spirit,... distributing to each person as he chooses**, not to provide ground for pride but **for the common good**. See 4:7 above.

8–10 Nine *charismata* (supernatural gifts; see v. 1N) from the Holy Spirit are mentioned:

(1) **Word of wisdom**, supernatural wisdom about how to solve a practical or spiritual problem. A homey example: my wife has what I playfully call the "gift of finding"; although she has plenty of *sekhel* (common sense) in knowing how to look for a lost item, not infrequently, in response to prayer, God reveals to her supernaturally where the missing item is located. (I provide her many opportunities to exercise her gift, since I seem to have the "gift" of losing.)

(2) **Word of knowledge**, supernatural knowledge relevant to understanding a situation. Example: a pastor expelling demons from a woman was told by the Spirit that the demons were connected with "smell of mother"; it seems unlikely that hours of questioning the subject would have revealed that in times of stress she would smell the pillows her deceased mother once used.

(3) **Faith** (or: "faithfulness") beyond what believers "normally" have, even though all faith is a gift from God (Ep 2:8–9) — "the faith which produces not only miracles, but martyrs" (Robertson & Plummer's *Commentary*).

(4) **Gifts of healing**. Nearly everyone is acquainted with inexplicable healings (doctors more than most people). Some of these are from God, and of these some come in response to "ordinary" prayer (Ya 5:14–16), while others result from the ministry of those who have one or more of the "gifts" (plural) of healing. To complicate matters, there are healings and miracles that are not from God but from other spirits, even from Satan (Mt 24:24; Ac 16:16–19; 2C 11:14; 2 Th 2:9; Rv 13:1–4, 12–15), not to mention ordinary impostors who neither produce genuine healings nor draw on any spirit more supernatural than their own spirit of greed. Nevertheless, healing was one of the chief ministries of Yeshua the Messiah when he walked the earth

(Mt 4:23–24), and he promised that we who believe in him would do "even greater works" (Yn 14:12). The New Testament does not teach that God will heal every illness, but it does teach that he will supernaturally heal some. This promise can stand up to objective research, of which there has been some but not much.

(5) **The working of miracles**. In a sense the events of everyday life are miracles, but the concept here seems to refer to "unusual" miracles, not "usual" ones. Spectacular miracles are reported more frequently in areas where the Gospel is relatively new. For example, in the 1960's reports came out of parts of Indonesia reached recently by the Gospel that water had been turned to wine and even that dead people had been raised to life. Verifying the truth of such reports is beyond the scope of a commentary, but the integrity of the Gospel demands avoiding credulity and applying evidential standards at least as high as for establishing other kinds of facts.

(6) **Prophecy** is speaking on behalf of God. The standard for judging a prophet is given in the *Torah*:

> "But the prophet who presumes to speak a word in my name, which I have not commanded him to speak, or who speaks in the name of other gods — that prophet shall die. And if you ask yourself, 'How are we to know if the word spoken is not from *Adonai?*' — when a prophet speaks in the name of *Adonai*, if the thing predicted does not come to pass, then it has not been spoken by *Adonai*; rather, the prophet has spoken it presumptuously, and you are not to be afraid of him." (Deuteronomy 18:20–22)

Significantly, this passage follows on Moshe's prediction that "a prophet like me" would arise, that prophet being Yeshua (see Ac 3:22&N).

Prophecy, then, is speaking on God's behalf, like the prophets of the *Tanakh*. Some, but not all, of their writings are predictive; but all are intended to inspire fear and awe of God. Today's prophets speak on God's behalf, but their prophecies do not thereby become Holy Scripture (many prophecies mentioned in the Bible did not become Holy Scripture either), but they are to be paid serious attention; see, however, paragraph (7) following. (Also see Ac 11:27N.)

(7) **The ability to judge between spirits**, popularly called "discernment of spirits," is the ability to tell whether a particular phenomenon is from the Spirit of God, from a person's own spirit, or from some demonic spirit; one might call it the supernatural ability to avoid being deceived. See paragraph (4) above for scriptural references. This particular gift is often needed in order to discern whether healings, miracles and prophecies are truly from God; it is also an indispensible part of the spiritual equipment of anyone who undertakes to expel demons.

(8) **The ability to speak in different kinds of tongues**. "Speaking in tongues" has become known more widely in the twentieth century than in centuries past, since there has been an entire movement within Christianity identified with it, namely, Pentecostalism, or, more recently, the Charismatic Movement among mainline denominations. The term means speaking in a language one has not learned.

The New Testament seems to mention or imply at least four **different kinds of tongues**:

(a) Speaking in ordinary human languages other than those one knows (Ac 2:4–11, 10:44–46, 19:6, and, some believe, by implication, 8:15–17, 9:17–20), as a sign that the Holy Spirit has come to dwell in God's people (Ac 1:8, 2:12–21, 10:47–48, 11:15–17). "Non-charismatics," those today who do not speak in tongues, and "anti-charismatics," those today who oppose speaking in tongues, understand this "sign" to be limited to the representative groups who received the Gospel — the Jews in Acts 2, the Samaritan "quasi-Jews" in Acts 8, the Gentiles in Acts 10–11, and the special group who believed in Yochanan the Immerser but knew nothing of Yeshua in Acts 19. These groups represent the spreading of the umbrella of God's people from the Jewish center, Jerusalem, to wider and wider circles of humanity, in keeping with the program of Ac 1:8. On the other hand, Charismatics and Pentecostals sometimes apply this same "sign" to individual believers and consider them to have been immersed (baptized) in the Holy Spirit only if they have spoken in tongues; for them Sha'ul's experience reported in Acts 9 is important because it is taken as the normative example of a single individual's receiving the Holy Spirit.

(b) Speaking in ordinary human languages other than those one has learned, not as a sign of receiving the Holy Spirit, but rather as a miracle from God. For example, one Pentecostal group reported in its denominational publication that one of their missionaries in Africa was saved from the soup pot of a cannibalistic tribe when he began to speak in the language of that tribe, a language he had never learned.

(c) Speaking publicly in a worship service in a language one has not learned, a language which may not be a human language at all but possibly a "tongue of angels" (13:1). This seems to be the "gift of tongues" concerning which Sha'ul gives rules in Chapter 14.

(d) Also in Chapter 14 Sha'ul distinguishes the public "gift of tongues" from speaking privately to God in a language one has not learned; the implication may be that some who speak in tongues privately to God do not have the "gift of tongues" suitable for public worship meetings.

(9) **The ability to interpret tongues**, to give the meaning in ordinary language of what is spoken by the "gift of tongues" (see 8(c) above) in a public worship service. From 14:5, 13 one can infer the following charismatic equation:

Tongues + Interpretation = Prophecy.

The best commentary on the *charismata* is 1 Ke 4:10: "As each one has received some spiritual gift (*charisma*), he should use it to serve others"; also see Ro 12:6–8&N.

The whole subject of the *charismata* is very controversial within the Body of the Messiah these days, and Jewish believers often seem to find themselves in the thick of the argument. Because of this, it seems wise to devote some space to giving its broad outlines. There are four fairly distinct positions:

(1) Narrow Charismatics: These hold that there is an experience known as immersion (baptism) in the Holy Spirit which is available to all believers and sometimes is a distinct experience subsequent to salvation; the necessary and sufficient sign or evidence that a believer has had this experience is that he has spoken in tongues. In

extreme cases these regard Non-Charismatics and Anti-Charismatics as second-class Christians or even as nonbelievers.

(2) Broad Charismatics: Same as (1), but having spoken in tongues is neither necessary nor sufficient as a sign of being immersed in the Spirit. The emphasis is more on the fact that the *charismata* are for the present day, in contrast with position (4) below. These are generally tolerant of Non-Charismatics and receive them in love.

(3) Non-Charismatics: These range from those whose viewpoint is the same as (2) but who have not personally received any of the *charismata* to those who think position (2) is mistaken but receive Charismatics in a spirit of tolerance and love as brothers who may in fact be right.

(4) Anti-Charismatics: These believe the Charismatics are wrong, that the *charismata* ceased in the first century, for "the perfect" (understood to be the canon of the New Testament) has replaced "the partial" (13:8–14:1a&N below). In extreme cases these regard Charismatics as second-class Christians or even as nonbelievers.

Those who oppose Charismatics often believe they rely too much on subjective experience. The objection is understandable, since Charismatics, who believe they have had a genuine experience with the Holy Spirit, would certainly be expected to take that experience seriously. On the other hand, it is possible for Anti-Charismatics to be influenced unduly by their own negative experiences with overzealous Charismatics, so that they end up throwing the baby out with the bathwater. As might be expected, each group stresses the verses of Scripture which support its case and offers harmonious explanations of verses that raise difficulties. All four positions have able spokesmen, who will generally agree that sometimes the emotions stimulated by the debate are *not* gifts of the Holy Spirit!

Since the Charismatic issue is not specifically Jewish, I will not develop further the cases for and against the above positions, except to observe that if "Jews ask for signs" (1:22&N) the question of the *charismata* may be significant in Jewish evangelism.

12–31 Believers have an organismic unity like that of a body; indeed, they are **parts of** such a body, the **body of the Messiah** (v. 27; compare 6:15; Ro 12:5; Ep 1:23, 2:16, 4:4–16; Co 1:18, 2:19). Therefore, all members of the Messiah's body, **whether Jews or Gentiles, slaves or free** (v. 13), have their places determined by God and have appropriate functions (ministries) which they should find and develop, trusting God for empowerment by the Holy Spirit. They should appreciate, not envy, others' ministries and gifts. The purpose of the gifts is not self-aggrandizement but building up the whole body in love.

13 Whether Jews or Gentiles (literally, "Greeks"). See Ga 3:28&N for references to Sha'ul's numerous other statements of the principle of Jewish-Gentile equality under the New Covenant, and a discussion of what this principle implies (and doesn't imply) for Messianic Judaism. Here the basis of the equality is stated to be that both **were immersed** by the same **Spirit** into the same **body**.

28 God has determined several distinct ministries. **First**, the most important group, are the **emissaries** ("apostles") — those sent by God to proclaim the Gospel and form new congregations of believers. **Second** are **prophets**, who speak for God (see vv. 8–10N, paragraph 6). **Third** are **teachers** to deepen believers' knowledge of God's truth. **Then**, after these in importance, are **those who work miracles** (same, paragraph 5) and **those with gifts of healing** (same, paragraph 4). Listed next are **those with** two gifts not mentioned specifically in vv. 8–10, the **ability to help** those in need and skill in **administration**; these seem to cover much the same ground as four gifts named in Ro 12:8 — counseling, giving, doing acts of mercy and leading. But exercise of those gifts would be manifestly improved if one also had the *charismata* listed above that are not mentioned here — wisdom, knowledge, faith, and discernment of spirits (vv. 8–10N, paragraphs 1, 2, 3 and 7). Finally, at the bottom of both this list (v. 30) and the one above, are the two showy *charismata* that are most easily abused — speaking in different kinds of **tongues** (see the four varieties listed in vv. 8–10N, paragraph 8) and interpretation (see vv. 8–10, paragraph 9). Sha'ul minimizes the importance of these two gifts as compared with the others, but at the same time that he deals with abuses involved in manifesting the gift of tongues, he instructs the Corinthians not to forbid speaking in tongues (14:39) and wishes that all would speak in tongues (14:5). Thus he strikes a balance worthy of imitation (11:1).

31 Eagerly seek the better gifts, especially prophecy (14:1); and yet **the best way of all**, literally, "a way according to excellence," is love.

CHAPTER 13

13:1–14:1a This hymn, which can stand alone yet fits its context perfectly, is the great "love chapter," just as Messianic Jews 11 is the great "faith chapter" and Chapter 15 below the great "resurrection chapter." Love is "the best way of all" (12:31) because it "fulfills the entire *Torah*" (Ro 13:8–10, Ga 5:14; see also Mt 22:34–40, Ya 2:8). The word in Greek for "love" is "*agapê*," defined in the New Testament (by passages such as this chapter, Yo 3:16, 17:23–26 and 1 Yn 2:5–4:21) as giving of and from oneself; love expresses itself in acts of benevolence, kindness and mercy in which heart, mind and will are united because they are motivated and empowered by God. Such love goes beyond what one can generate of oneself, because it has its origin in God. When such love is experienced by one person from another, the experience is of God's love channeled through that other.

Some Christian commentators stress the supposed uniqueness and superiority of *agapê* over the *ahavah* ("love") and *chesed* ("loving-kindness") of the *Tanakh*. But this is surely a false distinction, for the love of God is not different now from what it was then; nor is it more available now than before. This false differentiation has opened the way for Jewish critics such as Leo Baeck (in *The Essence of Judaism*) to present New Testament religion as romantic, based on mere feelings. Rather, the New Testament expositions of *agapê* clarify the nature of the very *ahavah* and *chesed* spoken of in the *Tanakh*.

1–3 Manifestations of the gifts of the Spirit may have value for others yet be without value for the person manifesting them unless accompanied by love. There is no ground for pride in possessing a gift from the Spirit. **I may give away everything I own**, and others may gain thereby, **but if I lack love, I gain nothing**. Since such love, as defined above, puts aside all concern with gain, we are faced with the paradox of love: to gain its benefits one must lose all concern for gaining them. Compare Lk 9:24, Yn 12:24–26.

My body to be burned *(ina kauthêsomai)*, as found in most modern English translations, or: "my body so that I can glory" (*ina kauchêsoô*), as in the UBS *Greek New Testament.* Both readings have strong and early manuscript evidence.

4–7 This description of love is not of its outward manifestations but of its inward properties. Sha'ul does not, however, define love as inward feelings, because love must act (1 Yn 2:5–4:21) — faith works itself out in love (Ga 5:6). It is precisely because love produces deeds that it fulfills the *Torah* (Ro 13:8–10&N).

13:8–14:1a Prophecies, tongues, knowledge and the other gifts **will pass** away **when the perfect comes** (that is, when Yeshua returns; but see last part of 12:8–10N). There will be no need then for such gifts; they are for this world only, but **what lasts** on into the next, says Sha'ul, following a common rabbinic pattern of comparing the two worlds, is **trust** (faith), **hope and love**. These are all inner spiritual qualities, but because love is an inner state that results in outward action, **the greatest of them is love**. For this reason, his final advice on the matter is, **"Pursue love."**

12 Now we see obscurely in a mirror. Compare the cave allegory in Plato's *Republic.* In the Talmud appears the following aggadic passage:

> "Abaye said the world contains 36 righteous men, but Raba said 18,000. No contradiction — the 36 see the Holy One, blessed be he, in a bright mirror, while the 18,000 contemplate him in a dim one." (Sanhedrin 97b, condensed)

13 Three things last: trust, hope, love. The formula of "three great things" is common in Jewish literature. The same three appear in Colossians 1:4–5. Compare Micah 6:8, and this example from the Mishna:

> "Rabban Shim'on ben-Gamli'el said, 'The world is sustained by three things: judgment, truth and peace, as it is said, "Execute the judgment of truth and peace in your gates" (Zechariah 8:16).'"(Avot 1:18)

See also Pirkey-Avot 1:2, quoted in Ro 12:8–21N

CHAPTER 14

1–5 Given the framework of **love** (Chapter 13), it is desirable to **keep on eagerly seeking the things of the Spirit** (12:1&N), **especially… to be able to prophesy**, for the gift of prophecy (on what it is, see 12:8–10N, paragraph 6) is greater than the gift of tongues; however, the latter, plus interpretation, equals prophecy (v. 5). Prophecy is greater because it **edifies the congregation**, whereas speaking in tongues **edifies** only oneself — although this is good, not bad ("…if I pray in a tongue, my spirit does pray," v. 14), so that Sha'ul can say, **I wish you would all speak in tongues**; and in this regard, as is so often the case, he himself sets the standard (v. 18). On the word "edify," see 10:1N.

6–25 Though the gift of tongues (12:8–10N, paragraph 8) has value, it can be abused in public, so that the congregation is not edified.

16 ***Amen***. The Jewish influence on Christian worship practice is evident. The word means, "I affirm it, so be it, in truth," and its congregational use is found throughout the *Tanakh*. Sha'ul assumes the largely Gentile Corinthian church has adopted the practice of using that Hebrew word. Also see Mt 5:18N, Ro 9:5N.

21 Sha'ul makes a *midrash* on this text from Isaiah; its *p'shat* (plain sense in context; see Mt 2:15N) has nothing to do with the gift of tongues. Here the ***Torah*** means the whole *Tanakh*, not just the Five Books of Moses (see Mt 5:17N).

23–25 Won't they say you're crazy? Some Christian groups seem oblivious to the effect their practices have on outsiders. They form a closed circle and encourage one another in a style which, rather than conveying love (Chapter 13) or even **judgment** to outsiders, conveys only weirdness. Such groups should reevaluate their practices in terms of evangelistic effectiveness: are people who could be won to faith being turned away by the oddness of it all? In this regard, Sha'ul is a sensible man (see also vv. 33, 40).

26–40 Only after teaching broadly and presenting general principles in 12:1–14:25 does Sha'ul give specific rules for the use of the verbal spiritual gifts (prophecy, tongues and interpretation) in congregational meetings. In so doing he follows his pattern at 8:1–11:1; there too the instructions came at the end of the discussion.

32–33 The prophets' spirits are under the prophets' control. This can mean either that each individual prophet ought not to let himself be carried away into unseemly behavior, or that the prophets as a group can exercise control as needed over individuals among their number. But clearly uncontrolled ecstatic utterance has no place in Messianic worship practice, **for God is not a God of unruliness but of *shalom*** (peace, wholeness, health, integrity).

33b–35 Wives... speak out. Or, "women... speak," which could imply that Sha'ul is prohibiting women from prophesying, preaching, teaching or praying (or possibly, given the context, from speaking in tongues) in a **congregational meeting**. But we know that there were women prophets (Ac 21:9), that in this very letter Sha'ul permits women to pray and prophesy in public meetings (11:5), and, of course, that not all women have **husbands** whom they can **ask at home**. The last point is decisive and shows that Sha'ul is answering a question (7:1) the Corinthians asked about wives' discussing with their husbands what is being said while it is being said. This would disturb decorum even if the wife were sitting next to her husband; but if the universal Jewish practice of the time (and of Orthodox congregations today) was followed, wherein women and men are seated separately in the synagogue, it would obviously be intolerable to have wives and husbands yelling at each other across the *m'chitzah* (dividing wall). Sha'ul places his instruction precisely here in the letter because it is here that he is dealing with matters of decorum and public order in congregational meetings; his advice seems curt and abrupt only if one ignores that he has already discussed the applicable general principles and that (by my assumption) his questioners are already familiar with the context of the problem, since they brought it up in the first place. If we could not supply such a framework for these verses, we might have to conclude, as some do, that Sha'ul demeans women (see 11:3–15&NN).

As the *Torah* also says. See v. 21N, Ro 3:19N and Mt 5:17&N. If Sha'ul means the Five Books of Moses, he may be thinking of Genesis 3:16 (compare Ep 5:22, 1 Ti 2:8–15). If he is thinking of the *Tanakh* as a whole, there are a number of places where a subordinate role for women is assumed or prescribed, although other places envision an equal or superior role; see the article on "Woman" in the *Encyclopedia Judaica* for references. The Talmud reports that Rabbi El'azar ben-'Azaryah (early 2nd century) gave a homily on the verse, "Assemble the people, the men and the women and the little ones" (Deuteronomy 31:10), in which he said, "If the men came to learn, the women came to hear" (Chagigah 3a). To "learn" in Judaism is to study by discussing and thus to understand fully, because one's questions get answered; whereas to "hear" is to listen to the interchange but not participate in it.

36–38 Did the word of God originate with you Gentiles? No, it originated with the Jewish people. This may be an additional reason for following Jewish worship practices as outlined in the preceding note. But the main point of these three verses is that the Corinthians have not arrived at a superior spiritual state giving them the right to invent practices inconsistent with genuine spirituality or with the praxis of other believers (compare 3:1–3, 4:7–8, 8:1b–3, 11:16). On "**command of the Lord,**" see 7:6N.

40 Sha'ul gives more specific guidelines like those of 7:10–15; 10:25–28; 11:6, 28, 33–34; and vv. 26–35 of this chapter. Then he adds "rules of order" such as may be needed to assure that **all things be done in a proper and orderly way**. All these contribute content to what I, for one, am willing to call the Oral *Torah* of the Messianic Community (see Ac 21:21N for more on this idea). Actually it is Written *Torah*, since it is written here in the New Testament.

CHAPTER 15

1–58 If Chapter 13 is the great "love chapter" of the New Testament, this is its great "resurrection chapter." Its *raison d'être* is that some Corinthians were saying that there is no such thing as bodily resurrection of the dead (v. 12). In this they were simply expressing a common Greek opinion — the Athenians too had mocked Sha'ul when he spoke of Yeshua's resurrection (Ac 17:31–32), just before his first visit to Corinth. Influenced by eastern philosophy, many regarded the body as evil or inferior, unworthy of eternal life (Ro 7:5N). Immortality of the soul, yes; but resurrection of the body, no — and this view is widely held today (on reincarnation see MJ 9:27&N). (The Jewish sect of the Sadducees also denied resurrection; see Mt 3:7&N, 22:23; Ac 23:8.)

1–2 Now, brothers, I must remind you of the Good News. Sha'ul immediately places the question of resurrection in the context of the Gospel (last mentioned at 14:36) because belief in the resurrection is an indispensible component of it, not a side issue (vv. 3–34). Only after reminding the Corinthians how important resurrection is can he address the difficulty which prevented some from believing in it, namely, their inability to imagine how it could happen (vv. 35–58).

How does the Gospel save? Here is Sha'ul's brief anatomy of the process. First it is **proclaimed**, then **received** and through further teaching internalized, so that one can take a **stand** on it, making it the foundation of one's life. Thus, by continuing to trust in it one goes on **being saved** (as at Ro 10:9–10&N), given one condition, to **keep holding fast to the message proclaimed** and not be diverted to "some other so-called 'good news,' which in fact is not good news at all" (Ga 1:6–7), in which case one's **trust will have been in vain** (compare Lk 8:13).

3–4 The essence of the Gospel is contained in these two verses, as we shall see, but the key point for Jewish people to grasp and for Messianic Jews to stress is that the Gospel is **in accordance with what the *Tanakh* says** (as Sha'ul himself emphasizes by saying it twice). That is, every major point of the Good News set forth in the New Covenant with Israel is spoken of or prophesied in the Hebrew Scriptures.

The Messiah died for our sins. First, because of our sins we are not right with God. "Your sins have made a separation between you and your God" (Isaiah 59:2). Second, the penalty for sin is the death of the sinner (Genesis 2:17; compare Ro 6:23). Third, only the death of something or someone sinless can atone for sin. Therefore there were animal deaths since Genesis 3:21 and animal sacrifices since Genesis 4:3–5, which later became institutionalized in the rituals of the Tabernacle and the Temple. Nevertheless, as explained in Messianic Jews 9–10&NN, these animal sacrifices were of temporary effectiveness only. A human death was needed to atone for human sin. But the death of a sinner would be ineffective; this is a major reason why Abraham was told not to sacrifice his son Isaac (Genesis 22:11–14) — Isaac's death would not have done anyone any good, since he was a sinner like the rest of us. However, the death of a sinless Messiah for our sins was foretold in Isaiah 52:13–53:8, 9b, 12b. **The Messiah died for our sins, in accordance with what the *Tanakh* says** — as Yeshua himself taught (Lk 24:25–27&N; see *JNT* Introduction, Section VII, for further *Tanakh* references).

And he was buried, as predicted in Isaiah 53:9a. Why is this an essential part of the Gospel? It shows that he was a human being who truly died and needed resurrection in order to live again, and that he was not some spiritual entity masquerading as human (a theory known as the docetic heresy, on which see Yn 19:34&N, 1 Yn 4:2&N).

And he was raised..., in accordance with what the *Tanakh* says in all three of its major sections — the *Torah* (Leviticus 23:9–15; see v. 20N), the Prophets (Isaiah 53:10–12a) and the Writings (Psalm 16:9–11, quoted at Ac 2:25–32 and 13:35–37): all are to be understood as referring to the Messiah's resurrection. But is general resurrection taught in the *Tanakh*? Yes, possibly at Job 19:25–27; certainly at Isaiah 26:14, "Your dead [God's dead] will live, my dead body will rise"; and even more unmistakably at Daniel 12:2, "And many of those who sleep in the dust of the earth will awake, some to everlasting life," which corresponds to Isaiah 26:14, "and some to shame and everlasting contempt." This double resurrection is the same as that taught by Yeshua

(Yn 5:29&N) and detailed in Rv 20:1–15&NN. Isaiah 66:24, quoted in this connection by Yeshua (Mk 9:44), is also generally understood to be speaking of resurrection.

On the third day. See 2 Kings 20:8 (in which King Hezekiah is raised up from terminal illness to go up to the Temple on the third day), Hosea 6:2 ("After two days he will revive us; on the third day he will raise us up, and we will live in his sight," used in the Talmud in connection with the End Times at Rosh Hashanah 31a and Sanhedrin 97a), and Jonah 1:17, 2:10 (Yeshua called the prophet's stay for three days in the belly of the fish "the sign of Jonah"; Mt 12:38–42&N, 16:4; Lk 11:29–30&N).

All four Gospels report all three events — Yeshua's death, his burial and his resurrection.

5–8 A rational person who is skeptical of Yeshua's resurrection needs compelling evidence that Yeshua actually fulfilled this aspect of the *Tanakh*'s prophetic description of the Messiah. In providing this evidence, Sha'ul speaks to one of the oldest philosophical questions about religion — can the content of faith be "proved"? His answer falls somewhere between a medieval theologian's "proof of the existence of God" and the existentialist's call for a "leap of faith." He does not assert that his data compel belief; but he does try to reduce the required "leap" to a tiny step which, instead of being in opposition to the rational and the objective, logically follows and builds upon them. In these four verses Sha'ul is implicitly challenging his readers to offer a better explanation for the observed phenomena than Yeshua's being the promised Messiah who rose from the dead. See Ac 26:8&N.

5 According to Lk 24:34 the resurrected Yeshua **was** first **seen by Kefa** (Peter), whom the Corinthians knew (1:12, 9:5), so that his report would command respect.

Then he was seen **by the Twelve** (Mt 28:16–20, Lk 24:33–51, Yn 20:19–29, Ac 1:3–9). The term, "the Twelve" means the inner circle of *talmidim* chosen by Yeshua (Mt 10:1–5, Mk 3:13–19, Lk 6:12–16); and it refers to the group as an entity, so that it applies when there were only eleven (after Y'hudah from K'riot hanged himself, Mt 27:5; also Ac 1:13, 23–26) and even when one of the group was absent (Yn 20:24). The report of the Twelve should carry more weight than Kefa's by itself.

6 **He was seen by more than five hundred brothers at one time, the majority of whom are still alive** some 20–25 years after the event took place, **though some have died**. The evidence of v. 5 is weighty, but because one can imagine twelve people agreeing to propagate a lie (as indeed had already been imagined, Mt 28:12–15), Sha'ul next presents the single most compelling piece of evidence for the truth of the Gospel that can be found in the entire New Testament, evidence which even the Orthodox Jewish scholar Pinchas Lapide has declared in print that he believes. (That is, Lapide believes Yeshua was in fact resurrected but does not believe him to be the Messiah; see his *The Resurrection of Jesus: A Jewish Perspective*; also see Ac 10:40–41&N.)

Some think this appearance of the resurrected Yeshua to five hundred refers to Mt 28:16–20, while others believe Sha'ul is writing about an appearance not documented elsewhere in the New Testament. In any case, Sha'ul's challenge to the Corinthians is this: "If you still doubt, there are a minimum of 250 people still alive who actually saw the resurrected Yeshua and can give you a first-hand report; you can talk personally to as many of them as you need to in order to be convinced." It is utterly implausible that Sha'ul would offer this opportunity for personal verification had it not been actually possible. He would not write to a skeptical readership that there were hundreds of witnesses if there weren't. Likewise it is utterly implausible that 500 people could conspire to perpetuate a lie so contrary to normal experience or be deceived in a way that would not break down under a skeptic's careful questioning.

For these reasons, Yeshua's resurrection must be acknowledged as an objective fact of history, not a vagary of "faith." That is the best rational explanation, both then and now, of the existence in Sha'ul's day of hundreds of people who Sha'ul could be absolutely confident would witness that Yeshua was in fact resurrected from the dead. No great "leap of faith" is required to believe it. All that is needed is the tiny step of acknowledging that Yeshua's resurrection stamps him as the Messiah promised by the *Tanakh*, worthy of eternal gratitude as Savior and allegiance as Lord. And without this tiny step there can be no New Covenant faith whatever (vv. 12–19).

7 The appearance to **Ya'akov** (James), whose mother was also Yeshua's mother, Miryam (Mt 13:55–56, Mk 6:3, Ga 1:19), is not mentioned elsewhere in the New Testament but is reported in one of the apocryphal books, the Gospel to the Hebrews (fragment 7). Ya'akov was not a follower of Yeshua before his execution (Mk 3:21, 31–35; Yn 7:5), but after coming to faith (Ac 1:14, 12:17&N) he became head of the Messianic community in Jerusalem (Ac 15:13; Ga 2:9, 12) and wrote one of the books of the New Testament (Ya 1:1).

All the emissaries. It is debated whether this phrase means that there were more than twelve, or that Ya'akov and Sha'ul are not to be counted as emissaries; see Ro 16:7N, Ep 4:11N.

8–9 **He was seen by me**, Sha'ul (9:1), not at his first encounter (Ac 9:4, 22:7, 26:14), but later (Ac 22:18 and 23:11, fulfilling Ac 22:14).

Even though I was born at the wrong time, that is, too late — after Yeshua had already lived, died, been resurrected and gone up to heaven.

The fact that Sha'ul **persecuted the Messianic Community** (Ac 8:3, 9:1–2; Ga 1:13, 23; Pp 3:6; 1 Ti 1:12–15) still affects his self-image. Could anything less than truly meeting the risen Lord have turned the leading opponent of Yeshua into his foremost advocate?

12–19 There are spokesmen within Christendom— Rudolf Bultmann comes to mind, with whom the term "demythologizing" is associated — who attempt to formulate a New Testament faith that does not acknowledge the resurrection of Yeshua as historical fact but consider it "true subjectively," whatever that means — perhaps, "true in terms of my own faith, so that I can act on it as if it were true, even though the event did not happen." This approach is an effort to meet the criticism of nineteenth- and twentieth-century naive empiricism (or, rather, graciously to accept defeat at its hands while salvaging something of the Gospel), but it is hard to see how such efforts at self-delusion can stand up to the crystal-clear claims and logic of these verses. For a refutation of the idea that Sha'ul's "Damascus road experience" was merely a concatenation of coincidences and misapprehensions see Ac 26:13–18N.

19 Although the Gospel does have benefits now (Mk 10:30a, 1 Ti 4:8), giving up everything in this world in order to gain the Messiah (Lk 9:23–25, Pp 3:8) and receive rewards in the *'olam haba* (4:4, 9:25; Mk 10:30b) would be foolish if there were no resurrection.

20 Sha'ul probably wrote this letter between *Pesach* (5:6–8) and *Shavu'ot* (16:8), during the season for presenting the **firstfruits** of the harvest at the Temple (Leviticus 23:9–15). Since we know that Sha'ul sees in the events and prescriptions of the *Tanakh* prefigurative events, examples and warnings pointing to God's later workings in history (9:9–10; 10:1–11; Ga 4:21–5:1), it is not surprising that he sees Yeshua's resurrection as the firstfruits of the larger harvest to come (v. 23; Yn 14:3, 19b–20; Ro 8:29).

21–22 A similar comparison between Adam and Yeshua is made at Romans 5:12–21&N. The comparison is continued in this chapter at vv. 45–49.

24 **Then the culmination** (Greek *telos*; see Ro 10:4N), which, because the word "then" is repeated, must come after Yeshua's return.

Every rulership,... authority and power in the spiritual realm which is not of God; compare 2C 10:3–4, Ep 6:12.

25 **Until he puts all his enemies under his feet**. This is a conflation of Psalm 110:1 ("until I make your enemies your footstool") and Psalm 8:7(6) (quoted in v. 27 and expounded on in MJ 2:5–18).

26 On **death** as the **last enemy**, see vv. 50–57.

27–28 These verses give specifics of the period spoken of in the *Tanakh* at Zechariah 14:9 ("*Adonai* will be king over all the earth; on that day *Adonai* will be One and his name One") and Daniel 7:14, referring to the Messiah ("His dominion is an everlasting dominion which will not pass away"). In his various books the conservative Christian scholar George Ladd contrasted the inbreaking of the Kingdom of God at Yeshua's first coming two thousand years ago with the fullness or consummation to come, when God will be **everything in everyone** (KJV: "all in all"). Using different terminology and making a different emphasis to say somewhat the same thing, the Orthodox Jew Pinchas Lapide and the Christian scholar Juergen Moltmann speak of the present era as a *preparatio messianica* (*Jewish Monotheism and Christian Trinitarian Doctrine,* Philadelphia: Fortress, 1981, pp. 80–81). At the end of history the Messiah's eternal rulership, in which the Messianic Community participates, is to merge with that of God the Father. Thus does Sha'ul sum up the final outworking of resurrection.

29–34 Several practical arguments for the reality of resurrection, following up on the theme of v. 19.

29 A controversial verse with uncertain significance; this is the only reference in the New Testament to such a practice.

32 **"Wild beasts,"** figuratively, for difficult opponents, as at Ac 19:23–41, or possibly literally, as reported in the New Testament apocryphal "Acts of Paul," written around the middle of the 2nd century.

33–34 The quotation is from Menander's comedy, *Thais*, and was probably a common Greek proverb in Sha'ul's day. Apparently the libertines (6:12) and gnostics (8:1) were also the ones who disbelieved the resurrection. Though the gnostics pursue knowledge, what they **lack** is **knowledge of God.**

35–49 Having proved the necessity of resurrection, Sha'ul can discuss his readers' concern about the practical details.

35–36 An imaginary **someone** can safely be called **stupid**; this is part of the style of Greek diatribes. Yeshua at Yn 12:24 used the same seed-sowing analogy. And the Talmud contains this passage:

> "The Samaritan Patriarch asked Rabbi Me'ir, 'I know that the dead will come back to life,... but when they do arise, will they be naked or clothed?' He replied, 'You may deduce the answer from a *kal v'chomer* argument [Mt 6:30N] based on a wheat grain — if a grain of wheat, which is buried naked, sprouts forth in many robes, then how much more so the righteous, who are buried in their clothing!'"(Sanhedrin 90b)

The "clothing" refers to righteous deeds (Isaiah 61:10, Rv 19:8).

45 Adam "became a living human being" (or: "a living soul") after God "breathed into his nostrils the breath of life"; the word for "breath," Hebrew *ruach*, can also be translated "spirit" or even "Spirit." Thus his life depended on God, which is why God could make death a penalty for sin (Genesis 2:17); whereas **the last "Adam"** (see vv. 21–22 above) is **a life-giving spirit** — he has life in himself (Yn 1:4, 5:26, 10:17–18).

49 **We will bear the image of the man from heaven**. Compare 2C 3:17–18.

51 **A secret**, Greek *mustêrion*, "a previously concealed truth now revealed" (see Ro 11:25N). Compare 1 Th 4:13–18 with vv. 51–57.

Not all of us will die. But we will all be changed. For a believer, death is no terror, but is "gain," because one goes to be with the Messiah (Pp 1:21, 23). Nevertheless, believers alive at the time Yeshua returns will not have the experience of dying at all.

52 The ***shofar***, Hebrew for "ram's horn," is sounded one hundred times on *Rosh-HaShanah*, the Jewish New Year. Within Judaism the *shofar* has multiple symbolism, including God's creation and kingship, his revelation at Sinai, prophetic warning, repentance, alertness, battle, Abraham's offering of Isaac (and its connection with God's mercy), the ingathering of God's people in exile, final judgment and resurrection (see Mt 24:31N). Also see 1 Th 4:16&N, Rv 8:2&N.

According to the *Alphabet Midrash of Rabbi Akiva*, seven *shofar*s announce suc-cessive steps of the resurrection process, with Zechariah 9:14 quoted as a proof text: "And *Adonai* the Lord will blow the *shofar*."

In 4 Ezra, a Jewish work completed around 120 C.E., one finds this picture of the End Times (compare Mattityahu 24):

> "When the age about to pass away is sealed, then the books will be opened before the firmament, and all will see it together… and the *shofar* will sound, at which all men, when they hear it, will be struck with sudden fear. At that time friends will war against friends like enemies, the earth and those living on it will be stricken with fear, and the springs of the fountains will stand still so that for three hours they will not flow. Whoever survives all these things I have foretold to you will be saved and will see my salvation and the end of my world. And the men who have been taken up, who from their birth have not tasted death, will appear. Then will the heart of the inhabitants of the world be changed and converted to a different spirit." (4 Ezra 6:20, 23–26)

56 This verse sums up what is taught at length in the book of Romans, especially at Ro 3:19–31, 5:12–21, 7:1–25.

57 Compare Ro 7:24–25.

CHAPTER 16

1–4 **The collection** may be for the Messianic Jewish community in Jerusalem, but a good case can be made that **God's people** (literally, "the saints" or "the holy ones") means all the Jewish people, Messianic or not — see Ro 15:25–27&NN, where Sha'ul teaches that Gentile believers have a duty to aid "the Jews" materially. Whichever is the case, Sha'ul had promised the Messianic Jewish leaders in Jerusalem that he would "remember the poor" (Ga 2:10). Sha'ul took an earlier such collection to Jerusalem (Ac 11:27–30, 12:25); this one may be the same as that spoken of in Romans and at Ac 24:17 (compare Ac 20:4, 16 with vv. 3, 8 here). In fundraising, as in other matters, Sha'ul was no slouch; see 2C 8:1–9:15 for his skillful and tactful "follow-up letter"; Ro 15:26–27a seems to imply that his efforts succeeded.

2 **Every week, on *Motza'ei-Shabbat*.** The Hebrew expression means, literally, "departure of the Sabbath"; it signifies Saturday night. It translates the Greek phrase which means, literally, "every one of a week," that is, every first day of the week. The question is: does this refer to Saturday night or to Sunday?

In favor of the idea that "every one of a week" means Sunday are these points:

(1) Gentiles did not keep *Shabbat*.

(2) By the Roman system of timekeeping days began at midnight.

(3) There is good documentation that the Gentile churches have observed Sunday as a day of worship since very early times. Specifically, Ignatius writes in the early second century of Sunday as "the Lord's Day," commemorating the day Yeshua rose from the grave. This we know to have been Sunday from Mt 28:1 and Lk 24:1;

Mk 16:2 pinpoints it as "just after sunrise" on the first day of the week, that is, Sunday morning. (But Rv 1:10 is speaking of the eschatological Day of Judgment, not Sunday; see note there.)

In favor of the idea that "every one of a week" means Saturday night are these points:

(1) The use of "one" rather than "first" shows that Sha'ul was thinking in Hebrew, not Greek (see the Hebrew of Genesis 1:5).

(2) In the Jewish calendar, days commence at sundown, so that the "first day of the week" refers to any time between sunset Saturday and sunset Sunday.

(3) In the early days of the Messianic Community, Jewish believers continued to observe *Shabbat* as a day of rest and met for Messianic worship in the evening after it was over.

(4) There were Jews, prominent ones, in the Corinthian congregation, so that Sha'ul would not have dealt with it as a wholly Gentile congregation.

(5) The only other use of this Greek phrase in connection with Sha'ul speaks of an evening event where he preached so long that Eutychus went to sleep and fell off the window ledge; this was probably Saturday night (see Ac 20:7&N).

(6) Sunday could not have been regularly celebrated by the early Jewish believers as *Shabbat* or as a *yom tov* ("festival," literally, "good day") because, since Judaism prohibits handling money on such days, Sha'ul would never have suggested taking up a collection then to a congregation with Jews in it.

I believe the reasons for Saturday night outweigh those for Sunday and accordingly translate the Greek phrase by "*Motza'ei-Shabbat.*"

While the New Testament does not abrogate *Shabbat* as the holy day of rest for Jews stipulated in the Fourth Commandment, it also contains no command concerning a proper day for Messianic worship. At the founding of the Messianic Community the believers met together every day (Ac 2:46). In conclusion, what makes sense to me is that a Messianic Jewish congregation can choose any day (or days) of the week for Messianic worship, but worship elements specific to *Shabbat* should be included only on *Shabbat* (Friday sundown to Saturday sundown).

8–9 ***Shavu'ot***, the Feast of Weeks, also known as Pentecost, had been invested with new meaning; because some twenty years earlier on this day God had poured out his Holy Spirit upon the Messianic Community in Jerusalem (Ac 2:4; see Ac 2:1N and Ac 2:4b–13N about the traditional and new significances of *Shavu'ot*).

The point here seems to be not merely that Sha'ul, an observant Jew (Ac 13:9N), intends to return in time to keep the holiday in Jerusalem, as prescribed in the *Torah* (as at Ac 20:16&N), but that he feels he has to justify his remaining in Ephesus until then, that is, during *Pesach*, which comes seven weeks earlier. He would normally plan to arrive in Jerusalem in time for *Pesach*, but he intends to forego being in Jerusalem for Passover **because a great and important door has opened for my work, and there are many people opposing me** — I need to deal with this difficult situation, even at the cost of disobeying the *Torah* command to be in Jerusalem for Passover. In effect Sha'ul issues a halakhic decision (see Mt 18:18–20&N, Yn 7:22–23&N, Ga 2:11–14&NN) that when one must choose between obeying the *mitzvah* of being in Jerusalem for a Pilgrim Festival and obeying the *mitzvah* of assuring the propagation of the Gospel, the latter is the more important and must be obeyed.

10–11 Timothy. See Ac 16:1–3. **Let no one treat him with disrespect**. Evidently this was a chronic problem for Timothy; see 1 Ti 4:12.

13 ***Mentsh***, Yiddish, from German *mensch*, "man," but meaning a person (male or female) of strong moral character, a truly human being, not just a male member of the human race. The Greek word here is "*andrizomai,*" defined by Arndt and Gingrich's *A Greek-English Lexicon of the New Testament* as to "conduct oneself in a manly or courageous way," which is precisely what "**behave like a *mentsh***" means.

19 Aquila and Prisca... the congregation that meets in their house. See Ac 18:1–3 (where she is called Priscilla), Ro 16:3–5&N.

21–24 In my own handwriting, signified in the *Jewish New Testament* by cursive type. Similarly at Ga 6:11–18, Co 4:18, 2 Th 3:17–18 and Pm 19.

22 Love. This is Sha'ul's only use of the Greek word "*phileô,*" which means having "brotherly affection" and is distinct from "*agapê*" (13:1&N, Yn 21:15–17&N). **A curse on him** (literally, "let him be anathema"), a phrase also found at Ga 1:8–9; compare 12:3 above. In context here, "**anyone**" refers to those Sha'ul can expect to regard his letter seriously; it means "anyone who counts himself a part of the Messianic community or understands what the Good News really is"; but it does not include random outsiders or casual inquirers still in the dilettante stage. I do not believe Sha'ul is lashing out in unprovoked anger; quite the contrary, in the light of his assurance of steadfast love and concern in the final words of the letter. Rather, he is giving a final warning: if anyone does not have even so much as brotherly affection for the Lord, let him understand that he is in danger of being cursed so as to be separated from God forever. Sha'ul understood the seriousness of his words — he said that he would be willing to invoke anathema on himself if it would help Jews trust in Yeshua (Ro 9:3; Ro 9:2–4aN).

"*Marana, ta*!" — our Lord, come! Greek *maranatha* is a transliteration of two Aramaic words which must have been a set expression in the Greek congregations. They may be read as either "*Marana, ta*!" ("Our Lord, come!"), which resembles Rv 22:20, or "*Maran ata*" (this can mean either "Our Lord has come" or "Our Lord is coming"). That our Lord Yeshua may come at any moment should spur the careless to heed Sha'ul's warning and encourage everyone to expect God's promises to be fulfilled. The rallying cry is consistent with the warm final greetings of vv. 23–24.

THE SECOND LETTER FROM YESHUA'S EMISSARY SHA'UL (PAUL) TO THE MESSIANIC COMMUNITY IN CORINTH:

2 CORINTHIANS

CHAPTER 1

1–2 This letter is written with much looser organization than 1 Corinthians (see vv. 15–17N, 13:1N). Nevertheless its contents can be outlined as follows:

CHAPTERS, VERSES	CONTENTS
1:1–11	Introductory greeting and thanksgiving.
1:12–7:16	I Review of Sha'ul's relationship with the Corinthians.
1:12–2:17	A. He defends his conduct.
3:1–6:10	B. The glory of the office of emissary. Sha'ul's boldness, sufferings and manner of life as an emissary.
6:11–7:16	C. Restoration of confidence and reconciliation with the Corinthians.
8:1–9:15	II The charitable collection for the Jerusalem poor.
10:1–13:10	III Vindication of Sha'ul's authority as an emissary as over against the false emissaries.
13:11–14	Concluding exhortation, greeting, blessing.

Sha'ul, that is, Paul (Ac 13:9&N). **Emissary**, usually rendered "apostle" (Mt 10:2–4N). **Messiah Yeshua**, usually rendered "Christ Jesus" (Mt 1:1N). **Timothy**, Sha'ul's companion and child in the faith (Ac 16:1–3&NN). **Messianic community**, usually rendered "church" (Mt 16:18N). **God's people**, often rendered "the saints." **Achaia** is the southern part of Greece; it includes Athens, Corinth and Cenchrea (all mentioned in Acts 17–18). ***Shalom***, a greeting meaning more than just "peace" (Mt 10:12&N). **Lord**, see Mt 1:20&N, 7:21&N.

3–7 Praised be God, Father of our Lord Yeshua the Messiah, compassionate Father, God of all encouragement and comfort, who…. This follows the liturgical formula for a Jewish *b'rakhah* (blessing); see Ep 1:3–14&N, 1 Ke 1:3–4&N. Notice that the praise is directed to God the Father, not to Yeshua the Messiah; Messianic faith does not "substitute Jesus for God." For more on *b'rakhot* see Mt 9:8N, 14:19N, 26:27–29N; Lk 5:26&N; 2 Ti 4:6–8N.

Encouragement and comfort. Both words are used in v. 3 to translate one Greek word, "*paraklêsis*"; in vv. 4–7 only one is used, as shorthand (see Yn 14:16&N, Ac 4:36&N). God encourages and comforts those who suffer. The Messiah called his followers to share in his sufferings (Lk 9:23, Ro 8:17–18, Co 1:24&N). New Testament believers, both Messianic Jews and Gentile Christians, are promised persecution and suffering (Mk 10:30, Yn 16:33&N); Westerners often find this hard to appreciate. Jews, both non-Messianic and Messianic, will suffer too, for Jeremiah 30:7 speaks of "the time of Jacob's trouble"; Gentile Christians must stand with them in their suffering, encouraging and comforting them. Messianic Jews share with Gentile Christians God's encouragement and comfort; it gives them supernatural strength to encourage others (vv. 4–7).

5 "Many are the afflictions of the righteous, but *Adonai* delivers him from them all" (Psalm 34:20(19)). "When my cares within me were many, your comforts would cheer my soul" (Psalm 94:19).

8 **Trials... in Asia**, modern Turkey, possibly in Ephesus (Ac 19:23–41, 1C 15:32).

11 A key verse on the effectiveness of prayer.

12–14 Those who wished to undermine Sha'ul's authority as an emissary of the Messiah apparently charged him with being insincere, deceptive, exploitative, unreliable, boastful and weak. He is forced (12:11) to defend himself against these charges throughout this letter — always, as he is at pains to stress, for the twin purposes of benefitting the Corinthians and upholding God's name, never in order to puff up himself.

15–17 More specifically, they charged that he had failed to keep his promise to visit them. This subject of visits is taken up intermittently — here, 2:1–3, 12–13; 7:5–7; 8:16–24; 12:14; 13:1. In this letter, more than in any of his others, he does not progress linearly from one subject to the next (see Ro 3:31N) but constantly moves back and forth in his writing between distance and presence, past and future, advice and praise, comfort and warning, abstraction and detail, theology and practice, reverence and irony, a firm hand and kid gloves. The effect is to create a many-layered texture of humanness. See 1:1–2N, 13:1N.

17 **Ready to say "Yes, yes," and "No, No," in the same breath**. Compare Mt 5:37.

19 **Sila** (Silas, Silvanus). See Ac 15:22&N.

20 All God's promises **find their "Yes" in connection with** Yeshua. Sometimes he fulfills them in his own person — "He has become wisdom for us" (1C 1:30); he is the last Adam, so that his resurrection guarantees ours (1 Corinthians 15, Ro 5:12–21). More than that, God fulfills all his other promises through him, because God does everything through him (Yn 1:1–5, Co 1:16–18, MJ 1:1–3).

Replacement theologians, who teach the traditional but mistaken Christian doctrine that the Church has replaced the Jews as God's people, misuse this verse in the following way: since God's promises find their "yes" in connection with Yeshua, and Yeshua came two thousand years ago,

> "all the Old Testament promises have in some mystical sense been fulfilled in the Messiah already, so that none remain for the Jews. But the verse does not say or mean that all the promises have been fulfilled already, but that whenever God's promises are fulfilled, they are fulfilled in, through or by Yeshua. He is the instrument through whom God the Father has fulfilled, is fulfilling and will fulfill every promise he has ever made to the Jewish people — including the promise that they will return from Exile to possess and live in the Land of Israel and the promise that the Kingdom will be restored, with the Son of David on the throne. A text which assures that God will fulfill every one of his promises to the Jews must not be turned into a pretext for cancelling them!" (from my *Messianic Jewish Manifesto*, pp. 111–112)

Because, in the view of Replacement theologians, all the promises God made in the *Tanakh* to the Jews have already found their "yes" in Yeshua, they must necessarily regard as a fluke the existence of the State of Israel and the fact that a third of the world's Jews now live here. For them this is a mere coincidence that has no connection with prophecy fulfillment.

However, this verse, rightly understood, has exactly the opposite meaning. Because all God's promises find their "yes" in Yeshua we can be confident that every one of God's as yet unfulfilled prophecies will be fulfilled, including the national salvation of Israel and the return of the Jewish people to the Land. Yeshua the Messiah, who embodies "the fullness of all that God is" (Co 2:9), guarantees the fulfillment of every one of God's promises. This is seen clearly in the relationship between Ro 8:28–39 and Romans 9–11 (see Ro 9:1–11:36N).

For another instance of Replacement theology's misconstruing Scripture see Mt 5:17&N; for additional references see Mt 5:5N.

The *"Amen,"* in effect, our "Yes" (in terms of vv. 17–19). On the word "***Amen***" see Mt 5:18&N; Ro 1:25&N, 9:5&N.

CHAPTER 2

3–4 I wrote, that is, in 1 Corinthians; see 7:8–12 and 10:1, 9 below.

5–10 See 1C 5:1–5&NN, 5:9–13&NN for the background.

11 The adversary, Satan, "the devil." See Mt 4:1&N.

13 Titus, mentioned 6 times in Chapters 7–8 and again in Chapter 12, also in Galatians 2 as a Gentile believer whom Sha'ul did not circumcise, in 2 Timothy 4, and in Ti 1:4 as the recipient of Sha'ul's letter.

15–16a The Good News is like a flower's fragrance. If a sweet-smelling flower smells bad to someone, the fault is not with the flower. Rather, there must be some disorder in his smelling apparatus. In the case of the Gospel, the disorder is called sin. So, if **to God we** who believe and proclaim the Good News **are the** sweet **aroma of the Messiah**, who lives in us, then **among those being saved, we are the** same **sweet smell of life leading to more life**. But **among those** in the process of **being lost, we are the** stinking **smell of death, leading only to more death**. Those bent on sin, those in the process of being eternally lost, cannot stand to hear the Good News and do not respond to it, except with redoubled antagonism or indifference (as seen in Rv 16:9, 11, 21; compare Ro 1:19–32; Ac 13:45, 14:4–5, 14:19, 16:20–24, 17:5–9, 17:32a, 18:9a).

2:16b–3:18 **Who is equal to such a task** as being a suitable channel for God to "spread everywhere the fragrance of what it means to know him" (2:14)? In other words, what can make people **competent to be workers proclaiming a New Covenant** (3:6a) even more glorious than the one Moses brought (3:6b–11)? The answer is that such **competence** is not produced by financial incentives (2:17), self-**recommendation** or **letters to or from** others (3:1), but **is from God** (3:5), through his **Spirit** (3:3, 6b, 8, 17–18). It is the *Ruach HaKodesh*, the Holy Spirit of God, who gives workers the **confidence** (3:4) to be sincere and **open** (3:12–13), who has the power to remove spiritual blindness (3:14–16), and who in doing so turns people into a living **letter** of recommendation **from the Messiah** himself, thus obviating the need for the usual kind (3:2–3).

17 **We** don't **go about huckstering God's message for a fee**. Quite the opposite — Sha'ul made the Good News available to the Corinthians free of charge (10:7, 11:7–12, 12:13; also 1C 9:12b–19, Ac 18:2–3), even though he was entitled to material support (1C 9:4–12a, Ga 6:6). The Mishna expresses the same attitude toward teaching *Torah*: "Do not make of it a crown with which to advance yourself or a spade with which to dig" (Avot 4:5, cited more fully at 1C 9:4N).

CHAPTER 3

1–3 Compare 1C 9:1–3; and see below, 10:13–16.

3 **You are a letter from the Messiah placed in our care** for safe delivery to God at the final Judgment (compare Pp 1:6, 1 Ke 1:5–8). The phrase translated, "placed in our care," is, literally, "worked by us." The Greek for "worked" (or: "ministered," "served") is "*diakoneô*"; related words appear five times in vv. 6–9 and again at 4:1; all are translated by a form of "work" in order to bring out the force of Sha'ul's repeated use of the word.

God wrote the *Torah* **on stone tablets** (Exodus 24:12, 31:18, 34:1; Deuteronomy 9:10–11); they are symbolized in Jewish decorative art by the familiar arch-shaped pair of panels containing the initial Hebrew words of the Ten Commandments.

On human hearts (literally, "on tablets [which are] hearts made of flesh"); the *Tanakh* uses the same imagery at Proverbs 3:3, 7:3 and Jeremiah 31:32(33), quoted in the following note. The prophet Ezekiel says that when God regathers the Jewish exiles and gives them the Land of Israel, he will "take the stony heart out of their flesh and will give them a heart of flesh" (11:19), "and I will put a new Spirit within you" (36:26). The contrast between stone and flesh (or the Spirit) is continued in vv. 6–11 and 14.

6–13 This passage is often understood to teach that the **New Covenant** has **more glory** than the *Torah*. Whether it does depends on how one defines "*Torah*." The Greek word for "law" or "*Torah*," "*nomos*," is not used at all here or anywhere in 2 Corinthians; so that if one is going to make such a statement about "the *Torah*" on the basis of this passage, one must limit the meaning of "*Torah*" to the elements given in the passage. And here Sha'ul talks only about a **written text** which was **engraved on stone tablets**, which **worked death**, which **worked to declare people guilty**, and which came with temporary **brightness** that was **already fading away** (see last three paragraphs of this note). It is with this **written text** that he contrasts the **New Covenant**, which is accompanied by the **Spirit**, who writes **on human hearts**, who **gives life**, who **works to declare people innocent**, and who **lasts**. He makes his point with a *kal v'chomer* argument (Mt 6:30&N), stated in three different ways (vv. 7–8, 9, 11; compare Yn 1:17 and Ro 7:6). But there is more to the *Torah* than a written text, so that what Sha'ul says here about a written text does not necessarily apply to all that the *Torah* is. (See paragraph below on the New Covenant.)

Nevertheless, what Sha'ul does say is startling enough. How is it that **the written text** of the *Torah* **brings death** (literally, as in KJV, "the letter killeth")? Since Sha'ul himself calls the *Torah* "holy" (Ro 7:12), how can he say that it kills? He does not answer this question in his letters to the Corinthians but assumes they are already knowledgeable on the subject, both in the present chapter and at 1C 9:19–23, 15:56. But elsewhere he explains that the *Torah* can be said to bring death for at least four reasons:

(1) It prescribes death as the penalty for sin (Ro 5:12–21).

(2) In defining transgression it increases sin (Ga 3:21–31), which leads to death.

(3) It provides an opportunity for sinful people to pervert God's holy *Torah* into legalism, that is, a dead system of rules intended to earn God's favor even when followed without trusting God (Ro 3:19–31&NN, 7:1–25&NN, 9:30–10:10&NN; see also 1C 9:19–23&NN).

(4) It does not have in itself (in its **written text engraved on stone tablets**, v. 7) the life-giving power of the Spirit which alone can make people righteous (Ro 8:1–11, Ac 13:38–39&N).

One must understand the shock a Jew experiences in hearing the *Torah* called an instrument of death, since in Jewish understanding the *Torah* ministers not death but life. Yeshua was well aware of Jewish regard for the *Torah* as an instrument of life (Yn 5:39). In the Midrash Rabbah Rabbi L'vi is cited as saying,

> "God sat on high, engraving for them tablets which would give them life."
> (Exodus Rabbah 41:1)

The prayer recited every time the *Torah* scroll is returned to the ark after being read in the synagogue quotes Proverbs 3:18:

"It is a tree of life to those who take hold of it."

Proverbs is speaking about wisdom; but since the *Torah* contains God's wisdom, the *Siddur* applies those words to the *Torah* itself.

Here is Sha'ul's explanation of how the *Torah*, whose "letter killeth," can be at the same time a tree of life: **but the Spirit**, the *Ruach HaKodesh*, the Holy Spirit of God, who lives in believers (Ro 8:9, 1C 3:16) and who is God himself (vv. 16–18 below), **gives life** (or: "enlivens," "makes alive"). The crucial thing for everyone to know is that the Spirit gives life (Yn 6:63, Ro 8:2) to sinners who are "dead in trespasses and sins" (Ep 2:1, KJV). But for Jews it is also important to understand that only **the Spirit** of God **gives life** to the *Torah* itself, that is, to its "letter." Or, more precisely, it is when people are filled with the Holy Spirit of God given by Yeshua the Messiah that the *Torah* becomes for them a tree of life and not a ministration of death.

All these things are clarified by Ro 8:1–11, which is the best commentary on this passage: "There is no longer any condemnation [as prescribed in the *Torah*] awaiting those who are in union with the Messiah Yeshua. Why? Because the *Torah* of the Spirit, which produces this life in union with Messiah Yeshua, has set me free from the '*torah*' of sin and death" (definable by this equation: God's "*Torah* of the Spirit" minus the Spirit equals "*torah*" of sin and death). "For what the *Torah* could not do by itself, because it lacked the power to make the old nature cooperate, God did by sending his own Son as a human being with a nature like our own sinful one. God did this in order to deal with sin, and in so doing he executed the punishment against sin in human nature, so that the just requirement of the *Torah* might be fulfilled in us who do not run our lives according to what our old nature wants but according to what the Spirit wants.... For the mind controlled by the old nature is hostile to God, because it does not submit itself to God's *Torah*.... But you, you do not identify with your old nature but with the Spirit — provided the Spirit of God is living inside you, for anyone who doesn't have the Spirit of the Messiah doesn't belong to him. However, if the Messiah is in you, then, on the one hand, your body is dead because of sin; but, on the other hand, the Spirit is giving life because God considers you righteous" (Ro 8:1–4, 7, 9–10).

The **New Covenant** spoken of in v. 6 is that of Jeremiah 31:30–33 (31–34), and the distinction Sha'ul draws is precisely the same as Jeremiah makes when he says that the new covenant will be "not like the covenant which I made with their fathers when I took them... out of... Egypt,... but I will put my *Torah* in their inward parts and write it on their hearts." See Mt 26:28&N, MJ 8:6–13&NN. Thus, it cannot be that Sha'ul is saying that the New Covenant is more glorious than the *Torah*, because the New Covenant *includes* the *Torah*, which God puts "in their inward parts" and writes "on their hearts." According to MJ 8:6&N, the New Covenant itself "has been made *Torah*." Sha'ul speaks of the "*Torah* as upheld by the Messiah" (literally, "*Torah* of Messiah") at Ga 6:2&N and makes a similar allusion at 1C 9:21&N; therefore the *Torah*, in some form, is still in force. The distinction is between letter and Spirit, not *Torah* and Spirit.

Workers serving a New Covenant, the essence of which is not a written text but the Spirit, literally, "workers" (or: "ministers"; see v. 3N) "of a new covenant, not of letter but of Spirit." Verses 6–13 are part of Sha'ul's defence of his office. He claims that as an emissary of the Messiah, his ministry is more glorious than that of **Moshe** — and not only that, but more glorious than at the very moment of Moses' greatest glory, when his face shone so brightly as he descended Mount Sinai (Exodus 34:29–30; compare Mt 17:2), after seeing God's glory (Exodus 33:18–34:8), that he put a veil over his face (Exodus 34:33, 35). But if one acknowledges that the New Covenant has come, bringing with it the Messiah himself and the very Spirit of God, whose glory obviously exceeds that of stone tablets, then one should see that the ministry of its **workers** has greater glory than that of Moses' ministry.

The *Tanakh* does not say that **the brightness was already fading away**, or that it ever faded away. Indeed, in Jewish tradition, Moses' face remained bright until he died. Where did Sha'ul get this idea? Was there another tradition within Judaism along the lines Sha'ul expresses? I do not know of one.

We are very open, that is, sincere (1:12–14, 18; 2:17; 6:11), **unlike Moshe**, who veiled his face. The Aramaic expression, "to cover the face," signifies shame and mourning, while an uncovered head (v. 18) signifies confidence and freedom. In Sha'ul's *midrash* here, he uses what Moses *did* as an acted parable symbolic of hiddenness and insincerity without implying that Moses *was* devious, hypocritical or ashamed himself. His point, rather, is that we who believe the Gospel have assurance that the glory and brightness of our eternal salvation will never fade, so we have neither need nor desire to hide it.

14–18 These verses must be read together with 4:3–6, which continue the discussion. Sha'ul mixes in a second metaphor: hardness of minds and hearts is combined with impaired vision and understanding. **Their minds**, the minds of unsaved Jewish people, **were made stonelike** (hard, unreceptive, stupefied; on this word, see Ro 11:7N), **for to this day**, Sha'ul's day, but still true in the present day, **the same veil remains over them**, so that **when they read the Old Covenant**, the Five Books of Moses, the *Torah*, they do not see that it points toward Yeshua the Messiah as its goal and fulfillment (Ro 10:4&N; on the illegitimacy of invidious comparisons between the Old and New Covenants see MJ 8:13&N). And the **veil lies over their heart**, singular, referring to the community as a whole, which resists being open to the truth of Yeshua and exerts social pressure against searching the scriptures to see if these things are so (Ac 17:9); although throughout history individual Jews have appeared who have been open to the Gospel and received it.

This passage is aimed directly at the resistance to Yeshua in the religion of non-Messianic Judaism. There is no animadversion here against Jews ethnically, racially, biologically, culturally, nationally as a people, or even religiously (in respect to other aspects of Judaism); least of all is there any implication that Jews with stonelike minds have less inherent mental ability. Rather, it is a spiritual veil, not a lack of intelligence, that prevents unsaved Jewish people from seeing that "the goal at which the *Torah* aims is the Messiah" (Ro 10:4). Yeshua himself made the same point to the religious stalwarts of his day: "You keep examining the *Tanakh* because you think that in it you have eternal life, and it keeps bearing witness to me! Yet you don't want to come to me in order to have life.... But don't think that I will be your accuser before the Father. Do you know who will accuse you? Moshe, the very one you have counted on! For if you really believed Moshe [that is, the *Torah*] you would believe me, because it was about me that he wrote. But if you don't believe what he wrote, how are you going to believe what I say?" (Yn 5:39–40, 45–47&N.)

Surprisingly, relatively few Jewish writers on the New Testament have voiced much objection to these verses. The only Jewish responses I have personally experienced have been either direct denial or amused but ironic acceptance — "If it's a veil that keeps us from seeing Jesus, we can live with that." Pitiful!

But there is hope. In fact, Sha'ul uses a verse from the *Torah* itself, from the very passage that speaks about Moses' veil, to point to what that hope is; it is the same hope that Sha'ul wrote about in Ro 10:11, where he quoted Joel 3:5(2:32), "Everyone who calls on the name of *Adonai* will be delivered." The Hebrew of Exodus 34:34 reads, "But when Moses went in before *Adonai* to speak to him, he took the veil off until he came out;" in v. 16 Sha'ul applies the verse midrashically to anyone seeking the Lord. In v. 15 it is **the Messiah** who takes away the veil, and one is reminded of Lk 24:25–27, 44–45, where Yeshua himself explained to his *talmidim* how the prophecies in the *Tanakh* apply to him. In v. 16 ***Adonai*** is the cause of the veil's removal, and in v. 17 it is explained that "***Adonai*" in this text means the Spirit.** It is the Spirit who has the specific ministry of convicting of "sin, righteousness and judgment" (Yn 16:7–11); it is he who makes a Jew or a Gentile willing and able to see Yeshua in the Jewish Scriptures.

17–18 Now, "*Adonai*" in this text means the Spirit, literally, "Now the Lord is the Spirit" (on "Lord" see Mt 1:20N, 7:21N). The phrase, "**in this text**," is not in this text; I have added it to clarify what I believe is Sha'ul's sense (see Section V of the Introduction to the *JNT*). This is an important verse for demonstrating the divinity of the Holy Spirit.

Where the Spirit of *Adonai* is, there is freedom to function within the framework of *Torah* without being enslaved by it. And thus **all of us,** not just Sha'ul and his co-workers, but all believers, **with faces unveiled**, with open hearts, not stonelike but sincere and unclouded, **see as in a mirror** (compare 1C 13:12, Exodus 33:18–34:8) **the glory of *Adonai*, and we are being changed into his very image, from one degree of glory to the next, by *Adonai* the Spirit** (literally, "by the Lord, who is the Spirit" or "by the Lord, that is, the Spirit"). This is how the Spirit "gives life" (v. 6).

CHAPTER 4

1–2 The background of this passage in relation to Sha'ul's defense of his ministry is 1:12–24. The reason I have written such a long note on these two verses is that Messianic Jews and Christian missions to Jews are frequently accused of using unethical means to "win converts." As a rule the charges lack evidence and are based on misunderstanding; but since they are often believed anyway, they deserve specific and intensive refutation. At the same time, it is good for us who are New Testament believers to be reminded of the standards we can legitimately be expected to observe.

Messianic Jews and Christian missions should refer to v. 2 both in defending against charges of unethical methods and in guiding their own behavior. On the one hand, there is no guarantee that people who call themselves Messianic or Christian or Bible-believing will in fact behave ethically; but on the other, there is no reason to put up with unsupported charges and rumors of ethical misconduct designed only to discredit Messianic Judaism, Christian missions and, most of all, the Gospel itself.

But first, the problem, which is that many official and self-appointed spokesmen for the Jewish community and for some streams of Christianity circulate reports intended to insulate Jewish people against the Gospel by creating the impression that Messianic Jews and Christian missions use **shameful underhanded methods, employing deception or distorting God's message**. More specifically, such charges have included the following:

(1) *Enticement to convert.* Messianic Jewish congregations and Christian missions are said to supply money, goods (food, clothing) and services (schooling, child care) — what Balfour Brickner, head of the Anti-Defamation League of the American Jewish Committee, has called "cajoleries" and "blandishments" — either making their receipt conditional upon the recipients' converting to Christianity or without making it clear that the recipients (especially minors) will be exposed to hearing the Gospel and being encouraged to convert. This charge is so widely believed in Israel that from time to time Israelis show up at the missions expecting help in emigrating in exchange for converting to Christianity. It produces such widespread fear of conversion that the unscrupulous can use it as a threat: "Unless you [the Israeli authorities, the Jewish Agency] do what I want [give me a house, a loan], I will convert to Christianity."

(2) *Preying on the disadvantaged.* Messianic Jewish congregations and Christian missions to the Jews are said to concentrate upon the disadvantaged — the young, the old, the poor, the physically handicapped, the psychologically distressed — and suit their techniques to them, rather than presenting their case openly and forthrightly in a rational manner that can be accepted or rejected by an adult in full possession of his intellectual, emotional, spiritual and financial powers.

(3) *Deceptive misuse of Jewish sancta.* Messianic Jewish congregations and Christian missions supposedly misuse "Jewish *sancta*," such as *kippah*, *tallit*, *t'fillin*, *Shabbat* candles, *Torah* scrolls, Passover materials, and Jewish liturgies, in order to create a "false" impression that these groups are Jewish and not Christian, with the intention of luring Jewish people to join them under the impression that they are not converting to Christianity.

At the same time, they often "Christianize" these "Jewish *sancta*," making them into parodies of what (non-Messianic) Judaism takes seriously, and thereby they insult (non-Messianic) Judaism. To appreciate the valence of this charge, consider how Christians might react to (non-Messianic) Jewish appropriation of communion or baptism rituals.

(4) *Insincere Christian conversion to Judaism.* A special case of the above is when Gentiles dress like Jews or even convert to Judaism while secretly remaining Christians with missionary intentions.

(5) *Distortion of the Tanakh.* Messianic Jewish congregations and Christian missions are charged with misusing the *Tanakh*, the Christian Old Testament, quoting verses out of context and even mis-translating or changing the text, in order to "prove" that Jesus is the Messiah and that the Church is the New Israel.

Before answering these serious accusations, I want to point out that Sha'ul was the target of the same or similar accusations: he was said to be "huckstering God's message for a fee" (2:17), engaging in self-puffery (3:1a), trading on letters of recommendation

(3:1b), corrupting people and taking advantage of them (7:2), and misleading them with "trickery" (12:16). His answer to these charges was that **God has shown us such mercy** by more and more changing us into his image (3:18) **that we do not lose courage** to behave uprightly **as we do the work** (see 3:3N) which God **has given us**, despite accusations, temptations and adverse conditions (all this is the theme of 4:1–6:13).

First, by way of direct defense against the charges, he writes: **Indeed, we refuse to make use of shameful underhanded methods, employing deception** (accusations 1–4 above) **or distorting God's message** (accusation 5). Second, by way of indirect defense through having a good offense: **On the contrary, by making very clear what the truth is, we commend ourselves to everyone's conscience in the sight of God.** See also 1 Th 2:3–12&N, where Sha'ul addresses similar accusations, and compare 2 Ti 2:15.

Next, there are two points that a believer angered by these charges must consider. First, are my own hands clean? Do I always **refuse to make use of shameful underhanded methods** and insist on **making very clear what the truth is**? If not, I have no case; I must repent and change my ways. The most common reason for slipping into such sub-Messianic behavior is fear — specifically, fear of opposition from the Jewish community (or others who oppose the Gospel) when they learn that I believe in Yeshua. If I give in to such fear I may mute my witness or distort it into something other than a forthright testimony about the Messiah. (On the specific fears that Israeli believers face and must overcome see Pp 1:27–28N.) But such fears, even when realistic, are not from God (2 Ti 1:7). They emanate either from the flesh, the "old nature" unregenerated by the Messiah (Ro 8:5–8), or from the pit, from Satan, the Adversary (2:11; see Yn 20:19&N on "fear of the Judeans"). It is precisely because of the temptation to succumb to fear of what nonbelievers will say or do that Sha'ul says he does **not lose courage**. His courage does not come from himself, for he is a breakable "clay jar" (v. 7), but from God, who makes us strong even when we are weak (12:9–10 below).

Second, it is not enough for a proclaimer of the Gospel merely to **refuse** the wrong; he must also manifest the **truth**. To "manifest" something means to make it **clear**. Some of the misunderstanding and mistrust of Messianic Jews and Christian missions is surely due to communication difficulties. In general, it is the interested party to a communication who is responsible for expressing himself clearly and paying close attention to what others say. In the present instance, the person telling the Good News of Yeshua is the interested party; motivated by the words of the Messiah in the Great Commission (Mt 28:18–20), he wants to spread the Gospel so that his hearers will understand and obey it (Ro 10:14–15). This is why it is up to him to make **clear what the truth is** and not up to those receiving the message, for initially they may be indifferent or opposed to it. Only later, if and when they develop a hunger for the Gospel, will they seek out the truth for themselves. Believers cannot blame unbelievers for misstating the Gospel; rather, the believers should express it so clearly that only the wilful can misunderstand it. Sha'ul makes **clear what the truth is** because he is strongly motivated: he knows that the truth sets people free (3:17, Yn 8:32). Those who work for the Messiah should imitate him (1C 11:1).

So then, what about these charges? Some are circulated even when provably false and known to be false by the circulators. Others may be documentable but are blown up out of all proportion to their frequency or importance. Surely *these* are shameful underhanded methods. In any case, let us consider the charges one by one:

(1) *Enticement to convert.* The Gospel enjoins hospitality and kindness; therefore believers can be expected to be friendly and give generously. But the friendliness and the giving are to be without expectation of anything in return (Mt 5:42, 46–47), least of all anything so intangible as trusting in God and his Messiah. Only the Holy Spirit of God, not believers, can move an unbeliever to undergo this radical change of heart.

In the past, Jews were sometimes forced or enticed to "convert" — that is, to make a public affirmation of adherence to Christianity — but many continued to be Jews secretly (the case of the "New Christians" or "Marranos" in medieval Spain is the best known instance; there are still secret Jews there 500 years later), while others refused to be forced and even gave up their lives *'al kiddush haShem* ("in sanctification of the Name" of God; see Ac 7:59–60N) rather than confess what they believed was a lie. Moreover, even aside from the tragedies caused by this practice, such a charade is ultimately ineffective anyway, since

> A man convinced against his will
> is of the same opinion still.

Besides, it demeans the Gospel to force it on anyone — the Good News either commends itself or it doesn't (see vv. 3–6).

Sometimes unbelievers shamelessly exploit the generosity of believers; they may even profess to be believers in order to deceive them. But unbelievers' abuse of believers' good will is not proof that believers make their hospitality conditional upon conversion.

And as for the potential *yordim* (Israeli expatriates) who show up at the mission door, they are politely informed that the missions do not trade aid for faith — if they are interested in the Gospel on its merits, welcome; but if they are interested only in a plane ticket to America, the mission cannot help them.

(2) *Preying on the disadvantaged.* This is an improper charge. When the Pharisees asked why Yeshua ate with "sinners" (the disadvantaged of their day; see Mt 9:10N), he answered, "The ones who need a doctor aren't the healthy but the sick" (Mt 9:12). The Good News is for everyone, including the disadvantaged.

The real reason for this charge, then, is to discredit the Gospel in the eyes of the very people likely to respond to it, namely, people who have come to the end of themselves or near it. There is no disputing that deeply committed non-Messianic Jews are unlikely to be convinced even by rational arguments for the Gospel; and often people in comfortable life situations feel no need for it. But this is not because the Gospel is irrational; rather, it is because non-Messianic Judaism inoculates its adherents against the Gospel, either openly or subliminally deprecating it, so that people deeply imbued with non-Messianic Judaism have had created in them, often in ways they cannot account for, nearly insurmountable barriers to open-minded consideration of the Gospel's claims and to genuine faith in God and his Son Yeshua.

It is a reasonable principle of evangelism, inferrable both from the practice of the New Testament believers and from effectiveness considerations, to concentrate proclamation of the Gospel on the people likely to accept it. Accordingly, if among

Jews the people likely to accept it are students (because they are questioning their received values), the elderly (because for them death is an imminent reality and they want to be right with God before it happens), the poor (because the Gospel can make them spiritually rich, and because they have little in this world attracting them which they must give up in order to follow Yeshua), the depressed (because the Gospel offers joy everlasting), and the physically and psychologically handicapped (because God through Yeshua can more than compensate for these handicaps or even cure them), then it is essential to present the Gospel in ways that meet the presented needs. But there is no shortage of rational appeals to be made on behalf of the Gospel, and it is deceptive or false to charge that such appeals are lacking; this is a "red herring."

(3) *Deceptive misuse of Jewish sancta.* When discussing this in *Messianic Jewish Manifesto* I made the point that Messianic Jews, since we too are Jews, have as much right to use Jewish *sancta* as non-Messianic Jews (pp. 167–175) — the latter do not have a patent on them. For example, why shouldn't Messianic Jews use *tallit* and *t'fillin* and say the prayers? They're Jews saying Jewish prayers in a Jewish way.

A more serious charge might be that Jewish *sancta* are sometimes used ignorantly. It is not that they are used without reverence, although according to non-Messianic Jewish *halakhah*, some things done in some places might, due to lack of knowledge, be improper and therefore "irreverent." Rather, the materials may be used foolishly. (In *Messianic Jewish Manifesto* I gave the example of a Messianic Jewish congregation that would unroll a *Torah* scroll and then read from the King James Version of the Bible because no one could read Hebrew; I suggested this might appear foolish to knowledgeable Jews.) I could point out that non-Messianic Jews sometimes do the same thing, likewise with good intentions but without knowledge. But I accept the criticism insofar as it constitutes a spur to being serious about our Jewishness.

A third aspect of the charge is deception. It is the responsibility of believers to inform inquirers that the Gospel is the Gospel. Messianic Jews often use the terms "Messianism" or "Messianic Judaism" instead of "Christianity," "Yeshua" instead of "Jesus," "congregation" or "community" instead of "church," and "Messiah" instead of "Christ." The purpose is to steer clear of the negative connotations attached to these words in the minds of many Jews, negative connotations due to history and not to the New Testament. Nevertheless, the communicator has an ethical responsibility not to mislead. Moishe Rosen, leader of Jews for Jesus, reports that early in his ministry a woman showed up at his mission and accepted "Yeshua," but on finding out that "Yeshua" is actually "Jesus," she never appeared again. If we use our own "minority terminology," we must explain why, not only so that no one will be misled, but also so that believers will truly understand the content and implications of their own faith.

The fourth aspect concerns "Christianizing" Jewish *sancta*. That is, for example, revising the Passover *Haggadah* so that the *afikoman* and the lamb shank refer to the Messiah, the third cup to communion, the deliverance from Egypt to the believer's deliverance from sin through the sacrifice of the Messiah, and so on. My answer is based first on the fact that Yeshua himself not only used Jewish *sancta* but often endowed them with new significance (Mt 26:28&N; Lk 22:17–20&NN; Yn 7:37–39&NN, 8:12&N). Also, since they are part of the heritage of Messianic as well as non-Messianic Jews, we have the right to invest them with meanings conforming to the truth of God as expressed in the New Testament — indeed, I would say we have more right than non-Messianic Jews have to exclude that truth.

Messianic Judaism in its present experimentalism, is introducing New Testament meanings in various ways. For example, there are a number of Messianic versions of the *b'rit-milah* ceremony and literally dozens of *Haggadot* for Passover. The one thing one might ask from all these experimenters is that they increase their knowledge of Judaism and of the New Testament's Jewish background, so that the revisions they make will draw deeply from the heart of the materials they are working with and not be merely superficial adjustments. There are signs that those concerned with Messianic Jewish liturgy are taking their task with increasing seriousness.

One last point: the charge of Christianizing Jewish *sancta* is inconsistent with the charge of using Jewish *sancta* to deceive non-Messianic Jews into thinking they are in a Jewish environment. Introducing New Testament meanings does not help convince a Jew that he has entered a (non-Messianic) Jewish environment but makes him question it. The critics can't have it both ways.

(4) *Insincere Christian conversion to Judaism.* I discussed whether Gentile Christians can convert to Judaism while retaining faith in Yeshua as the Messiah at 1C 7:18bN, Ga 5:2–4N and in my *Messianic Jewish Manifesto* (pp.175–180). It would be possible for a Gentile Christian to have, like Ruth, such a strong identification with the Jewish people that she wishes to be one of them, and for her to identify in this way despite non-Messianic Jewish rejection of Yeshua. Furthermore, she could convert in all honesty if she makes known the fact that she continues to believe that Yeshua is the Messiah. Some have done this.

But others have withheld that critical piece of information, and in so doing, they may have crossed the ethical barrier — although a judgment on this could depend on how seriously the ceremony of conversion to Judaism is taken in the local Jewish community. Where conversion to Judaism is commonly allowed for such casual reasons as outward legitimization of marriage between a Jew and a Gentile or, as in Israel, making it possible for a person to participate in the life of the State as a Jewish citizen, and the conversion process itself makes no demand that the convert deny Yeshua, then one is tempted to say that it is less critical for a Gentile Christian to volunteer that he retains his faith in Yeshua the Messiah. Against this, it is up to the believer to uphold the highest ethical standards, regardless of how the world around him functions.

As for Gentiles dressing like Jews, for example, wearing a *kippah* all the time like an Orthodox Jew or a long black coat like a Hasid (I know of instances of each!), one can judge for oneself the efficacy of such behavior. It is proper to "become as a Jew to the Jews," but that means empathizing, not imitating (see 1C 9:20aN). However, someone known to be a Gentile who wears a *yarmulke* at a Messianic Jewish synagogue service is deceiving no one; indeed, out of respect he would do the same in a non-Messianic synagogue.

(5) *Distortion of the Tanakh.* Misusing the *Tanakh* is a different kind of **shameful underhanded method**; the first four involve **employing deception**; this is **distorting God's message**. In a sense it is the most serious charge, because deception by bad practitioners of a true faith can be remedied without affecting the faith itself; but if

the content of that faith depends on distorting God's message, there may be nothing left to it after the error has been corrected.

Do Messianic Jews and Christians mis-translate or change the text of the *Tanakh*? The accusation usually concentrates on certain key verses, among which are Psalms 2:12, 22:17(16) and Isaiah 7:14. In general the problem is that either there is some question among scholars as to what the correct Hebrew text actually is, or there is division among scholars as to what the (agreed-on) text means. If a believer uses a verse of the *Tanakh* with which there is either of these difficulties and is unaware of it, while the person he is talking to either is aware of it or holds to a different view of the verse also without being aware of the difficulty, then the stage has been set for an unpleasant argument. To see how such arguments can be resolved, let us examine the three verses mentioned.

The beginning of Psalm 2:12 in Hebrew reads, "*Nashku-bar*," which Christian Bibles translate, "Kiss the Son," and Jewish Bibles translate variously, e.g., "Worship in purity," "Pay homage in good faith." "*Nashku*" normally means "kiss." The normal Hebrew word for "son" is "*ben*," but "*bar*" is the normal Aramaic word for it. The 12th-century Jewish scholar Avraham Ibn-Ezra writes,

> "'Serve the Lord' refers to HaShem, and 'Kiss the Son' refers to the Messiah; the meaning of *bar*, 'son,' is as we find it in Proverbs 31:2," [where "*bar*" appears three times, clearly meaning "son"]. (Cited in *The Messianic Outreach* 11:2 (1992), p. 17)

Because scholars differ on how to translate this one word, arguments arise among non-scholars. But if believers aware of the problem acknowledge it, there is no deception, no distorting of God's message. (The Greek of the Septuagint here means, "Accept correction," which fits the context.)

Likewise, whether Hebrew *almah* in Isaiah 7:14 means "virgin," as the Jewish translators of the Septuagint rendered it two centuries before Yeshua and as later quoted at Mt 1:23, or whether it means only "young woman" without reference to sexual purity is also debated by scholars, and the same caution applies. For more on this see Mt 1:23N.

Psalm 22:17(16) is considered by believers as virtually a prediction of the crucifixion of Yeshua. I myself would consider that to be not the *p'shat* (plain sense) of the text but a *remez* (hint) contained therein (see Mt 2:15N). The debate among scholars here is not over the meaning but over the text itself. The Masoretic text, used in Jewish Bibles, has the word "*k'ari*," so that the last line of the verse means, "Like a lion my hands and my feet." But the Hebrew text that the Septuagint translators used must have had the word "*karu*," so that the same line means, "They pierced my hands and my feet." It is easy to see how these two variants could have arisen, for confusing the letter *yud* with *vav* and adding or deleting *aleph* are frequent in early Hebrew. No matter which text was the original, no one questions that Psalm 22 speaks of a crowd ganging up against one individual; whether "they pierced" his hands and feet or crowded around like a lion at his hands and feet, they were a most unfriendly crew!

Leaving questions of text and translation, we turn to whether believers misinterpret verses, applying them to Yeshua when the original says nothing about him. Here the problem is usually confusion of levels of meaning. The *p'shat* of a *Tanakh* text never speaks about Yeshua by name, but it may at the level of *drash* (homily), *remez* (hint), or *sod* (secret meaning); further, it may contain a prediction about the Messiah which Yeshua realizes; or it may be a "type" (a "prefigurative historical event," 1C 10:6&N) of which Yeshua is the "antitype" (fulfillment). I said that the *p'shat* of Psalm 22:17 does not refer to Yeshua, but it does contain a *remez*; Hosea 11:1 is a similar text (see Mt 2:15&N). Isaiah 53 contains, in my judgment, many predictions about the Messiah which Yeshua fulfills; however, some (by no means all) Jewish commentators say that Isaiah was talking not about the Messiah but about the Jewish people. (A difficulty with this interpretation arises at Isaiah 53:8, which says, "He was cut off out of the land of the living; for the transgression of my people he was stricken"; "he" the Messiah can be put to death and stricken for the transgression of God's people the Jews, but how can "he" the Jewish people be put to death and stricken for their own transgression?) The conflict can be resolved, in my view, by noting that Yeshua identifies with and represents the Jewish people (see Mt 2:15&N and *Messianic Jewish Manifesto*, pp. 105–108).

On such matters of interpretation, presuppositions influence the results and differences of opinion remain. But when two people who have honestly examined the objective evidence reach different conclusions, they should not accuse each other of distorting God's message.

In the light of what has already been said, we can dispose quickly of the accusation of quoting verses out of context: nobody should. Whatever a verse can prove, it can prove in context; and if it cannot prove it in context, it cannot prove it at all.

But this leads me to raise an issue underlying this criticism which is rarely examined: is it proper to use the *Tanakh* to "prove" anything at all? That is, does the *Tanakh* carry an authority enabling it to prove something true or false? We are at once in the area of theology known as inspiration of Scripture. Did God really inspire the Bible? If he did, then its words mean something and can prove something. But if the Bible is only the product of men who lived long ago and wrote wisely, then what it says only stands alongside what other wise men have said and carries no special authority — it may provide a generally useful, uplifting, and comforting guide to ethical behavior, but it carries no weight in settling matters of fact such as whether Yeshua is the Messiah. If one holds to this "low view of Scripture," it follows logically that proof-texting is unacceptable, a **distorting of** the *Tanakh*, even though the *Tanakh* is no longer regarded as **God's message**.

But if one has a "high view of Scripture," that it truly constitutes **God's message** to humanity, that its authors were inspired by God, and that its words in the original languages, as communicated by the original authors and editors, carry God's authority, then proof-texting (when the verses are used in context) is an entirely proper and useful procedure.

More than that, even if one's debating partner has a "low view" of Scripture, those who have a "high view" need not mute it; on the contrary, they should rely openly on God's promise that his Word will perform its function: "See, the Word of God is alive! It is at work and is sharper than any double-edged sword — it cuts right through to where soul meets spirit and joints meet marrow, and it is quick to judge the inner reflections and attitudes of the heart" (MJ 4:12). Accordingly, believers can count on the powerful Word of God and on the Holy Spirit of God to use the texts of the *Tanakh* themselves to work in the hearts of nonbelievers, even those who discount Scripture, and bring them to a willing and loving knowledge of God and his Messiah Yeshua, the living Word.

In conclusion, believers who avoid the pitfalls of unethical behavior can hold their heads high in proclaiming the Gospel, confident that, like Sha'ul, they can say: **By making very clear what the truth is, we commend ourselves to everyone's conscience in the sight of God**.

3–4 Our Good News is veiled both to unsaved Jews (3:14–15) and to Gentiles **in the process of being lost** — the veil remains as long as they do not turn to *Adonai* (3:16–17). Why do they not turn to *Adonai*? **Because the god of this world**, the Adversary, Satan (2:11, see Mt 4:1N), **has blinded their minds** (3:14) with this "veil." Why? **In order to prevent them from seeing the light shining from the Good News about the glory of the Messiah**. As the perennial accuser and opposer of God's plans, Satan's desire is that people be lost, just as it is God's desire "that all should come to repentance" (2 Ke 3:9).

5 This verse answers, "No," to Sha'ul's earlier rhetorical question, "Are we starting to recommend ourselves again?" (3:1). **What we are proclaiming is not ourselves** as objects of worship, emulation or self-puffery, **but the Messiah Yeshua as Lord** (compare 1C 2:1–2), **with ourselves as slaves for you** (compare 1:24), helping you come to fuller knowledge of him; and we do this **because of** who **Yeshua** is.

6 The God who once said, "Let light shine out of darkness." Not a literal quotation from the *Tanakh*, but referring to Genesis 1:3, "And God said, 'Let there be light.'"The "quotation" in this form calls attention to the darkness both in creation and in human hearts before God speaks.

The verse is a florescent over-richness, like the last movement of Mozart's "Jupiter" Symphony, combining the major themes brought out since 3:7: brightness (3:7, 13), **light shining** (v. 4), **God's glory** (v. 4; 3:7–11, 18) **in the face** first of Moses (3:7, 11–13, 15), next of us (3:18) and now **of the Messiah Yeshua**; the contrast with veils (3:13–16, 18, vv. 3–4), **darkness** (v. 4) and blinding (v. 4) is implied.

7–18 Sha'ul and his companions' **power comes from God** (v. 7, compare 3:4–6); they are vulnerable **clay jars** who remain unbroken even under adverse conditions (vv. 8–9, compare 6:4–10, 11:22–33, 1C 4:9–13); they are dead yet filled with Yeshua's life (vv. 10–12a; compare Ro 6:2–11, 8:18–25, 1C 15:30–32; Ga 2:20, 6:14), because of their **trust** (vv. 13–14a). The purpose is both to bring **life** to **you** (vv. 12b, 14b–15a; compare v. 5, 1:24, 10:8, 11:7, 13:9, 1C 9:19) and to **bring glory to God** (v. 15b). But a third consequence, accomplished through daily renewal which enables us not to **lose courage** (v. 16; compare 3:18–4:1), is **for us an everlasting glory whose weight is beyond description** (vv. 16–18; compare Ro 8:17b–28). The Hebrew word for "glory," *kavod*, has the root meaning, "weight."

4:13–5:8 In addition to God's power through the Spirit for bearing up under adversity, **the**

Spirit enables us to trust (v. 13), and a major object of that trust is that we will be resurrected. This hope is not seen now but will last forever (v. 18). Three passages that contain similar ideas are 1C 15:35–52, Ro 8:17b–28 and Pp 1:18b–30.

4:18–5:7 Compare MJ 11:1, 7, 10, 13, 27.

CHAPTER 5

10 See 1C 3:8–15&N.

11–12 Sha'ul arms the people who are faithful to him so that they can answer **those who** elevate false emissaries because they judge by **a person's appearance rather than** "what is not seen" (4:18), **his inner qualities** (compare Yn 7:24).

13 **If we are insane**. Apparently some thought Sha'ul and his companions were, or he wouldn't have brought up the subject. As at Ac 26:24–29&NN he responds with a light touch: **it is for God's sake**; the implication is that he doesn't care all that much how people regard him (as at 6:8–10). Compare how Yeshua was regarded at Mk 3:20–21, Yn 10:20&N.

5:14–6:1a Sha'ul elaborates the ideas of this passage at Ro 3:24–26, 5:8–21, 7:24–8:13; 1C 15:22, 56.

All mankind was already dead (v. 14) spiritually and under sentence of physical and eternal death because of sin. Yeshua's death cancelled the sentence and turned spiritual death into spiritual life, through a **new creation** (v. 17). And all this has a purpose stated in v. 15.

God… through the Messiah has reconciled us to himself, made an at-one-ment and, in keeping with v. 15, **given us the work of** making known **that reconciliation** (v. 18), explained in v. 19 and in the **appeal** of vv. 20b–21. Reconciliation is the work of diplomats, so it is appropriate that the proclaimers of the Good News are called **ambassadors of the Messiah**. This high office is given a still more exalted title in 6:1, **God's fellow-workers**.

17 **If anyone is united with the Messiah, he is a new creation**. This verse is sometimes adduced to show that Jewish believers are no longer Jewish — because **the old has passed**. But Sha'ul is not talking about whether Messianic Jews are Jewish. He is talking about the fact that believers are now reconciled with God. Their old, unreconciled, sinful lives have passed into history. But they remain human beings with human characteristics and associations; they do not become abstract entities, divorced from their past. For evidence see Ro 11:13&N, Ga 2:13&N; also Ac 13:9N, Ga 3:28&N.

CHAPTER 6

1b–2 **We… urge you not to receive his grace and then do nothing with it** (literally, "to receive his grace in vain"), that is, and then not live for him (5:15). Thus begin the first notes of a new theme, heard again at v. 13b, "open wide your hearts," the significance of which blossoms in the charity appeal of Chapters 8–9. In line with this, v. 2 not only says what Sha'ul, imitating God, has done, but is an exhortation to the Corinthians to hear and help too.

3 Compare 1C 9:19, 23.

4–10 Compare 4:7–12, 11:22–33, 1C 4:9–13.

6:14–7:1 Sha'ul wants his **dear friends in Corinth** (v. 11) to **open wide** their **hearts** toward him (and others; see v. 1bN), as he has toward them, and not to **team** up with "pseudo-emissaries" (11:13) who are actually **unbelievers**; indeed this would be receiving God's grace in vain (v. 1b).

Verse 14 is sometimes used to support the principle that believers should not marry (**yoke** themselves **with**) **unbelievers**. One can surely make a *midrash* along these lines, but the plain sense of the text is not concerned with marriage. A believing widow is enjoined not to marry an unbeliever (1C 7:39). From a Jewish viewpoint intermarriage is usually understood to imply assimilation; see 1C 7:18&NN.

On "***Adonai-Tzva'ot***" (v. 18) see Ro 9:29N.

CHAPTER 7

5–7 This picks up the travel and visits narrative begun at 1:15–17&N. On **Titus**, see 2:13N.

8 **My letter**, probably 1 Corinthians but possibly another letter; compare 2:3–4.

10 Two ways of handling **pain** (or: "sorrow" or "sadness"). Ungodly sorrow, merely being sad or experiencing pain, has no virtue in it. It is concerned with self, not with God or with others who have been harmed; and it leads to self-hatred, self-pity, depression, despair and death. Godly sorrow, on the other hand, leads to repentance, *t'shuvah*, **turning from sin to God**, making restitution for wrongs, and resolving to act righteously. God is not interested in one's merely feeling sorry for having sinned, but in one's resolute turning from that sin and not doing it again when similarly tempted.

12 **The one who did the wrong** of living with his stepmother (1C 5:1). **The one wronged**, his father. See 2:5–10&N.

CHAPTER 8

8:1–10:1a The background of these two chapters appealing to the Corinthians to give generously to the brothers in Judea is 1C 16:1–4&NN. In addition, this section is connected with two themes enunciated elsewhere in this letter — the importance of the Corinthians' not receiving the grace of God in vain (6:1b–2&N), and Sha'ul's defence of his own ministry (10:1&N). The occasion for moving into the subject is Macedonia (v. 1), which he began discussing at 7:5.

Sha'ul's fundraising methods have much in common with those of today. But notice that although he has plenty of *sekhel* about practical matters, he brings everything — the gift itself, the motivations for giving, the remarks about the "fundraising committee," the allusions to the reactions of the recipients, even the "Jewish mother guilt trips" which he lays on the Corinthians — into the service of glorifying God.

1–5 He stirs up the Corinthians' envy of virtue by presenting the **congregations in** nearby but competitive **Macedonia** (v. 1) as a standard of comparison (v. 8). **Despite trials** and **poverty** they have been generous **beyond their means** without being nagged (vv. 2–3). They even **pleaded for the privilege** of giving (v. 4); further, their giving was not casual but an act of devotion **to the Lord** (v. 5).

6–8 Sha'ul's follow-up of his earlier nudging (1C 16:1–4) is to be carried out by an experienced man in the field, **Titus** (v. 6). Sha'ul again compliments the good qualities of the potential givers (v. 7) but says, in effect, "Put your money where your mouth is" (v. 8).

9 Here is a motivation for giving unique to believers in **the Lord Yeshua the Messiah. He was rich**, in that he had divine "glory... before the world existed" (Yn 17:5) and was "in the form of God," so that "equality with God" was available to him (Pp 2:6), yet **for your sakes he impoverished himself** (Pp 2:5–11), **so that he might make you rich** with the righteousness of God imputed to you. You should imitate his generosity in this more mundane way.

10–15 It is tempting to see Sha'ul as a Jewish mother, "**only giving an opinion**" as he urges mature expression of initial zeal as being **to your advantage** (vv. 10–11a). You should not be dissuaded by poverty or by fear that your gift will be inadequate (vv. 11b–12). And **relief for others should** not **cause trouble for you**; rather, there should be **reciprocity** (vv. 13–14), as when the Israelites were in the desert and each gathered just as much manna as he needed (v. 15).

16–24 Sha'ul is aware that the purity of **charitable work** can be clouded by misappropriation of funds and excessive administrative costs. He forestalls such criticism by entrusting these matters to a committee of three with credentials (vv. 16–19, 22–23) and **conduct** that are **above reproach** (vv. 20–21). But he does not let go of his main purpose, that the Corinthians respond appropriately (v. 24).

21 One need go no farther than the daily newspaper to read tragic stories of people who fail to make sure that their behavior not only is righteous but is seen by others as righteous. "Abstain from all appearance of evil" (1 Th 5:22, KJV).

CHAPTER 9

1 The Jewish mother again, **There is really no need for me to write you**. So why does he do it? By a figure of speech he indicates his awareness that underneath their laziness and slowness the Corinthians really do have the heart and the desire to do God's will. But at the same time he finds it necessary to prod them to act on these deeper and better motives.

2–4 Having offered the **Macedonians** as an example for emulation, he here presents the Corinthians themselves as an example he has used among others — and urges them to live up to their publicity (vv. 2–3), lest they **feel** bad at failing to meet the implicit quota and Sha'ul be **humiliated at having been so confident** about them (v. 4).

5 Another reason for sending the advance committee is to **prepare** the **gift**, so that **pressure** tactics will be unnecessary.

6 Next Sha'ul offers a more selfish reason for giving. He appeals to both exalted and ordinary motives but never to truly base or improper ones.

7–8 Sha'ul is concerned with the inner state of the giver and not merely with the fact of giving. The New Covenant emphasizes both the inner condition and the outward action; and that inner state is created not by oneself but by God.

8–11 Sha'ul urges the Corinthians not to fear for themselves, for God will supply plenty so that they may be generous (vv. 8–11; compare Mt 6:33, Pp 4:19).

9 Psalm 112 reads, in part:

> "Blessed is the man who fears *Adonai*,
> Who greatly delights in his commandments....
> Wealth and riches will be in his house....
> A good man shows favor....
> His heart is established....
> He has dispersed,
> He has given to the poor,
> His righteousness (***tzedakah***) remains forever."
> (Psalm 112:1, 3a, 5a, 8a, 9)

The Hebrew word "*tzedakah*" means both "righteousness" and "charity" (see Mt 6:1–4N).

12–14 Still another reason for giving: by so doing, you give the recipients a reason for praising God for having met their need through you (v. 12) and for having molded you into obedient believers (v. 13). As a result they will pray to God for you (v. 14).

15 **Thanks be to God for his indescribable gift**, namely, the opportunity to accomplish so much good for others, for yourselves, and for God's glory by giving to the Judean brothers!

CHAPTER 10

1–2 It is I, myself, Sha'ul. Why the emphasis? Because by some he is **considered timid** (or: "humble") and "weak" (v. 10) in person, so that only distance gives him the courage to be **intimidating** (or: "bold"). Sha'ul must put an end to such criticisms because they cause people to disrespect him and his authority (v. 8) as the Messiah's emissary and to turn to more glamorous "super-emissaries" (11:5) instead. The problem is not new in Corinth; see 1C 1:25–2:5, 4:14–21.

To overcome these attitudes Sha'ul has spent the last two chapters demonstrating how gentle, timid and humble he can be **when at a distance** — precisely the opposite of what his critics expect. In his **appeal** to the Corinthians to give generously to the Judeans, he leaned over backwards to show **meekness, forbearance** and tact; indeed, these qualities have characterized the entire letter up to this point. To those who deprecate such qualities he will explain that such "weakness" is true strength (12:9–10), and that he would rather boast about this kind of "weakness" than about what superficially appears to be strength (11:19–20, 30; compare 5:12, 1C 1:25–2:5).

Even then, he would boast only because these qualities are not natural in him but are evidence of how the Lord has changed him (3:18) — his only boasting will be about the Lord (10:17, 1C 1:31). The New Testament abounds with evidence that for Sha'ul in particular, such **meekness and forbearance** came only **from the Messiah**. The aggressive temper he displayed before he was saved (Ac 8:3, 9:1) was not done away with but stayed on in his "old nature" (vv. 3–5N) long afterwards (Ac 15:2, 39; 19:30–31; 23:3–5; Ga 5:12). He is well aware that he is "equal to such a task" as proclaiming the Good News (2:16b) and "competent" to be the Messiah's emissary (3:5) only because God makes him so.

Nevertheless, those who think Sha'ul is capable of being bold only when at a safe distance must be warned that he will not shrink from using his authority as the Messiah's emissary: **I beg you not to force me to be intimidating when I am with you**, which **I expect to be toward some** of you **who regard us as living in a worldly way**, unless you repent and change (compare v. 11; 13:2–4, 10; 1C 4:19–21).

In effect, in these two verses Sha'ul "bites the bullet"; he is now going to deal directly with those who carp at him, and a new element enters the tone of his letter. From here on, he makes use of irony, even sarcasm, as he ridicules his opponents, especially the "super-emissaries" (11:5, 12:11) who are actually "pseudo-emissaries" (11:13); and he indicates with increasing sharpness that he will not spare those who continue to sin. He has shown how gentle he can be; now he shows another side of himself, as he does his utmost to turn divisive troublemakers into faithful followers of the Messiah and his appointed emissary Sha'ul (1:1).

The phrase, "**as living in a worldly way**," is, literally, "as walking according to flesh." The term "flesh" (Greek *sarkos*) here, and often in Sha'ul's writings, means the "old nature," the emotional, mental and volitional qualities of a person before he has submitted himself to God, letting the Messiah change him. See Sha'ul's explanation of this at Ro 7:18–25a, 8:4b–13; and see Ro 7:5N.

3–5 Verse 3 is, literally, "For walking in flesh, we do not war according to flesh," that is, **for although we do live in the world**, in the body, in the flesh, and we do still have our "old nature" to contend with, nevertheless **we do not wage war in a worldly way**, the way unbelievers wage war, the way our "old nature" would wage war. See the similar declaration by David to Goliath at 1 Samuel 17:45.

First of all, the object of our warfare is different; as Ep 6:12–13 puts it, "We are not struggling against human beings, but against the rulers, authorities and cosmic powers governing this darkness, against the spiritual forces of evil in the heavenly realm," what Sha'ul here calls **strongholds** and **every arrogance**.

And secondly, **the weapons we use to wage war are not worldly**, they are not the weapons of aggressive hot-temperedness Sha'ul's old nature would be tempted to use; rather, they are the "war equipment God provides" (Ep 6:13) — truth, righteousness, the Good News, trust, salvation, the Spirit and the Word of God (Ep 6:14–17). These **have God's power for demolishing** demonic forces and the schemes which unredeemed human nature dreams up to prevent people from coming to a genuine **knowledge of God**; with these spiritual weapons **we take every thought captive**, even the most antagonistic and worldly, **and make it obey the Messiah**, forcing even anti-God ideas to "work for good" (Ro 8:28).

6–11 Sha'ul wants all of the Corinthians to let every rebellious thought be taken captive and made to obey the Messiah (v. 5b), and this means submitting to Sha'ul's authority as the Messiah's emissary. When that has happened, he will consider them to have **become completely obedient** (v. 6; compare 2:9). Only **then** will he **be ready to punish every** individual **act of disobedience**, because only then will punishment be valuable to them. Until that time, punishment would be counterproductive, since it would not be taken as the Lord's chastening (MJ 12:5–11) which works for good (Ro 8:28), but would be perverted into another grievance against Sha'ul. Grievance-collecting is a favorite pastime of spiritual babies, but Sha'ul wants his charges to grow up (compare 1C 3:1–4, 13:11, 14:20), not to be children or adolescent rebels, but mature adults capable of dealing rationally with those who are entitled to exercise authority (compare Mt 8:8–10, Ro 13:1–7, MJ 13:17).

But it is not as if he were going to wait indefinitely for the Corinthians to mature; he definitely plans to come, and when he does, he will not spare sinners (v. 11, 13:1–2). Meanwhile, because he has **the authority** (v. 8), he actively shepherds these recalcitrant sheep in the direction of becoming **completely obedient** (v. 6). He urges them to look deeper and consider that he is a brother in **the Messiah** (v. 7), whose **authority** is from **the Lord** and is intended **to build you up, not tear you down** (v. 8; compare 1:24; 4:5, 12–15; 11:7; 13:9; 1C 9:19). He deals with their imaginary grievances (v. 9; compare v. 1b, 2:3–4, 7:8–12) and counteracts their wrong attitude toward his weakness, starting with v. 10 and continuing to 12:12 (see vv. 1–2&N).

12–18 Expressing rich irony, Sha'ul does not **dare class or compare** himself with the "pseudo-emissaries" (11:13), not because they play this worldly game better than he (perhaps they do), or even because self-advertisement is ungodly (which it is), but because, for the reason given in v. 18, it is **simply stupid** (v. 12). Instead, knowing how risky boasting of any sort is, he limits his boasting to his own **area of work** (v. 13, 16b) and is guided by the rule of v. 17, which he has quoted to these people before (1C 1:31). Within that framework, he wants to boast only about the growing trust of the Corinthians themselves (v. 15), who are his "letter of recommendation" (3:1–3, 1C 9:1–3) because he led them to the Lord (v. 14, 1C 4:15). This is a difficult passage in the Greek, and other interpretations are possible.

CHAPTER 11

2b Compare 3:3a&N.

3b Genesis 3:1–7.

4 A demonic **spirit different from the** Holy Spirit, the *Ruach HaKodesh*, which **you received**. See Ga 1:6–9&N.
You bear with him. Compare v. 19.

6 **I may not be a skilled speaker**. Sha'ul is responding to the criticism of 10:10. Compare 1C 1:17, 2:1–5.

7–12 At 1C 9:4–19 Sha'ul gave several reasons for his **proclaiming the Good News to you free of charge**. Here a new reason is given at v. 12; also see below (12:13–15) for yet another. But the Corinthians are so sensitive about their pocketbooks — as is obvious from the way Chapters 8–9 are written — that Sha'ul cannot state explicitly to them at this time perhaps the most important reason why he will not accept their support. It is that he does not want them to feel that they have done God a favor and discharged their duty to God by giving money to Sha'ul. He will not permit them to attempt to earn a ticket to heaven by a legalistic work; only those less proud of their giving (vv. 8–9) can be entrusted to give. Further, Sha'ul is sparing the Corinthians the guilt they would feel if he accepted their commitment to support him, and they then failed to live up to that commitment — as seems to be highly probable, given their behavior in regard to the collection for the Judean brothers, as reported in Chapters 8–9.

12–15 **Pseudo-emissaries**, who of course are not really "super-emissaries" (11:5, 12:11) at all, are actually inspired by Satan, **the Adversary** (2:11, 12:7; see Mt 4:1N). The buffoonish red-suit-and-pitchfork image makes light of mankind's archenemy, who **masquerades as an angel of light**, perverting everything good to evil use in order to prevent people from trusting God. New Age religionists sometimes report encounters with beings of light; I wonder if they have read this passage.

16–21 **At least receive me as a fool**, as you receive these other fools, the false emissaries, **so that I too**, like them, **may do a little boasting**. Putting himself in the position of the Corinthians victimized by the false emissaries' superficial glamor, Sha'ul does a bit of controlled boasting himself in order to win them back (see 1C 9:19–23&NN). To do this, he must protest repeatedly (here, v. 23; 10:12, 18; 12:1, 6, 11) how foolish it is to boast; otherwise they would merely take him at his word and compare his claims with those of the others. But Sha'ul's real attitude toward such boasting (see 10:17) is summed up at Pp 3:8 — compared with knowing the Messiah Yeshua as his Lord, he regards all such boasts as garbage!

22–33 Compare 4:7–12, 6:4–10, 1C 4:9–13.

22–23 Are they Hebrews?... Israelites?... descendants of Avraham? So am I. Sha'ul identifies himself as a Jew, as do Messianic Jews today. See Ac 13:9N. And he does not call himself a "Christian" (see Ac 11:26N). But he does proclaim himself a **servant of the Messiah**; Messianic Jews must not, in their zeal to identify with their Jewishness, mute the fact that they serve Yeshua.

I'm speaking like a madman! See vv. 16–21N.

24–26 "Forty lashes less one," a set phrase in Jewish law. For certain offenses, the Oral *Torah* prescribes forty lashes. The practice was to give thirty-nine, allowing a margin of one for error in counting, lest the prescribed punishment be unjustly exceeded, which would be far worse than meting out slightly less. Why would **the Jews**, that is, a non-Messianic Jewish court, have ordered him to be lashed? Because of the strong reactions he stirred up as he proclaimed the Good News — which is to say, on trumped-up charges or for no good reason (compare Ac 13:50–51; 14:2–5, 19–20; 17:5–8, 13; 18:12–17; 19:9; 21:27–36; 24:2–9; 25:2–11). Is this evidence of a particularly virulent form of hardheartedness among Jews? It is indeed evidence of hardheartedness, but such is not unique to Jews; for Sha'ul's next remark is, "**Three times I was beaten with rods**"; this was a Roman punishment with which the Corinthians were familiar, so that he did not need to add, "by the Romans." Gentiles were quite capable of hardheartedness, venial behavior and disregard of justice where Sha'ul was concerned (see Ac 16:19–24, 19:23–34, 22:25–29, 25:9).

Once I was stoned by a mob of Jews and Gentiles (Ac 14:19). No wonder he speaks of being **exposed to danger from**, among other things, **my own people** and **Gentiles**.

30–33 This incident, reported at Ac 9:23–25, is an example of how **weak** and dependent on others Sha'ul was; about such things, **I will boast.** He begins here to answer those who criticize his "weakness" (10:10), referred to ironically at v. 21 above. The subject was reintroduced at v. 29, he puts "weakness" in proper perspective at 12:9–10, and he mentions it once again at 13:3–4.

CHAPTER 12

1–2, 5–7 Sha'ul has declared his program of showing just how stupid boasting is (see 11:16–21N). This is why when he says, "**I have to boast**," he adds that **there is nothing to be gained by it**.

I know a man, namely, myself, Sha'ul. Out of modesty he prefers to speak of himself in the third person when talking about his **visions and revelations**. That he is speaking of himself is clear from vv. 6b–7; so that when he says in v. 5, "**About such a man I will boast; but about myself I will not boast**," it is as if Sha'ul were two persons (compare Ro 7:14–25); or, perhaps more accurately, it is that he is now completely objective about his experience and utterly unattached to it.

2–4 The third heaven is not the air (the first heaven) or the sky where the stars are (the second heaven), but the "place" where God is, a spiritual realm. Other explanations are possible.

Snatched up. The term is used at only one other place in the New Testament, 1 Th 4:17, where believers are described being "snatched up to meet the Lord in the air."

Jewish writings too report instances of people's entering Paradise; a well-known instance is Chagigah 14a, which starts out,

> "Our Rabbis taught: 'Four men entered the *pardes* [Paradise; see below on "*Gan-Eden*"] — Ben-'Azzai, Ben-Zoma, Acher and Rabbi Akiva.'"

It tells of their experiences there; of interest is what it says Acher did as a result of his time in Paradise:

> "He mutilated the plants,"

meaning that he apostatized. He may have become a Messianic Jew, or he may have adopted some other religious position; scholarly opinions differ. After leaving non-Messianic Judaism, he was no longer called by his correct name, Elisha ben-'Avuyah, but by a word that means simply "another" or "different." For more on him see Ac 22:3N; also compare Mt 1:21N on the name "Yeshua" and its variant "Yeshu"; and see MJ 10:20N.

Whether he was in the body or outside the body I don't know, God knows. Some modern occult-oriented religions make much of "out-of-body experiences"; terms such as "astral projection" and "etheric body" are tossed about to impress the gullible. In my judgment, people sometimes have such experiences; but the experiences are rarely from God. They may be from Satan, masquerading as an angel of light (11:14). Or they may be a natural phenomenon about which little is known; Kirlian photography, which reportedly can produce pictures of amputated limbs, illustrates what I mean. In a number of books, some by Christians, people report "after-death experiences" in which they travel great distances outside their body in a few seconds, sometimes through a "tunnel of light" to a "place" corresponding sometimes to Paradise, sometimes to Hell and sometimes to locations on earth, where they may be "met" by Yeshua or someone else. Of course, these people then "return to their bodies," which may have been dead by clinical standards for many minutes; otherwise, obviously, there would be no report. In most discussions of such experiences and phenomena Sha'ul's main point is forgotten — these matters are not to be a source of pride. A person's reputation should be based only on what his words and deeds warrant (v. 6).

Gan-Eden. See Lk 23:43N.

7–10 What was Sha'ul's **thorn in** the **flesh**? Some think it was a physical incapacity, such as stuttering (10:10, 11:6), epilepsy (5:13, Ac 9:4), or weak vision (Ac 9:7, Ga 4:15); some, the emotional suffering resulting from not winning Jews to the Messiah as he would have liked (but see Ac 28:24&N); others, a recurring temptation, such as greed (Ro 7:8); and yet others take the following phrase, "**a messenger** [Greek *angelos*, "messenger, angel"] **from the Adversary**," to mean that his "thorn" was a demonic spiritual being especially dispatched by Satan (Mt 4:1N) **to pound away at** him (compare Mt 25:41, Rv 12:7, 9).

From vv. 8–9a we learn that the "messenger from the Adversary," whatever it was, even if it was a demon, was sent by God — the Adversary has no independent power; God is in control of the universe. We also learn that sometimes God's answer to prayer is not necessarily to grant the request as asked, but to change the person asking (3:18), so that he no longer wants what he wanted before (vv. 9b–10). On "**weak,**" see 10:1–2&N.

11 **I have behaved like a fool** to boast so much. See 11:16–21N. "**Super-emissaries.**" See 11:5, 13.

12 **The things that prove I am an emissary** are **signs, wonders and miracles** (see Mk 16:15–20, Yn 14:12), made possible by the power (v. 9) which the Spirit provides (Ro 15:19; 1C 2:4–5, 4:19; Ep 3:7, 20); because "the Kingdom of God is not a matter of words but of power" (1C 4:20).

13 See 11:7–12&N.

14 Sha'ul resumes talking about his plans; see 1:15–17&N.

CHAPTER 13

1–11 Sha'ul sums up the whole letter, which, as now becomes evident, has been written to the Corinthians with great care so as not to put them off, for he regards them as spiritual babies (1C 3:1–3) resembling skittish, squirrelly children or adolescents unable to concentrate. For this reason the letter's structure suits today's people, who are accustomed to message overload and multimedia presentations, rather than those of earlier eras, with their "linear," one-message-at-a-time communications.

Sha'ul has a number of loosely related "points" in his "sermon" (compare 1:1–2N):

(1) I am not a failure.
(2) I consider my weaknesses to be strengths.
(3) I do not operate in the flesh.
(4) I operate by God's power.
(5) Everything I do is for your sakes.
(6) As the Messiah's emissary I carry God's authority.
(7) I am straightforward and honest.
(8) My letters are to benefit you.
(9) You are worthwhile people with great strengths.
(10) Do not be misled by pseudo-emissaries.
(11) Our suffering and weakness are for your benefit and are part of my power.
(12) I will not hesitate to make use of my power when I am with you.

He never concentrates on any one of these points or themes for very long but keeps returning to them, placing each alongside others, in various sequences and contexts, hoping that as the Corinthians listen to the letter read aloud, some of his points, through sheer repetition, will sink in and motivate change. Only here, at the end of the letter, does he state its purpose concisely, in vv. 5–10, and especially in vv. 9–10: Sha'ul wants the Corinthians to **become perfect** without his having **to use** his **authority to deal sharply with** them, because **the Lord gave** him this authority **for building up and not for tearing down**.

1 **Any charge must be established by the testimony of two or three witnesses**. Sha'ul applies the biblical, Jewish evidential standard of Deuteronomy 19:15 in a non-Jewish legal context. Therefore it cannot be said, as some Christians do, that the *Torah*'s "civil law" was abolished by the New Testament.

12 No one is sure exactly what a **holy kiss** was. Surely it was some sort of physical expression of warmth and love involving a hug, an embrace, a kiss, touching, closeness — but entirely free of improper and unseemly overtones. In Israel, Arab men and Jewish men from Middle Eastern backgrounds often greet each other by kissing on both cheeks. See Ro 16:16N.

14 The wording of this benediction implies equality between the sources of **grace, love** and **fellowship** (Greek *koinônia,* which can also be rendered "communality," "commonness," "communion") — that is, between the Father (**God**), the Son (**the Lord Yeshua the Messiah**) and the Holy Spirit (**the *Ruach HaKodesh***). But this equality remains an implication and is not stated as a proposition. As pointed out elsewhere, *Adonai* is never called a "Trinity" in the New Testament. However, the three terms which appear here, along with equivalent terms, are used in various ways in both the New Testament and the *Tanakh* when speaking of God.

THE LETTER FROM YESHUA'S EMISSARY SHA'UL (PAUL) TO THE MESSIANIC COMMUNITY IN GALATIA:

GALATIANS

CHAPTER 1

1 Rabbi **Sha'ul** from Tarsus is Paul (Ac 13:9&N).

Emissary, Greek *apostolos*, "someone sent," usually rendered "apostle" (Mt 10:2–4N).

I received my commission, etc. The basis of Sha'ul's authority as an emissary of the Messiah Yeshua is one of the two main topics of this letter (see 1:10–2:14, 5:11, 6:12–14).

Who raised him from the dead. This shows that God's power and authority surpass those of any human claimant, and that Yeshua's power and authority did not cease when he died (compare Ro 1:3–4).

Also all the brothers with me. What Sha'ul writes to the Galatians on the very important issues raised in this letter carries not only his authority but that of all the fellow-believers with him.

2] **Messianic communities** or "congregations," Greek *ekklêsiai*, usually rendered "churches" (see Mt 16:18N).

Galatia, a region in what is today central Turkey where Sha'ul established congregations (Ac 13:51–14:23) and later returned to strengthen them (Ac 15:36, 16:1–6).

3a ***Shalom***. A greeting; denotes more than just "peace" (see Mt 10:12N).

3b–5 Together with v. 1, this epitomizes the Good News — Yeshua the Messiah's atoning death, forgiveness of sins, salvation, obedience to God's will, resurrection and continuing authority, all for God's glory. This is the standard against which to measure the false "supposedly 'Good News'" of vv. 6–9.

Amen. Intended to prompt a congregational response, when the letter is read aloud; see Ro 9:5N. The Galatians' "*Amen*" is a public statement of affirmation and agreement with Sha'ul's version of the Good News, contrasting with the version described in the following verses.

6–9 Is Sha'ul a martinet with an uncontrollable temper, or is he filled with venom against anyone whose opinions differ from his own? The answer depends on whether one believes there is such a thing as a true Gospel, God's **genuine Good News**, summed up in vv. 1 and 3b–5, answering the deepest questions of human existence. If in fact Yeshua

called Sha'ul **by** his **grace** to proclaim God's Good News, then this is the true Good News that saves. Any other "gospel" is **not good news at all** but misleading bad news, capable of drawing off to perdition people who began on the road to salvation. This unique truthfulness of God's Good News is a presupposition of the entire letter to the Galatians. Moreover, the idea that there is absolute truth which matters absolutely is the constant presumption of both the *Tanakh* and the New Testament. Any other view relegates the Bible to the category of "great literature" or "valuable historical evidence" or "wise sayings of great men." It is all of these, but, more than that, it is God's unique word to humanity, containing the only completely reliable guide toward everlasting life and away from everlasting death.

It becomes clear in what follows that the particular bad news to which the Galatians have been exposed is *legalism*. Legalism I define as the false principle that God grants acceptance to people, considers them righteous and worthy of being in his presence, on the ground of their obedience to a set of rules, apart from putting their trust in God, relying on him, loving him, and accepting his love for them.

On Sha'ul's use of the word "**curse**" (Greek *anathema*), see Ro 9:2–4a&N and 1C 16:22&N. As the man responsible for establishing the Galatian congregations on the right path, Sha'ul has no choice but to condemn in the strongest possible language those who try to destroy what is not merely his own work but God's work. Those who wilfully and in defiance of the truth choose for base reasons (2:3–5, 6:12–13) to preach a sub-gospel should not be spared; they have earned their punishment (5:7–10) and deserve accursedness if they will not repent; elsewhere Sha'ul teaches that repentance remains open to them (Ro 2:4, 10:13; 2 Ti 2:25; compare 2 Ke 3:9). Therefore I conclude that Sha'ul's animosity is not personal in this passage (whether the same is true at 5:12 is a separate question; see note there).

10 Sha'ul was evidently being accused by certain other Messianic Jews of **trying to win human approval**, in this case Gentile approval, by setting forth an "easy" Gospel which did not demand that Gentiles become Jews and thus be required to observe the *Torah* as non-Messianic Judaism understands it and as considerable numbers of Messianic Jews were practicing it.

Sha'ul's response is to establish from the start the dichotomy between winning human approval and winning **God's approval**: one cannot aim at both, and Sha'ul's interest is only in the latter (compare Ro 2:29). Or, to emphasize a different side of it, **if** Sha'ul **catered to people**, he **would not** in fact, indeed could not possibly, **be a servant of the Messiah**, since, no less than God the Father, the Messiah demands exclusive loyalty.

11–12 The Good News as I proclaim it was revealed directly (compare 2:2) by the risen **Yeshua**. The fact that it is **not a human product** and that **neither did** he **receive it from someone else nor was** he **taught it** means that he had no reason to try to win the approval of or cater to his teachers (v. 10); for those who had been his teachers, Rabban Gamli'el (Ac 22:3) and other non-Messianic Jews, had taught him something very different (vv. 13–14).

1:13–2:14 Sha'ul here provides evidence for what he has asserted in vv. 10–12. He certainly did not learn his Gospel in non-Messianic Judaism (vv. 13–14). Rather, it was

God's sovereign action to pick him, call him, reveal his Son directly and make him an emissary to the Gentiles (vv. 15–16). Even then, he did not go and study with those who were emissaries before him in order to prepare himself for his God-given task, but went off to Arabia for as long as three years (vv. 17–18) and began putting together his revolutionary version of the Gospel — revolutionary in that for the first time a Scriptural and theological basis was given for presenting the Gospel to Gentiles without their having to become Jews first (see v. 17N). From 1:18 through 2:14 Sha'ul further explains how his ministry developed independently of the leading Jewish believers, yet correctly and with their approval, so that under pressure from legalizers (2:3–5) and even from the foremost emissary, Kefa (2:11–14), he did not alter his version of the Gospel or add to the practices it requires. The ideas in this note are unpacked below in the notes to the separate verses.

13 Traditional Judaism. Literally just "Judaism," transliterating the Greek word "*Ioudaismos,*" which occurs in the New Testament only here and in the next verse; it means "the Jewish religion," and here it can only mean non-Messianic Judaism. I have added the adjective "traditional" to the text in order to make it absolutely clear that Sha'ul was not speaking about what is today called Messianic Judaism, that is, Judaism which accepts Yeshua as the Messiah and the New Testament as Holy Scripture alongside the *Tanakh*.

Some would take the absence in the Greek text of an adjective such as "traditional" or "non-Messianic" as evidence that the New Testament regards Judaism in all its forms as a religion distinct from Christianity, that Sha'ul considers himself now a Christian and no longer a Jew, and therefore that Messianic Judaism is Christianity and not Judaism. But Sha'ul, writing to the Gentiles in Galatia around 50 C.E., was addressing an altogether different issue than whether Judaism can have a Messianic form. His point was that the Galatians were not required to become Jews in order to join God's people and share in God's promises. It is clear from 2:13&N that he assumed Jews can be either Messianic or non-Messianic. It is only because many modern readers have been taught the opposite that I have added the term "traditional" to the text. Had Sha'ul intended to emphasize the Jewish unity of Messianic and non-Messianic Jews, he very well might have added "traditional" or "non-Messianic" before the word "Judaism" in these verses. But his job as emissary to the Gentiles (v. 16) was to stress a no less important unity, that of Messianic Jews with Messianic Gentiles on the ground of trusting in the Good News and being faithful to it (2:16). This he does throughout the entire letter, especially from 2:11 onwards, and most forcefully at 3:27–28&NN, where he writes that with the Messiah, "there is neither Jew nor Gentile."

I did my best to persecute God's Messianic Community and destroy it. Luke reports this at Ac 7:58–8:3; 9:1–2, 13–14; 22:4–5, 19–20; 26:9–12; and Sha'ul mentions it again himself at 1C 15:9, Pp 3:6 and 1 Ti 1:13–15. These passages confirm that he regarded his persecution of Jewish believers in Yeshua as a measure of his zeal for non-Messianic Judaism, although it was a zeal "not based on correct understanding" (Ro 10:2; compare 4:17–18 below).

One occasionally finds the same kind of zeal among non-Messianic Jews today. Some Christians magnify it above its real importance, letting it frighten them into not telling Jewish people about Yeshua. On the other hand, Jews involved in ecumenical dialogue with Christians find such zealotry, sometimes accompanied by intolerance of Christianity, an embarrassment; to protect Judaism's good name they tend to minimize it, correctly pointing out that very few Jewish zealots engage in physical violence against Christians and Messianic Jews — especially when compared with the violence that has emanated from Christendom against Jews over the centuries. Two incidents of modern persecution of Messianic Jews by Jewish zealots are the "deprogramming" of Ken Levitt, recounted by him with Ceil Rosen in their book, *Kidnapped For My Faith* (Van Nuys, California: Bible Voice, Inc., 1978), and the disruption of a concert of Messianic Jewish music by the Jewish Defense League, reported in Chapters 12–13 of David Rausch, *Messianic Judaism: Its History, Theology and Polity* (New York: The Edwin Mellen Press, 1982). Despite such opposition, believers continue to evangelize Jewish people, secure in the Lord Yeshua's promise that his Community will survive, and nothing will overcome it (Mt 16:18). Moreover, believers can pray that even the most acrimonious opponent will, like Sha'ul, himself come to Messianic faith.

14 The second measure of Sha'ul's zeal for **traditional Judaism** was how **rapidly** he **advanced** in it. In this he had every advantage (Pp 3:5–6), chief of which was that he studied with the leading teacher in Israel at the time, *Rabban* Gamli'el, under whom he was "trained in every detail of the *Torah* of our forefathers" (Ac 22:3). The phrase, "**the traditions handed down by my forefathers**," means the Oral *Torah* as set forth by the *P'rushim* (Pharisees; compare Mt 15:2–6, Mk 7:2–13&NN); whereas the similar phrase in Ac 22:3, by using the word "*Torah*" instead of "traditions," includes the written *Torah* as well. Sha'ul's point here in speaking of the Oral *Torah*, which includes many rules not mentioned in the written *Torah*, may be to show that he himself was far more observant than the very legalists he opposes in this letter.

Sha'ul's reason for advancing more rapidly than his fellow *talmidim* was that he **was more of a zealot for** the Oral Law **than most Jews** his **age**. The zeal for the Oral *Torah* of this outstanding "*yeshiva bocher*" was in keeping with his having been a *Parush* (Ac 23:6, Pp 3:5). Sha'ul had always been ambitious; what changed after he met Yeshua was the direction of his ambition (v. 23). His advancement in non-Messianic Judaism probably included both stricter observance of the details of its Law — being more *frum*, to use the Yiddish term derived from German *fromm* ("pious") — and faster promotion in its communal life. In connection with the latter, some have tried to prove that Sha'ul at the time of Stephen's death was already a member of the Sanhedrin (Ac 7:58&N, 8:1&N, 9:1–2N, 23:1&N, and especially Ac 26:10, where he says, "I cast my vote" in favor of putting believers to death). If so, he would have been a very youthful one, and this would evidence his rapid advancement.

If Sha'ul was so prominent, why is he not mentioned at all in any Jewish writings of the time? Yeshua's name appears in the Talmud, but Sha'ul's does not. This is not the place to examine the evidence in detail, but I will note that some students of this problem believe that it was because he was considered an apostate who damaged Israel that his name was expunged from official Jewish memory. The Messianic Jewish scholar H. L. Ellison believed that it was precisely because Sha'ul, as a believer, observed the Law so scrupulously that the non-Messianic Jewish community had to blot out all memory of him; see Acts 22:3N. Travers Herford, in his book, *Christianity in Talmud and Midrash*, builds a case that the Talmud makes a covert reference to Sha'ul at

Sotah 47a, where "Gehazi" (2 Kings 4–5, 8) is spoken of as having no place in the world to come (Mishna Sanhedrin 10:2) and as having refused to repent when offered the opportunity.

15–16 God… picked me out before I was born, as he did Jeremiah (Jeremiah 1:5; compare Isaiah 49:1); indeed it was "before the creation of the universe" (Ep 1:4); and he **called me** (Ac 9:4) **to reveal his Son to me** (Ac 9:5), **so that I might announce him to the Gentiles** (Ac 9:15, 22:21, 26:18–23; Ro 11:13).

1:17–21, 2:1–2 How the chronology of Sha'ul's life given here fits with that reported by Luke in the book of Acts is debated by scholars. One possible sequence is that Sha'ul came to faith on the way to Damascus (Ac 9:3–19) and stayed there with the Messianic Jewish believers briefly, evangelizing in the synagogues (Ac 9:20–22). He **immediately went off to Arabia** (v. 17); one does not know for how long, but according to v. 18 the upper limit has to be **three years**. **Afterwards** he **returned to Damascus**, where he continued evangelizing Jewish people until some of them hatched a murder plot, so that he had to escape by being lowered over the city wall in a basket (Ac 9:23–25, 2C 11:30–33; alternatively, he escaped from Damascus, went to Arabia, and returned three years later for a less traumatic visit).

Only then **did** Sha'ul **go up to Yerushalayim** (Ac 9:26–30), but just **for two weeks**. Sha'ul writes that he went **to make Kefa's acquaintance** (v. 18) but **did not see any of the other emissaries except Ya'akov** (v. 19); however, Ac 9:27 says that Bar-Nabba led him "to the emissaries," not to only two of them. A possible harmonization of these versions is that Sha'ul was introduced to all or most of the emissaries but spent no extended amount of time with them receiving instruction or discussing his version of the Good News (which is the focus here but not in Acts).

Next he **went to Syria and Cilicia**, specifically to Tarsus (Ac 9:30), where he remained a number of years, until Bar-Nabba brought him to be his assistant in Antioch (Ac 11:25–26). After some more time, Bar-Nabba and Sha'ul went to Jerusalem with the Antioch congregation's contribution for the relief of the Judean brothers (Ac 11:29–30, 12:25), so that Sha'ul's second visit there was only **after fourteen years** (2:1); and perhaps he would not have gone then had it not been for **a revelation** (2:2).

During this visit, he and **Bar-Nabba** (2:1) reached an agreement with the Jerusalem leaders on principles of Gentile evangelism, as described in 2:2–10. After this, he and Bar-Nabba evangelized the Galatians (Ac 13:2, 14:1–23), and Sha'ul wrote them this letter from Antioch either during the "some time" of Ac 14:28 or after the events of Ac 15:1–2; the latter seems more likely in the light of 2:11–14 below. At the time this letter was written, the Jerusalem Conference (Ac 15:3–29) had not yet happened; so that its more specific directives concerning how the Gospel was to be presented to Gentiles were announced to the Galatians by Sha'ul only at a later time (Ac 15:36, 16:4–6).

17 I immediately went off to Arabia. Phillip Goble, the Gentile author of several books on Messianic Judaism and a play about Sha'ul (*The Rabbi From Tarsus*, Tyndale Press, 1982) has said, "Christianity is simply transcultural Judaism." I believe that during this time in Arabia, away from the company of others and guided by the Holy Spirit, Sha'ul put together the outline of how the Gospel, hitherto confined within an ethnically

Jewish framework, could be made independent of Jewish culture and thus fully available not only to Jews, but also to Gentiles without their having to convert to Judaism (see v. 23; 2:2, 6–9; 5:2–4).

Sha'ul must have seen at once that the Pharisaic Judaism which he had learned from *Rabban* Gamli'el (Ac 22:3) had been shaken by the coming of Yeshua the Messiah. But it must have taken him considerable time to think about the various specific issues — the nature of atonement and forgiveness, the authority of the written and Oral *Torah*, the meaning of the Messianic prophecies, the role and future of the Jewish people, the preeminent requirement of trust for salvation, the role of ethics, and other essential theological matters — and to formulate and refine his views to what they were when he wrote his letters. As soon as he experienced God's call to be an emissary to the Gentiles, he must have realized that his need was not to be instructed in the Gospel as it had been presented to the Jews, but to think and meditate privately on its implications for Gentiles. No one could guide him in this, for he would be pioneering; but his training as a Jewish scholar by Gamli'el uniquely equipped him to investigate these matters in a fundamental way.

The development of Sha'ul's faith would have been a simpler process had the acceptance of Yeshua been for him, as it was for some of his fellow Jews, merely adding to traditional Judaism the belief that Yeshua is indeed the long-expected Messiah. And it would have been simpler if the acceptance of Yeshua had been for him what it doubtless was to many of the Gentiles he led to trust, namely, the acceptance of a new religion that displaced former pagan values and practices. To Sha'ul the revelation of Yeshua as the Son of God meant neither of these, but a radical reexamination of all his former beliefs, which issued in a conception of religion that differed from the other emissaries' Messianic Judaism perhaps even more than theirs differed from then-current non-Messianic Judaism. Only prolonged thought could enable him to see just how much of the old was to be abandoned, how much revised, how much retained unchanged. So although he wasted no time before plunging enthusiastically into evangelism (Ac 9:20, 22, 28), his real work was developing the implications of the Messiah's coming in the light of his deep knowledge of Judaism and in the light of God's call on him to communicate this Jewish truth to the non-Jewish world. (This paragraph, with minor changes, is taken from E. D. Burton's note to the same verse in his commentary written seventy years ago (*International Critical Commentary, Galatians*, Edinburgh: T. & T. Clark, 1971 (1st edition 1921), p. 56).

Thus Sha'ul was the perfect example of what Yeshua was talking about when he said, "Every *Torah*-teacher who has been made into a *talmid* for the Kingdom of Heaven is like a homeowner who brings out of his storage room both new things and old" (Mt 13:52&N). From his vast treasure of Jewish knowledge, his many years in the Gentile world, and his personal experience with the Messiah he developed the foundations of the transcultural Judaism which came to be known as Christianity.

A similar challenge awaits today's *Torah*-teacher, perhaps the most exciting challenge a Jewishly-educated Jew can take up. It is the challenge to apply what he knows of non-Messianic Judaism to the developing of Messianic Judaism, so that Messianic Judaism can deal meaningfully with every Jewishly important issue. Modern Messianic Judaism is awaiting its Rabbi Sha'ul.

However, the task is different in one respect. Christianity is transcultural Judaism, but Messianic Judaism is not merely reacculturated Christianity, even though some in the non-Messianic Jewish community suppose that it is; against this idea see Chapters 1–2 of my book, *Restoring the Jewishness of the Gospel*, or, equivalently, the Appendix to *Messianic Jewish Manifesto*. The accretions which two thousand years have laid upon today's Christianity make it necessary for Messianic Judaism's Rabbi Sha'uls (may there be many of them!) to penetrate as deeply into both non-Messianic Judaism and Christianity as Sha'ul penetrated into the religion of his day, not in order to syncretize, or even to synthesize, but simply to set forth the truth.

18 **Kefa** is Peter; see Mt 16:18N.

19 **Ya'akov the Lord's brother**. The brother of Yeshua (Mt 13:55, Mk 6:3, 1C 15:7) was not only the author of the New Testament book of Ya'akov (Ya 1:1) and head of the Messianic community in Jerusalem (Ac 12:17, 15:13, 21:18), but also one of the **emissaries**, as were Bar-Nabba and Sha'ul himself (Ac 14:4, 14; 1C 9:5–6). This means that there were more than twelve emissaries (see Ro 16:7), even though the role of the Twelve is unique (Mt 19:28, Rv 21:14); indeed Ep 4:11 suggests that the office of emissary continues to be a gift to the Messianic Community.

22 As further evidence that Sha'ul's version of the Good News was not taught him by others (vv. 11–12), he writes that **in Y'hudah**, where the greatest concentration of believers was, the **Messianic congregations didn't even know what** he **looked like**, much less had they instructed him in their version of the Gospel.

CHAPTER 2

1 **Bar-Nabba** (Ac 4:36&N) took an early interest in Sha'ul (Ac 9:27, 11:25) and accompanied him on the first of his four journeys (Acts 13–15); see also 1C 9:6, Co 4:10&N.

2–10 Having made the point that the **Good News** as he proclaims it **among the Gentiles** (v. 2) is something he learned from God, not from any human being, and especially not from the other emissaries (1:10–24), Sha'ul nevertheless insists (vv. 7–9) that its essence is the same as that of the Good News which the other emissaries proclaim to the Jews, "namely, this: the Messiah died for our sins, in accordance with what the *Tanakh* says; and he was buried; and he was raised on the third day, in accordance with what the *Tanakh* says" (1C 15:3–4).

What does make Sha'ul's message distinctive is his insistence that Gentiles do not have to become Jews in order to believe in Jesus. (Today the shoe is on the other foot: Messianic Jews are having to insist that a Jew need not become a *goy* in order to put his trust in Yeshua, the Jewish Messiah.) This point, irrelevant for Jews and therefore not part of the Gospel as it was presented to them, is essential for Gentiles; because it removes a major barrier, namely, the requirement, in addition to trusting God and the Good News, that Gentiles should leave one culture and join another. Sha'ul saw not only that this was unnecessary, but that insistence on it was a grave danger to **the truth of the Good News** (v. 5). Circumcision (vv. 3–5) quickly became the token of the entire controversy, precisely because when a Gentile allows himself to be circumcised, he obligates himself to obey the entire *Torah*, both written and oral; that is, he obligates himself to join the Jewish people as a Jew, to become fully Jewish (5:2–4&N).

3 **My Gentile companion Titus**, literally, "Titus, the one with me, being a Greek." Mentioned eight times in 2 Corinthians and once in 2 Timothy, he was the recipient of the New Testament letter that bears his name (Ti 1:4). The false brothers (vv. 4–5) wanted him **to undergo *b'rit-milah***, but the leaders of the Jerusalem Messianic community (vv. 6–10) **didn't force** him to do so. They believed, like Sha'ul, that it was unnecessary for Gentile followers of Yeshua to become Jews.

6–9 Sha'ul is at pains to show that although his distinctive form of the Good News has a different emphasis than the other emissaries' version, nevertheless, they accepted him, his work and his Gospel version with **the right hand of fellowship**. Those who insist on circumcision of Gentiles (vv. 3–5), therefore, do not have a better, purer, more Jewish Gospel at all, but a perversion of the Gospel (1:6–9) which denies its fruits to Gentiles and which is disapproved of by the very people to whose authority they appeal (v. 12, 5:11).

6 **Exactly what they were makes no difference to me**. Sha'ul is not demeaning the **acknowledged leaders** but calling attention to the fact that office, position, eminence, that is, **outward appearances**, do not matter. What does matter is the content and truth of the Gospel; and in this, these leaders, who Sha'ul knows were of great importance in the life of the Messianic Community, **added nothing to** him or to his message; on the contrary, they approved of him just as he was, placing upon him only the condition of v. 10.

7–9 **Just as Kefa had been for the Circumcised... the one working in Kefa to make him an emissary to the Circumcised... and they to the Circumcised**. Contrary to the claim by some in today's non-Messianic Jewish community that Jews should not be approached with the Gospel, let alone singled out for special attention, Scripture teaches precisely the opposite. The leading emissaries, the **acknowledged pillars of the community**, were specifically commissioned by God ("**the One working in Kefa**") to evangelize Jews (for which the term "**Circumcised**" is used because of the context, vv. 3–5).

9 **Ya'akov**, see 1:19&N. **Kefa**, see 1:18&N. **Yochanan** is the son of Zavdai (Mt 4:21), one of the Twelve (Mt 10:2), one of Yeshua's three closest companions (Mt 17:1, Mk 14:33), trusted, along with Kefa, for special tasks by both Yeshua (Lk 22:8) and the early Messianic Community (Ac 3:1–4, 11; 4:13, 19; 8:14), and regarded since earliest times as the author of five New Testament books.

10 See Ac 11:27–30, 12:25, 24:17; Ro 15:25–27; 1C 16:1–4; and 2C 8:1–9:15 for evidence not merely that Sha'ul **spared no pains** to **remember the poor** of Jerusalem, but that he regarded it as only just, a matter of principle, for Gentiles to give material support to Jews (Ro 15:25–27&NN). Presumably this aid was to benefit both the Messianic and the non-Messianic Jewish poor; there is no reason to suppose otherwise.

11 Sha'ul's confrontation with **Kefa** in **Antioch** (vv. 11–16, but see vv. 14b–21N) illustrates dramatically that Sha'ul ranked equally with the other emissaries, indeed with Kefa the leading emissary (a major purpose of the Book of Acts is to demonstrate the same thing). Hence the Greek word "*de*" at the beginning is rendered "**Furthermore**," not "but," as in most translations (see Ro 10:6–8&N for a discussion of "*de*"). "But" misses the point, for it implies that Sha'ul's primary concern is with Kefa, that Kefa was right in his earlier approval of Sha'ul's ministry (vv. 6–10) "but" (in contrast) was wrong in separating himself (v. 12). "Furthermore" makes the incident with Kefa the keystone in Sha'ul's defense of his own authority as an emissary, which has been the central issue since 1:10. He is saying here that his authority was so well-founded that he **opposed publicly** the leading emissary, Kefa. Sha'ul did so not in order to elevate himself, but because Kefa, a role model, was **clearly in the wrong** and the Galatians needed to be warned (see v. 14a&N).

12a From the community headed by Ya'akov, literally, "from Ya'akov." But what does that mean? One possibility is that these **certain people** were sent by Ya'akov, head of the Messianic Community in Jerusalem (see 1:19N). Yet clearly Ya'akov did not send them, because their insistence on observance of Jewish custom to the point of Jews' and Gentiles' not eating together contradicts Ya'akov's offering Sha'ul "the right hand of fellowship" (v. 9). It also contradicts what Ya'akov said at the Jerusalem Conference (Ac 15:4–29; compare also Ac 21:18ff.).

Another possibility is that they falsely represented themselves as having been sent by Ya'akov and as speaking on his behalf. It seems quite likely that indeed they did precisely that — otherwise Sha'ul would not have taken such pains in vv. 2–10 to show that the Jerusalem leaders approved his version of the Gospel, not theirs.

However, I have chosen not to push all of that into the translation, but only to say that **certain people** were **from the community headed by Ya'akov**. They came, but they were neither sent by him nor authorized to speak or act on his behalf.

They were probably the same, or from the same group, as the men who "came down from Judea to Antioch and began teaching the brothers, 'You can't be saved unless you get circumcised in the manner prescribed by Moshe,'" a doctrine which "brought them into no small amount of discord and dispute with Sha'ul and Bar-Nabba" (Ac 15:1–2) and which, at the Jerusalem Conference, resulted in a decision against them and in favor of Sha'ul and Bar-Nabba (Ac 15:20).

12b Before these people came, Kefa **had been eating with the Gentile believers**, literally, "with the Gentiles"; but the context of public confrontation implies that all (or nearly all) of those present were believers; for it is unlikely that Sha'ul would "air dirty laundry" before unbelievers.

This is important, for it is not to be thought that Kefa had abandoned Jewish tradition and now ignored keeping *kosher*, so that he ate with any and all Gentiles whenever he felt like it. His loyalty to *kashrut* had been such that nothing *treif* had ever touched his lips prior to his seeing Cornelius; for this we have his word, spoken while he was seeing a vision (Ac 10:12–15) and reported afterwards by him to other believers (Ac 11:5–10). There the meaning of Kefa's vision was not that the laws of *kashrut* had been abrogated, but that a new circumstance, the inclusion of Gentiles in the Messianic

Community, was to have an impact on *Torah* (see Ac 10:17–19&N, 10:28&N), so that keeping *kosher* became a less important *mitzvah* than preserving fellowship between Jewish and Gentile believers. Accordingly, the laws of *kashrut* remain; the Messianic Community has not ignored them (see Ac 21:20–21&NN) but rather has determined that Jewish-Gentile fellowship takes precedence over *kashrut* — just as circumcision of a boy on the eighth day takes precedence over not working on *Shabbat* (Yn 7:22–23&N).

I have heard the theory put forward by some Messianic Jews that Kefa and the other Jewish believers who ate with the Gentile believers ate *kosher* food with them — that either the Gentiles agreed to eat only *kosher* food, or special food was served to the Jewish believers. According to this theory, Kefa's fear of the Circumcision faction was only of their seeing him eating with Gentiles and supposing he was eating *treif* when he wasn't. (Eating with Gentiles was itself against custom, even if the food was *kosher*; but it did not violate *halakhah*; see Ac 10:28&N.) All this seems extremely unlikely to me. I understand the motivation for coming up with such a theory, namely, to show that the early Jewish believers did not stop being Jews; and one way of demonstrating this would be to show that they continued to observe the *Torah* in exactly the same way as before coming to faith. The flaw is in assuming that the *Torah* as set forth by non-Messianic Judaism is the standard by which to judge a Jew's Jewishness. If one realizes that it was the legalizers who had a distorted view of *Torah*, while the Jewish believers observed "the *Torah*'s true meaning, which the Messiah upholds" (6:2), then the motivation evaporates for developing a theory so contrary to any natural understanding of what Sha'ul reports was going on in Antioch.

The Messianic Jew Daniel Klutstein has offered an alternative understanding: the problem may not have been whether fellowship between Jewish and Gentile believers is more compelling than *kashrut* but whether it is more compelling than ritual purity. Today it is hard to appreciate how important purity was in first-century Jewish life, although the fact that one-sixth of the Talmud is devoted to this subject ought to give an indication. True, Orthodox Jews go to the *mikveh* on various occasions. But in the first century, homes of observant Jews frequently had a *mikveh* built in: to be able to maintain ritual purity at all times it was considered normal to have a private *mikveh*. Hundreds of them can be seen today at archeological sites in Yerushalayim, Tzippori and throughout Israel. Consider that Kefa went frequently to the Temple; he would not have been able to enter in a ritually impure state, but eating with Gentiles and being in their homes could render him impure and thus subject to criticism by the picky. A major point of Acts 10–11 is that Gentile believers in Yeshua were purified by God, so that Kefa learned to regard himself as ritually pure when eating with them. But before the overly critical Jews "from Ya'akov" he backed off and became a hypocrite or at least was intimidated into not being true to what he believed.

12c The faction that favored circumcision of Gentile believers, literally, "the Circumcision"; but this cannot here mean simply "the Jews," as it does in vv. 7–9; for all the principals — Sha'ul, Kefa, Bar-Nabba and the other Jewish believers — were Jews too. Rather, this is the group who insisted that Gentiles must become Jews before they can believe in Jesus, the group referred to in my translation at three other places as "the Circumcision faction" (see Ac 10:45&N, 11:2; Ti 1:10).

Kefa **withdrew and separated himself out of fear of** them. Why? What did the leading emissary have to be afraid of? Apparently, even though his explanation of Cornelius' conversion satisfied those of the Circumcision faction who heard him several years earlier (Ac 11:18), the issue had not died down but had grown more troublesome (vv. 3–4; Ac 15:1–2, 5; 21:20). Shall we look to Kefa's sanguine personality as an explanation, his desire to be a hail-fellow-well-met, accepted by everyone? Hardly, if his behavior in Acts 2–5 means anything at all. I think it was just a lapse, a moment of weakness — of which there are other examples in Kefa's life (Mt 26:75, Yn 21:7), as well as in Sha'ul's (Ac 23:2–5&N).

13 Jewish believers, Greek *Ioudaioi*, which is usually to be rendered "Jews" or "Judeans" (see Yn 1:19&N). But here "Judeans" is irrelevant, and the context makes it impossible that these *Ioudaioi* were non-Messianic Jews. Accordingly, we have here incontrovertible scriptural evidence that Jewish believers in Yeshua the Messiah are Jews, not ex-Jews as some claim.

Even Bar-Nabba, with Sha'ul an emissary specifically sent to the Gentiles (v. 9), who therefore, more than the others, should have known better.

14a Right in front of everyone. Since Kefa's public behavior was leading other believers astray, even the leaders, it was essential for Sha'ul to correct him publicly; see 1 Ti 5:20. The confrontation was a drama in which the central character was neither Kefa nor Sha'ul but **the truth of the Good News**.

14b–21 How much of this passage summarizes what Sha'ul said publicly to Kefa before the entire Messianic community of Antioch, and how much is Sha'ul's explanation to the Galatians, composed by him later for this letter? Three answers are given:

(1) Only to the end of v. 14 was said to Kefa, on the ground that only this much is truly confrontational in character, so that v. 15 onward is expository.

(2) The speech to Kefa extends through v. 16, on the ground that courtesy requires vv. 15–16 to explain Sha'ul's "outburst" in v. 14; but vv. 17–21 are commentary expressing Sha'ul's later reflections on the incident.

(3) Everything through v. 21 was said to Kefa, on two grounds. First, there is no reason why Sha'ul would not have wanted the Messianic community of Antioch to understand the issue as much as he now wants the Galatians to understand it, so that he would have made the incident with Kefa the occasion for a sermon. Second, his directly addressing the Galatians in 3:1 signals the transition from his remarks at Antioch.

The first seems least likely, because it is unthinkable that Sha'ul, the master at culturally adapting the Gospel, would use the language of v. 15 in speaking directly to Gentiles (see v. 15N). The second seems most likely because up through v. 16 the language is rhetorical, suited to public confrontation, while from v. 17 on the tone is calm, teacherly, suited to instructing the Galatians. Therefore I place the close-quote mark at the end of v. 16.

14b If you, A Jew, live like a *Goy* and not like a Jew, why are you forcing the *Goyim* to live like Jews? Kefa was a simple fisherman, a *guter Yid* (Yiddish: "a good Jew," with the sense, "a straightforward, honest man") whose loyalty to Jewish distinctives — to *kashrut*, for example (Ac 10:14) — was not the product of intellectual consideration or extended *Torah* study (Ac 4:14), but the naive expression of who he was. On the other hand, Sha'ul, the scholar and thinker who could talk circles around Kefa on any subject of *Torah*, and who used to be far more *frum* than Kefa ever dreamed of being (1:14&N), is "pulling intellectual rank" in the service of the Gospel: "Kefa, you observed *kashrut* without any exceptions most of your life. But you concluded, correctly, that with *Goyim* who are believers or are interested in the faith you should eat *treif* like a *Goy* if your insisting on *kosher* food would impede the communication of the Gospel. Now, with these impostors scrutinizing you, you go through the charade of always eating *kosher* and only with Jews. Why? From some holy motive? No, only to impress the people from Ya'akov's community who think the *Torah* as interpreted by the non-Messianic Jews is normative for Gentile believers. But I say that *Torah* so interpreted is normative for no one — not for Gentile believers, and not for Jewish believers either! And your past behavior and experience prove that you agree with me. Stop this charade! Stop this hypocrisy! Stop making the *Goyim* live like non-Messianic Jews — they don't have to! You know it, they are to know it, and the people from Ya'akov need to know it too."

Why are you forcing the *Goyim*, the Gentile believers here in Antioch, **to live like Jews?** This is an implied *kal v'chomer* argument (see Mt 6:30N): "Kefa, you used to be proud that you had never let a mouthful of *treif* food cross your lips (Ac 10:14). But you don't live according to the rules of non-Messianic Judaism any more. If you don't live by those rules, if you yourself live **not like a Jew**, how much more should you not force Gentiles to live by those rules!" The implication is that not only had Kefa hypocritically altered his own eating habits to conform with the wishes of the Judaizers, but he was now himself proselytizing on their behalf!

The terms used in this verse emphasize the strangeness of Kefa's behavior as much as its wrongness. For there are three Greek words which appear only here in the whole New Testament:

First, the phrase, "**like a *goy***" translates the Greek word "*ethnikôs*," which Sha'ul apparently invented for the occasion from *ethnos*, "pagan, heathen; Gentile, Non-Jew; nation; people, ethnic group"; a one-word translation of "*ethnikôs*" would be "Goyishly." I use the term "*Goy*" and its derivatives in my translation only to refer to Gentiles and only when one Jew is speaking to another. In modern Jewish English, "*Goy*" may have either a neutral or a pejorative overtone. Even though the expression, "*Goyishe* sinner," is pejorative in v. 15 (see note there), in this verse the word "***goy***" is used neutrally. See Mt 5:47N, 10:5N, 24:7N.

Second, the phrase, "**like a Jew**," "Jewishly," is Greek "*Ioudaikôs*," parallel to "*ethnikôs*" and formed from the word "*Ioudaios*" (here "Jew" and not "Judean"; see Yo 1:19N). Although "*Ioudaioi*" must mean "Jewish believers" in the previous verse (v. 13&N), and in this verse Kefa is called "*Ioudaios*" ("**a Jew**") without any reference to the nature of his faith, "*Ioudaikôs*" here can only mean "non-Messianic-Jewishly" — but it can't be translated that way in the text without losing the force of Sha'ul's rhetoric. See 1:13N on "non-Messianic Judaism." To live Messianic-Jewishly means sometimes to "live Goyishly" from the viewpoint of a non-Messianic Jew! Why? Because of the way in which the *Torah* has been modified under the New Covenant to take into account the inclusion of Gentiles in God's people. Thus the *Torah*-true Messianic Jew may break the laws of *kashrut* for the sake of preserving

Jewish-Gentile fellowship in the Body of the Messiah (and the *Torah*-true Messianic Gentile may sometimes choose to eat *kosher* for the same reason). What about the *Torah*-true non-Messianic Jew? According to Sha'ul and Messianic Judaism, there can be no such thing; for to deny that Yeshua is the Messiah is to deny the New Covenant, which "has been made *Torah*" (MJ 8:6b&N).

Third, the phrase, "**to live like Jews**" is Greek *Ioudaizein*, which gives us the English word "Judaize." Some Gentile Christians say that Messianic Jews are "Judaizers." Since non-Messianic Jews rarely use this word, it has for them a neutral or slightly positive overtone. But because the "villains" of the book of Galatians are commonly termed Judaizers, this word has a strongly negative valence in Christian circles; and for this reason it is necessary to defend Messianic Jews against the charge of being Judaizers.

In order to do so, the term must be defined; and it may quickly be determined that the word "Judaizer" is ambiguous, because it is applied indiscriminately to three distinct kinds of "villains" who are often confounded with each other; I call them (1) the Circumcision faction, (2) the assimilationists, and (3) the legalizers. Secondly, Messianic Jews are none of these; on the contrary, as history developed, it was the Church which produced analogues to each of them in *its* dealings with the Jews!

(1) *Circumcision faction.* The burden of the Circumcision faction was to insist that Gentiles cannot be saved by their inward faith in Yeshua the Messiah unless they undergo the outward procedure of converting to Judaism, symbolized for men by getting circumcised. As Sha'ul makes eloquently clear at 6:12–13, the Circumcision faction did not really care whether the Gentile proselytes then went on to fulfill their obligation (5:3) to observe the *Torah* as understood in non-Messianic Judaism, let alone whether their faith was genuine. In fact, Sha'ul did not consider members of the Circumcision faction to be believers at all (1:6–9).

The Church produced its own "circumcision faction," as it were. In the Middle Ages and on into modern times, some who called themselves Christians forced Jews to be baptized on pain of death (many Jews chose the latter; see Ac 7:59–60N), without the least interest in whether these Jews had inward faith.

(2) *Assimilationists.* The goal of the assimilationists was to get Gentile believers to follow certain Jewish customs, to assimilate into the Jewish community, to become culturally Jewish in greater or lesser degree. For them there was no such thing as "transcultural Judaism" (see 1:17N). In the present verse Sha'ul does not accuse Kefa of joining the Circumcision faction but of being an assimilationist, forcing Gentiles to observe *kashrut.*

The Church produced its own assimilationists as soon as Gentile believers began to exceed Jewish believers in number and power. As early as the middle of the second century, the Gentile-dominated Church was celebrating the Lord's resurrection not in accordance with the Jewish calendar on the third day of *Pesach*, but always on a Sunday — this is how Easter became separated from Passover, and an important purpose of the practice was to distance Christianity from Judaism. By the fourth century, Jews who became believers were required to agree to lengthy statements promising that they would give up all Jewish practices and associations. The fact that Messianic Judaism, indeed any distinctively Jewish form of Christianity, virtually disappeared from the scene of history between the fifth and eighteenth centuries is evidence of assimilationism in the Church. Even today, the vast majority of Gentile

Christians expect Jewish believers to assimilate to Gentile Christianity and either oppose or are indifferent to the development of a distinctive Messianic Judaism.

What motivated Kefa to press for assimilation? Fear, according to vv. 11–14a, fear of those whom the Gentiles perceived as more spiritual, more in touch with the right way to serve God. Sha'ul deals with this fear by providing Kefa and the Antioch Gentiles with fuller knowledge, so that those "from Ya'akov" will no longer be perceived as more spiritual and Kefa will no longer fear them. In the same way, it is my hope that the *Jewish New Testament* and this commentary will provide knowledge enabling similarly fearful Gentile Christians and Jewish believers to stop fearing persons hostile toward Messianic Judaism and thus stop making Messianic Jews assimilate to Gentile culture.

(3) *Legalizers.* I apply the term "legalizers" to those who (a) perverted the *Torah* into a legalistic system unrelated to trusting God (see v. 16bN), and (b) insisted that unless Gentiles obeyed this legalistic perversion of the *Torah*, they could not be saved. Legalizers would have taken Sha'ul's meaning at 5:3 below to be that Gentiles who get ritually circumcised must obey the whole *Torah* as it is expounded in non-Messianic Judaism. Further, since the *Torah* so understood is not merely an ethical and ceremonial code but a total embodiment of Jewish culture, the legalizers would have favored both goals of the other two groups, circumcision of Gentiles and their full cultural assimilation into the Jewish community.

The Church has produced its own legalizers, perverting God's gracious gift of salvation into their own set of rules and requiring everyone else to follow them on pain of exclusion. Such Christian legalizers, pestering Jewish and Gentile believers alike, are always a threat to the Gospel.

These three forms of "Judaizing" are not mutually exclusive. The same person can insist on all of them — outward signs, cultural assimilation, and legalistic obedience to a set of rules. A "Judaizer" could insist that Gentile believers in Yeshua get circumcised, adapt to Jewish culture and obey Jewish rules regardless of whether they have faith for doing so. A "Gentilizer" could insist that Jews get baptized whether they believe in Yeshua or not, adapt to Gentile church life and worship styles, and obey Gentile-Christian-determined rules of life whether they believe in them or not. Requiring any of these for salvation is a heresy, but they are three different heresies. However, in vv. 15–16 Sha'ul assumes that assimilationism normally leads to legalism, that it is but a short step from compelling Gentiles to follow Jewish customs (assimilationism) to teaching that their doing so will earn them favor with God (legalism).

The Greek word "*Ioudaizein*" can be rendered, "to Judaize, to Judaize oneself, to become a Jew, to convert to Judaism, to live like a Jew, to live as a Jew"; there is enough variety here to cover all three of these heresies. But all meanings of "*Ioudaizein*" assume that those who get "Judaized" are Gentiles, never Jews. In spite of this fact, one of the most tenacious and pernicious phenomena in Christendom is the application of the term "Judaizers" to Messianic Jews attempting to establish for Jewish believers a Jewish way of following the Jewish Messiah.

Messianic Jews, with very rare exceptions, are guilty of none of these heresies. They do not press Gentile Christians to get circumcised or convert to Judaism but usually discourage it on the basis of 1C 7:18 (however see my notes there and at 5:2–4 below). They do not force Gentile Christians to adopt Jewish practices, although Gentiles who voluntarily choose to are welcomed, provided their motives are sound, because they are "free in Christ" to make that choice. Finally, Messianic Jews do not claim that observance of customs developed in non-Messianic Judaism is either necessary for salvation or a sign of greater spirituality. Instead, Messianic Jews try to develop a Messianic mode of celebrating the Jewish festivals, a Messianic form of Jewish worship, and a Messianic Jewish lifestyle wherein Jewish believers can express both their Jewishness and their Messianic faith.

Yet for obeying the Great Commission (Mt 28:18–20), so often neglected by the Church in relation to the Jewish people, Messianic Jews are stigmatized among Gentile Christians as "Judaizers." Yet how can a Jew, who is already Jewish, be "Judaized"? This is a contradiction in terms, an absurdity. Nowhere in the New Testament are Jewish believers criticized for living like the Jews they are. On the contrary, when Sha'ul was accused of teaching Jews not to observe circumcision and the Mosaic Law, he demonstrated that the accusation was false (Ac 21:20–27&NN). Was Sha'ul therefore a "Judaizer" for encouraging Jewish believers to continue circumcising their children and observing the *Torah?*

Instead of calling Messianic Jews "Judaizers," Christians should root out all efforts to "Gentilize" Jewish believers. Why do some in the third world oppose Christian missions as "tools of Western imperialism"? Because missionaries sometimes fail to distinguish the transcultural Good News (see 1:17&N) from their own Western cultural baggage. When third-world Christians realize that they need not act like Americans or Europeans in order to be saved, they reject the imposed foreign patterns vigorously and establish vibrant national churches within their own cultural framework. It amazes me that many Gentile Christians who wisely oppose Westernizing the Gospel when presenting it to the non-Western world cannot see that the same principle compels them to refrain from Gentilizing the Gospel when presenting it to Jews; they seem to forget that the Gospel is "for the Jew especially" (Ro 1:16&N). Instead, they accuse those who present the Gospel in a Jewish way of "rebuilding the middle wall of partition" between Jewish and Gentile believers (Ep 2:14&N); they take the remark, "There is neither Jew nor Greek" (below, 3:28&N), to mean that in the Messianic Community there must be only Greeks and no Jews! One goal of the *Jewish New Testament* and this commentary is to bring into disrepute both the Gentilizing of Jewish believers and the labeling of Messianic Jews as Judaizers.

15–16 These two verses are the key to how Sha'ul regarded the Law of Moses; thus they are the key to the book of Galatians and to the book of Romans. He who seizes their true meaning can help repair the grave damage done to the unity of Jews and Gentiles in the Body of the Messiah by those who have misunderstood Sha'ul's view of *Torah.*

In these verses Sha'ul pivots from defending the authority behind his version of the Gospel (which he began in the very first verse of the letter and has made his central topic since 1:10) to explaining why under the New Covenant it is wrong to Judaize Gentile believers. From here to the end of the book of Galatians he will be attacking the Judaizers (see v. 14bN) and defending the true Gospel, according to which Gentiles need not become Jews in order to follow Yeshua the Messiah.

For comparative purposes, here is a literal translation of vv. 15–16:

[15] We, by nature Jews and not sinners from Gentiles, [16] but knowing that a person is not justified from works of law but through trust of Messiah Yeshua, even we unto Messiah Yeshua trusted, in order that we might be justified from trust of Messiah and not from works of law, because from works of law not will be justified all flesh.

15 "*Goyishe* sinners," literally, "sinners from Gentiles." I have added the words, "**so-called**," along with quotation marks, in order to show that Sha'ul was not employing this demeaning term himself but using the terminology of his opposition, the Circumcision faction (see vv. 11–12&NN). According to them Gentiles were by definition sinners, since they did not have the *Torah*. This equating of *Goyim* and sinners can be found in the Apocrypha (1 Maccabees 1:34, Tobit 13:6) and in the Gospels themselves (compare Lk 18:31–33 with Lk 24:7); while at Mt 9:10, 11:19; Lk 7:34, 37; 15:1–2 the *P'rushim* apply the word "sinners" in a similar way, but to a class of Jews rather than Gentiles. Formerly Kefa himself had held a low view of Gentiles, but his vision in Yafo changed his attitude (Ac 10:1–11:19). We don't have evidence for how Sha'ul thought about Gentiles before he came to faith, but it is clear from the whole book of Romans that as a Messianic Jew he went out of his way to emphasize the equality of Jews and Gentiles before God. See also vv. 17–18N.

16a Declared righteous by God, Greek *dikaioô,* "make righteous, justify." In order for a person to have fellowship with God, he must be righteous; because God is righteous, holy, without sin, and cannot tolerate sin in his presence. Theology distinguishes two kinds of righteousness: (1) behavioral righteousness, actually doing what is right, and (2) "forensic righteousness," being regarded as righteous in the senses (a) that God has cleared him of guilt for past sins, and (b) that God has given him a new human nature inclined to obey God rather than rebel against him as before.

Yeshua the Messiah has made forensic righteousness available to everyone by paying on everyone's behalf the penalty for sins which God's justice demands, death (see Ro 5:12–21&N). Forensic righteousness is appropriated by an individual for himself the moment he unreservedly puts his trust in God, which at this point in history entails also trusting in Yeshua the Messiah upon learning of him and understanding what he has done (1 Yn 2:23). The task of becoming behaviorally righteous begins with appropriating forensic righteousness by trusting in Yeshua; and it occupies the rest of a believer's life, being completed only at his own death, when he goes to be with Yeshua (Pp 1:23).

Libraries of books have been written on the subject of righteousness, both Jewish ethical treatises and volumes of Christian theology, since the question of how righteousness is attained sparked the entire Protestant Reformation. What is important to keep in mind here is the difference between these two kinds of righteousness. Each time the Greek word "*dikaioô*" or a cognate is encountered, it must be decided which of these two meanings of the word is meant. In the present verse and the next, all four instances of "*dikaioô*" refer to forensic righteousness. But in v. 21, the related word "*dikaiosunê*" refers to behavioral righteousness (see note there).

16b Legalistic observance of *Torah* commands. The Greek word "*nomos*" usually means "law"; it is also the normal New Testament word for Hebrew *Torah*, which can usually be translated by the phrase, "Law of Moses," or simply, "Law." Most Christians therefore suppose that "*erga nomou*," literally, "works of law," a term which appears three times in v. 16, must mean, "actions done in obedience to the *Torah*." But this is wrong. One of the best-kept secrets about the New Testament is that when Sha'ul writes "*nomos*" he frequently does not mean "law" but "legalism."

So that my defense of this interpretation will not appear to be special pleading, I make my case by quoting from two distinguished Gentile Christian scholars without any Messianic Jewish axe to grind. C. E. B. Cranfield, in his commentary on the book of Romans, writes:

> "...it will be well to bear in mind the fact (which, so far as we know, had not received attention before it was noted in [Cranfield's article in] the *Scottish Journal of Theology*, Volume 17, 1964, p. 55) that the Greek language of Paul's day possessed no word-group corresponding to our 'legalism,' 'legalist' and 'legalistic.' This means that he lacked a convenient terminology for expressing a vital distinction, and so was surely seriously hampered in the work of clarifying the Christian position with regard to the law. In view of this, we should always, we think, be ready to reckon with the possibility that Pauline statements which at first sight seem to disparage the law, were really directed not against the law itself but against that misunderstanding and misuse of it for which we now have a convenient terminology. In this very difficult terrain Paul was pioneering. If we make due allowance for these circumstances, we shall not be so easily baffled or misled by a certain impreciseness of statement which we shall sometimes encounter." (C. E. B. Cranfield, *The International Critical Commentary*, *Romans*, 1979, p. 853)

Cranfield is right — except for his speculation that he was the first. Forty-three years earlier Ernest De Witt Burton, in his classic commentary on Galatians, also made clear that in the present verse "*nomos*" means "legalism" and not God's *Torah*:

> "*Nomou* is here evidently used... in its legalistic sense, denoting divine law viewed as a purely legalistic system made up of statutes, on the basis of obedience or disobedience to which men are approved or condemned as a matter of debt without grace. This is divine law as the legalist defined it. In the apostle's thought it stands for a reality only in that it constitutes a single element of the divine law detached from all other elements and aspects of divine revelation; by such detachment it misrepresents the will of God and his real attitude towards men. By *erga nomou* Paul means deeds of obedience to formal statutes done in the legalistic spirit, with the expectation of thereby meriting and securing divine approval and award, such obedience, in other words, as the legalists rendered to the law of the Old Testament as expanded and interpreted by them. Though *nomos* in this sense had no existence as representing the basis of justification in the divine government, yet *erga nomou* had a very real existence in the thought and practice of men who conceived of the divine law after this fashion.... The translation of this phrase here and constantly... by 'the works of the law'... is

a serious defect of [versions that have it]." (E. Burton, *The International Critical Commentary, Galatians*, 1921, p. 120)

The phrase, "*erga nomou,*" found only in Sha'ul's writings, is used eight times, always in technical discussion of the *Torah* — here three times; 3:2, 5, 10; and Ro 3:20, 28. Two other uses of "*erga*" ("works") are closely associated with the word "*nomos*" ("law") — Ro 3:27, 9:32. Even when he uses *erga* by itself, the implied meaning is frequently "legalistic works" (5:19; Ro 4:2, 6; 9:11; 11:6; Ep 2:9; 2 Ti 1:9; Ti 3:5), although he uses it 17 times in a neutral way (Ro 2:6; 13:3, 12; 2C 11:15; Ep 2:10, 5:11; Co 1:21; 1 Ti 2:10; 5:10, 25; 2 Ti 3:17, 4:14; Ti 1:16; 2:7, 14; 3:8, 14).

I submit that in every instance "*erga nomou*" means not deeds done in virtue of following the *Torah* in the way God intended, but deeds done in consequence of perverting the *Torah* into a set of rules which, it is presumed, can be obeyed mechanically, automatically, *legalistically*, without having faith, without having trust in God, without having love for God or man, and without being empowered by the Holy Spirit.

"*Erga nomou,*" therefore, is a technical term coined by Sha'ul to meet precisely the need Cranfield has written about; it speaks of legalism, not Law. But because Sha'ul's subject is misunderstanding and perverting *Torah* into something it was never meant to be, *erga nomou* are, specifically, in context, "works of legalism in relation to the *Torah,*" exactly as Burton explained. Hence my rendering, **legalistic observance of *Torah* commands**.

Likewise, the term "*upo nomon*" ("under law"), which appears five times in this letter, never means simply "under the *Torah,*" in the sense of "subject to its provisions," "living within its framework." Rather, with one easily explainable variation, it is Sha'ul's shorthand for "living under the oppression caused by being enslaved to the social system or the mindset that results when the *Torah* is perverted into legalism" (but more on "*upo nomon*" in 3:23bN and 4:4–5N).

Christian scholars have discoursed at length about Sha'ul's supposedly ambivalent view of the *Torah*. Their burden has been to show that somehow he could abrogate the *Torah* and still respect it. Non-Messianic Jewish scholars, building on the supposedly reliable conclusion, gratuitously supplied by their Christian colleagues, that Sha'ul did in fact abrogate the *Torah*, have made it their burden to show that the logical implication of Sha'ul's abrogating the *Torah* is that he did not respect it either and thereby removed himself and all future Jewish believers in Yeshua from the camp of Judaism (the so-called "parting of the ways"). In this fashion liberally oriented non-Messianic Jews in the modern era have been able to have their cake and eat it too, to claim Jesus for themselves as a wonderful Jewish teacher while making Paul the villain of the piece.

But Sha'ul had no such ambivalence. For him the *Torah* of Moshe was unequivocally "holy" and its commands "holy, just and good" (Ro 7:12). And so were works done in true obedience to the *Torah*. But in order to be regarded by God as good, works done in obedience to the *Torah* had to be grounded in trust, never in legalism (see Ro 9:30–10:10&NN). If one keeps in mind that Sha'ul had nothing but bad to say for the sin of perverting the *Torah* into legalism, and nothing but good to say for the *Torah* itself, then the supposed contradictions in his view of the *Torah* vanish. Instead of being the villain who destroyed the backbone of Judaism and led Jews astray, he is the most authentic expositor of *Torah* that the Jewish people have ever had, apart from the Messiah Yeshua himself.

16c But through the Messiah Yeshua's trusting faithfulness, literally, as given above in vv. 15–16N, "except through trust of Messiah Yeshua." There are three issues here: (1) What is meant by "trust"? (2) What does the "of" mean in the phrase "of Messiah Yeshua"? That is, whose trust is Sha'ul speaking about, the Messiah's or ours? (3) Does the conjunction "but" at the beginning introduce a contrast or a limitation?

(1) *Trust.* The Greek word "*pistis*" is usually translated "faith" or "belief," but these English words can signify adherence to a creed, mere mental assent, whereas the biblical meaning, both in the New Testament and in the *Tanakh* (where the Hebrew word is "*emunah*"), is either (a) trust, reliance on someone or something, or (b) faithfulness, trustworthiness. A moment's thought shows that these two are really the same — if one has genuine and unreserved trust, reliance, faith, belief in someone, then one will be faithful to him and trustworthy in carrying out his commands — that is to say, faith implies faithfulness, trust implies obedience. Eugene Nida, developer of the "dynamic equivalence" approach to Bible translation, notes a tribe of Mexican Indians that has only one concept and one word in its language for these two ideas, and he comments that perhaps they are wiser than we. For more on *pistis* and *emunah* see Ac 3:16N.

It is so important for understanding the book of Galatians to be constantly reminded of both aspects of the word "*pistis*" that I have encumbered the style of the *Jewish New Testament* with the awkward phrase, "**trusting faithfulness**" (or some equally clumsy equivalent), every time "*pistis*" or a correlate appears in this letter.

(2) *Of Messiah Yeshua.* Romans 3:22N, which discusses the same issue and explains the grammatical concepts of subjective and objective genitive, is an essential introduction to what follows.

The major modern English versions take "*dia pisteôs Iêsou Christou*" ("through trust of Yeshua Messiah") and "*ek pisteôs Christou*" ("from faith of Messiah") both to be speaking of *our* trust *in* Yeshua the Messiah. This nearly always produces the translations, "through faith in Jesus Christ" and "by faith in Christ."

I feel a bit intimidated in taking on nearly all modern authorities and insisting that this understanding is wrong and that instead Sha'ul is writing about the trusting faithfulness to God and to God's promises which Yeshua the Messiah himself displayed in his own life. As before with "works of law" (v.16b), I will let Gentile scholars make my case for rendering "*dia pisteôs Iêsou Christou*" as **"the Messiah Yeshua's trusting faithfulness**."

Arndt and Gingrich's *A Greek-English Lexicon of the New Testament*, p. 668 (bottom), notes, "The *pistis Christou* in Paul is taken as a subjective genitive by…" and gives three scholarly references in German, although the authors of the lexicon themselves think otherwise. ("Subjective genitive" means that the faith/faithfulness is Yeshua's own faith in and faithfulness to God his Father, not our faith in Yeshua; see Ro 3:22N.)

More recently, George Howard, in his article, "Romans 3:21–31 and the Inclusion of the Gentiles" (*Harvard Theological Review* 63 (1970), pp. 223–233), writes,

"It is best to regard the genitive as a subjective genitive, meaning the 'faith of Jesus,' for the following reasons. (1) In passages that are clear when Paul uses *pistis* followed by a genitive noun of person he always implies the subjective genitive, *never* the objective (for example *tên pistin tou theou* [('God's faithfulness')] in Romans 3:3; *pisteôs tou patros êmôn Abraam* [('the trust which *Avraham avinu* had')] in Romans 4:12). (2) Galatians 2:16 shows that for Paul there is a difference between the ideas of faith *in* Christ and faith *of* Christ and that he is able to make himself clear by his use of grammar. (3) The Peshitta Syriac [version, 3rd century] always translates the phrase *pistis christou Iêsou* with the meaning of 'the faith of the Messiah' (especially is this clear in its rendition of Galatians 2:16 and Ephesians 3:12), showing how the ancient Syrian Church understood the construction. Some scholars do believe that *pistis christou Iêsou* is a subjective genitive, but by and large the phrase remains obscure." (p. 229)

In writing about Sha'ul's making "himself clear by his use of grammar," Howard is referring to the phrase in the middle of v. 16, "**we too have put our trust in Messiah Yeshua and become faithful to him,**" literally, "we unto Messiah Yeshua trusted." Here "unto," doubly translated in the *JNT* as "**in**" and "**to**," is the Greek word "*eis*" ("in, to, into, unto, toward"). The word is different, the grammar is different, and for this reason, says Howard, *the sense is therefore different.* Our trusting **in** Yeshua and being faithful **to** him means that we rely on him unreservedly, even to the point of being in "union with" him (v. 17), with the result that we too can now exercise the same trusting faithfulness as his. And what trusting faithfulness was that? The trusting faithfulness *of* Yeshua was the trust *in* God and the faithfulness *to* him which the Messiah exercised when he relied on God's promises to the extent of being willing to die for our sake, "a righteous person on behalf of unrighteous people" (1 Ke 3:18; compare Ro 5:6–8).

Thus Sha'ul in this verse dissects saving faith into its two component parts: (1) the trust in and faithfulness toward God which the Messiah had (mentioned twice), and (2) the trust in and faithfulness toward Yeshua — and, by implication, toward God the Father too (1 Yn 2:23) — which we have (mentioned once). Neither alone would suffice for someone to be declared righteous by God. In this way Sha'ul handles the paradox of free will, mentioned often in this commentary, that, as Rabbi Akiva put it in the Mishna (Avot 3:15), "All is foreseen" (hence the need for the Messiah's faithfulness, God having known and foreseen that we would all be faithless sinners), "and free will is given" (hence the need for us to put our trust in the Messiah by our own free choice).

Why must Sha'ul make the Messiah's objective act of faithfulness to God central? That is, why cannot Sha'ul be referring all three times to our faith in the Messiah? Because then Sha'ul would be asserting that God's declaring us righteous depends on nothing but our subjective choice of abstract "faith" over "works of law," without any explanation of why the former is preferred over the latter. The reason that "faith" (by which is meant not just any faith but faith specifically in the person and work of the Messiah Yeshua) is the only path to righteousness, and that "works of law" (that is, works of legalistic obedience to *Torah* commands) are not a path to righteousness, is that God objectively (that is, because he is holy and just) required someone to be faithful to him before he could declare him righteous. In a world where all have gone astray (see v. 16dN; compare Isaiah 53:6, Ro 3:10–18), Yeshua was that "someone." Yeshua's own trusting faithfulness to the promise which God gave Avraham (Genesis 12:1–3), Yeshua's faithfulness even unto death (Ro 3:24–26, 5:8; Pp 2:5–11), became the objective ground enabling God to make righteousness available to other human beings, provided only that they trust in and are faithful to Yeshua (or, equivalently, that they trust in and are faithful to God — according to Yn 14:6 and 1 Yn 2:23 the one necessarily implies the other). Yeshua's faithfulness, which we appropriate and become increasingly able to exercise when we come into union with him (v. 17) through our trust in him and faithfulness towards him, gives God objective ground for at once declaring us righteous forensically and in increments making us righteous behaviorally (v. 16aN) with Yeshua's own righteousness.

(3) "*But*": *contrast or limitation?* A person is not justified by works of law **but** through the Messiah's faithfulness. The Greek phrase translated "**but**" is "*ean mê.*" The other 51 times it appears in the New Testament, scholars agree that it introduces a limitation, so that it is properly translated "unless" or "except." Only here is it supposed to introduce a contrast, so that its meaning is "but rather." Clearly this singularity requires an explanation.

And here is the significance of rendering "*ean mê*" by "but": if it is rendered "unless," then a reader who disagrees with the points previously made in the comments on this verse — who thinks that "*erga nomou*" refers to *Torah* observance, not legalism, and that "*pistis Christou*" refers to our trust in Yeshua, not to Yeshua's trust in God — must still consider the possibility that "*ean mê*" means "unless," and that therefore Sha'ul is saying, "A person is not justified by works of law [*Torah* observance] *unless* [he does those works of law] through [his own] trust in the Messiah Yeshua." This is still a far more "pro-Law" statement than the verse is usually understood to be making.

Why do I not translate "*ean mê*" here as "unless"? Because in the Septuagint, "*ean mê*" is used several times to translate the Hebrew phrase "*ki-im*," which generally means "but rather." Thus there is evidence outside the New Testament that when Jews wrote Greek, "*ean mê*" could mean "but rather." If I am right that "*erga nomou*" refers to legalism, then "*ean mê*" here must mean "but rather" and not "unless." Why? Because Sha'ul in this letter is out to show that legalism and faith are incompatible: works of legalism by definition cannot be be done through trust. But if I am wrong about "*erga nomou*," if "works of law" really signify works of *Torah* observance, then I cannot allow that "*ean mê*" here means "but rather"; it must mean "unless." Why? Because Sha'ul neither believes nor says that *Torah* and faith are incompatible; therefore the normal New Testament meaning of "*ean mê*," "unless," which does not require any special explanation, is the one to expect.

16d No one will be declared forensically **righteous** (see v. 16aN). In quoting a few words from Psalm 143:2, Sha'ul, following normal rabbinic practice, intends the reader to call to mind the context. Here the relevant context is the following portion of Psalm 143, which makes exactly the same point as Sha'ul does in the present verse:

> "Hear my prayer, *Adonai*, give ear to my supplications!
> Answer me with your faithfulness, with your righteousness;
> And do not enter into judgment with your servant,
> For in your sight, no one living will be declared righteous."
> (Psalm 143:1–2)

The same phrase is cited, for the same reason, at Ro 3:20&N, where Sha'ul is dealing with the same issue. Romans 3:19–26 can be read as an expansion of Ga 2:15–16.

17–18 Through our union with the Messiah, Greek *en Christô*. The usual, literal translation, "in Christ," is not useful for the modern reader, for whom the idea of being "in" somebody has no meaning in the present context. The Greek preposition "*en*" can mean "in connection with," "in the sphere of," "in union with"; all of which convey the sense better. Our trust in the Messiah and faithfulness to him (see v. 16bN) unites us with him; according to Ro 6:1–8:13, we are united with his death, his resurrection and his life.

In typically rabbinic teaching fashion (see Ro 10:14–15&N), Sha'ul anticipates an objection the Judaizers might make. The objection is two-pronged. First, and easily disposed of: **Is the Messiah an aider and abetter of sin** (literally, "a minister of sin," "one who is in the service of sin")? The answer is Greek's most forceful negation, "*Mê genoito!*" literally, "May it not be!" but translated "**Heaven forbid!**" to convey its intensity (on this phrase see Ro 3:4N). For the idea of a Messiah who promotes or serves sin is Jewishly unthinkable, a contradiction in terms. Even if all who claim to trust in the Messiah were worse sinners than everyone else, it would be their own fault, not the Messiah's (compare Ro 3:3–4).

The second part of the objection might be stated by the Judaizers thusly: "You have been seeking to be righteous before God by uniting yourself with Yeshua; but instead of attaining righteousness, your condition is that of sinners (just like the *Goyim*, whom we call '*Goyishe* sinners' (v. 15&N)), because you don't observe the *Torah*." But Sha'ul answers by asserting that what the Judaizers regard as sin is not sin at all, not really transgression of the *Torah*. For the Judaizers apply the label, "sinner," not to those who disobey what is truly the *Torah*, but to those who do not submit to the system which results from perverting the *Torah* into legalism. That system, says Sha'ul, is not what the *Torah* really is. What is truly the *Torah* requires not legalism but trusting faithfulness. "The moment I realized that," says Sha'ul in v. 19, "I understood the *Torah* properly; and in that moment I destroyed for myself the bondage of legalism." Therefore, **if I build up again** the humanly-created legalistic set of rules whose power over me **I destroyed** when I realized that the *Torah* requires just one basic thing, trusting faithfulness, then I really do make myself a **transgressor**, a real transgressor of the true *Torah*, a real sinner, not merely someone whom Judaizers falsely call a sinner.

But from another point of view, **what I destroyed** was not only a legalistic system but also a form of idolatry, namely, ethnolatry, in which I took pride in being Jewish and insisted that keeping Jewish distinctives is essential to being part of God's people, even for Gentiles. Now, **if I build up again** that "ethnolatry," **I make myself a transgressor** of the true *Torah*, which says that because God is One (Deuteronomy 6:4), he is

God of both Jews and Gentiles (Ro 3:27–31) and therefore accepts the trusting faithfulness of Gentiles without requiring them to become Jews (a point on which Sha'ul expands in Romans 4).

19 **For it was through letting the *Torah* speak for itself that I died to its traditional legalistic misinterpretation**. The Greek is: *Egô gar dia nomou nomô apethanon*, literally, "For I through *nomos* to *nomos* died." A good general rule of interpretation is that if a word appears more than once in a passage, its meaning stays the same throughout the passage. Here we have an exception; the phrase means, "For I through *Torah* to legalism died." I know that because Sha'ul avoids the natural Greek word order in order to place two forms of the word "*nomos*" side by side. This signals the reader that something unusual is going on, specifically, that the sense of the first "*nomos*" differs from that of the second. My expanded translation brings out that the first "*nomos*" is the true *Torah*, the *Torah* understood properly as requiring trusting faithfulness; while the second is the perversion of the *Torah* into a legalistic system (see v. 16bN, vv. 17–18N).

So that I might live in a direct relationship with God, instead of being shut off from God by legalistic misinterpretation of the *Torah*. Literally, "so that to God I might live." There is a *Torah* to be observed (see 6:2 below), but it isn't the legalistic system made of it by much of the non-Messianic Jewish world.

20 **When the Messiah was executed on the stake as a criminal, so was I** executed on the stake as a criminal. Literally, "With Messiah I have been co-crucified" (see Mt 10:38N). The Messiah was not a sinner, let alone a criminal, but he was executed like one, the "stake" or "cross" being the electric chair of its day. "On the other hand," says Sha'ul, "I am a sinner, therefore in God's sight a criminal. By uniting myself with the Messiah through putting my trust in him, I share in his death (Ro 6:2); thus the penalty for my sin is paid, and I am dead."

My proud ego no longer lives, literally, "I no longer live"; that is, my old nature, with its evil desires, no longer controls me. One can regard all of Ro 6:1–8:13 as a *midrash* on this verse.

Because **the Messiah lives in me**, I am able to **live by the same trusting faithfulness that the Son of God had** (see v. 16cN), which enabled him to love me and give himself up for me. My entire life must be imbued by this spirit; anything else, anything less falls short of faith in and faithfulness to Yeshua the Messiah.

21 **I do not reject God's gracious gift**, literally, "God's grace," his *chesed* (Hebrew for "loving-kindness"). What is that gift? First, the death of the Messiah Yeshua on my behalf, which gives me forensic righteousness; and second, his life, which is making me actually righteous in my behavior (on the two kinds of righteousness see above, v. 16aN).

If the way in which one attains righteousness is through legalism, through any form of self-generated effort, and specifically, through legalistic following of *Torah* commands, **then the Messiah's death was pointless**, and so is his ongoing resurrected life. It is clear from the context two verses later (3:2–3) that the word "**righteousness**" (Greek *dikaiosunê*) here refers not only to being declared innocent but to becoming holy (the other three times in Galatians that Sha'ul uses "*dikaiosunê*" — 3:6, 21; 5:5 — he also means behavioral and not merely forensic righteousness). Such progress toward holiness does not result from an instant of trust followed by a lifetime of legalism, but from trusting faithfulness that endures until death.

CHAPTER 3

1 **You stupid Galatians!** Elsewhere Sha'ul displayed his amazement at their going astray (1:6) and his pain and confusion over what to do with them (4:19–20). Here, expressing his exasperation, he tries to arouse his charges with ridicule and shame. Yet all this is in the context of his loving them dearly; one piece of evidence for this is that he calls them "brothers," a favorite term of endearment among the early believers, no less than nine times in this letter (1:11; 3:15; 4:12, 28, 31; 5:11, 13; 6:1, 18).

Who has put you under a spell? The Judaizers (see 2:14bN), whom he sees as under demonic influence. The Adversary (Satan; see Mt 4:1N) uses human instruments to turn believers away from God's truth to "some other so-called 'Good News'"(1:6). In every chapter of this letter Sha'ul condemns these deceivers, often in very strong language (1:7–9; 2:3–5, 12; here; 4:17–18; 5:7–10, 12; 6:12–13).

Before your very eyes Yeshua the Messiah was clearly portrayed by me, Sha'ul, **as having been put to death** on the stake **as a criminal** (see Mt 10:38N) in your place. This is the central fact and the faith seed of born-again living. Its significance is unpacked in the next four verses, and more generally in the rest of the letter. The main implication is that the Judaizers' legalistic rule-following is a tragic exercise in futility (2:21): the Galatians should wake up from their stupor and not be taken in by it.

2 **I want to know from you just this one thing**. What Sha'ul does here is very Jewish — he announces that he is about to ask just one question and then asks five!

The Holy **Spirit**, the *Ruach HaKodesh*, was given through **trusting in** what was **heard** about the Messiah (Ac 1:8, 2:1–38; Yn 14:26, 15:26; Ro 10:17), not through legalistic rule-following.

Legalistic observance of *Torah* commands. See 2:16bN.

Trusting and being faithful. See 2:16cN.

4 **If that's the way you think, your suffering certainly will have been for nothing**. The highly elliptical Greek says only, "If indeed for nothing," which obviously requires interpretive expansion of some sort just to make sense; other interpretations are possible.

6–9 **Avraham** is the archetypical example of one who **trusted and was faithful**. Sha'ul picks precisely him because the Judaizers in all likelihood put him forward as their hero and example. Here are three of their points which Sha'ul addresses in these verses:

(1) Legalistically oriented Jews thought of Avraham as the archetypical legalist. They even tried to show that he obeyed the Oral Law — which didn't yet exist! For example, efforts are still made to prove that Avraham followed the rabbinic prohibition against serving milk with meat, even though Avraham, displaying lavish hospitality much like the Bedouins of 4,000 years later, served his three guests butter, milk and a dressed calf (Genesis 18:8). Rabbi Hertz's commentary on the

Pentateuch explains it thus: "The verse may be understood as meaning that the guests were given curd and milk to slake their thirst and refresh them (cf. Judges 4:19), and then followed the meal proper, which consisted of the calf. This procedure would be quite in accord with the dietary laws" of the Oral *Torah*, which allow dairy foods to be served before meat but not with or after it.

(2) Some Jews claimed Avraham as exclusively their father and not father to the Gentiles.

(3) For these two reasons, Jews thought of Avraham as having merit which provided benefits, even salvation, to his descendants. For an example, see Mt 3:9; see also Ro 11:28–29&N.

The notes to the separate verses show how Sha'ul demolishes these counterclaims of the Judaizers.

6 **It was the same with Avraham** as with Jews and Gentiles today — any legalistic rule-following he might have done availed him nothing. What counted was this: "**He trusted in God and was faithful to him, and that was credited to his account as** forensic **righteousness**" (Genesis 15:6; see above, v. 2:16aN). As Sha'ul makes even more clear at Romans 4, no actions which Avraham did apart from trust ever gave him an iota of righteousness-credit in his account with God. This destroys point (1) of vv. 6–9N.

7 This verse takes care of point (2): **It is those who live by trusting and being faithful**, both Jews and Gentiles, **who are really children of Avraham**. Even those physically descended from him — that is, Jews — are not truly his **children**, in the sense of being eligible to receive what God promised them, if they lack trust (see Ro 9:6b&N). Aspects of this idea are developed further in Romans 2 and 4, as well as later in this letter (3:26–4:7, 4:22–31).

8 Point (3), connected with the doctrine of *z'khut-avot*, the "merit of the fathers" (see Ro 11:28–29N), is overturned by this verse, wherein Sha'ul says that God gave a hint (*remez*, Mt 2:15N) **in advance** of his universalism (which ultimately found expression in the **Good News** of Yeshua) by telling Avraham, **"In connection with you** (Greek *en soi*, "in you," see 2:17–18N) **all the *Goyim*** (Greek *ethnê*, corresponding to Hebrew *goyim*, "Gentiles, nations") **will be blessed."** Thus Genesis 12:1–3, the seminal passage announcing the creation of the Jewish people, is seen by the emissary to the Gentiles as also the seminal passage for the creation of the Body of the Messiah, in which Jews and Gentiles are equal (see v. 28; this theme is elaborated in Ro 3:27–4:25, 9:25–10:21).

9 So the point of vv. 6–9, stated here, is to show that believing Gentiles are already **blessed along with Avraham**, already his children, because they **rely on trusting and being faithful**. By trusting and being faithful, they have done as much as Avraham, the father of the Jewish people, did. They have no need to add to their trust and faithfulness an alien culture, no need to become Jews or to observe Jewish rules. However, they, along with Jewish believers, are subject to the real *Torah*, "the *Torah*, as upheld by the Messiah" (6:2&N).

10–14 The key to this paragraph is in sorting out when the Greek word "*nomos*" means God's *Torah* and when it means legalistic perversion of it, as discussed in 2:16bN and 2:19N. In my judgment, most translations fail to make this essential distinction, are not "rightly dividing the word of truth" (2 Ti 2:15, KJV), and thus both misrepresent Sha'ul and foster antisemitism. The following expanded translation of vv. 10–13a is rendered along these traditional but mistaken lines:

> [10] For everyone who depends on trying to obey the *Torah* [in order to be declared righteous by God] lives under a curse; since it is written, "Cursed is everyone who does not keep on doing everything written in the Scroll of the *Torah*."
> [11] Also it is evident that no one comes to be declared righteous by God through trying to obey the *Torah*, since "The person who is righteous will live his life by trust." [12] Furthermore, the *Torah* is not based on trust but on the idea that "The one who does these things will attain life through them." [13] The Messiah redeemed us from the curse, which consists in having to live under the *Torah*....

From such a rendering, it is all too easy to reach the following antisemitic conclusions:
(1) According to v. 10, since the Jewish people depend on the *Torah*, but (by assumption) no one is capable of doing everything written in it, the entire Jewish people lives under God's curse.
(2) According to v. 11, by trying to obey the *Torah*, Jews are condemned to the impossibility of being considered righteous by God.
(3) According to vv. 11b–12, the *Torah* itself is defective, because it is not based on trust, but on legalism, on "doing these things," as proved by quoting one of the *Torah*'s own verses. (Logically, this reasoning impugns God himself; but antisemitic illogic arrives at a different consequence: that if Jews obey a defective *Torah*, then Jews themselves must be defective.)
(4) Finally, according to v. 13a, Jews are cursed already just by having to live under the *Torah*.

Fortunately, very few who claim to be Christians hold all of these false views, stated here in their most blatant and offensive form. But to hold even one of them, even in a weaker form, and even unintentionally, is a sin.

Since most people do not read the Greek text of the New Testament and are propelled in the direction of antisemitic conclusions by the translations generally available (which, in turn, are influenced by the conscious or unconscious theological presuppositions of their translators), it is all the more important to demonstrate, verse by verse, that Sha'ul's intended meaning, not found in the traditional renderings, is correctly expressed in the *Jewish New Testament*.

10 I take Sha'ul to be arguing as follows: Everyone — both legalists and those who trust — will agree that God's *Torah* requires obedience to all of its commands — or, looking at it from another angle, God does not gloss over sin. This Sha'ul proves here by quoting a verse from the *Torah* itself, Deuteronomy 27:26.

However, despite the contrary opinion of many Christian interpreters, his point is not that imperfect human nature is incapable of keeping all the commands of the *Torah*; for he neither says this nor proves it. On the contrary, the *Torah* itself, anticipating that people will fall short of complete obedience and thereby go out of fellowship with God, states what those who disobey *Torah* commands must do in order to restore such fellowship — they must repent, and sometimes they must bring a prescribed sacrifice. King David provides a good example: obviously he was less than perfectly obedient to all of the *Torah*'s commands — he committed adultery and murder. Nevertheless, God forgave him after he repented (2 Samuel 11:1–12:25; Psalms 32, 51). Not only does the *Torah* expect disobedience but it makes explicit provision for it, mentioning sin offerings in twenty chapters of Exodus, Leviticus and Numbers and some 120 times in the *Tanakh.*

Sha'ul proves not that the *Torah* can't be obeyed perfectly, but that legalists in particular, merely by being legalists, violate at least one of the *Torah*'s commands; and therefore, on the basis of Deuteronomy 27:26 and the other verses cited, they (1) do not attain life, (2) are not righteous, and (3) come under a curse.

11 Which is the command that legalists violate (v. 10N)? A good case can be made for its being nothing less than belief in the *Sh'ma*! The *Sh'ma* says, "Hear, O Israel, *Adonai* our God, *Adonai* is One" (Deuteronomy 6:4). But if legalists, posing as believers but actually being Judaizers, insist that Gentiles must submit themselves to the non-Messianic Jewish version of the *Torah*, then they are saying that God is God of Jews only, and not of Gentiles (compare Ro 3:29–30), and therefore that God is not one but two! This is a central issue in Galatians and Romans, perhaps *the* central issue.

Although legalists' violating the command of the *Sh'ma* is implied, I think what Sha'ul is referring to here is not that, but simply the command to trust in God, to base all one's actions on trusting God and being faithful to him. No verse is cited from the Five Books of Moshe, though in his similar argument in Romans, written later, Sha'ul makes a *midrash* on Deuteronomy 30:11–14 and uses it as a suggestive proof (see Ro 10:6–8&N). However, to prove that trust is essential for being declared righteous by God, he does in v. 11, as also in Ro 1:17, quote Habakkuk 2:4. This verse is not from the Five Books of Moses, but it is part of the *Tanakh*, God's Word, inspired "*Torah*" ("teaching," Mt 5:17N) and therefore authoritative.

12 Legalism is the exact opposite of trust. Verse 11 assumes this, but v. 12 proves it. The proof is that legalism uses a wrong hermeneutic. That is, instead of "letting the *Torah*" as a whole "speak for itself" (2:19) and thus guide behavior, legalism selects one verse, takes it out of context, and elevates it above the rest of the *Torah*, so that *it* replaces the *Torah* as the ultimate authority, it becomes "a canon within the canon." The verse is indeed part of the *Torah* and therefore has God's authority behind it, but only provided that it is understood along with and in relation to the rest of the *Torah*. By being removed from the modifying effects of the rest of the *Torah*, it becomes the basis for a heresy, the heresy called legalism. (The heresies based on Scripture verses taken out of context are beyond number, and the misery they cause is beyond measure.)

The heresy of legalism, when applied to the *Torah*, says that **anyone who does these things**, that is, anyone who mechanically follows the rules for *Shabbat*, *kashrut*, etc., **will attain life through them**, will be saved, will enter the Kingdom of God, will obtain eternal life. No need to trust God, just obey the rules! The problem with this simplistic ladder to Heaven is that legalism conveniently ignores the "rule" that trust must underlie all rule-following which God finds acceptable (see Section (3) of 2:16cN). But trust necessarily converts mere rule-following into something altogether different, in fact, into its opposite, genuine faithfulness to God. Therefore, "legalistic obedience to *Torah* commands" (that is, "works of law") is actually *dis*obedience to the *Torah*!

The false doctrine of legalism which Sha'ul is fighting is one which he himself once believed, and it must be presumed that he was not alone. While it is unfair, indeed antisemitic, to condemn all of first-century non-Messianic Judaism as legalistic, there can be no doubt that the legalistic heresy was a major way of relating to the *Torah*. Furthermore it remains a heresy sometimes seen within non-Messianic Judaism today. But it is not only a Jewish heresy; it is also a Christian heresy, and in fact it can be found in all religions, and in non-religions too, that is, among atheists, agnostics, and apathetics. The heresy says: "If I do this, this and this" (some self-determined agenda), "then God will accept me, he will applaud my deeds and be obligated to reward me for them. Whether I trust him, am faithful to him or even believe he exists is of no importance." Or, to state the same heresy, the same false hope, in secular language that avoids God-talk, "If I do such-and-such, everything will be all right." Psychologists and sociologists have a name for this approach to life: "magical thinking."

Legalism — that is, legalistic obedience to *Torah* commands — is disobedience to the *Torah*. One could be obeying every single *mitzvah* (except, by assumption, the *mitzvah* of trust), but if these things are being done without heartfelt trust in the God who is there, the only God there is, the God who sent his Son Yeshua to be the atonement for sin (v. 1), then all this outward "obedience" is hateful to God (Isaiah 1:14), and the person doing it, the legalist, "lives under a curse," because he is not "doing everything written in the Scroll of the *Torah*" (v. 10). He is not "doing" the trust which should motivate all doing (compare MJ 11:6). This leads to v. 13.

13 Everyone who hangs from a stake comes under a curse (Deuteronomy 21:22–23; on "stake" here see Ac 5:30N). The curse spoken of applies to legalists (vv. 9–12&NN) and is stated in v. 10, which quotes Deuteronomy 27:26. The elements comprising the content of the curse are detailed in Deuteronomy 28:15–68.

But those who are not legalists, those who do have trust, are not under the curse, because **the Messiah redeemed us** who trust in him and in God **from the curse pronounced in the *Torah*** at Deuteronomy 27–28. How? **By becoming cursed on our behalf**, in our place. This he did by his own choice (Yn 10:17–18), out of his love for us (Ro 5:6–8). That God's justice is consistent with the Messiah's atoning vicariously for our sins through undergoing death and being cursed, is not proved here, but it is proved elsewhere in both the *Tanakh* and the New Testament. See, for example, Isaiah 53:5–6, 12, quoted with further references at 1 Ke 2:24–25&N; also Ro 3:25–26&N.

What is proved by citing Deuteronomy 21:22–23 at the end of v. 13 is that the Messiah's being crucified implied his becoming cursed. The idea that the Messiah can be cursed contradicts some traditional Jewish notions about the Messiah, but not all. For the curses prescribed in Deuteronomy 28:15–68 are physical and emotional sufferings, not spiritual, and certainly not eternal removal from God's presence. The idea of a Messiah who suffers in sympathy and in company with the people of Israel is well known in Judaism. The *Tanakh* describes this most explicitly at Isaiah 53, which clearly pictures the Messiah undergoing the curse of suffering and death on behalf of others' sins (on whether Isaiah 53 applies to the Messiah see Mt 2:15N). For a number of quotations from later Jewish sources, see Chapters 12 and 17 of Raphael Patai's *The Messiah Texts*.

The following example of such a citation is from the Babylonian Talmud and assumes two Messiahs. The Messiah, son of Yosef, is thought of as suffering vicariously and dying for Israel, that is, being "cursed"; while the other, Messiah, son of David, is regarded as the one who will establish peace on earth.

> "'And the land shall mourn' (Zechariah 12:12). Rabbi Dosa and the other rabbis differed on what this verse means. The one said that they will mourn over *Mashiach Ben-Yosef*, who will be slain [in those days]; while the other said the mourning is over the *yetzer hara'* [the evil inclination], which will be slain…. The Rabbis taught that the Holy One, blessed be he, will say to *Mashiach Ben-David*, 'Ask anything of me, and I will give it to you, for it is written, "The Lord said unto me, 'You are my son, this day I have become your father; ask of me, and I will give you the nations as your inheritance'"(Psalm 2:7–8).' When *Mashiach Ben-David* sees that *Mashiach Ben-Yosef* has been slain, he will say to God, 'Master of the World! All I ask of you is life!' God will say to him, 'Even before you said, "life," your father David prophesied about you, as it is written, "He asked life of you, and you gave it to him"' (Psalm 21:5)." (Sukkah 52a)

The New Testament, of course, shows that *Mashiach Ben-Yosef* and *Mashiach Ben-David* are the same person, Yeshua, whose human descent was from King David, whose legal but not physical father was Yosef, and whose resurrection has made it possible for him to come twice and fill both roles. For more on Zechariah 12:10–14 see Yn 19:37&N, Rv 1:7&N.

14 The Messiah must come under the curse (v. 13) in order to pay the full penalty for sin required by God's justice. Why did he do this? Why did he trouble himself? Verse 14 gives the answer, so that **the Gentiles might receive the blessing announced to Avraham**, promised in Genesis 12:1–3, which is cited above in vv. 8–9; and not only the Gentiles, but also "**we**," which includes Jewish believers. How is this blessing appropriated? Once more, as at 2:17, Sha'ul brings out that it comes through being **in union with him**, so that when Yeshua receives what is promised to him, believers receive it too. And this, once again, comes about **through trusting and being faithful**, not through legalism.

What was promised, namely, the Spirit (see vv. 2, 5). However, the Greek says, literally, "the promise of the Spirit," which could alternatively mean, "what the Spirit promised," to wit, that all the *Goyim* would be blessed (v. 8).

15–17 Oath. Greek *diathêkê* does not mean "oath" but signifies either (1) "covenant," equivalent to Hebrew *b'rit*, or (2) "will, testament." Thus "**swears an oath**" (v. 15) is literally either "ratifies a covenant" or "draws a will"; likewise "**an oath sworn by God**" (v. 17) is literally "a covenant previously ratified" or "a will previously drawn." But, for the following reasons, neither "covenant" nor "will" is a good rendering here.

In the Bible, a covenant is made unilaterally by a superior party, either God or a conquering king, with the inferior party, God's people or the conquered vassals, who only submit to the terms announced. In the present case, God made promises to Avraham in a covenant. But in modern English one thinks of a covenant as a contract, drawn between equals and alterable by either party. I avoided the term "covenant" here because the modern connotations conflict with Sha'ul's point.

Likewise, even though the word "inheritance" appears in v. 18, I did not use "will" because a person can change his will by adding a codicil.

But an oath, once sworn, cannot be altered by anyone, not even by the one who swore it. And since God did swear an oath when he made the promises to Avraham (Genesis 22:16–17, MJ 6:13–18), the rendering "oath" is consistent with the biblical record.

16 In the *Tanakh* the term "**seed**" (Hebrew *zera'*), like English "posterity," is used in the singular as a collective noun to refer to all of a person's descendants. Thus the *p'shat* (simple sense, Mt 2:15N) of this text has "**seed**" referring to Avraham's descendants. But Sha'ul is not expounding the *p'shat*; rather, his emphasis on the singular form of the word allows the **seed** to sprout into a richly layered *midrash*:

(1) Israel is God's son.
(2) The Messiah is God's Son.
(3) Israel is descended from Avraham, is Avraham's seed, the children of Avraham.
(4) The true children of Avraham are those who trust.
(5) Those who trust in Yeshua are united with him by that trust — they are part of his Body, one with him, one, singular.
(6) In the thinking of the *Tanakh*, a king represents his people to the point of being one with them; and the king of Israel is treated as representing Israel, standing for them, being one with them.
(7) The Messiah Yeshua is the King of Israel, the promised Son of David, one with Israel.
(8) By trusting, Gentiles become identified with and in some sense a part of Israel.
(9) All of God's promises reach their culmination and fulfillment in the Messiah, who is Avraham's "seed."

All nine of these truths lead to this verse, and this verse leads to these nine truths, each of which is expressed at greater length elsewhere in Galatians and the rest of the Bible (see, *inter alia*, Hosea 11:1; Mt 2:15&N; Yn 17:20–26; Ro 9:6–13&NN; 2C 1:20&N; and below, 3:26–4:7&NN, 4:21–31&NN).

17 **The legal part of the *Torah* came into being** in the days of Moshe, **430 years later** than Avraham. In Judaism, the word "*Torah*" usually means one of the following: (1) the *Chumash* (Pentateuch, Five Books of Moses), (2) the *Tanakh* (the Hebrew Scriptures), (3) the *Tanakh* (Written Law) together with the Oral Law, or (4) all true religious teaching (see Mt 5:17N). In any of these senses the *Torah* includes the promises to Avraham. But here "the *Torah*" means none of these. Rather, Sha'ul is distinguishing the characteristic element of *Torah* that was received on Mount Sinai at the time of Moshe, its specifically legal portions, from the elements which existed previously. He is contrasting the *Torah*'s commandments with its promises, or, to use Jewish language from a couple of centuries later, contrasting *halakhah* (what to do, how to live) with *aggadah* (narrative).

Therefore, even if the legal part of the *Torah* had required legalistic obedience without trust, it could **not nullify an oath sworn** (or: "a covenant established"; see above,

vv. 15–17N) earlier **by God, so as to abolish the promise** to Avraham, which says that Gentiles will be blessed through Avraham (vv. 8–9) without having to become Jews or be subject to the *Torah* as non-Messianic Judaism expounds it.

18 If, contrary to fact, **the inheritance** (there is a punning connection in meaning with the word translated "oath" in vv. 15, 17, because that word, "*diathêkê*," can also be rendered "will"; see vv. 15–17N — inheritances come through wills) **comes from** (is promised in) **the legal part of the *Torah***, the halakhic part (see v. 17N), which sets up conditions to be met, then **it no longer comes from** an unconditional **promise. But** the fact is that **God gave it** not to Moshe but, earlier, **to Avraham through** an unconditional **promise** which affects Gentiles as well as Jews, and not through a legal code intended for Jews only.

Although I believe that in this verse "*nomos*" means "the legal portions of the *Torah*," since that specifically is what was promulgated at the time of Moshe, "*nomos*" here could instead mean "legalism" without significantly altering Sha'ul's argument, which would then be: "If the inheritance comes by legalism, that is, by meeting the condition of legalistically following the *Torah*'s prescriptions, then it no longer comes from an unconditional promise." In any case, "*nomos*" cannot simply mean "*Torah*" in the sense of the first five books of the Bible, because the very promise referred to is set forth in the *Torah* itself, in the book of Genesis.

19 So then, why the legal part of the *Torah* (see v. 17N)? Why was it needed at all, if the promise (v.18) is independent of it? **It was added** to the promise — and to the environment of Jewish history in particular and human history in general — **in order to create transgressions**, literally, "because of transgressions." The latter could mean, "in order to contain and limit transgressions," in order to keep the Jewish people from becoming so intolerably sinful that they would become irredeemable. But instead of this, I think it means, as Sha'ul explains in Romans 7, that a key purpose of the commandments was to make Jewish people ever aware of their sin — not that Jews were more sinful than Gentiles, but that, like Gentiles, Jews too "fall short of earning God's praise" (Ro 3:23). The *Torah* "creates" transgressions by containing commandments which people break, indeed, which rebellious human nature perversely wants to break (Ro 7:7–12&NN). But at least in some cases the guilt they feel causes them to despair of ever earning God's praise by their own works, so that they come to God in all humility to repent, seek his forgiveness, and trust him (see Ro 3:19–20&NN, 4:13–15&NN, 5:12–21&N, 7:5–25&NN).

Until the coming of the "seed," Yeshua (v. 16), **about whom the promise had been made**. From the time of Moshe until the coming of Yeshua, the *Torah* had this "consciousness-raising" role. The *Torah* still exists, is still in force (see 6:2N), and for those who have not yet come to trust in Yeshua it still has this function. But for those who do trust in Yeshua and are faithful to him, the *Torah* need no longer serve in this capacity. Sha'ul explains why in vv. 21–25.

It, the *Torah*, **was handed down** to Moshe on Mount Sinai **through angels**, a point made three times in the New Testament (see Ac 7:53&N) **and** through **a** human **mediator**, Moshe. An often heard Jewish objection to the New Testament's teaching is that Jews don't need Yeshua because they don't need a mediator between themselves and God. This verse refutes the claim with its reminder that Moshe himself served as such a mediator — as, for that matter, did the *cohanim* and the prophets. See MJ 8:6, 10:19–21; 1 Ti 2:5; Exodus 20:19; Deuteronomy 5:2, 5; and this citation from a Pseudepigraphic work dating from the first or second century B.C.E.:

> "Draw near to God and to the angel that intercedes for you, for he is a mediator between God and man…." (Testament of Dan 6:2)

20 It is said that this difficult verse has had some 300 different interpretations. Its literal translation: "Now the mediator is not of one, but God is one." My understanding of it is this: a mediator necessarily mediates between two parties, both of whom desire to affect the final outcome. In this case, Moshe mediated between God and the Israelites because they were afraid to have God speak to them directly (and perhaps they were hoping that through Moshe they could have a hand in shaping the *Torah*). Also angels served as mediators (v. 19). But God's promises to Avraham were unmediated. Sha'ul's point seems to be that because the promises of the *Torah* are unconditional and came directly from God without a mediator, they are superior to the legal portions of the *Torah*, which the legalists seize on. (It does not appear that the phrase, **"God is one,"** has to do with the *Sh'ma*, which seems irrelevant in context; contrast Ro 3:29–30&N.)

21–22 Does this mean that the legal part of the *Torah* stands in opposition to God's promises? Do they contradict each other? Do they say different things? Does the legal part of the *Torah* offer life through legalism while the earlier part of the *Torah*, with its unconditional promises to Avraham, offers life through trust? **Heaven forbid!** (On this strong negation see Ro 3:4N.) **For if the legal part of the *Torah* which God gave had had in itself the power to give life**, if it had somehow automatically imparted the Holy Spirit to legalists and turned them into people who trust God and are faithful to him, **then righteousness really would have come by legalistically following such a *Torah*.**

But such a thing is unimaginable. **Instead**, on the contrary, **the *Tanakh* shuts up everything under sin**, imprisoning all mankind (v. 23; compare Ro 11:30–32), **so that what had been promised might be given, on the ground of Yeshua the Messiah's trusting faithfulness**, only **to those who continue trustingly faithful** to him and to God. See 2:16cN, which explains why in this and the following verses the Greek word *"pistis"* is best translated not as "faith" but as "trusting faithfulness," and why the *pistis* spoken of is sometimes Yeshua's and sometimes ours, both being necessary for our salvation. Had Sha'ul meant here **on the ground** not **of… the Messiah's… faithfulness** to God but of our faithfulness to Yeshua, then the following phrase, "**to those who continue trustingly faithful**," would be superfluous. But as it is, Yeshua's faithfulness is described as applying only to those who, by being united with Yeshua, have acquired the same trusting faithfulness as his.

23a Before the time for this trusting faithfulness (Greek *pistis*; see 2:16cN) of Yeshua's **came, we were imprisoned**. The Greek word translated "**this**" in vv. 23–26 actually means "the." In Greek the definite article is sometimes unimportant and need not be translated at all; however, here I believe it refers not to *pistis* generally but specifically to the Messiah's own *pistis*, spoken of in the preceding verse. In other words, "the *pistis*" is **this** particular **trusting faithfulness** which the Messiah demonstrated in his lifetime, especially as he underwent the events leading up to his death. **Before the time for** it **came**, before God had presented humanity with this unsurpassable example of what trusting faithfulness really is, **we** Jews **were imprisoned** by a specific kind of sin, legalism, that arose from misconstruing the *Torah* (see v. 23bN). Gentiles were imprisoned by their sins too; see v. 22, Ro 1:16–2:16 and Ro 11:30–32, which develop this topic, the universality of sin and the reason for it, in other contexts.

An alternative sense would be: "Before the time came for us to trust [in Yeshua] and be faithful [to him], we were imprisoned." If the former interpretation is correct, as I believe it is, then Sha'ul is speaking of the period prior to the date of Yeshua's appearance on the scene of human history; if the latter, he could be speaking either of the time prior to the preaching of the Gospel in a particular region or to the time in a person's life before his coming to faith. Translations which eliminate the definite article, which say "Before faith came…" or "Before the time for faith came…," encourage the erroneous and antisemitic notion that prior to Yeshua no one had ever believed in God.

23b In subjection to the system which results from perverting the *Torah* — specifically, its legal parts (see v. 17N) — **into legalism**. (The discussion of 2:16bN and Ro 3:20bN is prerequisite and integral to what follows.) These thirteen English words translate two Greek words, "*upo nomon*," literally, "under law." The usual interpretation of this verse has Sha'ul saying that Jews were imprisoned by the Mosaic Law until Christ came but now are free from it — "so eat a ham sandwich!" However, "*upo nomon*," used ten times in the New Testament (here, 4:4, 5, 21; 5:18; Ro 6:14, 15; and three times in 1C 9:20), but only by Sha'ul, must be understood as a technical term which he coined in order to analyze one aspect of the concept of legalism. See the reasoning developed in 2:16bN and Ro 3:20bN in connection with the Greek phrase, "*erga nomou*" ("works of law").

Although the figurative use of the word "*upo*" and its English equivalent, "under," can be neutral and mean merely "within the framework of" (example: "under his tutelage"), it can also have a negative valence and connote oppression by meaning "in subjection to" or "burdened by." But when Sha'ul means "within the framework of *Torah*" he uses a different phrase, "*en nomô*" ("in law," Ro 2:12&N, 3:19&N); also note his unique use of the word "*ennomos*" ("en-lawed") at 1C 9:21&N. In writing "*upo nomon*" he is clearly bringing out the subjugative sense of the word, for the phrase always appears in the context of oppression — imprisonment (here), slavery (4:4, 5, 21; Ro 6:14–15), or being controlled by the evil desires of one's old nature (5:18). In 1C 9:20–22 Sha'ul labels four different groups of people with whom he tries to empathize; 1C 9:20bN explains why "those under law" in this passage are oppressed. (Ya'akov uses "*upo tou nomou*" ("under the law") in a negative context in the phrase, "convicted under the *Torah* as transgressors" (Ya 2:9); but unlike Sha'ul it is not for him a technical term inherently implying oppression.)

"*Upo nomon*" does not mean "subject to the legal part of the *Torah*" which has been the topic of discussion since v. 17, because the legal part of the *Torah* is not temporary — it is not abrogated by the Messiah's coming (Mt 5:17&N). It is true that specific elements of *Torah* have been transformed (especially the sacrificial system; see Messianic Jews 7–10), some punishments have been abolished for those who have become united with the Messiah (3:10–13&NN), the role of the Holy Spirit has been made expicit (Yn 14:26&N, 15:26; Ro 8:1–13&NN), the relationship of Gentiles to

Jews in the united Messianic Community has been spelled out (Ac 15:1–29&NN, Ep 2:11–22&NN), and the New Testament itself has been given as *Torah* (MJ 8:6b&N). Nevertheless most of the ordinances and statutes — the civic and ceremonial *mitzvot* as well as the ethical ones — remain the same, even if priorities among them have been rearranged (2:12bN, Yn 7:22–23). What has been brought to an end by Yeshua's death and resurrection is not the legal part of the *Torah* but the need for Jewish people to try to earn God's favor through **the system which results from perverting the *Torah* into legalism**. This is why nobody needs to be **in** oppressive **subjection to** it any more.

This oppressive legalistic system **kept** the Jewish people imprisoned **under guard** until Yeshua came. There were two aspects to this guardianship: protection and harshness. Prison is not a pleasant place, but it does provide a measure of protection from the outside world, from certain kinds of temptations, from angry people who might harm the prisoners. Sha'ul evokes the image of both aspects of imprisonment.

24 **The *Torah* functioned as a custodian until the Messiah came**. The word translated "custodian" is "*paidagôgos*," literally, "boy-leader." In ancient Greece a *paidagôgos* was a slave who conducted a boy to and from school. It is therefore not surprising that the KJV renders the phrase, "the law was our schoolmaster to bring us [Jews] unto Christ." But although the English word "pedagogy" is derived from it, the *paidagôgos* had no teaching functions (see Arndt and Gingrich, *A Greek-English Lexicon…*, *ad loc.*); and although the *Torah* had as one of its goals leading Jewish people to the Messiah, as Sha'ul explicitly says at Ro 10:4&N, that is not the import of the present verse. The *paidagôgos* actually would have been a harsh disciplinarian, hired to do a job, with the boy required to obey him. Thus the *Torah*, because it was perverted into legalism, served in the role of harsh disciplinarian for the Jewish people, providing some protection but generally making the Jewish person aware of many transgressions (see v. 19&N), **so that we** Jews **might** turn from legalistic rule-following and **be declared righteous** forensically (2:16aN) **on the basis of** our **trusting and being faithful** to Yeshua, whose trusting faithfulness to God the Father purchased our salvation.

25 Therefore, **now that the time for this** peerless example of **trusting faithfulness** which Yeshua displayed **has come**, which same trusting faithfulness we now have too because we are united with him (v. 26), **we** Jews **are no longer under** legalism of any sort, no longer **under a custodian**.

26 **This trusting faithfulness** which Yeshua demonstrated belongs not only to Jews ("we," v. 25), but to all of **you**, both Jewish and Gentile believers in him. If Jews and Gentiles exercise **this trusting faithfulness**, which belongs to both of us by virtue of our **union with the Messiah** (see 2:17–18N), then both Jews and Gentiles **are… children of God**, adopted as God's sons (4:5) on the ground of our **union with the Messiah** Yeshua, who himself is already God's Son.

27 Union with the Messiah comes about through being **immersed into the Messiah**. The Greek word for "**immersed**" is a form of "*baptizô*," usually rendered "baptized"; see Mt 3:1N on "Immerser." The word "*baptizô*" implies immersion so as to absorb the qualities of the immersing substance and thus be transformed. If you are an immersed believer, you have absorbed some of the qualities of the Messiah and are continually "being changed into his very image, from one degree of glory to the next, by *Adonai* the Spirit" (2C 3:18). This immersion into the Messiah comes about not merely through getting wet, but through prayer to God in which one repents of one's sinful way of life and accepts Yeshua the Messiah's atonement and Lordship. Here Sha'ul says this is equivalent to having **clothed yourself with the Messiah**.

28 Gentiles who by trusting in Yeshua and staying faithful to him have become children of God, who have immersed themselves into the Messiah, who have clothed themselves with the Messiah, are equal partners with Jews in the Body of the Messiah, declared righteous by God without their having to adopt any further Jewish distinctives. This is a point Sha'ul makes repeatedly in his writings; see Ro 3:22–23, 29–30; 4:9–12; 10:12; 11:32; 1C 12:13; Ep 2:11–22; 3:6; Co 3:11 — and these references do not exhaust the list; many other verses, especially in Romans, express the same idea. Therefore Jewish and Gentile believers must treat each other as equals before God, of equal worth as human beings. So must believing slaves and freemen, and likewise believing men and women. And that is really all this verse has to say.

However, the verse is misused in polemic against Messianic Judaism in the following way: "You Messianic Jews should not separate yourselves from us Gentile Christians by having Messianic synagogues! Don't you know that 'in Christ there is neither Jew nor Greek'? So be like us, give up your Jewish distinctives, stop observing the *Torah* and the Jewish holidays, put all that behind you; and worship with us in our Gentile-oriented congregations, living our Gentile lifestyle." The misuse is in concluding that because there is no distinction in God's sight between the forensic righteousness (2:16aN) of believing Gentiles and of believing Jews, therefore Jews are prohibited from observing God-given commandments. Such a conclusion defies both logic and the practice of the early believers.

Further, it defies the grammar of the sentence itself. The sentence contains three parallel pairs: **Jew... Gentile, slave... freeman, male... female**. Obviously there are still observable physical, psychological and social distinctions between **male** and **female** and between **slave** and **freeman** (even today there remain in the world tens of millions of slaves), even though **in union with the Messiah Yeshua** they **are all one**, so far as their acceptability before God is concerned. The same is true of **Jews** and **Gentiles**: the distinction remains; the verse does not obliterate it.

The Bible recognizes such differences between various groups. The *Torah* has commands which apply to the king but not to his subjects, to *cohanim* but not other Jews, to men but not women. The New Testament too has different commands for men and women, husbands and wives, parents and children, slaves and masters, leaders and followers, widows and other women (see 1C 11:2–16, 14:34–36; Ep 5:22–6:9; Co 3:18–4:1; 1 Ti 3:1–13, 5:3–16; MJ 13:7, 17; 1 Ke 3:1–7); and it makes special demands of pastors, elders, *shammashim* (deacons) and evangelists which are appropriate to their offices but are never regarded as undermining the equality of all believers before God.

Similarly there remain differences between Jews and Gentiles, differences in cultural background and religious heritage, differences in what God has promised them as a people (but not racial differences, as antisemites claim), and differences in what they are commanded to do. It is not for Gentile Christians to try to prevent

Jewish believers from taking cognizance of those differences and building their lifestyles in a way that reflects them, so long as the lesson of Galatians is heeded, which is that equality and fellowship in the Body of the Messiah between Jews and Gentiles must be nurtured and preserved. It is not that there is to be one race or one nationality, but one Messianic Community.

But nothing in the New Testament prevents a Jewish believer from choosing to worship with Gentile believers in a Gentile-oriented church; likewise nothing prevents a Gentile believer from choosing to worship with Jewish believers in a Messianic Jewish congregation. In either situation what the New Testament mandates is fellowship and equality between Jews and Gentiles in the Body.

Neither Jew nor Gentile, neither slave nor freeman, neither male nor female. The three pairs in this verse reflect the words spoken by (free) Jewish men in their morning prayers (see, for example, J. H. Hertz, *The Authorised Daily Prayer Book*, New York: Bloch Publishing Company, revised edition 1948, pp. 18–21):

> "Praised be you, *Adonai* our God, King of the universe, because you have not made me a Gentile.
>
> "Praised be you, *Adonai* our God, King of the universe, because you have not made me a woman.
>
> "Praised be you, *Adonai* our God, King of the universe, because you have not made me a slave."

(Likewise Gentiles and women were limited to certain parts of the Temple area; see Ep 2:14&N.) The implication that free Jewish men have special status with God is avoided by most Orthodox Jewish explanations of these prayers, although criticism from within Judaism has not been lacking. In any case, Sha'ul, with sweeping finality, says that in the Body of the Messiah, God has abolished such presumptive distinctions of status.

According to Messianic Jewish pastor Mark Kinzer, the witness to the world that the Messiah reconciles Jews and Gentiles requires them not to suppress their Jewish or Gentile identity, but to maintain their identities while relating to each other in love and thus manifesting unity. If Jewish or Gentile identity is suppressed, reconciliation is invisible and therefore is not a witness.

29 Whether Jewish or Gentile, **if you belong to the Messiah, you are seed of Avraham** in these senses:

(1) You are one with the Messiah who is the "seed" in the midrashic sense of v. 16.

(2) By having the same kind of trusting faithfulness that Avraham had, you prove yourself his spiritual descendants (vv. 7, 9).

(3) You are joined to Israel (6:16), who are Avraham's physical seed.

Thus you are **heirs according to the promise** of vv. 8, 18.

Are Gentiles full-fledged children of Avraham, or are they second-class children? Maimonides answered a comparable question from a Gentile convert to Judaism. In his "Letter to Ovadyah the Proselyte," he advised, "You are to say, 'our God and God of our fathers,' because Avraham is your father." The letter is quoted at length in Ro 4:16N. Sha'ul is equally insistent on the full equality of Gentile believers in the Messiah.

CHAPTER 4

3 **Elemental spirits of the universe** (the term is used again at v. 9, also at Co 2:8, 20). **We**, both Jews and Gentiles, **were slaves** to them. Gentiles served these demonic spirits as gods. Jews, though knowing the one true God, were sometimes led astray by demonic spirits, including the demonic spirit of legalism. Jews served this spirit whenever they perverted the *Torah* into a legalistic system (3:23b&N). That Jews too were bound by demonic spirits is indicated in Ep 2:3. See also vv. 8–10&N.

4–5 In a section of the Talmud that reviews a variety of Messianic speculations appears the following:

> "It was taught in the school of Eliyahu that the world is to exist for six thousand years. In the first two thousand there was desolation, for two thousand years the *Torah* flourished, and the next two thousand years is the Messianic age. But through our many iniquities all these years have been lost." (Sanhedrin 97a–97b)

The notes to the Soncino English edition say concerning the first 2,000 years that "desolation" means "no *Torah*." Concerning the second 2,000 years the notes state that "the *Torah* flourished" does not mean that the *Torah* ceases afterwards, but that the *Torah* is mentioned to distinguish this period from the next. While I agree that the *Torah* did not end when Yeshua the Messiah came, I believe the note is intended as a polemic against the common Christian teaching that the *Torah* has been abolished. On the third 2,000 years Soncino says, "I.e., Messiah will come within that period." This too is a polemic against the New Testament teaching that he came at the beginning of it (just as "desolation" and "*Torah*" began their eras). Finally, a note on the concluding sentence says, "He should have come at the beginning of the last two thousand years; the delay is due to our sins." In response to this daring remark obviously directed against the idea that Yeshua is the Messiah, one must proclaim that, in terms of the above teaching, the Messiah did indeed come at the beginning of the 2,000-year Messianic era, **when the appointed time arrived**.

God sent forth his son. At Pp 2:6–8 Sha'ul speaks of Yeshua's pre-human existence "in the form of God." **He was born from a woman**. That is, he took human form. This is as close as Sha'ul comes to saying anything about the virgin birth of Yeshua (reported explicitly in Mattityahu 1–2 and Luke 1–3; compare Ro 1:3–4).

Born into a culture in which legalistic perversion of the *Torah* was the norm. This lengthy phrase translates "*upo nomon*" ("under law") differently than at 3:23b (see note there), because the expression that fits most of the time misses the nuances when the focus of attention is on Yeshua the Messiah. For everyone else, "under law" is a technical term which means, "in subjection to the system which results from perverting the *Torah* into legalism," and perhaps even implying, "in subjection to an inner propensity to commit the sin of turning God's *Torah* of grace into a legalistic system." Of course

Yeshua had no such propensity, nor was he "in subjection to" anything, in the sense of being oppressed in spite of himself. He willingly submitted to God's will that he be born as a Jew, in a Jewish society pervaded by legalism (as Sha'ul himself experienced when he was younger; see 1:13–14).

Why was Yeshua born into such a society? **So that he might redeem those in subjection to this legalism.** ("In subjection to this legalism" again is a rendering of "*upo nomon.*") Yeshua had to submit himself to being in the same predicament as we humans are in order to redeem humanity; therefore, he was "born from a woman." Additionally, he had to submit to being in the special circumstances Jews are in — namely, being legally bound by a covenant to obey the *Torah* (Exodus 24:7) and at the same time being in a culture where the norm is to pervert that *Torah* into a legalistic system — in order to **enable us**, both Jews and Gentiles, **to be made God's sons**, adopted by God the Father (see Ro 8:14b–16&N). Romans 8:3 and MJ 2:14–18, 4:15 deal with the same subject and are essential commentary on this verse. Sha'ul's empathizing with the situations of various classes of unsaved people (1C 9:19–23&NN) may well be imitation of the Messiah (1C 11:1), as reflected in these two verses (and see v. 12&N).

6 ***Abba.*** See Mk 14:36&N, Ro 8:14b–16&N.

8–10 **Beings that in reality are non-gods**, i.e., idols, are one species of **elemental spirits** (v. 3&N). The Gentiles to whom Sha'ul is writing served them before they came to put their trust in Yeshua.

Judaism, as Conservative Jewish Rabbi Abraham Heschel eloquently pointed out in his writings, is a religion based on the sanctification of time. Jewish communal life thrives on celebrating biblically prescribed times. The **special days** come once a week — *Shabbat.* **Months** are noted at *Rosh-Chodesh*, the "head of the month," celebrated when the new moon becomes visible and commences a month of the Jewish calendar. **Seasons** include the three Pilgrim Festivals — *Pesach* (Passover), *Shavu'ot* (Weeks, Pentecost) and *Sukkot* (Tabernacles) — along with *Rosh-HaShanah* (New Year), *Yom-Kippur* (Day of Atonement), *Chanukkah* (Dedication, Lights), *Purim* (Lots) and other minor festivals and fasts. The **years** are the Sabbatical Year (every seven years), the Jubilee Year (every fifty years) and other years related to tithing; and there may be reference to the life-cycle events of *milah* (circumcision), *pidyon-haben* (dedication of the firstborn son), marriage and the ceremonies related to death. See also Co 2:16–17&NN.

But when Gentiles observe these Jewish holidays neither out of joy in sharing what God has given the Jewish people nor out of spiritual identification with them, but out of fear induced by Judaizers who have convinced them that unless they do these things, God will not accept them, then they are not obeying the *Torah* but subjugating themselves to legalism; and legalism is just another species of **those weak and miserable elemental** demonic **spirits**, no better than the idols left behind.

(An alternative interpretation, however, is that the "days, months, seasons and years" of this passage do not refer to the Jewish holidays at all but to pagan Gentile feasts, naturally and directly reflecting "those weak and miserable elemental spirits." According to this understanding Sha'ul was worried that his ex-pagan converts might be returning to these pagan festivals.)

Gentile Christians who choose to add a cultural identification with Jews to the spiritual identification they have already made by trusting in the Jewish Messiah, or who enjoy the beauty and significance of Jewish rituals, are, according to Romans 14 and 1 Corinthians 8, free to observe them. Moreover, Gentile Christians on their own have developed many adaptations of Jewish ceremonies. The very idea of a weekly Sunday church service is an adaptation of the Jewish *Shabbat* (see Ac 20:7&N, 1C 16:2&N). It is said that Christmas is celebrated on December 25 because *Chanukkah* begins on the 25th day of the Jewish month of Kislev. Erich Werner wrote an entire book detailing the Jewish roots of various Christian worship practices (*The Sacred Bridge: the Interdependence of Liturgy and Music in Synagogue and Church During the First Millennium*, 1959). During Holy Week, which memorializes the last days of Yeshua's life and his resurrection, Maundy Thursday commemorates the Last Supper, which was a Passover *Seder*; thus almost any Maundy Thursday ritual bears some relationship to that of *Pesach*. I have in my files about a dozen Christian *Haggadah*s (Passover liturgies); they display varying degrees of resemblance to the Jewish original. Whether their fidelity to the Jewish *Haggadah* is greater or less is of no religious significance. Whatever brings the Gentile Christian worshipper closer to God, or makes his behavior more godly, should be judged positively; the Jewishness of the ritual and ceremony is a matter of religious indifference. But a Gentile who supposes he earns God's approval by conforming his religious ceremonies to Jewish practice violates the message of Galatians by subjugating himself to legalism. There are many cults on the fringe of Christianity that foster such legalistic Judaizing of Gentiles.

Since Sha'ul is writing to correct a Gentile error, since he is writing to the Gentiles in Galatia, since he is the emissary to the Gentiles, his remarks here have no relevance whatever to Jewish believers, except as a caution to avoid legalism in general. That is, to use these verses as a wedge to drive Jewish believers away from celebrating *Shabbat*, Passover, the rest of the Jewish holidays and other Jewish customs, is to misappropriate them for a purpose that contradicts Sha'ul's teaching and practice. For we know that Sha'ul himself made substantial efforts as a believer to observe the Jewish holidays (Ac 20:16&N, 1C 16:8–9&N), and that the Jerusalem Messianic community surely did so. The New Testament does not oppose Messianic Jewish observance of Jewish holidays. Messianic Jews are, at the very least, free to observe all Jewish holidays and customs without interference by other Jewish or Gentile believers, and without being subjected to any accusations or guilt feeling connected with "Judaizing," since it is impossible to Judaize Jews (2:14bN). The degree to which, the circumstances under which, and the manner in which Messianic Jews might be obligated by *Torah* to observe the holidays and other Jewish customs is a subject worthy of investigation by believers (for more see *Messianic Jewish Manifesto*, Chapter V, entitled "Torah"). But the investigation must be conducted by believers free of anti-*Torah* bias.

I do not believe these verses prohibit the celebration of Christmas, Good Friday, Easter and other events of the Christian calendars followed by various Christian denominations. In contrast with the Jewish holidays, the Bible neither requires nor gives warrant for celebrating these holidays. Therefore the principles of Romans 14 and 1 Corinthians 8 govern: those who wish to celebrate, may; and those who prefer not to, may not — all so long as whatever is done honors the Lord and builds up the Messianic Community.

12 **I put myself in your place**. There is more about Sha'ul's practice of empathizing with others, of "becoming all things to all men," at 1C 9:19–23&NN.

13–15 For some speculation on what Sha'ul's **physical condition** was, see 2C 12:7N on his "thorn in the flesh."

17–18 On **zeal**, see Ro 10:2&N; also 1 Ke 3:13, "For who will hurt you if you become zealots for what is good?"

21 **In subjection to the system that results from perverting the *Torah* into legalism**. See 3:23bN.

22–23 See Genesis 16 and 21:1–21 for what the *Torah* **says** about **Avraham** and his **two sons**. **One**, Ishmael, was born **by the slave woman** Hagar. Avraham and Sarah's fear that God would not give them a child induced them to make use of their maidservant Hagar's childbearing capacity. Their way of forcing God's hand, of producing their own feeble pseudo-fulfillment of God's promise, was all too much **according to the limited capabilities of human beings** (literally, "according to flesh"; see Ro 7:5N).

On the other hand, the other **one**, Isaac, was born **by the free woman** Sarah **through the miracle-working power of God fulfilling his promise** (literally, "through the promise"), which he made to her at Genesis 18:9–15.

24a **To make a *midrash* on**, Greek *allêgoroumena*, "being allegorized." Hebrew *midrash* means "study, interpretation"; it derives from "*lidrosh*," "to search." Most of Jewish midrashic literature brings out ethical and devotional aspects of the Bible, sometimes drawing out and applying what is manifestly there, and sometimes imposing meanings on the texts, although the norm in Judaism is not to make a *midrash* that violates the *p'shat* (simple sense) of the text (see Mt 2:15N). Here Sha'ul goes beyond the *p'shat* of the Genesis texts, though without violating them. His application of them is bold and shocking; for although the Judaizers can claim physical descent from Sarah, Sha'ul calls them spiritual descendants of Hagar. Revelation 11:8 has an equally surprising reversal of traditional Jewish identifications. But such shocks are not limited to the New Testament — see Ezekiel 23, 34 and Hosea 1–2 for comparable examples in the *Tanakh*.

24b–25 **The two women are two covenants**. Sha'ul does not spell everything out but counts on his readers to get his point anyway. So the one covenant referred to **is from Mount Sinai**, the *Torah* of Moshe. It **bears children for slavery**, but not because it is bad (nowhere does the account in Genesis denigrate Hagar); hence there is no reason to demean the Mosaic Law on the basis of this passage. The Mosaic Law bears children for "slavery," to be enslaved to the "weak and miserable elemental spirits" (v. 9) of legalism, because people pervert the *Torah* into a legalistic system (vv. 21–23&NN). Who does this? **The present Yerushalayim**, that is, the non-Messianic Jewish community of the first century, both its establishment and the people loyal to that establishment. The Judaizers, the would-be Messianic Jews who insist that Gentiles become legalists, do the same thing. **She**, Hagar, the present Jerusalem, **serves as a slave, along with her children**, the legalists.

26–28 But the Yerushalayim above, corresponding to Sarah, **is free** (see 5:1N on "freedom"); **and she is our mother**, the mother of all who have the trusting faithfulness that Abraham and Yeshua had (2:16cN), whether Messianic Jews or Messianic Gentiles.

29–31 Non-Messianic Jews and Judaizers who pretend to be Messianic Jews (2:4–5) but actually come with a false gospel (1:6–9) may persecute genuine Messianic Jews and Messianic Gentiles (v. 29), but they themselves **will by no means… inherit** eternal life.

CHAPTER 5

1 The **freedom** which **the Messiah has freed us for** is the subject of this whole chapter, previewed at 3:1–5 (compare Romans 7–8). This freedom consists in a life of trust, faithfulness and love (vv. 5–6, 13b–14, 22), and it produces good fruit (vv. 22–23) because it is empowered by the indwelling Holy Spirit, with the old nature put to death (vv. 5, 16–18, 24–25). In contrast, the life of legalism (vv. 1–4, 13) produces all kinds of sin (vv. 15, 19–21, 26), because it is controlled by the old nature (vv.6, 13a, 16–18, 24). When we live by the Spirit all our circumstances help us (Ro 8:28), and our path continues growing brighter (1 Yn 2:8, 2C 3:17–18).

A yoke of slavery to legalism (see 2:16bN). In Judaism the "yoke of the *mitzvot*" is regarded as joyful to bear (Ac 15:10&N); and if the *Torah* is understood as requiring first of all trusting faithfulness, then, as Yeshua put it, "My yoke," the yoke of obedience to the *Torah*'s true meaning, as upheld by the Messiah (6:2&N), "is easy, my burden is light" (Mt 11:28–30&N). The yoke of the *mitzvot* becomes slavery only when the *Torah* is perverted into legalism (3:21–23&NN), as the Judaizers would have these Gentiles do.

2–4 It cannot be emphasized too strongly that the message of these verses is directed to Gentiles, specifically to Gentiles who have been told by the Judaizers that they not only must believe in Yeshua but also must become Jews in order to be acceptable to God. A Gentile who heeds them and gets circumcised loses the **advantage** of **the Messiah** and has **fallen away from God's grace** precisely because he is **trying to be declared** forensically **righteous** by God (2:16aN, 2:21N) **through legalism** (literally, "by law"; see 2:16bN).

The truth, says Sha'ul, is that now that the Messiah has come, a Gentile becomes part of God's expanded people, the Messianic Community, through trusting in God and his Son. This entails his turning from sin, seeking God's forgiveness, and being immersed into the Messiah (3:27&N). But it does not entail his becoming Jewish. So if he turns back to the earlier procedure for joining the people of God, he is denying the Messiah and the new procedure which he has inaugurated. What a tragedy that a Gentile believer, already declared righteous by God on the ground of his trust alone, by becoming dissatisfied and heeding the Judaizers' mistaken preaching that his trust is insufficient, would lose everything God has freely given him!

But none of this applies to Jewish believers. Sha'ul himself circumcised the Messianic Jew Timothy (Ac 16:1–3&NN). His actions during his last visit to Jerusalem were directed specifically at disproving the false charge that he told Jewish believers not to have their children circumcised (Ac 21:20–27&NN). The New Covenant through

Yeshua no more cancels *b'rit-milah*, the "covenant of circumcision" established by God with Avraham (Genesis 17:9–12), than the Sinai covenant through Moshe cancels God's promises to Avraham (3:15–18).

Thus it is **any** *Gentile* **man who gets** himself **circumcised** as a result of heeding the Judaizers who **is obligated to observe the entire *Torah***. It is interesting that even though Sha'ul disagrees with the legalistic system which non-Messianic Judaism made of the *Torah* he nevertheless respects the integrity of its initiation process.

When Sha'ul wrote, a Gentile initiated into God's people Israel had to (1) immerse himself in a *mikveh* for ritual purification, (2) offer a sacrifice at the Temple (a requirement which ended when the Temple was destroyed) and, if a man, (3) be circumcised. In other words, circumcision is part of an initiation rite which makes a Gentile part of the Jewish community. At that point he ceases to be a Gentile, becomes a Jew and voluntarily obligates himself to do everything a Jew is expected to do. And what is a Jew expected to do? Obey the *Torah*. In fact, at his initiation a Gentile convert to Judaism undertakes to observe the *Torah* even before he fully understands what his commitment means! (Compare Lk 20:18N.)

But this raises an interesting question. In a world containing more than one stream of Judaism, which version of the *Torah* is a proselyte expected to obey? For in the first century there were several streams of Judaism, just as there are today. Today if a Gentile becomes an Orthodox Jew, he obligates himself to obey the *Torah* as expounded in Orthodox Judaism, with the details of *halakhah* as developed in the Oral *Torah*. A Conservative Jewish proselyte is expected to obey *halakhah*, but with the interpretative variations developed in that movement. Reform Jews do not expect a convert to observe *halakhah* at all, since Reform Judaism grants its members freedom to follow or not follow specific customs. Likewise, it is reasonable to suppose that in the time of Sha'ul, if a Gentile was converted by Pharisees, they expected him to keep the "Tradition of the Elders" (Mk 7:3) as set forth by the Pharisees. But Sadducees or Essenes would naturally have expected a Gentile converted by them to follow their brand of Judaism.

In the light of the above, I want to raise a question which has implications for today. Could a Gentile believer, one not influenced by Judaizers or attempting to gain favor with God through legalistic works but sincerely wanting to join the Jewish people, convert to Messianic Judaism, get circumcised, and obligate himself to follow the *Torah* as Messianic Judaism expounds it without **fall**ing **away from God's grace**? In principle, I believe he could, although such a person would be the rare exception and not the rule. The following discussion of the issue, up to the final paragraph, is adapted from my book *Messianic Jewish Manifesto*, pp. 175–180.

Given that no Gentile needs to become Jewish in order to be saved (Ac 15:1–29), why would a Gentile Christian want to convert to Judaism? One can imagine conversions of convenience for the spouse of a Messianic Jew, or for a Gentile Christian living or wanting to live in the State of Israel; but no religion, Judaism included, looks favorably on converts with ulterior motives. Judaism rightly considers *yirat-HaShem*, "fear of God," as the only legitimate reason for converting. If a Gentile Christian's fear of God includes not only commitment to the Messiah, but equally a commitment to the Jewish people, including the desire to serve God and his Messiah as a Jew, does the New Testament allow him to convert to Judaism?

The main texts on the subject are 1C 7:17–20 and vv. 1–6 here. For years I understood them as absolutely prohibiting Gentile Christians from converting to Judaism, but the Orthodox Jewish philosopher Michael Wyschogrod wrote an article which changed my mind ("Judaism and Evangelical Christianity," in Marc H. Tanenbaum, Marvin R. Wilson and A. James Rudin, *Evangelicals and Jews in Conversation*, Grand Rapids, Michigan: Baker Book House, 1978, pp. 34–52). In it he notes that rabbis are required by *halakhah* to discourage potential converts in order to winnow out those who are insincere and suggests that Sha'ul's remarks are of this character, not absolute prohibitions.

Since Wyschogrod is a philosopher and not an historian, I had doubts. This "normal discouragement" is known from third-to-fifth century sources (Ruth Rabbah 2:16, Yevamot 47a–47b), but Sha'ul was writing in the first century, when Yeshua spoke of the *Torah*-teachers and *P'rushim* who "go about over land and sea to make one proselyte" (Mt 23:15). That is the opposite of "normal discouragement"!

Was there any first-century precedent for discouraging Gentiles from converting to Judaism? Yes; according to Josephus, Izates, King of Adiabene (near the Persian Gulf) from 36 to 60 C.E., was convinced of the truth of Judaism by a Jewish merchant named Ananias (Chananyah); his mother Helena, however, feared that if he got circumcised the people would not submit to his rule. Chananyah reassured him "that he might worship God without being circumcised, even though he did resolve to follow the Jewish law entirely; which worship of God was of a superior nature to circumcision." He was persuaded for the time being, but he had not lost his desire to convert completely; so when another Jew named El'azar (who evidently was more missionary-minded) saw him reading from the *Torah* and chided him for not doing what the *Torah* says, he had himself circumcised. This took place before he became king in 36 C.E. (See Josephus, *Antiquities of the Jews* 20:2:3–4; *Encyclopedia Judaica* 1:267–268, 924; compare Genesis Rabbah 46:10.)

This evidence convinces me that if a Gentile Christian wants to identify fully with the Jewish people, the New Testament in principle would permit him to become a Jew. He should accept the whole *Torah* as understood in the form of Judaism to which he is converting (this is implied by v. 3, where "*Torah*" evidently includes the Oral *Torah*), except where it conflicts with the New Covenant.

Most non-Messianic Jewish converting agencies have, at the very least, grave reservations about accepting into Judaism a Gentile who continues believing in Yeshua. Nevertheless a number of Gentile Christians have undergone Orthodox, Conservative or Reform Jewish conversion while retaining their faith. Sometimes this has been possible because the officiating rabbi simply did not ask whether they "still believe in Jesus"; while in several cases with which I am acquainted, the rabbi knew that the candidate retained his belief in Yeshua but permitted him to convert anyway. I know of an instance in which a Gentile Christian studied Orthodox Judaism for over a year; when he was about to enter the *mikveh* for the conversion ceremony he informed his rabbi that he still believed Yeshua is the Messiah. The rabbi was taken aback but allowed the ceremony to continue and eventually (after an unusual delay and several requests) mailed him a conversion certificate. A Jewish believer commented that even though this man had not concealed his faith, the rabbi had probably not understood him; instead of realizing he was serious, the rabbi had probably thought he was making a casual remark and that in the light of his year of Jewish study and practice his vestigial concern for Jesus would soon drop away. In other words, the man spoke, and the rabbi heard, but there was no real communication. I will leave the discussion here, unfinished as it is, adding only that while some Jews would regard any Gentile Christian conversion to Judaism as fraudulent if the convert continues to believe in Jesus, others respect whoever voluntarily and sincerely throws in his lot with the Jewish people, even if he does retain his faith in Yeshua.

Arnold Fruchtenbaum has pointed out another problem Messianic Judaism has with regard to conversion of Gentile Christians by non-Messianic Jewish rabbis, namely, that if we honor their conversions we are implicitly recognizing their authority in our own community. Doing that is something which ought to be discussed, not assumed.

In principle there is no reason why Messianic Judaism could not perform conversions. But the practical difficulties make it impossible at present. First, until Messianic Judaism has a clearer idea of what being Jewish in a Messianic setting means, it seems premature to convert Gentiles, enjoining them to **observe the entire *Torah*** before we ourselves have reached some consensus about what the "entire *Torah*," understood from a New Testament viewpoint, is! Second, no institutional arrangement exists whereby a Gentile could be converted and have his conversion recognized either by the Jewish community or by Christians — since the Jewish community does not regard Messianic Judaism as Jewish, and most Christians believe these verses prohibit conversion by a Gentile believer to any form of Judaism, even Messianic.

For Messianic Jews there is one final point, a sociological one: if many Gentile Christians were to convert to Judaism (whether through Messianic or non-Messianic rabbis), their numbers could overwhelm the born Jews in the movement, adding another problematic dimension to the relationship between Messianic Jews and the non-Messianic Jewish community.

In sum, Sha'ul in these verses is not addressing the Gentile believer who sincerely wants to cast in his lot with the Jewish people, but the Judaized Gentile, who undergoes circumcision because he thinks that by this legalistic work of his own he gains entry to God's "in-group" and attains a higher spiritual level of being. Verse 3 warns Gentiles influenced by the Judaizers that if they undergo conversion to Judaism, they obligate themselves to become Jewish completely, and at the same time they lose the benefits of having supposedly trusted in the Messiah. The Judaizers downplayed this obligation to obey the *Torah* because they didn't obey it themselves (6:12–13). But an instruction dealing with a specific problem cannot be generalized to apply to everyone everywhere throughout all time. Sha'ul does not absolutely rule out *all* Gentile conversion to Messianic Judaism, even though at present it is impractical.

5–6 **Neither being circumcised nor being uncircumcised matters**, so far as being accepted by God on the ground of trusting Yeshua is concerned. See 1C 7:19&N, where Sha'ul says the same thing; also 6:15 below; and see above, 3:28&N.

What matters is trust and faithfulness, expressing themselves through good deeds done in **love**. In both the *Tanakh* and the New Testament "love" refers to works, not mere feelings. Thus v. 6 powerfully refutes the idea that Christianity and Messianic Judaism elevate belief over action, creed over deed.

Good deeds, though always of value to those benefitted, will be of value to those who do them only if they spring from the **love** which comes through **the power of the**

Spirit, who works in us (v. 5). This is how, as others are helped, we ourselves progress toward **attaining** behavioral **righteousness** (see 2:16aN, 2:21N). The importance of our own holiness cannot be sidestepped by claiming that one should not be preoccupied with one's own spiritual progress but should be concerned with the well-being of others. The two are not mutually exclusive; one must indeed be concerned for others, but without countenancing sin in one's own life (see Yn 17:15–17, Ya 1:27).

7–10 Compare 1:6–9.

9 ***Chametz***, "leaven," is familiar to Jews from the Passover ritual; here it could stand for sin, wrong ideas or ungodly people ("One bad apple spoils the barrel"). See 1C 5:6–8N, where Sha'ul quotes the same popular proverb.

11 Apparently there was a group of people (call them the Out-of-Touch), whom we have not encountered prior to this verse, who had not kept up to date with what Sha'ul was actually saying and doing. They claimed he was **still preaching that circumcision is necessary** for Gentiles who wish to join God's people, as he had before he was saved. The Judaizers misappropriated this false rumor as evidence that Sha'ul himself approved their insisting on circumcision of Gentile believers.

Sha'ul's answer makes implicit reference to a second hitherto unmentioned group; I will call them the Super-Jews. They are zealous non-Messianic Jewish missionaries, the kind Yeshua said would "go about over land and sea to make one proselyte" (Mt 23:15). It is interesting that when Sha'ul wrote — in contrast with now — his proclaiming Yeshua as the crucified Jewish Messiah would have caused him no difficulties in the Jewish community, had he continued preaching that Gentiles who come to faith in Yeshua must then convert to Judaism. It was not because of his **preaching about the execution-stake** that the Super-Jews objected to and persecuted him. By itself, Sha'ul said, that **would cause no offense whatever**. Rather, it was his claim that Gentiles can join the people of God without getting circumcised. Sha'ul insisted that trust alone was sufficient, and for this the Super-Jews persecuted him. Their persecution refutes the Judaizers' false claim that Sha'ul is **still preaching that circumcision is necessary**.

12 **I wish**. Sha'ul's choleric personality leads him to make intemperate use of his gift for sarcasm, neither his first nor his last; for another, see Ac 23:2–5&N, and compare his behavior as a nonbeliever at Ac 8:3.

The people who are bothering you about getting circumcised are neither the Out-of-Touch nor the Super-Jews (v. 11&N), but the Judaizers.

Would go the whole way and castrate themselves, literally, "would indeed cut themselves off." The *Torah* declares a castrated *cohen* unfit to perform priestly duties (Leviticus 21:20); and, "He who has been wounded in the stones or has had his sexual organ cut off shall not enter the assembly of *Adonai*" (Deuteronomy 23:2). But there is also a punning reference to being cut off from one's people, a common sanction in the *Torah:* Sha'ul wishes these pests would be deprived of contact with the Messianic Community.

13 Until now Sha'ul has been preaching freedom; but here he issues a necessary caution against antinomianism, defined as abusing freedom by turning it into license.

14 **The whole of the *Torah* is summed up in one sentence**, Leviticus 19:18, which Sha'ul also used in this way at Ro 13:8–10&NN; compare Ya 1:27&N. Judaism contains a number of epitomes of *Torah*; one of the best-known passages naming several of them is in the Talmud:

> "Rabbi Simlai said, '613 commandments were given to Moses — 365 negative *mitzvot*, same as the number of days in the year, and 248 positive *mitzvot*, same as the number of parts in a man's body. David came and reduced them to eleven (Psalm 15), Isaiah to six (Isaiah 33:15), Micah to three (Micah 6:8), and Isaiah again to two — "Observe justice and do righteousness" (Isaiah 56:1). Then Amos came and reduced them to one, "Seek me and live" (Amos 5:4) — as did Habakkuk, "The righteous one will live by his trusting" (Habakkuk 2:4).'" (Makkot 23b–24a, abridged)

Also see Mt 7:12&N.

15 Factionalism is a major threat to the communal life of God's people; compare v. 26; Yn 17:21; 1C 1:10ff., 3:1ff.

16–17 This is essentially the same advice as in Ro 8:4–13. The term "**old nature**" renders Greek *sarx* ("flesh"; see Ro 7:5N). See Ro 8:4–13NN for the refutation of the idea that New Testament religion elevates the spiritual over the physical.

18 See 3:23bN.

19–21 There are believers who do not take these verses seriously, who think they can continue in adultery, fornication, *pharmakeia* (a Greek word which gives us our word "pharmacy" but combines the ideas of sorcery and drug use, as in the *JNT* rendering; see Rv 9:21N), and the other sins enumerated here without having to pay the price. They suppose that a loving God will accept them regardless of their sins, or that having once long ago professed their faith guarantees them entry to heaven. Sha'ul's response is brief and severe: **I warn you now as I have warned you before: those who do such things will have no share in** (literally, "will not inherit"; compare 3:29–4:7) **the Kingdom of God!** The phrase, "those who do such things," is the Greek word "*prassontes*" ("practicing"). It is not those who fall short of perfection who are excluded from the Kingdom, for that would exclude everyone, but those who wilfully continue to practice their sins instead of turning from them sincerely to seek God's forgiveness (1 Yn 1:9). While some of the listed sins can be performed alone, note how many involve abuse of other people and breakdown in human relationships (see v. 26&N).

22–23 **Fruit** does not come from efforts (of legalistic rule-following) but grows naturally (out of trust). "A tree is judged by its fruit," said Yeshua (Mt 12:33–37). Arguments for the objective truth of the Gospel are necessary, yet a most convincing form of evidence is the fruit of the Holy Spirit in the lives of believers.

In some Christian circles, an unseemly argument arises in which the **fruit of the Spirit** is set over against the gifts of the Spirit (see 1C 12:8–10&N), as if the one were better or more important than the other. The balanced New Testament believer will want both the fruit and the gifts of the Holy Spirit operating in his life, so that he can better serve God and his fellow human being.

Nothing in the *Torah* stands against such things. Or, "Against these things there is no law," in the sense that even legalism does not oppose them.

24 Likewise 2:20, 6:14; Ro 8:4–13.

25 See 3:5 and v. 16 above.

26 See v. 15 above. In contrast with the fruit of the Holy Spirit, the fruit of legalism and of the Judaizers' teaching is "feuding, fighting, becoming jealous and getting angry; selfish ambition, factionalism, intrigue and envy" (vv. 20–21).

CHAPTER 6

1 This follows on 5:26 without a break in the thought.

2 **The *Torah*'s true meaning, which the Messiah upholds**, Greek *ton nomon tou Christou*, "the law of the Messiah," a phrase found only once in the New Testament; although at 1C 9:21&N Sha'ul speaks of his being *ennomos Christou*, "en-lawed of Messiah" or "en-*Torah*ed of Messiah." But the phrase appears in the Midrash Rabbah on Ecclesiastes 11:8:

> "The *Torah* which a person learns in this world is 'vanity' in comparison with the *Torah* of the Messiah."

And its meaning there is essentially the same as in this verse: the *Torah* as it will be taught by the Messiah himself, the *Torah* as upheld by the Messiah.

Here the question is whether Yeshua instituted a new *Torah* different from the *Torah* given at Mount Sinai. In other words, is **fulfilling** "the law of the Messiah" different from fulfilling the Law of Moshe? I express my negative answer in my interpretive rendering, which by its wording excludes the common, but in my opinion mistaken, traditional Christian view that Jesus abrogated the supposedly legalistic *Torah* of Moshe and inaugurated in its place a "Law of Love."

This traditional view comes into direct conflict with one of the most firmly held tenets of Orthodox Judaism, the eternity or non-abrogability of the *Torah*. Each morning Orthodox Jews repeat in their prayers the *Yigdal* hymn, which affirms that

> "God gave the *Torah* of truth to his people
> Through his prophet, who was 'faithful in his house'
>
> "God will not alter his eternal Law
> Or exchange it for another."

The "prophet… faithful in his house" is Moshe (see Numbers 12:7 and the *midrash* on it in MJ 3:1–6&NN).

Yeshua himself reassured his hearers that he had not come to abolish the *Torah* (Mt 5:17). However, the eternity of the *Torah* does allow for changes in its historical manifestation and application to society; indeed Judaism itself provides numerous examples. Moreover, Jewish tradition includes a significant strand of expecting that when the Messiah comes, there will be a transformation of *Torah* (see Ac 6:13–14N, MJ 7:12&N). Messianic Judaism's search for common ground with non-Messianic Judaism on the subject of *Torah* must be carried out in this difficult terrain of change within sameness.

To become oriented in this terrain, it is useful to consult the section on "Eternity (or Non-abrogability)" in the *Encyclopedia Judaica*'s article on "*Torah*" (Volume 15, pp. 1244–1246). It points out,

> "In the [Hebrew] Bible there is no text unanimously understood to affirm explicitly the eternity or non-abrogability of the *Torah*; however, many laws of the *Torah* are accompanied by phrases such as, 'an everlasting injunction through your generations' (Lev. 3:17, *et al.*)."

But the rabbis interpreted Deuteronomy 30:12 ("It [the *Torah*] is not in heaven"; see Ro 10:6–8&N and Ac 9:4N) and Numbers 36:13 ("These are the commandments") to imply that the whole *Torah* has already been given. Thus the Babylonian Talmud can say, "A prophet is henceforth not permitted to innovate anything" (T'murah 16a), although he may suspend a law temporarily (Sifre Deuteronomy 175).

There is no reason why Messianic Judaism needs to accept this rabbinic impediment to change. Nevertheless, even if it is accepted for the sake of argument, it still should not apply to Yeshua. For Yochanan the Immerser was already "more than a prophet" (Mt 11:14), and he called Yeshua yet "more powerful than I" (Lk 3:15); therefore the Messiah (by *kal v'chomer*, see Mt 6:30N) was not subject to the supposed restrictions on prophets.

Such an answer is not implausible within the framework of Jewish tradition, for, the article adds,

> "The rabbis taught that the Torah would continue to exist in the world to come (e.g., Ecclesiastes Rabbah 2:1), although some of [the rabbis] were of the opinion that innovations would be made in the messianic era (e.g., Genesis Rabbah 98:9; Leviticus Rabbah 9:7)."

Both of these, along with other Jewish sources of the notion that the Messiah will alter the *Torah*, are quoted in Ac 6:13–14&N, where Stephen was accused of saying "that Yeshua from Natzeret will… change the customs Moshe handed down to us." In his defense Stephen did not say that the *Torah* had been abrogated, but upheld its sanctity and countercharged his accusers with disobeying it (Ac 7:1–53). Likewise, when Sha'ul was rumored to be "teaching all the Jews living among the *Goyim* to apostatize from Moshe, telling them not to have a *b'rit-milah* for their sons and not to follow the traditions," he demonstrated publicly that the gossip was groundless

(Ac 21:20–24&NN).

Pursuing this line of thought, the article continues,

> "With the rise... of Christianity and Islam, which argued that particular injunctions of the *Torah* had been abrogated, the question of the eternity or 'non-abrogatability' of the *Torah* became urgent. Saadiah Gaon... interpreted the verses, 'Remember ye the *Torah* of Moshe.... Behold, I will send you Elijah...' (Malachi 3:22–24(4:4–6)), as teaching that the *Torah* will hold valid until the prophet Elijah returns to herald the resurrection (*Beliefs and Opinions* 3:7)."

Luke, making use of the same passage in Malachi, wrote that Yochanan the Immerser came "in the spirit and power of Elijah to 'turn the hearts of fathers to their children'" (Lk 1:17); so that Yeshua could say that "Elijah has come already, and people did not recognize him" (Mt 17:12). In the light of these verses, the reasoning of this tenth-century sage is consistent with a Messianic Jewish approach.

But is it true that even "particular injunctions of the *Torah*," as opposed to the *Torah* as a whole, were abrogated by the New Testament? Some branches of Christianity teach that the ethical Law remains, while the civil and ceremonial statutes have been done away with. For Gentiles this may seem a satisfactory solution to the problem of the *Torah*, but for Jewish believers it isn't so simple as that. In my view, all supposed particular abrogations can be otherwise explained within the Jewish framework for understanding *Torah*. Some rules were transformed by their fulfillment; this is a process found already in the *Tanakh*, for example, when the Tabernacle was superseded by the Temple. In the New Testament, Yeshua's own sacrificial death fulfilled the function of the Temple sacrifice for sin and either superseded it or changed it into a memorial, as explained in Messianic Jews 7–10 (see especially MJ 7:12&N). Other rules were not abrogated but were re-prioritized — the obvious instance in the book of Galatians is *kashrut* (see 2:12bN). The biblical holidays (in a sense the term "Jewish holidays" detracts from their importance) were not abolished but were given new significance (Mt 26:26–29, Yn 7:37–39). Still other rules specify punishments for disobedience; for those united with the Messiah, these have not been abrogated but have been executed already (3:10–13&NN; Ro 6:2, 8:1).

Although non-Messianic Judaism does not recognize Yeshua's Messiahship and therefore necessarily must have some mistaken ideas about *Torah* after he has come, it seems to me that Messianic Judaism should take up at once the task of reconciling its view that the *Torah* includes the New Testament with such non-Messianic Jewish notions about *Torah* as are not mistaken. From this kind of study it may emerge that no "particular injunctions of the *Torah*" were actually "abrogated," in the sense that this term should be used in halakhic discussions.

The article notes that Maimonides, whose creed underlies the *Yigdal* hymn quoted above,

> "...contended that the eternity of the *Torah* is stated clearly in the Bible, particularly in Deuteronomy 13:1 ('thou shalt not add thereto, nor diminish from it') and Deuteronomy 29:28(29) ('the things that are revealed belong unto us and to our children forever, that we may do all the words of this Torah')."

But, far from being universally upheld, his opinion was criticized by two other prominent medieval Jewish philosophers, Chasdai Crescas and Joseph Albo. Similarly, the *Kabbalah* (the mystical, occult stream within Orthodox Judaism) produced an alternative view:

> "In the 13th century *Sefer ha-Temunah*, a doctrine of cosmic cycles or *shemittot* (cf. Deuteronomy 15) was expounded, according to which creation is renewed every 7,000 years, at which times the letters of the *Torah* reassemble, and the *Torah* enters the new cycle bearing different words and meanings. Thus, while eternal in its unrevealed state, the *Torah*, in its manifestation in creation, is destined to be abrogated. This doctrine... was exploited by the [17th century Messianic pretender and] heretic Shabbetai Zevi and his followers, who [taught] that 'the abrogation of the *Torah* is its fulfillment!'"

The Shabbeteans' view was close to the erroneous Christian doctrine that takes Ro 10:4 to mean that Yeshua brought the *Torah* to an end (see note there).

In the 19th century,

> "Achad Ha-Am called for the *Torah* in the Heart to replace the *Torah* of Moshe and of the rabbis, which, having been written down, had, in his opinion, become rigid and ossified in the process of time."

This notably anti-Christian apostle of cultural Zionism, alluding to the very passage in the *Tanakh* on which the New Covenant is founded (Jeremiah 31:30–33(31–34), quoted in MJ 8:6–12), actually repeated the argument Christian theologians used for centuries against Judaism!

After noting that the ideologists of Reform Judaism considered "the abrogation of parts of the traditional *Torah*... not a heresy at all but... necessary for the progress of the Jewish religion," the article concludes,

> "[I]t is not entirely untenable that the main distinction between Orthodox Judaism and non-Orthodox Judaism [today] is that the latter rejects the literal interpretation of the ninth principle of Maimonides' Creed that there will be no change in the *Torah*."

In my view, the *Torah* of Moshe and the *Torah* of the Messiah are the same. What is called "the perfect *Torah*, which gives freedom" (Ya 1:25, 2:12), "Kingdom *Torah*" (Ya 2:8), "the *Torah*... summed up in this one sentence: 'Love your neighbor as yourself'"(5:14; compare Ro 13:8–10, Mk 12:28–31), the "*Torah* that has to do with trusting" (Ro 3:27; compare Ro 9:32), and the *Torah* written on hearts by the New Covenant (Jeremiah 31:30–33(33–34), MJ 8:8–12) is the same *Torah* that Moshe received and promulgated. Apparent changes are not abrogations, but applications of the eternal *Torah* to the new historical situation resulting from the Messiah's first coming. The central requirement of the *Torah* remains unchanged, "trust and faithfulness expressing themselves in love" (5:6). Yes, there is a Law of Love; Moses brought it to God's people. What Yeshua said about it was, "If you love me, you will keep my commands" (Yn 14:15; compare 1 Yn 3:22); and Yeshua's "commands" are

God's *mitzvot*, *Torah* to be obeyed.

One considers the United States constitution to be "the same" as when it was promulgated, although it has been amended many times, and specific provisions have even had their meaning reversed by court interpretation. Similar processes — normal legal processes — have taken place within Judaism. One can say, for example, that the *Torah* was "amended" in the *Tanakh* itself when *Purim* was made a required festival centuries after Moshe. Rabbinic interpretation outlawed polygamy in most Jewish communities, made *chalitzah* (not taking a brother's childless widow as wife) the norm instead of the exception (see Mt 22:24&N), turned Sabbatical-year cancellation of debts into their protection (by the *prosbol* of Hillel; see Deuteronomy 25:9–11), and so on. Many of these changes were beneficial, by no means the kind Yeshua condemned when he criticized "your tradition" (Mk 7:5–13&NN).

It is tendentious to call the New Covenant's applications of the *Torah* "changes" or "abrogation" while not so regarding those of the rabbis. Not even the Orthodox Jewish ideology that the Oral *Torah* was given to Moshe at Mount Sinai along with the Written *Torah* can mask the inconsistency. For if there is any truth in that claim, then the Oral *Torah* given to Moshe must have included the fact that the New Covenant would itself be "given as *Torah*" (MJ 8:6b&N; possibly one should say, "be revealed as *Torah*"); perhaps this is the import of the "abuse [Moshe] suffered on behalf of the Messiah" (MJ 11:26). If one pursues this thought, then what passes now for Oral *Torah* must be checked for consistency with the New Testament, since the existing non-Messianic Jewish Oral *Torah* was produced by people who did not believe all of what the true Oral *Torah* contains — that is, the rabbis did not believe in the New Covenant and in Yeshua the Messiah. If there is anything in the existing Oral *Torah* not consistent with the New Testament, it will have to be modified or discarded.

The time has come for Jews to ignore anti-*Torah* Christian theology developed by people with an anti-Jewish bias, and to acknowledge instead that Yeshua the Messiah and the New Testament have not abolished, abrogated or "exchanged" the *Torah* of truth "for another" Law.

Instead of bringing a new *Torah*, Yeshua **upholds the *Torah*'s true meaning**. In so expounding it, he "fulfilled" it, that is, he "filled it full" (Mt 5:17&N). He insisted that the *Torah* not be subverted by human tradition (Mk 7:1–23&NN), that God's original intent be preserved (Mt 19:3–9), that its spirit take precedence over its letter (Mt 5:21–48, 12:1–15; Lk 10:25–37, 13:10–17; 2C 3:6), and that obedience to it now implies both following him (Mt 19:21) and being guided by the Holy Spirit (Yn 14:26, 15:26, 16:13). Sha'ul too made these same points (Ro 3:31; 7:6, 12, 14; 8:3; 2C 3:6; Ac 21:20–24).

What the *Torah* is *not*, either by God's intent or by its own nature, is legalism (see 2:16bN, 3:23bN). Rather, those who **bear one another's burdens**, thereby loving their neighbors as themselves (5:14), are **fulfilling the *Torah*'s true meaning, which the Messiah upholds** and does not abrogate. This is not a new *Torah*, "not... a new command. On the contrary, it is an old command, which you have had from the beginning" (1 Yn 2:7).

5 As explained in vv. 3–4, **each person will** have to **carry his own load** of guilt if he has failed to do the work which the Messiah has given him to do. There is no conflict with the exhortation in v. 2 to "bear one another's burdens"; there a different Greek word is used in urging the Galatians to act lovingly toward fellow-believers burdened by griefs, worries and illnesses.

6 Teachers of the Good News are to be supported by their fellow-believers. But Sha'ul himself made use of his entitlement only when he was certain that his doing so would not inhibit response to the Gospel itself (see Ac 18:3&N, 1C 9:1–18&NN, 2C 11:7–12&N).

7–8 The law of the harvest is not only that **a person reaps what he sows**, whether good or bad, but that the harvest is always greater than the planting — "thirty, sixty or a hundred times as much" (Mt 13:8, 23).

10 **Especially to the family of those who are trustingly faithful** (on "trustingly faithful" see 2:16cN). Love for neighbor means even love for enemies and for the unloveable (Lk 10:30–39, the parable of the Good Samaritan); at Yn 13:34–35&NN Yeshua enjoined his followers "to love one another as I have loved you." Such love only believers can give and receive, since it grows out of having the Holy Spirit.

11–18 **My own handwriting**. See 1C 16:21–24N. Normally Sha'ul's handwritten greeting is short, since its purpose is to assure his readers that the letter is really from him; this is proved by his calling attention to the **large letters** he uses and by 2 Th 3:17 in the light of 2 Th 2:2–3a&N. Here, however, after dictating the body of the letter and authenticating it, it seems that, with papyrus or parchment before him and quill in hand, he was moved by the intensity of his feelings to express once more (vv. 11–18) what he thought of the Judaizers and the evil they were doing. In these verses he is using highly charged, emotion-ridden language. This is important to keep in mind, because the very controversial v. 16 can be understood correctly only if it is remembered that Sha'ul was writing at white heat.

13 **Even those** Gentiles **who are getting circumcised**, becoming non-Messianic Jewish proselytes, and thus putting themselves *upo nomon*, "in subjection to the system which results from perverting the *Torah* into legalism" (see 3:23bN and 1C 9:20NN), obligating themselves "to observe the entire *Torah*" as a Jew (5:2–4&N) **don't keep the *Torah***, even thusly misunderstood. **On the contrary, they** don't follow that system's rules; the only reason they **want you to get circumcised** is not so that you will obey the *Torah*, but **so that they can boast of having gained your adherence** to them, personally (literally, "so that in your flesh they may boast").

15 **Neither being circumcised nor being uncircumcised matters**, repeated from 5:6 above (compare 1C 7:18–20) so that Sha'ul can bring in the new idea that has come to him in his white heat (see v. 11N), that **what matters is being a new creation** of God's because you trust Yeshua (compare 2C 5:17) and respond to the Holy Spirit (5:5, 16–25).

16 This controversial verse, with its expression, unique in the New Testament, "**the Israel of God**," has been misinterpreted as teaching what Replacement theology wrongly claims, namely, that the Church is the New Israel which has replaced the Jews, the so-called "Old Israel," who are therefore now no longer God's people. But neither this verse nor any other part of the New Testament teaches this false and antisemitic doctrine. Nor, in my view, does it teach, as has been proposed (perhaps in reaction), the contrary doctrine that the phrase refers only to Jews and that "Israel" can never mean Gentiles. To discover what it does teach, we must examine its Jewish background, the use of the word "Israel" in Sha'ul's time, and Sha'ul's purpose at this point in his letter. But we begin at the beginning.

And as many as order their lives by this standard. "**As many as**" means "all who" (see any lexicon); by context, the "all" Sha'ul has in mind are all those in Galatia, both Messianic Jews and Messianic Gentiles, who order their lives by the standard of being "a new creation" (v. 15), whose trusting faithfulness to God and Yeshua (2:16–3:9; 3:14, 22, 26–29) expresses itself freely (4:21–31, 5:13) in love (5:6, 13–15) by the Spirit (3:2, 5; 5:5, 16–25; 6:8). These alone constitute God's people in Galatia, God's Messianic Community. Others are self-excluded.

***Shalom* upon them**. On "*shalom*," which means so much more than just "peace," see Mt 10:12N. "*Shalom* upon them" (Hebrew *Shalom 'aleihem*) also means "Greetings to them." Thus, up to this point, the verse says little more than, "Greetings to the Messianic community in Galatia," and corresponds to similar sentiments which conclude his other letters.

Nothing remarkable so far, but the word sequence is odd. One would have expected, "*Shalom* and mercy upon as many as order their lives by this rule…." Sha'ul places the phrase, "as many as order their lives by this rule," at the beginning so that he can maximize the impact of what follows, namely, an allusion to the the main synagogue prayer, the *'Amidah* (Standing Prayer) or *Shmoneh-Esreh* (Eighteen Benedictions); it is the key to this verse.

The *'Amidah* was then and is now the central element of synagogue worship. "*Sim shalom*" ("Grant peace") was definitely one of the *'Amidah* prayers already in use in Yeshua's day; Abraham Millgram says it was part of the Temple liturgy, following immediately upon the priestly benediction of Numbers 6:24–26 (*Jewish Worship*, Philadelphia: The Jewish Publication Society of America, 1971, pp. 74, 103).

Sha'ul's Messianic Jewish readers and the Judaizers would have spotted the allusion immediately. And many of his Gentile readers would have noticed it too, because as "God-fearers" they had spent much time in synagogues. (See Ac 13:16&N, 46–48; 14:1, 6–7 for the evidence that many of the Gentile believers in Galatia had already been "God-fearers"; see Ac 10:2N, 13:16N on the term "God-fearers" itself.) Moreover, they probably continued using some of these prayers in their Messianic worship; if not, the Judaizers may have refreshed their memories.

In the following literal rendering of the first sentence of "*Sim shalom*," the *'Amidah*'s final blessing, the words quoted by Sha'ul are in boldface:

> Put ***shalom***, goodness and blessing, grace and kindness **and mercy upon** us **and upon** all **Israel**, your people.

By citing just these seven highlighted words, Sha'ul, with utmost economy, guides the reader's attention directly to the intended meaning of the verse. Further, his skill in wordplay is that of a virtuoso. He starts with the expected greeting, "***Shalom***" and skips to "**upon** us" (substituting "**them**" for "us"), thereby connecting the aforementioned greeting with the prayer, which becomes the new context. Only with the words, "**and mercy**," does the reader realize that Sha'ul has pivoted from greeting to *Amidah*; but, with rabbinic brevity (see Mt 2:6N) he does not quote the whole list of six blessings, just the first and last. Finally, the sequence of the words, "***Shalom* upon them and mercy**," differs from that in the *'Amidah* in order to preserve the integrity of the customary greeting, "*Shalom* upon them" ("*shalom 'aleihem*").

In the *'Amidah*, "us" refers to the congregation reciting the prayer; they are part of "all Israel," but by saying, "and upon all Israel," they ask God to extend the requested blessing of peace beyond themselves to the entire people of God. (The prayers in the synagogue liturgy are typically not merely for oneself or one's friends, but for all God's people.) The congregation is not "all Israel," but it is included in all Israel. Likewise, in this verse, "**them**" refers to the Messianic Community in Galatia, which is included in (i.e., is a subset of), but not identical with, **the Israel of God**. By adding, "**and upon the Israel of God**," Sha'ul extends his prayer to other believers outside Galatia.

He does not quote the words "your people" from the *'Amidah*, because it is unnecessary. As explained below, the word "Israel" itself already implies "God's people"; since Sha'ul is exercising "utmost economy," he has no need to belabor the obvious. Likewise, he does not have quote the word "all," because he is not focusing on whether the blessing should extend to "all" or only to "some" of God's Israel; without doubt he wished *shalom* and mercy upon *all* the Israel of God, whoever they are. But *who* is God's Israel? This is the question Sha'ul touches on by quoting from "*Sim shalom*" in such a way as to direct his readers' attention to a new application of the word "Israel," while stopping short of actually redefining it.

Israel. Before we can understand Sha'ul's purpose in changing the *'Amidah*'s "all Israel" to "the Israel of God," we must examine the crucial word "**Israel**." In Sha'ul's time this term was current only among those acquainted with Jewish writings, which means, for most practical purposes, that it was known only to Jews. Both Jewish and Gentile Greek-speakers said "*Ioudaioi*" when referring to the Jews (or "Judeans"; see Yn 1:19N) as a geographic, ethnic, national, political or socio-religious entity. But Jews reserved the word "**Israel**" to refer to themselves as God's people, the people of promise, whereas Gentiles did not use the term "Israel" at all — just as today the world uses the term "falashas" (actually a derogatory word in Amharic) to refer to the Ethiopian Jews, but they call themselves "Beta Israel" ("house of Israel"). For more see Ro 11:26aN; for a scholarly discussion with references, see G. Kittel, ed., *Theological Dictionary of the New Testament*, Volume 3, pp.356–391.

Thus "**Israel**" was Jewish jargon. The Judaizers exploited this fact in a crude appeal to the Gentiles' pride, so that their Gentile followers would think that by getting themselves circumcised they were joining God's fashionable elite, God's "in crowd." Therefore, as I see it, Sha'ul is teaching nothing at all here about what "the Israel of God" is. He is not defining it to be the Church, or the Jews, or some Jews and not others. Rather, he is using the word "Israel" as a synonym for "God's people," with "the Israel of God" being best defined as "those who are genuinely God's people," "God's 'Israel,' so to speak," in contrast with the Judaizers who may in *some* sense be "Israel" but are not "of God," not *God's* Israel. As insistently as possible I call attention to this metaphorical aspect of Sha'ul's use of the word "Israel," to the fact that he is not teaching but inveighing. In a sense, then, I agree with Today's English Version (The Good News Bible), which translates the last half of this verse, "mercy be… with all God's people," and with the Living Bible, which has, "mercy… upon those everywhere who are really God's own." But for the *Jewish New Testament* I would not want to omit the explicit reference to Israel or cloud the allusion to the *'Amidah.*

The entire momentum of Sha'ul's thought in the book of Galatians, rising to what I have called "white heat" (v. 11N), reaches its climax here. Even without a more precise definition for "the Israel of God," we may be certain that the central point of the verse is this: "The Judaizers want you Gentiles to think you must get circumcised in order to become part of God's people (5:3). But I say that Gentiles have only to trust in and remain faithful to God and his Messiah; if you are doing this, then, without circumcision, you are already part of God's people; you are *already*, so to speak, included in God's 'Israel.'" Using the "most Jewish" language possible, the phraseology of the *'Amidah,* he demolishes the Judaizers' last point of persuasion —*finito*! The tone of v. 17 shows that Sha'ul is fully aware of his accomplishment; and since nothing more of substance needs to be said, v. 18 ends the letter.

But interpreters have not been satisfied to let the matter rest. They have looked for a "deeper meaning," some deep truth concerning the nature of "the Israel of God." And that is their error. There isn't any deeper meaning! But we must pursue the matter as if there were in order to expose the mistakes.

And upon the Israel of God. "And" is Greek *kai,* which could, in theory, be understood as epexegetical, to be translated, "that is" or "in other words." In this case the traditional Christian misunderstanding would be correct; the verse would say: "Peace and mercy upon those who order their lives by this standard, that is, upon the Israel of God," namely, the Church. English versions which say essentially this in their rendering include the Revised Standard Version, the Phillips Modern English Version, and the Jerusalem Bible.

The consequence of this wrong interpretation has been immeasurable pain for the Jews. The conclusion was reached that the Church is now the "New Israel" and the Jews, the so-called "Old Israel," no longer God's people. If the Jews are no longer God's people, isn't it appropriate to persecute them? There are four reasons why this antisemitic conclusion is false and is not taught by this verse or any other: (1) the Greek grammar, (2) the Jewish background, (3) Sha'ul's purpose here, and (4) Sha'ul's teaching elsewhere.

(1) *Greek grammar.* The Greek grammar mitigates against translating this *kai* by "that is," because earlier in the verse the word "*kai*" appears twice where the context allows only the translation "and." It is unlikely that Sha'ul would use "*kai*" twice to mean "and" and once to mean "that is." The King James Version, the New Jerusalem Bible and the New American Standard Version correctly have "and."

(2) *Jewish background.* The Jewish background is Sha'ul's allusion to the *'Amidah.* In the *'Amidah* the phrase corresponding to "**and upon the Israel of God**" is "and on all Israel." The Hebrew particle "*ve-*" in the *'Amidah* can only mean "and." Sha'ul would not use in the position where "and" appears in the Hebrew of the *'Amidah* a Greek word which has "and" as one of its possible meanings while expecting his readers to understand "that is" instead.

(3) *Sha'ul's purpose here.* Sha'ul's purpose in the book of Galatians is polemic, not

didactic. He is destroying the arguments of the Judaizers, not teaching about the nature of Israel. This is clear from the fact that the word "Israel" appears only here in the whole book of Galatians. Thus whatever we learn in this verse about Israel is a byproduct, gleaned in passing and to be set alongside his reasoned discussion of the subject, which is found not in Galatians but in the book of Romans.

(4) *Sha'ul's teaching elsewhere.* In Romans, Sha'ul devotes three chapters to the subject of Israel (Chapters 9–11). There all eleven instances of the word "Israel" refer to the Jewish people, never to the Church. The climax of his teaching is that "all Israel" — the Jewish people as a whole — "will be saved" (Ro 11:26a; the note there shows that "Israel" in that verse does not mean the Church). And his purpose in those chapters is to prove that God can be counted on to keep his promises, both to the Jewish people and to all believers in Yeshua — which is precisely the opposite of the theology that says the Jews are no longer God's people, no longer the people of promise.

Traditional Roman Catholicism, Lutheranism and Covenant theology (Presbyterianism) are among the branches of Christendom that have perpetuated the idea that the Christians have replaced the Jews as "the New Israel," "the True Israel," "the Israel of God." But in reaction, the branch of fundamentalist Protestantism known as Dispensationalism has erred in the opposite direction. Taking the "**and**" before "**upon the Israel of God**" to mean that "**those who order their lives by this standard**" are entirely distinct from "**the Israel of God**," they propose a schema in which "the Israel of God" refers to Jews, but the Church and the Jewish people are forever separate in their histories and destinies. The Jews are seen as having a physical, non-spiritual, earthly destiny, while the Church is seen as having a heavenly, spiritual, non-earthly destiny. Intended to restore the Jewish people to a place in God's plan, the "separate but equal" status accorded them tends here, as in interracial contexts, toward "separate and inferior."

Further, in the case of a Jew who has accepted Yeshua as the Messiah, Dispensationalism has the curious effect of demanding that he decide whether he belongs to his own Jewish people, Israel, or to the Church. The psychological conflict is exacerbated by Dispensationalism's teaching that there will be a "Pre-Tribulation Rapture" of the Church, in which Christians will one day be removed to heaven from the scene of world history, while the Jews, Israel, will be left behind to suffer through "the time of Jacob's trouble." Is a Jewish believer, then, going to flee with the Christians or stay behind to suffer with the Jews? Is his fate to be "Jewish" suffering or "Christian" escape? For more on this, see 1 Th 4:13–18N.

If, as the Dispensationalists teach, the Church is not "the Israel of God," then precisely which Jews could Dispensationalists consistently understand to be "the Israel of God"? Messianic Jews? This would be consistent with Sha'ul's teaching that "not everyone from Israel is truly part of Israel," so that "only a remnant" will be saved (Ro 9:6, 27; 11:5). But Messianic Jews are already among "as many as order their lives by this standard," so that there is no need to mention them a second time. Non-Messianic Jews? Possibly, since Sha'ul's heart so ached for his unsaved brothers that he would have put himself under God's curse if it could have helped them (Ro 9:3–4, 10:1). But nothing in the letter to the Galatians prepares us for such a sentiment here; it simply doesn't fit into place. All Jews? Then there would have been no need for Sha'ul to invent the phrase, "the Israel of God"; he could have quoted "all Israel" from the *'Amidah* without modification.

The Dispensationalists are wrong; neither the Jewish people as a whole nor any subgroup of them constitute what Sha'ul means by "**the Israel of God**." This is clear from Ro 11:16–24, where Gentile believers are portrayed as wild olive branches grafted into the rich root of the cultivated olive tree which is Israel, the Jewish people. Since Gentile believers "have shared with the Jews in spiritual matters" (Ro 15:27), they are in some sense no longer "excluded from citizenship in Israel" (Ep 2:12&N); while unbelieving Jews, who are now broken-off branches, constitute some sort of "Israel in suspended animation," since they are capable, through trust, of being grafted back into their own olive tree. But none of this rather complex and subtle teaching about Israel is brought up in Galatians, and it is unreasonable to pack all this meaning into a single use of the word "Israel" (for more see Ro 11:23–24&N). In fact, since Sha'ul wrote Galatians before he wrote Romans, we cannot even be sure that he had yet thought all of this through.

The article on "Israel" in Kittel's *Theological Dictionary of the New Testament* referred to above says that "the expression [Israel of God in Ga 6:16] is in a sense to be put in quotation marks" (p. 388). I didn't do it in the *JNT*, but it's not a bad idea. Quotation marks would signal the reader that Sha'ul is not humorlessly declaring the Church to be the New or True Israel, having supplanted the Old; nor is he, with similar heavyhandedness, declaring the Church and Israel to be two different peoples of God. (It must be added that Sha'ul would also disagree with non-Messianic Jews who consider the Jewish people the only Israel there is, and the Church not Israel in any sense whatever.) Rather, he is indeed talking about genuine believers, both Jewish and Gentile — the Messianic Community — but polemically (not didactically), as a concerned pastor writing against the Judaizers who threaten his work for the Gospel. What he does teach about Israel here, in passing, contains elements of both the rejected views without agreeing with either. Believers are **the Israel of God**, God's people, God's "Israel," *so to speak*. Nevertheless, "Israel" refers to the Jewish people, not the Church. Only in Romans does he elucidate the anatomy of this paradox.

18 Brothers. As in eight other places in this letter, Sha'ul closes by reminding his hearers that they are all brothers in the Messiah. Therefore they should mend their doctrinal errors and become reconciled with one another.

The ***Amen*** at the end, like the one at 1:5, indicates that Sha'ul wants the congregation to respond to his final sentiment by saying, "***Amen***," the Hebrew word that means, "Let it be so." See Ro 9:5N.

THE LETTER FROM YESHUA'S EMISSARY SHA'UL (PAUL)
TO THE MESSIANIC COMMUNITY IN EPHESUS:

EPHESIANS

CHAPTER 1

1 Rabbi **Sha'ul** from Tarsus is Paul (Ac 13:9&N). **Emissary**, Greek *apostolos*, "someone sent," usually rendered "apostle" (Mt 10:2N). **To God's people**, literally, "to the holy ones," sometimes rendered, "to the saints." Some manuscripts lack "**in Ephesus**."

2 ***Shalom***. See Mt 10:12N.

3–14 These four paragraphs form a single sentence in the Greek text and are so rendered in KJV. Their form is that of a Jewish *b'rakhah* (benediction; for more see 2C 1:3–7&N, 1 Ke 1:3–4&N). This is signalled by the first words, **Praised be *Adonai*, Father of our Lord Yeshua the Messiah**, which echoes the initial phrases of the *'Amidah*, the central prayer of the synagogue liturgy, recited three times daily — *Barukh attah, Adonai, Eloheynu v'Elohey-avoteynu, Elohey-Avraham, Elohey-Yitzchak, v'Elohey-Ya'akov…* ("Praised be you, *Adonai*, our God and God of our fathers, God of Abraham, God of Isaac and God of Jacob…").

Other expressions are also reminiscent of the synagogue prayers. Two examples: **he chose us in love** (v. 4), which resembles the close of the *Ahavah* benediction immediately preceding the recital of the *Sh'ma*, "Praised be you, *Adonai*, who has chosen your people Israel in love"; and, **In all his wisdom and insight he has made known to us** (vv. 8–9), which recalls the fourth blessing of the *'Amidah*:

> "You favor humanity with knowledge and teach people understanding. Favor us with knowledge, understanding and insight from yourself. Praised be you, *Adonai*, gracious Giver of knowledge."

Moreover, the refrain in v. 6, **and would be worthy of praise commensurate with the glory of the grace he gave us** (literally, "unto praise of glory of the grace of him, which he graced us"), and its condensations in vv. 12 and 14, dividing the passage into three periods, function like the words, *Barukh attah, Adonai*, which close each of the nineteen *b'rakhot* of the *'Amidah*.

3 ***Adonai***. The Greek word "*theos*," which means "God," is used here for God's personal name, Hebrew *yud-heh-vav-heh*, written "*YHVH*," "Yahweh" or "Jehovah" in English and spoken aloud as "***Adonai***" (see Mt 1:20N). In the Septuagint "*YHVH*" is rendered by "*theos*" more than 250 times.

4 **He chose us... before the creation of the universe**. On predestination versus free will see Ro 9:19–21&N, Pp 2:12–13&N

5 **We would be his sons**. Compare Ro 8:15, 29; Ga 4:5.

6 **Grace**, Greek *charis* (which gives us the English words "charity" and "charismatic"), corresponds usually to the *Tanakh*'s Hebrew word "*chen*" ("favor, grace") and occasionally to "*chesed*" ("loving-kindness").

7 **Through the shedding of his blood, we are set free**. One of the Hebrew words corresponding to Greek *lutrôsis* ("redemption, ransom") is "*padut*," of which another form is "*pidyon*" (as in "*pidyon-haben*," redemption of the [firstborn] son, referred to at Lk 2:22–24&N). Moshe Ben-Maeir (1904–1978), a pioneer Israeli Messianic Jew, explained the connection between ransom and blood in a short commentary on Ephesians:

> "*Pidyon* has in it the idea of exchange, of substitution. In the *Torah* the Law of Ransom is stated at Exodus 13:13, 34:20. Every firstborn male and donkey must be ransomed. In Numbers 3, 22,000 Levites became substitutes for 22,000 of Israel's firstborn males, and the remaining 273, for whom there were no Levites, were ransomed by 1,365 shekels. In 1 Samuel 14, Jonathan came under sentence of death for transgressing a public oath his father made in his absence. Yet although King Saul condemned him to die, the sentence was not carried out, because the people objected. But law is law, not to be ignored. So they ransomed him, and thus legally prevented his being put to death.
>
> "We too, like Jonathan, have come under the sentence of death. Jonathan was condemned to death even though he had been unaware of King Saul's oath and order. We are condemned to death, even though we have not sinned after the manner of the first Adam (see Romans 5:12–14). Like Jonathan, we must either die or be ransomed. Jonathan and the Israel firstborn were ransomed with money. Money equals blood. One of the names for money in Hebrew is *damim*, plural of *dam*, blood, because it represents man's labor and risks. It is a Mishnaic term.
>
> "But money cannot redeem from eternal death. Man has nothing with which to ransom himself or others (Psalm 49:8–9(7–8)); God himself must redeem him from the power of the grave (Psalm 49:16(15)). But of God it is written, 'I have found a ransom' (Job 33:24); and that ransom is the blood of the Messiah." (Adapted from Moshe Ben-Maeir, *How A Jew Explains Ephesians*, Netivyah, P.O. Box 8043, Jerusalem 91080, 1978, pp. 23–25)

9 **He has made known to us his secret plan** (see 3:3–9). Greek *mustêrion* gives us the English word "mystery" but means "something previously concealed but now revealed." Hence the emphasis on God's foreordained purpose (vv. 4-5, this verse, v. 11, and 3:9, 11). Also see Ro 11:25N.

11–14 **We** Jews (vv. 11–12) are contrasted with **you** Gentiles (vv. 13–14). See 2:3N.

An inheritance (vv. 11, 14, 18; 5:5). Moshe Ben-Maeir called attention to an uncommon Hebrew word for the important concept of inheritance, "*morashah*," in the two places where it appears in the *Tanakh*: Deuteronomy 33:4, "Moshe commanded us a *Torah*, the inheritance of the congregation of Israel"; and Exodus 6:8, "I will bring you into the Land, which I swore to give to Avraham, Yitzchak and Ya'akov, and I will give it to you as an inheritance; I am *Adonai*." He wrote,

> "We Messianic Jews hold on to the *morashah* and have cast away neither the *Torah* nor our rights to *Eretz-Israel* [the Land of Israel]. We remain part and parcel of the chosen people." (*How A Jew Explains Ephesians*, pp. 31–33)

Verse 11 is speaking of Jews, whose inheritance is both spiritual (*Torah*) and physical (the Land). The *Torah* leads directly to Yeshua (Ro 10:4&N), through whom Gentiles share in the spiritual inheritance (vv. 13–14). Also through Yeshua the Jewish people receive the Land in perpetuity (2C 1:20&N).

17 **The God of our Lord Yeshua the Messiah** is **the glorious Father**, not Yeshua himself. Sha'ul distinguishes God from Yeshua without contradicting his view that in Yeshua, "bodily, lives the fullness of all that God is" (Co 2:9&N).

20–23a These verses introduce the theme of spiritual warfare, which returns at 2:2, 3:9–10 and 4:26–27 and is developed most fully at 6:10–18.

Verse 20 alludes to Psalm 110:1, cited frequently in the New Testament (see Mt 22:44N):

> "*Adonai* said to my Lord, 'Sit at my right hand,
> Until I make your enemies your footstool.'"

Verse 22 pivots on the last phrase to quote "**put all things under his feet**" from Psalm 8 (see MJ 2:6–10&NN for an application of Psalm 8 to Yeshua).

The somatic imagery continues, with Yeshua himself the **head** (v. 22; compare v. 10, 1C 11:3) and the Messianic Community **his body** (as at 2:16; 4:4, 12, 16; 5:30; Ro 12:5; 1C 10:17; Co 1:24, 2:19; the comparison is detailed at 1C 6:15–17, 12:11–27). In Ephesians the Messianic Community (Greek *ekklêsia*, usually rendered "church"; see Mt 16:18N) is also called a building (2:20–22, 1C 3:16–17) and compared with a wife (5:25–33, Rv 19:7–9).

23b **The full expression of him who fills all creation**, literally, "the fullness (Greek *plêrôma*) of him (God) who fills all things with everything." "*Plêrôma*" was a technical term used by Gnostics to refer to the totality of angels or "aeons" that supposedly mediated between God and humanity. Gnosticism itself was a philosophically oriented system of self-perfection through knowledge which offered a cheap substitute for both Judaism and Christianity — cheap in that, like many New Age and other modern variants, it skirted and minimized the issue of sin.

In Ephesians and Colossians Sha'ul counters the Gnostic heresy by co-opting its jargon to express biblical truth. We learn in these letters that Sha'ul prays for the believers in Ephesus to be "filled with all the *plêrôma* of God" (3:19); that "it pleased God to have his *plêrôma* live in his Son" (Co 1:19&N); that "in him [the Messiah], bodily, lives the *plêrôma* of all that God is" (Co 2:9); and that believers, corporately as the Messianic Community, constitute the Messiah's **body** and thus **the** ***plêrôma*** **of him who fills all creation** (this verse) — but unlike the Gnostics, Sha'ul discusses sin in the very next sentence. Therefore the aim of believers should be to "arrive… at the standard of maturity set by the Messiah's *plêrôma*" (4:13). Sha'ul takes the wind out of Gnosticism's sails by proclaiming that its aim of attaining the *plêrôma* cannot be reached by its means, but only by biblical means, only by joining the Body of the Messiah through trusting in and being faithful to Yeshua.

CHAPTER 2

2 **The ruler of the powers of the air** is the Adversary, Satan (see 6:11–12).

3 **We all once lived this way. All** of us did — "we" Jews too, just like "you" Gentiles, who "used to be dead" (v. 1). Thus Sha'ul introduces the topic of how Jews and Gentiles have been joined together into a single people of God through the Messiah. This discussion dominates Chapters 2–3, having been hinted at already through referring to God's "secret plan" (1:9) and the mention of "we" Jews and "you" Gentiles at 1:11–14&N. Earlier, in his letter to the Romans, which occupies itself with the same topic, Sha'ul in turn singled out for special attention both Jews (Ro 2:17ff.) and Gentiles (Ro 11:13ff.).

5–6 Compare Ro 5:6–8; 6:3–5, 11. Through being in union with the Messiah, believers share his position and so are **seated… with him in heaven** "at the right hand of God" (1:20).

8–10 **Grace** (favor, loving-kindness; see 1:6N), **trusting** (faith; see Ac 3:16N, Ga 2:16cN) and **actions** (works, deeds) are related thusly: God's **grace** is his unearned and unmerited favor and loving-kindness toward human beings. Included in this **grace** is the **gift** of having enough faith to believe the Good News of Yeshua the Messiah; yet this gift is not restricted to a few but is available to everyone (Ti 2:11). When a person is **trusting** in this Good News, that is evidence that God's **grace** has in fact come to apply individually to him. To the extent that we are **trusting**, God can mold us, so that we become **of God's making**, able to carry out the **good actions already prepared by God for us to do**. If we don't do these **good actions**, it shows that we are not believers after all. There is no such thing as faith apart from the works to which faith must lead; "faith without works is dead" (Ya 2:14–26); **trusting** that does not lead to **good actions** cannot save and is not a channel for God's **grace**.

On the other hand, works without faith cannot save the one who does them. Non-Messianic Judaism implicitly recognizes that good works alone do not buy salvation, as the British Messianic Jew Eric Lipson points out by writing that in Judaism,

> "Great stress is laid on doing good works, privately and corporately; but the prayers pleading for forgiveness (*s'lichot*) quote Isaiah's admission, 'All our righteous deeds are as filthy rags' [Isaiah 64:5(6)]. So Israel prays, '*Avinu malkenu*, our Father, our King, be gracious unto us and answer us, for we have done no good things of any worth. Deal with us in charity and loving-kindness and save us.'"(*The Hebrew Christian*, Spring 1984, p. 17)

No work is a good work in relation to rewarding its doer (even though others may benefit) if it does not stem from faith in God, which today entails trusting in his Son Yeshua the Messiah (Yn 14:6, 1 Yn 2:23). The crowds in the Galil asked Yeshua, "What should we do in order to perform the works of God?" His answer was, "Here's what the work of God is: to trust in the one he sent!" (Yn 6:28–29).

9 You were not delivered by your own actions; therefore no one should boast. "What room is left for boasting? None at all" (Ro 3:27, in response to Ro 3:21–26). "Therefore — as the *Tanakh* says — 'Let anyone who wants to boast, boast about *Adonai*'"(1C 1:31, quoting Jeremiah 9:23(24) in response to 1C 1:17–30).

11–22 These verses, often misused by Christians against Messianic Jews, are actually part of the charter for Messianic Judaism. They are fundamental to understanding both the nature of the *Torah*, which still exists and is binding on believers, and the relationship between Jews and Gentiles in the Messianic Community (1:22).

11 Farther on in this passage we will have occasion to remind ourselves that Sha'ul is speaking here to **Gentiles**, not Jews. On the word "Gentiles," Greek *ethnê,* equivalent to Hebrew *goyim,* see Mt 5:46N. Some Christians base on 1C 10:32 a false doctrine that once a Gentile comes to faith he is no longer a Gentile but a Christian (see note there). The present verse, like Ro 11:13&N, refutes that contention by calling Gentile Christians "**Gentiles**"; just as Ga 2:13, by calling Messianic Jews "Jews," contradicts the notion that a Jew who trusts in Yeshua is no longer Jewish (see note there).

Sha'ul here teaches two facts about Gentiles. First, being a Gentile is a matter of birth — **you Gentiles by birth**, literally, "you the Gentiles in flesh" — and is therefore not changed when a Gentile comes to believe the Gospel, although it does change if he becomes a Jewish proselyte (see Mt 23:15&N, Ga 5:2–4&N, Ac 16:1–3&NN).

Second, even though there is a real spiritual difference between Jews and Gentiles based on God's having dealt with them differently (as summarized in v. 12), the distinction popularly made was not based on this. Nor was it based on innate differences — there are none, "since all have sinned and come short of earning God's praise" (Ro 3:23). Rather, the Judaizers and their Gentile clients made external, artificial, "fleshly" distinctions. They used the fact that Gentiles were **called the Uncircumcised by those who, merely because of an operation on their flesh, are called the Circumcised** as an excuse for holding uncircumcised Gentiles in contempt, even though a godly believer is to refrain from boasting (v. 9&N; Mt 3:9&N; Ro 2:17–23&N, 3:27–31&NN; 1C 1:31&N). The Messiah has ended any imaginable ground for such invidious comparisons, as explained in vv. 13–16.

12 You Gentiles **were at that time** — "in your former state" (v. 11), when you were "dead because of your sins" (vv. 1–10) — lacking in five respects:

(1) You were **without any relationship to the Messiah**, since "Messiah" is entirely a Jewish concept. The word "Christ" has such a Gentile ring to Jews that they sometimes forget that the very idea of "Christ" is not Gentile but Jewish. The relationship to the Messiah is mentioned first because it is the direct means through which the other four deficiencies are remedied.

(2) **You were estranged**, excluded, alienated, **from the national life of Israel**. The Greek word translated "**national life**" is "*politeia*," which gives us English words like "polity" and "politics." Arndt and Gingrich's *A Greek-English Lexicon of the New Testament* offers as possible meanings "citizenship; commonwealth, state; way of life, conduct." But Gerhard Kittel's *Theological Dictionary of the New Testament* points out that in the Septuagint, "*politeia*"

> "does not mean civil rights, constitution, or state, [but] rather the pious order of life which, ordained by the Law of Moses, is inherited from the fathers. [With one exception it] is a religious and moral concept rather than a political concept; it denotes the 'walk' determined by the Mosaic Law." (Volume 6, p. 526)

The same article states that in the present verse "*politea*" means "civil rights" and is

> "used in the figurative sense of the privileged religious position of Israel as the recipient of the promise,"

corresponding to deficiency (3) below. But this conclusion strikes me as capricious, tendentious and antisemitic. Why should "*politea*" be deprived of its normal meaning, with its implication that Gentile Christians are joined to and obligated with the Jewish people.

My own understanding is very different. Gentiles should not think of their union with Israel as only a matter of rights and privileges. Rather, it implies an obligation to observe a godly way of life that has its origin in God's relationship with the Jewish people. More than that, it implies an obligation to relate as family to the Jewish community to whom their faith has joined them (Ro 11:17–24&NN, Ro 15:27&N).

When Ruth joined Israel, she said, "Your people shall be my people," even before she said, "Your God shall be my God" (Ruth 1:16). Gentile Christians should remember that being "no longer foreigners and strangers" but "fellow-citizens with God's people" (v. 19) means being fellows as well as citizens, i.e., being involved with the Jewish people, both Messianic and non-Messianic. Gentile Christians who regard Jewish Christians as the strangers and themselves as the rightful possessors, and those who accept Jewish believers but reject nonbelieving Jews, are not submitting to the message of these verses. Sha'ul does not say that Israel was estranged from the communal life of Gentiles, but the opposite, implying that Israel constitutes the norm and the center of gravity, not the Gentiles. In Ro 11:16–26, he portrays Gentiles as wild olive branches grafted into the cultivated olive tree which is Israel, the Jewish people, and cautions Gentile Christians against pride.

See also Ro 11:26a on "all Israel" and Ga 6:16&N on "the Israel of God," because these discuss the key word "**Israel**," which appears only here in the book of Ephesians.

(3) Because you Gentiles were estranged from the communal life of Israel, you were **foreigners to the covenants embodying God's promise**; these include the covenant with Avraham (see Galatians 3–4&NN, Romans 4&NN), the covenant with Moshe, and the New Covenant with Yeshua (see Messianic Jews 8&NN). The New Covenant was given not to Gentiles but to Israel; Gentiles are foreigners to it except through faith, which, as Sha'ul points out, makes them full participants.

(4–5) **You were in this world**, fourth, **without hope and**, fifth, **without God**; for apart from God there is only the false hope offered by false religions and non-religions, which sooner or later reveal themselves as disappointing illusions. Otto Rank, the Jewish psychoanalyst who broke with his teacher Sigmund Freud, wrote that everyone needs and produces illusions to sustain himself in a world without purpose. He could write such a peculiar thing because he did not believe in the God of Israel. Jean-Paul Sartre and Albert Camus, as atheists who were also existentialists, bravely faced up to the hypocrisy and self-deception of depending on illusions but gave no satisfactory remedy for the resulting hopelessness, other than suggesting that it is more "hopeful" to face the reality of hopelessness than to retreat into fantasy. But hopelessness cannot be palmed off as hope, nor is it reality, except for people without God. Through the centuries many people whose intellectual capacity and integrity match those of Rank, Sartre and Camus have found that the Bible not only fits the real world but provides a spiritual reality that does offer hope in an otherwise hopeless world.

In conclusion, the difference between Gentiles and Jews prior to the Messiah's coming was not merely the external fact that the latter were circumcised, but the spiritual and ontological fact that God dealt with them differently. God chose the Jewish people to receive certain promises and called them to exemplify God's involvement in human life and history. Through making the Bible known to the world, through presenting an example of dedication to God even when apart from Yeshua, but most of all through Yeshua the Messiah himself and his Jewish followers, the Jews have in a measure fulfilled that calling. By being joined to Israel, as explained in the following verses, believing Gentiles have a share in both the promises and the calling.

13 Far off… brought near. The language anticipates vv. 14 and 17.

Through the shedding of the Messiah's blood, literally, "by the blood of the Messiah." The things detailed in vv. 14–22 came about not through magical properties of Yeshua's blood but through his "bloody sacrificial death" atoning for all, Gentiles along with Jews (Ro 3:25&N, 29–30; Yn 3:16)

14 Although ***shalom*** means more than peace (Mt 10:12N), certainly peace is the main emphasis here. **He is our *shalom***. Not only does Yeshua make peace between Jews and Gentiles, but he himself *is* that peace. **He**, living in believing Jews and Gentiles, *is* what **has made us both one**, for our oneness is the one Messiah living in both.

The *m'chitzah* which divided us, literally, "the middle wall of the boundary fence." Hebrew ***m'chitzah*** means, literally, "that which divides something in half." In every Orthodox synagogue, a *m'chitzah*, a dividing wall, separates the men in the congregation from the women. Conservative and Reform Jewish practice happens to reflect New Testament truth about men and women, since these denominations have done away with the *m'chitzah* in the synagogue. Galatians 3:28&N makes the same point by saying that in the Messiah "there is neither Jew nor Gentile,... neither male nor female."

Actually, Sha'ul's imagery is probably not that of the synagogue but of the Temple. Surrounding the Temple was a wall with a sign "which forbade any foreigner to go in, on pain of death" (Josephus, *Antiquities of the Jews* 15:11:5; compare *Wars of the Jews* 5:5:2, 6:2:4). This was the "boundary fence" between Jews and Gentiles (there was also a court for women only). Just as the veil of the Temple was torn in two when the Messiah died (Mt 27:52), allowing everyone united with the Messiah to enter God's presence as into the Holy of Holies (a privilege previously reserved for the *cohen hagadol*, MJ 9:6–14, 10:19–22), so too the Messiah has removed the barrier preventing Gentiles from mixing with and being counted with God's people (except by converting to Judaism). Oddly, it was the false accusation that Sha'ul had brought the Gentile, Trophimus, beyond this barrier dividing the Court of the Gentiles from the Court of the Jews which inflamed the crowds in the Temple and led to Sha'ul's arrest there (Ac 21:27–32).

The King James Version, keeping fairly close to the Greek text, renders this, "the middle wall of partition." One of the most frequent and bothersome accusations made by uninformed Christians against Messianic Judaism is that Messianic Jews "are trying to build up again between Jews and Gentiles 'the middle wall of partition' which the Messiah has broken down." Without exception the charge is made by those who do not understand what Sha'ul is saying or what Messianic Judaism is really trying to accomplish.

Sha'ul's point is that Gentiles are no longer separated but can now join the Jewish people and be one with them as God's people through faith in the Jewish Messiah, Yeshua. The partition is down, the Gentiles can join us! The critics understand it the other way round: the partition is down, so that once Jews believe in their own Messiah they no longer have the right to maintain their Jewish identity but must conform to Gentile patterns. Amazing! And certainly not what Sha'ul himself did (Ac 13:9&N).

The object of Messianic Judaism is not to destroy fellowship between Jews and Gentiles in the Messiah's Body but to preserve it; a review of the notes at 1C 7:18b; Ga 1:13, 2:14b, 3:28 will suffice to show that. At the same time Messianic Judaism seeks to provide a framework in which Jewish believers can express their faith in Yeshua through and along with their Jewishness. The Scriptural warrant for this is not only Sha'ul's own practice but also his principle of presenting the Gospel in a way that minimizes the obstacles to its acceptance by its hearers (Ga 1:17, 1C 9:19–22&NN). Messianic Judaism ought to have been preserved continuously since the time of Yeshua, for there have always been believing Jews; there should have been no need to create it afresh. The movement is assertive today only because anti-Jewish pressure within the Church did away with and continued to oppose Jewish expressions of New Testament truth. That the New Covenant itself was made with Israel (v. 12, Jeremiah 31:30–33) adds irony to insult.

On the other hand, frequently those Gentiles who raise the bugaboo of the "middle wall of partition" are themselves the ones who are building it! For they would have Jews enter the Body of the Jewish Messiah only if they will conform to Gentile customs and ways and give up their Jewishness. Members of no other culture are put upon in this way, only Jews. Their idea of Sha'ul's remark that the Messiah **has made us both one** is that the "**one**" is Gentile!

15a The Messiah "has broken down the *m'chitzah* which divided us" (v. 14b) **by destroying in his own body the enmity occasioned by the *Torah*, with its commands set forth in the form of ordinances**. Following is a literal translation of vv. 14b–15a; the commas in brackets appear in some of the manuscripts which have punctuation but not in all:

> For he is our peace, the [person] having made the both [things] one, and the middle wall of the fence having broken, the enmity[,] in the flesh of him[,] the *Torah* of the commandments in decrees[,] having abolished, in order that the two [persons] he might create in himself into one new person....

Two questions call for attention here. First, some, considering the last two bracketed commas spurious, take "the enmity" as an explanation of what "the middle wall of the fence" is, so that Sha'ul is understood to be saying that Yeshua (1) broke the middle wall which is the enmity between Jews and Gentiles, and (2) abolished the *Torah*. However, many agree with me that "the enmity" goes not with "the middle wall" but with "the *Torah*."

Second, what is the grammatical significance of Sha'ul's placing "the *Torah*" in apposition with "the enmity"? If he means that the enmity is identical with the *Torah*, then when Yeshua abolished the enmity, he necessarily abolished the *Torah* too, in contradiction with his own statement at Mt 5:17. This makes little sense; and in fact, no one seriously considers the *Torah* to *be* enmity. My rendering offers another view, that since "the enmity" and "the *Torah*" are separated by the phrase, "in the flesh of him," the conceptual relationship is looser and requires more explicit specification — which I have provided in the words "**occasioned by**." **The enmity** is not **the *Torah***. Nor did the *Torah* "cause" the enmity directly — see Ro 7:5–14 for Sha'ul's own refutation of the idea that the *Torah* causes sin of any kind, and enmity between Jews and Gentiles is certainly sin. Rather, that passage shows that although the *Torah* is itself "holy" (Ro 7:12), it *occasions* sin (in this case enmity between Jews and Gentiles) by stimulating people's sinful propensities (see Ro 5:12–21&N).

This enmity between Jews and Gentiles had four components:

(1) Gentile envy of the special status accorded by God to Israel in the *Torah*.
(2) Jewish pride at being chosen.
(3) Gentile resentment of that pride.
(4) Mutual dislike of each other's customs. This is a common cause of friction between cultures, but in this instance, Jewish customs are different for a unique reason. They did not merely evolve; rather, they were the Jewish people's response to **the *Torah*, with its commands set forth in the form of ordinances**.

This is why it is appropriate to say that **the enmity** between Jews and Gentiles was **occasioned by the *Torah***.

The enmity was destroyed in the Messiah's body when he died for all sinners, Jews and Gentiles alike. Whoever catches a vision of himself as the undeserving object of God's grace, saved from eternally ongoing destruction by the Messiah's atoning death in his place, realizes that in comparison with this salvation the distinction between Jew and Gentile is insignificant. Isaiah, faced with a comparable display of God's holiness, said, "Woe is me, for I am undone!" (Isaiah 6:5). Jew and Gentile are equally undone before the Messiah; the Messiah destroys the enmity by showing Jew and Gentile equally needy at the foot of his execution-stake. This is what Sha'ul means by saying that in the Messiah "there is neither Jew nor Gentile" (Ga 3:28, Co 3:11).

Moreover, the cancelling of enmity between Jew and Gentile is not merely theoretical when both have been born again through trusting in Yeshua the Messiah. Inspiring examples can be found among Messianic Jews and truly believing Arab Christians in the Land of Israel today. Where the world expects hate or at best wary tolerance can be found a degree of trust and love from the Messiah that goes beyond politics; nothing testifies more eloquently to the truth of the Gospel. Arab and Jewish believers can express disagreement in dialogue over political issues while remaining united in the bond of the Messiah's love.

The Jerusalem Bible, prepared by Roman Catholics, is the one prominent English version that agrees with the *Jewish New Testament* on this passage. It translates 2:14b–15a, "destroying in his own person the hostility caused by the rules and decrees of the Law." Unfortunately, its note on v. 15 says that Jesus annulled the Law! And more unfortunately, the revised edition, the New Jerusalem Bible, reverts to a more traditional antisemitic rendering, "destroying in his own person the hostility, that is, the Law of commandments with its decrees."

Two other versions, Phillips and Moffatt, say that the Messiah destroyed the "hostility" or the "feud" of the Law, not the Law itself. Although these renderings express an unfriendly view toward the Law, at least they avoid asserting that the Law has been abolished.

But usually this verse is rendered so as to say that the Messiah did away with the *Torah*. Those who think so can give only lip service to Yeshua's own statement that he came not to destroy the *Torah* but to fill it up with its full meaning (Mt 5:17&N); only lip service to Yeshua's interpretations of specific commandments making them more stringent, not less so (Mt 5:21–48); only lip service to Sha'ul's assertion that "the *Torah* is holy; that is, the commandment is holy, just and good" (Ro 7:12); only lip service to his conclusion that the Gospel does not abolish *Torah* but confirms it (Ro 3:31). In order to arrive at such an opinion, other Pauline passages must be misconstrued as meaning that the *Torah* has been brought to an end (Ga 2:15–21&NN, 3:21–26&NN; Ro 9:30–10:10&NN).

The scholars who think this verse teaches that the Messiah abolished the *Torah* often offer arguments that either fail to convince or actually support the opposing view. By way of illustration, consider Francis Foulkes, *The Epistle of Paul to the Ephesians*, in the Tyndale Commentary series, pp. 82–83; my own responses are indented.

> "The law of commandments contained in ordinances [had to be] abolished.... Peter was sent to Cornelius and bidden to regard no longer the distinction between ceremonial cleanness and uncleanness (Acts 10)."

Not true: *kashrut* was not abolished (see Ga 2:11–16&NN), although the custom of regarding Gentile homes as unclean was indeed abolished; but the latter was not *Torah* anyhow (see Ac 10:28N).

> "The Church in its council at Jerusalem had agreed that there was no longer to

> be a barrier because the Jews had circumcision and all the other ordinances of the law, and the Gentiles did not (Acts 15)."

This does not mean that the *Torah* was abolished at the Jerusalem council, only that Gentiles did not need to become Jews in order to become Yeshua's disciples.

> "The Lord came not to destroy the law, but to fulfil (Mt 5:17)."

The last word means "fill up" (see Mt 5:17&N), but even rendering it "fulfil" gives no ground for thinking of the *Torah* as having been abolished when three words earlier in that verse Yeshua said he did *not* come to destroy the Law!

> "Much of it (e.g. the sacrificial ritual) was preparation for, and foreshadowing of, the Christ, and so was fulfilled by what He did when He came."

This kind of "fulfilling" does not abolish; one may say it transforms the older practice (MJ 7:11–12&NN) or gives new significance to it. For more on the sacrificial system see Messianic Jews 6–10&NN.

> "The moral demands and principles of the law were not lightened by Jesus, but made fuller and more far-reaching (Mt 5:21–48)."

Also this is not abolishing! In fact, Foulkes' remark here supports my earlier point about Mt 5:17.

> "In the discipline of obedience that its detailed regulations demanded, and as the revealer of right and wrong, it was intended to lead to Christ (Gal 3:24)."

My rendering of that verse is: "The *Torah* functioned as a harsh disciplinarian until the Messiah came," not "The Law was a schoolmaster leading us to Christ" (see note there). Even so, being led to Christ does not mean the Law is abolished.

> "In an absolute sense it cannot be said to be made of no effect in Christ (Rom 3:31)."

This is yet another argument *against* the *Torah*'s abolition by the Messiah, as noted in connection with Mt 5:21–48. Or, to make my point differently, if the Law is "in an absolute sense" *not* "of no effect," then (with the double negative removed) it is "in an absolute sense" of effect, effective, in force.

> "But as a code 'specific, rigid, and outward, fulfilled in external ordinances' (Westcott), and so serving to separate Jews and Gentiles, it was abolished (cf. Col 2:20–22)."

First, this description of the *Torah* is wrong; Cranfield and Burton do a better job — see Ga 2:16bN, where these scholars are quoted. What Westcott characterizes is not *Torah* but legalism; and if anything is "abolished" in this verse, it is not *Torah* but legalism. Second, Co 2:20–22 does not apply to *Torah* but to legalism; and the context is not Judaism but paganism, as implied by Sha'ul's use of the term, "elemental spirits," found in a similar context at Ga 4:1–11; see notes in both places and at Ro 14:1.

Elsewhere I have explained that while the *Torah* is not abolished, priorities within it are changed (Ga 6:2N). Surely that is what is done here; we know already from Ga 2:11–14&NN that fellowship between Jews and Gentiles in the Messianic Community is a more important *mitzvah* than any of the commands intended to separate Jews from Gentiles, such as *kashrut*. In this sense, fellowship is what rabbinic Judaism calls a "weighty" command, while the kinds of **commandments set forth in the form of ordinances** referred to here are, by comparison, "light" ones. Re-prioritization is not abolition. Where Jewish believers can carry out the "lighter" *mitzvot* without compromising their own relationship to believing Gentiles or otherwise transgressing "the *Torah*'s true meaning, which the Messiah upholds" (Ga 6:2), there is no reason not to do so — as Yeshua himself urged (Mt 23:23).

In this framework of thought one could understand the passage to be saying that for his Body, the Messianic Community, Yeshua abolished not the *Torah* in its entirety, but the *takkanot* (rabbinic ordinances) relating to the separation of Jews and Gentiles spiritually. The middle wall of the spiritual temple is done away with forever.

15b–22 The ideas of vv. 14–15a are restated, with focus on the oneness. The basic oneness is **union with himself**; this produces **from the two groups**, Jews and Gentiles, **a single new humanity** which is **a single body**. That body is both the physical body of the Messiah, **executed on a stake as a criminal** (see Mt 10:38N), and the Messianic Community (1:20–23a&N). Through the Messiah (Ro 8:9–11; Yn 14:26, 15:26) comes **one Spirit** (v. 18), and the word "**union**" appears three times in vv. 21–22. The theme of oneness returns for its fullest expression at 4:4–6; compare Yn 17:20–26, 1C 12:4–6.

In this entire passage Sha'ul is writing to Gentiles, and his object is to reassure them that they are fully God's people, that because of their faith in the Messiah and his work no barrier exists between them and Jews — Gentiles are not second-class citizens of the Kingdom. His purpose is not to downplay Jewish distinctives, but to "up-play" what God has now done for Gentiles. To find in these verses ground for opposing Messianic Judaism is simply to misappropriate them for a purpose Sha'ul never dreamed of.

17 Compare vv. 12–13.

20–22 The metaphor of the Messianic Community as a **building** is found also at 1 Ke 2:4–8. Yeshua as the **cornerstone** alludes to Psalm 118:22–23, which he himself quoted (Mt 21:42–43); see also Isaiah 28:16 (compare Ro 9:33). Corporately, the Messiah's Body is **growing into a holy temple** (as at 1C 3:16–17, 2C 6:16); while individually, each believer's body is already a temple for the Holy Spirit (1C 6:19).

CHAPTER 3

1 The letter was written from prison; compare 6:20.

3 The **secret plan** (see 1:9N) consists of two elements: (1) the bringing of Gentiles into the people of God on an equal footing, previously known but not nearly so clearly (v. 5&N), and (2) making known to spiritual beings in heaven, through the existence of the Messianic Community, the many-sided wisdom of God (vv. 9–10; see 1:20–23aN).

I have... written about it, about the first part of the mystery, **briefly**, at 2:11–22; verse 6 below summarizes that passage.

5 In the past there was less knowledge than now of the equality of Jews and Gentiles as God's people, but there was some knowledge, since at Ac 15:13–18 Ya'akov quotes the prophet Amos to make this very point.

13 See vv. 1–2.

14–21 This resumes Sha'ul's prayer of 1:17–19.

18 **The breadth, length, height and depth of the Messiah's love**. Like many Jews I think of myself as broadminded and recoil from the narrowness of bigots and fundamentalists of all religions and non-religions. Therefore it reassures me to find that Yeshua's **love** has **breadth;** one can see the breadth of his love throughout the Gospel narratives. In addition, since his **love** has **length** it continues forever, since it has **height** it carries one's spirit upward into the very presence of God, and since it has **depth** it meets anyone even in the most dire distress and depression. Compare Psalm 139.

21 **From generation to generation forever**. The language is that of the Psalms (*e.g.*, Psalms 48:13; 119:90; 145:4, 13).

CHAPTER 4

1 **Therefore**. Because of everything God has done in Chapters 1–3 Sha'ul calls on believers to do everything in Chapters 4–6, all of which is summed up in the phrase, "**lead a life worthy of the calling to which you have been called**." Compare Ro 8:1&N, 12:1&N.

2–6 First on the list of specific commands is to be a united body of believers. Yeshua's sole prayer specifically for those who would trust in him throughout the ages was that they should be one (Yn 17:21–23&N). Verses 2–3 indicate how we are to behave toward one another in order to realize this unity, while vv. 4–6 review the objective ground for that unity (see 2:15b–22&N), and vv. 7–13 explain how the Messiah himself forwards it by giving appropriate gifts.

Verses 4–6 may be a fragment of a creedal hymn (like the Jewish *Yigdal*, based on Maimonides' creed). Scholars find evidence of other early hymns in the New Testament; see 5:14&N; Yn 1:1–18&N; Ro 11:33–36&N; Pp 2:6–11&N; 1 Ti 1:17, 2:5–6, 3:16, 6:15–16; 2 Ti 2:11–13&N; Yd 24–25; and many examples in the book of Revelation (see references in Rv 4:11N).

7–11 Sha'ul's phrase, "**freely given**" (v. 7), is supported by a verse from Psalms quoted in v. 8, giving a basis in Scripture for the *midrash* on "freely given" in vv. 9–11.

7 Compare Ro 12:3–8, 1C 12:4–30.

8 **He gave gifts to mankind**. English translations of this line in Psalm 68:19(18) say that God "received gifts from men"; the Hebrew text, "*lakachta matanot ba'adam*," means, literally, "You took gifts in the man." Non-Messianic Jews sometimes complain that the New Testament misquotes the *Tanakh*, but Sha'ul is not alone in changing "took" to "**gave**." The Aramaic of the Targum on Psalms applies the "you" to Moshe and has: "You, prophet Moshe, ascended to the firmament, you took captives captive, you taught the words of the Law and gave them as gifts to the children of men." Likewise, the Peshitta (the Aramaic version of the Bible dating from the 1st–4th centuries C.E.) has, "You ascended on high, led captivity captive and gave gifts to the sons of men."

9 **The lower parts, that is, the earth**. The Messiah was a pre-existent being, the Word, co-equal with God, who, for the sake of mankind, came to earth as a man (Yn 1:1, 14; Pp 2:5–8). It would be less to the point if Sha'ul were saying here that Yeshua descended into Sh'ol after his death (Ac 2:27, 31; Ro 10:7; 1 Ke 3:18–20); but if this is indeed what he means, the phrase should be rendered "the lower parts of the earth" (as opposed to its upper parts).

10 In any case, the Messiah died. Saying he **went up** implies that he was resurrected. Then he **went up, far above all of heaven**, that is, to the very presence of God (compare Pp 2:9–11, Co 1:16–20). All this assures that we believers too will be resurrected in the future and that the Spirit is at work in our lives now (Yn 14:26, 15:26; 1C 15:1–58).

11 These are Yeshua's gifts to the Messianic Community. Because the Greek is ambiguous, some take the two terms "**shepherds**" (pastors) and "**teachers**" to be speaking of one office — "shepherd-teachers." Pastoring and teaching are overlapping yet distinguishable skills. **Emissaries** (apostles) found congregations. **Prophets** speak God's word. **Proclaimers of the Good News** (evangelists) communicate the Good News so that people turn from sin and accept God's forgiveness through the Messiah. **Pastors** carry on from there, discipling and counseling new and old believers in living the Messianic life. **Teachers** communicate and apply biblical truth. None is to boast about his position but to "equip God's people," as explained in vv. 12–13.

13–16 The New Covenant states that "they will not teach [each other], saying, 'Know *Adonai,'* because they will all know me" (Jeremiah 31:33(34)). This has not happened yet, and although the process has begun, we still need teachers (v. 12). How long? **Until we all arrive at the unity** (see vv. 2–6&N) **implied by trusting and knowing the Son of God**, and the other points of vv. 14–16 are fulfilled.

17–24 An analysis of what leads to immorality and amorality (e.g., **deceptive desires**, v. 22), and instruction in how to achieve right morality.

18 The conventional wisdom of our century is at odds with the Bible because it fails to see that **resisting God's will** suppresses **intelligence** and fosters **ignorance**.

27 **The adversary**. See Mt 4:1N.

30 **God's *Ruach HaKodesh***, rendered in most translations "the Holy Spirit of God." This phrase, which appears only here in the New Testament, explicitly equates the Holy Spirit with the Spirit of God. Also see MJ 3:2–4N.

CHAPTER 5

5 Compare Ga 5:19–21.

8 **Children of light**. The Essenes and other Jewish pietists used this term to denote God's elect. Compare also Yn 1:4–5, 8–9; 3:19–21; 12:36; 1 Yn 1:5–8.

14 The quotation is not from the *Tanakh*. "Like the Essenes, the early Christians used to sing hymns at dawn in praise of the 'Sun of Righteousness' (cf. Malachi 4:2). These lines may be from one such hymn. See also Yn 1:1–17." (Hugh Schonfield, *The Original New Testament*, p. 389).

5:18–6:9 Given a kernel of equality in that all are to **keep on being filled with the Spirit** (vv. 18–20) and to **submit to one another in fear of the Messiah** (v. 21), Sha'ul discusses three asymmetrical relationships: husband-wife (vv. 22–33), parents-children (6:1–4), and master-slave (6:5–9). Compare Co 3:16–4:1, 1 Ke 2:13–3:7.

5:22–25 **Wives should submit to their husbands as they do to the Lord** (compare 1C 11:3). **As for husbands, love your wives**. The asymmetry in the commands epitomizes the asymmetry in the marriage relationship. Sha'ul could have written, "Wives, love your husbands," and "Husbands, rule your wives." But men often find it all too easy to throw their weight around but hard to communicate love sensitively, in a self-giving fashion — for the standard Sha'ul sets is very high, **just as the Messiah loved the Messianic Community**, etc.

Likewise, women often find it easy and natural to express love but difficult to accept their husband's authority. Feminist objection to wifely submission is premised on the assumption that the husband does not obey the injunction to love his wife as the Messiah loved the Messianic Community (advice for a believing wife with an unbelieving husband is found at 1 Ke 3:1–6). In self-oriented marriages, arguments are between women who won't submit to their husbands and men who won't love their wives. In God-oriented marriages, arguments happen, but they have an altogether different character, because they are between men willing to go the second mile in loving and women willing to go the second mile in submitting. In such marriages Yeshua is the third partner; like a magnet over iron filings he orients things in the right direction.

Elsewhere Sha'ul says that "the head of a wife is her husband" (1C 11:3). Being the head, he is responsible to go first, to create the order of married life. But to do this he must be loving *first*, unconditionally, without waiting for or insisting on his wife's submitting first.

26b–27a A Jewish bride enters the ***mikveh*** (ritual bath) in order to be purified prior to the marriage ceremony, which is called *kiddushin* (literally, "being **set apart for God**").

Immersion. See Mt 3:1N, although the Greek word here and at Ti 3:5 is not "*baptismos*" but "*loutron*" ("washing").

27b Without spot, wrinkle or any such thing, as at Song of Songs 4:7, "You are altogether fair, my love, there is no blemish in you." Moreover, this is a condition required of sacrifices (v. 25b).

CHAPTER 6

4 Raise them with the Lord's kind of discipline and guidance, as did Avraham (Genesis 18:19). "The training you give a child does not leave him when he grows up" (Proverbs 22:6).

5–9 With the necessary changes, these verses apply to employer-employee relationships.

10–18 We are not struggling against human beings but against the unseen agents (1:20–23a&N) of **the Adversary**, Satan (Mt 4:1&N). This is why "the weapons we use to wage war are not worldly. On the contrary, they have God's power for demolishing strongholds" of demonic spirits (2C 2b–5&N). This description of **the armor and weaponry that God provides** confounds people who are used to fighting people by worldly methods and have no sensitivity to God's methods, which are: **truth, righteousness, readiness** grounded in **the Good News of *shalom*, trust, deliverance** (or: "salvation"), **the Word of God** given by **the Spirit**, and **prayers**. Unbelievers taken aback by the apparent triumphalism of the song, "Onward, Christian Soldiers," should understand that the "soldiers" in this song, that is, the believers in Yeshua, are not fighting to force non-Christians to convert, but to overcome demonic **principalities and powers** by God's prescribed methods.

17b Compare MJ 4:12–13.

18 A one-verse sermon on prayer; note the use three times of the word "**all**."

21 Tychicus. A believer from Asia Minor who accompanied Sha'ul to Jerusalem (Ac 20:4). Sha'ul sent him to Ephesus with this letter (this verse and 2 Ti 4:12) and the one to Colossae (Co 4:7) and perhaps to Titus in Crete (Ti 3:12).

THE LETTER FROM YESHUA'S EMISSARY SHA'UL (PAUL)
TO GOD'S PEOPLE LIVING IN PHILIPPI:

PHILIPPIANS

CHAPTER 1

1 Rabbi **Sha'ul** from Tarsus is Paul (Ac 13:9&N). He himself circumcised **Timothy** (Ac 16:1–3), who, as his closest co-worker (Ac 16:4–8, 17:14–15, 18:5, 19:22, 20:4), received two of Sha'ul's thirteen letters and is mentioned in eight others, also at MJ 13:23. **Philippi**, in Macedonia, was the first city in Greece evangelized by Sha'ul (Ac 16:9–40).

Congregation leaders and *shammashim*, which the King James Version renders "bishops and deacons," transliterating the Greek words "*episkopoi*" ("overseers, supervisors") and "*diakonoi*" ("those who serve"). Two terms similar to "*episkopoi*" are "*presbuteroi*" ("elders") and "*poimênoi*" ("shepherds," usually rendered "pastors"). In the New Testament these seem to be used sometimes interchangeably and sometimes not; those who think that they are not usually consider the office of *episkopos* higher, carrying responsibility for several congregations in a region rather than one (as with "bishops" today, as compared with "pastors"). In any case, these have responsibility for the spiritual progress of believers in their congregations and will have to render an account to God for them (MJ 13:17).

Two of the three major forms of congregational organization found in Christendom take their names from these Greek words: (1) the episcopal system, with a hierarchy of bishops largely controlled from the top (comparable with monarchy), (2) the opposite, the congregational system, wherein local congregations elect their own pastors and constitute the final authority (comparable with democracy), and (3) the presbyterian system, somewhere between, in which the congregation elects elders or "presbyters," who in turn appoint local pastors and elect general presbyters (something like a republic). The three major Christian denominations named for each of these systems are also examples of them (Episcopalian, Presbyterian, Congregational). All three systems can work and all can be abused. There is no scholarly consensus that the New Testament requires any one of them; the one agreed-on element of polity is that Yeshua is Lord.

The task of "deacons" is to care for the practical affairs of the Messianic Community, "serving tables" as distinct from "praying and serving the Word" (Ac 6:2, 4); Ac 6:1–6 tells how the first seven were appointed. The *Encyclopedia Judaica* describes the *shammash* (Yiddish *shammes*) as the

> "salaried beadle or sexton in the community, the synagogue, rabbinical court or a *chevrah* [cemetery committee]. A *shammash* performed a number of functions

varying in accordance with the measure of autonomy or the nature of the religious institutions he served: tax collector, bailiff, process server, secretary, messenger, almoner, all-around handyman, grave digger, or notary." (14:1292)

In the Messianic Community, the term "***shammashim***" does not mean salaried functionaries but persons appointed to serve without monetary remuneration in a spiritual office because of their spiritual qualifications. Sha'ul gives requirements for serving in the capacity of **congregation leader** at 1 Ti 3:1–7 and Ti 1:6–9; those for ***shammash*** are at Ac 6:3 and 1 Ti 3:8–13.

5 **You have shared** both financially (4:14–19, 2C 8:1–5, Ro 15:26) and by praying for my safety (v. 19, Pm 22) and for success in communicating the Gospel (Ro 6:19–20). Compare v. 7.

6 In an age when theology is done with slogans, one of the more sanguine and modest bumper stickers reads, "Be patient, God isn't finished with me yet." After someone has responded to God's call, God promises to continue making him ever more godly and holy, until **the Day of the Messiah Yeshua**'s return.

10 **So that you will be able to determine what is best**, instead of pursuing what is adequate yet falls short of the highest standard ("the good is the enemy of the best"), **and thus be pure and without blame for the Day of the Messiah** (compare v. 6).

11 Compare Ep 1:6 and last paragraph of Ep 1:3–14N.

12–14 Trusting in Yeshua the Messiah gives Sha'ul such strength (Co 1:26) and comfort (2C 1:3ff.) that, far from needing these himself from others, he from his prison cell can strengthen the brothers who are free and comfort those worrying about him with the assurance that the **Good News** is **advancing**, and that his own state is one of joy (v. 18b).

15–18a In God's providence, many have responded to the Good News of Yeshua the Messiah proclaimed by a hypocrite. It is the Gospel that saves, not the preacher. The insincere evangelist is storing up for himself judgment, but those who have come to Yeshua because of his words have entered eternal life.

21–24 Consider the charge that New Testament faith is otherworldly, selfish, oblivious to this world's pains. On the one hand, **death is gain** (v. 21); and v. 23 teaches that when a believer dies he is immediately **with the Messiah** in some unspecified way (according to 3:21 and 1C 15:35–58 he will later receive a resurrection body). This is **better by far** for Sha'ul himself than staying alive, precisely because eternal **life is the Messiah** (v. 21; Yn 1:4, 11:25, 14:6). Nevertheless, Sha'ul's choice is to remain alive "**because of you**" (v. 24), because the Philippians need him. Conclusion: precisely *because* of his Messianic faith Sha'ul does not ignore the needs of this world; though recognizing the benefits to himself of the *'olam haba*, he chooses to minister to others here in the *'olam hazeh*.

27–28 United in spirit... one accord. Unity is a major theme of this letter (2:2–16, 4:2; compare Yn 17:20–26), as well as of 1 Corinthians, 2 Corinthians, Galatians and Ephesians.

With its context, verse 28 is important for Messianic Jews. Sha'ul counsels boldness in communicating the truth of the Gospel. When, as Jews who trust in Yeshua the Messiah, we are **united in spirit, fighting with one accord** (using non-worldly weapons! — 2C 10:3–5&N, Ep 6:10–18&N) **for the faith of the Good News**, then we are enjoined to be **not frightened by anything the opposition does**. On the contrary, our boldness, reflecting our refusal to succumb to fear, **will be for them**, the opposition, **an indication** that our destiny is superior to theirs; one hopes also that it "will heap fiery coals of shame" on their head (Ro 12:21), leading them to repentance.

Wherever the Gospel is preached there is **opposition**, but a believer is **not** to be **frightened by anything** it **does**. This doesn't mean he must repress fear, but that by God-given strength he should not let it govern his behavior. He should overcome it by realizing that "God causes everything," even opposition, "to work together for the good of those who love God and are called in accordance with his purpose" (Ro 8:28).

The content of fear differs from place to place. Throughout the world Messianic Jews face rejection by family, friends and the Jewish community. In the State of Israel believers fear loss of their jobs, unpleasantness from Gospel-opposing neighbors and co-workers, violence from anti-Gospel zealots, governmental imposition of restrictions on evangelism. Non-permanent residents fear being expelled from the country, since the Interior Department need not give reasons for refusing to extend visas.

Nevertheless, many in the Land are brave witnesses who believe 1 Ke 4:14–16: "If you are being insulted because you bear the name of the Messiah, how blessed you are! For the Spirit of the *Sh'khinah*, that is, the Spirit of God, is resting on you!... If anyone suffers for being Messianic, let him not be ashamed; but let him bring glory to God by the way he bears this name." Sha'ul writes that when tempted to give in to fear he "does not lose courage" (2C 4:1–2&N). Let Messianic Jews and all believers everywhere continue to communicate the Good News about Yeshua "with humility and fear," (1 Ke 3:16) not of the opposition but of God, who will one day judge whether we obeyed his commission to make disciples of all nations (Mt 28:19), including our own. (For more on evangelism, fear and opposition to the Gospel in Israel see my *Messianic Jewish Manifesto*, pp. 221–227.)

CHAPTER 2

1–11 The supreme example of **looking out for** the **interests** of others (v. 4) was given by Yeshua's descent from **equality with God** to die for us (vv. 6–8). **In union with the Messiah** (vv. 1, 5), his **attitude** (v. 5) of **humility** (v. 3) can be ours. God rewards such obedience (vv. 8–11).

6–11 The material on these verses is largely based on Ralph P. Martin's *The Epistle of Paul to the Philippians* (Tyndale Commentary Series, Grand Rapids, Michigan: Eerdmans, 1959); he has also written a monograph on these six verses. The unusual Greek words in this passage suggest that Sha'ul may be quoting an Aramaic or Hebrew hymn used by the Messianic Jews in Israel when celebrating *Pesach* and Communion (compare the letter of Pliny the Younger quoted in Yn 1:1–18N). Its two sections tell of Yeshua's descent (vv. 6–8) and ascent (vv. 9–11). These each may be further divided: his pre-existence (vv. 6–7a), his life on earth (vv. 7b–8), his present exalted status (v. 9) and his future universal rulership (vv. 10–11).

6 **Though** prior to his incarnation Yeshua, the second Adam (Ro 5:15–18, 1C 15:45–49), **was**, like the first one, **in the form** or "image" **of God** (Genesis 1:26–27, 2C 4:4, Co 1:15, MJ 1:2), **he**, unlike the first Adam (Genesis 3:5–7) and unlike Satan (Mt 4:1–10&NN), **did not consider equality with God something to be possessed by force**. Not possessing by force could mean not retaining the equality with the Father which, as the Son of God, he already had. But more likely it means refraining from seizing what was not yet his, namely, rulership over all created beings, including humanity, who, because of sin, required his death on their behalf in order to be eligible to share in that rulership. For this reason he chose the Father's will over his own (Mt 26:39; MJ 10:7, quoting Psalm 40:9(8)), accepting the path of obedience and suffering for the sake of the promised reward (vv. 8–11; MJ 2:6–14, 5:8, 12:2).

The pre-existence of the Messiah was a familiar concept in rabbinic Judaism (Yn 1:1–18&NN), so that it is unnecessary to resort to the idea that Sha'ul is drawing on pagan notions of a "heavenly man" who descended and carried through a mission of redemption for mankind. The *Tanakh* provides more than sufficient ground for this passage in its material about Adam (Genesis 2:4–3:22) and the suffering Servant of *Adonai* (Isaiah 52:13–53:12); there is no need to resort to explanations that assume Hellenistic or Gnostic influence.

More problematical for Judaism is the Messiah's **equality with God**; on this, see vv. 9–11N below.

7–8 Of precisely what Yeshua **emptied himself** in order to do this is debated by theologians. The "kenosis theory" is that he gave up the attributes of God — omniscience, omnipotence, omnipresence, even consciousness of his eternal selfhood — in order to become a human being. My rendering attempts to express that his emptying himself consisted of three elements:

(1) He gave up his "equality with God" (v. 6), which may but does not necessarily imply that he had those attributes of God or that if he had them he fully gave them up.

(2) He took instead **the form** (same Greek word as in v. 6) **of a slave**, the Servant of *Adonai* (Isaiah 52:13–53:12), **by becoming like human beings are** — except that he was without sin (Ro 8:3; MJ 2:7, 14). "The Word became a human being and lived with us" (Yn 1:14); apart from his miracles and the Transfiguration (Lk 9:32) his pre-incarnation glory (Yn 17:5, 24) was hidden.

(3) He completed the emptying when **he humbled himself still more by becoming obedient even to death — death on a stake as a criminal**, the ultimate in degradation. "He has poured out his soul unto death" (Isaiah 53:12). Only for someone sinless can death be an act of obedience, not a foregone conclusion (Genesis 2:17; Ro 5:12–21N).

"**Obedient even to death**" might signify descent even farther, into the underworld, with obedience involving elements of voluntary enslavement to the demonic power of death (Ac 2:27, 31; Ro 10:6–8; 1C 15:54–57; Ep 4:8–10; MJ 2:14–15; 1 Ke 3:19).

Death by execution **on a stake as a criminal**, literally, "the death of the cross" (see Mt 10:38N). This was the most humiliating possible death in two contexts. In the Roman setting, it was reserved for criminals who were not Roman citizens; citizenship entitled even capital criminals to better treatment when being executed. In the Jewish setting, the victim of crucifixion came under a curse (Deuteronomy 21:23, quoted at Ga 3:13 in connection with Yeshua); for Jews this was "an obstacle" (1C 1:23) to regarding Yeshua as the Messiah. The curse of separation from God brought about by human sin (Isaiah 59:2) was endured by the sinless Savior (Mt 27:46) and thus removed as a barrier between human beings and God, as taught in Ro 5:9–11.

At the same time Yeshua's death both resembles and is distinct from what Jewish tradition understands as death *'al kiddush-HaShem*, martyrdom "for the sake of sanctifying the name" of God. On this see Ac 7:59–60N.

9–11 Because he was "obedient even to death" (v. 8), Yeshua was rewarded with exaltation after humiliation (compare his own teaching at Mt 18:4, 23:12; Lk 14:7–11, 18:9–14). **God has raised him to the highest place**, at his "right hand" (Psalm 110:1; see Mt 22:44N), where he shares "honor, glory and power" with the Father (Rv 5:13). Also God has **given him the name**, that is, the character and authority, **above every name** (v. 9). In vv. 10–11 Sha'ul reveals the extraordinary fact that this **name above every name** is ***Adonai***! He states, moreover, that the day is coming when **every tongue will acknowledge** it — angelic (**in heaven**), human (**on earth**) and demonic (**under the earth**).

Yeshua the Messiah is *Adonai* (Greek *kurios*). As explained at Mt 1:20N, the Greek word "*kurios*" can mean anything from the tetragrammaton *(YHVH*, "Jehovah," the personal name of God, rendered "*Adonai*" in the *Jewish New Testament)* to "Lord" (in the sense of God as universal ruler) to "lord" (in the human sense) to merely "sir" (a respectful form of address). Because Isaiah 45:23, which in its own context applies to *YHVH*, is quoted in v. 10 in reference to Yeshua, I believe this verse teaches that **Yeshua the Messiah is** *YHVH* and not only "Lord" in a lesser sense.

But in what sense "is" Yeshua *Adonai*? It is not that the Father "is" Yeshua, nor does Yeshua exhaust the full meaning of *YHVH* (the last line of v. 11 shows that neither of these can be meant), but that there is some intimate identity or unity or union between the Son and the Father. See comparable teaching at Yn 1:1&N, 18&N; 10:31&N; Co 2:9&N; Yeshua himself says more about this intimate identity as he prays to his Father in Yochanan 17.

Yet no matter what is said about this, it can be easily misconstrued so as to seem incompatible with the *Tanakh* and therefore incompatible with Judaism. Obviously, anyone who (1) speaks of the Father and the Son separately, (2) says "both" "are" *YHVH*, and (3) cleaves to the *Sh'ma* ("*YHVH* is one," Deuteronomy 6:4) is, at the very least, stretching language beyond its usual limits — although no more than when God, on the sixth day of creation, said, "Let *us* make man in *our* image" (Genesis 1:26). Since God himself transcends human limits, it is not surprising that his nature cannot be expressed fully by the normal use of language. Even though "the *Torah* uses everyday language" (B'rakhot 31a), so that there is no hidden meaning beyond the ken of ordinary readers, the fact that God transcends human limitation means that he exceeds what language can convey about him. The reader is forced to choose between exploring what "**Yeshua the Messiah is** *kurios*" means, and rejecting it by imposing his own limitations on God.

13 We come to the New Testament's most forthright and succinct statement of the paradox of human free will versus God's foreknowledge and/or predestination. **God is the one working among you** (plural) **both the willing and the working for what pleases him**. It would be a denial of God's own work not to do the work that pleases him (Ep 2:8–10&N), and we know from vv. 3–4 that what pleases him is believers' looking out for each other's interests.

The King James Version renders the first phrase, "It is God who worketh in you," suggesting that he is working inside each person, enabling each individual to will and do what pleases God. This interpretation too is legitimate.

The paradox of human choice is clearly seen in the *Tanakh* when Lamentations 5:21 ("Turn us, *Adonai*, to you; and we will turn.") is set alongside Zechariah 1:3 ("'Turn to me,' says *Adonai* of Heaven's Armies, 'and I will turn to you.'"). Rabbi Akiva expresses it even more succinctly: "All is foreseen and free will is given" (Avot 3:15). In this verse we see that God does not interfere with free will, but helps those who already seek to do his will to do it better.

14 ***Kvetching***, Yiddish for "petty complaining," translating the haunting Greek word "*gongusmoi*" ("murmurings").

16 **The Day of the Messiah**. The third reference to Yeshua's Second Coming in this letter (see 1:6, 10).

17 **Even if my lifeblood is poured out as a drink offering over the sacrifice and service of your faith**. Jacob poured out a drink offering of wine over the altar (Genesis 35:14). In Israel's sacrificial system the material of a drink offering was wine (Exodus 29:40; Leviticus 23:13; Numbers 15:5, 7, 10; 28:7; 29:40). In Yeshua's time wine was a metaphor for blood (Mt 26:27–29).

CHAPTER 3

1–3 Apparently there was a problem with Judaizers in Philippi as there was in Galatia (see Ga 2:14b&N); indeed, I believe this was the major cause of dissension in Philippi. Some suppose from the shift of tone in v. 1 that Sha'ul had planned to end his letter here but was suddenly apprised of new activity among the Judaizers and responded with the sharp warning which follows. But I think he had already decided to **repeat what** he had **written... before** (namely, the exhortation to humility of Chapter 2), by restating it negatively as a warning not to **boast** (v. 3), since humility excludes pride. Further, just as he used the Messiah himself as the supreme positive example (2:5–11), he uses the boasting Judaizers as a counterexample (vv. 2–9).

There is good reason to think that these Judaizers were not Jews by birth but fanatical Gentile proselytes preoccupied with physical circumcision, in which they took inordinate pride, regarding it as the necessary means of initiation into the people of God (see 1C 9:20b; Ga 5:2–4&N, 6:12–13&N). Against this hypothesis is raised the objection that Sha'ul would not list all his Jewish credentials (vv. 5–6) if the Judaizers had none themselves; hence the Judaizers must have been born Jews. My response comes from what Sha'ul himself writes. In effect, he asks, "Are they Jews? If so, they are Jews only by conversion, while I am 'an Israelite by birth' (v. 5), which is a more telling claim." Judaism forbids embarrassing a proselyte by reminding him of his non-Jewish origins (see also Ro 4:16N), but here Sha'ul effectively rules that protecting the faithful against those who prey on them is a weightier point of *halakhah*. Distressed at having to recommend himself, Sha'ul hastens to add that he does **not put confidence in human qualifications** and regards them as "garbage" (v. 8). He introduces them only because those who oppose him consider their own meager qualifications so impressive.

Mutilated... circumcised. Greek *katatomê... peritomê,* a play on words, literally, "cut down... cut around." Sha'ul is saying that circumcision does not provide the Judaizers with any spiritual advantage but results in their spiritual mutilation (compare Ga 5:12&N).

On the contrary, **the** spiritually **circumcised** are **we** who have "circumcised hearts and ears" (Ac 7:51&N, alluding to metaphors found in the *Tanakh*; see references there), we who have had the "foreskins of our old nature" removed (Co 2:11–13a&N), **we who worship by the Spirit of God and make our boast in the Messiah Yeshua,... not... in human qualifications** of any sort (vv. 4–9), literally, "not in flesh," not in "a circumcision... done by human hands" (Co 2:11).

An important question for Messianic Judaism is whether Sha'ul is teaching here that believing Gentiles are counted as **the Circumcised** and unbelieving Jews no longer are. The answer is that this is a verse with several levels of meaning, so that it teaches several things; but it is important not to get the levels confused. The *p'shat* (Mt 2:15N) is not that unbelieving Jews are not the Circumcised, or, as some Christians claim, that "Christians are the true Jews." Rather, he is saying that Gentiles who undergo an outward conversion to Judaism without an inward change of heart are certainly not the spiritually Circumcised, even though they claim to be.

Back to basics: Jews are Jews — have been, are, will be. Messianic Jews are Jews. Non-Messianic Jews are Jews. Messianic Jews and Messianic Gentiles — Jews and Gentiles who put their trust in Yeshua the Messiah — constitute the Body of the Messiah, the Messianic Community. By their faith Gentiles become Christians, not Jews; as Christians they become joined to Israel without becoming Jews. Gentiles can become non-Messianic Jews by conversion to non-Messianic Judaism.

Conclusions: A believing Gentile, spiritually circumcised but physically uncircumcised, has been grafted into Israel by faith (Ro 11:16–26&NN, Ep 2:11–16&NN), so that the promises given to Abraham apply to him as well (Ga 3:6–14&NN, 26–29&N). Yet he remains a Gentile and should not receive physical circumcision except possibly under very special circumstances (Ac 16:1–3&NN, 1C 7:17–20&NN, Ga 5:2–4&NN). On the other hand, a non-Messianic Jew, physically circumcised but spiritually uncircumcised because he does not trust in Yeshua the Messiah, is nevertheless a Jew; and even though he is a cut-off branch, he can be grafted back in again (Ro 11:16–24&NN). A Messianic Jew, circumcised both physically and spiritually, should take vv. 4–9 as a warning not to make this "double circumcision" into a ground for boasting, which is always a temptation; for in God's Messianic Community there is no first- and second-class citizenship based on whether one is circumcised (1C 7:19; Ga 5:6, 6:15) or Jewish (Ep 2:14) or on any other external criterion (Ga 3:28, Co 3:11). For a fuller discussion of these issues see Ro 2:28–29&N and Ga 6:16&N.

4–9 Gentiles who have accepted circumcision have less ground for boasting than Sha'ul (v. 4), who lists his external qualifications (vv. 5–6), seven of them in ascending order, only to dismiss them **as** not merely neutral but **a disadvantage in comparison with the supreme value of knowing the Messiah Yeshua as my Lord** (vv. 7–8), indeed, as **garbage** (literally, "dung"), so far as their usefulness for attaining **righteousness from God** (v. 9) is concerned.

5 **Circumcised the eighth day**, in accordance with the *Torah* (Genesis 17:8–12, Leviticus 12:3), not on a later occasion, which would have been a less faithful fulfillment of the command (see Ac 16:1–3, where Sha'ul himself circumcised Timothy as an adult, and discussion of circumcision in notes there and at Yn 7:22–23).

An Israelite by birth, not by conversion, like the Judaizers. See vv. 1–3N.

From the tribe of Binyamin. Many Jews by this time could not trace their genealogy, or were descended from proselytes. Presumably Sha'ul was named after King Sha'ul, also from the tribe of Benjamin.

A Hebrew-speaker, with Hebrew-speaking parents, literally, "a Hebrew of the Hebrews." My understanding is supported by many scholars; it can hardly mean "a Jew of Jews," since this has already been said twice; and nothing of substance is added if it is interpreted as meaning, "a real, genuine Hebrew." Contrary to what some scholars have asserted, Hebrew was still spoken by many Jews in the first century (Mk 5:41N). In an age when 85% of the Jews in the world were living in the Diaspora, being a Hebrew-speaker would confer higher status as a Jew.

In regard to the *Torah*, a *Parush*, a Pharisee; Sha'ul called the *P'rushim* "the strictest party in our religion" (Ac 26:5). Indeed, he was no ordinary *Parush* but was "trained at the feet of Gamli'el in every detail of the *Torah* of our forefathers" (Ac 22:3&N), Rabban Gamli'el I being the outstanding teacher among the *P'rushim* of that time. Moreover, wrote Sha'ul, "since I was more of a zealot for the traditions handed down by my forefathers than most Jews my age, I advanced in traditional Judaism more rapidly than they did" (Ga 1:14&N).

6 **In regard to zeal, a persecutor of the Messianic Community** (the *ekklêsia*, the Church). See the evidence at Ac 7:58; 8:1–3; 9:1–2, 13–14; 1C 15:9; Ga 1:13, 23; 1 Ti 1:12–15.

As a result of all these things, he was **in regard to the righteousness demanded by legalism, blameless**, which is far more than the Judaizers were (Ga 6:12–13) but far less than Z'kharyah and Elisheva were (Lk 1:6&N). On the very crucial decision to translate "*nomos*" as "legalism" and not "law" or "*Torah*," see Ga 2:16bN, especially the quotation from Cranfield's Commentary on Romans. Sha'ul was following all the rules as he had learned them, yet his heart was full of pride, which excluded trust, since trust requires humility, the opposite of pride. But trust is the primary requirement of the *Torah* (Ro 9:30–10:10&NN), and this Sha'ul lacked. Therefore he was by no means blameless in regard to the righteousness demanded by the *Torah* as it truly is, only in regard to the righteousness demanded by the system which results when the *Torah* is perverted into legalism. This matter is taken up again in v. 9.

7–8 Sha'ul does not mean that all the deeds which he did as a non-Messianic Jew were contemptuous, but that his pride in them he now regards as contemptuous.

9 **The Messiah's faithfulness** to God by being "obedient unto death" (2:6–8), not Sha'ul's faith in the Messiah (on this understanding see Ro 3:22N, Ga 2:16cN). Sha'ul's faith in the Messiah is adequately covered by the phrase, "**based on trust**," at the end of the verse. On the word "**righteousness**," see Ga 2:16aN. The present verse summarizes Sha'ul's teaching in Galatians and Romans on the subject of how people are made righteous by God.

11–14 **So that somehow I might arrive at being resurrected from the dead** (v. 11). It sounds as if Sha'ul were not sure; there is an apparent conflict with the certainty of 1 Yn 5:11 ("God has given us eternal life"). The common factor is that a believer cannot rest on his laurels — this is pride, lack of humility. He must **keep pursuing the goal** (v. 14; compare 1C 9:24–27, where Sha'ul uses the same imagery of running a race), or, as Yochanan puts it, he must "keep trusting in the person and power of the Son of God" (1 Yn 5:13).

17 **Brothers, join**. Another call to unity (1:27, 2:2; see also 4:2–3). **In imitating me**. Compare 1C 11:1.

18–19 Sha'ul seems to be referring not only to the Judaizers (vv. 2–3) but also to other **enemies of the Messiah's execution-stake**. Compare Ro 16:17–20.

20–21 This summarizes the teaching of 1 Corinthians 15.

CHAPTER 4

3 **Syzygos**. The word means "yokefellow" and thus may not be a proper name. **Clement**. Attempts have been made to show that this was Clement of Rome who wrote one of the first Christian documents outside the New Testament, the Letter to the Corinthians, confidently dated at 96 C.E. But the identification has no support, and Clement was a common name.

The Book of Life. A Jewish concept familiar from the High Holy Days liturgy; see Rv 20:12bN.

4 The injunction to **rejoice** (1:18; 2:17–18, 28; 3:1; 4:10) is not to indulge in casual pleasure or to bathe in a superficial gladness dependent on transient feelings, but to experience the abiding joy (1:4, 25; 2:2, 29; 4:1) that comes from trust in and commitment to Yeshua the Messiah.

6 Wise instruction for **prayer**, which is the remedy (v. 7) for **worry**. God cares about even the little things in life. Sometimes people are taught not to "bother" God with small or self-oriented requests. This is false humility.

8 The object is not retreat from an evil world, but sanity in it.

9 Sha'ul again makes himself an example (compare 3:17).

11–13 Christianity is accused of fostering both asceticism and greed. The teaching of these verses, based on personal experience (detailed at 2C 11:21–33), is that the Messiah offers **power** to cope with both penury and luxury, indeed power to **do all things**.

19 This is the ultimate assurance of God's providence and sufficiency.
Amen. See Ro 9:5N.

22 **The Emperor's household**. This indicates that Sha'ul was imprisoned in Rome when he wrote this letter.

THE LETTER FROM YESHUA'S EMISSARY SHA'UL (PAUL) TO GOD'S PEOPLE LIVING IN COLOSSAE:

COLOSSIANS

CHAPTER 1

1 As he often does, Sha'ul divides this letter into what God has done (Chapters 1–2) and what believers are obligated to do in gratitude (Chapters 3–4).

Sha'ul, **emissary**, **Timothy**. See Pp 1:1N.

2 **Colossae**, a town in Asia Minor whose **brothers** (believers) came to faith in Yeshua through the evangelizing efforts of someone other than Sha'ul (2:1), namely, Epaphras (v. 7&N).

4–5 **Trust, love, hope**. Compare 1C 13:13&N.

7 **Epaphras** is mentioned again at 4:12 and at Pm 23.

9 Sha'ul usually starts his letters by telling his readers in what manner he prays for them.

12 **People in the light**. See Ep 5:8N.

13b–23 Starting with the phrase, "**the Kingdom of his dear Son**," Sha'ul draws an exalted and multifaceted portrait of Yeshua the Messiah, in many ways comparable with the description of God found in the Jewish hymn, *Adon-'Olam*, attributed to the 11th-century poet Shlomo Ibn-Gvirol and sung (to any of 1,500 melodies) in most synagogue services:

"He is Lord of the universe, who reigned
Before anything had been created.
At the time when everything was made by his will,
Already then he was acknowledged as King.

"And after everything has ceased to be,
He alone, awesome, will still rule —
He who was, is, and will be
Glorious forever.

"He is One: there is no other
To compare with him, to place beside him —

Without beginning, without end;
Power and dominion are his.

"And he is my God — my Redeemer lives! —
The Rock of my suffering in time of trouble,
A banner guiding my way, a retreat when I flee,
The portion in my cup on the day I call.

"Into his hands I commit my spirit
When I sleep and when I wake —
And if my spirit, then also my body when I die:
Adonai is mine, and I will not fear."

The above hymn moves from God as transcendent and eternal Creator and Ruler to God as personal Guide and Protector. The present passage moves from Yeshua as eternal Creator and Ruler to Yeshua as Head of the Messianic Community and Reconciler of persons.

14 Although in Jewish understanding **redemption** (see Ep 1:7N) has a national dimension dating from the Exodus and extending to the Messianic Age, it also has an application to the individual defined by this verse. By implication the individual was enslaved to sin (compare Ro 6:16–23) but now has been redeemed from that slavery: **our sins have been forgiven**. This redemption is available from God but only **through his Son** Yeshua.

15 Yeshua, like Adam, **is the visible image of the invisible God** (Genesis 1:26–27, "Let us create man in our image.") See Ro 5:12–21 and 1C 15:44–49 for a more explicit comparison of Yeshua, "the last Adam," with the first one.

Such comparisons are not unknown in Judaism. A fourteenth-century *midrash* by Rabbi David ben-Amram of Aden says,

> "There were twenty-four good qualities in the world, but sins caused them all to disappear. In the future, at the End of Days, the Holy One, blessed be He, will restore them to Israel. And they are: the Image..." [and 23 others]. (Midrash HaGadol B'reshit, pp. 135–136; it can be found in Raphael Patai, *The Messiah Texts*, p. 263)

A note in *The Messiah Texts* explains that "the Image" refers to Genesis 1:26. Also compare 1C 15:49, 2C 4:4, MJ 1:3.

Supreme over all creation, Greek *protôtokos pasês ktiseôs,* alternatively and more literally, "firstborn of all creation." Verses 16–17 name three ways in which God is "supreme" and attribute them to Yeshua the Messiah; this is typical of how the New Testament shows the divine aspect of Yeshua's nature while avoiding the direct statement, "Yeshua is God" (see 2:9&N).

The Messiah is the firstborn of a new humanity through being the first to be resurrected from the dead; this is clearly the sense of "*protôtokos*" in v. 18. But this sense does not fit here because of what follows in vv. 16–17, even though it is consistent with the preceding allusion to Adam.

If one chooses "firstborn of" instead of "supreme over," the phrase, "firstborn of all creation," does not mean that Yeshua was the first created being but speaks of his eternal sonship. Yeshua's firstbornness does not merely antedate the creation of the material world but is an essential and eternal element of the inner nature of God. Timelessly and eternally the Word of God, who became flesh in Yeshua the Messiah (Yn 1:1, 14) is in the relationship of firstborn Son to the Father; this is a necessary part of the one God's description of himself.

Verses 15–20 are largely equivalent to MJ 1:2–3: The Word is God's

> "Son, to whom he has given ownership of everything and through whom he created the universe. This Son is the radiance of the *Sh'khinah*, the very expression of God's essence, upholding all that exists by his powerful word; and after he had, through himself, made purification for sins, he sat down at the right hand of *HaG'dulah BaM'romim* ["the Greatness on High"]."

17 He existed before all things, or: "He is over all things," **and he holds everything together** — the moment-to-moment existence of the physical and moral universe depend directly on his continuing oversight and providence.

18–20 Sha'ul shifts from Yeshua's relationship with the universe (vv. 15–17) to his relationship with the Messianic Community, thus picking up the theme introduced at v. 14; see vv. 13–23N.

18 He is head of the Body. The same metaphor as at Ep 1:22–23&N.

19 It pleased God to have his full being (Greek *plêrôma*) **live in his Son**. Compare 2:9&N. "*Plêrôma*" was a technical term used by the Gnostics and their antecedents to refer to the totality of the various spiritual "levels" and the beings or entities presumed to exist there; see Ep 1:23bN. Sha'ul uses the method of seizing on a characteristic distinctive of the heresy he is fighting and showing how it relates to and supports the Gospel. Thus he follows the pattern he described at 2C 10:4–5: "We demolish arguments and every arrogance that raises itself up against the knowledge of God; we take every thought captive and make it obey the Messiah."

21 Verses 25–27 and Ep 2:11–18 expand on this theme of how Gentiles, formerly separated from God, are reconciled to God and to God's people, the Jews, and made part of the Messianic Community through trusting in God and the Jewish Messiah. There is more on this subject at Romans 9–11, Galatians 3–4, Ep 3:5–6, Philippians 3.

24 The Messiah's afflictions. Either the "birth pangs of the Messiah" of Jewish tradition, or his present suffering due to the Messianic Community's present imperfections, but not his death pangs, because his atoning death is a completed work and does not require **completing**.

27 **The Messiah is united with you people**, with you believing Gentiles and not only with believing Jews. **In that rests your hope of glory**, of receiving everything good that God promises to those who are faithful.

29 **Striving with all the energy that he stirs up in me so mightily**, literally, "struggling according to the working of him who works powerfully in me." Compare Pp 2:13, Ep 2:8–9.

CHAPTER 2

2–3 **Understanding… fully knowing… secret truth… wisdom… knowledge….** All are Gnostic technical terms; see 1:19N above. On "**secret truth**" see Ro 11:25N, Ep 1:9N.

8 **Philosophy**. Here the word stands for the heretical Gnostic or pre-Gnostic alternative to the true understanding of who the Messiah is.

Human tradition here is pagan tradition, because it goes along with **the elemental spirits of the world** (see Ga 4:3N). Contrast it with Jewish tradition (including the Oral *Torah*; Mt 15:2–6, Mk 7:3–13, Ga 1:14) and with Messianic tradition (Ro 6:17; 1C 11:2, 23; 2 Th 2:15; 3:6).

9 **For in him**, in the Messiah Yeshua, **bodily**, in an actual human body and not merely in an imitation of one, as many pagan heretics taught (see 1 Yn 4:2&N, 2 Yn 7&N), **lives the fullness** (*plêrôma a*gain, see 1:19N) **of all that God is**. Literally, "Because in him dwells all the fullness of the divine nature, bodily." The Greek word "*theotês*" and two similar words, "*theiotês*" at Ro 1:20 and "*theion*" at Ac 17:29, each mean "deity, divinity, divine nature." Each occurs only once in the New Testament, each appears in a context where Sha'ul is dealing with pagan issues, and each, in the King James Version, is rendered, "Godhead." "Godhead" has a distinctly non-Jewish ring to it, because Judaism speaks of the personal God, not the abstract and impersonal "Godhead" of "philosophy" (v. 8). On the other hand, Reuben Alcalay's *The Complete Hebrew-English Dictionary* lists "Godhead" as one way to translate the Hebrew word *Sh'khinah* (on which see MJ 1:2–3N).

Stauffer, explaining "*theotês*" in Kittel's *Theological Dictionary of the New Testament* (Volume 3, p. 119), writes,

> "The [One God] of the Old Testament has attracted to Himself all divine power in the cosmos, and on the early Christian view He has given this fulness of power to Christ as the Bearer of the divine office."

Kleinknecht (*ibid*., p. 123) writes that "*theiotês*" is

> "that which shows God to be God, and gives Him the right to [receive] worship."

The *JNT* rendering expresses these truths in Jewish terminology.

This verse poses a challenge to non-Messianic Jews who attempt to reclaim Yeshua for Judaism by making him over into a great teacher, a wonderful man, or even a prophet, but yet a merely human figure and nothing more. **For in him, bodily**, in this human figure, Yeshua the Messiah, the Son of God, **lives the fullness of all that God is**. Underlying such a sweeping claim, though directed at pagans, not Jews, is the unshakeable foundation of the *Tanakh*.

> "For unto us a child is born; unto us a Son is given; and his name shall be called Wonder Counselor, Mighty God, Father of Eternity, Prince of Peace." (Isaiah 9:5(6))

> "'Behold, days are coming,' says *Adonai*, 'when I will raise to David a righteous offshoot. He will reign as king, prosper and execute justice and righteousness on earth. In his days Judah will be saved, and Israel will dwell safely. And here is the name by which he will be called: *Adonai Tzidkeinu* [*YHVH* our Righteousness].'"(Jeremiah 23:5–6)

See also Micah 5:1(2); Zechariah 12:10; 14:3–4, 9; Psalms 40:9–10; 45:6; 47:2, 7–8; 102:16; 110:1–4; Proverbs 30:4 for other indications in the *Tanakh* that the Messiah is divine as well as human.

A number of denominations outside the fringe of Christianity, including Jehovah's Witnesses, Christian Science, Mormonism, Unitarianism and Unity, have a view of the Messiah which is not exalted enough to square with what the New Testament says about him. This verse and others in the New Testament, such as Yn 1:1–18, 10:31, 17:5 and Pp 2:6–11, present the Messiah as divine, fully identified with God.

At the same time, this verse poses a no less pointed challenge to uncritical Christians who confuse Yeshua with God the Father. The New Testament almost never states, "Yeshua is God," but uses indirect expressions (Pp 2:11 is a rare exception, and Ro 10:9 may be another; see notes there). For example, even when Yeshua says, "I and the Father are one" (Yn 10:31&N), this is not the same as saying, "I am the Father." Such circumlocutions do not deny or detract from Yeshua's divinity; rather, they stimulate faithful but thoughtful definition of its character. Much of Christian theology has occupied itself with that enterprise, which is known as Christology (whether the Hebrew-Greek hybrid word "Messialogy" will obtain currency in Messianic Judaism remains to be seen). Nevertheless, few believers are clear on the difference between the Son and the Father. In the many tomes devoted to the subject one can find statements which express the truth well. But they are often buried in verbiage, expressed in language that minimizes the Jewish connection, and inaccessible to the ordinary believer because in most churches theology is rarely taught in depth. Therefore the opinions and resultant actions of the average Christian can easily remain unconformed to the Bible.

Messianic Judaism must take on itself the task of expressing the Messiah's human-divine character in Jewish language faithful to both the *Tanakh* and the New Testament. This will be a useful corrective to the paganism that has crept into much popular Christianity. Also it will help Jews attracted to New Covenant faith but trained to resist the concept of a Messiah who is more than human. See Yn 1:1N.

10 You have been made full, Greek *peplêrômenoi,* related to "*plêrôma*" in the preceding verse. The "fullness of all that God is" which is "in" the Messiah "bodily" (v. 9), will be in believers as well, because they are part of his Body (compare Yochanan 17; Ep 2:4–7, 19–22; 4:13–16).

The past tense is used to express a promise certain of fulfillment, a future truth as good as accomplished. Sha'ul does the same in v. 12 ("you were also raised up along with him"), Ro 8:30&N ("those whom he caused to be considered righteous, he also glorified"), and Ep 2:6 ("God raised us up with the Messiah Yeshua and seated us with him in heaven").

11–15 In Sha'ul's time, the three elements of a Gentile proselyte's initiation into Judaism were getting himself circumcised (men), immersing himself in a *mikveh* ("ritual bath") and offering a sacrifice at the Temple. (In today's Orthodox Judaism the last is moot because there is no Temple at which to sacrifice, but the other two remain as requirements for converts.) These three elements are set forth in these five verses as having been effected for Gentiles who trust in Yeshua, even though they have not become Jews (see following notes).

11–13a According to v. 11, **you** Gentile believers **were circumcised** spiritually, not physically, since it was **a circumcision not done by human hands, but… done by the Messiah**, the believer's spiritual *mohel* (Hebrew for "circumciser"). Using graphic language, Sha'ul explains that this spiritual circumcision consisted in the Messiah's **stripping away** not the literal foreskin but what it stands for, **the old nature's control over the body**. Verse 13a makes the metaphor explicit by equating "**foreskin**" with a person's **sins** and his **old nature**; one need only be present at a traditional Jewish *b'rit-milah* ceremony to understand very well the idea of "stripping away the foreskin." Such spiritualizing of ritual circumcision was not invented by the New Testament writers; the *Tanakh* does the same thing when it speaks of circumcised hearts (Leviticus 26:41; Deuteronomy 10:16; 30:6; Jeremiah 9:25; Ezekiel 44:7, 9) ears (Jeremiah 6:10) and lips (Exodus 6:12, 30); compare Ac 7:51&N.

However, an alternative understanding of the metaphor is possible. The Greek phrases rendered "**the old nature's control over the body**" and "**your old nature**" are, literally, "the body of the flesh" and "your flesh" (see Ro 7:5N). But Sha'ul could be thinking of the entire physical body as the "foreskin" of the believer's human spirit. The believer's body will be "stripped away" — it will die; but because he is united with the Messiah it will be replaced by a spiritual body like Yeshua's (1C 15:45–49&NN).

Before this "**circumcision**," **you were dead** (compare Ep 2:1–3, Ro 6:2). But **you were raised up along with him by God's faithfulness that worked when he raised Yeshua from the dead**. This is equivalent to the promise of Ro 8:11, that "if the Spirit of the One who raised Yeshua from the dead is living in you, then the One who raised the Messiah Yeshua from the dead will also give life to your mortal bodies through his Spirit living in you."

Most translators and commentators understand this passage differently; the Revised Standard Version is typical: "…you were… raised with him through your faith in the power of God, who raised him from the dead." This attributes your being raised up to your faith, not God's faithfulness. My reasons for rendering as I do are the same as at Ro 3:22&N: “faith of God” should be understood grammatically as a subjective genitive.

You were also raised up. By using the past tense Sha’ul expresses how certain he is that God, in his **faithfulness**, will fulfill his promise to resurrect believers. See v. 10&N.

This does not say that a believer’s old nature no longer has any influence on him, but that he can rule over it. In traditional rabbinic terminology, the *yetzer ra‘* (“evil inclination”) with which a person is born need not dominate the *yetzer tov* (“good inclination”; see Ro 5:12–21&N, 8:1–13).

When these verses are used to prove that Messianic Jews should not have their sons circumcised, the metaphor of spiritual circumcision is being tested beyond its strength. The verses do not say that spiritual circumcision has replaced physical circumcision for Messianic Jews, but that Gentile Christians are full members of God’s people through trusting God and his Messiah Yeshua, even though they have not taken the three steps necessary for conversion to non-Messianic Judaism. The verses say nothing about whether *b’rit-milah* is required, forbidden, or a matter of personal choice for Messianic Jews. However, that question is raised by Ac 16:1–3&NN, 21:20–21&NN.

This is the only passage in the New Testament where circumcision is identified with immersion (that is, with baptism; see Mt 3:1N). Sha’ul makes this identification because, as explained above, he is thinking in terms of Jewish initiation requirements and intends to reassure Gentile believers that they are fully initiated members of God’s people. But the comparison is with Gentile proselytization into Judaism, not with *b’rit-milah* for the sons of Jewish parents. It is not that immersion has now replaced circumcision, that Messianic Jews should baptize their baby sons instead of having a *b’rit-milah* for them. Rather, it is that, spiritually, all three of the Gentile proselyte initiation requirements — circumcision, immersion, and sacrifice — are fulfilled when one trusts in and is united with Yeshua.

Yeshua makes a spiritual circumcision of the heart, ears, and lips. It is accomplished at the time of one’s physical immersion in water, which is also a spiritual immersion by and into the Messiah, a union with him in his death (**you were buried along with him**; compare Ro 6:2). This union continues on through the present and into the future, culminating in resurrection (**you were raised up along with him**). The element of sacrifice enters in the discussion of his being executed on a stake in vv. 14–15. There is no clear dividing line between these three; for Sha’ul they are all one. Just as with proselytization into Judaism, the three requirements represent one spiritual event, entering God’s people.

13b God made you alive along with the Messiah by forgiving you all your sins. This connects immersion with sacrifice, and vv. 14–15 explain how, through the Messiah’s death on behalf of all, God was able to do this.

14 When a criminal was executed on a stake, it was customary to nail a list of his crimes on the stake; an example is the sign placed above Yeshua’s head (Yn 19:19–22). Some interpreters take this verse to mean that God removed not the charges against sinners but the *Torah* itself. Rather than repeat the many arguments against this view, I refer the reader to Ro 9:30–10:10&NN; Ga 2:16b&N, 3:23b&N; Ep 2:15a&N.

15 The spiritual **rulers and authorities** are the denizens of the demonic universe under the control of Satan. Compare 2C 10:3–5&N, Ep 6:10–18&N, 1 Ke 5:8, 1 Yn 4:4 and Mt 4:1–10&NN.

After **triumphing over** their enemies and **stripping** them **of their power**, it was customary for Roman victors to lead their captives in a procession and make a **public spectacle of them**; the same imagery is used at 2C 2:14.

Triumphing over them by means of the stake. But have the demonic powers been defeated? The theologian Oscar Cullman, writing shortly after World War II, compared the Stake (standing metaphorically for Yeshua's death) with D-Day, when the Allies' invasion of Normandy assured their ultimate victory. Yet the hell of war continued for another eleven months, until VE-Day, the day of Allied victory in Europe, to be compared with Yeshua's Second Coming.

16–23 So. The first word of v. 16 connects this passage with vv. 8–15, particularly with its keynote warning, sounded in v. 8, against being deceived into "following human tradition which accords with the elemental spirits of the world but does not accord with the Messiah." The rest of vv. 16–23 illustrates and explains exactly how such deception works.

The Colossian heresy involved not only Gnostic elements (1:14–19, 2:2–10) and Jewish initiation requirements (2:11–15), but Jewish-sounding rules applied pointlessly to Gentiles and in a legalistic way which has **no value at all in restraining people from indulging their old nature** (v. 23).

16 Don't let anyone pass judgment on you in connection with optional matters. Gentile believers are free to observe or not to observe rules about dining and Jewish holidays, as is clear from Romans 14&NN, 1 Corinthians 8&NN.

Eating and drinking, not "food and drink." Biblical *kashrut* says a good deal about which foods Jews may eat, and the Oral Law makes modest additions concerning drink (e.g., "*kosher* wine" is a rabbinic concept). But here it appears that Gentile Judaizers, perhaps like those in Corinth who put themselves "in subjection to a legalistic perversion of the *Torah*" (1C 9:20b&N), have set up arbitrary rules (Sha'ul brings examples at v. 21) about when and how to eat and drink, in order to "take... captive" (v. 8) their fellow Colossians. They probably included elements related to the laws of *kashrut* to give their pagan product a Jewish veneer. Also see Ga 2:14b&N for a discussion of (Jewish) Judaizers.

The list of holidays progresses from yearly to monthly to weekly. For more on them see Ga 4:8–10N.

A Jewish festival. The word "Jewish" is not in the text but is added because of the context. The major annual festivals are *Rosh-HaShanah*, *Yom-Kippur*, *Sukkot*, *Chanukkah*, *Purim*, *Pesach* and *Shavu'ot*.

Rosh-Chodesh, literally, "head of month," renders the Greek word for "new moon." *Rosh-Chodesh* commences when the new moon is first sighted visually; this is a day or two after its conjunction with the sun. In Sha'ul's day, word was brought to the rabbis in Jerusalem at the first sighting of the new moon; fires were lit on successive hilltops to signal *Rosh-Chodesh* to the Diaspora. Today *Rosh-Chodesh* is considered a minor festival and is celebrated in the synagogue with special prayers, although only relatively observant Jews are even aware of its existence. *Rosh-HaShanah* ("head of the year"), the New Year, is of course also a *Rosh-Chodesh*.

Shabbat. See Mt 12:1N.

17 **These are a shadow of things that are coming**, meaning the good things that will happen when Yeshua returns; or, alternatively, "These are a shadow of things which were yet to come," meaning the good things that happened when Yeshua came the first time but were still in the future when *kashrut* and the festivals were commanded.

These are a shadow. Most English versions (the New International Version is a welcome exception) deprecate the Jewish holidays by gratuitously adding the word "only" (or an equivalent): "These are *only* a shadow of things to come." But Sha'ul values Jewish practices; he himself observed them all his life (Ac 13:9&N). If one is going to add to the inspired text, the word to add is "definitely" or "indeed": "These are *definitely* a shadow of things to come." The festivals do *indeed* have value; since God commanded the Jewish people to observe them, they remind Jews of God and of what he has done. They are one of God's ways of bringing the Jewish people closer to himself.

With that understood, the rest of the verse falls into place: **but**, nevertheless, of even greater importance and value than a shadow is **the body** which casts the shadow, the reality behind it, because it **is of the Messiah**. See MJ 8:5, 9:23–24, 10:1 for a similar metaphorical comparison of shadow and substance, also MJ 10:1–18N. Lenski's commentary agrees with my point about the shadow, although his emphasis locates its value only in the past:

> "We should not think slightingly of the shadow. It was no less than the divine promise of all the heavenly realities about to arrive. The shadow proved the actuality and even the nearness of the realities, for only an actual body and one that is not far away casts a shadow. So the shadow called out all the faith and the hope of the Old Testament saints in the impending realities and guaranteed that faith and that hope in the strongest way. By faith Abraham saw Christ's day and was glad (John 8:56); Isaiah saw Christ's glory and spoke of it (John 12:41; Isaiah 53)." (R. C. H. Lenski, *The Interpretation of St. Paul's Epistles to the Colossians, to the Thessalonians, to Timothy, to Titus and to Philemon*, p. 126)

For Gentiles, however, Jewish practices are in most cases nothing more than a shadow, insofar as they do not arise out of their own national experience. (The exception would be the Gentile believer who has involved himself with Jewish life on a daily basis and absorbed naturally elements of the Jewish lifestyle without ascribing to them value for salvation or sanctification, since this contradicts the teaching of Galatians and Romans.) God gave the *Torah* to Israel in the context of Israel's peoplehood, and its details reflect what God knew Israel needed in order to grow spiritually. But rules concerning *kashrut* and celebrations are external impositions for non-Jews. Messianic Jews, since they are part of the Jewish people, have reason enough for observing these rules, which for them are pleasant shadows, even as through trust in Yeshua they have the substance as well. But since these shadows are irrelevant to Gentiles, since God did not give these commands to Gentiles, Sha'ul urges the Colossians not to be bound legalistically to them. For that matter, he elsewhere urges Jews as well not to fall into the trap of perverting the *Torah* into a legalistic system (Ga 2:16b&N, 3:23b&N).

18–23 There are critics of Messianic faith who draw a false contrast between Judaism and Christianity. They charge that Christianity requires **self-mortification** and **asceticism** because of its supposed otherworldliness; while the superior approach of Judaism is one of embracing this world with the object of improving it. Verses 18 and 23 should lay this canard to rest.

Elsewhere Sha'ul wrote, "I treat my body hard and make it my slave" (1C 9:27), meaning that he does not let himself be ruled by his impulses; and he counsels the Colossians similarly at 3:5 below (compare Ro 8:13&N). Sha'ul's approach to self-mastery is entirely Jewish in character, and so is his view of self-mortification and asceticism: these produce only **the outward appearance of wisdom** and stem from **false humility** (that is, from truly sinful pride disguised as humility) and have nothing to do with what the New Covenant requires. Moreover, **they have no value at all in restraining people from indulging their old nature**. In sum, the New Testament view is that asceticism fails to achieve its goal of squelching or confining the *yetzer ra'* (Ro 5:12–21N) but instead fosters its own virulent species of sin, pride.

Thus, for example, if Simeon Stylites (c. 390–459 C.E.) is considered a saint by the Roman Catholic Church, it is not because he lived for thirty years exposed to the elements on top of a fifty-foot pillar; but because, in spite of his odd and austere abode, he proved himself a champion of the poor, a wise counselor, a healer and worker of miracles, and an evangelist (although no friend of the Jews).

Man-made rules and teachings (v. 22, citing Isaiah 29:13, as did Yeshua at Mk 7:5–13&N). The God-given commandments in the *Tanakh* certainly do not fit this description. But requiring legalistic observance of rules (v. 21) is an all-too-human power-play by teachers who **vainly puff themselves up by their** sinful **worldly outlook** (v. 18; see vv. 16–17&NN).

19 Compare 1:18; Ep 1:22–23, 4:15–16, which employ the same imagery, with Yeshua the **Head** and his followers the **Body** (see Ep 1:20–23a&N). The use of the word "body" in v. 17&N is unrelated.

20 Elemental spirits. The same expression is used at 2:8 and Ga 4:3, 9; all three verses, like this one, have as their context Gentile observance of Jewish practices. See Ga 4:3N.

22 Things meant to perish by being used [not by being avoided!]. The phrase in brackets makes explicit Sha'ul's otherwise somewhat elliptical point; the brackets show that these words are not part of the Greek text.

CHAPTER 3

1–5 These verses resemble Yn 17:14–19; they counsel not otherworldliness and withdrawal but holiness in this world. They convey positively the same message as the negative warning of 2:16–23&NN. Compare Ro 6:1–23, 8:1–13. On Psalm 110, see Mt 22:44N.

5–9 With v. 5, Sha'ul turns from theory to practice, as in many of his letters. For other lists of sins, see Ro 1:29–31, 1C 6:9–10, Ga 5:19–21.

10 **Put on the new self**, as at Ep 4:24; compare 2C 5:17, Ga 6:15.

Fuller and fuller knowledge. Part of Sha'ul's anti-Gnostic polemic; see 1:19N, 2:2–3N.

The image of its Creator, see 1:15&N.

11 A literal translation of vv. 10b–11:

> …being renewed into full knowledge according to image of the one creating him, where Greek and Jew, circumcision and uncircumcision, barbarian, Scythian, slave, freeman have no place; rather Messiah is all things and in all.

Vincent writes:

> "The reference is probably shaped by the conditions of the Colossian church, where the form of error was partly Judaistic and ceremonial, insisting on circumcision, where the pretence of superior knowledge affected contempt for the rude barbarian, and where the distinction of master and slave had place as elsewhere." (M. R. Vincent, *Word Studies in the New Testament*, 1888)

Thus the meaning is not that among believers there is existentially no such thing as a Jew or a Gentile, but that such distinctions must not become a ground for **discrimination**. Here the basis of the equality among the many varieties of believers is stated to be that **in all** of them it is **the Messiah** who gives significance to **everything** (since he "is our life," v. 4). See Ga 3:28&N for references to Sha'ul's other statements about Jewish-Gentile equality and a discussion of what it means (and does not mean) for Messianic Judaism.

12 **God's chosen people**. This phrase is found at Ro 8:33 and Ti 1:1; see also Mt 24:31, Mk 13:27. As vv. 10–11 make clear, Gentiles who have committed themselves to God and the Jewish Messiah, Yeshua, have been grafted into Israel (Ro 11:17–24&NN) and, together with Jews who have made the same commitment, are co-sharers in what God has promised (see also Ep 2:11–3:11). However, this does not mean that — as an otherwise useful commentary says about this phrase — "Israel was God's chosen people, but under the new dispensation the Church has inherited that role." See Ro 11:16–26&NN and Ga 6:16&N for more on this subject, and the references at Mt 5:5N for other notes refuting Replacement theology.

15 ***Shalom*** here means something more like "wholeness" than "peace" (see Mt 10:12&N). The Messiah's wholeness or "oneness," his interest, is to do the judging, deciding, controlling and ruling in the **heart** of believers (compare Pp 2:1–13).

16–17 Compare the similar injunction at Ep 5:18–20, where "**the Word of God**" is replaced by "the Spirit."

3:18–4:1 Compare Ep 5:22–6:9&NN; this passage likewise offers counsel to the same three pairs of believers.

CHAPTER 4

5–6 Compare 1 Ke 3:15–17. The Good News of Yeshua should be communicated with prudence, tact, consideration and kindness; yet pointedly, not insipidly — the words rendered "**interesting**" or "engaging" mean, literally, "seasoned with salt" (compare Mt 5:13&N). Some people have the impression that believing in God and/or Yeshua is not so much un-Jewish as simply tedious, boring, dull. And there are believers who do their part to confirm this attitude by being tedious, boring and dull, seasoned with nothing. Caught up in their small world of church, Bible, and "fellowship," they fail to make **full use of every opportunity** to reach people who desperately need the Messiah in their life. Instead, their own lives seem dead. They seem unable to make their **conversation gracious and interesting** and do not **know how to respond to any particular individual**, because they, unlike Sha'ul (1C 9:19–23), do not try to understand people outside their own circle, whose background and experience are different. Communicating the Gospel involves listening as much as talking, and praying (vv. 2–4) more than either.

7 **Tychicus**. See Ep 6:21&N.

9 **Onesimus**. See Pm 10–11&N.

10 **Aristarchus** accompanied Sha'ul on his third journey through the province of Asia; he is mentioned at Ac 19:29, 20:4, 27:2 and Pm 24.

Mark (Ac 12:12&N) started out with Sha'ul on his first journey (Ac 12:25) but his premature and unauthorized departure (Ac 13:13) became the occasion for Sha'ul and **Bar-Nabba**'s later split (Ac 15:39&N). However, the Lord can heal such breaches of trust. Mark is here seen as Sha'ul's fellow-prisoner (Pm 24) and fellow-worker (this verse); later he worked closely with Kefa (1 Ke 5:13) and may have written the Gospel of Mark on the basis of material gleaned from him.

11 **Yeshua**. Greek *Iêsous* (see Mt 1:1N) appears in the New Testament as the name of two people besides the Messiah. One is the biblical Y'hoshua bin-Nun (Joshua son of Nun; Ac 7:45, MJ 4:8); the other is this man. Just as Sha'ul had the Gentile name Paul (Ac 13:9&N) and Yochanan the name Mark (v. 10, Ac 12:12&N), so this Diaspora Jew also had a Gentile name, **Justus**.

Among the Circumcision only these three turned out to be a comfort to Sha'ul in prison, as did the three Gentiles named in vv. 12–14. There is speculation that other Messianic Jews were unable to grasp and subscribe to Sha'ul's understanding of the *Torah* and therefore turned against him; this is but speculation. Gentile believers too turned against him (see two examples in 1 Ti 1:20).

12 **Epaphras**. See 1:7&N.

14 **Luke**, a fellow-prisoner who stuck with Sha'ul after **Demas** later fell away (Pm 24, 2 Ti 4:11). He wrote the Gospel of Luke and the Book of Acts; in the latter, the "we" passages (see Ac 16:10N) describe experiences Luke shared with Sha'ul but do not include this one.

15 **The congregation that meets in her home**. See Ro 16:5N.

16 On the basis of this verse a search has gone on for a presumably lost "Letter of Sha'ul to the Laodiceans."

17 **Archippus** may have been the interim shepherd of the Colossian congregation while Epaphras was with Sha'ul.

18 **This greeting I, Sha'ul, write with my own hand** to authenticate the letter. See Ga 6:11N.

THE FIRST LETTER FROM YESHUA'S EMISSARY SHA'UL (PAUL) TO THE MESSIANIC COMMUNITY IN THESSALONICA:

1 THESSALONIANS

CHAPTER 1

1 **Sha'ul** is Paul (Ac 13:9&N). **Sila** (Silas, Silvanus; see Ac 15:22N) and **Timothy** (Ac 16:1–3&NN) accompanied Sha'ul on his second journey (Ac 15:40–18:22).

The Thessalonians. Ancient Thessalonica is modern Salonika, in Macedonia, northern Greece.

3 Sha'ul has a very Jewish view of **trust** (or "faith") as being not merely a mental attitude or belief in a creed, but a firm reliance which **produces action**; compare Ac 3:16&N. Likewise **love** is not only a feeling; it results in **hard work**. And **hope** is not a vapid wish but the expectation, grounded in God's Word, that he will fulfill his promises to his people (see Ro 9:1–11:36N); as such, it produces **perseverance**, patience, endurance (compare Ro 5:2–5, 8:20–25; MJ 6:11).

"But for now, three things last — trust, hope, love; and the greatest of these is love" (1C 13:13). Here, however, Sha'ul mentions **hope** at the end of the list in order to emphasize it, because a major problem in the Thessalonian Messianic community was misunderstanding the nature of our hope in the Messiah's Second Coming, with impatience and laziness among the consequences (v. 10, 2:19, 3:13, 4:13–5:6; 2 Th 1:7–10, 2:1–12, 3:6–15).

5 The **Good News** is often communicated in a unbalanced way. We get dry **words** gospels, mushy ***Ruach*** (Spirit) gospels, fanatical and exhausting **total-conviction** gospels and hard-driving **power** gospels; none of them is complete. But the Good News is a balanced mix of all four, expressing itself practically in the quality of a believer's life (**how we lived for your sakes when we were with you**); and it results in imitation (v. 6; 1C 11:1), itself capable of becoming a pattern to be imitated and reproduced (vv. 7–9, 2 Ti 2:2).

9–10 Christianity is sometimes seen by non-Christians as idolatry, making something less than God (Yeshua, a man) into God. Sha'ul knew what idols were and how idolaters behaved, so it is no empty compliment when he writes that **you turned to God from idols to serve the true God, the one who is alive**, not a lifeless block of wood or stone. He then gives the proper perspective on **Yeshua**; he is God's **Son**, as the *Tanakh* indicates (at Isaiah 9:5(6), Psalm 2:7, Proverbs 30:4, Daniel 7:13), **whom he raised from the dead**, and who will, at his Second Coming, **appear from heaven**, where he is now "seated at the right hand of God" (Psalm 110:1). There he is interceding for us (MJ 7:25), and when he returns, he will **rescue us from the impending fury** (see Ro 1:18a&N). The words, "**of God's judgment**," are not in the Greek text but are implied. The references to end-time events here, at 2:19 and at 3:13 are all building up to the climactic teaching of 4:13–5:6.

CHAPTER 2

1 **Our visit to you was not fruitless**. See Ac 17:1–9.

2 **We had already suffered and been outraged in Philippi**. See Ac 16:16–40.

3–9 Accusations against those who proclaim the Good News have been around for a long time. Sha'ul catalogs ten of them here; they include (1) appealing **from error or** (2) **from impure motives**, (3) trying **to trick people**, (4) speaking **to win** their **favor**, (5) employing **flattering talk**, (6) putting on **a false front to mask** (7) **greed**, (8) seeking **human praise**, (9) using one's authority (**as emissaries of the Messiah**) to make one's **weight felt**, and (10) putting a **burden on** people by seeking material support from them. He answers these charges in vv. 7–12; see his similar defense at 2C 4:1–2&N. Believers must guard against allowing any of the charges to become true!

13 **God's Word... is at work**. Compare Pp 2:13, MJ 4:12.

14 **Judeans**. In all major English translations, the Greek word "*Ioudaiôn*" is rendered not "**Judeans**" as here, but "Jews." As a result, vv. 14–16 cease to be what they are, namely, a comparison of the Thessalonian congregation's suffering at the hands of their countrymen in Thessalonica with the Judean congregations' suffering at the hands of their countrymen the Judeans; and instead, despite Sha'ul's manifest love and zeal for his Jewish people (Ro 9:3–4, 10:1, 11:13–14), the passage reads as a virulently antisemitic outburst. The Revised Standard Version is typical:

> "...the Jews, who killed both the Lord Jesus and the prophets, and drove us out, and displease God and oppose all men by hindering us from speaking to the Gentiles that they may be saved — so as always to fill up the measure of their sins. But God's wrath has come upon them at last."

In fact, the New English Bible and the Living Bible (which is usually more sensitive to Jewish issues) hammer the point home by repeating "the Jews," even though the Greek text does not; and the Phillips version repeats it four times:

> "...you were sharing the experience of the Judaean Christian churches, who suffered persecution by the Jews. It was the Jews who killed their own prophets, the Jews who killed the Lord Jesus, and the Jews who drove us out...."

What this proves is that there is antisemitism not in Paul, as his Jewish critics claim, but in the Church! The Church has been so blind that it has not seen that the context of v. 14 is Judea, so that no other rendering than "Judeans" makes sense. Jews who thus criticize the New Testament as antisemitic can hardly be blamed for accepting as authoritative the Church's own interpretation of what Paul has written.

At Yn 1:19N I discuss at length the Greek word "*Ioudaioi*" and show that in a passage where the context is the Land of Israel it generally means "Judeans," the citizens of the province of Judea (however that province is delimited); whereas when the context is the Diaspora, it means "Jews" in a national or "peoplehood" sense. This alone would be reason enough for translating it "Judeans" here. (See also Ro 11:26aN and Ga 6:16N on the distinctive religious use of the term "Israel.")

But even if there were no general principle, the parallel construction in the sentence makes "Judeans" inescapably the only correct rendering. For Sha'ul, picking up the theme of suffering introduced at 1:6 and 2:2, says that **you** people in God's congregation in Thessalonica **suffered the same things from your countrymen** the Thessalonians as **God's congregations in Y'hudah did from theirs**. And what is the term used to name the countrymen of God's congregations in Judea? Jews? No, "**Judeans**."

The countrymen of the Judean believers were, of course, Jews. But so were the Judean believers themselves. Sha'ul is not talking about the Jewishness of the Judean believers' countrymen, but about the fact that the Jewish unbelievers from this area had a history of fighting the Jewish believers which goes right back to their role in having Yeshua executed (see v. 15N below); Sha'ul remained wary of them for many years (see Ro 15:31&N), with good reason (Ac 21:27&N). Sha'ul's purpose here seems to be to help the Thessalonians put their suffering in perspective. They are not suffering as severely or unremittingly as the Judean congregations, because the Judean nonbelievers are more dogged opponents (vv. 15–16) than those in Thessalonica.

The Judeans who. The final point has to do with punctuation. Other versions have a comma after "Jews" — "the Jews, who killed… the Lord Jesus." This punctuation gratuitously highlights the Church's traditional charge of deicide leveled against the Jews, because the function of such a comma is to make the predicate, "who killed the Lord Jesus," apply to *all* Jews. Without a comma, it reads, "the Jews who killed the Lord Jesus," so that the predicate specifies which *particular* Jews (or Judeans) are meant, namely, those who killed him, as opposed to those who didn't. The Greek text unambiguously requires the latter understanding, that is, no comma (as any standard Greek grammar will prove in its discussion of the use of the definite article with adjectival predicates). The fact that the United Bible Societies' critical Greek text has a comma here is beside the point, since the text originally was not punctuated at all — punctuation did not arrive in Greek until many centuries after the New Testament was written. I am not alone in raising this issue; see Frank D. Gilliard, "The Problem of the Antisemitic Comma Between 1 Thessalonians 2:14 and 15," in *New Testament Studies* 35 (1989), pp. 481–502.

15–16 "The Judeans who **killed the Lord Yeshua**." They did not actually kill him; the Roman governor Pontius Pilate allowed Yeshua to be executed by Roman soldiers. On the degree of Judean responsibility see Mt 27:25&N; Ac 2:22–23&N, 3:17&N.

And the prophets. Most of the prophets of the *Tanakh* prophesied in Judea. Here Sha'ul says, as did Yeshua (Mt 23:29–36, 35N; Lk 11:47–48) and Stephen (Ac 7:52&N),

that the Judeans' ancestors were so unwilling to hear the prophets that they killed them. The *Tanakh* provides evidence for this charge in a prayer said by "the Levites, Yeshua" (an earlier one), and others. It recites the history of the Israelites, lists some of God's blessings, and says: "Nevertheless they became disobedient, rebelled against you, thrust your *Torah* behind their backs, killed your prophets who had been warning them to return to you, and committed great blasphemies" (Nehemiah 9:5, 26).

And chased us out too. Before Sha'ul was saved, he was one of the chasers himself (Ac 8:3; 9:1–2; 1C 15:9; Ga 1:13, 23; Pp 3:6; 1 Ti 1:12–15).

Turning from past sins to present ones, Sha'ul says that **they** (the Judean unbelievers) **are displeasing God and opposing all mankind** by trying to prevent him from ministering the Good News of Yeshua among the Gentiles. Theirs is a dog-in-the-manger attitude, or, as Yeshua put it to some hypocritical *Torah*-teachers and *P'rushim*, "You are shutting the Kingdom of Heaven in people's faces, neither entering yourselves nor allowing those who wish to enter to do so" (Mt 23:13).

But God's fury will catch up with them in the end (alternatively: "and now retribution has overtaken them completely"). I don't consider this or Sha'ul's lengthier discussion at 2 Th 1:6–9 to be vindictiveness. On the contrary, I take it to be a way of countering the possible vindictiveness of his readers toward their persecutors, along the lines of Ro 12:19, where, quoting the *Tanakh* on the subject, he advises believers not to exercise vengeance themselves but to leave such matters to God. By implication he is giving the Thessalonians counsel similar to Yeshua's "Turn the other cheek" (Mt 5:38–42).

17 Compare 2C 1:13–2:4.

18 **The Adversary**, that is, Satan. See Mt 4:1N.

19 **When our Lord Yeshua returns**, literally, "at the coming of our Lord Yeshua," where the word "coming" is Greek *parousia*. Since Sha'ul's letters to the Thessalonians are among the first New Testament books written, this is chronologically the first use of this important word in the New Testament. It means "presence, being present," and was used for the arrival of a great personage, such as a king making a royal visit. King Yeshua's return will be *the* Royal Visit. See 4:13–18&NN.

20 Compare 2C 3:1–3.

CHAPTER 3

1–2 **We were... left in Athens alone; and we sent Timothy**. See 2:17–18; also Ac 17:13–15, 18:5, 19:22.

3 **Persecutions... are bound to come to us**, as Yeshua himself promised (Mt 24:4–13, Yn 16:33).

10 **Night and day we pray**. Sha'ul's advice is to pray regularly (5:17), and he follows his own advice. His frame of reference seems to be the synagogue, with its evening and morning prayers (*Ma'ariv* and *Shacharit* respectively). He mentions **night** first because Jewish days start at sunset. He uses the same expression at 2 Ti 1:3.

13 **Blameless, by reason of your holiness**. This anticipates 4:1–12.

At the coming of our Lord Yeshua. This anticipates 4:13–5:6; see 1:9–10N.

With all his angels (literally, "holy ones"); on angels see Ac 7:53N, Ga 3:19N, MJ 1:4–2:2&NN. On the basis of 4:16–17 it is tempting to understand the "holy ones" as the believers; but against this compare 2 Th 1:7 and see Rv 19:14&N.

CHAPTER 4

4–5 **To manage his sexual impulses in a holy and honorable manner**. The word translated "sexual impulses" is Greek *skevos*, "thing, object, instrument, vessel." I take "*skevos*" here to mean "instrument," referring obliquely to the male genitalia; I translate it figuratively.

But if "*skevos*" means "vessel," then, like "mountain of myrrh" and "garden" in Song of Songs 4:6, 12–16, it refers to the female genitals and makes possible three interpretations: (1) "to take a wife for himself in holiness and honor" (Revised Standard Version; this accords with rabbinic usage too); (2) "to live with his own wife in a way that is holy and honorable" (New International Version, margin); and (3) "to manage his sexual life with his wife in a holy and honorable manner," specifically addressing the importance of a husband's being considerate of his wife's sexual satisfaction (compare 1C 7:3–5, MJ 13:4). The message conveyed in my rendering is virtually equivalent to (3).

Contrast what Sha'ul writes with the commonly held opinion that he was a male chauvinist, also with the Victorian misimpression that the Bible is against sex. The Bible opposes not sex but **giving in to lustful desires, like the pagans who don't know God** and therefore commit adultery and fornication with impunity.

11–12 The tendency to laziness and dependency was deeply rooted in Thessalonica; see 2 Th 3:6–15 for Sha'ul's more detailed and strongly worded instructions on this matter.

13–18 Apparently some in Thessalonica expected the return of Yeshua and the end of history so imminently that they had stopped working (v. 11) — just like the cults that appear from time to time announcing that Jesus is coming back on such-and-such a date: "Sell all your goods! Head for the hills!" (What Yeshua's return has to do with selling one's possessions or living in the mountains is less than self-evident.)

Others in Thessalonica seemed to be unsure of the fate of believers in Yeshua who had died. Sha'ul was well aware that such uncertainty could wreak havoc with Messianic faith — see 1C 15:12–19&N.

Still others may have been diverted by some false teaching (see 2 Th 2:1–3). Hence the need for this interesting and surprising passage, discussed more fully in the following notes.

13 Believers in Yeshua do not need to **become sad** about their **brothers** in the faith who have died, because there is a **truth** from God which they can **know. Other people**, by contrast, since they **have nothing to hope for**, have every reason to be sad about the fate of those who have died. This does not mean that a believer will not grieve when a relative or friend passes; that is normal emotion, but it is the expression of one's own sense of loss, not concern for the one who has died.

For a believer, "death is gain," because he will "go off and be with the Messiah" (Pp 1:21–22), in the place he is preparing for his people (Yn 14:3). For this reason Sha'ul, facing execution, could write, "All that awaits me now is the crown of righteousness which the Lord, 'the Righteous Judge,' will award to me on that Day — and not only to me, but also to all who have longed for him to appear" (2 Ti 4:8).

Contrast the pitiable deathbed confession of doubt attributed to Rabbi Yochanan Ben-Zakkai, convener of the Yavneh Council (which established the parameters of Judaism after the destruction of the Temple and influences its character to this day):

> "Now I am being led before the supreme King of Kings, the Holy One, blessed be He, who lives and endures for ever and ever. If he is angry with me, he is angry for ever. If he imprisons me, he imprisons me for ever. If he puts me to death, he puts me to death for ever. I can't persuade him with words or bribe him with money. Moreover, there are two ways ahead of me: one leads to Gan-Eden [Paradise] and the other to Gey-Hinnom [Hell], and I do not know which one will take me. How can I do anything but weep?" (B'rakhot 28b)

14 The theme of Yeshua's being the "firstfruits of those who have died" (1C 15:20–23) is one of Sha'ul's consistent teachings; it appears in a number of his letters (Ro 6:5, 8; 8:11, 17, 23, 29–30; 2C 4:14; Co 1:18; 2:12).

Will take with him, Greek *axei sun avtô,* "will lead/bring/take with him." The text here and in the following verses leaves ambiguous whether Yeshua

(1) *will take back with him* on his return journey from earth to heaven those believers who have died and who are not yet with him,

(2) *will [collect and] take along with him*, as he reigns on earth, those believers who have died and are not yet with him, or

(3) *will bring along with him*, when he returns from heaven either to reign on earth or to collect living believers in a "rapture" (see vv. 15b–17&N), those believers who have died and are already with him where he is now.

But ancient notions of meeting a visitor, such as at Ac 28:15–16, where the believers met Sha'ul at Appian Market and Three Inns and accompanied him to Rome, suggest that believers who have died will meet Yeshua in the air (v. 17) and then accompany him as he descends to reign on earth. Actually, this is not so different from modern practice: we don't meet visitors in the air, but we do accompany them home from the airport.

A provocative question: Hosea 2:2 says, "Then shall the children of Judah and the children of Israel be gathered together; they will appoint themselves one head, and they will go up from the land (*va'alu min ha'aretz*)." Does this mean that they will make *aliyah* from the lands of their exile to the Land of Israel (so Rashi, Soncino, Keil & Delitzsch)? Or will the Jews be raptured from the Land of Israel while the Church stays behind?!!! (Compare Paragraph (3)(c) of vv. 15b–17N.)

15a **The Lord's own word**, probably something Yeshua said that is not recorded in the

Gospels (Yn 21:25). Alternatively, his guiding Sha'ul (1C 2:16) as he thought about the question troubling the Thessalonians, namely, what would be their share in the events of the Messiah's Second Coming.

15b–17 This event, the coming of Yeshua to raise first **those who have died** and afterwards us **who are left still alive**, is known in some Protestant circles as "the Rapture of the Church" (although the word "rapture," like the word "trinity," does not appear in the New Testament). Opinions differ as to when in the scheme of future history it will take place, or whether it will take place at all.

Eschatology, the branch of theology which deals with "last things," distinguishes at least these three events:

(1) The Millennium, the thousand-year earthly rule of Yeshua the Messiah spoken of at Rv 20:2–7&N.

(2) The Tribulation (see Rv 7:14&N), described most completely at Mt 24:15–31, and perhaps to be identified with "the time of Jacob's Trouble" (Jeremiah 30:7); see Rv 4:1N, 11:1–2N.

(3) The Rapture, described most completely in the present passage; see also 1C 15:51–53 and Rv 4:1N.

Since future history is not so easily discerned, there are a number of contradictory options concerning the timing of Millennium, Tribulation and Rapture, all of them supported in some measure by Scripture. The three major positions concerning the Millennium are:

(1) *The Millennium is Nonexistent.* This is the *Amillennial* position. There will be no earthly reign of the Messiah. The disembodied souls of martyred saints (Rv 6:9, 20:2) rule with Yeshua from heaven during the entire period from the first century until the Messiah's one and only future coming. This period is figuratively referred to in Rv 20:2–7 as "a thousand years." When Yeshua does return, he will judge mankind and then establish his glorious reign in the "new heaven and new earth" of Revelation 21–22.

(2) *The Millennium is Present.* This is the *Postmillennial* position. The Messiah is reigning now on earth through his spiritual presence in believers, making life better and better as the Gospel spreads throughout the world. But he will return bodily only after this figurative "millennium," whose length has already exceeded a thousand years. Popular in the nineteenth-century "age of progress," this position is more difficult to hold after the events of the twentieth century, which, to say the least, cast doubt on whether life on earth is improving. (The rash of expectation that Yeshua would return in 1000 C.E. was predicated on a version of postmillennialism that took the "thousand years" literally.)

(3) *The Millennium is Future.* This is the *Premillennial* position. After the Tribulation, Yeshua will return to earth bodily and rule for an extended period which may be a literal thousand years. At the end of this time Satan will rebel once more (Rv 20:7–10), the Great White Throne Judgment will take place (Rv 20:11–15), and the rulership of God and the Lamb in the new heaven and earth will be established (Revelation 21–22).

Premillennialists generally agree that the Tribulation is a short period, very possibly a literal seven years, immediately preceding the Millennium. But they are divided into three or four groups on the question of when, in relation to the Tribulation, the Rapture takes place. (Only in relation to the Premillennial position does the issue of when the rapture takes place arise; for Post- and Amillennialists, the Rapture is vaguely identified with the Messiah's one and only return.) Thus for Premillennialists there are these possibilities:

(a) *Pre-Tribulation Rapture*. The event of vv. 15–17 takes place prior to the Tribulation. Believers are removed so that they will not have to experience the time of the greatest trouble since earth began, and they return with the Messiah to rule on earth in glory. During the Tribulation itself, 144,000 Messianic Jews evangelize the world (Revelation 7). This position, held by Dispensationalists, is expounded in J. Dwight Pentecost, *Things To Come*, and in a rather sensational way by the popularizer Hal Lindsey in his book, *The Late Great Planet Earth*.

(b) *Mid-Tribulation Rapture*. The Rapture takes place after the three-and-a-half years of false peace brought about by the Anti-Messiah, and prior to the three-and-a-half years of judgment in the Tribulation (see Rv 11:3, 12:6).

(c) *Post-Tribulation Rapture*. The Rapture takes place after the Tribulation, so that the Church experiences it too. This is my own position, although I am not dogmatic about it. To me it is unthinkable that what New Testament faith offers is escape from suffering; on the contrary, "in this world you will have tribulation" (Yn 16:33, KJV). Nor is it thinkable that Messianic Jews are to be faced with the decision of whether to identify with their own people the Jews and stay to suffer, or with their own people the believers (the Messianic Community, the Church) and escape. For further discussion of this approach, see George Eldon Ladd, *The Blessed Hope*; Dave MacPherson, *The Unbelievable Pre-Trib Origin*; and most recently, *Israel, The Church and the Last Days*, by Messianic Jews Dan Juster and Keith Intrater (Shippensburg, PA: Destiny Image Publishers, 1990).

Messianic Jews seem to hold especially strong opinions about these things — perhaps because there is no certain way of determining who is right until events eliminate all but one possibility! For the *Jewish New Testament Commentary* it seems less important for me to stand unyieldingly for my own viewpoint than to observe that that there are several options, and any of them can be expressed in a way that honors the Jewishness of the New Testament. For broad and thorough discussion of these admittedly fascinating matters, consult Millard J. Erickson, *Contemporary Options in Eschatology*; R. Ludwigson, *A Survey of Bible Prophecy*; William E. Biederwolf, *The Second Coming Bible*; and J. Barton Payne, *Encyclopedia of Biblical Prophecy*. See also Rv 4:1&N, 20:1–15&NN; Mt 24:1–39&NN.

16 One of the ruling angels. Greek *archangelos*, usually rendered "archangel," is used in only one other place in the New Testament (Yd 9), where it refers to Mikha'el, whom the *Tanakh* calls "one of the first-ranked princes" and "the great chief prince" (Daniel 10:13, 12:1). See Rv 12:7&N.

God's *shofar*. What the King James Version calls "the trump of God" is not a winning bridge play, or even a metal musical instrument (see *Interpreter's Dictionary of the Bible*, Volume 3, pp. 472–473), but a ram's horn, such as is blown at *Rosh-HaShanah*, the Jewish New Year, also known as the Feast of *Shofar*s. In the

Tanakh the *shofar* was blown to introduce solemnity, to accompany celebration, to announce a memorable event, and/or to gather people together for war or other action (Exodus 19:16–19, 20:15(18); Leviticus 25:9; Joshua 6; Judges 3:27, 6:34; 2 Samuel 6:15; 1 Kings 1:34; etc.). That End-Time events will be announced by a *shofar* blast is part of a Jewish tradition which originates in the *Tanakh* (see Isaiah 27:31, Zephaniah 1:14–16, Zechariah 9:14) and is probably built on the *shofar* blasts which accompanied the giving of the *Torah* (Exodus 19–20). This tradition finds expression, for example, in the *'Amidah*, recited in every weekday synagogue service; its tenth blessing reads,

> "Sound the great *shofar* for our freedom, and raise the banner [or: "raise the miracle"] to gather our exiles, and gather us into one from the four corners of the earth. Blessed are you, *Adonai*, who gathers the dispersed of his people Israel."

See Mt 24:31&N, 1C 15:52&N, which speak of this same final *shofar* blast; and Rv 8:2&N, where the seven End-Time *shofar* judgments are introduced.

18 The remedy for excessive grief at the passing of loved ones who are believers is the reminder that these people are, in spirit, with Yeshua right now, and that they will be raised first at the Rapture. Grief at a loved one's death is normal, but inconsolable grief is unnecessary for believers.

CHAPTER 5

1–3 Only the Father knows the **times and dates when this will happen** (Mt 24:36), and **you have no need** to know them (Ac 1:7). You need only to be prepared (Mt 24:44, 25:13), since, using a comparison made by Yeshua himself (Mt 24:43), **the Day of the Lord will come like a thief in the night** (the analogy is also used at 2 Ke 3:10). The expression, "**the Day of the Lord**," is from the *Tanakh* (Amos 5:18–20; Isaiah 2:9; Zephaniah 1:7ff., 14ff.; 2:2–3; 3:8). See the same or similar expressions at Yn 6:39–40, 1C 1:8, Pp 1:6, 2 Th 1:10, 2 Ke 3:12, Yd 6, Rv 1:10&N.

3 The picture of **destruction** coming suddenly in the midst of apparent peace echoes the *Tanakh* (Isaiah 57:19–21; Jeremiah 6:14, 8:11; Ezekiel 13:10).

4–5 A play on words: **the Day** of Judgment won't **take** believers **by surprise**, since they **are not in the dark** about it; nor does the brightness of **day** surprise **people who belong to the light** (literally, "sons of light"; see Ep 5:8&N).

8 Imagery from Isaiah is also used at Ep 6:14, 17.

11 Compare 4:18.

12–13a On esteeming the elders of the congregation, compare MJ 13:17.
Confronting you in order to help you change. See 1C 4:14N.

17 Pray regularly. KJV has "Pray without ceasing," but this suggests praying in a mindless way, like reciting a Hindu mantra, which is not what Sha'ul means (compare Mt 6:7–8). He intends that believers should make prayer a regular habit, as it is for himself (3:10&N) and for Jews generally.

19–21 In the light of the current controversy over the charismatic movement (see 1C 12:8–10N), this passage, like 1 Corinthians 12–14, counsels a middle course. Prophetic messages are not to be rejected out of hand, but they are to be tested against Scripture, and by the other prophets (1C 14:32–33&N).

23 May the God of *shalom* make you completely holy. Compare the last verse of the *Kaddish*:

> "May he who makes peace in his high places (*'Oseh shalom bimromav*, quoted from Job 33:5) make peace for us and for all Israel; and say: *Amen*."

The essence of peace is not only the absence of war but holiness, which means living a life centered on and guided by God.

Whether a human being consists of three parts — **body, soul and spirit** — as this verse and MJ 4:12 suggest, or two ("body" and "soul" (Mt 10:28), physical and spiritual (1C 5:3), etc.), is less important than that the whole person, the entire "living soul" or "living being" (Genesis 2:7), should become holy. This will happen to believers, because **God is faithful and will do it**.

THE SECOND LETTER FROM YESHUA'S EMISSARY SHA'UL (PAUL) TO THE MESSIANIC COMMUNITY IN THESSALONICA:

2 THESSALONIANS

CHAPTER 1

1 See 1 Th 1:1N.

3 **Trust** in God and **love... for one another**. Yeshua called these the two greatest *mitzvot* (commandments; Mk 12:28–31).

4 In the rest of this chapter Sha'ul gives comfort and encouragement for the **persecutions and troubles** already spoken of at 1 Th 2:14.

6–9 Not vindictive. See 1 Th 2:15–16N.

7b–10; 2:1 These verses review the teaching of 1 Th 4:13–18&NN that believers will meet Yeshua "in the air" when he returns. They also lead up to 2:3b–12.

CHAPTER 2

2–3a Misinformation can come from **a spirit** other than the Holy Spirit (see 1 Th 5:19–22, 1 Yn 4:1, 1 Kings 22:22–23), **a spoken message**, that is, a sermon or teaching, or **a letter supposedly from us** but actually a forgery (see 3:17&N for Sha'ul's authentication of this letter). Alternatively, if this last phrase is translated "a letter from us, supposedly claiming..." then Sha'ul is referring to a genuine letter of his, perhaps 1 Thessalonians, which was being misinterpreted to imply **that the Day of the Lord has already come**. While a similar error is reported at 2 Timothy 2:14–18, it is hard to see how Sha'ul's message of 1 Th 1:10, 3:13 and especially 4:13–5:4 could be misunderstood in this way. In any case, **don't let anyone deceive you** (compare 2C 4:1–2&N).

3b–12 There is much speculation over exactly what this passage is talking about, since the events it speaks of have not yet occurred (in the view of Premillennialists; see 1 Th 4:15b–17N). The Thessalonians knew better what Sha'ul meant than we do, because he **used to tell** them **these things** (v. 5). Nevertheless, there is no shortage of opinions, all contradicting each other and all copiously supported by quotations from Scripture. My advice to those interested in pursuing these theories is first to read 1C 13:8–12, then to examine books on prophecy that present an overview of the subject, not just one perspective (for references to four such books see the end of 1 Th 4:15b–17N). My own notes here are suggestive, not dogmatic.

3 The proof that **the Day** of the Lord has **not come** is that **the Apostasy** (or "the rebellion"; Greek *ê apostasia* means literally "the standing away") **has** not **come and the man who separates himself from *Torah***, who is **destined for doom** (KJV: "the son of perdition"), **has** not **been revealed**.

On this **Apostasy** which precedes the second coming of Yeshua the Messiah, see 1 Ti 4:1–5&NN; on the moral decline which is part and parcel of such rebellion, see 2 Ti 3:1–9&NN. On the false teachers who will spearhead this evil movement, see 2 Ke 2:1–3a&NN and Yd 4–16&NN; and on the attitudes of those who welcome them, see 2 Ti 4:3–4&N. But already such false teachers are present; in fact, as Sha'ul himself said later, the Messianic Community itself spawns them (Ac 20:28–31). Yochanan agrees and calls them Anti-Messiahs (1 Yn 2:18–23, 4:1–6; 2 Yn 7), examples in advance of the final Anti-Messiah, whom Sha'ul here calls **the man who separates himself from *Torah***. In such false teachers, who have "the spirit of the Anti-Messiah" (1 Yn 4:3), "already this separating from *Torah* is at work secretly" (v. 7).

The man who separates himself from *Torah*. Greek *o anthrôpos tês anomias* means, literally, "the man of lawlessness" or "the man of wickedness." The two parts of the word "*anomia*" are "*a-*" ("apart from") and "*nomos*," which in a Jewish context does not usually refer to law in general but the *Torah* in particular. Obviously a man who sets himself apart from God's *Torah* is lawless and wicked as well. His separation from *Torah* (here, vv. 7–8) or avoiding *Torah* (v. 9) should not be understood narrowly, as if his sins were things like eating shrimp or driving on *Shabbat*. Here "***Torah***" means all of God's teaching, God's way of ordering the universe, and he wants none of it. He is truly anti-*Torah* in the broadest sense.

Who is this **man who separates himself from *Torah***? Clearly an evil figure, indeed, the very embodiment of evil. Such an apocalyptically evil figure is mentioned elsewhere in both the *Tanakh* and the New Testament. Isaiah speaks of a self-exalting individual (Isaiah 14:13–14), Daniel of the "little horn" and "the abomination that causes desolation" (Daniel 7, 9, 11–12); Yeshua of "false Messiahs" (Mt 24:4–28&NN, Mk 13:5–23, Lk 21:8–28); Yochanan not only of "Anti-Messiah" (1 Yn 2:18–19&N, 4:3) but also of two beasts and a false prophet (Revelation 11–20&NN).

With differing details, such a figure is also found in other early Jewish apocalyptic literature. For example:

> "The last leader of that time will be left alive. His entire army will be put to the sword; but he will be bound, and they will take him up to Mount Zion, and my Messiah will convict him of all his wicked deeds and will gather and set before him all the works of his armies. And after these things he will put him to death...." (2 Baruch 40:1–2)

As early as the first century (in *Targum Yonatan*, Isaiah 11:4) there is reference to an anti-Messianic figure called *Armilus* (Romulus, Rome). But it is in the post-Talmudic *midrashim* where one finds a sensational picture of the Anti-Messiah. In *Pirkei-Ha-Mashiach* he is called "*Satan Armilus*, whom the Gentiles call Antichrist."

He is six yards tall; his eyes are crooked and red, the soles of his feet are green, and he has two heads. This decidedly not jolly, green-footed giant claims to be the Messiah and God, rules the earth, gathers the world's armies against Israel, fights with ten kings over Jerusalem, kills *Mashiach Ben-Yosef*, and makes the stone impregnated by Satan from which he was born into an image for the Gentiles to worship. But God defeats him in the battle of Gog and Magog at the Valley of Arbel, and *Mashiach Ben-David* comes with deliverance for oppressed Israel. These fanciful accounts gained a significant place in medieval popular Jewry. See *Encyclopedia Judaica* 1:476–477, 11:1412–1415; and Raphael Patai, *The Messiah Texts*, pp. 156–164.

The evil and *hubris* of tyrants such as Hitler and Stalin are well anticipated by New Testament passages such as this one, yet these villains do not completely fulfill the prophecy of Anti-Messiah. Anyone who thinks the prophecy is fulfilled by the Pope must be reading his own anti-Catholic prejudice into the text. Who, then, is the **man who separates himself from *Torah***? He will "be revealed in his own time" (v. 6).

4 The man who separates himself from *Torah* will **sit in the Temple of God** (compare Mt 24:15). Although there are those who consider the Temple spoken of here to be metaphorical (individual believers, 1C 6:19; or the Messianic Community as a whole, 1C 3:16), that seems unlikely to me. After all, Sha'ul wrote when the Second Temple was still standing, and nothing in the passage suggests that his intent was other than to be taken literally. For this prophecy to be fulfilled, then, there has to be a Temple; but there hasn't been one since Titus destroyed the Second Temple in 70 C.E.

The seventeenth benediction of the *'Amidah*, recited thrice daily in the synagogue, includes these words:

> "…*Adonai*, our God,… restore the worship to the Holiest Place in your House…. Blessed are you, *Adonai*, who restores his *Sh'khinah* ["glorious presence"] to Zion."

This implicit prayer that God rebuild the Temple is made explicit in a meditation after the *'Amidah*:

> "May it be your will, *Adonai* our God and God of our fathers, that the Temple be speedily rebuilt in our days."

Reform Judaism, on the other hand, has no interest in a rebuilt Temple now or ever and doesn't expect one; neither does it expect a personal Messiah.

Since the seventh century, the site in Jerusalem which God authorized for the Temple has been occupied by the second most important mosque in Islam, the Dome of the Rock. Just how this particular piece of real estate might become available for Temple-building is not a topic on which I care to speculate. Teddy Kollek, the mayor of Jerusalem, writes in his autobiography,

> "I receive about twenty or thirty letters a year, mainly from Fundamentalist Christians of various churches, urging us to build the Temple, because they regard this as a prerequisite for the return of Christ. At press conferences I am

> often asked whether we plan to rebuild the Temple. I usually reply that according to Jewish tradition, the Temple already exists and will come down from heaven to its proper place when the Messiah comes — and that's a chance everyone has to take." (*For Jerusalem*, p. 230)

The Third Temple is the one which the man who separates himself from *Torah* will sit in, but it will probably last only a short time before it is destroyed. After that, the Messiah himself may build a Fourth Temple according to the pattern of Ezekiel 40–45. My city's distinguished mayor is partly right: *something* "will come down from heaven" — not the Temple but the New Jerusalem (Rv 21:2); it will have no Temple building, since the Temple will be God himself (Rv 21:22).

6–7 Sha'ul wrote to the Thessalonians, "**And now you know what** [in v. 7, "**who**"] **is restraining**." They knew, but we don't. According to Ernest Best (*The First and Second Epistles to the Thessalonians,* pp. 295–302), interpreters have suggested various candidates for the "restrainer": God, the Messiah, the Holy Spirit, the Roman Empire, the preaching of the Gospel, and some force hostile to God. There are arguments against all of these, but the last makes most sense to me, since the phrase, "**is out of the way**," can reasonably be applied to the Adversary, Satan, who holds sway in the world now (Ep 6:11–13, 1 Ke 5:8, 1 Yn 5:19) but will be dealt with in the future by God (Revelation 12–13, 20). At that time Satan will send forth the "man who avoids Torah" (vv. 9–11&N). Ernest Best offers this interpretative translation of vv. 6–7:

> "And now you are aware of the hostile occupying power so that the man of rebellion will be revealed at his proper time. For the mystery which is rebellion is already at work; only until the hostile power at present in occupation is out of the way. And then the Rebel will be revealed."

8 **The breath of his mouth**. Or: "the Spirit from his mouth."

9–11 **The Adversary** is Satan (Mt 4:1&N), the ultimate evil force who, as confirmed in Revelation 13, empowers the **man who avoids *Torah*** with supernatural powers **to deceive, in all kinds of wicked ways**. Eastern cults, pseudo-religious movements and drugs are some of these wicked ways. Although the scientific ideology of our age might be expected to inoculate against gullible acceptance of such panaceas, there has been over the past three decades a revolt against scientism accompanied by a naive and uncritical recourse to anything that claims contact with "the beyond."

According to an interesting book by McCandlish Phillips, *The Bible, The Supernatural and the Jews*, such quasi-religious movements contain Jews very much in disproportion to their numbers in the general population. He suggests as the reason for this well-documented phenomenon the fact that, no matter how much secular education we Jews may have or how alienated from our religion we may be, we are aware at some level that we are part of God's chosen people, and thus we are aware that there is indeed a "beyond" to be experienced. Since non-Messianic Judaism does not fill that inner craving for direct contact with God, and belief in Yeshua and the New Testament are considered forbidden, young Jews searching for the truth end up investigating all kinds of strange belief systems and experiences. Even if they abandon such weirdness for more "normal" escapes, such as materialism or politics, they **are headed for destruction because they** do **not receive the love of the truth that** can **save them**. (And all of this is no less true of Gentiles.) Messianic Judaism offers the solution to this problem — full acceptance of Jewishness coupled with full acceptance of the supernatural, but in God's way, not Satan's. For Jews and Gentiles alike this is the best prophylactic against going **astray** and believing **the Lie**.

13 **By giving you the holiness that has its origin in the Spirit and the faithfulness that has its origin in the truth**, Greek *en agiasmô pneumatos kai pistei alêtheias,* literally, "by holiness of spirit and faithfulness of truth." The Revised Standard Version renders this, "through sanctification by the Spirit and belief in the truth." But the constructions in Greek are parallel, and there is no reason why "*pneumatos*" should be a genitive of origin but "*alêtheias*" an objective genitive. See Ro 3:22N and Ga 2:16cN for the necessary background in understanding this point of Greek grammar. Furthermore, as explained there, I have found a systematic misreading of genitives as objective instead of subjective when related to the word "*pistis*" ("faith" or "faithfulness"), resulting several times in the rendering, "faith in Yeshua the Messiah," where it ought to be "Yeshua the Messiah's faithfulness."

15 **Hold to the traditions**. Both Christianity and Judaism have traditions which are not stated explicitly in Scripture. It is wrong to say, as some Protestants do, that Judaism has traditions but Christianity is free of them, as if this were a virtue. Not only is such a notion itself unscriptural, as proved by this verse, but, as a matter of fact, false, indeed impossible. A church group may have an ideology that upholds "Scripture only" and opposes tradition of any kind; but any observer— he need not be a professional sociologist— will have no difficulty discerning its traditions. Life without traditions simply does not exist.

Nevertheless, holding fast to traditions does not necessarily imply letting *rigor mortis* set in, failing to deal with new situations. While traditions conserve the wisdom of the past, the degree to which they should be modified to fit circumstances of the present is always a topic for discussion. This issue is at the root of the differences between Orthodox, Conservative and Reform Judaism. Messianic Judaism too, which upholds some non-Messianic Jewish traditions and some conveyed by the writers of the New Covenant Scriptures, has yet to join this debate in a productive way. It will have to do so because all religions, including both Judaism and Christianity, are rooted in tradition. Messianic Jews will have to make the point that believing in Yeshua does not imply giving up Jewish practices but may imply modifying them to take into account New Testament truth.

The traditions you were taught by us, by Sha'ul and his companions (1:1; compare 1C 11:2, 23). Sha'ul's authority, as the one who brought the Thessalonians to faith in God and the Messiah, is to be obeyed, both here and at 3:4. In neither place is he domineering over them; rather, this expected obedience is in the context of his fervent prayer for them and his reassurance that God is faithful (vv. 16–17; 3:3, 5).

CHAPTER 3

2 **That I may be delivered from wicked and evil people.** Compare the prayer composed in the second century by Y'hudah HaNasi, compiler of the Mishna, and recited by Orthodox Jews each morning:

> "May it be your will, *Adonai* my God and God of my fathers, to deliver me this day and every day from arrogant men and from arrogance, from a bad man, a bad companion and a bad neighbor,... be he a son of the covenant or not a son of the covenant."

6–15 **In the name of the Lord Yeshua the Messiah we command you.** Sha'ul dealt mildly with the problem of laziness at 1 Th 4:11–12. Here he takes a firmer hand (vv. 10–14); he has strong opinions on the subject (1 Ti 5:8). In this regard, he makes himself **an example to imitate** (vv. 7–9; compare 1C 9:4–19&NN, 10:33–11:1; 2C 11:7–15).

14–15 The practice of "shunning," found, for example, among the Amish in Pennsylvania, is based on passages such as this, 1C 5:4–13 and 2C 2:5–11. Popular journalistic accounts present it as cruel. Without judging the manner in which it is actually done, we can see from this and the other passages cited that its purpose should not be primarily punishment but ministry. On excommunication in Judaism, see Yn 9:22N. On the phrase, "**confront him... and try to help him change**," see 1C 4:14N.

17 See Ga 6:11N.

THE FIRST LETTER FROM YESHUA'S EMISSARY SHA'UL (PAUL) TO TIMOTHY:

1 TIMOTHY

CHAPTER 1

1 **Sha'ul** is Paul (Ac 13:9&N). **Emissary** or "apostle" (see Mt 10:2–4N).

The Greek word "*sôtêr*" may be rendered "**deliverer**" (Hebrew *go'el*) or "savior" (Hebrew *moshia'*). God as "deliverer" appears in the seventh blessing of the *'Amidah*:

> "Look on our affliction, plead our cause and deliver us quickly for your name's sake; for you are a mighty deliverer. Blessed are you, *Adonai*, deliverer of Israel."

In the first blessing of the *'Amidah*, God is spoken of as bringing a "deliverer" (*go'el*) in the future, but being himself "savior" (*moshia'*):

> "Blessed are you, ...God, ...who remembers the pious deeds of the Patriarchs, and who in love will bring a redeemer [*go'el*] to their children's children for your name's sake. King, helper, savior [*moshia'*] and shield! Blessed are you, *Adonai*, shield of Abraham."

Except for Lk 1:47 and Yd 25, where God is praised in the language of the *Tanakh*, only in this book (here, 2:3, 4:10) and sometimes in Titus is the word "*sôtêr*" applied to God the Father. Elsewhere in the New Testament it refers to Yeshua, the redeemer whom God has brought to the Patriarchs' children's children. For more on "*sôtêr*" see Lk 2:11N.

2 **Timothy**. See Pp 1:1N.

3a **When I was leaving for Macedonia**. This trip of Sha'ul's is not recorded in the book of Acts. Perhaps after being imprisoned in Rome (Acts 28) he was released and able to travel to the congregations he had started in Philippi, Thessalonica and Berea (Acts 16–17).

3b–4 Timothy was to **order certain people to stop teaching a different doctrine**, probably one with both Jewish and pre-Gnostic components (on the Gnostics see Ep 1:23N, Co 1:19N; on one way pagans misused Jewish practices see Co 2:16–23&NN). It did not focus on circumcision, as in Galatia, or on a wrong conception of the Messiah, as in Colossae, but on **myths** (called "Godless *bubbe-meises*" at 4:7 and "babblings" at 6:20)

and never-ending genealogies. The exact content of the heresy is not altogether clear, but its result is clear: people end up "majoring in minors," diverted to **speculating** about secondary matters and irrelevancies (compare 6:4) **instead of doing God's work, which requires** not useless information but ongoing **trust** in God and his Messiah, Yeshua.

Usually "**myths and never-ending genealogies**" is thought to refer to midrashic elaboration of the genealogies of the Patriarchs, such as can be found, for example, in the Book of Jubilees, written by a Pharisee around 125 B.C.E. But I propose that the error may also have included a variation of the Galatian heresy which, in lieu of requiring circumcision for Gentiles, attributed spiritual value to having blood ties with the Jewish people.

If those leading the movement were misguided Jewish believers, they were following the pattern of unjustifiable pride seen earlier in the antagonists of Yochanan the Immerser (Mt 3:9), Yeshua (Yn 8:39) and Sha'ul (2C 11:22, Pp 3:5–6). Also they were rejecting Sha'ul's teaching that Gentile believers are already children of Abraham through trusting (2:4; Ro 4:11–12, 16; Ga 3:29) and therefore have no need to produce a family tree with Jews in it.

But Gentiles could also spark such a movement, although their motivation would be a bit different. I have met quite a number of Gentile Christians who seem to be obsessed with discovering and proving that they have a Jewish family connection. I am not speaking of those who, by telling me about their Jewish great-grandfather, merely want to let me know that we have something in common, but those who have managed to convince themselves — lacking any hard evidence but sometimes claiming special revelation from God — that they really are Jewish. The most extreme instance of which I have personal knowledge was a church with nearly a thousand Gentiles whose pastor and many leaders claimed to have "heard from God" that they were Jewish, complete with knowledge of which tribe they belonged to (for more, see Rv 2:9N).

As a modern phenomenon, I think most of this can be explained either as an odd form of compensation for guilt at the Church's antisemitism, as the outworking of an individual's inner conflict with his own antisemitism, or as envy of the supposed spiritual benefit of being Jewish. In Sha'ul's time the motivation would have been a Gentile's feeling that he was not a full-fledged member of God's chosen people unless he could prove that he had some "Jewish blood."

The modern version of giving **attention to myths** and **speculating instead of doing God's work** is excessive concentration on God's plan for the future, so that people foolishly focus on doomsday and neglect good deeds here and now.

5–7 Sha'ul expands on what he said in vv. 3b–4. **The purpose of this order** to Timothy **is to promote love** (the chief commandment, Mk 12:28–32, Ro 13:8–10, 1 Corinthians 13), which has three components: **a clean heart, a good conscience** and **sincere trust**. The would-be **teachers of *Torah*** have not aimed at love; **by aiming amiss**, they **have wandered off into fruitless discussion**, they are "in over their heads" and simply don't understand what they're talking about.

Messianic Jews should carefully heed v. 7. A Messianic Jew attending a predominantly Gentile church may be singled out for special attention, either because he is considered "living proof that God is not finished with Israel" (Romans 11) or simply as the "token Jew." But one honor he should be cautious about accepting is an offer to teach the church about Judaism, unless he is both Jewishly knowledgeable and well acquainted with the history of the relationship between the Church and the Jewish people. "Not many of you should become teachers, my brothers, since you know that we" teachers "will be judged more severely" (Ya 3:1).

On the other hand, non-Messianic Jewish teachers are themselves often ignorant of the most important Jew in history, Yeshua the Messiah, and of his effect on *Torah*. Think how deficient would be the lectures of a psychology professor ignorant of Freud, or a physics professor ignorant of Einstein. One day there will be a supply of knowledgeable Messianic Jewish **teachers of *Torah***.

A question that may occur to some: why, when dealing with a predominantly Gentile congregation, should we understand Sha'ul's use of the Greek word *nomos* to mean "*Torah*" specifically, rather than "law" in general? My answer is that Sha'ul's whole way of thinking was Jewish, and he considered *Torah*, at least in its broad sense as God's teaching and his way of ordering the universe (see Mt 5:17N), an integral element of the Gospel for Gentiles as well as for Jews. What *Torah* requires of Gentiles is not the same as what it requires of Jews (Acts 15&NN), but Sha'ul taught Gentile believers to understand and operate with the Jewish concept of *Torah*, just as he taught them to understand and operate with the Jewish concept of Messiah and the Jewish concept of God. Later Church teaching has obscured the importance of the *Torah* concept, but the New Testament does not. For more, see my *Messianic Jewish Manifesto*, Chapter V ("*Torah*").

8 Misuses of the *Torah* include:

(1) Requiring Gentiles to observe aspects of the *Torah* that were meant only for Jews (Acts 15, 21; Ga 2:11–6:16; Co 2:16–23)

(2) Supposing that mere possession of the *Torah* guarantees personal salvation (Ro 2:17–3:31, 8:3; MJ 7:11–19)

(3) Regarding humanly determined traditions as *Torah* more authoritative than God's Word itself (Mt 15:1–20, Mk 7:1–23)

(4) Ignoring the New Testament's contribution to the understanding of the *Torah* (Mt 5:17–20, MJ 8:6)

(5) Using the *Torah* to lead people away from Yeshua instead of toward him, which is its purpose (Ro 10:4)

(6) Using the *Torah* as ground for boasting (Ro 3:27–31)

(7) Perverting the *Torah* into a legalistic system (Ro 3:19–26; Ga 2:16, 3:23)

(See notes to all these passages.) Proper uses, which **the *Torah* itself intends**, include building up Jewish peoplehood, trusting in Yeshua and living a holy life.

In the way the *Torah* itself intends. This phrase translates Greek *nomimôs*, "lawfully, according to law, legally." Since "*nomos*" here means "*Torah*" (v. 7N), the sense of "lawfully" is to be defined by the *Torah* itself, hence my rendering.

9 KJV renders the first part of this verse, "knowing this, that the law is not made for a righteous man, but for the lawless"; compare New English Bible: "it [the Law] is not aimed at good citizens." From this one might infer that good people don't need to study the *Torah* or observe its precepts, which is neither true nor Sha'ul's point. On the other hand, the Jerusalem Bible's "laws are not framed for people who are good" (similarly

New International Version, Today's English Version) is also off-target, because Greek *nomos* here does not mean "law" in a general sense, but ***Torah*** (v. 7N). For even though Sha'ul does switch sometimes from one meaning of "*nomos*" to another (as at Ro 7:21 and at several points in Galatians), in the present verse the sense is governed by Sha'ul's use of the Greek word "*dikaios*," which is for him a technical term, rendered here by the phrase, "**a person whom God has declared righteous**." "*Dikaios*" does not mean merely someone who is good, but someone who has committed himself to Yeshua and whom God therefore regards as innocent (see Ga 2:16aN; also Ro 1:17, 5:19, 8:1–4; Ga 3:11; MJ 12:23).

Psalm 37:30–31 says,

> "The mouth of the righteous speaks wisdom,
> and his tongue discourses justice.
> The *Torah* of God is in his heart."

So only in some of its aspects is the *Torah* **not for a person whom God has declared righteous**. In its role as that which prescribes punishment and condemnation for offenses, shows people their sinfulness and guilt before God, and guides them away from trying to prove how good they are and toward trusting in Yeshua the Messiah (Ro 2:12, 7:7–25, 9:30–10:4; Ga 3:17–25 and notes to these passages) the *Torah* **is for those who are heedless of *Torah*** in its role for the righteous.

The word for "**those who are heedless of *Torah***" is Greek *anomois* (see 2 Th 2:3N). Sha'ul enjoys harping on a word, using it over and over in a short passage. Here he uses "*nomos*" or a derivative five times in vv. 7–9. As with "*nomimôs*" in v. 8, the specific sense of this word is controlled by the context, in which "*nomos*" means "*Torah*," so that the rendering "lawless" captures only some of the sense. At 1C 9:21, "*anomois*" is translated, "those outside the framework of *Torah*," meaning a category of Gentiles (see note there). Here "*anomois*" seems to include Jews who live lives as if there were no *Torah*.

Those who are **heedless of *Torah***, Gentiles outside its framework or Jews who put themselves there, are, because they do not yet trust God and are still controlled by their old nature, **rebellious, ungodly and sinful, wicked and worldly** (compare Ro 7:7–8:13, Ga 5:13–26). From such a disposition flow all manner of vices, such as those listed; compare Mk 7:20–22; Ro 1:28–32; 1C 5:9–11, 6:9–10; 2C 12:20–21; Ga 5:19–21.

10 Sexual immorality — whether heterosexual or homosexual. See Ro 1:24–28N.

13a For documentation of Sha'ul's former life as a persecutor of God's Messianic Community, see Ac 7:58; 8:1–3; 9:1–2, 13–14; 22:4–5, 19–20; 26:9–12; 1C 15:9; Ga 1:13, 23; Pp 3:6.

13b–16 I received mercy because I acted in unbelief and thus did not understand what I was doing. Compare Lk 23:34, "Yeshua said, 'Father, forgive them; they don't understand what they are doing' "; likewise Kefa addressing his fellow-Jews at Ac 3:17. While some non-Messianic Jews are tolerant of Messianic Jews, others act against them in unbelief, not understanding what they are doing. They think that in opposing Messianic

Judaism they are serving God (compare Yn 16:2). They ignore Yeshua as an option for themselves. But God is very merciful; he can reach through all the sound and fury to the still, quiet place in every soul. Just as **our Lord's grace overflowed to** Sha'ul, who called himself **the number one sinner**, his forgiveness and mercy can overflow to anyone; indeed, Sha'ul knew that he would be **an example to those who would later come to trust in** Yeshua.

17 This verse, with its listing of God's attributes, has characteristics of a Jewish benediction or hymn (compare 2C 1:3–4&N).

King — eternal, literally, "King of the ages," equivalent to the Hebrew words "*Melekh-ha'olam*" in many Jewish blessings, which are usually rendered, "King of the universe," but can also be translated, "King of eternity."

Invisible. "No one has ever seen God" (Yn 1:18); yet, "Whoever has seen me has seen the Father" (Yn 14:9). An antinomy: both statements are true.

The only God there is. Sha'ul quotes the *Sh'ma* (Deuteronomy 6:4) below at 2:5.

Amen. See Ro 9:5N.

18–19 Prophecies. See 1C 12:10, 14:1–6. These prophecies were made about Timothy (see 4:14), and he should take courage from them to **fight the good fight**, as Sha'ul himself did (2 Ti 4:7), against wrong teaching. But essential weapons for the fight are **trust and a good conscience**; they are even more important than sound doctrine because they have to do with heart and spirit, not mind only.

20 Hymenaeus thought the resurrection had already come (2 Ti 2:17–18; compare 2 Th 2:3); **Alexander** was more likely to have been the metalworker who harmed and opposed Sha'ul (2 Ti 4:14–15) than the Ephesian Messianic Jew of Ac 19:33.

Sha'ul has **turned them over to the Adversary** (that is, to Satan; see Mt 4:1N), not for punishment alone but **so that they will learn not to blaspheme**. Satan is seen, then, not as an independent opponent of God but as a servant of God whose harsh methods can serve to train God's people, as at 1C 5:5&N. (Greek *paideuthôsin* "conveys the idea of stern punishment rather than instruction," J. N. D. Kelly, *The Pastoral Epistles*, p. 59; compare "*paidagôgos*" at Ga 3:24&N.)

CHAPTER 2

1–4 Sha'ul, who was neither passive nor selfish, did not **counsel prayers** for **quiet and peaceful lives** for ourselves, but **for** the deliverance (v. 4) of **all human beings, including** government leaders **and all in positions of prominence**.

> "Seek the peace of [Babylon, to which you have been exiled] and pray to the Lord for it. In the city's welfare you will find your welfare." (Jeremiah 29:7)

> "Rabbi Chanina, deputy *cohen gadol*, said, 'Pray for the welfare of the governing power; if people did not fear it they would swallow each other alive.'"(Mishna, Avot 3:2)

The Reform Jewish liturgy used in the United States contains the following prayer (in lieu of the traditional *Sim shalom*, on which see Ga 6:16N):

> "Grant us peace, Thy most precious gift, O Thou eternal source of peace, and enable Israel to be its messenger unto the peoples of the earth. Bless our country that it may ever be a stronghold of peace, and its advocate in the council of nations. May contentment reign within its borders, health and happiness within its homes. Strengthen the bonds of friendship and fellowship among all the inhabitants of our land. Plant virtue in every soul, and may the love of Thy name hallow every home and every heart. Praised be Thou, O Lord, Giver of peace." (*Union Prayer Book I*, [Cincinnati:] Central Conference of American Rabbis, 1972, p. 140)

Also compare Ro 13:1–7. On **God, our deliverer**, see 1:1N.

4 "'I take no pleasure in the death of the wicked,' says *Adonai*, 'but that he should turn from his ways and live'"(Ezekiel 18:23).

5a The theme of salvation for Gentiles as well as Jews appears in most of Sha'ul's letters. See Ro 3:29–30N, where, as here, Sha'ul derives from the *Sh'ma* his teaching that Gentiles and Jews alike have salvation available to them through trusting in the one God and his Messiah.

5b–6a There is but one Mediator between God and humanity, Yeshua the Messiah, himself human. This idea is resisted by non-Messianic Jews who urge that no human mediator is needed between God and mankind. The two-covenant theorists mentioned in Yn 14:6N, where Yeshua said, "No one comes to the Father except through me," would offer the variant that Jews come to God without a mediator but Gentiles approach him through Jesus. Some, taking for granted that the very idea of a mediator is in principle un-Jewish, think Sha'ul brought it in from Gnosticism (see Ac 8:10N, Co 1:19N) in order to make his Gospel more palatable to Gentiles.

Although Gnosticism posits various beings between God and man, the idea of a mediator between God and mankind is not only Jewish but inseparable from the history of Israel recorded throughout the *Tanakh*. Quite apart from the Jewish tradition that angels mediated at the giving of the *Torah* on Mount Sinai (Ac 7:53&N), Yeshua's role as mediator of the New Covenant (Mt 26:28; 1C 11:25; MJ 8:6, 9:15, 12:24) was foreshadowed by Moses, who is described as the mediator of the *Torah* not only at Ga 3:19&N, but also in the following extract from the fourth-century Midrash Rabbah:

> "Rabbi Yitzchak said: Our rabbis learned that if a cask is broken [before being delivered to the buyer], it is the middleman who bears the loss. God said to Moses, 'You were the middleman between me and my children; you broke the Tables [of the *Torah*, Exodus 32:19], so you must replace them.' How do we know this? Because it is written, 'Hew two tables of stone like the first…' [Exodus 34:1]." (Deuteronomy Rabbah 3:12)

A 9th-century *midrash* says:

> "Before Israel sinned, what does Scripture say of them? 'Before all Israel watching, the glory of the Lord appeared like a devouring fire on top of the mountain' (Exodus 24:17). According to Rabbi Abba bar-Kahana, the phrase, 'devouring fire,' means that seven realms of fire seemed to be devouring one another on the mountaintop. And Israel looked and felt neither fear nor terror. But after sinning, they couldn't even look at the face of God's intermediary, [as we learn from Exodus 34:29–35]." (Pesikta Rabbati 15:3)

In a footnote to his translation of Pesikta Rabbati (Yale University Press, 1968, p. 309), William G. Braude relates the word "intermediary" (Hebrew *sarsur*, rendered "middleman" above) to Deuteronomy 5:5, where Moses said of himself: "I stood between you and *Adonai* to declare to you the word of *Adonai*, since you were afraid of the fire and would not go up the mountain." If this is not mediation, what is?

Besides Moses, the *cohanim* were middlemen who presented the people's sacrifices to God; the prophets were middlemen who spoke God's words to the people; and the kings of Israel were middlemen in a more limited sense, ruling the people on God's behalf and representing them before God. Far from being "un-Jewish," human mediation between God and Israel is the norm in the *Tanakh*.

But none of this makes God any "farther away." Apparently the motivation of those who object that the concept of the Messiah as mediator between God and mankind is not Jewish is to affirm that a Jew need not "go through channels" to get to God. Agreed! — there are no Gnostic "aeons" or levels of attainment involved; nor need one approach God through saints, priests, a church hierarchy, or through rabbis. God is near to all who call on him.

Still, there is **but one Mediator**. One must address God through Yeshua; only then is there assurance that God is near, hearing our prayers. Why Yeshua? Because, on the one side, being **himself human** he is "near" our humanity; but being himself also divine, he is "near" the Father in a way that we are not. "No one has ever seen God; but the Only One, identical with God, the one at the Father's side" — Yeshua — "he has made him known" (Yn 1:18). He and the Father are one (Yn 10:31), in him lives the fullness of all that God is (Co 2:9), and he is right now "at God's right hand" interceding for his people (MJ 7:25–8:2).

In at least five ways is Yeshua a middleman for mankind, Jews and Gentiles alike. Besides being (1) prophet, (2) priest, (3) king and (4) mediator of the new covenant with Israel, he is (5) the **ransom on behalf of all**, as he himself said (Mk 10:45), bridging the gap we human beings have created between ourselves and God by our sins, the gap spoken of in Isaiah 59:1–2:

> "See, the hand of *Adonai* is not shortened, so that it cannot save; nor is his ear heavy, so that it cannot hear. Rather, your iniquities have made a separation between you and your God, and your sins have hidden his face from you, so that he will not hear."

Middlemen ease the way for others. Because Yeshua is without sin, so that Isaiah 59:2

does not apply to him as it does to us, he eases our way into the presence of God. We can approach God because he accepts us as if we had not sinned, provided we have put our trust in Yeshua, who ransomed us. The other mediators were "types," indicators pointing to him.

6b **Testimony to God's purpose** that all humanity should be delivered (v. 4). **At just the right time** in history. Compare Ga 4:4.

7 Till now I have been defending the idea that Jews as well as Gentiles are to be included in the "all" for whom Yeshua the Messiah is "mediator" and "gave himself as a ransom" (vv. 5–6NN). But Sha'ul's own object was exactly the opposite: no one questioned that Yeshua the Messiah was a mediator for Jews; rather, they disputed Sha'ul's right to be a **teacher of the *Goyim***, a **proclaimer** of the Good News that "God's purpose" (v. 6) was to deliver Gentiles too.

Sha'ul was divinely **appointed** to be **a proclaimer, even an emissary** of Yeshua (Ac 9:15, 13:47, 22:21). He frequently finds it necessary to defend this authority of his, nowhere more fully than in Galatians (see Ga 1:1N).

I am telling the truth, not lying! Compare similar protests at Ro 9:1, 2C 11:31, Ga 1:20. His point is that he, unlike those who spread "myths and genealogies" (1:4), is **trustworthy and truthful** when he teaches the Gentiles.

8–10 Advice to both **the men** and **women** (or: "wives"; see 3:11N) for public prayer (compare 1C 14:34–35&N). As at Ep 5:22–25&N, Sha'ul selects areas of likely failing in each of the sexes. Men must avoid hypocrisy (letting the work of one's **hands** not match one's **holy** words) and hostility (the inconsistency of hands lifted in prayer and in anger is like the inconsistency of curses and blessings coming from the same tongue, Ya 3:9–11); praying with uplifted hands is found in the *Tanakh* (Psalms 63:5(4), 134:2). Women will be able to pray better if they concentrate on **good deeds**, not external appearances (much the same teaching is found at 1C 11:3–16&NN and 1 Ke 3:1–6&NN).

Likewise, the women, when they pray. The last three words translate Greek *prosevchesthai* ("to pray") a second time, even though this term appears only in v. 8 and is not repeated in v. 9. The majority interpretation, that Sha'ul allows only men to pray and instructs women only about clothing, conflicts with his teaching at 1C 11:5. Although synagogue prayer is required of men and not women (Ga 3:28N, 1C 14:34–35N), the silence enjoined upon women in v. 11 applies to a specific kind of learning (see below), not to praying.

11–12 Greek *manthanetô* does not mean **learn** in the modern sense of acquiring information but is related to *mathetês,* disciple. Thus the context is the pattern of discipling and being discipled which existed in Judaism and was exemplified by Yeshua and his *talmidim* (on this word see Mt 5:1N). Orthodox Jews use the word "learn" to mean "studying *Torah,*" not merely to gain knowledge but to become more holy. This is close to the sense here.

One who disciples others has responsibility for their spiritual life and growth; women are not to have that kind of responsibility for men. Nevertheless, Timothy is to **let a woman learn** (be discipled) **in peace** (Greek *êsuchia*, "silence, restfulness"), without her being disturbed. The sense is not "in silence," as in most translations, implying she should keep her mouth shut, but "at rest"; compare Ac 22:2 and 2 Th 3:12, where the word is translated, "settle down." On the other hand, 1C 14:34–35 does teach against disturbing chatter by wives at congregational meetings. Although women may learn equally with men, Sha'ul does **not permit a woman to teach** (to disciple) **a man or exercise** a discipler's **authority over him**.

But in a well-led congregation (criteria for leaders is the topic of the next chapter) women may be given much authority and responsibility, including the discipling of women and the teaching of men; Sha'ul himself offers many examples — Lydia, the businesswoman who opened her home to him (Ac 16:14, 40), Priscilla, who taught Apollos (Ac 18:26), and Phoebe, who held a leadership position (Ro 16:1, and see 3:11N below) — to name but three.

13–15 The two reasons given for women's not being disciplers of men are Adam's chronological priority (compare 1C 11:8–9) and Eve's propensity for being deceived. Sha'ul does not say that Eve sinned, but that she **became involved in the transgression** (literally, "has become in transgression"), which I take to mean that she became mixed up in Adam's transgression. At Ro 5:12–21 Sha'ul teaches that it was Adam who sinned through directly disobeying God's command to him (Genesis 2:17, 3:1–7), and therefore he bears the primary responsibility for the "Fall" — the introduction of sin into human life. Although the Apocrypha gives us the verse, "Sin began with a woman, and thanks to her we must all die" (Sirach 25:24), the New Testament presents a different picture. Eve was not the sinner, Adam was, since it was he who disregarded God's command. Eve, rather, was "deceived" (2C 11:3) — when the serpent duped her, she **became involved in** Adam's **transgression**.

Sha'ul sees a role difference for men and women rooted in God's purpose. The eye of faith can accept this difference as not demeaning to women. Also, in the framework of faith, women's self-fulfillment is not limited. It must be admitted that Sha'ul's manner of argument does not appeal to the modern mind. But he was not writing for the modern mind. We owe it to the text to place ourselves in the shoes of his readers and not to measure his style against the assumptions of our age. For a broad discussion of the New Testament's teaching about the roles of the sexes which takes modern sociological observations and ideological movements such as feminism into account, see Stephen B. Clark, *Man and Woman in Christ*.

15 An obscure verse. Possibly Sha'ul is reducing the severity of vv. 11–14 (compare 1C 11:11–12) by mitigating the punishment Genesis 3:16 decreed for Eve's role in the Fall. There God said to her, "I will greatly multiply the pain of your childbearing — in pain will you bring forth children. You will turn away toward your husband, but he will rule over you." Verses 11–14 state that he still rules her. But now she is spared much of the emotional pain of motherhood (of "bringing forth" or raising children) — if not the physical pain of childbearing — through **trusting** and **loving** God **and living a holy life**.

Another possible meaning: God's purpose for women is motherhood; a woman who devotes herself to this is in harmony with God's plan. In any case, the verse certainly does not intend to teach that childbearing is an alternate "plan of salvation" for women, making trust in Yeshua unnecessary!

CHAPTER 3

1 **Congregation leader**, Greek *episkopos*, literally, "overseer" or perhaps its Latin-rooted English equivalent, "supervisor." Transliterated as "bishop" in English. See 1 Th 1:1N. Ambition to lead is not disparaged but praised.

2–7 Believers and nonbelievers alike have the right to judge congregational leaders by these criteria.

2 **Faithful to his wife**, literally, "husband of one wife," so that most of the discussion about this phrase has assumed its concern is not fidelity but numbers — at most one, at least one, or exactly one? Or at most one at a time?

At least one. No one seriously proposes this. Jacob, David and Solomon notwithstanding, polygamy would conflict with Sha'ul's own teaching at 1C 7:2 and with Yeshua's at Mt 19:3–9, where he cites God's original pattern as the model: "A man should be united with his wife," not with his wives, "and the two," not the many, "are to become one flesh" (Genesis 2:24).

Exactly one: a leader must be a married man. This fits well with the Jewish saying that a man without a wife is only half a man (a different application of Genesis 2:24).

> "Rabbi Tanchum said in the name of Rabbi Chanilai: 'Any man who has no wife lives without joy, without blessing and without goodness.'"(Yevamot 62b)

> "You can't compare a man with bread in his basket to one without." (Yoma)

And most directly,

> "Don't say, 'I won't get married.' Get married!" (*Avot diRabbi Natan*)

Traditional Jewish encouragement of marriage risks becoming callous toward those who remain single; contrast Yeshua's remarks at Mt 19:10–12 and Sha'ul's teaching in 1 Corinthians 7.

At most one at a time. This is possible; the question then is whether leaders may remarry after divorce or only after being widowed. In the light of the two clearly permitted reasons given in the New Testament for divorce, fornication (Mt 19:9) and desertion by an unbelieving spouse (1C 7:15), one may argue that it includes remarriage after divorce for those specific reasons. But then the standard for leaders is no different than for other believers, so why mention it?

At most one. This could be understood to exclude remarriage for any reason. But more importantly, it allows for unmarried pastors and *shammashim*. It does not *require* them to remain single, as does the Roman Catholic Church (see 4:3&N), but it *permits* them not to marry if they choose.

My own view is that the phrase, "husband of one wife," allows for single or married pastors and allows remarriage after being widowered or after divorce for either of the two specified reasons. But my rendering, "**faithful to his wife**," reflects my belief that Sha'ul's point here is not whether a leader may or must marry (or how many times), but the importance of his fidelity in marriage. Few things can bring a ministry to ruin more quickly and totally than the sexual misbehavior of its leaders. In an age when sexual immorality was even more rampant than today, Sha'ul stressed the importance of marital fidelity (likewise at v. 12 and 5:9). It is the shame of the Messiah's Body (v. 7, compare 1C 6:15–20) that not only are there well-publicized instances when this principle is violated, but known violations are sometimes not dealt with.

3 **He must not drink excessively**. The requirement is not that the leader abstain altogether but that he not make it his habit to get drunk. Wine has a role in Jewish religion, as the New Testament recognizes (Mt 26:27–29&N, Lk 22:17–20&NN). Also see below, 5:23&N.

4–5 **Having children who obey him** (a weaker requirement than at Ti 1:6&N). As at v. 2, does this mean a leader must have children? Or, rather, that if he has children, they should be obedient and not unruly, so that his **household** sets an example for the congregation? The latter is the usual interpretation. A reasonable inference is that family comes before ministry.

If a man can't manage his own household, how will he be able to care for God's Messianic community? One can turn this into a positive statement: a pastor gains valuable job experience from raising his own children.

6 **The Adversary** (Satan; see Mt 4:1N) **came under** God's **judgment** because of **pride**; see Isaiah 14:13–14, Ezekiel 28:1–19, Mt 4:1–10.

7 Leading a congregation is not like managing a business or holding public office. **The Adversary** doesn't care whether someone grows rich or powerful, but he does try with all his might to thwart the spread of the Good News and the advance of the Kingdom. For this reason his **trap** is ever set to **disgrace** those who are committed to doing God's work.

8 ***Shammashim***, "workers, deacons." See Pp 1:1N.

9 **Formerly hidden truth**. See Ro 11:25, Ep 1:9N. This points forward to v. 16.

11 Greek *gunaikas* can mean either "**wives**" or "women." If the former, Sha'ul is taking for granted that only men can be *shammashim* and is predicating their service on their wives' good behavior. But if the meaning is "women," he is allowing that the office of *shammash* can be filled by women as well as men. At Ro 16:1 Sha'ul calls Phoebe a *shammash*; his use of the masculine form of the Greek word "*diakonos*" suggests that he is in fact referring to the office and not just describing her as a worker. Against this idea stands v. 12, which says that a *shammash* **must be faithful to his wife** (see v. 2N) but says nothing about her being faithful to her husband (compare 5:9). However, this can be explained as brevity of expression, or as a statement of the rule for the more frequent case.

16 **Formerly hidden truth**. See v. 9N. The poetic form of this verse in the Greek suggests that Sha'ul is quoting an early Messianic hymn.

CHAPTER 4

1 **The** Holy **Spirit expressly states** in a prophecy, possibly that of Ac 20:28–31, which Sha'ul specifically directed to the believers in Ephesus, where Timothy was.

In the *acharit-hayamim*. The End Times are already here (1C 10:11N). So we need not say that **people will apostatize from the faith** only in the future (as at 2 Th 2:3) — they are doing it already.

What kinds of **deceiving spirits and things taught by demons** are they **paying attention to**? (On the reality of demons, see Mt 4:24N.) For the moment, confining ourselves only to religions, we may note:

(1) Eastern religions (and Western adaptations thereof), with their sub-biblical, impersonal concept of God and their tendency to depreciate the importance of human history and thus of human life.
(2) The older sub-Christian cults, including Jehovah's Witnesses, Mormonism, Christian Science and Unitarianism, all of which present an inadequate picture of Yeshua the Messiah.
(3) Non-Messianic Judaism, insofar as it denies the divine origin of the New Covenant and the Messiahship of Yeshua and stands in the way of Jews who affirm them.
(4) Secularism, humanism, atheism and agnosticism.
(5) Liberal Christianity, which, though using the Bible, denies fundamental biblical truths, and, most insidiously of all,
(6) Religion which passes itself off as affirming the Bible but in practice proves itself otherwise by its deeds.

Outside the realm of what should be called religion we see people turning to:

(7) Drugs, drink, illicit sex, pursuit of riches (see 6:7) and other self-centered activities.
(8) Various ideological movements without overt religious content that can capture a person as religion does; politics and environmentalism can function in this way, though they need not do so.
(9) The occult, including astrology, parapsychology, *kabbalah* (the occult tradition within Judaism).

Why do people turn to these substitutes for the truth and fail to see the Good News as good? Here are some of the most common reasons, along with the remedies:

(1) Having a false conception of God, of Yeshua and of what the Bible says. Often people who have never read the Bible as adults or have never read the New Testament have very strong opinions anyway. The solution is to read the Bible openmindedly, praying that God will reveal what is true.
(2) Being engaged in sin which one refuses to give up. The solution is to get one's priorities straight. Is it more important to continue the sin and go to eternal destruction, or to turn to God for forgiveness and receive assurance of everlasting life?
(3) Fear, for example, of being rejected by one's friends and community if one professes faith in Yeshua, or of poverty, or of having to live a "life that isn't fun." The remedy is to trust that God is in control and will open a life more fulfilling than one could ever have dreamed of, even if aspects of these fears prove well-grounded. Everything works for the good of those who trust God (Ro 8:28).

2 **Such** demonic **teachings come from the hypocrisy of liars**. The devil uses human

means. These false teachers are referred to at Ac 20:28–31; 2 Th 2:6; 2 Ke 3:1–3a&N; 1 Yn 2:18–23, 4:1–6; 2 Yn 7.

Consciences, like every other component of human nature, can be ruined. Kleptomaniacs and pathological liars are examples of people whose consciences don't function properly. Do those who habitually cheat on their taxes, or make under-the-table payments for favors, have seared consciences? Yes, if they have no awareness of the wrongness of what they are doing, or if they are convinced that they are an exception to the rule. But "let him who is without sin cast the first stone." We must examine the sensitivity of our own consciences, so that we may "go and sin no more" (Yn 8:8, 11, KJV).

3a They forbid marriage and require abstinence from various **foods**. Sha'ul favors self-discipline for the sake of the Kingdom of God (1C 9:24–27), but not asceticism. His own attitude toward marriage (1C 7:1–40) and eating (Ro 14:5–6, 14–17, 20; 1C 8:8, 13; 10:23–11:1; Co 2:16–23) is eminently sensible, avoiding both self-indulgence and self-denial. He evaluates these behaviors in terms of how they affect others and how they express commitment to Yeshua the Messiah.

Abstinence from foods does not mean observing *kashrut*, although the false teachers probably did incorporate elements of the Jewish dietary laws into their ascetic practices. See Ro 14:1N. Also compare Genesis 9:3–4.

3b–5 God created both **marriage** and **foods to be partaken of with thanksgiving**. Compare Ro 14:5–6 and the caution at 1C 10:30–31. In Jewish tradition there are blessings said at a wedding ceremony, and grace is both before and after meals. The *b'rakhah* before meals (Mt 14:19N) is short; afterwards, on a full stomach, one can be thankful at greater length for what one has just eaten. The first *b'rakhah* after the meal is:

> "Blessed are you, *Adonai* our God, king of the universe, who feeds the whole world with your goodness, grace, loving-kindness and mercy. You give food to everything that lives, because your loving-kindness endures forever. In your great goodness, we have never lacked food. For your great name's sake, may we never lack it ever, since you nourish, sustain and do good to all and provide food for all the creatures you created. Blessed are you, *Adonai*, giver of food to all."

The second *b'rakhah* includes thanks for the productive Land of Israel, the covenant and the *Torah*, and quotes the Scriptural basis for these blessings, "And you will eat and be satisfied, and you will bless *Adonai* your God for the good land which he has given you" (Deuteronomy 8:10). Subsequent *b'rakhot* include prayers for the restoration of Jerusalem, the return of the Jewish people to the Land, and the coming of the Messiah.

Everything created by God is good, but not everything created by God is food. Therefore, this verse does *not* abolish the Jewish dietary laws; see Ac 10:11–19&NN, Ga 2:12b&N).

The word of God and prayer make it holy. The means of sanctification are various, both in Judaism and in the New Testament. The blessing recited in connection with doing a *mitzvah* contains the phrase, "our God…, who has sanctified us with your commandments"; the commandments, a subspecies of the word of God, sanctify. See the article, "Kedushah" ("holiness," "sanctification"), in *Encyclopedia Judaica*, 10:866–875.

"Set them apart for holiness by means of the truth — your word is truth" (Yn 17:17); truth sanctifies.

"The Messiah loved the Messianic Community, indeed, gave himself up on its behalf, in order to set it apart for God, making it clean through immersion in the *mikveh*, so to speak" (Ep 5:26); immersion sanctifies.

"Yeshua suffered death outside the gate, in order to make the people holy through his own blood" (MJ 13:12); Yeshua's death for us sanctifies (see also MJ 10:10, 29; 1C 1:2).

"I have... the priestly duty of presenting the Good News of God, so that the Gentiles may be an acceptable offering, made holy by the *Ruach HaKodesh*" (Ro 15:15–16); the Holy Spirit sanctifies.

"May the God of *shalom* make you completely holy" (1 Th 5:23) — by whatever means he chooses!

7 ***Bubbe-meises***, Yiddish for "grandmother's stories," fables (1:4) told or believed only by silly, superstitious old women. It renders the Greek phrase, "*graô deis muthous*" ("old-womanish tales"; "*muthous*" underlies the English word "myths)."

8 **Physical exercise**, or "physical self-discipline" (compare v. 3) **does have some value** for the body (relevant for Timothy; see 5:23). Some make a religion of physical fitness, through health foods, jogging, sunbathing, saunas, bodybuilding, sports, massage. Care for one's body has an honorable place in Scripture: the body is the temple of the Holy Spirit, we are to honor God with our bodies. So we should take normal precautions but avoid neglecting, overindulging or idolizing our bodies. This parallels Jewish teaching on the role of the body.

10 **God is the deliverer** (1:1&N) **of all humanity** (2:4–7, Yn 3:16), **especially of those who trust**. The word "**especially**" reminds us that Ro 2:14–15 seems to allow the possibility that some who do not profess faith in Yeshua, perhaps because they do not have cognitive knowledge of the Gospel, may nevertheless be saved; but see the note there for the necessary cautions against using this concept to excuse not accepting Yeshua as the Messiah.

14 **Gift.** See Ro 12:6–8; 1C 12:4–11, 28–31. On ***s'mikhah*** (ordination) see Mt 21:23N.

16 Deeds and teachings, self and others: both matter.

CHAPTER 5

1 "You shall rise before the hoary head and honor the face of the old man; I am *Adonai*, your God" (Leviticus 19:32).

3 **Widows who are really in need**, literally, "who are real widows."

3–16 These verses balance Ac 2:44–46, 4:32–35, where believers shared their possessions with those in need. The first resort of the needy is to be their families, not the congregation; conversely, those with needy relatives should care for them (vv. 4, 8, 16).

5 "Let your widows trust in me" (Jeremiah 49:11).

8 Charity begins at home. Also, if believers should support related widows, how much more (Mt 6:30N) should they support themselves (2 Th 3:6–12, Ep 4:28).

9–10 **The list of widows**. Being a "real widow" (v. 3&N) is an office, so to speak, like *shammash*; and like *shammashim* widows must meet the qualifications set forth in order to be eligible for aid.

Was faithful to her husband, or: "was married only once" (see 3:2N).

One who has reared her children well, or "one who looks after children well." The former gives the literal sense of Greek *teknotrophein*, but conflicts with v. 4.

18 Compare 1C 9:7–9, Mt 10:10.

19 Although Sha'ul here reminds Timothy of a legal principle enunciated in the *Torah*, nevertheless some Christian theologians consider the "civil law" of the *Torah* to have been abrogated by the New Covenant!

20 In an age when people flee from authority, **rebuke** has fallen into disuse, and congregational discipline is frequently weak. Public rebuke, properly administered, is a form of God's love, but how many can see it that way? The subject is pursued in greater depth at MJ 12:5–13.

21 **The chosen angels**, as opposed to the fallen angels, will take part in the final judgment (Mt 25:31, Mk 8:38, Lk 9:26, Rv 14:10). Timothy should judge in a manner worthy of them; they will have a part in judging him (compare Lk 6:37–38).

23 **Water** was often impure, a disease-carrier; **wine** was less likely to be so. Wine itself was usually served diluted with three to six parts water. Medicinal and ceremonial use of wine has Scriptural support; getting drunk has Scriptural opposition. Normal use of wine at meals has Scriptural support, also use of strong drink for special festivals, and for easing final pain at death or in times of great grief. Obviously, these general principles would not apply to someone who has a problem with alcohol.

CHAPTER 6

4 **Controversies and word-battles**. Compare 1:4&N.

5–6 For how many people is **religion** discredited because those who profess it demonstrate by their lives that they consider it **a road to riches**! The sad thing is that by their greed they have been **deprived of the truth**, of the **riches** of **true religion**.

7 "I came naked from my mother's womb, and I will return there naked: *Adonai* gave, *Adonai* has taken away; blessed be the name of *Adonai*" (Job 1:21). Also see Psalm 49:17–18, Ecclesiastes 5:15 and in the Mishna, Pirkey-Avot 6:9 (quoted in Rv 14:13N).

8 "Give me neither poverty nor riches, but feed me with my proper share" (Proverbs 30:8).

9 Compare the "thorns" of Mt 13:7, 22; Lk 8:14. "Do not struggle to become rich; because you have understanding, forbear" (Proverbs 23:4). Also Proverbs 28:22.

10 It is not money itself but **the love of money** (v. 10) which is **the root of all the evils**. Or: "Loving money leads to all kinds of evils." Likewise, fundraising for religious purposes is not a sin. I trust people's gut reactions about such matters — greed and bad taste are hard to hide.

12 **Fight the good fight of faith**. Sha'ul did (2 Ti 4:6–8). The fight of faith is against sin, not against people (2C 10:3–5, Ep 6:10–13).

13 Sha'ul's only mention of Yeshua's trial before the Roman court. See Mt 27:11–14; Yn 18:33–38, 19:9–11.

15 **King of kings and Lord of lords**. "For *Adonai* your God is God of gods and Lord of lords" (Deuteronomy 10:17). See Rv 19:16&N.

17–19 The theme of **riches** (vv. 5–10) returns. Compare Jeremiah 9:22–23(23–24). "If riches increase, don't set your heart upon them" (Psalm 62:11(10)).

20–21 **Ungodly babblings and argumentative opposition**. Compare 1:4, 4:7, 6:4–5. On "**knowledge**," the keyword in Gnosticism, see 2C 8:1&N, Co 1:19&N.

THE SECOND LETTER FROM YESHUA'S EMISSARY SHA'UL (PAUL) TO TIMOTHY:

2 TIMOTHY

CHAPTER 1

1 Sha'ul's greetings often look forward to a major topic in his letter; see examples at the beginning of Romans, Galatians, Philippians and Titus. An error not dealt with in 1 Timothy has surfaced: it is being taught that the resurrection of believers has already happened (2:18; compare 2 Th 2:2–3). In anticipation of the discussion, Sha'ul hints that **God's will** still **holds forth a promise of** an as yet unrealized **life**.

3 **My prayers night and day**. See 1 Th 3:10&N, where Sha'ul uses the same expression.

5 **Lois and Eunice** were Jewish, but Timothy's father was not. It is because Jewishness is transmitted through the mother, not the father, that Sha'ul circumcised Timothy (Ac 16:1–3&NN).

6 Compare 1 Ti 4:14N; on ***s'mikhah*** (laying on of hands) see Mt 21:23N.

7 Compare Ro 8:15, 1 Ti 4:12, 1 Yn 4:18. It is easy not to **fan the flame of God's gift** but to wait passively for it to flash forth by itself. Such apathy and fear must be overcome by **the** Holy **Spirit, who produces not timidity, but** the means of conquering it — **power, love and self-discipline** (KJV's "a sound mind" is slightly off the point).

8 We should not be **ashamed of bearing testimony to** Yeshua (Ro 1:16, 10:8b–10N) or of associating with his workers, even if they happen to be in prison, **suffering disgrace**. Onesiphorus (v. 16) is our model; Sha'ul adds more on the subject at 2:3–7. This verse is relevant for Messianic Jews, since we often find ourselves regarded with contempt or suspicion by unbelievers. We should **accept** our **share** of this, knowing that **God will give** us **the strength for it**, since he has given us everything worthwhile that is ours (vv. 9–10).

9–10 Here is the Gospel in miniature. God **delivered us** (see 1 Ti 1:1N) from the penalty of eternal death due us for our sins; this is past. For the present, **he has called us to** live **a life of holiness**, not libertinism (3:2–5). This salvation is **not because of our deeds**; we did not earn it, we have no claim on God (Ro 1:16–8:39, Ep 2:8–10). Rather, it stems from **his own purpose**; this is what produced **the grace which he gave to us who are united with the Messiah Yeshua**. God's purpose existed, and his grace was assigned

before the beginning of time (see Ep 1:3–14, Rv 13:8), but to humanity it was a secret. **Only now,** at the time of his own choosing (Ro 5:6, Ga 4:4, 1 Ti 2:6), has he **made it public** (Ep 3:3–4, 9; Co 1:26) **through the appearing of Yeshua the Messiah our deliverer** (this is God's role, v. 9), **who abolished death** and **revealed** the **life and immortality** which will be ours in the future (compare 1:1, 2:18). This is the **Good News**, the Gospel, which anyone can appropriate for himself by trust, love and following its teaching (v.13).

11 As he often does, Sha'ul reaffirms his credentials as emissary to the Gentiles — provided the phrase, "**of the *Goyim*,**" lacking in some manuscripts, is not an adaptation from the parallel passage in 1 Ti 2:7.

12 A major resource of believers in times of persecution is confidence not that we can hold out, but that Yeshua the Messiah **can keep safe what he has entrusted to me** (or: "what I have deposited with him" — the Greek is not explicit). **That Day**, when Yeshua appears in glory to reward the faithful and execute judgment on unbelievers, is much on Sha'ul's mind in this letter (v. 18, 4:8), since he believes he is himself soon to die (4:7).

13–14 **The sound teachings**, equivalent to "the faith" (1 Ti 3:9, 16; 4:1, 6; Yd 3), are the **great treasure** to be kept **safe**. This requires the ***Ruach HaKodesh***, the Holy Spirit, who is in us.

15 It is but a short step from being ashamed (v. 8) to deserting the cause and its workers. Compare 4:10, 16. **Phygelus** and **Hermogenes** are not mentioned elsewhere in the New Testament.

16–18 **The household of Onesiphorus** lived in Ephesus (4:19). He exemplifies for Timothy what it means **not** to be **ashamed of** Sha'ul's **being in prison** (see v. 8).

May the Lord Yeshua **grant it to him to find mercy from *Adonai***. Since only his household is mentioned, Onesiphorus himself may himself have been no longer alive. If so, this is the unique instance of prayer for the dead in the New Testament. The practice was known in Judaism; this is proved by 2 Maccabees 12:39–45, written in the 1st century B.C.E. and alluded to in 4:8N below.

CHAPTER 2

2 Four generations in the tradition-passing process: **me** (Sha'ul), **you** (Timothy), **faithful people** and **others also** (compare Avot 1:1, quoted at Ac 6:13–14N). It is not enough to know or even to teach; one must make sure that at least some of those taught **will be competent to teach others also**; otherwise the movement dies. (I have heard of a school in South America where the students are graded by the examinations which *their* students write.) To do this will require a bold stand — which brings Sha'ul back to the subject of suffering disgrace (vv. 3–7; see 1:7–8, 15–16 above).

5 **According to the rules**. See 2C 4:1–2N.

6 Compare Lk 10:7, 1C 9:4–12, Ga 6:6.

8 Compare Ro 1:3–4, a similar epitome of the **Good News**. Sha'ul's phrase, "**who was raised from the dead**," looks forward to his refuting Hymenaeus and Philetus (vv. 17–18).

10 Compare 1C 9:19, 22b–23.

11–13 Like Pp 2:6–11 and 1 Ti 3:16, this is another hymn. Verse 11 (compare Ro 6:5) relates to the resurrection heresy of v. 18, vv. 12–13 to Timothy's fear. **If we persevere, we will rule with him**, according to Rv 3:21, 20:4. **If we disown him, he will disown us**, according to Mt 10:33, Lk 12:8–9. Even **if we are faithless, he remains faithful**, true to his promises; see Ro 3:3–4&N, 9:6a&N.

14–16 No need to be ashamed, compare above, 1:8, 16; 2:3–7. **Deals straightforwardly**, honestly (see 2C 4:1–2N), **with the Word of the Truth** (the Good News about Yeshua), without **word-battles** and **godless babbling** (compare v. 23; 1 Ti 6:4–5, 20–21). Examples in the modern context would include arguments over eternal punishment in hell with people who have no intention of repenting, or over Yeshua's virgin birth with unbelievers whose presuppositions exclude the possibility.

17 Hymenaeus Sha'ul had already excommunicated at 1 Ti 1:20, but apparently this did not put an end to his mischief. **Philetus** is not mentioned elsewhere.

18 Our resurrection has already taken place, spiritually, in immersion; no physical resurrection is to be expected. From Co 2:12 and Ro 6:5 one can see how such views start. They were held in Corinth too, but Sha'ul countered them, pointing out that faith without a hope of physical resurrection is useless (1 Corinthians 15). A somewhat similar teaching, that the Day of the Lord had already come, was current in Thessalonica (2 Th 2:2–3).

20–22 The "**pots**" metaphor is the same as at Ro 9:21. Also compare the ritual purification of pots spoken of at Mk 7:3–4 with the purity of heart spoken of here (v. 22).

23–26 On dealing with those who differ, and why.

CHAPTER 3

1–5 In the *acharit-hayamim* ("in the end of days"; compare 1 Ti 4:1) **there will come trying times** characterized by moral and spiritual decline. This will be accompanied by natural and social disasters, as is clear from the Messiah's own description of this period (Mattityahu 24–25, Mark 13, Lk 21:5–36), but here the emphasis is on the decadence of individuals.

In the rabbinic writings can be found similar descriptions of "the birth-pains of the Messiah" (compare Mt 24:8&N). One well-known saying from the Talmud suggests two equally likely possibilities:

"Rabbi Yochanan said: 'The Son of David will not come except in a generation which is either completely righteous or completely guilty.'"(Sanhedrin 98a)

But the more usual picture tends toward the latter, as is seen in this citation from the Mishna describing what can be expected when the Messiah is about to come:

"On the heels of the Messiah, *chutzpah* [insolence] will multiply, and honor will vanish. The vine will give its fruit, but wine will be costly. The government will be converted to *minut* [heresy, or Christianity specifically] without being admonished, and houses of learning will be prostituted. The Galil will be destroyed and the Golan [or: the leaders] devastated. The people of the frontier [or: the leaders] will go around begging, but no one will show them mercy. The wisdom of the *Torah*-teachers will degenerate, those who fear sin will be despised, and the truth will disappear. Youths will shame the faces of the old, and old men will stand up in the presence of children. 'The son dishonors the father, the daughter rises up against her mother, the daughter-in-law against her mother-in-law, and a man's enemies are the people of his own household.' (Micah 7:6) The face of the generation is like the face of a dog [shameless] — a son will not be embarrassed even before his own father. So on whom should we lean? On our Father who is in Heaven." (Sotah 9:15)

A *midrash* from before 500 C.E. gives this picture:

"And when the Holy One, blessed be He, sees that there is no righteous in the generation and no pious in the land, and no charity in the hands of man,... [then He] remembers his own charity, compassion and mercy, and helps Himself with His Great Arm,... whose length is like the length of the world from one end to the other.... Instantly Israel are redeemed among themselves, and the Messiah becomes visible to them." (*Sefer Hekhalot*, in A. Jellinek, *Bet HaMidrash* 5:189–190; quoted from Raphael Patai, *The Messiah Texts*, pp. 100–101)

Ever since Sha'ul penned his letter, commentators and preachers have applied this passage and v. 13 to their own times. Some day, the decadent generation then alive will in fact be the one in whose days Yeshua the Messiah returns. And who is to say that it will not be our own?

5 Most **religion** today is mere **outer form**, words and ritual without **power**; contrast 1C 2:4–5. Non-Messianic Judaism too must remain an **outer form of religion** lacking the spiritual **power** people want and need, so long as it continues to **deny** him who is the only way to the Father (Yn 14:6) and to the Holy Spirit (Ro 8:9–10), the source of that **power** (1:7 above).

6–7 Always learning but never able to come to full knowledge of the truth (compare 4:3, Yn 18:38a). A perfect description not only of **weak-willed women** (in today's world I can hope he would have written, "weak-willed people"), but of professional skeptics and others who, under the guise of "seeking the truth," keep avoiding it. The real reason they do this is that they are **heaped with sins** they do not want to give up and **swayed by various impulses** they do not want to face. See 1C 2:6–16, which can be read as a commentary on these two verses, and 1 Ti 4:1N.

8 **Jannes and Jambres** are not mentioned in the *Tanakh*, but they are identified in *Targum Yonatan* (Numbers 22:22) as sons of Balaam, and also as the magicians in Pharaoh's court who tried to equal the feats of Moses reported in Exodus 7:11–12; 8:3(7), 14–15(18–19); 9:11. They are described elsewhere as having been among the "mixed multitude" who followed the Israelites out of Egypt (Exodus 12:38), and as instigators of the golden calf debacle (Exodus 32:1). They appear in the Dead Sea Scrolls, in the writings of the pagans Pliny and Apuleius, and in Christian apocrypha. See *Encyclopedia Judaica* 7:711, 9:1277; H. Strack and P. Billerbeck, *Commentary to the New Testament from Talmud and Midrash*, 3:660–664. Editor James H. Charlesworth included a book of Jannes and Jambres, consisting of integrated manuscript fragments from the 1st to 3rd centuries, in *The Old Testament Pseudepigrapha*, New York: Doubleday & Co., 1985.

12 I once saw a sign on the marquee outside a theater that had been converted into a church: "If you were arrested for being a Christian, would there be enough evidence to convict you?" The **godly life** is the evidence.

15 Timothy was guided toward trust in Yeshua the Messiah **from childhood** by his Messianic Jewish mother Eunice and grandmother Lois (1:5). What a blessing to have such a head start in life! How few Jewish believers today have that advantage! Most of us discovered only as adults the unfortunately too-well-kept secret that **the Holy Scriptures**, which means, of course, the *Tanakh*, **can give the wisdom that leads to deliverance through trusting in Yeshua the Messiah**. A function of the *Jewish New Testament* is to point readers of the *Tanakh* in his direction, as the *Tanakh* itself intends (Lk 24:25–27, Ro 10:4&N).

16–17 **All Scripture is God-breathed**. Others have translated this, "All God-breathed Scripture is valuable…." As I have rendered it, we learn here that the entire *Tanakh*, every verse of it (***all*** **Scripture**), is inspired by God. Because of this, the Bible is incomparably more authoritative than anything else ever written or spoken. Opinions come a dime a dozen and a mile a minute, but assured truth from God about himself and humanity is found in the *Tanakh* and the New Testament, and nowhere else.

Because the Bible is God-breathed, it is **valuable** for the four pastoral purposes named. **Anyone who belongs to God** and who lets Scripture pastor him in all four of these ways (however, not apart from associating with the community of God's people; see MJ 10:24–25) **may be fully equipped for every good work**.

CHAPTER 4

1 See vv. 6–8N.

2 **Proclaim the Word**, that is, the Good News. See v. 5N. **Teaching; convict, censure…**

exhort. These correspond to the uses of Scripture named at 3:16.

3–4 Compare 3:7. **Myths**. Compare 1 Ti 1:4, 4:7.

5 **A proclaimer of the Good News**. The phrase translates Greek *evangelistos*, "evangelist," equivalent to Hebrew *m'vasser*. Philip is called this at Ac 21:8. Evangelists are among the gifts God has given to the Messianic Community (Ep 4:11). By the Great Commission (Mt 28:18–20&N), believers are commanded to proclaim the Good News to all nations, Gentiles and Jews alike.

6–8 In his last farewell Sha'ul uses phrases from his own past. **Poured out on the altar**, compare Pp 2:17. **Departure**, compare Pp 1:23. **I have fought the good fight**, compare 1 Ti 1:18, 6:12. **I have completed the course**, compare Ac 20:24, 1C 9:25, MJ 12:1–2. But finally, Sha'ul, ever Jewish, uses Jewish death language. The Jewish burial service contains these lines:

> "O True and Righteous Judge! Blessed be the True Judge, all of whose judgments are righteous and true."

The phrase, "**the Righteous Judge**," is found in connection with Y'hudah *HaMakkabi*'s prayer for fallen Jewish soldiers at 2 Maccabees 12:41 (see also 2 Maccabees 12:6). However, the Righteous Judge is **the Lord**, "the Messiah Yeshua, who will judge the living and the dead when he appears and establishes his Kingdom" (v. 1; compare Yn 5:22–30).

10–11 **Demas** and **Luke** (the author of the books of Luke and Acts) were fellow-workers with Sha'ul; see Co 4:14N. The tragedy of Demas' falling away could not be more poignantly expressed; see 1:15N. **Crescens**, otherwise unknown, and **Titus**, recipient in Crete of Sha'ul's letter, presumably were not deserters but dispatched by Sha'ul.

12–14 **Tychicus**, see Ep 6:21N. **Carpus**, otherwise unknown. **Alexander**, probably the same as at 1 Ti 1:20&N.

16 **May it not be counted against them**. Compare Lk 23:34, Ac 7:60.

19 **Priscilla and Aquila**, see Ac 18:2N, Ro 16:3N. **Onesiphorus**, see 1:16–18 above.

20 **Erastus** was sent with Timothy from Ephesus to Macedonia (Ac 19:22); he could be identical with the "city treasurer" of Corinth mentioned at Ro 16:23. **Trophimus** and Tychicus (above) represented the congregations in the province of Asia in the group which accompanied Sha'ul when he brought the contribution from the congregations he had founded to the Messianic Jews in Jerusalem (Ac 20:4, 21:29).

21 Irenaeus (c. 180 C.E.) writes that **Linus** succeeded Kefa (Peter) as leader of the Roman church, so that the Roman Catholic Church counts him the second Pope. By tradition **Claudia** was the wife of either Linus or **Pudens**.

THE LETTER FROM YESHUA'S EMISSARY SHA'UL (PAUL)
TO

TITUS

CHAPTER 1

1 **An emissary sent to promote... the trust and knowledge of truth which lead to godliness**, called "trust-grounded obedience" at Ro 1:5.
God's chosen people. See Co 3:12N.

2–3 **God, who does not lie** (compare Numbers 23:19), in contrast with the false teachers of vv. 10–16. On the rest of these verses, see 2 Ti 1:9–11&NN.

4 **Titus** was a Gentile co-worker of Sha'ul's who accompanied him to Jerusalem (Ga 2:1–3) and carried out various assignments (2C 2:13, 7:6–8:23, 12:18; 2 Ti 4:10).
In v. 3 it is God who is called **our Deliverer** (see 1 Ti 1:1N); here it is **the Messiah Yeshua**. This is typical of how the New Testament highlights Yeshua's divinity with roundabout language. Instead of saying, "Yeshua is God," it describes him with words that can apply only to God. It was precisely this sort of thing that those without faith could not grasp, even when they saw it (Mk 2:1–12; Yn 6:1–71, 9:1–41).

5–9 Compare 1 Ti 3:1–13. The organizational structure in Ephesus, where Timothy was when Sha'ul wrote to him, was more complex than that needed in Crete; *shammashim* are not mentioned here.

6 **Husband to one wife**, or: "faithful to his wife." See 1 Ti 3:2N.
With believing children. The requirement is not that a leader have children, but that if he has children they be believers (see 1 Ti 3:4–5&N). However, the criterion here is stronger than in the letter to Timothy: his children must not only "obey him with all proper respect" (1 Ti 3:4) but must be (literally) "having faith."

9 **Sound teaching** should not merely transfer data from head to head, it should **exhort and encourage**.

10 **The Circumcision faction**. This is not a synonym either for Messianic Jews or for non-Messianic Jews. Rather, it denotes, as in Galatia, a group which included Gentiles as well as Jews (this is clear from v. 12), whose distinctive was that they favored circumcising Gentile believers. Sha'ul was uncompromising in his opposition to them, because what they stood for negates the Gospel in relation to Gentiles. This was the central issue in the book of Galatians, and at Acts 15 the matter was settled once and for all. See Ac 10:45N, Ga 2:12cN and Appendix, p. 933.

11–13 Exactly how the false teachers might have made **dishonest gain** is not clear; however, in the ancient world Cretans were known for their avariciousness and for other negative qualities, **as one of their own prophets has said**, Epimenides of Cnossos, in the 6th century B.C.E. Starting with the claim that the tomb of Zeus was on their island, **Cretans** acquired a reputation for being **always liars** — etcetera.

If Sha'ul really means the plain sense of what he writes, he is simply prejudiced. But I cannot believe this cosmopolitan was a bigot. Nor do I think his anger at the false teachers was so uncontrolled that he vomited out genuinely held views which in a more guarded moment he would have suppressed for politics' sake (although the New Testament does record moments when Sha'ul lost control of himself — Ac 23:2–5&N, Ga 5:12&N). Most defences of Sha'ul here seem heavy-handed and unconvincing.

I offer two possible explanations. The first is to take this quotation, together with his own *coup de grace*, "**and it's true!**," as a light touch. Should he have said instead, "But I don't agree; some of my best friends are Cretans"? The citizen of the world who could write, "I owe a debt to both civilized Greeks and uncivilized people, to both the educated and the ignorant" (Ro 1:14), made an intentional overstatement, the humor of which removes the epithet from the realm of the real, insofar as its plain-sense application to Cretans in general is concerned, and leaves Sha'ul free to apply it entirely and only to the false teachers. If so, then the **reason** Titus is to be **severe** in rebuking the false teachers (v. 13) is not that Cretans lie, etc., (v. 12) but that **there are many... who delude... with their worthless... talk** (v. 11).

An alternative explanation, perhaps less "politically correct," is that lying, gluttony, etc., were indeed characteristic of society in Crete, not necessarily found in every single Cretan, but endemic to that culture; their own writers acknowledged it. Sha'ul therefore admonishes Titus to neutralize these factors by being especially severe when he rebukes the false teachers. Also see Appendix, p. 934.

14 Judaistic myths. The Greek word for "myths" is used at 1 Ti 1:4, 4:7&N; 2 Ti 4:4; 2 Ke 1:16. See 1 Ti 1:4N for a discussion of what the content of these myths may have been.

The Greek adjective *Ioudaikois* appears only here in the New Testament. I do not believe these myths were part of normative non-Messianic Judaism, but rather that they expressed the Circumcision faction's preoccupation with the trappings of Judaism. Therefore, the word usually used to translate it, "Jewish," is misleading and, in the ambience of the present world, antisemitic, insofar as it causes people to think less of normative non-Messianic Judaism. "Jewishy" would probably convey the sense best but is too informal; hence "**Judaistic**," that is, imitative of Judaism without actually emanating from normative Judaism.

The **commands** probably related to festivals and ascetic prohibitions along the lines of Ga 4:10, Co 2:16–23 and 1 Ti 4:3–6; see also Isaiah 29:13, Mk 7:5–7.

15 This seems a key verse for Messianic Jews to take into account when establishing the nature of *Torah* in the light of the New Testament. Is the import of "**Everything is pure**" to do away with the laws of *taharot* ("ritual purity") found in both the Written and Oral *Torah*? Is it to be applied only metaphorically, with "**pure**" and "**defiled**" having a spiritual sense that leaves the laws of *taharot* unaffected? Or is it to be taken as a statement about "priorities" within the framework of *Torah*, not altering the laws of *taharot* but establishing purity of **minds and consciences** as more important? (See Mt 23:23&N, Yn 7:22–23&N, Ga 2:12b&N.)

16 They claim to know God, but with their actions they deny him. (My seventh-grade teacher, Mrs. Uphoff, imprinted on the memory of everyone in her class the proverb, "What you are speaks so loudly I can't hear what you say.") Compare 2 Ti 3:5 (and meditate on the history of the Church *vis-à-vis* the Jewish people). These would-be leaders seem to have passed the point of no return. Sha'ul neither prays for them (compare 1 Yn 5:16b) nor says he has "turned them over to the Adversary, so that they will learn not to blaspheme" (1 Ti 1:20; compare 1C 5:5); rather, like the false prophets of 2 Kefa 2, **they are detestable and disobedient; they have proved themselves unfit to do anything good**.

CHAPTER 2

1 But you, Titus, in contrast with the false teachers who deny God by their actions and have proved themselves unable to do anything good (1:16), do not limit yourself to mere "talk" (1:10), even if it is **sound teaching**, but **explain what kind of behavior goes along with** it. Verses 2–10 outline what Titus should say and urge him to be an example (vv. 6–8). Compare Ep 5:21–6:9; Co 3:18–4:1; 1 Ti 5:1–2, 6:1–2.

11 God's grace, which brings deliverance (or: "salvation"), **has appeared to all people**. Nevertheless, not everyone is saved because not everyone has committed himself to this grace. However, because it has appeared to everyone, everyone has the opportunity to commit himself. Certainly everyone reading the New Testament has the opportunity to believe it. Compare Ro 1:19–20, 2:14–15.

12–13 Verse 12 restates "what kind of behavior goes along with sound teaching" (vv. 1–10), here and now, in this life; while v. 13 points to, literally, "the blessed hope," meaning **the blessed fulfillment of our certain hope, which is the appearing** at the End of Days **of the *Sh'khinah*** (manifest glory) **of God, and** (at the same time) **the appearing of our Deliverer, Yeshua the Messiah.**

An alternative rendering: "...the appearing of the *Sh'khinah* of the great God, which *Sh'khinah* is our Deliverer, Yeshua the Messiah." Messianic Jews 1:3 gives support by saying of Yeshua, "This Son is the radiance of the *Sh'khinah*."

Many translators and commentators believe the sense is as in the Revised Standard Version: "...the appearing of the glory of our great God and Savior, Jesus Christ." The verse then states clearly that Jesus is God. But I think that understanding forces a statement about Yeshua's divinity into a passage not concerned with it. Yeshua's divine nature is not compromised by rendering as I have done. As I have pointed out elsewhere, the New Testament usually uses more indirect language to express Yeshua's God-aspect.

14 He, Yeshua, **gave himself up on our behalf** (Mk 10:45; 2C 5:14–15; Ga 2:16, 20–21), **in order to free** (or: "ransom") **us** (see Ep 1:7N) **from all violation of *Torah*** (or "from all iniquity," "from all lawlessness"). Without this fact, vv. 1–12 would be good ethical advice devoid of purpose and promise.

Purify. Compare 1:15.

A people who would be his own, rendered "a peculiar people" in KJV; the same term (Hebrew *'am s'gulah*) is applied to Israel at Deuteronomy 14:2, 26:18; see also Exodus 19:5, Psalm 135:4. See 2 Ke 2:9&N.

15 Titus, like Timothy (1 Ti 4:12), needed reassurance of his ability and **authority**, so that he would not be overcome by inferiority feelings that would keep him from doing the Lord's work properly. In contrast, because he had once felt superior and self-sufficient, Sha'ul, before he could be a proper worker, had to reach the point of being able to ask, "Who is equal to such a task?" and answering himself, "Our competence is from God" (2C 2:16, 3:5).

CHAPTER 3

3–8 Compare Ep 2:3–10. The same relationship between individual salvation and good works is taught here (especially in v. 8) as throughout Sha'ul's letters.

5 ***Mikveh***, the Jewish ritual bath, renders Greek *loutron*, "washing," found in the New Testament only here and at Ep 5:26&N. The reference is clearly to immersion (baptism); see Mt 3:1N.

9–11 Controversies, genealogies, quarrels and fights about the *Torah*. See 1:14 above; 1 Ti 1:3b–4&N, 6:4; 2 Ti 2:14–16&N, 2:23. A congregation leader cannot tolerate divisiveness in a group with the task of "doing good deeds" (v. 8) by the power of the *Ruach HaKodesh* (v. 6); the unity for which the Messiah prayed (Yn 17:21) is essential if the group is serious and dedicated.

12 Artemas, not mentioned elsewhere. **Tychicus**, see Ep 6:2N1. **Nicopolis**, a city in Thrace near the boundary with Macedonia.

13 Zenas, not mentioned elsewhere.

***Torah* expert**. Same term, Greek *nomikos*, as at Mt 22:35; Lk 7:30, 10:25&N, 11:45–52, 14:3.

Apollos. An Alexandrian Jew, an eloquent speaker with a thorough knowledge of the *Tanakh*, whom Priscilla and Aquila instructed (Ac 18:24–19:1) and who had followers in Corinth (1C 1:12&N).

THE LETTER FROM YESHUA'S EMISSARY SHA'UL (PAUL)
TO

PHILEMON

1–2 The Letter to Philemon is unique among Sha'ul's writings in that it offers pastoral advice to someone who is not a pastor. It has been compared with the *Tanakh*'s book of Ruth in its rich human warmth and joy. It seems to have been written from prison at the same time as Colossians.

Sha'ul, Timothy. See Pp 1:1N.

A prisoner for the sake of the Messiah Yeshua, that is, incarcerated for proclaiming the Gospel (v. 13).

Philemon is a **fellow-worker** of Sha'ul's who hosts a **congregation** in his **home** (on house congregations, see Ro 16:5N); formerly he was master of the slave Onesimus (vv. 10, 16).

Apphia, not mentioned elsewhere, must have been a leader in the Messianic community of Colossae, like **Archippus** (see Co 4:17&N).

5–7 Interesting structure. **Love** (v. 5) looks forward to **love** in v. 7, where the phrase, "**refreshed the hearts**," anticipates v. 20. Likewise, **commitment** (v. 5) looks forward to **fellowship based on your commitment** in v. 6, which anticipates v. 17.

8–9 Sha'ul has the authority to **direct** but prefers to **appeal on the basis of** a **love** and sensitivity which pervades his entire plea (vv. 8–21).

10 **My son, of whom I became the father while here in prison**. Sha'ul brought him to trust in Yeshua the Messiah; his unpleasant prison surroundings did not prevent him from evangelizing. Compare 1C 4:15, 17. **Onesimus**, the runaway slave, had evidently sought refuge with Sha'ul but was not himself in prison. Had the authorities apprehended him, they would not have incarcerated him but would have returned him to his master, as required by law.

11 Literal translation: "Formerly he was useless to you, but now [he is] useful [Greek *evchrêstos*] to me and to you." The Greek name *Onêsimos* (v. 10) is another word for "useful." The *JNT* rendering makes explicit the Greek text's implicit wordplay.

12 **In returning him to you**. Onesimus was certainly the bearer of this letter.

14 I didn't want to do anything without your consent. Sha'ul's self-limitation is consistent with Jewish ethical standards, *derekh-eretz* (literally, the "way of [the] world,"), defined as "desirable behavior of a man toward his fellows, in keeping with natural practice and accepted social and moral standards, including the rules of etiquette and polite behavior" (*Encyclopedia Judaica* 5:1551).

19 As long as we're talking about debts, **I won't mention, of course....** This throwaway line is the archetypical "Jewish guilt trip," but Sha'ul is not using it to create guilt in Philemon. If he were, it wouldn't work! Rather, he trusts his relationship with Philemon is strong enough that the remark will touch a chord without offending. Delightful! Without doubt Philemon, like Onesimus, did **owe** Sha'ul his **very life**, his eternal life.

22 We do not know whether Sha'ul's hope to be released from prison soon and visit Onesimus was fulfilled.

23 Epaphras. See Co 1:7, 4:12–13.

24 Mark, Aristarchus. See Co 4:10&N. **Demas and Luke**, see Co 4:14, 2 Ti 4:10–11&N.

TO A GROUP OF

MESSIANIC JEWS (HEBREWS)

CHAPTER 1

1 This letter and those of Ya'akov, Kefa, Yochanan and Y'hudah are known as the General Letters, since they are thought of as being written to the entire Messianic Community, rather than to Gentiles only (like the majority of Sha'ul's) or to individuals (like the four Pastorals). However, there is a stream of biblical scholarship which holds that of these eight letters, all but Yochanan's three were written to Messianic Jews. For the present letter the argument is overwhelming.

Its Greek title, found on several of the oldest manuscripts, "*Pros Ebraious*" ("To Hebrews"), is not part of the original document but must nevertheless be very early. Clearly it is meant to indicate that the book concerns itself with topics of interest to believers in Yeshua who are Jewish — the *cahanut* ("priesthood"), the sacrificial system, angels, Malki-Tzedek (Melchizedek), Avraham (Abraham), Moshe (Moses), the Israelites in the wilderness, the biblical covenants, the *Tanakh*'s men of faith, the role of *Torah* in the New Covenant, and so on. More specifically, the author wrote to a particular community of Jewish believers whom he knew well and whose spiritual condition he monitored (5:11–12, 6:9–10, 10:32–34, 13:18–24). For these reasons and because in general my translation into modern English avoids archaisms and "churchy" language, I render the title as I do, "To a Group of Messianic Jews" (today one rarely hears Jews called "Hebrews"). For the following reasons I do not name its author.

Clement of Alexandria (around 200 C.E.) is quoted in Eusebius' *History of the Church* (324 C.E.) as stating "that the letter is Paul's and that it was written to Hebrews in the Hebrew language and translated [into Greek] by Luke." There is no other early evidence that Sha'ul wrote the letter or that it was originally written in Hebrew. Actually the Greek of Messianic Jews is the most elegant in the New Testament, and the most obvious use of this fact is to support the proposition that Greek is the language in which it was written. But it could mean only that the translator, whether Luke or another, had a good command of Greek. The fact that the diction differs from that of Romans and Corinthians could mean, not that Sha'ul didn't write this letter, but that he wrote it in Hebrew and the translator used his own polished style rather than Sha'ul's simpler one when rendering it into Greek.

Eusebius also quotes Origen (c. 280 C.E.), who was of the opinion that the ideas were Sha'ul's but not the authorship:

"…the thoughts are those of the emissary, but the language and composition that of one who recalled from memory and, as it were, made notes of what was said by his master."

The German Messianic Jew Dr. Joiachim Heinrich Biesenthal (1804–1886) wrote commentaries on the Gospels, Acts and Romans. In 1878 he published a commentary on this letter called *Das Trostschreiben des Apostels Paulus an die Hebräer,* in which he expressed the view that Sha'ul wrote it "in the dialect of the Mishna, the language of the schools," i.e., Hebrew. The Messianic Jewish commentator Yechiel Lichtenstein (see 3:13N) agreed, pointing out that Sha'ul's approach and subject matter in this letter differ from those in his other letters precisely because in those he wrote to Gentiles and in this to Jews; he was following his own advice in "becoming a Jew to the Jews" (1C 9:19–22&NN).

The majority of modern scholars believe Sha'ul did not write it. One reason is that in Rome, where the letter was known from an early date, Pauline authorship was rejected; additional reasons are well presented in other studies. I will mention only one piece of internal evidence, 2:3b, where the author writes, "This deliverance, which was first declared by the Lord, was confirmed to us by those who heard him." It is thought that Sha'ul could not have written these words, since he heard and saw Yeshua himself (Ac 9:3–6, 1C 15:8). But Sha'ul's advocates could answer that he was referring to the kind of "confirmation" he himself spoke of in Ga 2:1–2, 6–10, or that "those who heard him" refers to his earthly lifetime, not post-resurrection appearances.

Authorship candidates for whom there is no conflict with 2:3b include Apollos, an educated, courageous Hellenistic Jew who was clearly a charismatic leader (Ac 18:24–19:1; 1C 1:12, 3:4–5); Priscilla, who is mentioned in the New Testament before her husband Aquila four times out of six, notably in connection with teaching when "they took Apollos aside and explained to him the Way of God in greater detail" (Ac 18:26; also Ac 18:18, Ro 16:3, 2 Ti 4:19); Clement and Luke.

Some believe the letter was written in the 60's, shortly before the destruction of the Temple (if Sha'ul wrote it, it could not have been any later). Others date it anywhere from 70 to 100 C.E. The letter's references to the cultus allude not to the Temple but the earlier Tent of Meeting or Tabernacle. If the readers came from an Essene, Qumran or similar group who regarded the Temple establishment (the Sadducees and Pharisees) as corrupt and therefore centered their thoughts on the Tent of Meeting rather than the Temple, the author might have done this to take their sensitivities into account. But he might have done it because the Temple no longer existed. On the other hand, he writes of the Levitical *cahanut* as if it were still functioning (9:6–9), which it ceased to do in 70 C.E.

In days gone by, when the *Tanakh* was being written, **God spoke**: "Thus saith the Lord!" Some people claim to believe in God but not that he "spoke." A moment's reflection will cast a shadow on the viability of this position. If God did not "speak," if he has not revealed anything specific, if there are none of his words extant which can guide a person toward true knowledge about God, humanity and the relationship between them, then God is unconnected with life, irrelevant. Many secular people, agnostics and atheists seem willing to accept the hopelessness and meaninglessness of such a conclusion. I think they are wrong but closer to facing reality than those who believe in a God who has not spoken.

God spoke in many and varied ways, directly and indirectly, in dreams and stories, history and prophecy, poems and proverbs, **to the Fathers** of the Jewish people **through the prophets** from Moses to Malachi, and, before Moses, to Avraham, Isaac, Jacob and Joseph.

2–3 According to Jewish tradition Malachi was the last of the *Tanakh* prophets. For the next four centuries, to use the remark of an earlier prophet, "The word of *Adonai* was rare in those days; there was no frequent vision" (1 Samuel 3:1). **But in the *acharit-hayamim***, the *Tanakh*'s "latter days," which the New Testament regards as already here (1C 10:11&N), **he has spoken** again, not to Fathers long dead (v. 1), but **to us** in the 1st century C.E. (see 2:3N), **through his Son** (literally, "a son").

By implication, **his Son** is *better* than "the Prophets" (v. 1). A major purpose of the author is to show that Yeshua and everything connected with him are better than what was available previously. He uses this word, "better," twelve times in Messianic Jews to compare the Messiah and his era with what there was before. It appears first in v. 4, and last at 12:24, as the author summarizes this comparison of old and new (12:18–24).

There follow in vv. 2–3 seven features of God's **Son** which demonstrate his superiority:

(1) God **has given** him **ownership of everything** (compare Co 1:15b). Literally, God "has made him heir of all things." "Ask of me, and I will give you nations as an inheritance and the ends of the earth as your possession" (Psalms 2:8); compare Mt 4:8–9, 21:38; Ac 1:8. On the application of Psalm 2 to the Messiah, see v. 5aN below.

(2) God **created the universe through** him, as taught also at Yn 1:3, Co 1:16. That the universe was created through an intermediary — the Word (Yn 1:1–3), the *Sh'khinah* (see below), Wisdom, the *Torah* — is not an idea alien to Judaism, as shown by this quotation from Rabbi Akiva in the Mishna:

> "He used to say, '...God loves Israel, because he gave them a precious instrument [Hebrew *kli*, "instrument, vessel"]. But he enhanced that love by letting them know that the precious instrument they had been given was the very one through which the universe was created — as it is said, "For I give you good doctrine; do not forsake my *Torah*" (Proverbs 4:2).' " (Avot 3:14)

(3) **This Son is the radiance of**, literally, "the glory," best rendered Jewishly as **the *Sh'khinah***, which the *Encyclopedia Judaica* article on it (Volume 14, pp. 1349–1351) defines as

> "the Divine Presence, the numinous immanence of God in the world,... a revelation of the holy in the midst of the profane...."

The article continues:

> "One of the more prominent images associated with the *Shekhinah* is that of light. Thus on the verse, '...the earth did shine with His glory' (Ezekiel 43:2), the rabbis remark, 'This is the face of the *Shekhinah*' (*Avot diRabbi Natan* [18b–19a]; see also Chullin 59b–60a). Both the angels in heaven and

> the righteous in *olam ha-ba* ('the world to come') are sustained by the radiance of the *Shekhinah* (Exodus Rabbah 32:4, B'rakhot 17a; cf. Exodus 34:29–35)....
>
> "According to Saadiah Gaon [882–942 C.E.], the *Shekhinah* is identical with *kevod ha-Shem* ('the glory of God'), which served as an intermediary between God and man during the prophetic experience. He suggests that the 'glory of God' is the biblical term, and *Shekhinah* the talmudic term for the created splendor of light which acts as an intermediary between God and man, and which sometimes takes on human form. Thus when Moses asked to see the glory of God, he was shown the *Shekhinah*, and when the prophets in their visions saw God in human likeness, what they actually saw was not God Himself but the *Shekhinah* (see Saadiah's interpretation of Ezekiel 1:26, 1 Kings 22:19, and Daniel 7:9 in *Book of Beliefs and Opinions* 2:10)."

The point of these citations is not to suggest that Yeshua is a "created splendor of light," but to convey some of the associations of the expression, "the brightness of the glory" or **the radiance of the *Sh'khinah***. See also 2C 3:6–13&N, Rv 21:23.

On the etymology of "***Sh'khinah***" see Rv 7:15&N.

(4) The Greek word "*charactêr*" ("**very expression**"), used only here in the New Testament, delineates even more clearly than "*eikon*" ("image," 2C 4:4, Co 1:15a) that **God's essence** is manifested in the Messiah (Yn 14:9). Compare Numbers 12:8: Moses, unlike Miriam and Aaron, saw the *t'munah* ("likeness, representation"; in modern Hebrew, "picture") of *Adonai.*

Raphael Patai brings the following extraordinary paragraph from the works of the Alexandrian Jew Philo (20 B.C.E - 50 C.E.), noting that he "does not mention the Messiah by this name, but speaks of the 'Shoot' (rather infelicitously rendered in the Loeb Classical Library edition as the 'rising'),... who — remarkable words in the mouth of a Jewish thinker — 'differs not a whit from the divine image,' and is the Divine Father's 'eldest son'...." My own comments and references are in brackets.

> "I have heard also an oracle from the lips of one of the disciples of Moses which runs thus: 'Behold a man whose name is the rising' [more accurately, "shoot, sprout," Isaiah 11:1, Zechariah 6:12], strangest of titles, surely, if you suppose that a being composed of soul and body is here described. But if you suppose that it is that Incorporeal One [Yn 1:1, Pp 2:6], who differs not a whit from the divine image [the present verse; Co 1:15, 17], you will agree that the name 'rising' assigned to him quite truly describes him. For that man is the eldest son [Mk 6:3], whom the Father of all raised up [Ac 2:24, 32; 3:15; 4:10; Ro 8:11, 34], and elsewhere calls him his first-born [Mt 1:25; Lk 2:7; Ro 8:29; Co 1:15, 18], and indeed the Son [Mt 2:15] thus begotten [Yn 3:16] followed the ways of his Father [Yn 5:17–26, 36], and shaped the different kinds [Yn 1:3, Co 1:16–17], looking to the archetypal patterns which that Father supplied [MJ 8:1–5]." (Philo, *De Confusione Linguarum 4:45,* as cited in Rafael Patai, *The Messiah Texts*, pp. 171–172)

(5) Yeshua not only *is* the Word (Yn 1:1), but he *has* (says) a **powerful word** which "holds everything together" (Co 1:17&N), which **upholds** (or: "bears up under," "suffers") **all that exists**.

(6) The writer turns from the Messiah's cosmic functions to his functions in relation to humanity: **through himself**, he **made purification for sins**, which, as explained a little at a time throughout the rest of the book, no one else and nothing else could do.

(7) Finally, **after** that, **he sat down at the right hand of** God. Psalm 110:1 is quoted frequently in this book and elsewhere in the New Testament; see v. 13N and Mt 22:44&N. In the Hebrew of Psalm 110:1, as quoted in part at v. 13, it is God speaking: "*YHVH* said to my Lord, 'Sit at my right hand.'" "The right hand of God" is not a place but refers to the Messiah's exalted status and to his intimate involvement with God as *cohen gadol* interceding for those who trust in him (7:25–26).

God is referred to by a euphemism, "***HaG'dulah BaM'romim***" ("the Greatness in the heights"; KJV, "the majesty on high"). Long before Yeshua's time it became customary in Judaism not to use the personal name of God, *YHVH*, and the practice remains to this day. The phrase used here draws on 1 Chronicles 29:11, "For thine, *YHVH*, is the greatness (*HaG'dulah*) and the power (*HaG'vurah*) and the glory (*HaTif'eret*)," also echoed in a similar phrase at Mk 14:62 and in the Lord's Prayer (Mt 6:13&N). Moreover, in Greek both "*YHVH*" and "lord" would normally be rendered by the word "*kurios*" (see Mt 1:20N); by using a more elaborate expression than "*kurios*" the author signals clearly that he is speaking of *YHVH* and not an earthly lord. When he quotes Psalm 110:1 again at 8:1, he shortens the expression to "*HaG'dulah*." At 12:2 he uses a circumlocution, "the throne of God," and at 10:12, simply "God."

4 **So**, it is evident, since he is at God's right hand, that **he has become much better than angels** — even though "he was made, for a little while, lower than the angels" (2:9). Although today some non-Messianic Jews, reacting against Christianity, insist that Judaism has never expected the Messiah to be different from any other man, there can be no question that in the first century many Jews, both those attracted to Yeshua and those repelled by him, understood that the Messiah would be more than human. But how much more? As much as angels? Which angels? — Jewish angelology had become very complex during the six centuries before Yeshua; where among the angelic orders did the Messiah fit? The decisive answer given here is: nowhere. He is above them all — as the verses from the *Tanakh* cited in the rest of the chapter are intended to prove.

In one *midrash* the rabbis portray righteous people as better than angels (Genesis Rabbah 78:1), and this picture fits Yeshua well because "he did not sin" (4:15). But in another *midrash* the Messiah himself is so described — and, incidentally, it is also an instance of a Jewish application of Isaiah 52:13–53:12 to the Messiah:

> "'Behold, my servant shall (deal wisely) prosper.' This is King Messiah. 'He shall be exalted and extolled and be very high.' He shall be exalted beyond Avraham, and extolled beyond Moses, and raised high above the ministering angels." (*Yalkut Shim'oni* 2:53:3, on Isaiah 52:13; quoted in B. F. Westcott, *The Epistle to the Hebrews*, p. 16)

Yalkut Shim'oni itself is a collection of some 10,000 stories and comments from the Talmud and *midrashim*, arranged in biblical order in the 13th century by Rabbi Shim'on HaDarshan (Simon the Expositor, or Simon the Preacher).

Better. See paragraph (2) of vv. 2–3N.

The name God has given him which **is superior to** that of angels could mean his reputation but more likely signifies an actual name. Here, by context, it is "Son"; at Pp 2:9 "the name above every name" is "*Adonai*" (see Pp 2:9N).

A more literal translation of this verse would be, "He has become as much better than angels as the name he has inherited is superior to theirs." In two other places (7:22, 8:6) the author makes a similar comparison — A is as much greater than B as C is greater than D, or, expressed algebraically, A – B = C – D. In all three places my rendering attempts to give the meaning without the mathematics.

5–14 For to which of the angels did God ever say…? The writer obviously assumes that angels really exist (see discussion of this question in 13:2N) and proceeds to prove the proposition of v. 4, that the Messiah, as God's Son, is "much better than angels," by quoting seven texts from the *Tanakh*, each of which has its own richness of meaning (see notes on the individual passages below). He sums up with the conclusion, in v. 14, that angels are "merely spirits who serve, sent out to help those whom God will deliver," that is, believers in Yeshua.

5a You are my Son; today I have become your Father. Wasn't God always Yeshua's Father? Why did he have to "**become**" his Father? See 5:5&N, Ac 13:33–34&N.

In Judaism Psalm 2, quoted here, has been variously held to refer to Aaron, David, the people of Israel in Messianic times, *Mashiach Ben-David* and *Mashiach Ben-Yosef*. But the oldest reference, Psalms of Solomon 17:21–27, from the middle of the 1st century B.C.E., applies it to *Mashiach Ben-David*, as does the Talmud at Sukkah 52a.

The angels, collectively, are called "sons of God" at Job 1:6, 2:1, 38:7 and probably at Genesis 6:2; but to no angel did God say, "**You are my son**," as he did to Yeshua at his immersion (Mk 1:11, Lk 3:22); compare 5:5 and Ac 13:33, where the same verse is quoted. Other parts of Psalm 2 are applied to Yeshua at Ac 4:25; Rv 12:15, 19:15; and see above, numbered paragraph (1) in vv. 2–3N.

5b–6a I will be his Father and he will be my Son. Nathan prophesied to King David about his son Solomon and his descendants (2 Samuel 7:4–17). The rabbis applied it midrashically to the people of Israel, but the New Testament's application of it to the Messiah is a *chiddush* ("innovation") meant to show not only that Yeshua, as God's Son, is better than angels, but also that the entire prophecy, including the promise that the House of David will rule forever, is fulfilled in Yeshua, "descended from David physically" (Ro 1:3, Mt 1:1&N, Lk 3:23–38&N), but "Son of God spiritually" (Ro 1:4, Lk 1:35).

Moreover, this quotation, because it speaks of God's **Son**, and the next one, because it is introduced as referring to God's **Firstborn**, both strengthen the identification, often made in the New Testament, between Yeshua the Messiah and the people of Israel (see Mt 2:15N). There is a parallel between God's promise concerning the Messiah in v. 5b and his promise concerning Israel, "I will be their God, and they will be my people," quoted below (8:10) from Jeremiah 31:32(33), but originally made, in slightly different words, to Moses (Exodus 7:7). Earlier (Exodus 4:22) God had called Israel his son and also his firstborn. Furthermore, the New Testament is not innovating when it applies these concepts to the Messiah; the same is done in Psalm 89 (which recapitulates much of what is said in 2 Samuel 7):

> "He will call unto me, 'You are my Father,
> my God, and the rock of my salvation.'
>
> "I will also appoint him firstborn,
> the highest of the kings of the earth." (Psalm 89:27–28)

When God brings his Firstborn into the world, that is, into the *'olam hazeh*, this is preparation for bringing him also into the heavenly world to come, the *'olam haba*. This is the thrust of Chapters 1–2, where Yeshua's life on earth (the *'olam hazeh*) is in focus. But these lead us, through the Messiah's death, to Chapter 7, where he is seen as our *cohen gadol* in heaven (the *'olam haba*).

6b The Hebrew text of Psalm 97:7 says, "Worship him, all gods (*elohim*)." Since Judaism allows that *elohim* sometimes means "angels," the Septuagint's rendering, "**Let all God's angels worship him,**" is not surprising. What is surprising is that whereas in the original, the object of worship is *Adonai*, here it is the Son. This is another of the New Testament's indirect ways of identifying Yeshua with God (see Co 2:9N). Verse 4b parallels Pp 2:9; this parallels Pp 2:10–11. Needless to say, if angels worship the Son, the Son is "better than angels."

7 **Who makes his angels winds and his servants fiery flames**. This is the baseline against which is measured the portrait of the Son in this chapter's remaining three citations from the *Tanakh*.

Greek *pneumata*, equivalent to Hebrew *ruchot*, is rendered "spirits" in v. 14 but "**winds**" here because the sense of Psalm 104:4 in Hebrew is usually given as, "…who makes winds his messengers and fiery flames his servants." However, Hebrew grammar allows the possibility of reversing subject and predicate, and Judaism takes cognizance of it. A first-century pseudepigraphic work states:

> "O Lord… before whom (heaven's) hosts stand trembling,
> and at your word change to wind and fire…." (4 Ezra 8:20–21)

The angel of Judges 13 is described as having said to Manoah, Samson's father,

> "God changes us hour by hour;…
> sometimes he makes us fire, and sometimes wind."
> (*Yalkut Shim'oni* 2:11:3)

8–9 Psalm 45 is a wedding poem for David, Solomon or some other Israelite king. A Jewish commentator writes:

> "This Psalm came to be understood as referring to King Messiah (so the Targum), and his marriage as an allusion to his redemption of Israel" (A. Cohen's note to Psalm 45 in the Soncino Hebrew-and-English edition of the Hebrew Bible, *Psalms*, p. 140).

Your throne, O God. Cohen suggests instead, "Thy throne, given of God," and comments:

> "The Hebrew is difficult. A.V. and R.V., 'Thy throne, O God,' appears to be the obvious translation but does not suit the context."

Clearly the reason he thinks it "does not suit the context" is that even though he refers Psalm 45 to the Messiah, he is unwilling to allow that the psalmist may be prophesying the Messiah's divine character.

You rule your Kingdom with a scepter of equity; you have loved righteousness. The same idea is found in two psalms mentioned already: "Righteousness and justice are the foundation of his throne" (Psalms 89:15, 97:2), as well as in the Messianic passage, Isaiah 9:5–6(6–7): "to establish [the government on the Messiah's shoulder] with justice and righteousness, from henceforth for ever" (see Lk 1:79N).

The Messiah's **companions** (or: "partakers") are not angels (that would contradict the whole purpose of the quotation) but human beings who have put their trust in him (see 2:10–11, 3:14; Ro 8:17, 29). Alternatively, his **companions** are all human beings and not just the believers (see 2:14–17).

Therefore, O God, your God has anointed you — which suggests Yeshua's divinity. Or: "Therefore God, your God, has anointed you." The grammar makes either rendering a possibility.

10–12 In the Septuagint version, quoted here, these verses of Psalm 102 are spoken by God to someone whom he addresses as "**Lord**," possibly even meaning "*YHVH*" (Mt 1:20&N). In the Hebrew Bible as we have it now they are part of a human prayer to God, and no one is addressed directly.

13 Psalm 110:1 commences with, "*Adonai* said to my Lord,..." The most telling proof that the Son is better than angels is saved for last. This psalm is referred to also at v. 3; 5:6; 6:20; 7:17, 21; 8:1; 10:13 and 12:2. See numbered paragraph (7) of vv. 2–3N and Mt 22:44N.

14 In conclusion, **they**, the angels, are **all merely spirits** (see v. 7N) **who serve**, as opposed to the Son who rules. However, they serve not only him (Mt 4:11, 26:53; Yn 1:51), but his "companions" (v. 9) too, **those whom God will deliver**.

CHAPTER 2

1–4 The readers of this book are exhorted not less than five times to bestir themselves and not **drift away** through complacency, apathy or neglect (here, 3:6b–4:16; 5:11–6:12; 10:19–39; and 12:1–13:22).

1 If the Messiah is just another angel, there is little reason to take his Gospel seriously. But because he is God's Son and "much better than angels" (1:4, proved by 1:5–13), **Therefore, we must pay much more careful heed to the things we have heard**.

2 Although angels are inferior to the Messiah, and in the end even inferior to saved human beings (1:14), nevertheless their role is not negligible, because **through angels, God spoke** a **word**, the *Torah* (Judaism recognized the intermediary role of angels at Mount Sinai; see Ac 7:53N). In the *Torah*, **every violation and act of disobedience received its just deserts**, that is, the *Torah* specified the sanctions for violations of its laws. The actual punishments are meted out on earth through judgments of *b'tei-din* (Jewish courts) and acts of God; the final distribution of **just deserts**, as foretold in the *Tanakh* (see especially Daniel 12:3), will be at the Last Judgment (Rv 20:11–15).

3 **How will we escape** the condemnation pronounced in the *Torah* for our disobedience (compare Ga 3:10–13&NN) **if we ignore** the **deliverance** called **great** because it spares us the terrible condemnation we richly deserve? The implied answer, of course, is that we won't; because there is no other way to escape it (Ac 4:12).

The Lord Yeshua both initiated **this deliverance** (v. 10) and was the **first** to **declare** it. By referring to **those who heard him** as having **confirmed** the Gospel **to us,** the writer indicates that neither he nor his readers knew Yeshua personally during his earthly lifetime (also see 1:1N).

4 **Gifts of the *Ruach HaKodesh***, charismatic gifts of the Holy Spirit. See especially 1C 12:4–31&NN; also Ro 12:6–8&N, Ep 4:11&N.

5–18 Yeshua had to become human in order to deliver us. Yet, just as he is better than angels, so also he is better than other human beings.

5 **For.** This connects the thought with 1:14.

7–9a Hebrew *m'at* can mean only "a little bit," but Greek *brachu* can mean either "**a little** bit" (v. 7) or "**for a little while**" (v. 9). In v. 7, where he quotes Psalm 8:5 from the Septuagint, which uses the word "*brachu*," the writer adheres to the meaning of the Hebrew *m'at*, "a little bit." But there is no reason to suppose that "*brachu*" in v. 9 means the same thing. The author, a knowledgeable Jew of his time, did not distort the meaning of the Hebrew psalm when quoting it, but did make an interlingual *midrash* on the Greek word "*brachu*" which he could not have made with the Hebrew text alone. The writer makes his point through *midrash*, not through meaning something different in v. 7 than the Psalmist did.

Some manuscripts include after "**honor**" the missing line from Psalm 8, "You have set him over the works of your hands."

According to Genesis 1:28, God **put everything** on earth **in subjection under** the **feet** of mankind, not angels. Although this is **not yet** seen in relation to humanity as a whole, **we do see** it partly fulfilled in **Yeshua**.

9b–10 As the Son of God (1:4–14) and the Word of God (Yn 1:1–18), Yeshua was much higher than angels. But as man he was made **lower than angels,... so that... he might taste death**, experiencing evil and pain, **for all humanity** — something angels cannot do.

Because he suffered death, literally, "because of the suffering (Greek *to pathêma*) of the death (*tou thanatou*)." The word "*pathêma*" is used in the plural in v. 10 (**sufferings**, *pathêmatôn)* without "*thanatos*" to refer specifically to the sufferings of death, and this was a common euphemism. The author of this book uses "*pathêma*" and the related verb "*pathein*" ("to suffer") in this way a number of times; some instances are 2:18, 5:8, 9:26, 13:12.

10–13 As man, Yeshua had to suffer like us in order fully to identify with us. This is what uniquely qualifies him to be our mediator. By being identified fully both with God and with us he bridges the gap (Isaiah 59:1–2) and creates for us the unity with God that he himself has. Compare Yochanan 17. Verses 12–13 offer two proof-texts from parts of the *Tanakh* normally considered to have Messianic import.

14 This explicitly analyzes the Messiah's work in taking on himself the nature of humanity (compare Pp 2:6–8). "For the Messiah himself died for sins, a righteous person on behalf of unrighteous people, so that he might bring you to God" (1 Kefa 3:18). By doing this he tricked **the one who had power over death (that is, the Adversary**, Satan, as explained in Mt 4:1N). For Satan has the power of causing death but has no right to inflict it on someone who resists his temptations and does not sin (2:17–18, 4:14–16&N, Mt 4:1–11&NN), because death is the punishment for sin (Genesis 2:17; Ro 5:12–21N).

Did Yeshua **render** Satan **ineffective**? Although Satan continues to exercise power, his days are numbered and he will ultimately be destroyed. See Lk 10:18; Rv 12:9; 20:2, 10.

15 Not everyone admits his **fear of death**. Elizabeth Kubler-Ross writes as if death were merely a passage from one form of life to another; many religions teach the same thing. For nonbelievers that is a snare and a delusion. For believers it is true, better than she or those religions can imagine.

16–18 Yeshua did not **take hold of** (that is, either "take on the nature of" or "concern himself with") **angels**, because angels cannot die. He **takes hold of** not human beings generally but the **seed of Avraham**, because Jews, of all humanity, have in the *Torah* the most stringent conditions to fulfill in order not to sin and by not sinning escape death. If Yeshua could live as a Jew according to the *Torah* without committing any sin, so that he would not have earned the death penalty, he would deliver Jews from death and *a fortiori* (Mt 6:30&N) Gentiles as well.

Yeshua had to be made exactly like those to be rescued from death so that he would fully know and empathize with our experience and thereby, as our ***cohen gadol*** (high priest), be able to be fully **merciful** and (as brought forth in 3:1–6 and also at Ro 3:22, 24) **faithful, making a *kapparah*** ("atonement") **for the sins of the people**. The Messianic prophecy of Isaiah 53:12 predicted this seven hundred years in advance and also makes the best commentary: it is precisely because he "poured out his soul to death and was numbered with the transgressors" that he "bore the sin of many and will make intercession for the transgressors" (see 7:25&N).

17 The majority of the *mitzvot* set forth in the written *Torah* deal with the sacrificial system, including the *cahanut* (priesthood), in which all the *cohanim* (priests) and the ***cohen hagadol*** were members of the tribe of Levi (see 7:5–14). Thus it is very surprising, indeed revolutionary, to find that Yeshua, the Son of David, from the tribe of Judah, is spoken of as our ***cohen gadol***. Much of the rest of the book is occupied with explaining how this can be and why it is necessary (see 3:1–6, 4:14–5:10, 6:19–10:23).

18 **He suffered death**, literally, "he suffered." See vv. 9–10N above.

CHAPTER 3

1 Yeshua, like **Moshe** at Sinai, was **God's emissary**, conveying God's truth and God's wishes to the people of Israel. In this respect, Yeshua fulfills the role of being a prophet like Moses, as predicted in Deuteronomy 18:15–19 (see Ac 3:22&N). Also, like Moses, Yeshua intercedes for the people (7:25), and as such he is fulfilling the role of a ***cohen***, a priest, just as Moses did when the people worshipped the golden calf (Exodus 32:32) and at other times.

2–4 But Yeshua is not merely on the same level as Moses, the paragon of virtue within Judaism (**faithful in all God's house**), but better than Moses — just as he is better than angels (1:4&N) and better than other human beings in general (2:8, 4:15). Thus **Yeshua deserves more honor than Moshe**. Note the author's poetic play off the word "**house**."

The idea that the Messiah is better than *Moshe Rabbenu* can be inferred from traditional Jewish sources.

> "'And the spirit of God hovered over the face of the waters.' This phrase from Genesis 1:2 alludes to the spirit of the Messiah, because Isaiah 11:2 says, 'And the spirit of *Adonai* will rest upon him' [that is, upon the 'shoot of Jesse', which is a name for the Messiah]. Also we learn from the same text in Genesis 1:2 that this spirit of the Messiah comes through the merit of repentance; for in Lamentations 2:19 repentance is likened to water: 'Pour out your heart like water.'"(Genesis Rabbah 2:4)

This passage is also notable in that it equates the "spirit of the Messiah" (a term used at Ro 8:9&N) with the "spirit of God," who is the same as the *Ruach HaKodesh* ("Holy Spirit"; Ep 4:30&N).

> "At the beginning of the creation of the world king Messiah had already come into being, because he existed in God's mind even before the world was created." (Pesikta Rabbati 33:6)

Nothing like this is said in any Jewish source about Moses, but the same is taught about Yeshua by the New Testament (for example, at Yn 1:1–18&NN, 8:58–59&N; Co 1:15–17&NN).

The logic of vv. 3–4 leads to the conclusion that Yeshua is to be identified with

God, since he is **the one who built everything** (compare 1:2). As usual, the New Testament does not state outright that Yeshua is God but makes this identification indirectly (see 1:6b&N, Co 2:9&N).

5–6a A second reason why **Yeshua** is better than **Moshe** is that the latter was a **servant** but the former is a **Son**. For a comparison between son and servant, see Ga 4:1–7; also Yn 15:15.

For an extended comparison of the Messiah with Moses from a non-Messianic Jewish viewpoint, a comparison which is striking in how well it fits Yeshua, see Section 6 of the Introduction to Raphael Patai's *The Messiah Texts.*

3:6b–4:16 The second exhortation (see 2:1–4N), to enter God's End-Time *Shabbat* rest (4:9–10) by having a heart filled with courage, confidence and trust (vv. 6b, 12), makes use of a new passage of Scripture, Psalm 95:7–11, while retaining the Mosaic context of vv. 1–6a. As Yeshua was compared with Moses there, so here Yeshua's followers are compared with the people who followed Moses. The **Bitter Quarrel** or "rebellion" was when Israel repeatedly complained against God as Moses was leading them through the **wilderness**. These repeated "murmurings" are described in Numbers 11–16, from which the text in v. 2 was quoted. Verses 15–19 bring out the connection between the two *Tanakh* passages.

7 **Today, if you hear God's voice** (literally, "…his voice"). Psalm 95:7 is also used in a famous *midrash* about when the Messiah is to come:

> "Rabbi Joshua ben-L'vi met Elijah and asked him, 'When will the Messiah come?' 'Go and ask him!' 'Where is he?' 'At the entrance [to Rome], sitting among the lepers.' So he went, greeted him, and asked, 'Master, when will you come?' 'Today,' he answered. Upon returning to Elijah, Rabbi Joshua said, 'He lied to me. He told me he would come today, but he has not come.' Elijah replied, 'What he said to you was: "Today, if you will hear his voice."' "(Condensed from Sanhedrin 98a)

So it is with the real Messiah, Yeshua, and with all the greater poignancy. Yeshua will come today to anyone who will hear his voice and not rebel like the Israelites in the wilderness.

12 **To apostatize**. This transliterates the Greek word "*apostênai*" ("to go away, desert, stand apart, become apostate"). On whether it is possible for true believers to become apostate, see 6:4–6N.

13 In exhorting his readers to **keep exhorting each other**, the author is exemplifying the principle that the Messianic life pattern is not one in which the vast majority of passive believers let a few "ministers" do all the work. Rather, Yeshua gives his followers leaders whose task is "to equip God's people for the work of service that builds the Body of the Messiah" (Ep 4:11–16). Compare 10:24–25.

Every day, as long as it is called Today (as in Psalm 95). Between 1891 and 1904 the Institutum Delitzschianum in Leipzig, Germany, published a commentary on the New Testament by Yechiel Lichtenstein. So far as I know it is the only commentary on the entire New Testament by a Messianic Jew, apart from this one. It was written in Hebrew, with the Scripture text printed in block letters and the comments in Rashi script, like any rabbinic commentary. In it he points out that the urgency Sha'ul communicates in this verse is echoed by a well-known exhortation found in the Talmud:

> "Rabbi 'Eli'ezer said, 'Repent one day before you die.' His *talmidim* objected, 'Does one know in advance the day of one's death?' He replied, 'All the more reason to repent today, lest you die tomorrow! In this way, your entire life will be one of repentance.'"(Shabbat 153a)

15–19 See 3:6b–4:16N above, and compare especially Numbers 14:26–35.

CHAPTER 4

2 The **Good News** the Israelites heard was **the promise of entering his rest** in the Promised Land; the **Good News** which **has been proclaimed to us** is, of course, that we enter the rest that comes from knowing that our sins are forgiven.

3 The **rest** we are to **enter** is nothing less than the rest which God has been enjoying **since the founding of the universe**, even though he continues working (Yn 5:17).

3b–11 The seventh day (v. 4). Psalm 95, quoted at 3:8–11 and explained in the subsequent verses, was sung on *Shabbat* in the Temple and remains part of the *Shabbat* liturgy in the synagogue. Therefore it is natural for the author to make his point about rest by introducing a quotation from another *Shabbat*-related passage (used today in the home service before the Friday night meal), Genesis 2:1–3, and speaking in v. 9 of **a *Shabbat*-keeping** (see vv. 9–10N).

Although the author may be thinking of the rest that comes to believers after they die (Rv 14:13), it seems more likely to me that he has in mind Jewish traditions that equate a day with 1000 years and is therefore speaking of the **rest** that comes in the Messianic Age or Millennium. For example, in Sanhedrin 97a Rav Kattina teaches that six millennia of ordinary history will be followed by a millennium of *Shabbat*; the passage draws on Psalm 90:4 and is quoted in 2 Ke 3:3–9N, and see Rv 20:2–7&N.

6–8 The close reasoning and exact use of texts is typically rabbinic; compare Yeshua's logic at Mt 22:31–32&N. Verse 7 repeats the "**Today**" theme of 3:7, 13, 15.

8 Y'hoshua. Greek *Iêsous,* same as the Greek word for "Yeshua" (see Mt 1:1N); in fact, KJV renders the beginning of this verse, "If Jesus had given them rest." By leading God's people into the Promised Land, Y'hoshua bin-Nun (Joshua the son of Nun) prefigured the Messiah whose name he shares; and just as God's people Israel rested in *Eretz-Israel*, so God's Messianic Community rests in Yeshua.

9–10 A *Shabbat*-keeping, Greek *sabbatismos*, used only here in the New Testament. In the Septuagint, the related Greek word "*sabbatizein*" was coined to translate the Hebrew verb *shabat* when it means "to observe *Shabbat*." The usual translation, "There remains a Sabbath rest," minimizes the observance aspect and makes the role of God's people entirely passive.

Christians often assume that the New Testament does not require God's people to observe *Shabbat* and go on to claim that Sunday has replaced Saturday as the Church's day of worship (see 1C 16:2N). But this passage, and in particular v. 9, shows that *Shabbat*-observance is expected of believers. From Co 2:16–17, which says that *Shabbat* was a shadow of the things that were to come, but the substance comes from the Messiah, we learn that the essence of *Shabbat*-observance for believers is not following the detailed rules which *halakhah* sets forth concerning what may or may not be done on the seventh day of the week. Rather, as v. 10 explains, the ***Shabbat*-keeping** expected of God's people consists in resting from one's **own works, as God did from his**; it consists in trusting and being faithful to God (vv. 2–3). Although the specific "works" from which the readers of this letter were to rest were animal sacrifices (see 6:4–6N), by implication all self-struggle, in which one relies on one's own efforts instead of trusting God, is to be avoided; and in this the author is making the same point as Sha'ul does at Ro 3:19–4:25.

11 The same kind of disobedience. With this the author links his discussion of *Shabbat* (vv. 3–11) to his earlier discussion of the Israelites' disobedience in the desert (3:2–4:3). He also ties the concept of obedience to that of trusting and being faithful; compare the "trust-grounded obedience" of Ro 1:5, 16:25; and see Section (1) of Ga 2:16cN.

12–13 See, the Word of God is alive! The Bible does not merely speak in the dead tones of the past but applies living truth to the people of "Today" (3:7&N). When we read the Word of God with an open heart, mind and spirit, we let God penetrate deeply into our lives. **The inner reflections and attitudes of the heart** quickly come under judgment against the standards of Scripture; and there is no hope for us apart from entering God's rest, trusting in the ***cohen hagadol*** whom God has provided to intercede for us (7:25&N), and holding **firmly to what we acknowledge as true**.

But the Word of God is also Yeshua the Messiah (Yn 1:1&N, 14&N). When he returns to conquer the wicked at the End of Days, "he is called **the Word of God**,… and out of his mouth comes a sharp **sword**"; while **the eyes of him to whom we must render an account** are described as "like a fiery flame" (Rv 19:11–15). Actually, our account is rendered to God, but God has committed all judgment to Yeshua (Yn 5:22, Ac 17:31, Ro 2:16).

14–16 In the passage climaxing with vv. 12–13 the author has left his readers terrified of God's judgment. Now he reassures them that even though Yeshua will one day be our judge, now he is our intercessor and advocate (7:25, 1 Yn 2:1). **Therefore** — because he is our ***cohen gadol*** as well as our future judge — **let us approach the throne** to **find grace in our time of need**.

The subject of Yeshua as ***cohen gadol*** was introduced at 2:17. Here the author recapitulates what he said in 2:5–18, namely, that Yeshua had a human nature exactly like ours, enabling him **to empathize with our weaknesses, the only difference** between him and the rest of us **being that he did not sin.**

In every respect he was tempted just as we are. Yochanan calls the basic three kinds of temptations "the desires of the old nature, the desires of the eyes, and the pretensions of life" (1 Yn 2:15–17&N). Adam and Eve succumbed to them in the Garden of Eden (Genesis 3:1–6), whereas Yeshua resisted them when the Adversary tempted him (Mt 4:1–11&NN). Compare 2:14, 17–18; Ro 8:3&N.

Because Yeshua did not sin, he **passed through** Sh'ol (Hades) and such other "places" as house the dead and demonic beings (e.g., "dungeons lower than Sh'ol," 2 Ke 2:4&N; "the Abyss," Rv 9:1&N; and see 1 Ke 4:19–22&N). He **passed through to the highest heaven**, God's "abode," where he had been before (Yn 1:1; 17:5, 24; Pp 2:6–11).

Because we are his, united with him, we can follow him; and with him we can **confidently approach the throne from which God gives grace**. There may be an implied contrast with the mercy seat of the Tabernacle and Temple here on earth, which only the Levitical high priest could approach (see 9:5&N). Many Jewish people feel distant from God and his throne; this is often due to an overemphasis in some forms of Judaism on God's transcendence. New believers are frequently amazed to experience God's warm and loving nearness. They find that they need not merely recite prayers from a prayerbook; they find that God's love is not merely an abstract phenomenon without relevance to their hearts' needs. Like Moses and Avraham, we can experience God's **mercy** and **grace** (Greek *charis* and *eleos*, which correspond to what the last prayer of the *'Amidah* calls "*chen v'chesed v'rachamim*" ("grace, kindness and mercy"); see Ga 6:16N). The exhortation to hold firmly to the truth and to our hope and to approach God's throne boldly is alluded to again at 6:18–19 and expanded at 10:19–22, after Yeshua's work as ***cohen gadol*** has been thoroughly explained.

CHAPTER 5

1–10 The qualifications for the office of ***cohen gadol*** within the framework of the Levitical system of *cohanim* include ability to sympathize with the people and divine appointment (vv. 1–4). Yeshua meets these requirements (vv. 5–10).

2–3 The Levitical *cohanim* could empathize with those for whom they interceded because they shared the latter's human **weakness** in that both intercessor and interceded-for sinned. Yeshua did not sin, but he can sympathize because he suffered temptation without giving in to it.

4 **He is called by God, just as Aharon was**. See Exodus 28:1ff.; Leviticus 8:1ff.; Numbers 16:5, 17:5, 18:1ff.; Psalms 105:26. His successors too, Numbers 20:23ff., 25:10ff. Likewise others with a priestlike ministry, e.g., Samuel (1 Samuel 6:3ff.).

5 **Today I have become your father**. F. F. Bruce (*The Epistle to the Hebrews, ad loc.*) suggests that this refers to "the day of the Messiah's enthronement — the day when the Most High gave public notice that He had exalted the crucified Jesus as 'both Lord and

Christ' (Ac 2:36)." But see also 1:5&N and Ac 13:33–34&N, both of which cite the same passage from Psalm 2.

6 **To be compared with**, often rendered, "after the order of," as if there were an order of priests of which Malki-Tzedek was the founder; but this is not the meaning.

Malki-Tzedek (Melchizedek; the Hebrew name means "my king is righteousness") appears first at Genesis 14:18 as both priest of *El Elyon* ("Most High God") and king of Shalem, identified with Jerusalem (see 7:1–4 below). But in Judaism, kingship and priesthood were separated. Saul, the son of Kish, was the first king; after him came David, and all kings of Judah since then have been from the House of David (including Yeshua). On the other hand, the priestly line ran from Moses' brother Aaron. Thus at Zechariah 6:13 there is a reference to two persons; by context these must be King Zerubabbel (of the House of David) and Joshua the *cohen hagadol* (a descendant of Aaron). Yeshua is **to be compared with Malki-Tzedek** because in Yeshua, Jewish priest and Jewish king are united in one person. So far as is known, the author makes a *chiddush* ("innovation") in presenting the idea of king and priest combined in one person. But see Appendix, p. 934. On Psalm 110 see 1:13N.

7–10 This expands on 2:17 and 4:15, Yeshua's sympathizing with human beings because he became one of us, but, unlike us, was completely obedient to God.

Compare Yeshua's **prayers and petitions, crying aloud and shedding tears** in the Garden of Gat-Sh'manim, as reported at Mt 26:36–46 and Lk 22:39–46. You might think that he **was** *not* **heard because of his godliness**, since the **One who had the power to deliver him from death** did not do so. But he prayed that God's will be done, and according to the *Tanakh* (see 1C 15:3–4&N and Mt 26:24N), it was God's will that Yeshua die, the righteous for the unrighteous (1 Ke 3:18), so that he might become **the source of eternal deliverance to all who obey him**.

Yet "the Initiator" (or "Pioneer") "and Completer" of our own trusting (12:1) and of the **obedience** implied by that trusting (Ro 1:5, 16:26) did not pioneer the path of obedience for **all who obey him** by using divine power from heaven, **even though he was the Son** of God. Instead, he emptied himself of that power (Pp 2:6–8) and instead **learned obedience through his sufferings** (the Greek word for "sufferings" implies specifically the sufferings of death; see 2:9–10N). Only in this way was he **brought to the goal** of being "the firstborn [from the dead] among many brothers" (Ro 8:29, 1C 15:20) and our perfect ***cohen gadol*, to be compared with Malki-Tzedek**.

After he had been brought to the goal. This is usually translated, "having been made perfect"; see 7:11N. But Yeshua was not imperfect; rather, it was God's goal to have Yeshua made our perfect ***cohen gadol***, fully representative of and empathetic with the human condition (4:15). Through his heavenly priesthood **he became the source of eternal deliverance to all who obey him**, as explained further in Chapters 7–10.

11–14 The phrase, "to all who obey him" (v. 9), becomes the occasion for the third exhortation (see 2:1–4N), in which obedience to God is equated with spiritual maturity and with doing God's work — actively putting out energy for the Kingdom, as opposed to receiving doctrine passively. Listening to basic doctrine is **milk**, and **anyone who has to drink milk is still a baby**; compare Paul's use of the same metaphor at 1C 3:1–2.

What distinguishes the **mature** is that they have **experience in applying the Word** (Scripture), that is, in obeying God, in behaving ethically, in putting out as opposed to taking in. After some time doing this, their **faculties have been trained by continuous exercise to distinguish good from evil**. Those whose faculties are still undiscerning cannot make use of the **solid food** which the author is about to dispense, namely, the information concerning how Yeshua's high-priesthood goes beyond the Levitical priesthood and his personal death goes beyond the Temple and Tabernacle sacrificial system. So there are three stages: babyhood, in which one receives basic doctrine; moral maturity, in which one applies these basic doctrines so as to do good works; and spiritual maturity in which one is ready to receive more advanced doctrine (solid food). At Yn 4:31–34 Yeshua, who is of course both morally and spiritually mature, speaks of his "food" as doing God's will.

People who continually need to hear the "initial lessons about the Messiah" (6:1) remain spiritual babies, feeding on **milk, not solid food**. New believers (babies) ought to seek milk (1 Ke 2:2). And this milk is enough to orient people toward becoming morally mature and doing God's work. However, when believers become **sluggish in understanding**, due to their failure to grow up and do work — when they "ignore such a great deliverance" (2:3), display lack of trust (3:12) and disobey (4:11) — it becomes **hard to explain** things which mature workers need to know.

It should not be thought that solid food is more important than milk, that the doctrines of priesthood and sacrifice are more important than those of repentance, trust, purification, ordination, resurrection and judgment (6:1–2). Rather, each has its place in the life of the believer, according to his degree of maturity.

The Word about righteousness could well be the doctrine that people are declared righteous by God on the ground of their trust (Ro 3:20–21, Ga 2:16, Ep 2:8–10). This doctrine is dangerous in the hands of spiritual babies, who may use it to excuse their sins (Ro 3:7–8) and their lack of diligence in doing Kingdom work; it is only for the morally mature, those **whose faculties have been trained by continuous use to distinguish good from evil**.

The passage parallels Sha'ul's teaching at Ep 2:8–10, that faith is intended to be used in good works.

CHAPTER 6

1–2 The initial lessons about the Messiah can be presented as three pairs of doctrines constituting the **foundation** on which to build Messianic life. Being born again consists in **turning from works that lead to death** (repentance from sin) and **trusting God**. Both aspects are necessary: claiming to trust God without leaving one's sins behind is hypocrisy, because God is holy. Attempting to turn from sin without trusting God either fails, leads to pride in self-accomplishment, or both.

Two pairs of topics comprise the **instruction** a baby believer needs after coming to faith. The first pair deals with this world, the second with the world to come — biblical faith is neither altogether this-worldly nor altogether otherworldly.

Greek *baptismôn* is the normal New Testament word not for the immersion which accompanies coming to faith (Ac 2:37, 8:38, 16:32; see Mt 3:9N) but for **washings** or purifications, of which the initial immersion is but one. The Messianic Jewish readers would have been familiar with this subject, since the *Tanakh* speaks of such purifications at many places; also Yn 13:3–17 and below at 10:22. ***S'mikhah***, the laying on of hands (see Mt 21:23N), refers here to ordination of an individual for a particular task of ministry by the elders of a congregation, as with Sha'ul at Ac 13:1 and Timothy at 1 Ti 4:14; also see Mt 21:31N. Instruction about **washings** leads to the whole question of how to live a holy life in a sinful world, while ***s'mikhah*** introduces the subject of working for the Kingdom of God. Compare Ya 1:27, where "the religious observance that God the Father considers pure and faultless" is defined in essentially the same terms.

Without **resurrection of the dead** it becomes unclear how God is just (see the book of Job) and a believer's life becomes pointless (1C 15:18). The hope of eternal reward and the fear of **eternal punishment** are powerful motivators for believers to live holy lives and to work for the Kingdom of God.

Unlike Sha'ul at 1C 3:1, our author believes his readers do not need more "milk" (5:11–14); he assumes they understand these six basic doctrines and are prepared to **go on to maturity**, so he intends to explain the doctrine of Yeshua's high-priesthood and sacrifice and is satisfied that he need not **lay again the foundation**.

4–6 These verses have been commandeered into service of the most amazing variety of theological positions. Arminians (named after their supposed founder, Jacobus Arminius (1560–1609)) take them as proof that it is possible for someone who has once been a believer to fall away from faith irretrievably. Calvinists (after John Calvin (1509–1564)) interpret them in such a way as to make that a practical impossibility. The dispute between them has fueled many fires, but often forgotten is the author's purpose, which is not to deal abstractly with the "eternal security of the believer," but specifically with his readers' concern that unless the Levitical sacrifices required by the Five Books of Moses are offered their sins remain unforgiven. Whether they had in fact reintroduced sacrifices on their own cannot be determined from the evidence of this book. But it is obvious that they were fixated on the sacrificial system; and it becomes the author's task to show them that Yeshua's atoning death and his elevation to the office of *cohen gadol* has brought about "a transformation of *Torah*" (7:12) which alters the sacrificial system and priesthood.

Here is a review of the author's argument in these verses. He speaks of **people** who **have**

(1) **once been enlightened**, so that they know who Yeshua is and what he has done;
(2) **tasted the heavenly gift** of God's forgiveness;
(3) **become sharers in the *Ruach HaKodesh***, the Holy Spirit whom God gives only through his Son Yeshua (this terminology makes it impossible that the author is referring to pseudo-believers, because only true believers become sharers in the *Ruach HaKodesh*);
(4) **tasted the goodness** (compare Psalm 34:8) **of God's Word and**
(5) tasted **the powers of the *'olam haba***, which is interesting terminology for the gifts of the Holy Spirit as enumerated in 1C 12:8–10

When people who have experienced salvation in such a deep way **and then have fallen away** from faith by trusting not in Yeshua's own sacrificial death and high-priestly office but in animal sacrifices and the system of *cohanim* which the *Torah* set up to administer them — then **it is impossible to renew them so that they turn from their sin, as long as for themselves they keep** on **executing the Son of God on the stake all over again**. The reason is that they ignore what his death on the stake means, as proved by their trusting in animal sacrifices instead of his sacrifice. Thus they **keep holding him up to public contempt** by not glorifying his death as an atoning death but seeing it as having no special significance, so that his execution as a criminal becomes the dominant fact about it.

I am indebted to Jerome Fleischer, a Messianic Jew with a ministry in the San Francisco area, for pointing out to me that the author's purpose in these verses was not to provide fuel for the Calvinist-Arminian controversy of 1500 years later, but to turn his readers' concern away from animal sacrifices and toward the significance of Yeshua's final sacrifice. This is clear from the context of the following four chapters, which deal with precisely this question and which constitute the heart of the book.

However, it is possible to make a *midrash* on these verses which does deal with the Calvinist-Arminian controversy. Calvinism teaches the eternal security of the believer. It is possible to define "believer" tautologically, in such a way that no one so defined ever falls away; but then no one could be certain he is a "believer" until his life had ended. For it is manifestly possible for a person to trust the Messiah as fully as he knows how, by any imaginable subjective or objective measure of his ability to trust, and to experience subjectively all the benefits of faith, and still at some point later to fall away. If that happens, it is impossible, so long as he remains in such a state, to renew him again so that he turns from his sin. Why? Because God has given him everything he can give, yet he now refuses to accept his status as righteous with God, along with the implied responsibility of living a holy life. In vv. 7–8 these good gifts of God are compared to rain, intended to make a good crop grow; but if an evil crop comes, it is in due course burned — a reminder of the fate of the wicked on the Day of Judgment. But the New Testament's way of dealing with the security of the believer is different. Yochanan articulates it well: "The way we can be sure we know him is if we are obeying his commands" (1 Yn 2:3–6&N).

Some, insisting on the eternal security of one who has confessed the Messiah, understand this passage to say that carnal believers will be deprived of rewards (1C 3:8–15&N), or that they will spend the Millennial Age (Rv 20:2–7&N) in Outer Darkness (see Mt 22:13–14&N) instead of ruling with the Messiah.

9 The hellfire-and-brimstone of vv. 4–8 is balanced by a positive and comforting word: **we are confident that you** do not fall in the category of those who have fallen away and are close to being burned, but that you **have the better things that come with being delivered**.

10 There is no hint of "justification by works"; rather, the **work** and **service to his people** constitute "good actions already prepared by God" which those "delivered by grace through trusting" should do (Ep 2:8–10). The specific reference may be to 10:32–34 or the collection for the Jerusalem community (Ac 24:17&N, Ro 15:25–16:2&NN, 1C 16:1–4&N, 2C 8:1–9:15).

11–12 Keep showing the same diligence. Such action-oriented urging to "keep on keeping on" is found also at 1C 9:25–27, Pp 3:13–14, Ro 8:11–13, and below at 12:1–2. The point is reinforced by being expressed negatively in the advice not to be **sluggish** — a word found in the New Testament only at the beginning and end of this exhortation (5:11 and here).

Believers will surely realize their **hope** and receive **what has been promised**. This is the reason for the demonstration in vv. 13–19 of how certain God's promises are to those with **trust and patience**. Compare Ro 8:31–39, 9:1–11:36N.

13–20 **Avraham** was a man of great trust (11:8–19; compare Ro 4:1–22, Ga 3:6–18). The double security of **oath** and **promise** which God offered him **strongly encourages** us, who also have been given a **hope set before us** of going **right on through... the curtain of the Holy Place** in heaven to God himself (compare 10:22). This we will be able to do because we are united with Yeshua, and he has **entered** ahead of us as our **forerunner**. He has been able to enter because he **has become a *cohen gadol* forever, to be compared with Malki-Tzedek.** The author thus returns to the line of thought which he left at 5:10 in order to exhort his readers to diligence. He also is preparing the groundwork for his argument of 7:20–21.

CHAPTER 7

1–10 Yeshua "is to be compared with **Malki-Tzedek**" (Psalm 110:4, quoted at 5:6, 10; 6:20; 7:11, 17). He is also "**king of Shalem**"; the meanings of both phrases are given correctly in v. 2. Except for Psalm 110 he appears in the *Tanakh* only at Genesis 14:17–20. The author quotes from that passage before giving a *drash* on **how great he was** (v. 4); this *drash* is a step toward showing how great Yeshua is. See Appendix, p. 934.

2 **Shalem** — akin in Hebrew to the word *shalom*, **which means** not only "**peace**" but also "health, integrity, wholeness" (see Mt 10:12N) — is the city of Jerusalem. This is clear both from Psalm 76:3(2), where parallel lines of poetry identify Shalem (Salem) with Zion, and from traditional Jewish sources.

King of peace. In Isaiah 9:5–6(6–7), one of the most important *Tanakh* prophecies of the Messiah (see Lk 1:79N), he is called "prince of peace" (*sar-shalom*).

3 Not that Malki-Tzedek had no **father, mother, ancestry, birth or death**, but that the *Tanakh* contains no record of them. This fact enables the author to develop the *midrash* that Malki-Tzedek **continues as a *cohen* for all time, like the Son of God**, Yeshua, who had no human father (Mt 1:18–25) and who existed as the Word before his birth (Yn 1:1, 14) and continues to exist after his death. The *midrash* may be stated thus: the *Tanakh* presents Malki-Tzedek in no other way than as a *cohen*; and since the *Tanakh* is eternally true, Malki-Tzedek's existence as a *cohen* may be thought of as eternal. Such *midrash*-making is altogether Jewish in character; so that it is irrelevant to point out, as do literal-minded critics, that Malki-Tzedek surely was born of parents and died like other men. Traditional Jewish identification of Malki-Tzedek as a son of Shem (Babylonian Talmud, N'darim 32b) is likewise irrelevant; since the *Tanakh* is authoritative, while the traditions are not.

Note in passing a parallel the author does not use, presumably because it does not touch on his purpose: the use of bread and wine both by Malki-Tzedek and by Yeshua and all believers in communion (also see 13:11–14N).

4–11 These verses show five ways in which Malki-Tzedek is **great** (v. 4).

(1) He took a tithe of the spoils of battle from Avraham, even though

- (a) **Avraham** was the **Patriarch**, the father of all the Jews and thus the greatest of them;
- (b) Malki-Tzedek had no family connection with Avraham, whereas the Levitical priests receive tithes **from their own brothers**, from whom support is more naturally to be expected than from non-relatives; and
- (c) Malki-Tzedek was not specifically entitled to receive tithes from anyone, whereas the Levitical ***cohanim* have a commandment in the *Torah* to take a tenth of the income of the people** (vv. 4–6a).

The comparison of the Levitical priests with Malki-Tzedek leads later to their comparison with Yeshua.

(2) Malki-Tzedek **blessed Avraham**, which implies that Malki-Tzedek was greater than Avraham (vv. 6b–7).

(3) The Levitical priests receive tithes even though mortal, whereas Malki-Tzedek **is testified to be still alive**, that is, the text of the *Tanakh* does not tell us that he died (v. 8; see v. 3&N).

(4) An ordering of greatness is set forth as follows: Greatest, **Malki-Tzedek**, who received a tenth from Avraham; second greatest, **Avraham**, who paid it; third, **L'vi, who**, even though he **himself receives tenths, paid a tenth through Avraham, inasmuch as he was still in his ancestor Avraham's body when Malki-Tzedek met him**; fourth, L'vi's descendents, the *cohanim*, who are the ones who actually receive tenths, rather than L'vi; and least, the people of Israel, who pay them (vv. 9–10).

(5) The Jewish people "**were given the *Torah***" (Greek *nenomothetêtai,* see 8:6b&N) **in connection with the system of *cohanim* derived from L'vi.** But this system was not the final one, nor was it **possible** through it **to reach the goal** of being eternally in God's presence; this will be demonstrated in the next four chapters. This fact allows the possibility of and, more than that, shows the need for, **another, different kind of *cohen*, to be compared with Malki-Tzedek**, a *cohen* who by implication is greater than the greatest of the Levitical high priests, **Aharon**.

7 Compare Ac 20:35, "There is more blessing in giving than in receiving."

11 If it had been possible to reach the goal. Greek *teleiôsis* is often rendered "perfection," but here it means "reaching the goal" of being reconciled with God and able to be eternally in his presence, as Yeshua is now. (The same or a related Greek word appears at v. 19, 2:10, 5:9, 6:1, 9:9, 10:1, 10:14, 11:40, 12:23). In order for sinful human beings to reach this goal, they must indeed become "perfect" by having their sins forgiven by God. The author will later show that this can never come about through the Levitical priesthood but can come about through Yeshua's priesthood.

Some people might suppose that the goal can be reached through **the *Torah***. This is why the author offers as an argument for the possibility of reaching it **through the system of *cohanim* derived from L'vi** that **in connection with it, the** Jewish **people**

were given the *Torah*. But later, in v. 19, he destroys the validity of this argument by pointing out that "the *Torah* did not bring anything to the goal." This is the same point as Sha'ul makes when he observes that mere possession of *Torah* or legalistic observance of its commandments does not make a person righteous in God's sight, able to enter God's presence; but that "what *Torah* really does is show people how sinful they are" (Ro 3:20).

12 This is the only place where the New Testament speaks of a **transformation of *Torah*** (Greek *nomou metathesis*, which the Revised Standard Version renders, "a change in the law"). In Ac 6:14N I observed that the *Tanakh* itself records at least one change in the *Torah*, the addition of the festival of *Purim*; and also that a prominent Jewish tradition speaks of a change in *Torah* when the Messiah comes. The logical **necessity** for such a transformation is demonstrated by vv. 11–14; and the Scriptural basis for the transformation is found in Psalm 110:4, quoted at 5:6, 6:20 and v. 17 below.

The context makes it overwhelmingly clear that no change or transformation in *Torah* is envisioned other than in connection with the priesthood and the sacrificial system. The term "*metathesis*" implies retention of the basic structure of *Torah*, with some of its elements rearranged ("transformed"); it does not imply abrogation of either the *Torah* as a whole or of *mitzvot* not connected with the priesthood and the sacrificial system. As Yeshua himself said, "Don't think that I have come to abolish the *Torah*.... I have come not to abolish but to complete" (Mt 5:17&N).

14 **Our Lord** Yeshua the Messiah **arose out of** the tribe of **Y'hudah**, since Miryam his mother was a descendent of Y'hudah (if Lk 3:23–33 is her genealogy; see note there), and so was Miryam's husband Yosef (Mt 1:3–16).

15–19 A second reason for the "transformation of *Torah*" (v. 12) is that the Levitical priesthood set up by the *Torah* in the form that Moses received it from God was based on **a rule... concerning physical descent** from L'vi's son Gershon in the case of *cohanim* in general, and from Gershon's great-grandson Aharon in the case of the *cohen hagadol*. While Pinchas, Aharon's grandson, was given "the covenant of an everlasting priesthood" (Numbers 25:13), Yeshua by himself has an everlasting priesthood by **the power of an indestructible life** (as suggested midrashically by the life of Malki-Tzedek, v. 3&N). This sets aside the need for a system of passing on the priesthood from generation to generation, as is stated explicitly in vv. 23–25 below.

The contrast between a powerless **rule** and **power** itself is restated explicitly in vv. 18–19 and echoed elsewhere in the New Testament, for example, at Ro 8:3ff. and Ga 3:2–5.

19 **The *Torah* did not bring anything to the goal**. See v. 11N above.

20–28 **What is more**. In vv. 4–10 were given five ways in which Malki-Tzedek is greater than Avraham; in vv. 11–19 the author returned the focus from Malki-Tzedek to Yeshua, as he began to show how what Yeshua has brought is greater than what his predecessors brought. In vv. 20–28 he continues to show **more** ways in which Yeshua and what he has done is **better** (v. 22&N) than what has gone before him.

20–21 ***Adonai*** **has sworn and will not change his mind**. These verses must be read in the light of 6:13–20 (compare Ga 3:15–18).

The author approaches the *Tanakh* exactly as do the rabbis, singling out each word or phrase of the text of Psalm 110:4 to extract every ounce of significance. Here his attention is on "sworn"; in vv. 15–17, it was on "forever"; in vv. 11–14, on "to be compared with"; and in vv. 1–10, on "Malki-Tzedek."

22 Why the new **covenant, of which Yeshua has become guarantor**, is superior to the covenant with Moses at Sinai will be explained at 8:5–13&NN. On "**better**," see second paragraph of 1:2–3N and last paragraph of 1:4N.

23–25 Another reason Yeshua is better than the Levitical *cohanim* is that he **is alive forever**, so that he does not need to be replaced; **his position as *cohen*** is permanent, **it does not pass on to someone else**.

25 Isaiah 53:12 prophesies that the servant of *Adonai* (i.e., the Messiah) will "make intercession for the transgressors"; see 2:16–18&N. Romans 8:34 states that Yeshua is "at the right hand of God… pleading on our behalf"; and 1 Yn 2:1 that he is "the *Tzaddik*" ("the Righteous One"), who "pleads our cause with the Father." Other verses stress the universal necessity of approaching God only through him (Yn 14:6, Ac 4:12, 1 Yn 2:22–23).

26–28 Yet another point of Yeshua's superiority to the Levitical *cohanim* is that the latter **have the daily necessity of offering sacrifices for their own sins**, whereas Yeshua **offered one sacrifice, once and for all, by offering up himself** on behalf of sinners (9:14; Isaiah 53:12). Since he was **holy, without evil, without stain, set apart from sinners** (Ro 8:3&N), he did not need to make an offering for himself. The sacrificial process, as described in the *Torah*, emphasizes the need for both the *cohen* and the offerer to identify with the sacrifice; but here we see the ultimate identification; it is perfect, hence needs no repetition.

Jewish tradition condemns human sacrifice in the strongest language, recoiling in horror at the primitive notion that an innocent person should be put to death for the sake of an intangible supposed benefit to someone else. But the death of Yeshua breaks this rule by transcending its logic, as is so often the case when the supernatural events of Yeshua invade the natural world. It is true that the sacrifice of a sinful human being would be ineffective in paying even for himself, let alone for others, the just penalty of death which God demands for sin. (Or perhaps one should say that a sinner's own death does pay the just penalty for his own sin but still fails to restore him to fellowship with God in the *'olam haba*; that is, to use the language of Ro 6:9, death has eternal authority over the sinner.) God indicates this by specifying that sacrifices must be "without blemish" (the phrase appears 29 times in Leviticus and Numbers). Because the sacrifice of a sinful human being would not meet this criterion it would be ineffective, hence pointless, and therefore all the more repugnant. But the sacrifice of Yeshua, since he was sinless, first, was not needed for himself at all ("death has no authority over him," Ro 6:9), and, second, was effective for others, since he was a sacrifice "without blemish," as the *Torah* requires. The subject returns in Chapter 9. Finally, the horror of his human sacrifice was negated, indeed reversed and transformed into glory, by his resurrection.

The text which speaks about the swearing of the oath — Psalm 110:4, cited in v. 21 above — was **written** centuries **later than the *Torah*.**

Has been brought to the goal. See v. 11N.

CHAPTER 8

1 The author turns from Yeshua's credentials, character and status as ***cohen gadol*** (Chapter 7) to the nature of his work in the heavenly **Holy Place** as he sits (10:11–14&N, Psalm 110:1) or possibly stands (Ac 7:55–56&N) **at the right hand of** God. His being there was indicated earlier (1:3, 13).

On "***HaG'dulah***" ("the Greatness"), a euphemism for God, see numbered paragraph (7) of 1:2–3N.

2–6a That there is a **true Tent of Meeting** or Tabernacle in heaven is proved by the passage cited in v. 5. The Tent constructed in the Wilderness (Exodus 25–31, 35–39), long before there was any thought of a Temple, demonstrated that God dwells with his people; indeed, one of the Hebrew words the *Tanakh* uses for "tent" is "*mishkan*," which is related to both "*shakhen*" ("neighbor") and "*Sh'khinah*" ("God's immanent presence," see Paragraph (3) of 1:2–3N).

Not only is Yeshua himself better than the Levitical *cohanim*, as shown in Chapter 7, but **the work Yeshua has been given to do is far superior to theirs**, since the place where they serve **is only a copy and shadow of the heavenly original**, referred to in Rv 15:5 as "the Tent of Witness in heaven." The term, "**Tent of Meeting**," speaks of God's communicating with his people; whereas "Tent of Witness" bespeaks God's witness to his own righteousness (compare with Yn 5:37–40 and Ro 3:25–26).

4 There is no conflict between the Levitical priesthood established by the *Torah* of Moses and that of Yeshua as predicted by Psalm 110; it is not necessary to think of Yeshua's priesthood as superseding the Levitical one. The *Torah* says that earthly *cohanim* must be descendants of L'vi, and Numbers 25:12 speaks of God's "covenant of an everlasting priesthood" with Pinchas, the son of Aharon. But since Yeshua serves in heaven, he can be from the tribe of Y'hudah (7:13–14) and can also have an eternal ministry (7:23–25).

6a Is far superior to theirs, just as the covenant he mediates is better, literally, "is as far superior to theirs as the covenant he mediates is better." See second paragraph of 1:2–3N and last paragraph of 1:4N.

The covenant which Yeshua mediates is the New Covenant spoken of by Jeremiah in the passage quoted below (vv. 8–12). It is **better** than the covenant Moses mediated at Mount Sinai, as proved by vv. 6b–13.

Mediates. On whether the idea of a mediator between God and mankind is Jewish, see 1 Ti 2:5b–6aN.

6b–13 This passage is one of the New Testament's two most important discussions of the New Covenant in relation to the Covenant with Moses at Mount Sinai (the other is 2C 3:6–18). Non-Messianic Jews claim that God did not establish a New Covenant with

Israel through Yeshua — and indeed they must say this, even though it undermines ecumenical tolerance by attacking the foundation of Christian faith; because otherwise they have no excuse for not adhering to its terms and accepting Yeshua as the Messiah. When discussing the New Covenant in the context of these verses, they raise four objections, which I present with my answers. The first two are lightweight, but the third and fourth deserve careful rebuttal.

(1) *Objection*: "The covenant with Moses is eternal, so there is no ground for expecting a new one."
Answer: The covenant with Moses is indeed eternal (see v. 13N), but the conclusion that there is no new one does not logically follow. The eternal covenant with Avraham did not prevent God from making an eternal covenant with Moses, nor did the latter cancel the former (Ga 3:15–18&NN). Moreover, it is patently false that there is no ground for expecting a new covenant; this is proved by the Jeremiah text (vv. 8b–12), written six centuries before the time of Yeshua.

(2) *Objection*: "Who needs a new covenant? What you call the 'old' one is good enough for me."
Answer: This is not an argument but an expression of emotion. The Mosaic covenant is excellent, but the decisions whether it is "good enough" and whether one should reject the New Covenant should not be based on feelings, not even feelings of loyalty to the Jewish people. If God decided to establish a new covenant with the Jewish people, which, as the Jeremiah passage proves, he did promise to do, then one ought to agree that God did this for the benefit of Jews, not to hurt them, and one should welcome whatever God offers.

(3) *Objection*: "I welcome whatever God may offer, including a new covenant; and there is ground in the *Tanakh* for expecting one. But Jesus did not bring it, and the New Testament does not express it — as proved by the following four arguments, which are based on the very text you use to support your own view.

(a) "Jeremiah writes that the **new covenant** will be **over the house of Israel and over the House of Y'hudah**. It does not say that God will make his new covenant with Gentiles or with Christians."
Answer: Yeshua introduced the New Covenant not to a group of Gentiles (let alone to Christians — there weren't any), but to an exclusively Jewish company at a Passover *Seder* (Lk 22:15–20). More specifically, he announced this covenant to his twelve *talmidim*, who, Yeshua explained moments later, are in a special representative relationship with the twelve tribes of Israel as their judges (Lk 22:30; compare Mt 19:28, Rv 21:12–14). It is the twelve tribes of Israel of whom Jeremiah speaks collectively when he writes, "**the house of Israel and the house of Y'hudah**." Gentiles enter this covenant only by being "grafted in" to Israel (Ro 11:17–24; Ep 2:11–16).

(b) "God says he will put his ***Torah*** **in their minds and write it on their hearts**. It is no secret that Christians have done cruel things to Jews in Christ's name, things which are altogether alien to *Torah*, things which prove that *Torah* was far from their minds and hearts. I do not suppose it necessary to show how each one of the Ten Commandments has been violated by Christians in their dealings with Jews.

"However, I will pass over these things and take a different tack. I will grant that not all deeds done by Christians were necessarily authorized by Christ — some even adduced Christ's name to justify acts contrary to his teachings and to the Ten Commandments. Moreover, I know that there are Christians who love God and who desire to do good. But — and here is the point — this is not the same as having the *Torah* written on their hearts. For the *Torah* is the body of laws and instruction given to Moses for the Jewish people, consisting of both the Written and the Oral Law. Therefore, someone with the *Torah* written on his heart should be *shomer-mitzvot*, obedient to all the commandments of the Written and Oral Law; and this I do not see in Christians, not even in those whose character is exemplary."

Answer: First, concerning Christians who act against *Torah* in their dealings with Jews: God is indeed putting his *Torah*, his teaching, in the minds and hearts of his true followers by means of the *Ruach HaKodesh*, the Holy Spirit, whom Yeshua sent to teach us all the truth (Yn 16:13–15; on the relationship between the Holy Spirit and the *Torah*, see Ac 2:1N on the Jewish holiday *Shavu'ot*, and compare 2C 3:16–18, Ro 8:1–4). Having the *Torah* in one's mind and written on one's heart is Scriptural language for being holy. The path to holiness commences with trusting God and his son Yeshua, and following this path is a process, not an instantaneous event — believers do not suddenly become perfect. A genuine follower of Yeshua will have an inner desire to please God; so that as he understands more and more of what God wants and expects from him, he will be increasingly prepared and empowered by the Holy Spirit to do it. On the other hand, a professed follower of Yeshua still has free will and can resist "the finger of God" writing on his heart. Some who have acted against Jews have called themselves Christians but in fact have been unbelievers; while others have been believers who resisted God's will. None of this negates God's action (compare Ro 3:3–4), which he has been accomplishing according to the terms of the New Covenant ever since Yeshua inaugurated it, of writing his *Torah* on the heart of any willing person, Jewish or Gentile, who puts his trust in Yeshua the Messiah.

Second, your understanding of "*shomer-mitzvot*" is that of non-Messianic (and probably Orthodox) Judaism; my response is that any form of Judaism which fails to recognize that the New Covenant itself **has been given as *Torah*** (v. 6b&N) has a defective understanding of *Torah* and therefore of "*shomer-mitzvot.*" Someone with the *Torah* written in his heart puts his trust in Yeshua and should accept the New Testament's understanding of what *Torah* really is. That understanding does not give the Oral Law the authority which Orthodox Judaism grants it (although, unlike much Christian theology, the New Testament certainly does not denigrate the Oral Law, properly used; see 1 Ti 1:8&N). A person with the *Torah* in his mind and heart should indeed be *shomer-mitzvot*, but in a way consistent with the *p'rushei-Torah* (expositions of the Law) set forth by Yeshua and the other New Testament writers. My goal in the *Jewish New Testament Commentary* is, among other things, to help set forth the New Testament understanding of *Torah* in a way that a Jewish person can appreciate. Let me add that there is no reason why a Messianic Jew might not choose to be *shomer-mitzvot* in a sense that would include obedience to much of the Oral Law; nothing in the New Testament prevents it, and a number of passages lend support (Mt 5:19–20; 23:2, 23; Yn 7:37–39&NN; Ac 21:20; Ga 5:3).

But Christians and Messianic Jews should understand that everyone under the New Covenant has the *Torah* to observe. That is the plain sense of the phrase, "I will put my *Torah* in their minds and write it on their hearts." It is not some new *Torah*, different from Old Testament *Torah*. It is the one and only *Torah*, understood in the spirit of the Messiah, "as upheld by the Messiah" (Ga 6:2&N; 1C 9:21&N). Christian theology all too often tries to escape or water down the plain sense of what is said here, so that what is required is very little, usually a vague "sensitivity to God's will" that becomes impossible to pin down. Not infrequently the motivation for devising such theology has been to portray or create separation, spiritual distance and invidious comparison between the Church and the Jews. But other Christians have had a correct understanding, for example, A. Lukyn Williams:

> "God's words through Jeremiah do not announce the coming of a new Law, but of a new principle of keeping the Law, according to which God forgives the sinner, writes the Law on his heart, brings him into a new relation to Himself, and makes Himself known to him." (*Manual of Christian Evidences for Jews*, London: Society for Promoting Christian Knowledge, 1919, I:184.)

(c) "The text continues, '**None of them will teach his fellow-citizen or his brother, saying, "Know *Adonai*!"**' If so, why do you proselytize us? Moreover, the condition that **all will know** God remains unfulfilled; therefore what you offer is not what Jeremiah prophesied."
Answer: Like the individual process of becoming holy, the social process whereby everyone comes to know God is a gradual one. In the centuries since Yeshua's time on earth, the number of believers has grown enormously. The day will come when there will be no need for a believer to **teach his fellow-citizen or his brother**; but until that day arrives, and so long as there is anyone who has not accepted God's offer of forgiveness through Yeshua, there is need not to proselytize, which means to convert someone to another religion, but to evangelize, which means to communicate the Good News that God has provided a means for salvation, here and now, and for the eventual certain salvation of the Jewish people too (Ro 11:26a&N). Since Scripture says that there will be unbelievers right up until the time the Messiah returns, the consummation of the process, when **all will know** God, must not take place until the Messiah removes and punishes those who have made themselves resistant to God and the Gospel (Rv 20:11–15). Those who remain will all know God and will no longer need to teach others about him (Revelation 21–22).

(4) *Objection*: "The author's comments in vv. 6–8a and 13 denigrate both the people of Israel and God's covenant at Sinai. God would not impugn his own chosen people or his own covenant; the true new covenant will not be antisemitic, as is this book. Here are four antisemitic statements by the author of Messianic Jews:

(a) "He says the new covenant contains **better promises** than those in the covenant at Sinai (v. 6c); this directly impugns God and the Mosaic covenant."
Answer: This charge is false because it is based on a misuse of what the author says. See v. 6cN for a specific refutation.

(b) "The author says the first covenant was defective (v. 7)."
Answer: He does not say this, but the impression that he does is based on a mistranslation found in most versions. The first covenant is not itself faulty, but it has **given ground for faultfinding**. For details, see vv. 7–8aN.

(c) "The author says that God found fault with his own chosen people, the Jews (v. 8a)."
Answer: This is not a serious criticism. It was not the author of this book but Jeremiah, quoting God, who said that Israel **did not remain faithful to** God's **covenant** (v. 9). In noting that **God does find fault with the people** the author is only reporting the obvious. One of the glories of the *Tanakh* is that even though no human being — neither the individual heroes nor the Jewish people as a whole — is perfect but is shown as sinful and errant, nevertheless God loves them all. In the New Testament God finds plenty of faults with the members of the Messianic Community, and, as in the *Tanakh*, lovingly sets out to correct them.

(d) "The author calls the first covenant **old,... aging,... vanishing** (v. 13). This statement not only depreciates the Mosaic covenant and the God who made it, but, as we can see 2000 years later, it is false. The Mosaic covenant has not vanished. Rather, *'am-Israel chai* ("the people of Israel lives"); and we live by virtue of our covenant, the old-new one, fresh, not aging, not vanishing now or ever."
Answer: Good rhetoric, but see v. 13N.

In conclusion, we find that these objections to a New Covenant do not hold up. Instead of objecting, we should explore the New Covenant in order to understand its promises and conditions, so that we can obey it properly — with those of us who are Jewish doing so in the framework of staying Jewish, and those of us who are Gentile doing so in the framework of staying Gentile (see 1C 7:18&NN). This kind of exploration is a major purpose of the *Jewish New Testament* and the *Jewish New Testament Commentary*.

6b The New Covenant **has been given as *Torah***. This is a virtually unknown theological truth of far-reaching importance. First, although there are many, both Jews and Christians, who suppose that the New Testament abrogated the *Torah*, the New Testament here explicitly states that it has itself been given as *Torah*. Obviously, if the New Testament is *Torah*, then the *Torah* has not been abrogated. Instead, the New Testament has been given the same status as the *Torah* of Moses; that is, it has come to have the highest authority there is, the authority that accompanies promulgation by God himself. One might say that *Torah* has been expanded — or, better, that *Torah* has been made more explicit (compare Mt 5:17–48&NN).

Second, the fact that the New Covenant has been given as *Torah* means that a Jew is not *Torah*-true, he is not a *Torah*-observant Jew, unless he accepts the New Testament as *Torah*. A Jew who considers himself *shomer-mitzvot*, "an observer of [the] commandments," is deluding himself if he does not obey the New Covenant. Unless he trusts in Yeshua as Messiah and as his atonement for sin, he is disobeying *Torah*.

And third, it means that a Gentile grafted into Israel by his faith in Yeshua the Messiah (Ro 11:17–24, Ep 2:8–16) has himself come into the framework of Israel's *Torah*. Although what this *Torah* demands of him differs from what it demands of a Jew (see Ac 15:20&N), a Gentile Christian should never think of himself as "free from the Law," as many do.

That the New Covenant has become *Torah* is absolutely crucial for understanding the New Testament. Yet, so far as I know, not one existing translation brings out this truth; nor, to my knowledge, does any commentary so much as mention it. In fact, the issue is avoided altogether. To give a typical example, the Revised Standard Version in this verse says merely that the New Covenant "is enacted" on better promises.

A look at the Greek text will explain why the subject has been ignored. The phrase, "has been given as *Torah,*" is my rendering of the passive, perfect-tense verb, "*nenomothetêtai.*" This is a compound word formed from "*nomos*" and "*tithêmi.*" "*Tithêmi*" is a common word meaning "lay, put, place, make"; and in general — that is, when there is no specifically Jewish context — "*nomos*" may be translated "law." Thus "*nenomothetêtai*" in a non-Jewish context means simply "to make law"; when it is used in connection with the Roman Senate or the Athenian Areopagus (see Ac 17:19–22aN) it is quite properly rendered "to legislate, enact, establish as law."

But "*nomos*" is also the word used in the Septuagint and other Jewish literature written in Greek to render the Hebrew word "*Torah.*" Since the New Testament was written by Jews, the word "*nomos*" or any of its compounds must always be checked wherever it appears to see whether it refers to "law" in general or "*Torah*" in particular. (Not germane here are the meanings "legalism" and "the legal part of the *Torah*"; see Ro 3:20bN; Ga 2:16b&N, 3:17&N, 3:23b&N.) The word "*nomos*" appears 14 times in the book of Messianic Jews; and every time, without exception, it means "*Torah*" and never merely "law."

Also, every place in the New Testament or the Septuagint where there appears a compound word related to "*nenomothetêtai,*" it always has to do with "*Torah*" and never with "law." At Ya 4:12 the word "*nomothetês,*" the noun formed from the verb used in our verse, is used to describe God as the "one Giver of *Torah*, with the power to deliver and to destroy." At Ro 9:4 "*nomothesia,*" the verbal noun (gerund), is rendered "giving of the *Torah.*" In the Septuagint "*nomothetein,*" which is the active voice of the verb in our verse, is used more than a dozen times to mean "instruct," the context always implying "instruct in *Torah*" (and at the same time implying that instruction in *Torah* involves not only the legal component but the full range of God's "Teaching" — the literal translation of "*Torah*").

The word in our verse appears at only one other place in the New Testament, 7:11 above, where we read that the Jewish people "*nenomothetêtai,*" that is, "were given the *Torah.*" At 7:11, every translation, without exception, takes the "*nomos*" in "*nenomothetêtai*" to be not "law" in general but "*Torah*" in particular — no one thinks an early version of the Knesset (the legislative body of the State of Israel) met on Mount Sinai to pass laws. But in the present verse, even though "*nomos*" and its compound "*nenomothetêtai*" nowhere in the entire book of Messianic Jews refer to "law" in general, but always to "*Torah*" in particular, not one translator or commentator has grasped the point that the New Covenant **has been given as *Torah***.

I have enough paranoia to find this more than just an oversight. Although today there is likely no conscious ill intent, I am convinced that the failure to translate "*nenomothetêtai*" correctly is the evolved consequence of an earlier perverse unwillingness on the part of Christians to recognize and emphasize the Jewishness of the New Testament. This perversity resulted from the wrong theology that regards Christianity as a religion separate from Judaism, having superseded it, and which regards Judaism as a dead religion, whose Law, whose *Torah*, ceased to be operative when Yeshua came. Like the translation of "*telos*" in Ro 10:4 as "termination" instead of "goal," the failure to see that the New Covenant has been given as *Torah* reflects, even if unconsciously, the antisemitism which came to pervade the Christian Church during the centuries after it had drawn away from its Jewish roots (see Ro 10:4N). For more on refuting this erroneous theology, which became endemic in the Church, see references on Replacement theology in the last paragraph of Mt 5:5N.

I challenge non-Messianic Jews and Gentile Christians alike to recognize that the New Testament **has been given as *Torah***, to recognize the three implications of this fact stated in the three initial paragraphs of this note, and to draw the appropriate conclusions.

6c The **better promises** of the New Covenant were not invented by the author of the book of Messianic Jews but were announced by God in the *Tanakh* through the prophet Jeremiah (vv. 10–12). Having the *Torah* internalized is better than having it written out (v. 10; compare Ro 2:13–29), and it is better to have sins forgiven permanently than temporarily (v. 12; how this can happen is explained in 9:1–10:18).

7–8a If the first covenant, meaning the one with Moses at Sinai, **had not given ground for faultfinding**. Other translations render this as if something had been wrong with the first covenant itself, for example, the Revised Standard Version has, "if that first covenant had been faultless...." But vv. 8–9 show that the **fault** was not with the covenant but **with the people** of Israel who "did not remain faithful" to it (v. 9).

In Gerhard Kittel's *Theological Dictionary of the New Testament* (Volume 4, p. 572), one scholar observes that the Greek word "*amemptos*" used in v. 7 does not refer in the Septuagint to objective faults but "expresses a subjective judgment." If so, then this "subjectivity" points toward the Jeremiah quotation in vv. 8b–12, which says that the "fathers" broke the covenant, not that the covenant was objectively flawed. Another scholar then writes, "God does not reject the ancient covenant. The faithless Israelites are the occasion of new covenant action on the part of God. Their unfaithful conduct is an object of "*mempsesthai*" ["**faultfinding**," v. 8a], and they have robbed the old covenant of its significance." But even if the people of Israel in Jeremiah's time "robbed the old covenant of its significance" for themselves, they had neither the authority nor the capacity to abolish it, since it was God, not themselves, who had established it forever.

Thus the only "fault" in the **first covenant**, if one should even call it that, is that it does not contain in itself the power to keep the people faithful (compare vv. 15–19&N; also Ro 8:3ff., where Sha'ul says exactly the same thing about the *Torah*). In this regard, the **second** covenant is different, because its terms include God's putting his *Torah* in their minds and writing it on their hearts, providing power for obedience by the Holy Spirit within.

8b–12 This is the longest citation from the *Tanakh* in the New Testament, and appropriately so; for this prediction of Jeremiah's is the *Tanakh*'s clearest ground for the very existence of the "New Testament" (or "New Covenant" — "testament" and "covenant" are alternative renderings of the Greek word "*diathêkê*"; see vv. 9:16–17N, Ga 3:15–17N); see Section (3) of vv. 6b–13N above.

There are two words for "new" in Greek, "*kainos*" and "*neos*." "*Neos*" means something which has never before existed, whereas "*kainos*" carries overtones of freshness and renewal of something which has existed (see Mt 9:17N). The word used in Chapter 8 in the phrase, "New Covenant," is always "*kainos*," and this is as it should be, because in a very real way the New Covenant renews the Old Covenant — even though the author dwells more on the contrasts than on the similarities. The clearest illustration is that God's announcement, "**I will be their God and they will be my people**" (v. 10), was made first to Moses (Exodus 6:7, Leviticus 26:12), then to the Prophets (Jeremiah 32:38; Ezekiel 11:20, 37:27), and last to the New Testament writers, where it applies both to the present (here, 2C 6:16) and to the future (Rv 21:3&N).

The other three elements which Jeremiah specifies in vv. 10–12, although different from the provisions of the Old Covenant, nevertheless carry forward its purposes. By placing his *Torah* in people's minds and hearts (v. 10; compare Ezekiel 11:19, 36:26–27; 2C 3:16–18), God accomplishes precisely what the *Sh'ma* requires ("And these words which I command you this day are to be upon your hearts, etc," Deuteronomy 6:6–9). See also Section (3)(b) of vv. 6b–13N.

God's covenant people have always been expected to know God (v. 11; compare Judges 2:10; Hosea 4:1, 6; 6:6; 1C 8:3; Ga 4:9). God has made this knowledge available in various ways (1:1–3), and it will eventually become complete ("For the earth shall be full of the knowledge of *Adonai* as the waters cover the sea," Isaiah 11:9, Habakkuk 2:14), even though it isn't yet ("Now I know partly; then I will know fully, just as God has fully known me," 1C 13:12).

Finally, under the New Covenant God forgives and forgets people's sins (v. 12). According to the Bible, forgiveness of sins is the main issue of human history. It arises already at Genesis 2:17 and is not fully resolved until Rv 20:15 (see Ro 5:12–21N). The Old Covenant provided a way of having sins forgiven, in connection with the Levitical priesthood and sacrificial system; but the New Covenant provides a way that is better, through the heavenly priesthood and sacrificial system, as the author explains in the present section (7:1–10:18).

Thus even though the New Covenant is distinct from the Old, and its system of priesthood and sacrifice is better, God uses it to carry out faithfully his original covenantal purposes, the promises made earlier to the Jewish people.

9 **So I, for my part, stopped concerning myself with them**. The author quotes the Septuagint, whose translators had a different Hebrew text than the one we have now; it must have said "*bachalti*" ("I disdained them") instead of "*ba'alti*" ("I was a husband [or "lord"] to them"), as in our present Hebrew version. Rashi, cited in *Mikra'ot G'dolot*, makes the same point in his discussion of this verse of Jeremiah. The difference is not significant for understanding the New Covenant, but a cautionary note is apposite: God did not cease interesting himself in the Jewish people; rather, as explained above (3:15–4:11), God stopped concerning himself with the generation in the Wilderness, in

the sense that he did not permit them to enter the Promised Land; and by extension, when people turn away from him with sufficient stubbornness, he turns away from them (Ro 9:17–21&NN).

13 **By using the term, "new," he has made the first covenant "old."** The author is not criticizing the Mosaic Covenant but merely making explicit what Jeremiah implied. Sha'ul had already used the phrase, "Old Covenant," at 2C 3:14.

Is one to infer that the Jewish holidays, *Shabbat*, *kashrut*, civil laws, and moral laws of the Mosaic Covenant are **on the verge of vanishing altogether**? No, for the author could hardly have been unaware that the Mosaic Covenant presents itself as eternal; also the context shows that he is speaking only of its system of priests and sacrifices, not its other aspects. Since the laws concerning the cultus constitute the majority of the Mosaic prescriptions, it is not an inappropriate figure of speech to say that the Old Covenant itself is aging and about to disappear.

In this verse, the verb tenses are important. The Mosaic Covenant has already been **made... old**, but it is not already aged and it has not already vanished. It is **in the process of aging** and **on the verge of vanishing** in the same sense that "This world's leaders...are in the process of passing away" (2C 2:6). This world's leaders are still with us, and so is the Mosaic Covenant. Even Christians whose theology posits the abrogation or passage of the Mosaic Covenant in its entirety must therefore acknowledge that it has not yet vanished but still exists. Some have inferred from this language that at the time the author wrote, the Temple was still standing and the author was predicting what Yeshua had already prophesied (Mt 24:2, Mk 13:2, Lk 21:2), that the Temple would soon be destroyed by the Romans in 70 C.E., at which time the sacrifices would cease and the priesthood would be left without work to do. This is a possible interpretation, although against it is the fact that the author never refers to the Temple but always to the Tent (Tabernacle), which had passed out of existence a thousand years earlier. He is more interested in the system as the Mosaic Covenant specifies it than in its current mode of implementation (the instructions for making the Tent begin in Exodus 25, immediately after the establishment of the covenant at Exodus 24:1–8). No matter when the author wrote, his arguments do provide a rationale for Messianic Jews not to be distressed by the passing of the Temple and to carry on anyhow; in this sense, the role of the book of Messianic Jews is comparable with that of the Yavneh Council in non-Messianic Judaism (c. 90 C.E.), which transferred its focus from the Temple to the Written and Oral *Torah*. The book instructs Messianic Jews to center not on the Temple but on the Messiah and what he has done.

What is actually on the verge of vanishing is the old priesthood, not the old covenant — or, perhaps we may say, not God's unchangeable nature which stands behind the old covenant. The priesthood is the subject of the whole section (indeed, the sacrificial system is the subject of the whole letter), and it is this which is about to disappear or, at the very least, take on a very much transformed role (see 7:12&N). On this verse Paul Ellingworth, who has also written a commentary on Hebrews, says: "This refers to the replacement of the old cult by the new, not to a change in the ethical or civil requirements of the *Torah*!" The "old" *Torah* continues, and continues to have its same purpose, but there is now a new system of *cohanim*, as has already been said and will be explained further in the next two chapters.

CHAPTER 9

9:1–10:18 This section shows that the New Covenant's system of priesthood and sacrifice, in which Yeshua offered up himself once and for all in order to clear the way to the Holy of Holies for everyone, is better than the Old Covenant's system and effectively replaces it. The subject matter is the same as in *Seder Kodashim*, one of the six major divisions of the Talmud.

1–5 Both **Tent** and Temple consisted of an outer court (not mentioned in this passage), a **Holy Place**, and a **Holiest Place** (Holy of Holies), according to the pattern set forth in Exodus 25–31, 35–40. These verses provide only the minimal background necessary for vv. 6–10 and therefore end with one of the more tantalizing lines in Scripture; would that the author had chosen to **discuss these things in detail**!

2 **The *menorah*** ("candlestick, light") had seven branches and was made of gold; see Exodus 25:31–39, 37:17–24; variations are found in synagogues throughout the world, and the design rivals the six-pointed star for popularity as a Jewish symbol. The gold-covered acacia-wood **table** (Exodus 25:23–26, 37:10–16) had on it **the Bread of the Presence** (Exodus 25:30), one loaf to represent each of the twelve tribes, placed fresh every *Shabbat* (Leviticus 24:5–9); only *cohanim* were allowed to eat it (compare Mt 12:4, Mk 2:26, Lk 6:4).

3 The first curtain or "screen" (Exodus 26:36–37, 36:37–38) separated the Holy Place from the outer court, whereas **the second curtain** or "veil" (Exodus 26:31–33, 36:35–36; Mt 27:51) separated **the Holiest Place** from the Holy Place.

4 The Holiest Place **had** associated with itself **the golden altar for burning incense**. Critics have been quick to conclude that the author did not know what he was talking about, since the *Torah* clearly states that the golden altar was outside the curtain (Exodus 30:6, Leviticus 16:18, 1 Kings 6:22). Actually, the author knew his subject well. Although the incense altar was used daily for other purposes, it was used in a special way by the *cohen hagadol* on *Yom-Kippur*, when he would take from it a golden censer of coals and bring them into the Holiest Place (Exodus 30:10, Leviticus 16:12, 15). See paragraph after next.

Inside the Holiest Place was **the Ark of the Covenant** (described first at Exodus 25:10–22), the box in which were **the gold jar containing** a sample of **the manna** on which the Israelites lived for forty years in the Wilderness (Exodus 16:33); **Aharon's rod**, the dry almond branch **that sprouted** overnight as a sign to Korach and his rebels that Moses and Aaron were God's authorized representatives (Numbers 17:25); and **the** second set of **stone Tablets of the Covenant** that Moses brought down from Mount Sinai (Exodus 34:1–4, 28–29; Deuteronomy 10:1–5), which were in Solomon's Temple (2 Chronicles 5:10) but disappeared later, perhaps at the time of the Babylonian Exile (587 C.E.; see Rv 11:19N).

Earlier, in v. 2, the Greek text says that the table with showbread and the *menorah* were "in" the Holy Place. And in the latter part of the present verse, the Greek says that the manna, rod and tablets were "in" the ark. But the Greek expression for the relationship between the Holiest Place and the incense altar is not "in which" but "having," i.e., "having associated with itself." Like the ark the incense altar was *associated with* the Holiest Place. But the author did *not* make the mistake of *locating* the incense altar *in* the Holiest Place, which would have been an error; on the contrary, choosing his words carefully, he associated the incense altar with the Holiest Place *even though* it was outside. A diagram of the actual locations makes this even clearer; the figure shows that the incense altar was close to the Holiest Place, while the *menorah*, showbread and table were farther away.

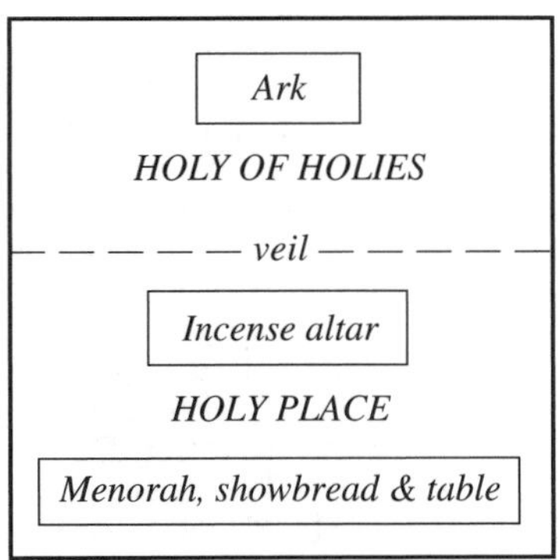

Also compare Rv 5:8, 6:9–10, 8:3–4, where the golden censer represents the prayers of believers in Yeshua.

5 **The lid of the Ark** was also known as the "mercy seat" (Hebrew *kapporet*), meaning the physical place where *Adonai* met the *cohen hagadol* on *Yom-Kippur* (Leviticus 16:2) and from which, in his mercy, he forgave the sins of the people of Israel. The Greek word for "mercy seat" is used in the New Testament at only one other place, Ro 3:23, where it is rendered, "*kapparah*" ("covering, atonement"): "God put Yeshua forward as the *kapparah* for sin." Thus the Tabernacle's mercy seat prefigured the eternal mercy seat, Yeshua.

Casting their shadow on the mercy seat were two figures, **the *k'ruvim*** (usually transliterated "cherubim"; see Exodus 25:18–22, 37:7–9). *K'ruvim* guarded the Garden of Eden (Genesis 3:24). God spoke to Moses "from between the *k'ruvim*" (Exodus 25:22, Numbers 7:89); and because the *Tanakh* speaks often of God's presence there (1 Samuel 4:4; Isaiah 37:16; Ezekiel 10:1–22; Psalms 80:1, 99:1), the author regards the *k'ruvim* as **representing the *Sh'khinah*** ("God's presence"; see Paragraph (3) of 1:2–3N).

6 The elements mentioned in vv. 2 and 4 already call to mind the **duties** of **the *cohanim*** in **the outer tent** (the Holy Place). They included keeping the *menorah* continually lit (Exodus 27:20–22, Leviticus 24:1–4), placing fresh loaves on the table (Leviticus 24:5–9) and burning incense on the incense altar (Exodus 30:7–9), as did Z'kharyah the father of Yochanan the Immerser (Lk 1:9–11).

7 The author mentions these activities only to contrast their regularity with the ***cohen hagadol***'s entry into the **inner** tent (the Holiest Place), which is permitted **only once a year** and is surrounded by other conditions. He must **bring** the **blood** of a slaughtered animal as a sin offering, as a reminder that death is the penalty for sin (he does not actually bring it into the Holiest Place itself, but slaughters a bull at the altar in the prescribed manner). He must **offer for himself**, since he too is a sinner; and his offering for **the people** is only for their **sins committed in ignorance**. These requirements are set forth in Leviticus 16.

8 **This arrangement showed that** during the time before Yeshua's first coming, when **the first Tent**, the Tabernacle established by the Mosaic Covenant, or any of its replacements, such as the First or Second Temple, **had standing, the way into the Holiest Place**, that is, into God's presence, **was still closed** to people in general and was open only to the *cohen hagadol*, and only once a year, and only if he came with blood.

Had standing. Some versions have "existed," but this is wrong. The author is referring to the time when the Tabernacle or Temple had status or position as an essential element in God's way of dealing with sin under the Mosaic Covenant. Compare 10:9.

Holiest Place, Greek *agia*, which can mean either "Holy Place" (as in vv. 1–2) or "Holiest Place" (compare Leviticus 16:2, which speaks of "the Holy Place inside the curtain"). Because of context *agia* must mean "Holy Place" at 10:1, and "Holiest Place" here and in vv. 12, 24, 25; 10:19, 22; 13:11. Only at 9:3 must the author use the explicit term "*agia agiôn*" ("Holy of Holies") for "Holiest Place" in order to avoid confusion.

9–10 **The present age** refers to the period after Yeshua's first coming, yet before the Mosaic Covenant's system of priesthood and sacrifice has altogether disappeared (8:13&N). The sacrifices go on, but, in the light of what Yeshua has accomplished, what they signify is **that the conscience** of **the person performing the service cannot be brought to the goal** (KJV: "be made perfect"; see 7:11&N) **by** obeying **regulations concerning the outward life** (on "**food and drink**" in the Temple see Leviticus 23; compare Co 2:16&N). And if so, how much less (Mt 6:30&N) can the sacrificial ritual bring the consciences of those for whom the service is performed to the goal of being, both in fact and in feeling, cleared of guilt.

Non-Messianic Judaism has never supposed that the mechanical performance of ritual acts causes God to forgive sin. Rather, since the destruction of the Temple, Judaism has taken a different tack, teaching that neither sacrifice nor priesthood is necessary for God to forgive sin. The author expresses the view that sacrifice and priesthood are indeed necessary, that the Mosaic system was **imposed until the time for God to reshape the whole structure**, literally, "until a time of re-formation," and thus prefigured the system established by Yeshua the Messiah.

11–15 Having described the Mosaic Covenant's system of priesthood and sacrifice, the author now addresses his readers' preoccupation with it by showing many ways in which the New Covenant's system and its priest/mediator are better; in vv. 13–14 he makes use of a *kal v'chomer* argument (see Mt 6:30&N):

(1) With Yeshua arrive **the good things that are happening already** (v. 11; some manuscripts have "the good things yet to come"). The entire discussion that follows,

through 10:18, demonstrates that these things are better than what came with the Mosaic Covenant's system of priesthood and sacrifice.

(2) Yeshua serves in a better **Tent**. It is **greater, more perfect**, and **not manmade (that is, it is not of this created world**) (v. 11). Moreover, it is not merely a copy of the true Tent, but the heavenly original (8:5, 9:24, 10:1).

(3) Yeshua, unlike the Mosaic *cohen hagadol* (v. 7a), has **entered into the Holiest Place** (literally, "the Holy Place," but the context implies "the Holiest Place"; see v. 8N on this) **once and for all** (v. 12a). His single, unique and eternally effective sacrifice and entry into the Holiest Place is discussed further at vv. 25–28, 10:10–18.

(4) Yeshua's **means** of entry into the Holy Place was better: **his own blood**, not **the blood of goats, calves** and **bulls** and the **ashes of a heifer** (vv. 12–13; the significance of blood is discussed at vv. 18–22). The blood of any other human being would not only have been an abomination itself, but would have accomplished nothing useful for others. But because Yeshua was sinless, he was **a sacrifice without blemish**, and God accepted his shed blood (see 7:26–28N).

Secondly, his sacrifice was **through the eternal Spirit** (v. 14), that is, authorized by God.

And finally, his death was necessary to **set people free from the transgressions** they have **committed under the first covenant** (v. 15). The ineffectiveness of animal sacrifices in comparison with Yeshua's sacrifice is taken up again at 10:1–4.

(5) What Yeshua's death accomplished is better than what the death of animals accomplishes: **setting people free forever** (v. 12) and **purifying our conscience from works that lead to death, so that we can serve the living God** (v. 14), versus not having our conscience brought to the goal (v. 9) and instead merely restoring **outward purity** (v. 13&N).

13 Restores their outward purity, so that they may enter the Temple; literally, "sanctifies toward the cleansing of the flesh." Also see v. 23N.

Ashes of a heifer. According to Numbers 19, anyone defiled by contact with or proximity to a corpse was ritually cleansed by **sprinkling** him with water containing the ashes of a perfect red heifer. According to Maimonides (*Yad-HaChazakah* 1, *Halakhah* 4), the *cohen hagadol* was sprinkled with this water in order to restore purity before entering the Holiest Place on *Yom-Kippur*; if so, this offers an explanation as to why these ashes are mentioned here.

A curious phenomenon that attracted the attention of the rabbis is that the ashes of the red heifer both purified and defiled. After the ceremony the person who had touched a corpse was no longer defiled (Numbers 19:11–12), but anyone touching the ashes was impure until evening (Numbers 19:7–8, 10). Yeshua has a similar dual role — see Yn 9:39, Lk 20:18.

Sprinkling is what cleansed; see also vv. 14, 19–22. At 10:19–22 the text uses the words "sprinkling" and "water" in an allusion to Ezekiel 36:16–38, which is the *haftarah* (prescribed reading from the Prophets) for *Shabbat Parah* ("heifer"), when Numbers 19 is the *Torah* reading.

At 13:11–13, a comparison is made between Yeshua and the animals "burned outside the camp"; the red heifer was one of those animals (Numbers 19:3, 5).

14 This verse mentions all three: **the Messiah, the eternal Spirit** and **God** (likewise 10:29). But our understanding of how these relate to the oneness of *Adonai* is not compressed into the word "trinity."

15 **Mediator of a new covenant**. Yeshua's relationship to the **new covenant** (see 8:6–13&NN) is, first, that **he is mediator** of it (see 1 Ti 2:5b–6aN), and second, that his **death** inaugurated it (see Mt 26:28N). However, his death has a function not only in relation to the New Covenant, but also in relation to **the first covenant**: it **sets people free from** their **transgressions** of it by being an effective death that pays the penalty for sin once and for all, whereas the death of animals offered as sin offerings gives temporary remission (see 10:1–14, Ac 13:38–39&N).

Promised eternal inheritance. These three words can be traced through the *Tanakh* as they outline one of its major themes. God promised Adam everlasting life, conditional on obedience (Genesis 2:9, 16–17; 3:22). God's covenant with Noah includes many promises and is called eternal (Genesis 9:16). God promised Avraham and his seed the Land of Israel for ever (Genesis 13:15), and the term "inherit" is first used in the Bible in connection with this promise (Genesis 15:7). God's promises to Avraham are reconfirmed in the covenant with Moses (see Ga 3:6–4:7&NN, which constitute an indispensable commentary on this verse), but people's sins disqualified them from receiving what had been promised. Those who accept Yeshua's once-for-all dealing with sin, as explained in these chapters, **may receive the promised eternal inheritance**.

16–17 Greek *diathêkê* may be translated "**covenant**," "**will**" or "testament"; the sense of these two verses depends on keeping in mind at least the first two meanings. A modern reader may be able more easily to grasp the author's argument by thinking in terms of wills, but the context (vv. 15, 18–22) is that of covenants as set forth in the *Tanakh*, where the Hebrew word "*b'rit*" must be translated "covenant" and cannot be rendered as "will." Although "will" is suggested by the last word of v. 15, "inheritance," the *Tanakh* uses "inheritance" to mean "that which is to be received" and knows nothing of wills.

There must necessarily be produced the evidence of its maker's death. For wills this is self-evident; but it is also true for God's covenants, insofar as sacrifices are stand-ins for the death of the one offering them. Noah offered sacrifices (Genesis 8:20, 9:9). In the case of Avraham there were actual sacrifices (Genesis 15:9, 17–18) as well as the symbolism of the blood shed at circumcision (Genesis 17:11). The author himself discusses the Mosaic sacrifices (Exodus 24:1–8) in vv. 18–22.

Now a will is one-sided, but a covenant is two-sided. Obviously it was not God, who set the terms of these covenants, who died. Rather, it was, in all instances, the receiver of God's covenant who died — not actually, but symbolically through identification with the shed blood. In the Mosaic Covenant, the dead animals represent the people of Israel as having died to their former uncovenanted, sinful way of life; while the sprinkled blood represents the new life offered through the covenant ("the life is in the blood," Leviticus 17:11). The necessary connection between deaths and covenants in the *Tanakh* is further suggested in the Hebrew phrase for "to make a covenant," "*likrot b'rit*," which means, literally, "to cut a covenant." On the day God cut a covenant with Avram that his descendants would inherit the Land, Avram cut animals in pieces and saw a burning lamp pass between them (Genesis 15:7–21).

19 **After Moshe had proclaimed** the Ten Commandments (Exodus 20) and the civil code of Exodus 21–23, and the people had responded, "We will do and obey everything *Adonai* has said," he inaugurated the covenant by **sprinkling** blood on the altar and on **the people** (Exodus 24:1–8). Leviticus 14:4, 6, 49, 51–52 report that in purification rituals **scarlet wool** and **hyssop** (see Yn 19:28–29N) were used, and living (i.e., running) **water** was mixed with the blood. The scroll of the covenant, from which Moses read to the people, is nowhere mentioned as having been sprinkled; but since it was made by human hands, it too needed cleansing, even though the words in it were from God himself.

21 Exodus 40:9–10 says that **the Tent and all the things used in its ceremonies** were purified with oil, but it does not mention **blood.** However, Josephus, in retelling the story, writes that Moses purified

> "the Tent and the vessels which belonged to it, both with oil that had first been incensed, and with the blood of bulls and rams." (*Antiquities of the Jews* 3:8:6)

22 **Everything is purified with blood**. See the numerous examples in **the *Torah*** at Exodus 29–30; Leviticus 1–9, 14–17. **Almost**. For exceptions, see Exodus 19:10; Leviticus 15:5ff.; 16:26, 28; 22:6; Numbers 31:22–24.

Without the shedding of blood there is no forgiveness of sins. This basic principle is minimized or overlooked entirely in modern non-Messianic Judaism.

On the one hand, those forms of non-Messianic Judaism which borrow from secular philosophy promulgate the idea that modern man has evolved past the kind of primitive religion that portrays God as requiring blood atonement. Thus Reform Judaism has removed from the *'Amidah* of its prayerbook all reference to the restoration of sacrifices.

On the other hand, although Orthodox Jews pray thrice daily for the rebuilding of the Temple, so that animal sacrifices can be offered in the manner the *Torah* requires, Orthodox Judaism attenuates their significance by emphasizing the efficacy of other factors in atonement. For example, at *Rosh-HaShanah*, the solemn New Year festival when Jews are supposed to examine the sin in their lives and seek God's forgiveness, one of the most revered and moving prayers in the liturgy is the *Un'tanneh Tokef*, quoted here in full:

> "We will celebrate the solemn holiness of this day, how awesome and fearsome it is. On this day your rulership is lifted up, your throne is established in mercy, and you sit upon it in truth. Truly you alone are judge, arbiter, discerner, witness, recorder, sealer, inscriber and reckoner; and you remember all forgotten deeds. You open the book of records and it reads itself, and everyone's signature is there.
>
> "The great *shofar* is sounded, the still small voice is heard, and the angels tremble with fear as they proclaim: 'Behold! The Day of Judgment!' Even the armies of heaven are to be brought to judgment, for in your sight even they are not innocent. You cause all who come into the world to pass before you like a flock of sheep. Like a shepherd seeking out his flock and causing them to pass under his staff, you cause every living soul to pass before you; you count, reckon and review every creature, determining its lifetime and inscribing its destiny.

> "On *Rosh-HaShanah* it is inscribed, and on *Yom-Kippur* it is sealed: how many will pass away and how many will be born, who will live and who will die; who will die prematurely and who will live out his days; who will perish by fire and who by water; who by sword and who by wild animals; who by hunger and who by thirst; who by earthquake and who by plague; who by strangling and who by stoning; who will have rest and who will wander about; who will be at peace and who will be tormented; who will be at ease and who will be bothered; who will become poor and who will become rich; who will be brought low and who will be raised up.
>
> "But repentance, prayer and charity (*tzedakah*) avert the harsh decree."

This prayer paints a terrifying picture of how gravely God views sin. It delineates heaven on the annual Day of Judgment (which gives but a foretaste of the final Day of *Adonai*; see Rv 1:10&N), when forgotten deeds are remembered and God apportions fates according to what everyone has done. At the end is an attempt to relieve the tension with the assurance that "repentance, prayer and charity avert the harsh decree." But this is a false hope. Although repentance, prayer and *tzedakah* (which means "righteousness" but came to have the secondary meaning "charity"; see Mt 6:1–4&N) are expected in a believer's life, they do not suffice to avert the harsh decree of eternal separation from God awaiting those who refuse the prompting by the Holy Spirit of God to trust in Yeshua the Messiah's blood atonement.

It is understandable that it was necessary for the survival of non-Messianic Judaism after the destruction of the Temple that it minimize the role of blood sacrifice. However, it is the *Torah* itself which proclaims the necessity of blood atonement for sin:

> "For the life of the flesh is in the blood; and I have given it to you upon the altar to make atonement for your souls; for it is the blood that maketh atonement by reason of the life." (Leviticus 17:11, Jewish Publication Society translation)

It is not supposed here that a magical power resides in blood (see Yn 6:35N, Ro 3:25bN). Rather, Leviticus 17:11 is one of the *Torah*'s clearest statements of the indissoluble connection between sin and death. Already at Genesis 2:17–21 it is clear that sin, defined as disobedience to God, requires the sinner's death (see Ro 5:12–21N). Animal sacrifice, which by implication is found as early as Genesis 3:11, is a reminder of the seriousness of sin (see 10:3 below) and at the same time a demonstration of God's mercy toward sinners (compare Ro 3:25–26).

In non-Messianic Judaism there is today no blood atonement. This contradicts the *Torah*, which says that "the blood maketh atonement by reason of the life." This discrepancy is implicitly acknowledged by some Orthodox Jews on *Yom-Kippur* in a ceremony called *kapparot* ("atonements"). Each person wrings a chicken's neck and swings the chicken around his head three times

> "while the following is pronounced: 'This is my substitute, my vicarious offering, my atonement; this chicken shall meet death, but I shall find a long and pleasant life of peace.' The fowl is thought to take on any misfortune which

might otherwise befall a person in punishment of his sins. After the ceremony, it is customary to donate the fowl to the poor, except for the intestines which are thrown to the birds." (*Encyclopedia Judaica* 10:756).

The paltriness of this substitute for the awesome, fearsome, never-ending bloodiness of the Temple sacrifices is obvious even to those performing the ritual. For if "it is impossible that the blood of goats and bulls should take away sin" (10:4 below), how much less will the blood of chickens?

In the light of the above, what is to be made of Scripture passages that seem to minimize the importance of animal sacrifices? For example, Isaiah 1:11–17 says, "I am full of the burnt offerings of rams and the fat of fed beasts; I do not delight in the blood of bulls, lambs or goats.... Who has required this of you?... Do not bring vain oblations any longer; it is an offering of abomination to me!" At Mt 12:7 Yeshua himself quoted Hosea 6:6: "I want compassion rather than animal-sacrifice." The answer is that animal sacrifices offered by people who lack compassion, whose "hands are full of blood," and who do not "seek justice, relieve the oppressed, judge the fatherless fairly or plead on behalf of the widow" (Isaiah 1:15–17; compare Ya 1:27) are not merely useless but are "an offering of abomination."

Micah has a representative Israelite say,

"With what shall I come before *Adonai*
and bow myself before God on high?
Shall I come before him with burnt offerings,
with yearling calves?
Will *Adonai* be pleased with even thousands of rams,
with tens of thousands of rivers of olive oil?
Am I to give my firstborn son for my transgression,
the fruit of my body for the sin of my soul?" (Micah 6:6–7)

The answer is one of the *Tanakh*'s best-known epitomes of the *Torah* (see Ga 5:14N):

"Man, it has been told you what is good,
and what *Adonai* requires of you —
just this: to do justice, to love mercy,
and to walk in humility with your God." (Micah 6:8)

Other similar passages are 1 Samuel 15:22, Amos 5:2ff. and Psalm 40:7–9(6–8) — which the author himself quotes at 10:5–7 in support of his own argument! Thus it is clear that the author does not regard such verses as downgrading the sacrificial system. Rather, he sees that God has never regarded sacrifices in themselves as capable of removing the guilt of sin in a permanent way (see 10:1–4). Only those whose hearts are right can offer blood sacrifices that will please God; "repentance, prayer and *tzedakah* (righteousness)" are necessary *preconditions* for acceptable sacrifice, but not *substitutes* for it.

That this is true throughout the *Tanakh*, not only at the beginning of Israel's history but at its end, is proved by quoting the last prophet, Malachi, who writes that in Messianic times, when *Adonai* suddenly comes to his Temple along with the "messenger of the covenant" (who should be understood as Yeshua the Messiah),

> "Then the offering of Judah and Jerusalem
> will be pleasant to *Adonai*,
> as in days of old,
> as in years long past." (Malachi 3:1–4)

What repentant, prayerful and righteous (or charitable) Judah and Jerusalem must offer God is "a sacrifice of praise continually" (13:15&N), thanking him that Yeshua has provided a once-for-all *kapparah*, a blood atonement for sin; because, as the present verse says, **without the shedding of blood there is no forgiveness of sins**. This kind of sacrificial offering will in truth "be pleasant to *Adonai*, as in days of old, as in years long past."

23 Why do **heavenly things require... sacrifices** at all? Surely they are not defiled, as are the **copies** (see 10:1N), such as the Tent and its implements. Hugh Montefiore, a Jewish Anglican, writes on this verse,

> "What our author meant was this: the purification of men's consciences, made by means of the heavenly cultus, needed a better sacrifice to make it effective than [the sacrifices] which sufficed for the earthly cultus, which was a mere copy of the heavenly." (*The Epistle To The Hebrews*, London: Adam and Charles Black, 1964, *ad loc.*)

The Messiah's blood made it possible for undefiled heavenly things to purify defiled sinners. For external cleansing, external sacrifices suffice (9:9–10); but for spiritual cleansing, spiritual ones are needed.

26 **To suffer death**, Greek *pathein*, literally, "to suffer." See 2:9b–10N.

27 God has so organized the universe that **human beings have to die once**, not "many times" (v. 26). This is the Bible's refutation of the concept of reincarnation, which is found in most Eastern religions and incorporated into a number of recent Western imitations. Reincarnation is based on the notion that although the body is obviously mortal, the soul is not; so that after one's body dies, the soul that was in it migrates, perhaps after an interval of time, to another body. The purpose of this migration is variously explained in these religions as purification, gaining experience or working out "karma." In Hinduism and Buddhism, karma is the spiritual force which attaches to a person's soul as a result of the ethical consequences of his actions. In general, karma causes the round of rebirths and deaths a soul endures until it achieves spiritual liberation; also the karma attached to a soul at a particular point in its evolution determines its specific destiny in its next existence.

The concept of reincarnation is attractive to people who are in some measure discontented with this life — which is to say, it is attractive to most people. And understandably so — it satisfies deep romantic needs to suppose that in a past life one might have been a general, a princess, a hermit, a great religious leader, or even a lion or a snail. Moreover, it builds on a nonbiblical notion, held by many, that only the soul is pure, the body is unclean, inferior, unworthy of being immortal (the same notion underlies gnostic and other philosophies that denigrate sex or promote various ascetic and, oddly, libertine practices; see 13:4N, Ro 7:5N, 1C 7:2–9&N, Co 2:18–23&N).

Quite apart from being false, belief in karma and reincarnation attenuates responsibility for one's actions. Anyone who believes in reincarnation cannot take sin seriously. This is because in his view the transgressions of this life can be made up in subsequent ones, and eventually every soul will achieve liberation from the "wheel of karma." In other words, there will be no Day of Judgment when sinners must account to God for their actions and receive what their deeds deserve (as taught in 10:25b–29; Yn 5:27–29; Ac 17:31; Ro 2:5–16; 1C 3:8b–15, 4:5; 2C 5:10); so that there is little motivation for ethical behavior here and now in this present existence. Moreover, a common vulgarization of the karma doctrine lets people excuse their present sins as the consequence of bad karma in past lives, so that they shouldn't be held responsible now ("my karma made me do it").

But our text is correct in proclaiming that first everyone dies; and then, **after this comes judgment**. Human life is nonrepeatable, one's actions in this life are judged after death, and there is no opportunity for amendment later. A great-uncle of mine who was a secular Jew and did not believe in an afterlife of any sort used to say it was his unbelief that motivated him to behave ethically in this life, since he would never have another chance to do so. I myself think that he was "living off the capital" of forbears who believed in the *'olam haba*. If one doesn't believe in afterlife, one perforce does not believe that there is a Judge who will reward and punish according to what one has done. The concept of a Day of Judgment (*Yom-HaDin*) is found throughout the *Tanakh*, as well as in Jewish tradition. I am not a fan of reductionism, but I am tempted to see ethics without God and judgment as reducible either to acting from learned patterns or seeking one's own advantage, and I question whether either deserves to be called ethics — even if "one's own advantage" is construed to include willing good for others.

Is it too extreme to say that belief in reincarnation among Hindus is one reason why Mother Theresa, a Christian, has a ministry of comforting persons left to die on the streets of Calcutta (for which she received the Nobel Peace Prize)? People who regard the miseries of this life as merely the outworking of karma acquired in past lives find it easy to regard unexplained suffering as just and have correspondingly little incentive to relieve it. There are, of course, other reasons for neglect — life in India is hard, and there may not be much poor people can do to help, even if they want to.

Reincarnation also does away with the idea of historical purpose. This is because it implies that the individual soul's journey from body to body is incomparably more important than anything a nation or a people might do. I call this the yo-yo theory of history; it asserts that the soul descends from the eternal unchanging world, takes on a body and appears in this illusory world of ordinary existence where nothing matters, lives a life without significance in relation to other people, and then goes back up into the eternal unchanging world, only to repeat the process. This yo-yo theory of history, in which nothing of moment ever happens, completely contradicts the *Tanakh*'s pervasive theme that history has a beginning (creation), a middle (revelation) and an end (redemption) — that God has created man for a purpose, and has revealed his choice of a people, Israel, through whom he will accomplish that redemptive purpose.

In sum, when compared with the alternatives, the idea expressed in this verse provides the most solid basis for a sound ethics and an intellectually satisfying philosophy of history, both of which are needed by anyone seriously seeking happiness and meaning in his life. For more, see my *Messianic Jewish Manifesto*, Chapter III, entitled "History."

28 Here is the clearest statement in the Bible of the relationship between Yeshua's first and second comings. His first coming fulfilled the prophecy of Isaiah 52:13–53:12, which predicted that the Messiah would die as an atonement for human sin and be raised from the dead, so that he could **appear a second time** to fulfill such prophecies as Isaiah 2:2–5 and 9:5–6 (6–7), which say that the Messiah will bring peace to the world and deliver his people Israel from oppression. However, since "not everyone from Israel is truly part of Israel" (Ro 9:6), only **those who are eagerly waiting for** Yeshua to return can have assurance that they will be delivered.

CHAPTER 10

1–18 "If the keynote of the last chapter was the efficacy of blood offered in sacrifice, the main theme of this chapter is the once-for-all character of [the Messiah's] saving death" (Hugh Montefiore, *The Epistle to the Hebrews*, p. 163).

Shadow... originals. The notion of earthly copies and heavenly originals is Hebraic and grounded in the *Tanakh* (see 8:2–6a&N; 9:1–5&N, 23–24), but here it is expressed in Hellenistic imagery drawn from Plato's *Republic*.

The *Torah* has in it a shadow of the good things to come, but not the actual manifestation (or "image") **of the originals**. The author does not belittle the *Torah* (compare Co 2:16–23&NN) but gives it its place in the unfolding of God's work in history. In respect to the sacrificial system, the Messiah's death and entry into the heavenly Holiest Place brings to humanity an **actual manifestation** here and now of what the *Torah* previewed, namely, the **good things** still **to come** when Yeshua returns.

But the argument does not extend to other components of the *Torah*. First of all, just as Sha'ul at Ga 3:17–25&NN uses the term "*Torah*" to refer to only its legal aspects, the author of this book frequently uses "*Torah*" in reference only to its "food and drink and various ceremonial washings" (9:10), not its moral elements. Secondly, nothing is said one way or another about Jewish rituals unconnected with the sacrificial system, such as *kashrut* or Jewish festivals. See 8:13N.

1–3 In Judaism the daily synagogue services are thought of as having replaced the daily Temple sacrifices. This connection is made clear in the *Siddur* itself, where the first part of the *shacharit* ("morning") service includes portions recalling the sacrifices (Hertz edition, pp. 34–41). Other portions of the liturgy are directly concerned with sin and forgiveness (the 5th and 6th blessings of the *'Amidah* and the *Tachanunim* ("supplications")). Thus, with the Temple no longer in existence, it is the daily synagogue service which serves as **a reminder of sins, year after year**. In fact, it makes sense for the Conservative and Reform Jewish movements to apply the term "Temple" to synagogues if synagogue prayers are equivalent to Temple sacrifices. But see 9:22&N on why they are not.

Yochanan Ben-Zakkai, who led the Synod of Yavneh (90 C.E.) in reorienting non-Messianic Judaism toward *halakhah* ("law") and away from the sacrificial system after the Temple had been destroyed, apparently continued to have **sins on** his **conscience**, even on his deathbed (see Talmudic source quoted in 1 Th 4:13N).

4 Compare Psalm 50:13.

5–7 It is sometimes claimed by opponents of the New Testament that in this passage the author distorts the *Tanakh* (see 2C 4:1–2&N) in order to prove that Yeshua is the Son of God. More specifically, they hold, first, that Psalm 40 does not refer to the Messiah at all, and second, that several of its lines are intentionally misquoted.

Following, for comparative purposes, is the Jewish Publication Society's rendering of Psalm 40:7–9(6–8):

"Sacrifice and meal-offering Thou hast no delight in;
Mine ears hast Thou opened;
Burnt-offering and sin-offering hast Thou not required.
Then said I: 'Lo, I am come
With the roll of a book which is prescribed for me;
I delight to do Thy will, O my God.'"

The answer to the first objection is that although the Psalm itself expresses its writer's gratitude at deliverance from trouble or sickness, our author, aware that the Messiah could have expressed his own conception of his task on earth with these words, uses the passage midrashically for this purpose. This procedure, legitimate if all understand that the text is being used in this elastic fashion, was common among Jewish writers of the time.

The answer to the second objection is that the author accurately quotes the Septuagint, the Greek version of the *Tanakh* prepared by Jewish translators more than two centuries before Yeshua was born; but it is necessary to examine three phrases more thoroughly.

You have prepared for me a body. The line differs significantly from the second line of the Hebrew text translated above, which is, literally, "You have dug my ears," and is usually understood to mean that God has opened this person's ears so that he will be able to hear the *Torah* better and thus be better able to carry out its commands. The sense of the Septuagint is essentially the same as that of the Hebrew, for the point in both is that the person is entirely ready to do God's **will** and obey his *Torah*. It is not known whether the Septuagint translators worked from a different Hebrew text or merely clarified the sense of the existing text, a common practice among the Targum translators.

In the scroll of the book it is written about me. The Hebrew of the corresponding line in Psalm 40 is: *Bim'gillat-sefer katuv 'alai*. The New Testament and my translation give a more obvious and defendable rendering of the Hebrew than the Jewish Publication Society version quoted above.

I have come to do your will. The Hebrew of Psalm 40:9(8) means, in full:

"I delight to do your will;
your *Torah* is in my inmost parts."

The objection is that the Psalmist equates delighting to do God's will with obeying the *Torah*, not with Yeshua's dying sacrificially, and that the author intentionally deletes the second line in order to avoid that conclusion. But, as I often point out, rabbinic citation of a *Tanakh* text always implies the context (see, for example, Mt 2:15N, Ro 10:6–8N). Therefore, we learn from this passage that Yeshua's relationship to the *Torah* is so intimate that he could speak of it as being "in my inmost parts." This accords with his own proclamation, at Mt 5:17–20, that he had not come to do away with the *Torah* or the Prophets, but to bring out their full meaning. We also learn that as "the firstborn among many brothers" (Ro 8:29), the Messiah himself was the first to receive God's New Covenant promise, as expressed by Jeremiah, "I will put my *Torah* in their minds and write it on their hearts" (v. 16b below). We who are Yeshua's followers, by being immersed into Yeshua (Ro 6:2), and to the degree that we are thus fully identified with him (Yn 15:1–10, 17:20–26), too have God's *Torah* in our own inmost parts and delight to **do** his **will**. The essence of *Torah*, then, is doing God's **will**; but it is a delight only if it arises out of fully trusting him (Ro 1:5, 17; Ep 2:8–10; Pp 2:12–13).

This extensive defense of the author's use of Psalm 40 has been necessary because of the word-by-word analysis which he makes in vv. 8–10. For example, God's **will** is mentioned in all three of those verses.

8–10 Notice that God does not take away the *Torah*; rather, **he takes away the first system** of sacrifices and priesthood **in order to set up the second** *within* the framework of the one eternal *Torah*.

Moreover, it is not necessary to suppose that this "taking away" prohibits all animal sacrifices by the Levitical priesthood. The author's point relates to only the sin offering: "an offering for sins is no longer needed" (vv. 15–18&N) because the second sin offering system is effectual in a way that the first never was (v. 10, 9:11–15&N). The other animal sacrifices and the Levitical priesthood could be continued without eclipsing the preeminent role of Yeshua's once-for-all sacrifice and eternal high-priesthood. Even the sin-offering ritual could theoretically be continued, but only if it were regarded as a memorial and not as effective in itself. Just as it was never more than "a shadow" (v. 1&N), so now, if it should be resumed (which would presuppose the rebuilding of the Temple at some future time; see 2 Th 2:4N), it could not be more than a reminder of the great deliverance provided in Yeshua's death as our final and permanently effective sin offering and his resurrection as our *cohen gadol*.

11–14 The point is the **once-and-for-all**-ness, the eternal effectiveness of Yeshua's sacrifice, as opposed to the repeated but only temporarily effective sacrifices of the first system (compare vv. 1–4, in cleansing consciences and making believers truly **holy**; also see 9:11–15&N). This is reinforced by the requoting of Psalm 110:1: Yeshua, after performing his ritual service, did what no Levitical *cohen gadol* ever did, he **sat down at the right hand of God**.

11 Every day... over and over. See Exodus 29:38.

14 Brought to the goal of being permanently forgiven. See 7:11N.

15–18 Having God's *Torah* written in one's heart and mind necessarily implies that God has forgiven one's sins, so that **an offering for sins is no longer needed**. Therefore the readers of this sermon should free themselves from their compulsion to offer animal sacrifices as sin offerings and instead be fully assured of the sufficiency of Yeshua's sacrifice of himself on their behalf. We moderns have no such compulsion, but we too should be convinced of the necessity of blood sacrifice for sin while having assurance that Yeshua's blood sacrifice fulfills that requirement. With this, the author's major argument is completed.

But the author is very specific in limiting what he says. **An offering for sins is no longer needed** and is ruled out. But the other sacrificial offerings remain part of God's order even after Yeshua's death, as proved by Sha'ul's activity in the Temple at Ac 21:26 and his own offering of sacrifices which he himself speaks of at Ac 24:17. With the destruction of the Temple, sacrificial offerings became impossible; but if the Temple is rebuilt, thank offerings, meal offerings, and praise offerings may be offered once again. The author of this letter does not proclaim the end of the sacrificial system in its entirety, only the end of animal sacrifices for sins.

19–39 The fourth exhortation (see 2:1–4N) has a tripartite form: two encouraging affirmations (vv. 19–25, 32–39) enclosing a stern warning (vv. 26–31).

19–21 After commencing the exhortation by addressing the **brothers**, the author summarizes the content of his argument, expressed at length in 2:17–3:6, 4:14–5:10, 6:13–10:18. The shed **blood of Yeshua**, that is, his death for us, **opened** for us **the way into the Holiest Place** in a manner more secure than the Levitical *cohen hagadol*'s entry was.

20 Through the curtain. Rabbi Elisha ben-'Avuyah (c. 120 C.E.) was known as "Acher" (Hebrew *acher* means "another," "different") after he left non-Messianic Judaism; whether he became a Gnostic, a Sadducee, a dualist or a Messianic Jew is debated. But one passage in the Talmud suggests that he had an understanding of the heavenly Holiest Place and its curtain not unlike that of our author. Acher, explaining a verse of Scripture to Rabbi Me'ir,

> "said, '... A scholar, even though he has sinned, has a remedy.' [Rabbi Me'ir] answered, 'Then you too, repent!' But he replied, 'I have already heard from behind the curtain, "'Return, you backsliding children' (Jeremiah 3:22) — except Acher!"'"(Chagigah 15a)

Elisha ben-'Avuyah meant that God had told him he was right and had no need to repent, but Meir understood him to be saying God had told him he was beyond hope of repenting. How had he "heard from behind the curtain"? Through having been taken up into Paradise, as explained in 2C 12:2–4N.

22–25 The exhortation to **trusting** (v. 22), **hope** (v. 23) and **love** (vv. 24–25) parallels 1C 13:13, also 1 Th 1:3&N.

22 Sprinkled… washed. See 9:13N. At *Shavu'ot* Moroccan Jews pour water on each other as a sign of purity, in keeping with Ezekiel 36:25–27, alluded to in this verse.

25 Not neglecting our congregational meetings (Greek *episunagôgên;* one could render the phrase, "not neglecting to synagogue ourselves together").

> "Hillel said, 'Do not separate yourself from the community.'"(Avot 2:4)

Many believers not only neglect to meet regularly with a congregation of believers but suppose it unnecessary. This is a very serious mistake, indeed a heresy which endangers their salvation (Yn 13:34–35; 1 Yn 3:10–11, 14, 18; 4:7–8), because biblical religion is socially oriented.

The *Tanakh* speaks of the *kahal* (assembly) and the *'edah* (congregation), the New Testament of the *ekklêsia* (called-out community, "church") and the Body of the Messiah, and both of the people of God. These are not mystical ideas. True, there is a worldwide spiritual unity of all believers throughout all time which transcends their physically gathering together. But the emphasis in the *Tanakh* is on the common historical destiny of God's people and their need to treat each other with justice and mercy. The New Testament is no less concerned with the group; it commands believers to love each other in real, practical ways and to build up the Body of the Messiah. This necessitates personal involvement, relationship, communication and working together for the Kingdom of God; and these are impossible challenges unless God's people meet together often.

In the last few decades, extreme forms of individualism spawned in the secular world have infected the Messianic Community and produced efforts to discredit the importance of believers' meeting together. Unabashed selfishness, championed by writers such as Ayn Rand and Robert Ringgren (*Looking Out For #1*), has become an acceptable part of popular culture. As the emptiness of outward conformity was exposed by sociologists like David Riesman (*The Lonely Crowd*), its opposite number, self-preoccupation, took its place; drug abuse and the turn toward Eastern religions are symptoms. First welcomed as a step toward consciousness-raising (Charles Reich, *The Greening of America*), such absorption with self was quickly recognized as escapist and destructive of the social fabric (Christopher Lasch, *The Culture of Narcissism*).

In addition to these influences from the secular world, believers often bring with them from their childhood a distaste for organized religion, which leads them to throw out the baby (fellowship, working together) with the bathwater (dead institutional forms, perfunctory attendance at meetings without genuine communion). Television preaching and home study materials further facilitate passive "blessing" without active involvement. Thus many professed believers suppose that their personal tie to God is the only element of their religious life that matters. But without purposeful contact with other believers, fruitful work for the Kingdom soon ceases, prayer becomes dry, the world shrinks, not only social conscience but even social awareness succumbs, and the person quickly withdraws into a world of his own in which costless discipleship and cheap grace prevail.

A different but related perversion of true congregational meeting consists in flitting from one *kehillah* (Hebrew, "congregation") to another without becoming committed to any. People who do this delude themselves if they suppose they are **not neglecting congregational meetings**, for such "butterflies" can neither become close to any one group nor work with other people toward a common goal. "Living stones being built into a spiritual house" (1 Ke 2:5) do not flit about from window to wall to ceiling. Paul did not spend long in any one place, but he was a faithful member of one local congregation (Antioch), who sent him on his journeys with the laying on of hands and evaluated what he accomplished; he did not proceed on his own initiative, and he did not interpret the Holy Spirit's command by himself (Ac 13:1–4, 14:25–15:2, 15:35–40). The time has come for God's people to understand that spirituality means what Dietrich Bonhoeffer called, in the title of his book, *Life Together*.

All of this should be easy for Jewish believers to understand, since Judaism fosters a strong communal feeling that fits well with the exhortation of this verse.

As you see the Day approaching. "**The Day**" is the Day of Judgment, and the phrase leads into the warning of vv. 26–31.

26–31 These verses recapitulate, in even stronger language, the exhortation of 6:4–8, with emphasis on fearing God. The modern tendency is to bowdlerize fear of God into "reverence for God" or minimize it by exalting love of God as a higher motivation for right behavior than fear of him. But doing so blunts the impact which the prospect of judgment ought to make (vv. 27, 30–31). There is a right reason for fearing God; there is such a thing as "holy fear" (11:7). "The fear of *Adonai* is the beginning of wisdom" (Proverbs 9:10).

Those who **deliberately continue to sin** (v. 26) are doing what the *Torah* calls sinning "with a high hand," and for such sins the Levitical system of sacrifices prescribed in the *Torah* does not atone (see Ya 2:10–11&N). **Think how much worse** it will be for those who highhandedly ignore Yeshua's atoning sacrificial death (v. 29)! This is the point of this passage.

However, in addition, v. 26 by its position emphasizes the seriousness of neglecting congregational meetings (v. 25&N), even though the specific sin actually referred to, as clarified by v. 29, is that of disregarding the Messiah's once-for-all sacrifice for sin and trusting in the Levitical system which only foreshadowed it (see 6:4–6N, 9:11–15&N, 10:1–18).

27 Raging fire. See 12:29&N.

29 The Son of God… the Spirit… God. See 9:14N.

32–39 The Messianic Jews to which this book was addressed had bravely **endured a hard struggle** for the sake of the Gospel (vv. 32–34a). Having proved their **courage** once, they are exhorted to continue to **hold out** for the **little time** necessary, in order to **receive** the **promised reward** (vv. 34b–37). The way to do this is not by returning to the familiar Levitical system but through **trusting** in Yeshua's once-for-all sacrifice (vv. 38–39). **Trusting** then becomes the subject of an entire *drashah* in itself (11:1–12:4).

38 As at Ro 1:17, Habakkuk 2:4 is cited to introduce a major discussion of **trusting**, a topic already mentioned at 3:12–4:3; 6:1, 12; and v. 22 above.

CHAPTER 11

1 **Trusting** or "faith," Greek *pistis*. See Ac 3:16&N and section (1) of Ga 2:16cN.

Being confident, Greek *upostasis* (literally, "that which stands under"), what gives present reality to **what we hope for**. See also v. 6&N.

2 The importance of **trusting** is that **"Scripture"** (here the word stands for "God") regards it as the sole basis for human **merit**, that is, for righteousness (see v. 7N) and thus for pleasing God (vv. 5–6). "Avraham put his trust in God, and it was credited to his account as righteousness" (Genesis 15:6, quoted at Ro 4:3).

Jewish writings contain similar catalogues of spiritual heroes. Judas Maccabeus' father Mattathias recalls the faithfulness under pressure of various Tanakhic figures in 1 Maccabees 2:51–61. The account in Sirach 44:1–50:21 commences with the phrase used by James Agee as a book title, "Let us now praise famous men." Compare 4 Maccabees 16:20–21, 18:11–13; likewise the martyrology recounting the execution by the Romans of ten rabbis in the second century C.E., recited in the *Musaf* service on *Yom-Kippur*.

3 In contrast to the rest of the chapter, which analyzes various "heroes of faith" chronicled in the *Tanakh*, this verse sets forth a basic function of **trusting**, namely, that **by trusting we understand** — or, as the 11th-century Christian theologian Anselm put it, *Credo ut intelligam* ("I believe in order to understand"). Those who refuse to take the tiny step necessary to trust in God cannot understand the most basic truths: the benevolent consequences of faith are not only emotional but affect the realm of the mind.

What is seen did not come into being out of existing phenomena but **was created through a spoken word of God**. "And God said…" (Genesis 1:1–3, 6, 9, 14, 20, 26); see also Psalm 33:6, 2 Ke 3:5&N. The Bible contradicts the philosophy of materialism. Incidentally, so does the "Big Bang" theory, which says that the entire universe began in an unimaginably great explosion some fifteen billion years ago, before which there was nothing (or, in terms of the theory itself, "before" which the concepts of time and matter are mathematically and physically undefined). A number of materialistic and atheistic scientists have confessed inability to cope emotionally and spiritually with these consequences of their own theory.

4 **Whereas Kayin**'s (Cain's) offering of field crops was rejected, **Hevel**'s (Abel's) animal **sacrifice** was accepted, **God giving him this testimony** in Genesis 4:3–10, which says that the voice of his blood cries out from the ground. Through Scripture, which mentions this voice, he **continues to speak**. Abel is referred to in the New Testament at Mt 23:35, 1 Yn 3:12. In Jewish writings the 6th-century *Tanchuma* (Balak 16) gives Abel second place in a list of "seven righteous men who built seven altars, from Adam to Moses" (Bruce, *The Epistle to the Hebrews*, p. 285).

There are those who accuse God of being unfair to Kayin. How could Kayin have known what to offer? If he didn't know, why did God punish him for it? My answer is that God's nature is such that he always gives those who err an opportunity to repent. This is exactly what he did in Genesis 4:6–7. Unfortunately Kayin, instead of rising to the occasion, "rose up against Abel his brother, and slew him" (Genesis 4:8). It was for this deliberate murder that he was punished (Genesis 4:9–15), not for making the wrong offering.

5 **Chanoch** (Enoch; Genesis 5:18, 21–24), like Elijah, is an object of rabbinic speculation, since both are reported to have been taken by God without dying. See Wisdom 4:10–14, Sirach 44:16, Enoch 70:1–4.

Was well pleasing to God. This is the Septuagint's rendering; the Hebrew text says he "walked with God."

6 This continues the definition of "**trusting**" begun in v. 1.

Whoever approaches God **must trust that he does exist**. This rules out atheism and agnosticism. But God answers people who are not sure whether God is there and are praying to find out if he is.

Although God is who he is for ever and for all, **he becomes** for some what he is not for others, **a rewarder of those who seek him out**. This idea rules out deism, the idea that God started the universe but now it runs by itself without his involvement, and it underlies the concepts of judgment, heaven and hell. The idea that it is more exalted to behave properly regardless of whether God will reward is prideful and anti-biblical; God does not require us to simulate a supposedly higher motive than he himself provides! In fact, such behavior is a form of self-righteousness.

7 **Noach**. See Genesis 5:28–10:1. **After receiving divine warning about things as yet unseen**, namely, of course, the Flood (Genesis 6:13–7:1; 2 Ke 3:20). Like Enoch (v. 5&N), Noah walked with God (Genesis 6:9).

Through this trusting, he put the world under condemnation. Righteous behavior condemns sin (Ro 12:20–21).

The righteousness that comes from trusting. Compare Ro 1:17, 3:22, 4:13, 9:30.

8–19 The *Tanakh* itself extols **Avraham**'s faith (Nehemiah 9:7–8), as does Sha'ul (Romans 4, Galatians 3). Our author devotes more space to him than to anyone else, giving no less than four instances of his **trusting**: his obeying God's call to leave home for an unknown land (v. 8), his steadfast hoping for the unseen heavenly city (vv. 9–10, 13–16), his trusting God to provide an heir through Sarah despite its natural impossibility (vv. 11–12), and his offering that heir as a sacrifice (vv. 17–19). The passage may also be divided into these two parts: faith for this life (vv. 8–12), and faith that transcends death (vv. 13–19).

8 Genesis 12:1–5.

9 After Avram arrived in the land of Cana'an God told him, "I will give this land to your seed" (Genesis 12:7). But later he said, "I will give it *to you* and your seed forever" (Genesis 13:15).

Avraham **lived as a temporary resident**, wandering **in** and out of **the Land** (Genesis 12:6–10; 13:1–12, 17–18; 14:13–16; 20:1; 21:34; 22:19; 23:4) which God had **promised** him (13:14–18; 15:7, 18–21; 17:8); so did **Yitzchak** (Genesis 26:3–4) and **Ya'akov** (Genesis 35:12, 27). But they all died without inheriting the land God had promised to them personally as well as to their descendants (v. 13).

Is the promise therefore unfulfillable? No, because Yeshua testified that Avraham, Yitzchak and Ya'akov are still alive (Mt 22:31–32&N). When their seed, the Jewish people, come into full possession of *Eretz-Israel*, as God has promised them, the Patriarchs will be alive to inherit with them.

But perhaps the promise that Avram will inherit the Land has been spiritualized in the New Covenant? Perhaps "the Land" now refers to heaven and not to a piece of real estate in the Middle East? No, because God instructed Avram, "Arise, and walk through the length and breadth of the Land, for I will give it to you" (Genesis 13:17). Obviously God did not mean him to walk through heaven. God keeps his promises, he does not renege on them by spiritualizing them into something else. See Mt 5:5&N, 2C 1:20&N.

10, 13–16 He was looking forward to the city with permanent foundations, etc. The author is thinking Jewishly, remaining conscious of several levels of meaning. He does not deny the simple sense (*p'shat*) of the promises concerning the Land of Israel, where Avraham, Yitzchak and Ya'akov lived as **aliens and temporary residents** (compare Genesis 23:4, 35:27, 47:9; Psalm 39:13(12); 1 Ke 2:11; and see v. 9N).

But at the same time he implies that Avraham understood a deeper level of meaning in God's promise, a meaning relating not only to the Land of Israel but to earth and heaven. This we learn from the author's citing the phrase, "**aliens and temporary residents on the earth**," from 1 Chronicles 29:15. The last three words could be rendered from the Greek as "in the Land," according to the context here. But in 1 Chronicles the Hebrew word "*'al*" means "on" not "in," and the context there makes it clear that "*ha'aretz*" means "the earth."

Avraham's awareness of the deeper meaning (*drash* or *remez*; see Mt 2:15N) gave him the faith to remain obedient to God in the face of not **receiving** during his lifetime **what had been promised**, namely, the Land of Israel. This is why he could **aspire to a better fatherland, a heavenly one** (compare Pp 3:20), namely, **the city with permanent foundations, of which the architect and builder is God** (v. 10), elsewhere called "the city of the living God, heavenly Jerusalem" (12:22; compare 13:14 and Ga 4:26).

11–12, 17–19 Avraham's faith was such that he trusted God to fulfill his promise, even if it required miracles, first, of making an aged couple able to have children (Genesis 17:19, 18:11–14, 21:2; compare Ro 4:17–22), and second, of resurrecting Isaac from the dead, a possible implication of the story of the *'Akedah* (the "binding" of Isaac for sacrifice by Avraham, Genesis 22:1–19); see vv. 17–19NN.

11 Some translations have this verse speaking of Sarah's faith, but there are arguments against this understanding. See F.F. Bruce's commentary, *ad loc*.

17 Avraham… offered up Yitzchak as a sacrifice. The story of the *'Akedat-Yitzchak*, the "Binding of Isaac," Genesis 22:1–19, is read in the synagogue as part of the liturgy for the second day of *Rosh-Hashanah* (some versions of the Siddur also include it in the first part of the daily morning prayers); and its *musaf* service contains this prayer:

> "Remember unto us, *Adonai* our God, the covenant, the loving-kindness and the oath which you swore to Avraham our father on Mount Moriah. May the binding (*'akedah*) with which Avraham our father bound his son Yitzchak on the altar appear before you, how he overcame his compassion in order to do your will with a perfect heart."

It is highly appropriate that the *'Akedah* should be remembered at this season, when Jewish people are concerned with sin and its punishment, death, as symbolized by sacrifices (see, for example, the *Un'tanneh Tokef* prayer quoted in 9:22N). Indeed, Rashi comments on Genesis 22:14 (on "this day"),

> "The Lord will see this *'akedah* to forgive Israel every year and rescue them from trouble; so that it will be said, 'On this day' in all coming generations, 'on the mountain of the Lord is seen' the ashes of Yitzchak heaped up and serving for atonement."

Verse 19N explains that the events of the *'Akedah* prefigure the atoning death of Yeshua the Messiah. The *'Akedah* is referred to again in the New Testament, at Ya 2:21–23.

19 In this verse the author focuses not on the ethical problem of human sacrifice (on which see 7:26–28N and 1C 15:3N, section on "the Messiah died for our sins"), but on the strong faith Avraham had, in the face of the fact that Isaac's survival was indispensable to the fulfillment of God's promise. This faith is evidenced in Avraham's confidence that both he and his son would come back from Mount Moriah: "I and the boy will go there, worship, and return to you" (Genesis 22:5).

God could even raise people from the dead. The Jewish doctrine of resurrection was not borrowed from Persian Zoroastrianism but is taught in the *Tanakh*; for details, see 1C 15:3N, section on "And he was raised." The *P'rushim* held this doctrine, whereas the *Tz'dukim* did not (see Mt 22:23–32&NN, Ac 23:8&N). The second *b'rakhah* of the *'Amidah*, recited three times a day by observant Jews, focuses on this central article of Orthodox Jewish faith (Reform Judaism denies physical resurrection and has altered this blessing accordingly). It says:

> You, Lord, are powerful forever. You revive the dead, you are strong to save. You sustain the living with loving-kindness, revive the dead with great compassion, support the falling, heal the sick, loose the bound and keep faith with those who sleep in the dust. Who is like you, O doer of mighty deeds? Who is a king like you, who puts to death, restores life and causes salvation to spring forth? You can be counted on to revive the dead. Blessed are you, reviver of the dead.

And or "And, as a result" of his faith, **figuratively speaking**, Avraham **did so receive him**; since Isaac was as good as dead until the angel stayed Avraham's hand (Genesis 22:11–12). Alternatively, Avraham received Isaac back from being virtually dead "as a figure" in advance of Yeshua the Messiah, who would actually be resurrected centuries later; compare Yeshua's words at Yn 8:56, "Avraham, your father, was glad that he would see my day; then he saw it and was overjoyed."

20 The **events** referred to in the **blessings** of Genesis 27:27–40 were **yet to come**, long after, when King Herod, an Idumean (that is, an Edomite, a descendant of **Esav**), would break Jacob's yoke on Esau (Genesis 27:40) and rule Jacob's descendants.

21 **Ya'akov, when he was dying, blessed each of Yosef's sons**, (Genesis 48), **leaning on his walking-stick**. The Masoretic text of Genesis 47:31 says that Jacob "leaned upon the head of the bed" (Hebrew *mittah*). The Greek of the Septuagint, quoted here, implies a different vowel-pointing of the same Hebrew consonants (*matteh*, which means "staff, walking-stick").

22 Although he lived as a highly honored Egyptian entitled to an elaborate tomb, **Yosef** believed the promises to Avraham that there would be an **Exodus** (on this word see Lk 9:31N). His instructions that his bones be carried to *Eretz-Israel* (Genesis 50:24–25) were carried out more than four centuries later (Genesis 50:26, Exodus 13:19, Joshua 24:32).

23–29 The author devotes more space to **Moshe** than to any of the other heroes of faith except Avraham.

23 **The parents of Moshe**, Amram and Yoch'eved (Exodus 6:20), hid him by placing him in a basket to float in the Nile, so that he wouldn't be killed according to Pharaoh's decree. In answer to their faith, Pharaoh's daughter found him there and raised him as her own son, even employing the child's own mother to nurse him (Exodus 2:1–10).

24–26 Moses had every possible advantage Egypt could offer. Jewish tradition maintains that as the adopted child of Pharaoh's daughter he may even have been in line for the throne. But he also had knowledge of God's revelation and of his own identity as an Israelite, and **chose being mistreated along with God's people rather than enjoying** the perquisites of his position, until finally (Exodus 2:11–15) he was forced to flee for his life.

26 **He had come to regard abuse suffered on behalf of the Messiah….** Moses did not know of Yeshua, nor is there evidence that he had specific knowledge of a coming Messiah, Savior or Son of God, although he did refer to a Star that would come out of Jacob (Numbers 24:17–19) and to a future prophet like himself (Deuteronomy 18:15, 18–19). But Yn 5:46 says that Moses nevertheless wrote about Yeshua. One may fairly say that Moses suffered on behalf of all God's promises, both those known to him at the time and those God would make in the future; and, after the fact, it is clear that this implies his suffering abuse on behalf of the Messiah. Sha'ul, in many ways the Moses of his day, suffered similarly (Ro 9:2–4a&N, 2C 11:22–33&NN).

He kept his eyes fixed on the reward, which was "not seen" (v. 1).

27 This refers not to the incident of Exodus 2:11–15 but to Moses' appearances before Pharaoh and to the Exodus itself (Exodus 5–11; 12:31–42, 51; 13:17–22).

28 Exodus 12:1–30.

29 Exodus 14:1–15:21.

30–31 These verses recount events from the time of Joshua (Joshua 6:1–20, 2:1–21, 6:21–25). **Rachav**'s (Rahab's) faith is referred to at Ya 2:25, and she was further rewarded by becoming an ancestor of King David and of Yeshua the Messiah (Mt 1:5–6, 16).

32 The author singles out the three best-known judges, a general, **David** the best-known king, **Shmu'el** (Samuel) the judge-prophet, and the other **prophets**.

Gid'on (Gideon, Judges 6:11–8:35) is remembered for the faith demonstrated when he accepted God's decision that he should reduce the size of the Israelites' army from 32,000 to 300 before defeating the Midianites' force of 50,000 (Judges 7).

General **Barak** (Judges 4–5), though not independent of Dvorah the judge and Ya'el, had faith of his own, for even though he knew that these women would get the glory for the victory instead of himself (Judges 4:9), he led the Israelites in conquering Sisera, Yavin and the Canaanites.

Shimshon (Samson, Judges 13–16) lived much of his life with his eyes not on the Lord. But after he was blinded he saw clearly enough to pray for strength to destroy the Philistines' temple; this is what qualifies him for the faith hall of fame (Judges 16:25–30).

At first glance **Yiftach** (Jephtha, Judges 11:1–12:7) seems an even less likely candidate, but his rash vow to sacrifice the first thing that came out of his house, which turned out to be his daughter, does not detract from the undiluted faith in God which this simple man demonstrated as he defeated the Ammonites.

33–36 Through trusting, Moses **conquered** the **kingdoms** of Sihon, king of the Amorites, and Og, king of Bashan (Numbers 21:21–35). Daniel **shut the mouths of lions** (Daniel 6:1–29). Chananyah, Misha'el and 'Azaryah (Shadrakh, Meishakh and 'Aved-n'go) **quenched the power of fire** (Daniel 1:6, 3:1–30). Elijah and Elisha were among those who **escaped the edge of the sword** (1 Kings 19:2ff., 2 Kings 6:31ff.). The widow of Tzarfat and the woman of Shunem **received back their dead resurrected** through Elijah and Elisha's ministries (1 Kings 17:8–24, 2 Kings 4:8–37). From the Apocrypha we learn how in the days of the Maccabees, the 90-year-old *Torah*-teacher El'azar willingly chose to die *'al kiddush haShem* ("to sanctify God's name"; see Ac 7:59–60N), rather than eat pork and appear publicly to have forsaken Judaism — he was among those **stretched on the rack and beaten to death, refusing to be ransomed, so that they would gain a better resurrection** (2 Maccabees 6:18–31). Yeshua himself was **mocked, whipped, chained and imprisoned** (Yn 19:1–3, Mk 15:1–9); compare also the prophets Mikhayahu (Micaiah, 1 Kings 22:24) and Yirmiyahu (Jeremiah 20:2, 7; 37:15).

37–38 Z'kharyah the son of Y'hoyadah the priest was **stoned** to death (2 Chronicles 24:21; compare Mt 23:35–37).

Being **sawed in two** was certainly a known form of torturing people to death (2 Samuel 12:31), and according to the first-century partly Jewish, partly Christian book, The Ascension of Isaiah, the prophet **Yesha'yahu** was killed in this way. The Talmud gives this description:

> "Rabbi Shim'on ben-'Azzai said, 'I found a genealogy scroll in Jerusalem, and it is written there… [that King] M'nasheh killed Yesha'yahu.' Raba said, 'Before killing him, M'nasheh staged a trial and said, "Your teacher Moshe said, 'For men shall not see me and live' [Exodus 33:20]; but you say, 'I saw *Adonai* sitting on a throne, high and lifted up' [Isaiah 6:1]." [Two similar contradictions are cited.] Yesha'yahu replied, "It is well known that you do not receive what people tell you; so if I answer your accusations, I will only turn you into a wilful murderer." So Yesha'yahu said a Name [of God, thought of as having supernatural power] and was swallowed up by a cedar. However, the cedar was brought and sawed in two; and when the saw reached his mouth he died; [this was his punishment] for having said, "I live among a people of unclean lips" [Isaiah 6:5].' "(Yevamot 49b)

Jeremiah 26:20–23 mentions the prophet Uriah as having been **murdered by the sword**, and Elijah speaks of others who suffered the same fate (1 Kings 19:10, Ro 11:3).

Went about clothed in sheepskins and goatskins, destitute, persecuted, mistreated, wandering about in deserts and mountains, living in caves and holes in the ground. The description fits Elijah and Elisha (1 Kings 19:13, 2 Kings 2:14), as well as the pious Jews who fled from the persecution of Antiochus IV in the time of the Maccabees (1 Maccabees 2:38). Yochanan the Immerser wore camel skins (Mt 3:4) and led a similar life, while Yeshua himself had "no home of his own" (Lk 9:58).

In other words, the people who trusted God were utterly unrewarded and unappreciated in their time by the rest of humanity; the reverse side of this coin is seen when our author writes that **the world was not worthy of them!** Worldly people, since they themselves do not truly trust God, cannot fully appreciate those whose lives are based utterly on trust, because their values are so different. But as soon as worldly people, by God's grace (Ep 2:8–9), take the tiniest step of faith themselves, then the great faith reported in this chapter takes on an altogether different significance for them and becomes a source of inspiration.

39–40 Chapter 11 is a homily on 10:35–39. In summarizing the two main themes of Chapter 11, vv. 39–40 hark back to the earlier passage, which expresses the necessity of continuing to trust God despite all obstacles and setbacks, physical or spiritual, in order to **receive** the reward which God has **promised**.

On the one hand, **all** the heroes of faith **had their merit attested because of their trusting**. (See vv. 2, 4, 5, 7.) For indeed the only meritorious acts there are, are those based on trusting in God, as expounded in Galatians and Romans (compare Isaiah 64:5(6)). The original readers of this letter are to renew their trust in Yeshua's atoning death; there is no other way for them to attain the reward of eternal life.

Nevertheless, on the other hand, these heroes of faith, even though they kept on trusting, **did not receive what had been promised** in their own lifetimes (v. 13), **because God**

had planned something better, namely, something **that would involve us** who came later; **so that only with us would they be brought to the goal** (or "perfected, made complete," as explained in 7:11N, Ro 10:4N). God's secret plan for history (Ro 11:25–26, 16:25–26; Ep 1:9, 3:9), involving the perfecting of human beings from all times, places and cultures (Rv 7:9–10), Gentiles as well as Jews (Ro 11:25–36; Ep 1:9–14, 2:1–3:11), is glorious beyond imagining (Ro 11:33–36, Ep 3:20–21). Only by trusting God can anyone enjoy its benefits.

CHAPTER 12

12:1–13:19 The last of the author's five exhortations (see 2:1–4N) is the longest. Chapter 12 largely emphasizes the negative, climaxing in the severe warnings of vv. 25–29; while Chapter 13 accentuates the positive.

1–13 In addition to completing the discussion of **trusting** begun at 10:35, verses 1–4 introduce the idea that believers in Yeshua are **running in a contest against sin** (vv. 1, 4), a contest which calls for **endurance** (vv. 1–3, 7). Having endurance means regarding the pains, setbacks and troubles which are inevitable in a believer's life (Ac 14:22, Yn 16:33) as **the discipline of *Adonai*** (vv. 5–13 constitute a sermon on this subject — the text is vv. 5–6, the three points are vv. 7–8, 9–10, 11–13). Only then will we be displaying the "trust-grounded obedience" (Ro 1:5, 16:26) which is the goal of the Gospel.

The contest has been **set before us** (v. 1); it is the "life of good actions already prepared by God for us to do" (Ep 2:10). Sha'ul (Paul) used sports metaphors when he wrote to Greeks (1C 9:24–27, Pp 3:12–14, 2 Ti 4:7–8), for whom athletic contests were an important part of life. But the author of this letter is writing to Jews, for whom, at the time, such contests smacked of Hellenistic paganism (see 1 Maccabees 1:10–15). Nevertheless, the rabbis made comparisons with gladiators (Exodus Rabbah 30:24), wrestlers (Genesis Rabbah 22:9) and other athletes. The sports-metaphor language of vv. 1–4 returns in vv. 11–13, where the author compares believers with athletes in training who care for their injuries in order to remain effective sportsmen.

2 **Looking away**, like a runner with his eye on the finish line, **to the initiator** (see Ep 2:8) **and completer of** our **trusting, Yeshua** — or, as in KJV, "Jesus, the author and finisher of our faith." The theme of Yeshua as beginning and end, *aleph* and *tav* is found at Rv 1:8, 21:6, 22:13. His "endurance" (v. 1) we are to emulate: **think about him** (v. 3; compare Pp 2:5). He, **in exchange for obtaining** the reward (10:35) of **the joy set before him, endured execution on a stake as a criminal** (see Mt 10:38N, Pp 2:8N), **scorning the shame**, as described in greater depth at Pp 2:6–11. Believers should scorn not those who put them to shame, but the shame itself (compare 1 Ke 4:16).

At the right hand of the throne of God, i.e., "in the place of honor by God's throne" (Living Bible). See paragraph (7) of 1:3N, 1:13 and Mt 22:44.

3–4 Compare 4:15, which says of Yeshua, "In every respect he was tempted just as we are, the only difference being that he did not sin."

Become despondent. This anticipates the *Tanakh* passage quoted in vv. 5–6.

7 **God is dealing with you as sons**. Israel collectively is God's son (Exodus 4:22, Hosea 11:1, Mt 2:15&N, Ro 9:4&N); but more than that, each believer, Jewish or Gentile, is individually God's son, by virtue of being united with God's only-begotten Son, Yeshua the Messiah (Ro 8:14–19, 29; Ga 4:1–7; Rv 21:7).

8 In rabbinic Judaism the Hebrew word "***mamzer***" is a technical term referring to the child of a marriage prohibited in Leviticus 18. Popularly it means "illegitimate son" and like "bastard" it can express strong contempt. See Yn 9:34&N.

9–11 The **discipline** of God, our **spiritual Father**, produces **holiness** (see v. 14) and **righteousness** (5:13; 10:38; 11:4, 7, 33).

12–13 The contrast with v. 1 is striking; the author no longer offers a pep-talk with advice to "keep running" but concerns himself with those who can barely walk because of physical and social disadvantage, emotional injury or being spiritually backslidden.

Strengthen your drooping arms, gradually increase your spiritual capacity for trust-grounded obedience to God (Ro 1:5).

Steady your tottering knees, get hold of your emotions, stop fearing the world.

Make a level path. "He leads me in straight paths for his name's sake" (Psalm 23:4). Make the physical and social environment such that you can work in it for good: place yourself where temptations are not excessive, and undertake tasks that can be accomplished.

For your feet. Of the wicked, Isaiah writes, "Their feet run to evil, they make haste to shed innocent blood" (Isaiah 59:7; compare Ro 3:15). But of God's servant he writes, "How beautiful upon the mountains are the feet of the bringer of Good News, announcing peace… and deliverance!" (Isaiah 52:7; compare Ro 10:15).

Someone who is hurt in any of these ways and neglects himself will have **what has been injured get wrenched out of joint**, "so that in the end, the person is worse off than he was before" (Mt 12:46). But if he gives his situation proper spiritual attention, **what has been injured will be healed**.

14–17 **Holiness without which no one will see the Lord**. The warning which climaxes at v. 29 begins here. Those who fail to heed it, who suppose that mere intellectual acknowledgment of God's existence and Yeshua's Messiahship, unaccompanied by good deeds and submissiveness to God, will "get them into heaven" are in for rude awakening and disappointment (compare Ya 2:19–20, Rv 20:15).

14 **Keep pursuing peace** (compare Psalm 34:15(14)) **with everyone** (compare Ro 12:18).

15 **Root of bitterness**. When presenting the covenant to "all Israel" (Deuteronomy 29:1), Moses warned "lest there be among you [anyone] whose heart turns away from *Adonai*… to serve other gods, …a root that bears gall and wormwood" (instead of "the peaceful fruit of righteousness," above, v. 11), "and it come to pass that when he hears the words of this curse" (Deuteronomy 28:15–68), "he blesses himself in his heart and says, 'I will have peace, even though I walk in the stubbornness of my heart….' *Adonai* will not be willing to pardon him" (Deuteronomy 29:17–20).

17 Even though he sought it with tears, his change of heart was to no avail. As rendered, this says that even though Esau had a change of heart between Genesis 25:27–34 and Genesis 27:30–41, it did not avail in getting his father Isaac to bless him with the blessing reserved for the firstborn son. But the Greek could mean, "Even though [Esau] sought with tears to have his father change his mind, his efforts were of no avail," partly because a blessing once given could not be withdrawn. No matter which understanding is correct, we learn that it is all but impossible to revoke the consequences of sin.

Even if the change of heart spoken of was Esau's, not Isaac's, there is no implication either here or in Genesis that Esau ever truly repented. His tears did not flow from the kind of pain that, "handled in God's way, produces a turning from sin to God which leads to salvation" (2C 7:10). Rather, his "repentance" (Greek *metanoia*, "change of mind, change of heart"; see Mt 3:2N) was only in valuing his rights as the firstborn (Genesis 27) instead of despising them (Genesis 25). Thus, although some translations suggest the idea, there is no basis for inferring from this passage that it can be "too late to repent," too late for a person to turn from sin to God. Such an attitude is only an excuse for continuing to sin. It is never too late, God's arms are always open, it is always "his purpose that… everyone should turn from his sins" (2 Ke 3:9)

18–29 As at 2:1–4, the author expresses in terms of a comparison between Mount Sinai (vv. 18–21) and spiritual **Mount Tziyon** (vv. 22–24) the many ways, spoken of or hinted at in earlier chapters, in which Messianic Judaism, with **Moshe** and **Yeshua**, is **better** (v. 24; see second paragraph of 1:2–3N) than non-Messianic Judaism, with Moshe but without Yeshua.

In both cases it is the same God revealing himself, his promises and his requirements. There is but one conclusion to be drawn: **See that you don't reject the One speaking** (vv. 25–29), the One who spoke through Moses then and through Yeshua now. As the *Sh'ma* succinctly puts it, "*Adonai* is One" (Deuteronomy 6:4); therefore anyone who rejects the God of Yeshua is necessarily rejecting the God of Moses (this point is made at many places in the New Testament, including Lk 16:29–31, 24:25–27; Yn 1:45, 5:45–46, 9:28–41; Ac 3:22–23, 26:22–23, 28:23–27; Ro 3:29–31, 10:4–10; 2C 3:6–16; MJ 3:1–6; Rv 15:3). And the penalty for rejecting God is fearful, since, even though he is merciful to those who trust in him, at the same time **our God is a consuming fire** (v. 29; compare Exodus 34:6–7, Mk 9:43–49, Rv 20:11–15).

18–21 The awesome appearance of Mount Sinai when God gave the *Torah* to the people of Israel demonstrated God's holiness. See Exodus 19:16–20, 20:15–18(18–21); Deuteronomy 4:10–13.

18 A theophany (an appearance of God to mankind) was often accompanied by **fire** (Exodus 13:21, Judges 13:20, 1 Kings 18:38), **darkness** (Genesis 15:12; Exodus 10:21–22, 14:20; 1 Kings 8:12; Joel 3:4(2:31); Amos 5:18) and **whirlwind** (Nahum 1:3; Job 37:9, 38:1; Zechariah 9:14).

19 The sound of a *shofar* will be heard in the end of days at the final manifestation of God (Isaiah 27:13, Zechariah 9:14), identified more specifically in the New Testament as the Messiah's second coming (Mt 24:31, 1C 15:52, 1 Th 4:16&N).

When God gave the Ten Commandments (Deuteronomy 5:6–18), called the Ten **Words** in the *Torah* (Deuteronomy 4:13), all the people of Israel heard his **voice**, and those **words made the hearers beg that no further message be given to them**, but only to Moses as their representative. This is described in Deuteronomy 4:10–13, 5:20–25 and 18:16–17 (which comes in the middle of Deuteronomy 18:15–19, where God promises to raise up a prophet like Moses; according to Ac 3:22–23&N Yeshua fulfills this prophecy).

21 **Moshe said, "I am quaking with dread."** Not only the people were frightened but Moses was too. However, by quoting a remark which Moses made not on Mount Sinai but upon returning and discovering the golden calf (Deuteronomy 9:14–19), the author of Messianic Jews shows us that as a result of Moses' personal experience with God, he developed a healthy fear of God (Proverbs 1:7, 9:10) which lasted not only while he was receiving the *Torah*, but also afterwards — indeed throughout his life. And the author's point is that it should be so with all of us — those who begin well with Yeshua should not slack off later.

22–24 The author lists eight things to which **you have come**.

22 **Mount Tziyon** is where King David placed the Ark of the Covenant (2 Samuel 6:2); in the New Testament, Yochanan sees Yeshua, the Lamb, "standing on Mount Tziyon" (Rv 14:1). Already in the *Tanakh* Mount Zion is identified with the whole of **the city of the living God**, Jerusalem:

> "*Adonai* is great, greatly to be praised
> in the city of our God — his holy mountain,
> beautifully situated, the joy of all the earth,
> Mount Zion, on the sides of the north —
> the city of the Great King." (Psalm 48:2–3(1–2))

But the identification transcends earthly Jerusalem and applies to the even better **heavenly Yerushalayim** (Ga 4:25–26, Rv 21:2), about which the author has more to say at 11:10, 13–16&N; 13:14. The idea that what is seen of spiritual truth here on earth is but the shadow of the heavenly original pervades this letter (8:5&N; 9:11&N, 23–24&N; 10:1&N).

Myriads of holy angels. God "came from the myriads of holy ones" in heaven to give the *Torah* on Mount Sinai (Deuteronomy 33:2). From 1:14, Daniel 7:10, Lk 2:13–15 and Rv 5:11–12 we learn that their **festive assembly** consists in ministering to God and to his people.

23 **A community**, Greek *ekklêsia;* see Mt 16:18N.

Firstborn. Yeshua is "supreme over all creation," literally, "firstborn of all creation" (Co 1:15&N). "Also he is head of the Body, the Messianic Community — he is the beginning, the firstborn from the dead; so that he might hold first place in everything" (Co 1:18). Finally, he is "the firstborn among many brothers" whose destiny is to be conformed to his pattern (Ro 8:29), in consequence of which they themselves are regarded by God as firstborn, with all the rights understood in Biblical times as pertaining thereto (v. 16 above). God originally assigned to Israel the status of firstborn (Exodus 4:22); in according it also to believers God strengthens the identification between the Messianic Community and Israel (see Ro 11:25–26&NN, Ga 6:16&N, Ep 2:11–16&NN).

Whose names have been recorded in heaven in the Book of Life (see Rv 20:12b&N).

A Judge who is God of everyone. There is no escaping God "the righteous Judge" (2 Ti 4:8&N); many New Testament and *Tanakh* passages attest to a final Day of Judgment for all; see Rv 20:11–15. God has entrusted the judging to Yeshua the Messiah (Yn 5:22&N, 27–30; Ac 17:31; Ro 2:16).

Spirits of righteous people (11:4, 7, 33) **who have been brought to the goal** (7:11N) along with us (11:39–40) by Yeshua, the Completer of our trusting (the one who brings our trusting to its goal, v. 2).

24 **The mediator of a new covenant, Yeshua**. Compare 7:22, 8:6–13.

The sprinkled blood of Yeshua. Compare 9:12–14, 19–21; 10:19–21; 13:13–15. **That speaks better things than that of Hevel** (see 11:4&N). Abel was the first to die (Genesis 4:3–10), Yeshua the last (since his death is timeless); Yeshua's blood brings life (Leviticus 17:11), Abel's brought only death. See 1 Ke 1:2N.

25 **How much less**. A *kal v'chomer* argument (Mt 6:30N), reinforced by v. 26.

26 **Even then**, on Mount Sinai, **his voice shook the earth**. Compare Judges 5:4–5; Psalms 68:9(8), 77:19(18), 114:7.

28 **Let us have grace**. Let us accept God's gracious gift of his Son, whose sacrificial death graciously atones for our sin — rather than continue adherence to the now defunct animal sacrifices for sin, or any other form of trying to persuade God to reward our works by considering us righteous. The animal sacrifices, though originally prescribed by God's grace, have become works righteousness now that Yeshua's sacrifice for sin has taken place, since they no longer avail for anything.

By accepting God's grace **we may offer service that will please God**. The Hebrew word " *'avodah*" means "work, labor, service"; but it is also used as a technical term signifying specifically the sacrificial "service" in the Tabernacle or Temple; compare 13:15, Ro 12:1. Chapter 13 summarizes the kind of service that will please God.

29 **Consuming fire**. See also 10:31, 12:18.

CHAPTER 13

1–19 The positive part of the author's final exhortation (see 12:1–13:19N) offers examples of the "service that will please God" (12:28). His readers are to do again good deeds like those of "earlier days" (10:32); compare vv. 3, 5–6 with 10:33–34.

1–2a Brotherly friendship, Greek *philadelphia*. Friendship toward "brothers," i.e., other believers.

Greek *philoxenias*, "friendship to **outsiders**." Hospitality toward nonbelievers.

2b Some people, without knowing it, have entertained angels. This matter-of-fact statement (like those of 1:5–2:16, 12:22) takes for granted that angels exist. Do they? Science cannot answer such a question, because science doesn't deal with metaphysics. Modern first-hand reports, of which there are many, are no more conclusive; since those inclined to disbelieve explain them away and are not convinced. The writers and characters of the Bible considered angels real, reporting encounters with them as straightforwardly as we would describe driving off in a car; therefore whoever can accept the Bible as God's revealed Word should have no difficulty acknowledging the reality of angels.

4 Marriage is honorable in every respect; and, in particular, sex within marriage is pure. It is commonly supposed by non-Christians and even by many Christians that the Bible opposes sexual activity of any kind. But the New Testament standard is set by passages such as this verse, 1C 7:2–9&N and Co 2:16–23, which express the same view (see also Ro 7:5N). This verse permits considerable variety in sexual activity between husband and wife, so long as both agree (1C 7:2–5); the notion that God requires the so-called "missionary position" is fiction, a limitation that Christians of the past imposed upon themselves. There are a number of popular books about the New Testament's approach to marriage, sex and family. On the other hand, although the Bible encourages sexual fulfillment, it does not condone promiscuity. Sexual activity is to be limited to the marriage relationship.

There is some uncertainty about the Greek text, so that an alternative reading is possible: "Let sex within marriage be pure." If this is correct, the author may be admonishing his Messianic Jewish readers to observe the laws of family purity, and specifically, the laws concerning the *niddah* ("menstruous woman"). The *Torah* says,

> "When a woman has a discharge, and her discharge is blood from her body, she is to be seven days in menstrual separation; anyone who touches her is ritually unclean until evening." (Leviticus 15:19)

The rest of Leviticus 15 details further stipulations.

> "If a man lies with a woman during her menstrual period, exposing her nakedness, baring her flow and exposing the source of her blood, both of them are to be cut off from among their people." (Leviticus 20:18)

Although Yeshua clearly ranked inward heart purity above outward ceremonial purity (Mk 7:1–23&NN), Sha'ul and the Messianic Jews of Jerusalem continued to observe details of ritual cleanliness (Ac 21:24&N, Ga 2:12bN).

5 Compare Mt 6:19–34; Pp 4:6, 11–13, 19; 1 Ti 6:6–10, 17–19.

6 Compare Psalm 27:1.

7 The references to "**your leaders**" here and at vv. 17, 24 suggest that Chapter 13 was appended as a covering letter accompanying the summary of sermons constituting Chapters 1–12 and was addressed to individuals in the congregation whom the author knew personally. Perhaps they had heard him give this series of sermons orally and had requested a written summary from him. The Greek phrasing seems to imply that the leaders mentioned in this verse had died, perhaps as a result of persecution.

Imitate their trust. It should be easier for the readers to imitate the trust of leaders they had known and loved than that of their distant forefathers (10:35–12:4). Compare Sha'ul at 1C 11:1, "Try to imitate me." The chief argument for imitating these leaders is **the results of their way of life**.

8 This connects with v. 7 at the point where those leaders "spoke God's message to you." You acted on the message then but are forsaking it now. If **Yeshua the Messiah is the same yesterday, today and forever**; if his sacrificial death remains the only true atonement; if holiness, "without which no one will see the Lord," (12:14) comes only through him; then why are you slacking off or seeking other paths to God (see v. 9&N)? Regain your former loyalty to Yeshua, and behave accordingly!

Moreover, Yeshua's being the same yesterday, today and forever means that he is still Jewish and will return as a Jew. The Messiah has not been transformed into a Christian (rather, the word "Christian" refers to people who are being transformed by him). Yeshua was born a Jew, died a Jew, and was resurrected a Jew. He is a Jew now, serving in heaven as a Jewish *cohen gadol* (2:17&N, also Rv 1:13&N). He will return as a Jewish king to occupy the throne of his Jewish ancestor David. His humanity makes him the savior of all, both Jews and non-Jews. But he has not himself been made over into a Gentile. See additional discussion on page 934.

9 **Do not be carried away by various strange teachings**. This is evidence that v. 8 warns against seeking ways apart from Yeshua for reaching God. Compare Ga 1:9, 3:1; 1C 2:2.

Foods. This has nothing to do with whether Messianic Jews should keep *kosher*, which is not at issue in this book. Moreover, scholars agree that the early Jewish believers observed *kashrut* (see Mk 7:19&N, Ac 10:17–19N, Ro 14:1–15:6N), and that the only question which they needed to solve concerned how Jewish believers should behave at the dining table with Gentile believers (Ga 2:11–16, especially Ga 2:12bN).

There are two possibilities for interpreting "**foods**" here. The more likely, based on the way in which v. 10 elaborates the subject, is that it refers once again to animal sacrifices, this time rather ironically — recall that the animal sacrifices were eaten by those who offered them.

The other is that some members of this community thought that eating certain foods would enhance their spirituality. As a former owner of health-food stores, I suggest that those who find such a notion improbable should spend an hour or two in a health-food store; they will discover that many people believe that eating in such-and-such a way will bring them to a higher spiritual plane. As with most lies, there is a kernel of truth: just as there are psychosomatic phenomena, wherein the body is affected by thoughts and emotions, so also there are "somatopsychic" phenomena, in which one's thoughts and emotions, and indirectly one's spiritual condition, are affected by the body. Just as drugs or coffee can affect one's state of mind, so can food. The most radical way to experience this is to note the difference in one's thoughts and emotions after fasting a number of days; a change of diet has comparable effects, though usually in reduced degree. But to grant these commonplace facts any great spiritual importance is to displace priorities; one's spiritual condition of sin is affected **by** God's **grace** appropriated by trusting, **not by foods. People who have made these the focus of their lives have not benefitted thereby**. Rather, faithfulness to God and to Yeshua should be the focus of everyone's life; this provides eternal benefits.

10 **We** believers **have an altar**. This altar is in heaven; on the heavenly altar Yeshua the Messiah made the once-for-all sacrifice of himself (8:2–5, 9:23–24, 10:1–14). But the altar is also "outside the camp" (v. 11), so that although **those who serve in the Tent**, the Levitical *cohanim*, representing the pre-Yeshua dispensation and nonbelievers, may eat the thank offerings and peace offerings, they **are not permitted to eat** the sin offerings, because the **bodies** of those animals **are burned outside the camp**. Since Yeshua was a sin offering, nonbelievers **are not permitted to** partake of him unless and until they put their trust in Yeshua.

It seems to me that while it is inappropriate for nonbelievers to participate in the *se'udat-ha'Adon* (the Lord's meal, Communion), in which bread and wine "are" or represent the body and blood of the Messiah, there is no direct reference to it here. Rather, the metaphorical "eating" is of the spiritual truth available through the *Ruach HaKodesh* to those who have trusted Yeshua.

11–14 The author evokes at least five images here:

(1) *Sin offering*: **Yeshua suffered death** (see 2:9–10N), and this had the significance of **a sin offering** in two ways. First, just as **the *cohen gadol* brings the blood of** the **animals into the Holy Place**, so Yeshua **suffered death in order to make the people holy through his own blood**. Second, just as the **bodies** of the **animals** used for **a sin offering are burned outside the camp**, so Yeshua's death took place **outside the gate** of the city of Jerusalem, which replaced the "camp" in the wilderness. See Mishna Sanhedrin 6:4, quoted in Ac 7:58N.

(2) *Impurity*: Just as lepers and other people declared impure had to remain **outside the camp** in **disgrace**, so **Yeshua** was wrongfully regarded as impure and **suffered death** (see 2:9–10N) with **disgrace** by being executed as a criminal on a stake **outside the gate** at Gulgolta.

(3) *Separation*: Being **outside the camp** in **disgrace** implies not only impurity but separation from the Jewish people. Yeshua is indeed separated; however, his separation is in fact not *from* the Jewish people, due to impurity, but *unto* God, due to his holiness; so that his separation from the Jewish people is wrongful, illusory and not disgraceful. Moreover, he can **make the** Jewish **people holy through his own blood**, ending their very real and justified separation from God due to sin (as he also can end the justified and real separation of Gentiles from God due to sin). Messianic Jews, who **go out to him who is outside the camp** to **share his disgrace**, remain, like him, part of the Jewish people, even though, like him, we may not be so regarded. Like Yeshua, we experience the pain of exclusion; but we must stand with him and not seek respect or inclusion on any terms except God's.

(4) *Red heifer*: The reference to Yeshua's making **the people holy through his own blood** recalls 9:11–14, which mentions the red heifer. The body of the red heifer too was **burned outside the camp**; by suggestion, then, Yeshua is also our "red heifer." See 9:13N.

(5) *Permanent city*: Having mentioned the **gate** of the city, the author returns to the language of 11:9–10, 13–16; 12:22 in reminding us believers that **we have no permanent city here** but **seek the one to come**, heavenly Jerusalem. There is no implication of otherworldliness, in the sense of neglecting the needs of this world; rather, we live simultaneously in both the *'olam hazeh* and the *'olam haba*.

15–16 Modern man is not accustomed to using the word "**sacrifice**" except metaphorically, but the author here may be referring to real, physical thank-offerings. This would be consistent not only with the context of vv. 10–14, but also with the End-Time prophecies of Jeremiah 33:11, the Messianic prophecies of Malachi 3:1–4 and with rabbinic Jewish understanding as seen in the Midrash Rabbah:

> "Rabbi Pinchas, Rabbi L'vi and Rabbi Yochanan said in the name of Rabbi Menachem of Gallia, 'In the time to come all sacrifices will be annulled except for the sacrifice of thanksgiving.'"(Leviticus Rabbah 9:7)

But for two reasons it seems at least equally likely that he is in fact speaking of metaphorical sacrifice, like Sha'ul at Ro 12:1–2. First, **lips that acknowledge his name** should **offer God a** spiritual **sacrifice** which consists in **praise**; compare Psalm 51:19(17), recited in the synagogue before the *'Amidah*: "*Adonai*, open my lips and I will declare your praise." Second, **doing good and sharing with others** are spiritual **sacrifices** with which **God is well pleased**.

17 Obey your present **leaders** (compare v. 7&N) **and submit to them**. Many who call themselves believers in the Bible are unwilling to live by this verse of inspired Scripture; possibly because of fear and distrust of authority figures or excessive individualism (read self-centeredness), they are rebellious, undisciplined, and unwilling to be part of a team in order to accomplish the work of the Body of the Messiah. Compare Jeremiah 6:17, "I set watchmen over you, saying, 'Hearken…!' But they said, 'We will not hearken.'"Such people should acknowledge this attitude as sin and seek the Body's help and counsel in overcoming it.

On the other hand, there are leaders who misuse this verse to exploit their charges, brainwashing or forcing them to submit to unreasonable and ungodly demands.

But the verse itself encourages cooperation between leader and led for the good of the led and the glory of the Lord. On the one hand, your leaders have work to do: **they keep watch over your lives** (or: "over your souls"; compare Ezekiel 3:17–18, 33:1–6). Moreover, they are not their own bosses: **they will have to render an account** of their stewardship to the "great Shepherd of the sheep, our Lord Yeshua" (see vv. 18–21&N). On the other hand, you who are being led can **make it a task of joy for them, not one of groaning**; and it is to your **advantage** to do so.

18–21 The author requests his readers to pray that he **be restored to** them; imprisonment may be preventing it (vv. 18–19; compare Pp 1:14–26, Ep 6:18–20, Pm 22–24); and he in turn prays for them (v. 21). He fixes the direction of his brief prayer by summing up the six key points of his letter:

(1) God is a **God of *shalom*.** By reconciling sinful mankind to himself through Yeshua God has taken the initiative in restoring peace, integrity and wholeness (see 7:2, 12:14; Mt 10:12&N).
(2) Yeshua has been **brought up from the dead**. He is alive, our *cohen gadol* forever making intercession for us at the right hand of God (see 1:3; 2:5–18; 7:15–17, 24–28; 9:24–28; 13:8).
(3) Yeshua is **the great Shepherd**, or, as he calls himself in the best explanation of this phrase, Yn 10:1–18, "the good shepherd." That passage also speaks of **the sheep**, both Jews and Gentiles. Isaiah 53:6 too compares God's people with sheep: "All we like sheep have gone astray, we have turned each one to his own way; but *Adonai* has laid on him," Yeshua, "the iniquity of us all." Kefa puts all of this together: "For you used to be like sheep gone astray, but now you have turned to the Shepherd, who watches over you" (1 Ke 2:25). He guides each of his sheep "into the paths of righteousness" (7:2; 12:11; Psalm 23:1, 3); he initiates and completes our deliverance and our trust (2:10, 5:9, 12:2); and it is to him that all leaders, who themselves are his sheep and may yet go astray, "will have to render an account" (above, v. 17).
(4) **Yeshua** is **our Lord** (1:2–4, 8–13; 3:6), who disciplines us for our benefit (12:5–10) and expects obedience (5:9).
(5) Yeshua has come to have this role in God's administration of world history because he gave his **blood** to atone for the sins of mankind (1:3, 2:9–15, 9:12–10:14).
(6) Through this **blood** Yeshua also inaugurated **an eternal covenant**, the New Covenant (7:22, 8:5–13, 10:15–18), the *b'rit chadashah* promised by Jeremiah 31:30–33(31–34).

22 Bear with my message of exhortation; for I have written you only briefly. This supports the idea that the author is summarizing a series of sermons he previously gave orally to some of the **brothers**.

23–24 These verses lend weight to the theory that Sha'ul is the author of Messianic Jews (see 1:1N); for although he spent his last days imprisoned in **Italy** (2 Ti 4:6–8), by then his co-worker and **brother** in the Lord **Timothy** (see Pp 1:1N), who had at one time been imprisoned with him (Pm 1:1), had **been released**, so that Sha'ul could write 2 Timothy to him.

On the other hand, "**I will bring him with me**" suggests that the author was not in prison when he wrote this letter but was free to move about.

THE LETTER FROM

YA'AKOV (JAMES)

CHAPTER 1

1 **Ya'akov** was not only **a slave of the Lord Yeshua the Messiah** but also his brother, as well as leader of the Messianic community in Jerusalem. See Mt 13:55, Ac 12:17N.

"The Twelve Tribes" refers to Jews and is not merely a metaphor for Christians, as some Christian commentators maintain. This is clear from the style of the letter generally, and particularly from the fact that they had synagogues (2:2&N). Not that Gentile Christians were excluded from reading it, but that the leader of the Messianic Jewish community in Jerusalem is addressing fellow Jewish believers **in the Diaspora,** outside Israel; compare Yn 7:35&N, 1 Ke 1:1&N, and this citation from the Talmud (Shabbat 16a): "Rabbi [Judah haNasi] went to the Diaspora," where the Greek word "*diaspora*," which means "dispersion," appears in Hebrew transliteration. Possibly Ya'akov is writing Messianic Jews who knew him personally in Jerusalem but fled Sha'ul's persecution (Ac 8:1–3) or the later one of Acts 12 (44 C.E.). But it seems more likely that these were Jews already living in the Diaspora when they came to faith, for whom Ya'akov's words carry his authority as the Lord's brother and leader of the Jerusalem community.

Shalom! See Mt 10:12N.

2–4 **Regard temptations** (or: "testings") **as joy**, because **the testing of your trust produces perseverance**, as at Ro 5:2–5.

5 Compare Proverbs 2:3–6.

6–8 Compare 3:10–12; 4:1b, 5–6a, 8b; Mt 7:15–20; Ro 7:23; 1 Ke 2:11.

9–11 Ya'akov has more to say about the poor and **the rich** at 2:1–9, 5:1–6; compare 1C 7:22.

The *sharav* is the hot, dry wind which blows across Israel from the deserts east of the Land in the spring and (less often) in the fall. **The sun rises with the *sharav*.** Weather like this made Jonah faint and want to die (Jonah 4:8). Compare Isaiah 40:7 ("The grass withers, the flower fades when a wind from *Adonai* blows upon it"); Psalm 102:4, 11.

13 Satan tempted (or: "tested") Job (Job 1–2) and Yeshua (Mt 4:1–11), but **God tempts no one**. Genesis 22:1 must be understood as God's means of strengthening Abraham's faith (compare MJ 11:17–19, 12:5–10; and see below, 2:17–24), not as tempting him to sin.

14 His own desire, known in Judaism as the *yetzer ra'* ("evil inclination"); see Ro 5:12–21N. The genesis of sinful acts is treated similarly by the rabbis; see, for example, *The Gates of Repentance,* by Rabbi Jonah of Gerona (a cousin of Maimonides):

> "One who commits a transgression has been seized by lust and incited thereto by the evil inclination (*yetzer*, with *ra'* understood)."

Repentance halts at once the vicious sequence described in vv. 14–15.

15 Sin gives birth to death, an example of Ya'akov's striking manner of expression. Contrast with v. 18: God "gave birth to us," i.e., new birth (Yn 3:3).

17 Heavenly lights... variation... darkness caused by turning. Astronomical language: either eclipse or phases of the moon. Ya'akov's cosmology was more Copernican than Ptolemaic; the Roman Catholic Church's condemnation of Galileo (recently corrected) was inconsistent with this verse. The meaning, of course, is that God does not change (Malachi 3:6, 1 Yn 1:5).

18 Having made his decision of his own free will, by grace and not because he owed it to us, God **gave birth to us through a Word that can be relied upon** (compare Ro 10:17). The Word of truth is Yeshua the Messiah; this is taught most clearly by the Gospel of Yochanan (see Yn 1:1, 14; 3:5–8; 15:26; 16:7–15; also 1 Yn 5:4–8). We are **a kind of firstfruits of all that** God **created**, as can be inferred from Ro 8:19–23, 29; 1C 15:20&N, 23.

19 Let every person be quick to listen but slow to speak (compare 3:3–12), **slow to get angry** (compare Ecclesiastes 7:9). Can modern psychology match this advice for improving interpersonal relations? When someone does or says something that would normally provoke quick angry speech, invite him to explain more clearly what he has done or said; listen carefully to him, trying to understand him and his situation; and respond in love, aware that, like you, he was "made in the image of God" (3:9, Genesis 1:27).

20 The history of Jewish-Christian relations is riddled with the sad consequences of believers' failure to heed this verse. If Jews have tenaciously refused to trust in Yeshua, it is partly because frustrated Christians have attempted to **accomplish God's righteousness** through their own **anger**. It cannot be done. Jews receive God's righteousness through Gentile believers' mercy not their anger (Ro 11:31&N), through their humility not their arrogance (Ro 11:16–22).

21–27 Having received the new birth through a Word of God (v. 18), we should **receive** it (v. 21) and **do it** (v. 22). True religion involves not **only hearing** but doing (vv. 22–27). The entire letter emphasizes deed over creed, action over profession; and this is the usual Jewish approach to religion, morals and life. See Rv 1:3N and references there.

23–25 Someone who looks at his face in a mirror, who looks at himself, goes away and immediately forgets what he looks like — instead of grooming himself to face the day — is failing to use the mirror properly, that is, actively instead of passively. **The perfect *Torah*** (or: "the complete *Torah*," Mt 5:17&N) is the believer's perfect, complete mirror; it perfectly, completely reflects his ungroomed (i.e., sinful) condition — as Sha'ul puts it, "what *Torah* really does is show people how sinful they are" (Ro 3:20). The believer uses the perfect mirror's assessment of his spiritual condition to correct and groom his behavior; and as with the bathroom mirror, he **continues** to use it this way throughout his life.

The perfect *Torah*, which gives freedom, literally, "a perfect [or: "completed"] law of the freedom." Ya'akov speaks again at 2:12 of the "*Torah* which gives freedom," having earlier spoken of it as "Kingdom *Torah*" (2:8&N). At the same time he regards it as the God-given standard which no one may transgress (2:9–11), speak against or judge (4:11–12).

The perfect *Torah*. Yechiel Lichtenstein (see MJ 3:13N) comments, again alluding to Mt. 5:17:

> "The Messiah perfected it, since the Lord said that he came to make the *Torah* complete."

***Torah* which gives freedom**. He continues,

> "It means that the believer in Yeshua no longer serves God like a slave, out of fear, but like a son serving his father, out of love. The Spirit of the Messiah freed him and gave him a new spirit." (*Commentary to the New Testament*, *ad loc.*)

Lichtenstein is correct; but some Christians misuse this verse, along with Ro 7:3, to proclaim their joy in being "free from the Law," by which they mean "free from the supposedly oppressive rules and regulations prescribed for Jews by the *Torah* of Moses." Actually, the situation is precisely the opposite: it is the *Torah* which, because it is perfect, gives freedom! Only rebellious antinomians seek to be free from rules and regulations; the wise understand that only within a framework of law is true freedom possible.

Moreover, the *b'rit chadashah* itself, the New Covenant, the New Testament, "has been made *Torah*" (MJ 8:6b&N; see also Ac 6:13–14&N, 1C 9:20&NN, Ga 6:2&N), and no believer is free from it. The "perfect" or "completed" *Torah*, then, is the *Torah* which includes the New Covenant. Within the framework of this perfect *Torah*, Messianic Jews observing the *mitzvot* given to the Jewish people at Sinai serve God in full freedom of spirit, while the same perfect *Torah* gives Messianic Gentiles equal freedom not to observe them (Ac 15:20–21&NN, 28–29). Be warned, however, that this perfect *Torah* is just as capable as the pre-New Covenant *Torah* of being perverted into an oppressive legalism (see Ga 3:23b&N).

But is the *Torah* of Moses, then, incomplete, less than perfect? Of course not. It was God's perfect, complete and sufficient revelation to mankind at the point in history when it was given. Later, "when the appointed time arrived, God sent forth his Son" (Ga 4:4) to initiate the New Covenant and provide further revelation and instruction (*Torah*), adding to and completing, in the light of the history which had transpired since Sinai, the *Torah* which was already perfect. And there is promise of yet fuller revelation in the End of Days, when the Messiah returns, and we see him not as in a mirror, obscurely, but as he truly is (1C 13:12, 1 Yn 3:2).

26 **Anyone who thinks he is religiously observant**. Greek *thrêskos* in this verse and *thrêskeia* ("religious observance") in the next (as well as the same or related words in Co 2:18, 23, the only other places in the New Testament where they appear) connote zeal in performing religious acts, whether in connection with true religion or false. In Jewish terms one could say, equivalently, "Anyone who thinks he is *dati*" ("religious") or "*frum*" (Yiddish, "pious") or "*shomer-mitzvot*" ("one who observes the commandments" of the *Torah*) **but does not control his tongue** (see 1:19–21, 3:3–12; also Psalms 34:14(13), 39:2(1), 141:3) **is deceiving himself**.

27 This verse, apparently based on Isaiah 1:15–16 (quoted below in 4:8N), sums up the burden of all the Prophets, who zealously insisted that true religion must consist not in mere external observances but in good deeds flowing from a sound spiritual condition. In reducing the *Torah* to two commandments — the one enjoining a practical expression of self-giving love toward those who can offer little or nothing in return, the other concerning the inward spiritual and outward ethical purity prerequisite to right action — Ya'akov entered a time-honored Jewish tradition of epitomizing the *Torah*, as is seen from the well-known Talmud passage, Makkot 23b–24a, quoted in Ga 5:14N. This verse, like the book of Galatians, is a warning to believers who become enamored of specific observances at the expense of "the weightier matters of the *Torah* — justice, mercy, trust" (Mt 23:23).

CHAPTER 2

1–9 This section is concerned with how believers, specifically Messianic Jews, are to treat non-Messianic Jews inquiring about New Covenant faith.

1 **The faith of our Lord Yeshua**. Or "the faithfulness of our Lord Yeshua," according to Ro 3:22N, Ga 2:16cN.

Favoritism. Compare Deuteronomy 1:17, Job 34:19, Ac 10:34.

2–3 Your synagogue. This is a Messianic synagogue, a congregation of believers in Yeshua, predominantly Jewish, expressing their New Covenant faith in a way retaining most or all of the prayers, customs and style of non-Messianic synagogues. The word in Greek is "*sunagôgê*"; it appears 57 times in the New Testament. Fifty-six times it refers to a Jewish place of congregational assembly and is translated "synagogue" in virtually all English versions. Yet in the present verse KJV and the Revised Standard Version render it "assembly," and other versions translate it by "church," "meeting," "place of worship" and other avoidances of the word "synagogue." This reflects the translators' unwillingness to acknowledge the Jewishness of New Covenant faith and the overall antisemitic bias that has infected Christianity over the centuries (see Ro 10:4&N). The New Jerusalem Bible prepared by Roman Catholics does use the word "synagogue," but adds in a note, "James is writing to Jewish Christians; it is possible that they may even have still been attending Jewish synagogues, or it may be his word for the Christian 'assembly' for liturgical services." "Even... still... attending Jewish synagogues" — how backward of them! And how backward of Sha'ul, who made it his "usual practice" to do so (Ac 17:2)!

Ya'akov is talking neither about a Christian church service nor a gathering of Jewish nonbelievers but a Messianic synagogue. He would not refer to "**your synagogue**" and assume his readers were in charge of seating visitors if the synagogue was not controlled by the Messianic Jews. There is no reason why "synagogue," with its unmistakably Jewish connotation, should have been "his word for the Christian 'assembly'" in general, since the term the New Testament uses 112 times for that is "*ekklêsia*" (usually rendered "church" in other versions; see Mt 16:18N); Ya'akov himself employs it at 5:14. The idea that this synagogue was Messianic simply did not occur to the Jerusalem Bible note-writer. Rendering *sunagôgê* "assembly" or "church" instead of "synagogue" robs Messianic Jews of their identity.

This verse establishes a solid New Testament basis for modern-day Messianic synagogues, provided they do not exclude Gentile believers. To do so would "raise the middle wall of partition" once again, in violation of Ep 2:11–16&NN. A Messianic synagogue, while committed to preserving and developing a Jewish rather than a Gentile mode of expressing New Covenant faith, must be open to participation by believing Jews and Gentiles alike.

5 **God has chosen the poor to be rich**, as Yeshua himself said (Mt 5:3).

Kingdom. The Kingdom of God (see Mt 4:1N), in which "Kingdom *Torah*" (v. 8) prevails.

6–7 Why treat **the rich** nonbelieving Jews in some special way when they are **the ones who oppress you and drag you** possibly **into** a *beit-din*, a Jewish religious **court**, and **insult the good name of him to whom you belong**, namely, "our Lord Yeshua, the glorious Messiah" (v. 1)? Alternatively, these verses speak of any **rich** person, Jewish or Gentile, and any **court**.

8 **Kingdom *Torah***, usually rendered "the royal law" (but "law of the Kingdom" in Today's English Version), since Greek *basilikos*, like English "royal," means "of or pertaining to the king." The *Torah* of and pertaining to King Yeshua is precisely that which holds in the "Kingdom" of God mentioned in v. 5.

Kingdom *Torah* is not a new *Torah* given by the Messiah (see 1:25N and references there). It does not make the Mosaic Law obsolete, even though, as Ga 5:14&N puts it (compare Ro 13:8–10), "the whole of the *Torah* is summed up in this one sentence: **Love your neighbor as yourself**." Rather, Ya'akov means that Kingdom *Torah* is in essence nothing other than the *Torah* of Moses carried out, by the power of the Holy Spirit, **in conformity with** its own **passage that says, "Love your neighbor as yourself**." Yeshua was pointing in this direction when he said that this is one of the two *mitzvot* ("principles," Mt 22:36&N) on which all of the *Torah* and the Prophets depend (Mt 22:40). Here the principle says that the poor, including the "widows and orphans" of 1:26, as well as the rich are counted as "neighbors" to be loved as oneself; Yeshua meant the same at Lk 10:25–37 in the parable of the man from Shomron.

If you... attain the goal of Kingdom *Torah*. This is usually understood to mean, "If you fulfill it, if you observe it and obey it." But Greek *teleite* also allows the translation, "If you complete Kingdom *Torah*," if you bring it to its goal (see Ro 10:4N, MJ 7:11N). That would mean that the believers would accomplish the purpose of Kingdom *Torah* by obeying the *Torah* of Moses, interpreted **in conformity with the passage that says, "Love your neighbor as yourself**," that is, in such a way as to take into account the coming of Yeshua the Messiah and the New Covenant. If, as many think, Ya'akov's letter was the first book of the New Testament to be written, then one could say that the other New Testament characters and writers in effect followed his recommendation and completed Kingdom *Torah* (or reported its completion) in such passages as Ac 10:28, 34–35; 15:19–29; Ro 3:19–31; 11:16–22; Ga 2:11–16; 3:28; MJ 7:12–15; 8:6; 10:14–18 (see notes there and at Ac 21:21). And this would be in keeping with Yeshua's commission to his *talmidim* at Mt 18:18, "Whatever you prohibit on earth will be prohibited in heaven, and whatever you permit on earth will be permitted in heaven," a commission first given to Kefa along with "the keys to the Kingdom of Heaven," which is the same **Kingdom** as mentioned here and in v. 5 (Mt 16:19&N).

Although obeying and interpreting *Torah* are thought of in Judaism as quite distinct, since the rabbinical authorities are the only authorized interpreters who may establish *halakhah*, it is nevertheless clear that there is a sense in which any obedience at all requires a measure of interpretation, at least the measure necessary to understand what it is that must be obeyed. Moreover, a Messianic believer attempting to "attain the goal of Kingdom *Torah*" is not given free rein to do what is right in his own eyes; the proviso that the *Torah* is to be accomplished according to the principle of neighborly love sets boundaries. But this canon of interpretation might lead to a different *halakhah* from that of non-Messianic Judaism. The issues that might be raised in the resulting *machloket* ("dispute") are beyond the scope of this commentary.

9 **Your actions constitute**. Greek *ergazesthe*, related to "*erga*" ("actions"), which appears twelve times in vv. 14–26. Thus **if you show favoritism**, then, no matter how much faith you claim to have, **your actions constitute sin**. It is this theme, what sort of actions must accompany genuine faith, which is picked up and given detailed treatment in vv. 14–26.

Your actions constitute sin, since you are convicted under the *Torah* as transgressors. The *Torah* condemns favoritism in another context with these words: "Do not respect persons in judgment, but hear the small as well as the great; do not be afraid of the face of any man, for the judgment is God's" (Deuteronomy 1:17). Sha'ul too relates sin to transgression of the *Torah* (see Ro 4:15, 7:7–12), as does Yochanan ("sin is violation of *Torah*," 1 Yn 3:4; or, in KJV, "sin is the transgression of the law").

10–11 **A person who keeps the whole *Torah*, yet stumbles at one point, has become guilty of breaking them all**, that is, of breaking all the points of the Torah, thus, breaking all of the *Torah* — as illustrated by v. 11.

These verses are sometimes taken as proof that if a person violates a single commandment of the *Torah* even once, he has placed himself permanently in the category of sinner and therefore has no hope of a restored relationship with God except by throwing himself on the grace of Yeshua. Moreover, it is sometimes inferred further that since everyone sins (Isaiah 53:5, Ro 3:23&N) and sooner or later must violate at least one commandment of *Torah*, it was inherently impossible under the Mosaic Law for anyone to be in a right relationship with God. This inference is wrong; it contradicts Lk 1:6 (see note there).

It is true that no one can have a right relationship with God apart from Yeshua. But it is not true that once violating a commandment means that one has broken the *Torah* permanently and irremediably. That is not what this verse is saying. And it is certainly not true that the Mosaic Law as given was unfulfillable.

Rather, these verses agree with the normal Jewish understanding, found in the writings of the rabbis, that if one withholds one's willingness to accept the authority of any part of the *Torah*, one has abrogated the authority of the whole *Torah*. It is useful to quote here from the commentary of Yechiel Lichtenstein (see MJ 3:13N) on v. 10 (my own expansion of what he wrote is in brackets):

> "This refers to what is called by the Jews and the sages of Israel an *avaryan* ["transgressor, criminal"; literally, "one who has passed beyond"]. It is as if he has offended in all points and is guilty of all. The opinion of Ya'akov is the same as that of Resh Lakish [a fourth-century rabbi often quoted in the Talmud], who said in Sanhedrin 111a, '"*Sh'ol...* has opened her mouth without measure"(Isaiah 5:14) for him who leaves undone even one statute.'" [The remark of Resh Lakish gains significance from a wordplay: the Hebrew words meaning "without measure" in Isaiah are "*b'li chok*," which would normally be translated, "lacking a statute."]

> "See also Makkot 24a." [The passage, quoted at Ga 5:14N, tells how in Psalm 15 King David reduced the 613 commandments of the *Torah* to eleven and concluded, "He who does these things shall never be moved." The Talmud comments, "Whenever Rabban Gamli'el [see Ac 5:34&N, 22:3&N] came to this passage he used to weep, saying, 'Only someone who practices all these [eleven virtues of Psalm 15] shall not be moved; but anyone falling short in any of them will be moved.'"]

> "Also see *Yalkut Shim'oni* on Leviticus 4:2 ['If a soul shall sin by ignorance against any of the commandments...'], where it says, 'One who transgresses one commandment is as if he had transgressed them all.'"[The relevant passage of the medieval *midrash*, *Yalkut Shim'oni*, is this: "*Zayit Ra'anan* says, 'Whosoever transgresses by ignorance any of the commandments is as if he had transgressed all of God's commandments.' Why is this? Because one who sins consciously knows what sin he committed and what sin he did not commit, so that he takes care not to sin; but one who sins in ignorance is as if he transgresses all the commandments, because he does not take care to keep them. Therefore it is written, 'If a soul shall sin in ignorance against any of the commandments...' (Leviticus 4:2) and, 'Who can understand his errors?' (Psalm 19:12) If it is true for unconscious sin, how much more so for conscious sin! The Holy One, blessed be he, says, 'You sin in this world because the *yetzer* [(evil) impulse]

> governs you; but in the world to come, I will take it away from you;' as it is said in Ezekiel 36:26, 'And I will take away the stony heart out of your flesh, and I will give you a heart of flesh.'"(*Commentary to the New Testament, ad loc.*)

A representative non-Messianic Jewish teaching on this subject can also be found in the medieval work, *Gates of Repentance*, by Rabbi Yonah of Gerona:

> "Listen to this and understand it, for it is an important principle: It is true that sometimes righteous people fail and commit sin, since 'There is no one on earth so righteous that he always does good and never sins' (Ecclesiastes 7:20). However, they subdue their *yetzer* [(evil) inclination] a hundred times. And if they do fall into sin once, they do not repeat it; rather, having become loathsome in their own eyes, they repent. But everyone who does not take care to avoid a known sin and does not take it upon himself to guard against it, then, even though it may be a relatively minor transgression, and even though he may take care to avoid all the other transgressions of the *Torah*, nevertheless the sages of Israel call him 'an apostate in respect to one thing' (Babylonian Talmud, Chullin 4b–5a). He is counted with the rebels, and his transgression is too great to forgive. For if a servant says to his master, 'I will do everything you tell me, except for one thing,' he has already broken off his master's yoke and is doing what is right in his own eyes. Concerning this, it is said, 'Cursed is he who does not confirm the words of this *Torah*, to do them' (Deuteronomy 27:26); and the meaning of that verse is that whoever does not fulfill all the words of the *Torah*, from beginning to end." (Gate 1, Paragraph 6)

Ya'akov in vv. 10–11 is teaching along similar lines, as is clear from the Greek verb tenses: **If you don't commit adultery**, that is, if you make it your ongoing practice (present tense) to obey the command not to commit adultery, **but do murder**, making it your ongoing practice and continuing mindset to disobey this command, then **you have become** (perfect tense) — you have once and for all put yourself in the category of being — **a transgressor of the *Torah***, what Lichtenstein in his commentary referred to as an *avaryan* and the Talmud as "an apostate in respect to one thing." The *Tanakh* calls such rejection of the authority of the *Torah* "sinning with a high hand." Moreover, any society regards acceptance of some of its laws and rejection of others as tantamount to rejection of its whole legal system. Compare 4:11–12 below.

Concerning whether the Mosaic Law can be fulfilled, note that the *Torah* itself prescribed sacrifices coupled with repentance as the means whereby sinners could be reconciled with God. Such reconciliation was not "permanent" (this is the point of the entire book of Messianic Jews; see especially Chapters 9 and 10) but was effectual "temporarily." It is just not true that under the Mosaic Law a person who failed to obey a single commandment had destroyed any possibility of getting right with God — as some Christian theologies teach. See Ro 9:30–10:10&NN.

12–13 *Torah* which gives freedom. See 1:25N.

Love, the fruit of the Spirit (Ga 5:22), does freely what God's *Torah* requires (v. 8&N, Ro 13:8–10). This is what Jeremiah 31:30–33(31–34) meant in promising that under the New Covenant, the *Torah* would be written on the hearts of God's people (see MJ 8:6b–13&NN). But there is always the risk that such freedom will be perverted into license; see Ga 5:13–14.

In these two verses Ya'akov reminds his readers that even though under the New Covenant the *Torah* gives freedom, nevertheless, the *Torah* still sets the standard for **judgment**, and God's people **will be judged by** it (see Ro 2:12–13). Oversimple comparisons between Christianity and Judaism assume that the Old Testament portrays God as stern and unremittingly judgmental, with the New Testament offering a God of mercy. Actually the *Tanakh*'s God is merciful too (Exodus 34:6–7, Psalm 62:12), while under the New Covenant **judgment will be without mercy toward one who doesn't show mercy** himself. Ya'akov relieves the stark severity by stating that the **mercy** (or love, v. 8) which a person shows toward others **wins out over**, that is, prevents, God's adverse **judgment** toward him. The same idea is found in Yeshua's words at Mt 6:14, 18:21–35, and in the Talmud:

> "Whoever shows mercy toward others, Heaven will show mercy toward him; but whoever shows no mercy toward others, Heaven will show no mercy toward him." (Shabbat 151a)

Another way to understand the problematic Greek at the end of v. 13 is: "God's mercy wins out over his judgment." Certainly for believers in Yeshua God's mercy wins out over his judgment: while there will be a judgment on believers' works, their salvation is assured entirely because of Yeshua's atoning death, which is the ultimate expression of God's mercy. While the overall biblical picture makes it impossible to say that God's attribute of mercy is more important or stronger than his attribute of justice, the present verse corresponds to individual passages in the *Tanakh* such as Hosea 11:8–9, where God is quoted in the first person:

> "My heart is turned within me, all my compassion is kindled. I will not execute the fierceness of my anger, I will not turn to destroy Efrayim; for I am God and not a man, the Holy One in the midst of you, so I will not come as an enemy."

But this interpretation seems less relevant to the context of Chapter 2, in which Ya'akov is not teaching about God's nature but urging his readers to be merciful themselves.

14–26 Opponents of New Testament faith claim that it offers "cheap grace" — salvation by merely affirming in one's mind certain facts or ideas about Yeshua, or through merely feeling good in one's heart toward God, without doing good deeds. This passage is the classic disproof of that allegation.

Its context is vv. 1–13. The topic of faith ("the faith of our Lord Yeshua") is introduced in v. 1 and mentioned again in v. 5. The first nine verses demonstrate that faith is inconsistent with showing favoritism, while vv. 12–13 imply that faith necessarily produces mercy. The present passage expands these ideas into the general principle that genuine faith proves itself by being expressed in good works. Thus mental or emotional **faith by itself** (v. 17) or **faith alone** (v. 24), **unaccompanied by** the right kinds of **actions, is dead** (vv. 17, 26), **barren** (v. 20), no better than the so-called "faith" demons have (v. 19) because they know the reality of the spirit world. But only **by actions** is **faith made complete** (v. 22) and capable of giving God ground to **declare** a person **righteous** (v. 24).

The Greek word translated "**faith**" in this passage is "*pistis*," usually rendered "trust" in the *Jewish New Testament* for reasons given in Ac 3:16N and Ga 2:16cN. The word "faith" is used here because Ya'akov is really speaking about not all of trust, but just a part of it, the confessional, intellectual part. Ya'akov brings this out by using restrictive modifiers: **such faith** (v. 14; literally, "the faith"), **faith by itself** (v. 17), **faith without actions** (v. 26; compare v. 20) and **faith alone** (v. 24); moreover, he points out specifically that actions must be added to this limited part of faith in order for faith to be **made complete** (or "made perfect," v. 22; see 1:23–25N).

Ya'akov is sometimes mistakenly thought to contradict Sha'ul, particularly Ep 2:8–9 and Ro 3:28. This is why Martin Luther regarded the book of Ya'akov as "a right strawy epistle." Nothing could be farther from the truth. Ya'akov is in full agreement with Sha'ul, once it is understood that the "faith alone" which Ya'akov decries as barren and dead is only part of the genuine faith or trust which Sha'ul authoritatively declares is sufficient.

In Ephesians, after Sha'ul writes, "For you have been delivered by grace through trusting,… not… by your own actions" (Ep 2:8–9), he affirms the importance of good works by adding, "For we are of God's making, created in union with the Messiah Yeshua for a life of good actions already prepared by God for us to do" (Ep 2:10).

In Romans, the problem is largely one of translation. The KJV, which is typical, renders Ro 3:28, "Therefore we conclude that a man is justified by faith without the deeds of the law." Two false propositions are frequently inferred: (1) a person's good works are irrelevant and do not affect God's decision to count him righteous; and (2) faith alone, understood either as mental belief in a creed or as some inner emotional state in relation to God, is all that is needed for salvation. The *Jewish New Testament*, by bringing out clearly the true sense of Ro 3:28, makes it impossible to reach either of those conclusions: "Therefore, we hold the view that a person comes to be considered righteous by God on the ground of trusting, which has nothing to do with legalistic observance of *Torah* commands."

It is not without significance that Ya'akov in his argument that genuine faith must result in good works employs the identical verse about Abraham (Genesis 15:6, quoted in v. 23) that Sha'ul uses at Ro 4:3 to prove the complete sufficiency of faith without legalistic observances.

Ya'akov and Sha'ul are in complete harmony; both understand genuine faith as consisting of an inward acknowledgement of God's truth which is expressed and flows outward in the form of good works. Ya'akov's point is that if good works are subtracted from genuine faith, what is left is barren and dead. Sha'ul's point is that if legalistic observances are added to or substituted for genuine faith, that result too is barren and dead.

Not in Romans, Ephesians or anywhere else does Sha'ul demean the importance of works in the life of faith. On the contrary, such verses as Ga 5:6, 1 Ti 5:8 and Ti 3:2 express the importance of expressing one's faith through good works; indeed, in a fully Jewish way, his letters contain whole chapters full of advice on which good works to do, and when and how to do them.

In vv. 14–20 Ya'akov employs deep irony. After giving an example of the shallow intellectual faith that can ignore obvious human need (vv. 14–17), he shows up the inability of such "faith" to prove its existence (v. 18), characterizes it as no better than that of demons (v. 19), and calls a person who holds such faith **foolish** (v. 20). But then he asks whether such a person might be willing to learn something (v. 20), and, assuming the possibility of a positive answer, leaves irony behind to offer two examples from Scripture — Abraham (vv. 21–24) and Rahab (vv. 25–26) — demonstrating that true faith must be accompanied by actions.

18 But someone will say that you have faith and I have actions. Ya'akov introduces an imaginary third party, "**someone**," coming to defend an imaginary "**you**" who answers "Yes" to the questions of v. 14 and believes that intellectual faith without good works can save him: **someone will say that *you*** are the one who has genuine **faith, and** that ***I***, Ya'akov, **have** only **actions** without faith and am trying to save myself by my works (which would indeed contradict Sha'ul at Ro 3:28). My answer to "**you**" (and indirectly to "**someone**") is: **Show me this faith of yours without the actions!** You won't be able to, since genuine faith is perceived not through talk, but through the deeds that issue from it. However, for my part, I, Ya'akov, **will show you my faith *by* my actions**, and you will have to conclude that I am not trying to save myself by my works; rather, my works grow out of my faith and prove that it is genuine faith.

Introducing imaginary adversaries is a recognized strategy in Jewish pedagogy; see practically anywhere in the Talmud. For an extended example in Sha'ul's writing, see Ro 10:14–11:11 and Ro 10:14–15N.

19 You believe that "God is one"? Ya'akov's challenge to his imaginary adversary is: "You may affirm the *Sh'ma*, the central creedal statement of Judaism, recited twice daily by every observant Jew. **Good for you!** — so what? **The demons believe it too**; for Satan and his minions are thoroughly familiar with Scripture and do not dispute its truth (see Mt 4:1–11&NN). But such intellectual affirmation is not saving faith, so **the thought makes them shudder with fear**. For unlike believers joyfully anticipating their eternal glorification with God, they know that an irremediable and dreadful fate in hell awaits them at the Last Judgment (Revelation 20). Also, unlike human skeptics, they know that this hell, with its lake of fire and brimstone, is real and not merely a scare tactic used to frighten the gullible."

20, 24, 26 Faith apart from actions is barren, etc. See vv. 14–26N.

21 *Avraham avinu*... offered up his son Yitzchak, Genesis 22:1–19. See MJ 11:17–19&NN.

Abraham was **declared righteous because of actions**. On this Yechiel Lichtenstein writes (with my comments in brackets),

> "It means that his faith was revealed through his actions, as is immediately explained in the following verse; and this corresponds to Genesis 22:12, 'Now I know that you fear God.' See the Ramban's commentary there. [The Ramban (*R*abbi *M*oshe *B*en-*N*achman, Nachmanides, 12th century) wrote that God was already aware of Abraham's faith in potentiality, but his willingness to sacrifice

Isaac made Abraham's faith concrete and brought him to full merit before God.] Paul said in Ro 4:2, 'For if Abraham came to be considered righteous by God because of works, then he has something to boast about. But this is not how it is before God.' The meaning is that Paul interprets the words, 'I know' in Genesis 22:12 as Rashi does, that God can now glorify himself with Abraham before mankind. [Rashi commented, ' "Now I know" — henceforth I have something to answer Satan and the nations who wonder what is my love towards you. Now I have a point of attack, for they see "that you fear God." '] But in any case, Paul admits that Abraham was declared righteous because of his actions — as written in Genesis 26:5, 'Abraham obeyed my voice and kept my charge, commandments, statutes and laws.' This is what the Holy One, blessed be he, said to Isaac." (*Commentary to the New Testament, ad loc.*)

23 **God's friend**. A friend is not one who merely declares his loyalty but who proves it by his deeds. On the subject of friendship Yeshua told his *talmidim*, "No one has greater love than a person who lays down his life for his friends. You are my friends, if you do what I command you" (Yn 15:13–14). Abraham's offering his son Isaac resembles God's offering his son Yeshua (see Yn 3:16).

25 **Rachav the prostitute**. See Joshua 2:8–21, 6:25. She is also mentioned at MJ 11:31 as one of the heroines of faith; and her example is even more striking than that of Abraham, for her works prior to her "conversion" were unarguably wicked. Mekhilta to Exodus 18:1 reports that she had been a prostitute for forty years from age 10, but then she joined herself to the Jewish people and became a proselyte. Her faith was genuine, for she not only affirmed the God of Israel (Joshua 2:11), but did actions demonstrating her faith **when she welcomed the messengers and sent them out by another route**. This was the beginning of a complete change of lifestyle. Mattityahu 1:5 names her as an ancestor of Yeshua the Messiah.

CHAPTER 3

1 **Not many of you should become teachers**. Compare 1 Ti 3:1–13 and Ti 1:5–14. **We will be judged more severely**. See MJ 13:17.

8 **The tongue... is an... evil thing**. *Lashon hara'* (literally, "tongue of the evil") in Judaism refers to gossip, backbiting, rumormongering, slander and other misuses of speech. The Talmud condemns it severely:

> "If one speaks *lashon hara'*, it is as though he denied God.... The sin of *lashon hara'* is weighed equally with the sins of idolatry, sexual immorality and murder." (Arakhin 15b)

The three sins named are those for which, according to the Talmud (Sanhedrin 74a, quoted in Ac 15:20a), a Jew is supposed to give up his life rather than commit.

Zelig Pliskin (a non-Messianic Jew) has written an interesting book on the laws of *lashon hara'* called *Guard Your Tongue*, based on the writings of Rabbi Israel Meir Kagan, known as the *Chafetz Chaim* ("desirer of life," from Psalm 34:13–14(12–13), "Which of you is a desirer of life, and wants long life to enjoy what is good? Then keep your tongue [*lashon*] from evil [*ra'*], and your lips from uttering lies." The *Chafetz Chaim* died in 1934 at the age of 95.) He points out that even true statements may be *lashon hara'* if relating them can cause damage. A sample of his amusing yet practical advice:

> "Beware of *loshon hora* when speaking on the telephone. If the person with whom you are conversing insists on relating *loshon hora*, you should rebuke him. If this is not possible, find an excuse to hang up — 'Excuse me, something has just come up' (the *loshon hora*) — and discontinue the conversation." (pp. 31–32)

Out of the heart proceed all kinds of evils (Mk 7:20–23), and the first place they go is to the tongue (v. 6).

Full of death-dealing poison. Compare Psalm 140:4(3), quoted at Ro 3:13.

10–12 See 1:6–8&N.

13–18 Compare 1:5–8, 13–18. There are two kinds of **wisdom**. That which is **worldly, unspiritual** and **demonic** produces **jealousy** (or "bitter zeal") **and selfish ambition**, followed by **disharmony and every foul practice** (see, for example, the lists at Ro 1:28–31, Ga 5:19–21). **But the wisdom from above** is "from the Father," with whom "there is neither variation nor darkness" (1:17); it is extolled at Proverbs 8:22ff.

18 Compare Isaiah 32:17, MJ 12:11.

CHAPTER 4

1 **Your desires battling inside you**. See 1:6–8&N.

3 **You pray with the wrong motive**. There is a heresy current among believers which, feeding off the excessive individualism and greed rampant in popular Western ideologies, purports to give God's approval to selfish prayer. It beckons: "You are a child of God. He is a loving Father who would deny his children nothing. Therefore you can pray for anything you want, and God will give it to you. You want a new car? a bigger house? fancy clothes? Just 'ask, and it will be given to you' (Lk 11:10)." Besides misusing Scripture, raising false hopes and making prayer a magic charm indistinct from witchcraft, this teaching ignores the fact that a truly loving father does not give his children whatever they ask for; fathers know better than their children what they actually need and act accordingly. The present verse refutes this selfish philosophy masquerading as biblical teaching; compare Ya'akov's scathing condemnation of the arrogant rich at 4:13–5:6, and see Isaiah 1:15–16, quoted in v. 8N below. For a right perspective see Mt 6:19–34, especially 6:33; also Yn 16:33, 1 Ke 4:2 and 1 Yn 5:14. Ya'akov gives his own instruction about prayer at 1:5–8, 5:13–20.

4 **Unfaithful wives**. In the *Tanakh* Israel's unfaithfulness to God her *Ba'al* (the Hebrew word means both "lord" and "husband") is often expressed in terms of adultery and whoredom; see Ezekiel 23; Hosea 1–2, 9:1. Yeshua means the same thing when he calls his generation "wicked and adulterous" (Mt 12:39, 16:4); compare Rv 2:22. On the rest of the verse, the best commentary is 1 Yn 2:15–17; compare also Ga 1:4, and what is said about **the world** in Yochanan 14–17.

5–6 **Do you suppose the *Tanakh* speaks in vain when it says that there is a spirit in us which longs to envy?** Yechiel Lichtenstein writes,

> "The commentators have had great difficulty with this reference to the *Tanakh*. What verse is it? What does it mean? Who is the subject of it? Some say it speaks about God. Others say it speaks about the Holy Spirit. But according to all commentators, it is not found in Scripture. In my opinion, the spirit it refers to is not God's but Satan's, as in Ep 6:12. The evil spirit is the evil impulse (*yetzer hara'*) in us. Ya'akov refers to it in v. 7: 'Take a stand against the Adversary, and he will flee from you.' Jews today still call Satan *der ruach* [Yiddish for "the spirit"; Lichtenstein was writing around 1900]. I believe Ya'akov is referring to Genesis 4:7, where God says to Cain, 'Sin lies at the door, and his desire shall be toward you, but you are to rule over him.' This is understood by all to be speaking about Satan, who is the evil impulse in man; for example, in the Talmud (Bava Batra 16a), 'He is Satan, the evil impulse.' The evil impulse is used by satanic angels to cause man to sin." (*Commentary to the New Testament, ad loc.*)

As Lichtenstein indicated, a different sense is possible for the Greek text of vv. 5–6a: "Or do you suppose that the *Tanakh* speaks in vain when it says that the Spirit, whom God has caused to live in us, longs for us even to the point of jealousy? And he gives greater grace." But this fits the context less well. Rather, I agree with Lichtenstein: **There is a spirit in us which longs to envy** and thus inclines us to fight each other (vv. 1–2); because that spirit absorbs the worldly (v. 4), demonic (Satanic) wisdom which fosters bitter jealousy and envy (3:14–16). **The *Tanakh* speaks** directly of that spirit, the *yetzer ra'* at Genesis 6:5, 8:21 (see Section D of Ro 5:12–21N). **But the grace he**, God, **gives** to overcome through the power of the Holy Spirit in us **is greater** than Satan's spirit inclining us to jealousy and quarrels; for "he who is in you," the Holy Spirit, "is greater than he who is in the world," Satan (1 Yn 4:4).

7 **Take a stand against the Adversary**, Satan (see Mt 4:1N), who "stalks about like a roaring lion looking for someone to devour" (1 Ke 5:8–9). Although he is "the god of this world" (2C 4:4), Yeshua has overcome the world (Yn 16:33). Therefore, if you use Scripture properly (2 Ti 2:15, Mt 4:1–11) and employ the other means of spiritual warfare that are available (2C 10:3–5, Ep 6:10–18), **he will flee from you**. The verse carries the same message as Genesis 4:7 (see vv. 5–6N above).

8 **Come close to God, and he will come close to you**, as in Zechariah 1:3 ("'Turn to me,' says *Adonai* of Hosts, 'and I will turn to you.'"), Malachi 3:7, 2 Chronicles 15:2. Here the initiative for reconciliation is ours; elsewhere Scripture places it in God's hands, as

at Lamentations 5:21 ("Turn us to you, *Adonai*, and we will be turned.") and Ep 2:4–10. Yochanan 3:16 expresses both sides equally: "God... gave..., so that everyone who trusts...."; similarly MJ 10:20, 22 ("He [Yeshua] inaugurated it.... Therefore, let us approach....") and Ro 3:22 ("a righteousness that comes from God... to all who continue trusting").

Clean your hands... purify your hearts. Compare Isaiah 1:15–16:

> "When you spread out your hands, I will hide my eyes from you; even when you make many prayers, I will not hear — for your hands are full of blood. Wash yourselves, make yourselves clean; put away the evil of your doings from before my eyes; cease to do evil, learn to do good; seek justice, relieve the oppressed, judge the fatherless, plead for the widow."

Also Psalm 24:4(3):

> "Who shall ascend into the mountain of *Adonai?*
> Who shall stand in his holy place?
> He who has clean hands and a pure heart."

Double-minded people. See 1:6–8&N.

9–10 These verses explain what is meant by purifying one's heart (v. 8).

10 Compare Job 5:11, 22:29; Mt 23:12; Lk 14:11, 18:14; 1 Ke 5:6.

11–12 **Stop speaking against each other!** See vv. 1–2. One who **speaks against or judges a brother** is arrogating to himself the position of **a judge**, that is, of God, who has **the power to deliver and to destroy**. Yechiel Lichtenstein writes, in his *Commentary to the New Testament* (*ad loc.*),

> "The most important part of the *Torah* is, 'Love your neighbor as yourself' (above, 2:8). In saying this, the *Torah* does not distinguish the righteous neighbor from the wicked one.... The Lord taught that the neighbor could be a Samaritan,"

that is, someone who is usually the object of adverse prejudgment (Lk 10:37&N). Compare Mt 7:1–5; Ro 2:1–3, 12–16; 14:4, 10–12.

If you judge *Torah*, you are not a doer of what *Torah* says. This is essentially the same point as at 2:10–11&N.

Giver of *Torah*, Greek *nomothetês*, related to the word "*nenomothetêtai*" in the phrase, "this covenant [the New Covenant] has been given as *Torah*," at MJ 8:6b&N.

13–16 Planning is an important ingredient of today's managerial society, but it is easy for planners to forget that they stand only as God permits — not only their plans, but they themselves. Hence, **"If *Adonai* wants it to happen, we will live" to do this or that**. If we don't live, what good will the plans do? — as in Yeshua's story about the rich man who built new barns (Lk 12:16–21). "Don't boast about tomorrow, because you don't know what today may bring forth!" (Proverbs 27:1) For more on **boasting**, see 1C 1:31&N.

17 Anyone who knows the right thing to do and fails to do it is committing a sin of omission far more serious than the sin of those who are uninformed — as is clear from Lk 12:47–48, 2 Ke 2:21. Romans 14:23 makes a related yet distinct point, likewise 1C 8:13. In this specific situation the sin is to announce plans as if we could control all the circumstances, failing to acknowledge that God is in charge and our plans depend on his will.

CHAPTER 5

1–6 These verses continue the thought of 4:13–17; compare Mt 6:19–20. Commentaries which understand this condemnation to be directed at nonbelieving Jews (like 2:6–7) not only feed antisemitism by lending supposed biblical support to the caricature of the miserly and oppressive Jew, but also misunderstand the prophetic task. In the *Tanakh*, Psalm 73 and Isaiah 5:8 are similarly critical of the arrogant rich without excluding them from God's people Israel, and there are other similar passages in the Prophets. This paragraph, which addresses **the rich** directly, must be understood as meant for rich believers, who will read it, not for unbelievers, who won't. (However, its truth applies to them as well.)

3 This is the *acharit-hayamim* ("the end of days"), **and you have been storing up wealth!** Yechiel Lichtenstein remarks,

> "This is an ironical way of writing, 'You have heaped treasure for a time when it will deteriorate.' So it will be in the end of days (*ketz-hayamim*). [In contrast,] Ya'akov says that his hope is... that the Lord will speedily return — as in v. 8, 'the Lord's return is near.'"(*Commentary to the New Testament*, *ad loc.*)

4 The wages you have fraudulently withheld. Compare Leviticus 19:13, "The wages of him who is hired shall not stay with you all night until morning"; also Deuteronomy 24:14–15, Malachi 3:5.

The outcries have reached the ears of *Adonai-Tzva'ot*, like those of Abel's blood (Genesis 4:10) and of the Israelites in Egypt (Exodus 3:7). God saw the sin in these cases and dealt with it; likewise he will not ignore injustice toward workers.

7–8 "Fruit of the earth." The quotation is from the *b'rakhah* said before eating berries or vegetables, "Blessed are you, *Adonai* our God, King of the universe, creator of the fruit of the earth." Compare Mt 26:27–29&N.

The fall and spring rains, called in the Hebrew Bible, respectively, *yoreh* and *malkosh*. The reference is to the climatic pattern in Israel, where the bulk of the rainfall comes between November and March. Substantial rains in October (the *yoreh*) and April (the *malkosh*) are rare, but they are of great benefit to crops. Dan Levine, a Messianic

Jewish friend: "The spiritual *yoreh* was at *Shavu'ot* [Acts 2&NN], the *malkosh* is coming soon." Or, as Ya'akov puts it, **The Lord's return is near**, following up his remark that "this is the *acharit-hayamim*" (v. 3&N).

9 This repeats the warning of 4:11–12.

10–11 As an example of suffering mistreatment and being patient, brothers, take the prophets. Compare Mt 5:11–12, 23:29–37; MJ 11:32–38.

The perseverance (see 1:12) **of Iyov** (Job), **and you know what the purpose of *Adonai* was**. The purpose was, as Milton put it in "Paradise Lost," "to justify the ways of God to man." Job's troubles began when God chose to answer Satan's challenge by permitting him to touch Job's possessions and person, except that he could not take Job's life (Job 1–2). Job persevered in the face of all his losses and pains, magnified by the unhelpful advice of his "friends" (Job 3–37). In the end, God vindicated himself and proved to Job that only God had the power and wisdom to deal with Satan (referred to indirectly as Behemoth and Leviathan, Job 38–42).

12 Yeshua taught similarly at Mt 5:33–37. This verse follows on the ideas of 4:13–17&NN; if we do not know what tomorrow will bring, we dare not take an oath, because it is such a serious commitment.

13–20 Here, along with 1:5–8 and 4:3, is Ya'akov's teaching on prayer. Verses 14–20 deal with healing.

14–15 The Lord heals the sick among his people, according to this passage, in response to **the prayer offered with trust**. Healing was one of Yeshua's three main ministries (Mt 4:23–24), and he promised that his followers would do yet greater works than he did (Yn 14:12). In addition, the Holy Spirit, whom he has sent to his followers (Yn 15:26), grants to some gifts of healing (1C 12:9, 30).

Rub olive oil on him. Anointing with oil is not merely a ceremony. In biblical times, olive oil was medicine (Isaiah 1:6, Lk 10:34), and being anointed with oil was considered physically pleasant (Psalms 23:5, 133:2–3).

16 This verse is taken by Roman Catholics as scriptural ground for their sacrament of confession to a priest. Comparison of this verse with modern secular psychology reveals these three points:

(1) **Sins**. Apart from such psychologists as Menninger and Mowrer, secular psychology obscures personal responsibility for sins by calling them "neuroses" or "problems."

(2) **Openly acknowledge**. Communication of one's inner life is basic to psychoanalysis and other forms of verbal psychotherapy.

(3) **Pray for each other**. Secular psychology offers group therapy and doctor-patient relationships but nothing having healing power comparable with that of praying to God. But sinners must repent of sin in order to have their prayers heard (Isaiah 59:1–2).

(4) **So that you may be healed**. "Healing" of sin involves not only confessing but also being genuinely sorry, intending to stop sinning, and actually stopping.

The prayer of a righteous person is powerful and effective. This statement, followed by reference to the prophet Elijah, calls to mind the following *aggadah* from the Talmud:

"Eliyahu frequently visited the academy of Rabbi [Y'hudah HaNasi]. One day, when it was *Rosh-Chodesh*, Rabbi waited for Eliyahu, but he didn't come. Next day, Rabbi asked him, 'Why didn't you come?' Eliyahu replied, 'I had to wake up Abraham, wash his hands, wait while he prayed, then make him lie down again; likewise with Isaac and Jacob.' 'But couldn't you have awakened all of them at the same time?' 'I knew that if they prayed together, their prayers would be so powerful that they would bring the Messiah before his time.'

"'Are there any like them in this world?' asked Rabbi. 'There is Rav Chiyya and his sons,' replied Eliyahu. Rabbi proclaimed a fast, and Rav Chiyya and his sons were called down [to the *bimah*, the pulpit of the synagogue]. As he prayed [from the second blessing of the *'Amidah*], 'He causes the wind to blow,' the wind blew. He continued, 'he causes the rain to fall,' and rain fell. As he was about to say, 'he makes the dead come alive,' the universe trembled, and in heaven it was asked, 'Who has revealed our secret to the world?' 'Eliyahu,' they replied. Eliyahu was brought and beaten with sixty fiery lashes; so he went, disguised himself as a flaming bear, entered [the synagogue] and scattered them." (Bava Metzia 85b)

Compare Leviticus 26:8, Deuteronomy 32:30, Psalm 91:7.

17–18 See 1 Kings 17:1, 18:42–45. These do not mention Eliyahu's prayer, but an *aggadah* in the Talmud does:

"Eliyahu prayed and received the keys to the rain and stopped the heavens." (Sanhedrin 113a)

19–20 Causing a brother to turn from sin is the greatest form of healing, since it **saves him from** spiritual **death**. Compare Ezekiel 33:14–16, 1 Yn 5:16–17 and 1 Ke 4:8&N.

THE FIRST LETTER FROM YESHUA'S EMISSARY KEFA:

1 KEFA (1 PETER)

CHAPTER 1

1 **Kefa** is the name Yeshua gave Shim'on Bar-Yochanan when he called him to be his *talmid* (Yn 1:42&N, Mt 4:18N); in most English versions it is written, "Cephas," following the Greek transliteration of the Aramaic word. Yeshua, upon Shim'on's being first to acknowledge him as the Messiah, revealed the significance of the name: "You are Kefa [which means 'Rock'], and on this rock I will build my Community, and the gates of Sh'ol will not overcome it"(Mt 16:17–18&NN). The New Testament emphasizes that significance by usually rendering the name in Greek as "*Petros*" ("rock"), normally transliterated "Peter" in English.

Emissary. Greek *apostolos*, usually transliterated "apostle," equivalent to Hebrew *shaliach*, "someone sent." See Mt 10:2– 4N.

To: God's chosen people, literally, "God's elected ones," meaning Israel, **living as aliens in the Diaspora**. Kefa directs his letter primarily to Jewish believers (including Jewish proselytes who later accepted Yeshua), since he was "an emissary to the Circumcised" (Ga 2:7–8). However, the spiritual content of his Gospel, salvation by trust (vv. 3–9), was identical with that of Sha'ul, the "emissary to the Gentiles" (Ga 2:6–9&NN). However, Gentiles who have not converted to Judaism but have trusted in the Jewish Messiah and thrown in their lot with the Jewish believers are counted along with them, since by their trust such Gentiles have been grafted into Israel (Ro 11:17–24, Ep 2:11–16). What the phrase does not mean is simply "the Church," as opposed to "the Jews"; since the word "**Diaspora**" (Greek for "dispersion" from the Land of Israel) would then be inapplicable. Compare Ya'akov's similar greeting, "To: The Twelve Tribes in the Diaspora" (Ya 1:1&N).

Living as aliens in the Diaspora. By using this phrase Kefa indirectly acknowledges that God has promised the Land of Israel to the Jewish people and will eventually accomplish *kibbutz-hagaluyot*, "the ingathering of the exiles" from the Diaspora to *Eretz-Israel* (see Mt 5:5N). This hope, now partly realized, has been kept alive in the eleventh blessing of the *'Amidah:*

> "Sound the great *shofar* for our freedom, raise a banner [or: "a miracle"] to gather our exiles and gather us together from the four corners of the earth. Blessed be you, *Adonai,* who gathers the dispersed of his people Israel."

Pontus, Galatia, etc. These places are all in present-day Turkey.

2 This verse names what Christian theology calls "the three persons of the Trinity"; and, even though non-Messianic Jews find it a stumblingblock, Messianic Judaism must not finesse the fact that God expresses distinct aspects of his absolute unity through **the Father**, the Holy **Spirit**, and **Yeshua the Messiah**. Here it is the Father who has **chosen** and exercised **foreknowledge**, the Holy Spirit who has **set** believers **apart** from sin, and **Yeshua the Messiah** who is to be the object of **obedience** and is the one whose blood is sprinkled.

Set apart by the Spirit for obedience to Yeshua the Messiah. Yechiel Lichtenstein writes,

> "It also relates to the word '**chosen**.' The meaning is that because they have trust, God helps them by his Holy Spirit, so that they will obey the Gospel and commit themselves to it with all their heart. Thus are they set apart from sin." (*Commentary to the New Testament, ad loc.)*

This is the "trust-grounded obedience" of Ro 1:5, 16:26. Thus believers in Yeshua, like the Jewish people, were **chosen** to show God to the world.

Yeshua the Messiah and… sprinkling with his blood. Sprinkling is mentioned six times in the New Testament, the other five instances are in Messianic Jews 9–12. Under the Mosaic Covenant, blood represents both death and life, because "the life is in the blood" (Leviticus 17:11). "According to the *Torah*, almost everything is purified with blood; indeed, without the shedding of blood there is no forgiveness of sins" (MJ 9:22). The shed blood brings forgiveness, the sprinkled blood purifies. See MJ 9:11–23&NN.

Under the New Covenant, the significance of shedding and sprinkling blood is the same as in the *Tanakh*; but instead of being literal, the sprinkling is accomplished inwardly through trust (Ro 3:25). Our hearts are "sprinkled clean from a bad conscience" (MJ 10:22, Ezekiel 36:25) with Yeshua the Messiah's "blood shed on behalf of many people, so that they may have their sins forgiven" (Mt 26:28), with his "blood, poured out for you" on the execution-stake (Lk 22:20) memorialized in the Communion service (1C 11:25–26). Through this heart sprinkling, "the blood… of… Yeshua purifies us from all sin" (1 Yn 1:7); so that "the sprinkled blood" of Yeshua, bringing life and forgiveness, "speaks better things than that of Hevel [Abel]," whose blood brought only death (MJ 12:24&N).

3–4 **Praised be God, Father of our Lord Yeshua the Messiah, who….** This is the liturgical formula for commencing a *b'rakhah* (Jewish benediction); for similar formulas see 2C 1:3–4&N, Ep 1:3–14&N. For example, the initial *b'rakhah* of the *'Amidah* begins, "Praised be you, *Adonai*, our God and God of our fathers…." The "who" in this formula signals a list of praiseworthy things God has done. In this case, he has **caused us to be born again to a living hope, to an inheritance… kept safe for you in heaven**. See Abraham Millgram, *Jewish Worship* (Philadelphia: The Jewish Publication Society of America, 1971), pp. 91–96. At 2:9 Kefa writes that the reason believers are "a chosen people" is so that they may declare the praises of God; here in vv. 1–4 he makes himself an example by doing exactly that — declaring the praises of God.

Born again. See Yn 3:3N. Here the Greek word "*anagennêsas*" can only mean "caused us to be born again"; at Yn 3:3 "*gennêthê anôthen*" can also be rendered "born from above."

Through the resurrection of Yeshua you have been **born again to a living hope**. At Ro 6:4–11, 8:9–25 Sha'ul explains how it works. "Yeshua said..., 'I AM the Resurrection and the Life! Whoever puts his trust in me will live, even if he dies; and everyone living and trusting in me will never die. Do you believe this?'"(Yn 11:25) Kefa did.

An inheritance (see Ep 1:11N) **that cannot decay, spoil or fade**. Compare Mt 6:19–21, Ya 5:2–3.

5 **A deliverance ready to be revealed at the Last Time**, when the Messiah returns (v. 7). See vv. 10–12N.

10–12 There are scholars who hold that the prophets of the *Tanakh* spoke only to their own times, that they always understood the significance of what they said, and that their utterances contained only moral content and were never of predictive value or intent. These verses contradict that opinion. So does Daniel, who reports that an angel told him about the future and then instructed, "But you, Daniel, shut up the words and seal the book until the Time of the End." Daniel then declares, "I heard, but I did not understand. So I said, 'O my lord, what will be the end of these things?' And he replied, 'Go on your way, Daniel, for the words are closed up and sealed until the Time of the End'"(Daniel 12:4, 8–9). Compare also Jeremiah 32. Therefore people seeking the truth, like the Jews of Berea who "checked the *Tanakh* every day to see if the things Sha'ul was saying were true" (Ac 17:11), should search the *Tanakh* to see if it points to Yeshua the Messiah. The Messianic prophecies already fulfilled by him show that it does (see Section VII of the Introduction to *JNT*, Mt 26:24N).

11 **The Spirit of the Messiah**, present in the Prophets centuries before Yeshua was born, is the Holy Spirit, the *Ruach HaKodesh* (compare Ro 8:9).

12 **Not for their own benefit but for yours**. Compare MJ 11:39–40&N.

13–16 **Get your minds ready for work** (v. 13a). Be mentally prepared for opposition, distractions, temptations and unexpected setbacks. This, having a clear hope for future reward (v. 13b) and refusing to **be shaped by the evil desires you used to have when you were still ignorant** of Yeshua the Messiah (v. 14) are necessary in order to heed Kefa's main exhortation, namely, to **become holy yourselves in your entire way of life** (v. 15).

17 **The Father judges according to each person's actions**, and not by "faith alone" (Ya 2:24), since "faith by itself, unaccompanied by actions, is dead" (Ya 2:17). See 1C 3:8–15&N, Ya 2:14–26&NN, Rv 20:12b&N.

Your temporary stay on earth. See MJ 11:9–10, 13–16&NN.

18 **The worthless way of life which your fathers passed on to you**. This is neither pagan idolatry nor the Mosaic Law as set forth in the *Tanakh*, but the perversion of the *Torah* into an oppressive, legalistic **way of life which your fathers**, the Jewish establishment, those guiding the direction of the Jewish lifestyle, **passed on to you** Jews who have come to believe in Yeshua the Messiah. (See Ro 3:20b&N, Ga 3:23b&N. This

interpretation assumes that Kefa is addressing Messianic Jews and Messianic Gentiles identifying with them, rather than Gentiles retaining a pagan mindset, whose former "worthless way of life" would have consisted in idol-worship and gross immorality. See v. 1N above, on "God's chosen people.")

Kefa is repeating what he said to the legalizers at the Jerusalem Conference, "Why are you putting God to the test now by placing a yoke on the neck of the *talmidim* which neither our fathers nor we have had the strength to bear?" (Ac 15:10&N).

The ransom... did not consist of anything perishable like silver or gold. Compare Isaiah 52:3, "You shall be redeemed without money"; also Ya 5:2–3&N.

19 **Bloody sacrificial death**, literally, "blood." See Yn 6:51–66&N, Ro 3:25bN.

A lamb without defect or spot. Starting with the lamb offered by each family at the time of the Exodus (Exodus 12:5), all sacrifices had to be without blemish, Leviticus 22:18–25, MJ 9:11–15&N. Yochanan the Immerser calls Yeshua "God's lamb! The one who is taking away the sin of the world!" (Yn 1:29). Yeshua was a lamb offered as a sin offering to atone for our sins according to the *Torah* (Ro 3:25–26&NN, 8:3–4&N); he was also the final Passover lamb (Lk 22:7&N, 1C 5:6–8&N). In the past he died; in the present we share his life (Yn 6:51–66&N, 1C 11:23–26); and in the future he will return as "the slaughtered Lamb" (Rv 5:6&N; Isaiah 53:7, quoted at Ac 8:32) who, because he was without sin (Isaiah 53:9, quoted below at 2:22), is worthy to open the scroll with seven seals and to rule the Kingdom of God as "the Lion of the tribe of Judah, the Root of David" (Rv 5:5&N). In him the Lamb and the Lion "lie down together" (Isaiah 11:6–7) by virtue of being one and the same person, Yeshua the Messiah.

20 **God knew him**, Yeshua the Messiah, **before the founding of the universe** This corresponds to the Jewish teaching that God created the Messiah before he created the world. For New Testament teaching on the Messiah's pre-existence, see Yn 1:1&N, 14; Ep 1:3–6; 3:11; Co 1:15–17&NN; MJ 1:1–3&NN; Rv 5:5–6&NN.

But revealed him in the *acharit-hayamim* ("the end of days") **for your sakes**, as Sha'ul said at Ep 1:8–10, 3:3–11.

22 Compare Yn 13:34–35.

23–25 The preeminent Christian theologian of the twentieth century, Karl Barth, notes that the eternal **Word** comes to New Covenant believers in three forms:

(1) Yeshua the Messiah. **You have been born again through... the living Word of God that lasts forever**. "In the beginning was the Word, and the Word was with God, and the Word was God. He was with God in the beginning.... The Word became a human being and *lived* with us" (Yn 1:1–2, 14).

(2) Scripture, which Kefa quotes (Isaiah 40:6–8) as authenticating itself: **The grass withers, and the flower falls off; but the Word of *Adonai* lasts forever**. Compare MJ 4:12–13; Ya 1:10–11, 4:14.

(3) The preachings of God's people, equated with the first two forms. **Moreover, this "Word" is the Good News which has been proclaimed to you**. Compare Ro 10:17.

See 2:1–3&N.

CHAPTER 2

1–3 Be like newborn babies, thirsty for the pure milk of the Word of God, which here can mean (1) the written Word, then only the *Tanakh* (1:24), (2) the Gospel (1:25), which implies the future New Testament, (3) Yeshua (1:23, 2:4), (4) true doctrine (as in MJ 5:11–6:2), or (5) all of the above (an understanding which works well here; see 1:23–25&N).

Alternate renderings: "Be in your speech like newborn babies, thirsty for pure milk" to flow from you; or: "Be like newborn babies, thirsty for pure spiritual milk." All three are possible translations of the Greek text because the word "*logikos*," the adjective formed from "*logos*" ("word"), can mean (1) "pertaining to a word (or words, or the Word)," as in the *JNT* rendering, (2) "pertaining to speech," as in my first alternate rendering, or (3) "logical, reasonable," as in Ro 12:1 and my second alternate rendering; this is the sense most versions give, but of the three possibilities it seems to me the one most weakly and vaguely related to the context.

If my first alternate rendering is correct, then the sense of vv. 1–3 is that because ***Adonai* is good**, a believer should earnestly desire to have the pure milk of the **good**ness which he has **tasted** in God's **Word** affect his own words, so that his speech consists of kindnesses and blessings instead of **malice,... deceit, hypocrisy and envy** (compare Ya 1:19–22, 26; 3:1–12).

4–8 The "**chosen**" theme appears first at 1:2 and is seen again at 2:9. See notes to these verses. A second theme developed in these verses is the "**stone**"; the same three Messianic "stone" prophecies are found also at Mt 21:42; Mk 12:10–11; Lk 20:17; Ac 4:11; Ro 9:32–33, 10:11, 13.

8 Humanly **disobeying** the Word, **as had been planned** by God. Once again we hear human free choice and God's foreordination in the same breath — as also at 1:2; see Ro 9:19–21&N, Pp 2:13&N.

9 A chosen people, the King's *cohanim*, a holy nation, a people for God to possess (KJV "a peculiar people"). In the *Tanakh* these terms are applied to the Jewish people, Israel. Kefa applies them to the readers of his letter, who, according to 1:1N, are, firstly, Messianic Jews and, secondly, Messianic Gentiles who truly identify with them (compare Ro 1:16). Many Christian theologians have used this verse as evidence that the Church (the Christians) has replaced Israel (the Jews). If I am right about who the readers of this letter were, then these Christian theologians are wrong. Even if I am wrong about the readers, Replacement theology is inconsistent with Ro 11:17–26, Ep 2:11–22, and other references at Mt 5:5N. I would put it this way: Christians are indeed a chosen people, priests for the King, a holy "nation" (in a metaphorical sense), a people set aside for God to possess — not by way of superseding the Jews as God's people, but by way of being joined to them by faith in the same God and in the Jewish Messiah. A so-called "Christian" who opposes or looks down on the Jews as merely God's "former" people has missed the point altogether and is probably not a Christian at all.

On what it means to be God's **chosen people,** see Ac 13:17N. The Bible resolves doubts and questions about election by stating its true purpose: **in order for you to declare the praises of the One who called you out of darkness into his wonderful light**, namely, God. The word "Jew" in Hebrew is "*Y'hudi*," related to the words "*hod*" ("praise") and "*todah*" ("thanks"). To be a Jew, then, is to be one who praises and thanks God (see Ro 2:28–29N); the very name of the Jewish people reflects God's purpose in choosing us. Gentiles grafted into Israel, and therefore sharing Israel's spiritual life through her Messiah, are chosen for the same purpose.

10 Sha'ul makes a *midrash* on these same phrases, applying them not to Jews, as does Hosea, but to Gentiles (Ro 9:24b–26&NN). Here Kefa applies them to his Messianic Jewish and Messianic Gentile readers. Again, as at v. 9&N, there is no implication that the Gentiles or the Christians have replaced the Jews as God's people.

11 **Aliens and temporary residents** not only in the Diaspora (1:1&N) but on earth (see MJ 11:9–10, 13–16&N).

Not to give in to the desires of your old nature. See Ro 8:3–13&NN.

12 **Live such good lives among the pagans** (or "Gentiles") **that even though they now speak against you as evildoers, they will, as a result of seeing your good actions, give glory to God**. That is, let your deeds be your testimony, as Yeshua counseled in the Sermon on the Mount (Mt 5:16; see also 4:16 below and Yn 13:34–35). **On the day of his coming**, literally, "on the Day of visitation" or "overseeing"; compare Mt 7:21–23. Messianic Jews living amidst opposition from some of their non-Messianic Jewish brothers can apply this verse midrashically to their situation.

The message of this verse is applied in vv. 13–17 to the question of how believing citizens should relate to a government run by unbelievers, in vv. 18–25 to how believing slaves should relate to unbelieving masters, and in 3:1–6 to how believing wives should relate to unbelieving husbands.

13–17 See Ro 13:1–7&NN.

16 See Ga 5:13&N, Ya 2:12&N.

18–25 Kefa's advice to the household servants of 2000 years ago that they should bear up even under undeserved punishment can be applied, with the necessary changes, by today's employees. (One obvious and necessary change is that employees today have better means for improving their working conditions than were available to slaves seeking redress from their masters.) Compare Ep 6:5–8, Co 3:22–25. In this **the Messiah** serves as our **example** (v. 21), since he fulfills the prophecies of Isaiah concerning the "suffering servant." The main such passage is Isaiah 52:13–53:12; vv. 22–25 quote it four times.

23 **To him who judges justly**, or "righteously." God is referred to in the Jewish burial service as the "Righteous Judge," as in 2 Ti 4:6–8&N.

But handed them over to him who judges justly. The following is a modification of Yechiel Lichtenstein's note on this:

"The meaning here is not as in the Talmud, 'Let Heaven judge him,' that is, 'Let Heaven destroy my enemies.' For Yeshua preached the opposite: 'Love your enemies! Pray for those who persecute you!' (Mt 5:44). Not only that, but in the moment of utmost extremity, as he was hanging from the stake, he practiced what he preached, praying, 'Father, forgive them; they don't understand what they are doing' (Lk 23:34; compare Stephen at Ac 7:60). Thus the meaning here is that Yeshua gave his case over into the hand of the Righteous Judge, confident that God would decide to accept his prayer for them — as written in Lk 22:42, 'Not my will but yours be done.'"(*Commentary to the New Testament, ad loc.*)

Handed them over. The Greek text does not give a direct object for the verb, "handed over." Thus an alternative understanding of this verse would have it tell us that Yeshua, confident that his enemies' **insults** were nothing compared to God's eventual vindication, "handed himself over to him who judges justly." But since the rest of the verse gives two ways Yeshua did not deal with his enemies, it seems reasonable that Kefa would satisfy our curiosity and tell us how Yeshua did deal with them, thereby clarifying how Yeshua is an "example" in whose steps we should follow (v. 21).

24 Deuteronomy 21:22–23 reads, in part, "If a man has committed a sin for which the penalty is death, and he is put to death, and you hang him on a stake, then his body is not to remain all night on the stake; rather, you are to bury him that day, for he who has been hanged is cursed by God." In relation to Yeshua, **the stake** is the execution-stake on which he was wrongly put to death as a criminal (see Mt 10:38N). This is clear from Ga 3:13, which says that although the Messiah was undeserving of punishment (compare v. 22), he "redeemed us from the curse pronounced in the *Torah* by becoming cursed on our behalf; for the *Tanakh* says, 'Everyone who hangs from a stake comes under a curse.'"On rendering Greek *xulon* as "stake," and not "tree" as in KJV, see Ac 5:30N.

25 **Shepherd**, Greek *poimên,* often translated "pastor."

Who watches over you. KJV has "bishop of your souls." Greek *episkopos* means "one who looks over," hence "supervisor, overseer." "Bishop" merely transliterates the Greek. In those Christian denominations which have them, the job of bishops is to oversee the work of the pastors of local congregations. But in the New Testament, "overseer," "pastor" and "elder" are used more or less interchangeably; see 1 Ti 3:1&N.

"Of your souls" is a literal translation; but the Hebrew way of thinking — Kefa's way of thinking — does not separate souls from persons; therefore, to say that Yeshua watches over your soul means simply that he watches over you.

CHAPTER 3

1–2 **In the same way** as citizens with their government (2:13–17) and slaves with their masters (2:18–25), believing **wives** should exemplify the principle of 2:12 with their

husbands by submitting to them. Compare 1C 7:12–16, Ep 5:22–24, Co 3:18, 1 Ti 2:9–15.

Don't be a *noodge* or a *nudnik* (Yiddish for "nag" and "bore"). For **they will be won over** to being curious about the Yeshua they already know you believe in, not by your preachments, but **by your conduct, without your saying a word, as they see your respectful and pure behavior**. Then, when you have an interested audience, you can speak! This is equally true for husbands.

But there is no guarantee here of a spouse's salvation; compare 1C 7:16.

6 **Honoring him as her lord**. Midrash Tanchuma on the *Torah* portion, *Chayyey-Sarah*, 29a:

> "Abraham's wife honored him and called him 'lord,' for it is written that Sarah said, 'My lord is old' (Genesis 18:12). But, conversely, God commanded Abraham to honor his wife by calling her 'princess'; for that is the meaning of her Hebrew name *'Sarah'* (Genesis 17:15)."

You are her daughters. As Abraham is the father of all believers (Ya 2:21–23; Ro 4:12, 16; Ga 3:7–9, 29), his wife **Sarah** is appropriately singled out as the mother of believing women, in that she is an example for them, just as Abraham is for all believers. In Hebrew being a "daughter of " or a "son of " someone or something implies having that person or thing's qualities (see Mt 1:1N on "son of"). This is expressed by the prayer a father recites over his daughter before the *Erev-Shabbat* (Friday evening) meal, "May God make you like Sarah, Rivkah, Leah and Rachel," the four Mothers of Israel; he then blesses her with the Aaronic benediction (Numbers 6:24–26).

Do not succumb to fear. This is a call to give up neurotic anxiety. The anxious feelings may not go away, but one can gain a right perspective on them, not by suppressing them and denying their existence, but by acknowledging them while at the same time experiencing that God's peace, his *shalom*, a fruit of the Holy Spirit (Ga 5:22), is stronger: as is God's power, love and self-control (1 Ti 1:7). Seek God's rulership instead of dwelling on anxious thoughts and worries (Mt 6:25–26, 33). The basic fear is of death, but Yeshua has abolished death (2 Ti 1:10) and set believers free from this fear (MJ 2:15).

7 **Husbands, conduct your married lives** (the term includes the sexual aspect but is not limited to it) **with understanding**. This fits with Co 3:19 ("Husbands, love your wives and don't treat them harshly") and Ep 5:25–33.

Respect her as a fellow-heir of the gift of life; compare Ep 5:21.

If you don't, your prayers will be blocked. This is a portentous warning. A man who does not respect his wife might try to retreat into prayer; but he will be unable to have a good spiritual life so long as he does not love, understand and honor his wife. Any husband who has attempted to pray privately while in the midst of a fight with his wife should agree.

14 **Even if you do suffer for being righteous, you are blessed!** Compare Mt 5:10–12.

15–16 These verses tell when, how, and to whom a believer should proclaim the Gospel

Compare this advice from the Mishna:

> "Rabbi El'azar said, 'Be diligent to learn *Torah*, and know what to answer a skeptic [Hebrew *apikoros*, transliterating the Greek word for "follower of the philosopher Epicurus"].'"(Avot 2:14)

(1) *When should you proclaim the Gospel* — and when not? Although you should be **always ready to give a reasoned answer**, you normally need to speak only when someone **asks you to explain the hope you have in you**. Not everyone asks. Believers who feel compelled to introduce the topic of their faith into every conversation with an unbeliever can relax!

On the other hand, if someone wants to hear about the faith, a believer should not remain silent or avoid the subject. "But my life is my testimony, I don't need words." No, the relationship between words and deeds in witnessing to your faith is that your actions, attitudes and lifestyle are to show unbelievers that the Holy Spirit is at work in your life (2:12, 3:1), so that they begin to ask questions: "Why don't you get angry when people mistreat you?" "Everyone else cheats; how come you don't?" "What is it that makes you so happy all the time?" or, paraphrasing v. 15, "The world is such a difficult and depressing place, and you have had your share of misfortunes, yet you retain hope. Why?"

When they ask such questions, you should be ready to give a reasoned answer. You cannot carry out the Great Commission to make disciples of all nations (Mt 28:19–20) without both aspects of witness — words and deeds. Words without deeds are empty and hypocritical, as Kefa recognizes when he writes that we must **keep a clear conscience** and display **good behavior**. But deeds without words do not explain what people need to know about Yeshua in order to be saved. As Sha'ul put it, "How can they trust in someone if they haven't heard about him? And how can they hear about someone if no one is proclaiming him?… Trust comes from what is heard, and what is heard comes through a word proclaimed about the Messiah" (Ro 10:14, 17).

There are times when one should not wait to be asked. Sometimes it may be necessary to proclaim the Gospel to people who do not want to hear it. There may be no possibility of delay, the urgency of the situation may compel witness.

> "There is a point when deference, that is, respect for a person's wish to be left alone and not evangelized, must defer to decisive action. Precisely what is that point? It is when we are dealing with a matter of life and death. Suppose you claim you can fly without wings. So long as we are merely discussing flying, I'll respect your point of view. But the moment you step out the window onto the ledge, believe me, *true* respect — respect for your life — demands my resolute conviction to get you back inside! Why can't we believers keep our views to ourselves? Why can't we mind our own business? Because we're dealing with a matter of life and death." (Adapted from Avi Snyder, "With All Due Respect," in *Jews for Jesus Newsletter*, Volume 6 (1983)).

(2) *How should you proclaim the Gospel* to those who want to know? With **a reasoned answer**. A reasoned answer draws on objective evidence and uses rational

arguments. More than that, a reasoned answer about Messianic faith must be consistent with Scripture; and, in my opinion, it should actively make use of Scripture — even when addressed to people who do not believe the Bible to be inspired by God; for the Word of God has power of its own (MJ 1:2, 4:12). Moreover, when you anchor your message in your own reasoning, it's your word against his; but if you quote the Bible, whose text is the same for him as for you, then he has to take his case to God (to whom he must turn anyway, sooner or later). Also you, no longer under pressure to defend yourself, can turn your energy to defending God and what he has done through Yeshua.

A reasoned answer *may* include such subjective aspects of your personal testimony as how much better you feel since knowing Yeshua, or ways in which God has blessed you, for these things are facts concerning you. But it *must* deal primarily with the facts that concern everyone, including your questioner — God exists, God made us, we sinned, we are under sentence of death, God sent Yeshua to atone for our sin, God resurrected him, he is coming back, we must trust in God and in his Messiah in order to be saved and have eternal life, Israel's national salvation comes only through Yeshua the Messiah.

Kefa says more about how to proclaim the Gospel. You should do it **with humility and fear, keeping a clear conscience**. How tempting it is when engaging in evangelism to set humility aside! After all, aren't your answers right and theirs wrong? (It is tempting to think so.) Therefore you must be better than they are! No, you are *not* better. But you *are* saved "by grace through trusting, and even this is not your accomplishment but God's gift…; therefore no one should boast" (Ep 2:8–9). One reason for being humble is that you should be embarrassed by the fact that the lives of even the most saintly believers fall short of their preaching, let alone the lives of the worst! We preach a Gospel of perfection, and none of us is perfect. Therefore, if we are without humility, we contradict our own message. See also v. 8, 5:5–6.

And fear. The fear we should have is not that the person we are talking to will react negatively to our message or to us. Our job is to proclaim the truth of the Gospel; whether he receives it or not is his responsibility (Ezekiel 33:7–9). Nor are we to fear persecution, as Kefa reiterates throughout this letter (1:6; 2:12, 19–25; 3:14, 17; 4:12–19; 5:9–10). Rather, we are to fear God, who holds us to account for both our words and our deeds (compare Ro 11:17–24).

Keeping a clear conscience. You keep your conscience clear by displaying only the **good behavior flowing from your union with the Messiah**. As noted, this is the "deeds" side of your witness. See Ac 24:16&N.

(3) *To whom should you proclaim the Gospel*? To **anyone who asks you about the hope you have in you**, Jew or Gentile, young or old, poor or rich, since everyone needs salvation (Ro 3:23) and no one comes to the Father except through Yeshua (Yn 14:6).

But not everyone who raises a question about your faith is asking about the hope you have in you. "Are savages who have never even heard of the Bible going to go to hell because they don't believe in Jesus?" "You don't really believe that Mary was a virgin, do you?" These are not questions about the hope you have in you. You are not being invited to share the source of your purposefulness and joy. Yeshua cautioned, "Don't give to dogs what is holy, and don't throw your pearls to the pigs. If you do, they may trample them under their feet, then turn and attack you" (Mt 7:6).

What kind of answer should you give to questions like these? It depends. Discernment, the ability to judge between spirits, is a gift of the *Ruach HaKodesh* (1C 12:8–10&N) which helps you know how to respond to different questioners; pray for the gift of discernment (Lk 11:13, 1C 12:31). Sometimes people who are nearly ready to receive the Gospel raise a few such questions as a sort of "last fling" against it before capitulating to God. They should be given the "reasoned answer" Kefa recommends, such as: "God, the Righteous Judge, will determine fairly the fate of everyone, including the savages, on the basis of the way they responded to the truth they understood. But your fate will be determined by how you respond to the Gospel preached to you." (For more on this, see Ro 2:11–16&NN.) "Yes, I believe in the virgin birth; let us study the Bible together and see why." You would then turn to the opening chapters of Mattityahu and Luke; and your questioner, who I have assumed to be open to a reasoned answer, would study with you.

But other people asking the same questions have hardened hearts (see Ro 9:17–21&NN), are resisting the Gospel with all their might, have no intention of accepting it, and are not interested in reasoned answers. They fall in a different category, one the *Tanakh* calls "fool." Concerning them, Proverbs 26:4–5 offers this seemingly contradictory advice:

> "Do not answer a fool according to his folly,
> lest you become like him yourself.
>
> "Answer a fool according to his folly,
> lest he be wise in his own eyes."

The former verse means that you should not let yourself be dragged down to his emotional and spiritual level by engaging in heated but fruitless debate. The latter tells you that even though an opinionated person is not open to changing his mind, he should be shown that his ideas are not as unassailable as he thinks. Moreover, both verses taken together also imply that when reasoned argument is of no avail ("My mind is made up, don't confuse me with the facts"), you should confront the objector or heckler in a different manner altogether.

In such a case you might answer his question with one of your own. In response to the question about savages going to hell, you could ask, "Do you believe in hell?" If he answers that he doesn't, you add, "Then why ask a question about something that doesn't exist? Are you just baiting me?" Or suppose the question about the virgin birth came from someone who you know is a married man with a mistress. Under some not-too-difficult-to-imagine circumstances you might be able to say something like this: "You are not really concerned with how the Messiah was born but with justifying your own unbelief, and the real reason you won't trust in Yeshua for salvation is that you don't want to give up your sin of adultery." A man like this is hardened against the Gospel because he has a vested interest in continuing to engage in his sin; but there is always the possibility that a strong answer like this will break him, so that he will see himself for what he really is and begin to recognize his need for a Savior. But remember that when you speak such penetrating truth, do so in love (Ep 4:15). Live righteously, and pray for such people, that they will be no longer "fools" but wise with the wisdom of God (1C 1:17–31); for "The prayer of a righteous person is powerful and effective" (Ya 5:16).

There are many books on "how to witness," some specifically on "how to witness to the Jews." Some are written well, some offensively; some of the material offered is good, some irrelevant. "Of making many books there is no end, and much study is a weariness of the flesh" (Ecclesiastes 12:12). We might sum up the subject of witnessing much as did the writer of Ecclesiastes did in his book: "The end of the matter, when all is said and done: Fear God, and keep his commandments; for that is the whole of man. For God will bring every work into judgment, including every secret thing, whether good or bad" (Ecclesiastes 12:13–14). So I advise all believers to live a Messianic life, know the truth, speak in love and humility, discern who is open, and trust the Lord to work in people's hearts, including yours.

19–22 Instead of trying to weigh critically the many interpretations of this difficult passage, I present one approach. The **imprisoned spirits** are the "angels who sinned" (2 Ke 2:4) and "abandoned their proper sphere" (Yd 6). That is, they are the *b'nei-ha'elohim* ("sons of God" or "sons of the angels"), also called *nefilim* ("fallen ones"), who fell to earth from their proper sphere, heaven, and "came in to the daughters of men" **in the days of Noach** (Genesis 6:2–4).

When Yeshua **went and made a proclamation** to them, he was doing what the rabbinic *midrashim* say Enoch did after he "walked with *ha-elohim*," which means that he walked either with "God" or with "the angels" (Genesis 5:24).

Interpreters who believe the **imprisoned spirits** were the souls of human beings who died before Yeshua came (see 4:6&N) usually regard this **proclamation** as a salvation message, the implication being that dead people (or some of them) have (or once had) the possibility of being saved. But if the proclamation was to angels, it was not a salvation message, for these angels God has "kept in darkness, bound with everlasting chains for the Judgment of the Great Day" (Yd 6). Rather, the proclamation must have been Yeshua's announcement that, "Stripping the [evil angelic] rulers and authorities [that is, the ones still at large] of their power, he made a public spectacle of them, triumphing over them by means of the stake" (Co 2:15&N).

In the days of Noach, the **water** of the Flood which drowned most of humanity was the **means** (inasmuch as the **ark** floated on it) by which **a few people — to be specific, eight** (Noah, his three sons, and the wives) — **were delivered. This** water **also prefigures what delivers us now, the water of immersion** (or "baptism," Hebrew *t'vilah*; see Mt 3:1N). The water of the Red Sea was similarly understood by Sha'ul to prefigure immersion (1C 10:1–13&NN). Kefa points out that the essence of immersion is **not** the physical **removal of dirt from the body**, but the spiritual transaction which accompanies the physical event, **one's pledge to keep a good conscience** (v. 16) **toward God**. Believers have the power to keep such a pledge only **through the resurrection of Yeshua the Messiah**, for this is what made it possible for him to send the Holy Spirit to them (Yn 14:16, 16:7; Ac 1:8), after going **into heaven** to intercede for them (MJ 7:25) **at the right hand of God** (see Mt 22:42N, Ac 7:55–56&N).

Thus Kefa compares the believers with Noah and his family, both being righteous minorities persecuted by wicked neighbors, and both being delivered from the forces of darkness through trusting God and obeying him.

CHAPTER 4

1–2 Compare Ro 12:1–2.

3–4 The letter as a whole is meant for Messianic Jews and Messianic Gentiles who identify with them (1:1N, 2:9N). But just as earlier Kefa addresses the Jewish believers specifically (1:18&N), so here he speaks to the Gentile believers.

Today's world is not so different from Kefa's. Many believers face the same kinds of temptation, ridicule and rejection by their friends and family, who **think it strange that you** try to follow God's priorities instead of theirs.

5–6 According to Yn 5:21 and Ro 2:16, Yeshua the Messiah is the one **who stands ready to judge** "the quick and the dead" (KJV). **This is why he** (or "it"; see below) **was proclaimed to those who have** since **died** (literally, "to the dead"; see below); namely, **it was so that, even though physically they would receive the judgment common to all men**, death, nevertheless **they might live by the Spirit in the way that God has provided**. That is, as a result of trusting in Yeshua, they might, by the power of the *Ruach HaKodesh*, live holy lives of joy before death; and also, after death, they might have the joy of eternal life with God, also by the *Ruach HaKodesh*. The passage, like 1 Th 4:13–18, provides believers with comfort over friends who have died, as well as an answer to pagans mocking them for exchanging worldly enjoyment merely for the grave (vv. 3–4).

Some have interpreted v. 6 to mean that Yeshua proclaimed the Gospel to persons who had already died (or to their spirits, 3:19), so that they had an opportunity to be saved. To those who prefer to lead selfish and sinful lives, ignoring God, this "second chance theory" has appeal. However, the only support in the New Testament for such an understanding comes from verses at least equally problematical (3:19–22&N above, 1C 15:29&N). On the contrary, MJ 9:27, agreeing with v. 5, says that "human beings have to die once, but after this comes judgment," not another opportunity to accept the Gospel. Persons who believed as much of God's truth as had been revealed and then died before Yeshua came joined those who would be saved through Yeshua's atoning death later on; this is clear from Messianic Jews 11, especially MJ 11:39–40.

8 **Love covers many sins**. Two alternative interpretations: (1) Love makes you willing to forgive others' sins and overlook their faults. (2) At the final judgment, God will forgive many of your sins if you keep loving (compare Lk 7:47, Mt 25:31–46). See also Ya 5:20.

10 **Spiritual gift**, Greek *charisma*. See 1C 12:8–10&N.

13–14 Do not only brace for afflictions, but **rejoice** in them, sharing **the fellowship of the Messiah's sufferings** (compare Co 1:24). For just as the ***Sh'khinah*** (God's manifest glory, MJ 1:2–3N) once rested on the Temple in Jerusalem, now **the Spirit of the *Sh'khinah* is resting on you**, since "your body is a temple for the *Ruach HaKodesh* who lives inside you" (1C 6:19). The *Sh'khinah* was **revealed** as **his**, Yeshua's, ***Sh'khinah*** at his first coming (Yn 1:14–15); it is the same as "the glory to be revealed" (5:1&N) at his second coming (Ti 2:12). The term "***Sh'khinah***" refers only to God; its use in connection with the Messiah and the Spirit exemplifies again the New Testament's tendency to speak indirectly about the divinity of Yeshua and the *Ruach HaKodesh.*

14, 16 Because you bear the name of the Messiah (literally, "in the name of the Messiah"). **For being Messianic. By the way you bear this name** (v. 16; literally, "by this name" or "in this name"). **Messianic** is Greek *Christianos*; most versions resemble KJV, "if any man suffer as a Christian." See Ac 11:26N, 26:28N, the only other places in the New Testament where "*Christianos*" appears.

CHAPTER 5

1 Kefa writes **the elders** humbly, **as a fellow-elder**, not as a superior, even though he personally was a **witness to the Messiah's sufferings**.

The glory to be revealed, as at Ro 8:18, "I don't think the sufferings we are going through now are even worth comparing with the glory that will be revealed to us in the future." Alternatively: "the *Sh'khinah* to be revealed," as at 4:13–14&N.

2–3 Shepherd the flock. Kefa is faithfully transmitting Yeshua's command to him at Yn 21:16.

Exercising oversight… willingly. Some elders take too little responsibility, so that their congregations remain weak and undisciplined. If it is true that the Messiah wants followers who will follow, all the more does he want leaders who will lead — but **not as *machers***. The word "*macher*" is Yiddish for "big shot, real operator," with the overtone of trying to take charge; the perfect New Testament example is Diotrephes (3 Yn 9–10). The Greek word so rendered here is "*katakurieuontes*" ("lording it over", "trying to show one's authority," "domineering").

7 Compare Psalm 55:23(22).

8 **The Adversary** is Satan, who is real (Mt 4:1N) and should be resisted (v. 9, Ya 4:8).

12–14 At one point Yochanan **Mark** abandoned Sha'ul and Bar-Nabba (Ac 13:5, 13), with the result that Sha'ul and Bar-Nabba split over whether to take him with them again, and Sha'ul took **Sila** instead (Ac 15:22&N, 15:39&N).

Babylon was a common euphemism for Rome among Jewish writers seeking to avoid censorship and worse (see Midrash Rabbah on Song of Songs 1:6, Megillah 6b, Makkot 24a). "Rome was called Babylon because it was the worst kingdom" (Yechiel Lichtenstein on this verse).

Shalom aleikhem, "Peace be upon you," a common Hebrew greeting then and now. See Mt 10:12N.

THE SECOND LETTER FROM YESHUA'S EMISSARY KEFA:

2 KEFA (2 PETER)

CHAPTER 1

1 **Shim'on** bar-Yochanan and **Kefa** are names for Peter the **emissary** (apostle). See Mt 4:18, 10:2–4, 16:17–18&NN; Yn 1:42&N; 1 Ke 1:1N.

To: Those who... have been given the same kind of trust as ours, namely, Messianic Gentiles (Kefa's first letter was written to Messianic Jews, 1 Ke 1:1&N). "**Ours**," in the plural, refers to Messianic Jews in general (see, e.g., Ep 1:11–14&N, 2:3N). Messianic Gentiles are considered righteous by God because of their **trust**, which is **the same** as that of Messianic Jews (see references in Ro 1:16N). Kefa had made this discovery earlier (Ac 10:1–11:18&NN) and made it part of his life (Ac 15:7–11&NN), even though on at least one occasion he needed reminding about it (Ga 2:11–21&NN).

The righteousness of our God consists in his forbearance in regard to sins committed before Yeshua came, and his making people righteous on the ground of Yeshua's faithfulness to God when dying on behalf of sinners (see Ro 3:25–26&NN). The righteousness **of our Deliverer Yeshua the Messiah** is the sinlessness which made his dying on behalf of sinners a genuine atonement. As Kefa puts it elsewhere, "The Messiah himself died for sins, once and for all, a righteous person on behalf of unrighteous people, so that he might bring you to God" (1 Ke 3:18; see also 1 Ke 2:21–24, Ro 8:3, MJ 4:15).

5–11 **Try your hardest** and **try even harder** to add these qualities to your **faith**. Faith saves, but not if so-called "believers" are merely passive spectators of their salvation, for then they are **barren and unfruitful** (Ya 2:14–26&NN), and fail to make their **being called and chosen a certainty**. Instead, they deceive themselves into thinking they are saved when they are not (see MJ 6:4–6&N). The only way to be certain one **will enter the eternal Kingdom of our Lord and Deliverer Yeshua the Messiah**, is by letting God act through you as you develop the **qualities** named in vv. 5–7. For similar chains of qualities see Ro 5:2–4, 8:29–30, and in the Apocrypha, Wisdom of Solomon 6:17–20.

14–15 **As our Lord Yeshua the Messiah has made clear to me**. Yeshua indicated how Kefa would die at Yn 21:18–19, though without saying when. Here Kefa knows it will be **soon**. According to tradition, Kefa was crucified upside down, saying he did not deserve to be crucified right side up like his Lord.

Exodus. The Greek word "*exodos*" ("departure") appears three times in the New Testament, each time, of course, recalling the original Exodus of the Israelites. In this verse the world and heaven are implicitly compared with Egypt and the Promised Land. See Lk 9:31N.

Like Moshe in Deuteronomy 31:24–33:29, Kefa before he is to die makes known his "last will" for God's people.

16–18 Also like Moshe, Kefa encountered God on a **holy mountain**. Three of the four Gospel writers report this event, the Transfiguration of Yeshua, when Kefa, Ya'akov and Yochanan saw the **majesty** of the Messiah made manifest (Mt 17:1–9, Mk 9:2–10, Lk 9:28–36). The words, **"This is my Son, whom I love; with him I am well pleased,"** were also heard when Yeshua was immersed by Yochanan the Immerser (Mt 3:17, Mk 1:11, Lk 3:22); and they allude to Psalm 2:7, "You are my Son; today I have become your Father," itself quoted at Ac 13:33 and at MJ 1:5, 5:5.

Kefa testifies here to his own personal experience with Yeshua the Messiah (1) in order to establish his credentials as a reliable interpreter of prophecy (vv. 19–21&NN), and (2) to contrast the historical veracity of the events of Yeshua's life, death and resurrection with the **cunningly contrived myths** and "fabricated stories" (2:3) used by the false prophets. The Greek word "*sophismenos*" ("cunningly contrived"), could be rendered by the English word which it generated, "sophisticated."

On **the *Sh'khinah***, God's glorious presence, see numbered paragraph (3) of MJ 1:2–3N.

19–21 General principles concerning the right way to interpret Scripture are set forth here in order to establish the standard against which the false prophets of Chapter 2 may be judged.

19 Kefa had **the prophetic Word** set forth by the writers of the *Tanakh* concerning God's "valuable and superlatively great promises" (v. 4) **made very certain**. First, his direct experience with Yeshua and his glory (vv. 16–18) made him confident. And second, since many of the words of the Prophets concerning the Messiah had already been fulfilled at Yeshua's first coming, Kefa could be certain that the rest would be fulfilled at his second coming (this Kefa had known long before; see Ac 3:21). The import of Kefa's having "the prophetic Word made very certain" is that he, not the false teachers of Chapter 2, is the one whose interpretations of prophecy should be trusted.

"**The Day**" refers to Yeshua's second coming (compare Ro 13:12, 1 Ke 2:12), but there is also an underlying hint at the Day of Judgment (3:10, Yd 6). As **the Day dawns**, then, **the Morning Star** is Yeshua the Messiah. This seems to be a reference to Numbers 24:17, "There shall come a star out of Jacob," taken in Judaism as pointing to the Messiah (for example, Testament of Levi 17:3, Testament of Judah 24:1–5). Rabbi Akiva acclaimed the leader of the Second Rebellion (132–135 C.E.), Bar-Kosiba, as the Messiah and called him Bar-Kochva, "Son of a Star," in allusion to this verse. In the twelfth century the *Ramban* (Nachmanides) wrote:

> "'There shall step forth a star out of Jacob.' Because the Messiah will gather together the dispersed of Israel from all the corners of the earth, Balaam compares him [metaphorically] to a star that passes through the firmament from the ends of heaven, just as it is said about [the Messiah]: 'and behold, there came

with the clouds of heaven one like unto a son of man,' etc. [Daniel 7:13]." (*Commentary on the Torah*, translated by C. B. Chavel, Volume IV, p. 283)

See also Malachi 3:20(4:2), Mt 2:2&N, Lk 1:78, Rv 22:16.

20 **No prophecy of Scripture** (i.e., the *Tanakh*; but see 3:16&N) **is to be interpreted by an individual on his own**. Or: "No prophecy of Scripture comes from an individual's own decision" — but this rendering makes v. 20 say the same thing as v. 21 and does not contribute to the ground being laid in vv. 19–21 for the argument against the false prophets of Chapter 2.

A prophecy of Scripture must be interpreted not on the basis of thoughts rooted in a person's old nature, such as those of the false prophets of Chapter 2, but on the basis of what the Holy Spirit makes clear about its meaning, since Yeshua sent the Spirit to guide believers into the truth (Yn 16:13). But since he sent the Holy Spirit to the believers as a community, be cautious of those who offer "the true word" but avoid subjecting their opinions to the scrutiny of other believers. Much false teaching both in Kefa's day and our own arises from people's developing their own idiosyncratic interpretations, supposedly hearing the Holy Spirit, but without examining other views or admitting that their own could be mistaken. Prophecies are not to be subjected to eisegesis (putting one's own preconceived ideas in), but to exegesis (getting the writer's ideas out). Moreover, the exegete ought not to make interpretation of prophecy a vehicle for self-aggrandizement and self-exaltation, gaining a reputation at the expense of perverting Holy Writ.

21 **Never has a prophecy come as a result of human willing**. This is why prophecy should not be interpreted on the basis of one's own preconceptions, one's own willing and thinking (v. 20). Just as **people moved by the *Ruach HaKodesh*** (compare Ac 1:16, MJ 1:1) **spoke a message from God**, so people moved by the *Ruach HaKodesh* should interpret the message from God.

CHAPTER 2

1–23 This chapter is the first century's picture of the "sleaze factor" at work. Then, just as now, immoral and greedy persons misled God's people by assuming the role of teachers and had a devastating effect on the morale and reputation of the Messianic Community. Compare Yd 4–16.

1 **But among the people there were also false prophets**. Kefa continues the parallel begun in 1:20 between the time when he was writing and the time of the Prophets.

3 **Fabricated stories**. See 1:16.

4–8 Compare Yd 5–7, also 1 Ke 3:19–20.

4 **The angels who sinned** are the *b'nei-ha'elohim* ("sons of God" or "sons of angels"; Genesis 6:2), also called *nefilim* ("fallen ones"; Genesis 6:4), who fell from heaven, which was "their proper sphere" (Yd 6), and "came in to the daughters of men" (Genesis 6:2, 4). But now they are "imprisoned spirits" (1 Ke 3:19&N), whom God has **put… in gloomy dungeons lower than Sh'ol to be held for judgment**, "in darkness, bound with everlasting chains for the Judgment of the Great Day" (Yd 6). In these descriptions Kefa and Y'hudah are not using their imagination, but drawing on elaborations of the Genesis narrative which can be found in earlier Jewish writings, such as 1 Enoch, written in the first century B.C.E.:

> "…the Watchers called and said to me, 'Enoch, scribe of righteousness, go, declare to the Watchers of heaven who have left the high heaven, the holy eternal place, and have defiled themselves with women, and have done as the children of people do, and have taken for themselves wives: "You have caused great defilement on the earth. You will have neither peace nor forgiveness of sin…."' Enoch went and said [to the leader of the rebellious Watchers]: ''Aza'zel, you will have no peace. A severe judgment has gone forth against you: they will put you in bonds.'
>
> "…the Lord said to Rafa'el, 'Bind 'Aza'zel hand and foot, and cast him into the darkness: make a pit in the desert in Duda'el, throw him in it, hurl rough jagged rocks on him, cover him with darkness, let him dwell there for ever, and cover his face so that he won't be able to see light. On the day of the great judgment he will be cast into the fire.'"(1 Enoch 12:4–13:1, 10:4–6)

5–9 On **the Flood** see Genesis 6–9; on **S'dom, 'Amora** and **Lot**, see Genesis 19, and compare Yd 7. In urging his hearers to be alert and ready for **the Day of Judgment**, Yeshua too used the cautionary examples of the Flood (Mt 24:37–39), Sodom and Gomorrah (Mt 10:15, 11:23–24; Lk 10:12), and both together (Lk 17:26–30). Kefa makes further use of the example of the Flood at 3:3–7 below; 1 Ke 3:20 and MJ 11:7 also mention it. None of these passages requires the reader to take a stand on whether the Flood is historical or legendary.

10b–13a See Yd 8–10 and Yd 9N.

15–16 **Bil'am Ben-B'or** (Balaam, son of Beor) was bribed by Balak, the king of Moab, to "curse Jacob and denounce Israel" (Numbers 22:6, 23:7) when they were on their way to the Promised Land; but Bil'am was **rebuked for his sin** when God spoke through his donkey (Numbers 22:22ff.). Bil'am then spoke a blessing on Israel which included the Messianic promise of the "star out of Jacob" (Numbers 24:17; see above, 1:19N).

According to the Mishna,

> "The characteristics of the *talmidim* of Bil'am the wicked are an evil eye [i.e., stinginess or greed; see Mt 6:22–23&N], a haughty spirit and a proud soul…. [They] inherit Gey-Hinnom and descend to the pit of destruction." (Avot 5:19)

For more on Bil'am see Rv 2:14N.

17 Compare Yd 12–13.

Waterless springs promise good but are in fact useless. They falsely raise our hopes and then deliver nothing. Compare Jeremiah 2:13:

> "For my people have committed two evils: they have forsaken me the fountain of living waters, and they have hewed for themselves cisterns, broken cisterns, that can hold no water."

20 **Their latter condition has become worse than their former**. Compare Mt 12:43–45, MJ 6:4–8.

21 See Rv 1:3N and references there.

22 **"The pig washed itself, only to wallow in the mud!"** This must be a proverb familiar to Kefa's readers. Compare the Jewish expression, "to enter the *mikveh* while [still] touching the corpse." Though the ritual bath can cleanse ceremonial impurity, immersion is ineffective if one continues holding onto the source of the defilement.

CHAPTER 3

1 **This** is the **second letter**, 1 Kefa, of course, being the first. **Reminders**. See 1:12–13.

2 **Predictions** (literally, "words spoken previously") **of the holy prophets**, either those of the *Tanakh* or recent New Covenant prophets (Ac 11:27&N). The rest of the chapter suggests the latter, even though at 1:19 "the prophetic Word" refers to the *Tanakh*.

Kefa regards **the command given by the Lord and Deliverer through your emissaries** as having as much authority over believers' lives as **the predictions of the holy prophets**, as is also clear from v. 15&N.

3–9 Kefa answers **scoffers** who, scorning the believer's conviction that Yeshua will return, ask, **"Where is this promised 'coming' of his**, heralding the Day of Judgment when the false teachers of Chapter 2 will be judged? **For... everything goes on just as it has since the beginning of creation**." A modern group of **scoffers** are persons who adhere to scientism, the system of thought which places science on a pedestal and effectively converts it into a theology. According to scientism the laws of nature are given and fixed, and God will not, or cannot, interfere with them or intervene in human history. Such a statement transgresses the limits of what science itself has a right to say; and responsible scientists do not abuse their profession to spread such ideas, even if they hold them. According to the Bible, the "laws of science" are not forever fixed but are merely a current description of how God currently runs the universe. Science can discover present patterns of uniformity but can say nothing about whether God might suddenly change them. For example, any scientific argument for the evolution of man from lower animals must presuppose God's nonintervention; but science, by its own standards, has no way to know whether God did or did not create the human species by fiat. Nor can science determine whether it is a **fact that it was by God's Word that long ago there**

were heavens (see MJ 11:3 and its note, which compares the "Big Bang" theory of cosmological origins), **and there was land which arose out of water and existed between the waters, and that by means of these things** — God's Word and water — **the world of that time was flooded with water and destroyed** (contrast v. 7, where the means are God's Word and fire). In vv. 5–6 the Greek allows other renderings: People don't **overlook the fact** but "wilfully forget," not that it was **by means of these *things***, but that it was "through these [evil] ones," the people who lived before the Flood (2:5), that **the world of that time was... destroyed.**

Feelings run strong on issues of this kind. People **want so much to be right** that they **overlook the fact** which might make them alter their opinions — the wish is father to the thought. But the reason people feel so strongly is not mainly out of intellectual conviction but because they are **following their own desires**. They have a vested interest, usually in some sort of sin. A truly intellectual conviction can be countered with intellectual arguments and influenced by objective evidence. When people let their desires and feelings control their thinking, only a confrontation with those desires and feelings offers any prospect of attitudinal change. It is these the Psalmist refers to when he writes, "The fool has said in his heart, 'There is no God'"(Psalms 14:1, 53:1).

It was by God's Word, Yeshua (Yn 1:1, 14), **that long ago there were heavens and... land which arose out of water** (Genesis 1:6–13, Yn 1:3, Co 1:16, MJ 1:2). **By that same Word**, Yeshua, **the present heavens and earth, having been preserved, are being kept**, since it is he who "holds everything together" (Co 1:17, MJ 1:3). On the Day of the Lord they will come to an end (vv. 10–12), to be replaced by a "new heavens and a new earth" (v. 13, Rv 21:1–8&N).

But in this passage God as Creator is a less important theme than God as Judge. The **present heavens and earth... are being kept for fire until the Day of Judgment** (v. 7), which is the same as the Day of the Lord (v. 10&N) and the Day of God (v. 12). The **scoffers,... following their own desires**, do not *want* Yeshua or **this promised "coming" of his** (vv. 3–4), because they know that when it happens he will judge them. Kefa holds out for these people their one and only hope, repentance: **The Lord... is patient...; for it is not his purpose that anyone should be destroyed, but that everyone should turn from his sins** (v. 9).

Water... fire. God promised never again to destroy the world by water (Genesis 9:15); but he also said, "Behold, *Adonai* will come with fire" (Isaiah 66:15). Immersion in water and fire are also contrasted at Mt 3:11–12&N.

Yeshua's second coming is intimated in the *Tanakh*. Isaiah 53:7–9 speaks of the Messiah's death: "Like a lamb brought to be slaughtered.... He was cut off out of the land of the living.... For they made his grave among the wicked, his tomb among the rich." But afterwards, in vv. 10–12, even though he has died, "he shall see his seed, he shall prolong his days, and the purpose of *Adonai* shall prosper in his hand.... Surely I will give him a portion with the great." Also Psalms 8 and 110 are shown in the New Testament to be speaking of the Messiah's return to earth after sitting at God's right hand until his enemies are brought into subjection beneath his feet (Mt 22:41–46; 1C 15:23–27; MJ 2:5–17, 7:17–8:1).

In the New Testament, all four Gospels report Yeshua's own promise to return (Mt 24:3, 27–30; Mk 14:61–62; Lk 21:27; Yn 14:3), as does Rv 22:7, 12, 20. As he left the Mount of Olives to be in heaven, two angels promised his *talmidim*, "This

Yeshua, who has been taken away from you into heaven, will come back to you in just the same way as you saw him go into heaven" (Ac 1:11). All the New Testament letter-writers teach his second coming — Sha'ul (1 Th 4:13–18; 2 Th 2:1, 8–9; compare below, vv. 15–16), the author of Messianic Jews (MJ 9:28), Ya'akov (Ya 5:7–8), Yochanan (1 Yn 2:28), Y'hudah (Yd 21) and Kefa (here).

Moreover, the expectation was not only that he would come back, but that he would do so "soon" (Rv 22:6), even "very soon" (Rv 22:7). This is why Sha'ul could write, "There is not much time left;... the present scheme of things in this world won't last much longer" (1C 7:29, 31). When Kefa penned this letter, believers had waited thirty-five years or so for Yeshua to return; today the delay has been nearly two thousand years. Did prophecy fail?

Kefa's negative answer, intended not only to refute the false prophets but also to comfort his **dear friends**, is that **with the Lord, one day is like a thousand years and a thousand years like one day**. This idea, taken from Psalm 90:4, is not a mere *deus ex machina* for shoring up a mistaken prediction. Rather, it has deep roots in Judaism, specifically in connection with dating the Messianic Era. A famous example is found in the Talmud, in Tractate Sanhedrin:

> "Rav Kattina said, 'The world will exist for six thousand years, then for one thousand it will be desolate, as it is said, "The Lord alone will be exalted in that day"' (Isaiah 2:11). Abaye said, 'It will be desolate two thousand, as it is said, "After two days he will revive us; on the third day, he will raise us up, and we will live in his sight"' (Hosea 6:2).
>
> "It has been taught in accordance with Rav Kattina, 'Just as every seventh year is a year of *sh'mittah* [letting the land lie fallow], so it is with the world: one thousand years out of seven are to be fallow — as proved by the following three texts taken together [in which the key word is "day"]: "The Lord alone will be exalted in that day" (Isaiah 2:11); "A psalm and song for the day of *Shabbat*" (Psalm 92:1), meaning the day that is entirely *Shabbat;* and, "For a thousand years in your sight are but as yesterday when it is past"' (Psalm 90:4).
>
> "The school of Eliyahu teaches: 'The world exists for six thousand years — two thousand of them *tohu* ["void"]; two thousand, *Torah*; and two thousand, the era of the Messiah. But because of our numerous iniquities many of these years have been lost.' "(Sanhedrin 97a–97b)

According to Jewish tradition, there were 2,000 years without *Torah* — spiritual *tohu* — between the creation of Adam and the time when Abraham, aged 52, began convincing people to worship the one true God.

The second 2,000 years supposedly lasted from then until 172 years after the destruction of the second Temple, that is, until 244 C.E. That was the year 4000 by the Jewish calendar, but no significant event in Jewish history took place then. However, biblical chronology has a number of uncertainties, so that not all agree that the Jewish calendar accurately dates the biblical beginning of creation. James Ussher, Archbishop of Armagh, Ireland, writing in the 17th century, placed the creation according to Genesis at 4004 B.C.E., exactly 4,000 years before Yeshua's supposed birthdate (see Mt 2:1N).

Concerning the third 2,000 years, a footnote to this passage in the Soncino English edition of the Talmud says, "Messiah will come within that period. He should have come at the beginning of [it]; the delay is due to our sins." It should be obvious that the Messiah who "should have come at the beginning" of the last 2,000-year period is in fact Yeshua, who did come then. The delay is not of his coming but of our recognizing him, and this delay is indeed "due to our sins." For more on predicting when the Messiah is to come, see Mt 24:36N.

Yet, as Kefa points out, there is a delay in his second coming; and this is, in a different sense, "due to our sins": **The Lord is not slow in keeping his promise...; on the contrary, he is patient with you; for it is... his purpose that everyone should turn from his sins**, literally, "that everyone should come to repentance" (see Mt 3:2N). On the Lord's patience in this regard, compare Ro 2:4&N.

For more on the End Times generally see vv. 10&N, 12&N; Mt 24:1–39&NN; 1 Th 4:15b–17N; Rv 1:1N. For more on the Millennium in the New Testament and in Judaism see Rv 4:1N, 20:2–7&N.

10 Even though the second coming seems delayed, nevertheless **the Day of the Lord will come like a thief**, says Kefa. Like Sha'ul teaching on the same subject (1 Th 5:1–8) and Yochanan reporting his vision (Rv 3:3, 16:15), he alludes to Yeshua's own words about the suddenness of his reappearance (Mt 24:35–44, Lk 12:35–49).

The Day of the Lord is spoken of frequently in the *Tanakh*; examples include Isaiah 13:9, 61:2; Jeremiah 46:10; Joel 1:15; Zephaniah 1:14–16; Malachi 3:2, 3:23(4:5)). There it is called the Day of *Adonai*, a day of judgment and vengeance, but also a day of salvation and comfort. The role of Yeshua the Messiah on that Day is taught in the New Testament (Yn 5:22–27, Ac 17:31, Ro 2:14–16&N), so that the Day of the Lord can as well refer to Yeshua as to the Father (since *kurios* can mean either "Lord" or "*Adonai*"; see Mt 1:20&N, 7:21&N).

The cataclysmic picture of that Day which Kefa gives here and in vv. 7, 12 is founded in the *Tanakh*. **The heavens will disappear** (Isaiah 13:10, 34:4; Ezekiel 32:7–8; Joel 3:4(2:31), 4:15(3:15); compare Mt 24:29, Rv 6:12–13) **with a roar** (Isaiah 29:5b–6), **the elements will melt and disintegrate, and the earth and everything in it will be burned up** (Isaiah 30:30, 66:15–16; Micah 1:4; Nahum 1:5–6; Zephaniah 1:18, 3:8; Psalm 97:3, 5). Compare also similar pictures in such Jewish writings, dating from before Yeshua, as Sibylline Oracles 3:83–92, 4:171–182; 1 Enoch 1:6, 52:6–9; 4 Ezra 13:10–11.

Both Kefa and Sha'ul agree that the purpose of prophecy is not to titillate the ears of believers (2 Ti 4:3), or to make them speculate about "times and dates" (1 Th 5:1), but to make them ask **what kind of people** they **should... be**, and to answer, with Kefa, that they **should lead holy and godly lives**. Many believers preoccupy themselves with future events, seemingly enjoying the proclamation of apocalyptic doom as an escape from the command to concern themselves with living holy lives in the *'olam hazeh* ("this world"), rather than pie in the sky in the *'olam haba* ("the world to come").

12 **As you wait for the day of God** (which is the same as the "Day of the Lord," v. 10&N)

and work to hasten its coming. The idea of working to hasten the coming of the Messiah is deeply rooted in Jewish tradition, but it often surprises both Jews and Christians to find the concept in the New Testament as well. Many Christians would be glad to sit back passively and **wait for the Day of God**; it is hard to motivate them to **work to hasten its coming**; and learning they are supposed to surprises them. On the other hand, Jews who think of the New Testament as fatalistic and otherworldly are equally amazed to discover Kefa's orientation toward action and ethical behavior ("You should lead godly and holy lives," v. 11). Moreover, there is reciprocity: not only are we to hasten the End, but, as we learn from MJ 10:25b ("And let us do this all the more as you see the Day approaching"), the End hastens us!

On the present verse Yechiel Lichtenstein writes:

> "Kefa says the believers can hasten the Day. In the Talmud compare Sanhedrin 98a, which applies Isaiah 60:22 ('I, *Adonai*, will hasten it in its time') to the Messiah's coming:
>
> > 'Rabbi Y'hoshua ben-L'vi pointed out a contradiction — "hasten it" implies *before*, not "*in* its time." Rabbi Y'hoshua's solution: God means, "If they deserve him, I will hasten it; but if they do not deserve him, his coming will be in its time." ' "

See Mt 21:2–7N and MJ 3:7N for related citations from Sanhedrin 98a. Lichtenstein continues,

> "Kefa also says in vv. 4–10 that at the second coming of the Messiah, heaven and earth will pass away. Yet in Revelation 20–21 there are a thousand years between the Messiah's coming and the remaking of heaven and earth, during which time he has to reign as king in Jerusalem." (*Commentary to the New Testament*, *ad loc.*)

The reason for the discrepancy is that Kefa is less concerned than Revelation 19–21 to set out End-Time events in chronological sequence. See 1 Th 4:15b–17N.

What **work** can believers do to **hasten** the Messiah's **coming**? Here is the answer of Joseph Hoffman Cohn, son of the founder of the American Board of Missions to the Jews (now Chosen People Ministries), written in 1921:

> "Many of His true children are earnestly looking for the early return of our Lord, and they are putting forth every effort to hasten His coming. To all such we would say that there is no surer way of hastening this blessed fulfillment of His promise than by evangelizing the Jews. The reasons for this are many, but… of special interest here… [is that] it was only to Jews that our Lord said in Matthew 23:39, 'For I say unto you, Ye shall not see me henceforth, till ye shall say, Blessed is he that cometh in the name of the Lord.' Which, if we interpret Scripture aright, means to us that whenever the Jews as a nation accept Him as Lord and Savior, then He will come. And who does not long for His appearing? And who does not realize that unless He does soon appear, this world

> is doomed to a horrible cataclysm the like of which has not been duplicated in history?" (Reprinted in *The Chosen People*, June 1984, p. 12)

In non-Messianic Judaism, "hastening the end" has a somewhat different flavor. According to Chapter 7 of Raphael Patai's *The Messiah Texts*, it means forcing God's hand. A number of legends recounted there tell how *Hasidim* and Kabbalists impatient for the Messiah tried to compel him to come by means of "the powers of saintliness they had acquired by years of ruthless mortification of their flesh." In each case, of course, they were prevented — by death, by Satan, or by some sin which they committed.

In one of these legends — as retold by Zalman Shazar, third president of the State of Israel — the 14th-century rabbi Joseph Della Reina ("of the Queen") attempts, with the help of the prophet Elijah, to destroy Satan (disguised as a black dog) by using God's secret names. But he doesn't follow Elijah's instructions to the letter, and thus fails in his task. Later he goes astray, having illicit sexual relations with none other than the Queen of France (hence his name), and ultimately commits suicide. (*The Messiah Texts*, pp. 68–73)

In a story by the famous Hasidic teacher, Rabbi Nachman of Bratslav (1772–1811), Satan, disguised as a merchant, prevents a rabbi's son from meeting with a great *tzaddik* (holy man). In the end the son dies. The rabbi again encounters the merchant, who tells him, "Now I have dispatched your son.... Had he and the *tzaddik* met and joined forces, the Messiah would have come." (See also Ya 5:16N.)

Other stories tell of Hasidic rabbis who decide during their lifetime that they will refuse to enter heaven after death unless the Messiah agrees to come.

> "Since, in the Hasidic world view, merits must without fail get their reward, such a refusal on the part of a great saint causes an intolerable disruption in the heavenly order of things, which must instantly be remedied by letting the Messiah commence his mission. But this pious blackmail, too, is doomed to failure. 'Those in heaven' manage to play a trick on the soul of the saint and entice it to enter heaven against its will." (*The Messiah Texts*, p. 66)

In still other stories, such as the one quoted in Lk 15:15N, *hasidim* seeking to hasten the end are given the opportunity of appearing personally before the Holy One, blessed be he, to present their petition; but instead of seizing the moment to request redemption they ask for lesser benefits.

Also in the category of "hastening the end" is the tradition that if the whole Jewish people would keep *Shabbat* properly just once, the Messiah would come. It is based on a passage in Jeremiah:

> "...if you diligently hearken to me, says *Adonai*, to bring no burden in through the gates of this city on *Shabbat*, but instead hallow *Shabbat* by not doing work, then into the gates of this city shall enter kings and princes sitting on the throne of David...." (Jeremiah 17:24–25)

And finally, again the Talmud:

"Rav said, 'All the forecast dates [for redemption] have come and gone. Now the matter [of when the Messiah will come] depends only on repentance and good deeds.'"(Sanhedrin 97b).

13 New heavens and a new earth. See Revelation 21–22 for a description of them.

15–16 This is the only place in the New Testament where one of its authors refers to another of its authors as such. In fact, with the phrase, "**the other Scriptures**," Kefa gives Sha'ul's letters the status of Holy Writ.

Kefa commends **Sha'ul** as **our dear brother**; there is no conflict between them, some nineteenth-century scholars to the contrary notwithstanding. It is possible, however, says Kefa, to **distort** what Sha'ul writes. The most common distortion is in the direction of antinomianism; this happens especially when Sha'ul's letters are read apart from their *Tanakh* and Gospels-Acts background. Much of this commentary is occupied with correcting some of these distortions.

18 The final advice is to **keep growing in the grace and knowledge**, not of Sha'ul (vv. 15–16) or Kefa (1:13–19), but **of our Lord and Deliverer, Yeshua the Messiah**. Compare 1C 1:12&N.

THE FIRST LETTER FROM YESHUA'S EMISSARY YOCHANAN:

1 YOCHANAN (1 JOHN)

CHAPTER 1

1–4 This prologue, like the one the same author wrote for his Gospel, seems to be composed as poetry; see Yn 1:1–18&N. **The Word**, who **existed from the beginning**, is **Yeshua the Messiah** (Yn 1:1–18&NN). Believers (**you... us**) have **fellowship** (Greek *koinônia,* "commonness, communion, community") with God (**the Father... his Son**; compare Yochanan 17).

1:5–2:2 This section deals with the relationship of a believer both to sin in general (what theologians call the "sinful nature of man") and also to particular sins. These verses give a threefold message: (1) There is an absolute call to put away sin. (2) It is impossible to live without sinning. (3) Nevertheless, one has no right to give up the battle against sin. The following famous quotation from the Mishna is appropriately cited in connection with many New Testament passages, but I have saved it for this one:

> "He [Rabbi Tarfon, 2nd century C.E.] used to say, 'You are not obligated to complete the task, but you are still not free from working at it.'"(Avot 2:16)

5–10 Because **there is no darkness** in God, **if we claim to have fellowship** (v. 3) with him but **are walking in darkness**, then **we are lying** with our words and also with our actions (**not living out the truth**). Only when we let the **light** of **God** shine into our whole life, permitting even its secrets to be judged by him, can we be purified from our sinful habits and be made more holy.

As a rule, people do not want to let in God's light (Yn 3:19–21), but instead of saying so, they claim they don't need it. Yochanan gives two examples: **If we claim not to have sin**, not to have a nature which tends to sin, not to have a *yetzer ra'* ("evil inclination"; see Ro 5:12–21N) ever rearing its ugly head, **we are deceiving ourselves, and the truth is not in us.** Likewise, **If we claim we have not been sinning**, that our acts have been above reproach, and we have not committed actual sins, **we are making him out to be a liar, and his Word is not in us**. Either of these claims, if true, would provide an excuse for not letting God judge our inmost heart, in accordance with the prayers of Psalms 19:13–15(12–14), 139:23–24.

In Yochanan's day it was especially the Gnostics who, misusing Romans 6 and 8, said that since the Messianic believer has the Spirit of the Messiah in him, he cannot sin any more. Yochanan agrees that the Spirit of the Messiah cleanses us and gives us strength to overcome sin, in keeping with Ezekiel 36:27, "I will put my Spirit in you and cause you to follow my statutes, and you will keep my judgments and do them." Nevertheless, we still commit sin, as v. 10 reminds us; this follows along with what is said about the days of the Messiah in Jeremiah 31:29(30), "Everyone will die for his own iniquity." Isaiah 65:20 too speaks of sinners in the Messianic Era, and in the Lord's Prayer believers are told to pray, "Forgive us what we have done wrong" (Mt 6:12).

This is also the answer to the objection raised in the sixteenth century by Rabbi Yitzchak of Troki's *Chizzuk-Emunah*, which says — citing Deuteronomy 30:6, Zephaniah 3:13, Jeremiah 3:17, Ezekiel 36:25–27 — that Yeshua cannot be the Messiah because in the days of the Messiah there will be everlasting righteousness, and iniquity will cease. Eventually this will be the case (Revelation 21–22); but in the present segment of the days of the Messiah there are sinners. Nevertheless, the Messiah "will justify many" (Isaiah 53:12), and by his death he atones for sin (v. 7, 2:2).

The objection that here Yochanan contradicts what he writes at 3:6, 9 ("…no one who remains united with him continues sinning…. No one who has God as his Father keeps on sinning….") is answered in the notes to those verses.

Believers commit sins. They are not to be confronted by self-righteous fellow sinners passing judgment (Mt 7:1–5, Ro 2:1–4) but by God's own Word, which sets the standard for holiness. Then they will not make the mistake of the rich young ruler who asserted that he had kept the Ten Commandments from his youth (Mt 19:20). Instead of deceiving ourselves with excuses we should be **walking in the light** (v. 7), trying to do what pleases God. And we should **acknowledge our sins** as we commit them, even though we do not intend to commit them (v. 9). The Greek word "*omologeô*" ("**acknowledge**, confess") is, literally, "say the same thing." If we say the same thing about our sins as God does, namely, that our sins are truly sinful; and if we have the kind of godly sorrow that leads to repentance (2C 7:10–11); then **the blood**, by which is meant the bloody sacrificial death (Ro 3:25b&N), **of Yeshua** continually **purifies us from all sin**. Our identification with his atoning death (Ro 6:3, Ga 2:20) empowers that death to go on helping us put to death our *yetzer ra'* (Ro 6:16–23, 8:12–13, and Section D of Ro 5:12–21N), which is what we must do if we are to conduct our life the way Yeshua did (2:6). Also, **since he is trustworthy and just** (Ro 3:25–26), **he will forgive** our sins **and purify us from all wrongdoing**. Compare Yn 13:1–17.

Acknowledging of sin, then, as Yochanan uses the term, is not merely a verbal transaction but in every respect the full equivalent of repentance, *t'shuvah* (see Mt 3:1N). The relationship between repentance and blood sacrifice is correctly set forth in these verses. Repentance is the *sine qua non* of forgiveness; with this non-Messianic Judaism agrees, as is clear from the Mishna:

> "A sin-offering and a trespass-offering atone for sins committed wittingly. Death or *Yom-Kippur* atones, provided a person repents. Repentance atones for minor transgressions against the *Torah*'s positive commands and for any transgression against its negative commands; for more serious transgressions repentance suspends punishment until *Yom-Kippur* arrives and atones.
>
> "If a person says, 'I will sin and repent, I will sin and repent,' God will not give him an opportunity to repent! If he says, 'I will sin, and *Yom-Kippur* will atone,'

> then *Yom-Kippur* will not atone! *Yom-Kippur* atones for transgressions from man towards God; but for transgressions between a man and his fellowman, *Yom-Kippur* does not atone until he has conciliated his fellowman.... Rabbi Akiva said, '...Who cleanses you [from your transgressions]? Your Father in heaven, as it is said, "I will sprinkle clean water on you, and you will be clean" (Ezekiel 36:25). And it also says, "*Mikveh-Israel*" [which can be translated either "the hope of Israel," referring to God, or "the ritual-bath of Israel"] (Jeremiah 17:13). Just as the ritual bath cleanses the unclean, so does the Holy One, blessed be he, cleanse Israel.'"(Yoma 8:8–9)

But at the same time that repentance is proclaimed as essential before God can grant forgiveness, the justice of and necessity for a blood sacrifice is clear both from the *Torah* (see Leviticus especially; but also Isaiah 1:16–17, Malachi 3:2–4) and the New Testament (see the book of Messianic Jews especially).

CHAPTER 2

1–2 To avoid the inference from 1:9 that Yochanan condones sin, or supposes that one may intentionally indulge in sin and expect forgiveness, Yochanan specifically says, **I am writing you these things so that you won't sin**. Compare Ro 3:8, 6:1ff.; and the Mishna cited in 1:5–10N.

Some Bible-believers are so aware of the evil of sin that when confronted with its inevitability they can neither cope nor advise. Not so the New Testament. Yochanan wants the best from his readers (**so that you won't sin**), but nevertheless prepares them for less than the best (**but if anyone does sin**).

The *Tzaddik*, literally, "the Righteous One." See Mt 13:17N on the concept of the *tzaddik* in Judaism.

Who pleads our cause with the father, as stated in MJ 7:25.

He is the *kapparah*, "atonement, expiation, propitiation"; the Greek word is "*ilasmos*," related to "*ilastêrion*" at Ro 3:25&N; see also 1:5–10N above. On *Yom-Kippur* (the Day of Atonement) it is through Yeshua, **the *kapparah*** (atonement) that sins are forgiven. On *Yom-Kippur* Jews who have not yet accepted Yeshua into their lives may understandably be uncertain as to whether God has truly forgiven their sins.

3–6 Two ways not to have the truth: (1) to claim not to have sin (1:8), and (2) to say "**I know him**" but not **obey his commands** (as Ya 2:14–26 teaches). In the *Tanakh* the word "know" can mean "have intimate experience"; here "knowing Yeshua" means having intimate spiritual experience with him, to the degree that one obeys his commands from the heart. Anything less is not true knowledge; there is a difference between giving mental assent to Yeshua's Messiahship and knowing him. Elsewhere Yochanan reports that Yeshua said, "If you love me, you will keep my commands," and "If you keep my commands, you will stay in my love" (Yn 14:15, 15:10; compare Yn 14:21, 15:14). **This is how we are sure that we are united with him**, and this answers the question raised by the "eternal security of the believer" in MJ 6:4–6N.

7–8 Yechiel Lichtenstein, observing that Yeshua's **command** to love (v. 10) is both **old** and **new**, notes that while Moses commanded, "Love your neighbor as yourself" (Leviticus 19:18), we do not learn from this to love our friend to the point of being willing to die for him.

Indeed, Rabbi Akiva taught the opposite, that our own life comes before our friend's life. He gives the example of two men walking in the desert with water sufficient for one to survive if he drinks all of it, but both will die if they split it between them. Akiva concluded that the owner of the water should drink it, because you should love your neighbor *as* yourself, not *more* than yourself.

But our Lord said, "I am giving you a new command: that you keep on loving each other. In the same way that I have loved you, you are also to keep on loving each other" (Yn 13:34). Our Lord's love was to the point of dying for us (Mk 10:45, Ro 5:8), and we are to love each other "in the same way." So this commandment is both old, since Moses already said to love your neighbor, and new, enjoining us "to lay down our lives for the brothers" (3:16).

9 **Brother**. Here and throughout this book, "fellow member of God's people."

12–14 **Children... young people... fathers** — believers of increasing degrees of maturity in the faith. In other words, Yochanan has something to say to everyone.

For his sake, literally, "for the sake of his name" or "by his name."

15–17 Because his readers have experienced the positive results of faith (vv. 12–14) and therefore have an alternative to this world's order of things, Yochanan can tell them, **Do not love the world or the things of the world** (compare Yn 17:14–19).

The three main kinds of temptations were present already in the Garden of Eden, as is clear from Genesis 3:6: "When the woman saw that the tree was good for food" (**the desires of the old nature** or "flesh," Ro 7:5N), "and that it was a delight to the eyes" (**the desires of the eyes**), "and a tree to be desired to make one wise" (**the pretensions of life**), "she took of the fruit and ate." Satan later used the same temptations with Yeshua, but he resisted them (Mt 4:1–11&NN, MJ 4:14–16&N). Yochanan's readers and we are to do the same.

18–19 **An anti-Messiah** or "antichrist" **is coming**. See 2 Th 2:3N on the Man of Lawlessness and his role in the drama of End-Time history; see also Revelation 12–13. Yochanan is less concerned with this unique anti-Messianic figure than with the practical danger to believers from the **many anti-Messiahs** who **went out from us, but they weren't part of us**, who deny that Yeshua is the Messiah (vv. 22–23&N) or that he came as a flesh-and-blood human being (4:2–3&N, 2 Yn 7&N). See also 3:7–10N.

20 **You have received the Messiah's anointing**, literally, "you have an anointing"; but, because of the context, this could be rendered, "you have been 'Messiah-ed.'" ***HaKadosh*** ("the Holy One") is understood here to mean God the Father (see Rv 3:7N). Because the Holy One has 'Messiah-ed' you with the real Messiah, Yeshua, **you know all this** about the danger of anti-Messiahs (vv. 18–19).

22–23 This passage invites comparison with Yeshua's own statements — "If you knew me you would know my Father too" (Yn 8:19), "I and the Father are one" (Yn 10:30), and "I am the Way — and the Truth and the Life; no one comes to the Father except through me" (Yn 14:6). All these verses refute the Two-Covenant theory (see Yo 14:6&N), which says that Jews and Christians each have their own independent but equally valid covenants with God, so that Jews do not need to relate to the New Testament or to Yeshua.

Even though Yochanan is writing primarily to Gentile believers, he makes his statement universal: **Everyone**, Jew and Gentile alike, **who denies the Son** — which, in context (v. 22), means denying Yeshua's Messiahship — **is also without the Father**. Thus does the New Testament directly contradict a central tenet of non-Messianic Judaism, that a Jew can have God as his Father while rejecting Yeshua. On the contrary, it is **the person who acknowledges the Son** who **has the Father as well**, as taught in Yn 14:6, cited above. But **Everyone who denies the Son is also without the Father**. Nothing could be clearer.

Ecumenical dialogue which attempts to overlook this basic contradiction between non-Messianic Judaism on the one hand, and Messianic Judaism and Christianity on the other, must ignore, distort or defuse this verse. Such dialogue will be built on a facile and superficial bowdlerization of New Testament faith, and any agreement emerging from it will necessarily have sidestepped what the Bible presents as serious and true answers to the ultimate questions of life. On the other hand, the *dinim* (halakhic decisions) of Rabbi Moshe Feinstein (1895–1986), an American Orthodox Jewish community leader, prohibited Jews from engaging in religious dialogue with Christians at all. In a way, his rulings recognized the irreconcilability of the opposing claims, more honest than denaturing the claims themselves. But recognizing irreconcilability is not the same as recognizing truth, and prohibiting discussion of a subject is not the way to arrive at the truth about it.

Some segments of the Orthodox Jewish community carry this approach even further by prohibiting the reading of the New Testament itself. Obviously, persons who subject themselves to this *din* have less opportunity to learn whether the New Testament's claims are true; although there are instances of Orthodox Jews who happened to come across a New Testament, read it secretly, and discovered it to be not the hateful book of lies it was purported to be, but the book of love and salvation which it is.

27 **You have no need for anyone to teach you**. Both "**you**'s" are plural and refer to the believing community as a whole; there is no ground here for a hyper-individualistic understanding of the Gospel wherein the views of other believers and the gathering of believers together are considered unimportant (see MJ 10:25&N). On "**messianic anointing**" see v. 20N.

CHAPTER 3

2 **We are God's children now** (compare Ro 8:15); **and** although **it has not yet been made clear what we will become**, there are clues, such as Ro 8:29–30. **We do know**, from 1C 15:35–54, **that when he appears** to collect his people (2:28; Yn 14:3; 1 Th 4:13–18), **we will be like him**.

We will see him as he really is (compare 1C 13:12). On this Yechiel Lichtenstein comments:

> "Isaiah 5:28 says, 'For they shall see eye to eye when the Lord shall bring again Zion.' On this basis Yochanan proved here that **when he appears, we will be like him**. The proof that we will see him is that since in the flesh it is impossible to see God — as it is written, 'Man shall not see me and live' (Exodus 33:20) — so it must be that '**we will be like him**' means that we will be comparable with him. And this is so, for we will have a spiritual body like his — as Paul said in Philippians 3:21, 'He will change the bodies we have in this humble state and make them like his glorious body.' Likewise the sages cited in the book, *Mivchar-HaPninim* ("The Choice Pearls") said, 'If I knew, I would be,' that is, 'If I knew God, I would already be like him.'"(*Commentary to the New Testament, ad loc.*)

4 **Sin is** defined as **violation of *Torah***; conversely, "where there is no law, there is also no violation" (Ro 4:15&N).

6, 9 **No one who remains united with him continues sinning.... No one who has God as his Father keeps on sinning.... That is, he cannot continue sinning.** The Greek verb in the present tense, as used here, implies ongoing action. A number of English versions (among them KJV, the New English Bible, and the Jerusalem Bible) confuse readers by seeming to imply that believers are exempt from sin. For example, the Revised Standard Version: "No one who abides in him sins.... No one born of God commits sin; ...and he cannot sin."

Yochanan is not saying that once a person confesses faith in Yeshua he will never again commit sin; this is already clear from 1:5–2:2. On the contrary, his point is that a believer should never intend to sin, that he should never be a habitual sinner, that he should not continue to reserve for himself an area of life devoted to sinful practices. Instead of being defensive and self-excusing, he should acknowledge his sins (1:9) and renounce them. He should not exempt any part of his life from continuous self-scrutiny.

No one who has God as his Father keeps on sinning, because the seed planted by God remains in him. "The seed planted by God" is, literally, "his seed." It refers to the seed of the Gospel (Mt 13:1–23), the once-for-all spiritual awareness of who God is and what God wants from his human creatures. The context cannot justify interpreting "his seed" as not God's seed but the person's own seed; from this error spring pagan-style heresies demanding sexual asceticism.

7–10 **Don't let anyone deceive you. Everyone who does not continue doing what is right** and does not **keep loving his brother is not from God**, but **from the Adversary**, Satan. The anti-Messiahs (2:19) are such deceivers (4:2); what they preach may sound good, but their actions belie their words. Yeshua promised that false Messiahs and false prophets would come and deceive "even the chosen, if possible" (Mt 24:23–26&N), but "you will recognize them by their fruit" (Mt 7:15–20).

8 The first four editions of the *JNT* inadvertantly omitted the last half of the verse, which reads: "It was for this very reason that the son of God appeared, to destroy these doings of the Adversary."

12 See Genesis 4:1–15 and MJ 11:6N.

14 **We have passed from** spiritual **death to** spiritual **life**. Romans 8:6 explains what this means: "Having one's mind controlled by the old nature is death, but having one's mind controlled by the Spirit is life and *shalom*." The proof of our having passed from death to life is not in our beliefs and professions, but in the fact that **we keep loving the brothers**.

Is still under the power of death, literally, "remains in the death."

15–18 With v. 15 compare Mt. 5:21–26. With vv. 17–18 compare Ya 2:14–17. Yochanan, like all the New Testament writers, retains the customary Jewish emphasis on the importance of deeds. While Ya'akov speaks of deeds as necessary expressions of faith, Yochanan stresses deeds as necessary expressions of love. Similarly Sha'ul at Ga 5:6.

19–21 Our consciences can be misguided (1C 8:7–13), but if in fact we are loving our brothers with deeds of kindness, and not merely with our feelings, then we can quiet our consciences.

With these verses compare Psalm 139:23–24:

> "Search me, O God, and know my heart! Try me and know my thoughts!
> See if there is any wicked way in me, and lead me in the everlasting way!"

23 **The person and power**, literally, "the name." See Mt 28:19N; Ac 2:38N, 3:16N.

CHAPTER 4

1 **Don't trust every spirit. On the contrary, test the spirits to see whether they are from God** (compare 1 Th 5:19–22). This is an important principle for our age. After years of having lost touch with the spiritual realm altogether, many people are rediscovering it but have not the discernment to know which spirits "are from God." Not every inner voice or feeling is from God. Some are merely from ourselves, either consequences of being overtired or overwrought, or expressions of our own wishes and fears. Others are truly from the spiritual realm, but, unfortunately, from Satan and his demons, not from God and his angels. By the same token, not every prophet or religious teacher is from God; yet some are.

Verses 2–3 give one criterion by which to **test the spirits**. Another is that "spirits from God" can be expected to give wholehearted support to everything the Bible says.

2 **Every spirit which acknowledges**. Yechiel Lichtenstein writes, "Yochanan did not say 'believes,' because a person cannot be recognized by his thoughts, only by his confession."

Yeshua the Messiah came as a human being. One of the earliest heresies was that of the Docetists, who taught that the Messiah only appeared to be a human being. They considered human flesh on too low a plane for so exalted a figure as the Son of God. This heresy persists explicitly in "theosophy" and in sects based on Eastern religious teachings which speak of "the Christ" as a spiritual entity which, in effect, masqueraded as human but was actually "a far higher being." It persists in a far more widespread fashion in the implicit popular theology of much of the Christian Church, which in emphasizing Yeshua's divinity practically ignores his humanity and portrays him as if he floated around the Holy Land several feet off the ground. For a Jew there may be difficulty in regarding the Messiah as divine, but none whatever in regarding him as human; quite the contrary, the idea of a Messiah who is not a human being is virtually meaningless within the thought-framework of Judaism.

3 **The Anti-Messiah**. See 2:18–19N.

4 **He who is in you is** the *Ruach HaKodesh* (the Holy Spirit). **He who is in the world** is "Your enemy, the Adversary," Satan, who "stalks about like a roaring lion looking for someone to devour" (1 Ke 5:8).

4–6 **False prophets** were promised by Yeshua (Mt 7:15, 24:11, 24; Mk 13:22; Lk 6:26); and see 2 Ke 2:1.

The world listens to them. True then, and true now. Any number of false prophets, basing their pronouncements on their own imaginations (since they are **from the world**), on demonic influences (Ac 13:6–12, 16:16–18) and on what people want to hear (2 Ti 4:3–4) are available to distract and miseducate the public. You can find them in the media, on the streets, in the schools and universities, in many homes, and, yes, in the pulpits.

Among the false prophets whom the world will listen to will be some who have "gone out from us", (2:19), who have at one time or another claimed to be Messianic but have renounced their faith. It is useful to see that Yochanan recognized such a category of people. His advice is to beware of their errors, but not to become preoccupied with trying to win them back (compare 1 Ti 1:20). Rather, we should take as our guideline that **whoever knows God listens to us; whoever is not from God doesn't listen to us**; like Yochanan, we can be satisfied with that.

8 **God is love** (also v. 16). This simple sentence embodies the profoundest religious truth; yet it can be perverted into a callow slogan, in which God is pictured as some sort of floating fuzz-ball of love, accepting everything and judging nothing. This is wrong for two reasons: (1) God's love is not mere feeling, but action, as the familiar Yn 3:16 teaches: God so *loved* the world *that he sent* his only-begotten Son to die for us sinners who needed rescue (compare v. 12 below and 3:16–18 above). (2) God is not only love; he is also justice, pouring out wrath on those who reject his mercy (Ro 1:18–2:16, 3:19–20). Believers must proclaim not only God's love, but also his hatred for sin and his intolerance of human pride that presumes on God: God is not mocked (Ga 6:7).

C. S. Lewis points out an interesting relationship between consciousness of self and love as spoken of in this chapter:

"There is no reason to suppose that self-consciousness, the recognition of a creature by itself as a 'self,' can exist except in contrast with an 'other,' a something which is not the self. It is against an environment, and preferably a social environment, an environment of other selves, that the awareness of Myself stands out. This would raise a difficulty about the consciousness of God if we were mere theists: being Christians, we learn from the doctrine of the Blessed Trinity that something analogous to 'society' exists within the Divine Being from all eternity — that God is Love, not merely in the sense of being the Platonic form of love, but because, within Him, the concrete reciprocities of love exist before all worlds and are thence derived to the creatures." (*The Problem of Pain*, New York: Macmillan Publishing Co., paperback edition 1962, p. 29)

10 ***Kapparah*** ("atonement"). See 2:1–2N.

12 People saw Yeshua, Yeshua as the Word "is" God (Yn 1:1, 14), and yet Yochanan writes that **no one has ever seen God**. New Testament faith is not so simplistic as some make it out to be. See Yn 1:18N.

19–21 These verses come against making religion a matter of "words and talk" instead of "actions" and "reality" (3:17–18&N).

CHAPTER 5

4 **Overcomes the world**, in the sense of 2:16–17.

6 **He is the one who came by means of water and blood, Yeshua the Messiah.** Contrary to Gnostic teachings, he did not "receive the heavenly Christ" upon emerging from the Jordan; rather, it was Yeshua, already the Messiah, who was immersed; and his immersion in **water** symbolized his death and resurrection (see Ro 6:3–6). Likewise, he did not imitate being human but died a real death on the execution-stake; otherwise he would not have atoned for our sin. The **blood**, which is shorthand for Yeshua's death (Ro 3:25bN), witnesses that he is the Son of God (vv. 5, 9–13).

The Spirit bears witness, because the Spirit is the truth. Compare Yn 15:26, 2 Yn 1N.

7–8 **There are three witnesses — the Spirit, the water and the blood — and these three are in agreement.** One cannot claim to accept the witness of the Holy Spirit if one rejects the witness of the water and the blood to the true character of Yeshua, as set forth in v. 6.

The KJV, following the Textus Receptus, has: "For there are three that bear record in heaven, the Father, the Word, and the Holy Ghost: and these three are one. And there are three that bear witness in earth, the spirit, and the water, and the blood: and these three agree in one." Concerning this uniquely clear reference to the Trinity, Bruce Metzger writes: "That these words are spurious and have no right to stand in the New Testament is certain." His reasons: (1) the passage is absent from all but four Greek manuscripts, none earlier than the fourteenth century C.E., (2) it was unknown to the

Greek fathers, who would otherwise have seized on it in the fourth-century Trinitarian controversies, (3) it is not found in versions or quotations of any kind prior to the fourth century, (4) if the passage were original, no good reason can be found to account for its omission, and (5) the passage makes an awkward break in the sense. (*A Textual Commentary on the Greek New Testament*, New York: United Bible Societies, Corrected Edition 1975, pp. 715–717)

9 **God's witness** is given at Mt 3:16–17, 17:5.

12 Compare 2:22–23.

13 **You have eternal life**. You have it already, here and now, **you who keep trusting in the person and power** (literally, "in the name"; see 3:23N) **of the Son of God**. Compare Yn 11:25–26.

14–15 Compare 3:22–23, Mk 11:24.

16 **Sin that does lead to death**. Judaism distinguishes between unconscious sin, for which sacrifices atone, and deliberate, "high-handed" sin, for which only death atones. In the context of this letter, those who deliberately choose not to "keep trusting in the person and power of the Son of God" (v. 13), who do not obey God's commands (vv. 2–3) and who do not love their brothers (4:21), "do not have the life" (v. 12).

A believer's responsibility to **a brother committing a sin** is not only to **ask** God to **give him life**, but also to "go and show him his fault" (Mt 18:15–17), to "set him right, but in a spirit of humility" (Ga 6:1), to "turn" him "from his wandering path" (Ya 5:19–20).

18–20 Three things **we know. Everyone who has God as his Father does not go on sinning** (see 3:6, 9N),… **and the evil one does not touch him**, but he can tempt him. **The whole world lies in the power of the Evil One** (see Lk 4:5–6).

He is the genuine God and eternal life. It is possible to understand this as stating that **Yeshua the Messiah… is the genuine God**. But the verse's purpose does not appear to be declaring the divinity of Yeshua, but setting forth that **the Son of God has come and has given us discernment, so that we may know who** among the various prophets teaching this, that and the other **is genuine**. Not only that, **we are united with the One who is genuine**, that is, we are united with God; and also we are **united with his Son Yeshua the Messiah. He**, not the Evil One (v. 18) but the Genuine One, the One whose Son is Yeshua, **is the genuine God and eternal life**.

21 In the light of the summary of v. 20, the final warning is to **guard yourselves from false gods**, from anything which might distract you from true life, from Yeshua, from God.

THE SECOND LETTER FROM YESHUA'S EMISSARY YOCHANAN:

2 YOCHANAN (2 JOHN)

1 **The Elder** writes in the same style as the writer of 1 Yochanan and the Gospel of Yochanan, so it is assumed that he is Yochanan.

The chosen lady. This seems to be a disguised way of referring to a local congregation, the object being to avoid the scrutiny of the Roman censor. Likewise "your chosen sister" (v. 13). Further evidence is v. 12, "I would rather not use paper and ink."

Truth. Yochanan uses this word five times in the first four verses; it seems to be a coded way of referring to the Gospel.

5 Compare 1 Yn 2:3–4, Yn 13:34–35.

6 **Love** toward God **is this: that we should live according to his commands**. Compare 1 Yn 5:3. **This is the command** — to love one another (v. 5); it includes all the commands (Ro 13:8–10&N, Ga 5:14&N).

7 **Many deceivers have gone out into the world**, as prophesied by Yeshua (Mt 24:5, 11, 23–26; Mk 13:5–6, 21–22; Lk 21:8), by Sha'ul (1 Ti 4:1–3; 2 Ti 3:1–9, 4:3–4), by Kefa (2 Ke 2:1–25), and by Y'hudah (Yd 4–16).

They **do not acknowledge Yeshua the Messiah's coming as a human being**. In 1 Yochanan the writer refers to Yeshua's incarnation, to his having come in the past as a human being (1 Yn 4:2&N, 5:6–8&NN). This verse could refer to the same thing, or to his being incarnated right now while in heaven at God's right hand, or to his future appearance in the flesh, or to all of the above. If Yochanan is speaking about the future, then he is insisting that the Messiah will return to earth bodily and denying the theology which says that Yeshua's coming is to be realized only spiritually in the spreading influence of the Gospel.

Anti-Messiah. See 1 Yn 2:18–19N.

9 **Have God… have both the Father and the Son**. The phrasing implies that **God** includes **both the Father and the Son**. Compare 1 Yn 2:22–23&N.

10–11 **Don't even say "Shalom!"** (on this word see Mt 10:12N) **to him**. This seems a rather extreme form of inhospitality, but v. 11 gives the reason for it. Yechiel Lichtenstein writes,

> "Some say it refers to the **deceivers** of v. 7, who come as brothers but lead people astray with their false teachings. It is not said about any other kind of believer, for everyone is to be received courteously, even pagans." (*Commentary to the New Testament, ad loc.*)

On the one hand, it is appropriate to engage in dialogue with persons who do not acknowledge Yeshua as the Messiah because of conflicting religious commitments, but who are open to the possibility of change. On the other hand, it is wrong to let oneself be strung along by those who claim to honor him but misuse Scripture in the service of "some other supposedly 'Good News,' which is not good news at all" (Ga 1:6–7). Even politeness toward such a self-appointed teacher, deceiver and anti-Messiah (v. 7) can be misinterpreted as support; this is why **the person who says, "Shalom!" to him shares in his evil deeds**.

THE THIRD LETTER FROM YESHUA'S EMISSARY YOCHANAN:

3 YOCHANAN (3 JOHN)

1 **The Elder**. See 2 Yn 1&N.

Gaius. A common name in the New Testament; see 1C 1:14–17N. Because of Yochanan's language in v. 7, I take it that this Gaius was a Messianic Jew.

Truth. Used five times in vv. 1–4, 12; see 2 Yn 1&N.

7 **For the sake of *HaShem***, literally, "for the sake of the name." "*HaShem*," like "*Adonai*" (see Mt 1:20N), is a Jewish euphemism for "*YHVH*," God's personal name. Hence Yochanan means "for the sake of God." Alternatively, "the name" may be a code for "Yeshua," reflecting the danger of referring to him explicitly in a written message (2 Yn 1&N). Also see Ac 5:41&N.

They, Messianic Jews, **went out without accepting anything from the *Goyim***, that is, from pagans; Messianic Gentiles are surely not counted as *Goyim* in this context. And that is as it should be, since the middle wall of partition has been broken down (Ep 2:11–16&NN), and in the Messiah there is neither Jew nor Gentile (Ga 3:28&N). **It is we, therefore, who should support such people**, we Jews and Gentiles who believe in Yeshua. In colloquial language, we should put our money where our mouth is.

9–10 ***Macher***, Yiddish for "big shot, real operator"; see 1 Ke 5:3&N. **Diotrephes** is the perfect example of one. Not only **doesn't** he **recognize** Yochanan's **authority**, but he uses against him the weapon of *lashon hara'*, **gossip** which is not only **spiteful** but **groundless** (see Ya 3:8&N). He won't submit to the other **brothers' authority either**; indeed he will not have anyone around him who accepts the biblical principle of submission to authority (Ep 5:21, MJ 13:17). Unless Diotrephes is stopped, only blind followers will be left in this congregation; and he will turn it into a cult, in the modern sense of the term.

12 **Demetrius** may have given ordinances to the community which were not accepted by Diotrephes and his claque. Or he may have brought the letter to Gaius. According to an early Christian writing, Kefa ordained as first bishop in Philadelphia a man called Demetrius (*Apostolic Constitutions* 7:46).

You know that our testimony is true. Compare Yn 21:24.

13 **I don't want to write with pen and ink**. See 2 Yn 1N.

THE LETTER FROM

Y'HUDAH (JUDE)

1 **Y'hudah** is traditionally understood to be **the brother of Ya'akov** and of Yeshua (Mt 13:55, Mk 6:3, 1C 9:5). If so, he might call himself **a slave of Yeshua the Messiah** in order to avoid exploiting his blood relationship with the Lord. But some scholars think that this Y'hudah is a relatively unknown person who mentioned his better-known brother (also unknown to us) in order to help his readers identify him.

No clue is given as to the intended audience; the heresy described makes Asia Minor a likely destination.

3a **I was busily at work writing to you about the salvation we share**. As with many books mentioned in the *Tanakh* that have not survived, our curiosity about Y'hudah's soteriological treatise cannot be satisfied.

3b–4 **Keep contending earnestly for the faith which was once and for all passed on to God's people**. This, along with v. 17 ("the words spoken… by the emissaries of our Lord"), suggests that the letter was written in the latter part of the first century when "the faith" had begun to crystallize. This use of Greek *pistis* to mean a systematized body of doctrine is unusual (see Ac 3:16N, Ga 2:16cN), but even here we should not limit "the faith" to its intellectual aspects; it includes and implies not only doctrine to be believed, but the entire Messianic way of life to be observed and obeyed (Ro 1:5, "the obedience that comes from trusting").

This is clear from v. 4: what the **ungodly people do** is not merely pass on mistaken information, but **pervert God's grace into a license for debauchery and disown our only Master and Lord**. They no longer recognize Yeshua's right to command obedience but teach instead a perversion of Ro 3:28 and Ep 2:8–9, that a person is considered righteous by God on the ground of professing faith in Yeshua regardless of what sort of works he does. Such an attitude quickly results in debauchery, as well as other kinds of antinomianism, since it removes the ethical and moral component of faith/faithfulness/trusting. In Y'hudah's time various kinds of Gnostics taught in this way; our age too has its share of false teachers (see 2 Ti 4:3–4, 1 Yn 4:4–6&N).

Written about long ago. See vv. 14–15.

5–7 Three examples warn that God does not tolerate those who "pervert God's grace" (vv. 3b–4&N). **The Lord who once delivered the people… later destroyed them**.

Compare Ro 11:19–22, MJ 3:7–4:11&NN. On v. 6 see 2 Ke 2:4&N. On v. 7 see 2 Ke 2:5–9N.

9 Although modern Jewish popular ideology holds that **angels** are a Christian invention reflecting a departure from pure monotheism, actually the *Tanakh* speaks of them often, and post-*Tanakh* Judaism developed an intricate angelology which helps to explain this verse. Moreover, the tantalizing brevity of the *Tanakh*'s account of Moses' death together with the fact that "to this day no one knows where he is buried" (Deuteronomy 34:5–6) gave rise to numerous elaborations (see Rv 6:9&N, 11:3–6&N, and especially 12:7&N).

Here Y'hudah reportedly alludes to a story included in the Testament of Moses, a Jewish writing from the beginning of the first century C.E.; although some portions of it have survived, the relevant ones have not. However, elements of the legend are found elsewhere. Deuteronomy Rabbah 11:10 reports a dispute an hour before Moses' death between Samma'el — regarded in Judaism as the angel of death and often identified with **the Adversary** (Satan, the accuser; see Mt 4:1N) — and **Mikha'el** (Michael; who, on the basis of Daniel 10:13, 21; 12:1, is regarded in Jewish tradition as Israel's defender and Satan's opponent; see Rv 12:7&N). *Targum Yonatan* says that Moses' tomb was put under Mikha'el's authority. The Testament of Moses must have added that God assigned Mikha'el to bury Moses' corpse, but when Satan claimed it as his Mikha'el **took issue with the Adversary, arguing over the body of Moshe**. Yet even though he was **one of the chief angels** (on this phrase see 1 Th 4:16N), Mikha'el **did not dare bring against** Satan **an insulting charge**, because he recognized that Satan's role as accuser was given to him by God. (This is portrayed clearly in Job 1–2; the New Testament, like the *Tanakh*, does not consider Satan an independent force for evil, but a servant of God with limited authority.) Rather, in keeping with the warning, "*Adonai* says, 'Vengeance is my responsibility; I will repay'"(Deuteronomy 32:25, Ro 12:19), he **said** only, "**May *Adonai* rebuke you**," echoing God's own rebuke of Satan (Zechariah 3:1–2).

For more on **Mikha'el** see Rv 12:7N. Also compare 2 Ke 2:10–13 with vv. 8–10.

11 **The** rebellious **road of Kayin** took him "out from the presence of *Adonai*" (Genesis 4:16) because he refused to accept God's advice and did not take advantage of any of the five or six opportunities God gave him to repent (Genesis 4:1–16). Cain's road led him to murder his brother Abel, but murder was not the road itself. See MJ 11:4N.

They have given themselves over for money to the error of Bil'am (Balaam). See 2 Ke 2:15–16N.

Numbers 16 reports **the rebellion of Korach** (Korah) against God's appointed leader Moses as a major threat to the community of Israel, eliminated only when God had the earth swallow up Korach and his 250 co-conspirators. Because the false prophets similarly wish to take on themselves the authority in the Body of the Messiah which God has given to others, Y'hudah says they **have been destroyed**.

12–13 Compare 2 Ke 2:17&N.

Waterless clouds carried along by the winds. Compare Proverbs 25:14, "One who boasts of gifts that he fails to give is like clouds and wind without rain."

In Jewish culture, meals have always been **festive gatherings meant to foster love**; among believers in Yeshua this is seen at Ac 2:42 and 1C 11:21.

14–15 Y'hudah quotes 1 Enoch 1:9. 1 Enoch, a compilation of writings by several authors who lived in the last two centuries B.C.E., is one of the Pseudepigrapha, Jewish books attributed to famous biblical figures, such as **Chanoch** (Enoch, Genesis 5:18–24), **in the seventh generation starting with Adam** (Genesis 5:1). Such attribution was not deceptive but either honorific or a means of identifying the message of the actual author with the character and activity of the supposed one; compare the writer of an historical novel or documentary who puts words in the mouth of George Washington.

Y'hudah's quoting a non-canonical book does not make 1 Enoch inspired Scripture, nor does it disqualify Y'hudah's letter. Sha'ul quoted pagan authors at Ac 17:28–29 and Ti 1:12, and no one supposes that their works should be included in Holy Writ or Sha'ul's excluded.

17–18 The majority of scholars hold that 2 Kefa is an expansion of Y'hudah's letter, but these verses suggest that Y'hudah drew on 2 Kefa, since Y'hudah not only excludes himself from **the emissaries of our Lord Yeshua the Messiah**, but in reciting what **they told you** he seems to be quoting 2 Ke 3:3. A third possibility is that both books partly depend on a common source.

19 Compare Ro 8:9–13.

20–21 Y'hudah contrasts "**you, dear friends**," genuine believers, with the ungodly libertines of vv. 4–19, and prescribes four things to do. On **faith** see vv. 3b–4N.

22–23 There are a number of textual variants of these two verses; several of them mention only two kinds of people who have left the "most holy faith" (v. 20), but the preponderant evidence favors three:

(1) Those **who are disputing** have closed themselves off to the truth. One can neither teach nor save them, only **rebuke** them, praying that God will help them to change.

(2) **Others**, who have been swept along by the libertine disputers, are themselves relatively innocent but in grave danger of falling away. **Save** them, **snatching them out of the fire**, then ground them in the principles of truth.

(3) **Yet others** have fallen into sin but have not lost their basic teachability, so that they may be restored. To them, **show mercy, but with fear, hating even the clothes stained by their vices** — love the sinner, but hate the sin. "You who have the Spirit should set him right, but in a spirit of humility, keeping an eye on yourselves so that you won't be tempted too" (Ga 6:1).

24–25 In addressing God as **the one who can keep you from falling**, the closing prayer follows the theme of vv. 22–23. This passage is one of the greatest of the New Testament doxologies, comparable with Ro 11:33–36, 16:25–27; Rv 4:10–11, 5:12–13, 15:3–4. On ***Sh'khinah*** see Paragraph (3) of MJ 1:2–3N.

THE
REVELATION
OF YESHUA THE MESSIAH TO YOCHANAN (JOHN)

CHAPTER 1

1 The book of Revelation, the last book in the New Testament, polarizes readers. Some see in it the key to the universe, or at least the key to the future. Others find it completely opaque or dismiss it as nonsense. Some regard its highly picturesque language as absolutely literal, others as entirely symbolic, and still others as sometimes one and sometimes the other, or even both at once. There are four major approaches to its interpretation:

(1) *Futurist.* The book of Revelation is an explicit forecast of a future yet to unfold.
(2) *Preterist.* The prophecies of Revelation were fulfilled in the first century. (Latin *praeter* means "before.")
(3) *Historical* or *Presentist.* The prophecies of Revelation are being fulfilled now, during the period between Yeshua's resurrection and his second coming.
(4) *Idealist.* The book of Revelation does not refer to history at all but is a timeless allegory of the conflict between good and evil.

To add to the confusion, some commentators combine two or more of these approaches at once.

Given no more information than this, it should be obvious that Revelation is the most difficult book in the Bible on which to comment. Dealing with the historical assertions and theological opinions found in the other 26 books of the New Testament is hard enough; but when the subject matter touches on the future, it's everyone for himself! Making sense of such a book is a great challenge, and I am not the first to whom it has given pause — John Calvin wrote an extensive commentary on the whole Bible, Old Testament and New, except for Revelation. On the other hand, there are those so eager to read their own pre-formed opinions into Revelation that they ignore what it actually says; or they engage in what Arnold Fruchtenbaum, a Hebrew Christian scholar, calls (in his commentary on Revelation, *Footsteps of the Messiah*) "newspaper exegesis," that is, seeing in every current event a sensational fulfillment of some biblical prophecy.

I myself do not hold strong views about the book of Revelation. I do not have a distinctly preferred pair of spectacles through which I see it. If readers perceive that my remarks shift from one perspective to another, and if they find this disturbing, I apologize in advance — I can't give more than I've got. Fortunately, much of what I have to say about this book does not depend on which of the above four viewpoints is correct.

In KJV the book is called "The Revelation of Saint John the Divine," but the text calls it **the revelation which God gave to Yeshua the Messiah,... communicated...**

by sending his angel to his servant Yochanan. Hence the *Jewish New Testament* properly calls it "The Revelation of Yeshua the Messiah to Yochanan." The Greek word for "revelation" is "*apokalupsis*" ("unveiling"), which gives the book its other popular title, "The Apocalypse," and raises the question of how this book relates to a category of Jewish writing called "apocalyptic literature."

George Eldon Ladd calls Jewish apocalyptic "tracts for hard times." Biblical imagery and symbolic language are used to express the idea that this world offers no hope for improvement; but history will end with a cosmic catastrophe, at which time the apparently victorious wicked will be punished and the downtrodden righteous rewarded. Such books as The Assumption of Moses, 1 Enoch, 4 Ezra and The Apocalypse of Baruch are examples. Moreover, Isaiah 26–29, Zechariah 12–14, and Daniel 7–12 offer a biblical pattern for these later, extra-biblical books.

The book of Revelation is sometimes said to be merely another example of Jewish apocalyptic, but there are these differences:

(1) Most of the Jewish apocalypses were written pseudonymously, in the names of heroes long dead. Revelation's author uses his own name, reflecting the fact that in New Testament times God had restored prophecy (Ac 11:27&N), and Yochanan was a prophet (v. 3).

(2) Jewish apocalypses are pseudo-predictive — the author writes from a viewpoint in the past and "predicts" history that has already taken place. But Yochanan stands in his own time and looks forward to God's future consummation of his redemptive purpose.

(3) The Jewish apocalypses are entirely pessimistic about the past and present. Revelation's author looks to the past work of Yeshua as the ground for present hope.

Moreover, the book of Revelation is highly distinctive in the way it uses the *Tanakh*. There are very few direct quotations, but no less than five hundred allusions to the *Tanakh*, especially the books of Exodus, Isaiah, Jeremiah, Ezekiel, Zechariah and Daniel. In fact, they are so numerous and frequent that I have not attempted to note very many of them either in the text of the *JNT* or in this commentary; the interested reader should consult other commentaries on Revelation. But the overall effect of so many *Tanakh* references and allusions is to anchor every part of the book in the God-inspired words of Israel's Prophets.

Yochanan. Tradition takes him to be the emissary Yochanan, the same as the author of the Gospel and the three letters bearing this name. To this it is objected that the style of Greek used in Revelation is far rougher and more Hebraic than that of the other four books, which all resemble each other. One possibility is that the fisherman from the Galil, for whom Greek was a second or third language, wrote the visions of Revelation himself, as commanded (v. 11), and did not permit alterations (22:18–19); whereas for the Gospel and his letters he had a native Greek-speaker to help edit and translate. Another possibility is that this was a different Yochanan, known to history as an elder in the congregation at Ephesus (although Yochanan the emissary also is identified with Ephesus; see 2:1N).

What must happen very soon. Compare Daniel 2:28–29. To what degree the New Testament writers regarded the End as imminent is debatable. Contrast, for example, 1C 7:29–31 with 2 Ke 3:2–10. Yet they did urge believers to stay alert, for the Messiah may return without warning, like a thief in the night (Mt 24:32–25:30, Mk 13:32–37, 1 Th 5:2–3, 2 Ke 3:10).

> "Without doubt the early church lived in expectancy of the imminent return of the Lord; but so should every generation of believers. The New Testament expresses a tension between imminence and perspective; the time is near, yet the end is delayed (Mt 24:42–44, Lk 19:11ff.)." (G. E. Ladd, *Revelation*, p. 292).

A more strained rendering of the Greek, especially in view of v. 3 ("For the time is near"), is, "what must happen rapidly"; i.e., once the events described commence, it won't take long for all of them to occur.

Yeshua uses **his angel** to mediate the vision. Angels play a significant role in the book of Revelation.

2 **The Word of God** is the Gospel (6:9); it does not come back void (Isaiah 55:11); it is the "sword" which comes from the Messiah's mouth, by which he conquers and rules (v. 16&N; 19:15).

The testimony of Yeshua the Messiah. See 1:9N.

3 **Blessed**. This is the first of seven blessings, the others being at 14:12–13, 16:15, 19:9, 20:6, 22:7, 22:14. See v. 4N on "seven."

Reader... hearers. Like Sha'ul (Co 4:16), Yochanan expected what he wrote to be read aloud to the congregations.

Hearers... obey. In both Messianic and non-Messianic Judaism, learning is supposed to lead to doing. Compare Exodus 24:7, Ro 10:14–21, MJ 6:4–8, Ya 1:22–25, 2 Ke 2:20–21.

> "Rabbi David Hoffman (1843–1921), the leading Orthodox rabbinical authority in Germany during his era, [wrote in a *responsum*:] 'The *Torah* of Israel is not only a song and rhetoric which one studies only to understand the religion of Israel. Rather, the purpose of Jewish religious learning is *lilmod v'la'asot*, to study and to observe, and one who learns and does not observe, it would be better if he had not learned.'"(Aron and David Ellenson, "The Dilemma of Jewish Education: To Learn and To Do," in *Judaism*, Spring 1984)

Prophecy. The author of the book of Revelation claims to be a prophet. The term puts the book of Revelation on a par with the *Tanakh* — both are inspired by God.

The time is near. See v. 1N on "very soon."

4 **Seven** is the number of completion and perfection in the *Tanakh*. God ended his work of creation on the seventh day (Genesis 2:1–3). This is why the day of rest, *Shabbat* (the Hebrew word means "rest"), is the seventh day of the week (Exodus 20:8–10); the year of *sh'mittah* ("remission"), when the land rests, is the seventh year (Leviticus 25:3–7); and the year of *yovel* ("jubilee"), in which both the land and possession of it rest, comes after seven years of *sh'mittah* (Leviticus 25:8–17). Sevenfold vengeance was to be taken on anyone who might kill Cain (Genesis 4:15). Noah took seven of each clean animal on board the ark (Genesis 7:2). From Pharaoh's dream of seven fat and seven lean cows Joseph predicted seven years of plenty and seven of famine (Genesis 41). The number seven appears over and over in connection with sacrifices and temple ritual; here are

two examples: the blood of a sin offering was sprinkled seven times before *Adonai* (Leviticus 4:3–4); the leper appeared before a *cohen* on the seventh day to be examined and pronounced clean (Leviticus 13:5–6). The festivals of *Pesach* and *Sukkot* each last seven days; and seven weeks intervene between *Pesach* and *Shavu'ot*, on which day seven lambs were offered (Leviticus 23). If Israel is unrepentant she will be punished sevenfold for her sins (Leviticus 26:18–28). Jericho fell after Israel had marched around the city seven times, and seven *cohanim* had blown seven *shofars* (Joshua 6:4–15). Chanah, celebrating her fertility at the birth of Samuel, prayed, "The barren has borne seven" (1 Samuel 2:5; contrast Jeremiah 15:9). Solomon took seven years to build the first Temple (1 Kings 6:38). The Shunammite woman's child sneezed seven times before opening his eyes when Elisha raised him from the dead (2 Kings 4:35). After Israel's male population has been decimated, "seven women shall take hold of one man" (Isaiah 4:1). It will take seven days to consecrate the altar of the End-Time temple (Ezekiel 43:25–26).

Seven is also the number of fullness and completion in the book of Revelation, speaking of God's perfection and the finality of his coming judgment on mankind. Yochanan writes about **seven Messianic communities** and **the sevenfold Spirit**, seven gold *menorahs* (v. 12), seven stars (v. 16), seven flaming torches (4:5), seven seals (5:1), a Lamb with seven horns and seven eyes (5:6), seven angels with seven *shofars* (8:2), seven thunders (10:3), a dragon with seven crowns on his seven heads (12:3) — which are also seven hills and seven kings (17:9–10), and seven angels with the seven last plagues in seven gold bowls (15:1, 7); moreover, he pronounces seven blessings (above, v. 3&N). These references are only to the first mention of each; altogether "seven" and "seventh" appear nearly sixty times in this book.

There were more than **seven Messianic communities in the province of Asia** (present-day Turkey), but those named in v. 11 represent them all.

Grace and *shalom* to you — the same greeting as Sha'ul gives in nine of his letters.

The One who is, who was and who is coming. This is based on God's self-identification in Exodus 3:14, "I am who I am," or, "I will be who I will be." Compare MJ 13:8. In the *Siddur* a line from the popular Jewish hymn, *Adon-'Olam*, reads: "*V'hu hayah v'hu hoveh v'hu yihyeh l'tif'arah*" ("He was, and he is, and he will be, into glorious eternity"). The substitution of "is coming" for "will be" seems to allude to Yeshua's return.

The sevenfold Spirit. Although I believe the reference is to the Holy Spirit, for reasons given in the next paragraph, the literal translation, "the seven spirits" (here and at 3:1, 4:5, 5:6), has strong arguments in its favor. The spirits could be seven angels attending God **before his throne** (Judaism recognized seven archangels — Mikha'el, Gavri'el, Rafa'el, Uri'el, Suri'el, Fanu'el and Yechi'el; see 8:2N). At MJ 1:14 angels are called "spirits who serve," which is consistent with describing the Lamb's seven eyes (5:6) as "the seven spirits sent out into all the earth." Messianic Jews 1:7 quotes Psalm 104:4, "...who makes his angels winds [Hebrew *ruchot*, also translatable as "spirits"] and his servants fiery flames." The rendering "seven spirits" would make 4:5 parallel to Psalm 104 (with the terms reversed): "...before the throne were seven flaming torches, which are the seven spirits of God."

However, the above understanding presents a major difficulty in that it means the author, who opposes angel-worship (19:10, 22:8–9), has sandwiched into his divine greeting, between God and Yeshua, a reference to seven created beings. Moreover, two passages from the *Tanakh* suggest a special relationship between the Holy Spirit and the number seven — Isaiah 11:2, which gives seven attributes of the Spirit, and Zechariah 4:2–10, in which some of the "seven"-imagery of Revelation is associated with the Spirit.

5–6 The original readers were greatly encouraged in their struggle against persecution by these three aspects of **Yeshua the Messiah**:

(1) He is **the faithful witness** (or "the faithful martyr"; see 2:13&N). He witnessed unto the point of his own death, and especially *through* his own death, that God is in control of history. Compare Yn 1:18, "the Only Son…, the one at the Father's side — he has made him known"; and Isaiah 55:3–4, "…the sure mercies of David. Behold I have given him for a witness."

(2) He is **the firstborn** (or "foremost, chief") of those who get raised **from the dead**. This means that faithful believers too can look forward to being resurrected and having eternal fellowship with God, even if in this world they receive no reward and die ignominiously. Compare Ro 6:5; 1C 15:20, 23.

(3) He is **the ruler of the earth's kings**, the "King of Kings" (17:14, 19:16) who will one day subject to himself even the most unbridled and oppressive governments (1C 15:24–25).

Moreover,

(4) He **loves us**.

(5) He **has freed us from our sins at the cost of his blood** (that is, by his bloody, sacrificial death; see Ro 3:24N).

(6) He has **caused us to be a kingdom**, a community subject to him who loves us.

(7) He has caused us to be ***cohanim*** ("priests," Mt 2:4N) for God, his Father.

For these seven reasons, **to him be the glory and the rulership forever and ever**.

On hearing this read (v. 3&N), the congregation is to respond by saying, "***Amen***" (see paragraph on "*Amen*" in Ro 9:5N and Mt 5:18N).

7 This verse states the theme of the book of Revelation, the second coming of Yeshua the Messiah in a way that the world will be unable to ignore. When predicting his own second coming Yeshua himself combined the same phrases from Daniel and Zechariah (Mt 24:30).

Those who pierced him. The allusion is to Zechariah 12:10, in which *Adonai* says, "They will look to me, whom they pierced; and they will mourn him as one mourns an only son." The 19th-century Messianic Jewish commentator Yechiel Lichtenstein (see MJ 3:13N) writes,

> "It can be seen that the mourners will be the people of Israel, first, because Zechariah writes of the families of Israel — the families of David, L'vi, Shim'i, Natan, and 'all the rest' (Zechariah 12:10–14), and second, because the phrase 'they will look' refers to 'the House of David and the inhabitants of Jerusalem' (Zechariah 12:8–11, 13:1)."

Thus this great Messianic prophecy from the *Tanakh* speaks of the day when the entire Jewish people will recognize Yeshua, pierced on the execution-stake, as the Messiah and as fully identified with God, "me, whom they pierced." But in a midrashic sense the phrase, "**those who pierced him**," is not limited to Jews, nor does it mean only the Jews and Gentiles historically responsible for Yeshua's physical death. Rather, it includes all who have not acknowledged his atoning sacrificial death, who by their sins participated in and continue to participate in piercing him. See Yn 19:37&N, where this verse of Zechariah is also quoted.

Lichtenstein's note continues,

> "Some say they will weep because there is no longer any opportunity to repent, but this is wrong. True, there will be an obstacle to repentance, the unbelief of the majority of Israel in their Messiah and Savior, so that he will not be able to come and save them. But this is precisely why God 'will pour on [them] the spirit of grace' (Zechariah 12:10), enabling them to recognize Yeshua as their Savior."

I would put it this way: The tribes of Israel **will mourn** Yeshua, experiencing deep grief over centuries of having rejected him as a nation; this grief will open the way to repentance and accepting him as Messiah and savior of the Jewish people. Some translations render this, "will wail because of him," implying that the Jewish people will experience neither grief nor repentance but only the anguish of judgment. But the Greek text here quotes the Septuagint word for word, which in turn translates Hebrew *safdu 'alav* ("will mourn on him") word for word. In Hebrew "to mourn on someone" does not mean "to wail because of him"; it is simply how Hebrew says "to mourn him." Mourning generally includes both grief over the death itself and sorrow at what one failed to do in relation to the deceased. There is no ground for supposing Yochanan meant anything other than what Zechariah meant.

Lichtenstein again:

> "The Talmud offers an astonishingly similar interpretation:
>
> > "'The land will mourn, each family by itself' (Zechariah 12:12). Why do they mourn? Rabbi Dosa and the Rabbis give different answers. One says it is because *Mashiach ben-Yosef* [the Messiah, the son of Joseph] has been killed, while the other says it is because the *yetzer hara'* [the evil inclination] has been killed. The former is a good explanation, because we have Zechariah 12:10, "They will look to me, whom they pierced; and they will mourn over him as one mourns over an only son."' (from Sukkah 52a)
>
> "Of course, '*Mashiach ben-Yosef*' is Yeshua ben-Yosef (son of Joseph) from Nazareth.
>
> "Moreover, when Zechariah 13:1 continues, 'On that day there will be opened for the house of David and the inhabitants of Jerusalem a fountain to cleanse them from sin and impurity,' it refers to Yeshua's second coming; for it conveys the same idea as Sha'ul's statement in Ro 11:25–26,

'It is in this way that all Israel will be saved. As the *Tanakh* says, "Out of Tziyon will come the Redeemer; he will turn away ungodliness from Ya'akov; and this will be my covenant with them,... when I take away their sins.'

"At Acts 1:11 one learns that just as the Messiah was taken from the Mount of Olives **with the clouds**, so he will return there in the same manner [and this too the prophet knew — see Zechariah 14:4]. What is said here, that **every eye will see him** in perfection coming down on earth, is in keeping with Mattityahu 24:30, which says that the mourning will be after 'the sign of the Son of Man will appear in the sky.'"(*Commentary on the New Testament, ad loc.*)

All the tribes (or "clans" or "families") **of the Land** of Israel **will mourn him**. This alludes to more of Zechariah's prophecy about the people of Israel — "All the Land will mourn, each family by itself" (Zechariah 12:12; the Septuagint translates "family" by the Greek word for "tribe"). Every other translation of this verse reads, "All the tribes of the *earth* will mourn him." This may indeed happen, but in context Zechariah is referring to the Land of Israel, and there is no reason to suppose that Yochanan is altering or spiritualizing the original. Indeed the contrary is true, since both Zechariah and Revelation speak of Israel's future acknowledgement of her pierced Messiah. See Mt 5:5N for more on why Greek *gê* should be rendered "Land" and not "earth."

Yes, *Amen*. Compare 22:20, where the hearers are again encouraged to affirm Yeshua's soon coming. Therefore the sense is, "Yes, that is how it will be," or, "Yes, we want it that way." See last paragraph of vv. 5–6N.

8 **The "A" and the "Z,"** literally, "the Alpha and the Omega," that is, the one who existed at the beginning and who will exist at the end. Here and at 21:6&N the phrase refers to God the Father; but at 22:13&N it refers to Yeshua. It means the same thing as **the One who is, who was and who is coming** (on which see v. 4N).

***Adonai*, God of heaven's armies**. The Greek is *kurios o theos o pantokratôr,* literally, "Lord, the God, the ruler of all." In the Septuagint at Amos 3:13, 4:13 this phrase renders Hebrew *YHVH Elohey-Tzva'ot* ("*YHVH*, God of hosts"). These "hosts" are the angelic armies of heaven, both the good and the evil, over which God rules; and since they are the most powerful of God's creatures, the title epitomizes God's absolute dominion over the universe. Readers are thus reassured that no matter what demonically evil things might happen to them, God remains in control. This is why the Septuagint writers rendered "*tzva'ot*" ("of hosts") into Greek as "*pantokratôr*," which means "ruler over all" but is often translated, "the Almighty." Thus the KJV's phrase here in v. 8, "the Lord, God,... the Almighty," renders the Greek well but does not take account of its Hebrew source in the *Tanakh*. The reference to God's armies of angels highlights Revelation's concern with God's final judgment, in which — as is clear from the book itself — the angels play a major role; for example, see 19:14&N, where "the armies of heaven" are seen following Yeshua on his white horse to defeat the forces of the beast.

9 On believers' sharing Yeshua's **kingship**, see 3:21, 5:10&N, 20:4&N, and 2 Ti 2:12.

The island called Patmos is off the coast of Turkey.

For having proclaimed the message of God and borne witness to Yeshua. Literally, "on account of the word of God and the testimony of Yeshua." There are two genitives here ("word of God," "testimony of Yeshua"), and the question is whether these are subjective genitives ("word which God gave," "testimony which Yeshua gave") or objective genitives ("message about God" and "testimony about Yeshua" which believers proclaim). For background to this grammatical problem see Ro 3:22N, Ga 2:16cN.

As translated here, "the message of God" could be either subjective or objective, while the second is objective. But a good case, based on 1:5, 3:14 and 22:20, can be made for rendering the second too as subjective in all six instances where the phrase appears in Revelation (v. 2, here, 12:17, twice in 19:10, and 20:4). Even though the grammar then makes "the testimony" that given by Yeshua and not by the believer, the believer still has an active role: here, for example, Yochanan can be understood as having been exiled to Patmos not "for having... borne witness to Yeshua" but "on account of [proclaiming] the testimony which Yeshua gave."

10 **I came to be, in the Spirit**. Alternative understandings: (1) Yochanan's body remained where it was, but in his spirit he saw visions; (2) the Holy Spirit came over him, with the result that he saw visions; or (3) the Holy Spirit caused him to be physically present (with this possibility compare Ezekiel 11:1, Ac 8:39–40, 2C 12:2).

On the Day of the Lord. If this is what Greek *en tê kuriakê êmera* means, as I believe it does, Yochanan is reporting the unique experience of having seen God's final Judgment. If it means "on the Lord's Day," that is, Sunday, the day on which Yeshua was resurrected (Mt 28:1, Mk 16:2, Lk 24:1) — and this is the majority understanding — then Yochanan is mentioning a relatively minor detail, the day of the week on which his visions took place.

I think my translation is supported by the context, since the whole book of Revelation is about the Last Judgment, which over and over in the *Tanakh* is called in Hebrew "*yom-YHVH*" ("the Day of *Adonai*," "the Day of the Lord"). On the other hand, Ignatius, who claimed to be a disciple of the emissary Yochanan, wrote letters only two decades or so after Revelation was written, in which he uses "*kuriakê*" to mean Sunday — as does modern Greek. This only shows how quickly the Jewish roots of the New Testament were forgotten or ignored.

(Even if "on the Lord's Day" is correct, *Shabbat* is not thereby moved from Saturday to Sunday; nor does "the Lord's Day" replace or abrogate *Shabbat* (Mt 5:17); nor is Sunday mandatory as a day of worship for Christians or Messianic Jews. On this see Ac 20:7N, 1C 16:2N.)

The interpretative problem arises because the Greek adjective "*kuriakê*" is rare; it appears in the New Testament at only one other place, 1C 11:20, which speaks of "a meal of the Lord," that is, pertaining to the Lord; in context it means a meal eaten in a manner worthy of Yeshua or of God, a "lordly" or godly meal.

According to Yechiel Lichtenstein's commentary (see MJ 3:13N), the late second-century writer Irenaeus mentioned a church tradition that the Messiah will return during *Pesach* and believed that *en tê kuriakê êmera* refers not to Sunday but to the first day of *Pesach*. This calls to mind the *Seder* ritual of opening the front door for Elijah the prophet, forerunner of the Messiah.

Actually, when the events of Yeshua's ministry are arrayed in relation to the Jewish calendar set forth in Leviticus 23, Numbers 28 and Deuteronomy 16, his return should be expected at *Rosh-HaShanah* ("New Year"), the biblical Feast of *Shofars* ("Trumpets"). The Jewish calendar is divided into the spring and fall holidays, corresponding to Yeshua's first and second comings. The first spring festival is *Pesach* ("Passover"), when Yeshua's atoning death took place (Mattityahu 26–27). The next is *Shavu'ot* ("Weeks," "Pentecost"), when the Holy Spirit was given to his *talmidim* (Yn 7:39, 14:26, 15:26, 16:7–15, 17:5; Ac 2:1–4&NN). The long summer break corresponds to the present period when Yeshua is not on earth. According to Mt 24:31, 1C 15:52 and 1 Th 4:16–17 (see notes there and at 8:2 below, and compare Isaiah 27:13), Yeshua's second coming will be announced by *shofars*; this corresponds to the first fall holiday, the Feast of *Shofars*. Interpreters expecting a Millennium (4:1N) see it in relation to the Ten Days of Repentance between *Rosh-HaShanah* and *Yom-Kippur* (the "Day of Atonement"), which itself corresponds to the Day of Judgment (20:11–15). Finally, the new heaven and earth (21:1–22:17&NN) hold the position of the year's last holiday, the joyous pilgrim festival of *Sukkot* (Yn 7:2N, 7:37&N), which all the nations of the world will one day celebrate (Zechariah 14:16–19), just as through the New Covenant the nations of the world are invited to join Israel through faith in Israel's Messiah, Yeshua.

11 See the letters to these seven churches in Chapters 2–3.

12 **Seven gold *menorahs*** ("candlesticks"). Exodus 25:31–40 speaks of the seven-branched *menorah* which stood outside the second curtain in the Tabernacle. The ten gold *menorahs* in Solomon's Temple (1 Chronicles 28:15) were carted off to Babylon (Jeremiah 52:19). Zechariah 4:2 speaks of a single gold *menorah* with seven *nerot* ("lamps," "candles").

According to v. 20, "The seven *menorahs* are the seven Messianic communities" of v. 11. With Yeshua's warning to the community in Ephesus, "I will remove your *menorah* from its place — unless you turn from your sin!" (2:5), compare his remark in the Sermon on the Mount that believers are light for the world (Mt 5:15–16); see also 2C 4:6.

13 **Son of Man**. Yeshua's preferred title for himself as the Messiah; see Mt 8:20N.

Yeshua fulfills three main offices set forth in the *Tanakh* — prophet, priest and king. Yeshua served as a prophet during his life on earth (Mt 21:11). At present he serves as high priest in heaven (MJ 2:17–3:6, 4:14–5:10, 6:20–10:21); this is signified by his **wearing a long robe and a gold band around his chest**, the clothing of the *cohen hagadol* (Exodus 28). The rest of the description in vv. 14–15 suggests his future role as judge and Messianic king.

14 At Daniel 7:9–10 it is "an Ancient of Days," God the Father, who is described in similar language. Thus we see here Yeshua's identification with God.

Eyes like a fiery flame against unholiness; see 2:18, 19:11–12.

15 **Voice like the sound of rushing waters** (literally, "...of many waters"), loud and majestic.

16 **Seven stars**. See v. 20.

A sharp double-edged sword came from his mouth. This imagery is found Isaiah 49:1–3, where Yeshua the Messiah and the people of Israel are identified with each other (see Mt 2:15N). This **sword** is the Word of God (6:9, Ep 6:17). With it Yeshua, in his role as judge and king, strikes down nations (19:15); for earlier he had warned that people would be judged by it (Yn 12:48–49). The Word of God is well-suited for judging, since it can discern the truth in people's hearts (MJ 4:12–13&N).

17 **I fell down at his feet like a dead man**. A common reaction to seeing the *Sh'khinah*, the divine glory (see MJ 1:2–3N); compare Isaiah 6:5, Ezekiel 1:28; also 19:10 below and Daniel 8:17.

Yeshua says, "**I am the First and the Last**," here, at 2:8, and at 22:13 (see v. 8N above). At Isaiah 44:6, 48:12 it is God the Father who so describes himself. Many titles and descriptions which the *Tanakh* applies only to *YHVH* are in the New Testament applied to Yeshua (for another example, see 3:7&N). Since the New Testament distinguishes Yeshua from God the Father, we conclude: (1) Yeshua is to be identified with *YHVH*, with God; yet (2) Yeshua is not the Father. See Yn 1:1N, 20:28N; Co 2:9N.

18 **The Living One**; compare the phrase, "*El Chai*" ("the Living God"), at Joshua 3:10, Psalms 42:3, 84:3.

I was dead, literally, "I became dead" — by being executed on the stake. **But look! I am alive forever and ever** (compare v. 5).

And I hold the keys to death and Sh'ol, the abode of the dead. Since keys are a symbol of authority (Mt 16:19), the meaning is that Yeshua can release the dead (compare Hosea 13:14, Yn 10:17–18&N, 1C 15:1–58). But this authority is God's alone; compare these passages from the Talmud:

> "Rabbi Yochanan said, 'The Holy One, blessed be he, has retained three keys in his own hands and not entrusted them to the hand of any messenger — the key to the rain, the key to childbirth, and the key to revival of the dead.... [We know this is true about] the key to reviving the dead because it is written, "You will know that I am *Adonai* when I have opened your graves" (Ezekiel 37:13).'" (Ta'anit 2a–2b)

> "Elijah prayed to be given the key to the raising of the dead but was told, 'Three keys have not been entrusted to an agent: those of birth, rain and resurrection. Is it to be said that two are in he hands of the *talmid* [Elijah] and only one in the hands of the Rabbi? Bring me the other [the key to the rain, which he already had (1 Kings 17:1; see Ya 5:17–18&N)], and take this one [temporarily, to raise the widow's son (1 Kings 17:17–23)].'"(Sanhedrin 113a)

Thus in having authority over death and Sh'ol, Yeshua is shown to have authority reserved to God and is thus identified with God.

19 **Both what is now, and what will happen afterwards**. This phrase can be used to support the Futurist, Preterist and Historical approaches to the book of Revelation, or a combination of them (see v. 1N).

20 Angels. Difficult. Alternative possibilities:
(1) They are guardian-angels; but then it is odd that Yochanan is to write them letters (2:1, 8, etc.).
(2) They are the pastors of the Messianic communities; but there is no precedent for calling pastors "angels."
(3) They are "messengers" (an alternative meaning for Greek *angeloi*) from the communities; but if so, why address them rather than the communities themselves?
In any case the letters of Chapters 2–3 are meant for the seven Messianic communities mentioned therein.

CHAPTER 2

2:1–3:21 Like the days of creation in Genesis 1, the seven letters of Chapters 2–3 to the Messianic communities named in 1:11 share a common form. Each commences with "Here is the message from," followed by a characterization of Yeshua the Messiah based on specifics found in 1:12–18. Next the congregation is praised for its virtues (except Laodicea) and warned about its faults (except Smyrna and Philadelphia). Yeshua then gives promises of good things, especially to "those winning the victory"; often they are related specifically to the congregation's situation — the Philadelphians, with "little power" (3:8) will be "pillars" (3:12); those in Pergamum who avoid "food… sacrificed to idols" (2:14) will have "hidden manna" (2:17); the people of Smyrna who are suffering and being persecuted to death (2:9–10a) will have life as their crown and not be hurt by the second death (2:10b–11). Finally, he closes each letter with an admonition reminiscent of the Gospels (Mt 11:15&N): "Those who have ears, let them hear what the Spirit is saying to the Messianic communities."

1 Angel. See 1:20N.

Ephesus had the most important Messianic community in the province of Asia. It was already a religious center, home of the pagan goddess Artemis (Ac 19:35), and a focus for magic (Ac 19:19). The congregation had been founded by Aquila and Priscilla (Ac 18:18), and with Sha'ul's guidance it quickly became an evangelistic center (Ac 19:10). Timothy later took Sha'ul's place (1 Ti 1:3), and tradition has it that Yochanan the emissary lived here (Irenaeus, Eusebius).

The seven stars… the seven gold *menorahs*. See 1:12–13, 16, 20 and 1:12N.

4 You have lost the love you had at first — not the strong emotions, which cannot be expected to last, but the zeal for God, which can be renewed by repentance and rededication.

5 Remove your *menorah*, so that you will cease to exist as a part of the Messiah's body, even though you may continue as an institution or social grouping.

6 **Nicolaitans**. A heretical sect which encouraged idolatry and sexual sin; see vv. 14–15. Writing in the late second century, Irenaeus speculated that they were followers of Nicholas, the Jewish proselyte who was appointed *shammash* in the Jerusalem community (Ac 6:5) but, by implication, later went astray. There is no evidence for his hypothesis.

7 **To him who wins the victory** (or: "to him who overcomes"). The victory is over evil, temptation and apathy. According to 3:21&N Yeshua himself is our role-model.

To eat from the Tree of Life means to have eternal life. Genesis 2:9; 3:22, 24 shows that this was true in the original ***Gan-Eden*** ("Garden of Eden" or "Paradise," Lk 23:43N). It is also true in **God's *Gan-Eden***, which is the New Jerusalem (21:2; 22:2, 14, 19). In the *Tanakh* the term "tree of life" is used at Proverbs 3:18, 11:30, 13:12 and 15:4 to describe wisdom, the fruit of the righteous, desire fulfilled, and a wholesome tongue — all of which may be seen as aspects of eternal life.

8 **Smyrna** was a wealthy seaport, a competitor of Ephesus, and a center of emperor-worship.

The First and the Last, who died and came alive again. See 1:17–18&NN.

9 Yochanan writes about Gentiles **who call themselves Jews but aren't — on the contrary, they are a synagogue of** Satan, **the Adversary** (see Mt 4:1N). Perhaps they, like the Gentile Judaizers of the book of Galatians, adopted a smattering of Jewish practices and tried to force them on Gentile Christians. They may have subjected themselves to a legalistic perversion of the *Torah* (see 1C 9:20&N). They apparently organized a pseudo-Messianic synagogue. Their false doctrine probably led them to wrong and immoral behavior, since false doctrine usually does. They probably drew Gentile Christians away from the truth and thereby threatened the Messianic community.

Virtually all the commentators ignore the obvious and straightforward interpretation that Yochanan is talking here about Gentiles who pretend to be Jews. The same kind of expression is used in v. 2: "...you tested those who call themselves emissaries but aren't — and you found them to be liars." It obviously refers to false apostles, and there the commentators accept the literal sense without demur. But here they opt for the metaphorical interpretation that Yochanan is talking about Jews who reject Yeshua as the Messiah instead of the literal understanding that these are non-Jews who lie and say they are Jews but in fact are Gentiles. In this way a verse which says nothing about Jews is given a virulently antisemitic significance. The result is that over the centuries Jews have had the epithet "synagogue of Satan" hurled at them by Christians who thought they understood the Bible.

But nowhere in the New Testament are unbelieving Jews called non-Jews, although Ro 2:28–29 is sometimes mistakenly brought as evidence to the contrary (see note there). Nor does anything in the present context call for a violent outburst against Jews. A good rule of interpretation is that when the literal sense makes good sense, seek no other sense. The only explanation I can see for its nearly universal disregard in this case is the anti-Jewish mindset that infected the Church, including its theologians and commentators, so that even those without antisemitic feelings rejected the *p'shat* in favor of imposing on the text their own *drash* (see Mt 2:15N). For another instance of this process, see Ro 10:4&N.

In the first century, the Jewish religion was highly regarded; many Gentiles became Jewish proselytes. It is not surprising that other Gentiles preferred a short-cut, reaping the advantage of Jewish identification without the burden of adherence to *Torah*. Sha'ul had already encountered such types in Galatia (see Ga 6:12–13).

Should it nevertheless be thought improbable that Gentiles would call themselves Jews, Hebrews or Israelites, consider the following modern examples. The "British Israelites" regard the British as the Ten Lost Tribes. The Mormons not only consider themselves to be the Ten Lost Tribes but regard themselves as Jews and everyone else (real Jews included) as Gentiles! A sect of mostly American-born blacks consider themselves the true Hebrews; several thousand of them are living in Israel. All of these are outside the pale of Christianity. In addition, scattered about are well-meaning Gentile Christians whose strong identification with and love for the Jewish people has made them believe — without a shred of evidence — that they are actually Jewish themselves (see 1 Ti 1:3b–4N). In fact, some years ago a congregation was expelled from the American Lutheran Church because, along with a general drift into weirdness, its pastor and dozens of its members claimed to have heard from God that they were really Jews; many even said they knew which tribe they belonged to.

Without exception this phenomenon of Gentiles imagining and asserting they are Jewish when they are not leads to strange patterns of doctrine and practice. Such people are not accepted by Jews as Jewish; nor, as this verse shows, are they to be accepted by Christians as Christian. Isolated and self-defensive, they can easily become prideful, neither obeying the *Torah* nor showing brotherly love to Yeshua's real followers. It is easy to see why Yeshua does not regard them as harmlessly neutral but pegs them as **a synagogue of the Adversary**.

10 **Ten days**, that is, a short time. It is impossible to recover what **ordeal** is referred to.

11 **The second death**, eternal death in the lake of fire, according to 20:6, 14; 21:8.

12–13a **Pergamum** was a center for pagan worship of many deities, hence it is called the site of **the Adversary** Satan's **throne**, with the result that the sins of vv. 14–15 are widespread.

Sharp double-edged sword. See 1:16&N.

13b **You did not deny trusting me**, or "You did not deny that I had been faithful." See Ro 3:22N.

Antipas, unknown except here, was apparently one of the early believers who died at the hands of the Roman overlords *'al kiddush HaShem* (see Ac 7:59–60N; Greek *marturos* can be translated either "**witness**" or "martyr"). Some twenty to forty years later the same Roman government put to death the ten Jewish martyrs recalled in the *Musaf* liturgy on *Yom-Kippur*, among them Gamli'el II and Rabbi Akiva.

14 **The teaching of Bil'am** (Balaam). Although God did not allow Bil'am to do what **Balak** had hired him for, namely, to curse Israel (Numbers 22–24; see 2 Ke 2:15–16N), Bil'am made up for the king of Moab's disappointment by counseling Israel to engage in idolatry and harlotry (Numbers 25:1–3, 31:16). Bil'am's counsel was indirect — he **taught Balak to set a trap for the children of Israel, so that they would eat food which had been sacrificed to idols and commit sexual sin**. The issue here is not eating meat used in pagan rituals, as at 1C 8:1–13, 10:21, but actually participating in idolatrous feasts and sexual sin, thus violating the *mitzvot* laid down for Gentile believers at Ac 15:28–29.

An alternative understanding here and at v. 20, based on the *Tanakh*'s frequent figurative use of the word translated "sexual sin": the Israelites ate food sacrificed to idols, thus joining in idolatrous worship and *thereby* "committing adultery" against God — that is, they became apostate.

15 Nicolaitans. See v. 6N.

17 Hidden manna. The biblical data are that God fed Israel in the wilderness with "bread from heaven" (Exodus 16:4, 35; Yn 6:31–35), which was called manna (Exodus 16:15, 31), and that a pot of it was preserved in the ark of the covenant (Exodus 16:32–34, MJ 9:4). The Talmud says that in the third heaven "mills grind manna for the righteous" (Chagigah 12b). According to 2 Baruch 29:8, in the Messianic Era "the treasury of manna will again descend from on high, and those alive then will eat of it." When the first Temple was destroyed, Jeremiah (2 Maccabees 2:4–8) or an angel (2 Baruch 6:5–10) rescued the ark with its pot of manna, and they are being kept for the days of the Messiah, when God's people will again eat manna. Yochanan here uses the language of such traditions to show that believers in him will be admitted to the Messianic Banquet, "the marriage supper of the Lamb" (19:9).

In the ancient world a **white stone** was used as an admission ticket to public festivals; believers will be admitted to the Messianic feast. On it is **written** either their own **new name** or that of the Messiah (19:12); this reflects the quantum jump in purity and identification with Yeshua attained by **those winning the victory**.

18 Thyatira was a small town noted for its trade guilds, and these held meals probably dedicated to a pagan god. A believer whose livelihood depended on his membership in a guild was thus faced with the problem of whether he could in good conscience participate.

Yeshua remains the **Son of God** (see Mt 4:3N) even after his resurrection and ascension into heaven. He is the same yesterday, today and forever (MJ 13:8&N).

Eyes like a fiery flame... feet like burnished brass. See 1:14–15.

20 That Izevel woman, that is, someone who resembles King Ahab's queen, Izevel (Jezebel). She supported idolatry and came dangerously close to eliminating true worship of God (1 Kings 16:30–33; 18:4, 13, 22; 2 Kings 9:22). Evidently the "**Izevel woman**" injects occultism and other demonic practices into the Messianic community.

22–23 Those who join in **the sins connected with what** the Jezebel woman **does** are in turmoil; they are struggling with how to be loyal to the Messiah and at the same time function in their social and business environment (see v. 18N). But **her children** have no such ambivalence; trained by her, they are fully committed to her teachings. Hence their punishment, death, is worse than hers, **a sickbed** (literally, "a bed"; but see Exodus 21:18).

24 "Deep things." Various Gnostic philosophies appealed to people's pride by promising spiritual knowledge deeper than that available to ordinary mortals. Many modern cults and movements make the same empty promises.

26–27 Psalm 2 is understood as referring to the Messiah as early as in the first century B.C.E. Pseudepigraphic work, Psalms of Solomon 17:21–27. The believers will reign with the Messiah when he returns — compare 20:4, 6; also Mt 5:5, 19:28; 1C 6:2. Psalm 2 is also cited at 11:18, 12:5 and 19:15.

28 The morning star. Literally, this would be Venus, the brightest object in the sky after the sun and the moon. Here it means either great glory; or, as in 22:16, the Messiah himself, whose coming was foretold by Bil'am: "A star shall step forth out of Jacob" (Numbers 24:17). See 2 Ke 1:19&N.

CHAPTER 3

1 The people of **Sardis** were spiritually apathetic, as a result of their luxurious, loose way of life.

The sevenfold Spirit of God. See 1:4N.

The seven stars. See 1:16, 20.

You have a reputation for being alive, but in fact you are dead! Today this statement about hypocrites describes people (Jews, Christians, other) who support charitable works but have no spiritual connection with the living God (Isaiah 64:5(6)); people who feel close to God or have correct theological doctrine but produce no evangelistic or social action fruit (Ya 2:17); people whose lack of faith in God and ignorance or rejection of Yeshua produce dead religious formalism, social clubbiness, fortress mentality defensiveness, and/or pride in self-accomplishment; and people who try to fill their spiritual vacuum with sensual gratification.

2–5 The Sardis congregation was severely backslidden; Yeshua prescribes the only possible cure: spiritual revival.

3 I am coming like a thief, that is, suddenly and unexpectedly. The way to be prepared for it is to be ready and alert always, that is, always leading a godly life. Yeshua gives the same warning at 16:15; compare his remarks at Mt 24:42–50 and Lk 12:39–46; also 1 Th 5:2–8 and 2 Ke 3:8–13, which speak of the Day of the Lord itself coming like a thief.

4–5a Soiled their clothes... clothed in white. Throughout the Bible white, clean clothes refer to the righteous deeds God gives his people to do so that they may exercise and express their faith (19:8, Isaiah 61:10, Ep 2:10); also see below at 3:18; 4:4; 6:11; 7:9, 13–14; 16:15; 19:14. Contrast the outwardly righteous works which people without faith organize for themselves to do; these God calls "filthy rags" (Isaiah 64:5(6), cited above, v. 1N).

5 **I will not blot his name out of the Book of Life**. Compare Pp 4:3. On "**Book of Life**" see 20:12bN.

I will acknowledge him individually before my Father and before his angels. Compare Mt 10:32–33, Lk 12:8–9, Yn 10:3.

7 Of the seven cities **Philadelphia** was the one founded most recently. Its congregation was in a healthy condition, for Yeshua only praised it.

HaKadosh means "the Holy One." At 6:10 the term designates God the Father. Moreover, in the Talmud, the Prayerbook and other Jewish writings, it is common to refer to God as "*HaKadosh, barukh hu*" ("the Holy One, blessed be he"). But here (and possibly at 1 Yn 2:20) this title refers to Yeshua. (So there is no need for a "blessed be he," because here the Holy One is talking about himself.) Thus Yeshua is to be identified with God, yet he is not the Father (see 1:17N).

Yeshua is also **the True One**, the one who is faithful and trustworthy.

At Isaiah 22:20–22, Elyakim was given "the **key of** the house of **David**," that is, full authority to act on behalf of King Hezekiah in his household. Likewise Yeshua, "the Root and Offspring of David" (5:5, 22:16), has full authority (Mt 28:18) to act on behalf of God, our King. Yeshua does not permit others to usurp this authority (see v. 9), yet he voluntarily shares "the keys of the Kingdom of Heaven" with those who commit themselves to him (Mt 16:19). Two others named Elyakim appear in the genealogies of Yeshua (Mt 1:13, Lk 3:30). For other "keys" Yeshua has in his possession see 1:18&N.

8 **I know that you have but little** worldly **power**, but much spiritual power, since **you have obeyed my message and have not disowned me**.

9 **Those who call themselves Jews but aren't**. On these Gentile pretenders, see 2:9N.

I will cause them to come and prostrate themselves at your feet, and they will know that I have loved you. In his remarks on this phrase the non-Jewish commentator George Eldon Ladd notes verses from the *Tanakh* in which it is prophesied that the pagan nations of the world will come and bow before Israel (Isaiah 45:14, 49:23, 60:14; Ezekiel 36:23, 37:28), and then writes,

> "These and many other passages look forward to a day of the triumph of Israel over the nations; sometimes it is expressed in terms of the humiliation of the gentiles before Israel, sometimes in the conversion of the gentiles to the faith of Israel." (*Revelation*, Eerdmans, 1972, pp. 60–61)

On the term "Israel" see Ro 11:17–26&NN, Ga 6:16&N, Ep 2:11–16&NN.

10 **The time of trial** (or: "temptation") **coming upon the whole world** is spoken of in the *Tanakh* at Daniel 12:1; in other books of the New Testament at Mt 24:4–28, Mk 13:5–23, 2 Th 2:1–12; and in Revelation throughout Chapters 6–18. Premillennialists call this period the Tribulation (on these two terms see 4:1N, 7:14&N, 11:1–2N; 1 Th 4:15b–17N).

I will keep you from the time of trial. Those who believe in a "Pre-Tribulation Rapture" (see 4:1N, 1 Th 4:15b–17N) understand Yeshua to be saying here that he will remove ("rapture") the faithful from the earth before the *time* of the trial begins. Others are satisfied to take it in a general sense to mean that God will seal his people against harm when the trial comes (9:4) and will warn them to flee impending judgment (18:4).

The people living on earth. There are two equivalent Hebrew phrases in the *Tanakh*. "*Yoshvei-tevel*" appears in the *Tanakh* five times. Four times it means "inhabitants of the habitable world," all human beings (Isaiah 18:3, 26:9, Psalm 33:8, Lamentations 4:12); but at Isaiah 26:18 it seems to exclude God's people and refer to the world's pagans. "*Yoshvei-ha'aretz*" ("inhabitants of the Land" or "...of the earth") appears over 20 times and can mean: (1) all human beings (Isaiah 24:6, 26:21; Jeremiah 25:30; Psalm 33:14), (2) the pagan tribes of Cana'an (Exodus 23:31, Joshua 2:9, Jeremiah 47:2, Nehemiah 9:24), or (3) the Jews in their Land, Israel (Jeremiah 6:12; 10:18; Hosea 4:1; Joel 1:2, 14; 2:1).

Here, by context, "the people living on earth" are, as at Isaiah 26:18, all humans on earth except those devoted to the Lord, in other words, all pagans, all who follow the beast (13:3, 8) and do not turn to God. This expression has the same meaning also at 6:10; 8:13; 13:8, 14; and 17:8 (13:12, 17:2 and Ac 17:26 are similar); but at 11:10&N it probably refers to Jewish people living in Israel.

The pagans will be **put... to the test** of experiencing God's judgment upon the earth (Chapters 6–18). Some will pass the test by repenting (11:13), which is God's fervent desire (2 Ke 3:9); but most will not (9:20–21; 16:8–11, 21).

12 **I will make those winning the victory pillars** (leaders, Ga 2:6–9) **in the Temple of my God**. In Solomon's Temple were two pillars named Bo'az and Yakhin (1 Kings 7:21). Compare 1 Ke 2:5, where believers are said to be "living stones,... being built into a spiritual house." Later in Yochanan's vision there is a Temple in heaven (7:15, 11:19, 14:15, 15:5, 16:1), and Yeshua ministers there as *cohen gadol* (MJ 2:17&N). But in **the New Yerushalayim coming down out of heaven** (see 21:2&N), God himself will be the Temple, so it is not surprising that its pillars will be believers.

I will write on him the name of my God. People signify by the names they bear whom they belong to. In the *Tanakh*, God put his name (*YHVH*) on the people of Israel by having the *cohanim* recite the Aaronic blessing (Numbers 6:24–27). The faithful bear the name of God (here, 22:4) and the name of the Messiah (14:1), including his **own new name** (2:17, 19:12). Likewise, the followers of the beast signify that they belong to him by bearing his name (13:17).

The name of my God's city. This signifies citizenship in that city (see 21:2N).

14 Sha'ul worked hard for **Laodicea**'s congregation (Co 2:1, 4:13), greeted them as brothers (Co 4:15), and even wrote them a letter (Co 4:16). Perhaps the fact that their letter is now lost is a sign of how little good it did them. Here Yeshua finds the Laodiceans worthy only of blame and exhortation; he does not praise them for anything.

The word "***Amen***," from the Hebrew word meaning "truth," confirms the truth of a previous statement (see Mt 5:18N, Ro 9:5N). Compare "the God of *Amen*" (Isaiah 65:16). Yeshua is **the Ruler** (Greek *archê*) **of God's creation**, literally, "the beginning of God's creation," who as the Word of God began it and continues to uphold and rule it (Genesis 1:2, Yn 1:1–3, Co 1:17, MJ 1:3). But the word "*archê*" as used at 21:6 and 22:13 suggests a philosophical understanding of Yeshua as the supertemporal one, "the 'A' and the 'Z'"(1:8&N). Thus in relation to the Laodiceans, Yeshua is **the**

Amen, confirming how serious is their spiritual condition. He is **the faithful and true witness** (see 19:11N) whose testimony on the subject cannot be controverted. And he is **the Ruler of God's creation**, capable of bringing judgment upon them if they do not repent.

15 While "**hot**" is best, believers who feel threatened by people hostile to the Gospel and are more at ease with the apathetic, the indifferent, the complacent and the nominal should conform themselves to Yeshua's preference for "**cold**" over "**lukewarm**." "Zeal for God but not according to knowledge" (Ro 10:2) is more fertile ground for the Gospel than zeal for nothing.

And now a *drash:* what about people who are "cool" (in the slang sense current since my high school days)? Someone seeking to be "cool" wants to be well regarded by the "in-crowd." If his referent "in-crowd" consists of believers in Yeshua, then — "cool" is **hot**.

16–17 Yeshua's strong words of judgment are meant to jar the Laodiceans from their complacency, so that they will repent (vv. 18–20). To their false claim of spiritual well-being (**I am rich**) they add the spiritual pride of the "self-made man" (**I have gotten rich** by my own efforts) and a false and dangerous (Ya 4:13–16) sense of self-sufficiency (**I don't need a thing**). Compare Hosea 12:9–10, where Efrayim (the Northern Kingdom, Israel) says, "I have become rich, I have found wealth for myself, in all my labors they will find no iniquity in me that is sin"; and in consequence God promises to make them dwell in tents (as nomads).

18 Yeshua here does not command but offers his **advice**. Being infinitely wise, he knows the Laodiceans are far too undisciplined to obey orders. Likewise, observe his courtesy at v. 20.

Of course one does not **buy** for money Yeshua's spiritual **gold** which makes people truly **rich**; it is free (22:17, Isaiah 55:1, Ro 3:24). But Yeshua is catering to the psychology of people who measure everything in monetary terms, who think that if you don't **buy** it, it isn't **worth** anything.

Laodicea had a famous medical college where "Phrygian powder" was used to make **eyesalve**. Yeshua can heal not only the physically blind (Yn 9:1–7), but also the spiritually blind; however, these must first admit that they cannot see (Yn 9:39–41).

White clothing. See 3:4–5aN.

19 **I rebuke and discipline everyone I love**. Compare MJ 12:6. Yeshua still loves the errant Laodiceans; this is why he criticizes them in vv. 15–18. Because God loves Israel he criticizes them throughout the *Tanakh*; this is one of the glories of biblical truth.

Exert yourselves, and turn from your sins. Repentance is not a gift placed in waiting hands. The excuse, "I'm not ready to repent yet," often hides such a passivist theology of repentance. Yeshua, however, has a different idea, a Jewish idea: it takes effort to lift oneself out of apathy and turn from sin.

20 God's readiness to receive repentant sinners, well known from the *Tanakh* (for example, Zechariah 1:3: "Thus says *Adonai* of Heaven's Armies: 'Return to me, and I will return to you.'") and restated in the New Testament (Ac 2:38), is the ground for what Yeshua says in this verse. **Look, I am standing at the door, knocking**. Yeshua does not barge in or bang at the door, but courteously stands there knocking, waiting to be invited in. He does not force his way into people's hearts, either those of believers who have turned away from him like the Laodiceans, or those of nonbelievers who have not yet received him. On the other hand, he does not stand silently, so that no one could suspect his presence, but he makes his presence insistently yet not intrusively felt through the behavior of believers, through the preaching of the Gospel, through the conformity of history to prophecy, through nature, through conscience. He waits until **someone hears** Yeshua's still small **voice** prompting belief and trust, removes the intellectual and emotional barricades, and **opens the door** to faith and the first steps of repentance. Then, when thus invited, **I will come in and eat with him, and he will eat with me**. It might be added that unlike most guests Yeshua provides the food, the spiritual nourishment that gives the strength needed for exerting oneself to take the more difficult steps of repentance. The metaphor of meal-sharing (compare Lk 15:2, Yn 14:23, Ac 11:3) is appropriate to Jewish and to most oriental cultures, where table fellowship implies affection, intimacy and mutual confidence. In short, Yeshua is promising to be intimately and truly present with anyone who genuinely asks him, Jew or Gentile alike.

21 Yeshua presents himself as the model for anyone who wants to **win the victory** over evil, temptation and apathy. Compare Pp 2:6–11, and also MJ 2:9–11, 18; 4:15–16. There too the Messiah is depicted as having overcome temptation, and we are invited to "approach" God's throne boldly when we have need. Here Yeshua promises that believers who overcome will actually **sit** with him on the **throne** (see 20:11N) which he shares with God the Father.

CHAPTER 4

1 Futurists who are also Dispensationalists find in this verse an indication of the Church's Pre-Tribulation Rapture (on the terminology and theological background of this note see 1:1N, 1 Th 4:15b–17N). Clearly at this point Yochanan's visions shift from earth to heaven (there are many shifts in the book of Revelation; see R. H. Charles's commentary, Volume 1, p. 109), but nothing is said about removing believers. The Pre-Tribulationists' interpretation requires three assumptions:

(1) The sequence of Yochanan's visions corresponds to the sequence of events in future history.
(2) The Messianic Community (the Church, the Body of the Messiah) does not appear at all in Chapters 4–18.
(3) Those believers who come to faith during the Tribulation are not part of the Messianic Community.

Against these assumptions it may be argued:

(1) The text gives no reason to suppose that the sequence of Yochanan's visions is the same as the order in which the events depicted occur; therefore one should not assume it. On the contrary, 12:1–5&N provides a counterexample. Moreover, if, as may be the case, a given event is depicted by more than one vision, then a direct

chronological correspondence is also impossible logically.

(2) It is not true that the Messianic Community is absent from Chapters 4–18. It is true that the Greek word "*ekklêsia*" (usually translated "Church" and in the Jewish New Testament translated "Messianic Community"; see Mt 16:18N) does not appear after 3:22 until 22:16. But from this fact one might also infer that the Church does not take part in the marriage supper of the Lamb (19:7–9) or in the Millennium and Last Judgment (Chapter 20).

Believers are clearly present throughout the visions of Chapters 6–18 — see 6:9 (the martyred souls under the altar), 7:1–8, 14:1–5 (the 144,000 from the tribes of Israel), 7:9–10, 13–14 (the huge crowd from all nations dressed in white robes), 11:13 (those who give glory to the God of Israel after the two witnesses are resurrected), 12:17 (the rest of the woman's children, who obey God's commands and bear witness to Yeshua), 13:8–10 (those whose names are written in the Book of Life), 14:12–13 (God's people, who observe his commands and exercise Yeshua's faithfulness), 15:2–3 (those defeating the beast, who sing the song of Moses and the song of the Lamb), 18:4 (God's people called to come out of Babylon).

In most cases these believers are on earth, not in heaven. The descriptions applied to them in these verses are exactly those appropriate to members of the Messianic Community. However, the next assumption excludes them from being members of the Messianic Community; therefore assumption (3) must be addressed.

(3) The argument that Tribulation believers do not belong to the Messianic Community depends on drawing a rigid distinction between Israel and the Church, as do all Pre-Tribulation theologies with which I am acquainted. It is assumed that during the present era — what Dispensationalists call the "parenthesis" or "Church Age," defined as the period between Pentecost (Acts 2) and the Tribulation — God's clock with Israel has stopped at the end of the 69th week of Daniel 11:26–27 and he is now dealing only with the Church. After the Rapture, Israel's clock will again begin to tick, as Daniel's 70th week, the Tribulation, unfolds.

There is circular reasoning here; for if it is only believers who come to faith during the "Church Age" who are counted as part of the Messianic Community, and the "Church Age" is defined as ending with the Tribulation, then by definition no one who comes to faith during or after the Tribulation is in the Messianic Community, even though by every other criterion their faith is identical with that of Messianic Community members.

Moreover, for the following three reasons Israel (the Jewish people) is not as fully distinct from the Messianic Community as the Pre-Tribulationists would have one think:

(a) Gentile believers have been grafted into Israel, that is, into the Jewish people (Ro 11:17–24). Thus there is an indissoluble connection; they are not to be ungrafted at some future date unless they cease to have faith.

(b) The New Covenant, even though it creates the Messianic Community, has been made, not with the Messianic Community, but with Israel, (Jeremiah 31:30–33(31–34), MJ 8:8–12). The Messianic Community, if separated from the Jewish people, is deprived of its constitutional basis for existence.

(c) Sha'ul, a member of the Messianic Community when he wrote his letters, writes that he is an Israelite (2C 11:22, Ro 11:1). He does not say he was formerly an

Israelite and has now left Israel to join the Messianic Community. Rather, like every other Jewish believer, he is both.

But if Sha'ul and other Jewish believers are members both of Israel and of the Messianic Community, Pre-Tribulationists must answer this question: when the rapture takes place, do Jewish believers in Yeshua stay behind with the rest of physical Israel, or do they join the rest of the Messianic Community with Yeshua in the air? They can't be in both places at once. Is it a matter of our personal choice? Do we have to choose whether to be more loyal to the Jewish people or to our brothers in the Messiah? This is an absurd question, absurd because the situation proposed will never arise. The Jewish believer does not abandon his people. He never has to choose between loyalty to the Jews and loyalty to the Messianic Community, except in worldly relationships — that is, in order to follow the Jewish Messiah, he may have to choose rejection by the Jewish community as presently constituted in the world.

Some Dispensationalists are not unnerved by this question but answer unequivocally, "It is not a matter of individual choice. Jews who accept Jesus are raptured along with other Christians. Only unbelieving Jews will remain behind to face the terrors of the Tribulation." But when told this Messianic Jews very often *are* unnerved. This is not what they bought into when they came to faith. They were told, "Now you're a Jew who has accepted his Messiah." They were not told, "Now you have abandoned your Jewish people and will spend eternity without them." Yet this is the clear implication of the Pre-Tribulation Rapture position, based, as it is, on the idea of two eternally separate peoples of God.

Israel and the Messianic Community are two, yet they are one. Overemphasizing the "one"-ness led Christian theologians to conclude that the Church had replaced the Jews as God's people. But overemphasizing the "two"-ness yields errors just as serious, and, in their own way, just as potentially antisemitic. Messianic Judaism should set for itself the task of elucidating correctly the relationship between the Jewish people and the Messianic Community of Jews and Gentiles by means of "olive tree theology" (Ro 11:23–24N, 11:26aN; Ga 6:16N).

2a Instantly I was in the Spirit. Yochanan was already in the Spirit (1:9). This seems to refer to his experiencing a change of circumstances within his vision.

2b–8 Although both *Tanakh* and New Testament teach that God is invisible (Exodus 33:20, Yn 1:18, 1 Ti 1:17), both report that people have seen God (to be specific, God the Father; God the Son is described differently in Chapter 5). Indeed, Yochanan's vision closely resembles several found in the *Tanakh*. Exodus 24:9–11 says that Moses, two sons of Aaron and seventy elders "saw the God of Israel" on "a paved work of sapphire stone as clear as heaven," very much like the **sea of glass, clear as crystal** of v. 6a (also see 15:2). The *k'ruvim* Ezekiel saw closely resemble the **living beings** of vv. 6b–8a (Ezekiel 1:5–11; 10:12, 14–15); he also saw a man on a throne with surroundings similar to those Yochanan describes in vv. 2–6a (Ezekiel 1:22, 26–28; 10:1). The prophet Mikhayahu (Micaiah) said, "I saw *Adonai* sitting on his throne and all the army of heaven standing by him on his right hand and on his left" (1 Kings 22:19,

2 Chronicles 18:18). Isaiah wrote, "I saw *Adonai* sitting on a throne, high and lifted up" (Isaiah 6:1). He too saw winged beings (*s'rafim*) who worshipped God in language like that of v. 8b, crying to each other, "Holy, holy, holy is *Adonai* of heaven's armies" (Isaiah 6:2–3), a phrase which is part of the *Kedushah* ("Sanctification" of God) in the synagogue prayers (see the third blessing of the *'Amidah*).

4 **Twenty-four elders**. Who are they? Four possibilities:
(1) Representatives of the 24 divisions of *cohanim* (see Lk 1:5N).
(2) The twelve emissaries of Yeshua plus the twelve founders of the tribes of Israel; if so, they represent all of redeemed humanity.
(3) A special group of angels, since at 5:10 they refer to the redeemed as "them" and not "us."
(4) Unspecified representatives of saved humanity in the *'olam haba*. In this regard it is interesting that Yochanan's description, including the **gold crowns** and the worship of vv. 10–11, closely resembles the imagery used by Rav in the Talmud to depict saved human beings in the age to come:

> "In the *'olam haba*… the righteous sit with their crowns upon their heads and feast on the *Sh'khinah*." (B'rakhot 17a)

(On "*Sh'khinah*" see Paragraph (3) of MJ 1:2–3N.)

5 **Voices**. Or: "rumblings"; see Ac 2:4b–13&N. **The sevenfold Spirit of God**. See 1:4N.

6 **In front of the throne was what looked like a sea of glass, clear as crystal**. The description resembles that of Exodus 24:10 and Ezekiel 1:22, 26.

8b See 1:4N, 1:8N.

11 This wonderful New Testament *Hallel* ("doxology," "expression of praise") is the first of several in the book of Revelation; others are found at 5:9–10, 12, 13; 7:10, 12; 11:15, 17–18; 12:10–12; 14:7, 8; 15:3–4; 16:5–6, 7; 19:1–2, 5, 6–8. See also Ro 11:33–36; 1 Ti 1:17, 3:16; Yd 24–25; and in the *Tanakh*, of course, the whole book of Psalms.

CHAPTER 5

1 **Scroll**, or, possibly a book with pages. See 10:8–11N. Most of the rest of the book of Revelation describes God's judgments, revealed when the scroll's **seven seals** are removed.

5 **The Lion of the tribe of Y'hudah**. This description of the Messiah draws on Jacob's blessing upon his son Judah, which has been understood in Judaism as a Messianic prophecy:

> "Y'hudah is a lion's cub.
> My son, you stand over the prey.
> He stoops down, crouching like a lion,
> a mighty lion — who will dare make him get up?
>
> "The scepter will not depart from Y'hudah,
> or the ruler's staff from between his feet,
> until he comes to whom it belongs [or: "until Shiloh comes"],
> and the peoples obey him." (Genesis 49:9–10)

Within the Messianic Community many peoples obey Yeshua, to whom the scepter belongs (compare Isaiah 9:5–6(6–7); MJ 1:8, 7:14).

The Root of David. (See also 22:16&N.) This draws on Isaiah 11:1–10, which commences with, "There will come forth a rod from the stem of Yishai" (Jesse, King David's father), "and a branch will grow out of his roots." This description of the Messiah is followed by details about his rule (compare Isaiah 9:5–6(6–7)) and the Messianic Age of peace which he establishes. The passage concludes with: "On that day nations [or: "Gentiles"] will seek the root of Yishai, which stands as a banner [or: "as a miracle"] "for the peoples; and his dwelling-place will be glorious."

Of particular interest are the two verses which follow, where there is an astonishingly clear prophecy of the present and future ingathering of the Jewish people:

> "In that day *Adonai* will set his hand again a second time to recover the remnant of his people, …the dispersed of Judah from the four corners of the earth." (Isaiah 11:11–12)

The description does not fit either the Exodus from Egypt or the return from Babylon and "that day" can only be the Messianic Age, which has not yet fully come. Both the rabbis and the writers of the New Testament adhere to the principle that a biblical citation implies its context. Therefore Yochanan, by alluding to Isaiah 11, affirms that God will yet fulfill his promises to restore the Jewish people to our Land, Israel. I stress this because it is sometimes claimed that the New Testament cancels the promises God made to the Jewish people. Quite the contrary: of the Jewish people the New Testament says, "With respect to being chosen they are loved for the Patriarchs' sake, for God's free gifts and his calling are irrevocable" (Ro 11:28–29; see Mt 5:5N for references on refuting Replacement theology).

By his incarnation, obedient life and atoning death Yeshua has **won** the victory over human sin which gives him **the right to open the scroll and its seven seals**.

6 **A Lamb that appeared to have been slaughtered.** The allusion is to Isaiah 53:7–8, "Like a lamb brought to be slaughtered… he was cut off out of the land of the living." Philip expounded this passage to the Ethiopian eunuch as being about Yeshua (Ac 8:26–39). Yochanan 1:29 speaks of "God's lamb… taking away the sin of the world." See also Mt 26:26–29; Ro 8:3–4; 1C 5:6–8, 11:23–26; MJ 9:11–10:20; 1 Ke 1:19.

The **Lion of Y'hudah** is a **Lamb… slaughtered**. The juxtaposition of these contrasting descriptions of the Messiah in vv. 5–6 is one of the clearest expressions in the New Testament of the dual functioning of Yeshua, who came first as a **Lamb** sacrificed for sin, and returns (6:16–17) as a **Lion** to execute judgment, rule the world and bring peace. Jewish tradition, unable or unwilling to reconcile these two roles in one person, invented the idea of *Mashiach Ben-Yosef* who dies and a different *Mashiach Ben-David* who rules.

Seven horns. In the *Tanakh* horns symbolize power; seven is the number of completeness (1:4N). Hence Yeshua has complete power (compare Mt 28:18, Yn 17:1–2). In the Apocrypha at 1 Enoch 90:9 the Maccabees are symbolized by "horned lambs." In Testament of Joseph 19:8 is imagery similar to that of this verse: the Messiah is designated a lamb who goes forth from the midst of horns with a lion on his right.

Seven eyes, which are the sevenfold Spirit of God (see 1:4N) **sent out into all the earth**. Compare Zechariah 4:10, a difficult verse, which apparently says that the seven lamps of Zechariah 4:2 (see 1:12&N above) represent "the eyes of *Adonai*" which "rove to and fro throughout the whole earth," preventing anything from impeding the building of the second Temple under Z'rubavel. If the Lamb has "seven eyes," he has complete knowledge to match his complete power.

7 The Messiah's normal position in the present age is at **the right hand of the One sitting on the throne** (Psalm 110:1; Mt 22:44; Ac 2:34–35, 7:56; MJ 1:3).

8 **Harp**. The usual instrument of praise in the book of Psalms.

Gold bowls filled with incense are also among the accoutrements of worship in the *Tanakh*; they symbolize **the prayers of God's people** (compare 6:9–10, 8:3).

9a **A new song**, as in Psalms 33:3, 98:1, 144:9, 149:1.

9b–13 These verses, like 1:12–16, repeat elements of the Daniel 7:9–14 vision, in which an "Ancient of Days," served by "a thousand thousands and ten thousand times ten thousand" is visited by "one like a son of man," to whom is given "dominion, glory and a kingdom, that all the peoples, nations and tongues should serve him." The context there and in Revelation thus shows that the phrase, "**every tribe, language, people and nation**" (and its variations at 7:9, 10:11, 11:9, 13:7, 14:6 and 17:15), refers to the Gentile nations of the world.

10 **You made them into a kingdom for God to rule, *cohanim* to serve him**. The language comes from Exodus 19:6, Isaiah 61:6. See 1 Ke 2:9&N; also compare 1:6 above.

They will rule over the earth in the Millennium (20:4) and on the new earth (22:5); see also Mt 5:5; 1C 4:8.

12–13 God the Father, **the One sitting on the throne**, already has **power, honor**, etc., from time immemorial. He grants these attributes to **the Lamb**, who is **worthy to receive** them because he did not grasp at them (Pp 2:5–11). They henceforth **belong** both to him and to his Father **forever and ever.** See also 7:12, and compare Yochanan 17.

Every creature will acknowledge God's universal rule (Pp 2:9–11&N, Co 1:20), but demons and the wicked will not enjoy its benefits (20:11–15&NN, Ya 2:19).

CHAPTER 6

1–20 Six of the seven seals are broken in this chapter; the scroll itself is open when the seventh seal is broken, at 8:1.

1–8 The breaking of the first four seals releases the "four horsemen of the Apocalypse," who represent, respectively, (1) war in its aspect of subjecting peoples one to another, (2) war in its aspect of hate between nations and individuals, (3) inequitable economic distribution (or, less likely, general scarcity of goods), and (4) the death which results from the first three (**war, wild animals** = hate, **famine** = inequitable distribution) and from disease (= **plagues**).

This section is apparently related to Leviticus 16:14–26 and Ezekiel 14:12–20, which speak of similar judgments. Compare also the ravagers at Jeremiah 15:3, 24:10, 29:17; Ezekiel 5:17, 14:21; and the four horses at Zechariah 6:2–3. **The four living beings** were introduced at 4:6 above.

2 Some consider the **rider** on the **white horse** to be the Messiah depicted as a **conqueror** (as at 19:11ff.) in the sense that his Gospel conquers the world. But this makes him only one rider among many; moreover, the rest of the "four horsemen of the Apocalypse" bring judgment, not relief. Better to see this rider as bringing judgment in the form of war and conquest.

6 The rich are cushioned by their wealth from the effects of economic inequality and scarcity; but the poor, who must pay **a day's wages** (literally, "a denarius"; see Mt 20:2) for starvation rations, are brusquely ordered not to **meddle with** (or "damage") **the** olive **oil or the wine**, now luxuries far beyond their means.

Yechiel Lichtenstein (see MJ 3:13N) comments:

> "Weighing the bread is a sign of a curse, according to Leviticus 26:26, 'They shall dole out your bread by weight; you will eat, but you will not be satisfied.'" *(Commentary to the New Testament, ad loc.)*

8 **A pallid, sickly-looking horse** (or: "a green horse"). Lichtenstein comments,

> "The greenness is a sign of death. Death causes the face to turn green, as it says in the Talmud, referring to the angel of death: '…they throw in the mouth of the dying the drop which caused his death, and his skin and face become green' ('Avodah Zarah 26b)."

9 **Underneath the altar the souls**. This odd image should be understood in the light of rabbinic literature. According to a work attributed to the second-century Rabbi Natan HaBavli,

> "*HaKadosh* ["the Holy One"], blessed be he, took the soul of Moses and stored it under the Throne of Glory…. Not only the soul of Moses is stored under the Throne of Glory, but the souls of the righteous are also stored there.

> "Rabbi Akiva used to say,... 'Whoever is buried beneath the altar is as though he were buried beneath the Throne of Glory.' "(*Avot diRabbi Natan* 12:4, 26:2)

According to the Talmud, the third-century Rabbi Abba Arikha, known as Rav, taught that the archangel Michael offers a sacrifice on the heavenly altar in the heavenly temple (M'nachot 110a). The Tosafot, medieval commentators on the Talmud, said about this passage that this sacrifice consists of the souls of the righteous, of *Torah*-scholars. Similarly Shabbat 152b. On **the altar** itself, see 8:3N.

Put to death... for bearing witness. The Greek word for "witness" is "*marturia*," from which is derived the English word "martyr." See Ac 7:59–60N on the Jewish concept of death *'al kiddush HaShem* ("to sanctify the Name" of God).

10 ***HaKadosh*,... how long... before you... avenge our blood?** People who oppose vengeance on principle can appeal to both Yeshua's example and his teaching (Mt 5:42, 26:51–54; Lk 23:34). Yet the Scriptures make room for vengeance. The martyrs recognize that while vengeance is not properly within the human domain, it is a proper function of God. As Ro 12:19 puts it,

> "Never seek revenge, my friends; instead, leave that to God's anger; for in the *Tanakh* it is written, *'Adonai* says, "Vengeance is my responsibility; I will repay."' [Deuteronomy 32:25]"

Moreover, just as the voice of Abel's blood cries out to God from the ground (Genesis 4), righteousness demands payment (vengeance) for murder or wrongful death. Psalm 79:10 and Lk 18:7–8a suggest that the martyrs here are praying for vindication rather than vengeance. But a similar prayer in the Pseudepigraphic book 1 Enoch 47:1–4 is for vengeance.

11 **White robe**. See 3:4–5aN.

12–17 The description of the breaking of the **sixth seal** alludes to descriptions of the end of the world found in Isaiah 2:10–12, 2:19, 13:10, 34:4, 50:3; Jeremiah 4:23–29; Joel 3:4(2:31), 4:15(3:15); Nahum 1:5–6; Haggai 2:6 (compare Mt 24:29, Lk 23:30).

The fury of the Lamb will be fearful because the Lamb is also a Lion (see 5:5–6&NN). According to Yn 5:22, Ac 17:31, Ro 2:16 and 2C 5:10 God has entrusted judgment to this Lion/Lamb. It will take place on **the Great Day**, also known as the Day of the Lord (1:10&N above, 2 Th 2:2, 2 Ke 3:10, and more than a dozen places in the *Tanakh*), the Day of our Lord Yeshua the Messiah (1C 1:8), the Day of our Lord Yeshua (2C 1:14), the Day of the Messiah (Pp 1:10), the Great Day of *Adonai-Tzva'ot* (16:14 below, Isaiah 2:12, Jeremiah 46:10), the Day of Anger (Ro 2:5; Zephaniah 1:18, 2:2–3; Lamentations 2:22), and the Day of Judgment (Mt 10:15, 2 Ke 2:9, 1 Yn 4:17 and five other places in the New Testament).

On the Great Day... who can stand? Those of the world who glory in their power will realize that it was all an illusion. Even weak people who manipulate and try to gain power in small ways will be revealed for what they are. Only those who restrict "praise, honor, glory and power" to God and the Lamb (5:13), will survive **their fury**.

CHAPTER 7

2–3 The servants of our God are **sealed on their foreheads** so that certain plagues, such as the one from the fifth trumpet (9:4), will not affect them. Yechiel Lichtenstein writes: "From 14:1 it seems that on the seal was written the name of the Lamb and of his Father." See also Ezekiel 9:4, where a mark is set on the foreheads of those who oppose the abominations done in Jerusalem.

4 144,000. Whether this number is to be taken literally or figuratively, the obvious question is: why exactly this number? The answer is usually along these lines: there are twelve tribes of Israel and twelve emissaries; there are Ten Commandments; squaring the former and cubing the latter bespeaks perfection, the perfection and fullness of Israel. Yechiel Lichtenstein (MJ 3:13N) offers an intriguing explanation:

> "Israel numbered 7,200,000 at the time of the destruction of the Second Temple. The *t'rumah* [the offering to *cohanim* from the firstfruits] is normally one fiftieth (Mishna, T'rumot 4:3), which here comes to 144,000. At Ro 11:16 Paul remarked that 'if the *challah* offered as firstfruits is holy, so is the whole loaf.' Thus the meaning is that if the firstfruits of Israel, the 144,000 Messianic Jews who put their trust in Yeshua, is holy, then the whole loaf, all of Israel, is holy. Therefore Paul continues, 'In this way all Israel will be saved. As the *Tanakh* says, "Out of Zion will come the Redeemer; he will turn away ungodliness from Jacob" (Ro 11:26).' This is in accordance with my comment on 1:7, which says that when the sign of the son of man is seen in heaven, the children of Israel will repent, recognize the Messiah, and mourn because they pierced him unjustly. That is when all Israel will be saved. Yet the condition for this is the prior salvation of 144,000." (*Commentary to the New Testament*, on Rv 7:9)

Although there is no way of knowing exactly how many Jews there were in 70 C.E. scholars agree that the number was between five and ten million. The number of Messianic Jews then, as now, was surely in six figures (see Ac 21:20N), but it would be sheer speculation to fix it at 144,000.

From every tribe of the people of Israel. The plain sense, the *p'shat*, of this phrase is "from among the entire Jewish people." But many commentators say it refers to the Church. In Ro 2:28–29N I suggest that even where the *p'shat* of a text refers to Jews, there may be a midrashic application to the entire Body of the Messiah. Moreover, at Ga 6:16 and Ep 2:11–13 (see notes there and at Ro 11:26a) "Israel" is used in a way that does include saved Gentiles, new creations formerly distant but now brought near and grafted in (Ro 11:17–24). However, the case that the **144,000 from every tribe of the people of Israel** means "the Church" is harder to make here; because v. 9 below speaks of "a huge crowd, too large for anyone to count from every nation, tribe, people and language." Apparently, this innumerable crowd of saved Gentiles is to be contrasted with the delimited number of saved Jews in the present verse. Furthermore, to emphasize the fact that these 144,000 are Jews vv. 5–8 lists the twelve tribes; this would have no immediate relevance to the Church. See also 14:1–5&NN, where the number 144,000 reappears.

One objection sometimes made to interpreting these 144,000 as Jews is that there is supposedly no reason why Jews would be singled out for special protection. Such thinking contradicts the whole of salvation history as set forth in the *Tanakh* and reflects an unawareness on the part of Gentile Christian commentators that they have been joined to Israel, that is, to the Jewish people. God, by his grace, has singled out the Jewish people for special protection for thousands of years. After centuries of dispersion and persecution, culminating in the Holocaust, we would not exist at all without such protection. This protection is promised over and over by the Prophets, even when Israel becomes sinful and breaks covenant; though it is not always promised to the entire people, but rather only to a remnant (see Ro 9:27–29, 11:1–32) — such as the 144,000. Moreover, the sealing of the Jewish people from judgment corresponds specifically to God's promise at Zechariah 9:14–16 (see 8:2N on "*shofars*").

The Jehovah's Witnesses used to claim that their adherents constituted the 144,000. When their membership came to exceed this number, they simply revised their theology! Such a blatant appeal to pride at being among the supposed spiritual elite is a favorite tactic of cults.

5–8 No matter who the 144,000 are, there is a problem with these verses, in that the listing of the twelve tribes is very strange: (1) Dan is missing, (2) Efrayim is missing but included in **Yosef**, who was Efrayim's father, (3) **M'nasheh** is counted twice, since **Yosef** was also his father, (4) **Y'hudah**, not **Re'uven**, is mentioned first, and (5) **L'vi** is included, even though this tribe is sometimes not counted, since it was not assigned a portion in the Land. Efrayim and **M'nasheh** were the two sons of **Yosef**, and their descendants were at first counted as half-tribes; but over time they became elevated to the status of tribes because Yosef, after saving his family from starvation, was treated like the firstborn and given a double portion (Genesis 48:22).

On these verses Yechiel Lichtenstein writes in his *Commentary to the New Testament*:

> "Rabbi Yitzchak of Troki's *Chizzuk-Emunah* accused Yochanan of not knowing the number of the tribes. This is nonsense, since Yochanan in his book demonstrates wonderful knowledge of the *Tanakh*.
>
> "Some say Dan is excluded because he sinned by worshipping idols (Judges 18:30, 2 Kings 10:29); as proof they quote 1 Chronicles 2–7, where the tribe of Dan is not mentioned. But this is not a valid proof, because Z'vulun is not mentioned there either; and the reason in both cases is that the author, Ezra, wrote in his book only what he found in the scrolls available to him. This is why the subjects there often follow one another without logical connection — there are missing links.
>
> "Concerning Dan, Ya'akov, when blessing his sons, said, 'Dan will judge his people as one of the tribes of Israel' (Genesis 49:16). Moreover, Ezekiel 48:32 attributes one gate to Dan, one to Yosef, since Joseph includes Efrayim and M'nasheh in respect to the heritage, and one to L'vi."

Here is Lichtenstein's solution to the problem:

> "It seems to me that a scribal error was made when the book of Revelation was being prepared for transmission to the world. Instead of 'M'nasheh' we should read 'Dan.' Yochanan also mentioned Y'hudah before Re'uven, because the Messiah came out of Y'hudah (see 1 Chronicles 2–7, where Y'hudah is also mentioned first, and the Jewish commentators on it). Next he mentions Re'uven, because he was the firstborn of the tribal patriarchs. But after this Yochanan paid no more attention to the subject."

In other words, when Yochanan proofread the manuscript of his book he failed to notic anomalies in the tribal listing. It is always tempting to attribute a difficult reading t scribal error, but I am not sure this explanation should be invoked so quickly here.

Shim'on is missing from Moses' blessing of the tribes in Deuteronomy 33. Ther too corruption of the manuscript is offered as a possible reason, although a mor specific one is that his tribe had no extended area of its own — his inheritance o 19 cities was spread through the territory of Y'hudah (Joshua 19:2–9).

It is suggested that Dan is absent from the present list because the Anti-Messiah is t come from this tribe. This idea can be found in the second-century church fathe Irenaeus; in Jewish tradition it can be traced back to the Pseudepigraphic Testaments o the Twelve Patriarchs, written around 100 B.C.E., where Dan is told:

> "In the last days you will depart from the Lord.... For I have read in the book of Enoch the righteous that your prince is Satan." (Testament of Dan 5:4–7)

But for this idea there is no biblical evidence.

Another reason for Dan's omission might be this tribe's poor reputation due to it weakness for idol-worship. The Midrash Rabbah explains Numbers 2:25, "The standar of the camp of Dan is to be on the north side," thusly:

> "'The north.' From there comes darkness [since the sun is in the south]. Why is this relevant to Dan? Because Dan darkened the world by idolatry. For [King] Jeroboam made two calves of gold. And idolatry is darkness, as it is said, 'Their works are in the dark' (Isaiah 29:15). Jeroboam went about all over Israel, but they would not receive his teaching, except for the tribe of Dan, as it is said, 'The king took counsel, made two calves of gold... and set the one in Dan' (1 Kings 12:28–29). This is why the Holy One commanded that Dan should set up his camp on the north." (Numbers Rabbah 2:10)

If it is meant literally that 12,000 from each tribe are to be selected, it can b objected that no one will know who belongs to which tribe, since genealogies no longe exist. One answer: God, who will be doing the choosing, will know.

9 **A huge crowd... dressed in white robes**. See vv. 13–17. **From every nation, trib people and language**. See 5:9b–13N.

10 **Victory**. Greek *sôtêria* usually means "salvation" or "deliverance," but KJV's "Salvation to our God..." is awkward, since God does not need to be saved. Here (and at 12:10, 19:1) the sense is as at Psalm 98:2: "His right hand and his holy arm have gotten him [God] the victory." The Hebrew word there is the verb related to "*yeshu'ah*" ("salvation").

11–12 "***Amen***" always refers back to something said previously (Mt 5:18N). The first "*Amen*" of **the elders and the four living beings** in v. 12 is their response to the shout of the crowd at v. 10. The second one is a signal to that crowd to respond by affirming the elders' and living beings' own words of praise (see Ro 9:5N).

To our God. Or: "come from our God." See v. 10N.

14 **The Great Persecution** (KJV, "great tribulation"); compare Daniel 12:1, also Mt 24:21–22&N. Verses 14–17 offer comfort to any believer undergoing persecution.

They have washed their robes and made them white with the blood of the Lamb. The metaphor, which only gains power from being contradictory when taken literally, means that those who did not capitulate under persecution have become clean and are regarded by God as sinless (compare Isaiah 1:18) because they have remained faithful to Yeshua, who shed his blood for them (see 1:7&N).

15 **His Temple**. According to Jewish tradition, God has a temple in heaven. Compare the book of Messianic Jews, in which Yeshua is presented as a *cohen* serving God in heaven. See also MJ 8:2–6a&N, which refers to the Tent (Tabernacle) in heaven and gives references in Exodus.

Will put his *Sh'khinah* upon them. Or: "will spread his tent over them," giving protection. The Greek word "*skênôsei*" ("will spread his tent, will dwell") is related to the Hebrew words "*mishkan*" ("tent, tabernacle") and "*Sh'khinah*" ("dwelling," used in rabbinic Judaism to mean "God's manifest glory dwelling with mankind"; see MJ 1:2–3N). Compare Ezekiel 37:27, where, in the valley of dry bones, God says, "*V'hayah mishkani 'aleihem*" ("and my tent will be upon them").

17 **The Lamb** can be **at the center of the throne** because he is identified with God. **Springs of living water**. See 21:6N. **Wipe away every tear**. See 21:4N.

CHAPTER 8

1 After **the seventh seal** the scroll (5:1) is not mentioned again, but what follows is a description of its contents.

2 **The seven angels who stand before God**. Seven "Angels of the Presence" have a well-documented history in Jewish literature (see 1:4N), possibly commencing with Isaiah 63:9, which mentions "an angel of his [God's] presence" (compare Lk 1:19, "I am Gavri'el," the angel answered him, "and I stand in the presence of God."), and Ezekiel 9:2, which speaks of "six men... with slaughter weapons, and one man among them clothed in linen with a writer's ink well at his side," to whom God speaks.

In the Apocrypha, Rafa'el identifies himself as "one of the seven holy angels" (Tobit 12:15). 1 Enoch 20 gives the names and functions of seven "holy angels who watch": Uri'el, Rafa'el, Ragu'el, Mikha'el, Saraka'el, Gavri'el and Remi'el. The first four are called "ministering angels" ("*mal'akhey-hasharet*") in the Talmud, the *siddur*, and the *kabbalah*; compare the fact that in vv. 7–12 four angels are singled out to announce the four "non-woe" *shofar* judgments. See also 1:4N on "the sevenfold Spirit" and v. 4&N below. On whether angels exist at all, see MJ 13:2bN.

Shofars ("ram's horns"), not trumpets. The idea that the Great Judgment of the Last Days is heralded by blasts on the *shofar* has its roots in the *Tanakh*. "*YHVH* will be seen over them, his arrow will go forth like lightning, and *Adonai YHVH* will sound the *shofar* and will move in the stormwinds of the south.... And *YHVH* their God will save them [Y'hudah and Efrayim] on that day as the flock of his people" (Zechariah 9:14, 16). Similarly God protects Israel at 7:1–8 before setting the *shofar* judgments in motion "on that day," half an hour afterwards (8:1). Compare Isaiah 27:13, Joel 2:1, Zephaniah 1:16 and, in the Pseudepigrapha, Psalms of Solomon 11 and 4 Ezra 6:23–26. In the New Testament see Mt 24:31&N, 1C 15:52&N and 1 Th 4:16&N.

3 It is not clear from the Greek grammar whether this verse speaks of two altars or one. The temple in Jerusalem had two — one for burnt offerings and another for incense. But, as R. H. Charles puts it, "since there could be no animal sacrifices in heaven" (this is also consistent with MJ 9:18–10:20), there is only **the altar** for **incense**. Moreover, the rabbinic citations in 6:9N mention only one altar.

4 **The smoke of the incense** added by **another angel** accompanies **the prayers of all God's people** (not only those of the martyrs, as at 6:9–10); both rise to God together — but it is not clear just what this means. Nevertheless, compare Exodus Rabbah 21:4:

> "What is the meaning of 'O Thou that hearest prayer' (Psalm 65:3)? Rabbi Pinchas in the name of Rabbi Me'ir and Rabbi Yirmiyahu in the name of Rabbi Chiyya bar-Abba said, 'When the people of Israel pray, you do not find them all praying at the same time, but each assembly prays separately, first one and then another. When they have all finished, the angel appointed over prayers collects all the prayers that have been offered in all the synagogues, weaves them into garlands and places them upon the head of God.'"

Also Testament of Levi 3:5–6:

> "In [the heaven next to the highest heaven] are the angels of the presence of the Lord, who minister and make propitiation to the Lord for all the sins of ignorance of the righteous. And they offer to the Lord a sweet-smelling savor, a reasonable and bloodless offering."

The prayers are evidently for judgment to begin, and God answers at once (v. 5 through 14:20); but see also 6:10N.

7–12 The first four *shofar* judgments affect nature directly and people indirectly (compare

Mt 24:4–8) and resemble the plagues of Egypt (see Psalm 105:29, 32), while the last three plagues (v. 13) affect people directly (compare Mt 24:13–22).

The idea that the End-Time plagues will recapitulate those of Egypt can be found in the Midrash Rabbah:

> "'Behold, tomorrow about this time I will cause it to rain a very grievous hail such as has not been in Egypt from the day it was founded until now' (Exodus 9:18).... However, there will be one like it in the time to come. When? In the days of Gog and Magog, as it is written,... 'A torrential rain, and great hailstones, fire and sulfur' (Ezekiel 38:2, 22)." (Exodus Rabbah 12:2)

Compare below at 11:19, 16:21, 20:7.

Consider the function of the Egyptian plagues. The well-known song, "*Dayenu*" ([It would have been] "Enough for us"), from the Passover *Haggadah*, says that God through the plagues judged both the Egyptians and their gods (compare 9:20). He did this by turning against the Egyptians the very things they worshipped. They worshipped the Nile River; it became blood. They worshipped beetles (scarabs); they got lice and locusts. They worshipped frogs and found them in bed. They worshipped the weather and had their crops destroyed by hail.

If these verses in Revelation are to be understood literally, then, since God uses nature to accomplish his purposes, one can imagine asteroids plunging into the earth, other materials from outer space darkening the skies and infecting the water, and heat flashes setting fire to the vegetation; and one can seek scientific explanations for such phenomena. But if these are graphic but figurative ways of describing God's judgment and the terror it will evoke, such speculations and researches are irrelevant. There are intelligent, well-informed, God-fearing New Testament scholars taking each approach.

10–11 **Bitterness**, literally, "wormwood, absinthe"; compare Jeremiah 9:15, 23:15: "I will feed this people wormwood and give them water of gall to drink."

13 **A lone eagle**, representing swiftness, or "a lone vulture," representing pursuit of carrion (as at Mt 24:28&N, Lk 17:37).

Woe! Woe! Woe! The remaining *shofar* judgments are directed not at nature but at **the people living on earth** (the pagan world hostile to God; see 3:10N) in order to get them to repent (9:20–21), while the sealed are spared (9:4; 7:1–8). These three "woes" are announced by **the remaining** *shofar* **blasts**, and are described at 9:1–12, 9:13–11:14 and 11:15–18:24 respectively. Just as the seventh seal (v. 1&N) included the seven "*shofar*" judgments, so the seventh *shofar* blast includes the seven "bowl" judgments, which begin at 16:1.

CHAPTER 9

1 The **star** is not Satan (despite Isaiah 14:12, Lk 10:17), but an angel, who still has **the key** at 20:1. **The Abyss** is not *Sh'ol* (as at Ro 10:7), but a place where demonic beings are imprisoned (vv. 2–11, 11:7, 17:8, 20:2–3). In the Apocrypha, God is called, "You who close and seal the Abyss with your fearful and glorious name" (Prayer of Manasseh 3).

2 **Like the smoke of a huge furnace** or volcano, evoking images of Sodom (Genesis 19:28) and of Sinai; there too a *shofar* sounded (Exodus 19:18–19).

3 Demonic monsters are released which fly like **locusts** (Exodus 10:12–20; Joel 1:4, 2:4–14) and sting like **scorpions** (Ezekiel 2:6, Lk 11:12).

4 **The people who did not have the seal of God on their foreheads**. See 7:1–8&NN.

5 "**Five months**" may mean "a few months, a short time."

6 Compare 6:16, Jeremiah 8:3, Hosea 10:8, Job 3:21, Lk 23:30.

7–9 The descriptions are from Joel 1:4–6, 2:4–5.

11 "The locusts have no king, yet all of them march in rank" (Proverbs 30:27). Here they have **as king over them the angel of the Abyss**, probably not the same angel as in v. 1.

In our language, "Destroyer." Literally, "in Greek, he has the name '*Apolluôn*.' " Hebrew "*Abaddon*" and Greek "*Apolluôn*" both mean "Destroyer."

12 See 8:13&N.

13–19 The fifth *shofar* brought suffering, the sixth brings death.

16 **Two hundred million**. Perhaps a literal number, but compare Psalm 68:18: "The chariots of God are twice ten thousand, thousands upon thousands."

18 **Fire... and sulfur**. See 14:10aN.

19 Those who interpret literally take this as a description of some modern invention. On literal and figurative interpretation see 8:7–12N.

20 The locusts in Joel 2:4–10 were intended to bring about repentance (Joel 2:11–14); likewise here, but the people refused.

Idols, though themselves not real (1C 8:4, Psalm 115:4–8), have real **demons** behind them (1C 10:19–20). Moreover, not every idolatry involves bowing to statues (see Ep 5:5, Co 3:5, 1 Yn 5:21&N). On this and **plagues** see 8:7–12N.

21 **Nor did they turn**.... Compare 16:9, 11, 21. All the sins named are connected with idolatry (v. 20).

Misuse of drugs in connection with the occult. Greek *pharmakeia*, usually translated "sorceries," "witchcraft" or "magic arts," is here rendered by this longer phrase in order to focus on the fact that using potions and drugs is an essential part of the word's meaning — as is clear from the derived English words "pharmaceuticals" and "pharmacy." The usual renderings suggest to many people a setting so removed from the fabric of their lives that the text does not speak to them. The reason I employ this lengthy expression is that the *Jewish New Testament* is a product of the 1980's, when the Western world has seen an explosion of drug abuse, and I want readers to understand that this subject is dealt with in the Bible.

Spiritually speaking, there are four distinct categories of drug misuse: (1) taking drugs in order to explore spiritual realms, (2) taking drugs in order to engage in "sorcery, witchcraft and magic arts" while under their influence, (3) giving drugs to other people in order to gain control over them, which is another form of "sorcery, witchcraft and magic arts," and (4) taking drugs for pleasure. The last is a misuse because the drugs in question — besides whatever temporary enjoyment they provide, and apart from their adverse medical and psychological effects — open a person to supernatural or spiritual experiences; but these experiences are almost always demonic and not from God, since the Holy One of Israel reveals himself through his Word (Ro 1:16–17, 10:8–17), not through drugs. (I know of one instance where God overruled LSD and spoke to someone under its influence; he became a believer immediately, was instantly sober and never used drugs again.)

Just as a virgin who has sexual intercourse can never again be a virgin, so a person is not the same after having taken mind-altering drugs. His range of experience has been broadened, but not every experience is edifying (1C 10:23). As Sha'ul puts it:

> "You say, 'For me, everything is permitted'? Maybe, but not everything is helpful. 'For me, everything is permitted'? Maybe, but as far as I am concerned, I am not going to let anything gain control over me. 'Food is meant for the stomach and the stomach for food'? Maybe, but God will put an end to both of them. Anyhow, the body is not meant for sexual immorality" [or for drugs] "but for the Lord, and the Lord is for the body."(1C 6:12–13)
>
> "I want you to be wise concerning good, but innocent concerning evil." (Ro 16:19)

From other New Testament passages where "*pharmakeia*" and its cognates appear, we learn that those who misuse drugs "have no share in the Kingdom of God" (Ga 5:20), so that they remain outside the holy city, New Jerusalem; and instead, "their destiny is the lake burning with fire and sulfur, the second death" (below, 21:8, 22:5). (At 18:23 *pharmakeia* has a different meaning.)

So much for the Bad News. The Good News is that when a pride-filled, weak-willed, uncaring, despairing drug-user trusts Yeshua the Messiah, God can turn him into a person of faith and right action.

CHAPTER 10

1 **Legs** (as in most versions; KJV, "feet"). This is a good proof that the Jewish author, Yochanan, thought in Hebrew. In Greek, "*podes*" means "feet," and "*skelê*" means "legs." But Hebrew has only one word, "*raglayim*," which can mean either. The text

here has "*podes,*" but feet cannot be **like columns** (or "pillars"), only legs can. Either the author, thinking in Hebrew but writing in Greek, believed "*podes*" was the appropriate Greek rendering of "*raglayim*"; or the author thought and wrote in Hebrew, but someone else, equally unacquainted with Greek nuances, translated "*raglayim*" as "*podes*" instead of "*skelê.*" (I know from living in Israel that this specific confusion does occur: even my own children, bilingual in Hebrew and English, used to call feet "legs.")

2 **His right foot on the sea and his left foot on the land**, symbolizing the fact that this angel's mission involves the whole world.

3 **Thunderclaps sounded with voices**. Compare 1:15, 4:5; and see Ac 2:4b–13&N.

4 **The seven thunders** are aspects of divine wrath which God orders concealed and not revealed. Sha'ul mentioned a similar experience at 2C 12:3–4. Compare Daniel 12:9.

6 **No more delay**. Compare Ro 9:28, 2 Ke 3:9.

7 **The hidden plan** ("mystery"; see Ro 11:25N) **of God** is **the Good News**, the Gospel. It includes both judgment, as described in the book of Revelation, and the overall outworking of history, including the salvation of the Jewish people and of others who come to faith, as outlined at Ro 11:25–36, 16:25; Ep 1:9–10; 3:3–11; and Co 1:26–27; compare Mt 13:11. God **proclaimed it to his servants the prophets** (the phrase echoes Daniel 9:6), even though, since they lived centuries earlier, they did not fully understand it (Daniel 12:8ff.); compare Ga 3:8.

8–11 On eating the scroll, compare Jeremiah 15:16, Ezekiel 2:8–3:3; also Psalms 19:11(10) 119:103 on its words' being **sweet as honey**. On the bitterness, see Ezekiel 3:4–11; also compare Yeshua weeping over Jerusalem (Mt 23:37–38, Lk 19:41) — there is no joy in preaching the wrath of God.

CHAPTER 11

1–14 Although some take this passage as referring symbolically to the Church, many see it as a graphic way of saying that after the Anti-Messiah and his minions do all in their power to destroy the Gospel witness to the Jewish people (v. 7) and to destroy the Jewish people themselves (v. 2b), then "All Israel will be saved" (Ro 11:26a&N). Verses 1–2&N show that the focus is on Jews, not Gentiles.

1–2 **Measuring** symbolizes reserving a city either for preservation (Ezekiel 40:3–48:35, Zechariah 2:5–9(1–5)) or for destruction (2 Kings 21:12–14, Isaiah 34:11, Lamentations 2:8). Verses 2, 8 and 13a suggest that Jerusalem, the capital of the Jewish nation and therefore a figure for the Jewish people (as at Isaiah 40:1–2, Mt 23:37–39&N, Lk 2:38), deserves judgment and destruction. But v. 13b shows that its destiny is repenting and being preserved.

The Temple of God. In addition to the Tent of Meeting (the Tabernacle) and the

heavenly original after which it was modeled (see 15:5&N, MJ 8:2–6a&N), Scripture mentions six literal temples:
(1) Solomon's, the First Temple (1 Kings 5–8).
(2) Z'rubavel's, the Second Temple (Haggai 1–2, Ezra 3:4–13).
(3) Herod's, called the rebuilt Second Temple or, by some, the Third Temple (Mt 21:12ff., 24:1–2; Yn 2:19–20).
(4) A future temple in the days of Anti-Messiah (Daniel 9:27, 11:45, 12:7; Mt 24:15; 2 Th 2:3–4; and here).
(5) A future temple in the days of the Messiah (Ezekiel 40–48, Zechariah 6:12–15).
(6) The temple in heaven (below at 7:15; 11:19; 14:15, 17; 16:17).
Besides, there are three figurative ones:
(1) The Messianic Community (1C 3:16–17, 2C 6:16, Ep 2:21).
(2) The physical body of a believer (1C 6:19).
(3) God and the Lamb (in the New Jerusalem; Revelation 21:22).

The **people... worshipping** in the Temple are Jews, and perhaps not all the Jews but the believing Jewish remnant (see Ro 9:6N, 9:27–29N, 11:1–6N, 11:26aN); since **the court outside the Temple**, known as the Court of the Gentiles (see Ep 2:14N) is to be left out and not measured. In fact, the role of the ***Goyim*** (see Mt 5:46N) here is to **trample over the holy city**, Jerusalem (as at Lk 21:24&N), while the remnant is spared. At v. 9 Gentiles prevent the burial of the two witnesses.

42 months (also at 13:5). This is apparently identical with the "1,260 days" of v. 3 and 12:6 (compare Daniel 12:11–12, where "1,290 days" and "1,335 days" are mentioned) and the "season and two seasons and half a season" of 12:14 below (and Daniel 7:25, 12:7).

Related, but pertaining rather to a period twice as long, seven years, are Daniel 8:14 ("2,300 evenings and mornings") and Daniel 9:25–27 (referring to 7 weeks of years, 62 weeks of years and 1 week of years). A Talmudic passage cited in Mt 24:1–39N speaks of a seven-year period during which various plagues occur. Also see 13:1–8N.

3–6 My (the Messiah's) **two witnesses** are identified with **the two olive trees** of Zechariah 4:3 and **the two *menorah*s standing before the Lord of the earth**. Zechariah 4:2 speaks of one *menorah* with seven branches, while Zechariah 4:14 identifies the two olive branches with "the two anointed ones who stand by the Lord of the whole earth."

These two witnesses testify about Yeshua, spread his Good News among the Jewish people in Jerusalem, prophesy and perform miracles; during this time they enjoy God's special protection (vv. 5–6). Then the beast from the Abyss kills them (v. 7). Their bodies lie in the main street of Jerusalem for three-and-a-half days (vv. 8–9), after which they rise from death and go up into heaven (vv. 11–12).

In the context of Zechariah 3–4 the two "anointed ones" are Joshua the *cohen hagadol* and Z'rubavel the governor. Various midrashic traditions identify them as Aaron and Moses (Exodus Rabbah 15:3), Aaron and David (Numbers Rabbah 14:13, 18:16), Aaron and the Messiah (*Avot diRabbi Natan* 30b), possibly *Mashiach Ben-Yosef* and *Mashiach Ben-David* (Pesikta Rabbati 8:4; the text is ambiguous). In the Talmud Rabbi Yitzchak calls the scholars of *Eretz-Israel* "anointed ones" (*b'nei-yitzhar*, literally, "sons of clear oil") because they debate amicably, and those of Babylon "olive trees" because their disputes are bitter (like uncured olives; Sanhedrin 24a).

So then, who are the two witnesses? Often they are said to be Moses and Elijah, since these appeared with Yeshua at the Transfiguration (Mt 17:1–8). The problem with this understanding is that the witnesses must die (v. 7), and human beings die only once (MJ 9:27).

The case for Elijah is a good one. He has not yet died (2 Kings 2:1, 9–12), he is expected to return before the Messiah comes (Malachi 3:23–24(4:5–6)), and he has already **shut up the sky, so that no rain falls** (1 Kings 17:1, 18:42–45; Lk 4:25; Ya 5:17–18&N).

While Moses did **turn the waters into blood and strike the earth with every kind of plague** (Exodus 7:17–12:30; 1 Samuel 4:8), Scripture says that he died, so that he cannot die again. Nevertheless Jewish tradition is not satisfied to let him rest in peace. To prove he is still alive one Talmudic rabbi used the principle of interpretation called *g'zerah shavah*. The term means "analogy" (literally, "equal decision") and operates by inferring that if a word has a particular meaning in one passage of Scripture it must have the same meaning in a second passage. (The rabbis saw that this technique could easily be misused to reach conclusions contrary to Scripture and therefore prohibited its further use; only the instances cited by the early interpreters are recognized.)

> "It has been taught that Rabbi Eli'ezer the Elder said, 'Over an area [about two miles square], the size of the camp of Israel, a *bat-kol* [heavenly voice] proclaimed, "So Moses died there, the great sage of Israel." But others say that Moses never died. For although the *Tanakh* says, "So Moses died there" (Deuteronomy 34:5), it elsewhere says, "And he was there with *Adonai*" (Exodus 34:28). Just as in the latter passage the word "there" means "standing and ministering," so likewise in the former it means "standing and ministering."' "(Sotah 13b)

In any case, perhaps only because Moses' death was unusual (Deuteronomy 34:5–6; Yd 9&N; below, v. 12N), there is a popular belief that he and Elijah will return:

> "Rabbi Yochanan Ben-Zakkai… [taught that God] said, 'Moses, I swear to you that in the time to come, when I bring Elijah the prophet to [Israel], the two of you will come together.'"(Deuteronomy Rabbah 3:17)

Yochanan himself is sometimes suggested as one of the witnesses, on the basis of Yn 21:20–24. But the two witnesses had lived and were already in heaven in the fifth century B.C.E., when Zechariah prophesied (see Zechariah 4:11–14).

Besides Elijah, only one person has been taken into heaven without dying — Enoch (Genesis 5:21–24; MJ 11:5). Both lived before 500 B.C.E., and both were prophets (**they will prophesy**; see Yd 14). Since they have never died, they can yet undergo the death of v. 7. If the "two witnesses" are two literal persons and we are not dealing with a figurative expression, I nominate Enoch and Elijah.

Meanwhile, believers in Jerusalem have grown used to being presented with other candidates. They appear every few months, often **dressed in sackcloth** like the Prophets of the *Tanakh* (Isaiah 20:2; compare 2 Kings 1:8, Zechariah 13:4, Mt 3:4), and claiming to be "in the spirit and power of Elijah" (Lk 1:17) or even to be Elijah himself. Whatever the spirit, till now the power (vv. 5–6) has not been in evidence.

Fire comes out of their mouth and consumes their enemies. At Jeremiah 5:14, the prophet addresses Israel: "Therefore thus says *Adonai*, God of the armies of heaven: 'Because you speak this word, I will make my words fire in your mouth, and this people wood, and it will consume them.' " See also 2 Kings 1:10, 12; Lk 9:54.

7 **The beast** seems to be the same as the Anti-Messiah (1 Yn 2:18–19&N). See 13:1–18&NN, 14:8–11&NN. **The Abyss.** See 9:1N.

8 **The city where their Lord was executed on a stake** can only be Jerusalem. "Their" refers to the Jewish people, as does the city itself (vv. 1–2N). The author, speaking to his own people, uses hard language. Their **spiritual condition** is that of **"S'dom"** (compare Isaiah 1:10), where sexual sin and misuse of people were rife (Genesis 19), and **"Egypt,"** where false religion, hatred of the one true God and antisemitism flourished (Exodus 1–15).

9 **Some from the nations, tribes, languages and peoples**, that is, from the Gentiles (see 5:9b–13N), are so hostile to God, his Word and his Prophets that they prevent the burial of the two witnesses whose bodies lie exposed in the main street of Jerusalem to dogs and flies, and, more importantly, to shame (19:21N, Psalm 69:2–4, 1 Kings 13:22; Josephus' *Wars of the Jews* 4:5:2).

10 **The people living in the Land.** I believe this refers here not to the pagans of the earth, as elsewhere in Revelation, but to Jews living in Israel. This conclusion is based on the facts that (1) the Hebrew antecedents of the Greek expression frequently mean this (see 3:10N), and (2) a Gentile reaction to the death of the witnesses has been given already in v. 9.

Yochanan foresees a time when Jewish opposition to the Gospel is intensified by the appearance of **these two prophets**. From the point of view of believers, they evangelize the non-Messianic Jews of the Land, testifying to Yeshua and proclaiming the Good News. But the non-Messianic Jews' evaluation is that the two prophets **tormented** them. For this reason they not only reject the witnesses' message but, instead of sitting *shiv'ah* (Yn 11:19–20N), they **celebrate and send each other gifts** — like the Jews of Shushan after slaying Haman's sons (Esther 9:22). The difference, of course, is that Haman and his sons were truly oppressors, whereas the Messiah's witnesses offer deliverance.

11–12 The resurrection and ascension of the witnesses, similar to Yeshua's own, causes **great fear** in their **enemies**, because this demonstrates in power (1C 2:14, 4:20, 6:14, 15:54–57) that our God reigns. The Word of *Adonai* is powerful (Isaiah 55:10–11; MJ 1:3) and indestructible (Isaiah 40:8; 1 Ke 1:23–25); it cannot be silenced by killing those who speak it.

They went up to heaven in a cloud, not only like Yeshua (Ac 1:9–11), but also, according to Josephus, like Moses. Notice how Josephus deals with the contrary witness of Deuteronomy 34:5–6:

> "As [Moses] was going to embrace El'azar [the *cohen hagadol*] and Y'hoshua [*bin-Nun*], while he was still talking with them, all of a sudden a cloud stood over him, and he disappeared in a certain valley — although he wrote in the holy books that he died. This he did out of fear that people might say that because of his extraordinary virtue he went to God." (Josephus, *Antiquities of the Jews* 4:8:48)

See also vv. 3–6N, 6:9N, Yd 9N.

13 The **earthquake** is a frequent form of judgment in the Last Days (6:12, 8:5, 11:19, 16:18; Ezekiel 38:19–20). It kills **seven thousand people** (about 1.3% of Jerusalem's present population) and causes widespread damage (**a tenth of the city collapsed**). The result, for the survivors, is nothing less than salvation, the fulfillment of God's promise through Sha'ul that "all Israel will be saved" (Ro 11:26a&N). "Jews ask for signs" (1C 1:22). At Mt 16:1–4, the *P'rushim* asked Yeshua for a sign, but he promised none "except the sign of Jonah," whose being vomited from the stomach of the fish is a type of resurrection. The two witnesses' resurrection and ascension, along with the simultaneous earthquake (**in that hour**), are correctly understood by the Jewish people as signs from God — **the rest were awestruck**. Even while grieved at the death of 7,000 people, they handled their pain in God's way (2C 7:10&N) — it led them to repentance, so that they **gave glory to the God of heaven**. Throughout the book of Revelation, only those in a right relationship with God give him glory (1:6; 4:9, 11; 5:12–13; 7:12; 15:4; 19:1, 7). Conversely, those who are not in a right relationship with God glorify themselves (18:7) instead of God (14:7, 16:9) — compare the hardened pagans of Ro 1:21: "Although they know who God is, they do not glorify him as God or thank him." This mass repentance breaks the back of the Jewish national establishment's centuries-long opposition to the Gospel. May it come speedily, in our days.

14 See 8:13&N.

15–17 When **the seventh angel** sounds **his *shofar***, then **The kingdom of the world has become the Kingdom of our Lord and his Messiah**, and *Adonai* has **begun to rule**. The active reign of God on earth, the Messianic Kingdom, promised at 1:5–8 and 6:10, now begins to become real. Between these verses and Chapter 19 are the various judgments and other events associated with the overthrow of the system of this world and the inauguration of the Messiah's rulership. This is why essentially the same cry is heard again at 19:6: "*Halleluyah*! *Adonai*, God of heaven's armies, has begun his reign!"

18 This is a *midrash* on the whole of Psalm 2, contrasting God's righteous judgment and **rage** with that of **the *Goyim***, the pagan nations opposed to God and his ways.

19 **The Temple of God**. See vv. 1–2N.

In heaven... the Ark of the Covenant. The earthly ark, mentioned in the New Testament at MJ 9:4–5&NN, is first described at Exodus 25:10–22. Initially kept behind the Tabernacle's curtain and later inside the Holy of Holies in Solomon's temple, this chest was afterwards apparently either removed by Shishak, king of Egypt, when he "took away the treasures of the house of the Lord" (1 Kings 14:25), or destroyed along with the temple by the Babylonians (compare Jeremiah 3:16).

Extra-biblical narratives say that the ark was hidden "in its place" (Talmud, Yoma 53b) or elsewhere. Yoma 52b says it was King Josiah who hid it; but in the Apocrypha, 2 Maccabees 2:4–8 tells that Jeremiah rescued the ark and brought it to a cave on Mount Sinai to be preserved until God gathers his people together in Messianic times (see 2:17N). Mention of the ark in the present verse accords with this tradition, since Israel's salvation, a Messianic event, is reported above at v. 13.

If the earthly ark symbolized God's presence guiding his people, the appearance of the heavenly ark symbolizes God's being about to fulfill the rest of his covenanted promises.

CHAPTER 12

1–5 Whether favoring literal or figurative interpretation of the book of Revelation, nearly all commentators agree that these verses depict the birth of Yeshua the Messiah and his ascension to heaven after being resurrected. This means that Revelation is not simply a presentation of future events in chronological order, since this passage flashes back to past history.

1 The **woman** is not Miryam, Yeshua's mother, but Israel, in its normal sense, the Jewish people, because the imagery is from Isaiah 66:7–10 (compare also Isaiah 26:17, Micah 4:10). Because of v. 17 this cannot be the "extended Israel" concept which includes Gentile Christians (see 7:4N on "from every tribe of the sons of Israel").

Although Israel is on earth, Yochanan sees her **in heaven**, symbolizing the fact that God protects and preserves the Jews; this is made more explicit at vv. 6, 13–16. Moreover, Mikha'el is Israel's angelic protector (v. 7&N). There is an obvious resemblance between the woman and "heavenly Jerusalem" (Ga 4:26, MJ 12:22–24).

Twelve stars. Some think this means the twelve signs of the zodiac. While writers draw on materials from their own culture, and Judaism became embroiled with astrology well before Yochanan lived, it is clear that his purposes have nothing to do with astrology. At 21:12–14 the number twelve refers to the tribes of Israel and the emissaries of Yeshua, and this understanding is adequate to the context here too.

She screamed in the agony of labor. See Mt 24:8N on the "birth pains" of the Messiah.

3–4 The **dragon** is Satan, the Adversary (see v. 9N); its **seven heads and ten horns** also equate it with the "fourth beast" of Daniel 7:7, 24 (see 13:1N). It **stood in front of the woman**, opposing Yeshua, ready to **devour the child the moment it was born**.

Stars. Possibly natural stars (6:13, 8:12; Mt 24:29), but more likely "his angels" (v. 7; compare 1:20, 9:1), who rebelled with Satan against God (see 2 Ke 2:4N).

5 **A male child**. Compare Isaiah 66:7; see v. 17&N. **Who will rule all the nations with a staff of iron**. This phrase from Psalm 2, in its entirety about the Messiah, is also quoted at 2:26–27&N and 19:15; see also 11:18&N.

6 See vv. 14–17&N.

7 **Mikha'el, one of the ruling angels** (see 1 Th 4:16N, Yd 9&N). In Jewish popular thought, angels are a Christian invention reflecting a departure from pure monotheism. Actually, angels are frequently mentioned in the *Tanakh*, although **Mikha'el** (Michael) and Gavri'el (Gabriel; see Lk 1:19N) are the only ones it identifies by name. Post-*Tanakh* Judaism developed an elaborate angelology.

At Daniel 10:13, after Daniel had fasted three weeks, Gavri'el explains his delay in coming: "The prince of the kingdom of Persia withstood me for twenty-one days, until Mikha'el, one of the first-ranked angels, came to my aid, and I was no longer needed there with the kings of Persia." At Daniel 10:21, Gavri'el tells Daniel about "Mikha'el, your prince"; and "your" is plural — Mikha'el is the Jewish people's prince or guardian angel, who fights alongside Gavri'el against the angels of Persia and Greece. Daniel 12:1, speaking of the End of Days, adds, "At that time Mikha'el, the great prince who stands [guard] for the children of your people, will arise; and there will be a period of trouble greater than any which has been from the time nations began until then; but at that time your people — that is, everyone whose name is found written in the book — will be delivered." (This verse is alluded to at 20:15, Mt 24:21.) Here Mikha'el is seen with his heavenly armies, defeating the dragon.

The *aggadah* names many other angels, for example, Rafa'el and 'Aza'zel, referred to in the quotation from 1 Enoch in 2 Ke 2:4N. (See also 1:4N on "the sevenfold Spirit" and 8:2N.) Moreover, the tradition expands the roles of Mikha'el and Gavri'el. According to Pesikta Rabbati 46:3, they are two of the four angels surrounding God's throne; but the Talmud states that Mikha'el is greater than Gavri'el (B'rakhot 4b). Mikha'el was the angel who called on Avraham not to sacrifice Yitzchak (*Midrash Va-Yosha* in A. Jellinek, *Beit-HaMidrash* 1:38, referring to Genesis 22:11). According to Exodus Rabbah 18:5, it was Mikha'el who smote Sennacherib and the Assyrian army (2 Kings 19:35); the passage adds that

> "Mikha'el and Samma'el [identified with Satan; see Yd 9N] both stand before the *Sh'khinah*; Satan accuses, while Mikha'el points out Israel's virtues, and when Satan wishes to speak again, Mikha'el silences him."

Esther Rabbah 7:12 says it was Mikha'el who defended the Jews against each of Haman's accusations. When the Messiah comes, Mikha'el and Gavri'el will accompany him and will fight the wicked (*Alphabet Midrash of Rabbi Akiva*).

One of the most moving passages in the Midrash Rabbah occurs at its close. When the time came for Moses to die, Samma'el, the angel of death, came to take his soul. But Moses objected, reciting a long list of his accomplishments to prove that he need not surrender his soul to Samma'el. Finally it was God himself who

> "came down from the highest heavens to take away the soul of Moses; and with him were three ministering angels, Mikha'el, Gavri'el and Zagzag'el. Mikha'el prepared his bier, Gavri'el spread out a fine linen cloth by the pillow under his head, and Zagzag'el put one at his feet. Then Mikha'el stood at one side and Gavri'el at the other. The Holy One, blessed be he, summoned Moses' soul; but

it replied, 'Master of the Universe, I beg you, let me stay in Moses' body.' Whereupon God kissed Moses, taking his soul away with a kiss of his mouth; and God, if one may say so, wept. And the *Ruach HaKodesh* said, 'Since then there has not arisen in Israel a prophet like Moses' (Deuteronomy 34:10). Blessed be the Lord forever. *Amen* and *Amen*." (Condensed from Deuteronomy Rabbah 11:10)

Though compiled in the fourth century C.E., the writers of the Midrash Rabbah did not recognize that Yeshua was the "prophet like Moses" and had already "arisen in Israel"; see Ac 3:22–23N. Y'hudah 9 alludes to this tradition concerning Mikha'el's role in Moses' death; see notes there and at 11:3–6 above.

In the kabbalistic (Jewish occult) literature the status of Mikha'el is further exalted. He is associated or even identified with the angel Metatron, himself sometimes equated with the Messiah. Mikha'el is given a role in redemption and becomes a personification of grace. He is sometimes portrayed as bringing before God the souls of the righteous (see 6:9&N).

9–10 Is the New Testament merely warmed-over Greek mythology? If not, why does it have a chapter about a **great dragon**? Yochanan answers here and at 20:2 by identifying the dragon (Greek *drakô*) in Jewish terminology as:

(1) **That ancient serpent**, Greek *ophis*, used in the Septuagint at Genesis 3 to translate Hebrew *nachash*, the serpent in the Garden of Eden.

(2) **The Devil**, Greek *diabolos*, "slanderer, accuser," the Septuagint's word for "Satan"; this is precisely his role at Job 1–2.

(3) **Satan (the Adversary)**. I render Greek *Satanas* twice, first by a transliteration, then by a translation; see Mt 4:1N.

(4) **The deceiver of the whole world**. Compare 20:2–3 below.

(5) **The accuser of our brothers**. Satan's accusing God's people is familiar in non-Messianic Judaism; one may say that antisemitism is one of its manifestations.

Moreover, the *Tanakh* uses "monster language" of its own when speaking of Satan:

(1) *Rahav* ("Rahab" — no connection with the woman who sheltered the spies in Jericho), meaning Egypt, but with Satan's power lurking beneath (Isaiah 51:9, Psalm 39:10, Job 26:13).

(2) *Livyatan* ("Leviathan, sea monster"; Isaiah 27:1; Psalms 74:14, 104:26; Job 40:25–41:26(41:1–34)); the description in the last passage makes it clear that Leviathan is no natural sea monster.

(3) *Behemot* ("Behemoth, hippopotamus"; but in Job 40:15–24 a supernatural being).

(4) *Tanin* ("dragon, crocodile"; Isaiah 51:9, Psalm 74:13, Job 7:12).

(5) *Nachash* ("serpent"; Genesis 3:1–19, Isaiah 27:1, Amos 9:3, Job 26:13).

In the Septuagint "*drakôn*" (which underlies the English word "dragon") is used frequently to translate "*tanin*," "*nachash*" and "*livyatan*"; the KJV Old Testament uses "dragon" twenty times.

In v. 3 above this dragon is also identified with the "fourth beast" of Daniel 7:7, 24.

The great dragon was thrown out. Compare Lk 10:18, where Yeshua says, "I saw Satan fall like lightning from heaven."

He was hurled down to earth. What does he do here? Answer: "Your enemy, the

Adversary, stalks about like a roaring lion looking for someone to devour" (1 Ke 5:8). This is confirmed in vv. 12–17, 13:7. What should we do about it? "Stand against him…" (1 Ke 5:9–10, Ya 4:7; compare Ep 6:10–17, also 13:10 and 14:12 below).

The coming of **God's victory** (or "salvation"; see 7:10N) is the subject of the next six chapters; the cry is repeated at 19:1.

11 Our brothers **defeated** Satan, the Accuser, **because of** God's gracious act on behalf of mankind, the shedding of **the Lamb's blood** (see Ro 3:25bN), and also **because of… their** fearlessly doing their part, giving **witness** to this act of God and his son Yeshua, **even when facing death**. See Ac 7:59–60N on being martyred *'al kiddush HaShem.*

12 **His time is short**. After unknown ages in heaven (Isaiah 14:11–15), **the Adversary** spends a relatively short interlude on earth before being banished to "the lake of fire and sulfur" (20:10), "the fire prepared for the Adversary and his angels" (Mt 25:41). During this time **he is very angry** — see 1 Ke 5:8 and vv. 9–10N above.

13–16 **He went in pursuit of the woman**, that is, went to persecute the Jewish people (v. 1N), and perhaps the Messianic Jews in particular. The precise meaning of the details is not clear; the general sense is that God foils Satan's most demonic attempts to destroy Israel.

17 **The rest of her children** are Gentile Christians. They **obey God's commands**, not the 613 *mitzvot* but the *Torah* with the necessary changes (MJ 7:11, 8:6; Ac 15:22–23; Yn 13:34; Ro 13:8–10) that give us "the *Torah*'s true meaning, which the Messiah upholds" (Ga 6:2). See notes to these passages. **And**, like Messianic Jews, they **bear witness to Yeshua** (see v. 11N). R. H. Charles uses convoluted reasoning to equate the woman with the Church and "the rest of her seed" with all believers; nevertheless, even he says that the phrase "originally" meant "Gentile Christians." *Revelation*, Volume 1, p. 315. See also Isaiah 66:8.

18 **The dragon stood on the seashore** to call forth the two beasts of 13:1, 11, his instruments for persecuting both Israel and Gentile believers.

CHAPTER 13

1–8 These verses and 11:7, 17:24 place this chapter in the context of Daniel 7. The **beast** is a composite of Daniel's four beasts. Like the dragon (12:3–4&N), it has the **ten horns and seven heads** of Daniel's "fourth beast" (v. 1, Daniel 7:7); although unlike the dragon, it also resembles the other three (**lion… bear… leopard**; v. 2, Daniel 7:4–6). It comes **up out of the sea** (v. 1, Daniel 7:3). It speaks **arrogant blasphemies** (vv. 5–6 Daniel 7:8, 20, 25). It has **authority to act for 42 months** (v. 5, Daniel 7:25). Daniel himself explains,

> "The fourth beast will be a fourth kingdom upon earth, which will be different from all kingdoms. It will devour the whole earth, tread it down and break it

> in pieces. The ten horns are ten kings which will arise out of this kingdom, and another king will arise after them, and he will be different from the former ones, and he will subdue three kings. He will speak great words against the Most High, he will wear out the holy people of the Most High, and he will think to change times and laws; and they will be given into his hand for a season, seasons and half a season. But they will sit in judgment, and his dominion will be taken away, to be consumed and destroyed in the end. And the kingdom and dominion, and the greatness of the kingdoms under the whole heaven will be given to the people of the holy ones of the Most High, whose kingdom is an everlasting kingdom, and all dominions will serve and obey him. Here is the end of the matter." (Daniel 7:23–27)

Many scholars regard Daniel's prophecy as fulfilled in 168–164 B.C.E. by the Seleucid king Antiochus IV, who "changed times and laws," even causing pigs to be offered to idols in place of the daily sacrifice, an abomination which desolated the Temple (Daniel 9:27, 11:31, 12:11) for three-and-a-half years ("a season, seasons and half a season"), until the Maccabees recaptured and rededicated it, an event memorialized by the festival of *Chanukkah* (see Yn 10:22N). But since Yeshua renewed the prophecy two centuries later, there must be a later fulfillment as well. See 17:8&N.

In the *Tanakh*, "horn" often means "king." Many identify "another king" arising from the ten with the second beast (vv. 11–12&N).

The four beasts of Daniel are four kingdoms; and most scholars identify them as Babylon, Persia, Greece and Rome. Since all are ancient history, futurists (see 1:1N) expect the beast of vv. 1–8 to be a revived Roman Empire, or a nation covering the same territory, or a nation in which the brutal and depraved spirit of the Roman Empire finds expression. C. I. Scofield, expressing the Dispensationalist view, regards the head with **a fatal wound** (v. 3) as the restored Roman Empire, which is "dead" now but will live again, to everyone's **amazement**. A few years ago the "newspaper exegetes" (1:1N) saw the fulfillment of this prophecy in the ten members of the European Common Market. The fact that the Common Market now comprises more than ten participating nations does not necessarily disprove the futurist approach.

Non-futurists sometimes make this beast an allegory of all Satanic power mobilized against God's people on earth, especially governmental power (as opposed to religious).

3–4, 8 **The whole earth followed after the beast** and **worshipped** it, except for believers in Yeshua, **those whose names are written in the Book of Life** (see 20:12bN) **belonging to the Lamb**, Yeshua, **slaughtered before the world was founded** (God planned his atoning death before creating the world; 5:6&N, Ep 1:3–12, Co 1:14–23).

4 **Who is like the beast**? This beast-worship litany is a parody of the name of the angel Mikha'el (Hebrew, meaning "Who is like God"), who defeated the dragon (12:7–9), and of the Song of Moses (see 15:3&N):

> "Who is like you, *Adonai*, among the gods?
> Who is like you, glorious in holiness,
> fearful in praises, doing wonders?" (Exodus 15:11)

The **authority** of **the beast** comes through **the dragon**, but the ultimate source of all authority is God (Isaiah 45:6–7; Job 1:12, 2:6).

6 **And his *Sh'khinah*, and those living in heaven**, literally, "and his tent, those tenting in heaven." See 7:15N.

7 **Everyone living on earth**. See 3:10N.

8 **Book of Life**. See 20:12bN.

9 See note at beginning of Chapter 2.

11–12 **Another beast**. This second beast is the "false prophet" (16:13, 19:20, 20:10). It is the "Anti-Messiah" (1 Yn 2:18); as a travesty of the real Messiah, it has **two horns, like those of a lamb** (5:6&N). It is the "man who separates himself from *Torah*" (2 Th 2:3–10&NN), who fulfills Yeshua's prophecy that "'the abomination which causes devastation' spoken about through the prophet Daniel" will one day "stand in the Holy Place" of a rebuilt temple (Mt 24:15, citing Daniel 9:27, 11:31, 12:11). It is the "other king" which arises from the ten (Daniel 7:23–27, quoted in v. 1N). Non-futurists see this beast as symbolizing organized, institutional religion enforcing **worship** of **the first beast**.

13–14 **Miracles** pose two problems: (1) Do they happen at all? (2) If they do, are they signs from God? Whether miracles happen depends on how one defines a miracle. Without entering into subtleties, I will define a miracle as an event outside the ordinary which involves supernatural intervention. Although this displaces the locus of uncertainty onto what is meant by "supernatural intervention," the Bible, most religions and many nonreligious sources agree that miracles so defined do occur.

The Bible takes some miracles as signs from God, but others are acknowledged as having demonic origin. Thus the second beast **deceives the people living on earth**, just as the magicians in Pharaoh's court deceived him into discounting the God of Israel (Exodus 7:11, 22; 8:3(7); in the New Testament compare Ac 13:6b–9, 16:16–18, 19:13–16). However, God sets limits to demonic and Satanic capacity to perform miracles (Job 1:12, 2:6; Mt 24:24), just as he did as in Moses' day (Exodus 8:14–15(18–19), 9:11; see also Deuteronomy 18:9ff.).

Fire... from heaven. This mimics Elijah's miracle (2 Kings 1:10–13); compare Lk 9:54. The word "fire" appears more than twenty times in the book of Revelation, generally signifying judgment. Thus the beast even mimics God's judgment.

16–17a **A mark on his right hand or on his forehead**. Compare 20:4, which says "and," not "or": "those who had not worshipped the beast or its image and had not received the mark on their foreheads *and* on their hands." This makes mockery of *t'fillin* (see Mt 23:5N), which Orthodox and Conservative Jews wear in the synagogue on the hand and forehead to obey Deuteronomy 6:8, "You shall bind them [that is, God's *mitzvot*] for a sign on your hand, and they shall be for frontlets between your eyes."

This "mark of the beast" (16:2, 19:20; also 14:9–11) also mimics the sealing of the

144,000 (7:2–3&N). Some suggest that this "mark" refers to a computerized credit-card system coupled with a transmitter-identifier implanted in people's foreheads and hands or some other high-technology development. Regardless of whether such speculations are true or fanciful, the mark points to a time of complete totalitarian control over economic life by religious elements.

17b–18 **The number of its name**. In both Hebrew and Greek each letter of the alphabet corresponds to a number — the first nine letters correspond to 1 through 9, the next nine to 10 through 90, and the last few letters to the hundreds. The number of a word or name is the sum of the numerical equivalents of its letters.

In Jewish interpretation, *gematria* (the Hebrew word derives from the Greek word "*geômetria*," which underlies English "geometry") is a system of deducing the *sod* ("secret"; see Mt 2:15N) of a text by positing a meaningful connection between words whose numbers are either identical or related by simple arithmetic. Example: in rabbinic literature, God is sometimes called the "Place" ("*Makom*"). Why this should be is not evident, so *Gematria* explains it in this way: the letters of "*YHVH*" — *yud*, *heh*, *vav* and *heh* — are equivalent to 10, 5, 6 and 5. The sum of the squares of these four numbers is 186, which is the same as the number of "*Makom*" — *mem*, *kuf*, *vav*, *mem* (40 + 100 + 6 + 40).

Those who understand should count the number of the beast, for it is the number of a person, and its number is 666. This has evoked even more speculation than the beast's mark. Who is the beast? Certain forms of the name of the Roman Emperor Nero have that number; moreover, a first-century cult expected him to be resurrected after his death in 68 C.E. Napoleon and other historical figures have been suggested. Moreover, if one uses other languages and manipulates the numerical correspondences, then, as George E. Ladd writes, "Almost anything can be done with these numbers.... If A = 100, B = 101, C = 102, etc., the name Hitler totals 666." Thus **wisdom is needed**, so that one will remain alert but not be misled.

The number could be entirely symbolic. The name of Messiah in Greek, *Iêsous,* equals 888; 7 is regarded as the perfect number; and triple repetition symbolizes absolute ultimacy (as in Isaiah 6:3, "Holy, holy, holy is *Adonai* of Hosts."). Therefore 888 means that Yeshua is absolutely and ultimately beyond perfection, while 666 means that the beast in every respect falls short of perfection and is therefore absolutely and ultimately imperfect and evil.

CHAPTER 14

1–20 In this chapter God is shown working behind the scenes of history, preparing rewards for his people and punishments for those who disobey him. Believers are warned against falling away and encouraged to remain faithful.

1 **The** slain **Lamb** (5:6&N) is seen **on Mount Tziyon** (Mount Zion), the highest point in Jerusalem. In 4 Ezra the seer is told that he

"whom the Most High is keeping many ages and through whom he will deliver his creation [i.e., the Messiah] will stand on the summit of Mount Zion. Yes, Zion shall come and be seen by everyone, prepared and built, just as you saw the mountain cut out without hands. But he, my Son, will reprove the nations who have come for their ungodliness." (4 Ezra 13:26, 36–37).

Here "Zion" refers to the heavenly Jerusalem; see MJ 12:22&N.

The 144,000 are the Messianic Jews of 7:4&N. Their **foreheads** are "sealed" (7:2–3&N, 9:4) with both the Lamb's **name** and **his Father's name** (contrast 13:16–17). One of the two *t'fillin* is worn on the forehead and contains the Father's name, *YHVH* (see 13:16–17aN); it symbolizes complete devotion and open profession. These 144,000 will be equally open and devoted about proclaiming the name of the Lamb, Yeshua.

4 **The ones who have not defiled themselves with women, for they are virgins**. These are not male celibates, despite the explicit mention of women. Rather, they are people of both sexes who are faithful to God and his Son, as the rest of vv. 4–5 makes clear. Fornication is a common biblical metaphor for idolatry — for several examples from the *Tanakh* see Ezekiel 16, 23 and Hosea 1–5. Here in the book of Revelation, misdirected worship is explicitly called whoring at v. 8 below, as well as at 17:2, 4; 18:3, 9; 19:2.

On celibacy itself, R. H. Charles writes, "The superiority of the celibate life, though un-Jewish and un-Christian, was early adopted from the Gnostics and other Christian heretics," such as Marcion, the religions of Isis and Mithra and the Vestal Virgins in Rome (*Revelation*, Volume 2, p. 9). For more concerning this subject see 1C 7:1–9&NN.

5 **On their lips no lie was found**. This is prophesied of Yeshua at Isaiah 53:9 and of Israel's remnant at Zephaniah 3:13.

6–13 The three angels exhort God's people to remain faithful (vv. 6–7, 12; compare 13:9b, 10b), so as to avoid the judgment against **Babylon the Great** (vv. 8–11, v. 8N). They must persevere, observe God's *mitzvot* and **exercise Yeshua's faithfulness** (v.12), the same faithfulness Yeshua had (see Ro 3:22&N, Ga 2:16c&N). Note that works and faith go hand in hand (Ro 3:27–28&N, Ep 2:8–10&N, Ya 2:14–26&NN), and that the works of the righteous go with them for reward (v. 13; compare Ro 2:6–16, 1C 3:8–15). Verse 13 is a reassurance when any believer dies.

6–7 **The Good News** of v. 6 *is* what the angel says in v. 7. It is not the whole of the Gospel but the aspect relevant here.

8 **She has fallen! She has fallen! Babylon the Great!** This cry, combining Isaiah 21:9 with Daniel 4:21, is repeated at 18:2, when the destruction of Babylon is being detailed (Chapters 17–18). In the *Tanakh* Babylon epitomizes evil. Already in Genesis 11 it is the site of the Tower of Babel. In Isaiah 14 the king of Babylon is a thinly veiled stand-in for Satan (especially Isaiah 14:12–16). Following are discussions of four possible meanings for "**Babylon**" here and at 16:19; 17:5; 18:2, 10, 21.

(1) *Literal Babylon.* Babylon was located on the Euphrates River (16:12) and was criss-crossed by canals ("sitting on many waters," 17:1, alluding to Jeremiah 51:13,

"O you who dwell on many waters, abundant in treasures, your end has come, and the measure of your greed."). But against a literal interpretation is 17:15, which interprets the "waters" figuratively, and Jeremiah's prophecy that Babylon's "desolation" would be "everlasting" (Jeremiah 25:12; also Isaiah 13:19–22 and most extensively Jeremiah 50:1–51:64), along with the fact that Babylon in the first century C.E. was hardly worthy of the attention Yochanan gives it, since it was neither a center of Gospel activity (see 1 Ke 5:13N) nor the major world power center it had once been.

(2) *Rome.* The arguments in favor of Babylon as a codeword for Rome are weighty. Rome was widely known as the city set on seven hills (17:9). Caution militated against portraying the evils of Rome's oppressive rule too directly. "Babylon" was a common euphemism for "Rome" in the Pseudepigrapha (2 Baruch 11:1, 67:7; Sibylline Oracles 5:143, 159) and in rabbinic writings. Midrash Rabbah on Song of Songs 1:6.4 states directly, "One calls Rome 'Babylon.'"Yechiel Lichtenstein on 1 Ke 5:13 remarks that "Rome is called 'Babylon' since it is always described as the worst kingdom." Because Rome's political power has declined since the book of Revelation was written, making the literal understanding of Rome less relevant, there are Protestants who equate **Babylon** with Rome and Rome with Roman Catholicism, turning the passage into an anti-Catholic polemic.

(3) *The wicked world-system*, ruled in the spiritual realm by Satan and ultimately in the physical world by the anti-Messiah. Viewing Babylon allegorically as the evil world-system accords with the extensive description of the rule of the anti-Messiah in Chapters 12–13 and the return of this imagery in the immediate context (vv. 9–11).

(4) *The ungodly in general.* This less specific understanding of Babylon the Great as the ungodly in general as over against the godly would derive from a hermeneutic that interprets the whole book along such figurative lines (see 1:1N).

The wine of God's fury, here and at v. 10: see vv. 14–20N below.

10a Fire and sulfur, which KJV renders "fire and brimstone." Because this expression is used to describe Christian preachers who vividly portray the tortures of hell, it is sometimes thought foreign to Judaism. Actually the destiny of evildoers is described in this way throughout the *Tanakh*. Four examples: Genesis 19:24 (God's destruction of Sodom), Isaiah 34:8–10 (the coming "day of vengeance" against Edom), Ezekiel 38:22 (prophecy against Gog) and Psalm 11:6 (the fate of the wicked). The phrase is found in Revelation also at 9:17–18, 19:20, 20:10, 21:8. See 19:20N.

10b–11 Before the holy angels... forever. The idea that the judgment of the wicked is eternally on display before the righteous is found in a Pseudipegraphic Jewish work:

> "This cursed valley [Gey-Hinnom (Gehenna, hell; see Mt 5:22N)] is for those who are cursed forever.... Here they will be gathered together and here will be their place of judgment. In the last days there will be upon them the spectacle of righteous judgment in the presence of the righteous forever." (1 Enoch 27:1–3)

13 What they have accomplished follows along with them. The Mishna puts it this way:

> "In the hour of a person's departure, neither silver nor gold nor precious stones nor pearls accompany him, only *Torah* and good works." (Avot 6:9)

14–20 As a whole, the passage echoes Joel 4:9–13(3:9–13), in which grape harvesting and wine pressing are used as a metaphor for judgment in the context of the eschatological war, and Isaiah 63:1–6, in which God treads the winevat in his fury, pressing out the lifeblood of the peoples. The same metaphor is found at Jeremiah 25:15, 28–31.

Judgment is also symbolized by the harvest at Jeremiah 51:33 and Hosea 6:11. Also see Yeshua's own parable of the wheat and the weeds, especially Mk 4:29 and Mt 13:39–42; both there and here the Messiah is the reaper at the final judgment, using angels as his instruments. Moreover, here it is the Messiah who treads the winepress (see below, 19:15).

14 On the cloud was someone like a Son of Man. The prophecy of Daniel 7:13 is made to refer to Yeshua; compare Mt 24:30–31&NN, Mk 14:61–62&N.

20 Outside the city of Jerusalem, in the valley of Y'hoshafat (the name means "God judges"), mentioned in Joel 4:2, 12(3:2, 12). Jewish authorities understand this as Kidron Valley (Yn 18:1) or the Hinnom Valley (see 10b–11N, Mt 5:22N).

Blood flowed… as high as the horses' bridles for two hundred miles. Compare the Midrash Rabbah:

> "They [the Romans under Hadrian] slew the inhabitants [of Betar, after Bar-Kosiba, its defender, had been killed] until the horses waded in blood up to the nostrils, and the blood rolled along stones of the size of forty *se'ah* and flowed into the sea a distance of four miles." Lamentations Rabbah 2:2:4.

CHAPTER 15

1 Seven angels have "seven bowls" (16:1) containing **the seven plagues**. These bowls are poured out on the earth (16:2–21); and **with them, God's fury is finished**.

2–4 Those defeating the beast (13:1–8&N, 13:11–12&N), **its image** (13:14–15), **and the number of its name** (13:17–18&N) are seen **standing by the sea of glass** (see 4:6N), just as the Israelites stood by the Red Sea after their Egyptian pursuers were drowned in it. At that time the Israelites sang **the song of Moshe** (Exodus 15:1–18; see 13:4&N), which is included in its entirety in the daily morning synagogue service and liberally quoted again in the twice-daily blessing after the *Sh'ma*. The victors over the beast will sing the Song of Moses, signifying that true believers in Yeshua fully identify with the Jewish people.

The song of the Lamb, as given in vv. 3b–4, is not sung to or about the Lamb, but by the Lamb to God — just as the Song of Moses was sung by Moses and not to him. Just as the victorious Jewish people learned and sang the song which Moses sang (Exodus 15:1), so the victorious believers in heaven learn and sing the song which the Lamb sings. Like the Song of Moses the Song of the Lamb exults in the just ways of God, using the language of the *Tanakh* as found in Jeremiah 10:7; Amos 3:13, 4:13; Malachi 1:11; Psalms 86:9–10, 92:6(5), 98:1, 111:2, 139:14, 145:17; 1 Chronicles 16:9, 12. But unlike the Song of Moses it also brings out that in the final judgment God is revealed as **king of the nations**, king of the whole world, as prophesied in Zechariah 14:9, so that **all nations will come and worship before** him — as predicted in the continuation of that passage (Zechariah 14:16–20).

5 **The sanctuary (that is, the Tent of Witness).** The word "tent" appears only here in Revelation. If there was a Hebrew original underlying our Greek text, this phrase, unique in ancient literature, could be explained as a corruption of "the Temple of God in heaven," which appears with the same verb ("**was opened**") at 11:19. If the phrase stands as translated, the "sanctuary" is the Holy of Holies, which was also the location (or "tent") of the ark of the Covenant (MJ 9:4&N), called the ark of the Testimony throughout Exodus 25–40. Verse 8 supports this rendering, for we read that the smoke from God's *Sh'khinah* filled the sanctuary; in Exodus and Ezekiel God's glory inhabited the sanctuary. These final "bowl" plagues come from God's ultimate holiness.

7–8 Messianic Jews 9:5 understands "the *k'ruvim*..., casting their shadow on the lid of the Ark," as "representing the *Sh'khinah*," in the earthly Holy of Holies. Thus it is no surprise to find that in heaven **the sanctuary was filled with smoke from God's *Sh'khinah*** (see Paragraph (3) of MJ 1:2–3N). At 13:6, the beast insulted God's "name and his *Sh'khinah*, and those living in heaven" and "was allowed to make war on God's holy people and to defeat them." Now the tables are turned, with God's people victorious, and God's **fury** about to be poured out on those who follow the beast.

CHAPTER 16

1 **The seven bowls of God's fury**, introduced in 15:1, 7–8, contain the third set of seven judgments in the book of Revelation, the others being the seal judgments of 5:1–9, 6:1–17, 8:1ff., and the *shofar* judgments of 8:2–11:15ff. The bowl judgments are poured out in this chapter.

2 Like the plague of boils which affected only the Egyptians (Exodus 9:8–11), these **disgusting and painful sores** appear only on unbelievers, **the people who had the mark of the beast and worshipped its image**. According to v. 11, despite the pain of these sores, their hearts, like Pharaoh's, remain hard — they never turn from their sins to glorify God (v. 9) but curse him to the end (v. 21).

5 **O *HaKadosh***, "O Holy One." Rabbinic writings often refer to God as *HaKadosh, barukh hu*, "the Holy One, blessed be he"; as, for example, in the well-known *'Aleinu* prayer recited near the end of each synagogue service: "We bend the knee, bow and acknowledge before the supreme King of kings, *HaKadosh, barukh hu* [the Holy One, blessed be he],... that he is our God, there is none else." Here too the reference is to God the Father, but at Ac 2:27, 13:35, quoting Psalm 16:10, the term applies to the Messiah.

6 This verse and 17:6, 16 echo Isaiah 49:26, where God says to Israel, "I will feed your oppressors with their own flesh, and they will be drunk on their own blood." The nations that fight against God's people will shed each other's blood in internecine warfare. Compare Ezekiel 38:21–22, Haggai 2:21–22 and Zechariah 14:12–13 (which also suggests the first and fifth bowl judgments).

9 Here is the New Testament's most cogent description of the normal behavior of hardened sinners. **They cursed the name of God... instead of turning from their sins**, the result of which would have been **to give him glory**. Although God **had the authority over these plagues**, these unbelievers, in their irrationality, instead of entreating the only one who could help them, curse him. They recognize that God controls the plagues but blame him instead of themselves, since, being amoral and materialistic, they see no causal connection between their own sinful behavior and these events as judgment. They remain unrepentant throughout the chapter (see vv. 11, 21 and v. 2N).

12–16 The War of Armageddon (Hebrew ***Har Megiddo***, v. 16&N), the final earthly battle, is demonically inspired (vv. 13–14). In v. 14 it is called **the war of the Great Day of *Adonai-Tzva'ot*** ("the Lord of Heavenly Armies" or "*YHVH* of Hosts"; see 1:8N). In this conflict the **kings of the whole inhabited world** (vv. 12, 14, 16) come against God's people; but God, through his Messiah Yeshua (v. 15), wins the victory (19:11–21&NN) after "Babylon the Great" has been destroyed (v. 19&N; compare Zechariah 12, 14).

12 The River **Euphrates** was the center of the major pagan civilizations that pressed against Israel in *Tanakh* times, and when Revelation was written it was the center of the Parthian kingdom which continually warred with Rome. Think of the Euphrates as the launching point of attack, whether of angel-mediated judgment (9:14), **the kings from the east** (v. 12), or **the whole inhabited world** (v. 14).

15 **I am coming like a thief**. Yeshua interjects his own personal warning into the vision of the bowl judgments. Quoting his own words (3:3&N) he cautions believers to **keep their clothes clean** (compare 3:4–5a&N).

16 **The place which in Hebrew is called *Har Megiddo*** ("Mount Megiddo") or possibly "*'Ir Megiddo*" ("City of Megiddo"). The Greek word here is "*Armageddon*" — there is no Greek letter to represent the Hebrew "h" sound, and "n" is often added to Greek renderings of foreign words. But in Zechariah 12:10–11, which also places Megiddo in the context of the Last Days, the Hebrew word is actually "*Megiddon*":

> "...they will look on Me whom they have pierced, and they will mourn for him as one mourns for an only son.... On that day the mourning in Jerusalem will be as great as the mourning of Hadad-Rimmon in the valley of *Megiddon*."

Hadad-Rimmon was the place in the Valley of Yizre'el (Jezreel) near Megiddo where king Yoshiyahu (Josiah) fell at the hands of Pharaoh Nekhoh in 609 B.C.E. (2 Kings 23:29–30).

The city of Megiddo, which overlooks the Yizre'el Valley and guards a major pass on the ancient *Via Maris* ("Way of the Sea") connecting Egypt with Syria, has seen many battles and much mourning. The archeological remains, spanning a period from the Chalcolithic Age (4th millennium B.C.E.) to the Persian conquest (7th century C.E.), consist of twenty levels, indicating the city was destroyed and rebuilt many times. In this valley Dvorah and Barak defeated the Canaanites (Judges 4–5; Megiddo is mentioned at Judges 5:19) and Gid'on the Midianites (Judges 6–8). In modern times both Napoleon (1799) and General Allenby (1918) defeated the Turks near Megiddo. The hundred square miles of the Yizre'el Valley would provide more than enough space for the conflict envisioned in the book of Revelation.

However, the final war may not take place at *Har Megiddo* at all, but in Jerusalem, at *Har Migdo*, the "mount of his choice fruit," i.e., the mountain of God's blessing, Mount Zion. Mount Zion has already been mentioned at 14:1; moreover, the imagery resembles Joel's picture of the Day of *Adonai*, when God's power goes forth from Mount Zion against the forces of evil (Joel 2:1–11, 4:16–17 (3:16–17); compare also Isaiah 31:4–9). The next passage (vv. 17–21) resembles 14:14–20, which also draws on imagery from Joel 4 (see 14:14–20N). Strengthening the case further Zechariah 12:11, cited above, mentions Jerusalem along with *Megiddon*.

19 **Babylon the Great** (see 14:8N) **was split into three parts**, that is, destroyed, as detailed in the next two chapters. The judgment imagery is taken from the Prophets; see 14:14–20N.

Made her drink the wine from the cup of his raging fury. Compare Jeremiah 25:15, 25:26–31.

21 **The people cursed God for the plague of hail**. See v. 2N, v. 9N, 8:7N, Exodus 9:22–35.

CHAPTER 17

1–2 **The judgment**, except for v. 16, is described in Chapter 18.

Sitting by many waters. See 14:8N on Babylon.

Great whore… The kings of the earth went whoring with her. Nahum 3:4 calls Nineveh, another of Israel's nemeses, "the charming and bewitching harlot who sells nations with her lewd practices and families by her witchcrafts." Compare 18:3, 7, 12–23. Isaiah 23:17 says that Tyre "will play the harlot with all the kingdoms of the world on the face of the earth."

The people… have become drunk. See 18:3; also Jeremiah 51:7, quoted in v. 4N.

3 **Beast… having… ten horns**. See 12:3–4N, 13:1–8N.

4 **Gold cup**. Jeremiah 51:7: "Babylon was a gold cup in the hand of *Adonai* that made all the earth drunk; the nations have drunk of her wine; therefore the nations are mad."

Cup filled with obscene and filthy things. At 18:6 this cup becomes the cup of God's raging fury, as at 14:10, 16:19.

5 Contrast this name with that written on the forehead of the redeemed (see 14:1&N, 22:5&N).

Babylon the Great. See 14:8N.

6 **On seeing her, I was altogether astounded**, since a whore does not usually dress so magnificently (v. 4; see G. E. Ladd, *Revelation, ad loc.*)

7–14 See 13:1–8&NN, and compare Daniel 7:19–25.

8 The beast **once was** (in the form of Antiochus IV "Epiphanes"), **now is not** in such an evil form, **and will come** as the anti-Messiah — as explained in 13:1–8N. Since the beast pretends to the position of God, the angel sarcastically describes him in language similar to that used to describe God, "the One who is, who was and who is coming" (1:4&N). This beast, Satan, **will come up from the Abyss** and be "set free for a little while" (20:2–3, 7–8), **but he is on his way to destruction** in "the lake of fire and sulfur" (20:9–10).

The people living on earth (those in v. 2; see 3:10N) **whose names have not been written in the Book of Life** (see 20:12bN) **since the founding of the world** are to be contrasted with "God's people… who testify about Yeshua" (v. 6). Also compare 13:3–4, 8; Ep 1:3–12; and Co 1:14–23.

9 **Seven hills**. See 14:8N on Babylon.

10 **Seven kings — five have fallen, one is living now, and the other is yet to come**. A difficult verse in a difficult book. If "Babylon" means Rome or the Roman Empire (see 14:8N), the **fallen** could be the first five emperors, of whom Nero was the last. After three emperors who ruled for a very short time each came Vespasian, who would be the sixth, ruling from 69 to 79 C.E., and **living now**. Titus would be **yet to come**. In his commentary on Revelation R. H. Charles considers Nero to be the "beast" of this chapter, expected to return from the dead leading the kings of the east against Rome (see 13:17b–18N).

12 **Ten horns**. See v. 3N.

14 **He is Lord of lords and King of kings**. See 19:16N.

16 **They will hate the whore**. The ten horns and the beast, who are evil, hate the whore, who is also evil. Those who are good love even those who, unlike themselves, are evil. But those who are evil hate not only the good but also even those who are like themselves, evil.

And consume her with fire (also 18:8). The same punishment as for the daughter of a *cohen* who profanes her father by playing the whore, Leviticus 21:9.

17 **God put it in their hearts to do what will fulfill his purpose**. In the *Tanakh* God often uses the wicked to accomplish his purposes; see Exodus 10:1, Habakkuk 1:5–11. This verse is a strong statement of God's sovereignty, like Ro 9:6–29&NN. Though much is said in the book of Revelation about Satan and his power, there is no dualism, not the slightest suggestion that Satan is on a par with God. **God's words** must **accomplish their intent** (compare Isaiah 55:10–11, Mt 24:35, Ro 8:28).

18 The Great City. See 14:8N.

CHAPTER 18

1–24 The judgment against **Babylon** (see 14:8N) is against her pride, ruthlessness, greed (1 Ti 6:9–10) and materialism. It is a just judgment (15:3; 16:5, 7; 18:10, 20; 19:2), praised by God's people but mourned by the worldly and wicked who share her values.

Much in this chapter resembles the lamentation in Ezekiel 27–28 over the commercial center and port of Tzor (Tyre). It is highly significant that Tyre is often understood as a surrogate for Satan's realm of activity and its king for Satan himself (this identification is based especially on Ezekiel 28:11–19). By analogy, the destruction of Babylon in this chapter is really the destruction of Satan's kingdom; the destruction of Satan himself in Chapter 20 invokes "Gog and Magog" as described in Ezekiel 38–39, which also resembles Ezekiel 27–28.

21 The size of a great millstone. The name "Gat-Sh'manim" ("Gethsemane," Mt 26:36&N) means "oil press," that is, a stone mill for grinding olives into pulp for their oil. Until quite recently the Arabs in the villages here in Israel used such presses for the same purpose, and many of the millstones are still around. They are circular with a hole in the center about 9 inches square; diameter averages about five feet, thickness a foot and weight well over a ton.

23 The voice of bridegroom and bride (a phrase found at Jeremiah 7:34, 16:9, 25:16, 33:1) **will never again be heard in you**, but they will be heard soon at the inauguration of God's reign (19:7–9&N).

24 Compare 6:9–11, 16:5–7, 17:6, 19:2; also Mt 23:35.

CHAPTER 19

1–6 ***Halleluyah*****!** Hebrew for "Praise *Yah*!" ("Praise the Lord!"), rendered in the Greek text as *Allelouia*, and found in the Bible 22 times in Psalms 104–150 and 4 times in these six verses. The **huge crowd in heaven** praises God for judging Babylon the Great and for actively beginning to rule his Kingdom (v. 6).

6 ***Halleluyah*****! *Adonai*, God of heaven's armies** (see 1:8N), **has begun his reign** (or: "has become King"). God's universal rule is a major theme of the *Tanakh* (Psalms 103:19, 145:13; Isaiah 2:2–4, 9:5–6(6–7), 11:6–9; Micah 4:1–4; Zechariah 14:9). On the one hand, the New Testament presents the "Kingdom" or "rulership" of God (see Mt 3:2N on "Kingdom of Heaven") as a reality present at this moment through trusting in Yeshua the Messiah (Mt 5:3, 10; 11:11; 12:28; 25:34; 26:29; Lk 17:21;

Ro 14:17; 1C 4:20; Co 1:13). On the other hand, it also describes the Kingdom as a future promise yet to be fully manifested (Mt 6:10, 7:21; Lk 22:30, 23:42; 1C 6:9–10; Ga 5:21; 2 Ke 1:11). The present verse inaugurates God's kingly **reign**, although its establishment requires several stages: first is the wedding feast of the Lamb (vv. 7–9), climaxed by the return of the Messiah (vv. 11–15); then Satan must be chained (20:1–3, 7–10), judgment must take place (20:11–15), and only then does Yeshua actually rule (21:3–4, 22:3–5); compare 1C 15:23–28.

The "Hallelujah Chorus" in George F. Handel's oratorio, *The Messiah*, consists of the KJV renderings of this verse and phrases from 11:15 and 19:16. Messianic prophecies from the *Tanakh* and other Bible verses about Yeshua constitute its entire libretto.

7 **The wedding of the Lamb** (Yeshua the Messiah), **and his bride** or "wife" (the Body of all believers throughout history, the Messianic Community). Although in the *'olam haba* individual resurrected believers will not marry (Mt 22:30), the Messianic Community as a whole is the Bride of the Messiah. Similar imagery of the Messiah as bridegroom and the inauguration of the Kingdom as wedding is found also at Mt 22:1–14, 25:1–13; Mk 2:18–20; Yn 3:28–30; Ro 7:1–4; 1C 6:13–20; 2C 11:2 and Ep 5:25–33.

The *Tanakh* similarly pictures Israel as the wife of *YHVH* — see Isaiah 54:1–8, 62:4–5; Jeremiah 31:31(32); Ezekiel 16; and the whole book of Hosea, especially Chapters 1–3. Midrash Rabbah to Song of Songs 4:10 names ten places in the *Tanakh* which speak of Israel directly or allegorically as a bride.

Arnold Fruchtenbaum, a Jewish believing scholar whose theology might be categorized as a modified Dispensationalism, distinguishes radically between the "wife of Jehovah," Israel, and the "bride of the Messiah," the Messianic Community; see his commentary on Revelation called *The Footsteps of the Messiah*, Appendix III ("The Wife of Jehovah and the Bride of Christ").

My view is that the distinction between the Church and the Jewish people is less sharp and more subtle than Dispensationalism has generally depicted it (see Ro 11:23–24&N), and that Yeshua the Messiah sometimes represents and sometimes is intimately identified with the Jewish people (see Mt 2:15&N). For these reasons I see no significant substantive distinction to be made between the bride of the Messiah and the wife of *YHVH*. Rather, the Bible employs a variety of metaphors to express the future intimacy of God with his people; different ones are used at 21:2–3, 22:3–5.

8 **Fine linen, bright and clean** contrasts with the garish dress of the harlot (17:4). "**Fine linen" means** or "results from" (literally, "is") **the righteous deeds**, etc.

10 **I fell at his feet to worship him**, etc. Compare Ac 10:25–26&N. The early believers sometimes were led astray into angel-worship, but this was condemned (Co 2:18). Perhaps Yochanan, in awed confusion, thought the voice of the angel was that of the Messiah and reports his embarrassment at his mistake.

The testimony of Yeshua is the Spirit of prophecy. A difficult phrase. I think the author is explaining why he was instructed not to worship the angel; compare Kefa's similar remark to Cornelius (Ac 10:25–26&N). Yochanan and his **brothers** have in themselves Yeshua's **testimony** or "evidence," that is, what Yeshua said about himself and his Messianic Community (similarly at 1:2b, 22:16). This evidence which believers have in them is **the Spirit of prophecy** (Greek *prophêteia,* "speaking forth" on behalf of God), that is, the Holy Spirit, who speaks forth God's truth whenever they live a godly, Messianic life and communicate the Good News to others.

11–16 At Ti 2:13&N we are taught "to expect the blessed fulfillment of our certain hope, which is the appearing of the *Sh'khinah* of our great God and the appearing of our Deliverer, Yeshua the Messiah." The present verses describe this eagerly awaited Second Coming.

In the *Tanakh YHVH* wars victoriously over his enemies (Isaiah 13, 31, 63:1–6; Ezekiel 38–39; Joel 4:9–21(3:9–21); Zechariah 14); here we see that it is through Yeshua the Messiah that he does this. Moreover, Yeshua's work upon his return is not only to reward the righteous (vv. 6–10) but also to conquer and judge the wicked, as seen from Mt 13:41–42, 25:41–46; Ro 2:5–6, 8–9, 16; 1 Th 1:7–9, 2:8. The first time, God did not send his Son into the world to judge but to save (Yn 3:17); however, God has entrusted all judgment to the Son (Yn 5:22), and this takes place at his Second Coming.

11 **A white horse**, different from the one at 6:2&N, with a different rider.

Faithful and True — words applied to the Messiah also at 3:14. The two words mean virtually the same thing, since the Hebrew idea of truth was not correspondence to reality (as in Greek thought), but reliability. The "God of truth" (*Elohim emet*, Jeremiah 10:10) is not primarily the God who reveals eternal verities, but the God who can be trusted to keep his covenant. When Yochanan in his Gospel wrote that "grace and truth came through Yeshua the Messiah" (Yn 1:17), he meant that in the life, death and resurrection of the Messiah, God's faithfulness was revealed in fulfillment of his covenant. Likewise, the return of Yeshua will be the faithful reappearance of him who has already appeared among men; this time he comes to bring God's covenant promises to their final and full consummation. (Adapted from George E. Ladd, *Revelation*, *ad loc.*)

12–15 **His eyes were like a fiery flame** (1:14).... **the name by which he is called is, "THE WORD OF GOD"** (1:2, 6:9, 20:4).... **Out of his mouth comes a sharp sword** (1:16; 2:12, 16). The sword here and at v. 21 is the Word of God (see 1:2N, 1:16N). See MJ 4:12–13&N for the same three metaphors (Word of God, sword, eyes).

12 **A name written which no one knew but himself**. Yeshua has three public names in vv. 11–16; each reveals aspects of his nature (see Yn 1:12N on how names were understood in antiquity). Yet even on the day of the eschatological battle there are elements which remain hidden.

13 **Soaked in blood**. This could be the blood of the enemies' armies (vv. 19, 21), Yeshua's own blood shed on the execution-stake or the blood of martyred believers (6:9–10&N, 12:11&N). Most interpreters opt for the first.

14 **The armies of heaven**, the angels. God is called "*Adonai*, God of heaven's armies" many times in the book of Revelation (see 1:8&N). "*Adonai* my God will come, and all holy ones with him" (Zechariah 14:5). Yeshua returns with angels (Mk 8:38, Lk 9:26, 1 Th 3:13, 2 Th 1:7). However, the believers too accompany him as he overcomes his enemies (17:14 above; also Mt 24:31, 1 Th 4:15b–17&N).

15 **He will rule them with a staff of iron**. See 2:26–27N, 11:18&N, 12:5. **Winepress**, etc. See 14:14–20N.

16 **KING OF KINGS AND LORD OF LORDS** (in reverse order at 17:14). A title expressing Yeshua's rulership over all creation (1C 15:25–28&NN, Pp 2:9–11&N, MJ 2:8&N). It is equivalent to the phrase "King of kings of kings" which the *Siddur* (prayerbook) applies to *YHVH* in this song which introduces *Shabbat* in many Jewish homes:

> "*Shalom 'aleikhem, mal'akhey-hasharet, mal'akhey-Elyon,*
> *miMelekh-malkhey-ham'lakhim, HaKadosh, barukh hu.*
> *Bo'akhem l'shalom,… barkhuni l'shalom,… tzetkhem l'shalom….*"
>
> "Welcome, ministering angels, messengers from the Most High,
> from the King of kings of kings, the Holy One, blessed be he.
> Come in peace,… bless me with peace,… go in peace…."

The extra "kings of" in Yeshua's title is necessary because the ruler of Persia styled himself "king of kings" — and truly so, since Esther 1:1 says that Achashverosh (Ahasuerus, Xerxes) ruled 127 countries (and, by implication, their kings as well). See also citation of Avot 3:1 in 20:11–15N below.

17–21 This is the Battle of Armageddon (see 16:16&N); the Messiah defeats the anti-God forces, both the instigators in the spiritual realm (v. 20) and their human followers (v. 21).

17–18 **Birds** of carrion **feast** on their **flesh** (vv. 17–18). The imagery is from the book of Ezekiel 39:17–20, although Ezekiel is speaking of the battle of Gog and Magog, which does not appear in Revelation until 20:8&N. See v. 21N.

19 Compare Psalm 2:2, Joel 4:9–17(3:9–17); see 14:14–20N, 16:16N.

20 Here is God's answer to the logical conundrum, "How do you throw away the trash can?" **The beast… and with him the false prophet** (see 13:1–18&NN, 14:8–11&NN) are **thrown alive into the lake of fire that burns with sulfur** (compare Ezekiel 38:22), "prepared for the Adversary and his angels" (Mt 25:41). At 20:10 Satan himself joins these "angels" of his to be "tormented forever and ever"; compare Daniel 7:11, and see 12:12N, 14:10aN. Death and Sh'ol themselves are thrown into this lake of fire, as there is no longer any need for them (20:13–14&N). And in the final judgment of humanity, "Anyone whose name was not found written in the Book of Life was hurled into the lake of fire" (20:15&N).

Compare Mt 3:10–12; 5:22, 29–30; 10:28 ("Do not fear those who kill the body but are powerless to kill the soul. Rather, fear him who can destroy both soul and body in Gey-Hinnom"; and see Lk 12:4–5); 13:40–43; 18:8–9; 23:15, 33; 25:46. Also note Mk 9:43, 48 ("If your hand makes you sin, cut it off! Better that you should be maimed but obtain eternal life, rather than keep both hands and go to Gey-Hinnom, to unquenchable fire…, where their worm does not die, and the fire is not quenched." There Mark is citing the most important *Tanakh* reference to eternal fiery punishment, Isaiah 66:24 (quoted below in 21:1–8N). In Lk 16:23–24 torment by fire is experienced by the dead already in Sh'ol, even before the lake of fire. In Lk 17:29–30 fire and sulfur are cited as God's means of punishment and destruction in the days of Sodom (Genesis 19). See also 2 Th 1:8, MJ 12:29, 2 Ke 3:7, Yd 7.

21 **And all the birds gorged themselves on their flesh**. In Judaism, following biblical practice, the honored dead are buried. Not to be buried is a disgrace (see 2 Kings 9:34), and being torn apart by buzzards and dogs is the ultimate disgrace (note Yeshua's figurative use of this fact at Mt 24:28&N).

Elijah prophesied about Ach'av (Ahab), the king of the Northern Kingdom (Israel), and his wife Izevel (Jezebel):

> "*Adonai* also said of Izevel, 'The dogs will eat Izevel by the wall of Yizre'el. Any of Ach'av's people that die in the city the dogs will eat, and the birds flying around will eat those who die in the field.'"(1 Kings 21:23–24)

Elisha later confirmed that

> "The dogs will eat Izevel in the area of Yizre'el, and no one will bury her." (2 Kings 9:10)

God fulfilled the prophecy about Izevel at 2 Kings 9:32–37. Yehu (Jehu, later the king) had her thrown to her death from a high window of her castle. But even he wanted to show her dead body the respect of burial:

> "Go, take care of this cursed woman, and bury her; for she is a king's daughter. So they went to bury her; but all they found of her was the skull, the feet and the palms of her hands."

Yehu then recognized that Elijah and Elisha's prophecies about her had come true. See also above, 11:8–10&NN.

CHAPTER 20

1–10 Now that Satan's front-men have been taken care of (19:21), the Messiah attends to Satan himself.

1 **An angel… who had the key to the Abyss**. See 9:1N.

2–7 A thousand years, the Millennium. Depending on their overall approach to the book of Revelation (see 1:1N), interpreters are divided over whether this period is symbolic (Amillennialists) or historical; and if historical, possibly present (Postmillennialists) or definitely future (Premillennialists); and if future, literally 1,000 years (most Dispensationalists) or not. Amillennialism sees Chapter 20 as recapitulating the events described in earlier chapters, rather than describing a chronologically later period. Postmillennialism understands the Millennium as the present historical age, with the Body of the Messiah establishing righteousness on earth in increasing measure (in which case Chapter 19 does not speak of the Messiah's victorious return, but of the triumph of good over evil at the end of the age). Premillennialism alone expects a future Millennium in which the Messiah himself will rule on earth, and I share this opinion. But I also agree with Lance Lambert, a Messianic Jew living in Jerusalem, who writes:

> "It is my belief that there will be a millennium. It would not alter my faith or joy in the Lord if there were no such period. I find myself unable to hold such a conviction in an argumentative or hotly dogmatic spirit. If we are honest, both views present us with problems which are not easily answered. The vital need is to be ready for the Lord's coming and for all that will follow it." (*Till the Day Dawns*, Eastbourne: Kingsway Publications, 1982, p. 160)

For more on the different eschatological positions, including the varieties of Premillennialism, see 4:1N, 1 Th 4:15b–17N.

A millennium of sorts appears in the lengthy collection of opinions about Messianic times found in Chapter 11 of Babylonian Talmud tractate Sanhedrin:

> "Rav Kattina said, 'The world will exist for six thousand years, then for one thousand years it will lie desolate....'"(Sanhedrin 97a)

This passage and a related one are quoted fully and discussed in 2 Ke 3:3–9N.

Likewise, although the events leading up to the Messianic Age are described differently in the Zohar (the central text of Jewish mysticism compiled in the 13th century), it tells us:

> "Happy are those left alive at the end of the sixth millennium to enter into [the millennium of] the *Shabbat*." (Zohar 1:119a)

With this compare MJ 4:1–11&NN.

Traditional Judaism has other views of how long the "Days of the Messiah" will last. In the following passage ellipses stand for the Scripture verses the rabbis bring in support of their estimates.

> "It was taught: Rabbi Eli'ezer said: 'The days of the Messiah will be forty years....' Rabbi El'azar ben-'Azaryah said: 'Seventy years....' Rabbi [Y'hudah the Prince] said: 'Three generations....' ...
>
> "Another taught: Rabbi Eli'ezer said: 'The days of the Messiah will be forty

years....' Rabbi Dosa said: 'Four hundred years....' Rabbi said: 'Three hundred sixty-five years, like the days of the solar year....' Abimi ben-Rabbi Abbahu taught: 'The days of Israel's Messiah will be seven thousand years....' Rav Y'hudah said in Shmu'el's name, 'The days of the Messiah will last as long as from the Creation until now....' Rav Nachman ben-Yitzchak said, 'As long as from Noach's days until our own.'"(Sanhedrin 99a)

This chapter of Revelation portrays the Millennium and the events at its close as distinct from the period following, when there will be "a new heaven and a new earth" (Chapters 21–22); a similar differentiation is found in the *Tanakh* in Ezekiel 36–48 (see v. 8N below). Likewise, traditional Judaism sometimes makes a distinction between the Days of the Messiah and the *'olam haba* ("the world to come"):

"Rabbi Chiyya ben-Abba said in Rabbi Yochanan's name: 'All the prophets prophesied [the good things] only for the Days of the Messiah; but as for the *'olam ha-ba*, "no eye but yours, God, has seen what He has prepared for him who waits for Him" (Isaiah 64:3(4)).'"(Sanhedrin 99a; similarly B'rakhot 34b)

However, in the following passage specifying the length of the Messianic Era, eschatological events which the New Testament assigns to different periods are conflated. This excerpt from a first-century C. E. Jewish book pseudepigraphically attributed to Ezra the Scribe is remarkable for the sheer quantity of ideas similar to those elaborated in the New Testament: it refers to the Messiah as the Son of God (Mt 3:17), speaks of his death (Mt 27:50), mentions "those with him" (whether angels or saints returning to rule, v. 6 below; and see 19:14N), and alludes to the New Jerusalem (21:1–2), resurrection (vv. 4–6, 12 below), the doing away with what is corruptible (1C 15:42–54), the throne of judgment (vv. 11–15), judgment on the basis of deeds (vv. 14–15; Mt 25:34–46), the Abyss (9:1, 2, 11; 11:7; 17:8; vv. 1–3 above), torment and Gey-Hinnom (14:10, 19:20, vv. 9–15 below, 21:8; Mt 5:22, 5:29–30, 10:28, 18:9, 23:15, 23:33; Mk 9:44–47), the final Paradise (21:1–22:9), and a seven-year period (Daniel 9:24–27; also compare above, 12:14, with Daniel 7:25, 12:7).

"Ezra, ...the time will come when the signs I have told you about will come to pass, that the city now unseen will appear and the land now concealed be revealed. Everyone delivered from the predicted evils will see My wonders. My Son the Messiah will be disclosed, along with those who are with him, and he will gladden the survivors four hundred years [variant readings: 1,000 years, 30 years (close to the length of Yeshua's life)]. After those years My Son the Messiah will die, and all in whom there is human breath. Then the world will be turned into the primeval silence for seven days, as it was at the first beginnings, so that no one is left.

"After seven days the age not yet awake will be roused, and what is corruptible will perish. The earth will restore those who sleep in her, and the dust will restore those who rest in it. The Most High will be revealed upon the throne of judgment, and then comes the End. Compassion will pass away, pity be distant, longsuffering withdrawn; only judgment will remain, truth stand, faithfulness triumph. Recompense will follow, the reward will be made manifest. Acts of righteousness will awake and acts of iniquity not sleep. Then the Abyss of torment will appear, and in contrast the place of refreshment; the furnace of Gey-Hinnom will be manifested, and in contrast the Paradise of delight.

"Then the Most High will say to the nations that have been raised [from the dead]: 'Look now and consider whom you have denied, whom you have not served, whose commandments you have despised! Look, now, before you: here delight and refreshment, there fire and torments!' Thus will he speak to them in the Day of Judgment. For thus shall the Day of Judgment be: a day on which there is no sun, moon, stars; no clouds, thunder, lightning, wind, rainstorm, cloud-rack; no darkness, evening, morning; no summer, fall, winter; no heat, frost, cold, hail, rain, dew; no noon, night, dawn, shining, brightness or light — except for the splendor of the brightness of the Most High, whereby all shall be destined to see what has been determined for them. And its duration shall be, as it were, a week of years. Such is my Judgment and its prescribed order; I have shown these things only to you." (4 Ezra 7:25–44)

2 **The dragon, that ancient serpent**, etc. (see 12:9–10N) must be **chained**, his powers severely limited for a period; afterwards he "must be set free for a little while" (vv. 3, 7) to deceive the nations (vv. 3, 8) and Israel (v. 9a) before his final defeat and eternal punishment (vv. 9b–10). The ideas of binding demonic beings and of punishing them with eternal fire are also found in the Jewish apocrypha (Tobit 8:3) and pseudepigrapha (1 Enoch 10:4–17, 18:12–19:2, 21:1–6, 54:4–6; Testament of Levi 18:12; Jubilees 48:15–16), and in Christian apocrypha (Acts of Pilate 22:2). See also 2 Ke 2:4&N, which quotes 1 Enoch 10:4–6.

4 **Then I saw thrones, and those seated on them received authority to judge.... They came to life and ruled with the Messiah for a thousand years**. Compare Daniel's prophecy:

"As I looked, thrones were placed,... and millions... sat in judgment.... And the time came when the holy ones possessed the kingdom." (Daniel 7:9–10, 22)

According to G. E. Ladd,

"[Revelation 20:4–6] is the only passage in the entire Bible which teaches a temporal *millennial* kingdom, and there is only one other passage in the New Testament which may envisage a temporal reign of Christ between his parousia [coming] and the *telos* [consummation, final goal]: I Cor. 15:23–24." (*Revelation*, p. 267)

But elsewhere Yeshua promises to share his rulership with believers (2:26–28, 3:21, 5:9–10; Mt 19:28; 1C 6:2).

Also those who had not worshipped the beast.... Greek *kai* could mean not "**also**" but "in other words," in which case there is only one group ruling with the Messiah, not two.

5–6 The first resurrection is the coming to life of God's holy people, as described in vv. 4 and 6. The second resurrection is not mentioned as such; it is implied by the parenthetical remark that **the rest of the dead did not come to life until the thousand years were over** (see v. 12), at which time they are alive only long enough to experience **the second death** (see v. 14N, 2:11), which **has no power** over the believers.

They will be *cohanim*, "priests," **of God and of the Messiah**. "You [the people of Israel] shall be for me [God] a kingdom of *cohanim* and a holy nation" (Exodus 19:6). "You [believers in Yeshua] are... the King's *cohanim*" (1 Ke 2:9, alluding to Exodus 19:6, Isaiah 61:6). These promises reach their fulfillment here.

8 To deceive the nations in the four quarters of the earth, God and Magog, to gather them for battle. Compare the structure of Ezekiel 36–48 with Revelation 20–22. Ezekiel 36–37 speaks of Israel's salvation, with David ruling over them (compare this chapter, vv. 1–6). In Ezekiel 38–39 Gog from Magog interrupts this rule with an eschatological battle, in which the nations come against the Kingdom (compare this chapter, vv. 7–10). The final order is described in Ezekiel 40–48 in terms of a rebuilt temple in a new Jerusalem (compare Revelation 21–22). In both places a temporal kingdom is followed by an eternal kingdom after a final war.

Ezekiel writes that Gog, from the land of Magog, the chief prince of Meshekh and Tuval, will come with armies from a number of other places against the Jewish people regathered into the Land of Israel from the other nations and living at peace in unwalled towns. Those nations are the same in Ezekiel 38 as in Ezekiel 27, in the lament against the king of Tyre, who is, as is clearest from Ezekiel 28:11–19, a stand-in for Satan.

9 Fire came down from heaven. Compare Ezekiel 38:22, 39:6.

10 This is the final event in the long and wicked history of the one who originated rebellion against God. Already at the beginning, after enticing Adam and Eve to commit the first human sin, God knew and said what the end would be:

> "I will put enmity between you [the serpent] and the woman [Eve], and between your seed [all who sin and rejoice in the sin of others, whether angelic (Ep 6:10–13) or human (Ro 1:32)] and her seed [her descendants, *i.e.*, humanity; but more particularly, the unique "seed" spoken of in Ga 3:16&N, Yeshua]; he [the Hebrew is singular, referring to Yeshua, not plural] will bruise [or: crush] your head, and you will bruise their heel [the Hebrew is plural; humanity can be injured, Yeshua cannot]." (Genesis 3:15)

This prediction of Satan's ultimate downfall is fulfilled in stages. Thus when Yeshua said, "Now is the time for this world to be judged, now the ruler of this world will be expelled" (Yn 12:31), he was speaking of how his death on the execution-stake would defeat the Adversary (compare Revelation 12). The Messianic Community also has a part in causing Satan's ruin, as Sha'ul writes, "God, the source of *shalom*, will soon crush the Adversary under your feet" (Ro 16:20). In vv. 1–3 above that Adversary is chained in the Abyss, and here he is **hurled into the lake of fire and sulfur** (on this see v. 15N) to be **tormented forever and ever**.

11–15 Everyone is to face God's judgment. Although God is a God of mercy, he is also a God of judgment. This is taught equally by the *Tanakh*, the New Testament, and Jewish tradition.

The Prophets speak of this judgment as the Day of *YHVH*; see Isaiah 2:12, 13:6–13 (a verse of which is alluded to in Mt 24:29); Ezekiel 30:3; Joel 1:15, 2:1, 3:4(2:31) (quoted at Ac 2:20), 4:14(3:14); Amos 5:18–20; Obadiah 15; Zephaniah 1:17–18; Zechariah 14:1–9 and Malachi 4:5(3:23) (alluded to at Mt 17:10–11).

> "The prominent feature of these passages is a dramatic sense of doom, underlined by a few characteristic motives, such as a darkness and wailing.... The warning is given that the Day of the Lord is near.... The wicked will be punished, justice established, mankind confounded, and its destiny somehow definitely changed.... God will... act — suddenly, decisively, and directly, in a single day, with vehemence and terror." (*Encyclopedia Judaica* 5:1387–8)

In the New Testament can be found the terms "Day of God" (2 Ke 3:12), "Great Day of *Adonai-Tzva'ot*" (16:14 above), Day of the Messiah Yeshua (Pp 1:6, 10; 2:16), and the ambiguous phrase, "Day of the Lord," which can mean either "Day of *YHVH*" or "Day of the Lord [Yeshua the Messiah]" (1C 1:8, 5:5; 2C 1:14; 1 Th 5:2–3; 2 Th 2:1–2; 2 Ke 3:10). (Also see 1:10&N, where the Greek expression is unique, making my rendering, "Day of the Lord," controversial.)

Moreover, God judges not only outward deeds, but the inner man. In the New Testament we see this when Yeshua confronts the *P'rushim* (Lk 12:1–5, Mt 23:23–28) and in the whole tenor of his Sermon on the Mount (Mattityahu 5–7); also compare Yn 2:23–25; Ro 2:16; MJ 4:13, 10:30. The *Tanakh* too speaks of secret deeds and motives when it says: "God will bring every work into judgment, concerning every hidden thing, whether it be good or evil" (Ecclesiastes 12:14). Compare also Psalm 139. The Oral *Torah* affirms this:

> "Rabbi [Y'hudah HaNasi, 135–219 C.E.] said, '... Pay attention to three things and you will not come under the power of transgression: know what is above you — an all-seeing eye, an all-hearing ear, and all your deeds recorded in a book'"(Avot 2:1)

So there is no room either for the common misunderstanding on the part of both Christians and Jews that the Old Testament portrays God as stern, judgmental and lacking mercy, with the New Testament picturing him as so merciful that he overlooks judgment and even justice; or for the opposite mistake of thinking that the New Testament, with its talk of hellfire, focuses on judgment more than the *Tanakh*.

Quoting Hosea 10:8, which depicts how the inhabitants of Samaria will feel when God judges them by having Assyria carry them away, Yeshua warns that the Day of

God's judgment will be fearful: "Then they will begin to say to the mountains, 'Fall on us!' and to the hills, 'Cover us!'"(Lk 23:30).

The Bible gives a symmetrical picture of salvation history. In its first two chapters, at the beginning of history, a sinless world is described; and at the beginning of the third chapter (Genesis 3:1–7) Satan the serpent (see above, v. 2) entices Eve and Adam into sin, resulting in damage both to humanity and to the world (Ro 8:19–22). God's plan from the very beginning was to remedy this damage through the death and resurrection of Yeshua the Messiah, the slaughtered Lamb (5:6, 9; 13:8; Ep 1:4–7; Yn 1:29); 1,256 chapters of the Bible deal with the outworking of this plan. Now, at the end of history, here in the third-to-last chapter of the Bible, sin is judged, with Satan (v. 10) and the wicked (v. 15) condemned to the lake of fire; while the final two chapters of Revelation present a newly created world and a humanity restored to Eden-like sinlessness. This is what is meant when God says (21:6), "I am the 'A' and the 'Z,' the Beginning and the End." There is but one asymmetry: Satan and the first man, Adam, cause sin at the beginning; while God the Father and the second man, Yeshua, cause sinlessness at the end (1C 15:45–49, Ro 5:12–21).

11 The One sitting on the **throne** is Yeshua. Although he shares the throne with God the Father (3:21), it is through Yeshua alone that God renders the final judgment (see also v. 12aN). According to Yochanan's Gospel,

> "The Father does not judge anyone, but has entrusted all judgment to the Son.... [The Father] has given him authority to execute judgment, because he is the Son of Man. Don't be surprised at this; because the time is coming when all who are in the grave will hear his voice and come out, those who have done good to a resurrection of life and those who have done evil to a resurrection of judgment." (Yn 5:22, 27–29)

What the Gospel calls the "resurrection of life" is in this chapter called the first resurrection, for believers only; while the "resurrection of judgment" applies to "the rest of the dead" (v. 5), who experience the second death (v. 14). See Yn 5:22N and compare Ac 17:31.

Earth and heaven fled from his presence and no place was found for them, because they are corrupted by sin, unholy and impure (Ro 8:19–22). Although in the present age the impure defiles the pure, when God himself appears in glory his purity banishes the impure, for his holiness cannot abide that which is corrupted by sin (see Mt 9:20&N). The only remedy is "a new heaven and a new earth, for the old heaven and the old earth had passed away" (21:1).

12a I saw the dead, both great and small, standing in front of the throne.

> "All of us will stand before God's judgment seat.... For we must all appear before the Messiah's court of judgment, where everyone will receive the good or bad consequences of what he did while he was in the body... on a day when God passes judgment on people's inmost secrets. (According to the Good News as I proclaim it, he does this through the Messiah Yeshua.)" (Ro 14:10, 2C 5:10, Ro 2:16)

12b Books… another book, the Book of Life. There seem to be two elements in the Final Judgment. First, there is judgment for eternal salvation (v. 5) or damnation (vv. 14–15) on the basis of being written in the Book of Life. Second, there is judgment according to works **from what was written in the books** (plural); this concept appears in the *Tanakh* at Daniel 7:9–10. From these books God judges all our deeds (see Ro 2:6&N), both public and secret, and even our innermost thoughts (see vv. 11–15N, v. 12aN). For the saved this judgment determines rewards (1C 3:8–15&N), while for the lost it determines degrees of punishment (Lk 12:47–48). But third, in traditional Judaism there is yet another meaning to these **books** — they determine what a person will experience in this world, not in the world to come.

The Hebrew term "*sefer-chayim*" ("book of life," "book of the living") appears in the *Tanakh* only at Psalms 69:28–29(27–28),

> "Add iniquity to their iniquity,
> don't let them come into Your righteousness.
> Let them be blotted out of the book of life
> And not be written with the righteous."

(Incidentally, this is a continuation of the passage quoted at Ro 11:9–10.)

The first reference to such a book is in Exodus 33:32–33. After the Israelites made the golden calf, Moses prayed that God would forgive them for this great sin, "and if not, then I pray that you blot me out of your book which you have written" (compare what Sha'ul writes at Ro 9:2–4a&N). *Adonai's* response to Moses was, "Whoever has sinned against me, him will I blot out of my book."

Other places in the *Tanakh* referring to a book containing individual destinies in the *'olam haba* are Malachi 3:16 ("a book of remembrance was opened") and Daniel 12:1 ("every one whose name shall be found written in the book"); while Psalm 139:16 ("your book") seems to refer to the *'olam hazeh*. In the New Testament the term "Book of Life" appears at Pp 4:3 and MJ 12:23 (and compare Lk 10:20), as well as six times in Revelation (3:5; 13:8; 17:8; 20:12, 15; 21:27), always signifying eternal salvation. There are other references in the Pseudepigrapha (Jubilees 30:22, which mentions a second book, the book of those who will be destroyed, with the possibility of having one's name transferred to it from the Book of Life; 1 Enoch 104:7; 108:3, 7; 1 Baruch 24:1) and in early Christian literature (Vision of Hermas 1:24, Similitude 2:12). In the Mishna it is spoken of in Pirkey-Avot 2:1 (quoted above in vv. 11–15N), 3:17.

From God's answer to Moses in Exodus, together with 3:1–5 above, we learn that it is possible to fall from grace, to have one's eternal destiny changed from salvation to condemnation, in consequence of unrepented sin in one's life, even though such passages as Ep 1:3–14 and 1 Ke 2:9 suggest that salvation is predestined. One way to deal with this antinomy is to suppose that everyone's name is initially written in the Book of Life — babies who die before the age of responsibility go to heaven. But upon reaching the age of responsibility, everyone sins (Ro 3:23); and only those who turn to God through Yeshua the Messiah (Yn 14:6) can know that they are saved. A name is not removed from the Book of Life unless the person has committed the unpardonable sin, the sin against the Holy Spirit, of finally and definitively rejecting God and his Son Yeshua (Mt 12:32&N).

The term "book of life" finds a prominent place in the liturgy for the High Holy Days. Thus the final blessing of the *'Amidah* is expanded so as to conclude:

> "May we and all your people, the house of Israel, be remembered and inscribed in the book of life, blessing, peace and prosperity, so that we will have a life of goodness and peace. Blessed are you, *Adonai*, the maker of peace."

Some Messianic Jews take exception to the customary greetings for *Rosh-HaShanah* — "*Shanah tovah tikatevu*" ("May you be inscribed [in the book of life] for a good year") — and *Yom-Kippur* — "*Chatimah tovah*" ("[May you have] a good sealing [of your destiny in the book of life]") — on the ground that as believers in Yeshua our names are already written in the Book of Life. This is unnecessary scrupulousness, for here the "book of life" is not concerned with eternal salvation but with life in this world. The tradition is that on *Rosh-HaShanah* God opens the heavenly books and judges people according to their works, writing in them who will die and what kind of life the living will enjoy during the coming year. The Ten Days of Penitence, *Rosh-HaShanah* through *Yom-Kippur*, are thought of as offering an opportunity for repentance that will influence God to change these fates for the better. But on *Yom-Kippur* these fates are fixed or "sealed." All of this is portrayed most clearly in the important High Holy Days prayer *Un'tanneh Tokef* (literally, "Let us recount the authority" of this day), quoted in full at MJ 9:22N.

13–14 All the dead who have not participated in the first resurrection are now resurrected and judged (see vv. 5–6N above). There is no longer any need for **Sh'ol**, where the dead are held for judgment, since this *is* the judgment. Nor is there need for **death**, the punishment for sin, since sin is now being banished from the universe, as foretold by Sha'ul at 1C 15:54–55. Likewise **the sea**, a biblical metaphor for death, destruction and turmoil (see Isaiah 57:20, Ezekiel 28:8, Psalm 107:25–28), harboring fearsome, Satanic creatures such as Leviathan (Isaiah 27:1, Psalm 104:27, Job 40:25–41:26(41:1–34)) and the beast of 12:18–13:8 above, releases its dead for judgment, so that, having served its purpose, it too disappears (21:1).

15 This is the event foretold by the parable of the sheep and the goats in Mt 25:31–46:

> "Then he will also speak to those on his left, saying, 'Get away from me, you who are cursed! Go off into the fire prepared for the Adversary and his angels!' … They will go off to eternal punishment, but those who have done what God wants will go to eternal life." (Mt 25:41, 46)

The "eternal life" spoken of is depicted in 22:1–22:5.

It is possible that **the lake of fire** is meant literally, to the degree that the wicked, in resurrected physical bodies, will experience physically the torment of burning and stench forever. Or it may be a metaphor for the eternal pain of knowing that one is forever to be denied the bliss of being present with the God of the universe and must be separated from him, to burn forever with frustration, anger and regret; Jean-Paul Sartre's play, "No Exit," is one man's expression of this understanding. For more on **the lake of fire**, see 19:20N.

Anyone whose name was not found written in the Book of Life was hurled into the lake of fire. (On "Book of Life" see v. 12bN.) This is the climactic moment for the wicked. Yet it is not God who has determined their fate, but they themselves, by their deeds that fall short of God's holiness, and by their lack of trusting Him for salvation through Yeshua the Messiah. "The Lord... is patient with you; for it is not his purpose that anyone should be destroyed, but that everyone should turn from his sins" (2 Ke 3:9). And compare Ro 2:1–8, especially vv. 5b–6: "...by your unrepentant heart you are storing up anger for yourself on the Day of Anger, when God's righteous judgment will be revealed; for he will pay back each one according to his deeds," as taught in Psalm 62:13(12) and Proverbs 24:12. God's desire is that the wicked should turn from his evil ways.

> "Therefore I will judge you, O house of Israel, every one according to his ways, says *Adonai*, God. Repent and turn from all your transgressions, lest iniquity be your ruin. Cast away from you all the transgressions which you have committed against me and get yourselves a new heart and a new spirit! Why will you die, O house of Israel? For I have no pleasure in the death of anyone, says *Adonai*, God; so turn, and live!" (Ezekiel 18:30–32)

> "For God so loved the world that he gave his only Son, so that everyone who trusts in him may have eternal life, instead of being utterly destroyed. For God did not send the Son into the world to judge the world, but rather so that through him, the world might be saved. Those who trust in him are not judged; those who do not trust have been judged already, in that they have not trusted in the one who is God's only Son." (Yn 3:16–18)

The Judaism of today tends to finesse or minimize the punishment to be meted out to the wicked. Orthodox Judaism speaks of a probationary period (like the Roman Catholic purgatory) of not more than eleven months for members of the House of Israel. In this sense Judaism does not take sin seriously, in terms of its consequences to the individual sinner.

To those who cannot relate to vv. 11–15 because they find the doctrine of eternal punishment for the wicked too fearsome, or because they cannot accept that God would be "so mean — it's against his loving nature," the *Tanakh* replies, "The fear of *Adonai* is the beginning of wisdom" (Psalm 111:10). Justice and mercy, holiness and love are qualities which God balances in his own way, which may not be the way we would choose.

> "My thoughts are not your thoughts, says *Adonai*,
> and my ways are not your ways.
> As the heavens are higher than the earth,
> so are my ways higher than your ways
> and my thoughts higher than your thoughts." (Isaiah 55:8–9)

> "There is a way which seems right to a man,
> but at its end are the ways of death." (Proverbs 14:12).

CHAPTER 21

1–8 The judgment of Chapter 20 is one side of a coin; this is the other. The sinless conditions of the Garden of Eden are restored (see last paragraph of 20:11–15N). It is the time when "the creation," which "has been groaning as with the pains of childbirth," will be "set free from its bondage to decay" to "enjoy the freedom accompanying the glory that God's children will have" (Ro 8:19–23). It is the restoration spoken of in Ac 3:21, in which Yeshua "has to remain in heaven until the time comes for restoring everything, as God said long ago, when he spoke through the holy prophets." It is the fulfillment of Isaiah's prophecy:

> "Behold, I create new heavens and a new earth;
> the former things will not be remembered or come to mind.
> Rather, you will be glad, you will rejoice forever over what I create,
> for, behold, I create Jerusalem a rejoicing, and her people a joy;
> and I will rejoice in Jerusalem and take joy in my people —
> no longer shall there be heard in her the sound of weeping or crying."
> (Isaiah 65:17–19)

The interconnection between new creation and judgment is even clearer in the words of Isaiah 66:22–24:

> "For as the new heavens and the new earth, which I will make, are to remain before me, says *Adonai*, so will your seed and your name remain. And it will come to pass that every new moon and every *Shabbat* all flesh will come to worship before me, says *Adonai*. And they will go out and look at the carcasses of the people who rebelled against me, for their worm will not die, and their fire will not be quenched, and all flesh will regard them with disgrace."

1 **The sea was no longer there**. See 20:13–14&N. Early *JNT* editions have "There was no longer any sea." The change reflects my conclusion that the author, whose viewpoint is the Land of Israel, is not saying that there will no longer be oceans on the earth but that the Mediterranean Sea will no longer be the Land's western boundary. (Is my being a surfer influencing my exegesis?)

The Bible depicts creation as war. Light conquers darkness (Genesis 1:1–5, Yn 1:1–5), but the sea is allied with the darkness. (This metaphor does not require our text to refer to all the oceans; the Mediterranean suffices.) Therefore the sea has to be contained, limited — this is done on the second day of creation (Genesis 1:6–10; see also Job 38:8–11, Isaiah 27:1, and possibly Isaiah 51:9–52:12). The sea is active in bringing destruction and death through the flood of Noach, an event mentioned five times in the New Testament (Mt 24:37–38, Lk 17:26–27, MJ 11:7, 1 Ke 3:20, 2 Ke 2:5). But the sea is under God's control, as seen most clearly in the Exodus, where God's "strong hand and outstretched arm" turn the Red Sea into a means of salvation for the Israelites, though a means of destruction for the Egyptians. God has promised never again to use water as a means of universal destruction

(Genesis 9:11), but equally he has promised that he *will* use fire for that purpose (2 Ke 3:10–12). The Lake of Fire (20:15) is a fiery sea of eternal destruction; it conquers finally and universally what the Red Sea conquered temporally and locally — namely, sin. Water is powerful, but fire is more powerful; hence Yochanan the Immerser says he immerses in water but another is coming, Yeshua, who will immerse in the Holy Spirit and in fire (Lk 3:16–17).

2 **The holy city, New Yerushalayim**, "the Jerusalem above" which "is our mother" (Ga 4:26), "the city with permanent foundations, of which the architect and builder is God" (MJ 11:10, 16), "the city of the living God, heavenly Yerushalayim" (MJ 12:22&N), the permanent city to come (MJ 13:14), is seen **coming down out of heaven from God, prepared like a bride beautifully dressed for her husband**, as described in 21:9–22:5 below. The wedding imagery here, at v. 9 and at 22:17 identifies the New Jerusalem with God's people (compare 19:7–9; also in the New Testament Mt 9:15, 25:1–13; Yn 3:27–30; 2C 11:2; Ep 5:21–33; and in the *Tanakh* Isaiah 54:1–8; Jeremiah 3:1, 20; Hosea 1–2). Contrast "the great whore,… Babylon" (17:1, 5).

3 This important verse tells the final fulfillment of one of the most frequently repeated covenant promises in the *Tanakh*, that God will dwell with his people and be their God, with full fellowship restored as in the Garden of Eden. See Genesis 17:7; Exodus 6:7, 29:45; Leviticus 26:11–12 (which is particularly related to this verse); Numbers 15:41; Deuteronomy 29:12(13); 2 Samuel 7:24; Jeremiah 7:23, 11:4, 24:7, 30:22, 31:33(34), 32:38; Ezekiel 11:20, 34:24, 36:28, 37:23, 27; Zechariah 8:8; MJ 8:10; and v. 7 below.

"***Sh'khinah***" and "**he will live**" translate the Greek words "*skênê*" ("tent, tabernacle, lodging") and "*skênôsei*" ("he will dwell"); and both are related to the Hebrew word "*shakhan*" ("to dwell"), from which is derived "*Sh'khinah*," referring to the glorious manifesting presence of God who can dwell among men (see 7:15N). Thus God will dwell with them, be the *Sh'khinah* and the Tabernacle with them, be the glory (*kavod* = *Sh'khinah*) in the midst of them (Zechariah 2:9(10)). "But will God indeed dwell with man on earth?" (2 Chronicles 6:18). Yes, he will.

Peoples or "people"; the manuscripts vary. Here are Bruce M. Metzger's remarks on this:

> "It is extremely difficult to decide between the reading *laoi* [peoples], which is supported by [several very important early manuscripts], and the reading *laos* [people], which is supported by [a larger number of mostly less important sources]. Has the author followed the prophetic Scriptures that consistently speak of the one people of God (e.g., Jeremiah 31:32(33), Ezekiel 37:27, Zechariah 8:8)? In that case, *laoi* was introduced by copyists who pedantically conformed the word to the preceding *autoi* [they]. Or [on the other hand], did the author deliberately modify the traditional concept, substituting 'the many peoples of redeemed humanity for the single elect nation, the world for Israel' (Swete)? In that case, *laos* betrays the hand of the emendator, who conformed the reading to the imagery of the Old Testament. Chiefly on the basis of what was taken to be very slightly superior manuscript evidence a majority of the

Committee [who put together the UBS edition of the Greek New Testament] preferred *laoi*." (*A Textual Commentary on the Greek New Testament*, London & New York: United Bible Societies, 1975, p. 763)

If the correct reading is "**peoples**," it confirms not only that God "made every nation living on the entire surface of the earth, and he fixed the limits of their territory and the periods when they would flourish" (Ac 17:26), but that God will save entire non-Jewish **peoples**, corporately; compare Isaiah 19:25.

God-with-them. This phrase tells us of the consummation of Isaiah 7:14, which foresees that the Messiah is to be called Immanu'el ("God with us"); see Mt 1:23&N.

4 **Wipe away every tear… no longer any death**, as written at Isaiah 25:8.

6 **I am the "A" and the "Z," the Beginning and the End**, here and at 22:13. See 1:8N and the last paragraph of 20:11–15N. Compare Ro 11:36&N.

Beginning, Greek *archê*, "beginning, ruler, initiator, beginner," that is, he who stands above and beyond time, who created and rules everything (see 3:14N).

To anyone who is thirsty I myself will give water free of charge from the Fountain of Life. Thirst represents spiritual need, water spiritual satisfaction. Compare Psalm 36:9 ("For with you is the fountain of life"); Proverbs 13:14 ("The teaching of the wise is a fountain of life"), 14:27 ("The fear of *Adonai* is a fountain of life"); Mt 5:6, 10:42; Yn 4:5–14, 7:37–39; and especially Rv 7:17; 22:1, 17.

7 **He who wins the victory**. The phrase occurs seven times in Chapters 2–3; see 2:7N, 3:21N. "They defeated him," won the victory over the dragon, "because of the Lamb's blood and because of the message of their witness" (12:11).

8 See 9:21N and 22:15N.

21:9–22:5 The vision of the **new Yerushalayim** resembles that of Ezekiel 40–48. Compare v. 10 with Ezekiel 40:2, v. 11 with Ezekiel 43:2, vv. 12–13 with Ezekiel 48:31–34, v. 15 with Ezekiel 40:3, 5, v. 27 with Ezekiel 44:9, 22:1 with Ezekiel 47:1, 22:2 with Ezekiel 47:12. See vv. 1–8N above.

9–10 **The bride, the wife of the Lamb,**… the New **Yerushalayim**. See v. 2&N.

12–14 **Inscribed on the gates were the names of the twelve tribes of Israel…. twelve foundation-stones, and on these were the twelve names of the twelve emissaries of the Lamb** (compare Ep 2:20). The twelve tribes of Israel are mentioned in the New Testament at Mt 19:28 and Lk 22:30, where the emissaries are to judge them; at Ac 26:7 as a synonym for the entire Jewish people; at Ya 1:1 in the greeting; and at 7:4–8 above (by name). The twenty-four elders of 4:4 may represent the tribes plus the emissaries. See notes in all these places. Conclusion: there is no Church apart from the Jewish people and no Israel apart from the New Covenant. See related discussions in Ro 11:26aN, Ga 6:16N, and Ep 2:11–13&NN.

15–21 A cubical city 1500 miles on a side — can one imagine it projecting so far from the earth without setting up gravitational and other forces that would destroy it? Gold resembling glass — whatever can that mean? A wall of diamond 216 feet high? On the one hand, the world's largest cut diamond weighs less than 5 ounces; on the other, this wall is minuscule in relation to the city. Each gate made of a single pearl — from what size oyster? It is all a dramatic way of saying that the new heaven and earth and the New Jerusalem are beautiful, valuable, wondrous and glorious beyond anything we can know or imagine.

19–20 Compare the judgment breastplate of the *cohen hagadol*, which also had twelve different stones. They represented the twelve tribes of Israel, whose judgment Aaron was to "bear on his heart before *Adonai* continually" (Exodus 28:15–21, 29–30). Also see Isaiah 54:11–12.

23–26 This section draws on the imagery of Isaiah 60:

> "Arise, shine, for your light has come, and the glory of *Adonai* has risen upon you.... Nations will walk at your light, and kings at the brightness of your rising.... The wealth of the nations will come to you.... Your gates will be open continually — day and night they will not be shut, so that people can bring you the wealth of the nations, and their kings in procession.... The sun will no more be your light by day, nor will the moon give light to you for brightness, but *Adonai* will be for you an everlasting light, and your God your glory." (Isaiah 60:1–5, 11, 16, 19–20)

The nations (or "Gentiles") **will walk by its light**. There are not unregenerate nations living outside the city. Rather, as George E. Ladd says in his comment on this verse,

> "In the divine consummation, the redeemed will consist of peoples from every nation and tribe and people and tongue (7:9) who will not lose their national identity. John's language means no more than the statements of the prophets: 'and many peoples shall come and say: "Come, let us go up to the mountain of the Lord, to the house of the God of Jacob"' (Isaiah 2:3).... This is the affirmation of the universality of the knowledge of God, as promised in Jeremiah's presentation of the New Covenant (Jeremiah 31:30–33(31–34))." (*Revelation*, p. 284)

27 See 20:12bN, 22:15N.

CHAPTER 22

1 **The river of the water of life..., flowing from the throne of God and the Lamb**. "There is a river, whose streams make glad the city of God, the holiest dwelling-place of the Most High. God is in the midst of her...." (Psalm 46:5–6; compare Zechariah 14:8–9) See also 3:21N.

2–3a **The Tree of Life** was in the Garden of Eden (Genesis 2:9), but after sinning, Adam and Eve had to be kept from it (Genesis 3:22) and the way to it guarded by a *keruv* ("cherub," Genesis 3:24). Here in restored Eden, the tree of life too is restored. Like the other phenomena of the new creation (see 21:14–21N) it is unlike anything we now know, **producing twelve kinds of fruit, a different kind every month.** Moreover, **the leaves of the tree** are **for healing the nations — no longer will there be any curses**. Here "healing" seems to mean "making whole." The "curses" are evils that come upon nations — both Israel and the Gentile nations — due to their continued and unrepented sins; most of the biblical prophets pronounced curses at one time or another.

3b–5 The central theme of existence in the redeemed world will be worship **of God and of the Lamb** Yeshua the Messiah, who share the **throne**. **His servants will** be fully focused and completely satisfied when they **worship him** (which is not always the case today!), because (1) having unimpeded fellowship with God, **they will see his face**, and (2) **his name will be on their foreheads**, meaning that God will have made them fully his own (see also 7:2–3&N, 13:16–17a&N, 14:1&N, 17:5). **Night**, with its darkness symbolizing God's absence (Yn 1:5–9, 3:19–21; 1 Yn 1:5–7, 2:7–11), **will no longer exist,... because *Adonai*, God, will shine upon them.** Moreover, the physical and the spiritual will be intimately interconnected, since God's immediate presence will make them **need neither the light of a lamp nor the light of the sun. And**, as promised at 3:21 and 1C 6:2–3, **they will reign** over the universe with the Messiah and with God **as kings forever and ever.**

6–21 This is the epilogue to the Book of Revelation.

6, 7, 10, 12 **Soon... very soon... near... soon**. See 1:1N on "what must happen very soon." The repetition adds to the urgency.

8–9 See 19:10&N.

10–11 Contrast these verses with Daniel 12:9–10, where the prophet was told, "Daniel, go your way, for the words are shut up and sealed until the time of the end." (See also Isaiah 8:16; Daniel 8:26, 12:4). Here Yochanan is told, "**Don't seal up the words of the prophecy in this book, because the time of their fulfillment is near.**" Moreover, in Daniel 12:10 Daniel is told, "Many will purify themselves." But here, "**Whoever keeps acting wickedly, let him go on acting wickedly,**" because he is past the point of being able to repent (see Yn 12:39&N); yet compare v. 17 below, still an invitation to repent.

12 **My rewards are with me to give to each person according to what he has done**. See first paragraph of 20:12bN.

13 **I am the "A" and the "Z"** ("the Alpha and the Omega"; see 1:8&N), **the Beginning and the End.** Repeated from 21:6; see 3:14N.

The First and the Last. Quoted from Isaiah 44:6, where *Adonai* says it:

"Thus says *Adonai*, the King of Israel, and its redeemer *Adonai* of Hosts [heavenly armies]: I am the first, and I am the last, and beside me there is no God."

By applying this text to himself Yeshua once again identifies himself as *Adonai*.

14–15 These verses may be the words of Yeshua (as this version has it), or of Yochanan.

Those who wash their robes, who obtain forgiveness for their sins. How? "With the blood of the lamb" (7:14), that is, through the atoning work of Yeshua the Messiah, so that their robes are "white" (7:14; see also 3:4, 19:7–8, Isaiah 1:18).

To eat from the Tree of Life and go through the gates into the city is to enjoy eternal life in fellowship with God.

Outside, in the lake of fire (20:12b, 21:8, 21:27), **are** unrepentant sinners. They are outside not only in the future, but outside even now, to the extent that the Kingdom of God has broken through into this world in the hearts and lives of the saved.

Homosexuals, Greek *kunes* ("dogs"). One can imagine literal wild dogs slavering over the wicked excluded from the city (compare Mt 15:26&N, Lk 16:21). But Deuteronomy 23:18–19 illustrates the figurative use of the word "dog" in the Bible to mean "male (homosexual) prostitute":

"No daughter of Israel is to be a female prostitute (*k'deshah*), nor is a son of Israel to be a male prostitute (*kadesh*). You are to bring neither the wages of a female prostitute (*zonah*) nor the wages of a dog (*kelev*) into the house of *Adonai* your God in payment of any vow; both of them are an abomination to *Adonai* your God."

On the New Testament's attitude toward homosexuality see Ro 1:24–28&N.

Those who misuse drugs in connection with the occult. See 9:21N.

16 I, Yeshua, have sent my angel to give you this testimony for the Messianic communities, as stated in 1:1–2.

The Root and Offspring of David. King David sprang from this Root, because Yeshua pre-existed David (Micah 5:1(2), Yn 8:58), and through Yeshua everything, including David's ancestor Adam, was made (Yn 1:1–2, 14). But Yeshua is also David's offspring; in particular, he is the promised Son of David who would be the Messiah (see Mt 1:1&N). Yeshua's Davidic ancestry is referred to in the rest of the New Testament also at Mt 1:6, 9:27, 15:22, 21:9; Lk 1:32, 2:4, 3:31; Ro 1:3; 2 Ti 2:8. In Revelation the term "Root of David" is found also at 5:5&N.

The bright Morning Star. See 2:28&N, 2 Ke 1:19N.

17 As in vv. 14–15, either Yeshua or Yochanan may be speaking here. No matter which, both the Holy **Spirit** and the **Bride**, the Messianic Community, identified also with the New Jerusalem (21:2&N), agree with Yeshua in reiterating his call to the **thirsty** to **take the water of life free of charge** (see 21:6&N).

18–19 The warning of either Yeshua or Yochanan follows the form of Deuteronomy 4:2, which reads:

> "Don't add anything to the word which I am commanding you, and don't take anything away from it, so that you may keep the *mitzvot* of *Adonai* your God which I am commanding you."

Yochanan's warning refers to the Book of Revelation, not to the whole Bible. However, it is a warning which I or anyone who deals with the Word of God must keep in mind at all times. It is my fervent hope that both my translation and my commentary have not distorted what God meant us to know, for work of this kind mediates eternal destinies. My prayer is that the eternal destinies of the readers of this commentary will be with God and his son Yeshua, and that my work has not distanced anyone from him but brought people closer.

20–21 The congregation is instructed to say "***Amen***" (Ro 9:5&N) at the close of the public reading of the book (1:3). The two final sentences, one for heaven and one for earth, set the tone for those inspired to do the Lord's will. So I echo the words of Yochanan: **Come, Lord Yeshua**, and **May the grace of the Lord Yeshua be with all.**

INDEX

This index will be more user-friendly if the reader considers how it was made. A computer produced an alphabetical list of all 18,000-or-so individual words used in the book and a separate list of capitalized word sequences enabling me to find names of persons and titles of books. I made a combined list, pruned it to 7,000 entries and printed a raw index showing the pages on which each appears. After learning such fascinating trivia as that the words "of" and "the" appear on every page, and "in" on every page but one, I combined related words into a single entry and developed conceptual entries such as "Hastening the End" and "Spiritual gifts." However, most of the entries consist of single keywords.

An index entry for a noun normally covers the keyword in both nominative and possessive cases and in both singular and plural number. Example: the entry "Criminal" includes "Criminal," "Criminal's," "Criminals" and "Criminals'." Noun keywords may be singular or plural and have no asterisk.

An asterisk (*) appears after entries covering both the keyword and related forms of it. Thus the entry "Ownership*" covers "owner," "owners," "owners'," "ownership," "owned," "owning" and "owns." This particular entry does not cover "own," because that word is often only distantly related to the idea of ownership: "his own approach to life." My choice of "Ownership" as the keyword to list in the index and my decision not to cover "own" are applications of common sense and personal preference.

A few entries are followed by "passim," meaning that the term appears frequently throughout the book. Other words which appear on many pages are simply not listed at all — the invisible "passim." In the latter category are such books of the Bible as Genesis, Isaiah and Acts.

The conceptual entries involved programming the computer to find words in close proximity. For "Hastening the End" I instructed it to find every instance where the word "hasten" in any of its forms appears within six words of "coming," "salvation" or "end" in any of its forms. This instruction finds most instances of "hastening the End" but probably overlooks some; also it may refer the reader to a page which meets the conditions but has nothing to do with hastening the End. Similarly the entry "Fall of man" lists page 189, where a passage with the words "fall" and "man" is irrelevant to the fall of man. Thus the conceptual entries entail the likelihood of some reader frustration. He can compensate by using the vast number of keyword entries to arrive at what he is looking for by alternate routes.

The index also functions as a brief dictionary and glossary. In parentheses after some entries is an explanation of what the word means or who the person is. Some of these entries give the page numbers for both the entry term and the explanation term, others for the entry term only.

APPENDIX

The following paragraphs, added since the first printing in 1992, are too long for inclusion in the main body of the commentary.

Mattityahu (Matthew) 1:23 (see pp. 6–8). As I said at the top of page 7, I am embarrassed by a mistake uncorrected in the first four editions of this Commentary, in which I misquoted Rashi as having written:

> " 'Behold, the *'almah* shall conceive and bear a son and shall call his name *Immanu'el.*' This means that our creator will be with us. And this is the sign: the one who will conceive is a girl (*na'arah*) who never in her life has had intercourse with any man. Upon this one shall the Holy Spirit have power."

What happened is that I relied on the commentary *The Prophet Isaiah*, written by the Hebrew Christian Victor Buksbazen (The Spearhead Press, Collingswood, NJ, 1971). I assumed that in his remarks on Isaiah 7:14 (page 150) he had given an accurate translation of Rashi's comment, and that he correctly cited *Mikra'ot G'dolot* as the source. (*Mikra'ot G'dolot* is considered the definitive edition of the Masoretic text of the *Tanakh*; it was published together with a collection of commentaries thereon, Rashi's among them, by Daniel Bomberg in 1525.)

In fact, the Hebrew text of Rashi as it appears in *Mikra'ot G'dolot* says something quite different and far less supportive of the case I am making that in Isaiah 7:14 " *'almah*" means "virgin." Following is a literal translation of Rashi's remarks in *Mikra'ot G'dolot*.

Isaiah: God gives you (plural) a sign.
Rashi: He gives it to you (plural) by himself upon you against your will.
Isaiah: Pregnant.
Rashi: In the future she will be like we found with Manoach's wife, that was spoken to her by the angel and she became pregnant and gave birth to a son, and it was written, and he will say to her; here you are pregnant, etc.
Isaiah: The young girl [*'almah*].
Rashi: My wife pregnant this year? and it will be the fourth year of King Achaz?
Isaiah: And she will call his name.
Rashi: The Holy Spirit will descend upon her.
Isaiah: Immanu'el.
Rashi: This will be to say that God is with us. And this is the sign that after the *na'arah* who will have never prophesied in all her life and with him (the son) will come the Holy Spirit. And that has been said in [Talmud tractate] Sotah, "and he will draw near to the prophetess," etc. We never find a prophet's wife is called a prophetess unless she prophesied. And there are some who understand this to be

> referring to Chizkiyahu (Hezekiah). But this is impossible. After you count the years you will find that Chizkiyahu would have been born nine years before his father's kingship began. And there are some who interpret this to mean that this is the sign, that she was an *'almah* for whom it was not appropriate that she give birth — or, with Hebrew r'uyah translated differently, the 'almah was not suited to giving birth, i.e., she was too young.

Contrary to Buksbazen's citation, Rashi never explicitly says that the *na'arah* has never in her life had intercourse with any man (i.e.: is a virgin). Rather, he simply defines the *'almah* as a *na'arah* and then says that some interpret this to mean either that it was improper for her to give birth (presumably because she was unmarried, in which case what would be proper is that she would be a virgin) or that she was too young to be physically capable of giving birth (in which case, unless she had been abused, she would be a virgin).

I regret misrepresenting Rashi. Nevertheless, even without the Rashi paragraph at the beginning of this note (at the top of page 7 in earlier editions), I believe the overall case I have made on pp. 6–8 for understanding the *'almah* of Isaiah 7:14 as a virgin remains convincing. (A friend says that Rashi did write the paragraph as quoted, but it is not in *Mikra'ot G'dolot*. However, until someone directs me to a genuine Rashi source for it, the matter remains as I have left it in this Appendix note.)

Mattityahu (Matthew) 5:3 (see p. 23). According to Elazar (Larry) Brandt, a Messianic Jewish friend, the Beatitudes are actually *Tanakh* phrases in the form of blessings representing the messianic age. At the end of them, Yeshua says, "How blessed *you* are when people insult *you* and persecute *you* and tell all kinds of vicious lies about *you* because *you* follow *me*" (v. 11; italics added). By pronouncing this blessing in the context of messianic blessings, he is saying, in code, that he is the Messiah — which must have surprised and shocked his hearers.

This understanding supports my interpretation of v. 17 as the theme sentence for the Messiah's interpretation of Torah. Previously I did not have ground for assuming that Yeshua's premise in his Sermon on the Mount was "I am the Messiah," so that my understanding of v. 17 "came from nowhere." Now I see that it is the logical implication of the "I am the Messiah" premise, communicated in code by the Beatitudes.

Mattityahu (Matthew) 5:5 (see pp. 23–24). Further evidence that the Land of Israel belongs forever to the Jewish people: Psalm 105:7–11 shows God using words and phrases of great certainty — "everlasting covenant," "swore," "oath," etc. — to speak of this promise. At Messianic Jews 6:17–18 the author speaks of God's promise and his oath as "two unchangeable things, in neither of which God could lie." At 47 places in the *Tanakh* God swears to give the Land to Israel. This is the kind of language the Bible uses to assure us that the promise of the Land to the Jews is eternal and irrevocable.

Mattityahu (Matthew) 5:22, 28, 32, 34, 39, 44 (see pp. 27–30). These verses all begin with "But I tell you." The Greek word translated "but" is "*de*," which can be rendered either "but" or "and"; see Ro 10:6–8N, which is the basis for what follows. Yeshua is not here abrogating the Law (v. 17&N); so his "but" does not introduce something that contradicts or contrasts with the ideas of the prior "You have heard" (vv. 21, 27, 33, 38, 43) or "It was said" (v. 31). Yeshua is not telling his audience that they have heard something which is wrong that he is now about to correct. Rather, his "but" completes and "fills" (v. 17&N) the full sense of the *Torah* which they have already heard. At vv. 22, 28 and 34 "*de*" can successfully be rendered "and" or "moreover," to bring out how Yeshua's remark carries forward and completes the thought of the previous verse. However, in vv. 32, 39 and 44 "but" does the job better while also remaining satisfactory in the other three verses.

Mattityahu (Matthew) 8:26–27 (see p. 36). Calming wind and waves recalls Psalm 107:28–29, "Then they cried out to *Adonai* in their trouble, and he brought them out of their distress. He stilled the storm to a whisper, and the waves of the sea were hushed. They were glad when it grew calm, and he guided them to their desired haven." Seeing that Yeshua's miracle reflects this psalm shows how the New Testament sets about establishing Yeshua's divinity.

Mattityahu (Matthew) 15:21–28 (see p. 52). Here is a teaching on this passage by Joseph Shulam: The Syrophoenician woman knew that Yeshua was the Son of David (v. 22), i.e., the Messiah. Yeshua puts this piece of information in the context of Ezekiel 34; see Ezekiel 34:24. Thus his answer about coming only to the lost sheep of Israel (v. 24) reflects Ezekiel 34:12, 16; in effect he says, "If, as you say, I am the Son of David, the shepherd who was King of Israel, I was sent to find my lost sheep and am not sent to you. So I'm surprised that you recognize me." It's a straightforward Middle-Eastern style friendly joke, not an insult. But his remark also reflects the biblical truth that God cares for his own people first — as Sha'ul put it, "Let us do good unto all, especially unto them who are of the household of faith" (Ga 6:10). However, God does not neglect the others, as we learn from I Kings 7:7ff., where the prophet Elijah asks to be fed first, yet the widow of Tzarfat, coming second, gains a miraculous lasting food supply.

Mattityahu (Matthew) 16:23 (see p. 55). Another of Shulam's teachings: When Yeshua says, "Get behind me, Satan!" He could be talking to Satan, conceived of as speaking through Kefa; if so, Yeshua is telling Satan not to be an obstacle to him but to get behind him, out of the way. Or Yeshua could be addressing Kefa; it could refer to Peter as an adversary (a *soten/satan)* who is opposing Yeshua, so that Yeshua is saying: "*Bo acharai*" (come after me), and see that the things I have predicted for myself will indeed happen, contrary to what you are saying, and that this will be for the benefit of all concerned. This interpretation is based on the fact that the Hebrew *achar* means both "behind" and "after" or "following," with the implication that the translator of the incident into Greek misunderstood it. The context certainly does not support an interpretation I occasionally hear, that Yeshua is actually inviting Satan to become his follower (with the universalistic doctrinal implication that eventually even Satan will be "saved").

Mattityahu (Matthew) 23:15 (see p. 70). Orthodox Judaism has a strand that clearly calls for missionary activity on behalf of Judaism, as seen in the following citation from the *Rambam*'s *Sefer HaMitzvot*:

"The sages say that this Commandment [to love *Adonai* your God with all your heart, soul and might] also includes an obligation to call upon all mankind to serve Him (exalted be He) and to have faith in Him. For just as you praise and extol anybody whom you love, and call upon others also to love him, so, if you love the Lord to the extent of the conception of His true nature to which you have attained, you will undoubtedly call upon the foolish and ignorant to seek knowledge of the Truth which you have already acquired.

"As the *Sifre* says [on Deuteronomy 6:5]: 'And thou shalt love the Lord thy God: this means that you should make Him beloved of man as Abraham your father did, as it is said, "And the souls they had gotten in Haran" [Genesis 12:5].' That is to say, just as Abraham, being a lover of the Lord — as Scripture testifies, 'Abraham My friend' [Isaiah 41:8] — by the power of his conception of God and out of his great love for Him, summoned mankind to believe, you too must so love Him as to summon mankind unto him." [*Maimonides: The Commandments*, translated by Charles B. Chavel Volume 1, Commandment 3, page 5]

Mattityahu (Matthew) 27:2 (see p. 82). **They put him in chains.** Literally, "binding him." The *'Akedat-Yitzchak* ("Binding of Isaac") plays a prominent role in Judaism; see MJ 11:17–19&N and Ya 2:21–23. In the present verse we see that Yeshua literally underwent an *'akedah.*

Mark 14:28 (see p. 99). **But after I have been raised, I will go ahead of you into the Galil** In *The Voice of the Martyrs, Inc.* newsletter, November 1993, page 1, Richard Wurmbrand writes

> " 'Galilee' is the name of the northern region of Israel and also of a slope of Jerusalem's Mount of Olives. After His resurrection, Jesus first met some of His disciples in the latter place."

Luke 24 portrays the risen Yeshua on the Mount of Olives, while Yochanan 21 describe[s] his appearance in the Galil (i.e., in the north). The present text, as well as those a[t] Mk 16:7 and Mt 28:10, 16 can be interpreted either way.

Luke 1:15 (see pp. 103–104). **Other liquor** (Greek *sikera*, related to Hebrew and Yiddish *shikker*, which means "drunk") can only be barley beer, says Jeff Spivak, an Israel[i] Messianic Jewish student of the Second Temple period. He says that since the technology did not exist to make anything stronger than wine, barley beer was the only other alcoholic drink in common use then.

Luke 2:6 (see p. 107). **There was no space for them at the inn** (*Jewish New Testament*). **There was no space for them in the living-quarters** (*Complete Jewish Bible*). The *CJB* version is the correct one. Jeff Spivak also pointed out to me that a small, poor village like Bethlehem would not have had an inn. Rather, in most homes (as in rural Arab homes even today), the animals were kept downstairs, while the upper part of the house consisted of a work-room where the children slept, a separate bedroom for the parents, and a guest room (the last two only if the owner was rich enough to afford them). In a pinch the space for animals underneath the living quarters would have afforded guests some privacy.

Luke 23:26–31 (see pp. 147–148). "**For if they do these things when the wood is green, what is going to happen when it's dry?"** The Greek behind this enigmatic English sentence literally reads, "For if in the green tree they do these things, [then] in the dry what may happen?" But David Bivin and Roy Blizzard, in their book *Understanding the Difficult Words of Jesus*, point out that Greek "do... in" renders too literally a Hebrew phrase that is here better translated "do... to." Thus the sentence should be rendered, "If they do these things to the green wood, what will they do to the dry?" They refer to the passage in Ezekiel 21:1–12 (20:45–21:8), where green and dry trees refer to the righteous and the wicked and note that Yeshua is using a *kal v'chomer* statement to say, "If they do this to a righteous one, what will happen to the wicked?" — or, even more explicitly, "If they do this to me (the Righteous One), what will happen to them?"

Romans 11:25 (see pp. 417–418). Metaphorically speaking, the situation has now reversed itself: hardness has come on the Church until the full number of Jews (or: until the Jewish world in its fullness) has come in.

1 Corinthians 11:17–34 (see p. 475). Joseph Shulam points out that in the century before Yeshua the Qumran Community had a communion meal in honor of the Messiah whom they expected soon, and who was "represented" at such meals by a member of the community. "The Rule Annexe" to "The Scroll of the Rule" has the following passage, as translated by Geza Vermes and quoted in A. Dupont-Sommer, *The Essene Writings from Qumran* (Gloucester, Mass.: Peter Smith, 1973, pp. 108–109); I have eliminated the brackets indicating interpolations by the translator:

> "And when they gather for the Community table or to drink wine, and arrange the Community table and mix the wine to drink, let no man stretch out his hand over the first-fruits of bread and wine before the Priest; for it is he who shall bless the first-fruits of bread and wine, and shall first stretch out his hand over the bread. And afterwards, the Messiah of Israel shall stretch out his hands over the bread. And afterwards, all the Congregation of the Community shall bless, each according to his rank.
>
> "And they shall process according to this rite at every meal where at least ten persons are assembled."

From this we learn that the concept of a public ceremonial meal in honor of the Messiah and involving bread and wine was a tradition within the Jewish world prior to Yeshua's advent. The earliest biblical mention of a bread-and-wine meal, of course, is Malki-Tzedek's presentation of these elements to Avraham in Genesis 14. Therefore this kind of a Communion service should not be regarded as a peculiarly Christian invention.

We can also infer that the writer was dealing with a problem in Qumran not unlike the one in Corinth — there was a need to prevent people from grabbing the food without regard for order or for each other.

Finally, note that Qumran used the ten-person definition of *minyan* (see Ac 16:12–13N).

Even though a bread-and-wine ceremonial meal antedates Yeshua, it seems unreason able to me to suppose that this could have been anything like the morsel of bread and th sip of wine offered at Communion Services in churches today. Bread was the staff of life especially when served with oil or spices or both (as in the Middle East today); and surel enough was served to satisfy hunger. Even if it wasn't a full meal, one should think o it as at least a snack! The wine too was nourishing as well as refreshing. Though ceremo nial and rich in symbolism, the Lord's Supper was a real meal, not a symbolic one See Ac 2:42N on "Breaking bread" in the main part of the Commentary.

Titus 1:10–13 (see p. 654–655). Verse 10 speaks of the Circumcision faction, and the not speaks of this group in Crete as being composed of both Jews and Gentiles. In fact, from v. 12 one must conclude that it was primarily Gentile, since that verse refers to th (Gentile) Cretans' own prophets, whereas the Jews' own prophets are those whose word are recorded in the *Tanakh*. Also: v. 11 speaks of silencing the Circumcision faction, an v. 13 of being severe and rebuking those who have followed this false teaching. Appar ently the same group — Gentile Cretan Circumcision faction people — are being silence and rebuked in both verses.

Titus 1:11–13 (see p. 655). In his wide-ranging and fascinating book, *Gödel, Escher, Bach an Eternal Golden Braid*, on the similarity of thought patterns in the mathematics, a and music of these three men, Douglas Hofstadter writes (p. 17) that Epimenides

> "was a Cretan who made one immortal statement: 'All Cretans are liars.' A sharper version of the statement is simply 'I am lying'; or, 'This statement is false'....It...rudely violates the usually assumed dichotomy of statements into true and false, because if you tentatively think it is true, then it immediately backfires on you and makes you think it is false. But once you've decided it is false, a similar backfiring returns to you to the idea that it must be true. Try it!"

Therefore it is logically impossible that Sha'ul meant the "plain sense" of Epimenides epigram. Sha'ul is not serious in quoting Epimenides, because Epimenides was no serious when he spoke. This is the ground for the "two possible explanations" I hav offered in my note.

Messianic Jews (Hebrews) 5:6, 7:1–10 (see pp. 675, 679–680). Joseph Shulam has show that among the Dead Sea Scrolls the one-page document known as 1Q Melch is uniqu in early Jewish literature in presenting a picture of Malki-Tzedek very similar to that o the author of the New Testament book of Messianic Jews (Hebrews). This fact strength ens the contention made by some scholars that the author of Messianic Jews, whoever h was (see 1:1N), was familiar with the Qumran Community and its ideas.

Messianic Jews (Hebrews) 13:8. Yeshua the Messiah is the same yesterday, today an forever. So, if he ever was a Jew, he was resurrected a Jew; and he is one to this day. H was born a Jew, lived a Jew, died a Jew, and rose from the dead a Jew. He is alive an Jewish now, and remains a Jew forevermore. The following additional "proof texts" (would rather call them "discussion texts") in support of this proposition are offered fo your consideration:

Yeshua walked with his *talmidim* toward Beit-Anyah. "Then, raising his hands, he said a *b'rakhah* over them" (Lk 24:50). What blessing is spoken with lifted hands? The Aaronic Benediction (Numbers 6:24-26). It is given in this manner by the *cohanim* in synagogues to this day, as it was in the Temple centuries before Yeshua was born. Our *cohen gadol* (as Yeshua is referred to throughout this letter) gave his priestly blessing in the same way. In fact, another name for the Aaronic Benediction is "The Lifting up of Hands" (see Alfred Edersheim, *Sketches of Jewish Social Life in the Days of Christ*, Chapter XVI).

Sha'ul the emissary tells us that while he was on the road to Damascus, Yeshua spoke to him from heaven in Hebrew (Ac 26:14). Sha'ul, a Jew who was born a Roman citizen (Ac 22:27-28), was fluent in Greek (Ac 21:37) and possibly many other languages, but Yeshua spoke to him in Hebrew, the language of the Jews.

Sha'ul did not become a believer until well after Yeshua's death and resurrection, yet an important part of his message is that Yeshua is a descendant of the Jewish king David (Ro 1:3, 2 Ti 2:8). Many years after his resurrection, Yeshua testified that he is "the Root and Offspring of [king] David" (Rv 22:16). In a time yet future, two of his titles will be "Lion of the tribe of Y'hudah," and "Root of David" (Rv 5:5).

In Mt 26:27-29 Yeshua indicates that he will be celebrating the Passover *seder* with his *talmidim* in his Father's kingdom.

The standard Yeshua will use at the judgment is *Torah*. To those who fall short of being *Torah*-true, he will say, "Get away from me, you workers of lawlessness!" (Mt 7:22-23); the Greek word translated "lawlessness" is *anomia*; it can also be translated "absence of *Torah*."

NOTES

NOTES

ABOUT THE AUTHOR

David H. Stern was born in Los Angeles in 1935, the great-grandson of two of the city's first twenty Jews. He earned a Ph.D. in economics at Princeton University and was a professor at UCLA, mountain-climber, co-author of a book on surfing and owner of health-food stores.

In 1972 he came to faith in Yeshua the Messiah, after which he received a Master of Divinity degree at Fuller Theological Seminary and did graduate work at the University of Judaism.

He was married in 1976 to Martha Frankel, also a Messianic Jew, and together they served one year on the staff of Jews for Jesus. Dr. Stern taught Fuller Theological Seminary's first course in "Judaism and Christianity," organized Messianic Jewish conferences and leaders' meetings, and served as an officer of the Messianic Jewish Alliance of America.

In 1979 the Stern family made *aliyah* [immigrated to Israel]. They now live in Jerusalem with their two children and are active in Israel's Messianic Jewish community.

This commentary is a companion to Dr. Stern's *Jewish New Testament,* which is his translation of the New Testament from the original first-century Greek into enjoyable modern English. This translation brings out the essential Jewishness of the New Testament by its use of Hebrew names and Jewish terminology and by its correction of antisemitic renderings found in other translations.

The *Jewish New Testament Commentary* discusses, verse by verse, Jewish issues raised in the New Testament — questions Jews have about Yeshua, the New Testament and Christianity; questions Christians have about Judaism and the Jewish roots of their faith; and questions Messianic Jews have about their own identity and role.

The *Jewish New Testament* and *Jewish New Testament Commentary* are available singly in hard or soft cover or as a boxed, hardcover matched set. Both are available on CD-ROM. In addition, the *Jewish New Testament* is available on 16 audio cassettes.

Dr. Stern is also author of *Messianic Jewish Manifesto*, which outlines the destiny, identity, history, theology and program of today's Messianic Jewish movement, and of *Restoring the Jewishness of the Gospel*, an abridgement of the "*Manifesto*" meant for those unaccustomed to thinking of the Gospel as Jewish.

Finally, in 1998, Dr. Stern published the *Complete Jewish Bible*, his stylistically modified adaptation of an existing Jewish translation of the *Tanakh* ("Old Testament") bound together with the *Jewish New Testament.*